Hilary Hamilton

# THESAURUS

## OF WORDS AND PHRASES

# THESAURUS

## OF WORDS AND PHRASES

BY

PETER MARK ROGET, M.D., F.R.S.

ENLARGED BY

JOHN LEWIS ROGET, M.A.

NEW EDITION REVISED AND ENLARGED BY

SAMUEL ROMILLY ROGET, M.A.

---

REVISED AND AUTHORIZED AMERICAN EDITION

---

GROSSET & DUNLAP
A FILMWAYS COMPANY
Publishers • New York

National Library of Australia cataloguing in publication data

Roget, Peter Mark, 1779-1869,
Thesaurus of words and phrases/by John Louis Roget, New ed./revised and enlarged by Samuel Romilly Roget.— published, New York; Grosset & Dunlap, Inc.
ISBN 0 333 17573 5

1. English language—Synonyms and antonyms. I. Roget, John Lewis, ed. II. Roget, Samuel Romilly, ed. III. Title.

ROGET: THESAURUS

AUTHORIZED EDITION

REVISED

1941



ISBN: 0-448-01607-9

*1980 PRINTING*

PRINTED IN THE UNITED STATES OF AMERICA

# WHAT ROGET CAN DO FOR YOU

As Mark Twain said: "The difference between the right word and the almost right word is the difference between lightning and the lightning bug." To find precisely the correct word is the problem of every writer and speaker—and that is where ROGET'S THESAURUS is invaluable.

Suppose you are an advertising copywriter seeking a new substitute for the much over-used "fascination." How to go about finding a fresh eye-catching simile? It's quite simple. First look in the alphabetical index which occupies the last third of the book.

There on page 486 you find "fascinate: *influence* 615." Turn back in the body of the book to section 615, which you will easily find from the numbers on the upper corner of each page.

And here is a vast store of welcome variants for "fascination": *temptation, enticement, allurement, cajolery, blandishment, magnetism*—and any number of additional choices—including that dashing word *bewitchery*. Surely one of these will fit your needs better than the weary and outworn "fascination."

Perhaps you're a minister wrestling with the knotty problem of how to strengthen next Sunday's sermon on "sin." What to do about it? Look up "sin" in ROGET. You find in the index "sin: 945, 947." Back again to the body of the book (sections 945 & 947), and there is a magnificent collection of all the virtues and most of the vices arrayed in parallel columns: *Immorality, infamy, depravity, knavery, lust,* and *pollution* vie for space with *morality, integrity, nobleness,* and *self-control*. You find that sinners may range in degree from *naughty* and *undutiful* to *base, sinister, satanic, depraved,* and even *irreclaimable*.

But then you may be neither a preacher nor a copywriter. The problem may be that of a student confronted with an assignment to write a composition about the evolution of the modern dance. You know, of course, all about *jitterbugging*, the *Shag*, and the *Big Apple*. But, after all, these represent only the last ten years of popular dancing. What of the centuries before? What were the names of the dances your grandparents enjoyed? Before the dictionary or encyclopedia can be used, at least their names must be known.

So look again in the index of ROGET under "dance" and find on page 453 "dance: *sport* 840." Turning to section 840 you discover an all-inclusive list of dance-names. The *morris dance* of medieval England is here; the *fandango, pavan,* and the *polka*. The *bolero* and *tango* from Spain; the *Charleston*, the *cakewalk, jazz,* and the *blues*. The *gavotte, mazurka, quadrille,* and *lancers* are found in the merry company of the *turkeytrot, shimmy,* and *rhumba*. Here truly is a stimulating introduction to the dance in all its manifold varieties from the *polonaise* to the *cancan!*

When you run through this list, not only will the right word automatically catch your eye but the rich array of colorful names will suggest fresh ideas that are sure to help you in your thinking and writing.

Briefly, the simplest and best way to use ROGET is this:

1. Look up in the index at the back of the book the word for which you want a substitute.
2. Note the category number of the group which seems to fit your needs best.
3. Turn back to this number which you will find at the top of a page in the main part of the book. And there you will find the right word, the exact word for your purpose.

This, then, is *your* ROGET, a book you will want to keep always in reach when writing or preparing a speech. You will be amazed at how easily you get the knack of its use—and how enormously valuable and profitable it will prove.

# FOREWORD

## TO THE

## AUTHORIZED AMERICAN EDITION

IT IS fitting that a new American edition of Roget's Thesaurus, issued by the American Company of its original London publishers, should have some account of its origin and progress.

Early in the nineteenth century the idea of the utility of a list of words classified according to the ideas that they express occurred to Dr. Peter Mark Roget, and his first draft was completed in 1805. It was added to from time to time, but it was not until Dr. Roget was over seventy years of age and had retired from the active secretaryship of the Royal Society that he was able to devote three or four years to the work of expansion.

It was first published in London by Longman, Brown, Green and Longmans in 1852, and went into a second edition in 1853. Two years later the "third and cheaper edition enlarged and improved" appeared, and was followed by the fourth edition in the same year. The fifth edition was issued in 1857, and since then edition has followed edition almost every year, and occasionally two or three times in one year, until seventy-seven printings have been called for, totalling more than two hundred thousand books.

The merits of the Thesaurus, its scholarship and erudition, were appreciated from the first, and successive improvements and enlargements by the author, the author's son and grandson, have caused it to maintain its great reputation.

In the course of years there have been several competing editions printed in America, all based on the London editions, but from none of these did the author or his representatives derive any pecuniary advantage.

The present edition, edited and revised by Willard Jerome Heggen, is the first one to be issued in America with the sanction and approval of Samuel Romilly Roget, the author's grandson, and holder of the existing British copyright.

It is worthy of note that it took three generations of the Roget family to compile and perfect this Thesaurus, and that after eighty years it is still published in London by the same firm, and from the same address in Paternoster Row, as when issued originally.

# PREFACE

Since the preface of March 17, 1879, was written, Mr. John L. Roget continued to revise periodical reprints of the Thesaurus until his death in 1908. It then devolved upon the undersigned, his son, to carry on this task, and it has been his endeavour to follow the same lines in making such additions that have seemed suitable from time to time. The opportunity has now, however, presented itself for a rather more complete revision, owing to the necessity of resetting the entire work, and in the edition that is now presented not only have a few hitherto unnoticed errors been corrected but some hundreds of new words and phrases have been added throughout the book, some of which have only recently become a part of the language as the result of progress in the various arts of peace and the unfortunate necessities of war. Many additional entries of words already represented have also been made, where the meanings have widened out or where for other reasons it has been thought advisable, but in practically no case has a word been removed, as archaic and even obsolete words are often sought for by authors. A few examples of alternative and obsolete spelling have been removed, but no alteration whatever has been made with the general arrangement and classification of the categories.

The editor would at all times welcome practical suggestions from users of the Thesaurus, and would take this opportunity of expressing his thanks for much kind help already afforded in this direction.

S. R. Roget

July 1925

# PREFACE

## TO

## THE FIRST EDITION

## (1852)

It is now nearly fifty years since I first projected a system of verbal classification similar to that on which the present Work is founded. Conceiving that such a compilation might help to supply my own deficiencies, I had, in the year 1805, completed a classed catalogue of words on a small scale, but on the same principle, and nearly in the same form, as the Thesaurus now published. I had often during that long interval found this little collection, scanty and imperfect as it was, of much use to me in literary composition, and often contemplated its extension and improvement; but a sense of the magnitude of the task, amidst a multitude of other avocations, deterred me from the attempt. Since my retirement from the duties of Secretary of the Royal Society, however, finding myself possessed of more leisure, and believing that a repertory of which I had myself experienced the advantage might, when amplified, prove useful to others, I resolved to embark in an undertaking which, for the last three or four years, has given me incessant occupation, and has, indeed, imposed upon me an amount of labour very much greater than I had anticipated. Notwithstanding all the pains I have bestowed on its execution, I am fully aware of its numerous deficiencies and imperfections, and of its falling far short of the degree of excellence that might be attained. But, in a Work of this nature, where perfection is placed at so great a distance, I have thought it best to limit my ambition to that moderate share of merit which it may claim in its present form; trusting to the indulgence of those for whose benefit it is intended, and to the candour of critics who, while they find it easy to detect faults, can at the same time duly appreciate difficulties.

P. M. Roget

April 29th, 1852

# EDITOR'S PREFACE

(1879)

(*Slightly Abridged*)

The First Edition of Dr. Roget's Thesaurus was published in the year 1852, and a second in the ensuing spring. On the issue of the third, in 1855, the volume was stereotyped. Since that time until now, the work has been reprinted in the same form and with little alteration, in rapidly succeeding editions, the printing of which has worn out the original plates.

During the last years of the author's life, which closed, at a very advanced age, in the month of September, 1869, he was engaged in the task of collecting additional words and phrases, for an enlarged edition which he had long projected. This he did not live to complete, and it became my duty, as his son, to attempt to carry the design into execution.

The result of the author's labours was embodied in a copy of the Thesaurus, in which the margins and spaces about the letterpress were closely covered with written words and phrases, without any very precise indication of the places in the text where additions or alterations were intended to be made. On a careful examination of these *addenda,* I came to the conclusion that, in order to introduce them with advantage, it would be necessary to make some slight changes; without, however, interfering at all with the framework of the book, and but little with the details of its system. In this proceeding my course has been mainly determined by the following considerations.

Any attempt at a philosophical arrangement under categories of the words of our language must reveal the fact that it is impossible to separate and circumscribe the several groups by absolutely distinct boundary lines. Many words, originally employed to express simple conceptions, are found to be capable, with perhaps a very slight modification of meaning, of being applied in many varied associations. Connecting links, thus formed, induce an approach between the categories; and a danger arises that the outlines of our classification may, by their means, become confused and eventually merged. Were we to disengage these interwoven ramifications, and seek to confine every word to its main or original import, we should find some secondary meaning has become so firmly associated with many words and phrases, that to sever the alliance would be to deprive our language of the richness due to an infinity of natural adaptations.

Were we, on the other hand, to attempt to include, in each category of the Thesaurus, every word and phrase which could by any possibility be appropriately used in relation to the leading idea for which that category was designed, we should impair, if not destroy, the whole use and value of the book. For, in the endeavour to enrich our treasury of expression, we might easily allow ourselves to be led imperceptibly onward by the natural association of one word with another, and to add word after word, until group after group would successively be absorbed under some single heading, and the fundamental divisions of the system be effaced. The small cluster of nearly synonymous words, which had formed the nucleus of a category, would be lost in a sea of phrases, and it would become difficult to recognize those which were peculiarly adapted to express the leading ideas.

These considerations were material in dealing with the new and multitudinous store of words and phrases which the author had accumulated. Many of these were altogether new to the Thesaurus. Many were merely repetitions in new places of words already included in its pages. With reference to cases similar to the latter, the author had declared it to have been a general rule with him 'to place words and phrases which appertain more especially to one head, also under other heads to which they have a relation,' whenever it appeared to him 'that this repetition would suit the convenience of the inquirer and spare him the trouble of turning to other parts of the work.' But, with the now increased mass of words, it became a question, in many cases, whether such repetition would still prove convenient. Where categories might by that course be unduly swollen, or where they might, by reason of their being separated from each other by subtile distinctions or faint lines of demarcation, be thereby too nearly assimilated, I thought it would often be better to confine words of the kind referred to to their primary headings. The necessity of keeping the book within reasonable dimensions had also to be borne in mind.

Under these circumstances, the best method of ensuring the ready accessibility of the multitude of words now to be dealt with, and at the same time preserving unimpaired the unity of the several categories, appeared to me to lie in the copious use of references from one place in the book to another. Relying on this contrivance as a means of opening more widely the resources of the collection, by making the groups of words mutually suggestive, and thereby leading not only to more varied forms of expression, but to kindred ideas, I have added largely to the references already inserted by the author. I have also ventured occasionally to substitute a reference for a group of words, when the identical group existed in another place, and could thus be made immediately available.

In order, at the same time, to make the value of the references more appreciable, I have (whenever it has appeared to me to be necessary) inserted, in a parenthesis, a word indicating the nature of the group or category referred to. Any one using the book will thereby be enabled to judge whether it will be worth his while to turn to the place in question.

The cross references may also be looked upon as indicating in some degree the natural points of connection between the categories, and the ramification of the ideas which they embody. As would be the case under any classification of language, a large proportion of the expressions, to find which recourse is had to the Thesaurus, lie on an ill-defined border land between one category and another; and it is not always easy, even with the aid of a carefully compiled index, to determine under which of several allied headings they should be sought. In the present edition, when the inquirer has once started on his voyage of discovery, the references enable him to pass freely from one division to another without recurring to the Index.

Many new words have also been inserted which were not contained in the author's manuscript.

Except in a very few cases, where distinct ideas were obviously united under one head, I have not had the presumption to meddle with the author's division into categories; but, within each category, I have endeavoured to carry somewhat further the sorting of words according to the ideas which they convey.

With these objects in view, I have supplied the work with a new and elaborate Index, much more complete than that which was appended to the previous editions. Although, in the original design of his work, the author appears to have conceived the process of search for a required expression as one in which the system of classification would be first consulted, and the Index afterwards called in aid if necessary, I believe that almost everyone who uses the book finds it more convenient to have recourse to the Index first.

From the peculiar nature and use of the Thesaurus, its Index will be found to differ, in some of its essential functions, from an alphabetical table of contents. The present Index does not merely afford an indication of the place where every given word or topic occurs or is dealt with in the text; but it is intended as a guide to other expressions which may be found there. The word we look out in this Index is not that which we require, but that which we wish to avoid. It is, therefore, not necessary that every word there given should be a repetition of one in the text. It may even happen that the word selected as a guide, though suggestive of the group wanted, is wholly unfit to be comprised within it.

The new Index contains not only all the *words* in the book (without needless repetition of conjugate forms), but likewise the *phrases,* all of which had been excluded from the Index to the previous editions. It is hoped that these additions, although they increase the bulk of the book, will have the effect of extending its usefulness in at least a corresponding degree.

Some changes of detail have also been made, where the form of the work seemed susceptible of improvement, and there was no reason to suppose that the author would have disapproved of the alteration. In the previous editions, the *phrases* were in general placed in separate paragraphs, under the heading **Phr.**, in each of the subdivisions assigned to the different grammatical parts of speech. In the present edition, *words* and *phrases* are placed together, and the heading **Phr.** is only employed in the case of phrases which have no convenient place in such an arrangement. Much space has been saved, and many repetitions have been avoided, by the use of lines and hyphens, where words or phrases in the same group have syllables or parts in common, and by references from one part of speech to another. These abbreviations may be best explained by examples, of which the following are a few:—

'with -relation, - reference, - respect, - regard- to'; is meant to include the phrases 'with relation to,' 'with reference to,' 'with respect to,' 'with regard to.'

'root –, weed –, grub –, rake- -up, - out;' includes 'root up,' 'root out,' 'weed up,' 'weed out,' 'grub up,' 'grub out,' 'rake up,' 'rake out.'

'away from –, foreign to –, beside- the -purpose, - question, - transaction, - point;' includes 'away from the purpose,' 'foreign to the purpose,' 'beside the purpose,' 'away from the question,' 'foreign to the question,' 'foreign to the transaction,' 'beside the question,' 'away from the point,' 'beside the transaction,' 'foreign to the point,' 'away from the transaction,' 'beside the point.'

'raze - to the ground'; includes 'raze,' and 'raze to the ground.'

'campan-iform, -ulate, -iliform;' includes 'campaniform,' 'campanulate,' and 'campaniliform.'

'goodness &c. *adj.*'; 'badly &c. *adj.*'; 'hindred &c. *v.*'; include all words similarly formed from synonyms of 'good,' 'bad,' and 'hinder,' respectively, given under the headings **Adj.** and **V.** in the same categories where the abbreviations occur.

The participle 'to' before a verb has in all cases been rejected, the heading **V.** being thought sufficiently distinctive; the use of capitals for the initial letters of the first words of paragraphs has been abandoned, as giving those words undue importance; and the title of each category has been kept distinct from the collection of words under its heading.

I should be ungrateful were I not to acknowledge the assistance derived, both by my father and myself, from various suggestions made by well-wishers to the work, some of whom have been personally unknown to either of us; and also to record my thanks to several kind friends, and to Messrs. Spottiswoode and Co.'s careful reader, for valuable aid during the passage of the sheets through the press.

JOHN L. ROGET

March 17th, 1879.

# PLAN OF CLASSIFICATION

| Class | Section | Nos. |
|---|---|---|
| I. ABSTRACT RELATIONS | I. Existence | 1 to 8 |
| | II. Relation | 9— 24 |
| | III. Quantity | 25— 57 |
| | IV. Order | 58— 83 |
| | V. Number | 84— 105 |
| | VI. Time | 106— 139 |
| | VII. Change | 140— 152 |
| | VIII. Causation | 153— 179 |
| II. SPACE | I. Generally | 180— 191 |
| | II. Dimensions | 192— 239 |
| | III. Form | 240— 263 |
| | IV. Motion | 264— 315 |
| III. MATTER | I. Generally | 316— 320 |
| | II. Inorganic | 321— 356 |
| | III. Organic | 357— 449 |
| | **Division** | |
| IV. INTELLECT | (I.) Formation of Ideas | 450— 515 |
| | (II.) Communication of Ideas | 516— 599 |
| V. VOLITION | (I.) Individual | 600— 736 |
| | (II.) Intersocial | 737— 819 |
| | **Section** | |
| VI. AFFECTIONS | I. Generally | 820— 826 |
| | II. Personal | 827— 887 |
| | III. Sympathetic | 888— 921 |
| | IV. Moral | 922— 975 |
| | V. Religious | 976—1000 |

# TABULAR SYNOPSIS OF CATEGORIES

## CLASS I. ABSTRACT RELATIONS

### I. EXISTENCE

| | | |
|---|---|---|
| 1°. ABSTRACT | 1. Existence. | 2. Inexistence. |
| 2°. CONCRETE | 3. Substantiality. | 4. Unsubstantiality. |
| 3°. FORMAL | *Internal.* | *External.* |
| | 5. Intrinsicality. | 6. Extrinsicality. |
| 4°. MODAL | *Absolute.* | *Relative.* |
| | 7. State. | 8. Circumstance. |

### II. RELATION

| | | |
|---|---|---|
| 1°. ABSOLUTE | 9. Relation. | 10. Irrelation. |
| | 11. Consanguinity. | |
| | 12. Correlation. | |
| | 13. Identity. | 14. Contrariety. |
| | 15. Difference. | |
| 2°. CONTINUOUS | 16. Uniformity. | 16*a*. Non-uniformity |
| 3°. PARTIAL | 17. Similarity. | 18. Dissimilarity. |
| | 19. Imitation. | 20. Non-imitation. |
| | 20*a*. Variation. | |
| | 21. Copy. | 22. Prototype. |
| 4°. GENERAL | 23. Agreement. | 24. Disagreement. |

### III. QUANTITY

| | | |
|---|---|---|
| 1°. SIMPLE | *Absolute.* | *Relative.* |
| | 25. Quantity. | 26. Degree. |
| 2°. COMPARATIVE | 27. Equality. | 28. Inequality. |
| | 29. Mean. | |
| | 30. Compensation. | |
| | *By Comparison with a Standard.* | |
| | 31. Greatness. | 32. Smallness. |
| | *By Comparison with a similar Object.* | |
| | 33. Superiority. | 34. Inferiority. |
| | *Changes in Quantity.* | |
| | 35. Increase. | 36. Decrease. |
| 3°. CONJUNCTIVE | 37. Addition. | 38. Non-addition. Subduction. |
| | 39. Adjunct. | 40. Remainder. |
| | | 40*a*. Decrement. |
| | 41. Mixture. | 42. Simpleness. |
| | 43. Junction. | 44. Disjunction. |
| | 45. Vinculum. | |
| | 46. Coherence. | 47. Incoherence. |
| | 48. Combination. | 49. Decomposition. |

| | | |
|---|---|---|
| 4°. CONCRETE | 50. Whole. | 51. Part. |
| | 52. Completeness. | 53. Incompleteness. |
| | 54. Composition. | 55. Exclusion. |
| | 56. Component. | 57. Extraneous. |

## IV. ORDER

| | | |
|---|---|---|
| 1°. GENERAL | 58. Order. | 59. Disorder. |
| | 60. Arrangement. | 61. Derangement. |
| 2°. CONSECUTIVE | 62. Precedence. | 63. Sequence. |
| | 64. Precursor. | 65. Sequel. |
| | 66. Beginning. | 67. End. |
| | 68. Middle. | |
| | 69. Continuity. | 70. Discontinuity. |
| | 71. Term. | |
| 3°. COLLECTIVE | 72. Assemblage. | 73. Non-assemblage. Dispersion. |
| | 74. Focus. | |
| 4°. DISTRIBUTIVE | 75. Class. | |
| | 76. Inclusion. | 77. Exclusion. |
| | 78. Generality. | 79. Speciality. |
| 5°. CATEGORICAL | 80. Rule. | 81. Multiformity. |
| | 82. Conformity. | 83. Unconformity. |

## V. NUMBER

| | | |
|---|---|---|
| 1°. ABSTRACT | 84. Number. | |
| | 85. Numeration. | |
| | 86. List. | |
| 2°. DETERMINATE | 87. Unity. | 88. Accompaniment. |
| | 89. Duality. | |
| | 90. Duplication. | 91. Bisection. |
| | 92. Triality. | |
| | 93. Triplication. | 96. Quadruplication. |
| | 94. Trisection. | |
| | 95. Quaternity. | 97. Quadrisection. |
| | 98. Five, &c. | 99. Quinquesection, &c. |
| 3°. INDETERMINATE | 100. Plurality. | 100*a*. Fraction. |
| | | 101. Zero. |
| | 102. Multitude. | 103. Fewness. |
| | 104. Repetition. | |
| | 105. Infinity. | |

## VI. TIME

| | | | |
|---|---|---|---|
| 1°. ABSOLUTE | | 106. Time. | 107. Neverness. |
| | | *Definite.* | *Indefinite.* |
| | | 108. Period. | 109. Course. |
| | | 108*a*. Contingent Duration. | |
| | | 110. Diuturnity. | 111. Transientness. |
| | | 112. Perpetuity. | 113. Instantaneity. |
| | | 114. Chronometry. | 115. Anachronism. |
| 2°. RELATIVE | 1. *to Succession* | 116. Priority. | 117. Posteriority. |
| | | 118. Present time. | 119. Different time. |
| | | 120. Synchronism. | |
| | 2. *to a Period* | 121. Futurity. | 122. Preterition. |
| | | 123. Newness. | 124. Oldness. |
| | | 125. Morning. | 126. Evening. |
| | | 127. Youth. | 128. Age. |
| | | 129. Infant. | 130. Veteran. |
| | | 131. Adolescence. | |
| | 3. *to an Effect or purpose* | 132. Earliness. | 133. Lateness. |
| | | 134. Occasion. | 135. Intempestivity. |
| 3°. RECURRENT | | 136. Frequency. | 137. Infrequency. |
| | | 138. Periodicity. | 139. Irregularity. |

## VII. CHANGE

| | | |
|---|---|---|
| 1°. SIMPLE | 140. Change. | 141. Permanence. |
| | 142. Cessation. | 143. Continuance. |
| | 144. Conversion. | 145. Reversion. |
| | 146. Revolution. | |
| | 147. Substitution. | 148. Interchange. |
| 2°. COMPLEX | 149. Changeableness. | 150. Stability. |
| | *Present.* | *Future.* |
| | 151. Eventuality. | 152. Destiny. |

## VIII. CAUSATION

| | | |
|---|---|---|
| 1°. CONSTANCY OF SEQUENCE | 153. *Constant Antecedent.* Cause. | 154. *Constant Sequent.* Effect. |
| | 155. *Assignment of Cause.* Attribution. | 156. *Absence of Assignment.* Chance. |
| 2°. CONNECTION BETWEEN CAUSE AND EFFECT | 157. Power. | 158. Impotence. |
| | *Degrees of Power.* | |
| | 159. Strength. | 160. Weakness. |
| 3°. POWER IN OPERATION | 161. Production. | 162. Destruction. |
| | 163. Reproduction. | |
| | 164. Producer. | 165. Destroyer. |
| | 166. Paternity. | 167. Posterity. |
| | 168. Productiveness. | 169. Unproductiveness. |
| | 170. Agency. | |
| | 171. Energy. | 172. Inertness. |
| | 173. Violence. | 174. Moderation. |
| 4°. INDIRECT POWER | 175. Influence. | 175a. Absence of Influence. |
| | 176. Tendency. | |
| | 177. Liability. | |
| 5°. COMBINATIONS OF CAUSES | 178. Concurrence. | 179. Counteraction. |

---

# CLASS II. SPACE

## I. SPACE IN GENERAL

| | | |
|---|---|---|
| 1°. ABSTRACT SPACE | | 180a. Inextension. |
| | 180. *Indefinite.* Space. | 181. *Definite.* Region. |
| | | 182. *Limited.* Place. |
| 2°. RELATIVE SPACE | 183. Situation. | |
| | 184. Location. | 185. Displacement. |
| 3°. EXISTENCE IN SPACE | 186. Presence. | 187. Absence. |
| | 188. Inhabitant. | 189. Abode. |
| | 190. Contents. | 191. Receptacle. |

## II. DIMENSIONS

| | | |
|---|---|---|
| 1°. GENERAL | 192. Size. | 193. Littleness. |
| | 194. Expansion. | 195. Contraction. |
| | 196. Distance. | 197. Nearness. |
| | 198. Interval. | 199. Contiguity. |
| 2°. LINEAR | 200. Length. | 201. Shortness. |
| | 202. Breadth. Thickness. | 203. Narrowness. Thinness. |
| | 204. Layer. | 205. Filament. |
| | 206. Height. | 207. Lowness. |
| | 208. Depth. | 209. Shallowness. |

**2°. LINEAR**—*continued*...

| | | |
|---|---|---|
| **2°. Linear**—*continued* | 210. Summit. | 211. Base. |
| | 212. Verticality. | 213. Horizontality. |
| | 214. Pendency. | 215. Support. |
| | 216. Parallelism. | 217. Obliquity. |
| | 218. Inversion. | |
| | 219. Crossing. | |
| **3°. Centrical** — 1. *General* | 220. Exteriority. | 221. Interiority. |
| | 222. Centrality. | |
| | 223. Covering. | 224. Lining. |
| | 225. Investment. | 226. Divestment. |
| | 227. Circumjacence. | 228. Interjacence. |
| | 229. Circumscription. | |
| | 230. Outline. | |
| | 231. Edge. | |
| | 232. Inclosure. | |
| | 233. Limit. | |
| 2. *Special* | 234. Front | 235. Rear. |
| | 236. Laterality. | 237. Contraposition. |
| | 238. Dextrality. | 239. Sinistrality. |

## III. FORM

| | | |
|---|---|---|
| **1°. General**........... | 240. Form. | 241. Amorphism. |
| | 242. Symmetry. | 243. Distortion. |
| **2°. Special**............ | 244. Angularity. | |
| | 245. Curvature. | 246. Straightness. |
| | 247. Circularity. | 248. Convolution. |
| | 249. Rotundity. | |
| **3°. Superficial**........ | 250. Convexity. | 252. Concavity. |
| | 251. Flatness. | |
| | 253. Sharpness. | 254. Bluntness. |
| | 255. Smoothness. | 256. Roughness. |
| | 257. Notch. | |
| | 258. Fold. | |
| | 259. Furrow. | |
| | 260. Opening. | 261. Closure. |
| | 262. Perforator. | 263. Stopper. |

## IV. MOTION

| | | |
|---|---|---|
| **1°. Motion in General** | 264. Motion. | 265. Quiescence. |
| | 266. Journey. | 267. Navigation. |
| | 268. Traveller. | 269. Mariner. |
| | 270. Transference. | |
| | 271. Carrier. | |
| | 272. Vehicle. | 273. Ship. |
| **2°. Degrees of Motion** | 274. Velocity. | 275. Slowness. |
| **3°. Conjoined with Force**............ | 276. Impulse. | 277. Recoil. |
| **4°. With Reference to Direction**..... | 278. Direction. | 279. Deviation. |
| | 280. Precession. | 281. Sequence. |
| | 282. Progression. | 283. Regression. |
| | 284. Propulsion. | 285. Traction. |
| | 286. Approach. | 287. Recession. |
| | 288. Attraction. | 289. Repulsion. |
| | 290. Convergence. | 291. Divergence. |
| | 292. Arrival. | 293. Departure. |
| | 294. Ingress. | 295. Egress. |
| | 296. Reception. | 297. Ejection. |
| | 298. Food. | 299. Excretion. |
| | 300. Insertion. | 301. Extraction. |
| | 302. Passage. | |
| | 303. Overstep. | 304. Shortcoming. |

| | | |
|---|---|---|
| 4°. WITH REFERENCE TO DIRECTION—*cont.* . . | 305. Ascent. | 306. Descent. |
| | 307. Elevation. | 308. Depression. |
| | 309. Leap. | 310. Plunge. |
| | 311. Circuition. | |
| | 312. Rotation. | 313. Evolution. |
| | 314. Oscillation. | |
| | 315. Agitation. | |

---

## CLASS III. MATTER

| | | |
|---|---|---|
| I. MATTER IN GENERAL . . . . . . . | 316. Materiality. | 317. Immateriality. |
| | 318. World. | |
| | 319. Gravity. | 320. Levity. |

### II. INORGANIC MATTER

| | | | |
|---|---|---|---|
| 1°. SOLIDS . . . . . . . . . . . . . | | 321. Density. | 322. Rarity. |
| | | 323. Hardness. | 324. Softness. |
| | | 325. Elasticity. | 326. Inelasticity. |
| | | 327. Tenacity. | 328. Brittleness. |
| | | 329. Texture. | |
| | | 330. Pulverulence. | |
| | | 331. Friction. | 332. Lubrication. |
| 2°. FLUIDS | 1. *In General* | 333. Fluidity. | 334. Gaseity. |
| | | 335. Liquefaction. | 336. Vaporization. |
| | 2. *Specific* . . . | 337. Water. | 338. Air. |
| | | 339. Moisture. | 340. Dryness. |
| | | 341. Ocean. | 342. Land. |
| | | 343. Gulf. Lake. | 344. Plain. |
| | | 345. Marsh. | 346. Island. |
| | 3. *In motion* | 347. Stream. | |
| | | 348. River. | 349. Wind. |
| | | 350. Conduit. | 351. Air-pipe. |
| 3°. IMPERFECT FLUIDS . . . | | 352. Semiliquidity. | 353. Bubble. |
| | | 354. Pulpiness. | 355. Unctuousness. |
| | | | 356. Oil. |
| | | | 356*a*. Resin. |

### III. ORGANIC MATTER

| | | | |
|---|---|---|---|
| 1°. VITALITY | 1. *In General* . . . . | 357. Organization. | 358. Inorganization |
| | | 359. Life. | 360. Death. |
| | | | 361. Killing. |
| | | | 362. Corpse. |
| | | | 363. Interment. |
| | 2. *Special* | 364. Animality. | 365. Vegetability. |
| | | 366. Animal. | 367. Vegetable. |
| | | 368. Zoology. | 369. Botany. |
| | | 370. Cicuration. | 371. Agriculture. |
| | | 372. Mankind. | |
| | | 373. Man. | 374. Woman. |

**7. Sensation**

(1) *General* ............
375. Sensibility. — 376. Insensibility.
377. Pleasure. — 378. Pain.

(2) *Special*

1. *Touch* ..
379. Touch.
380. Sensations of Touch. — 381. Numbness.

2. *Heat* ...
382. Heat. — 383. Cold.
384. Calefaction. — 385. Refrigeration.
386. Furnace. — 387. Refrigerator.
388. Fuel.
389. Thermometer.

3. *Taste* ...
390. Taste. — 391. Insipidity.
392. Pungency.
393. Condiment.
394. Savouriness. — 395. Unsavouriness.
396. Sweetness. — 397. Sourness.

4. *Odour* ..
398. Odour. — 399. Inodorousness.
400. Fragrance. — 401. Fetor.

5. *Sound* ..

(i.) *Sound in General.*
402. Sound. — 403. Silence.
404. Loudness. — 405. Faintness.

(ii.) *Specific Sounds.*
406. Snap. — 407. Roll.
408. Resonance. — 408*a*. Non-resonance.
409. Sibilation.
410. Stridor.
411. Cry. — 412. Ululation.

(iii.) *Musical Sounds.*
413. Melody. Concord. — 414. Discord.
415. Music.
416. Musician.
417. Musical Instruments.

(iv.) *Perception of Sound.*
418. Hearing. — 419. Deafness.

6. *Light* ...

(i.) *Light in General.*
420. Light. — 421. Darkness.
422. Dimness.
423. Luminary. — 424. Shade.
425. Transparency. — 426. Opacity.
427. Semitransparency.

(ii.) *Specific Light.*
428. Colour. — 429. Achromatism.
430. Whiteness. — 431. Blackness.
432. Gray. — 433. Brown.
434. Redness. — 435. Greenness.
436. Yellowness. — 437. Purple.
438. Blueness. — 439. Orange.
440. Variegation.

(iii.) *Perceptions of Light.*
441. Vision. — 442. Blindness.
443. Dimsightedness.
444. Spectator.
445. Optical Instruments.
446. Visibility. — 447. Invisibility.
448. Appearance. — 449. Disappearance.

## Class IV. INTELLECT

### Division (I.). Formation of Ideas

|  | | |
|---|---|---|
| I. Operations of Intellect in General | 450. Intellect. | 450*a*. Absence of Intellect. |
| | 451. Thought. | 452. Incogitancy. |
| | 453. Idea. | 454. Topic. |
| II. Precursory Conditions and Operations | 455. Curiosity. | 456. Incuriosity. |
| | 457. Attention. | 458. Inattention. |
| | 459. Care. | 460. Neglect. |
| | 461. Inquiry. | 462. Answer. |
| | 463. Experiment. | |
| | 464. Comparison. | |
| | 465. Discrimination. | 465*a*. Indiscrimination. |
| | 466. Measurement. | |
| III. Materials for Reasoning | 467. Evidence. | 468. Counter-evidence. |
| | 469. Qualification. | |
| | *Degrees of Evidence.* | |
| | 470. Possibility. | 471. Impossibility. |
| | 472. Probability. | 473. Improbability. |
| | 474. Certainty. | 475. Uncertainty. |
| IV. Reasoning Processes | 476. Reasoning. | 477. Intuition. Sophistry. |
| | 478. Demonstration. | 479. Confutation. |
| V. Results of Reasoning | 480. Judgement. | 481. Misjudgement. |
| | 480*a*. Discovery. | |
| | 482. Over-estimation. | 483. Under-estimation. |
| | 484. Belief. | 485. Unbelief. Doubt. |
| | 486. Credulity. | 487. Incredulity. |
| | 488. Assent. | 489. Dissent. |
| | 490. Knowledge. | 491. Ignorance. |
| | 492. Scholar. | 493. Ignoramus. |
| | 494. Truth. | 495. Error. |
| | 496. Maxim. | 497. Absurdity. |
| | *Faculties.* | |
| | 498. Intelligence. Wisdom. | 499. Imbecility. Folly. |
| | 500. Sage. | 501. Fool. |
| | 502. Sanity. | 503. Insanity. |
| | | 504. Madman. |
| VI. Extension of Thought — 1°. *To the Past* | 505. Memory. | 506. Oblivion. |
| VI. Extension of Thought — 2°. *To the Future* | 507. Expectation. | 508. Inexpectation. |
| | | 509. Disappointment. |
| | 510. Foresight. | |
| | 511. Prediction. | |
| | 512. Omen. | |
| | 513. Oracle. | |
| VII. Creative Thought | 514. Supposition. | |
| | 515. Imagination. | |

## Division (II.). Communication of Ideas

**I. Nature of Ideas Communicated**

516. Meaning. 517. Unmeaningness.
518. Intelligibility. 519. Unintelligibility.
520. Equivocalness.
521. Metaphor.
522. Interpretation. 523. Misinterpretation.
524. Interpreter.

**II. Modes of Communication**

525. Manifestation. 526. Latency.
527. Information. 528. Concealment.
529. Disclosure. 530. Ambush.
531. Publication.
532. News. 533. Secret.
534. Messenger.
535. Affirmation. 536. Negation.
537. Teaching. 538. Misteaching. 539. Learning.
540. Teacher. 541. Learner.
542. School.
543. Veracity. 544. Falsehood.
545. Deception.
546. Untruth.
547. Dupe. 548. Deceiver.
549. Exaggeration.

**III. Means of Communication**

*1°. Natural Means*

550. Indication.
551. Record. 552. Obliteration.
553. Recorder.
554. Representation. 555. Misrepresentation.
556. Painting.
557. Sculpture.
558. Engraving.
559. Artist.

*2°. Conventional Means*

*1. Language generally*

560. Language.
561. Letter.
562. Word. 563. Neology.
564. Nomenclature. 565. Misnomer.
566. Phrase.
567. Grammar. 568. Solecism.
569. Style.

*Qualities of Style.*

570. Perspicuity. 571. Obscurity.
572. Conciseness. 573. Diffuseness.
574. Vigour. 575. Feebleness.
576. Plainness. 577. Ornament.
578. Elegance. 579. Inelegance.

*2. Spoken Language*

580. Voice. 581. Aphony.
582. Speech. 583. Stammering.
584. Loquacity. 585. Taciturnity.
586. Allocution. 587. Response.
588. Interlocution. 589. Soliloquy.

*3. Written Language*

590. Writing. 591. Printing.
592. Correspondence. 593. Book.
594. Description.
595. Dissertation.
596. Compendium.
597. Poetry. 598. Prose.
599. The Drama.

## CLASS V. VOLITION

### Division (I.). INDIVIDUAL VOLITION

**I. VOLITION IN GENERAL**

1°. *Acts*....

| | |
|---|---|
| 600. Will. | 601. Necessity. |
| 602. Willingness. | 603. Unwillingness. |
| 604. Resolution. | 605. Irresolution. |
| 604*a*. Perseverance.<br>606. Obstinacy. | 607. Tergiversation. |
| | 608. Caprice. |
| 609. Choice. | 609*a*. Absence of Choice.<br>610. Rejection. |
| 611. Predetermination. | 612. Impulse. |
| 613. Habit. | 614. Desuetude. |

2°. *Causes*..

| | |
|---|---|
| 615. Motive. | 615*a*. Absence of Motive.<br>616. Dissuasion. |
| 617. Plea. | |

3°. *Objects*..

| | |
|---|---|
| 618. Good. | 619. Evil. |

**II. PROSPECTIVE VOLITION**........

1°. *Conceptional*..

| | |
|---|---|
| 620. Intention. | 621. Chance. |
| 622. Pursuit. | 623. Avoidance. |
| | 624. Relinquishment. |
| 625. Business. | |
| 626. Plan. | |
| 627. Method. | |
| 628. Mid-Course. | 629. Circuit. |
| 630. Requirement. | |

2°. *Subservience to Ends*...

1. *Actual Subservience.*

| | |
|---|---|
| 631. Instrumentality. | |
| 632. Means. | |
| 633. Instrument. | |
| 634. Substitute. | |
| 635. Materials. | |
| 636. Store. | |
| 637. Provision. | 638. Waste. |
| 639. Sufficiency. | |
| 641. Redundance. | 640. Insufficiency. |

2. *Degree of Subservience.*

| | |
|---|---|
| 642. Importance. | 643. Unimportance. |
| 644. Utility. | 645. Inutility. |
| 646. Expedience. | 647. Inexpedience. |
| 648. Goodness. | 649. Badness. |
| 650. Perfection. | 651. Imperfection. |
| 652. Cleanness. | 653. Uncleanness. |
| 654. Health. | 655. Disease. |
| 656. Salubrity. | 657. Insalubrity. |
| 658. Improvement. | 659. Deterioration. |
| 660. Restoration. | 661. Relapse. |
| 662. Remedy. | 663. Bane. |

3. *Contingent Subservience.*

| | |
|---|---|
| 664. Safety. | 665. Danger. |
| 666. Refuge. | 667. Pitfall. |
| 668. Warning. | |
| 669. Alarm. | |
| 670. Preservation. | |
| 671. Escape. | |
| 672. Deliverance. | |

|  |  |  |  |
|---|---|---|---|
| II. PROSPECTIVE VOLITION—*cont.* | 3°. *Precursory Measures* | 673. Preparation. | 674. Non-preparation. |
| | | 675. Essay. | |
| | | 676. Undertaking. | |
| | | 677. Use. | 678. Disuse. |
| | | | 679. Misuse. |
| III. ACTION | 1°. *Simple* | 680. Action. | 681. Inaction. |
| | | 682. Activity. | 683. Inactivity. |
| | | 684. Haste. | 685. Leisure. |
| | | 686. Exertion. | 687. Repose. |
| | | 688. Fatigue. | 689. Refreshment. |
| | | 690. Agent. | |
| | | 691. Workshop. | |
| | 2°. *Complex* | 692. Conduct. | |
| | | 693. Direction. | |
| | | 694. Director. | |
| | | 695. Advice. | |
| | | 696. Council. | |
| | | 697. Precept. | |
| | | 698. Skill. | 699. Unskilfulness. |
| | | 700. Proficient. | 701. Bungler. |
| | | 702. Cunning. | 703. Artlessness. |
| IV. ANTAGONISM | 1°. *Conditional* | 704. Difficulty. | 705. Facility. |
| | 2°. *Active* | 706. Hindrance. | 707. Aid. |
| | | 708. Opposition. | 709. Co-operation. |
| | | 710. Opponent. | 711. Auxiliary. |
| | | 712. Party. | |
| | | 713. Discord. | 714. Concord. |
| | | 715. Defiance. | |
| | | 716. Attack. | 717. Defence. |
| | | 718. Retaliation. | 719. Resistance. |
| | | 720. Contention. | 721. Peace. |
| | | 722. Warfare. | 723. Pacification. |
| | | 724. Mediation. | |
| | | 725. Submission. | |
| | | 726. Combatant. | |
| | | 727. Arms. | |
| | | 728. Arena. | |
| V. RESULTS OF ACTION | | 729. Completion. | 730. Non-completion. |
| | | 731. Success. | 732. Failure. |
| | | 733. Trophy. | |
| | | 734. Prosperity. | 735. Adversity. |
| | | 736. Mediocrity. | |

## Division (II.). INTERSOCIAL VOLITION

|  |  |  |
|---|---|---|
| I. GENERAL | 737. Authority. | 738. Laxity. |
| | 739. Severity. | 740. Lenity. |
| | 741. Command. | |
| | 742. Disobedience. | 743. Obedience. |
| | 744. Compulsion. | |
| | 745. Master. | 746. Servant. |
| | 747. Sceptre. | |
| | 748. Freedom. | 749. Subjection. |
| | 750. Liberation. | 751. Restraint. |
| | | 752. Prison. |
| | 753. Keeper. | 754. Prisoner. |
| | 755. Commission. | 756. Abrogation. |
| | | 757 Resignation. |
| | 758. Consignee. | |
| | 759. Deputy. | |

II. Special

760. Permission. 761. Prohibition.
762. Consent.
763. Offer. 764. Refusal.
765. Request. 766. Deprecation.
767. Petitioner.

III. Conditional

768. Promise. 768*a*. Release.
769. Compact.
770. Conditions.
771. Security.
772. Observance. 773. Non-observance.
774. Compromise.

IV. Possessive Relations

1°. *Property in General*

775. Acquisition. 776. Loss.
777. Possession. 777*a*. Exemption.
778. Participation.
779. Possessor.
780. Property.
781. Retention. 782. Relinquishment.

2°. *Transfer of Property*

783. Transfer.
784. Giving. 785. Receiving.
786. Apportionment.
787. Lending. 788. Borrowing.
789. Taking. 790. Restitution.
791. Stealing.
792. Thief.
793. Booty.

3°. *Interchange of Property*

794. Barter.
795. Purchase. 796. Sale.
797. Merchant.
798. Merchandise.
799. Mart.

4°. *Monetary Relations*

800. Money.
801. Treasurer.
802. Treasury.
803. Wealth. 804. Poverty.
805. Credit. 806. Debt.
807. Payment. 808. Non-payment.
809. Expenditure. 810. Receipt.
811. Accounts.
812. Price. 813. Discount.
814. Dearness. 815. Cheapness.
816. Liberality. 817. Economy.
818. Prodigality. 819. Parsimony.

---

## Class VI. AFFECTIONS

I. AFFECTIONS GENERALLY

820. Affections.
821. Feeling.
822. Sensibility. 823. Insensibility.
824. Excitation.
825. Excitability. 826. Inexcitability.

## II. PERSONAL

| | | |
|---|---|---|
| 1°. PASSIVE | 827. Pleasure. | 828. Pain. |
| | 829. Pleasureableness. | 830. Painfulness. |
| | 831. Content. | 832. Discontent.<br>833. Regret. |
| | 834. Relief. | 835. Aggravation. |
| | 836. Cheerfulness. | 837. Dejection. |
| | 838. Rejoicing. | 839. Lamentation. |
| | 840. Amusement. | 841. Weariness. |
| | 842. Wit. | 843. Dulness. |
| | 844. Humorist. | |
| 2°. DISCRIMINATIVE | 845. Beauty. | 846. Ugliness. |
| | 847. Ornament. | 848. Blemish. |
| | | 849. Simplicity. |
| | 850. Taste. | 851. Vulgarity. |
| | 852. Fashion. | |
| | | 853. Ridiculousness. |
| | | 854. Fop. |
| | | 855. Affectation. |
| | | 856. Ridicule. |
| | | 857. Laughing-stock. |
| 3°. PROSPECTIVE | 858. Hope. | 859. Hopelessness.<br>860. Fear. |
| | 861. Courage. | 862. Cowardice. |
| | 863. Rashness. | 864. Caution. |
| | 865. Desire. | 866. Indifference. |
| | | 867. Dislike. |
| | | 868. Fastidiousness. |
| | | 869. Satiety. |
| 4°. CONTEMPLATIVE | 870. Wonder. | 871. Expectance. |
| | 872. Prodigy. | |
| 5°. EXTRINSIC | 873. Repute. | 874. Disrepute. |
| | 875. Nobility. | 876. Commonalty. |
| | 877. Title. | |
| | 878. Pride. | 879. Humility. |
| | 880. Vanity. | 881. Modesty. |
| | 882. Ostentation. | |
| | 883. Celebration. | |
| | 884. Boasting. | |
| | 885. Insolence. | 886. Servility. |
| | 887. Blusterer. | |

## III. SYMPATHETIC

| | | |
|---|---|---|
| 1°. SOCIAL | 888. Friendship. | 889. Enmity. |
| | 890. Friend. | 891. Enemy. |
| | 892. Sociality. | 893. Seclusion. |
| | 894. Courtesy. | 895. Discourtesy. |
| | 896. Congratulation. | |
| | 897. Love. | 898. Hate. |
| | 899. Favourite. | |
| | | 900. Resentment. |
| | | 901. Irascibility. |
| | | 901*a*. Sullenness. |
| | 902. Endearment. | |
| | 903. Marriage. | 904. Celibacy.<br>905. Divorce. |

| | | |
|---|---|---|
| 2°. Diffusive | 906. Benevolence. | 907. Malevolence. |
| | | 908. Malediction. |
| | | 909. Threat. |
| | 910. Philanthropy. | 911. Misanthropy. |
| | 912. Benefactor. | 913. Evil doer. |
| 3°. Special | 914. Pity. | 914a. Pitilessness. |
| | 915. Condolence. | |
| 4°. Retrospective | 916. Gratitude. | 917. Ingratitude. |
| | 918. Forgiveness. | 919. Revenge. |
| | | 920. Jealousy. |
| | | 921. Envy. |

## IV. MORAL

| | | |
|---|---|---|
| 1°. Obligations | 922. Right. | 923. Wrong. |
| | 924. Dueness. | 925. Undueness. |
| | 926. Duty. | 927. Dereliction. |
| | | 927a. Exemption. |
| 2°. Sentiments | 928. Respect. | 929. Disrespect. |
| | | 930. Contempt. |
| | 931. Approbation. | 932. Disapprobation. |
| | 933. Flattery. | 934. Detraction. |
| | 935. Flatterer. | 936. Detractor. |
| | 937. Vindication. | 938. Accusation. |
| 3°. Conditions | 939. Probity. | 940. Improbity. |
| | | 941. Knave. |
| | 942. Disinterestedness. | 943. Selfishness. |
| | 944. Virtue. | 945. Vice. |
| | 946. Innocence. | 947. Guilt. |
| | 948. Good Man. | 949. Bad Man. |
| | 950. Penitence. | 951. Impenitence. |
| | 952. Atonement. | |
| 4°. Practice | 953. Temperance. | 954. Intemperance. |
| | | 954a. Sensualist. |
| | 955. Asceticism. | |
| | 956. Fasting. | 957. Gluttony. |
| | 958. Sobriety. | 959. Drunkenness. |
| | 960. Purity. | 961. Impurity. |
| | | 962. Libertine. |
| 5°. Institutions | 963. Legality. | 964. Illegality. |
| | 965. Jurisprudence. | |
| | 966. Tribunal. | |
| | 967. Judge. | |
| | 968. Lawyer. | |
| | 969. Lawsuit. | |
| | 970. Acquittal. | 971. Condemnation. |
| | 973. Reward. | 972. Punishment. |
| | | 974. Penalty. |
| | | 975. Scourge. |

## RELIGIOUS

| | | |
|---|---|---|
| 1°. Superhuman Beings and Regions | 976. Deity. | |
| | 977. Angel. | 978. Satan. |
| | 979. Jupiter. | 980. Demon. |
| | 981. Heaven. | 982. Hell. |
| 2°. Doctrines | 983. Theology. | |
| | 983a. Orthodoxy. | 984. Heterodoxy. |
| | 985. Revelation. | 986. Pseudo-revelation. |
| 3°. Sentiments | 987. Piety. | 988. Impiety. |
| | | 989. Irreligion. |

## SYNOPSIS OF CATEGORIES

| | | |
|---|---|---|
| 4°. ACTS | 990. Worship. | 991. Idolatry |
| | | 992. Sorcery. |
| | | 993. Spell. |
| | | 994. Sorcerer. |
| 5°. INSTITUTIONS | 995. Churchdom. | |
| | 996. Clergy. | 997. Laity. |
| | 998. Rite. | |
| | 999. Canonicals. | |
| | 1000. Temple. | |

## ABBREVIATIONS, &c.

| | | |
|---|---|---|
| **Adj.** | *adj.* | Adjectives, Participles, and Words having the power of Adjectives. |
| **Adv.** | *adv.* | Adverbs and Adverbial Expressions. |
| **Int.** | *int.* | Interjections. |
| **Phr.** | *phr.* | Phrases. |
| **V.** | *v.* | Verbs. |

The numbers are those of the headings, or Categories.

Words in italics within parentheses are not intended to explain the meanings of the words which precede them, but to indicate the nature of allied group of words under the numbers which follow them.

See also the Editor's Preface, p. xi.

# THESAURUS

OF

# WORDS AND PHRASES

## CLASS I

## Words expressing ABSTRACT RELATIONS

## Section I. EXISTENCE

### 1°. Being, in the Abstract

**1. Existence.—N.** existence, being, entity, *ens, esse,* subsistence, quiddity.

reality, realness, actuality; positiveness &c. *adj.*; fact, matter of fact, sober reality; truth &c. 494; actual existence.

presence &c. (*existence in space*) 186; coexistence &c. 120.

stubborn fact; not a -dream &c. 515; no joke.

substance, essence, prime constituent, hypostatis.

[Science of existence], ontology.

**V.** exist, be; have -being &c. *n.*; subsist, live, breathe, stand, obtain, be the case; occur &c. (*event*) 151; have place, rank, prevail; find oneself, pass the time, vegetate.

consist in, lie in, reside in, inhere in.

come into -existence &c. *n.*; arise &c. (*begin*) 66; come forth &c. (*appear*) 446.

become &c. (*be converted*) 144; bring into existence &c. 161; coexist, preexist, endure &c. 141.

**Adj.** existing &c. *v.*; existent, subsistent, under the sun; in -existence &c. *n.*; extant; afloat, on foot, current, prevalent, rife, in force, -vogue; undestroyed.

real, actual, positive, absolute; true &c. 494; substan-tial, -tive; self-existing, -ent.

**2. Inexistence.—N.** inexistence; nonexistence, -subsistence; nonentity, *nil*; negativeness &c. *adj.*; nullity; nihil-ity, -ism; *tabula rasa,* blank; abeyance; absence &c. 187; no such thing &c. 4; nothingness, oblivion, *non esse.*

annihilation; extinction &c. (*destruction*) 162.

**V.** not -exist &c. 1; have no -existence &c. 1; be null and void; cease to -exist &c. 1; pass away, perish; be –, become extinct &c. *adj.*; die out; disappear &c. 449; melt away, dissolve, leave not a rack behind, leave no trace; go, be no more; die &c. 360.

annihilate, render null, nullify; abrogate &c. 756; destroy &c. 162; take away; remove &c. (*displace*) 185.

**Adj.** inexistent, non-existent &c. 1; negative, blank, null and void; missing, omitted; absent &c. 187; visionary &c. 515.

unreal, potential, virtual; baseless, *in nubibus*; unsubstantial &c. 4; vain.

un-born, -created, -begotten, -conceived, -produced, -made.

perished, annihilated &c. *v.*; extinct, exhausted, gone, lost, departed; defunct &c. (*dead*) 360; *spurlos versenkt.*

fabulous, ideal &c. (*imaginary*) 515; supposititious &c. 514.

**Adv.** negatively, virtually, &c. *adj.*

well-founded, -grounded; un-ideal, -imagined; not -potential &c. 2.

**Adv.** actually &c. *adj.*; in -fact, - point of fact, - reality; indeed; *de* -, *ipso-facto*.

## 2°. Being, in the Concrete

**3. Substantiality.—N.** substantiality, *hypostasis*; person, thing, object, article; something, a being, an existence; creature, body, substance, flesh and blood, stuff, *substratum*; matter &c. 316; physical nature.

[Totality of existences], world &c. 318; *plenum*.

**Adj.** substan-tive, -tial, concrete; hypostatic; personal, bodily; tangible &c. (*material*) 316; real, corporeal, evident.

**Adv.** substantially &c. *adj.*; bodily, essentially.

**4. Unsubstantiality.—N.** un-, in-substantiality; nothingness, nihility.

nothing, naught, *nil*, nullity, zero, cipher, no one, nobody; never -, ne'er -a one; no such thing, none in the world; nothing -whatever, - at all, - on earth; not a -particle &c. (*smallness*) 32; all -talk, - moonshine, - stuff and nonsense, matter of no import.

thing of naught, man of straw, John Doe and Richard Roe; *nominis umbra*, nonentity, figurehead, lay figure; flash in the pan, *vox et præterea nihil*.

shadow; phantasm, phantom &c. (*fallacy of vision*) 443; dream &c. (*imagination*) 515; *ignis fatuus* &c. (luminary) 423; 'such stuff as dreams are made on'; air, thin air; bubble &c. 353; 'baseless fabric of a vision'; mockery.

hollowness, blank; vacuity, void &c. (*absence*) 187.

inanity, fool's paradise, fatuity, stupidity, emptiness of mind.

**V.** vanish, evaporate, fade, sink, fly -, die -, melt- away, dissolve, disappear &c. 449, become extinct, become invisible.

**Adj.** unsubstantial; fleeting; base-, ground-less; ungrounded; without -, having no- foundation.

visionary &c. (*imaginary*) 515; immaterial &c. 317; spectral &c. 980; dreamy; shadowy; ethereal, airy, imponderable, tenuous, vague.

vacant, vacuous; empty &c. 187; eviscerated; blank, hollow; nominal; null; inane.

**Phr.** there's nothing in it.

## 3°. Formal Existence

### *Internal conditions*

**5. Intrinsicality.—N.** intrinsicality, inbeing, inherence, inhesion, immanence; subjectiveness; *ego*; essence; essentialness &c. *adj.*; essential part, essential stuff, substance, quintessence, incarnation, quiddity, gist, pith, core, kernel, marrow, sap, life-blood, backbone, heart, soul, life, flower; important part &c. (*importance*) 642.

principle, nature, constitution, character, ethos, type, quality, crasis, *diathesis*.

habit; temper, -ament; spirit, humour, grain, disposition, streak, tendency &c. 176.

### *External conditions*

**6. Extrinsicality.—N.** extrinsicality, objectiveness, *non ego*; extraneousness &c. 57; accident; letter of the law.

**Adj.** derived from without; objective; extrin-sic, -sical; extraneous &c. (*foreign*) 57; modal, adventitious, additional, supervenient, fortuitous; a-, ad-scititious; incidental, casual, accidental, unessential, non-essential, accessory.

implanted, ingrafted, instilled, inculcated.

outward &c. (*external*) 220.

**Adv.** extrinsically &c. *adj.*

endowment, capacity; capability &c. (*power*) 157; moods, declensions, features, aspects; peculiarities &c. (*specialty*) 79; idiosyncrasy; idiocrasy; diagnostics.

**V.** be –, run- in the blood; be born so; be -intrinsic &c. *adj.*

**Adj.** derived from within, subjective; idiocratic, idiosyncratic, intrin-sic, -sical; fundamental, cardinal, normal; inherent, essential, natural; in-nate, -born, -bred, -dwelling, -grained, -wrought; radical, incarnate, thoroughbred, hereditary, inherited, immanent; congen-ital, -ite; connate, running in the blood; coeval with birth, genetic, ingenerate, -genite; indigenous; in the -grain &c. *n.*; bred in the bone, instinctive; inward, internal &c. 221; to the manner born; virtual.

characteristic &c. (*special*) 79, (*indicative*) 550; invariable, incurable, ineradicable, fixed, settled, constant, unchanging.

**Adv.** intrinsically &c. *adj.*; at bottom, in the main, in effect, essentially, practically, virtually, substantially, *au fond*; fairly.

### 4°. Modal Existence

*Absolute*

**7. State.—N.** state, condition, category, estate, lot, case, trim, mood, pickle, plight &c. 735; temper; aspect &c. (*appearance*) 448.

constitution, habitude, *diathesis*; frame, fabric &c. 329; stamp, set, fit, mould.

mode, modality, schesis; fettle; form &c. (*shape*) 240.

tone, tenor, turn; trim, guise, fashion, light, complexion, style, character.

**V.** be in –, possess –, enjoy –, labour under- a -state &c. *n.*; be on a footing, do, fare; come to pass.

**Adj.** conditional, modal, formal; structural, organic.

**Adv.** conditionally &c. *adj.*; as -the matter stands, – things are; such being the case &c. 8.

*Relative*

**8. Circumstance.—N.** circumstance, situation, phase, position, posture, attitude, place, point; terms; *régime*; footing, standing, status.

occasion, juncture, conjuncture; contingency &c. (*event*) 151.

predicament; emergen-ce, -cy; exigency, crisis, pinch, pass, push; turning point; crossroads.

bearings, how the land lies.

**Adj.** circumstantial; given, conditional, provisional; critical; modal; contingent, incidental; adventitious &c. (*extrinsic*) 6.

**Adv.** in the circumstances &c. *n.*, under the conditions &c. 7; thus, in such wise.

accordingly; that –, such- being the case; that being so, since, seeing that.

as matters stand; as -things, – times- go.

conditionally, provided, if, in case; if -so, – so be, – it be so; if it so -happen, – turn out; in the event of; in such a -contingency, – case, – event; provisionally, unless, without.

according to -circumstances, – the occasion; as it may -happen, – turn out, – be; as the -case may be, – wind blows; *pro re natâ*.

## Section II. RELATION

### 1°. Absolute Relation

**9. Relation.—N.** relation, bearing, reference, connection, apposition, interconnection, concern, cognation; applicability, appositeness; correlation

**10.** [Want, or absence of relation.] **Irrelation.—N.** irrelation, dissociation; inapplicability; inconnection; multifariousness; disconnection &c. (*dis-*

&c. 12; analogy; similarity &c. 17; affinity, intimacy, friendship; homology, alliance, homogeneity, association, rapport; approximation &c. (*nearness*) 197; filiation &c. (*consanguinity*) 11; interest; relevancy &c. 23; relationship, relative position; relativity; interrelation &c. 12.

comparison &c. 464; ratio, proportion.

link, tie, bond, bond of union.

**V.** be-related &c. *adj.*; have a relation &c. *n.*; relate –, refer- to; bear upon, regard, concern, touch, affect, have to do with; pertain –, belong –, appertain- to; have respect to; answer to; interest.

bring -into relation with, – to bear upon; connect, associate, draw a parallel; link &c. 43.

**Adj.** relative; correlative &c. 12; cognate; relating to &c. *v.*; relative to, in relation with, referable *or* referrible to; belonging to &c. *v.*; appurtenant to, in common with.

related, connected; implicated, associated, affiliated, akin, allied to; collateral, cognate, congenial, kindred, affinitive, *en rapport*, in touch with.

approxima-tive, -ting; approaching; proportion-al, -ate, -able; allusive, comparable.

in the same -category &c. 75; like &c. 17; relevant &c. (*apt*) 23.

**Adv.** relatively &c. *adj.*; pertinently &c. 23.

thereof; as -to, – for, – respects, – regards; about; concerning &c. *v.*; anent; relating –, as relates- to; with -relation, – reference, – respect, – regard- to; in respect of; while speaking –, *à propos*- of; in connection with; by the -way, – by; whereas; for –, in -as much as; in point of, as far as; on the -part, – score- of; *quoad hoc*; *pro re natâ*; under the -head &c. (*class*) 75- of; in the matter of, *in re*.

**Phr.** 'thereby hangs a tale.'

*junction*) 44; inconsequence, independence; incommensurability; irreconcilableness &c. (*disagreement*) 24; heterogeneity; unconformity &c. 83; irrelevancy, impertinence, *nihil ad rem*; intrusion &c. 24.

**V.** have no -relation &c. 9 to, – bearing upon, – concern &c. 9 with, – business with; not -concern &c. 9; have -nothing to do with, – no business there; intrude, &c. 24.

bring –, drag –, haul –, lug- in head and shoulders.

**Adj.** irrelative, irrespective, unrelated, irrelated; arbitrary; independent, unallied; un-, dis-connected; adrift, isolated, insular; extraneous, strange, alien, foreign, outlandish, exotic.

not comparable, incommensurable, heterogeneous; unconformable &c. 83.

irrelevant; rambling &c. 279; inapplicable; not -pertinent, – to the purpose; impertinent, inapposite, beside the mark, *à propos de bottes*; away from –, foreign to –, beside- the -purpose, – question, – transaction, – point; misplaced &c. (*intrusive*) 24.

remote, far fetched, out of the way, forced, neither here nor there, quite another thing; detached, segregated, segregate.

multifarious; discordant &c. 24.

incidental, parenthetical, *obiter dictum*, episodic.

**Adv.** parenthetically &c. *adj.*; by the -way, – by; *en passant*, incidentally; irrespectively &c. *adj.*; without reference, – regard- to; in the abstract &c. 87; *a se*.

---

**11.** [Relations of kindred.] **Consanguinity.**—**N.** consanguinity, relationship, kindred, blood; parentage &c. (*paternity*) 166; filiation, affiliation; lineage, agnation, connection, cognation, alliance; family -connection, – tie; ties of blood; blood relationship; nepotism.

kins-man, -folk; people; kith and kin; rela-tion, -tive; connection; sib; next of kin; uncle, aunt, nephew, niece; cousin, -german; first –, second- cousin; cousin -once, – twice &c.- removed; near –, distant- relation; brother, sister, one's own flesh and blood.

family, patriarch, matriarch; fraternity; brother-, sister-, cousin-hood; race, stock, generation; sept &c. 166; stirps, side; strain; breed, clan, tribe.

V. be -related &c. *adj.* – to; claim -relationship &c. *n.*- with.

Adj. related, akin, consanguineous, matrilinear, patrilineal, of the blood, family, allied, collateral; cog-, ag-, con-nate; kindred; affiliated, affine; fraternal, avuncular.

intimately –, nearly –, closely –, remotely –, distantly- related, – allied; german.

**12.** [Double or reciprocal relation.] **Correlation.**—**N.** reciprocalness &c. *adj.*; recipro-city, -cality, -cation; mutuality, correlation, correspondence, interdependence; interchange &c. 148; exchange, barter; interrelation, interconnection; alternation, see-saw.

V. reciprocate, alternate; interchange &c. 148; exchange; counterchange; interact, correspond, mutualize, give and take.

Adj. reciprocal, mutual, commutual, correlative; alternate; interchangeable; international; correspondent, complementary, analogous.

Adv. *mutatis mutandis*; *vice versâ*; each other; by turns &c. 148; reciprocally &c. *adj.*; to and fro &c. 314.

**13. Identity.**—**N.** identity, sameness, oneness, ditto, homogeneity; unity, coincidence, coalescence; convertibility; equality &c. 27; selfness, self, oneself; identification.

monotony, tautology &c. (*repetition*) 104.

synonym.

fac-simile &c. (*copy*) 21; *alter ego* &c. (*similar*) 17; *ipsissima verba* &c. (*exactness*) 494; same; self –, very –, one and the- same; very –, actual- thing; no other.

V. be -identical &c. *adj.*; match, coincide, coalesce.

treat as –, render- -the same, –identical; identify; recognize the identity of.

Adj. identical; self, ilk; the -same &c. *n.*; self same; synonymous; one and the same.

coincid-, coalesc-ent, -ing; indistinguishable; one; equivalent &c. (*equal*) 27; much -the same, – of a muchness; unaltered.

Adv. identically &c. *adj.*; on all fours; *ibid-*, *-em*.

**14.** [Non-coincidence.] **Contrariety.**—**N.** contrariety, contrast, foil, antithesis, oppositeness; counterpole; contradiction; antagonism &c. (*opposition*) 708; counteraction &c. 179.

inversion &c. 218; the -opposite, – reverse, – inverse, – converse, – antipodes, – other extreme &c. 237.

antonym.

V. be -contrary &c. *adj.*; contrast with, oppose; differ *toto cœlo*.

invert, reverse, turn the tables &c. 218.

contra-dict, -vene; antagonize &c. 708.

Adj. contrar-y, -ious, -iant; opposite, counter, dead against; ad-, con-, reverse; opposed, antithetical, contrasted, antipodean, antagonistic, opposing; conflicting, inconsistent, contradictory, at cross purposes; negative; hostile &c. 708.

differing *toto cœlo*; diametrically opposite; as opposite as -black and white, – light and darkness, – fire and water, – the poles, as different as chalk from cheese; 'Hyperion to a satyr'; quite the -contrary, – reverse; no such thing, just the other way, *tout au contraire*.

Adv. contrarily &c. *adj.*; *contra*, contrariwise, *per contra*, on the contrary, nay rather; topsy-turvy; *vice versâ*; on the other hand &c. (*in compensation*) 30.

**15. Difference.**—**N.** difference, unlikeness; heterogeneity; vari-ance, -ation, -ety; diversity, dissimilarity &c. 18; disagreement &c. 24; disparity &c. (*inequality*) 28; distinction, contradistinction; distinctness; discrepancy, divergence, contrast &c. 18; nonconformity, incompatibility, antithesis.

discord &c. 713.

modification, moods and tenses.

nice –, fine –, delicate –, subtle- distinction; shade of difference, *nuance;* discrimination &c. 465; *differentia.*

different thing, something else, variant, apple off another tree, horse of another colour, another pair of shoes; this that or the other.

**V.** be -different &c. *adj.*; differ, vary, ablude, mismatch, contrast; diverge –, depart –, deviate- -from; divaricate; differ -*toto cœlo,* – *longo intervallo.*

disagree &c. 713.

vary, modify &c. (*change*) 140.

discriminate &c. 465.

**Adj.** differing &c. *v.*; different, diverse, divided, heterogeneous; distinguishable; varied, modified; divergent, incongruous, diversified, various; discrepant, dissentient, differential; divers, all manner of; variform &c. 81; discordant &c. 713.

other, another, not the same; unequal &c. 28; unmatched; widely apart.

distinctive, characteristic; discriminative; distinguishing.

**Adv.** differently &c. *adj.*

**Phr.** *il y a fagots et fagots; quot homines tot sententiæ;* one man's meat is another man's poison.

## 2°. Continuous Relation

**16. Uniformity.** — **N.** uniformity; homogene-ity, -ousness; continuity, stability, consistency; connatural-ity, -ness; homology; accordance; conformity &c. 82; agreement &c. 23.

regularity, constancy, even tenor, routine; monotony, evenness, sameness, dead level; steadiness, equability, unity.

**V.** be -uniform &c. *adj.*; accord with &c. 23; run through.

become -uniform &c. *adj.*; conform to &c. 82.

render uniform &c. *adj.*; assimilate, level, smooth, dress.

**Adj.** uniform; homo-geneous, -logous; of a piece, consistent, steady; connatural; monotonous, changeless, dreary, even, invariable, equable, level, regular, stereotyped, unchanged, unvarying; methodical &c. 60; habitual &c. 613.

**Adv.** uniformly &c. *adj.*; uniformly with &c. (*conformably*) 82; in harmony with &c. (*agreeing*) 23; in a -rut, – groove.

always, ever &c. 112; invariably, without exception, never otherwise; by clock-work; endlessly &c. 112.

**Phr.** *ab uno disce omnes.*

**16a.** [Absence or want of uniformity.] **Non-uniformity.** — **N.** diversity irregularity, unevenness; multiformity &c. 81; unconformity &c. 83; roughness &c. 256; heterogeneity, heteromorphism.

**Adj.** diversified, varied, irregular, uneven, rough &c. 256; multifarious; multiform &c. 81; of various kinds; all -manner, – sorts, – kinds- of.

**Adv.** in all manner of ways, here there and everywhere.

---

## 3°. Partial Relation

**17. Similarity.**—**N.** similarity, resemblance, likeness, similitude, sem-

**18. Dissimilarity.**—**N.** dissimil-arity, -itude; unlikeness, diversity, disparity

blance; affinity, approximation, parallelism; parity; agreement &c. 23; ana-logy, -logicalness; correspondence, equality &c.

connatural-ness, -ity; brotherhood, family likeness.

alliteration, rhyme, pun.

repetition &c. 104; sameness &c. (*identity*) 13; uniformity &c. 16.

analogue; the like; match, *pendant*, fellow, companion, pair, mate, twin, double, counterpart, brother, sister; one's second self, *alter ego*, chip of the old block, *par nobile fratrum, Arcades ambo*, birds of a feather, *et hoc genus omne.*

parallel; simile; type &c. (*metaphor*) 521; image &c. (*representation*) 554; photograph; close –, striking –, speaking –, faithful &c. *adj.* – likeness, – resemblance.

**V.** be -similar &c. *adj.*; look like, resemble, bear resemblance, favour; savour –, smack- of; approximate; parallel, match, rhyme with; take after; imitate &c. 19; run in pairs.

render -similar &c. *adj.*; assimilate, approximate, bring near; connaturalize, make alike; rhyme, pun.

**Adj.** similar; resembling &c. *v.*; like, alike; twin.

analog-ous, -ical; parallel, of a piece; such as, so.

connatural, congeneric, allied to; corresponding, cognate; akin to &c. (*consanguineous*) 11.

approximate, much the same, near, close, something like, such like; a show of; mock, *pseudo*, simulating, representing.

exact &c. (*true*) 494; lifelike, faithful, realistic; true to -nature, – the life; the -very image – picture- of; for all the world like, *comme deux gouttes d'eau*; as like as -two peas, – it can stare; *instar omnium*, cast in the same mould, ridiculously like.

**Adv.** as if, so to speak; as –, as if- it were; *quasi*, just as, *veluti in speculum.*

dissemblance; divergence, inequality, difference &c. 15; novelty; variation, variety, originality, disguise.

**V.** be -unlike &c. *adj.*; vary &c. (*differ*) 15; bear no resemblance to, differ *toto cœlo.*

render -unlike &c. *adj.*; vary &c. (*diversify*) 140.

**Adj.** dissimilar, unlike, disparate; of a different kind &c. (*class*) 75; unmatched, unique; new, novel; unprecedented &c. 83; original.

nothing of the kind; no such –, quite another- thing; far from it, other than, cast in a different mould, *tertium quid*, as like a dock as a daisy, 'very like a whale'; as different as -chalk from cheese, – Macedon and Monmouth; *lucus a non lucendo.*

diversified &c. 16*a*.

**Adv.** otherwise, *alias.*

---

**19. Imitation.—N.** imitation; copying &c. *v.*; transcription; repetition, mimeograph, mimeotype, duplication, reduplication; quotation; reproduction.

mockery, mimicry, mime, simulation, impersonation; representation &c. 554; semblance, simulacrum; pretence; copy &c. 21; assimilation.

paraphrase, parody &c. 21.

plagiarism; forgery &c. (*falsehood*) 544.

imitator, echo, cuckoo, parrot, ape, monkey, mocking-bird, mimic, impersonator; copyist.

**V.** imitate, copy, mirror, reflect, reproduce, repeat, borrow; do like, echo, re-echo, catch; transcribe; match, parallel.

**20. Non-Imitation.—N.** no imitation, genuineness, originality; creativeness.

**Adj.** unimitated, uncopied; unmatched, unparalleled; inimitable &c. 33; *unique*, original, primordial, primary, pristine, underived, first-hand, archetypal, prototypal.

---

mock, take off, mimic, ape, simulate, personate, impersonate; forge; act &c. (*drama*) 599; represent &c. 554; counterfeit, duplicate; portray, parody, travesty, caricature, burlesque.

follow –, tread- in the- -steps, – footsteps, – wake- of; pattern after, take pattern by; follow -suit, – the example of; walk in the shoes of, take a leaf out of another's book, strike in with; take –, model -after; emulate.

**Adj.** imitated &c. *v.*; mock, mimic; counterfeit, false, pseudo; modelled after, moulded on, paraphrastic; literal; imitative, apish; second-hand; imitable; sham &c. 545.

**Adv.** literally, to the letter, strictly, precisely, *verbatim, literatim, sic, totidem verbis,* word for word, *mot à mot.*

**Phr.** like master like man.

**20a. Variation.—N.** variation; alteration &c. (*change*) 140.
modification, moods and tenses; modulation.
divergency &c. 291; deviation &c. 279; aberration; innovation.
**V.** vary &c. (*change*) 140; deviate &c. 279; diverge &c. 291.
**Adj.** varied &c. *v.*; modified; dissimilar &c. 18; diversified &c. 16*a*.

**21.** [Result of imitation.] **Copy.—N.** copy, fac-simile, counterpart, *effigies,* effigy, symbol, image, form, likeness, similitude, semblance, resemblance, cast, electrotype, stereotype, tracing, ectype; imitation &c. 19; model, representation, adumbration, study; counterfeit presentment, portrait &c. (*representment*) 554.

duplicate; transcript, -ion; reflex, -ion; shadow, echo; chip of the old block; reprint, reproduction, casting, engraving, replica; transfer; second edition &c. (*repetition*) 104; *réchauffé;* apograph, fair copy, revise.

parody, caricature, cartoon, burlesque, travesty, paraphrase.

servile -copy, – imitation; counterfeit &c. (*deception*) 545; *pasticcio.*

**Adj.** faithful; lifelike &c. (*similar*) 17.

**22.** [Thing copied.] **Prototype.—N.** prototype, original, model, pattern, founding, precedent, standard, scantling, type, arche-, anti-type; protoplast, copy-book, module, exemplar, example, ensample, specimen; paradigm; guide; templet; lay-figure.

text, copy, manuscript, MS., design; fugleman, keynote.

die, mould; matrix, engraving, last, plasm; pro-, proto-plasm; mint; seal, punch, *intaglio,* negative, stamp.

**V.** be –, set- an example; set a copy; standardize.

### 4°. General Relation

**23. Agreement. — N.** agreement; ac-cord, -cordance; unison, harmony, syntony; concord &c. 714; concordance, concert, understanding, convention, *entente -cordiale, consortium,* consensus of opinion, pact, mutual understanding, unanimity.

conformity &c. 82; conformance; uniformity &c. 16; consonance, consentaneousness, consistency; congruity, -ence; keeping; congeniality; correspondence, concinnity, parallelism, apposition, union.

fitness, aptness &c. *adj.*; relevancy;

**24. Disagreement. — N.** disagreement; dis-cord, -cordance; disunion, dissonance, dissidence, discrepancy· unconformity &c. 83; incongru-ity, -ence; discongruity, *mésalliance, oxymoron;* jarring &c. *v.*; clash, collision, dissension &c. 713; conflict &c. (*opposition*) 708; controversy &c. 720; falling out, wrangle, argument.

disparity, mismatch, misfit, disproportion; disproportionateness &c. *adj.*; variance, divergence, repugnance.

unfitness &c. *adj.*; inaptitude, impropriety; inapplicability &c. *adj.*; in-

pertinen-ce, -cy; sortance; case in point; aptitude, coaptation, propriety, applicability, admissibility, commensurability, compatibility, suitability; cognation &c. (*relation*) 9.

adaptation, adjustment, arrangement, graduation, accommodation; reconcil-iation -ement; assimilation; attunement.

consent &c. (*assent*) 488; concurrence &c. 178; co-operation &c. 709.

right man in the right place, very thing; quite –, just- the thing.

**V.** be -accordant &c. *adj.*; agree, accord, harmonize; correspond, tally, respond; meet, suit, fit, befit, do, adapt itself to; fall in –, chime in –, square –, quadrate –, consort –, comport- with; dovetail, assimilate; fit like a glove; fit to a -tittle, – T; match &c. 17; become one.

consent &c. (*assent*) 488.

render -accordant &c. *adj.*; fit, suit, adapt, accommodate; graduate; adjust &c. (*render equal*) 27; dress, regulate, readjust; accord, harmonize, reconcile; fadge, dovetail, square.

**Adj.** agreeing, suiting &c. *v.*; in accord, accordant, concordant, consonant, congruous, consentaneous, correspondent, corresponding, homologous, congenial; becoming; harmonious, reconcilable, conformable; in -accordance, – harmony, – keeping, – unison, &c. *n.*- with; at one with, of one mind, of a piece; consistent, compatible, proportionate, answerable; commensurate; on all fours.

apt, apposite, pertinent, pat; to the -point, – purpose; happy, felicitous, germane, *ad rem*, in point, bearing upon, applicable, relevant, admissible.

fit, adapted, *in loco*, *à propos*, appropriate, seasonable, sortable, suitable, idoneous, deft; meet &c. (*expedient*) 646.

at home, in one's proper element.

**Adv.** *à propos of*; pertinently &c. *adj.*; *pro rata*.

**Phr.** *rem acu tetigisti*, the cap fits.

consistency, inconcinnity; irrelevancy &c. (*irrelation*) 10.

misjoin-ing, -der; syncretism, intrusion, interference; *concordia discors*.

fish out of water.

**V.** disagree; clash, quarrel, jar &c. (*discord*) 713; interfere, intrude, come amiss; not concern &c. 10; mismatch; *humano capiti cervicem jungere equinam*.

**Adj.** disagreeing &c. *v.*; discordant, discrepant; at -variance, – war; hostile, antagonistic, repugnant, factious, contradictory, dissentious, incompatible, irreconcilable, inconsistent with; unconformable, exceptional &c. 83; intrusive, incongruous; disproportionate, -ed; unharmonious; unconsonant; divergent, repugnant to.

inapt, unapt, inappropriate, inept, infelicitous, improper; unsuit-ed, -able; inapplicable; un-fit, -fitting, -befitting; unbecoming; ill-timed, ill-adapted, unseasonable, *mal à propos*, inadmissible; inapposite &c. (*irrelevant*) 10.

uncongenial; ill-assorted, -sorted, -matched; mis-matched, -mated, -joined, -placed; unaccommodating, irreducible, uncommensurable, unsympathetic.

out of -character, – keeping, – proportion, – joint, – tune, – place, – season, – its element; at -odds, – variance with.

**Adv.** in -defiance, – contempt, – spite-of; discordantly &c. *adj.*; *à tort et à travers*.

---

## Section III. QUANTITY

### 1°. Simple Quantity

**25.** [Absolute quantity.] **Quantity.**— **N.** quantity, magnitude; size &c. (*dimensions*) 192; amplitude, mass,

**26.** [Relative quantity.] **Degree.**— **N.** degree, grade, extent, measure, proportion, amount, ratio, stint, standard

amount, *quantum*, measure, measurement, substance, strength.

[Science of quantity.] Mathematics, Mathesis.

[Definite or finite quantity] arm-, hand-, mouth-, spoon-, thimble-, capful; stock, batch, lot, dose, ration, quotum, quota, pittance, driblet, part, portion &c. 51.

**Adj.** quantitative, some, any, more or less.

**Adv.** to the tune of.

height, pitch; reach, amplitude, range, scope, size, calibre; gradation, shade; tenor, compass; sphere, station, rank, standing; rate, way, sort.

point, mark, step, stage &c. (*term*) 71; intensity, strength &c. (*greatness*) 31.

**V.** compare, graduate, calibrate, measure.

**Adj.** comparative; gradual, shading off, gradational; within the bounds &c. (*limit*), 233.

**Adv.** by degrees, gradually, inasmuch, *pro tanto*; how-ever, -soever; step by step, bit by bit, little by little, inch by inch, drop by drop, gradatim; by -inches, – slow degrees, – little and little; in some -degree, – measure, to some extent; just a bit.

## 2°. Comparative Quantity

**27.** [Sameness of quantity or degree.] **Equality.—N.** equality, parity, co-extension, symmetry, balance, poise; evenness, monotony, level.

equivalence; equi-pollence, -poise, -librium, -ponderance; par, quits; not a pin to choose; distinction without a difference, six of one and half a dozen of the other; identity &c. 13; similarity &c. 17; isotropism; coequality.

equalization, equation; equilibration, co-ordination, adjustment, readjustment.

drawn -game, -battle, draw, stalemate; neck and neck race; tie, dead heat.

match, peer, compeer, equal, mate, fellow, brother; equivalent.

**V.** be -equal &c. *adj.*; equal, match, reach, keep pace with, run abreast; come –, amount –, come up- to; be –, lie- on a level with; balance; cope with; come to the same thing; level off.

render -equal &c. *adj.*; equalize, level, dress, balance, equate, handicap, give points, trim, adjust, poise; fit, accommodate; adapt &c. (*render accordant*) 23; strike a balance; establish –, restore- equality, – equilibrium; readjust; stretch on the bed of Procrustes.

**Adj.** equal, even, level, monotonous, coequal, symmetrical, coordinate; on a -par, – level, – footing- with; up to the mark; equiparent.

equivalent, tantamount; quits; homologous; synonymous &c. 522; resolvable into, convertible, much at one, as broad as long, neither more nor less; much the same –, the same thing –, as good- as; all -one, – the same; equi-pollent, -ponderant, -ponderous, -balanced; equalized &c. *v.*; drawn; half and half; isochronous; isoperimetrical.

**28.** [Difference of quantity or degree.] **Inequality.—N.** inequality; dis-, im-parity; odds; difference &c. 15; ill-balanced; unevenness; inclination of the balance, partiality; shortcoming; casting – make- weight; superiority &c. 33; inferiority &c. 34.

**V.** be -unequal &c. *adj.*; countervail; have –, give the advantage; turn the scale; kick the beam; topple, -over; over-match &c. 33; not come up to &c. 34.

**Adj.** unequal, uneven, disparate, partial; un-, over-balanced; top-heavy, lop-sided.

**Adv.** *haud passibus æquis.*

**Adv.** equally &c. *adj.*; *pari passu, ad eundem, cæteris paribus*; *in equilibrio*; to all intents and purposes.

**Phr.** it -comes, -adds up, – amounts- to the same thing.

**29. Mean.**—**N.** mean, medium, intermedium, average, run of the mill, normal, balance; mediocrity, generality, rule, ordinary -run, -ruck; golden mean &c. (*mid-course*) 628; middle &c. 68; compromise &c. 774; neutrality; middle point, middle course.

**V.** split the difference; take the -average &c. *n.*; reduce to a -mean &c. *n.*; strike a balance, pair off.

**Adj.** mean, intermediate; medial; middle &c. 68; average, normal, standard; neutral; middling, moderate.

mediocre, middle-class; *bourgeois*, commonplace &c. (*unimportant*) 643.

**Adv.** on an average, in the long run; taking -one with another, – all things together, – it for all in all; *communibus annis*, in round numbers.

**30. Compensation.**—**N.** compensation, equation; commutation; indemnification; compromise &c. 774; neutralization, nullification; counteraction &c. 179; reaction; measure for measure; retaliation &c. 718; equalization &c. 27; redemption, recoupment, recompense.

set-off, offset; make- casting-weight; counterpoise, equipoise, ballast; indemnity, reparation &c. 790; equivalent, *quid pro quo*; bribe, hush-money, tribute &c. 784; amends &c. (*atonement*) 952; counterclaim, counterbalance, equiponderance, countervail, cross demand.

**V.** make -amends, – compensation; com-pensate, -pense; indemnify; counter-act, -vail, -poise; equiponderate; balance; out-, over-, counter-balance; set off, offset, cancel; hedge, square, give and take; make up -for, – lee way; cover, fill up, neutralize, nullify; equalize &c. 27; make good; redeem &c. (*atone*) 952; recoup, pay &c. 973.

**Adj.** compensat-ing, -ory; amendatory, reparative, countervailing &c. *v.*; in the opposite scale; equivalent &c. (*equal*) 27.

**Adv.** in -return, – consideration; but, however, yet, still, notwithstanding; neverthe-, nath-less; although, though; al-, how-beit; in spite of, despite; maugre; at -all events, – any rate; be that as it may, for all that, even so, on the other hand, at the same time, *quoad minus*, *quand même*, however that may be; after all, – is said and done; taking one thing with another &c. (*average*) 29.

## Quantity by Comparison with a Standard

**31. Greatness.**—**N.** greatness &c. *adj.*; magnitude; size &c. (*dimensions*) 192; multitude &c. (*number*) 102; immensity, enormity; infinity &c. 105; might, strength, intensity, fulness; importance &c. 642; fame &c. 873.

great quantity, quantity, deal, power, sight, pot, volume, world; mass, heap &c. (*assemblage*) 72; stock &c. (*store*) 636; peck, bushel, load, cargo; cart –, wagon –, car –, truck –, ship- load; flood, spring tide; abundance &c. (*sufficiency*) 639.

principal –, chief –, main –, greater –,

**32. Smallness.**—**N.** smallness &c. *adj.*; littleness &c. (*small size*) 193; tenuity; paucity; fewness &c. (*small number*) 103; meanness, insignificance &c. (*unimportance*) 643; mediocrity, moderation.

small quantity, *modicum, minimum*; vanishing point; material point, electron, atom, particle, molecule, corpuscle, point, dab, fleck, speck, dot, mote, jot, iota, ace; *minutiæ*, details; look, thought, idea, *soupçon*, whit, tittle, shade, shadow; spark, *scintilla*, gleam; touch, cast; grain, scruple,

major –, best –, essential- part; bulk, mass &c. (*whole*) 50.

**V.** be -great &c. *adj.*; run high, soar, loom up, tower, bulk large, transcend; rise –, carry- to a great height; know no bounds; scale, overtop, ascend.

enlarge &c. (*increase*) 35, (*expand*) 194.

**Adj.** great; greater &c. 33; large, considerable, fair, above par; big, massive, huge &c. (*large in size*) 192; ample; abundant &c. (*enough*) 639; Herculean &c. 159; full, intense, strong, sound, passing, heavy, plenary, deep, high; signal, at its height, in the zenith.

world-wide, wide-spread, extensive; wholesale; many &c. 102.

goodly, noble, precious, mighty; sad, grave, serious; far gone, arrant, downright; utter, -most; crass, gross, arch, profound, intense, consummate; rank, unmitigated, red-hot, desperate; glaring, flagrant, stark staring; thorough-paced, -going; roaring, thumping, thundering, strapping, whacking; extraordinary; important &c. 642; unsurpassed &c. (*supreme*) 33; complete &c. 52.

vast, immense, enormous, extreme; inordinate, excessive, extravagant, exorbitant, outrageous, preposterous, unconscionable, swingeing, monstrous, over-grown; towering, stupendous, prodigious, astonishing, incredible; terrific, frightful; marvellous &c. (*wonder*) 870; grand.

unlimited &c. (*infinite*) 105; unapproachable, unutterable, indescribable, ineffable, unspeakable, inexpressible, beyond expression, fabulous.

un-diminished, -abated, -reduced, -restricted.

absolute, positive, stark, decided, unequivocal, essential, perfect, finished.

remarkable, of mark, marked, pointed, veriest; noticeable, uncommon, noteworthy, eminent &c. 873.

**Adv.** [in a positive degree] truly &c. (*truth*) 494; decidedly, unequivocally, purely, absolutely, seriously, essentially, fundamentally, radically, downright, in all conscience; for the most part, in the main.

[in a complete degree] entirely &c. (*completely*) 52; abundantly, &c. (*suf-*

granule, globule, minim, sup, sip, sop, spice, drop, droplet, sprinkling, dash, smack, tinge, tincture; inch, patch, scantling, dole; scrap, shred, tag, splinter, rag, tatter, cantlet, flitter, gobbet, mite, bit, morsel, crumb, seed, fritter, shive; snip, -pet; snick, snack, snatch, slip, scrag; chip, -ping; shiver, sliver, driblet, clipping, paring, shaving, hair.

nutshell; thimble-, spoon-, hand-, cap-, mouth-ful; fragment; fraction &c. (*part*) 51; drop in the ocean, drop in the bucket.

animalcule &c. 193.

trifle &c. (*unimportant thing*) 643; mere –, next to- nothing; hardly anything; just enough to swear by; the shadow of a shade.

finiteness, finite quantity.

**V.** be -small &c. *adj.*; lie in a nutshell.

diminish &c. (*decrease*) 36, (*contract*) 195.

**Adj.** small, little, tiny, weeny; diminutive &c. (*small in size*) 193; minute; minikin, fine, inconsiderable, dribbling, paltry &c. (*unimportant*) 643; faint &c. (*weak*) 160; slender, light, slight, scanty, scant, limited; meagre &c. (*insufficient*) 640; sparing; few &c. 103; low, so-so, middling, tolerable, no great shakes; below –, under- -par, – the mark; at a low ebb; half-way; moderate, modest; tender, subtle; petty, shallow, skin-deep.

inappreciable, evanescent, infinitesimal, homœopathic, very small, atomic, molecular, ultra-, -microscopic.

petty, shallow &c. 499.

mere, simple, sheer, stark, bare; near run.

**Adv.** [in a small degree] to a small extent, on a small scale; a -little, -wee, – tiny bit; slightly &c. *adj.*; imperceptibly; miserably, wretchedly; insufficiently &c. 640; imperfectly; faintly &c. 160; passably, pretty well, well enough.

[in a certain or limited degree] partially, in part; in –, to a certain degree; to a certain extent; comparatively; some, rather; in some -degree, -measure; some-thing, -what; simply, only, purely, merely; at –, at the- -least,

*ficiently*) 639; widely, far and wide.

[in a great or high degree] greatly &c. *adj.*; much, muckle, well, indeed, very, very much, a deal, no end of, most, not a little; pretty, – well; enough, in a great measure, passing richly; to a -large, – great, – gigantic- extent; on a large scale; so; never –, ever- so; ever so much; by wholesale; mightily, mighty, powerfully; with a witness, *ultra*, in the extreme, extremely, exceedingly, intensely, exquisitely, acutely, indefinitely, immeasurably; beyond -compare, – comparison, – measure, – all bounds; incalculably, infinitely.

[in a supreme degree] pre-eminently, superlatively &c. (*superiority*) 33.

[in a too great degree] immoderately, unduly, monstrously, grossly, preposterously, inordinately, exorbitantly, excessively, enormously, out of all proportion, with a vengeance.

[in a marked degree] particularly, remarkably, singularly, curiously, uncommonly, unusually, peculiarly, notably, signally, strikingly, pointedly, mainly, chiefly; famously, egregiously, prominently, glaringly, emphatically, strangely, wonderfully, amazingly, surprisingly, astonishingly, incredibly, marvellously, awfully, stupendously.

[in an exceptional degree] peculiarly &c. (*unconformity*) 83.

[in a violent degree] furiously &c. (*violence*) 173; severely, desperately, tremendously, extravagantly, confoundedly, deucedly, devilishly, with a vengeance; *à* –, *à toute- outrance*.

[in a painful degree] painfully, sadly, grossly, sorely, bitterly, piteously, grievously, miserably, cruelly, woefully, lamentably, shockingly, frightfully, dreadfully, fearfully, terribly, horribly, distressingly, balefully.

– most; ever so little, as little as may be, *tant soit peu*, in ever so small a degree; thus far, *pro tanto*, within bounds, in a manner, after a fashion.

almost, nearly, well nigh, short of, not quite, all but; near –, close- upon; *peu s'en faut*, near the mark; within an -ace, – inch- of; on the brink of; scarcely, hardly, barely, only just, no more than.

[in an uncertain degree] about, thereabouts, somewhere about, nearly, say; be the same -more, – little more- or less.

[in no degree] no- ways, – wise; not -at all, – in the least, – a bit, – a bit of it, – a whit, – a jot, – a shadow; in no -wise, – respect; by no -means, – manner of means; on no account, at no hand.

## Quantity by Comparison with a Similar Object

**33. Superiority.—N.** supremacy, superiority, majority; greatness &c. 31; advantage, odds, pull; preponderance, -ation; predominance, vantage ground, coign of vantage, prevalence, partiality; personal superiority; sovereignty &c. 737; nobility &c. (*rank*) 875; Triton among the minnows, *primus inter pares, nulli secundus*, superman; captain &c. 745.

supremacy, pre-eminence; primacy, lead, *maximum*; record; climax, crest, top; culmination &c. (*summit*) 210; transcendence; *ne plus ultra*; lion's share, Benjamin's mess; excess; bisque,

**34. Inferiority.—N.** inferiority, minority, subordinancy; shortcoming, deficiency; handicap; *minimum*; smallness &c. 32; imperfection, shabbiness.

[personal inferiority] commonalty &c. 876; subordinate, substitute, sub.

**V.** be -inferior &c. *adj.*; fall –, come- short of; not -pass, – come up to; want.

become –, render- smaller &c. (*decrease*) 36, (*contract*) 195; hide its diminished head, retire into the shade, yield the palm, play second fiddle, take a back seat; bow.

**Adj.** inferior, smaller; small &c. 32;

surplus &c. (*remainder*) 40, (*redundance*) 641.

**V.** be -superior &c. *adj.*; exceed, excel, transcend; out-do, -balance, -weigh, -rival, -Herod, outrank, pass, surpass, surmount, get ahead of; overtop, -ride, -pass, -balance, -weigh, -match; top, o'er-top, cap, beat, win out, cut out; beat hollow; outstrip &c. 303; eclipse, throw into the shade, take the shine out of, put one's nose out of joint; have the -upper hand, – whip hand of, – advantage; turn the scale, play first fiddle &c. (*importance*) 642; preponderate, predominate, prevail; precede, take precedence, come first; come to a head, culminate; beat &c. all others, bear the palm; break the record, take the cake.

become –, render- -larger, &c. (*increase*) 35, (*expand*) 194.

**Adj.** superior, greater, major, higher; exceeding &c. *v.*; great &c. 31; distinguished, *ultra*; vaulting; more than a match for.

supreme, greatest, maximal, maximum, utmost, paramount, preeminent, foremost, crowning; first-rate &c. (*important*) 642, (*excellent*) 648; unrivalled; peer-, match-less; none such, second to none, *sans pareil*; un-paragoned, -paralleled, -equalled, -approached, -surpassed; superlative, inimitable, *facile princeps*, incomparable, sovereign, without parallel, *nulli secundus*, *ne plus ultra*; beyond -compare, – comparison; culminating &c. (*topmost*) 210; transcendent, -ental; *plus royaliste que le Roi*.

increased &c. (*added to*) 35; enlarged &c. (*expanded*) 194.

**Adv.** beyond, more, over; over –, above- the mark; above par; upwards –, in advance- of; over and above; at the top of the scale, on the crest, at its height.

[in a superior or supreme degree] eminently, egregiously, preeminently, surpassing, prominently, superlatively, supremely, above all, of all things, the most, to crown all, *par excellence*, principally, especially, particularly, peculiarly, *a fortiori*, even, yea, still more.

**Phr.** 'we shall not look upon his like again.'

minor, less, lesser, deficient, minus, lower, subordinate, secondary; second-rate &c. (*imperfect*) 651; sub, subaltern; thrown into the shade; weighed in the balance and found wanting; not fit to hold a candle to.

least, smallest &c. (*see* little, small &c. 193); lowest.

diminished &c. (*decreased*) 36; reduced &c. (*contracted*) 195; unimportant &c. 643.

**Adv.** less; under –, below- -the mark, – par; at -the bottom of the scale, – a low ebb, – a disadvantage; short of, under.

---

## Changes in Quantity

**35. Increase—N.** increase, augmentation, addition, enlargement, extension; dilatation &c. (*expansion*) 194; multiplication; increment, accretion; accession &c. 37; production &c. 161; development, growth; aggrandizement, aggravation, intensification; rise; ascent &c. 305; anabasis; ex-aggeration, -acerbation; spread &c. (*dispersion*) 73; flood-, spring-, -tide; gain, produce, profit &c. 618; booty, plunder &c. 793.

**V.** increase, augment, add to, enlarge; dilate &c. (*expand*) 194; grow,

**36. Non-Increase, Decrease.—N.** decrease, diminution; lessening &c. *v.*; subtraction &c. 38; reduction, abatement, declension; shrinkage &c. (*contraction*) 195; coarctation; abridgment &c. (*shortening*) 201; extenuation.

subsidence, catabasis, wane, ebb-, neap-tide, decline; descent &c. 306; decrement, reflux, depreciation; erosion, wear and tear, deterioration &c. 659; anticlimax; mitigation &c. (*moderation*) 174.

**V.** decrease, diminish, lessen; abridge

wax, mount, swell, get ahead, gain strength; advance; run –, shoot- up; rise; ascend &c. 305; sprout &c. 194.

aggrandize; raise, exalt; deepen, heighten; lengthen; thicken; strengthen; intensify, enhance, inflate, magnify, double, redouble; multiply; aggravate, exaggerate; ex-asperate, -acerbate; add fuel to the flame, *oleum addere camino*, superadd &c. (*add*) 37; spread &c. (*disperse*) 73.

**Adj.** increased &c. *v.*; on the increase, undiminished; additional &c. (*added*) 37; increasing &c. *v.*; growing, crescent, intensive, cumulative.

**Adv.** *crescendo*, increasingly.

**Phr.** *vires acquirit eundo.*

---

&c. (*shorten*) 201; shrink &c. (*contract*) 195; drop –, fall –, tail- off; fall away, waste, wear, erode; wane, ebb, decline; descend &c. 306; subside; deliquesce, melt –, die -away; retire into the shade, hide its diminished head, fall to a low ebb, run low, languish, decay, crumble, consume away.

bate, abate, dequantitate; discount; depreciate; extenuate, lower, weaken, attenuate, fritter away; mitigate &c. (*moderate*) 174; belittle, minimize; dwarf, throw into the shade; keep down, reduce &c. 195; shorten &c. 201; subtract &c. 38.

**Adj.** unincreased &c. (*see* increase &c. 35); decreased &c. *v.*; decreasing &c. *v.*; on the -wane &c. *n.*; deliquescent.

**Adv.** *diminuendo*, *decrescendo*, decreasingly.

## 3°. Conjunctive Quantity

**37. Addition.—N.** addition, annexation, adjection; junction &c. 43; super-position, -addition, -junction, -fetation; accession, reinforcement; increase &c. 35; increment, supplement; accompaniment &c. 88; interposition &c. 228; insertion &c. 300; summation &c. 85; adjunct &c. 39.

**V.** add, annex, adject, affix, attach, superadd, subjoin, superpose; clap –, saddle- on; tack to, postfix, append, tag; ingraft; saddle with; sprinkle; introduce &c. (*interpose*) 228; insert &c. 300.

become added, accrue; ad-, supervene; add up &c. 85.

reinforce, strengthen, swell the ranks of; augment &c. 35.

**Adj.** added &c. *v.*; additional; supplement, -al, -ary; suppletory, subjunctive; adjec-, adsci-, asci-titious; additive, extra, spare, further, fresh, more, new, ulterior, other, auxiliary, supernumerary, accessory.

**Adv.** in addition, more, plus, extra; and, also, likewise, too, furthermore, further, item; and -also, – eke; else, besides, to boot, *et cætera*; &c.; and so -on, – forth; into the bargain, *cum multis aliis*, over and above, moreover.

with, withal; including, inclusive, as well as, not to mention, let

**38. Non-Addition. Subduction.—N.** sub-traction, -duction; deduction, retrenchment; removal; ab-, sub-lation; abstraction &c. (*taking*) 789; garbling &c. *v.*; mutilation, detruncation; amputation, severance; abs-, ex-, re-cision; curtailment &c. 201; minuend, subtrahend; decrease &c. 36; abrasion.

**V.** sub-tract, -duct; rebate, de-duct, -duce; bate, retrench; remove, withdraw; take -from, – away; detract.

garble, mutilate, amputate, sever, detruncate; cut -off, – away, – out; expurgate; abscind, excise; pare, thin, prune, decimate; abrade, scrape, file; geld, castrate, emasculate, unman, spay, caponize; eliminate.

diminish &c. 36; curtail &c. (*shorten*) 201; deprive of &c. (*take*) 789; weaken.

**Adj.** subtracted &c. *v.*; subtractive. tailless, acaudal.

**Adv.** in -deduction &c. *n.*; less, short of; minus, without, except, excepting, with the exception of, barring, bar, save, exclusive of, save and except, with a reservation.

---

alone; together –, along –, coupled –, in conjunction- with; conjointly; jointly &c. 43.

**39.** [Thing added.] **Adjunct.—N.** adjunct; addit-ion, -ament; *additum*, affix, appendage, annex; augment, -ation; increment, reinforcement, supernumerary, accessory, item; garnish, sauce; accompaniment &c. 88; adjective, *addendum*, accession, complement, supplement; continuation; extension, subscript, tag, appendix, postscript, interlineation, interpolation, insertion.

rider, codicil, off-shoot, episode, side issue, corollary; piece; flap, lapel, label, tab, strip, fold, lappet, apron, skirt, embroidery, trappings, *cortège*; tail, suffix &c. (*sequel*) 65; wing.

**Adj.** additional &c. 37.

**Adv.** in addition &c. 37.

**40.** [Thing remaining.] **Remainder.—N.** remainder, residue; remains, *remanet*, remnant, rest, relic, relict; leavings, heel-tap, odds and ends, cheese-parings, candle ends, orts; *residuum*; dottle, dregs &c. (*dirt*) 653; refuse &c. (*useless*) 645; stubble, result, educt; fag-end, stub; ruins, wreck, skeleton, stump; *alluvium*.

surplus, overplus, excess; balance, complement; superfluity &c. (*redundance*) 641; surviv-al, -ance; afterglow.

**V.** remain; be -left &c. *adj.*; exceed, survive; leave.

**Adj.** remaining, left; left -behind, – over; residu-al, -ary; over, odd; unconsumed, sedimentary; surviving; net; exceeding, over and above; outlying, -standing; cast off &c. 782; superfluous &c. (*redundant*) 641.

**40a.** [Thing deducted.] **Decrement.—N.** decrement, discount, rebate, defect, loss, deduction, eduction, tare; drawback; waste, wastage; reprise.

**41.** [Forming a whole without coherence.] **Mixture.—N.** mix-, admix-, commix-ture, -tion, mingling; commixion, immixture, interfusion, intermixture, alloyage, matrimony; junction &c. 43; combination &c. 48; entanglement, interlacing; miscegenation, interbreeding.

impregnation; in-, dif-, suf-, trans fusion; infiltration; seasoning, sprinkling, interlarding; interpolation &c. 228; adulteration, sophistication.

[Thing mixed] tinge, tincture, touch, dash, smack, sprinkling, spice, seasoning, infusion, *soupçon*.

[Compound resulting from mixture] alloy, brass, bronze, pewter &c.; amalgam, *magma*, blend, half-and-half, *mélange*, *tertium quid*, miscellany, *ambigu*, medley, mess, hash, hotchpotch, hodgepodge, *pasticcio*, patchwork, odds and ends, all sorts; jumble &c. (*disorder*) 59; salad, sauce, mash, *omnium gatherum*, gallimaufry, ragout, *olla podrida*, *olio*, salmagundi, *potpourri*, Noah's ark; texture, mingled yarn; mosaic &c. (*variegation*) 440.

half-blood, -caste, -breed, Eurasian; mulatto; terc-, quart-, quinteron &c.; quad-, octo-roon; *griffo*, *zambo*; cross, hybrid, mongrel &c. 83.

**42.** [Freedom from mixture.] **Simpleness.—N.** simpleness &c. *adj.*; purity, homogeneity.

elimination; sifting &c. *v.*; purification &c. (*cleanness*) 652.

**V.** render -simple &c. *adj.*; simplify; sift, winnow, bolt, eliminate; narrow down; get rid of, exclude &c. 55; clear; purify &c. (*clean*) 652; disentangle &c. (*disjoin*) 44.

**Adj.** simple, uniform, of a piece, homogeneous, single, pure, clear, sheer, neat; Attic.

un-mixed, -mingled, -blended, -combined, -compounded; elementary, undecomposed; un-adulterated, -sophisticated, -alloyed, -tinged, -fortified; pure and simple.

free –, exempt- from; exclusive.

**Adv.** simply &c. *adj.*; only.

**V.** mix; join &c. 43; combine &c. 48; com-, im-, inter-mix; mix up with, mingle; com-, inter-, be-mingle; shuffle &c. (*derange*) 61; pound together; hash –, stir- up; knead, brew; impregnate with; interlard &c. (*interpolate*) 228; inter-twine, -weave &c. 219; associate with, miscegenate, interbreed.

be mixed &c.; get among, be entangled with.

instil, imbue; in-, suf-, trans-fuse; infiltrate, dash, tinge, tincture, season, sprinkle, besprinkle, attemper, medicate, blend, cross; alloy, amalgamate, compound, adulterate, sophisticate, infect.

**Adj.** mixed &c. *v.*; implex, composite, half-and-half, linsey-wolsey, hybrid, mongrel, heterogeneous; motley &c. (*variegated*) 440; miscellaneous, promiscuous, indiscriminate; miscible.

**Adv.** among, amongst, amid, amidst, with; in the midst of, in the crowd.

**43. Junction.—N.** junction; joining &c. *v.*; joinder, union; con-nection, -junction, -jugation, compendency, annex-ion, -ation, -ment; coalition; astriction, attachment, compagination, vincture, ligation, alligation; accouplement; marriage &c. (*wedlock*) 903; infibulation, inosculation, symphysis, anastomosis, confluence, communication, concatenation; concurrence, meeting, reunion; assemblage &c. 72.

copulation, coition, intercourse.

joint, joining, juncture, chiasma, pivot, hinge, articulation, commissure, seam, suture, gusset, stitch, splice; link &c. 45; mitre, mortise.

closeness, tightness &c. *adj.*; coherence &c. 46; combination &c. 48.

**V.** join, unite; con-join, -nect; associate; put –, lay –, clap –, hang –, lump –, hold –, piece –, tack –, fix –, bind up- together; embody, re-embody; roll into one.

attach, fix, affix, saddle on, fasten, bind, paste, secure, clinch, twist, make -fast &c. *adj.*; tie, pinion, string, strap, sew, lace, stitch, tack, baste, knit, button, buckle, hitch, lash, truss, bandage, braid, splice, swathe, gird, tether, moor, picket, harness, chain; fetter &c. (*restrain*) 751; lock, latch, belay, brace, hook, grapple, leash, couple, accouple, link, yoke, bracket; marry &c. (*wed*) 903; bridge over, span.

pin, nail, bolt, hasp, clasp, clamp, screw, rivet; impact, solder, braze, cement, set; weld –, fuse- together; wedge, rabbet, mortise, mitre, jam, dovetail, enchase; graft, ingraft, inosculate; en-, in-twine; inter-link, -lace,

**44. Disjunction.—N.** dis-junction, -connection, -unity, -union, -association, -engagement, -sociation; discontinuity &c. 70; inconnection; abstraction, -edness; isolation; insul-arity, -ation; oasis; separateness &c. *adj.*; severalty; *disjecta membra*; dispersion &c. 73; apportionment &c. 786.

separation; parting &c. *v.*; detachment, segregation; divorce, sejunction, seposition, diduction, diremption, discerption; elision; *cæsura*, division, subdivision, break, fracture, rupture; compartition; dis-memberment, -integration, -location; luxation; sever-, dis-sever-ance; scission; re-, ab-scission; circumcision; lacer-, dilacer-ation; dis-, ab-ruption; avulsion, divulsion; section, resection, cleavage; fission; separability; separatism.

fissure, breach, rent, split, rift, crack, slit, slot, incision.

dissection, anatomy; decomposition &c. 49; cutting instrument &c. (*sharpness*) 253; saw.

**V.** be -disjoined &c.; come –, fall- -off, – to pieces; peel off; get loose.

dis-join, -connect, -engage, -unite, -sociate, -pair; divorce, part, dispart, detach, uncouple, separate, cut off, rescind, segregate; set –, keep- apart; insulate, isolate; throw out of gear; cut adrift; loose; un-loose, -do, -bind, -tie, -hitch, -chain, -lock &c. (*fix*) 43, -pack, -ravel; disentangle; set free &c. (*liberate*) 750.

sunder, divide, subdivide, sectionalize, sever, dissever, abscind; cut; segment; in-cide, -cise; circumcise; saw, snip, nib, nip, cleave, rive, rend, slit,

-twine, -twist, -weave; entangle; twine round, belay; tighten; trice –, screw-up.

be -joined &c.; hang –, hold- together; cohere &c. 46.

Adj. joined &c. *v.*; joint; con-joint, -junct; corporate, compact; hand in hand.

firm, fast, close, tight, taut, taught, tense, secure, set, intervolved; in-separable, -dissoluble, -secable, -severable.

Adv. jointly &c. *adj.*; in conjunction with &c. (*in addition to*) 37; fast, firmly &c. *adj.*; intimately.

split, splinter, chip, crack, snap, break, tear, burst; rend &c. -asunder, – in twain; wrench, rupture, shatter, shiver, cranch, crunch, craunch, chop; rip up; hack, hew, slash; whittle; haggle, hackle, discind, lacerate, scamble, mangle, gash, hash, slice, shave.

cut up, carve, quarter, dissect, anatomize; take –, pull –, pick –, tear- to pieces; tear to tatters, – piecemeal; divellicate; skin &c. 226; dis-integrate, -member, -branch, -band; disperse &c. 73; dis-locate, -joint; break up; mince; comminute &c. (*pulverize*) 330; distribute, apportion &c. 786.

---

part, – company; separate, leave; alienate, estrange.

Adj. disjoined &c. *v.*; discontinuous &c. 70; bipartite, multipartite, abstract; digitate; disjunctive; isolated &c. *v.*; insular, separate, disparate, discrete, apart, asunder, far between, loose, free; unattached, -annexed, -associated, -connected; distinct; adrift; straggling; rift, reft, cleft, split.

[capable of being divided] scissile, partible, divisible, separable, severable, detachable.

Adv. separately &c. *adj.*; one by one, severally, apart; adrift, asunder, in twain; in the abstract, abstractedly.

**45.** [Connecting medium.] **Vinculum.—N.** vinculum, link, *nexus*; connec-tive, -tion; junction &c. 43; bond of union, copula, intermedium, hyphen; bracket; bridge, stepping-stone, isthmus.

bond, tendon, tendril; fibre; cord, -age; riband, ribbon, rope, guy, cable, line, halser, hawser, painter, moorings, wire, chain; string &c. (*filament*) 205.

fastening, tie; liga-ment, -ture; strap; bowline, halliard, tackle, lanyard, rigging, shrouds; standing –, running- rigging; traces, harness; yoke; band, -age; brace, roller, fillet; inkle; with. withe, withy; thong, braid; girder, tie-beam; girt, cinch, girth, girdle, cestus, garter, braces, suspenders, halter, noose, lasso, lariat, surcingle, knot, hitch, running knot, frog.

pin, corking pin, nail, brad, tack, skewer, staple, cleat, clamp; cramp, screw, button, buckle, clasp, hasp, hinge, hank, catch, latch, bolt, ring, latchet, pawl, tag; tooth; stud; hook, – and eye; morse, lock, holdfast, padlock, rivet; anchor, grappling-iron, drawbar, coupler, drawhead, coupling, treenail, trennel, stake, pale, pile, post, bollard.

cement, glue, gum, paste, size, wafer, solder, lute, putty, bird-lime, mortar, stucco, plaster, grout.

shackle, rein &c. (*means of restraint*) 752; suspender &c. 214; prop &c. (*support*) 215.

V. bridge over, span; connect &c. 43; hang &c. 214.

**46. Coherence.—N.** co-, ad-herence, -hesion, -hesiveness; concretion, accretion; con-, ag-glutination, -glomeration; aggregation; consolidation, set, cementation; sticking, soldering &c. *v.*; connection.

**47.** [Want of adhesion, non-adhesion, immiscibility.] **Incoherence.—N.** non-adhesion; immiscibility; incoherence; looseness &c. *adj.*; laxity; relaxation; loosening &c. *v.*; freedom; disjunction &c. 44; rope of sand.

tenacity, toughness; stickiness &c. 352; insepara-bility, -bleness; bur, remora.

conglomerate, concrete &c. (*density*) 321.

**V.** cohere, adhere, stick, cling, cleave, hold, take hold of, hold fast, close with, embrace, clasp, hug; grow –, hang- together; twine round &c. (*join*) 43.

stick like -a leech, – wax; stick close; cling like -ivy, – a bur; adhere like -a remora, – Dejanira's shirt.

glue; ag-, con-glutinate; cement, lute, paste, gum; solder, weld; cake, coagulate, consolidate &c. (*solidify*) 321; agglomerate.

**Adj.** co-, ad-hesive, -hering &c. *v.*; tenacious, tough; sticky &c. 352.

united, unseparated, sessile, inseparable, inextricable, infrangible; compact &c. (*dense*) 321.

**V.** make -loose &c. *adj.*; loosen slacken, relax; un-glue &c. 46; detach &c. (*disjoin*) 44.

**Adj.** non-adhesive, immiscible; incoherent, detached, loose, slack, baggy, lax, relaxed, flapping, streaming; dishevelled; segregated, like grains of sand; un-consolidated &c. 321, -combined &c. 48; non-cohesive.

---

**48. Combination.**—**N.** combination; mixture &c. 41; alloy; junction &c. 43; union, unification, synthesis, incorporation, amalgamation, embodiment, coalescence, crasis, fusion, blend, blending, absorption, centralization, federation.

compound, amalgam, composition, *tertium quid*; resultant, impregnation.

**V.** combine, unite, incorporate, alloy, intertwine &c. 41; amalgamate, embody, absorb, re-embody, blend, merge, fuse, melt into one, consolidate, coalesce, centralize, impregnate; put –, lump- together; federate, associate; fraternize; cement a union, marry, wed, couple, pair, ally.

**Adj.** combined &c. *v.*; conjunctive, conjugate, conjoint, allied, confederate; impregnated with, ingrained, inoculated.

**49. Decomposition.**—**N.** decomposition, analysis, diæresis, dissection, resolution, catalysis, electrolysis, hydrolysis, photolysis, dissolution; dispersion &c. 73; disjunction &c. 44; disintegration, decay, rot, putrefaction, putrescence, caries, necrosis, corruption &c. (*uncleanness*) 653.

**V.** decom-pose, -pound; analyze, disembody, dissolve; resolve –, separate- into its elements; electrolyze; dissect, decentralize, break up; disintegrate; disperse &c. 73; unravel &c. (*unroll*) 313; crumble into dust; decay &c. *n.*; deteriorate &c. 659.

**Adj.** decomposed &c. *v.*; catalytic analytical.

---

## 4°. Concrete Quantity

**50. Whole.** [Principal part.]—**N.** whole, totality, integrity; totalness &c. *adj.*; entirety, *ensemble*, collectiveness; unity &c. 87; completeness &c. 52; indivisibility, indiscerptibility; integration, embodiment; integer, integral.

all, the whole, total, aggregate, one and all, gross amount, sum, sum-total, *tout ensemble*, length and breadth of, Alpha and Omega, 'be all and end all,' lock, stock and barrel.

bulk, mass, lump, tissue, staple, body, torso, *compages*; trunk, bole, hull, hulk, skeleton; greater –, major

**51. Part.**—**N.** part, portion; dose, item, particular; aught, any; division, ward; subdivision, section; chapter, verse; article, clause, count, paragraph, passage; phrase; number, volume, book, fascicule; sector, segment; fraction, fragment; cantle, -t; frustum; detachment, parcel, unit, class &c. 75.

piece, lump, bit; cut, -ting; chip, chunk, collop, slice, scale, shard; lamina &c. 204; moiety; small part; morsel, scrap, crumb; particle &c. (*smallness*) 32; instalment, dividend; share &c. (*allotment*) 786.

–, best –, principal –, main- part; essential part &c. (*importance*) 642; lion's share, Benjamin's mess; the long and the short; nearly –, almost- all.

V. form –, constitute- a whole; integrate, embody, amass; aggregate &c. (*assemble*) 72; amount to, come to.

Adj. whole, total, integral, entire; complete &c. 52; one, individual.

un-broken, -cut, -divided, -severed, -clipped, -cropped, -shorn; seamless; undiminished; un-demolished, -dissolved, -destroyed, -bruised.

in-divisible, -dissoluble, -dissolvable, -discerptible.

wholesale, sweeping, comprehensive.

Adv. wholly, altogether; totally &c. (*completely*) 52; entirely, all, all in all, considering all things, in a body, collectively, all put together; in the -aggregate, – lump, – mass, – gross, – main, – long run; *en masse*, on the whole, as a whole, bodily, *en bloc*, *in extenso*, throughout, every inch; substantially.

*débris*, odds and ends, oddments, *detritus*; *excerpta*; member, limb, lobe, lobule, arm, wing, scion, branch, bough, joint, link, offshoot, ramification, twig, stipule, tendril, bush, spray, sprig; runner; leaf, -let; stump; constituent, ingredient, component part &c. 56.

compartment; department &c. (*class*) 75; county &c. (*region*) 181.

V. part, divide, break &c. (*disjoin*) 44; partition &c. (*apportion*) 786.

Adj. fractional, fragmentary; sectional, aliquot; divided &c. *v.*; in compartments, multifid, incomplete, partial, divided &c. 44.

Adv. partly, in part, partially; piecemeal, part by part; by -instalments, – snatches, – inches, – driblets; bit by bit, inch by inch, foot by foot, drop by drop; in -detail, – lots.

---

52. **Completeness.**—N. completeness &c. *adj.*; completion &c. 729; integration; integrality.

entirety; universality; totality; perfection &c. 650; solid-ity, -arity; unity; all; *ne plus ultra*, ideal, limit.

complement, supplement, makeweight; filling up &c. *v.*

impletion; satur-ation, -ity; high water; high –, flood –, spring- tide; fill, load, bumper, bellyful; brimmer; sufficiency &c. 639.

V. be -complete &c. *adj.*; come to a head.

render -complete &c. *adj.*; complete &c. (*accomplish*) 729; fill, charge, load, replenish; make-up, – good; piece –, eke- out; supply deficiencies; fill -up, – in, – to the brim, – the measure of; saturate &c. 869.

go the whole -hog, – length, go all lengths.

Adj. complete, entire; whole &c. 50; perfect &c. 650; full, good, absolute, thorough, plenary; solid, undivided; with all its parts.

exhaustive, radical, sweeping, thorough-going; dead.

regular, consummate, unmitigated, sheer, unqualified, unconditional, free; abundant &c. (*sufficient*) 639.

53. **Incompleteness.**—N. incompleteness &c. *adj.*; deficiency, short -measure, – weight; shortcoming &c. 304; insufficiency &c. 640; imperfection &c. 651; immaturity &c. (*non-preparation*) 674; half measures.

[part wanting] defect, deficit, shortage, ullage, defalcation, omission, *caret*; interval &c. 198; break &c. (*discontinuity*) 70; non-completion &c. 730; missing link.

V. be -incomplete &c. *adj.*; fall short of &c. 304; lack &c. (*be insufficient*) 640; neglect &c. 460.

Adj. incomplete; imperfect &c. 651; unfinished; uncompleted &c. (*see* complete &c. 729); defective, deficient, wanting; failing; in -default, – arrear; short, – of; hollow, meagre, lame, half-and-half, perfunctory, sketchy; crude &c. (*unprepared*) 674.

mutilated, garbled, mangled, docked, lopped, truncated; bobtailed, cropped, bobbed, shingled.

in -progress, – hand; going on, proceeding.

Adv. incompletely &c. *adj.*; by halves.

Phr. *cætera desunt*; *caret*.

---

brimming; brim-, top-ful; chock –, choke- full; as full as -an egg is of meat, – a vetch, – a tick; saturated, crammed; replete &c. (*redundant*) 641; fraught, laden; full-laden, -fraught, -charged; heavy laden.

completing &c. *v.*; supplement-al, -ary; ascititious.

**Adv.** completely &c. *adj.*; altogether, outright, wholly, totally, *in toto,* quite; over head and ears; effectually, for good and all, nicely, fully, through thick and thin, head and shoulders; neck and -heel, – crop; all out; in -all respects, – every respect; at all points, out and out, to all intents and purposes; *toto cœlo*; utterly, clean, – as a whistle; to the -full, – utmost, – backbone; hollow, stark; heart and soul, root and branch; down to the ground.

to the top of one's bent, as far as possible, *à outrance.*

throughout; from -first to last, – beginning to end, – end to end, – one end to the other, – Dan to Beersheba, – head to foot, – head to heels, – top to toe, – top to bottom; *de fond en comble*; *à fond, a capite ad calcem, ab ovo usque ad mala,* fore and aft; every -whit, – inch; *cap-à-pie,* to the end of the chapter; up to the -brim, – ears, – eyes; as . . . as can be.

on all accounts; *sous tous les rapports*; with a -vengeance, – witness.

**54. Composition.—N.** composition, constitution, crasis, synthesis; make-up; combination &c. 48; inclusion, admission, comprehension, reception; embodiment, formation, conformation, production.

compilation &c. 72; (*musical*) composition &c. 415; painting &c. 556; writing &c. 590; typography &c. 591.

**V.** be -composed, – made, – formed, – made up- of; consist of, be resolved into.

include &c. (*in a class*) 76; subsume; synthesize; contain, hold, comprehend, take in, admit, embrace, embody; involve; implicate, drag into.

compose, constitute, form, make; make –, fill –, build- up; weave, construct, fabricate; compile; write, draw; set up (*printing*); enter into the composition of &c. (*be a component*) 56.

**Adj.** containing, constituting &c. *v.*

**55. Exclusion.—N.** exclusion, non-admission, omission, exception, rejection, repudiation; exile &c. (*seclusion*) 893; preclusion, lock out, ostracism, prohibition; disbarment, expulsion, ban.

separation, segregation, seposition, elimination, coffer-dam.

**V.** be excluded from &c.

exclude, bar, ban; leave –, shut –, thrust –, bar- out; reject, repudiate, spurn, blackball; ostracize, boycott; lay –, put –, set -apart, – aside; relegate, segregate; throw overboard; strike -off, – out; neglect &c. 460; banish &c. (*seclude*) 893; separate &c. (*disjoin*) 44.

pass over, omit; garble; eliminate, weed, winnow.

**Adj.** excluding &c. *v.*; exclusive.

excluded &c. *v.*; unrecounted, not included in; inadmissible; preventive, interdictive.

**Adv.** exclusive of, barring; except; with the exception of; save, bating.

**56. Component.—N.** component; component –, integral –, integrant- part; element, constituent, ingredient, leaven, part and parcel; contents; appurtenance; feature; member &c. (*part*) 51; personnel.

**V.** enter into, – the composition of; be a -component &c. *n.*; be –, form- part of; merge –, be merged- in; be

**57. Extraneousness.—N.** extraneousness &c. *adj.*; extrinsicality &c. 6; exteriority &c. 220; alienism.

foreign -body, – substance, – element; alien, stranger, intruder, interloper, foreigner, tramontane, *novus homo,* new comer, immi-, emi-grant; creole, Afrikander; outsider, outlander, tenderfoot.

implicated in; share in &c. (*participate*) 778; belong –, appertain- to.

form, make, constitute, compose.

**Adj.** forming &c. *v.*; inclusive; inherent &c. 5.

**Adj.** extraneous, foreign, alien, ulterior; exterior, external, outside, outlandish; oversea; tra-, ultra-montane.

excluded &c. 55; inadmissible; exceptional.

**Adv.** in foreign -parts, – lands; abroad, beyond seas, overseas.

## Section IV. ORDER

### 1°. Order in General

**58. Order.**—**N.** order, regularity &c. 80; uniformity, symmetry, *lucidus ordo*; harmony, music of the spheres.

gradation, progression; series &c. (*continuity*) 69.

subordination; course, even tenor, routine; method, disposition, arrangement, array, system, economy, discipline; orderliness &c. *adj.*

rank, place, &c. (*term*) 71.

**V.** be –, become- in order &c. *adj.*; form, fall in, draw up; arrange –, range –, place- itself; adjust; fall into –, take- -one's place, – rank; rally round; arrange &c. 60.

**Adj.** orderly, regular; in -order, – trim, – apple-pie order, according to Cocker, – its proper place, neat, neat as a pin, tidy, *en règle,* well regulated, correct, methodical, uniform, symmetrical, ship-shape, business-like, systematic; habitual; unconfused &c. (*see* confuse &c. 61) arranged &c. 60.

**Adv.** in order; methodically &c. *adj.*; in -turn, – its turn; step by step; by regular -steps, – gradations, – stages, – intervals; *seriatim,* systematically, by clockwork, *gradatim*; at stated periods &c. (*periodically*) 138; O.K.

**59.** [Absence, or want of Order, &c.] **Disorder.**—**N.** disorder; derangement &c. 61; irregularity; anomaly &c. (*unconformity*) 83; anar-chy, -chism; want of method; dishevelment, untidiness &c. *adj.*; disunion; discord &c. 24.

confusion; confusedness &c. *adj.*; disarray, jumble, mix-up, huddle, litter, lumber; *cahotage*; farrago; mess, muss, mash, muddle, hash; hotchpotch; *imbroglio,* chaos, *omnium gatherum,* medley; mere -mixture &c. 41; fortuitous concourse of atoms, *disjecta membra, rudis indigestaque moles.*

complexity; complexness &c. *adj.*; com-, im-plication; intri-cacy, -cation; perplexity; network, maze, labyrinth; wilderness, jungle; involution, ravelling, entanglement; coil &c. (*convolution*) 248; sleave, tangled skein, knot, Gordian knot, kink, web; wheels within wheels.

turmoil; ferment, &c. (*agitation*) 315; to do, trouble, pudder, pother, row, disturbance, convulsion, tumult, pandemonium, uproar, riot, rumpus, stour, scramble, *fracas,* embroilment, *mêlée,* spill and pelt, rough and tumble; whirlwind &c. 349; bear garden, Babel, Saturnalia, Donnybrook Fair, confusion worse confounded, most admired disorder, *concordia discors*; Bedlam –, hell- broke loose; bull in a china shop; all the fat in the fire, *diable à quatre,* Devil to pay; pretty kettle of fish; pretty piece of -work, – business.

slattern, slut, sloven, draggle-tail.

**V.** be -disorderly &c. *adj.*; ferment, play at cross purposes.

put out of order; derange &c. 61; ravel &c. 219; ruffle, rumple; bungle, botch.

**Adj.** disorderly, orderless; out of -order, – place, – gear, – whack; irregular, desultory; anomalous &c. (*unconformable*) 83; acephalous, disorganized, straggling; un-, im-methodical; unsymmetric; unsystematic; untidy, slovenly, bedraggled, messy; dislocated; out of sorts; promiscuous, indiscriminate; chaotic, anarchical, lawless; unarranged &c. 60; confused, tumultuous, turbulent, tempestuous; deranged &c. 61; topsy turvy &c. (*inverted*) 218; shapeless &c. 241; disjointed, out of joint.

com-plex, -plexed; intricate, complicated, perplexed, involved, ravelled, entangled, knotted, tangled, inextricable; irreducible.

troublous; riotous &c. (*violent*) 173.

**Adv.** irregularly &c. *adj.*; by fits and -snatches, – starts; pell-mell; higgledy-piggledy; helter-skelter, harum-scarum; in a ferment; at -sixes and sevens, – cross purposes; upside down &c. 218.

**Phr.** the cart before the horse, chaos is come again.

**60.** [Reduction to Order.] **Arrangement.—N.** arrangement; plan &c. 626; preparation &c. 673; dispos-al, -ition; col-, al-location; distribution; sorting &c. *v.*; assortment, allotment; grouping; apportionment, *taxis*, taxonomy, *syn-taxis*, graduation, organization, grading; re-organization, rationalization.

analysis, classification, division, digestion; systematism.

[Result of arrangement] order, orderliness, form, array; digest, synopsis &c. (*compendium*) 596; *syntagma*, table, atlas; register &c. (*record*) 551; score &c. 415; cosmos, organism, architecture.

[Instrument for sorting] sieve &c. 260; file, card index.

**V.** reduce to –, bring into- order; introduce order into; rally.

arrange, dispose, place, form; put –, –, place- in order; straighten up, up; set out, collocate, allocate, pack, marshal, range, size, rank, array, group, parcel out, allot, space, distribute, deal; cast –, assign- the parts; dispose of, assign places to; assort, sort; sift, riddle; put –, set- -to rights, – into shape, – in trim, – in array.

class, -ify; divide; file, string together, thread; register &c. (*record*) 551; list, catalogue, tabulate, index, alphabeticize, graduate, digest, grade, codify; orchestrate, score.

methodize, regulate, systematize, standardize, co-ordinate, organize, settle, fix, apportion.

unravel, disentangle, ravel, card; disembroil.

**Adj.** arranged &c. *v.*; embattled, in battle array; cut and dried; methodical, orderly, regular, systematic, tabular.

**61.** [Subversion of Order; bringing into disorder.] **Derangement.—N.** derangement &c. *v.*; disorder &c. 59; evection, discomposure, disturbance; dis-, de-organization; involvement; dislocation; perturbation, interruption; shuffling &c. *v.*; inversion &c. 218; corrugation &c. (*fold*) 258; insanity &c. 503.

**V.** derange; dis-, mis-arrange; dis-, mis-place; mislay, discompose, disorder, de-, dis-organize; embroil, unsettle, disturb, confuse, trouble, perturb, jumble, tumble; huddle, shuffle, muddle, toss, hustle, fumble, riot; bring –, put –, throw- into -disorder &c. 59; break the ranks, disconcert, convulse; break in upon.

unhinge, dislocate, put out of joint, throw out of gear.

turn topsy-turvy &c. (*invert*) 218; bedevil; complicate, involve, perplex, confound; im-, em-brangle; tangle, en-tangle, ravel, tousle, dishevel, ruffle, rumple &c. (*fold*) 258; dement.

litter, scatter; mix &c. 41.

**Adj.** deranged &c. *v.*; syncre-tic, -tistic.

## 2°. Consecutive Order

**62. Precedence.—N.** precedence; coming before &c. *v.*; the lead, *le pas*; superiority &c. 33; importance &c. 642; anteced-ence, -ency; anteriority &c. (*front*) 234; precursor &c. 64; priority &c. 116; precession &c. 280; anteposition, preference.

**V.** precede; come -before, – first; forerun, head, lead, take the lead; lead the -way, – dance; introduce, usher in; have the *pas*; set the fashion &c. (*influence*) 175; lead off, kick off, open the ball; take –, have- precedence; outrank; have the start &c. (*get before*) 280.

place before; prefix; premise, prelude, preface.

**Adj.** preceding &c. *v.*; pre-, antecedent; anterior; prior &c. 116; before; former, foregoing; before-, above-mentioned; aforesaid, said; precurs-ory, -ive; prevenient, preliminary, prefatory, introductory; prelus-ive, -ory; proemial, preparatory.

**Adv.** before; in advance &c. (*precession*) 280.

**Phr.** *seniores priores.*

**63. Sequence.—N.** sequence, coming after; going after &c. (*following*) 281; consecution, succession; posteriority &c. 117.

continuation; prolongation, order of succession; successiveness; Elijah's mantle.

secondariness; subordinancy &c. (*inferiority*) 34.

**V.** succeed; come -after, – on, – next; follow, ensue, step into the shoes of; alternate.

place after, suffix, append.

**Adj.** succeeding &c. *v.*; sequent; sub-, con-sequent; sequacious, proximate, next; consecutive &c. (*continuity*) 69; alternate, amœbæan.

latter; posterior &c. 117.

**Adv.** after, subsequently; behind &c. (*rear*) 235.

---

**64. Precursor.—N.** precursor, antecedent, precedent, predecessor; forerunner, van-courier, *avant-coureur*, pioneer, prodrome, *prodromos*, outrider; leader, bell-wether; herald, harbinger; dawn.

prelude, preamble, preface, prologue, foreword, *avant-propos*, *protasis*, prolusion, proem, *prolepsis*, *prolegomena*, prefix, introduction; lead, heading, frontispiece, groundwork; preparation &c. 673; overture, voluntary, *exordium*, symphony, *ritornello*; premises.

prefigurement &c. 511; omen &c. 512.

**Adj.** precursory; prelu-sive, -sory, -dious; proemial, introductory, prefatory, prodromous, inaugural, preliminary; precedent &c. (*prior*) 116.

**65. Sequel.—N.** sequel, suffix, successor; tail, queue, train, wake, trail, rear; retinue, suite; appendix, postscript, subscript; epilogue; conclusion; peroration; codicil; continuation, *sequela*; appendage &c. 39; tail –, heelpiece; tag, more last words; colophon, *feliciter explicit.*

follower, after-glow, -growth, -crop, -taste, -math.

after-part, -piece, -course, -thought, -game; *arrière pensée*, second thoughts.

---

**66. Beginning.—N.** beginning, commencement, opening, outset, incipience, inception, inchoation; introduction &c. (*precursor*) 64; *alpha*; initial; foundation; inauguration, *début, le premier pas*, embarcation, rising of the curtain; zero hour; exordium, curtain raiser; maiden speech; prelude; outbreak, onset, brunt; initiative, move, first move; gambit, narrow –, thin-

**67. End.—N.** end, close, termination; desinence, conclusion, *finis*, *finale*, period, term, *terminus*, last, *omega*; extreme, -tremity; gable –, butt –, fag-end; tip, nib, point; tail &c. (*rear*) 235; verge &c. (*edge*) 231; tag, epilogue, peroration; *bonne bouche*; bitter end, tail end; terminal; *apodosis*; appendix.

consummation, *dénouement*; finish &c. (*completion*) 729; fate; doom, -sday;

end of the wedge; fresh start, new departure; forefront.

origin &c. (*cause*) 153; source, rise; bud, germ &c. 153; egg, rudiment; genesis, birth, nativity, cradle, infancy, incunabula; start, starting-point &c. 293; dawn &c. (*morning*) 125.

title-page; head, -ing, caption; van &c. (*front*) 234, *feliciter incipit.*

en-trance, -try; inlet, orifice, mouth, chops, lips, porch, portal, portico, *propylon*, door; gate, -way; postern, wicket, threshold, vestibule; skirts, border &c. (*edge*) 231; tee.

first -stage, – blush, – glance, – impression, – sight.

rudiments, elements, outlines, *principia*, grammar, *protasis*; alphabet, ABC.

**V.** begin, commence, inchoate, rise, arise, originate, institute, conceive, initiate, open, dawn, set in, take its rise, enter upon, start; enter; set out &c. (*depart*) 293; embark in.

usher in; lead -off, – the way; take the -lead, – initiative; inaugurate, head; stand -at the head, – first, – for; lay the foundations &c. (*prepare*) 673; found &c. (*cause*) 153; set -up, – on foot, – agoing, – abroach, – the ball in motion; apply the match to a train; launch, broach; open -up, – the door to; set -about, – to work; make a -beginning, – start; handsel; take the first step, lay the first stone, cut the first turf; break -ground, – the ice, – cover; pass –, cross- the Rubicon; open -fire, – the ball; ventilate, air; undertake &c. 676.

come into -existence, – the world; make one's *début*, take birth; burst forth, break out; spring –, crop- up.

begin -at the beginning, – *ab ovo*, – again, – *de novo*; start afresh, make a fresh start, shuffle the cards, resume, recommence.

**Adj.** beginning &c. *v.*; initi-al, -atory, -ative; inceptive, introductory, incipient; proemial, inaugural; incho-ate, -ative; embryonic, rudimental; primogenial; primeval &c. (*old*) 124; rudimentary, aboriginal; natal, nascent.

first, foremost, front, leading, head; maiden.

begun &c. *v.*; just -begun &c. *v.*

**Adv.** at –, in- the beginning &c. *n.*; first, in the first place, *imprimis*, first and foremost; *in limine*; in -the bud, – embryo, – its infancy; from -the beginning, – its birth; *ab -initio*, – *ovo*, – *incunabulis*, primarily, originally.

crack of doom, day of Judgement, fall of the curtain, wind-up; goal, destination; limit, stoppage, end all, determination; expiration, expiry; death &c. 360; end of all things; finality; eschatology.

break up, *commencement de la fin*, last stage, turning point; *coup de grâce*, death-blow; knock-out.

**V.** end, close, finish, terminate, conclude, be all over; expire; die &c. 360; come –, draw- to a -close &c. *n.*; have run its course; run out, pass away.

bring to an -end &c. *n.*; put an end to, make an end of; determine; get through; achieve &c. (*complete*) 729; stop &c. (*make to cease*) 142; shut up shop.

**Adj.** ending &c. *v.*; final, terminal, definitive, conclusive; crowning &c. (*completing*) 729; last, ultimate; hindermost; rear &c. 235; caudal.

contermin-ate, -ous, -able.

ended &c. *v.*; at an end; settled, decided, over, played out, set at rest.

penultimate; last but -one, – two, &c.

unbegun, uncommenced; fresh.

**Adv.** finally &c. *adj.*; in fine; at the last; once for all.

---

**68. Middle.—N.** middle, midst, mediety; mean &c. 29; medium, middle term; centre &c. 222, mid-course &c. 628; *mezzo termine*; *juste milieu* &c. 628; half-way house, nave, navel, omphalos; nucle-us, -olus.

equidistance, bisection, half-distance; middle-distance, equator, diaphragm, midriff; interjacence &c. 228.

**Adj.** middle, medial, mesial, mean, mid; middle-, mid-most; middling; mediate; intermediate &c. (*interjacent*) 228; equidistant; central &c. 222; mediterranean, equatorial.

**Adv.** in the middle; in the thick; mid-, half-way; midships, *in medias res.*

**69.** [Uninterrupted sequence.] **Continuity.—N.** continuity; consecu-tion, -tiveness &c. *adj.*; succession, round, suite, progression, series, train, chain; cat-, concat-enation; catena; scale; gradation, course, constant flow, perpetuity.

procession, column; retinue, *cortège*, cavalcade, rank and file, line of battle, array.

pedigree, genealogy, lineage, race &c. 166.

rank, file, line, row, range, tier, string, thread, team; suit; colonnade.

**V.** follow in –, form- a series &c. *n.*; fall in.

arrange in a -series &c. *n.*; string together, catenate, file, thread, graduate, tabulate.

**Adj.** continu-ous, -ed; consecutive; progressive, gradual; serial, successive; immediate, unbroken, entire; linear; in a -line, – row &c. *n.*; uninter-rupted, -mitting; unremitting; perennial, evergreen; constant.

**Adv.** continuously &c. *adj.*; *seriatim*; in a -line &c. *n.*; in -succession, – turn; running, gradually, step by step, *gradatim*, at a stretch; in -file, – column, – single file, – Indian file.

**70.** [Interrupted sequence.] **Discontinuity.—N.** discontinuity; disjunction &c. 44; anacoluthon, *non sequitur*; interruption, break, fracture, flaw, fault, split, crack, cut; gap &c. (*interval*) 198; solution of continuity, *cæsura*; broken thread; parenthesis, episode; rhapsody, patchwork; intermission; alternation &c. (*periodicity*) 138; dropping fire.

**V.** be -discontinuous &c. *adj.*; alternate, intermit.

discontinue, pause, interrupt; intervene; break, – in upon; interpose &c. 228; break –, snap- the thread; disconnect &c. (*disjoin*) 44.

**Adj.** discontinuous, unsuccessive, broken, interrupted, *décousu*; dis-, un-connected, discrete, disjunctive; fitful &c. (*irregular*) 139; spasmodic, desultory, intermit-ting &c. *v.*, -tent; alternate; recurrent &c. (*periodic*) 138; few and far between.

**Adv.** at intervals; by -snatches, – jerks, – skips, – catches, – fits and starts; skippingly, *per saltum*; *longo intervallo.*

---

**71. Term.—N.** term, rank, station, stage, step; degree &c. 26; scale, remove, grade, link, peg, round –, rung- of the ladder, *status*, position, place, point, mark, *pas*, period, pitch; stand, -ing; footing, range.

**V.** hold –, occupy –, fall into- a place &c. *n.*

## 3°. Collective Order

**72. Assemblage.—N.** assemblage; col-lection, -location, -ligation; compilation, levy, gathering, ingathering, mobilization, meet, foregathering, muster, *attroupement*; con-course, -flux, -gregation, -tesseration, -vergence &c. 290; meeting, *levée*, *réunion*, drawing room, at home; conversazione &c. (*social gathering*) 892; assembly, congress, eisteddfod; conven-tion, -ticle;

**73. Non-assemblage. Dispersion.—N.** dispersion; disjunction &c. 44; divergence &c. 291; scattering &c. *v.*; dissemination, broadcasting, diffusion, dissipation, distribution; apportionment &c. 786; spread, respersion, circumfusion, interspersion, spargefaction.

waifs and estrays, flotsam and jetsam, *disjecta membra*.

**V.** disperse, scatter, sow, dissemi-

gemote; conclave, &c. (*council*) 696; posse, *posse comitatûs*; Noah's ark.

miscellany, *collectanea*, symposium; museum, menagerie, &c. (*store*) 636.

crowd, throng, multitude; flood, rush, deluge; rout, rabble, mob, press, crush, *cohue*, jam, horde, body, tribe; crew, gang, knot, squad, band, party; swarm, shoal, school, covey, flock, herd, drove, kennel; array, bevy, galaxy; *corps*, company, troop, *troupe*; army, force, regiment, &c. (*combatants*) 726; host &c. (*multitude*) 102; populousness.

clan, brotherhood, association &c. (*party*) 712.

volley, shower, storm, cloud.

group, cluster, Pleiades, clump, pencil; set, batch, lot, pack; budget, *dossier*, assortment, bunch; parcel; pack-et, -age; bundle, *fasciculus*, fascine, bale; ser-on, -oon; faggot, wisp, truss, tuft; shock, rick, fardel, stack, sheaf, swath, gavel, haycock, stook.

accumulation &c. (*store*) 636; congeries, heap, lump, pile, *rouleau*, tissue, mass, pyramid; drift; snow-ball, -drift; acervation, cumulation; amassment, glom-, agglom-eration; conglobation; conglomeration, -ate; coacervation, coagmentation, aggregation, concentration, congestion, *omnium gatherum*, *spicilegium*, black hole of Calcutta; quantity &c. (*greatness*) 31.

collector, gatherer; whip, -per in.

**V.** [be or come together] assemble, collect, muster; meet, unite, join, rejoin; cluster, flock, swarm, surge, stream, herd, crowd, throng, associate; con-gregate, -glomerate, -centrate; centre round, *rendezvous*, resort; come –, flock –, get –, pig- together; forgather; huddle; reassemble.

[get or bring together] assemble, muster, mobilize; bring –, get –, put –, draw –, scrape –, lump- together; col-lect, -locate, -ligate; get –, whip- in; gather; hold a meeting; con-vene, -voke, -vocate; rake up, dredge; heap, mass, pile; pack, put up, truss, cram; acervate; ag-glomerate, -gregate; compile; group, aggroup, concentrate, unite; collect –, bring- into a focus; amass, accumulate &c. (*store*) 636; collect in a drag-net; heap Ossa upon Pelion.

**Adj.** assembled &c. *v.*; closely packed, dense, serried, crowded to suffocation, teeming, swarming, populous; as thick as hops; all of a heap, fasciculated; cumulative.

**Phr.** the plot thickens.

nate, radiate, diffuse, shed, spread, ted, bestrew, overspread, dispense, disband, disembody, demobilize, dismember, distribute; apportion &c. 786; blow off, let out, dispel, cast forth, draught off; strew, straw, strow; spirtle, cast, sprinkle, spatter; issue, deal out, retail, utter; re-, inter-sperse; set abroach, circumfuse.

turn –, cast- adrift; scatter to the winds; sow broadcast.

spread like wildfire, disperse themselves.

**Adj.** unassembled &c. (*see* assemble &c. 72); dispersed &c. *v.*; sparse, dispread, broadcast, sporadic, widespread; far-flung; epidemic &c. (*general*) 78; adrift, stray; dishevelled, streaming.

**Adv.** *sparsim*, here and there, *passim*.

**74.** [Place of meeting.] **Focus.—N.** focus; point of- convergence &c. 290; corradiation; centre &c. 222; gathering-place, resort; haunt; retreat; *venue*, *rendezvous*; rallying point, headquarters, home, club; *dépôt* &c. (*store*) 636; tryst, trysting-place; place of -meeting, – resort, – assignation; *point de* –, *lieu de- réunion*; issue.

**V.** bring to- a point, – a focus, – an issue; focus.

## 4°. Distributive Order

**75. Class.—N.** class, category, *categorema*, head, order, sec tion; division, subdivision; department, province, domain, sphere.

kind, sort, genus, species, variety, branch, family, race, tribe, caste, sept, clan, breed; *clique, coterie*; type, kit, sect, set; assortment; feather, kidney; suit; range; gender, sex, kin.

manner, description, denomination, persuasion, connection, designation, character, stamp; predicament; conviction &c. 484.

similarity &c. 17.

**76. Inclusion.** [Comprehension under, or reference to a class.]—**N.** inclusion, admission, incorporation, comprehension, reception.

composition &c. (*inclusion in a compound*) 54.

**V.** be -included in &c.; come –, fall –, range- under; belong –, pertain- to; range with; merge in.

include, compromise, comprehend, contain, admit, embrace, receive; enclose &c. (*circumscribe*) 229; incorporate, cover, embody, encircle.

reckon –, enumerate –, number- among; refer to; place –, arrange- under, – with; take into account.

**Adj.** includ-ed, -ing &c. *v.*; inclusive; comprehensive, all-embracing; congen-er, -erous: of the same -class &c. 75.

**Phr.** *et hoc genus omne*, &c.; *et cætera.*

**77. Exclusion.***—**N.** exclusion &c. 55.

---

**78. Generality.** — **N.** general-ity, -ization; universality; catholic-ity, -ism; miscel-lany, -laneousness; dragnet.

every-one, -body; all hands, all the world and his wife; any body, N or M, all sorts; *tout le monde.*

prevalence, run.

**V.** be -general &c. *adj.*; prevail, obtain, be going about, stalk abroad.

render -general &c. *adj.*; generalize; spread, broadcast.

**Adj.** general, usual, current, generic, collective; broad, comprehensive, sweeping; encyclopedical, panoramic, widespread &c. (*dispersed*) 73.

universal; catho-lic, -lical; common, world-wide; œ-, e-cumenical; transcendental; prevalent, prevailing, rife, epidemic, besetting; all over, covered with.

every, all; indeterminate, indefinite, unspecified, impersonal.

customary &c. (*habitual*) 613.

**Adv.** what-ever, -soever; to a man, one and all, without exception.

generally &c. *adj.*; always, for better

**79. Speciality.**—**N.** speciality, *spécialité*; individ-uality, -uity; particularity, peculiarity; idiocrasy &c. (*tendency*) 176; personality, characteristic, mannerism, idiosyncrasy, attribute, specificness &c. *adj.*; singularity &c. (*unconformity*) 83; reading, version, lection; state; *trait*; distinctive feature; technicality; *differentia.*

particulars, details, minutiæ, items, counts.

I, self, I myself, *ego*; my-, him-, her-, it-self.

**V.** specify, particularize, individualize, realize, specialize, designate, differentiate, determine, define, denote, indicate, itemize, detail.

descend to particulars, enter into detail, come to the point.

**Adj.** special, particular, individual, specific, proper, personal, intimate, original, private, respective, definite, concrete, determinate, especial, certain, esoteric, endemic, partial, party, peculiar, marked, appropriate, several, characteristic, diagnostic, exact, exclusive; singular &c. (*exceptional*) 83;

* The same set of words is used to express *Exclusion from a class* and *Exclusion from a compound.* Reference is therefore made to the former at 55. This identity does not occur with regard to *Inclusion*, which therefore constitutes a separate category.

for worse; in general, generally speaking; speaking generally; for the most part; in the long run &c. (*on an average*) 29.

---

idiomatic; typical, representative, distinctive.

this, that; yon, -der.

**Adv.** specially &c. *adj.*; in particular, *in propriâ personâ*; *ad hominem*; for my part.

each, apiece, one by one; severally, respectively, each to each; *seriatim*, in detail, bit by bit; *pro hac vice*, – *re natâ*.

namely, that is to say, *videlicet*, viz.; to wit; i.e., e.g.

### 5°. Order as regards Categories

**80. Rule.**—**N.** regularity, uniformity &c. 16; clock-work precision; punctuality &c. (*exactness*) 494; routine &c. (*custom*) 613; formula; system; rut; canon, convention, maxim; rule &c. (*form, regulation*) 697; key-note, standard, model; precedent &c. (*prototype*) 22; conformity &c. 82.

nature, principle; law; order of things; normal –, natural –, ordinary –, model- -state, – condition; standing -dish, – order; normality; Procrustean law; law of the Medes and Persians; hard and fast rule.

**Adj.** regular, uniform, symmetrical, constant, steady; according to rule &c. (*conformable*) 82; customary &c. 613; orderly &c. 58.

**81. Multiformity.**—**N.** multi-, omniformity; variety, diversity; multifariousness &c. *adj.*

**Adj.** multi-form, -fold, -farious, -generous; multiplex, variform, manifold, many-sided, multiplicate; omni-form, -genous, -farious; polymorphic; protean; heterogeneous, motley, mosaic; epicene, indiscriminate, desultory, irregular, diversified, different, divers; all manner of; of -every description, – all sorts and kinds; *et hoc genus omne*; and what not? *de omnibus rebus et quibusdam aliis.*

---

**82. Conformity.**—**N.** conform-ity, -ance; observance.

naturalization; conventionality &c. (*custom*) 613; agreement &c. 23.

example, instance, specimen, sample, quotation; exemplification, illustration, case in point; object lesson.

conventionalist, formalist, Philistine.

pattern &c. (*prototype*) 22.

**V.** conform to, – rule; accommodate –, adapt- oneself to; rub off corners.

be -regular &c. *adj.*; move in a groove; follow –, observe –, go by –, bend to –, obey- -rules, – precedents; comply –, tally –, chime in –, fall in-with; be -guided, – regulated- by; fall into a -custom, – usage; follow the -fashion, – multitude; pass muster, do as others do, *hurler avec les loups*; do at Rome as the Romans do; go –, swim- with the -stream, – current, – tide; tread the beaten track &c. (*habit*) 613; rubber-stamp; keep one in countenance.

exemplify, illustrate, cite, quote, put

**83. Unconformity.**—**N.** non-conformity &c. 82; un-, dis-conformity; unconventionality, informality, abnormity, anomaly; anomalousness &c. *adj.*; exception, peculiarity, &c. 79; infraction –, breach –, violation –, infringement- of -law, – custom, – usage; eccentricity, *bizarrerie*, oddity, *je ne sais quoi*, monstrosity, rarity; freak of Nature.

individuality, idiosyncrasy, singularity, originality, mannerism.

aberration; irregularity; variety; singularity; exemption; salvo &c. (*qualification*) 469.

nonconformist; nondescript, character, original, nonsuch, monster, prodigy, wonder, miracle, curiosity, missing link, flying fish, black swan, *lusus naturæ*, *rara avis*, queer fish; mongrel; half-caste, -blood, -breed; *métis*, cross breed, hybrid, mule, mulatto, sacatra, marabou; *tertium quid*, hermaphrodite, gynander, androgyn.

phœnix, chimera, hydra, sphinx, minotaur; griff-in, -on; centaur; hippo-

a case; produce an- instance &c. *n.*

**Adj.** conformable to rule, adaptable, compliant, consistent, agreeable; regular &c. 80; according to -regulation, - rule, - Cocker; *en règle, selon les règles,* well regulated, orderly; symmetric &c. 242.

conventional, commonplace &c. (*customary*) 613; of -daily, - every day- occurrence; in the natural order of things; ordinary, common, - or garden, prosaic, habitual, usual.

in the order of the day; naturalized.

typical, normal, formal; canonical, orthodox, sound, strict, rigid, positive, uncompromising, Procrustean; point device.

*secundum artem,* ship-shape, technical.

exemplary, illustrative, in point.

**Adv.** conformably &c. *adj.*; by rule; agreeably to; in -conformity, - accordance, - keeping- with; according to; consistently with; as usual, *ad instar, instar omnium; more -solito, - majorum.*

for the sake of conformity; of -, as a matter of- course; *pro formâ,* for form's sake, by the card; according to plan.

invariably &c. (*uniformly*) 16.

for -example, - instance; *exempli gratiâ; e.g.; inter alia.*

**Phr.** *cela va sans dire; ex pede Herculem, noscitur a sociis.*

---

griff, -centaur; sagittary; kraken, cockatrice, wyvern, roc, liver, dragon, sea-serpent; mermaid; unicorn; Cyclops, 'men whose heads do grow beneath their shoulders'; Teratology.

fish out of water; neither -one thing nor another, - fish flesh nor fowl nor good red herring; one in a -way, - thousand; out-cast, -law; Ishmael, pariah; oasis.

**V.** be -unconformable &c. *adj.*; leave the beaten -track, - path; infringe -, break -, violate- a -law, - habit, - usage, - custom; drive a coach and six through; stretch a point; have no business there; baffle -, beggar- all description.

**Adj.** unconformable, exceptional; abnorm-al, -ous; anomal-ous, -istic; out of -order, - place, - keeping, - tune, - one's element; irregular, arbitrary; lawless, informal, aberrant, stray, wandering, wanton; peculiar, exclusive, unnatural, eccentric, crotchety, egregious; out of the -beaten track, - common, - common run, - pale of; misplaced; funny.

un-usual, -accustomed, -customary, -wonted, -common; rare, singular, unique, curious, odd, extraordinary, strange, monstrous; wonderful &c. 870; unexpected, unaccountable; *outré,* out of the way, remarkable, noteworthy; queer, quaint, nondescript, none such, *sui generis*; original, unconventional, Bohemian, unfashionable; un-described, -precedented, -paralleled, -exampled, -heard of, -familiar; fantastic, new-fangled, grotesque, *bizarre*; outlandish, exotic, *tombé des nues,* preternatural; denaturalized.

heterogeneous, heteroclite, amorphous, mongrel, amphibious, epicene, half-blood, hybrid; androgyn-ous, -al; unsymmetric &c. 243.

qualified &c. 469.

**Adv.** unconformably &c. *adj.*; except, unless, save, barring, beside, without, save and except, let alone.

however, yet, but.

**Int.** what -on earth! - in the world!

**Phr.** never was -seen, - heard, - known- the like.

## Section V. NUMBER

### 1°. Number, in the Abstract

**84. Number.**—**N.** number, symbol, numeral, figure, cipher, digit, integer; counter; round number; formula; function; series.

sum, total, aggregate, difference, complement, subtrahend; product; multipli-cand, -er, -cator; coefficient, multiple; dividend, divisor, factor, quotient, sub-multiple, fraction; mixed number; numerator, denominator; decimal, circulating decimal, repetend, common measure, aliquot part; reciprocal; prime number; totitive, totient.

permutation, combination, variation; election.

ratio, proportion; progression; arithmetical –, geometrical –, harmonical- progression; percentage.

figurate –, pyramidal –, polygonal- numbers.

power, root, exponent, index, logarithm, antilogarithm; modulus; differential, integral, fluxion, fluent.

**Adj.** numeral, complementary, divisible, aliquot, reciprocal, prime, fractional, decimal, figurate, incommensurable.

proportional, exponential, logarithmic, logometric, differential, fluxional, integral.

positive, negative; rational, irrational; surd, radical, real, imaginary, impossible.

**85. Numeration.—N.** numeration; numbering &c. *v.*; pagination; tale, tally, recension, enumeration, summation, reckoning, computation, supputation; calcu-lation, -lus; algorithm, rhabdology, dactylonomy; measurement &c. 466; statistics.

arithmetic, analysis, algebra, fluxions; differential –, integral –, infinitesimal- calculus; calculus of differences.

[Statistics] dead reckoning, muster, poll, census, capitation, roll-call, recapitulation; account &c. (*list*) 86.

[Operations] notation, addition, subtraction, multiplication, division, proportion, rule of three, practice, equations, extraction of roots, reduction, involution, evolution, approximation, interpolation, differentiation, integration.

[Instruments] abacus, swan-pan, logometer, sliding –, slide- rule, tallies, Napier's bones, calculating –, adding- machine, difference engine; cash register.

arithmetician, calculator, abacist; mathematician, actuary, statistician, surveyor, geodesist.

**V.** number, count, tell; call –, run- over, take an account of, enumerate, call the roll, muster, poll, recite, recapitulate; sum; sum –, cast- up; tell off, score, cipher, compute, calculate, set a price, reckon, – up, estimate; suppute, add, subtract, multiply, divide, extract roots.

check, prove, demonstrate, balance, audit, overhaul, take stock; affix numbers to, page, foliate, paginate.

amount –, come- to.

**Adj.** numer-al, -ical; arithmetical, analytic, algebraic, statistical, numerable, computable, calculable; commensur-able, -ate; incommensur-able, -ate.

**86. List.—N.** list, catalogue, enumeration, inventory, schedule; register &c. (*record*) 551; account; bill, – of costs; syllabus; terrier, tally, file; almanac, calendar, index, table, atlas, contents, card index; rota, ticket; book, ledger; synopsis, *catalogue raisonné*; *tableau*; scroll, manifest, invoice, bill of lading; prospectus, *programme*; bill of fare, *menu*, *carte*; score, census, statistics, returns; Red –, Blue –, Domesday- book; *cadastre*; directory, gazetteer, dictionary, glossary, lexicon, thesaurus, gradus.

roll; check –, chequer –, bead- roll, – of honour; muster -roll, – book; roster, panel; cartulary, diptych.

**V.** list, enrol, schedule, register &c. *n.*; indent, post, docket; matriculate.

**Adj.** cadastral, listed &c. *v.*

## 2°. Determinate Number

**87. Unity.—N.** unity; oneness &c. *adj.*; individuality; solitude &c. (*seclusion*) 893; isolation &c. (*disjunction*) 44; unification &c. 48.

one, unit, ace; item; individual; solo, none else, no other, naught beside.

**V.** be -one, – alone &c. *adj.*; dine with Duke Humphrey.

isolate &c. (*disjoin*) 44.

render one; unite &c. (*join*) 43, (*combine*) 48.

**Adj.** one, sole, single, solitary, only-begotten; individual, apart, alone; kithless.

un-accompanied, -attended; *solus*, single-handed; singular, odd, unique, unrepeated, azygous, first and last; isolated &c. (*disjoined*) 44; insular; unitary.

lone; lone-ly, -some; desolate, dreary.

in-secable, -severable, -discerptible; compact, irresolvable.

**Adv.** singly &c. *adj.*; alone, by itself, *per se*, only, apart, in the singular number, in the abstract; one -by one, – at a time; simply; one and a half, *sesqui-*.

**Phr.** *natura il fece, e poi roppe la stampa.*

**88. Accompaniment.—N.** accompaniment; appurtenance, adjunct &c. 39; context.

coexistence, concomitance, company, association, companionship; part-, copart-nership; coefficiency.

concomitant, accessory, coefficient; companion, attendant, fellow, associate, consort, spouse, colleague, *fidus Achates*; part-, co-part-ner; satellite, hanger on, shadow; escort, *entourage*, suite, *cortège*; convoy, follower &c. 65; attribute.

**V.** accompany, coexist, attend, convoy, chaperon; hang –, wait- on; go hand in hand with; synchronize &c. 120; bear –, keep- company; row in the same boat; bring in its train, associate –, couple- with.

**Adj.** accompanying &c. *v.*; concomitant, fellow, twin, joint; associated –, coupled- with; accessory, attendant, *obbligato*.

**Adv.** with, withal; together –, along –, in company- with; hand in hand, side by side; cheek by -jowl, – jole; arm in arm; there-, here-with; and &c. (*addition*) 37.

together, in a body, collectively.

---

**89. Duality.—N.** dual-ity, -ism; duplicity; bi-plicity, -formity; span, polarity.

two, deuce, couple, couplet, doublet, brace, pair, cheeks, twins, Castor and Pollux, *gemini*, Siamese twins; fellows; yoke, conjugation, dyad, distich.

**V.** [unite in pairs] pair, couple, bracket, yoke; conduplicate, mate.

**Adj.** two, twain; dual, -istic; binary, binomial; twin, biparous; dyadic; conduplicate; duplex &c. 90; *tête-à-tête*; paired; dihedral.

coupled &c. *v.*; conjugate.

both, – the one and the other.

**90. Duplication.—N.** duplication; doubling &c. *v.*; gemi-, ingemi-nation; reduplication; iteration &c. (*repetition*) 104; renewal.

**V.** double; re-double, -duplicate; geminate; repeat &c. 104; renew &c. 660; duplicate, copy &c. 21.

**Adj.** double; doubled &c. *v.*; bicameral, bicapital, bi-fold, -form, -lateral,

**91.** [Division into two parts.] **Bisection.—N.** bi-section, -partition; di-, subdi-chotomy; halving &c. *v.*; dimidiation; *hendiadys*.

bifurcation, forking, branching, furcation, ramification, divarication; fork, prong; fold.

half, moiety.

**V.** bisect, halve, divide, split, cut in

-farious, -facial; two-fold, -sided, -headed, -edged &c.; duplex; double-faced; twin, duplicate, ingeminate; second; dual &c. 89.

**Adv.** twice, once more; over again &c. (*repeatedly*) 104; as much again, twofold.

secondly, in the second place, again.

two, cleave, dimidiate, dichotomize, divaricate.

go halves, divide with.

separate, fork, bifurcate; branch -off, ~ out; ramify.

**Adj.** bisected &c. *v.*; cloven, cleft; bipartite, biconjugate, bicuspid, bifid; bifur-cous, -cate, -cated; semi-, demi-hemi-.

**92. Triality.—N.** triality, trinity,* triplicity.

three, triad, triplet, trey, trio, ternion, trinomial, leash; tierce; triennium; trefoil, triangle, trident, tripod, triumvirate, *troika*.

third power, cube.

**Adj.** three; tri-form, -nal, -nomial; tertiary; triune.

**93. Triplication.—N.** tripli-cation, -city; trebleness, trine, trilogy.

**V.** treble, triple, triplicate, cube.

**Adj.** treble, triple; tern, -ary; triplex, triplicate, threefold, trilogistic; third; trinal; trihedral.

**Adv.** three -times, – fold; thrice, in the third place, thirdly; trebly &c. *adj.*

**94.** [Division into three parts.] **Trisection. — N.** tri-section, -partition, -chotomy; third, – part.

**V.** trisect, divide into three parts; trifurcate.

**Adj.** trifid; trisected &c. *v.*; tri partite, -chotomous, -sulcate.

---

**95. Quaternity.—N.** quaternity, four, tetrad, quartet, quaternion, square, quadrature, quarter, quadruplet; quadrilateral, quadrangle, quatrefoil; *quadriga*.

**V.** reduce to a square, square.

**Adj.** four; quat-ernary, -ernal; quadratic; quartile, quartic, tetractic, tetrad, tetrahedral; quadrennial; quadrivalent.

**96. Quadruplication.—N.** quadruplication.

**V.** multiply by four, quadruplicate, biquadrate.

**Adj.** fourfold; quad-ruple, -ruplicate, -rible; quadruplex; fourth.

**Adv.** four times; in the fourth place, fourthly.

---

**97.** [Division into four parts.] **Quadrisection.—N.** quadri-section, -partition; quartering &c. *v.*; fourth; quart, -er, -ern; farthing (*i.e.* fourthing); quarto.

**V.** quarter, divide into four parts, quadrisect.

**Adj.** quartered &c. *v.*; quadri-fid, -partite.

**98. Five, &c.—N.** five, cinque, quint, quincunx, quintuplet, quintet, pentagon, pentameter, Pentateuch; six, half-a-dozen, sextet, hexagon, hexameter; seven, Heptarchy; eight, octet, octagon, octave; nine, three times three; ten, decade; eleven; twelve, dozen; thirteen; long –, baker's- dozen.

twenty, score; twenty-four, four and twenty, two dozen; twenty-five, five and twenty, quarter of a hundred; forty, two score; fifty, half a hundred; sixty, three score, sexagenarian; seventy, three score and ten, septuagenarian; eighty, four score, octogenarian; ninety, four score and ten, nonagenarian.

**99. Quinquesection, &c.—N.** division by -five &c. 98; quinquesection &c.; fifth &c.; decimation.

**V.** decimate, quinquesect.

**Adj.** quinque-fid, -partite; quinquarticular; octifid; decimal, tenth, tithe, teind; duodecimal, twelfth; sexa-gesimal, -genary; hundredth, centesimal; millesimal &c.

---

* *Trinity* is hardly ever used except in a theological sense; *see* Deity 976.

hundred, centenary, hecatomb, century; hundredweight, cwt.; one hundred and forty-four, gross; bicentenary, tercentenary &c.

thousand, chiliad; myriad, millennium, ten thousand; lac, lakh, one hundred thousand, plum; million; thousand million, *milliard*.

billion, trillion &c.

**V.** centuriate.

**Adj.** five, quinary, quintuple; fifth; senary, sextuple; sixth; seventh; octuple; eighth; ninefold, ninth; tenfold, decimal, denary, decuple, tenth; eleventh; duo-denary, -denal; twelfth; in one's 'teens, thirteenth.

vices-, viges-imal; twentieth; twenty-fourth &c. *n.*

cent-uple, -uplicate, -ennial, -enary, -urial; secular, hundredth; thousandth; millenary &c.

### 3°. Indeterminate Number

**100.** [More than one.] **Plurality.—N.** plurality; a -number, – certain number; one or two, two or three &c.; a few, several; multitude &c. 102.

**Adj.** plural, more than one, upwards of, some, certain; not -alone &c. 87.

**Adv.** *et cætera*, &c., etc.

**Phr.** *non deficit alter.*

---

**100a.** [Less than one.] **Fraction.—N.** fraction, fractional part, fragment; part &c. 51.

**Adj.** fractional, fragmentary, partial.

**101. Zero.—N.** zero, nothing naught, nought, duck's egg, goose egg; cipher, none, nobody; not a soul; *âme qui vive*; absence &c. 187; unsubstantiality &c. 4.

**Adj.** not -one, – any.

**102. Multitude.—N.** multitude; numerousness &c. *adj.*; numer-osity, -ality; multiplicity; profusion &c. (*plenty*) 639; legion, host; great –, large –, round –, enormous- number; a quantity, numbers, array, sight, army, sea, galaxy; scores, peck, bushel, school, shoal, swarm, draft, bevy, cloud, flock, herd, drove, flight, covey, hive, brood, litter, farrow, fry, nest; mob, crowd &c. (*assemblage*) 72; lots, loads, heaps; all the world and his wife.

[Increase of number] greater number, majority; multiplication, multiple.

**V.** be -numerous &c. *adj.*; swarm –, teem –, crawl –, creep -with; crowd, swarm, come thick upon; outnumber, multiply; people; swarm like -locusts, – bees; be alive with.

**Adj.** many, several, sundry, divers, various, not a few; a -hundred, – thousand, – myriad, – million, – thousand and one; some -ten or a dozen, – forty or fifty &c.; half a -dozen, – hundred &c.; very –, full –, ever so- many; numer-ous, -ose; profuse, in profusion; manifold, multiplied, multitudinous, multiferous, multiple, multinomial, teeming, crawling, populous, peopled, crowded, thick, studded; galore.

thick coming, many more, more than one can tell, a world of; no end -of, – to; *cum multis aliis*; thick as -hops, – hail; plenty as blackberries; numerous as the -stars in the firmament, – sands on

**103. Fewness.—N.** fewness &c. *adj.*; paucity, small number; small quantity &c. 32; scarcity, sparsity; rarity; infrequency &c. 137; handful; maniple; minority, exiguity.

[Diminution of number] reduction; weeding &c. *v.*; elimination, sarculation, decimation.

**V.** be -few &c. *adj.*

render -few &c. *adj.*; reduce, diminish the number, weed, eliminate, thin decimate.

**Adj.** few; scarce; scant, -y; thin, rare, thinly scattered, few and far between; exiguous; infrequent &c. 137; *rari nantes*; hardly –, scarcely- any; to be counted on one's fingers; reduced &c. *v.*; unrepeated.

**Adv.** here and there.

the sea-shore, – hairs on the head; and -what not, – heaven knows what; endless &c. (*infinite*) 105.

**Phr.** their name is 'Legion.'

**104. Repetition.—N.** repetition, iteration, reiteration, duplication, ding-dong, alliteration; *epistrophe*; harping, recurrence, succession, run; batto-, tauto-logy; monotony, tautophony; rhythm &c. 138; pleonasm, redundancy, diffuseness.

chimes, repetend, echo, *ritornello*, burden of a song, *refrain*; rehearsal; encore; *réchauffé*, *rifacimento*, recapitulation.

cuckoo &c. (*imitation*) 19; reverberation &c. 408; drumming &c. (*roll*) 407; renewal &c. (*restoration*) 660.

twice-told tale; old -story, – song, chestnut; second –, new- edition; reprint, new impression; return game, return match, reappearance, reproduction; periodicity &c. 138.

**V.** repeat, iterate, reiterate, reproduce, parrot, echo, re-echo, drum, harp upon, battologize, hammer, redouble.

recur, revert, return, reappear; renew &c. (*restore*) 660.

rehearse; do –, say- over again; ring the changes on; harp on the same string; din –, drum- in the ear; conjugate in all its moods, tenses and inflexions, begin again, go over the same ground, go the same round never hear the last of; resume, return to, recapitulate, reword.

**Adj.** repeated &c. *v.*; repetition-al, -ary; recur-rent, -ring; ever recurring, thick coming; frequent, incessant, redundant, pleonastic, tautological.

monotonous, harping, iterative; mocking, chiming; retold; aforesaid, -named; above-mentioned, said; habitual &c. 613; another.

**Adv.** repeatedly, often, again, afresh, anew, over again, once more; ditto, *encore, de novo, bis, da capo.*

again and again; over and over, – again; many times over; time and again, – after time; year after year; day by day &c.; many –, several –, a number of- times; many –, full many- a time; times out of number, year in and year out, morning, noon and night; frequently &c. 136.

**Phr.** *ecce iterum Crispinus, toujours perdrix*, cut and come again; tomorrow and tomorrow.'

**105. Infinity.—N.** infini-ty, -tude, -teness &c. *adj.*; perpetuity &c. 112.

**V.** be -infinite &c. *adj.*; know –, have- no -limits, – bounds; go on for ever.

**Adj.** infinite; immense; number-, count-, sum-, measure-less; innumer-, immeasur-, incalcul-, illimit-, intermin-, unfathom-, unapproach-able; exhaustless, inexhaustible, indefinite; without -number, – measure, – limit, – end; incomprehensible; limit-, end-, bound-, termless; un-told, -numbered, -measured, -bounded, -limited; illimited; perpetual &c. 112.

**Adv.** infinitely &c. *adj.*; *ad infinitum.*

## Section VI. TIME

### 1°. Absolute Time

**106. Time.—N.** time, duration; period, term, stage, space, span, spell, season; the whole -time, – period; course &c. 109.

**107. Neverness.*—N.** 'neverness' absence of time, no time; *dies non*, Tib's eve; Greek Kalends.

**Adv.** never; at no -time, – period

* A term introduced by Bishop Wilkins.

intermediate time, while, *interim*, interval, bit, pendency; inter-vention, -mission, -mittence, -regnum, -lude; respite. on no occasion, never in all one's born days, nevermore, *sine die*.

era, epoch, æon, cycle; time of life, age, year, date; decade &c. (*period*) 108; moment, &c. (*instant*) 113; reign &c. 737.

glass –, ravages –, whirligig –, noiseless foot- of time; scythe.

**V.** continue, last, endure, go on, hold out, remain, stay, persist, abide, run; intervene; elapse &c. 109.

take –, take up –, fill –, occupy- time.

pass –, pass away –, spend –, while away –, consume –, talk against –, kill- time; tide over; use –, employ- time; tarry &c. 110; seize an opportunity &c. 134; waste time &c. (*be inactive*) 683.

**Adj.** continuing &c. *v.*; on foot; permanent &c. (*durable*) 110.

**Adv.** while, whilst, during, pending; during the -time, – interval; in the course of; for the time being, day by day; in the time of, when; mean-time, -while; in the -meantime, – *interim*; *ad interim*, *pendente lite*; *de die in diem*; from -day to day, – hour to hour &c.; hourly, always; for a -time, – season; till, until, up to, yet; the whole –, all the- time; all along; throughout &c. (*completely*) 52; for good &c. (*diuturnity*) 110.

here-, there-, where-upon; then; *anno*, – *Domini*; A.D.; *ante Christum*; A.C.; before Christ; B.C.; *anno urbis conditæ*; A.U.C.; *anno regni*; A.R.; once upon a time, one fine morning.

**Phr.** time -runs, – runs against; *tempus fugit*.

**108.** [Definite duration, or portion of time.] **Period.—N.** period; second, minute, hour, day, week, sennight, octave, month, moon, quarter, semester, year, *lustrum*, *quinquennium*, decade, *decennium*, indiction, lifetime, generation, epoch, era, cycle.

century, age, *millennium*; *annus magnus*.

**Adj.** horary; hourly, annual &c. (*periodical*) 138.

**108a. Contingent Duration.—Adv.** during -pleasure, – good behaviour; *quamdiu se bene gesserit*.

**109.** [Indefinite duration.] **Course.—N.** course –, progress –, process –, succession –, lapse –, flow –, flux –, effluxion, stream –, tract –, current –, sweep –, tide –, march –, step –, flight- of time; duration &c. 106.

[Indefinite time] aorist.

**V.** elapse, lapse, flow, run, proceed, advance, pass; roll –, wear –, press –, drag- on; flit, fly, slip, slide, glide, crawl; run -its course.

out; expire; go –, pass- by; be -past &c. 122.

**Adj.** elapsing &c. *v.*; aoristic; progressive, transient &c. 111.

**Adv.** in due -time, – season; in -course, – process, – the fulness- of time; in time.

**Phr.** *labitur et labetur*; *truditur dies die*; *fugaces labuntur anni*; 'tomorrow and tomorrow and tomorrow creeps in this petty pace from day to day.'

**110.** [Long duration.] **Diuturnity.—N.** diuturnity; a -long –, length of- time; an age, a century, an eternity,

**111.** [Short duration.] **Transientness.—N.** transientness &c. *adj.*; evanescence, impermanence, fugacity, transi-

æons; slowness &c. 275; perpetuity &c. 112; blue moon.

dura-bleness, -bility; persistence, lastingness &c. *adj.*; continuance, assiduity, endurance, standing; permanence &c. (*stability*) 150; survi-val, -vance; longevity &c. (*age*) 128; distance of time.

protraction –, prolongation –, extension- of time; delay &c. (*lateness*) 133.

**V.** last, endure, stand, remain, abide, continue, brave a thousand years.

tarry &c. (*be late*) 133; drag -on, – its slow length along, – a lengthening chain; protract, prolong; spin –, eke –, draw –, lengthen- out; temporize; gain –, make –, talk against- time.

out-last, -live; survive; live to fight again.

**Adj.** durable; perdurable; lasting &c. *v.*; of long -duration, – standing; permanent, chronic, long-standing; intransi-ent, -tive; intransmutable, persistent; life-, live-long; longeval, long-lived, macrobiotic, diuturnal, sempervirent, evergreen, perennial; unin-, ter-, unre-mitting; perpetual &c. 112.

lingering, protracted, prolonged, spun out &c. *v.*; long-pending, -winded; slow &c. 275.

**Adv.** long; for -a long time, – an age, – ages, – ever so long, – many a long day; long ago &c. (*in a past time*) 122; *longo intervallo.*

all the -day long, – year round; the livelong day, as the day is long, morning, noon and night; hour after hour, day after day, &c.; for good; permanently &c. *adj.*

**112.** [Endless duration.] **Perpetuity.** —**N.** perpetuity, eternity, timelessness; everness,* aye, sempiternity, immortality, athanasia; everlastingness &c. *adj.*; perpetuation; infinite duration.

**V.** last –, endure –, go on- for ever; have no end.

eternize, eternify, perpetuate, immortalize.

**Adj.** perpetual, eternal, eterne; everlasting, -living, -flowing; continual, constant, sempiternal; co-eternal; endless, unending; ceaseless, incessant, uninterrupted, indesinent, unceasing; interminable, having no end; unfad-

toriness, volatility, caducity, mortality, span; flash in the pan, nine days' wonder, bubble, May-fly; spurt; temporary arrangement, interregnum.

velocity &c. 274; suddenness &c. 113; changeableness &c. 149.

**V.** be -transient &c. *adj.*; flit, pass away, fly, gallop, vanish, fade, fleet, melt away, evaporate; pass away like a -cloud, – summer cloud, – shadow, – dream.

**Adj.** transi-ent, -tory, -tive; passing, evanescent, fleeting; flying &c. *v.*; fug-acious, -itive; shifting, slippery; spasmodic.

tempor-al, -ary; provis-ional, -ory; cursory, short-lived, ephemeral, deciduous; perishable, mortal, precarious; impermanent.

brief, quick, brisk; cometary, meteoric, extemporaneous, summary; pressed for time &c. (*haste*) 684; sudden, momentary &c. (*instantaneous*) 113.

**Adv.** temporarily &c. *adj.*; *pro tempore*; for -the moment, – a time; awhile, *en passant, in transitu*; in a short time; soon &c. (*early*) 132; briefly &c. *adj.*; at short notice; on the -point, – eve -of; *in articulo*; between cup and lip.

**Phr.** one's days are numbered; the time is up; here to-day and gone to-morrow; *non semper erit æstas; eheu! fugaces labuntur anni; sic transit gloria mundi.*

---

**113.** [Point of time.] **Instantaneity.** —**N.** instantane-ity, -ousness; sudden-, abrupt-ness.

moment, instant, second, minute; twinkling, trice, flash, breath, crack, jiffy, *coup*, burst, flash of lightning, stroke of time.

epoch, time; time of -day, – night; hour, minute; very -minute &c., – time, – hour; present –, right –, true –, exact –, correct- time.

**V.** be -instantaneous &c. *adj.*; twinkle, flash.

**Adj.** instantaneous, momentary, extempore, sudden, instant, abrupt;

* Bishop Wilkins.

ing, evergreen, amaranthine; never-ending, -dying, -fading; deathless, immortal, undying, imperishable.

**Adv.** perpetually &c. *adj.*; always, ever, evermore, aye; for -ever, – aye, – evermore, – ever and a day, – ever and ever; in all ages, from age to age; without end; world –, time- without end; *in sæcula sæculorum*; to the -end of time, – crack of doom, – 'last syllable of recorded time'; till doomsday; constantly &c. (*very frequently*) 136.

**Phr.** *esto perpetua!; labitur et labetur in omne volubilis ævum.*

subitaneous, hasty; quick as -thought,* – lightning, – a flash; rapid as electricity.

**Adv.** instantaneously &c. *adj.*; in –, in less than- no time; *presto, subito, instanter*, suddenly, at a stroke, like- a shot, – greased lightning; in a trice, in a moment &c. *n.*; eftsoons, in the twinkling of -an eye, – a bed post; at one jump, in the same breath, *per saltum, uno saltu*; at –, all at- once; in one's tracks; plump, slap; 'at one fell swoop'; at the same -instant &c. *n.*; immediately &c. (*early*) 132; extempore, on the -spot, – spur of the moment, – dot; just then; slap- dash &c. (*haste*) 684; before you could -turn round, – say -knife, – Jack Robinson.

**Phr.** touch and go; no sooner said than done.

**114.** [Estimation, measurement, and record of time.] **Chronometry.—N.** chrono-, horo-metry, -logy; date, epoch; style, era, age.

almanac, calendar, ephemeris; register, -try; chronicle, annals, journal, diary, chronogram.

[Instruments for the measurement of time] clock, watch; chrono-meter, -scope, -graph; repeater, alarum; time-keeper, -piece; dial, sun-dial, *gnomon, pendule*, horologe, pendulum, hourglass, water clock, clepsydra.

mean –, Greenwich –, solar –, sidereal –, local –, summer- time; daylight saving.

chrono-grapher, -loger, -logist; annalist.

**V.** fix –, mark- the time; date, register, chronicle; measure – beat –, mark- time; bear date.

**Adj.** chrono-logical, -metrical, -grammatical; isochronal.

**Adv.** o'clock; *a.m., p.m.*

**115.** [False estimate of time.] **Anachronism.—N.** ana-, meta-, para-, prochronism; *prolepsis*, misdate; anticipation, antichronism.

disregard –, neglect –, oblivion- of time.

intempestivity &c. 135.

**V.** mis-, ante-, post-, over-date; anticipate; take no note of time.

**Adj.** misdated &c. *v.*; undated; overdue; out of date; anachronous &c. *n.*

## 2°. Relative Time

### 1. *Time with reference to Succession*

**116. Priority.—N.** priority, antecedence, anteriority, pre-existence, precedence &c. 62; precession &c. 280; precursor &c. 64; the past &c. 122; premises.

**V.** precede, come before; forerun; antecede, go before &c. (*lead*) 280; pre-exist; dawn; premise, presage &c. 511.

be -beforehand &c. (*be early*) 132;

**117. Posteriority.—N.** posteriority; succession, sequence; following &c. 281; subsequence, supervention; futurity &c. 121; successor; sequel &c. 65; remainder, reversion.

**V.** follow &c. 281 –, come –, go- after; ensue, result; succeed, supervene; step into the shoes of.

**Adj.** subsequent, posterior, following, after, later, succeeding, postliminious,

* See note on 264.

steal a march upon, anticipate, forestall; have –, gain- the start.

**Adj.** prior, previous; preced-ing, -ent; anterior, antecedent; pre-existing, -existent; foresighted; former, foregoing; afore –, before-, above-mentioned; aforesaid, said; introductory &c. (*precursory*) 64; pre-war.

**Adv.** before, prior to; earlier; previously &c. *adj.*; afore, ere, theretofore, erewhile; ere –, before- -then, – now; erewhile, already, yet, beforehand; aforetime, on the eve of, in anticipation.

**118. The Present Time.—N.** the present -time, – day, – moment, – juncture, – occasion; the times, existing time, time being; twentieth century; nonce, crisis, epoch, day, hour.

age, time of life.

**Adj.** present, actual, instant, current, latest, existing, that is.

**Adv.** at this -time, – moment &c. 113; at the -present time &c. *n.*; now, at present.

at this time of day, to-day, now-a-days; already; even –, but –, just-now; on the present occasion; for the -time being, – nonce; *pro hâc vice*; on the -nail, – spot; on the spur of the -moment, – occasion.

until now; to -this, – the present day.

postnate; successive &c. 63; postdiluvial, -an; *puisné*; posthumous; post-war, future &c. 121.

**Adv.** subsequently, after, afterwards, since, later; at a -subsequent, – later- period; next, in the sequel, close upon, thereafter, thereupon, upon which, eftsoons; from that -time, – moment; after a -while, – time; in process of time.

postcenal, postcibal, postprandial, after-dinner.

---

**119.** [Time different from the present.] **Different Time.—N.** different –, other- time.

[Indefinite time] aorist.

**Adj.** aoristic.

**Adv.** at that –, at which- -time, – moment, – instant; then, on that occasion, upon.

when; when-ever, -soever; upon which, on which occasion; at -another, – a different, – some other, – any- time; at various times; some –, one- -of these days, – fine morning, – day; sooner or later; some time or other; once upon a time, once.

---

**120. Synchronism.—N.** synchronism; coexistence, coincidence; simultaneousness &c. *adj.*; concurrence, concomitance, unity of time, interim.

[Having equal times] isochronism, syntony.

contemporary, coetanian.

**V.** coexist, concur, accompany, go hand in hand, keep pace with; synchronize, isochronize.

**Adj.** synchron-ous, -al, -ical, -istical; simultaneous, coexisting, coincident, concomitant, concurrent; coev-al, -ous; contempora-ry, -neous; coetaneous; coterminous, coeternal; isochronous.

**Adv.** at the same time; simultaneously &c. *adj.*; together, in concert, during the same time; in the same breath; *pari passu*; in the interim.

at the -very moment &c. 113; just as, as soon as; meanwhile &c. (*while*) 106.

**121.** [Prospective time.] **Futurity.—N.** futur-ity, -ition; future, hereafter, time to come; approaching –, coming –, after- -time, – age, – days, – hours, – years, – ages, – life; morrow, to-morrow, by and by; millennium, doomsday, day of judgment, crack of doom, remote future.

**122.** [Retrospective time.] **Preterition.—N.** preterition; priority &c. 116; the past, past time; days –, times- -of yore, – of old, – past, – gone by; bygone days, good old days; old –, ancient –, former -times; fore time; yesterdays; the olden –, good old- time; auld lang syne; eld.

approach of time, advent, time drawing on, womb of time; destiny &c. 152; eventuality.

heritage, heirs, posterity, descendants.

prospect &c. (*expectation*) 507; foresight &c. 510.

**V.** look forwards; anticipate &c. (*expect*) 507, (*foresee*) 510; forestall &c. (*be early*) 132.

come –, draw- on; draw near; approach, await, threaten; impend &c. (*be destined*) 152.

**Adj.** future, to come; coming &c. (*impending*) 152; next, near; near –, close- at hand; eventual, ulterior; expectant, prospective, in prospect &c. (*expectation*) 507.

**Adv.** prospectively, hereafter, on the knees of the gods, in future; to-morrow, the day after to-morrow; in -course, – process, – the fulness- of time; eventually, ultimately, sooner or later; *proximo*; *paulo post futurum*; in after time; one of these days; after a -time, – while.

from this time; hence-forth, -forwards; thence; thence-forth, -forward; whereupon, upon which.

soon &c. (*early*) 132; on the -eve, – point, – brink- of; about to; close upon.

---

antiquity, antiqueness, *status quo*; time immemorial; distance of time; remote -age, – time; ancient history; remote past; rust of antiquity; ancientness.

pale-ontology, -ography, -ology; palætiology,* archæology; archaism, antiquarianism, mediævalism, pre-Raphaelitism; retrospection, looking back, memory &c. 505.

*laudator temporis acti*; mediævalist, pre-Raphaelite; antiqu-ary, -arian; archæologist &c.; Oldbuck, Dryasdust.

ancestry &c. (*paternity*) 166.

**V.** be -past &c. *adj.*; have -expired &c. *adj.*, – run its course, – had its day; pass; pass –, go- -by, – away, – off; lapse, blow over.

look –, trace –, cast the eyes- back; exhume.

**Adj.** past, gone, gone by, over, passed away, bygone, foregone; elapsed, lapsed, preterlapsed, expired, no more, run out, blown over, that has been, whilom, extinct, never to return, exploded, forgotten, irrecoverable; obsolete &c. (*old*) 124; extinct as the dodo.

former, pristine, *quondam*, *ci-devant*, late; ancestral.

foregoing; last, latter; recent, overnight; past, preterite, preter-perfect, -pluperfect, past perfect.

looking back &c. *v.*; retro-spective, -active; archæological &c. *n.*

**Adv.** formerly; of -old, – yore; erst, whilom, erewhile, time was ago, over; in -the olden time &c. *n.*; anciently, long -ago, – since; a long -while, – time- ago; years –, ages- ago; some time -ago, – since, – back.

yesterday, the day before yesterday; last -year, – season, – month &c.; *ultimo*; lately &c. (*newly*) 123.

retrospectively, ere –, before –, till- now; hitherto, heretofore; no longer; once, – upon a time; from time immemorial; in the memory of man; time out of mind; already, yet, up to this time; *ex post facto*.

**Phr.** time was; the time -has, – hath- been.

## 2. *Time with reference to a particular Period*

**123. Newness.—N.** newness &c. *adj.*; neologism, neoterism; novelty, recency; immaturity; youth &c. 127; gloss of novelty.

**124. Oldness.—N.** oldness &c. *adj.*; age, antiquity; cobwebs of antiquity;

maturity, ripeness; decline, decay; senility &c. 128.

* Whewell.

innovation; renovation &c. (*restoration*) 660.

modernist, neologist, neoteric.

modernism, modernity; mushroom; latest fashion, *dernier cri*.

upstart, *parvenu*, *nouveau riche*.

**V.** renew &c. (*restore*) 660; modernize.

**Adj.** new, novel, recent, fresh, green; young &c. 127; evergreen; raw, immature; virgin; un-tried, -handseled, -used, -trodden, -beaten; fledgling.

late, modern, neoteric; new-born, -fashioned, -fangled, -fledged; of yesterday; just out, brand –, span-new, up to date, topical; vernal, renovated; innovatory.

fresh as -a rose, – a daisy, – paint; spick and span.

**Adv.** newly &c. *adj.*; afresh, anew, lately, just now, only yesterday, the other day; latterly, of late.

not long –, a short time- ago.

---

seniority, eldership, primogeniture; archaism &c. (*the past*) 122; thing –, relic- of the past; megatherium.

tradition, prescription, custom, folklore, immemorial usage, common law.

**V.** be -old &c. *adj.*; have -had, – seen- its day; become -old &c. *adj.*; age, fade.

**Adj.** old, olden, ancient, antique; of long standing, time-honoured, venerable; eld-er, -est; first-born.

prime; prim-itive, -eval, -igenous; primordi-al, -nate; aboriginal &c. (*beginning*) 66; diluvian, antediluvian; pre-historic; patriarchal, preadamite; palæocrystic; fossil, paleozoic, preglacial, ante-mundane; archaic, classic, mediæval, pre-Raphaelite, ancestral, black-letter.

immemorial, traditional, prescriptive, customary, whereof the memory of man runneth not to the contrary; inveterate, rooted.

antiquated, of other times, rococo, of the old school, after-age, obsolete; fusty, moth-eaten; out of -date, – fashion; stale, old-fashioned, behind the -age, – times; exploded; gone out, – by; *passé*, outworn, run out; disused; senile &c. 128; time-worn; crumbling &c. (*deteriorated*) 659; second-hand.

old as -the hills, – Methuselah, – Adam, – history; Anno Domini.

**Adv.** since the -world was made, – year one, – days of Methuselah.

**125. Morning.** [Noon.]—**N.** morning, morn, matins, forenoon, *a.m.*, prime, dawn, daybreak, daylight, sun-up, peep –, break- of day; aurora, Eos; first blush –, prime- of the morning; twilight, crepuscule, sunrise, cockcrow.

spring; vernal equinox.

noon; mid-, noon-day; noontide, meridian, prime.

summer, midsummer; summer solstice.

**Adj.** matin, matutinal; vernal, æstival.

**Adv.** at -sunrise &c. *n.*; with the lark, when the morning dawns.

**126. Evening.** [Midnight.]—**N.** evening, eve; decline –, fall –, close- of day; eventide, evensong, vespers; candlelight; nightfall, curfew, dusk, twilight, blind man's holiday; eleventh hour; sun-set, -down; going down of the sun, cock-shut, dewy eve, gloaming, bed-time.

afternoon, *post meridiem*, *p.m.*

autumn; fall, – of the leaf; autumnal equinox, Indian summer, harvest-time.

midnight; dead –, witching time- of night; winter, – solstice.

**Adj.** vespertine, autumnal, nocturnal, wintry, brumal, hiemal.

**127. Youth.**—**N.** youth; juven- -ility, -escence; juniority; infancy; baby-, child-, boy-, girl-, youth-hood; *incunabula*; minority, immaturity, nonage, teens, tender age, bloom.

cradle, nursery, leading-strings, pupilage, puberty, *pucelage*.

**128. Age.**—**N.** age; oldness &c. *adj.*; old –, advanced- age; sen-ility, -escence; years, anility, grey hairs, climacteric, grand climacteric, declining years, decrepitude, hoary age, caducity, superannuation; second childhood, -ishness; dotage; vale of years,

prime –, flower –, spring-tide –, seed-time –, golden season- of life; heyday of youth, school days; rising generation, younger generation.

**Adj.** young, youthful, juvenile, green, callow, budding, sappy, *puisné*, beardless, unfledged, unripe, under age, in one's teens; *in statu pupillari*; younger, junior.

---

decline of life, 'sear and yellow leaf'; three-score years and ten; green old age, ripe old age; longevity; time of life.

seniority, eldership; elders &c. (*veteran*) 130; firstling; *doyen*, dean, father; primogeniture; nostology.

**V.** be -aged &c. *adj.*; grow –, get- old &c. *adj.*; age; decline, wane.

**Adj.** aged; old &c. 124; elderly, senile; matronly, anile; in years; ripe, mellow, run to seed, declining, waning, past one's prime; grey, -headed; hoar, -y; venerable, time-worn, antiquated, *passé*, effete, doddering, decrepit, superannuated; advanced in -life, – years; stricken in years; wrinkled, marked with the crow's foot; having one foot in the grave; doting &c. (*imbecile*) 499.

old-, eld-er, -est; senior; first-born.

turned of, years old; of a certain age, no chicken, old as Methuselah; gerontic; ancestral; patriarchal &c. (*ancient*) 124.

**129. Infant.**—**N.** infant, babe, baby; nurse-, suck-, year-, wean-ling; *papoose*, *bambino*.

child, bairn, little- one, – tot, – mite, chick, brat, chit, pickaninny, kid, urchin; bant-, brat-ling; elf.

youth, boy, lad, slip, sprig, stripling, youngster, cub, unlicked cub, younker, callant, whipster, whipper-snapper, schoolboy, hobbledehoy, hopeful, cadet, minor, master.

scion; sap-, seed-ling; tendril, olive-branch, nestling, chicken, duckling; larva, caterpillar, chrysalis, cocoon; tadpole, whelp, cub, pullet, fry, callow; codlin, -g; *fœtus*, calf, colt, pup, foal, kitten; lamb, -kin.

girl; lass, -ie; wench, miss, damsel, *demoiselle*, damozel; maid, -en; virgin; nymph; colleen; minx, baggage, school-girl; tomboy, flapper, hoyden.

**Adj.** infant-ine, -ile; puerile; boy-, girl-, child-, baby-, kitten-ish; baby; new-born, unfledged, new-fledged, callow.

in -the cradle, – swaddling clothes, – long clothes, – arms, – leading strings; at the breast; in one's teens; young &c. 127.

**130. Veteran.**—**N.** veteran, old man, seer, patriarch, greybeard, dugout, grand-father, -sire; grandam, beldam; gaffer, gammer; hag, crone; pantaloon; sexage-, octoge-, nonage-, cente-narian; old stager; dotard &c. 501.

preadamite, Methuselah, Nestor, Rip van Winkle, old Parr; elders; forefathers &c. (*paternity*) 166.

---

**131. Adolescence.**—**N.** adolescence, pubescence, majority; adultness &c. *adj.*; manhood, virility, maturity; flower of age; prime –, meridian- of life.

man &c. 373; woman &c. 374; adult, no chicken.

**V.** come -of age, – to man's estate, – to years of discretion; attain majority, assume the *toga virilis*; have -cut one's eye-teeth, – sown one's wild oats, settle down.

**Adj.** adolescent, pubescent, of age; of -full, – ripe- age; out of one's teens, grown up, mature, full- blown, – grown, in one's prime, in full bloom, manly, virile, adult; womanly, matronly; marriageable, nubile;

### 3. *Time with reference to an Effect or Purpose*

**132. Earliness.—N.** earliness &c. *adj.*; morning &c. 125.

punctuality; promptitude &c. (*activity*) 682; haste &c. (*velocity*) 274; suddenness &c. (*instantaneity*) 113.

prematurity, precocity, precipitation, anticipation; prevenience, a stitch in time.

**V.** be -early &c. *adj.*, – beforehand &c. *adv.*; keep time, take time by the forelock, anticipate, forestall; have –, gain- the start; steal a march upon; gain time, draw on futurity; bespeak, secure, engage, pre-engage.

accelerate; expedite &c. (*quicken*) 274; make haste &c. (*hurry*) 684.

**Adj.** early, prime, timely, in time, punctual, forward; prompt &c. (*active*) 682; summary.

premature, precipitate, precocious; prevenient, anticipatory; rathe.

sudden &c. (*instantaneous*) 113; unexpected &c. 508; impending, imminent; near, – at hand; immediate.

**Adv.** early, soon, anon, betimes, rathe; eft, -soons; ere –, before- long; punctually &c. *adj.*; to the minute; in time; in -good, – military, – pudding, – due- time; time enough.

beforehand; prematurely &c. *adj.*; precipitately &c. (*hastily*) 684; too soon; before -its, – one's- time; in anticipation; unexpectedly &c. 508.

suddenly &c. (*instantaneously*) 113; before one can say 'Jack Robinson,' at short notice, extempore; on the spur of the -moment, – occasion; at once; on the -spot, – instant; at sight; off –, out of- hand; à *vue d'œil*; straight, -way, -forth; forthwith, incontinently, summarily, instanter, immediately, briefly, shortly, quickly, speedily, apace, before the ink is dry, almost immediately, presently, at the first opportunity, in no long time, by and by, in a while, directly.

**Phr.** touch and go, no sooner said than done.

**133. Lateness.—N.** lateness &c. *adj.*; tardiness &c. (*slowness*) 275.

de-lay, -lation; cunctation, procrastination; detention; deferring &c. *v.*; filibuster, postponement, adjournment, prorogation, retardation, respite, reprieve, stay; protraction, prolongation, moratorium; contango; demurrage; remand; Fabian policy, *médecine expectante*, chancery suit; leeway; high time.

**V.** be -late &c. *adj.*; tarry, wait, stay, bide, take time; dawdle &c. (*be inactive*) 683; linger, loiter, saunter, lag behind; bide –, take- one's time; hang -about, – around, – back, – in the balance; gain time; hang fire; stand –, lie-over.

put off, defer, delay, lay over, suspend; shift –, stave- off; waive, retard, remand, postpone, adjourn; procrastinate; dally; prolong, protract; spin –, draw –, lengthen- out; prorogue; keep back; tide over; push –, drive- to the last; let the matter stand over; reserve &c. (*store*) 636; temporize; consult one's pillow, sleep upon it.

shelve, table, lay on the table.

lose an opportunity &c. 135; be kept waiting, dance attendance; kick –, cool- one's heels; *faire antichambre*; wait impatiently; await &c. (*expect*) 507; sit up, – at night.

**Adj.** late, tardy, slow, behindhand, belated, postliminious, posthumous, backward, unpunctual; dilatory &c. (*slow*), overdue 275; delayed &c. *v.*; in abeyance.

**Adv.** late; late-, back-ward; late in the day; at -sunset, – the eleventh hour, – length, – last, – long; ultimately; after –, behind- time; too late; too late for &c. 135.

slowly, leisurely, deliberately, at one's leisure; *ex post facto*; *sine die*.

**Phr.** *nonum prematur in annum*.

---

**134. Occasion.—N.** occasion, opportunity, opening, room, scope, field; suitable –, proper- -time, – season; high time; opportuneness &c. *adj.*; tempestivity.

**135. Intempestivity.—N.** intempestivity; unseasonableness; unsuitable –, improper-time; unreasonableness &c. *adj.*; evil hour; *contretemps*; intrusion; anachronism &c. 115.

crisis, turn, juncture, emergency, conjuncture; turning point, given time.

nick of time; golden –, well-timed –, fine –, favourable- opportunity; clear stage, fair field; *mollia tempora*; *fata Morgana*; spare time &c. (*leisure*) 685.

**V.** seize &c. (*take*) 789 –, use &c. 677 –, give &c. 784- an -opportunity, – occasion; improve the occasion.

suit the occasion &c. (*be expedient*) 646.

strike the iron while it is hot, *battre le fer sur l'enclume*, make hay while the sun shines, take time by the forelock, *prendre la balle au bond*.

**Adj.** opportune, timely, well-timed, timeous, timeful, seasonable.

providential, lucky, fortunate, happy, favourable, propitious, auspicious, critical; suitable &c. 23; *obiter dicta*.

**Adv.** opportunely &c. *adj.*; in -proper, – due- -time, – course, – season; for the nonce; in the -nick, – fulness- of time; all in good time; just in time, at the eleventh hour, now or never.

by the -way, – by; *en passant*, *à propos*; *pro -re natâ*, – *hac vice*; *par parenthèse*, parenthetically, by way of parenthesis; while -speaking of, – on this subject; extempore; on the spur of the -moment, – occasion; on the spot &c. (*early*) 132.

**Phr.** *carpe diem*; *occasionem cognosce*; one's hour is come, the time is up; that reminds me.

**V.** be -ill timed &c. *adj.*; mistime, intrude, come amiss, break in upon; have other fish to fry; be -busy, – engaged, – tied up, – occupied.

lose –, throw away –, waste –, neglect &c. 460- an opportunity; allow –, suffer- the -opportunity, – occasion- to -pass, – slip, – go by, – escape, – lapse; waste time &c. (*be inactive*) 683; let slip through the fingers, lock the stable door when the steed is stolen.

**Adj.** ill-, mis-timed; untimely, intrusive, unseasonable; out of -date, – season; inopportune, timeless, untoward, *mal à propos*, unlucky, inauspicious, unpropitious, unfortunate, unfavourable; unsuited &c. 24; inexpedient &c. 647.

unpunctual &c. (*late*) 133; too late for; premature &c. (*early*) 132; too soon for; wise after the event.

**Adv.** inopportunely &c. *adj.*; as ill luck would have it, in an evil hour, the time having gone by, a day after the fair.

**Phr.** after meat mustard, after death the doctor.

---

## 3°. Recurrent Time

**136. Frequency.—N.** frequency, oftness; repetition, &c. 104.

**V.** recur &c. 104; do nothing but; keep, – on.

**Adj.** frequent, many times, not rare, thickcoming, incessant, perpetual, continual, constant, recurrent, repeated &c. 104; habitual &c. 613; hourly, &c. 138.

**Adv.** often, often to be met with, oft; oft-, often-times; frequently; repeatedly &c. 104; unseldom, not unfrequently; in -quick, – rapid- succession; many a time and oft; daily, hourly &c.; every -day, – hour, – moment &c.

perpetually, continually, constantly, incessantly, without ceasing, at all times, daily and hourly, night and day,

**137. Infrequency.—N.** infrequency, infrequence, rareness, rarity; fewness &c. 103; seldomness, uncommonness.

**V.** be -rare &c. *adj.*

**Adj.** un-, in-frequent; uncommon, sporadic, rare, – as a blue diamond; few &c. 103; scarce; almost unheard of, unprecedented, which has not occurred within the memory of the oldest inhabitant, not within one's previous experience.

**Adv.** seldom, rarely, scarcely, hardly; not often, unfrequently, infrequently, unoften; scarcely –, hardly- ever; once in a blue moon.

once; once -for all, – in a way; *pro hac vice*; like angels' visits, few and far between.

---

**day and night, day after day, morning noon and night, ever and anon.**

most often; commonly &c. (*habitually*) 613.

sometimes, occasionally, at times, now and then, from time to time, there being times when, *toties quoties*, often enough, again and again &c. 104.

**138. Regularity of recurrence. Periodicity.—N.** periodicity, intermittence; beat; oscillation &c. 314; pulse, pulsation; rhythm; alter-nation, -nateness, -nativeness, -nity.

bout, round, revolution, rotation, turn.

anniversary, birthday, jubilee, centenary, bi-, ter-centenary.

[Regularity of return] rota, cycle, period, stated time, routine; days of the week; Sunday, Monday &c.; months of the year; January &c.; feast, fast, saint's day &c.; Christmas, Easter, New Year's Day &c. 998; quarter-, Lady-, Midsummer-, Michaelmas-day; May Day, the King's Birthday; leap year; seasons.

punctuality, regularity, steadiness.

**V.** recur in regular -order, – succession; return, revolve, rotate; come -again, – in its turn; come round, – again; beat, pulsate; alternate; intermit.

**Adj.** periodic, -al; serial, recurrent, cyclic-, -al, rhythmic-, -al. even; recurring &c. *v.*; inter-, re-mittent; alternate, every other.

hourly; diurnal, daily; quotidian, tertian, weekly; hebdomad-al, -ary; bi-weekly, fortnightly; monthly, menstrual, catamenial; yearly, annual; biennial, triennial, &c.; bissextile; centennial, secular; paschal, lenten, &c.

regular, steady, punctual, constant, methodical, regular as clockwork.

**Adv.** periodically &c. *adj.*; at -regular intervals, – stated times; at -fixed, – established- periods; punctually &c. *adj.*; *de die in diem*; from day to day, day by day.

by turns; in -turn, – rotation; alternately, every other day, off and on, ride and tie, round and round.

**139. Irregularity of recurrence.—N.** irregularity, uncertainty, unpunctuality; fitfulness &c. *adj.*

**Adj.** irregular, uneven, uncertain, unpunctual, capricious, erratic, desultory, fitful, flickering; rambling, rhapsodical; spasmodic, unsystematic, unequal, variable, halting.

**Adv.** irregularly &c. *adj.*; by fits and starts &c. (*discontinuously*) 70.

---

## Section VII. CHANGE

### 1°. Simple Change

**140.** [Difference at different times.] **Change.—N.** change, alteration, mutation, permutation, variation, modification, modulation, inflexion, mood, qualification, innovation, *metastasis*, deviation, shift, turn; diversion; break.

transformation, transfiguration; metamorphosis; metabolism; transmutation; transubstantiation; metagenesis, transanimation, transmigration, me-

**141.** [Absence of change.] **Permanence.—N.** stability &c. 150; quiescence &c. 265; obstinacy &c. 606.

permanence, -cy, persistence, fixity, fixity of purpose, endurance, durability; standing, *status quo*; maintenance, preservation, conservation; conservatism; *laissez-faire*; law of the Medes and Persians; standing dish.

**V.** let -alone, – be; persist, remain,

tempsychosis; version; metathesis; transmogrification; catalysis; *avatar*; alterative.

conversion &c. (*gradual change*) 144; revolution &c. (*sudden or radical change*) 146; inversion &c. (*reversal*) 218; displacement &c. 185; transference &c. 270.

changeableness &c. 149; tergiversation &c. (*change of mind*) 607.

**V.** change, alter, vary, wax and wane; modulate, diversify, qualify, tamper with; turn, shift, veer, jibe, tack, chop, shuffle, swerve, dodge, warp, deviate, turn aside, evert, intervert; pass to, take a turn, turn the corner, resume.

work a change, modify, vamp, revamp, superinduce; trans-form, -mute, -ume, -figure &c. *n.*; metamorphose, ring the changes; convert, resolve; revolutionize; chop and change; patch, re-shape.

innovate, introduce new blood, shuffle the cards, spin the wheel; give a -turn, - colour- to; influence, turn the scale; shift the scene, turn over a new leaf.

recast &c. 146; reverse &c. 218; disturb &c. 61; convert into &c. 144.

**Adj.** changed &c. *v.*; new-fangled; changeable &c. 149; transitional; modifiable; alterative.

**Adv.** *mutatis mutandis.*

**Int.** *quantum mutatus!*

**Phr.** 'a change came o'er the spirit of my dream'; *nous avons changé tout cela; tempora mutantur et nos mutamur in illis; non sum qualis eram.*

stay, tarry, rest; hold, - on; last, endure, bide, abide, aby, dwell, maintain, keep; stand, - still, - fast; subsist, live, outlive, survive; hold -, keep- one's -ground, - footing; hold good.

**Adj.** stable &c. 150; persisting &c. *v.*; permanent; established, fixed; durable; unchanged &c. (change &c. 140); unrenewed; intact, inviolate; persistent; monotonous, uncheckered; unfailing.

un-destroyed, -repealed, -suppressed; conservative, *qualis ab incepto*; prescriptive &c. (*old*) 124; stationary &c. 265.

**Adv.** *in statu quo*; for good, finally; at a stand, -still; *uti possidetis*; without a shadow of turning.

**Phr.** as you were!; *j'y suis j'y reste; esto perpetua; nolumus leges Angliæ mutari*; let sleeping dogs lie.

---

**142.** [Change from action to rest.] **Cessation.—N.** cessation, discontinuance, desistance, desinence.

inter-, re-mission; sus-pense, -pension; interruption, hitch; hartal; stop; stopping &c. *v.*; closure, stoppage, halt; arrival &c. 292.

pause, rest, lull, respite, truce, armistice, drop; interregnum, abeyance.

closure &c. 261.

dead -stop, - stand, - lock; checkmate; comma, colon, semicolon, period, full stop; end &c. 67; death &c. 360; *cæsura.*

**V.** cease, discontinue, desist, stay; break -, leave- off; hold, stop, pull up, stall, stop short, check; stick, deadlock, hang fire; halt; pause, rest.

have done with, give over, surcease,

**143. Continuance in action.—N.** continu-ance, -ation; run; extension, prolongation; maintenance, perpetuation; persistence &c. (*perseverance*) 604*a*; repetition &c. 104.

**V.** continue, persist; go -, jog -, keep -, carry -, run - hold- on; abide, keep, pursue, stick to; endure; take -, maintain- its course; keep up.

sustain, uphold, hold up, keep on foot; follow up, perpetuate, prolong; maintain; preserve &c. 604*a*; harp upon &c. (*repeat*) 104.

keep going, - alive, - at it, - the pot boiling, - the ball rolling, - up the ball; plod-, plug- along; slog on; die in harness; hold on -, pursue- the even tenor of one's way.

let be; *stare super antiquas vias*;

shut up shop; give up &c. (*relinquish*) 624.

hold –, stay- one's hand; rest on one's oars, repose on one's laurels.

come to a -stand, – standstill, – dead lock, – full stop; arrive &c. 292; go out, die away, peter out; wear -away, – off; pass away &c. (*be past*) 122; be at an end.

intromit, interrupt, suspend, interpel; inter-, re-mit; put -an end, – a stop, – a period- to; bring to a stand, -still; stop, cut out, cut short, arrest, avast; stem the -tide, – torrent; pull the check string; switch off.

**Int.** halt! hold! stop! enough! avast! have done! a truce to! scft! leave off! shut up! give over! chuck it!

*quieta non movere*; let things take their course.

**Adj.** continuing &c. *v.*; uninterrupted, unintermitting, unremitting, unvarying, unshifting; unreversed, unstopped, unrevoked, unvaried; sustained; undying &c. (*perpetual*) 112; inconvertible.

follow-up.

**Int.** carry on! right away!

**Phr.** *vestigia nulla retrorsum*; *labitur et labetur.*

---

**144.** [Gradual change to something different.] **Conversion.—N.** conversion, reduction, transmutation, transformation, development, resolution, assimilation; assumption; naturalization.

chemistry, alchemy; progress, growth, lapse, flux.

passage; transit, -ion; transmigration, shifting &c. *v.*; conjugation; convertibility.

crucible, alembic, caldron, retort, test tube &c.

convert, neophyte, proselyte, pervert, renegade, deserter, apostate, turncoat.

**V.** be converted into; become, get, wax; come –, turn- -to, – into; turn out, lapse, shift; run –, fall –, pass –, slide –, glide –, grow –, ripen –, open –, resolve itself –, settle –, merge- into; melt, grow, come round to, mature, mellow; assume the -form, – shape, – state, – nature, – character- of; illapse; assume a new phase, undergo a change.

convert –, resolve- into; make, render; mould, form &c. 240; remodel, new model, refound, reform, reorganize; assimilate –, bring –, reduce- to; transform.

**Adj.** converted into &c. *v.*; convertible, resolvable into; transitional; naturalized.

**Adv.** gradually &c. (*slowly*) 275; *in transitu* &c. (*transference*) 270.

**145. Reversion.—N.** reversion, return; revulsion; reaction.

turning point, turn of the tide; *status quo ante bellum*; calm before a storm.

alternation &c. (*periodicity*) 138; inversion &c. 218; recoil &c. 277; regression &c. 283; restoration &c. 660; relapse &c. 661; vicinism, atavism, throwback.

**V.** revert, turn back, return; relapse &c. 661; recoil &c. 277; retreat &c. 283; restore &c. 660; undo, unmake; turn the -tide, – scale; escheat.

**Adj.** reverting &c. *v.*; revulsive, reactionary.

**Adv.** *à rebours*, wrong side out.

**146.** [Sudden or violent change.] **Revolution.—N.** revolution, *bouleversement*, subversion, break up; destruction &c. 162; sudden –, radical –, sweeping –, organic- change; clean sweep, *coup d'état*, overthrow, *débâcle*; counter-revolution, rebellion &c. 742.

transilience, jump, leap, plunge, jerk, start; explosion; spasm, convulsion, throe, revulsion; storm, earthquake, eruption, upheaval, cataclysm.

legerdemain &c. (*trick*) 545.

**V.** revolutionize; new model, remodel, recast; strike out something new, break with the past; change the face of, unsex; revert &c. 742.

**Adj.** unrecognizable.

Revolutionary, Bolshevik &c. 742.

**147.** [Change of one thing for another.] **Substitution.—N.** substitution, subrogation, commutation; supplanting &c. *v.*, supersession, metonymy &c. (*figure of speech*) 521.

[Thing substituted] substitute, *succedaneum*, make-shift, temporary expedient, shift, *pis aller*, stop-gap, jury-mast, *locum tenens*, warming-pan, dummy, goat, scape-goat; double; changeling; *quid pro quo*, alternative; remount; representative &c. (*deputy*) 759; palimpsest.

price, purchase-money, consideration, equivalent.

**V.** substitute, put in the place of, change for; make way for, give place to; supply –, take- the place of; supplant, supersede, replace, cut out, serve as a substitute; step into –, stand in- the shoes of; make a shift –, put up- with; borrow of Peter to pay Paul; commute, redeem, compound for.

**Adj.** substituted &c. *v.*; vicarious, subdititious; substitutional.

**Adv.** instead; in -place, – lieu, – the stead, – the room- of; *faute de mieux*.

**148.** [Double or mutual change.] **Interchange.—N.** inter-, ex-change; com-, per-, inter-mutation; reciprocation, transposal, transposition, shuffling; reciprocity, castling [at chess]; hocus-pocus.

interchange-ableness, -ability.

barter &c. 794; tit for tat &c. (*retaliation*) 718; cross fire, battledore and shuttlecock; *quid pro quo*.

**V.** inter-, ex-, counter-change; bandy, transpose, shuffle, change hands, swap, trade, permute, reciprocate, commute; give and take, return the compliment; play at -puss in the corner, – battledore and shuttlecock; retaliate &c. 718; barter &c. 794.

**Adj.** interchanged &c. *v.*; reciprocal, mutual, commutative, interchanged &c. *v.*; interchangeable, intercurrent.

**Adv.** in exchange, *vice versâ*, *mutatis mutandis*, backwards and forwards, by turns, turn and turn about, turn about; each –, every one- in his turn.

---

## 2°. Complex Change

**149. Changeableness.—N.** changeableness &c. *adj.*; mutability, inconstancy; versatility, mobility; instability, unstable equilibrium; vacillation &c. (*irresolution*) 605; fluctuation, vicissitude; alternation &c. (*oscillation*) 314.

restlessness &c. *adj.*; fidgets, disquiet; dis-, in-quietude; unrest; agitation &c. 315.

moon, Proteus, chameleon, kaleidoscope, quicksilver, shifting sands, weathercock, harlequin, Cynthia of the minute, April showers; wheel of Fortune; transientness &c. 111.

**V.** fluctuate, vary, waver, flounder, flicker, flitter, flit, flutter, shift, shuffle, shake, totter, tremble, vacillate, wamble, turn and turn about, ring the changes; sway –, shift- to and fro; change and change about; oscillate

**150. Stability.—N.** stability; immutability &c. *adj.*; unchangeableness &c. *adj.*; constancy; stable equilibrium, immobility, soundness, vitality, stabiliment, stabilization, stiffness, ankylosis, solidity, *aplomb*.

establishment, fixture; rock, pillar, tower, foundation, leopard's spots, Ethiopian's skin, law of the Medes and Persians.

stabilimeter, stabilizator.

permanence &c. 141; obstinacy &c. 606.

**V.** be -firm &c. *adj.*; stick fast; stand –, keep –, remain- firm; weather the storm.

settle, establish, stablish, ascertain, fix, set, stabilitate, stabilize; retain, stet, keep hold; make -good, – sure; fasten &c. (*join*) 43; set on its legs, float; perpetuate.

&c. 314; vibrate –, oscillate- between two extremes; alternate; have as many phases as the moon.

**Adj.** change-able, -ful; changing &c. 140; mutable, variable, checkered, ever changing, kaleidoscopic, prote-an, -iform; versatile.

unstaid, inconstant; un-steady, -stable, -fixed, -settled; fluctuating &c. *v.*; restless; mercurial; agitated &c. 315; erratic, fickle; irresolute &c. 605; capricious &c. 608; touch-and-go; inconsonant, fitful, spasmodic; vibratory; vagrant, wayward, wavering; desultory; afloat; alternating; alterable, plastic, mobile; fleeting, transient &c. 111.

**Adv.** see-saw &c. (*oscillation*) 314; off and on.

---

settle down; strike –, take- root; take up one's abode &c. 184; build one's house on a rock.

**Adj.** unchangeable, immutable; unalter-ed, -able; not to be changed, constant; permanent &c. 141; invariable, undeviating; stable, durable; perennial &c. (*diuturnal*) 110.

fixed, steadfast, firm, fast, steady, balanced; confirmed, valid, fiducial, immovable, irremovable, riveted, rooted; settled, established &c. *v.*; vested; incontrovertible, stereotyped, indeclinable.

tethered, anchored, moored, at anchor, on a rock, firm as a rock; firmly -seated, – established &c. *v.*; deep-rooted, ineradicable; inveterate; obstinate &c. 606.

transfixed, stuck fast, aground, high and dry, stranded.

indefeasible, irretrievable, intransmutable, incommutable, irresoluble, irrevocable, irreversible, reverseless, inextinguishable, irreducible; indissol-uble, -vable; indestructible, undying, imperishable, indelible, indeciduous; insusceptible, – of change.

**Int.** *stet.*

*Present Events*

**151. Eventuality.—N.** eventuality, event, occurrence, incident, affair, transaction, proceeding, fact; matter of –, naked- fact; phenomenon; advent.

business, concern; circumstance, particular, casualty, happening, accident, adventure, passage, crisis, pass, emergency, contingency, consequence &c. 154.

the world, life, things, doings, affairs, matters; things –, affairs- in general; the times, state of affairs, order of the day; course –, tide –, stream –, current –, run –, march- of -things, – events; ups and downs of life; chapter of accidents &c. (*chance*) 156; situation &c. (*circumstances*) 8.

**V.** happen, occur; take -place, – effect; come, become of; come -off, – about, – round, – into existence, – forth, – to pass, – on; pass, present itself; fall; fall –, turn- out; run, be on foot, fall in; be-fall, -tide, -chance; prove, eventuate, draw on; turn –, crop –, spring –, cast- up; super-, sur-vene; issue, emanate, arrive, ensue,

*Future Events*

**152. Destiny.—N.** destiny &c. (*necessity*) 601; hereafter, future –, post existence; future state, next world, world to come, after life; futurity &c. 121; everlasting -life, – death; prospect &c. (*expectation*) 507.

**V.** impend; hang –, lie –, hover- over; threaten, loom, await, come on, approach, stare one in the face; fore-, pre-ordain; predestine, doom, foredoom, foreshadow, have in store for.

**Adj.** impending &c. *v.*; destined; about to -be, – happen; coming, in store, to come, going to happen, instant, at hand, near; near –, close- at hand; overhanging, hanging over one's head, imminent; brewing, preparing, forthcoming; in the wind, on the cards, in reserve; that -will, – is to- be; in prospect &c. (*expected*) 507; looming in the -distance, – horizon, – future; unborn, in embryo; in the womb of -time; – futurity; on the knees of the gods; pregnant &c. (*producing*) 161.

**Adv.** in -time, – the long run; all in good time; eventually &c. 151; what-

arise, start, hold, take its course; pass off &c. (*be past*) 122.

meet with; experience; fall to the lot of; be one's -chance, – fortune, – lot; find; encounter, undergo; pass –, go- through; endure &c. (*feel*) 821.

ever may happen &c. (*certainly*) 474; as -chance &c. 156- would have it.

**Adj.** happening &c. *v.*; going on, doing, current; in the wind, afloat; on -foot, – the *tapis*; at issue, in question; incidental.

eventful, momentous, signal; stirring, bustling, full of incident.

**Adv.** eventually, ultimately, in -the event of, – case; in the course of things; in the -natural, – ordinary- course of things; as -things, – times- go; as the world -goes, – wags; as the -tree falls, – cat jumps; as it may -turn out, – happen.

**Phr.** the plot thickens.

## Section VIII. CAUSATION

### 1°. Constancy of Sequence in Events

**153.** [Constant antecedent.] **Cause.—N.** cause, origin, source, principle, element; occasioner, prime mover, engine, turbine, motor, *primum mobile*; *vera causa*; author &c. (*producer*) 164; main-spring, agent; dynamo, generator, battery (electric); leaven; groundwork, foundation &c. (*support*) 215.

spring, fountain, well, font; fountain –, spring- head; *fons et origo*, genesis; descent &c. (*paternity*) 166; remote cause; influence.

pivot, hinge, turning-point, lever; key; kernel, core; proximate cause, *causa causans*; last straw that breaks the camel's back.

ground; reason, – why; why and wherefore, rationale, occasion, derivation; final cause &c. (*intention*) 620; *le dessous des cartes*; undercurrents.

rudiment, egg, germ, embryo, fœtus bud, root, *radix*, radical, etymon, nucleus, seed, stem, stalk, stock, *stirps*, trunk, tap-root; latent organism.

nest, cradle, nursery, womb, *nidus*, birth-, breeding-place, hot-bed.

caus-ality, -ation; origination; production &c. 161.

**V.** be the -cause &c. *n.*- of; originate; give -origin, – rise, – occasion- to; cause, occasion, sow the seeds of, kindle, suscitate; bring -on, – to pass, – about; produce; create &c. 161; set -up, – afloat, – on foot; found, broach,

**154.** [Constant sequent.] **Effect.—N.** effect, consequence, sequela; derivative, -tion; result; result-ant, -ance; upshot, issue, *dénouement*; outcome; termination, end &c. 67; development, outgrowth, fruit, crop, harvest, product, bud, blossom, florescence, ear.

production, produce, product, finished product, work, handiwork, fabric, performance; creature, creation; offspring, -shoot; first-fruits, -lings; *prémices*.

**V.** be the -effect &c. *n.*- of; be -due, – owing- to; originate -in, – from; rise –, arise –, take its rise –, spring –, proceed –, emanate –, come –, grow –, bud –, sprout –, germinate –, issue –, flow –, result –, follow –, derive its origin –, accrue- from; come -to, – of, – out of; depend –, hang –, hinge –, turn- upon.

take the consequences, sow the wind and reap the whirlwind.

**Adj.** owing to; resulting from &c. *v.*; resultant; derivable from; due to; caused &c. by, 153; dependent upon; derived –, evolved- from; derivative; hereditary.

**Adv.** of course, it follows that, naturally, consequently; as a –, in- consequence; through all, all along of, necessarily, eventually.

**Phr.** *cela va sans dire*, thereby hangs a tale.

institute, lay the foundation of, inaugurate; lie at the root of.

procure, induce, draw down, open the door to, superinduce, evoke, entail, operate; elicit, provoke.

conduce to &c. (*tend to*) 176; contribute; promote; have a -hand in, – finger in- the pie; determine, decide, turn the scale, give the casting vote; have a common origin; derive its origin &c. (*effect*) 154.

**Adj.** caused &c. *v.*; causal, original; prim-ary, -itive, -ordial; aboriginal; radical; inceptive, embry-onic, -otic; *in -embryo, – ovo*; seminal, germinal; formative, productive &c. 168; at the bottom of; connate, having a common origin.

**Adv.** because &c. 155; behind the scenes.

**155.** [Assignment of cause.] **Attribution.—N.** attribution, theory, etiology, ascription, reference to, rationale; accounting for &c. *v.*; palaetiology,* imputation, derivation from.

fil-, affil-iation; pedigree &c. (*paternity*) 166.

explanation &c. (*interpretation*) 522; reason why &c. (*cause*) 153.

**V.** attribute –, ascribe –, impute –, refer –, lay –, point –, trace –, bring home- to; put –, set- down- to; charge –, ground- on; invest with, assign as cause, charge with, blame, lay at the door of, father upon; saddle with; affiliate; account for, derive from, point out the -reason &c. 153; theorize; tell how it comes; put the saddle on the right horse.

**Adj.** attributed &c. *v.*; attributable &c. *v.*; refer-able, -rible; due to, derivable from; owing to &c. (*effect*) 154; putative.

**Adv.** hence, thence, therefore, for, since, on account of, because, owing to; on that account; from -this, – that- cause; thanks to, forasmuch as; whence, *propter hoc*.

why? wherefore? whence? how -comes, – is, – happens- it? how does it happen?

in -some, – some such- way; somehow, – or other.

**Phr.** that is why; *hinc illæ lachrymæ*; *cherchez la femme*.

**156.** [Absence of assignable cause.] **Chance.**†**—N.** chance, indetermination, accident, fortune, hazard, hap, haphazard, chance-medley, random, luck, *raccroc*, casualty, fortuity, contingence, coincidence, adventure, hit; fate &c. (*necessity*) 601; equal chance; lottery, raffle, tombola, sweepstake; toss up &c. 621; turn of the -table, – cards; hazard of the die, chapter of accidents; cast –, throw- of the dice; heads or tails, wheel of Fortune, whirligig of chance; *sortes, – Virgilianæ, -biblicæ*.

probability, possibility, contingency, odds, long odds, run of luck; main-chance.

theory of -probabilities, – chances; book-making; assurance; speculation, gamble, gaming &c. 621.

**V.** chance, hap, turn up; fall to one's lot; be one's -fate &c. 601; stumble on, light –, blunder –, hit- upon; take one's chance &c. 621.

**Adj.** casual, fortuitous, accidental, haphazard, random, stray, adventitious, adventive, causeless, incidental. contingent, uncaused, undetermined, indeterminate; possible &c. 470; unintentional &c. 621.

**Adv.** by -chance, – accident; casually; perchance &c. (*possibly*) 470; for aught one knows; as -good, – bad, – ill-luck &c. *n.*- would have it; as it may -be, – chance, – turn up, – happen; as the case may be.

## 2°. Connection between Cause and Effect

**157. Power.—N.** power; poten-cy, -tiality; puissance, might, force; energy &c. 171; dint; right -hand, – arm;

**158. Impotence.—N.** impotence; in-, dis-ability; disablement, impuissance, imbecility, caducity; incapa-city,

* Whewell, 'History of the Inductive Sciences,' book xviii, vol. iii., p. 397 (3rd edit.).

† The word *Chance* has two distinct meanings: the first, the absence of assignable *cause*, as above; and the second, the absence of *design*—for the latter see 621.

ascendency, sway, control; pre-potency, -pollence; almightiness, omnipotence; authority &c. 737; strength &c. 159.

ability; ableness &c. *adj.*; competency; effi-ciency, -cacy; validity, cogency; enablement; vantage ground; influence &c. 175; horse power; dynamometer.

pressure; elasticity; gravity, electricity, magnetism, galvanism, voltaic electricity, voltaism, electro-magnetism, electrostatics, electrification, electric current &c.; attraction, repulsion; *vis -inertiæ, – mortua, – viva*; potential –, dynamic –, kinetic –, electrical –, chemical –, atomic- energy; friction, suction.

capability, capacity; *quid valeant humeri quid ferre recusent*; faculty, quality, attribute, endowment, virtue, gift, property, qualification, susceptibility.

V. be -powerful &c. *adj.*; gain -power &c. *n.*

belong –, pertain- to; lie –, be- in one's power; can.

give –, confer –, exercise- power &c. *n.*; empower, enable, invest; in-, en-due; endow, arm; strengthen &c. 159; compel &c. 744.

Adj. powerful, puissant; potent, -ial; capable, able; equal –, up- to; cogent, valid; effect-ive, -ual; efficient, efficacious, adequate, competent; multi-, pleni-, omni-, armi- potent; mighty, ascendent; almighty.

electric, electrical &c.

forcible &c. *adj.* (*energetic*) 171; influential &c. 175; productive &c. 168.

Adv. powerfully &c. *adj.*; by -virtue, – dint- of.

---

-bility; inapt-, inept-itude; indocility; invalidity, inefficiency, incompetence, disqualification.

*telum imbelle, brutum fulmen*, blank cartridge, flash in the pan, *vox et præterea nihil*, dead letter, bit of waste paper, dummy; scrap of paper.

inefficacy &c. (*inutility*) 645; failure &c. 732.

helplessness &c. *adj.*; prostration, paralysis, palsy, ataxia, apoplexy, syncope, sideration, *deliquium*, collapse, exhaustion, softening of the brain, emasculation, inanition, senility &c. 128; castrato, eunuch.

cripple, old woman, muff, mollycoddle, milksop.

V. be -impotent &c. *adj.*; not have a leg to stand on.

*vouloir -rompre l'anguille au genou, – prendre la lune avec les dents.*

collapse, faint, swoon, fall into a swoon, drop; go by the board; end in smoke &c. (*fail*) 732.

render -powerless &c. *adj.*; deprive of power; decontrol; dis-able, -enable; disarm, incapacitate, disqualify, unfit, invalidate, undermine, deaden, cramp, tie the hands; double up, prostrate, paralyze, muzzle, cripple, becripple, maim, lame, hamstring, draw the teeth of; throttle, strangle, *garrotte*; ratten, silence, sprain, clip the wings of, render *hors de combat*, spike the guns; take the wind out of one's sails, scotch the snake, put a spoke in one's wheel; break the -neck, – back; un-hinge, -fit; put out of gear.

unman, unnerve, devitalize, attenuate, enervate; emasculate, spay, caponize, castrate, geld; effeminize.

shatter, exhaust; weaken &c. 160.

Adj. powerless, impotent, unable, incapable, incompetent; ineff-icient, -ective; inept; un-fit, -fitted; un-, dis-qualified; unendowed; in-, un-apt; crippled, decrepit, disabled &c. *v.*; armless.

harmless, unarmed, weaponless, defenceless, *sine ictu*, unfortified, indefensible, vincible, pregnable, untenable.

para-lytic, -lyzed; palsied, imbecile; nerve-, sinew-, marrow-, pith-, lust-less; emasculate, disjointed; out of -joint, – gear; un- -nerved, -hinged; water-logged, on one's beam ends, rudderless; laid on one's back; done up, dead beat, exhausted, shattered, demoralized; gravelled &c. (*in difficulty*) 704; helpless, unfriended, fatherless; without a leg to stand on, *hors de combat*, laid on the shelf;

null and void, nugatory, inoperative, good for nothing; dud; invertebrate; ineffectual &c. (*failing*) 732; inadequate &c. 640; inefficacious &c. (*useless*) 645.

**159.** [Degree of power.] **Strength.** —**N.** strength; power &c. 157; energy &c. 171; vigour, force; main –, physical –, brute- force; spring, elasticity, tone, tension, tonicity.

stoutness &c. *adj*; lustihood, stamina, nerve, muscle, sinew, thews and sinews, *physique*; pith, -iness; virility, vitality.

athlet-ics, -icism; gymnastics, feats of strength.

adamant, steel, iron, oak, heart of oak; iron grip; grit, bone.

athlete, gymnast, tumbler, acrobat; Atlas, Hercules, Antæus, Samson, Cyclops, Goliath, Titan; tower of strength; giant refreshed.

strengthening &c. *v.*; invigoration, refreshment, refocillation.

[Science of forces] dynamics, statics.

**V.** be -strong &c. *adj.*, – stronger; overmatch.

render -strong &c. *adj.*; give -strength &c. *n.*; strengthen, invigorate, brace, nerve, fortify, buttress, sustain, harden, case-harden, steel; gird; screw –, wind –, set- up; gird –, brace- up one's loins; recruit, set on one's legs; vivify; refresh &c. 689; refect; reinforce &c. (*restore*) 660.

**Adj.** strong, mighty, vigorous, forcible, hard, adamantine, stout, robust, sturdy, hardy, powerful, potent, puissant, valid.

resistless, irresistible, invincible, proof against, impregnable, unconquerable, indomitable, inextinguishable, unquenchable; incontestable; more than a match for; over-powering, -whelming; all-powerful; sovereign.

able-bodied; athletic, gymnastic; Herculean, Cyclopean, Atlantean; muscular, husky, brawny, wiry, well-knit, broad-shouldered, sinewy, strapping, stalwart, gigantic.

man-ly, -like, -ful; masculine, male, virile, in the prime of manhood.

un-weakened, -allayed, -withered, -shaken, -worn, -exhausted; in full -force, – swing; in the plenitude of power.

**160. Weakness.**—**N.** weakness &c. *adj.*; debility, atony, relaxation, languor, enervation; impotence &c. 158 infirmity; effeminancy, feminality; fragility, flaccidity; inactivity &c. 683.

declension –, loss –, failure- of strength; delicacy, invalidation, decrepitude, asthenia, adynamy, cachexy, *cachexia*, anæmia, bloodlessness, sprain, strain.

reed, thread, rope of sand, broken reed, house -of cards, – built on sand.

soft-, weak-ling; infant &c. 129; youth &c. 127.

**V.** be -weak &c. *adj.*; drop, crumble, give way, totter, tremble, shake, halt, limp, fade, languish, decline, flag, fail, have one foot in the grave.

render -weak &c. *adj.*; weaken, enfeeble, debilitate, shake, deprive of strength, relax, enervate; un-brace, -nerve; cripple, unman, &c. (*render powerless*) 158; cramp, reduce, sprain, strain, blunt the edge of; dilute, impoverish; decimate; extenuate; reduce -in strength, – the strength of; invalidate; *mettre de l'eau dans son vin.*

**Adj.** weak, feeble, debile; impotent &c. 158; relaxed, unnerved &c. *v.*; sap-, strength-, power-less; weakly, unstrung, flaccid, adynamic, asthenic; nervous.

soft, effeminate, feminate, womanish.

frail, fragile, shattery, frangible, brittle &c. 328; flimsy, unsubstantial, gimcrack, gingerbread; rickety, cranky; creachy; drooping, tottering &c. *v.*; broken, lame, halt, game, withered, shattered, shaken, crazy, shaky, tumble-down; palsied &c. 158; decrepit; C3.

languid, poor, poorly, infirm; faint, -ish; sickly &c. (*disease*) 655; dull, slack, evanid, spent, short-winded, effete; weatherbeaten; decayed, rotten, worn, seedy, languishing, wasted, washy, wishy-washy, laid low, pulled down, the worse for wear.

un-strengthened &c. 159, -supported, -aided, -assisted; aidless, defenceless &c. 158.

stubborn, thick-ribbed, made of iron, deep-rooted; strong as -a lion, – a horse, – brandy; sound as a roach; in -fine, – high- feather; in fine fettle; like a giant refreshed.

**Adv.** strongly &c. *adj.*; by -force &c. *n.*; by main force &c. (*by compulsion*) 744.

**Phr.** 'our withers are unwrung.'

on its last legs; weak as a -child, – baby, – chicken, – cat, – rat; weak as -water, – water gruel, – gingerbread, – milk and water; colourless &c. 429.

**Phr.** *non sum qualis eram.*

---

### 3°. Power in Operation

**161. Production.—N.** production, creation, construction, formation, fabrication, manufacture; building, architecture, erection, edification; coinage; organization; *nisus formativus*; putting together &c. *v.*; establishment; workmanship, performance; achievement &c. (*completion*) 729; effect &c. 154.

flowering, fructification, fruition.

bringing forth &c. *v.*; parturition, birth, birth-throe, child-birth, delivery, confinement, *accouchement*, travail, labour, midwifery, obstetrics; geniture; gestation &c. (*maturation*) 673; evolution, development, growth; genesis, fertilization, breeding, conception, germination, generation, *epigenesis*, pro-creation, -generation, -pagation; fecundation, impregnation; spontaneous generation; *arche-genesis, -biosis; bio-, abio-, homo-, xeno-genesis.**

authorship, publication; works, *œuvre, opus.*

edifice, building, structure, fabric, erection, pile, tower, flower, fruit.

**V.** produce, perform, operate, do, make, gar, form, construct, fabricate, frame, contrive, manufacture; weave, forge, coin, carve, chisel; build, raise, edify, rear, erect, put together; set –, run- up; establish, constitute, compose, organize, institute, get up; achieve, accomplish &c. (*complete*) 729.

flower, sprout, blossom, burgeon, bear fruit, fructify, spawn, teem, ean, yean, farrow, drop, calf, pup, whelp, kitten, kindle; bear, lay, bring forth, give birth to, lie in, be brought to bed of, evolve, pullulate, usher into the world.

make productive &c. 168; create; beget, conceive, get, generate, fecun-

**162.** [Non-production.] **Destruction. —N.** destruction; waste, dissolution, breaking up; di-, dis-ruption; consumption; disorganization.

fall, downfall, ruin, perdition, crash, smash, havoc, *délabrement, débâcle*; break -down, – up; prostration; desolation, *bouleversement*, wreck, crack-up, crash, wrack, shipwreck, cataclysm; Caudine Forks, Sedan.

extinction, annihilation; destruction of life &c. 361; knock-out, knock-down blow; doom, crack of doom.

destroying &c. *v.*; demo-lition, -lishment; biblioclasm; overthrow, subversion, suppression; abolition &c. (*abrogation*) 756; sacrifice; ravage, devastation, *sabotage, razzia*; incendiarism; revolution &c. 146; extirpation &c. (*extraction*) 301; *commencement de la fin*, road to ruin; dilapidation &c. (*deterioration*) 659.

**V.** be -destroyed &c.; perish; fall, – to the ground; tumble, topple; go –, fall- to pieces; break up; crumble, – to dust; go to -the dogs, – the wall, – smash, – shivers, – wreck, – pot, – wrack and ruin; go -by the board, – all to smash, – to pieces, – under; be all -over, – up- with; totter to its fall.

destroy; do –, make- away with; nullify; annul &c. 756; sacrifice, demolish; tear up; over-turn, -throw, -whelm; upset, subvert, put an end to; seal the doom of, do for, dish, undo; break –, cut- up; break –, cut –, pull –, mow –, blow –, beat- down; suppress, quash, put down; cut short, take off, blot out; dispel, dissipate, dissolve; consume; abolish.

smash, – to smithereens, quell, squash, squelch, crumple up, shatter,

* Huxley.

date, impregnate; pro-create, -generate, -pagate; engender; bring –, call- into -being, – existence; breed, hatch, develop, bring up.

induce, superinduce; suscitate; cause &c. 153; acquire &c. 775.

**Adj.** produc-ed, -ing &c. *v.*; productive of; prolific &c. 168; creative; formative; gen-etic, -ial, -ital; fertile, pregnant; *enceinte*, big –, fraught-with; with child, in the family way, teeming, parturient, in the straw, brought to bed of; puerper-al, -ous.

architectonic; constructive.

---

shiver; batter; tear –, crush –, cut –, shake –, pull –, pick- to pieces; nip; tear to -rags, – tatters; crush –, knock- to atoms; pulverize; ruin; strike out; throw –, knock- -down, – over; lay by the heels; fell, sink, swamp, scuttle, wreck, crash, shipwreck, engulf, submerge; lay in -ashes, – ruins; sweep away, erase, expunge, strike out, delete, efface, raze; level, – with the -ground, – dust.

deal destruction, lay waste, ravage, gut; disorganize; dismantle &c. (*render useless*) 645; devour, swallow up, desolate, devastate, sap, mine, blast, confound; exterminate, extinguish, quench, annihilate; snuff –, put –, stamp –, trample- out; lay –, trample- in the dust; prostrate; tread –, crush –, trample- under foot; lay the axe to the root of; make -short work, – a clean sweep, – mincemeat- of; cut up root and branch; fling –, scatter- to the winds; throw overboard; strike at the root of, sap the foundations of, spring a mine, blow up; ravage with fire and sword; cast to the dogs; eradicate &c. 301.

**Adj.** destroyed &c. *v.*; perishing &c. *v.*; trembling –, nodding –, tottering- to its fall; in course of -destruction &c. *n.*; extinct.

destructive, subversive, ruinous, incendiary. deletory; destroying &c. *v.*; suicidal; deadly &c. (*killing*) 361.

**Adv.** with -crushing effect, – a sledge-hammer.

**Phr.** *delenda est Carthago.*

**163. Reproduction.**—**N.** reproduction, renovation; restoration &c. 660; renewal; new edition, reprint &c. 21; revival, regeneration, palingenesia, revivification; apotheosis; resuscitation, reanimation, resurrection, resurgence, reappearance, atavism; Phœnix; reincarnation.

generation &c. (*production*) 161; multiplication.

**V.** reproduce; restore &c. 660; revive, renovate, renew, regenerate, revivify, resuscitate, reanimate, refashion, stir the embers, put into the crucible; multiply, repeat, resurge.

crop up, spring up like mushrooms.

**Adj.** reproduced &c. *v.*; renascent, reappearing; reproductive; resurgent; progenitive; Hydra-headed.

**164. Producer.**—**N.** producer, creator, deviser, designer, originator, inventor, author, founder, generator, mover, architect; grower, constructor, maker &c. (*agent*) 690.

**165. Destroyer.**—**N.** destroyer &c. (destroy &c. 162); cankerworm &c. (*bane*) 663; iconoclast; assassin &c. (*killer*) 361; executioner &c. (*punish*) 975; Hun, Vandal, nihilist, anarchist.

**166. Paternity.**—**N.** paternity; parentage; fatherhood; consanguinity &c. 11.

parent, father, sire, dad, daddy, papa, governor, *pater*, *paterfamilias*, *abba*; genitor, progenitor, procreator, begetter; ancestor; grand-sire, -father; great-grandfather.

**167. Posterity.**—**N.** posterity, progeny, breed, issue, offspring, brood, litter, seed, farrow, spawn, spat; family, children, grandchildren, heirs; great-grandchild.

child, son, daughter; kid; infant &c. 129; bantling, scion; shoot, sprout, olive branch, sprit, branch; off-shoot,

house, stem, trunk, tree, stock, *stirps*, pedigree, lineage, line, family, tribe, sept, race, clan; genealogy, descent, extraction, birth, ancestry; forefathers, forbears, patriarchs.

motherhood, maternity; mother, dam, mamma, *materfamilias*; grandmother; matriarch.

**Adj.** paternal, parental; maternal; family, ancestral, linear, matrilinear, patrilineal, patriarchal.

-set; ramification; descendant; **heir**, -ess; heir -apparent, – presumptive; chip of the old block; heredity; rising generation.

straight descent, sonship, line, lineage, filiation, primogeniture.

**Adj.** filial.

---

**168. Productiveness.—N.** productiveness &c. *adj.*; fecundity, fertility, luxuriance, uberty.

pregnancy, pullulation, fructification, multiplication, propagation, procreation; superfetation.

milch cow, rabbit, hydra, warren, seed-plot, land flowing with milk and honey; second crop, after-crop, -growth, -math; fertilization.

**V.** make -productive &c. *adj.*; fructify; procreate, generate, fertilize, spermatize, impregnate; fecund-ate, -ify; teem, pullulate, multiply; produce &c. 161; conceive.

**Adj.** productive, prolific; teem-ing, -ful; fertile, fruitful, frugiferous, fruit-bearing; fructiferous; fecund, luxuriant; pregnant, uberous.

procre-ant, -ative; generative, life-giving, spermatic; originative; multiparous; omnific; propagable.

parturient &c. (*producing*) 161; profitable &c. (*useful*) 644.

**169. Unproductiveness.—N.** unproductiveness &c. *adj.*; infertility, sterility, infecundity; impotence &c. 158; unprofitableness &c. (*inutility*) 645.

waste, desert, Sahara, wild, wilderness, howling wilderness.

**V.** be -unproductive &c. *adj.*; hang fire, flash in the pan, come to nothing.

**Adj.** unproductive, inoperative, barren, addle, unfertile, unprolific, arid, sterile, unfruitful, acarpous, infecund; *sine prole*; fallow; teem-, issue-, fruitless; unprofitable &c. (*useless*) 645; null and void, of no effect.

---

**170. Agency.—N.** agency, operation, force, working, strain, function, office, maintenance, exercise, work, swing, play; inter-working, -action, procuration, procurement.

causation &c. 153; instrumentality &c. 631; influence &c. 175; action &c. (*voluntary*) 680; *modus operandi* &c. 627.

quickening –, maintaining- power; home stroke.

**V.** be -in action &c. *adj.*; operate, work; act, – upon; perform, play, support, sustain, strain, maintain, take effect, quicken, strike.

come –, bring- into -operation, – play; have -play, – free play; bring to bear upon.

**Adj.** operative, efficient, efficacious, practical, effectual.

at work, on foot; acting &c. (*doing*) 680; in -operation, – force, – action, – play, – exercise; acted –, wrought- upon.

**Adv.** by the -agency &c. *n.*- of; through &c. (*instrumentality*) 631; by means of &c. 632.

**171.** Physical **Energy.—N.** energy, physical energy, force; keenness &c. *adj.*; intensity, vigour, strength, elasticity; go; pep, live wire, high pressure; backbone, mettle, fire, vim.

**acri-mony, -tude, -dity; causticity,**

**172.** Physical **Inertness.—N.** inertness, dulness &c. *adj.*; inertia, *vis inertiæ*, inertion, inactivity, torpor, languor; dormancy, quiescence &c. 265; latency, inaction, passivity.

mental inertness; sloth &c. (*inac-*

virulence, poignancy; harshness &c. *adj.*; severity, edge, point; pungency &c. 392.

cantharides; Spanish fly; seasoning &c. (*condiment*) 393, stimulant, excitant.

activity, agitation, effervescence; ferment, -ation; ebullition, splutter, perturbation, stir, bustle; voluntary energy &c. 682; quicksilver.

resolution &c. (*mental energy*) 604; exertion &c. (*effort*) 686; excitation &c. (*mental*) 824.

**V.** give -energy &c. *n.*; energize, stimulate, kindle, excite, activate, exert; sharpen, pep up, intensify; inflame &c. (*render violent*) 173; wind up &c. (*strengthen*) 159.

strike, – into, – hard, – home; make an impression.

**Adj.** strong, energetic, forcible, active; strenuous, forceful, mettlesome, enterprising, go ahead; intense, deep-dyed, severe, keen, vivid, sharp, acute, incisive, trenchant, brisk, vigorous, live.

rousing, irritating; poignant; virulent, caustic, corrosive, mordant, harsh, stringent; double-edged, – shotted, – distilled; drastic, escharotic; racy &c. (*pungent*) 392; sarcastic &c. 932; irenic.

potent &c. (*powerful*) 157; radio-active.

**Adv.** strongly &c. *adj.*; *fortiter in re*; with telling effect.

**Phr.** the steam is up; *vires acquirit eundo.*

tivity) 683; inexcitability &c. 826; irresolution &c. 605; obstinacy &c. 606; permanence &c. 141.

**V.** be -inert &c. *adj.*; hang fire, smoulder.

**Adj.** inert, inactive, passive, pacific; torpid &c. 683; sluggish, stagnant, dull, heavy, flat, slack, tame, slow, blunt; lifeless, dead, uninfluential.

latent, dormant, smouldering, unexerted.

**Adv.** inactively &c. *adj.*; in -suspense, -abeyance.

**173. Violence.—N.** violence, inclemency, vehemence, might, impetuosity; boisterousness &c. *adj.*; effervescence, ebullition; turbulence, bluster; uproar, riot, row, rumpus, *le diable à quatre*, devil to pay, all the fat in the fire.

severity &c. 739; ferocity, rage, berserk, fury; exacerbation, exasperation, malignity; fit, paroxysm, orgasm; force, brute force; outrage; *coup de main*; strain, shock, shog; spasm, convulsion, throe; hysterics, passion &c. (*state of excitability*) 825.

out-break, -burst; burst, bounce, dissilience, discharge, volley, explosion, blow up, blast, detonation, rush, eruption, displosion, torrent.

turmoil &c. (*disorder*) 59; ferment &c. (*agitation*) 315; storm, tempest, rough weather; squall &c. (*wind*) 349; earthquake, volcano, thunderstorm.

fury, dragon, demon, tiger, beldame, Tisiphone, Megæra, Alecto, madcap, wild beast; fire-eater &c. (*blusterer*) 887.

**V.** be -violent &c. *adj.*; run high; ferment, effervesce; romp, rampage; run -wild, – riot; break the peace;

**174. Moderation.—N.** moderation; lenity &c. 740; temperance, temperateness, gentleness &c. *adj.*; sobriety; quiet; mental calmness &c. (*inexcitability*) 826.

moderating &c. *v.*; relaxation, remission, mitigation &c. 834; tranquillization, alleviation, assuagement, appeasement, contemporation, pacification.

measure, *juste milieu*, golden mean &c. 29.

moderator; lullaby, sedative, lenitive, demulcent, rose-water, balm, soothing syrup, poppy, opiate, anodyne, milk, opium, laudanum, 'poppy or mandragora'; wet blanket; palliative, calmative.

**V.** be -moderate &c. *adj.*; keep within -bounds, – compass; sober –, settle- down; keep the peace, remit, relent; shorten sail.

moderate, soften, mitigate, temper, accoy; at-, con-temper; mollify, lenify, dull, take off the edge, blunt, obtund, sheathe, subdue, chasten; sober –, tone –, smooth- down; censor, blue-

rush, tear; rush head-long, -foremost; run amuck, raise a storm, make a riot; make –, kick up- a row, – a fuss; bluster, rage, roar, riot, storm; boil, – over; fume, foam, come in like a lion, wreak, bear down, ride rough-shod, out-Herod Herod; spread like wildfire.

break –, fly –, burst- out; bounce, shock, strain; break-, pry-, force-, prize- open.

render -violent &c. *adj.*; sharpen, stir up, quicken, excite, incite, urge, lash, stimulate; irritate, inflame, exacerbate, kindle, suscitate, foment; accelerate, aggravate, exasperate, convulse, infuriate, madden, lash into fury; fan –, add fuel to- the flame; *oleum addere camino.*

explode, go off, displode, fly, detonate, thunder, blow up, flash, flare, erupt, burst; let -off, – fly; discharge, detonize, fulminate.

**Adj.** violent, vehement, forcible; warm; acute, sharp; rough, rude, ungentle, bluff, boisterous, wild, vicious; brusque, abrupt, waspish; impetuous; rampant.

turbulent; disorderly; blustering, raging &c. *v.*; troublous, riotous; tumultu-ary, -ous; obstreperous, uproarious; extravagant, unmitigated; ravening, tameless; frenzied &c. (*insane*) 503; desperate &c. (*rash*) 863; infuriate, towering, furious, outrageous, frantic, hysteric, in hysterics.

fiery, flaming, scorching, hot, red-hot, ebullient.

savage, fierce, ferocious, fierce as a tiger.

excited &c. *v.*; un-quelled, -quenched, -extinguished, -repressed, -bridled, -ruly; headstrong; un-governable, -appeasable, -mitigable; un-, in-controllable; insup-, irre-pressible.

spasmodic, convulsive, explosive; detonating &c. *v.*; volcanic, meteoric; stormy &c. (*wind*) 349.

**Adv.** violently &c. *adj.*; amain; by -storm, – force, – main force; with might and main; tooth and nail, *vi et armis*, at the point of the -sword, – bayonet; at one fell swoop; with a high hand, through thick and thin; in desperation, with a vengeance; *à –, à toute outrance*; head-long, -foremost, -first; like a bull at a gate.

pencil, weaken &c. 160; lessen &c. (*decrease*) 36; check; palliate.

tranquillize, assuage, appease, dulcify, swage, lull, soothe, compose, still, calm, cool, quiet, hush, quell, sober, pacify, tame, damp, lay, allay, rebate, slacken, smooth, alleviate, rock to sleep, deaden, smother; throw -cold water on, – a wet blanket over; slake; curb &c. (*restrain*) 751; tame &c. (*subjugate*) 749; smooth over; pour oil on the -waves, – troubled waters; pour balm into, *mettre de l'eau dans son vin.*

go out like a lamb, 'roar you as gently as any sucking dove.'

**Adj.** moderate; lenient &c. 740; gentle, mild; cool, sober, temperate, reasonable, measured; tempered &c. *v.*; calm, unruffled, quiet, tranquil, still; slow, smooth, untroubled; tame; peaceful, -able; pacific, halcyon.

un-exciting, -irritating; soft, bland, oily, demulcent, lenitive, anodyne; hypnotic &c. 683; sedative; assuaging.

mild as mother's milk; milk and water; gentle as a lamb.

**Adv.** moderately &c. *adj.*; gingerly; *piano*; under easy sail, at half speed; within -bounds, – compass; in reason.

**Phr.** *est modus in rebus.*

## 4°. Indirect Power

**175. Influence.—N.** influence; importance &c. 642; weight, pressure, preponderance, prevalence, sway, pull; predomi-nance, -nancy; ascendency; control, dominance, reign; authority

**175a. Absence of Influence.—N.** impotence &c. 158; inertness &c. 172; irrelevancy &c. 10.

**V.** have no -influence &c. 175.

**Adj.** uninfluential; unconduc-ing,

&c. 737; capability &c. (*power*) 157; interest; spell, magic, magnetism.

footing; purchase &c. (*support*) 215; play, leverage, vantage ground.

tower of strength, host in himself; protection, patronage, auspices.

**V.** have -influence &c. *n.*; be -influential &c. *adj.*; carry weight, actuate, sway, bias, weigh, tell; have a hold upon, magnetize, bear upon, gain a footing, work upon; take -root, – hold; strike root in.

run through, pervade; prevail, dominate, predominate, subject; out-, over-weigh; over-ride, -bear, – come; gain head; rage; be -rife &c. *adj.*; spread like wildfire; have –, get –, gain- -the upper hand, – full play.

be -recognized, – listened to; make one's voice heard, gain a hearing; play a -part, – leading part- in; lead, control, rule, master; get the mastery over; make one's influence felt, cut ice with; take the lead, pull the strings; turn –, throw one's weight into- the scale; set the fashion, lead the dance.

**Adj.** influential; important &c. 642; weighty; prevailing &c. *v.*; prevalent, rife, rampant, dominant, regnant, predominant, in the ascendant, hegemonical; authoritative, recognized, telling, with authority.

**Adv.** with telling effect.

-ive, -ting to; powerless &c. 158; irrelevant &c. 10.

---

**176. Tendency.—N.** tendency; apt-ness, -itude; proneness, proclivity, bent, turn, tone, bias, set, warp, leaning to, predisposition, inclination, conatus, propensity, susceptibility; liability &c. 177; quality, nature, temperament; characteristic, idio-crasy, -syncrasy; cast, vein, grain; humour, mood; drift &c. (*direction*) 278; con-duciveness, -ducement; applicability &c. (*utility*) 644; subservience &c. (*instrumentality*) 631.

**V.** tend, contribute, conduce, lead, dispose, incline, verge, bend to, warp, turn, trend, affect, carry, redound to, bid fair to, gravitate towards; promote &c. (*aid*) 707.

**Adj.** tending &c. *v.*; conducive, working towards, in a fair way to, calculated to; liable &c. 177; subservient &c. (*instrumental*) 631; useful &c. 644; subsidiary &c. (*helping*) 707.

**Adv.** for, whither.

**177. Liability.—N.** lia-bility, -bleness; possibility, contingency; suscepti-vity, -bility.

**V.** be -liable &c. *adj.*; incur, lay oneself open to; run the –, stand a- chance; lie under, expose oneself to, open a door to.

**Adj.** liable, subject; in danger &c. 665; open –, exposed –, obnoxious- to; answerable, responsible, accountable, amenable; unexempt from; apt to; dependent on; incident to.

contingent, incidental, possible, on the cards, within range of, at the mercy of.

## 5°. Combinations of Causes

**178. Concurrence.—N.** concurrence, co-operation, coagency; coincidence, consilience; union; agreement &c. 23; consent &c. (*assent*) 488; alliance; concert &c. 709; partnership &c. 712; collaboration, conformity.

**V.** con-cur, -duce, -spire, -tribute;

**179. Counteraction.—N.** counteraction, opposition; contrariety &c. 14; antagonism, polarity; clashing &c. *v.*; collision, interference, resistance, renitency, friction; reaction; retroaction; repercussion &c. (*recoil*) 277; counterblast; neutralization &c. (*compensa-*

agree, unite, harmonize; hang –, pull- together &c. (*co-operate*) 709; help to &c. (*aid*) 707.

keep pace with, run parallel to; go –, go along –, go hand in hand- with.

**Adj.** concurring &c. *v.*; concurrent, conformable, joint, co-operative, concordant, coincident, concomitant, harmonious; in alliance with, banded together, of one mind, at one with; parallel.

**Adv.** with one consent.

*tion*) 30; *vis inertiæ*; check &c. (*hindrance*) 706.

voluntary -opposition &c. 708, – resistance &c. 719; repression &c. (*restraint*) 751.

**V.** counteract; run counter, clash, cross; interfere –, conflict- with; jostle; go –, run –, beat –, militate- against; stultify; antagonize, frustrate, oppose &c. 708; withstand &c. (*resist*) 719; hinder &c. 706; repress &c. (*restrain*) 751; react &c. (*recoil*) 277.

undo, neutralize, cancel; counterpoise &c. (*compensate*) 30; overpoise.

**Adj.** counteracting &c. *v.*; antagonistic, conflicting, retroactive, renitent, reactionary; contrary &c. 14.

**Adv.** although &c. 30; in spite of &c. 708; *malgré*; against.

# CLASS II

## WORDS RELATING TO SPACE

## SECTION I. SPACE IN GENERAL

### 1°. ABSTRACT SPACE

**180.** [Indefinite space.] **Space.—N.** space, extension, extent, superficial extent, expanse, stretch; capacity, room, accommodation, scope, range, latitude, field, way, expansion, compass, sweep, play, swing, spread.

spare –, elbow –, house- room; stowage, roomage, margin; opening, sphere, arena; lee-, sea-, head-way.

open –, free- space; wide open spaces; void &c. (*absence*) 187; waste; wild-, wilder-ness; up-, bottom-, moor -land; *campagna*, *veld*, prairie, steppe.

abyss &c. (*interval*) 198; unlimited space; infinity &c. 105; world, wide world; ubiquity &c. (*presence*) 186; length and breadth of the land.

proportions, acreage; acres, – roods and perches; square -inches, – yards &c.

**Adj.** spacious, roomy, extensive, expansive, capacious, ample; wide-spread, vast, world-wide, uncircumscribed; boundless &c. (*infinite*) 105; shore-, track-, path-less; large &c. 192.

**Adv.** extensively &c. *adj.*; wherever; everywhere; far and -near, – wide; right and left, all over, all the world over; throughout the -world, – length and breadth of the land; under the sun, in every quarter; in all -quarters, – lands; here, there and everywhere; from -pole to pole, – China to Peru, – Indus to the pole, – Dan to Beersheba, – end to end; on the face of the earth, in the wide world, from all points of the compass; to the -four winds, – uttermost parts of the earth.

---

**180a. Inextension.—N.** in-, non-extension; point; atom &c. (*smallness*) 32; pinprick; limitation &c. 229.

**181.** [Definite space.] **Region.—N.** region, sphere, sphere of influence, corridor, ground, soil, area, realm, hemisphere, quarter, district, beat, orb, circuit, circle; pale &c. (*limit*) 233; com-, de-partment; domain, tract, territory, terrain, country, canton, county, shire, province, *arrondissement*, diocese, parish, township, borough, constituency, *commune*, ward, wapentake, hundred, riding, lathe, garth, soke, tithing, bailiwick; empire, kingdom, principality, duchy, grand –, arch- duchy, palatinate; republic, commonwealth, dominion, colony, state, island.

arena, precincts, *enceinte*, walk, march; patch, plot, enclosure, &c. 232; close, *enclave*, field, court; street &c. (*abode*) 189.

clime, climate, zone, meridian, latitude.

**Adj.** territorial, local, parochial, provincial, insular.

**182.** [Limited space.] **Place.—N.** place, lieu, spot, point, dot; niche, nook, &c. (*corner*) 244; hole; pigeonhole &c. (*receptacle*) 191; compartment; premises, precinct, station, confine; area, court, yard, court-yard, quadrangle, square, compound; abode &c. 189; locality &c. (*situation*) 183.

ins and outs; every hole and corner.

**Adv.** somewhere, in some place, wherever it may be, here and there, in various places, *passim*.

## 2°. Relative Space

**183. Situation.—N.** situation, position, locality, *locale*, *status*, latitude and longitude; footing, standing, standpoint, post; stage; aspect, attitude, posture, *pose*.

place, site, base, station, seat, *venue*, whereabouts, environment, neighbourhood; bearings &c. (*direction*) 278; spot &c. (*limited space*) 182.

top-, ge-, chor-ography; map &c. 554.

**V.** be -situated, - situate; lie; have its seat in.

**Adj.** situ-ate, -ated; local, topical, topographical &c. *n.*

**Adv.** *in -situ*, - *loco*; here and there, *passim*; here-, there-, whereabouts; in place, here, there.

in -, amidst- such and such- -surroundings, - *environs*, - *entourage*.

**184. Location.—N.** loca-tion, -lization; lodgment; de-, re-position; stow-, pack-age; collocation; packing, lading; establishment, settlement, installation; fixation; insertion &c. 300.

anchorage, roadstead, mooring, mooring mast, encampment, camp, bivouac.

plantation, colony, settlement, cantonment, encampment, reservation; colonization, domestication, situation; habitation &c. (*abode*) 189; cohabitation; 'a local habitation and a name'; indenization, naturalization.

**V.** place, situate, locate, localize, make a place for, put, lay, set, seat, station, lodge, quarter, post, install; store, house, stow; establish, fix, pin, root; graft; plant &c. (*insert*) 300; shelve, pitch, camp, lay down, deposit, reposit; cradle; moor, tether, picket; pack, tuck in; embed; vest, invest in.

billet on, quarter upon, saddle with; load, lade, freight; pocket, put up, bag.

inhabit &c. (*be present*) 186; domesticate, colonize, populate, people; take -, strike- root; anchor; cast -, come to an- anchor; sit -, settle-down; settle; take up one's -abode, - quarters; plant -, establish -, locate- oneself; squat, perch, hive, *se nicher*, bivouac, burrow, get a footing; encamp, pitch one's tent; put up -at, - one's horses at; keep house.

indenizen, naturalize, adopt.

put back, replace &c. (*restore*) 660.

**Adj.** placed &c. *v.*; situate, posited, ensconced, embedded, embosomed, rooted; domesticated; vested in, unremoved.

moored &c. *v.*; at anchor.

**185. Displacement.—N.** displacement, elocation, transposition.

ejectment &c. 297; exile &c. (*banishment*) 893; removal &c. (*transference*) 270; unshipment.

misplacement, dislocation &c. 61; fish out of water.

**V.** dis-place, -plant, -lodge, -nest, -establish; misplace, unseat, disturb; exile &c. (*seclude*) 893; ablegate, set aside, remove; take -, cart- away; take -, draft- off; lade &c. 184, unship.

unload, empty &c. (*eject*) 297; transfer &c. 270; dispel.

vacate; depart &c. 293.

**Adj.** displaced &c. *v.*; un-placed, -housed, -harboured, -established, -settled; house-, home-less; out of -place, - a situation.

misplaced, out of its element.

## 3°. Existence in Space

**186. Presence.—N.** presence; occupancy, -ation; attendance; whereness.

permeation, pervasion; diffusion &c. (*dispersion*) 73.

**187.** [Nullibiety.*] **Absence.—N** absence; inexistence &c. 2; non-residence, absenteeism; non-attendance, *alibi*.

* Bishop Wilkins.

ubi-ety, -quity, -quitariness; omnipresence.

bystander &c. (*spectator*) 444.

**V.** exist in space, be -present &c. *adj.*; assist at; make one -of, – at; look on, attend, remain; find –, present- oneself; show one's face; fall in the way of, occur in a place; lie, stand; occupy.

people; inhabit, dwell, reside, stay, sojourn, live, room, abide, bunk, lodge, nestle, roost, perch; take up one's abode &c. (*be located*) 184; tenant, occupy.

resort to, frequent, haunt; revisit.

fill, pervade, permeate; be -diffused, – disseminated- through; over-spread, -run; run through; meet one at every turn.

**Adj.** present; occupying, inhabiting &c. *v.*; moored &c. 184; residential, resi-ant, -dent, -dentiary; domiciled.

ubiquit-ous, -ary; omnipresent.

peopled, populous, full of people, inhabited.

**Adv.** here, there, where, everywhere, aboard, on board, at home, afield; on the spot; here, there and everywhere &c. (*space*) 180; in presence of, before; under the -eyes, – nose- of; in the face of; *in propriâ personâ*.

emptiness &c. *adj.*; void, *vacuum*; vac-uity, -ancy; *tabula rasa*; exemption; *hiatus* &c. (*interval*) 198; no man's land.

truant, absentee.

nobody; nobody -present, – on earth; no one; not a soul; *âme qui vive*.

**V.** be -absent &c. *adj.*; keep -away, – out of the way; play truant, absent oneself, stay away.

withdraw, make oneself scarce, vacate; go away, slip out, slip away, retreat &c. 293.

**Adj.** absent, not present, away, nonresident, gone, from home; missing; lost; wanted, wanting; omitted; nowhere to be found; inexistent &c. 2.

empty, void; blank, vac-ant, -uous; untenanted, -occupied, -inhabited; tenantless; desert, -ed; devoid; un-, uninhabitable.

exempt from, not having.

**Adv.** without, *minus*, nowhere; elsewhere; neither here nor there; in default of; *sans*; behind one's back.

**Phr.** the bird has flown, *non est inventus*.

---

**188. Inhabitant. — N.** inhabitant; habitant, resident, -iary; dweller, indweller; occup-ier, -ant, farmer, planter; householder, lodger, boarder, paying guest; inmate, tenant, renter, incumbent, sojourner, *locum tenens*, commorant; settler, squatter, backwoodsman, colonist; islander; denizen, citizen; burgher, oppidan, cockney, cit, townsman, burgess; villager; cot-tager, -tier, -ter; compatriot.

native, indigene, aboriginal, aborigines, autochthones; Briton, Englishman, John Bull; new comer &c. (*stranger*) 57.

garrison, crew; population; people &c. (*mankind*) 372; colony, settlement; household.

**V.** inhabit &c. (*be present*) 186; indenizen &c. (*locate oneself*) 184.

**Adj.** indigenous; enchorial; national, nat-ive, -al; autochthonous; British, English; colonial; domestic; domicil-

**189.** [Place of habitation, or resort.] **Abode.—N.** abode, dwelling, lodging, -s; diggings, domicile, residence, address, habitation, where one's lot is cast, local habitation, berth, seat, lap, sojourn, housing, quarters, headquarters, resiance, tabernacle, throne, ark.

home, fatherland, mother country, country &c. 181; home-stead, -stall; fireside, chimney corner; hearth, – stone; household gods, *lares et penates*, roof, household, housing, *dulce domum*, paternal domicile; native -soil, – land, blighty.

nest, *nidus*, snuggery; arbour, bower &c. 191; lair, den, cave, hole, hiding-place, cache, cell, *sanctum sanctorum*, aerie, eyry, rookery, hive; *habitat*, haunt, covert, resort, retreat, perch, roost; nidification.

bivouac, camp, encampment, cantonment, castrametation; barrack, casemate, casern.

lated, -ed; naturalized, vernacular, domesticated; domiciliary.

in the occupation of; garrisoned –, occupied- by.

---

tent &c. (*covering*) 223; building &c. (*construction*) 161; chamber &c. (*receptacle*) 191.

tenement, messuage, farm, farm-house, grange, *hacienda.*

cot, cabin, log cabin, shack, hut, *châlet*, croft, shed, booth, stall, hovel, bothy, shanty, igloo, tepee, wigwam; pen &c. (*inclosure*) 232; barn, bawn; kennel, sty, dog-hole, cote, coop, hutch, byre; cow-house, -shed; stable, dove-cote, shippen.

house, mansion, place, villa, cottage, box, lodge, hermitage, *rus in urbe*, folly, rotunda, tower, *château*, castle, pavilion, hotel, court, manor-house, capital messuage, hall, palace, alcazar; country seat; kiosk, bungalow; temple &c. 1000; home of rest, alms-, poor-, work-house, asylum; boarding-, lodging-house; flat, maisonette, duplex, penthouse, suite of rooms, apartments, rooms, room, building &c. 161; Mansion House, town hall, Capitol.

assembly-room, auditorium, coliseum, meeting-house, pump-room, spa, health resort, watering-place; club; theatre &c. 840; drill hall, gymnasium, church &c. 1000; Houses of Parliament &c. 696; school &c. 542; inn; hostel, -ry; hotel, tavern, caravansary, khan, hospice; public-, ale-, pot-, mug-house; gin-palace, gin-mill; coffee-, eating-house; canteen, *restaurant*, *rôtisserie*, cafeteria, grill-room, *buffet*, *café*, *estaminet*, *posada*, *bodega*; bar; saloon, speakeasy, shebeen.

hamlet, village, thorp, dorp, ham, kraal; borough, burgh, town, county-seat, – town, city, capital, metropolis; suburb, quarter, parish &c. 181; ghetto; province, country.

street, place, terrace, parade, esplanade, promenade, pier, embankment, road, villas, row, walk, lane, alley, court, quadrangle, quad, wynd, close, yard, passage, rents, mansions, buildings, mews.

square, polygon, circus, crescent, mall, *piazza*, arcade, colonnade, peristyle, cloister; gardens, grove, residences; block of buildings, market-place, *place.*

anchorage, roadstead, roads; dock, basin, wharf, quay, port, harbour; dry-, graving-, floating-dock.

garden, park, pleasure-ground, pleasance, demesne.

**V.** take up one's abode &c. (*locate oneself*) 184; inhabit &c. (*be present*) 186.

**Adj.** urban, oppidan, metropolitan; suburban; provincial, rural, rustic; countrified; regional, parochial, domestic; cosmopolitan; palatial.

**190.** [Things contained.] **Contents.—N.** contents; cargo, lading, freight, shipment, load, bale, burden; cart-, ship-load; cup –, basket –, &c. (*receptacle*) 191- of; inside &c. 221; stuffing, ullage.

**V.** load, lade, ship, charge, fill, stuff.

**191. Receptacle.—N.** receptacle, container; inclosure &c. 232; recipient, receiver, reservatory.

compartment; cell, -ule; follicle; hole, corner, niche, recess, nook; crypt, stall, pigeon-hole, cove, oriel; cave &c. (*concavity*) 252.

capsule, vesicle, cyst, pod, calyx, *cancelli*, utricle, bladder, udder.

stomach, paunch, *venter*, abdomen, ventricle, crop, craw, ingluvies, maw, gizzard, bread-basket, belly, little Mary; mouth.

pocket, pouch, fob, sheath, scabbard, socket, bag, vanity bag. compact, sac, sack, saccule, despatch –, attaché-, tachy- case, wallet, scrip, card-, note- case, billfold, poke, kit, knap-, haver-, ruck-sack, sachel, satchel, reticule, budget, net; ditty-, -box, -bag, kitbag; portfolio; saddlebags, holster; quiver &c. (*magazine*) 636.

chest, box, coffer, caddy, case, casket, pyx, pix, *caisson*, desk, *bureau*, reliquary, shrine; trunk, portmanteau, band-box, *valise*, suitcase, hand-, traveling-, overnight-, Gladstone-, carpet-bag, brief case; boot, imperial; *vache*; cage, manger, rack.

vessel, vase, bushel, barrel; canister, jar; pottle, basket, punnet, pannier, buck-basket, hopper, maund, creel, cran, crate, cradle, bassinet, wisket, whisket, *jardinière*, *corbeille*, hamper, wastepaper basket, dosser, dorser, tray, hod, scuttle, utensil, spittoon, cuspidor.

[For liquids] cistern &c. (*store*) 636; vat, caldron, barrel, cask, puncheon, keg, rundlet, tun, butt, firkin, hogshead, kilderkin, carboy, amphora, ampulla, bottle, jar, leather bottle, decanter, ewer, cruse, carafe, crock, kit, canteen, flagon; demijohn; flask, -et; stoup, noggin, vial, phial, *ampoule*, cruet, caster; gourd; urn, *épergne*, salver, *patella*, *tazza*, *patera*; pig-, big-gin; tea-, coffee-pot, percolator, *samovar*; tyg, nipperkin, pocket-pistol; tub, bucket, pail, skeel, pot, tankard, jug, pitcher, toby, mug, pipkin; gal-, gall-ipot, pannikin; matrass, receiver, retort, alembic, bolthead, can, kettle; bowl, basin, jorum, punch-bowl, cup, goblet, chalice, tumbler, glass, wineglass, rummer, beaker, tass, horn, saucepan, skillet, posnet, tureen, terrine, *casserole*, sauce-, gravy-boat.

plate, platter, paten, dish, vegetable –, *entrée*- dish, trencher, calabash, porringer, potager, saucer, pan, crucible.

shovel, trowel, spoon; table-, dessert-, tea-, egg-, salt-spoon; spatula, ladle; dipper; baler; watch-glass, thimble.

closet, commode, cupboard, cellaret, *chiffonnière*, locker, bin, bunker, *buffet*, press, safe, sideboard, drawer, chest of drawers, till, *scrutoire*, *secrétaire*, *éscritoire*, davenport, book-case, cabinet, canterbury; corner cupboard, wardrobe.

chamber, apartment, room, cabin; office, court, hall, atrium; suite of rooms, flat, story; saloon, *salon*, parlour; presence-chamber; sitting-, drawing-, reception-, state-, living-, work-room; gallery, cabinet, closet, cubicle; pew, box; *boudoir*; *adytum*, *sanctum*; bed-room, dormitory, dressing-room; refectory, dining-room, *salle-à-manger*; nursery, school-room; library, study; studio; billiard-, bath-, smoking-room; den, canteen, mess, officers' mess; gun-, ward-, mess-room.

attic, loft, garret, cockloft, clerestory; cellar, vault, hold, cockpit; *entresol*; mezzanine floor; ground-floor, *rez-de-chaussée*; basement, kitchen, cook-house, galley, pantry, scullery, offices; store-room &c. (*depository*) 636; lumber-room; dust-hole, -bin; dairy, laundry, coach-house; *garage*; *hangar*; out-, pent-house; lean-to.

portico, porch, piazza, verandah, lobby, court, hall, vestibule, corridor, passage; ante-room, -chamber; lounge; *foyer*, *loggia*.

conservatory, green-house, glass-house, vinery, bower, arbour, summer-house, alcove, grotto, hermitage, pergola.

lodging &c. (*abode*) 189; bed &c. (*support*) 215; carriage &c. (*vehicle*) 272.

**Adj.** capsular; saccu-lar, -lated; recipient; ventricular, cystic, vascular, vesicular, cellular, camerated, locular, multilocular, poly-gastric; marsupial; siliqu-ose, -ous.

## Section II. DIMENSIONS

### 1°. General Dimensions

**192. Size.—N.** size, magnitude, dimension, bulk, volume; largeness &c. *adj.*; greatness &c. (*of quantity*) 31; expanse &c. (*space*) 180; amplitude, mass; proportions.

capacity; ton-, tun-nage; calibre, scantling.

turgidity &c. (*expansion*) 194; corpulence, obesity; plumpness, &c. *adj.*; *embonpoint*, corporation, flesh and blood, lustihood.

hugeness &c. *adj.*; enormity, immensity, monstrosity.

giant, Brobdingnagian, Antæus, Goliath, Gog and Magog, Gargantua, monster, mammoth, Cyclops; whale, porpoise, behemoth, leviathan, elephant, hippopotamus; colossus; tun, lump, bulk, block, loaf, mass, clod, nugget, bushel, thumper, whopper, spanker, strapper; Triton among the minnows.

mountain, mound; heap &c. (*assemblage*) 72.

largest portion &c. 50; full-, life-size.

**V.** be- large &c. *adj.*; become -large &c. (*expand*) 194.

**Adj.** large, big; great &c. (*in quantity*) 31; considerable, bulky, voluminous, ample, massive, massy; capacious, comprehensive; spacious &c. 180; mighty towering, fine, magnificent.

corpulent, stout, fat, plump, squab, full, lusty, strapping, bouncing; portly, burly, well-fed, full-grown; stalwart, brawny, fleshy; goodly; in good -case, - condition; in condition; chopping, jolly; chub-, chubby-faced.

lubberly, hulky, unwieldy, lumpish, gaunt, spanking, whacking, whopping, thumping, thundering, hulking; overgrown; puffy &c. (*swollen*) 194.

huge, immense, enormous, mighty; vast, -y; amplitudinous, stupendous; monst-er, -rous; gigantic, elephantine;

**193. Littleness.—N.** littleness &c. *adj.*; smallness &c. (*of quantity*) 32; exiguity, inextension; parvi-tude, -ty; duodecimo; Elzevir edition, epitome, microcosm; rudiment; vanishing point; thinness &c. 203.

dwarf, pigmy, atomy, Liliputian, midget, chit, pigwidgeon, urchin, elf; doll, puppet; Tom Thumb, Hop-o'-my thumb, Humpty-dumpty; man-, mannikin; *homunculus*, dapperling, fingerling, dandiprat, cock-sparrow, scalawag.

animalcule, monad, mite, insect, emmet, fly, midge, gnat, shrimp, minnow, worm, maggot, entozoon; *bacillus*, microbe, micro-organism, *bacteria*; *infusoria*; microbe; grub; tit, tomtit, runt, mouse, small fry; millet-, mustard-seed; barley-corn; pebble, grain of sand; mole-hill, button, bubble.

point; atom &c. (*small quantity*) 32; fragment &c. (*small part*) 51; powder &c. 330; point of a pin, mathematical point; *minutiæ* &c. (*unimportance*) 643.

micro-graphy, -meter, -scope; vernier; scale.

**V.** be -little &c. *adj.*; lie in a nutshell; become small &c. (*decrease*) 36, (*contract*) 195.

**Adj.** little; small &c. (*in quantity*) 32; minute, diminutive, microscopic; inconsiderable &c. (*unimportant*) 643; exiguous, puny, tiny, wee, petty, minikin, miniature, pigmy, elfin; under sized; dwarf, -ed, -ish; spare, stunted, limited; cramp, -ed; pollard, Liliputian, dapper, pocket; port-ative, -able; duodecimo; dumpy, squat; compact, handy; short &c. 201.

impalpable, intangible, evanescent, imperceptible, invisible, inappreciable, infinitesimal, homœopathic; atomic, corpuscular, molecular; rudiment-ary, -al; embryonic.

weazen, scant, scraggy, scrubby;

giant, -like; colossal, Cyclopean, Brobdingnagian, Gargantuan, Titanic; infinite &c. 105.

large as life; plump as a -dumpling, – partridge; fat as -a pig, – a quail, – butter, – brawn, – bacon.

thin &c. (*narrow*) 203; granular &c. (*powdery*) 330; shrunk &c. 195.

Adv. in a -small compass, – nutshell; on a small scale.

---

**194. Expansion. — N.** expansion; increase &c. 35 -of size; enlargement, extension, augmentation; ampli-fica-tion, -ation; aggrandizement, spread, increment, growth, development, pullulation, swell, dilation, dilatation, rarefaction; turg-escence, -idness, -idity; obesity &c. (*size*) 192; dropsy, tumefaction, intumescence, swelling, tumour, *diastole*, distension; puff-ing, -iness; inflation; pandiculation.

dilatability, expansibility.

germination, growth, upgrowth; accretion &c. 35.

over-growth, -distension; hypertrophy, tympany.

bulb &c. (*convexity*) 250; plumper; superiority of size.

V. become -larger &c. (large &c. 192); expand, widen, enlarge, extend, grow, increase, incrassate, swell, gather; fill out; deploy, take open order, dilate, stretch, spread; mantle, wax; grow –, spring- up; bud, bourgeon, shoot, sprout, germinate, put forth, vegetate, pullulate, open, burst forth, flower, blow &c. 734; gain –, gather- flesh; outgrow; spread like wildfire, overrun.

be larger than; surpass &c. (*be superior*) 33.

render -larger &c. (large &c. 192); expand, spread, extend, aggrandize, distend, develop, amplify, spread out, widen, magnify, rarefy, inflate, puff, puff out, blow up, stuff, pad, cram; exaggerate; fatten; bloat, augment.

Adj. expanded &c. *v.*; larger &c. (large &c. 192); swollen; expansive; wide-open, -spread; fan-shaped; flabelliform; overgrown, exaggerated, bloated, fat, turgid, tumid, hypertrophied, dropsical; pot-, swag-bellied; œdematous, obese, puffy, pursy, blowzy, distended; patulous; bulbous &c. (*convex*) 250; full-blown, -grown, -formed; big &c. 192.

**195. Contraction.—N.** contraction, reduction, diminution; decrease &c. 36-of size; defalcation, decrement; lessening, shrinkage; collapse, emaciation, attenuation, tabefaction, consumption, marasmus, atrophy; systole, neck, hour-glass.

condensation, compression, constraint, compactness; compendium &c. 596; squeezing &c. *v.*; strangulation; corrugation; astringency, constringency; astringents, sclerotics; contractility, compressibility; coarctation.

inferiority in size.

V. become -small, – smaller; lessen, decrease &c. 36; grow less, dwindle, shrink, contract, narrow, shrivel, collapse, wither, lose flesh, wizen, fall away, waste, wane, ebb; decay &c. (*deteriorate*) 659.

be smaller than, fall short of; not come up to &c. (*be inferior*) 34.

render smaller, lessen, diminish, contract, draw in, narrow, coarctate; constrict, constringe; condense, compress, boil down, deflate, exhaust, empty; squeeze, corrugate, crush, crumple up, warp, purse up, pack, stow; pinch, tighten, strangle; cramp; dwarf, bedwarf; shorten &c. 201; circumscribe &c. 229; restrain &c. 751; fold &c. 258.

pare, reduce, attenuate, rub down, scrape, file, grind, chip, shave, shear.

Adj. contracting &c. *v.*; astringent; shrunk, contracted &c. *v.*; strangulated, tabid, wizened, stunted; tabescent; marasmic; waning &c. *v.*; neap; compact.

unexpanded &c. (expand &c. 194); inswept; contractile; compressible; smaller &c. (small &c. 193).

---

**196. Distance.—N.** distance; space &c. 180; remoteness, farness; far- cry

**197. Nearness.—N.** nearness &c. *adj.*; proximity, propinquity; vicinity,

to; longinquity, elongation; offing, background; removedness; parallax; reach, span, stride; drift.

out-post, -skirt; horizon, sky-line; aphelion; foreign parts, *ultima Thule*, *ne plus ultra*, antipodes; long range, giant's stride.

dispersion &c. 73.

V. be -distant &c. *adj.*; extend –, stretch –, reach –, spread –, go –, get –, stretch away- to; range, outrange, outreach.

remain at a distance; keep –, stand- -away, – off, – aloof, – clear of.

Adj. distant; far -off, – away; remote, telescopic, distal, wide of; stretching to &c. *v.*; yon, -der; ulterior; trans-marine, -pontine, -atlantic, -alpine; tramontane; ultra-montane, -mundane; hyperborean, antipodean; inaccessible, out of the way; unapproach-ed, -able; incontiguous.

Adv. far -off, – away; afar, -off; off; away; a -long, – great, – good- way off; wide away, aloof; wide –, clear- of; out of -the way, – reach; abroad, yonder, farther, further, beyond; *outre mer*, over the border, far and wide, over the hills and far away; from pole to pole &c. (*over great space*) 180; to the -uttermost parts, – ends- of the earth; out of -hearing, – range, nobody knows where, *à perte de vue*, out of the sphere of, wide of the mark; a far cry to.

apart, asunder; wide -apart, – asunder; *longo intervallo*; at arm's length.

---

-age; neighbourhood, adjacency; contiguity &c. 199.

short -distance, – step, – cut; earshot, close quarters, stone's throw; bow –, gun –, pistol- shot; hair's breadth, span; close-up.

purlieus, neighbourhood, vicinage, *environs*, *alentours*, suburbs, confines, *banlieue*, borderland; whereabouts.

bystander; neighbour, borderer.

approach &c. 286; convergence &c. 290; perihelion.

V. be -near &c. *adj.*; adjoin, hang about, trench on; border –, verge upon; stand by, approximate, tread on the heels of, cling to, clasp, hug; cuddle, huddle; hang upon the skirts of, hover over; burn; abut.

bring –, draw- -near &c. 286; converge &c. 290; crowd &c. 72; place -side by side &c. *adv.*

Adj. near, nigh; close –, near- at hand; close, neighbouring, propinquent, bordering upon; adjacent, adjoining, limitrophe; proxim-ate, -al; at hand, handy; near the mark, near run; home, intimate.

Adv. near, nigh; hard –, fast- by; close -to, – upon, – up; at the point of; next door to; within -reach, – call, – hearing, – earshot, – range; within an ace of; but a step, not far from, at no great distance; on the -verge, – brink, – skirts- of; in the -environs &c. *n.*; at one's -door, – feet, – elbow, – finger's end, – side; on the tip of one's tongue; under one's nose; within a -stone's throw &c. *n.*; in -sight, – presence- of; at close quarters; cheek by -jole, – jowl; beside, alongside, side by side, *tête-à-tête*; in juxtaposition &c. (*touching*) 199; yard-arm to yard-arm; at the heels of; on the confines of, at the threshold, bordering upon, verging to; in the way.

about; here-, there-abouts; roughly, in round numbers; approxim- -ately, -atively; as good as, well nigh.

**198. Interval.**—**N.** interval, interspace; separation &c. 44; break, gap, opening; hole &c. 260; chasm, *hiatus*, cæsura; inter-ruption, -regnum; interstice, *lacuna*, cleft, mesh, crevice, chink, rime, creek, cranny, crack, chap, slit, slot, fissure, scissure, rift, flaw, breach, fracture, rent, gash, cut, leak, dike, ha-ha.

**199. Contiguity.**—**N.** contiguity, contact, proximity, apposition, juxtaposition, touching &c. *v.*; abutment, osculation; meeting, appulse, appulsion, *rencontre*, rencounter, syzygy, coincidence, conjunction, coexistence; adhesion &c. 46.

border-land; frontier &c. (*limit*) 233; tangent.

gorge, defile, ravine, cañon, *crevasse*, abyss, abysm; gulf; inlet, frith, strait, gully, gulch, nullah; pass; notch; furrow &c. 259; yawning gulf; *hiatus -maxime, - valde- deflendus*; parenthesis &c. (*interjacence*) 228; void &c. (*absence*) 187; incompleteness &c. 530.

V. gape &c. (*open*) 260.

Adj. with an interval, far between.

Adv. at intervals &c. (*discontinuously*) 70; *longo intervallo*.

V. be -contiguous &c. *adj.*; join, adjoin, abut on, march with, border; tick, graze, touch, meet, osculate, kiss, come in contact, coincide; coexist; adhere &c. 46.

Adj. contiguous; touching &c. *v.*; in -contact &c. *n.*; conterminous, end to end, osculatory; pertingent; tangential.

hand to hand; close to &c. (*near*) 197; with no -interval &c. 198.

## 2°. Linear Dimensions

**200. Length.**—N. length, longitude, span, extent, mileage.

line, bar, rule, stripe, streak, spoke, radius.

lengthening &c. *v.*; pro-longation, -duction, -traction; ten-sion, -sure; extension.

[Measures of length] line, nail, inch, hand, palm, foot, cubit, yard, ell, fathom, rod, pole, perch, furlong, mile, league; chain, metre, kilo-, centi-, milli- &c. -metre.

pedometer, perambulator, odometer, odograph, speedometer, cyclometer, log, telemeter, range finder; scale &c. (*measurement*) 466.

V. be -long &c. *adj.*; stretch out, sprawl; extend -, reach -, stretch- to; make a long arm, 'drag its slow length along.'

render -long &c. *adj.*; lengthen, extend, elongate; stretch; pro-long, -duce, -tract; let -, pay -, draw -, spin- out; drawl.

enfilade, look along, view in perspective.

Adj. long, -some; lengthy, lank, wire-drawn, outstretched; lengthened &c. *v.*; sesquipedalian &c. (*words*) 577; interminable, no end of.

line-ar, -al; longitudinal, oblong.

as long as -my arm, - to-day and to-morrow; unshortened &c. (shorten &c. 201).

Adv. lengthwise, at length, longitudinally, endlong, along; *tandem*; in a line &c. (*continuously*) 69; in perspective.

from -end to end, - stem to stern, - head to foot, - the crown of the head to the sole of the foot. - top to toe, - head to heels; fore and aft.

**201. Shortness.**—N. shortness &c. *adj.*; brevity; littleness &c. 193; a span.

shortening &c. *v.*; abbrevia-tion, -ture; abridgment, concision, retrenchment, curtailment, decurtation; reduction &c. (*contraction*) 195; epitome &c. (*compendium*) 596.

abridger, abstractor, epitomiser.

elision, ellipsis; conciseness &c. (*in style*) 572.

V. be -short &c. *adj.*; render -short &c. *adj.*; shorten, curtail, abridge, abbreviate, take in, reduce; compress &c. (*contract*) 195; epitomize &c. 596.

retrench, cut short, obtruncate; scrimp, cut, chop up, hack, hew; cut -, pare- down; clip, snip, dock, lop, prune; shear, shave, mow, reap, crop; snub; truncate, pollard, stunt, nip, nip in the bud, check the growth of; [in drawing] foreshorten.

Adj. short, brief, curt; compendious, compact; stubby, scrimp; shorn, stubbed; stumpy, thickset, podgy, stocky, pug; squab, -by; squat, dumpy; little &c. 193; curtailed of its fair proportions; short by; oblate; concise &c. 572; summary.

Adv. shortly &c. *adj.*; in short &c. (*concisely*) 572.

**202. Breadth. Thickness.—N.** breadth, width, latitude, amplitude; diameter, bore, calibre, radius; superficial extent &c. (*space*) 180.

thickness, crassitude; corpulence &c. (*size*) 192; dilatation &c. (*expansion*) 194.

**V.** be -broad &c. *adj.*; become –, render- -broad &c. *adj.*; expand &c. 194; thicken, widen.

**Adj.** broad, wide, ample, extended; discous; fan-like; out-spread, -stretched; wide as a church-door.

thick, dumpy, squab, squat, thickset, tubby; thick as a rope, stubby &c. 201.

**203. Narrowness. Thinness. —N.** narrowness &c. *adj.*; closeness, exility; exiguity &c. (*little*) 193.

line; hair's –, finger's -breadth; strip, streak, vein.

thinness &c. *adj.*; tenuity; emaciation, macilency, *marcor*.

shaving, slip &c. (*filament*) 205; threadpaper, skeleton, shadow, scrag, anatomy, spindle-shanks, barebones, lantern jaws, mere skin and bone.

middle constriction, stricture, neck, waist, isthmus, wasp, hour-glass; ridge, *ghaut*, pass; ravine &c. 198.

narrowing, coarctation, angustation, tapering; contraction &c. 195.

**V.** be -narrow &c. *adj.*; narrow, taper, contract &c. 195; render -narrow &c. *adj.*

---

**Adj.** narrow, close; slender, thin, fine; *svelte*; thread-like &c. (*filament*) 205; finespun, taper, slim, gracile, slight, slight-made; scant, -y; spare, delicate, incapacious; contracted &c. 195; unexpanded &c. (expand &c. 194); slender as a thread, capillary.

emaciated, lean, meagre, gaunt, macilent; lank, -y; weedy, skinny, scrawny, scraggy; starv-ed, -eling; attenuated, shrivelled, wizened, pinched, peaky, skeletal, spindling, spindle- -legged, -shanked; extenuated, tabid, marcid, bare-bone, raw-boned; herring-gutted; worn to a shadow, lean as a rake; thin as a -lath, – whipping post, – wafer; hatchet-faced; lantern-jawed.

**204. Layer.—N.** layer, stratum, course, bed, zone, *substratum*, floor, flag, stage, story, tier, slab, escarpment, table, tablet, panel, plaque; board, plank; trencher, platter.

plate; lam-ina, -ella; sheet, flake, foil, wafer, scale, coat, peel, pellicle, ply, thickness, membrane, film, leaf, slice, shive, cut, rasher, shaving, integument &c. (*covering*) 223.

stratification, lamination, scaliness, nest of boxes, coats of an onion.

**V.** slice, shave, pare, peel; plate, coat, veneer; cover &c. 223.

**Adj.** lamell-ar, -ated, -iform; laminated, -iferous; micaceous; schist-ose, -ous; scaly, filmy, membranous, flaky, squamous; folia-ted, -ceous; stratified, -form; tabular, discoid, spathic.

**205. Filament.—N.** filament, line; fibre, fibril; funicle, vein, hair, capillament, *cilium*, tendril, gossamer; hairstroke; harl.

wire, string, thread, packthread, cotton, sewing-silk, twine, twist, whipcord, cord, rope, cable, yarn, hemp, oakum, jute, wool, worsted.

strip, shred, slip, spill, list, band, fillet, *fascia*, ribbon, riband, tape, roll, lath, slat, strake, splinter, shiver, shaving.

beard &c. (*roughness*) 256; ramification; strand.

**Adj.** fil-amentous, -aceous, -iform; fibr-ous, -illous; thread-like, wiry, stringy, ropy; capill-ary, -iform; funicular, wire-drawn; anguilliform; flagelliform; hairy &c. (*rough*) 256; ligulate.

---

**206. Height.—N.** height, altitude, elevation, ceiling; eminence. pitch; loftiness &c. *adj.*; sublimity.

tallness &c. *adj.*; stature, procerity; prominence &c. 250.

**207. Lowness.—N.** lowness &c. *adj.*; debasement, depression; prostration &c. (*horizontal*) 213; depression &c. (*concave*) 252.

molehill; lowlands; bottomlands;

colossus &c. (*size*) 192; giant, grenadier, giraffe.

mount, -ain; hill, butte, monticle, fell, knap; cape; head-, fore-land; promontory; ridge, hog's back, dune; rising –, vantage- ground; down; moor, -land; Alp; up-, high-lands; heights &c. (*summit*) 210; knoll, hummock, hillock, barrow, mound, mole, *kopje*; steeps, bluff, cliff, craig, tor, peak, pike, clough; escarpment, edge, ledge, brae; dizzy height.

tower, pillar, column, pylon, obelisk, monument, steeple, spire, minaret, *campanile*, belfry, turret, roof, dome, cupola, pagoda, pyramid; sky scraper; Eiffel tower.

pole, pikestaff, maypole, flagstaff; mast, top –, topgallant- mast.

ceiling &c. (*covering*) 223.

high water; high –, flood –, spring- tide.

altimetry &c. (*angle*) 244; altimeter, height-finder, hypsometer, barograph.

**V.** be -high &c. *adj.*; tower, soar, command; hover; cap, culminate; overhang, hang over, impend, beetle; bestride, ride, mount; perch, surmount; cover &c. 223; overtop &c. (*be superior*) 33; stand on tiptoe.

become -high &c. *adj.*; grow, – higher, – taller; upgrow; rise &c. (*ascend*) 305.

render -high &c. *adj.*; heighten &c. (*elevate*) 307.

**Adj.** high, elevated, eminent, exalted, lofty, supernal; tall; gigantic &c. (*big*) 192; Patagonian; towering, beetling, soaring, hanging [gardens]; elevated &c. 307; upper; highest &c. (*topmost*) 210; monticolous, perching, hill-dwelling.

up-, moor-land; hilly, mountainous, alpine, sub-alpine, heaven-kissing; cloud-topt, -capt, -touching; aerial.

overhanging &c. *v.*; incumbent, overlying; super-incumbent, -natant, -imposed; prominent &c. 250.

tall as a -maypole, – poplar, – steeple; lanky &c. (*thin*) 203.

**Adv.** on high, high up, aloft, up, above, aloof, overhead; up –, above- stairs; in the clouds; on -tiptoe, – stilts, – the shoulders of; over head and ears; breast high.

over, upwards; from top to bottom &c. (*completely*) 52.

basement, ground-floor; *rez-de-chaussée* &c. 211; hold; feet, heels.

low water; low –, ebb –, neap –, spring- tide.

**V.** be -low &c. *adj.*; lie -low, – flat; underlie; crouch, slouch, wallow, grovel; lower &c. (*depress*) 308.

**Adj.** low, neap, debased; nether, -most; flat, level with the ground; lying low &c. *v.*; crouched, subjacent, squat, prostrate &c. (*horizontal*) 213.

**Adv.** under; be-, under-neath; below; down, -wards; adown, at the foot of; under-foot, -ground; down –, below-stairs; at a low ebb; below par.

---

**208. Depth.—N.** depth; deepness &c. *adj.*; profundity, depression &c. (*concavity*) 252.

hollow, pit, shaft, well, crater, abyss; gulf &c. 198; bowels of the earth, bottomless pit, hell.

soundings, depth of water, water, draught, submersion; plummet, sound, probe; sounding -rod, – line, – machine; lead; submarine, diving bell, bathysphere; diver.

**V.** be -deep &c. *adj.*; render -deep &c. *adj.*; deepen.

plunge &c. 310; sound, heave the lead, take soundings; dig &c. (*excavate*) 252.

**209. Shallowness.—N.** shallowness &c. *adj.*; shoals; mere scratch.

**Adj.** shallow, superficial; skin –, ankle –, knee- deep; just enough to wet one's feet; shoal, -y

---

**Adj.** deep, -seated; profound, sunk, buried; submerged &c. 310; sub-aqueous, -marine, -terranean, -terrene; underground.

bottom-, sound-, fathom-less; unfathom-ed, -able; abysmal; deep as a well, deep-sea.

knee-, ankle-deep.

**Adv.** beyond –, out of- one's depth; over head and ears, over one's head.

**210. Summit.**—**N.** summit, -y; top, vertex, apex, zenith, pinnacle, acme, acropolis, culmination, meridian, utmost height, *ne plus ultra*, height, pitch, maximum, climax, apogee; culminating –, crowning –, turning- point; turn of the tide, fountain head; water-shed, -parting; sky, pole.

tip, -top; crest, crow's nest, cap, truck, peak, nib; end &c. 67; crown, brow; head, nob, noddle, pate.

high places, heights.

top-, top-gallant mast, sky scraper; quarter –, hurricane- deck.

architrave, frieze, cornice, coping, coping-stone, zoophorus, capital, headpiece, capstone, epistyle, sconce, pediment, entablature; tympanum; ceiling &c. (*covering*) 223.

attic, loft, garret, house-top, upper story, roof.

**V.** culminate, cap, crown, top; overtop &c. (*be superior to*) 33.

**Adj.** highest &c. (high &c. 206); top; top-, upper-most; tip-top; culminating &c. *v.*; meridi-an, -onal; capital, head, polar, supreme, supernal, top-gallant.

**Adv.** a-top, at the top of – the tree, – the heap.

**211. Base.**—**N.** base, -ment; plinth, dado, wainscot, baseboard; foundation &c. (*support*) 215; substructure, *substratum*, sump, ground, earth, pavement, floor, paving, flag, carpet, ground-floor, deck; footing, groundwork, basis; hold, bilge, orlop deck.

bottom, nadir, foot, sole, toe, hoof, keel, kelson, root.

**Adj.** bottom; under-, nether-most; fundamental; founded –, based –, grounded –, built- on.

**212. Verticality.** — **N.** verticality; erectness &c. *adj.*; perpendicularity; right angle, normal; azimuth circle.

wall, palisade, precipice, cliff, steep, bluff.

elevation, erection; square, plumbline, plummet.

**V.** be -vertical &c. *adj.*; stand -up, – on end, – erect, – upright; stick –, cock-up.

render -vertical &c. *adj.*; set –, stick –, raise –, cock- up; erect, rear, raise, pitch, raise on its legs.

**Adj.** vertical, upright, erect, perpendicular, normal, plumb, straight, bolt upright; rampant; straight –, standing-up &c. *v.*; rectangular, orthogonal.

**Adv.** vertically &c. *adj.*; up, on end; up –, right- on end; *à plomb*, endwise; on one's legs; at right angles.

**213. Horizontality.**—**N.** horizontality; flatness; level, plane; stratum &c. 204; dead -level, – flat; level plane.

recumbency; lying down &c. *v.*; reclination, decumbence; de-, discumbency; proneness &c. *adj.*; accubation, supination, resupination, prostration; azimuth.

plain, floor, platform, bowling-green; cricket-ground; court; gridiron; baseball diamond; hockey rink; tennis-, croquet-ground, – lawn; billiard table; terrace, estrade, esplanade, *parterre*, table-land, *plateau*, ledge.

spirit-, level; T-square.

**V.** be -horizontal &c. *adj.*; lie, recline, couch; lie -down, – flat, – prostrate; sprawl, loll; sit down.

render -horizontal &c. *adj.*; lay, – down, – out; level, flatten, even, raze, equalize, smooth, align; prostrate, knock down, floor, fell, ground.

**Adj.** horizontal, level, even, plane;

flat &c. 251; flat as a -billiard table, - bowling green; alluvial; calm, - as a mill-pond; smooth, - as glass.

re-, de-, pro-, ac-cumbent; lying &c. *v.*; prone, supine, couchant, jacent, prostrate.

Adv. horizontally &c. *adj.*; on -one's back. - all fours, - its beam ends.

**214. Pendency.**—**N.** pend-, dependency; suspension, hanging &c. *v.*

pendant, drop, tippet, tassel, lobe, tail, train, flap, lappet, skirt, pig-tail, queue, pendulum.

peg, knob, button, hook, nail, stud, ring, staple, tenterhook; davit; fastening &c. 45; spar, horse.

chande-, gase-, electro-lier.

**V.** be -pendent &c. *adj.*; hang, depend, swing, dangle, droop, sag; swag; daggle, flap, trail, flow.

suspend, hang, sling, hook up, hitch, fasten to, append.

**Adj.** pend-ent, -ulous; pensile; hanging &c. *v.*; dependent; suspended &c. *v.*; lowering, overhanging, beetling, decumbent; loose, flowing.

having a -peduncle &c. *n.*; pedunculate, tailed, caudate.

---

**215. Support.**—**N.** support, ground, foundation, base, basis; *terra firma*; bearing, fulcrum, *point d'appui*, caudex, purchase, footing, hold, -*locus standi*; landing, - stage, - place; stage, platform; block; rest, resting-place; groundwork, *substratum*, sustentation, subvention; floor &c. (*basement*) 211.

supporter; aid &c. 707; prop, stand, anvil, fulciment; hod, stay, shore, skid, rib, sprag, truss, bandage; sleeper; stirrup, stilts, shoe, sole, heel, splint, lap; bar, rod, boom, sprit, outrigger.

staff, stick, crutch, alpenstock, bourdon; *bâton*, maulstick, colstaff, cowlstaff, staddle; stalk, ped-icel, -icle, - uncle.

post, pillar, shaft, column, pilaster; pediment, pedestal; plinth, shank, leg, socle, zocle; buttress, jamb, mullion, abutment; pile, baluster, banister, stanchion, king post; balustrade.

frame, -work, body, *chassis*, *fuselage*; scaffold, skeleton, beam, rafter, girder, lintel, joist, cantilever, travis, trave, corner-stone. summer, transom; rung, round, step, sill.

columella, back-bone; key-stone; axle, -tree; axis; arch, ogive, mainstay.

trunnion, pivot, rowlock; peg &c. (*pendency*) 214; tie-beam &c. (*fastening*) 45; thole pin.

board, ledge, shelf, hob, bracket, trevet, trivet, arbor, rack, hatrack; mantel, -piece, -shelf; slab, console; counter, dresser; flange, corbel; table, trestle, teapoy; shoulder; perch; horse; easel, desk; retable, predella.

seat, throne, dais; divan, musnud; chair, bench, form, stool, camp-stool, sofa, settee, davenport, stall, miserere, arm -, easy -, elbow -, rocking- chair; couch, day bed, *fauteuil*, woolsack, ottoman, settle, squab, bench, box, dicky; saddle, pannel, pillion; side -, pack- saddle; pommel.

bed, berth, pallet, tester, crib, cot, bassinet, hammock, shakedown, camp bed, bunk, truckle-bed, cradle, litter, stretcher, bedstead; four-poster, French bed; bedding, mattress, *paillasse*; pillow, bolster; mat, rug, cushion.

stool, footstool, hassock, faldstool, *prie-dieu*; tabouret; tripod. Atlas, Persides, Atlantes, Caryatides, Hercules.

**V.** be -supported &c.; lie -, sit -, recline -, lean -, loll - rest - stand -, step -, repose -, abut -, bear -, be based &c.- on; have at one's back; be-stride, -straddle.

support, bear, carry, hold, sustain, shoulder; hold -, back -, bolster –, shore- up; up-hold, -bear; prop; under-prop, -pin, -set; bandage, &c. 43; brace, truss; cradle, pillow.

give –, furnish –, afford –, supply –, lend- -support, – foundations; bottom, found, base, ground, embed.

maintain, keep on foot; aid &c. 707.

**Adj.** support-ing, -ed, &c. *v.*; atlantean, columellar; sustentative, fundamental, basal.

**Adv.** astride on, astraddle; pick-a-back.

**216. Parallelism.—N.** parallelism; coextension, concentricity, collimation.

**V.** be –, lie- parallel to; collimate.

**Adj.** parallel; coextensive, collateral, concentric, concurrent.

**Adv.** alongside, abreast &c. (*laterally*) 236.

---

**217. Obliquity.—N.** obliquity, inclination, skew, slope, slant; crookedness &c. *adj.*; slopeness; leaning &c. *v.*; bevel, bezel, ramp, tilt; bias, list, twist, swag, cant, lurch; distortion &c. 243; bend &c. (*curve*) 245; tower of Pisa.

acclivity, rise, ascent, grade, gradient, *glacis*, rising ground, hill, bank, declivity, downhill, dip, fall, devexity; gentle –, rapid- slope; easy -ascent, – descent; shelving beach; *talus*; *montagne Russe*; *facilis descensus Averni.*

steepness &c. *adj.*; cliff, precipice &c. (*vertical*) 212; escarpment, scarp.

[Measure of inclination] clinometer, theodolite, level, sextant, quadrant, protractor; angle, sine, cosine, tangent &c. hypothenuse.

diagonal; zigzag, chevron.

**V.** be -oblique &c. *adj.*; slope, slant, lean, incline, shelve, stoop, decline, descend, bend, heel, careen, sag, swag, seel, slouch, cant, sidle.

render -oblique &c. *adj.*; sway, bias; slope, slant; incline, bend, crook; cant, tilt; distort &c. 243.

**Adj.** oblique, inclined; sloping &c. *v.*; tilted &c. *v.*; recumbent, clinal, skew, askew, slant, aslant, bias, plagiedral, indirect, wry, awry, ajee, crooked; knock-kneed &c. (*distorted*) 243; bevel, out of the perpendicular.

uphill, rising, ascending, acclivous; downhill, falling, descending; declining, declivous, devex, anticlinal; steep, abrupt, precipitous, break-neck.

diagonal; trans-verse, -versal; athwart, antiparallel; curved &c. 245.

**Adv.** obliquely &c. *adj.*; on –, all on- one side; askew, askant, askance, aslope, asquint, edgewise, at an angle; side-long, -ways; slope-, slant-wise; by a side wind.

**218. Inversion.—N.** in-, e-, sub-, re-, retro-, intro-version; contraposition &c. 237; contrariety &c. 14; reversal; turn of the tide.

overturn; somer-sault, -set; summerset; *culbute*; revulsion; *pirouette.*

transposition, transposal, anastrophy, *metastasis*, *hyperbaton*, *anastrophe*, *hysteron-proteron*, hypallage, *synchysis*, *tmesis*, parenthesis; *metathesis*; palindrome; Spoonerism.

pronation and supination.

**V.** be -inverted &c.; turn –, go –, wheel- -round, – about, – to the right about; turn –, go –, tilt –, topple-over; capsize, turn turtle.

in-, sub-, retro-, intro-vert; reverse; up-, over-turn, -set; turn -topsy turvy &c. *adj.*; *culbuter*; transpose, put the cart before the horse, turn the tables.

**Adj.** inverted &c. *v.*; wrong side -out, – up; inside out, upside down; bottom –, keel- upwards; supine, on one's head, topsy turvy, *sens dessus sens dessous.*

inverse; reverse &c. (*contrary*) 14; opposite &c. 237.

topheavy, unstable.

**Adv.** inversely &c. *adj.*; hirdie-girdie; heels over head, head over heels.

**219. Crossing.**—**N.** crossing &c. *v.*; inter-section, – lacement, – twinement, -digitation; decussation, transversion; convolution &c. 248.

reticulation, meshwork, network; inosculation, anastomosis, intertexture, mortise.

net, *plexus*, web, mesh, twill, skein, sleeve, felt, lace; wicker; mat, -ting; plait, trellis, wattle, lattice, grating, *grille*, gridiron, tracery, fretwork, filigree, reticle; tissue, netting, mokes.

cross, crucifix, rood, crisscross, crux; chain, wreath, braid, cat's cradle, knot; entanglement &c. (*disorder*) 59.

[woven fabrics] cloth, linen, muslin, cambric, drill, homespun, tweed, broadcloth &c.

**V.** cross, decussate; inter-sect, -lace, -twine, -twist, -weave, -digitate, -link.

twine, entwine, weave, inweave, twist, wreathe; anastomose, inosculate, dovetail, splice, link.

mat, plait, plat, braid, felt, twill; tangle, entangle, ravel; net, knot; dishevel, raddle.

**Adj.** crossing &c. *v.*; crossed, matted &c. *v.*; transverse.

cross, cruciform, crucial; reti-form, -cular, -culated; areolar, cancellated, mullioned, latticed, grated, barred, streaked; textile, secant, plexal; interfretted.

**Adv.** across, thwart, athwart, transversely, crosswise.

## 3°. Centrical Dimensions*

### 1. *General*

**220. Exteriority.** — **N.** exteriority; outside, exterior; surface, superficies; skin &c. (*covering*) 223; *superstratum*; disk, disc; face, facet.

excentricity; circumjacence &c. 227.

**V.** be -exterior &c. *adj.*; lie around &c. 227.

place -exteriorly, – outwardly, – outside; put –, turn- out.

**Adj.** exter-ior, -nal; extraneous, outer, -most; out-ward, -lying, -side, -door; round about &c. 227; extramural.

superficial, skin-deep; frontal, discoid.

extraregarding; eccentric; outstanding; extrinsic &c. 6.

**Adv.** externally &c. *adj.*; out, without, over, outwards, *ab extra*, out of doors; *extra muros.*

**221. Interiority.**—**N.** interiority; inside, interior, endocrine; interspace, subsoil, *substratum.*

contents &c. 190; substance, pith, marrow; backbone &c. (*centre*) 222; heart, bosom, breast, abdomen; vitals, viscera, entrails, bowels, belly, intestines, guts, chitterlings, womb, lap; gland, cell; internal organs, *penetralia*, recesses, innermost recesses; cave &c. (*concavity*) 252.

inhabitant &c. 188.

**V.** be -inside &c. *adj.*, – within &c. *adv.*

place –, keep- within; enclose &c. (*circumscribe*) 229; intern; embed &c. (*insert*) 300.

**Adj.** inter-ior, -nal; inner, inside, intimate, inward, intraregarding; in-, inner-most; deep-seated; visceral, intes-

* That is, Dimensions having reference to a centre.

in the open air; *sub -Jove, - dio*; *à la belle étoile, al fresco.*

tine, -tinal; inland; subcutaneous; interstitial &c. (*interjacent*) 228; inwrought &c. (*intrinsic*) 5; enclosed &c. *v.*

home, domestic, indoor, intramural, vernacular; endemic.

**Adv.** internally &c. *adj.*; inwards, within, in, inly; here-, there-, where-in; *ab intra*, withinside; in –, within- doors; at home, in the bosom of one's family.

**222. Centrality.—N.** centrality, centricalness, centre; middle &c. 68; focus &c. 74.

core, kernel; nucleus, nucleolus; heart, pole, axis, pivot, fulcrum, bull's eye; hub, nave, navel; *umbilicus*, spine, backbone, marrow, pith; hot-bed; concentration &c. (*convergence*) 290; centralization; symmetry.

centre of -gravity, – pressure, – percussion, – oscillation, – buoyancy &c. metacentre.

**V.** be -central &c. *adj.*; converge &c. 290.

render central, centralize, concentrate; bring to a focus.

**Adj.** centr-al, -ical; middle &c. 68; axial, pivotal, focal, umbilical, concentric; middlemost, nuclear, centric, centraidal; spinal, vertebral.

**Adv.** middle; midst; centrally &c. *adj.*

**223. Covering.—N.** covering, cover; canopy, tilt, awning, baldachin, tent, marquee, *tente d'abri*, umbrella, parasol, sunshade; veil (*shade*) 424; shield &c. (*defence*) 717; pall.

roof, dome, cupola, mansard roof; ceiling; thatch, tile; pan-, pen-tile; tiling, shingles, slates, slating, leads; shed &c. (*abode*) 189.

top, lid, covercle, door, *operculum*, eyelid, blind, curtain.

bandage, plaster, lint, wrapping, dossil, finger stall.

coverlet, counterpane, sheet, quilt, comforter, eiderdown; tarpaulin, blanket, rug, drugget, linoleum, oilcloth; housing.

in-, tegument; skin, pellicle, fleece, fell, fur, ermine, miniver, sable, sealskin &c.; leather, morocco, calf, pigskin, elk, kid, cowhide &c.; shagreen, hide; pelt, -ry; cuticle, *dermis*, scarf-skin, *epidermis*.

clothing &c. 225; mask &c. (*concealment*) 530.

peel, crust, bark, rind, *cortex*, husk, shell, coat.

capsule; ferrule; sheath, -ing; pod, cod; casing, case, theca, *elytron*; *involucrum*; wrapp-ing, -er, envelope, vesicle; dermatology, conchology.

armour, -plate, armouring; veneer, facing; pavement; scale &c. (*layer*) 204; coating, paint, stain; varnish &c. (*resin*) 356*a*; anointing &c. *v.*; inunction; incrustation, superposition, obduction, ground, enamel, whitewash, plaster, stucco, rough cast, pebble dash, compo; rendering; cerement; ointment &c. (*grease*) 356.

**V.** cover; super-pose, -impose; over-lay, -spread; wrap &c. 225; incase; face, case, veneer, pave, paper; tip, cap, bind, revet.

coat, paint, varnish, pay, incrust, stucco, cement, dab, plaster, tar; wash; be-, smear; be-, daub; anoint, do over; gild, plate,

**224. Lining.—N.** lining, inner coating; coating &c. (*covering*) 223; stalactite, -agmite.

filling, stuffing, wadding, padding, bushing.

wainscot, *parietes*, wall, brattice.

**V.** line, stuff, incrust, wad, pad, fill.

**Adj.** lined &c. *v.*

electroplate, japan, lacquer, lacker, enamel, whitewash; lay it on thick.

over-lie, -arch; conceal &c. 528.

Adj. covering &c. *v.*; cutaneous, dermal, cortical, cuticular, tegumentary, skinny, scaly, squamous; covered &c. *v.*; imbricated, loricated, armour-plated, iron-clad; under cover, hooded, cloaked, cowled.

**225. Investment.—N.** investment; covering &c. 223; dress, clothing, raiment, drapery, costume, attire, guise, toilet, *toilette*, trim; habiliment; vesture, -ment; garment, garb, palliament, apparel, wardrobe, wearing apparel, clothes, things.

array; tailoring, millinery; best bib and tucker; finery &c. (*ornament*) 847; full dress &c. (*show*) 882; garniture; theatrical properties.

outfit, equipment, *trousseau*; uniform, khaki, regimentals; academicals, canonicals &c. 999; livery, gear, harness, turn out, accoutrement, caparison, suit, rigging, trappings, traps, slops, togs, toggery; masquerade.

dishabille, morning dress, lounge suit, tea-gown, *kimono*, *négligé*, dressing-gown, *peignoir*, wrapper, undress; shooting-coat; smoking-jacket, mufti; rags, tatters, old clothes; mourning, weeds; duds; slippers.

robe, tunic, dolman, *paletot*, habit, gown, coat, coatee, frock, blouse, middy, sagum, *toga*, smock-frock; frock-, dress-, morning-, tail-coat; dress-suit, – clothes, swallow-tail coat, dinner-, Eton-jacket.

cloak, pall; mantle, mantlet, mantua, shawl, *pelisse*, veil, yashmak; cape, tippet, kirtle, plaid, muffler, comforter, Balaclava helmet, haik, huke, chlamys, mantilla, tabard, housing, horse-cloth, burnous, *roquelaure*; *houppelande*; sur-, top, over-, great-coat; *surtout*, spencer, cardigan, sweater, blazer; mackintosh, waterproof, slicker, raincoat, oilskin, trench coat, ulster, monkey-, pea-, pilot-jacket, redingote; wraprascal, poncho, cardinal, pelerine, talma.

jacket, jumper, vest, jerkin, waistcoat, doublet, *camisole*, gabardine; stays, *corsage*, corset, corselet, bodice; stomacher; skirt, petticoat, slip, farthingale, kilt, jupe, crinoline, bustle, hobble skirt, *panier*, apron, pinafore; loin cloth.

trousers; breeches, trews, pantaloons, unmentionables, inexpressibles, overalls, pyjamas, smalls, small-clothes; tights, pants, shorts, drawers; knickerbockers, knickers, plus fours, bloomers, divided skirt; phil-, fill-ibeg.

**226. Divestment.—N.** divestment; taking off &c. *v.*

nudity; bareness &c. *adj.*; undress; dishabille &c. 225, altogether; nu-, denu-dation; decortication, depilation, excoriation, desquamation; moulting; exfoliation.

baldness, alopecia, acomia.

**V.** divest; uncover &c. (*cover* &c. 223); denude, bare, strip; undress, unclothe, disrobe &c. (dress, enrobe, &c. 225); uncoif; dismantle; uncase; put –, take –, cast- off; shed, doff; husk, peel, pare, decorticate, desquamate, excoriate, skin, scalp, flay, bark, expose, lay open; exfoliate, moult, mew; cast the skin.

**Adj.** divested &c. *v.*; bare, naked, nude; un-dressed, -draped, -clad, -clothed, -appareled; exposed; in dishabille; *décolleté*; bald, threadbare, ragged, callow, roofless.

in -a state of nature, – nature's garb, – buff, – native buff, – birthday suit; *in puris naturalibus*; with nothing on, stark naked; bald as a coot, bare as the back of one's hand; out at elbows; barefoot; bareback; leaf-, nap-, hairless, shaved, clean shaven, tonsured, beardless, bald-headed, acomous.

head-dress, -gear; cap, *béret*, tam o' shanter, glengarry, topee, sombrero; hat; cocked –, high –, tall –, top –, silk –, opera –, crush -hat, *gibus*, beaver, castor, bonnet, tile, wideawake, billy-cock; bowler; soft felt –, straw –, leghorn -hat, panama; toque; wimple; night-, mob-, skull-cap, biretta; hood, cowl, coif; capote, calach; scull-cap; kerchief, snood; head, *coiffure*; crown &c. (*circle*) 247; *chignon*, pelt, wig, front, peruke, periwig; caftan, turban, fez, *tarboosh*, taj, shako, csako, busby; *képi*, forage cap, bearskin; helmet &c. 717; mask, domino.

body clothes; linen; shirt, sark, smock, shift, *chemise*, *lingerie*; night-gown, -shirt; bed-gown, *sac de nuit*; jersey, guernsey; underwear, undies, underclothing, -waistcoat.

neck-erchief, -cloth; tie, ruff, collar, cravat, stock, handkerchief, bandana, scarf; bib, tucker; dicky; boa; girdle &c. (*circle*) 247; cummerbund.

shoe, pump, brogue, boot, slipper, sandal, galoche, goloshes, arctics, rubber boots, overshoes, patten, clog, sabot; high-low; Blücher –, Wellington –, Hessian –, jack –, top- boot; Balmoral; legging, puttee, buskin, greave, galligaskin, moccasin, *gamache*, gambado, gaiter, spatter-dash, spat, antigropelos; stocking, hose, gaskins, trunk-hose, sock, hosiery.

glove, gauntlet, mitten, cuff, muffettee, wristband, sleeve.

swaddling cloth, baby-linen, *layette*; pocket-handkerchief.

shroud &c. 363.

clothier, tailor, milliner, *costumier*, sempstress, seamstress, snip; dress-, habit-, breeches-, shoe-maker; cordwainer, cobbler, Crispin, hosier, hatter; draper, linendraper, haberdasher, mercer.

**V.** invest; cover &c. 223; envelop, lap, involve; in-, en-wrap; wrap; fold –, wrap –, lap –, muffle- up; overlap; sheathe, swathe, swaddle, roll up in, shroud, circumvest.

vest, clothe, array, dress, dight, drape, robe, enrobe, attire, tire, garb, habilitate, apparel, accoutre, rig, fit out; bedizen, deck &c. (*ornament*) 847; perk; equip, harness, caparison; dress up.

wear; don; put –, huddle –, slip- on; mantle.

**Adj.** invested &c. *v.*; habited; dight, -ed; clad, *costumé*, shod, *chaussé*; *en grande tenue* &c. (*show*) 882.

sartorial.

**227. Circumjacence.—N.** circum-jacence, -ambience; environment, encompassment; atmosphere, medium; surroundings, *entourage*.

outpost; border &c. (*edge*) 231; girdle &c. (*circumference*) 230; outskirts, *boulevards*, suburbs, purlieus, precincts, *faubourgs*, *environs*, *banlieue*, neighbourhood, vicinity.

**V.** lie -around &c. *adv.*; surround, beset, compass, encompass, environ, inclose, enclose, encircle, circle, embrace, circumvent, lap, gird; begird, girdle, engird; skirt, twine round; hem in &c. (*circumscribe*) 229; besiege, invest, blockade.

**Adj.** circum-jacent, -ambient, -fluent;

**228. Interjacence.—N.** inter-jacence, -currence, -venience, -location, -digitation, -penetration; permeation.

inter-jection, -polation, -lineation, -spersion, -calation; embolism.

inter-vention, -ference, -position; in-, ob-trusion; insinuation; insertion &c. 300; dovetailing; infiltration; intromission.

intermedi-um, -ary; go-between, agent, middleman, medium, bodkin, intruder, interloper; parenthesis, episode; fly-leaf.

partition, *septum*, diaphragm, midriff; party-wall, panel, vail, bulkhead, brattice, *cloison*; half-way house.

**V.** lie –, come –, get- between; inter-

ambient; surrounding &c. *v.*; circumferential, surburban.

**Adv.** around, about; without; on – every side, – all sides; right and left, all round, round about; in the neighbourhood.

---

vene, slide in, interpenetrate, permeate.

put between, introduce, intromit. import; throw –, wedge –, edge –, jam –, worm –, foist –, run –, plough –, work- in; inter-pose, -ject, -calate, -polate, -line, -leave, -sperse, -weave, -lard, -digitate; let in, dovetail, splice, mortise; insinuate, smuggle; infiltrate, ingrain.

interfere, put in an oar, thrust one's nose in; intrude, obtrude; have a finger in the pie; introduce the thin end of the wedge; thrust in &c. (*insert*) 300.

**Adj.** inter-jacent, -current, -venient, -vening &c. *v.*, -mediate, -mediary, -calary, -stitial, -costal, -mural, -planetary, -stellar; embolismal.

parenthetical, episodic; mediterranean; intrusive; embosomed; merged, mean, middle, medium, median.

**Adv.** between, betwixt; 'twixt; among, -st; amid, -st; 'mid, -st; in the thick of; betwixt and between; sandwich-wise; parenthetically, *obiter dictum.*

**229. Circumscription.**—**N.** circumscription, limitation, inclosure; confinement &c. (*restraint*) 751; circumvallation, encincture; envelope &c. 232.

**V.** circumscribe, limit, bound, confine, enclose; surround &c. 227; compass about; imprison &c. (*restrain*) 751; hedge –, wall –, rail- in; fence –, hedge- round; embar; picket, corral.

enfold, bury, incase, pack up, enshrine, inclasp; wrap up &c. (*invest*) 225; embosom.

**Adj.** circumscribed &c. *v.*; begirt, lapt; circumambient; buried –, immersed- in; embosomed, in the bosom of, imbedded, encysted, mewed up; imprisoned &c. 751; land-locked, in a ring fence.

**230. Outline.**—**N.** outline, circumference; peri-meter, -phery; ambit, circuit, lines, *tournure, contour*, profile, *silhouette*, lineaments; bounds, coastline.

zone, belt, girth, band, baldric, zodiac, girdle, tire, cingle, clasp, girt; *cordon* &c. (*inclosure*) 232; circlet &c. 247.

**V.** outline, delineate, *silhouette*, circumscribe &c. 229; profile, block out.

**Adj.** outlined &c. *v.*; circumferential, perimetric, peripheral.

**231. Edge.**—**N.** edge, verge, brink, brow, brim, margin, border, confines, skirt, rim, felloe, felly, flange, side, mouth; jaws, chops, chaps, *fauces*; lip, muzzle.

threshold, door, porch; portal &c. (*opening*) 260; coast, shore, strand, beach, bank, wharf, quay, dock.

frame, fringe, flounce, frill, list, trimming, edging, skirting, hem, selvedge, welt; furbelow, valance, exergue.

**Adj.** border, marginal, skirting; labial, labiated, marginated.

**232. Inclosure.**—**N.** inclosure, enclosure, envelope; case &c. (*receptacle*) 191; wrapper; girdle &c. 230.

pen, fold, croft, sty; pen-, in-, sheep-fold; paddock, pound, corral, kraal; yard, compound; net, seine net.

wall; hedge, -row; *espalier*; fence &c. (*defence*) 717; pale, paling, balustrade, rail, railing, gunwale; quickset hedge, park paling, circumvallation, *enceinte*, ring fence.

barrier, barricade; gate, -way; door, hatch, *cordon*; prison &c. 752.
dike, dyke, ditch, fosse, moat, trench.

**V.** inclose; circumscribe &c. 229.

**233. Limit.**—**N.** limit, boundary, bounds, confine, *enclave*, term, bourn, verge, kerb-stone, curbstone, but, pale; termin-ation, -us; stint, frontier, precinct, marches.

boundary line, landmark, benchmark; line of -demarcation, – circumvallation; pillars of Hercules; Rubicon, turning-point; *ne plus ultra*; sluice, flood-gate.

**V.** limit, bound, confine, define, circumscribe, demarcate, delimit, encompass.

**Adj.** definite; contermin-ate, -able, terminable, limitable; terminal, frontier, border, bordering, boundary.

**Adv.** thus far, – and no further.

2. *Special*

**234. Front.**—**N.** front; fore, – part; foreground; forefront, face, disk, disc, frontage, *façade*, *proscenium*, facia, frontispiece; priority, anteriority; obverse [of a medal].

fore –, front- rank, first line; van, -guard; advanced guard; outpost, scout.

brow, forehead, visage, physiognomy, phiz, features, countenance, map, mug; rostrum, beak, bow, stem, prow, prore, jib, bowsprit; forecastle.

pioneer &c. (*precursor*) 64; metoposcopy.

**V.** be –, stand- in front &c. *adj.*; front, face, confront, breast, brave; bend forwards; come to the -front, – fore.

**Adj.** fore, forward, anterior, front, frontal.

**Adv.** before; in -front, – the van, – advance; ahead, right ahead; fore-, head-most; in the foreground; before one's -face, – eyes; face to face, *vis-à-vis*.

**235. Rear.**—**N.** rear, back, posteriority; rear -rank, – guard; background, *hinterland*.

occiput, nape, scruff, chine; heels; tail, rump, croup, buttock, posteriors, bottom, seat, backside, scut, breech, *dorsum*, loin; dorsal –, lumbar- region; hind quarters.

stern, poop, after-part, counter; postern, heel-, tail-piece, crupper.

wake; train &c. (*sequence*) 281.

reverse; other side of the shield.

**V.** be -behind &c. *adv.*; fall astern; bend backwards; bring up the rear; follow &c. 622; tail, shadow.

**Adj.** back, rear; hind, -er, -most, -ermost; post-ern, -erior; dorsal, after; caudal, lumbar; mizzen.

**Adv.** behind; in the -rear, – ruck, – back-ground; behind one's back; at the -heels, – tail, – back- of; back to back.

after, -most, aft, abaft, astern, sternmost, aback, rear-, hind-, back-ward.

---

**236. Laterality.**—**N.** laterality; side, flank, beam, quarter, lee; hand; cheek, jowl, jole, wing; profile; temple, *parietes*, loin, haunch, hip.

gable, -end; broadside; lee side.

points of the compass; East, Orient, Levant; West, occident; orientation.

**V.** be -on one side &c. *adv.*; flank, outflank; sidle; skirt, border.

**Adj.** lateral, sidelong; collateral;

**237. Contraposition.**—**N.** contraposition, opposition; polarity; inversion &c. 218; opposite side; antithesis; reverse, inverse; counterpart; antipodes; opposite poles, North and South.

**V.** be -opposite &c. *adj.*; subtend.

**Adj.** opposite; reverse, inverse; antipodal, subcontrary; fronting, facing, diametrically opposite.

Northern, Septentrional, Boreal, arc

parietal, flanking, skirting; flanked; sideling.

many-sided; multi-, bi-, tri-, quadrilateral.

East-ern, -ward, -erly; orient, -al, auroral, Levantine; West-ern, -ward, -erly; occidental, Hesperian; equatorial.

Adv. side-ways, -long; broadside on; on one side, abreast, abeam, alongside, beside, aside; by, - the side of; side by side; cheek by jowl &c. (*near*) 197; to -windward, - leeward; laterally &c. *adj.*; right and left; on her beam ends.

tic; Southern, Austral, antarctic, polar.

Adv. over, - the way, - against; against; face to face, *vis-à-vis*; as poles asunder.

---

**238. Dextrality.** — **N.** dextrality; right, - hand; dexter, offside, starboard.

**Adj.** dextral, right-handed; ambidextral, dexterous, dextrorsal &c.

**239. Sinistrality.**—**N.** sinistrality; left, - hand; *sinister*, nearside, larboard, port.

**Adj.** sinistral, sinister, sinistrorsal &c., left-handed, sinistromanual, sinistrous.

## Section III. FORM

### 1°. General Form

**240. Form.**—**N.** form, figure, shape; con-formation, -figuration; make, formation, frame, construction, design, cut, set, build, trim, cut of one's jib; stamp, type, cast, mould; fashion; contour &c. (*outline*) 230; structure &c. 329.

feature, lineament, outline, turn; phase &c. (*aspect*) 448; posture, attitude, *pose*.

[Science of form] morphology.

[Similarity of form] isomorphism.

forming &c. *v.*; form-, figur-, efformation; sculpture.

**V.** form, shape, figure, fashion, efform, carve, cut, chisel, hew, cast; rough-hew, -cast; sketch; block -, hammer- out; trim; lick -, put- into shape; model, knead, work up into, set, mould, sculpture; cast, stamp; build &c. (*construct*) 161.

**Adj.** formed &c. *v.*

[Receiving form] plastic, fictile, full-fashioned &c.

[Giving form] plasmic &c.

[Similar in form] isomorphous &c.

**241.** [Absence of form.] **Amorphism.** —**N.** amorphism, informity, uncouthness; unlicked cub, rough diamond; *rudis indigestaque moles*; disorder &c. 59; deformity &c. 243.

disfigure-, deface-ment, deformation; mutilation.

**V.** [Destroy form] deface, disfigure, deform, mutilate, truncate; derange &c. 61.

**Adj.** shapeless, amorphous, malformed, formless; un-formed, -hewn, -fashioned, -shapen; rough, rude, Gothic, barbarous, rugged, in the rough; misshapen &c. 243.

---

**242.** [Regularity of form.] **Symmetry.** —**N.** symmetry, shapeliness, finish; beauty &c. 845; proportion, eurythmy, eurythmic, uniformity, parallelism; bi-, tri-, multi-lateral symmetry; centrality &c. 222.

**243.** [Irregularity of form.] **Distortion.**—**N.** dis-, de-, con-tortion; knot, mop, warp, buckle, screw, twist; crookedness &c. (*obliquity*) 217; grimace; deformity; mal-, malcon-formation; monstrosity, misproportion, want

arborescence, branching, ramification.

Adj. symmetrical, shapely, well set, finished; beautiful &c. 845; classic, chaste, severe.

regular, uniform, balanced; equal &c. 27; parallel, coextensive.

arbor-escent, -iform; dendr-iform, -oid; branching; ramous, ramose.

---

of symmetry, *anamorphosis*; ugliness &c. 846; teratology.

**V.** distort, contort, twist, warp &c. *n.*; wrest, writhe, make faces, deform, misshape.

**Adj.** distorted &c. *v.*; out of shape, irregular, unsymmetric, awry, wry, askew, crooked, sinuous; anamorphous; not -true, - straight; on one side, crump, deformed; mis-shapen, -begotten; mis-, ill-proportioned; ill-made; grotesque, crooked as a ram's horn; hump-, hunch-, bunch-, crook-backed; bandy; bandy-, bow-legged; bow-, knock-kneed; splay-, club-footed; taliped; round-shouldered; snub-nosed; curtailed of one's fair proportions; scalene, stumpy &c. (*short*) 201; gaunt &c. (*thin*) 203; bloated &c. 194.

**Adv.** all manner of ways.

## 2°. Special Form

**244. Angularity.—N.** angular-ity, -ness; aduncity; angle, cusp, bend; fold &c. 258; notch &c. 257; fork, bifurcation.

elbow, knee, knuckle, ankle, groin, crotch, crutch, crane, fluke, scythe, sickle, zigzag, kimbo.

corner, nook, recess, niche, oriel.

right angle &c. (*perpendicular*) 212; obliquity &c. 217; angle of 45°, mitre; acute -, obtuse -, salient -, re-entrant -, spherical -, solid -, dihedral- angle.

angular -measurement, - elevation, - distance, - velocity; trigon-, goni-ometry; altimetry; clin-, graph-, goni-ometer; theodolite; transit circle; sextant, quadrant; dichotomy.

triangle, trigon, wedge; rectangle, square, lozenge, diamond; rhomb, -us; quadr-angle, -ilateral; parallelogram; quadrature; poly-, penta-, hexa-, hepta-, octa-, deca-gon.

Platonic bodies; cube, rhomboid; tetra-, penta-, hexa-, octa-, dodeca-, icosa-hedron; prism, pyramid; parallelopiped.

**V.** bend, fork, bifurcate, crinkle, divaricate, branch, ramify.

**Adj.** angular, bent, crooked, aduncous, uncinated, aquiline, jagged, serrated; falc-iform, -ated; furcular, furcated, forked, bifurcate, crotched; zigzag; dovetailed; knock-kneed, crinkled, akimbo, kimbo, geniculated; oblique &c. 217.

fusiform, wedge-shaped, cuneiform; tri-angular, -gonal, -lateral; quadr-angular, -ilateral; rectangular, square, foursquare, multilateral; polygonal &c. *n.*; cubical, rhomboidal, pyramidal.

**245. Curvature.—N.** curv-ature, -ity, -ation; incurv-ity, -ation; bend; flexure, -ion; conflexure; crook, hook, bought, bending; de-, inflexion; arcuation, devexity, turn; deviation, *détour*, sweep; curl, -ing; bough; recurv-ity, -ation; sinuosity &c. 248; aduncity.

curve, arc, arch, arcade, vault, dome, bow, crescent, *meniscus*, half-moon, lunule, horse-shoe, loop, crane-neck;

**246. Straightness.—N.** straightness, rectilinearity, directness; inflexibility &c. (*stiffness*) 323; straight -, right -, direct-, bee- line; short cut.

**V.** be -straight &c. *adj.*; have no turning; not -incline, - bend, - turn, - deviate- to either side; go straight; steer for &c. (*direction*) 278.

render straight, straighten, rectify; set -, put- straight; un-bend, -fold.

para-, hyper-bola; catenary, festoon; conch-, cardi-oid; caustic, instep; tracery.

V. be -curved &c. *adj.*; sweep, swag, sag; deviate &c. 279; turn; re-enter.

render -curved &c. *adj.*; bend, curve, incurvate; de-, in-flect; crook; turn, round, arch, arcuate, arch over, loop the loop, concamerate; bow, coil, curl, recurve, frizzle.

Adj. curved &c. *v.*; curvi-form, -lineal, -linear; devex, devious; recurv-ed, -ous; *retroussé*; crump; bowed &c. *v.*; vaulted; hooked; falc-iform, -ated; semicircular, crescentic; lun-iform, -ular; semilunar, meniscal; conchoidal; cord-iform, -ated; cardioid; heart-, bell-, pear-, fig-shaped; reniform; lenti-form, -cular; bow-legged &c. (*distorted*) 243; oblique &c. 217; circular &c. 247.

**247.** [Simple circularity.] **Circularity.** —**N.** circularity, roundness; rotundity &c. 249.

circle, circlet, clasp, ring, washer, areola, hoop, roundlet, *annulus*, amulet, bracelet, armlet, armilla; ringlet; eye, loop, wheel; cycle, orb, orbit, rundle, zone, belt, *cordon*, band; sash, girdle, cestus, cincture, baldric, fillet, *fascia*, wreath, garland; crown, corona, coronet, chaplet, snood, necklace, collar; noose, lasso, lariat.

ellipse, oval, ovule; ellipsoid, cycloid; epi-cycloid, -cycle; semi-circle; quadrant, sextant, sector.

V. make -round &c. *adj.*; round.

go round; encircle &c. 227; describe a circle &c. 311.

Adj. round, rounded, circular, annular, orbicular; oval, ovate; elliptic, -al; ovoid, egg-shaped; pear-shaped &c. 245; cycloidal &c. *n.*; spherical &c. 249.

**248.** [Complex circularity.] **Convolution.**—**N.** winding &c. *v.*; con-, in-, circum-volution; wave, undulation, tortuosity, anfractuosity; sinu-osity, -ation, sinuousness; meandering, circuit, circumbendibus, twist, twirl, windings and turnings, *ambages*; torsion; inosculation; reticulation &c. (*crossing*) 219.

coil, roll, curl, buckle, spire, spiral, helix, corkscrew, worm, volute, whorl, rundle; tendril; scollop, scallop, escalop; kink.

serpent, snake, eel, maze, labyrinth.

V. be -convoluted &c. *adj.*; wind, twine, turn and twist, twirl; wave, undulate, meander; inosculate; entwine, intwine; twist, coil, roll; wrinkle, curl, crisp, twill; frizz, -le; crimp, crape, indent, scollop, scallop; wring, intort; contort; wreathe &c. (*cross*) 219.

Adj. convoluted; winding, twisted &c. *v.*; tortile, tortive; wavy; und-ated, -ulatory; circling, snaky, snake-like, serpentine; serpent-, anguill-, verm-iform; vermicular; mazy, tortuous, anfractuous, sinuous, flexuous, wavy, sigmoidal.

involved, intricate, complicated, perplexed; labyrinth-ic, -ian, -ine; circuitous; peristaltic; dædalian, curly.

wreathy, frizzly, crapy, buckled; ravelled &c. (*in disorder*) 59.

spiral, coiled, helical, turbinated.

Adv. in and out, round and round.

-curl &c. 248, -ravel &c. 219, -wrap.

Adj. straight; rectiline-ar, -al; direct, even, right, true, in a line; unbent &c. *v.*; un-deviating, -turned, -distorted, -swerving; straight as an arrow &c. (*direct*) 278; inflexible &c. 323.

**249. Rotundity.**—**N.** rotundity; roundness &c. *adj.*; cylindricity; spher-icity, -oidity; globosity.

cylin-der, -droid; barrel, drum; roll, -er; *rouleau*, column, rolling-pin, rundle; chimney-pot, drain-pipe.

cone, conoid; pear-, egg-, bell-shape.

sphere, globe, ball, boulder, bowlder; spher-, ellips-, ge-, glob-oid, oblong –, oblate- spheroid; drop, spherule, globule, vesicle, bulb, bullet, pellet, *pelote*, clew, pill, marble, pea, knob, pommel, knot.

V. render -spherical &c. *adj.*; form into a sphere, sphere, roll into a ball; give -rotundity &c. *n.*; round.

Adj. rotund; round &c. (*circular*) 247; cylindr-ic, -ical, -oid; columnar, lumbriciform; conic, -al; spher-ical, -oidal; glob-ular, -ated, -ous, -ose; egg-, bell-, pear-shaped; ov-oid, -iform; gibbous; campaniform, -ulate, -iliform; fungiform, bead-like, moniliform, pyriform, bulbous; *teres atque rotundus*; round as -an orange, – an apple, – a ball, – a billiard ball, – a cannon ball.

### 3°. Superficial Form

**250. Convexity. — N.** convexity, prominence, projection, swelling, gibbosity, bilge, bulge, protuberance, protrusion; excrescency, camber.

intumescence; tumour, tumor; tubercle, -osity; excrescence; hump, hunch, bunch, gnarl, lump.

tooth, knob, elbow, process, *apophysis*, condyle, bulb, node, nodule, nodosity, tongue, *dorsum*, boss, embossment, bump, clump; sugar-loaf &c. (*sharpness*) 253; bow; mamelon.

pimple, wen, wheal, *papula*, postule, pock, proud flesh, growth, goitre, *sarcoma*, carbuncle, corn, bunion, wart, furnuncle, polypus, adenoid, fungus, fungosity, *exostosis*, bleb, blister, blain; boil &c. (*disease*) 655; bubble, blob.

papilla, nipple, teat, pap, breast, dug, mammilla; proboscis, nose, neb, beak, snout, nozzle, snozzle; Adam's apple; belly, paunch, corporation; withers, back, shoulder, lip, flange.

peg, button, stud, ridge, rib, jutty, trunnion, snag.

cupola, dome, bee-hive; arch, balcony, eaves; pilaster.

relief, relievo, *cameo*; *basso-*, *mezzo-*, *alto-rilievo*; low-, bas-, high-relief.

hill &c. (*height*) 206; cape, promontory, mull; fore-, head-land; point of land, naze, ness, mole, jetty, hummock, ledge, spur.

V. be -prominent &c. *adj.*; project, bulge, protrude, bag, belly, pout, bouge, bunch; jut –, stand –, stick –, poke- out; stick –, bristle –, start –, cock –, shoot- up; swell –, hang –, bend- over; beetle.

render -prominent &c. *adj.*; raise emboss, chase.

**251. Flatness.—N.** flatness &c. *adj.*; smoothness &c. 255.

plane; level &c. 213; plate, platter, table, tablet, slab.

V. render flat, flatten, squash; level &c. 213.

Adj. flat, plane, even, flush, scutiform, discoid; level &c. (*horizontal*) 213; smooth; flat as -a pancake, – a fluke, – a flounder, – a board, – my hand.

**252. Concavity.—N.** concavity, depression, dip; hollow, -ness; indentation, *intaglio*, cavity, antrum, dent, dint, dimple, follicle, pit, *sinus*, *alveolus*, *lacuna*; excavation, trench, sap, mine, tunnel, burrow; trough &c. (*furrow*) 259; honeycomb.

cup, basin, crater, punch-bowl; cell &c. (*receptacle*) 191; socket, faucet.

valley, vale, dale, dell, gap, dingle, combe, bottom, slade, strath, glade, grove, glen, cave, cavern, cove; grot, -to; alcove, *cul-de-sac*, blind alley; gully &c. 198; arch &c. (*curve*) 245; bay &c. (*of the sea*) 343.

excavator, sapper, miner.

V. be -concave &c. *adj.*; retire, cave in.

render -concave &c. *adj.*; depress hollow; scoop, – out; gouge, dig, delve, excavate, dent, dint, mine, sap, undermine, burrow, tunnel, stave in.

Adj. depressed &c. *v.*; concave, hollow, stove in; dished; spoon-like; retiring; retreating; cavernous; porous &c. (*with holes*) 260; cellular, spongy, spongious; honeycombed, alveolar; infundibul-ar, -iform; funnel-, bell-shaped; campaniform, capsular; vaulted, arched.

**Adj.** convex, prominent, protuberant, underhung, undershot; projecting &c. *v.*; bossed, bossy, nodular, bunchy; clav-ate, -ated; hummocky, *moutonné*, mammiform; papul-ous, -ose; hemispheric, bulbous; bowed, arched; bold; bellied; tuber-ous, -culous; tumorous; cornute, knobby, odontoid; lenti-form, -cular; gibbous.

salient, in relief, raised, *repoussé*; bloated &c. (*expanded*) 194.

**253. Sharpness.—N.** sharpness &c. *adj.*; acuity, acumination; spinosity.

point, spike, spine, *spiculum*, tine; needle, pin; tack, nail; prick, -le; spur, rowel, barb; spit, cusp; horn, antler; snag; tag; thorn, bristle.

nib, tooth, incisor, tusk; spoke, cog, ratchet.

crag. crest, *arête*, cone, peak, sugar-loaf, pike, *aiguille*; spire, pyramid, steeple.

beard, *chevaux de frise*, porcupine, hedgehog, brier, bramble, thistle; comb, awn, bur.

wedge; knife-, cutting- edge; blade, edge-tool, cutlery, knife, penknife, whittle, razor; scalpel, bistoury, lancet; chisel; ploughshare, coulter; hatchet, axe, pick-axe, mattock, pick, adze, bill; bill-hook, cleaver, cutter; skiver; scythe, sickle, scissors, shears; sword &c. (*arms*) 727; bodkin &c. (*perforator*) 262.

sharpener, hone, strop; grind-, whet-stone; steel, emery.

**V.** be -sharp &c. *adj.*; taper to a point; bristle with.

render -sharp &c. *adj.*; sharpen, point, aculeate, acuminate, whet, barb, spiculate, set, strop, grind.

cut &c. (*sunder*) 44.

**Adj.** sharp, keen; acute; aci-cular, -form; acu-leated, -minated; pointed; tapering; conical, pyramidal; mucron-ate, -ated; spindle-, needle-shaped; spiked, spiky, ensiform, peaked, salient, cusp-ed; -idate, -idated; corn-ute, -uted, -iculate; prickly; spiny, spinous; thorny, bristling, muricated, pectinated, studded, thistly, briery; craggy &c. (*rough*) 256; snaggy; digitated, two-edged, fusiform; denti-form, -culated; toothed; odontoid; star-like; stell-ated, -iform; arrow-headed; arrowy, barbed, spurred, sagittal; spear-shaped, hastate; horned; conical.

cutting; sharp-, knife-edged; sharp –, keen- as a razor; sharp as a needle; sharpened &c. *v.*; set.

**254. Bluntness.—N.** bluntness &c. *adj.*

**V.** be –, render- blunt &c. *adj.*; obtund, dull; take off the -point, – edge; turn.

**Adj.** blunt, obtuse, dull, bluff.

---

**255. Smoothness.—N.** smoothness &c. *adj.*; polish, gloss; lubric-ity, -ation.

down, velvet, silk, satin; slide; bowling green &c. (*level*) 213; glass, ice; asphalt, pavement, flags.

roller, steam-roller; iron, flat-iron, tailor's goose; sand-, emery-paper; burnisher, turpentine and bees-wax.

**V.** smooth, -en; plane; file; mow, shave; level, roll; macadamize; polish, burnish, planish, levigate, calender, glaze; iron, hot-press, mangle; lubricate &c. (*oil*) 332.

**256. Roughness.—N.** roughness &c. *adj.*; tooth, grain, texture, ripple; asperity, rugosity, salebrosity, corrugation, nodosity; arborescence &c. 242.

brush, hair, beard, shag, mane, whisker, mutton-chops, *moustache*, *mustachio*, imperial, Van Dyke, tress, lock, curl, ringlet, *fimbriæ*, *cilia*, *villi*; eye-lashes, eye-brows, love-lock.

plum-age, -osity; plume, *panache*, crest; feather, tuft, tussock, fringe, toupee.

wool, velvet, plush, nap, pile, floss,

**Adj.** smooth; polished &c. *v.*; even; level &c. 213; plane &c. (*flat*) 251; sleek, glossy; silken, silky; lanate, downy, velvety; glabrous, slippery, glassy, lubricous, oily, soft; unwrinkled; smooth as -glass, – ice, – velvet, – oil; slippery as an eel; woolly &c. (*feathery*) 256.

---

fluff, fur, down; byssus, moss, bur.

**V.** be -rough &c. *adj.*; go against the grain.

render -rough &c. *adj.*; roughen, rough cast, knurl; ruffle, crisp, crumple, crinkle, corrugate, engrail; set on edge, stroke –, rub- the wrong way, rumple.

**Adj.** rough, uneven; scabrous, knotted; nodular; rug-ged, -ose, -ous; asperous, crisp, salebrous, gnarled, unpolished, unsmooth, rough-hewn; knurled, cross-grained, crag-gy, -ged; crankling, scraggy, jagged, unkempt, prickly &c. (*sharp*) 253; arborescent &c. 242; leafy, well wooded; feathery; plum-ose, -igerous; tufted, fimbriated, hairy, bristly, ciliated, filamentous, hirsute; crin-ose, -ite; bushy, hispid, villous, pappous, bearded, pilous, shaggy, shagged; fringed, befringed; set-ous, -ose, -aceous; 'like quills upon the fretful porcupine'; rough as a -nutmeg grater, – bear.

downy, velvety, flocculent, woolly; lan-ate, -ated; lanugin-ous, -ose; tomentous.

**Adv.** against the grain, in the rough, on edge.

**257. Notch.**—**N.** notch, dent, nick, cut; indent, -ation; serration; dimple.

embrasure, battlement, machicolation; saw, tooth, crenelle, scallop, scollop, vandyke.

**V.** notch, nick, cut, pink, mill, score, dent, indent, jag, scarify, scotch, crimp, scollop, crenulate, vandyke.

**Adj.** notched &c. *v.*; crenate, -d; dentate, -d; denticulate, -d; toothed, palmated, serrated.

**258. Fold.**—**N.** fold, plicature, pleat, plait, ply, crease; tuck, gather; flexion, flexure, joint, elbow, doubling, duplicature, wrinkle, rimple, crinkle, crankle, crumple, rumple, rivel, ruck, ruffle, dog's ear, corrugation, frounce, flounce, lapel; pucker, crow's feet.

**V.** fold, double, plicate, pleat, plait, crease, wrinkle, crinkle, crankle, curl, smock, cockle up, crocker, rimple, rumple, frizzle, frounce, rivel, twill, corrugate, ruffle, crimple, crumple, pucker; turn –, double- -down, – under; tuck, ruck, hem, gather.

**Adj.** folded &c. *v.*

**259. Furrow.**—**N.** furrow, groove, rut, *sulcus*, scratch, streak, *striæ*, crack, score, incision, slit; chamfer, fluting.

channel, gutter, trench, ditch, dike, dyke, moat, fosse, trough, kennel; ravine &c. (*interval*) 198.

**V.** furrow &c. *n.*; flute, groove, carve, corrugate, plough; incise, chase, enchase, grave, engrave, etch, bite in, cross-hatch.

**Adj.** furrowed &c. *v.*; ribbed, striated, sulcated, fluted, canaliculated; bisulc-ous, -ate; trisulcate; corduroy.

**260. Opening.**—**N.** hole, foramen; puncture, blow-out, perforation; pin-, key-, loop-, port-, peep-, mouse-, pigeon-hole; eye, – of a needle; eyelet; slot.

opening; apert-ure, -ness; hiation,

**261. Closure.**—**N.** closure, occlusion, blockade; shutting up &c. *v.*; obstruction &c. (*hindrance*) 706; gag; embolism; contraction &c. 195; infarction; con-, ob-stipation; blind -alley, – corner; *cul-de-sac*, *cæcum*; imper-foration

yawning, oscitancy, dehiscence, patefaction, pandiculation; gap, chasm &c. (*interval*) 198.

embrasure, window, casement, light; sky-, fan-light; lattice; bay-, bow-window; oriel; dormer, lantern, *abat-jour*.

out-, in-let; vent, vomitory; *embouchure*; orifice, mouth, sucker, muzzle, throat, gullet, placket, weasand, wizen, nozzle, *œsophagus*.

portal, porch, gate, ostiary, postern, wicket, trap-door, hatch, door; arcade; gate-, door-, hatch-, gang-way; lich-gate.

way, path &c. 627; thoroughfare; channel, passage, tube, pipe; water-pipe &c. 350; air-pipe &c. 351; vessel, tubule, canal, gut, fistula; adjutage, ajutage; chimney, smoke stack, flue, tap, funnel, gully, tunnel, main; mine, pit, adit, shaft; gallery.

alley, aisle, glade, lane, vista.

bore, calibre; pore; blind orifice.

por-ousness, -osity; sieve, cullender, colander; grater, shredder; cribble, riddle, screen; honeycomb.

apertion, perforation; piercing &c. *v.*; terebration, empalement, pertusion, puncture, acupuncture, penetration.

opener, key, master-key, *passe-partout*.

**V.** open, ope, gape, dehisce, yawn, bilge; fly open.

perforate, pierce, empierce, tap, bore, drill; mine &c. (*scoop out*) 252; tunnel; trans-pierce, -fix; enfilade, impale, spike, spear, gore, spit, stab, pink, puncture, lance, trepan, trephine, stick, prick, riddle, punch; stave in.

cut a passage through; make -way, – room- for.

un-cover, -close, -rip; lay –, cut –, rip –, throw- open.

**Adj.** open; perforated &c. *v.*; perforate; wide open, agape, ajar; un-closed, -stopped; oscitant, gaping, yawning; patent.

tubular, cannular, fistulous; per-vious, -meable; foraminous; vesi-, vas-cular; porous, follicular, cribriform, honeycombed, infundibular, riddled; tubul-ous, -ated, piped.

opening &c. *v.*; aperient.

**Int.** *open sesame!*

**262. Perforator.** — **N.** perforator, piercer, borer, auger, gimlet, stylet, drill, wimble, awl, bradawl, scoop, terrier, corkscrew, dibble, trocar, trepan, trephine, probe, bodkin, needle, stiletto, broach, reamer, rimer, warder, lancet; punch, -eon; spikebit, gouge; spear &c. (*weapon*) 727.

---

-viousness &c. *adj.*, -meability; stopper &c. 263; *operculum*.

**V.** close, occlude, plug; block –, stop –, fill –, bung –, cork –, button –, stuff –, shut –, dam- up, obturate; blockade; obstruct &c. (*hinder*) 706; bar, bolt, stop, seal, plumb; choke, throttle; ram down, tamp, dam, cram; trap, clinch; put to –, shut- the door; batten down the hatches.

**Adj.** closed &c. *v.*; shut, operculated; unopened.

unpierced, imporous, cæcal; imperforate, -vious, -meable; impenetrable; un-, im-passable; invious; path-, way-less; untrodden.

unventilated; air-, water-tight; hermetically sealed; tight, snug.

---

**263. Stopper.**—**N.** stopper, stopple, plug, cork, bung, spike, spill, stop-cock, tap; rammer; ram, -rod; piston; stop-gap; wadding, stuffing, padding, stopping, dossil, pledget, tompion, tourniquet, obturator; wad.

cover &c. 223; valve, slide valve; vent-peg, spigot.

janitor, door –, gate- keeper, porter, commissionaire, *concierge*, warder, beadle, Cerberus, usher, guard, sentry, sentinel; ostiary.

# Section IV. MOTION

## 1°. Motion in General

**264.** [Successive change of place.*] **Motion.—N.** motion, movement, move; motivity, motility, going &c. *v.*; unrest.

stream, current, flow, flux, run, course, stir; conduction, evolution; kinematics.

step, rate, pace, tread, stride, gait, clip, port, footfall, cadence, carriage, velocity, angular velocity; progress, locomotion; journey &c. 266; voyage &c. 267; transit &c. 270.

restlessness &c. (*changeableness*) 149; mobility; movableness, motive power; laws of motion; mobilization.

**V.** be -in motion &c. *adj.*; move, go, hie, gang, budge, stir, pass, flit; hover -round, – about; shift, slide, slither, glide; roll, – on; flow, stream, run, drift, sweep along; wander &c. (*deviate*) 279; walk &c. 266; change –, shift- one's -place, – quarters; dodge; keep -going, – moving.

put –, set- in motion; move; impel &c. 276; propel &c. 284; render movable, mobilize.

**Adj.** moving &c. *v.*; in motion; motile, transitional; motory, motive; shifting, movable, mobile, mercurial, unquiet; restless &c. (*changeable*) 149; nomadic &c. 266; erratic &c. 279.

**Adv.** under way; on the -move, – wing, – tramp, – march.

---

**265. Quiescence.—N.** rest; stillness &c. *adj.*; quiescence; stag-nation, -nancy; fixity, immobility, catalepsy; indisturbance; quietism.

quiet, tranquillity, calm; repose &c. 687; peace; dead calm, anticyclone; statue-like repose; silence &c. 403; not a -breath of air, – mouse stirring; sleep &c. (*inactivity*) 683.

pause, lull &c. (*cessation*) 142; stand, – still; standing still &c. *v.*; lock; dead -lock, – stop, – stand; full stop; fix; embargo.

resting-place; bivouac; home &c. (*abode*) 189; pillow &c. (*support*) 215; haven &c. (*refuge*) 666; goal &c. (*arrival*) 292.

**V.** be -quiescent &c. *adj.*; stand –, lie- still; keep quiet, repose, hold the breath.

remain, stay; stand, lie to, ride at anchor, remain *in situ*, mark time, tarry; bring –, heave –, lay- to; pull –, draw- up; hold, halt; stop, – short; rest, pause, anchor; cast –, come to an- anchor; rest on one's oars; repose on one's laurels, take breath; stop &c. (*discontinue*) 142.

stagnate, vegetate; *quieta non movere*; let -alone, – well alone; abide, rest and be thankful; keep within doors, stay at home, go to bed.

dwell &c. (*be present*) 186; settle &c. (*be located*) 184; alight &c. (*arrive*) 292.

stick, – fast; stand, – like a post; not stir a -peg, – step; be at a -stand &c. *n.*

quell, becalm, hush, stay, lull to sleep, lay an embargo on; put the brake on.

**Adj.** quiescent, still; motion-, move-less; fixed; stationary; at -rest, – a stand, – a stand-still, – anchor; stock-still; immotile; standing still &c. *v.*; sedentary, untravelled, stay-at-home; becalmed, stagnant, quiet; un-moved, -disturbed, -ruffled; calm, restful; cataleptic; immovable &c. (*stable*) 150; sleeping &c. (*inactive*) 683; silent &c. 403; still as -a statue, – a post, – a mouse, – death.

**Adv.** at a stand &c. *adj.*; *tout court*; at the halt.

**Int.** stop! stay! avast! halt! hold, – hard! whoa!

**Phr.** *requiescat in pace.*

* A thing cannot be said to *move* from one place to another, unless it passes in succession through every intermediate place; hence motion is only such a change of place as is *successive*. 'Rapid, swift, &c., as thought' are therefore incorrect expressions.

**266.** [Locomotion by land.] **Journey.** —**N.** travel; travelling &c. *v.*; wayfaring, campaigning.

journey, excursion, expedition, tour, trip, grand tour, circuit, peregrination, discursion, ramble, pilgrimage, *trek*, course, ambulation, march, walk, hike, promenade, constitutional, stroll, saunter, tramp, jog-trot, turn, stalk, perambulation; noctambulation; somnambulism, sleep walking; outing, ride, drive, airing, jaunt.

equitation, horsemanship, riding, *manège*, ride and tie.

roving, vagrancy, pererration; marching and countermarching; nomadism; vagabond-ism, -age; gadding; flit, -ting; migration; e-, im-, de-, inter-migration.

plan, itinerary, guide; hand-, road-book; Baedeker, Murray, Bradshaw, time table.

procession, parade, cavalcade, caravan, file, *cortège*, column.

[Organs and instruments of locomotion] vehicle &c. 272; locomotive &c. 271; legs, feet, pegs, pins, trotters.

traveller &c. 268.

**V.** travel, journey, course; tour; take –, go- a journey; take –, go out for- -a walk &c. *n.*; have a run; take the air.

flit, take wing; migrate, emigrate, *trek*; rove, prowl, roam, range, patrol, pace up and down, traverse; scour –, traverse- the country; peragrate; per-, circum-ambulate; nomadize, wander, ramble, stroll, saunter, hover, go one's rounds, straggle; gad, – about; expatiate.

walk, march, step, tread, pace, plod, wend; promenade; trudge, tramp; stalk, stride, straddle, strut, foot it, stump, bundle, bowl along, toddle; paddle; tread –, follow –, pursue- a path.

take horse, ride, drive, trot, amble, canter, prance, fisk, frisk, *caracoler*; gallop &c. (*move quickly*) 274; motor, cycle, taxi; go by -car, – train, – tram, – bus, – plane.

peg –, jog –, wag –, shuffle- on; stir one's stumps; bend one's -steps, – course; make –, find –, wend –, pick –, thread –, plough- one's way; coast, slide, glide, skim, skate, ski; march in procession, file off, defile.

go –, repair –, resort –, hie –, betake oneself- to.

**Adj.** travelling &c. *v.*; ambulatory, itinerant, peripatetic, peram-

**267.** [Locomotion by water, or air.] **Navigation.**—**N.** navigation; aquatics; boating, cruising, yachting; ship &c. 273; oar, scull, sweep, punt-pole, paddle, – wheel, screw, propeller, stern wheel, sail, canvas.

natation, swimming; fin, flipper, fish's tail.

aerial navigation, air service, airways, airmanship, aero-donetics, -dynamics, -mechanics, -station, -statics, -nautics; ballooning, balloonry; balloon &c. 273; flying, flight, aviation, volitation; wing, pinion, *aileron*.

voyage, sail, cruise, passage, circumnavigation, *periplus*; head-, stern-, lee-way.

mariner, aeronaut &c. 269.

**V.** sail; put to sea &c. (*depart*) 293; take ship, get under way; spread -sail, – canvas; gather way, have way on; make –, carry- sail; plough the -waves, – deep, – main, – ocean; walk the waters.

navigate, warp, luff, scud, boom, kedge; drift, course, cruise, coast; hug the -shore, – land; circumnavigate.

ply the oar, row, paddle, pull, scull, punt, steam.

swim, float; buffet the waves, ride the storm, skim, *effleurer*, dive, wade.

fly, aviate, be wafted, hover, soar, drift, glide, plane, sideslip, *volplane*, pique, dive, spin, roll, loop, flutter; take -wing, – a flight; wing one's -flight, – way.

**Adj.** sailing &c. *v.*; seafaring, nautical, maritime, naval; sea-going, coasting; afloat; navigable, aquatic, natatory.

volitant, volant, aerostatic, aerial, aeronautic; alar, alate, pennate.

**Adv.** under -way, – sail, – canvas, – steam; on the wing.

bulatory, roving, rambling, gadding, discursive, vagrant, migratory, nomadic; circumforane-an, -ous; somnambular, nocti-, mundivagant; locomotive, automotive, self-moving.

way-faring, -worn; travel-stained.

**Adv.** on -foot, – horseback, – Shanks's mare; by the Marrowbone stage; *in transitu* &c. 270; *en route* &c. 282.

**Int.** come along!

**268. Traveller.—N.** traveller, wayfarer, voyager, itinerant, passenger.

tourist, excursionist, globe-trotter; explorer, adventurer, mountaineer, Alpine Club; peregrinator, wanderer, rover, straggler, rambler; bird of passage; gad-about, -ling; vagrant, scatterling, landloper, waifs and estrays, wastrel, stray; loafer; tramp, -er, hobo, beachcomber, vagabond, nomad, Bohemian, gipsy, Arab, Wandering Jew, Hadji, pilgrim, palmer; peripatetic; somnambulist, sleep walker, noctambulist; emigrant, fugitive, refugee, *émigré*.

runner, courier, King's messenger; Mercury, Iris, Ariel, comet.

pedestrian, walker, foot-passenger; cyclist; wheelman.

rider, horseman, equestrian, cavalier, jockey, rough rider, trainer, breaker, huntsman.

driver, coachman, whip, Jehu, charioteer, postilion, post-boy, carter, wagoner, drayman, truckman; cab-man, -driver; *voiturier, vetturino, condottiere*; engine-driver; stoker, fireman, guard, brakeman, conductor; chauffeur, automobilist, motorist, motor –, truck –, taxi- driver.

**269. Mariner.—N.** sailor, mariner, navigator, argonaut; sea-man, -farer, -faring man; yachtsman; tar, jack tar, salt, gob, sea-dog, shellback, able seaman, A.B.; man-of-war's man, bluejacket, marine, jolly; midshipman, middy, reefer; captain, commander, master mariner, skipper, mate; ship-, boat-, ferry-, water-, lighter-, barge-, longshore- man, hoveller; bargee, gondolier; oar-, -sman; rower; boat-, cock-swain; coxswain; steersman, helmsman, pilot; crew; lascar.

aerial navigator, aeronaut, balloonist, Icarus, aviator, pilot, observer, flyer, airman.

---

**270. Transference.—N.** transfer, -ence; trans-, e-location; displacement; *meta-stasis, -thesis*; removal; re-, a-motion; relegation; de-, as-portation; extradition, conveyance, draft; carrying, carriage; convection, -duction, -tagion, infection; transfusion; transfer &c. (*of property*) 783.

transit, transition; passage, ferry, gestation; portage, porterage, carting, cartage; shovelling &c. *v.*; vect-ion, -ure, -itation; shipment, freight, wafture; trans-mission, -port, -portation, -umption, -plantation, -lation; shift-, dodg-ing; dispersion &c. 73; transposition &c. (*interchange*) 148; traction &c. 285.

[Thing transferred] drift, alluvium, detritus, *moraine*; gift, legacy, bequest, lease; freight, mails, cargo, luggage, baggage, goods.

**V.** trans-fer, -mit, -port, -place, -plant; convey, assign, carry, bear, fetch and carry; carry –, ferry- over; hand, pass, forward; shift; conduct, convoy, bring, fetch, reach.

send, delegate, consign, mail, post, relegate, turn over to, pass the buck, deliver; ship, embark; waft; switch, shunt; transpose &c. (*interchange*) 148; displace &c. 185; throw &c. 284; drag &c. 285.

shovel, lade, dip, ladle, bale, decant, draft off, transfuse.

**Adj.** transferred &c. *v.*; drifted; movable; port-able, -ative; conductive; contagious, infectious.

transferable, assignable, conveyable, devisable, negotiable, transmissible.

**Adv.** from -hand to hand, – pillar to post.

on –, by- the way; on the -road, – wing; as one goes; *in transitu, en route, chemin faisant, en passant*, in mid-progress.

**271. Carrier.—N.** carrier, porter, red cap, bearer, messenger, postman, tranter, conveyer; stevedore; coolie; conductor, locomotive, tractor, caterpillar tractor, motor.

beast of burden, cattle, horse, steed, nag, palfrey, Arab, blood horse, thorough-bred, galloway, charger, courser, racer, hunter, jument, pony, filly, colt, foal, barb, roan, jade, hack, *bidet*, pad, cob, tit, punch, roadster, goer; race-, pack-, draft-, cart-, dray-, post-horse, mount; Shetland pony, sheltie; garran; jennet, genet, bayard, mare, stallion, gelding; stud.

Pegasus, Bucephalus, Rozinante.

ass, donkey, jackass, mule, hinny; sumpter -horse, – mule; reindeer; camel, dromedary, mehari, llama, elephant; carrier pigeon.

carriage &c. (*vehicle*) 272; ship &c. 273.

**Adj.** equine, asinine.

**272. Vehicle.—N.** vehicle, conveyance, carriage, car, caravan, van, furniture van, pantechnicon; wagon, wain, dray, cart, lorry.

carriole; sledge, sled, sleigh, bobsleigh, toboggan, *luge*, truck, tram; limber, tumbrel, pontoon; barrow; wheel-, hand- -barrow, – cart, trolley; perambulator; Bath –, wheel –, sedan-chair, jinriksha, rickshaw; ekka; chaise; palan-keen, -quin; litter, horse-litter, brancard, crate, hurdle, stretcher, ambulance; velocipede, hobby-horse, coaster, scooter, go-cart; cycle; bi-, tri-, quadri-cycle; tandem, safety; skate, roller skate; ski, snow-shoe.

equipage, turn-out; coach, chariot, *quadriga*, chaise, phaëton, break, brake, mail-phaëton, wagonette, drag, curricle, tilbury, whisky, landau, *barouche*, victoria, brougham, clarence, calash, *calèche*, britzska, *araba*, kibitka; berlin; sulky, *désobligeant*, sociable, *vis-à-vis*, *dormeuse*; jaunting –, outside- car; *tarantass*; runabout; shay.

post-chaise; diligence, stage; stage –, mail –, hackney –, glass- coach; stage-wagon; car, omnibus, bus, fly, *cabriolet*, cab, hansom, shofle, four-wheeler, growler, *droshki*, drosky.

dog-cart, trap, gig, whitechapel, buggy, four-in-hand, unicorn, random, tandem; shandredhan, *char-à-banc*.

automobile, motor-, auto-, touring-, racing-, cycle-, side-, steam-, electric-

**273. Ship.—N.** ship, vessel, sail; craft, bottom.

navy, marine, fleet, flotilla, squadron; shipping.

man of war &c. (*combatant*) 726; transport, tender, store-ship; merchant ship, merchantman; packet, liner; whaler, slaver, collier, coaster, tanker, freighter, freight steamer, cargo boat, lighter; fishing-, pilot- boat; trawler, drifter; cable ship; hulk; yacht; floating palace, ocean greyhound.

ship, bark, barque, brig, snow, hermaphrodite brig; brigantine, barquentine; schooner; topsail –, fore and aft –, three masted- schooner; *chasse-marée*; sloop, cutter, corvette, clipper, foist, yawl, dandy, ketch, smack, lugger, barge, hoy, cat-, -boat, buss; sail-er, -ing vessel, wind-jammer; steam-er, -boat, -ship; mail –, paddle –, screw –, sternwheel- steamer; tug; train-ferry; line of steamers &c.

boat, pinnace, launch, motor-boat, picket-boat; hydroplane; life-, long-, jolly-, bum-, fly-, cock-, ferry-, canal-boat, dory, dugout, galliot; shallop, gig, funny, skiff, dingy, scow, cockle-shell, wherry, coble, punt, cog, lerret; eight-, four-, pair- oar; randan; outrigger; float, raft, pontoon; prame, ice-yacht.

state barge, bucentaur.

catamaran, coracle, gondola, carvel, caravel; felucca, caique, canoe; trireme;

car; motor-, -omnibus, – bus, – cab, – cycle; limousine, landaulette, cabriolet, *coupé*, *voiturette*, runabout, electromobile, taxi, -cab.

train; passenger –, express –, freight –, subway –, special –, corridor –, parliamentary –, luggage –, goods-train, *train de luxe*; 1st-, 2nd-, 3rd-class- -train, – carriage, – compartment; Pullman –, sleeping-, club-, observation-, dining-, restaurant-car; mail-, luggage-, brake-van, coach, car, carriage; rolling stock; horse-box, cattle-truck.

tramcar, trolley-omnibus, trackless trolley.

shovel, spoon, spatula, ladle, hod, hoe; spade, spaddle, loy; spud; pitch-fork.

**Adj.** vehicular.

---

galley, – foist, oilander, dogger, hooker, howker; argosy, carack; galliass, galleon; galliot, polacca, polacre, corsair, tartane, junk, lorcha, praam, proa, prahu, saick, sampan, xebec, dhow; dahabeah; nuggar, cayak, pirogue.

submarine, submersible.

aircraft (*combatant*) &c. 726; flying machine, air mail, aero-, air-, mono-, bi-, tri-, hydroplane, plane, cabin plane, transport plane, *avion*, flying boat, glider, *aviette*, helicopter; balloon, air-, fire-, gas-, Mongolfier-, pilot-, captive-, free-, kite-, dirigible- balloon, air-ship, *Zeppelin*, blimp; kite, parachute.

nacelle, car, gondola, aileron; hangar, airport, landing field, airdrome; catwalk, controls, rudder, tail.

**Adj.** marine, maritime, naval, nautical, seafaring, sea-, ocean going, seaworthy.

aerial, aeronautical, air-worthy, flying &c. *n.*

**Adv.** afloat, aboard; on -board, – ship board, – board ship.

## 2°. Degrees of Motion

**274. Velocity.**—**N.** velocity, speed, celerity; swiftness &c. *adj.*; rapidity, eagle speed; expedition &c. (*activity*) 682; pernicity; acceleration; haste &c. 684.

spurt, rush, dash, race, steeplechase; smart –, lively –, swift &c. *adj.* –, rattling –, spanking –, strapping- -rate, – pace; round pace; flying, flight.

gallop, canter, trot, round trot, run, scamper; hand –, full- gallop; swoop.

lightning, light, electricity, wind; cannon-ball, rocket, arrow, dart, quicksilver; telegraph, express train; torrent; swallow flight.

eagle, antelope, courser, race-horse, gazelle, greyhound, hare, doe, squirrel.

Mercury, Ariel, Camilla, Harlequin.

[Measurement of velocity] speedometer, log, -line, tachometer.

**V.** move quickly, trip, fisk; speed, hie, hasten, sprint, spurt, post, spank, scuttle; scud, -dle, scurry; scour, – the plain; scamper; run, – like mad; fly, race, run a race, cut away, cut and run, shoot, tear, whisk, whiz, sweep, skim, brush; cut –, bowl- along; rush

**275. Slowness.**—**N.** slowness &c. *adj.*; languor &c. (*inactivity*) 683; drawl; creeping &c. *v.*, lentor.

retardation; slackening &c. *v.*; delay &c. (*lateness*) 133; claudication.

jog-, dog-trot, walk; mincing steps; slow -march, – time.

slow -goer, – coach, – back; lingerer, loiterer, sluggard, tortoise, snail; dawdle &c. (*inactive*) 683.

**V.** move -slowly, &c. *adv.*; creep, crawl, lag, slug, walk, drawl, linger, loiter, saunter; plod, trudge, stump along, lumber; trail; drag; dawdle &c. (*be inactive*) 683; grovel, worm one's way, steal along; jog –, rub –, bundle- on; toddle, waddle, wabble, slug; traipse, slouch, shuffle, halt, hobble, limp, claudicate, shamble; flag, falter, totter, stagger; mince, step short; march in -slow time, – funeral procession; take one's time; hang fire &c. (*be late*) 133.

retard, relax; slacken, check, moderate, rein in, curb; reef; strike –, shorten –, take in- sail; put on the drag, apply the brake; clip the wings; reduce the

&c. (*be violent*) 173; dash -on, – off, – forward; bolt; trot, gallop, bound, flit, spring, dart, boom; march in double-time; ride hard, get over the ground, scorch.

hurry &c. (*hasten*) 684; accelerate, put on; quicken; quicken –, mend- one's pace; clap spurs to one's horse; make -haste, – rapid strides, – forced marches, – the best of one's way; put one's best leg foremost, stir one's stumps, wing one's way, set off at a score; carry –, crowd- sail; go off like a shot, go ahead, gain ground; outstrip the wind, fly on the wings of the wind.

keep -up, – pace- with; outstrip &c. 303.

**Adj.** fast, speedy, swift, rapid, quick, fleet; nimble, agile, expeditious; express; active &c. 682; flying, galloping &c. *v.*; light-, nimble-footed; winged, eagle-winged, mercurial, electric, telegraphic; light-legged, light of heel; swift as -an arrow &c. *n.*; quick as -lightning &c. *n.*, – thought.*

**Adv.** swiftly &c. *adj.*; with -speed &c. *n.*; apace; at -a great rate, – full speed, – railway speed; full -drive, – gallop; post-haste, in full sail, tantivy; trippingly; instantaneously &c. 113; like a shot.

under press of -sail, – canvas, – sail and steam; *velis et remis*, on eagle's wing, in double quick time; with -rapid, – giant- strides; *à pas de géant*; in seven league boots; whip and spur; *ventre à terre*; as fast as one's -legs, – heels- will carry one; as fast as one can lay feet to the ground, at the top of one's speed; by leaps and bounds; with haste &c. 684; in- high – gear, – speed.

**Phr.** *vires acquirit eundo.*

speed, decelerate; slacken -speed, – one's pace, lose ground; back -water, – pedal, put the engines astern, throttle down.

**Adj.** slow, slack; tardy; dilatory &c. (*inactive*) 683; gentle, easy; leisurely; deliberate, gradual; insensible, imperceptible; languid, sluggish, apathetic, phlegmatic, slow-paced, tardigrade, snail-like; creeping &c. *v.*

**Adv.** slowly &c. *adj.*; leisurely; *piano, adagio*; *largo, larghetto*; at half speed, under easy sail; at a -foot's, – snail's, – funeral- pace; slower than molasses in January; in slow time; with -mincing steps, – clipped wings; *haud passibus æquis*; in- low –, gear, – speed.

gradually &c. *adj.*; *gradatim*; by -degrees, – slow degrees, – inches, – little and little; step by step; inch by inch, bit by bit, little by little, *seriatim*; consecutively.

## 3°. Motion Conjoined with Force

**276. Impulse.—N.** impulse, impulsion, impetus; momentum; push, pulsion, thrust, shove, jog, jolt, brunt, booming, boost, throw; explosion &c. (*violence*) 173; propulsion &c. 284.

percussion, concussion, collision, occursion, clash, encounter, cannon, *carambole*, appulse, shock, crash, bump; impact; *élan*; charge &c. (*attack*) 716; beating &c. (*punishment*) 972.

blow, dint, stroke, knock, tap, rap, slap, smack, pat, dab; fillip; slam, bang; hit, whack, thwack, clout; cuff &c. 972; squash, dowse, whap, swap, punch, thump, swipe, jab, pelt, kick, punce, calcitration; *ruade*; arietation; cut, thrust, lunge, yerk.

**277. Recoil.—N.** recoil; re-, retroaction; revulsion; rebound, *ricochet*; re-percussion, -calcitration; kick, *contrecoup*; springing back &c. *v.*; elasticity &c. 325; reflection, reflex, reflux; reverberation &c. (*resonance*) 408; rebuff, repulse; return.

ducks and drakes; boomerang; spring; reactionist, reactionary.

**V.** recoil, resile, react; spring –, fly –, bound- back; rebound, reverberate, repercuss, recalcitrate, echo, *ricochet.*

**Adj.** recoiling &c. *v.*; re-fluent, -percussive, -calcitrant, -actionary; retroactive.

**Adv.** on the -recoil &c. *n.*

* See note on 264.

hammer, sledge-hammer, mall, maul, mallet, flail; ram, -mer; battering-ram, monkey, pile-driver, punch, bat, tamper, tamping iron; cudgel &c. (*weapon*) 727; axe &c. (*sharp*) 253.

[Science of mechanical forces] mechanics, dynamics &c.

**V.** give an -impetus &c. *n.*; impel, push; start, give a start to, set going; drive, urge, boom; thrust, prod, foin; cant; elbow, shoulder, jostle, justle, hustle, hurtle, shove, jog, jolt, bean, encounter; run –, bump –, butt- against; knock –, run- one's head against; impinge.

strike, knock, hit, bash, tap, rap, bat, slap, flap, dab, pat, thump, beat, bang, slam, dash; punch, thwack, whack; hit –, strike- hard; swap, batter, dowse, baste; pelt, patter, skelter, buffet, belabour, tamp; fetch one a blow, swat; poke at, pink, lunge, yerk; kick, calcitrate; butt; strike at &c. (*attack*) 716; whip &c. (*punish*) 972; propel &c. 284.

come –, enter- into collision; collide; foul; fall –, run- foul of.

throw &c. (*propel*) 284.

**Adj.** impelling &c. *v.*; im-pulsive, -pellent; booming; dynamic, -al; impelled &c. *v.*

## 4°. Motion with Reference to Direction

**278. Direction.**—**N.** direction, bearing, course, set, drift, tenor; tendency &c. 176; incidence; bending, trending &c. *v.*; dip, tack, aim, collimation; steer-ing, -age.

point of the compass, cardinal –, half –, quarter- points; North, East, South, West; N by E, ENE, NE by N, NE &c.; rhumb, azimuth, line of collimation.

line, path, road, range, quarter, line of march; alignment; straight shot, bee-line.

**V.** tend –, bend –, point- towards; conduct –, go- to; point -to, – at; bend, trend, verge, incline, dip, determine.

steer –, make- -for, – towards; aim –, level- at; take aim; keep –, hold- a course; be bound for; bend one's steps towards; direct –, steer –, bend –, shape- one's course; align –, one's march; go straight, – to the point; march -on, – on a point.

ascertain one's -direction &c. *n.*; *s'orienter*, see which way the wind blows; box the compass.

**Adj.** directed &c. *v.*, – towards; pointing towards &c. *v.*; bound for; aligned –, alligned- with; direct, straight; un-deviating, -swerving; straightforward; North, -ern, -erly, &c. *n.*

directable &c. *v.*

**Adv.** towards; on the -road, – high

**279. Deviation.** — **N.** deviation; swerving &c. *v.*; obliquation, warp, refraction; flection, flexion; sweep; de-flection, -flexure; declination.

diversion, digression, departure from, aberration, drift, sheer; divergence &c. 291; zigzag; *détour* &c. (*circuit*) 629.

[Desultory motion] wandering &c. *v.*, vagrancy, evagation; by-paths and crooked ways.

[Motion sideways, oblique motion] sidling &c. *v.*; *échelon*, leeway; knight's move (at chess).

**V.** alter one's course, deviate, depart from, turn, trend; bend, curve &c. 245; swerve, heel, bear off.

intervert; deflect; divert, – from its course; put on a new scent, shift, shunt, switch, wear, draw aside, crook, warp. short circuit.

stray, straggle; sidle, edge; diverge &c. 291; tralineate, digress, divagate, wander; wind, twist, meander, meander around Robin Hood's barn; veer, tack, sheer; turn -aside, – a corner, – away from; wheel, steer clear of; ramble, rove, drift; go -astray, – adrift; yaw, dodge; step aside, ease off, make way for, shy.

fly off at a tangent; glance off; turn, wheel –, face- about; turn –, face- to the right about; wabble &c. (*oscillate*) 314; go out of one's way &c. (*perform a circuit*) 629: lose one's way.

road- to; *versus*, to; hither, thither, whither; directly; straight, – forwards, – as an arrow; point blank; in a -direct, – straight- line -to, – for, – with; in a line with; full tilt at, as the crow flies.

before –, near –, close to –, against- the wind; windwards, in the wind's eye.

through, *via*, by way of; in all -directions, – manner of ways; *quaquaversum*, from the four winds.

**Adj.** deviating &c. *v.*; aberrant, errant; ex-, dis-cursive; devious, desultory, loose; rambling; stray, erratic, vagrant, undirected; circuitous, indirect, zigzag; crab-like.

**Adv.** astray from, round about, wide of the mark; to the right about; all manner of ways; circuitously &c. 629.

obliquely, sideling, like the move of the knight on a chessboard.

---

**280.** [Going before.] **Precession.—N.** precession, leading, heading; precedence &c. 62; priority &c. 116; the lead, *le pas*; van &c. (*front*) 234; precursor &c. 64.

**V.** go -before, – ahead, – in the van, – in advance; precede, forerun; usher in, introduce, herald, head, take the lead; lead, – the way, – the dance; get –, have- the start; steal a march; get -before, – ahead, – in front of; outstrip &c. 303; take precedence &c. (*first in order*) 62.

**Adj.** foremost, first, leading &c. *v.*

**Adv.** in advance, before, ahead, in the van; fore-, head-most; in front.

**Phr.** *seniores priores.*

---

**281.** [Going after.] **Sequence.—N.** sequence, run; coming after &c. (*order*) 63; (*time*) 117; following; pursuit &c. 622.

follower, attendant, satellite, shadow, dangler, train.

**V.** follow; pursue &c. 622; go –, fly- after.

attend, beset, dance attendance on, dog, be-dog; tread -in the steps of, – close upon; be –, go –, follow- in the -wake, – trail. – rear- of; trail, follow as a shadow, hang on the skirts of; tread –, follow- on the heels of, tag after.

lag, get behind.

**Adj.** following &c. *v.*

**Adv.** behind; in the -rear &c. 235, – train of, wake of; after &c. (*order*) 63, (*time*) 117.

---

**282.** [Motion forwards; progressive motion.] **Progression.—N.** progress, -ion, -iveness; advancing &c. *v.*; advance, -ment; ongoing; flood-tide, headway; march &c. 266; rise; improvement &c. 658.

**V.** advance; proceed, progress; get -on, – along, – over the ground; gain ground; jog –, rub –, wag- on; go with the stream; keep –, hold on- one's course; go –, move –, come –, get –, pass –, push –, press- -on, – forward, – forwards, – ahead; press onwards, step forward; make –, work –, carve –, push –, force –, edge –, elbow- one's way; make -progress, – head, – way, – headway, – advances, – strides, – rapid strides &c. (*velocity*) 274; go –, shoot- ahead; distance; make up leeway.

**Adj.** advancing &c. *v.*; pro-gressive, -fluent; advanced.

**283.** [Motion backwards.] **Regression.—N.** regress, -ion; retro-cession, -gression, -gradation, -action; *reculade*; retreat, withdrawal, retirement, remigration; recession &c. (*motion from*) 287; recess; crab-like motion.

re-fluence, -flux; backwater, regurgitation, ebb, return; resilience; reflexion (*recoil*) 277; *volte-face.*

counter -motion, – movement, march; veering, tergiversation, recidivation, backsliding, fall, relapse; deterioration &c. 659.

turning-point &c. (*reversion*) 145.

**V.** re-cede, -grade, -turn, -vert, -treat, -tire; retro-grade, -cede; back, – down, – out, crawl; withdraw; rebound &c. 277; go –, come –, turn –, hark –, draw –, fall –, get –, put –, run- back; lose ground; fall –, drop- astern; back water, put about; veer, – round; double.

**Adv.** forward, onward; forth, on ahead, under way, *en route* for, on -one's way, – the way, – the road, – the high road- to; in -progress, – mid progress; *in transitu* &c. 270.

**Int.** Forward, march!

**Phr.** *vestigia nulla retrorsum.*

wheel, counter-march; ebb, regurgitate; jib, shrink, shy.

turn -tail, – round, – upon one's heel, – one's back upon; retrace one's steps, dance the back step; sound –, beat- a retreat; go home.

**Adj.** receding &c. *v.*; retro-grade, -gressive; re-gressive, -fluent, -flex, -cidivous, -silient; crab-like; reactionary &c. 277; counter-clockwise.

**Adv.** back, -wards; reflexively, to the right about; *à reculons, à rebours.*

**Phr.** *revenons à nos moutons,* as you were.

---

**284.** [Motion given to an object situated in front.] **Propulsion.—N.** pro-pulsion, -jection; *vis a tergo*; push &c. (*impulse*) 276; e-, jaculation; ejection &c. 297; throw, fling, toss, shot, discharge, shy.

[Science of propulsion] gunnery, ballistics, archery.

missile, projectile, ball, *discus*, javelin, hammer, quoit, brickbat, shot, bullet; arrow, shaft; gun &c. (*arms*) 727.

shooter, shot; gunner, gun-layer; archer, toxophilite; bow-, rifle-, marksman; good –, crack- shot; sharpshooter &c. (*combatant*) 726.

**V.** propel, project, throw, fling, cast, pitch, chuck, toss, jerk, heave, shy, hurl; flirt, fillip.

dart, lance, tilt; e-, jaculate; fulminate, bolt, drive, sling, pitchfork.

send; send –, let –, fire- off; discharge, shoot; launch, send forth, let fly; dash.

put –, set- in motion; set agoing, start; give -a start, – an impulse- to; push, impel &c. 276; trundle &c. (*set in rotation*) 312; expel &c. 297.

carry one off one's legs; put to flight.

**Adj.** propelled &c. *v.*; propelling &c. *v.*; pro-pulsive, -jectile.

**285.** [Motion given to an object situated behind.] **Traction.—N.** traction; drawing &c. *v.*; draught, pull, haul; rake; 'a long pull, a strong pull and a pull all together'; towage, haulage.

**V.** draw, pull, haul, lug rake, drag, draggle, tug, tow, trail, trawl, train, take in tow.

wrench, jerk, twitch.

**Adj.** drawing &c. *v.*; tractive, tractile; ductile.

---

**286.** [Motion towards.] **Approach.—N.** approach, approximation, appropinquation; access; appulse; afflux, -ion; advent &c. (*approach of time*) 121; pursuit &c. 622; convergence &c. 290.

**V.** approach, approximate; near; get –, go –, draw- near; come, – near, – to close quarters; move –, set in- towards; drift; make up to; gain upon; pursue &c. 622; tread on the heels of; bear up; make the land; hug the -shore, -coast, – land.

**Adj.** approaching &c. *v.*; approximative; convergent; affluent; impending, imminent &c. (*destined*) 152.

**287.** [Motion from.] **Recession.—N.** recession, retirement, withdrawal; retreat; retrocession &c. 283; departure &c. 293; recoil &c. 277; flight &c. (*avoidance*) 623.

**V.** recede, go, move from, retire, ebb, withdraw, shrink; come –, move –, go –, get –, drift- away; depart &c. 293; retreat &c. 283; move –, stand –, sheer- off; swerve from; fall back, stand aside; run away &c. (*avoid*) 623.

remove, shunt, side track, switch off

**Adj.** receding &c. *v.*

---

**Adv.** on the road.

**Int.** come hither! approach! here! come! come near!

**288.** [Motion towards, actively.] **Attraction.—N.** attract-ion, -iveness; pull; drawing to, pulling towards, adduction, magnetism, gravity, attraction of gravitation; lure, bait, decoy.

loadstone, -star; magnet, siderite, magnetite.

**V.** attract; draw –, pull –, drag- towards; adduce.

lure, bait, decoy.

**Adj.** attracting &c. *v.*; attrahent, attractive, adducent, adductive.

**289.** [Motion from, actively.] **Repulsion.—N.** repulsion; driving from &c. *v.*; repulse; abduction.

**V.** repel; push –, drive – &c. 276. from; chase, dispel; retrude; abduce, abduct; send away, repulse, dismiss.

keep at arm's length, turn one's back upon, give the cold shoulder; send packing; send -off, – away- with a flea in one's ear, – about one's business.

**Adj.** repelling &c. *v.*; repellant, repulsive; abducent, abductive.

**290.** [Motion nearer to.] **Convergence.—N.** con-vergence, -fluence, -course, -flux, -gress, -currence, -centration; appulse, meeting; corradiation.

assemblage &c. 72; resort &c. (*focus*) 74; asymptote.

**V.** converge, concur; come together, unite, meet, fall in with; close -with, – in upon; centre -round, – in; enter in; pour in.

gather together, unite, concentrate, bring into a focus.

**Adj.** converging &c. *v.*; con-vergent, -fluent, -current; centripetal; asymptotical.

**291.** [Motion further off.] **Divergence.—N.** diverg-ence, -ency; divarication, ramification, radiation; separation &c. (*disjunction*) 44; dispersion &c. 73; deviation &c. 279; aberration, declination.

**V.** diverge, divaricate, radiate; ramify; branch –, glance –, file- off; fly off, – at a tangent; spread, scatter, disperse &c. 73; deviate &c. 279; part &c. (*separate*) 44; splay apart.

**Adj.** diverging &c. *v.*; divergent, radiant, centrifugal; aberrant.

---

**292.** [Terminal motion at.] **Arrival.—N.** arrival, advent; landing; de-, disem-barkation; reception, welcome, *vin d'honneur*.

home, goal, bourn; landing-place, -stage; resting –, stopping -place; destination, harbour, haven, port; terminal, terminus, railway station, depot, airport; halt, halting -place, – ground; anchorage &c. (*refuge*) 666.

return, recursion, remigration; meeting; ren-, en-counter.

completion &c. 729.

**V.** arrive; get to, come to; come; reach, attain; come up, – with, – to; overtake; make, fetch; complete &c. 729; join, rejoin.

light, alight, dismount; land, go ashore; debark, disembark; put -in, – into; visit, cast anchor, pitch one's tent; sit down &c. (*be located*) 184; get to one's journey's end; make the

**293.** [Initial motion from.] **Departure.—N.** departure, decession, decampment; embarkation; take-off; outset, start; removal; exit &c. (*egress*) 295; exodus, Hejira, flight.

leave-taking, *congé*, valediction, valedictory, adieu, farewell, good-bye, stirrup-cup.

starting -point, – post; point –, place- of -departure, – embarkation; port of embarkation.

**V.** depart; go, – away; take one's departure, set out; set –, march –, put –, start –, be –, move –, get –, whip –, pack –, go –, take oneself- off; start, issue, march out, debouch; go –, sally- forth; sally, set forward; be gone.

leave a place, quit, vacate, evacuate, abandon; go off the stage, make one's exit; retire, withdraw, remove; go -one's way, – along, – from home; take -flight, – wing; spring, fly, flit, wing

land; be in at the death; come –, get- -back, – home; return; come in &c. (*ingress*) 294; make one's appearance &c. (*appear*) 446; drop in; detrain; outspan.

come to hand; come -at, – across; hit; come –, light –, pop –, bounce –, plump –, burst –, pitch- upon; meet; en- ren-counter; come in contact.

**Adj.** arriving &c. *v.*; homeward-bound; terminal.

**Adv.** here, hither.

**Int.** welcome! hail! all hail! good-day, – morrow; greetings! hullo! well!

one's flight; fly –, whip- away; take off, hop off; embark; go -on board, – aboard; set sail; put –, go- to sea; sail, take ship; hoist blue Peter; get under way, weigh anchor; strike tents, break camp, decamp; walk one's chalks, make tracks, cut one's stick; cut and run; take leave; say –, bid- -good-bye &c. *n.*; disappear &c. 449; abscond &c. (*avoid*) 623; entrain, saddle –, harness –, hitch- up; inspan.

**Adj.** departing &c. *v.*; valedictory; outward bound.

**Adv.** whence, hence, thence; with a foot in the stirrup; on the -wing, – move.

**Int.** begone! &c. (*ejection*) 297; to horse! all aboard! farewell! adieu! good-bye, – day! *au revoir! auf Wiedersehen!* fare you well! so long! God -bless you, – speed! *bon voyage!*

**294.** [Motion into.] **Ingress.—N.** ingress; entrance, entry; introgression; influx; intrusion, inroad, incursion, invasion, irruption; pene-, interpenetration; illapse, import, importation, infiltration; immigration; admission &c. (*reception*) 296; insinuation &c. (*interjacence*) 228; insertion &c. 300.

inlet; way in; mouth, door &c. (*opening*) 260; path &c. (*way*) 627; conduit &c. 350; immigrant, visitor, incomer, newcomer, colonist.

**V.** have the *entrée*; enter; go –, come –, pour –, flow –, creep –, slip –, pop –, break –, burst- -into, – in; set foot on; burst –, break- in upon; invade, intrude, butt in, horn in, crash; insinuate itself; inter-, penetrate; infiltrate; find one's way –, wriggle –, worm oneself- into.

give entrance to &c. (*receive*) 296; insert &c. 300.

**Adj.** incoming, ingressive &c. *n.*; inward bound.

**Adv.** inward.

**295.** [Motion out of.] **Egress.—N.** egress, exit, issue; emer-sion, -gence; disemboguement; out-break, -burst; e-, pro-ruption; emanation; evacuation; ex-, trans-udation; extravasation, perspiration, sweating, leakage, percolation, distillation, oozing; gush &c. (*water in motion*) 348; outpour, -ing; effluence, effusion; efflux, -ion; drain; dribbling &c. *v.*; defluxion; drainage; out-come, -put; discharge &c. (*excretion*) 299.

export; expatriation; e-, re-migration; *débouche*; exodus &c. (*departure*) 293; emigrant, migrant, *émigré*, colonist.

outlet, vent, spout, tap, sluice, floodgate; pore; vomitory, out-gate, sallyport; way out; mouth, door &c. (*opening*) 260; path &c. (*way*) 627; conduit &c. 350; air-pipe &c. 351.

**V.** emerge, emanate, issue; go –, come –, move –, pass –, pour –, flow- out of; pass off, evacuate; migrate.

ex-, trans-ude; leak; run, – out, – through; per-, trans-colate; seep; strain, distil; perspire, sweat, drain, ooze; filter, filtrate; dribble, gush, spout, flow out; well, – out; pour, trickle &c. (*water in motion*) 348; effuse, extravasate, disembogue, discharge itself, debouch; come –, break- forth; burst- out, – through; find vent, escape &c. 671.

**Adj.** effused &c. *v.*; outgoing, outward bound.

**Adv.** outward.

**296.** [Motion into, actively.] **Reception.** —**N.** reception; admission, admittance, *entrée*, importation; initiation; intro-duction, -mission, -ception; immission, ingestion, imbibition, absorption, ingurgitation, inhalation; suction, sucking; eating, drinking &c. (*food*) 298; insertion &c. 300; interjection &c. 228.

**V.** give -entrance to, – admittance to, – the *entrée*; intro-duce, -mit; usher, admit, receive, import, initiate, bring in, open the door to, throw open, ingest, absorb, imbibe, inhale, infiltrate; let –, take –, suck- in; re-admit, -sorb, -absorb; snuff up; swallow, ingurgitate: engulf, engorge; gulp; eat, drink &c. (*food*) 298.

**Adj.** admit-ting &c. *v.*, -ted &c. *v.*; admissible; absorbent; introductory, introceptive, intromittent, initiatory.

---

**297.** [Motion out of, actively.] **Ejection.**—**N.** ejection, emission, effusion, rejection, expulsion, eviction, extrusion, trajection; discharge.

egestion, evacuation, vomition, disgorgement, voidance, eruption, eruptiveness; ruc-, eruc-tation, blood-letting, venesection, phlebotomy, paracentesis; tapping, drainage; clear-ance, -age, voidance; vomiting, excretion &c. 299.

deportation; banishment &c. (*punishment*) 972; rogue's march; relegation, extradition; dislodgment.

**V.** give -exit, – vent- to; let –, give –, pour –, send- out; des-, dis-patch; exhale, excern, excrete, disembogue, secrete, secern; extravasate, shed, void, evacuate, egest, emit; open the -sluices, – floodgates; turn on the tap; extrude, detrude; effuse, spend, expend; pour forth; squirt, spirt, spill, slop; perspire &c. (*exude*) 295; breathe, blow &c. (*wind*) 349.

tap, draw off; bale –, lade- out; let blood, broach.

eject, reject; expel, discard; cut, send to Coventry, boycott, ostracize; *chasser*; banish &c. (*punish*) 972; throw &c. 284 -out, – up, – off, – away, – aside; push &c. 276 -out, – off, – away, – aside; shovel –, sweep- -out, – away; brush –, whisk –, turn –, send- -off, – away; discharge; send –, turn –, cast- adrift; turn –, bundle- out; throw overboard; give the sack to; send -packing, – about one's business, – to the right about; strike off the roll &c. (*abrogate*) 756; turn out- neck and heels, – head and shoulders, – neck and crop; pack off; send away with a flea in the ear; send to Jericho; bow out, show the door to, dismiss, fire, sack.

turn out of -doors, – house and home; evict, oust; exorcise, un-house, -kennel; dislodge; un-, dis-people; depopulate; relegate, deport.

empty; drain, – to the dregs; sweep off; clear, – off, – out, – away; suck, draw off, extract; clean out, make a clean sweep of, clear decks, purge.

em-, dis-, disem-bowel; eviscerate, gut; unearth, root -out, – up; averruncate; weed –, get out; eliminate, get rid of, do away with, shake off; exenterate.

vomit, spew, puke, keck, retch; belch, – out, eruct, eructate; cast –, bring- up; disgorge; expectorate, salivate, clear the throat, hawk, spit, sputter, splutter, slobber, drool, drivel, slaver, slabber.

unpack, unlade, unload, unship; break bulk.

be let out; ooze &c. (*emerge*) 295.

**Adj.** emitt-ing, -ed &c. *v.*

**Int.** begone! get you gone! get –, go- -away, – along, – along with you! go your way! away, – with! off with you! go, – about your business! be off! avaunt! aroynt! get out! beat it!

**298.** [Eating.] **Food.—N.** eating &c. *v.*; deglutition, gulp, epulation, mastication, manducation, rumination, gastronomy, gastrology; panto-, hippo-, ichthyo-phagy &c.; gluttony &c. 957; carnivorousness, vegetarianism.

mouth, jaws, mandible, mazard, chops.

drinking &c. *v.*; potation, draught, libation; carousal &c. (*amusement*) 840; drunkenness &c. 959.

food, *pabulum*; aliment, nourishment, nutriment; susten-ance, -tation; nurture, subsistence, provender, feed, fodder, provision, ration, keep, commons, board; commissariat &c. (*provision*) 637; prey, forage, pasture, pasturage; fare, cheer; diet, -ary; regimen; belly timber, staff of life; bread, -and cheese; proteins, carbohydrates, vitamines.

comestibles, eatables, victuals, edibles, *ingesta*; grub, prog, tack, hard tack, meat; bread, -stuffs; cereals; viands, cates, delicacy, dainty, creature comforts, contents of the larder, flesh-pots; festal board; ambrosia; good -cheer, – living.

*hors-d'œuvre*; soup, pottage, *potage*, broth, *bouillon*, *consommé*, *purée*, *borsch*, stock, skilly, gumbo; fish, – cakes, – pie; joint, *rôti*, *pièce de résistance*, *relevé*, hash, *réchauffé*, stew, *ragoût*, fricassee, mince, *salmi*, *goulash*, *bouillabaisse*, remove, *entrée*, *croquette*, *rissole*, sausage, curry, bubble and squeak; haggis, collops, giblets; poultry, game &c.; biscuit, bun, scone, rusk, pancake, pie, pastry, pasty, patty, *patisserie*, tart, turnover, *vol-au-vent*, *soufflé*, dumpling, pudding, duff, *compote*, fritters, cake, napoleon, *blancmange*, custard, jelly, jam, sweets &c. 396; *entremet*; oatmeal, porridge, hasty pudding, gruel; eggs, omelet, cheese, matzoon, savoury; vegetable, salad, *mayonnaise*, fruit; sauce, condiment &c. 393; kickshaws.

table, *cuisine*, bill of fare, *menu*, *prix fixe*, ordinary, *a la carte*; cover.

meal, repast, feed, spread; mess; dish, plate, course, side dish; regale; regale-, refresh-, entertain-ment; refection, collation, picnic, feast, banquet, junket, breakfast; lunch, -eon; *déjeuner*, bever, tiffin, tea, dinner, supper, snack, whet, bait, dessert; pot-luck, *table d'hôte*, *déjeuner à la fourchette*; hearty –, square –, substantial – full- -meal; blow out; light refreshment; pemmican.

mouthful, bolus, gobbet, tid-bit, morsel, sop, sippet.

drink, beverage, liquor, broth, soup; potion, dram, draught, drench, swill; nip, peg, sip, sup, gulp.

wine, champagne, spirits, *liqueur*, beer, porter, stout, ale, malt liquor, julep, Sir John Barleycorn, stingo, heavy wet, bitter, lager-beer, cider; grog, toddy, flip, purl, punch, negus, cup, bishop, posset, wassail; bitters, *apéritif*, high-ball, cocktail; whisky, rum, absinthe; gin &c. (*intoxicating liquor*) 959; coffee, chocolate, cocoa tea, *maté*, the cup that cheers but not inebriates.

eating-house &c. 189.

**299. Excretion.—N.** excretion, discharge, emanation; ejection &c. 297; exhalation, extrusion, secretion, effusion, extravasation, *ecchymosis*, evacuation, cacation, defecation, dysentery, dejection, *fæces*, excrement; perspiration, sweat; sud-, exud-ation; *diaphoresis*; sewage.

saliva, spittle, rheum; ptyalism, salivation, catarrh, diarrhœa; *ejecta*, *egesta*, *sputum*, *sputa*; *excreta*; lava; *exuviæ* &c. (*uncleanness*) 653.

hemorrhage, bleeding; catamenia, menses; outpouring &c. (*egress*) 295; leucorrhea.

**V.** excrete &c. (*eject*) 297; emanate &c. (*come out*) 295.

**Adj.** excretory, fæcal, secretory; ejective, eliminant.

**V.** eat, feed, fare, devour, swallow, take; gulp, bolt, snap; fall to; despatch, dispatch; discuss; take –, get –, gulp-down; lay –, tuck- in; lick, pick, peck; gormandize &c. 957; bite, champ, munch, cranch, craunch, crunch, chew, masticate, nibble, gnaw, mumble.

live on; feed –, batten –, fatten –, feast- upon; browse, graze, crop, regale; carouse &c. (*make merry*) 840; eat heartily, do justice to, play a good knife and fork, banquet.

break -bread, – one's fast; breakfast, lunch, dine, take tea, sup.

drink, – in, – up, – one's fill; quaff, sip, sup; suck, – up; lap; swig; swill, tipple &c. (*be drunken*) 959; empty one's glass, drain the cup; toss -off, – one's glass; wash down, crack a bottle, wet one's whistle.

cater, purvey &c. 637.

**Adj.** eatable, edible, esculent, comestible, alimentary; cereal, cibarious; dietetic; culinary; nutri-tive, -tious; succulent; drinkable, pot-able, -ulent; bibulous.

omn-, carn-, herb-, frug-, gran-, gramin-, phyt-ivorus; ichthyophagous.

prandial.

**300.** [Forcible ingress.] **Insertion.—N.** insertion, implantation, intercalation, embolism, introduction; interpolation, insinuation &c. (*intervention*) 228; planting &c. *v.*; injection, inoculation, importation, infusion; forcible -ingress &c. 294; immersion; submersion, -gence; dip, plunge; bath &c. (*water*) 337; interment &c. 363.

**V.** insert; intro-duce, -mit; put –, run- into; import; inject; interject &c. 228; infuse, instil, inoculate, impregnate, imbue, imbrue.

graft, ingraft, bud, plant, implant; dovetail.

obtrude; thrust –, stick –, ram –, stuff –, tuck –, press –, drive –, pop –, whip –, drop –, put- in; impact; empierce &c. (*make a hole*) 260.

embed; immerse, immerge, merge; bathe, soak &c. (*water*) 337; dip, plunge &c. 310.

bury &c. (*inter*) 363.

insert &c.- itself; plunge *in medias res.*

**Adj.** inserted &c. *v.*

**301.** [Forcible egress.] **Extraction.—N.** extraction; extracting &c. *v.*; removal, elimination, extrication, eradication, evolution.

evulsion, avulsion; wrench; expression, squeezing; extirpation, extermination; ejection &c. 297; export &c. (*egress*) 295; distillation.

extractor, corkscrew, forceps, pliers.

**V.** extract, draw, pit; take –, draw –, pull –, tear –, pluck –, pick –, get- out; wring from, wrench; extort; root –, weed –, grub –, rake- up, – out; eradicate; pull –, pluck- up by the roots; averruncate; unroot; uproot, pull up, extirpate, dredge.

remove; educe, elicit; evolve, extricate; eliminate &c. (*eject*) 297; eviscerate &c. 297.

express, squeeze –, press- out; distil.

**Adj.** extracted &c. *v.*

---

**302.** [Motion through.] **Passage.—N.** passage, transmission; permeation; pene-, interpene-tration; transudation, infiltration; *osmosis*, osmose, endos-, exos-mose; intercurrence; ingress &c. 294; egress &c. 295; path &c. 627; conduit &c. 350; opening &c. 260; journey &c. 266; voyage &c. 267.

**V.** pass, – through; perforate &c. (*hole*) 260; penetrate, permeate, thread, thrid, enfilade; go -through, – across; go –, pass- over; cut across; ford, cross; pass and repass, work; make –, thread –. worm –, force- one's way; make –, force- a passage; cut one's way through;

find its -way, – vent; transmit, make way, clear the course; traverse, go over the ground.

**Adj.** passing &c. *v.*; intercurrent; osmotic &c. *n.*

**Adv.** *en passant* &c. (*transit*) 270.

**303.** [Motion beyond.] **Overstep.**—**N.** trans-cursion, -ilience, -gression; infraction, intrusion; trespass; en-croach-, infringe-ment; extravagation, transcendence; redundance &c. 641; ingress &c. 294.

**V.** transgress, surpass, pass; go- be-yond, – by; show in –, come to the-front; shoot ahead of; steal a march –, gain- upon.

over-step, -pass, -reach, -go, -ride, -leap, -jump, -skip, -lap, -shoot the mark; out-strip, -leap, -jump, -go, -step, -run, -ride, -rival, -do; beat, – hollow; distance; leave in the -lurch, – rear; go one better, throw into the shade; exceed, transcend, surmount; soar &c. (*rise*) 305.

encroach, intrude, trespass, infringe, invade, trench upon, intrench on; strain; stretch –, strain- a point; pass the Rubicon.

**Adj.** surpassing &c. *v.*

**Adv.** beyond the mark, ahead.

**304.** [Motion short of.] **Shortcoming.**—**N.** shortcoming, failure; delinquency; falling short &c. *v.*; de-fault, -falcation; leeway; labour in vain, no go.

incompleteness &c. 53; imperfection &c. 651; insufficiency &c. 640; non-completion &c. 730; failure &c. 732.

**V.** come –, fall –, stop- -short, – short of; not reach; want; keep within -bounds, – the mark, – compass.

break down, stick in the mud, col-lapse, come to nothing; fall -through, – to the ground, – down; cave in, end in smoke, fizzle out, miss the mark, fail; lose ground; miss stays, slump.

**Adj.** unreached; deficient; short, – of; *minus*; out of depth; perfunctory &c. (*neglect*) 460.

**Adv.** within -the mark, – compass, – bounds; behindhand; *re infectâ*; to no purpose; far from it.

**Phr.** the bubble burst.

---

**305.** [Motion upwards.] **Ascent.**—**N.** ascent, ascension; rising &c. *v.*; rise, upgrowth; leap &c. 309; acclivity, hill &c. 217; stair, stairs, stair-case, -way, flight of -steps, – stairs; ladder, com-panion, – way; lift, elevator &c. 307.

rocket, lark; sky-rocket, -lark; Alpine Club.

**V.** ascend, rise, mount, arise, uprise; go –, get –, work one's way –, start –, spring –, shoot- up; zoom; aspire.

climb, clamber, ramp, scramble, swarm, *escalade*, surmount; scale, – the heights.

tower, soar, hover, spire, plane, swim, float, surge; leap &c. 309.

**Adj.** rising &c. *v.*; scandent, buoyant; super-natant, -fluitant; excelsior.

**Adv.** uphill.

**306.** [Motion downwards.] **Descent.**—**N.** descent, descension, declension, declination; fall; falling &c. *v.*; drop, cadence; subsidence, lapse; come-down, downfall, tumble, slip, tilt, trip, lurch; cropper, *culbute*; titubation, stumble; fate of Icarus; dive, nose-dive, *volplane*.

*avalanche*, *débâcle*, land-slip, -slide.

declivity, dip, hill; decline, drop.

**V.** descend; go –, drop –, come-down; fall, gravitate, drop, slip, slide, glissade, dive, plunge, settle; decline, slump, set, sink, droop, come down a peg.

dismount, alight, light, get down; swoop; stoop &c. 308; fall prostrate, precipitate oneself; let fall &c. 308.

tumble, trip, stumble, titubate, lurch, pitch, swag, topple; topple –, tumble- -down, – over; tilt, sprawl, plump down, come a cropper.

**Adj.** descending &c. *v.*; descendent, declivitous; downcast; decur-rent, -sive; labent, deciduous; nodding to its fall.

**Adv.** down, -hill, -wards.

**307. Elevation.**—**N.** elevation; raising &c. *v.*; erection, lift; sublevation, upheaval; sublimation, exaltation; prominence &c. (*convexity*) 250.

lever &c. 633; crane, derrick, windlass, capstan, winch, dredger, lift, elevator, escalator, dumb waiter.

**V.** heighten, elevate, raise, lift, erect; set –, stick –, perch –, perk –, tilt- up; rear, hoist, heave; up-lift, -raise, -rear, -bear, -cast, -hoist, -heave; buoy, weigh, mount, give a lift; exalt, sublimate; place –, set- on a pedestal.

take –, drag –, fish- up; dredge.

stand –, rise –, get –, jump- up; spring to one's feet; hold -oneself, – one's head- up; draw oneself up to his full height.

**Adj.** elevated &c. *v.*; standing up; stilted, attollent, rampant.

**Adv.** on -stilts, – the shoulders of, – one's legs, – one's hind legs.

**308. Depression.**—**N.** lowering &c. *v.*; depression; dip &c. (*concavity*) 252; abasement; detrusion; reduction.

over-throw, -set, -turn; upset; prostration, subversion, precipitation.

bow; courtesy, curtsy; genuflexion, *kowtow*, obeisance, *salaam*.

**V.** depress, lower; let –, take- -down, – down a peg; cast; let -drop, – fall; sink, debase, bring low, abase, slash, reduce, detrude, pitch, precipitate.

over-throw, -turn, -set; upset, subvert, prostrate, level, fell; cast –, take –, throw –, fling –, dash –, pull –, cut –, knock –, hew- down; raze, – to the ground; humiliate, trample in the dust, pull about one's ears.

sit, – down; couch, squat, crouch, stoop, bend, bow, courtsey, curtsy; bob, duck, dip, genuflect, kneel; *kowtow, salaam*, make obeisance, prostrate oneself; bend, bow- the -head, – knee; incline the head; bow down; cower; recline &c. (*be horizontal*) 213.

**Adj.** depressed &c. *v.*; at a low ebb; prostrate &c. (*horizontal*) 213; detrusive.

**309. Leap.**—**N.** leap, jump, hop, spring, bound, vault, saltation.

dance, caper, gambol; curvet, caracole; *gam-bade, -bado*; capriole, demivolt; buck, – jump; hop, skip and jump.

kangaroo, jerboa, chamois, goat, frog, grasshopper, flea.

**V.** leap; jump -up, – over the moon; hop, spring, bound, vault, ramp, cut capers, gambol, trip, skip, dance, caper; curvet, *caracole*; foot it, bob, bounce, flounce, start, frisk &c. (*amusement*) 840; jump about &c. (*agitation*) 315; trip it on the light fantastic toe, dance oneself off one's legs.

**Adj.** leaping &c. *v.*; saltatory, frisky.

**Adv.** on the light fantastic toe.

**310. Plunge.**—**N.** plunge, dip, dive, header; ducking &c. *v.*; submergence, immersion, diver.

**V.** plunge, dip, souse, duck; dive, plump; take a -plunge, – header, make a plunge; bathe &c. (*water*) 337.

sub-merge, -merse; immerse, douse, sink, engulf, send to -the bottom, – Davy Jones' locker.

get out of one's depth; go -to the bottom, – down like a stone; founder, welter, wallow.

**311.** [Curvilinear motion.] **Circuition.**—**N.** circuition, circulation; turn, curvet; excursion; circum-vention, -navigation, -ambulation; north-west passage; ambit, gyre, lap, circuit &c. 629.

turning &c. *v.*; wrench; evolution; coil, helix, spiral; corkscrew.

**V.** turn, bend, wheel; go –, put- about; heel; go –, turn -round, – to the right about; turn on one's heel; make –, describe- a -circle, – complete circle; encircle; go –, pass- through -180°, – 360°.

circum-navigate, -aviate, -ambulate, -vent; put a girdle round the earth, go the round, make the round of.

turn –, round- a corner; double a point.

wind, circulate, meander; whisk, twirl; twist &c. (*convolution*) 248; make a *détour* &c. (*circuit*) 629.

**Adj.** turning &c. *v.*; circuitous; circum-foraneous, -fluent; devious, roundabout, circum-ambient, -flex, -navigable.

**Adv.** round about.

**312.** [Motion in a continued circle.] **Rotation.—N.** rotation, revolution, gyration, circulation, roll; circum-rotation, -volution, -gyration; volutation, circination, turbination, *pirouette*, convolution.

verticity; whir, whirl, swirl, eddy, vortex, whirlpool, gurge; cyclone, tornado; surge; *vertigo*, dizzy round; Maelstrom, Charybdis; Ixion; wheel of Fortune.

wheel, screw, propeller, whirligig, rolling stone, windmill; top, teetotum, merry-go-round; roller; cog-, fly-wheel, spit; jack; caster.

axis, axle, spindle, spool, pivot, pin, hinge, pole, swivel, gimbals, arbor, bobbin, mandrel, shaft.

[Science of rotatory motion] trochilics, gyrostatics.

**V.** rotate; roll, – along; revolve, spin; turn, – round; circumvolve; circulate, gyre, gyrate, wheel, whirl, swirl, twirl, trundle, troll, bowl; slew round.

roll up, furl; wallow, welter; box the compass; spin like a -top, – teetotum.

**Adj.** rotating &c. *v.*; rota-tory, -ry; circumrotatory, trochilic, vertiginous, gyratory; vortic-al, -ose.

**Adv.** head over heels, round and round, like a horse in a mill.

**313.** [Motion in a reverse circle.] **Evolution.—N.** evolution, unfolding, development; eversion &c. (*inversion*) 218.

**V.** evolve; un-fold, -roll, -wind, -coil, -twist, -furl, -twine, -ravel; disentangle; develop.

**Adj.** evolving &c. *v.*; evolved &c. *v.*

---

**314.** [Reciprocating motion, motion to and fro.] **Oscillation.—N.** oscillation; vibration, libration; motion of a pendulum; nutation; undulation; pulsation; pulse; throb; seismic disturbance.

alternation; coming and going &c. *v.*; ebb and flow, flux and reflux, ups and downs; wave, vibratiuncle, swing, beat, shake, wag, see-saw, dance, lurch, dodge; fluctuation; vacillation &c. (*irresolution*) 605.

seismometer, vibroscope, seismograph.

**V.** oscillate; vi-, li-brate; alternate, undulate, wave; sway, rock, swing; pulsate, beat; wag, -gle; nod, bob, courtesy, curtsy; tick; play; chatter, wamble, wabble; teeter, dangle, swag.

fluctuate, dance, curvet, reel, quake; quiver, quaver, shake, flicker; wriggle; roll, toss, pitch; flounder, stagger, totter, waddle; move –, bob- up and down &c. *adv.*; pass and repass, ebb and flow, come and go, shuttle; vacillate &c. 605.

brandish, shake, flourish.

**Adj.** oscillating &c. *v.*; oscill-, undul-, puls-, libr-atory; vibrat-ory, -ile; pendulous, shutterwise, seismic.

**Adv.** to and fro, up and down, backwards and forwards, see-saw, zigzag, wibble-wabble, in and out, from side to side, like buckets in a well.

**315.** [Irregular motion.] **Agitation.—N.** agitation, stir, tremor, shake, ripple, jog, jolt, jar, jerk, shock, succussion, trepidation, quiver, quaver, dance; jactit-ation, -ance; shuffling &c. *v.*; twitter, flicker, flutter.

disquiet, perturbation, commotion, turmoil, turbulence; tumult, -uation; hubbub, rout, bustle, fuss, racket, *subsultus*, staggers, megrims, epilepsy, fits, twitching, vellication, St. Vitus' dance.

spasm, throe, throb, palpitation, convulsion, paroxysm; tetanus.

disturbance &c. (*disorder*) 59; restlessness &c. (*changeableness*) 149.

ferment, -ation; ebullition, effervescence, hurly-burly, *cahotage*; tempest, storm, ground swell, heavy sea, whirlpool, vortex &c. 312; whirlwind &c. (*wind*) 349.

V. be -agitated &c.; shake; tremble, – like an aspen leaf; quiver, quaver, quake, shiver, twitter, twire, dither, dodder; twitch, writhe, toss, shuffle, tumble, stagger, bob, reel, sway; wag, -gle, wiggle; wriggle, – like an eel; squirm; dance, stumble, shamble, flounder, totter, flounce, flop, curvet, prance.

throb, pulsate, beat, palpitate, go pit-a-pat; flutter, flitter, flicker, bicker; bustle.

ferment, effervesce, foam; boil, – over; bubble, – up; simmer.

toss –, jump- about; jump like a parched pea; shake to its -centre, – foundations; be the sport of the winds and waves; reel to and fro like a drunken man; move –, drive- from post to pillar and from pillar to post; keep between hawk and buzzard.

agitate, shake, convulse, toss, tumble, bandy, wield, brandish, flap, flourish, whisk, jerk, hitch, jolt; jog, -gle; jostle, buffet, hustle, disturb, stir, shake up, churn, jounce, wallop, whip, vellicate.

Adj. shaking &c. *v.*; agitated, tremulous; de-, sub-sultory; shambling; giddy-paced, saltatory, convulsive, jerky, unquiet, restless, all of a twitter.

Adv. by fits and starts; subsultorily &c. *adj.*; *per saltum*; hop, skip and jump; in -convulsions, – fits, pit-a-pat.

# CLASS III

## Words relating to MATTER

## Section I. MATTER IN GENERAL

**316. Materiality.—N.** material-ity, -ness; materialization; corpor-eity, -ality; substantiality, material existence, incarnation, flesh and blood, *plenum*; physical condition.

matter, body, substance, brute matter, stuff, element, principle, protoplasm, plasma, *parenchyma*, material, *substratum*, hyle, *corpus*, *pabulum*; frame.

object, article, thing, something; still life; stocks and stones; materials &c. 635.

[Science of matter] physics; somatology, -ics; natural –, experimental- philosophy; physical science, *philosophie positive*, materialism, hylism; materialist, physicist.

V. materialize, incorporate, incarnate, substantiate, embody.

Adj. material, bodily; corpor-eal, -al; physical; somat-ic, -oscopic; sensible, tangible, ponderable, palpable, substantial; fleshly incarnate.

objective, impersonal, neuter, unspiritual, materialistic.

**317. Immateriality.—N.** immateriality, -ness; incorporeity, dematerialization, unsubstantiality, spirituality; inextension; astral plane.

personality; I, myself, me; *ego*, spirit &c. (*soul*) 450; astral body; immaterialism; spiritual-ism, -ist; subliminal –, subconscious- self.

V. disembody, spiritualize, dematerialize.

Adj. immateri-al, -ate; incorpor-eal, -al; asomatous, unextended; un-, disembodied; extramundane, supersensible, unearthly; pneumatoscopic; spiritual &c. (*psychical*) 450; aery.

personal, subjective.

---

**318. World.—N.** world, creation, nature, universe; earth, globe, wide world; *cosmos*; terraqueous globe, sphere; macro-, mega-cosm; music of the spheres.

heavens, sky, welkin, empyrean; starry -heaven, – host; firmament; vault –, canopy- of heaven; celestial spaces.

heavenly bodies, stars, luminaries, nebulæ; galaxy, milky way, galactic circle, *via lactea*.

sun, orb of day, Apollo, Phœbus; photo-, chromo-sphere; solar system; planet, -oid, asteroid; comet; satellite; moon, orb of night, Diana, Luna; aerolite, meteor; falling –, shooting- star; meteorite.

constellation. zodiac, signs of the zodiac, Charles's wain, Great Bear Southern Cross, Orion's belt, Cassiopeia's chair, Pleiades &c.

colures, equator, ecliptic, orbit.

[Science of heavenly bodies] astronomy; urano-graphy, -logy; cosmo-logy, -graphy, -gony; *eidouranion*, orrery; geography; geodesy

&c. (*measurement*) 466; star-gazing, -gazer; astronomer; cosmogonist, geodesist, geographer; observatory.

**Adj.** cosmic, cosmical, mundane; terr-estrial, -estrious, -aqueous, -ene, -eous; telluric, earthly, geotic, geodetic, cosmogonal, under the sun; sub-lunary, -astral.

solar, heliacal; lunar; celestial, heavenly, empyreal, sphery; starry, stellar; sider-eal, -al; astral; nebular.

**Adv.** in all creation, on the face of the globe, here below, under the sun.

**319. Gravity.—N.** gravi-ty, -tation; weight; heaviness &c. *adj.*; specific gravity; ponderosity, pressure, load; bur-den, -then; ballast, counterpoise; lump –, mass –, weight- of.

lead, millstone, mountain, Ossa on Pelion.

weighing, ponderation, trutination; weights; avoirdupois –, troy –, apothecaries'- weight; grain, scruple, drachm, ounce, pound, lb., load, stone, hundredweight, cwt., ton, quintal, carat, pennyweight, tod, gramme, kilogramme &c.

[Weighing instrument] balance, scales, steelyard, beam, weighbridge, spring balance, weighing machine.

[Science of gravity] statics.

**V.** be -heavy &c. *adj.*; gravitate, weigh, press, cumber, load.

[Measure the weight of] weigh, poise.

**Adj.** weighty; weighing &c. *v.*; heavy, – as lead; ponder-ous, -able; lump-ish, -y; cumber-, burden-some; cumbrous, unwieldy, massive.

in-, superin-cumbent.

**320. Levity.—N.** levity; lightness &c. *adj.*; imponderability, imponderableness, buoyancy, volatility.

feather, dust, mote, down, thistledown, flue, cobweb, gossamer, straw, cork, bubble; float, buoy; ether, air.

leaven, ferment, barm yeast, enzyme.

**V.** be -light &c. *adj.*; float, swim, be buoyed up.

render -light &c. *adj.*; lighten, levitate; leaven.

**Adj.** light, subtile, subtle, airy; imponder-ous, -able; astatic, weightless, ethereal, sublimated; uncompressed, volatile; buoyant, floating &c. *v.*; barmy, frothy; portable.

light as -a feather, – thistle down, – air.

fermenting &c. *n.*

---

## Section II. INORGANIC MATTER

### 1°. Solid Matter

**321. Density.—N.** density, solidity; solidness &c. *adj.*; impenetra-, impermea-bility; incompressibility; imporosity; cohesion &c. 46; constipation, consistence, spissitude.

specific gravity; hydro-, areo-meter.

condensation; solid-ation, -ification; consolidation; concretion, caseation, coagulation; petrifaction &c. (*hardening*) 323; crystallization, precipitation; deposit, precipitate, silt; inspissation; thickening &c. *v.*

indivisibility, indiscerptibility, indissolvableness.

solid body, mass, block, knot, lump; con-cretion, -crete, -glomerate; cake.

**322. Rarity.—N.** rarity; tenuity; absence of -solidity &c. 321; subtility; sponginess, compressibility.

rarefaction, expansion, dilatation, inflation, subtilization.

ether &c. (*gas*) 334.

**V.** rarefy, expand, dilate, subtilize, attenuate, thin.

**Adj.** rare, subtile, thin, fine, tenuous, compressible, flimsy, slight; light &c. 320; cavernous, spongy &c. (*hollow*) 252.

rarefied &c. *v.*; unsubstantial; uncom-pact, -pressed.

---

clot, stone, curd, coagulum, grume; bone, gristle, cartilage.

**V.** be -dense &c. *adj.*; become –, render- solid &c. *adj.*; solid-ify, -ate; concrete, set, take a set, consolidate, congeal, coagulate; curd, -le; fix, clot, cake, candy, precipitate, deposit, cohere, crystallize; petrify &c. (*harden*) 323.

condense, thicken, inspissate, incrassate; compress, squeeze, ram down, constipate.

**Adj.** dense, solid; solidified &c. *v.*; cohe-rent, -sive &c. 46; compact, close, serried, thickset; substantial, massive, lumpish; impenetrable, impermeable, imporous; incompressible; constipated; concrete &c. (*hard*) 323; knot-ted, -ty; gnarled; crystal-line, -lizable; thick, grumous, stuffy.

un-dissolved, -melted, -liquefied, -thawed.

in-divisible, -discerptible, -frangible, -dissolvable, -dissoluble, -soluble, -fusible.

**323. Hardness.—N.** hardness &c. *adj.*; rigidity, renitence, inflexibility, temper, callosity, durity.

induration, petrifaction; lapid-ification, -escence; vitri-, ossi-, corni-fication; crystallization.

stone, pebble, flint, marble, rock, fossil, crag, crystal, quartz, granite, adamant; bone, cartilage; heart of oak, block, board, deal board; iron, steel; cast –, wrought- iron; nail; brick, concrete; cement.

**V.** render -hard &c. *adj.*; harden, stiffen, indurate, petrify, temper, ossify, vitrify.

**Adj.** hard, rigid, stubborn, stiff, firm; starch, -ed; stark, unbending, unlimber, unyielding; inflexible, tense; indurate, -d; gritty, proof.

adamant-ine, -ean; concrete, stony, rocky, lithic, granitic, vitreous; crystalline; horny, corneous; bony; oss-eous, -ific; cartilaginous; hard as a -stone &c. *n.*; stiff as -buckram, – a poker.

**324. Softness.—N.** softness, pliableness &c. *adj.*; flexibility; pli-ancy, -ability; sequacity, malleability; flabbiness; duct-, tract-ility; extend-, extensibility; plasticity; inelasticity, flaccidity, laxity.

clay, wax, butter, dough, pudding; cushion, pillow, feather-bed, pad, down, padding, wadding.

mollification; softening &c. *v.*

**V.** render -soft &c. *adj.*; soften, mollify, mellow, relax, temper; mash, knead, squash, *massage*.

bend, yield, relent, relax, give.

**Adj.** soft, tender, supple; pli-ant, -able; flex-ible, -ile; lithe, -some; lissom, limber, plastic; ductile; tract-ile, -able; malleable, extensile, sequacious, inelastic, mollient.

yielding &c. *v.*; flabby, limp, flimsy.

flaccid, flocculent, downy; spongy, œdematous, medullary, doughy, argillaceous, mellow.

soft as -butter, – down, – silk; yielding as wax; tender as a chicken.

**325. Elasticity. — N.** elasticity, springiness, spring, resilience, renitency, buoyancy.

india-rubber, caoutchouc, gutta-percha, whalebone, gum elastic.

**V.** be -elastic &c. *adj.*; spring back &c. (*recoil*) 277.

**Adj.** elastic, tensile, springy, ductile, resilient, renitent, buoyant.

**326. Inelasticity.—N.** want of –, absence of- elasticity &c. 325; inelasticity &c. (*softness*) 324.

**Adj.** inelastic &c. (*soft*) 324.

---

**327. Tenacity.—N.** tenacity, toughness, strength; cohesion &c. 46; sequacity; stubbornness &c. (*obstinacy*) 606; viscidity &c. 352.

leather; gristle, cartilage.

**328. Brittleness.—N.** brittleness &c. *adj.*; frag-, friab-, frangib-, fiss-ility; frailty; house of -cards, – glass.

**V.** be -brittle &c. *adj.*; live in a glass house.

**V.** be -tenacious &c. *adj.*; resist fracture.

**Adj.** tenacious, tough, cohesive, adhesive, strong, resisting, sequacious, stringy, gristly, cartilaginous, leathery, coriaceous, tough as whit-leather; stubborn &c. (*obstinate*) 606.

break, crack, snap, split, shiver, splinter, crumble, break short, burst, fly, give way; fall to pieces; crumble -to, – into- dust.

**Adj.** breakable, brittle, frangible, fragile, frail, friable, delicate, gimcrack, shivery, fissile; splitting &c. *v.*; lacerable, splintery, crisp, crimp, short brittle as glass.

**329.** [Structure.] **Texture.—N.** structure, organization, anatomy, frame, mould, fabric, construction; frame-work, carcass, architecture; stratification, cleavage.

substance, stuff, *compages, parenchyma*; constitution, staple, organism.

[Science of structures] organ-, oste-, my-, splanchn-, neur , angi-, aden-ology; angi-, aden-ography.

texture; inter-, con-texture; tissue, grain, web, surface; warp and -woof, – weft; tooth, nap &c. (*roughness*) 256; fineness –, coarseness- of grain.

[Science of tissues] histology.

**Adj.** structural, organic; anatomic, -al.

text-ural, -ile; fine-, coarse-grained; fine, delicate, subtile, gossamery, filmy; coarse; home-spun; linsey-woolsey.

**330. Pulverulence.—N.** [State of powder.] pulverulence; sandiness &c. *adj.*; efflorescence; friability.

powder, dust, sand, shingle; sawdust; grit; attrition; meal, bran, flour, *farina*, spore, sporule; crumb, seed, grain; particle &c. (*smallness*) 32; thermion; limature, filings, *débris, detritus*, scobs, magistery, fine powder; *flocculi*.

smoke; cloud of -dust, – sand, – smoke; puff –, volume -of smoke; sand –, dust- storm.

[Reduction to powder] pulverization, comminution, attenuation, granulation, disintegration, subaction, contusion, trituration, levigation, abrasion, detrition, multure; limation; filing &c. *v.*

[Instruments for pulverization] mill, millstone, grater, rasp, file, pestle and mortar, nutmeg-grater, teeth, molar, grinder, chopper, grindstone, kern, quern, muller.

**V.** come to dust; be -disintegrated, – reduced to powder &c.

reduce –, grind- to powder; pulverize, comminute, granulate, triturate, levigate; scrape, file, abrade, rub down, grind, grate, rasp, pound, bray, bruise; con-tuse, -tund; beat, crush, cranch, craunch, crunch, muller, scranch, crumble, disintegrate; attenuate &c. 195.

**Adj.** powdery, pulverulent, granular, mealy, floury, farinaceous, branny, furfuraceous, flocculent, dusty, sandy, sabulous; aren-ose, -arious, -aceous; gritty; efflorescent, impalpable.

pulverizable; friable, crumbly, shivery; pulverized &c. *v.*; attrite; in pieces.

**331. Friction.—N.** friction, attrition; rubbing &c. *v.*; erasure; con-frication, -trition; affriction, abrasion, arrosion, limature, frication, rub; elbow-grease; rosin; massage.

**V.** rub, scratch, abrade, scrape, scrub,

**332.** [Absence of friction. Prevention of friction.] **Lubrication.—N.** smoothness &c. 255; unctuousness &c. 355.

lubri-cation, -fication; anointment; oiling &c. *v.*

fray, rasp, graze, curry, scour, polish, rub out, erase, gnaw; file, grind &c. (*reduce to powder*) 330; *massage*.

set one's teeth on edge; rosin.

**Adj.** anatriptic, abrasive.

synovia; lubricant, graphite, glycerine, oil &c. 356; saliva; lather.

**V.** lubri-cate, -citate; oil, grease lather, soap; wax.

**Adj.** lubricated &c. *v.*

## 2°. Fluid Matter

### 1. *Fluids in General*

**333. Fluidity.—N.** fluidity, liquidity; liquidness &c. *adj.*; gaseity &c. 334; liquefaction &c. 334.

fluid, inelastic fluid; liquid, liquor; lymph, humour, juice, sap, serum, blood, serosity, gravy, rheum, ichor, sanies.

solu-bility, -bleness.

[Science of liquids] hydro-logy, -statics, -dynamics, hydraulics &c.

**V.** be -fluid &c. *adj.*; flow &c. (*water in motion*) 348; liquefy &c. 335.

**Adj.** liquid, fluid, serous, juicy, succulent, sappy; fluent &c. (*flowing*) 348.

liquefied &c. 335; uncongealed; soluble, hydrostatic &c. *n.*

**334. Gaseity.—N.** gaseity, gaseousness; vapourousness &c. *adj.*; flatulence, -lency; volatility, aeration, gasification.

elastic fluid, gas, air, vapour, ether, steam, fume, reek, *effluvium*, *flatus*; cloud &c. 353.

[Science of elastic fluids] pneumat-ics, -ostatics; aero-statics, -dynamics &c.

gas-, gaso-meter.

**V.** gassify, aerate, aerify; emit vapour &c. 336.

**Adj.** gaseous, aeriform, ethereal, aerial, airy, vaporous, volatile, evaporable; flatulent; aerostatic &c. *n.*

**335. Liquefaction.—N.** liquefaction; liquescen-ce, -cy, deliquescence; melting &c. (*heat*) 384; colliqu-ation, -efaction; thaw; de-, liquation; lixiviation, dissolution.

solution, apozem, lixivium, infusion, decoction, flux.

solvent, diluent, menstruum, alkahest, *aqua fortis*.

**V.** render -liquid &c. 333; liquefy, run, deliquesce; melt &c. (*heat*) 384; solve; dissolve, resolve; liquate; hold in solution; leach, lixiviate.

**Adj.** lique-fied &c. *v.*, -scent, -fiable; deliquescent, soluble, colliquative; solvent.

**336. Vaporization. — N.** vapor-, volatil-ization; gasification; e-, vaporation; distillation, cohobation, sublimation, exhalation; volatility.

vaporizer, still, retort, spray, atomizer; fumigation, steaming.

**V.** render -gaseous &c. 334; vaporize, volatilize; distil, sublime; evaporate, exhale, smoke, transpire, emit vapour, fume, reek, steam, fumigate.

**Adj.** volatilized &c. *v.*; reeking &c. *v.*; volatile; evaporable, vaporizable.

### 2. *Specific Fluids*

**337. Water.—N.** water; serum, serosity; lymph; rheum; diluent.

dilution, maceration, lotion; washing &c. *v.*; im-, mersion; humectation, infiltration, spargefaction, affusion, irrigation, *douche*, balneation, bath.

deluge &c. (*water in motion*) 348; high water, flood-, spring-tide

**338. Air.—N.** air &c. (*gas*) 334; common –, atmospheric- air; atmosphere, stratosphere, isothermal layer, troposphere, Heaviside layer.

open, – air; sky, welkin; blue, – sky; cloud &c. 353.

weather, climate, rise and fall of the barometer, isobar.

**V.** be -watery &c. *adj.*; reek.

add water, water, wet; moisten &c. 339; dilute, dip, immerse; merge; im-, sub-merge; plunge, souse, duck, drown; soak, steep, macerate, pickle, wash, sprinkle, sparge, lave, bathe, affuse, splash, swash, douse, slosh, drench; dabble, slop, slobber, irrigate, inundate, deluge; syringe, inject, gargle; infiltrate, percolate.

**Adj.** watery, aqueous, aquatic, lymphatic; balneal, diluent; drenching &c. *v.*; diluted &c. *v.*; weak; wet &c. (*moist*) 339.

**Phr.** the waters are out.

**339. Moisture.—N.** moisture; moistness &c. *adj.*; hum-idity, -ectation; madefaction, dew; *serein*; marsh &c. 345; Hygromet-ry, -er.

**V.** moisten, wet; humect, -ate; sponge, damp, dampen, bedew; imbue, imbrue, infiltrate, saturate; seethe, sop; soak, drench &c. (*water*) 337.

be -moist &c. *adj.*; not have a dry thread; perspire &c. (*exude*) 295.

**Adj.** moist, damp; watery &c. 337; undried, humid, wet, dank, muggy, dewy; roric; roscid; juicy.

wringing wet; wet -through, – to the skin; saturated &c. *v*

swashy, soggy, dabbled; reeking, seething, dripping, soaking, soft, sodden, sloppy, muddy; swampy &c. (*marshy*) 345; irriguous.

**341. Ocean.—N.** sea, ocean, main, deep, brine, salt water, waters, waves, billows, high seas, offing, great waters, watery waste, 'vasty deep,' briny ocean, herring pond, steamer track, the seven seas; wave, tide &c. (*water in motion*) 348.

hydrograph-y, -er, oceanography; Neptune, Thetis, Triton, Naiad, Nereid; sea-nymph, Siren, mer-maid, -man; trident, dolphin.

**Adj.** oceanic; mar-ine, -itime; pelagic, -ian; sea-going, -worthy; hydrographic.

**Adv.** at –, on- sea; afloat; on the high seas.

[Science of air] pneumatics, aero-logy, -scopy, -graphy; meteorology, climatology; eudio-, baro-, aero-meter; aneroid baro-graph, -scope; weather-gauge, -glass, -cock.

exposure to the -air, – weather; ventilation; aero-station, -nautics, -naut &c. 267 and 269.

**V.** air, ventilate; fan &c. (*wind*) 349.

**Adj.** containing air, flatulent, effervescent; windy &c. 349.

atmospheric, airy; aeri-al, -form; pneumatic; meteorological; weather-wise.

**Adv.** in the open air, out of doors, *à la belle étoile, al fresco*; *sub -Jove, – dio.*

**340. Dryness.—N.** dryness &c. *adj.*; siccity, aridity, drought, ebb-, neap-tide, low water.

drying, ex-, de-siccation; evaporation; dehydration; arefaction, dephlegmation, drainage.

drier, desiccator.

**V.** be -dry &c. *adj.*; render -dry &c. *adj.*; dry; dry –, soak- up; sponge, swab, wipe; ex-, de-siccate, dehydrate, anhydrate; drain, parch.

be fine, hold up.

**Adj.** dry, anhydrous, arid, waterless; dried &c. *v.*; undamped; juice-, sap-less; sear; husky; rainless, without rain, fine; dry as -a bone, – dust, – a stick, – a mummy, – a biscuit; desiccated; dehydrated; water-proof, -tight.

**342. Land.—N.** land, earth, ground, dry land, *terra firma.*

continent, mainland, peninsula, delta; tongue –, neck- of land; isthmus, oasis; promontory &c. (*projection*) 250; highland &c. (*height*) 206.

coast, shore, scar, strand, beach; bank, lea; sea- board, -side, -shore, -bank, -coast, -beach; rock-, iron-bound coast; loom of the land; derelict; innings; *alluvium*, alluvion.

soil, glebe, clay, loam, marl, cledge, chalk, gravel, mould, subsoil, clod, clot; rock, crag, cliff.

acres; real estate &c. (*property*) 780; landsman, land-lubber, farmer.

geography &c. 318; agriculture &c. 371.

**V.** land, come to land; set foot on -the soil, - dry land; come -, go- ashore.

**Adj.** earthy; continental, midland; littoral, riparian, ripuarian; alluvial; terrene &c. (*world*) 318; landed, predial, territorial.

**Adv.** ashore; on -shore, - land.

**343. Gulf. Lake.—N.** land covered with water, gulf gulph, bay, inlet, bight, estuary, arm of the sea, fiord, armlet; frith, firth, ostiary, mouth; lagune, lagoon; indraught; cove, creek; natural harbour; roads; strait, narrows; Euripus; sound, belt, gut, kyles.

lake, loch, lough, mere, tarn, plash, broad, pond, pool, lin, puddle, well, artesian well, tank, sump; standing -, dead -, sheet of- water; fish -, mill-pond; race; ditch, dike, dyke, dam; reservoir &c. (*store*) 636.

**Adj.** lacustrine; land locked.

**344. Plain.—N.** plain, table land, mesa, face of the country; open -, country; basin, downs, waste, weary waste, desert, tundra, wild, steppe, pampas, savanna, prairie, champaign, heath, common, wold, veld; moor, -land, uplands, fell; bush; *plateau* &c. (*level*) 213; *campagna.*

meadow, mead, haugh, pasturage, park, field, lawn, green, plat, plot, grass-plat, greensward, sward, grass, turf, sod, heather; lea, ley, lay; grounds.

**Adj.** campestrian, champaign, alluvial.

**345. Marsh.—N.** marsh, swamp, morass, marish, moss, fen, bog, quagmire, slough, sump, wash; mud, squash, slush.

**Adj.** marsh, -y; swampy, boggy, plashy, poachy, quaggy, soft; muddy, sloppy, squashy, spongy; paludal; moor-ish, -y; fenny.

**346. Island.—N.** island, isle, islet, eyot, ait, holm, reef, atoll, breaker; archipelago; islander.

**Adj.** insular, sea-girt.

### 3. *Fluids in Motion*

**347.** [Fluid in motion.] **Stream.—N.** stream &c. (*of water*) 348, (*of air*) 349.

**V.** flow &c. 348; blow &c. 349.

**348.** [Water in motion.] **River.—N.** running water.

jet, spirt, squirt, spout, splash, swash, rush, gush, *jet d'eau*; sluice, chute.

water-spout, -fall; fall, cascade, force, foss; lin, -n; ghyll, Niagara; cata-ract, -dupe, -clysm; *débâcle*, inundation, deluge.

rain, -fall; *serein*; shower, scud; downpour, cloud burst; driving -, pouring -, drenching- rain; hyeto-logy, -graphy; rainy season, monsoon; predominance of Aquarius, reign of St. Swithin; mizzle, drizzle, *stillicidium*, plash; dropping &c. *v.*

stream, course, flux, flow, profluence; effluence &c. (*egress*) 295; defluxion; flowing &c. *v.*; current, tide, race.

spring; fount, -ain; rill, rivulet, gill,

**349.** [Air in motion.] **Wind.—N.** wind, draught, *flatus*, *afflatus*, air; breath, - of air; puff, whiff, zephyr; blow, drift; *aura*; stream, current; under-current.

gust, blast, breeze, squall, gale, half a gale, storm, tempest, hurricane, whirlwind, tornado, samiel, cyclone, typhoon; simoon; harmattan, monsoon, trade wind, sirocco, *mistral*, *bise*, *föhn*, tramontane, levanter; capful of wind; fresh -, stiff- breeze; keen blast; blizzard.

windiness &c. *adj.*; ventosity; rough -, dirty -, ugly -, stress of- weather; dirty-, windy-, mackerel- sky; mare's tail; thick -, black -, white- squall.

anemography, aerodynamics; wind-gauge, anemometer, weather cock vane.

gullet, rillet; stream-, brook-let; runnel, sike, burn, beck, brook, stream, river; reach; tributary.

body of water, torrent, rapids, flush, flood, swash, spate; spring –, high –, full-tide; bore; eagre, *hygre*; fresh, -et; undertow, indraught, reflux, undercurrent, eddy, vortex, gurge, whirlpool, Maelstrom, regurgitation, overflow; confluence, corrivation.

wave, billow, surge, swell, ripple; roller, ground swell, surf, breaker, white horses; comber, beach-comber; rough –, heavy –, cross –, long –, short –, chopping –, choppy- sea, choppiness; tidal wave.

[Science of fluids in motion] Hydrodynamics; Hydraul-ics &c.; rain-gauge &c.

water-bearer, – carrier, Aquarius.

irrigation &c. (*water*) 337; pump; watering-pot, – cart; hydrant, standpipe, hose, sprinkler, drencher; fire engine, squirt, syringe.

**V.** flow, run; meander; gush, pour, spout, roll, jet, well, issue; drop, drip, dribble, plash, squirt, spurt, spirtle, trill, trickle, distil, percolate; stream, overflow, inundate, deluge, flow over, splash, swash; guggle, murmur, babble, bubble, purl, gurgle, sputter, regurgitate; ooze, flow out &c. (*egress*) 295.

rain, – hard, – in torrents, – cats and dogs, – pitchforks; come down in sheets; pour with rain, drizzle, mizzle, spit, sprinkle, set in.

flow –, fall –, open –, drain- into; discharge itself, disembogue.

[Cause a flow] pour; pour out &c. (*discharge*) 297; shower down; irrigate, drench &c. (*wet*) 337; spill, splash.

[Stop a flow] stanch; dam, -up &c. (*close*) 261; obstruct &c. 706.

**Adj.** fluent; dif-, pro-, af-fluent; tidal; flowing &c. *v.*; meand-ering, -ry, -rous; fluvi-al, -atile; streamy, showery, rainy, drizzly, drizzling, pluvial, pluviose, stillicidous.

suf-, insuf-, per-, in-, af-flation; blowing, fanning &c. *v.*; ventilation.

sneezing &c. *v.*; sternutation; hiccup, -cough; catching of the breath; breathing &c.

Eolus, Eurus, Boreas, Zephyr, cave of Eolus.

air-pump, lungs, bellows, blow-pipe, fan, blower; pulmotor, ventilator, punkah, aspirator, exhauster, ejector.

**V.** blow, waft; blow -hard, – great guns, – a hurricane &c. *n.*; whistle, roar, howl, ring in the shrouds; stream, issue.

respire, breathe, in-, ex-hale, puff; whif, -fle; gasp, wheeze; snuff, -le; sniff, -le; sneeze, cough, belch.

fan, ventilate; in-, per-flate; blow –, pump- up.

**Adj.** blowing &c. *v.*; windy, airy, æolian, flatulent; breezy, gusty, squally; stormy, tempestuous, blustering; boisterous &c. (*violent*) 173.

pulmon-ic, -ary.

---

**350.** [Channel for the passage of water.] **Conduit.**—**N.** conduit, channel, duct, watercourse, race; head –, tail-race; adit, aqueduct, canal, trough, flume, gutter, pantile; dike, canyon, ravine, gorge, hollow, main, gully, moat, ditch, drain, sewer, culvert, *cloaca*, sough, kennel, siphon, *piscina*; pipe &c. (*tube*) 260; funnel; tunnel &c. (*passage*) 627; water –, waste- pipe; emunctory, gully-hole, artery, aorta, vein, blood vessel; lymphatic; throat, alimentary canal, intestine; pore, spout, scupper; ad-, a-jutage;

**351.** [Channel for the passage of air.] **Air-pipe.**—**N.** air-pipe, – shaft, – way, – passage, – tube; shaft, flue, chimney, funnel, vent, blow-hole, nostril, nozzle, throat, weasand, *trachea*; *bronch-us, -ia*; larynx, tonsils, wind-pipe, spiracle; venti-duct, -lator; louvre, blow-pipe &c. (*wind*) 349; pipe &c. (*tube*) 260.

---

hose; gar-, gur-goyle; penstock, weir; flood-, water-gate; sluice, lock, valve; rose; waterworks.

**Adj.** vascular &c. (*with holes*) 260.

## 3°. Imperfect Fluids

**352. Semiliquidity.—N.** semiliquidity; stickiness &c. *adj.*; visc-idity, -osity; gumm-, glutin-, muc-osity; spiss-, crass-itude; lentor; adhesiveness &c. (*cohesion*) 46.

inspiss-, incrass-ation; thickening, coagulation.

jelly, aspic, mucilage, gelatin, isinglass; colloid, mucus, phlegm; pituite, lava; glair, starch, gluten, albumen, milk, cream, protein; syrup, treacle; gum, size, glue, paste; wax, bee's-wax; emulsoid, emulsion, soup; squash, mud, slush, slime, ooze; moisture &c. 339; marsh &c. 345.

**V.** inspiss-, incrass-ate; coagulate, gelatinize, gelatinify, gel, jell, emulsify, thicken; mash, squash, churn, beat up.

**Adj.** semi-fluid, -liquid; half-melted, -frozen; milky, muddy &c. *n.*; lact-eal, -ean, -eous, -escent, -iferous; emulsive, curdled, thick, succulent, uliginous.

gelat-, album-, mucilag-, glut-inous; gelatine, mastic, amylaceous, ropy, clammy, clotted; vis-cid, -cous; sticky, tacky; slab, -by; lentous, pituitous; mu-cid, -culent, -cous.

**353.** [Mixture of air and water.] **Bubble.** [Cloud.]—**N.** bubble; foam, froth, head, fume, spume, lather, suds, spray, surf, yeast, barm, spindrift.

cloud, vapour, fog, mist, haze, steam; scud, rack, *nimbus*; *cumulus*, woolpack, *cirrus*, *stratus*; *cirro-*, *cumulo-stratus*; *cirro-cumulus*; mackerel sky, mare's tail, dirty sky.

[Science of clouds] nephelognosy, nephology.

effervescence, fermentation; bubbling &c. *v.*

nebula; cloudiness &c. (*opacity*) 426; nebulosity &c. (*dimness*) 422.

**V.** bubble, boil, foam, froth, spume, mantle, sparkle, guggle, gurgle; effervesce, ferment, fizzle; aerate; cloud, overcast, befog.

**Adj.** bubbling &c. *v.*; frothy, nappy, effervescent, sparkling, *mousseux*, up, fizzy, with a head on.

cloudy &c. *n.*; vaporous, nebulous, overcast; nubiferous, nephological; foggy, brumous.

---

**354. Pulpiness.—N.** pulpiness &c. *adj.*; pulp, paste, dough, sponge, curd, pap, rob, jam, pudding, mush, fool, poultice, grume, *papier mâché*.

**Adj.** pulpy &c. *n.*; pultaceous, grumous.

**V.** pulp, pulpify, mash.

---

**355. Unctuousness.—N.** unctuousness &c. *adj.*; unctuosity, lubricity; ointment &c. (*oil*) 356; anointment; lubrication &c. 332.

**V.** oil &c. (*lubricate*) 332.

**Adj.** unctuous, oily, oleaginous, adipose, sebaceous; fat, -ty; greasy; waxy, butyraceous, soapy, saponaceous, pinguid, lardaceous; slippery.

**356. Oil.—N.** oil, fat, butter, cream, grease, tallow, suet, lard, dripping, margarine, oleomargarine, exunge, blubber; glycerine, stearine, elaine, oleagine; soap; soft soap, wax, cerement; paraffin, spermaceti, adipocere; petroleum, mineral –, rock –, crystal- oil, kerosene, vegetable –, colza –, olive –, linseed –, cotton seed –, rape –, nut –, fusel- oil; animal –, neat's foot –, signal –, train- oil; ointment, unguent, liniment, salve, pomade, pomatum, brilliantine, spike –, nard.

**356a. Resin.—N.** resin, rosin, colophony; gum; lac, shellac, sealing-wax; amber, -gris; bitumen, pitch, tar, asphalt, -e, -um; varnish, copal, mastic, magilp, lacquer, japan.

**V.** varnish &c. (*overlay*) 223.

**Adj.** resinous, bituminous, pitchy, tarry.

# SECTION III. ORGANIC MATTER

## 1°. VITALITY

### 1. *Vitality in general*

**357. Organization.—N.** organized -world, – nature; living –, animated- nature; living beings; organic remains, organism; fossils; animal and vegetable kingdom, *fauna* and *flora*, biota.

prot-oplasm, -ein; albumen; structure &c. 329; organ-ization, -ism.

[Science of living beings] biology; natural history,* organic –, bio-chemistry, anatomy, physiology, embryology, morphology, evolution, Darwinism, Lamarkism, zoology &c. 368; botany &c. 369; naturalist, biologist &c.

**Adj.** organ-ic, -ized.

**358. Inorganization. — N.** mineral -world, – kingdom; unorganized –, inorganic –, brute –, inanimate- matter.

[Science of the mineral kingdom] mineralogy; geo-logy, -gnosy, -scopy; metall-urgy, -ography; lithology; orycto-logy, -graphy.

**V.** turn to dust, pulverize.

**Adj.** in-organic, -animate; unorganized; azoic; mineral.

---

**359. Life.—N.** life; vi-tality, -ability; animation; vital -spark, – flame, – force.

respiration, wind; breath -of life, – of one's nostrils; life-blood; Archeus; existence &c. 1.

vivification, vitalization; revivification &c. 163; Prometheus; life to come &c. (*destiny*) 152.

[Science of life] physiology, etiology, embryology, biology; animal economy.

nourishment, staff of life &c. (*food*) 298.

**V.** be -alive &c. *adj.*; live, breathe, respire; subsist &c. (*exist*) 1; walk the earth; strut and fret one's hour upon a stage; be spared.

see the light, be born, come into the world; fetch –, draw- -breath, – the breath of life; quicken; revive; come to, – life.

give birth to &c. (*produce*) 161; bring to life, put life into, vitalize; vivi-fy, -ficate; reanimate &c. (*restore*) 660; keep -alive, – body and soul together, – the wolf from the door; support life.

have nine lives like a cat.

**360. Death.—N.** death, dying &c. *v.*; de-cease, -mise; dissolution, departure, *obit*, release, rest, *quietus*, fall; loss, bereavement.

end &c. 67 –, cessation &c. 142 –, loss –, extinction –, ebb- of -life &c. 359.

death-warrant, -watch, -rattle, -bed; stroke –, agonies –, shades –, valley of the shadow –, jaws –, hand- of death; last -breath, – gasp, – agonies; dying -day, – breath, – agonies; swan song, *chant du cygne*; *rigor mortis*; Stygian shore; crossing the bar, the great adventure.

King -of terrors, – Death; Death, Angel of Death; mortality; doom &c. (*necessity*) 601.

*euthanasia*; happy release; break up of the system; natural -death, – decay; sudden –, violent- death; untimely end, watery grave; suffocation, *asphyxia*; heart failure; fatal disease &c. (*disease*) 655; death-blow &c. (*killing*) 361:

necrology, bills of mortality, obituary; death-song &c. (*lamentation*) 839.

**V.** die, expire, perish; meet one's -death, – end; pass away, be taken; yield –, resign- one's breath; resign

* The term *Natural History* is also used as relating to all the objects in Nature whether organic or inorganic, and including therefore *Mineralogy*, *Geology*, *Meteorology*, &c.

**Adj.** living, alive; in -life, – the flesh, – the land of the living; on this side of the grave, above ground, breathing, quick, animated, viable; lively &c. (*active*) 682; alive and kicking; tenacious of life.

vital; vivi-fying, -fied &c. *v.*; Promethean.

**Adv.** *vivendi causâ.*

---

one's -being, – life; end one's -days, – life, – earthly career; breathe one's last; cease to -live, – breathe; depart this life; be -no more &c. *adj.*; go –, drop –, pop -off; lose –, lay down –, relinquish –, surrender- one's life; drop –, sink- into the grave; close one's eyes; fall –, drop- dead, – down dead; break one's neck; give –, yield- up the ghost; be all over with one.

pay the debt to nature, shuffle off this mortal coil, take one's last sleep; go the way of all flesh; join the -greater number, – majority, – choir invisible; awake to life immortal; come –, turn- to dust; cross the Stygian ferry; go to -one's long account, – one's last home, – Davy Jones's locker, – the wall; receive one's death warrant, make one's will, die a natural death, go out like the snuff of a candle; come to an untimely end; catch one's death; go off the hooks, kick the bucket, peg out; go West; hop the twig, turn up one's toes; die a violent death &c. (*be killed*) 361; make the supreme sacrifice.

**Adj.** dead, lifeless; deceased, demised, departed, defunct; late, gone, no more; ex-, in-animate; out of the world, taken off, released; departed this life &c. *v.*; dead and gone; bereft of life, stone dead, dead as -a door nail, – a door post, – mutton, – a herring, – nits; launched into eternity, gathered to one's fathers, numbered with the dead, gone to a better land, behind the veil, beyond the grave, – mortal ken.

dying &c. *v.*; mori-bund, -ent, Acherontic; hippocratic; *in -articulo, – extremis*; in the -jaws, – agony- of death; going, – off; *aux abois*; on one's -last legs, – death bed; at -the point of death, – death's door, – the last gasp; near one's end, given over, booked, fey; with one foot in –, tottering on the brink of- the grave.

still-born; mortuary; deadly &c. (*killing*) 361.

**Adv.** *post -obit, – mortem.*

**Phr.** life -ebbs, – fails, – hangs by a thread; one's -days are numbered, – hour is come, – race is run, – doom is sealed; Death -knocks at the door, – stares one in the face; the breath is out of the body; the grave closes over one; *sic itur ad astra.*

**361.** [Destruction of life; violent death.] **Killing.**—**N.** killing &c. *v.*; homicide, manslaughter, murder, assassination, trucidation, occision; lynching, effusion of blood; blood, -shed; gore, slaughter, carnage, butchery; *battue*, gladiatorial combat.

massacre; *fusillade, noyade, pogrom*; Thuggee, thuggism.

death blow, finishing stroke, *coup de grâce, quietus*; execution &c. (*capital punishment*) 972; judicial murder; martyrdom.

butcher, slayer, murderer, Cain, assassin, cut-throat, garrotter, *bravo*, thug, racketeer, gunman, mobster, gangster, Moloch, *matador, sabreur*; *guet-à-pens*; gallows, executioner &c. (*punishment*) 975; man-eater.

regicide, parricide, fratricide, infanticide, aborticide &c.

suicide, *felo-de-se, suttee, hara-kiri*, Juggernaut; immolation, holocaust.

suffocation, strangulation, garrotte; hanging &c. *v.*

deadly weapon &c. (*arms*) 727; Aceldama; the potter's field, the field of blood.

fatal accident, violent death, casualty.

[Destruction of animals] slaughtering; phthiozoics;* sport, -ing; the chase, venery; hunting, coursing, shooting, fishing; pig-sticking; sports-, hunts-, fisher-man; hunter, Nimrod; slaughterer, knacker, slaughter-house, shambles, *abattoir*.

**V.** kill, put to death, slay, shed blood; murder, assassinate, butcher, slaughter; victimize, immolate; massacre; take away –, deprive of- life; make away with, put an end to; despatch, decimate; burke, settle do, – to death, – for.

strangle, garrotte, hang, lynch, throttle, choke, stifle, suffocate, stop the breath, smother, asphyxiate, drown.

sabre; cut -down, – to pieces, – the throat; jugulate; stab, run through the body, bayonet; put to the -sword, – edge of the sword.

shoot, – dead; blow one's brains out; brain, knock on the head; stone, lapidate; give –, deal- a death blow; give a -*quietus*, – *coup de grâce*.

behead, bowstring &c. (*execute*) 972.

hunt, shoot &c. *n.*

cut off, nip in the bud, launch into eternity, send to one's last account.

bump off, rub out, sign one's death warrant, strike the death knell of.

give no quarter, pour out blood like water; run amuck, wade knee-deep –, imbrue one's hands- in blood.

die a violent death, welter in one's blood; dash –, blow- out one's brains; commit suicide; kill –, -make away with –, put an end to- oneself.

**Adj.** killing &c. *v.*; murd-, slaught-erous; sanguin-ary, -olent; blood-stained, -thirsty; homicidal, red-handed; bloody, -minded; ensanguined, gory, sanguineous.

mortal, fatal, lethal; dead-, death-ly; mort-, leth-iferous; unhealthy &c. 657; internecine; suicidal.

sporting; piscator-ial, -y.

**Adv.** in at the death.

**362. Corpse.—N.** corpse, corse, carcass, bones, skeleton, dry-bones; defunct, relics, *reliquiæ*, remains, mortal remains, dust, ashes, earth, clay; mummy; carrion; food for- worms, – fishes; tenement of clay, this mortal coil.

shade, ghost, *manes*, apparition &c. 980.

organic remains, fossils.

**Adj.** cadaverous, corpse-like; unburied &c. 363.

**363. Interment.—N.** interment, burial, sepulture, entombment; in-, humation; obs-, ex-equies; funeral, wake, pyre, funeral pile; cremation.

funeral -rite, – solemnity; knell, passing bell, tolling; dirge &c. (*lamentation*) 839; cypress; *obit*, dead march, muffled drum; coroner, mortician, undertaker, mute, mourner, professional mourner, pall-bearer; elegy; funeral -oration, – sermon; epitaph.

grave clothes, shroud, winding-sheet, cere-cloth; cerement.

coffin, shell, sarcophagus, urn, pall, bier, hearse, catafalque, cinerary urn.

grave, pit, sepulchre, tomb, vault, crypt, catacomb, mausoleum, *Golgotha*, house of death, narrow house, long home; cemetery, necropolis, boneyard; burial-place, -ground; grave-, church-yard; God's acre; mortuary, tope, cromlech, dolmen, menhir, barrow, tumulus, cairn;

* Bentham, 'Chrestomathia.'

ossuary; bone-, charnel-, dead-house; *morgue*; lich-gate; crematorium.

sexton, grave-digger.

monument, memorial, cenotaph, shrine; grave-, head-, tomb-stone: *memento mori*; hatchment, stone, cross.

exhumation, disinterment; necropsy, autopsy, *post-mortem* examination.

V. inter, bury; lay in –, consign to- the -grave, – tomb; en-, in-tomb; inhume; lay out, prepare for burial, embalm, mummify; conduct a funeral, hold services; toll the knell; put to bed with a shovel.

exhume, disinter, unearth.

Adj. buried &c. *v.*; burial; fune-real, -brial; mortuary, sepulchral, cinerary; elegiac; necroscopic.

Adv. *in memoriam*; *post-obit*, *-mortem*; beneath –, under- the sod.

Phr. *hic jacet*, *ci-gît*, *requiescat in pace*.

## 2. *Special Vitality*

**364. Animality.**—N. animal life; anima-tion, -lity, -lization; breath.

flesh, – and blood; corporeal nature; *physique*; strength &c. 159.

V. animalize, incorporate.

Adj. fleshly, incarnate, carnal, corporeal, human.

**365. Vegetability.**—N. vegetable life; vegeta-tion, -bility; herbage.

V. vegetate, germinate, sprout, shoot; cultivate.

Adj. vegetable &c. 367; rank, lush.

**366. Animal.***—N. animal, – kingdom; *fauna*; brute creation.

beast, brute, creature, created being; creeping –, living- thing; dumb -animal, – creature.

flocks and herds, live stock; domestic –, wild- animals; game, *feræ naturæ*; beasts of the field, fowls of the air, denizens of the day.

vertebrate, bi-, quadru-ped, mammal, marsupial, bird, reptile, batrachian, amphibian, fish, crustacean, shell fish, articulate, mollusc, worm, insect, zoophyte; protozoon, animalcule &c. 193.

horse &c. (*beast of burden*) 271; cattle, kine, ox; bull, -ock; steer, stot; cow, milch cow, calf, heifer, shorthorn; sheep; lamb, -kin; ewe –, pet- lamb; ewe, ram, tup; pig, swine, boar, hog, shoat, sow; tag, teg, wether.

dog, bitch, hound; pup, -py; whelp, cur, mutt, mongrel; house-, watch-, sheep-, shepherd's-, sporting-, fancy-, lap-, toy-, bull-, badger-dog; mastiff; blood-, grey-, stag-, deer-, fox-, otter-hound; harrier, beagle, spaniel, pointer,

**367. Vegetable.***— N. vegetable – kingdom; *flora*, verdure.

plant; tree, shrub, bush; creeper; vine; herb, -age; grass.

annual; per-, bi-, tri-ennial; exotic.

timber; primeval –, virgin- forest; wood, -lands; hurst, frith, holt, weald, park, chase, greenwood, brake, grove, copse, coppice, *bocage*, *tope*, clump of trees, thicket, spinet, spinney; under-, brush-wood; boscage, scrub; the oak and the ash and the bonny ivy tree.

bush, jungle, prairie; heath, -er; fern, bracken; furze, gorse, whin broom; grass, turf, grassland, greensward, green, lawn, meadow; pas-ture, -turage; turbary; sedge, rush, weed; fungus, mushroom, toadstool; lichen, moss, conferva, mould; seaweed &c.; growth, crop.

foliage, leafage, branch, bough, ramage; spray &c. 51; leaf, frond, flag, petal, shoot, tendril.

flower, blossom, bud, bloom, bine; flowering plant; tree, sapling, pollard; timber-, fruit-tree; palm-, gum-tree; pulse, legume.

* Extended lists of names of specific varieties of animals, vegetables, &c., are beyond the scope of this work; see Introduction, p. xxv.

setter, retriever; Newfoundland; water -dog, - spaniel; pug, poodle; dachshund; Pinscher; turnspit; terrier; fox –, Skye-terrier; Dandie Dinmont; collie.

cat; puss, -y; kitten; grimalkin; gib-, tom-cat; mouser; fox, Reynard, vixen, stag, deer, hart, buck, doe, roe, antelope.

bird; poultry, fowl, cock, hen, chicken, chanticleer, partlet, rooster, dunghill cock, barn-door fowl; feathered -tribes, – songster; singing –, dicky- bird; canary; finch; auk, dodo, moa, roc, phœnix.

snake, serpent, viper, adder; newt, eft; asp, vermin.

**Adj.** animal, zoological.

equine, bovine, vaccine, canine, feline; fishy; piscator-y, -ial; molluscous, porcine, vermicular.

**Adj.** veget-able, -ous; herb-aceous, -al; botanic; sylvan, silvan; arbor- ary, -eous, -escent, -ical; dendritic, dendriform; woody, grassy; ver-dant, -durous; floral, mossy; lign-ous, -eous; wooden, leguminous; end-, ex-ogenous.

---

**368.** [The science of animals.] **Zoology.**—**N.** zoo-logy, -nomy, -graphy, -tomy; anatomy; comparative anatomy; animal –, comparative- physiology; morphology.

anthrop-, ornith-, ichthy-, herpet-, ophi-, malac-, helminth-, entom-, oryct-, paleont-ology; ichthy- &c. -otomy; taxidermy.

zo- &c. -ologist.

**Adj.** zoological &c. *n.*

**369.** [The science of plants.] **Botany.**—**N.** botany; phyto-graphy, -logy, -tomy; vegetable physiology, herborization, dendr-, myc-, fung-, alg-ology; flora, pomona; botanist &c.; botanic garden &c. (*garden*) 371; *hortus siccus*, *herbarium*, herbal.

herb-ist, -arist, -alist, -orist, -arian &c.

**V.** botanize, herborize.

**Adj.** botanical &c. *n.*

**370.** [The economy or management of animals.] **Cicuration.**—**N.** taming &c. *v.*; cicuration, zoohygiantics; domestication, -ity; *manège*; veterinary art; breeding, pisciculture, apiculture &c.

menagery, vivarium, zoological garden, zoo; bear-pit; aviary, apiary, hive; aquarium, fishery, fish hatchery; duck-, fish-pond; stud-farm; stock farm, dairy.

[Destruction of animals] phthisozoics* &c. (*killing*) 361.

neat-, cow-, shep-herd, shepherdess; grazier, drover, cowboy, cowkeeper; trainer, breeder, groom, ostler &c. 746; veterinary surgeon, vet, horse doctor; farrier; keeper; gamekeeper.

cage &c. (*prison*) 752; hen-coop, bird-cage, cauf; sheep-fold &c. (*inclosure*) 232.

**V.** tame, domesticate, acclimatize, breed, tend, break in, train, corral, round up; cage, bridle &c. (*restrain*) 751; ride &c. 266.

drive, yoke, harness. hitch; groom,

**371.** [The economy or management of plants.] **Agriculture.**—**N.** agriculture, cultivation, husbandry, farming; georgics, geoponics; tillage, tilth, agronomy, gardening, spade husbandry, vintage; hort-, arbor-, silv-, citr-, vit-, flor-iculture; intensive culture; landscape gardening; forestry, afforestation.

husbandman, horticulturist, citriculturist, gardener, florist; agricult-or, -urist; yeoman, farmer, cultivator, tiller of the soil, ploughman, sower, reaper; woodcutter, backwoodsman, forester; vine grower, vintager; Boer; Triptolemus.

field, meadow, garden; botanic –, winter –, ornamental –, flower –, kitchen –, truck –, market –, hop- garden; nursery; green-, hot-, glass-house; conservatory, cucumber frame, *cloche*, bed, border, seed-plot; grass-plat, lawn; park &c. (*pleasure ground*) 840; *parterre*, shrubbery, plantation, avenue,

* Bentham.

curry-comb; milk; shear; hatch; incubate.

**Adj.** pastoral, bucolic; tame, domestic, domesticated, broken in, gentle, docile.

*arboretum*, pinery, *pinetum*, orchard; vineyard, vinery; orangery; farm &c. (*abode*) 189.

**V.** cultivate; till, – the soil; farm, garden; sow, plant; reap, mow, cut; manure, dress the ground, dig, delve, dibble, hoe, plough, plow, harrow, rake, weed, lop and top, force, transplant, thin out, bed out, prune, graft.

**Adj.** agr-icultural, -arian, -estic.

arable; predial, rural, rustic, country, bucolic, Bœotian; horticultural.

**372. Mankind.—N.** man, -kind; human -race, – species, – nature; humanity, mortality, flesh, generation.

[Science of man] anthropo-logy, -graphy, -sophy; ethno-logy, -graphy; humanitarianism.

human being; person, -age; individual, creature, fellow creature, mortal, body, somebody, one; such a –, some- one; soul, living soul; earthling; party, head, hand; *dramatis personæ*.

people, persons, folk, public, society, world; community, – at large; general public; nation, -ality; state, realm; common-weal, -wealth; republic, body politic; million &c. (*commonalty*) 876; population &c. (*inhabitant*) 188.

cosmopolite; lords of the creation; ourselves.

**Adj.** human, mortal, personal, individual, national, civic, public, cosmopolitan; anthropoid.

**373. Man.—N.** man, male, he; manhood &c. (*adolescence*) 131; gentleman, sir, master; yeoman, wight, swain, fellow, guy, blade, *beau*, chap, gaffer, goodman; husband &c. (*married man*) 903; Mr., mister, *monsieur*, *sahib*, *Herr*, *señor*, *signor*; boy &c. (*youth*) 129; Adonis.

[Male animal] cock, drake, gander, dog, boar, stag, hart, buck, horse, entire horse, stallion; gib-, tom-cat; he-, Billy-goat; ram, tup; bull, -ock; capon, ox, gelding; steer, stot.

**Adj.** male, he, masculine; manly, virile; un-womanly, -feminine.

**374. Woman.—N.** woman, she, female, petticoat, skirt, moll, broad.

feminality, feminity, muliebrity; womanhood &c. (*adolescence*) 131; feminism; gynecology, gyniatrics, gynics.

womankind; the -sex, – fair; fair –, softer- sex; weaker vessel; the distaff side.

dame, madam, *madame*, mistress, Mrs., lady, *mem-sahib*, *Frau*, *señora*, *signora*, *donna*, *belle*, matron, dowager, goody, gammer; good -woman, – wife; squaw; wife &c. (*marriage*) 903; matron-age, -hood.

Venus, nymph, wench, *grisette*; little bit of fluff; girl &c. (*youth*) 129.

*inamorata* (love) &c. 897; courtesan &c. 962.

spinster, old maid, virgin, bachelor girl, new woman, Amazon.

[Female animal] hen, slut, bitch, sow, doe, roe, mare; she-, Nanny-goat; ewe, cow; lioness, tigress; vixen.

*gynecæum*, harem, *seraglio*, *zenana*, *purdah*.

**Adj.** female, she; feminine, womanly, ladylike, matronly, maidenly; womanish, effeminate, unmanly, gynecic.

## 2°. Sensation

### (1.) *Sensation in general*

**375. Physical Sensibility.—N.** sensibility; sensitiveness &c. *adj.*; physical sensibility, feeling, perceptivity, anaphylaxis, susceptibility, æsthetics; moral sensibility &c. 822.

sensation, impression, effect; consciousness &c. (*knowledge*) 490.

external senses.

**V.** be -sensible &c. *adj.* -of; feel, perceive.

render, -sensible &c. *adj.*; excite, stir, sharpen, cultivate, tutor.

cause sensation, impress; excite –, produce- an impression.

**Adj.** sens-ible, -itive, -uous; æsthetic, perceptive, sentient; conscious &c. (*aware*) 490; impressionable, responsive, alive to.

acute, sharp, keen, vivid, lively, impressive, thin-skinned.

**Adv.** to the quick.

**376. Physical Insensibility.—N.** insensibility, physical insensibility; obtuseness &c. *adj.*; palsy, paralysis, *anæsthesia*, *analgesia*, *narcosis*, *hypnosis*, twilight sleep, stupor, coma, trance, catalepsy; sleep &c. (*inactivity*) 683; moral insensibility &c. 823; numbness &c. 381.

anæsthetic agent, general –, local- anæsthetic, opium, ether, chloroform, cocaine, novocaine, chloral; nitrous oxide, laughing gas; refrigeration.

**V.** be -insensible &c. *adj.*; have a -thick skin, – rhinoceros hide.

render -insensible &c. *adj.*; blunt, pall, obtund, benumb, deaden, paralyze; anæsthetize, drug, dope; put under the influence of chloroform &c. *n.*; hypnotize; stupefy stun, narcotize.

**Adj.** insensible, unfeeling, senseless, comatose, dazed, impercipient, callous, thick-skinned, pachydermatous; hard, -ened; case-hardened; proof; obtuse, dull; anæsthetic; paralytic, palsied, numb, dead.

**377. Physical Pleasure.—N.** pleasure; physical –, sensual –, sensuous- pleasure; bodily enjoyment, animal gratification, sensuality; hedonism, luxuriousness &c. *adj.*; dissipation, round of pleasure; titillation, *gusto*, creature comforts, comfort, ease; pillow &c. (*support*) 215; luxury, lap of luxury; purple and fine linen; bed of -down, – roses; velvet, clover; cup of Circe &c. (*intemperance*) 954.

treat; diversion, divertisement, entertainment; refreshment, regale; feast; *délice*; dainty &c. 394; *bonne bouche*.

source of pleasure &c. 829; happiness &c. (*mental enjoyment*) 827.

**V.** feel –, experience –, receive- pleasure; enjoy, relish; luxuriate –, revel –, riot –, bask –, swim –, wallow- in; feast on; gloat -over, – on; smack the lips.

live -on the fat of the land, – in comfort &c. *adv.*; bask in the sunshine, *faire ses choux gras*.

give pleasure &c. 829.

**378. Physical Pain.—N.** pain; suffering, -ance; bodily – physical- -pain, - suffering; mental suffering &c. 828; dolour, ache; aching &c. *v.*; smart; shoot, -ing; twinge, twitch, gripe, head-, ear-, tooth-ache; *migraine*, neuralgia, neuritis, lumbago, gout, sciatica; hurt, cut; sore, -ness; discomfort, *malaise*; *tic douloureux*.

spasm, cramp; nightmare, *ephialtes*; crick, stitch, kink; thrill, convulsion. throe; throb &c. (*agitation*) 315; pang.

sharp –, piercing –, throbbing –, shooting –, gnawing –, burning- pain; anguish, agony.

torment, torture; rack; cruci-ation. -fixion; martyrdom; martyr, toad under a harrow, vivisection.

**V.** feel –, experience –, suffer –, undergo- pain &c. *n.*; suffer, ache, smart, bleed; tingle, shoot; twinge, twitch, lancinate; writhe, wince, make a wry face; sit on -thorns, – pins and needles.

give –, inflict- pain; pain, hurt, chafe, sting, bite, gnaw, gripe, stab, grind;

**Adj.** enjoying &c. *v.*; luxurious, voluptuous, sensual, hedonistic, comfortable, cosy, snug, in comfort, at ease.

agreeable &c. 829; grateful, refreshing, comforting, cordial, genial; sensuous; palatable &c. 394; sweet &c. (*sugar*) 396; fragrant &c. 400; melodious &c. 413; lovely &c. (*beautiful*) 845.

**Adv.** in -comfort &c. *n.*; on -a bed of roses &c. *n.*; at one's ease.

pinch, tweak; grate, gall, fret, prick, pierce wring, convulse; torment, torture; rack, agonize; crucify; ex-, cruciate; break on the wheel, put to the rack; flog &c. (*punish*) 972; grate on the ear &c. (*harsh sound*) 410.

**Adj.** in -pain &c. *n.*, – a state of pain; pained &c. *v.*

painful; aching &c. *v.*; biting, poignant; sore, raw, tender, with exposed nerve.

---

## (2.) *Special Sensation*

### 1. *Touch*

**379.** [Sensation of pressure.] **Touch.—N.** touch; tact, -ion, -ility; feeling; palp-ation, -ability; manipulation; brush, tick, graze, contact &c. 199.

[Organ of touch] hand, finger, fore-finger, thumb, paw, feeler, *antenna.*

**V.** touch, feel, handle, finger, thumb, paw, fumble, grope, grabble; twiddle, tweedle; pass –, run- the fingers over, massage, rub, knead; palpate, stroke, manipulate, wield; throw out a feeler.

**Adj.** tact-ual, -ile; tangible, palpable; lambent.

**380. Sensations of Touch.—N.** itching &c. *v.*; titillation, formication, *aura.*

**V.** itch, tingle, creep, thrill, sting; prick, -le; tickle, titillate.

**Adj.** itching &c. *v.*

**381.** [Insensibility to touch.] **Numbness.—N.** numbness &c. (*physical insensibility*) 376; pins and needles.

local anæsthetic, cocaine, novocaine &c.; morphia.

**V.** benumb &c. 376; freeze, dull deaden.

**Adj.** numb; benumbed &c. *v.*; intangible, impalpable.

### 2. *Heat*

**382. Heat.—N.** heat, caloric; temperature, warmth, fervour, calidity; incal-, incand-, recal-, decal-escence; glow, flush, blush; fever, hectic.

phlogiston; fire, spark, scintillation, flash, flame, blaze; arc; bonfire; firework, pyrotechny; wild-fire; sheet of fire, lambent flame; devouring element; conflagration.

summer, dog-days, canicule; baking &c. 384 –, white –, tropical –, Afric –, Bengal –, summer –, blood- heat; heat wave, sirocco, simoon; broiling sun; isolation; warming &c. 384.

sun &c. (*luminary*) 423; fire worshipper &c. 991; furnace &c. 386.

geyser, hot spring, volcano.

[Science of heat] pyrology; therm-

**383. Cold.—N.** cold, -ness &c. *adj.*; frigidity, gelidity, algidity, inclemency, *fresco.*

winter; depth of –, hard- winter; Siberia, Nova Zembla; Ant-, arctic, North –, South- Pole.

ice; snow, – flake, – crystal, – drift; sleet; hail, -stone; rime, frost; hoar –, white –, hard –, sharp- frost; icicle, thick-ribbed ice; fall of snow, snow storm, heavy fall, *avalanche;* ice-berg, -floe; floe, berg; *glacier; névé, serac.*

[Sensation of cold] chilliness &c. *adj.*; chill; shivering &c. *v.*; goose-skin, -flesh; *rigor,* horripilation, chattering of teeth; frostbite, chilblain.

**V.** be -cold &c. *adj.*; shiver, starve, quake. shake, tremble, shudder, didder,

ology, -otics; thermometer &c. 389.

V. be -hot &c. *adj.*; glow, incandesce, flush, sweat, swelter, bask, smoke, reek, stew, simmer, seethe, boil, burn, singe, scorch, scald, grill, broil, blaze, flame; smoulder; parch, fume, pant.

heat &c. (*make hot*) 384; thaw, fuse, melt, give.

**Adj.** hot, heated, warm, mild, genial, tepid, lukewarm, unfrozen; therm-al, -ic; calorific; ferv-ent, -id; ardent; aglow.

sunny, torrid, tropical, estival, canicular; close, sultry, stifling, stuffy, suffocating, oppressive; reeking &c. *v.*; baking &c. 384.

red –, white –, smoking –, burning &c. *v.* –, piping- hot; like -a furnace, – an oven; hot as -fire, – pepper; hot enough to roast an ox.

fiery; incand-, incal-escent; candent, ebullient, glowing, smoking; on fire; blazing &c. *v.*; in -flames, – a blaze; alight, afire, ablaze; un-quenched, -extinguished; smouldering; in a -heat, – glow, – fever, – perspiration, – sweat; sudorific; swelter-ing, -ed; blood-hot, -warm; warm as -a toast, – wool; recalescent, thermogenic, pyrotechnic, feverish, febrile, inflamed.

volcanic, plutonic, igneous; isother-mal, -mic, -al.

**Phr.** Not a breath of air.

quiver; perish with cold; chill &c. (*render cold*) 385.

Adj. cold, cool; chill, -y; gelid, frigid, algid; fresh, keen, bleak, raw, inclement, bitter, biting, niveous, cutting, nipping, piercing, pinching; clay-cold; starved &c. (*made cold*) 385; shivering &c. *v.*; aguish, *transi de froid*; frostbitten, -bound, -nipped.

cold as -a stone, – marble, – lead, – iron, – a frog, – charity, – Christmas; cool as -a cucumber, – custard.

icy, glacial, frosty, freezing, wintry, brumal, hibernal, boreal, arctic, antarctic, polar, Siberian, hyemal; hyperbore-an, -al; ice-bound; frozen out.

un-warmed, -thawed, -heated; isocheimal, -chimenal.

**Adv.** coldly, bitterly &c. *adj.*; *à pierre fendre.*

---

**384. Calefaction.**—**N.** increase of temperature; heating &c. *v.*; cale-, tepe-, torre-faction; melting, fusion; liquefaction &c. 335; burning &c. *v.*; kindling, combustion; in-, ac-cension; con-, cremation; scorification; cauter-y, -ization; ustulation, calcination; in-, cineration; cupellation; carbonization.

ignition, inflammation, adustion, flagration; de-, con-flagration; empyrosis, incendiarism; arson; *auto-da-fé*; suttee.

boiling &c. *v.*; coction, ebullition, estuation, elixation, decoction.

furnace &c. 386; blanket, flannel, fur, muffler, wrap; wadding &c. (*lining*) 224; clothing &c. 225.

match &c. (*fuel*) 388; incendiary, pyromaniac; *pétroleur*, *pétroleuse*; cauterant, caustic, lunar caustic, apozem, moxa.

sunstroke, *coup de soleil*; insolation, sunburn.

pottery, ceramics, crockery, porcelain. china; earthen-, stone-ware; pot-

**385. Refrigeration.**—**N.** refrigeration, infrigidation, reduction of temperature; cooling &c. *v.*; con-gelation, -glaciation; ice &c. 383; solidification &c. (*density*) 321; refrigerator &c. 387.

**V.** cool, fan, refrigerate, refresh, ice; congeal, freeze, glaciate; benumb. starve, pinch, chill, petrify, chill to the marrow, nip, cut, pierce, bite, make one's teeth chatter; damp.

Adj. cooled &c. *v.*; frozen out, cooling &c. *v.*; frigorific.

**Extinction.**—**N.** *extincteur*; fire, – engine, – extinguisher, – annihilator, – brigade, – man; sprinkler, hose, hydrant, standpipe.

incombusti-bility, -bleness &c. *adj.*

**V.** Quench, damp; blow-, put –, stamp – out; extinquish.

go –, burn-out.

Adj. incombustible; un-, unin-flammable; fire-proof.

---

mug, *terra-cotta,* brick, clinker; cinder, ash, *scoriæ*; embers, dross, slag, products of combustion, coke, carbon, charcoal.

inflamma-, combusti-bility.

[Transmission of heat] diathermancy, transcalency.

**V.** heat, warm, chafe, stive, foment; make -hot &c. 382; sun oneself, bask in the sun.

fire; set -fire to, - on fire; kindle, enkindle, light, ignite, strike a light; apply the -match, - torch- to; re-kindle, -lume; fan -, add fuel to- the flame; poke -, stir -, blow- the fire; make a bonfire of; burn at the stake.

melt, thaw, fuse; liquefy &c. 335.

burn, inflame, roast, toast, fry, grill, singe, parch, bake, torrefy, scorch; brand, cauterize, sear, burn in; corrode, char, carbonize, calcine, incinerate; smelt, cupel, scorify; reduce to ashes; burn to a cinder; commit -, consign- to the flames.

boil, digest, stew, cook, seethe, scald, parboil, simmer; do to rags.

take -, catch- fire; blaze &c. (*flame*) 382.

**Adj.** heated &c. *v.*; molten, sodden; *réchauffé*; heating &c. *v.*

inflammable, burnable, inflammatory, combustible; diatherm-al -anous; burnt &c. *v.*; volcanic.

**386. Furnace.—N.** furnace, blast furnace, fire-box, stove, incinerator, destructor, crematorium, crematory, kiln, oven, oast-house; hot-, bake-, wash-house; laundry; conservatory; hearth, focus; athanor, hypocaust, reverberatory; volcano; forge, fiery furnace; *tuyère,* brasier, salamander, heater, warming-pan, foot-warmer, hot-water bottle; radiator; boiler, geyser, caldron, seething caldron, pot; urn, kettle; chafing-dish; retort, crucible, alembic, still; saggar.

fire-place, -dog, -irons; hearth, ingle, grate, range, kitchener; kitchen range; oil-, gas-, electric, -cooker, -stove; fireless cooker; fire; galley; ca-, cam-boose; poker, tongs, shovel, hob, trivet; and-, grid-iron; frying-, stew-pan &c.

hot -, Turkish -, Russian -, vapour -, shower -, warm- bath; *calidarium, tepidarium, sudatorium,* sudatory; *hammam.*

**387. Refrigerator.—N.** refrigerator, -y; *frigidarium*; cold storage; refrigerating-plant, - machine; ice-house, -pail, -bag, -chest, -pack; cooler, damper; wine-cooler, freezing mixture.

*See* 385.

---

**388. Fuel.—N.** fuel, firing, combustible, coal, wallsend, anthracite, bituminous coal, slack, culm, cannel coal, lignite, briquette, coke, carbon, charcoal, turf, peat, fire-wood, bobbing, faggot, log, Yule log ember, cinder &c. (*products of combustion*) 384; kindling wood, tinder, touch-wood; fumigator, sulphur, brimstone; incense; port-fire; fire-barrel, -ball, -brand

fuel oil gas, gasoline.

brand, torch, fuse; wick; spill, match, safety match, light, lucifer, congreve, vesuvian, vesta, fusee, locofoco; linstock; illuminant.

candle &c. (*luminary*) 423; oil &c. (*grease*), 356; petrol, gasoline, methylated -, spirit; gas, acetylene.

**Adj.** carbonaceous; combustible, inflammable.

**V.** stoke, fire, feed, add fuel to the flames.

**389. Thermometer.—N.** thermo-meter, -scope, -stat, -pile, differential thermometer; pyro-, calori-meter; radio micrometer &c.

## 3. *Taste*

**390. Taste.—N.** taste, flavour, gust, *gusto*, relish, savour; sapor, sapidity; twang, smack, smatch; after-taste, tang.

tasting; de-, gustation.

palate, tongue, tooth, stomach.

**V.** taste, savour, smatch, smack, flavour, twang; tickle the palate &c. (*savoury*) 394; smack the lips.

**Adj.** sapid, saporific; gusta-ble, -tory; strong; flavoured, spiced, savoury; palatable &c. 394.

**391. Insipidity.—N.** insipidity; tastelessness &c. *adj.*

**V.** be -tasteless &c. *adj.*

**Adj.** void of -taste &c. 390; insipid; jejune; taste-, gust-, savour-less; ingustible, mawkish. milk and water, weak, stale, flat, vapid, *fade*, wishy-washy, mild; untasted.

---

**392. Pungency.—N.** pungency, piquancy, poignancy, *haut-goût*, strong taste, twang, race, tang.

sharpness &c. *adj.*; acrimony, acridity; roughness &c. (*sour*) 397; unsavouriness &c. 395.

nitre, saltpetre; mustard, cayenne, caviare; seasoning &c. (*condiment*) 393; brine.

dram, cordial, nip, pick-me-up, bracer, potion.

nicotine, tobacco, snuff, quid; segar; cigar, -ette, gasper, fag; cheroot; weed; fragrant –, Indian- weed; pipe, clay pipe, churchwarden, brier, meerschaum, hookah, hubble-bubble.

**V.** be -pungent &c. *adj.*; bite the tongue.

render -pungent &c. *adj.*; season, spice, salt, pepper, pickle, brine, devil, curry.

smoke, chew, take snuff.

**Adj.** pungent, strong; high-, full-flavoured; high-tasted, -seasoned; gamy; sharp, stinging, rough, *piquant*, racy; biting, mordant; spicy; seasoned &c. *v.*; hot, – as pepper; peppery, vellicating, escharotic, meracious; acrid, acrimonious, bitter; rough &c. (*sour*) 397; unsavoury &c. 395.

salt, saline, brackish, briny; salt as -brine, – a herring, – Lot's wife.

**393. Condiment.—N.** condiment, flavouring, salt, mustard, pepper, cayenne, curry, seasoning, sauce, spice, cinnamon, chillies, relish, *sauce piquante*, caviare, pot-herbs, onion, garlic, pickle, chutney, nutmeg &c.

**V.** season &c. (*render pungent*) 392.

**394. Savouriness.—N.** savouriness &c. *adj.*; relish, zest.

tit-bit, dainty, delicacy, ambrosia, nectar, *bonne bouche*; game, turtle, venison.

**V.** taste good, be -savoury &c. *adj.*; tickle the -palate, – appetite; flatter the palate.

render -palatable &c. *adj.*

relish, like, smack the lips.

**Adj.** savoury, well-tasted, to one's taste, tasty, good, palatable, nice, dainty, delectable; tooth-ful, -some;

**395. Unsavouriness.—N.** unsavouriness &c. *adj.*; amaritude; acri-mony, -tude; roughness &c. (*sour*) 397; acerbity, austerity; gall and worm-wood, rue, quassia, aloes; sickener.

**V.** be -unpalatable &c. *adj.*; sicken, disgust, nauseate, pall, turn the stomach.

**Adj.** un-savoury, -palatable, -sweet; ill-flavoured, un-appetizing, -eatable, inedible; bitter, – as gall; acrid, acrimonious; rough.

offensive, repulsive, nasty; sickening

gustful, appetizing, lickerish, delicate, delicious, exquisite, rich, luscious, ambrosial.

**Adv.** *per amusare la bocca.*

**Phr.** *cela se laisse manger.*

&c. *v.*; nauseous; loath-, ful-some; unpleasant &c. 830.

---

**396. Sweetness.**—**N.** sweetness, dulcitude, saccharinity.

sugar, cane-, beet-sugar; saccharine, glucose, syrup, treacle, molasses, honey, manna; confection, -ery; sweets, grocery, conserve, preserve, *confiture,* jam, marmalade, julep; sugar-candy, -plum; licorice, liquorice, plum, lollipop, *bonbon, jujube,* comfit, sweetmeat, caramel, toffee, butterscotch.

nectar; hydromel, mead, metheglin, honeysuckle, *liqueur,* sweet wine.

pastry, pie, tart, puff, pudding, cake.

dulc-ification, -oration.

**V.** be -sweet &c. *adj.*

render -sweet &c. *adj.*; sugar, saccharize, sweeten; edulcorate; dulc-orate, -ify; candy; mull.

**Adj.** sweet, sugary; sacchar-ine, -iferous; dulcet, honied, candied, luscious, nectarious, melliferous; sweetened &c. *v.*

sweet as -a nut, – sugar, – honey.

**397. Sourness.**—**N.** sourness &c. *adj.*; acid, -ity; acetous fermentation; acerbity.

vinegar, verjuice, crab, alum.

**V.** be –, turn- -sour &c. *adj.*; set the teeth on edge.

render -sour &c. *adj.*; acid-ify, -ulate.

**Adj.** sour; acid, -ulous, -ulated; acerb; tart, crabbed; acet-ous, -ose; sour as vinegar, sourish, acescent, sub-acid; styptic, hard, rough; unripe, green.

---

4. *Odour*

**398. Odour.**—**N.** odour, smell, odorament, scent, effluvium; eman-, exhal-ation; fume, essence, trail, nidor, redolence.

sense of smell; scent; act of -smelling &c. *v.*

**V.** have an -odour &c. *n.*; smell, – of, – strong of; exhale; give out a -smell &c. *n.*; scent.

smell, scent; snuff, – up; sniff, nose, inhale.

**Adj.** odor-ous, -iferous; smelling, strong-scented; redolent, graveolent, nidorous, pungent.

[Relating to the sense of smell] olfactory, quick-scented.

**399. Inodorousness.**—**N.** inodorousness; absence –, want- of smell.

**V.** be -inodorous &c. *adj.*; not smell.

deodorize.

**Adj.** inodor-ous, -ate; scentless; without –, wanting- smell &c. 398.

deodoriz-ed, -ing.

---

**400. Fragrance.** — **N.** fragrance, aroma, redolence, perfume, *bouquet*; sweet smell, aromatic perfume.

perfumery; incense; musk, frankincense; pastil, -le; myrrh, perfumes of Arabia, chypre; otto, ottar, attar; bergamot, balm, civet, *pot-pourri,* pulvil; nosegay, *boutonnière*; scent, -bag; *sachet,* scent-bottle, smelling bottle, *vinaigrette*; toilet water, *eau de Cologne*; thurible, censer, thurification.

perfumer; incense bearer.

**401. Fetor.**—**N.** fetor, fetidness; bad &c. *adj.*; -smell, – odour; stench, stink; mephitis, foul –, mal- odour; *empyreuma*; mustiness &c. *adj.*; rancidity; foulness &c. (*uncleanness*) 653.

stoat, polecat, skunk; assafœtida, fungus, garlic; stink-pot, -bomb.

**V.** have a -bad smell &c. *n.*; smell; stink, – in the nostrils, – like a polecat; smell -strong &c. *adj.*, – offensively.

**Adj.** fetid; strong-smelling; high, bad, strong, fulsome, offensive, noisome, rank, rancid, reasty, tainted, musty.

**V.** be -fragrant &c. *adj.*; have a -perfume &c. *n.*; smell sweet, scent, perfume, thurify, embalm.

**Adj.** fragrant, aromatic, redolent, spicy, balmy, scented; sweet-smelling, -scented; perfum-ed, -atory; thuriferous; fragrant as a rose, muscadine, ambrosial.

fusty, frouzy; olid, -ous; nidorous; smelling, stinking; putrid &c. 653; suffocating, mephitic; empyreumatic.

---

## 5. *Sound*

### (i.) Sound in General

**402. Sound.**—**N.** sound, noise, strain; accent, twang, intonation, tone, tune; cadence; sonority, sonorousness &c. *adj.*; audibility; resonance &c. 408; voice &c. 580.

[Science of sound] acou-, acu-stics; catacoustics, cataphonics; phon-ics, -etics, -ology, -ography; dia-coustics, -phonics.

telephone, phonograph &c. 418.

**V.** produce sound; sound, make a noise; give out –, emit- sound; phonetize, phonate; resound &c. 408.

**Adj.** sounding; soniferous; sonorific; resonant, audible, acoustic, auditory, distinct; stertorous; phonic, sonant; phonetic.

**403. Silence.**—**N.** silence; stillness &c. (*quiet*) 265; peace, hush, lull, rest; muteness &c. 581; solemn –, awful –, dead –, deathlike- silence.

**V.** be -silent &c. *adj.*; hold one's tongue &c. (*not speak*) 585.

render -silent &c. *adj.*; silence, still, hush; stifle, muffle, gag, stop; muzzle, put to silence &c. (*render mute*) 581.

**Adj.** silent; still, -y; calm, quiet; noise-, sound-, speech-less; hushed &c. *v.*; mute &c. 581; aphonic.

soft, solemn, awful, deathlike, silent as the grave; inaudible &c. (*faint*) 405.

**Adv.** silently &c. *adj.*; *sub silentio*; in perfect silence.

**Int.** hush! 'sh! silence! soft! whist! tush! chut! tut! *pax!* mum's the word! hold your tongue! shut up! be silent! be quiet! stop that noise! hold your row! dry up! peace, be still!

**Phr.** one might hear a -feather, – pin- drop.

**404. Loudness.**—**N.** loudness, power; loud noise, din; clang, -or; clatter, noise, bombilation, roar, uproar, racket, static, grinders, hubbub, *fracas, charivari*, trumpet blast, blare, flourish of trumpets, fanfare, *tintamarre*, peal, swell, blast, alarum, boom; resonance &c. 408.

vociferation; pandemonium, hullaballoo &c. 411; lungs; Stentor; megaphone; siren.

artillery, cannon, gunfire, shellburst, bomb; thunder.

**V.** be -loud &c. *adj.*; peal, swell, clang, boom, thunder, fulminate, roar; resound &c. 408; speak up, shout &c. (*vociferate*) 411; bellow &c. (*cry as an animal*) 412; give tongue.

rend the -air, – skies; fill the air; din –, ring –, thunder- in the ear;

**405. Faintness.**—**N.** faintness &c. *adj.*; faint sound, whisper, breath; under-tone, -breath; murmur, hum, rustle, buzz, purr; plash; sough, moan, sigh, susurration; tinkle; 'still small voice.'

hoarseness &c. *adj.*; raucity.

silencer, soft pedal, damper, mute, *sourdine*.

**V.** whisper, breathe, murmur, purl, hum, gurgle, ripple, babble, flow; tinkle; mutter &c. (*speak imperfectly*) 583.

steal on the ear; melt in –, float on- the air.

muffle, mute, deaden, damp, stifle.

**Adj.** inaudible; scarcely –, just- audible; low, dull; stifled, muffled; hoarse, husky; gentle, soft, faint; floating; purling, flowing &c. *v.*;

pierce –, split –, rend- the -ears, – head; deafen, stun; *faire le diable à quatre*; make one's windows shake; awaken –, startle- the echoes; make the welkin ring.

**Adj.** loud, sonorous; high-, big-sounding; blatant; deep, full, powerful, noisy, clangorous, multisonous, *fortissimo*; thundering, deafening &c. *v.*; trumpet-tongued; ear-splitting, -rending, -deafening; piercing; obstreperous, rackety, uproarious; enough to wake the -dead, – seven sleepers.

shrill &c. 410; clamorous &c. (*vociferous*) 411; stentor-ian, -ophonic.

**Adv.** loudly &c. *adj.*; aloud; at the top of one's voice, lustily, in full cry.

**Phr.** the air rings with.

whispered &c. *v.*; liquid; soothing; dulcet &c. (*melodious*) 413.

**Adv.** in a whisper, with bated breath, *sotto voce*, between the teeth, aside; *pian-o, -issimo*; *à la sourdine*; *con sordine*; out of earshot, inaudibly &c. *adj.*

(ii.) Specific Sounds*

**406.** [Sudden and violent sounds.] **Snap.**—**N.** snap &c. *v.*; rapping &c. *v.*; de-, crepitation; smack, clap, report; thud; burst, explosion, discharge, detonation, blow-out, back-fire, firing, salvo, volley, pistol-shot.

squib, cracker, gun, rifle, pop-gun.

**V.** rap, snap, tap, knock; click; clash; crack, -le; crash; pop; slam, bang, clap, thump, plump; toot; back-fire, explode, burst on the ear.

**Adj.** rapping &c. *v.*

**Int.** crash! bang!

**407.** [Repeated and protracted sounds.] **Roll.**—**N.** roll &c. *v.*; drumming &c. *v.*; tattoo; ding-dong; tantara; rataplan; whirr; rat-a-tat; rub-a-dub; pit-a-pat; quaver, clutter, *charivari*, racket; cuckoo; repetition &c. 104; peal of bells, devil's tattoo; reverberation &c. 408.

drumfire, barrage.

machine gun.

**V.** roll, drum, rumble, rattle, clatter, rustle, roar, drone, patter, clack.

hum, trill, shake; chime, peal, toll; tick, beat.

drum –, din- in the ear.

**Adj.** rolling &c. *v.*; monotonous &c. (*repeated*), 104; like a bee in a bottle.

**408. Resonance.**—**N.** resonance; ring &c. *v.*; ringing &c. *v.*; tintinnabulation; reflection, reverberation, clangor.

low –, base –, bass –, flat –, grave –, deep –, pedal- note; bass; *basso, – profondo*; bari-, bary-tone; *contralto*.

**V.** re-sound, -verberate, -echo; ring, ding, sing, jingle, gingle, chink, clink; tink, -le; chime; gurgle &c. 405; plash, guggle, echo, ring in the ear.

**Adj.** resounding &c. *v.*; resonant, tinnient, tintinnabulary; deep-toned, -sounding, -mouthed; hollow, sepulchral; gruff &c. (*harsh*) 410.

**408a. Non-resonance.** — **N.** thud, thump, dead sound; non-resonance; muffled drums, cracked bell; silencer, damper; mute, *sourdine*.

**V.** sound dead; stop –, damp- the -sound, – reverberations; deaden, muffle.

**Adj.** non-resonant, dead, muted, muffled.

**409.** [Hissing sounds.] **Sibilation.**—**N.** sibilation; hiss &c. *v.*; sternutation; high note &c. 410.

goose, serpent, snake.

* [The author's classification of sounds has been retained, though it does not entirely accord with the theories of modern science.—Ed.]

**V.** hiss, buzz, whiz, rustle; fizz, -le, sizzle, swish; wheeze, whistle, snuffle; squash; sneeze.

**Adj.** sibilant; hissing &c. *v.*; wheezy.

**410.** [Harsh sounds.] **Stridor.**—**N.** creak &c. *v.*; creaking &c. *v.*; discord &c. 414; stridor; harshness, roughness, sharpness &c. *adj.*; cacophony.

acute –, high- note; *soprano*, treble, tenor, *alto*, falsetto, *voce di testa*; shriek, cry &c. 411.

piccolo, fife, penny -whistle, – trumpet.

**V.** creak, grate, jar, burr, pipe, twang, jangle, clank, clink; scream &c. (*cry*) 411; yelp &c. (*animal sound*) 412; buzz &c. (*hiss*) 409.

set the teeth on edge, *écorcher les oreilles*; pierce –, split- the -ears, – head; offend –, grate upon –, jar upon- the ear.

**Adj.** creaking &c. *v.*; strident, stridulous, harsh, coarse, hoarse, horrisonous, raucous, metallic, rough, gruff, grum, sepulchral.

sharp, high, acute, shrill, high-pitched; trumpet-toned; piercing, ear-piercing; cracked; discordant &c. 414; cacophonous.

**411. Cry.**—**N.** cry &c. *v.*; voice &c. (*human*) 580; bark &c. (*animal*) 412.

vociferation, outcry, hullaballoo, chorus, clamour, hue and cry, plaint; lungs; stentor.

**V.** cry, roar, shout, bawl, brawl, halloo, halloa, hail, hoop, whoop, yell, bellow, howl, scream, screech, screak, shriek, shrill, squeak, squeal, squall, whine, whinny, pule, pipe, yaup.

cheer, hurrah; hoot; grumble, moan, groan.

snore, snort; grunt &c. (*animal sounds*) 412.

vociferate; raise –, lift up- the voice; call –, sing –, cry- out; exclaim; rend the air; thunder –, shout- at the -top of one's voice, – pitch of one's breath; *s'égosiller*; strain the -throat, – voice, – lungs; give a -cry &c.

**Adj.** crying &c. *v.*; clam-ant, -orous; vociferous; stentorian &c. (*loud*) 404; open-mouthed.

**412.** [Animal sounds.] **Ululation.**—**N.** cry &c. *v.*; crying &c. *v.*; ululation, latration, belling; reboation; call, note; bark, howl, yelp; twittering, woodnote; insect cry, fritinancy, drone; screech; cuckoo.

**V.** cry, ululate, howl, roar, bellow, blare, rebellow, bark, yelp; bay, – the moon; yap, growl, yarr, yawl, snarl, howl; grunt, -le; snort, squeak; neigh, bray; mew, mewl; purr, caterwaul, pule; bleat, low, moo; troat, croak, crow, screech, caw, coo, gobble, quack, cackle, gaggle, guggle; chuck, -le; cluck; clack; cheep, chirp, chirrup, twitter, sing, cuckoo; pout, wail, hum, buzz; hiss, blatter; hoot.

**Adj.** crying &c. *v.*; blatant, latrant; re-, mugient; deep-, full-mouthed.

**Adv.** in full cry.

### (iii.) Musical Sounds

**413. Melody. Concord.**—**N.** melody, rhythm, measure; rhyme &c. (*poetry*) 597.

pitch, *timbre*, intonation, tone, overtone.

scale, gamut; diapason; diatonic –, chromatic –, enharmonic- scale; key, clef, chords,

modulation, temperament, syncope, syncopation, preparation, suspension, resolution.

**414. Discord.**—**N.** discord, -ance; dissonance, cacophony, caterwauling; harshness &c. 410; consecutive fifths.

[Confused sounds] Babel, pandemonium; Dutch –, cat's- concert, marrow-bones and cleavers.

**V.** be -discordant &c. *adj.*; jar &c (*sound harshly*) 410.

**Adj.** discordant; dis-, ab-sonant; out of tune, tuneless; un-musical, -tunable; un-, im-melodious; un-, in-harmonious;

staff, stave, line, space, brace; bar, rest; *appogia-to, -tura; acciaccatura,* shake, *arpeggio.*

note, musical note, notes of a scale; sharp, flat, natural; high note &c. (*shrillness*) 410; low note &c. 408; interval; semitone; second, third, fourth &c.; diatessaron.

breve, semibreve, minim, crotchet, quaver; semi-, demisemiquaver; sustained note, drone, burden.

tonic; key-, leading-, fundamental- note; supertonic, mediant, dominant; sub-mediant, -dominant, organ-, pedal-point; octave, tetrachord; major –, minor- -mode, – scale, – key; Doric mode, passage, phrase.

concord, harmony; unison, -ance; chime, homophony; euphon-y, -ism; tonality; consonance; concent; part.

orchestration, harmonization, – phrasing.

[Science of harmony] harmon-y, -ics; thorough-, fundamental-bass; counterpoint; faburden.

piece of music &c. 415; composer, harmonist, contrapuntist.

**V.** be -harmonious &c. *adj.*; harmonize, chime, symphonize, transpose; put in tune, tune, accord, string; score, arrange, orchestrate.

**Adj.** harmoni-ous, -cal; in -concord &c. *n.*, – tune, – concert; unisonant, concentual, symphonizing, isotonic, homophonous, assonant, consonant.

measured, rhythmical, diatonic, chromatic, enharmonic.

melodious, musical; tuneful, tunable; sweet, dulcet, canorous; mell-ow, -ifluous; soft; clear, – as a bell; silvery; euphon-ious, -ic, -ical; symphonious; enchanting &c. (*pleasure-giving*) 829; fine-, full-, silver-toned.

**Adv.** harmoniously &c. *adj.*

sing-song; cacophonous; jarring, harsh &c. 410.

---

**415. Music.**—**N.** music, classical –, modern –, descriptive- music; concert, recital; strain, tune, air, *motif*; melody &c. 413; *aria, arietta*; piece of music, *sonata*; *rond-o, -eau*; *pastorale, cavatina,* roulade, *fantasia, toccata, concerto,* overture, symphony, symphonic poem, tone poem, prelude, voluntary, *intermezzo,* variations, *cadenza*; cadence; fugue, canon, serenade, *nocturne, notturno,* rhapsody, romance, *aubade,* dithyramb; opera, operetta; oratorio; composition, movement; stave.

instrumental music; full-, orchestral- score; minstrelsy, tweedledum and tweedledee, band, orchestra &c. 416; concerted piece, *potpourri,* medley, *capriccio,* incidental music; improvisation; peal.

vocal music, vocalism; chaunt, chant; psalm, -ody; hymn; song &c. (*poem*) 597; canticle, canzonet, *cantata, bravura, coloratura*; lay, ballad, ditty, carol, barcarolle, pastoral, recitative, *recitativo, solfeggio,* tonic sol-fa.

Lydian measures; slow -music, – movement; *adagio* &c. *adv.*; minuet; siren strains, soft music, lullaby; *berceuse,* cradle song, dump; dirge &c. (*lament*) 839; pibroch; martial music, march, funeral-, dead- march; dance music; waltz &c. (*dance*) 840; rag-time, syncopation, jazz.

solo, duet, *duo, trio*; quartet; quintet, sextet, septet; part song, descant, glee, madrigal, catch, round, chorus, *chorale*; antiphon, -y; accompaniment, second –, alto –, tenor –, bass- part; score, thorough bass; counterpoint.

composer &c. 413; musician &c. 416.

**V.** compose, perform &c. 416; attune.

**Adj.** musical; instrumental, orchestral, vocal, choral, lyric, operatic; harmonious &c. 413.

**Adv.** *adagio*; *largo*, *larghetto*, *andan-te*, *-tino*; *alla capella*; *maestoso*, *moderato*; *allegr-o*, *-etto*; *spiritoso*, *vivace*, *veloce*; *prest-o*, *-issimo*; *pian-o*, *-issimo*, *fort-e*, *-issimo*, *sforzando*; *con brio*; *capriccioso*; *scherz-o*, *-ando*; *legato*, *sostenuto*, *staccato*, *crescendo*, *diminuendo*, *rallentando*, *affettuoso*, *arioso*; *parlante*, *cantabile*; *obbligato*; *pizzicato*, *tremolo*, *vibrato*.

**416. Musician.** [Performance of Music.]—**N.** musician, *artiste*, *virtuoso*, performer, player, minstrel; bard &c. (*poet*) 597; instrumental-, organ-, accompan-, pian-, violin-, flaut-, harp-ist; harper, fiddler, fifer, trumpeter, piper, drummer; catgut scraper.

band, orchestra, waits.

vocal-, melod-ist; singer, warbler; songst-, chaunt-er, -ress; *diva*, *cantatrice*, coloratura, soprano, mezzo-soprano, alto, contralto, tenor, baritone, bass, *basso*, *-profondo*.

choir, quire, chorister; chorus, – singer; choral society, festival, *eisteddfod*.

nightingale, philomel, thrush; siren; Orpheus, Apollo, the Muses, Erato, Euterpe, Terpsichore; tuneful -nine, – quire.

composer &c. 413.

performance, virtuosity, execution, touch, expression, solmization.

**V.** play, pipe, strike –, tune- up, sweep the chords, tickle –, paw- the ivories, vamp, tweedle, fiddle; strike the lyre, beat the drum; blow –, sound –, wind- the horn; grind the organ; touch the -guitar &c. (*instruments*) 417; thrum, strum, twang, drum, beat –, keep- time, conduct.

execute, perform; accompany; sing –, play- a second; compose, write music, set to music, arrange, harmonize, orchestrate.

sing, chaunt, chant, hum, warble, carol, chirp, chirrup, lilt, purl, quaver, trill, shake, twitter, whistle; sol-fa; intone.

have -an ear for music, – a musical ear, – a correct ear, – absolute pitch.

**Adj.** playing &c. *v.*; musical, lyric.

**Adv.** *adagio*, *andante* &c. (*music*) 415.

**417. Musical Instruments.**—**N.** musical instruments; band; string- brass-, drum and fife-, military-, bugle-, German-, dance-, jazz-band, orchestra, string quartet; orchestrion, orchestrelle.

[Stringed instruments] mono-, poly-chord; harp, lyre, lute, archlute, theorbo; mandol-a, -in, -ine; guitar; *ukulele*; psaltery, zither; bandore, cither, -n; gittern, rebeck, *bandurria*, banjo, zither banjo, *balalaika*, *samisen*; plectrum.

viol, -in, Cremona, Stradivarius; fiddle, kit; *vielle*, *viola*, – *d'amore*, – *di gamba*; tenor, *violoncello*, cello; bass, bass-, base-viol; double-bass, *contrabasso*, *violone*, hurdy-gurdy; strings, catgut; bow, fiddlestick.

piano, -forte; grand –, concert grand –, baby –, upright –, cottage- piano; pianino, pianette; harpsi-, clavi-, clari-, mani-chord; *clavier*, spinet, virginals; dulcimer, *cymbalo*; Eolian harp; piano-organ, -player, electric piano, player-piano, pianola.

[Wind instruments] organ, church –, pipe –, American- organ; harmoni-um, -phon; accordion, seraphina, concertina; melodeon; barrel- organ; humming top.

flute, fife, piccolo, flageolet, penny-whistle, reed instrument; clari-net, -onet; bass clarionet; saxophone; basset horn, *corno di bassetto*; musette, shawm, oboe, hautboy, *cor Anglais*, *corno Inglese*, bassoon, double bassoon, *contrafagotto*; bag-, union-pipes; ocarina, Pandean pipes; calliope; sirene, pipe, pitch-pipe; sourdet; whistle, catcall.

horn, bugle, key bugle, cornet, *cornet-à-pistons*, cornopean, clarion, trumpet, trombone, ophicleide, serpent; English-, French-, bugle-, sax-, flugel-, alt-, helicon-, post-horn; sackbut, euphonium, bombardon, tuba, bass tuba.

[Vibrating surfaces] cymbal, bell, gong, peal of bells, *carillon*; tambour, -ine; drum, tom-tom, tab-or, -ret, -ourine, -orin; *sistrum*; *grande caisse*, bass-, big-, side-, kettle-drum; *tympani*; war drums; tymbal timbrel, castanet, bones; musical-glasses, -stones; harmonica, sounding-board, rattle; gramophone, phonograph.

[Vibrating bars] reed, tuning-fork, triangle, Jew's harp, musical box, harmonicon, xylophone, marimba, *celeste*.

sord-ine, -et; *sourd-ine, -et*; mute.

### (iv.) Perception of Sound

**418.** [Sense of sound.] **Hearing.—N.** hearing &c. *v.*; audition, auscultation; eavesdropping; audibility; acoustics &c. 402.

acute –, nice –, delicate –, quick –, sharp –, correct –, musical -ear; ear for music.

ear, auricle, lug, acoustic organs, auditory apparatus, ear-drum, tympanum; ear-, speaking-trumpet, megaphone; telephone, radiophone, stethoscope, phonograph, gramophone, microphone.

hearer, auditor, listener, eavesdropper; audi-tory, -ence.

**V.** hear, overhear; hark, -en; list, -en; give –, lend –, bend- an ear; give attention; catch a sound, prick up one's ears; give -a hearing, – audience- to.

hang upon the lips of, be all ear, listen with both ears.

become audible; meet –, fall upon –, catch –, reach- the ear; be heard; ring in the ear &c. (*resound*) 408.

**Adj.** hearing &c. *v.*; auditory, auricular, aural, auditive, acoustic.

**Adv.** *arrectis auribus.*

**Int.** hark, – ye! hear! list, -en! *Oyez!* attention! lend me your ears!

**419. Deafness.—N.** deafness, hardness of hearing, surdity; inaudibility.

**V.** be -deaf &c. *adj.*; have no ear; shut –, stop –, close- one's ears; turn a deaf ear to.

render deaf, stun, deafen.

**Adj.** deaf, earless, surd; hard –, dull- of hearing; deaf-mute, stunned, deafened; stone deaf; deaf as -a post, – an adder, – a beetle, – a trunk-maker.

inaudible &c. 405; out of hearing

## 6. *Light*

### (i.) Light in General

**420. Light.—N.** light, ray, beam, stream, gleam, streak, pencil; sun-, moon-beam; dawn, aurora.

day; sunshine; light of -day, – heaven; sun &c. (*luminary*) 423, day-, broad day-, noontide- light; noon-tide, -day; glare.

**421. Darkness.—N.** darkness &c. *adj.*; blackness &c. (*dark colour*) 431; obscurity, gloom, murk; dusk &c. (*dimness*) 422; tenebrosity, umbrageousness.

Cimmerian –, Stygian –, Egyptian- darkness; night; midnight; dead of –.

glow &c. *v.*; afterglow, sunset; glimmering &c. *v.*; glint; play –, flood- of light; phosphorescence, lambent flame.

flush, halo, glory, nimbus, aureole, *aureola.*

spark, *scintilla*; *facula*; sparkling &c. *v.*; emication, scintillation, flash, blaze, coruscation, fulguration; flame &c. (*fire*) 382; lightning, *ignis fatuus*, &c. (*luminary*) 423, radio-activity.

lustre, sheen, shimmer, reflection; gloss, tinsel, spangle, brightness, brilliancy, splendour; ef-, re-fulgence; ful-gor, -gidity; dazzlement, resplendence, transplendency; luminousness &c. *adj.*; luminosity; lucidity; renitency; radi-ance, -ation; irradiation, illumination, phosphorescence, luminescence.

radiation, radiant heat, infra-red rays, visible radiation, ultra-violet –, actinic- rays, actinism; X –, Roentgen-rays; phot-, heli-ography; optical instruments &c. 445.

[Science of light] optics; photo-logy, -metry; di-, cat-optrics.

[Distribution of light] *chiaroscuro*, *clair-obscur*, clear-obscure, breadth, light and shade, black and white, tonality, half-tone, mezzotint.

reflection, refraction, dispersion, double refraction, polarization, diffraction, interference.

illuminant &c. 423.

**V.** shine, glow, glitter, phosphoresce; glis-ter, -ten; twinkle, gleam; flare, – up; glare, beam, shimmer, glimmer, flicker, sparkle, scintillate, coruscate, flash, fulgurate, blaze; be -bright &c. *adj.*; reflect light, daze, dazzle, bedazzle, radiate, shoot out beams.

clear up, brighten.

lighten, enlighten; light, – up; irradiate, shine upon; give –, hang out- a light; cast –, throw –, shed- -lustre, – light- upon; illum-e, -ine, -inate; relume, strike a light; kindle &c. (*set fire to*) 384.

**Adj.** shining &c. *v.*; lumin-ous, -iferous; luc-id, -ent, -ulent, -ific, -iferous; illuminating, light, -some; bright, vivid, splendent, nitid, lustrous, shiny, brilliant, beamy, scintillant, radiant, lambent; sheen, -y; glossy, witching time of- night; blind man's holiday; darkness -visible, – that can be felt; palpable, obscure; Erebus.

shade, shadow, umbra, penumbra; sciagraphy; *silhouette*; radiograph, skiagraph.

obscuration; ad-, ob-umbration; obtenebration, offuscation, caligation; extinction; eclipse, total eclipse; gathering of the clouds.

shading; distribution of shade; *chiaroscuro* &c. (*light*) 420.

noctivagation, noctograph, noctuary. obscurantist.

**V.** be -dark &c. *adj.*

darken, obscure, shade; dim; tone down, lower; over-cast, -shadow; cloud, eclipse; ob-, of-fuscate; ob-, ad-umbrate, cast into the shade; be-cloud, -dim, -darken; cast –, throw –, spread- a -shade, – shadow, – gloom.

extinguish; put –, blow –, snuff- out; doubt.

**Adj.** dark, -some, -ling; obscure, tenebrous, tenebrious, sombrous, pitch dark, pitchy; caliginous; black &c. (*in colour*) 431.

sunless, lightless &c. (*see* sun, light, &c. 423); sombre, dusky; unilluminated &c. (*see* illuminate &c. 420); nocturnal; dingy, lurid, gloomy; murk-y, -some; shady, umbrageous; overcast &c. (*dim*) 422; cloudy &c. (*opaque*) 426; darkened &c. *v.*

dark as -pitch, – a pit, – Erebus.

benighted; noctivag-ant, -ous.

**Adv.** in the -dark, – shade; at night.

**422. Dimness.**—**N.** dimness &c. *adj.*; darkness &c. 421; paleness &c. (*light colour*) 429.

half-light, *demi-jour*; partial -shadow, – eclipse; shadow of a shade; glimmer, -ing; nebulosity; cloud &c. 353; eclipse.

aurora, dusk, twilight, gloaming, blind man's holiday, shades of evening, crepuscule, cockshut time; break of day, daybreak, dawn.

moon-light, -beam, -shine; star-, owl's-, candle-, rush-, fire-light; farthing candle.

**V.** be –, grow- -dim &c. *adj.*; flicker, twinkle, glimmer; loom, lower; fade; darken; pale, – its ineffectual fire.

burnished, glassy, sunny, orient, meridian; noon-day, -tide; cloudless, clear; un-clouded, -obscured.

garish; re-, tran-splendent; re-, effulgent; ful-gid, -gent; relucent, splendid, blazing, in a blaze, ablaze, rutilant, meteoric, phosphorescent; aglow.

bright as silver; light –, bright- as -day, – noonday, – the sun at noonday.

optical, actinic; photo-genic, -graphic; heliographic, radioactive.

render -dim &c. *adj.*; dim, bedim, obscure.

**Adj.** dim, dull, lack-lustre, dingy, darkish, shorn of its beams; dark 421.

faint, shadowed forth; glassy; bleary; cloudy; misty &c. (*opaque*) 426; muggy, fuliginous; nebul-ous, -ar; obnubilated, overcast, crepuscular, twilight, muddy, lurid, leaden, dun, dirty; looming &c. *v.*

pale &c. (*colourless*) 429; confused &c. (*invisible*) 447.

---

**423.** [Source of light &c.] **Luminary.** —**N.** luminary; light &c. 420; flame &c. (*fire*) 382.

spark, *scintilla*; phosphorescence.

sun, orb of day, day star, Phœbus, Apollo, Helios, Phaethon, Hyperion, Ra, Aurora; star, orb, meteor; falling –, shooting- star; blazing –, dog- star; Sirius, canicula, Aldebaran; morning star, Lucifer, Phosphor, evening star; Hesperus, Venus, planet, moon &c. 318; constellation, galaxy; northern light, *aurora -borealis, – australis*, zodiacal light; mock sun, parhelion.

lightning; fork –, sheet –, summer- lightning, St. Elmo's fire; phosphorus; *ignis fatuus*; Jack o' –, Friar's- lantern; Will o' the wisp, fire-drake, *Fata Morgana*.

glow-worm, fire-fly.

radium, luminous paint.

[Artificial light] gas; gas –, lime –, electric –, head –, search –, spot –, flash –, flood –, foot-light; lamp, oil –, gas –, arc –, incandescent- lamp; flare; lant-ern, -horn; dark lantern, bull's eye, projector; candle, *bougie*, tallow –, wax- candle; dip, farthing dip; taper, rush-light; oil &c. (*grease*) 356; wick, burner; Argand, moderator, duplex; torch, *flambeau*, link, brand; cresset; gase-, chande-, electro-lier; candelabrum, *girandole*, sconce, lustre, candle-stick.

firework, fizgig; pyrotechnics; Roman candle, Véry light, star shell, parachute light; rocket, lighthouse &c. (*signal*) 550.

**V.** illuminate &c. (*light*) 420.

**Adj.** self-luminous, incandescent; phosphor-ic, -escent; luminescent, fluorescent, radiant &c. (*light*) 420.

**424.** **Shade.**—**N.** shade; awning &c. (*cover*) 223; parasol, sunshade, umbrella; screen, curtain, shutter, blind, gauze, veil, mantle, mask; cloud, mist, gathering of clouds; smoke screen; smoked glasses, coloured spectacles; blinkers, blinders.

umbrage, glade; shadow &c. 421.

**V.** draw a curtain; put up –, close- a shutter; veil &c. *v.*; cast a shadow &c. (*darken*) 421; screen, obstruct the view.

**Adj.** shady, umbrageous, bowery.

---

**425.** **Transparency.** — **N.** transparen-ce, -cy; translucen-ce, -cy; diaphaneity; luc-, pelluc-, limp-idity.

transparent medium, glass, crystal, mica; lymph, water.

**V.** be -transparent &c. *adj.*; transmit light.

**Adj.** transparent, pellucid, lucid, diaphanous; trans-, tra-lucent; limpid, clear, serene, crystalline, clear as crys-

**426.** **Opacity.**—**N.** opacity; opaqueness &c. *adj.*

film; cloud &c. 353.

**V.** be -opaque &c. *adj.*; obstruct the passage of light; ob-, of-fuscate.

**Adj.** opaque, impervious to light.

dim &c. 422; turbid, thick, muddy, opacous, obfuscated, fuliginous, cloudy, hazy, foggy, vaporous, nubiferous, muggy.

tal, vitreous, transpicuous, glassy, hyaline.

smoky, fumid, murky, dirty.

**427. Semitransparency.—N.** semitransparency, opalescence, milkiness, pearliness; gauze, muslin; film; mist &c. (*cloud*) 353; frosted glass.

**Adj.** semi-transparent, -pellucid, -diaphanous, -opacous, -opaque; opal-escent, -ine; pearly, milky, frosted, mat; misty.

## (ii.) Specific Light

**428. Colour.—N.** colour, hue, tint, tinge, dye, complexion, shade, tincture, cast, livery, coloration, chromatism, glow, flush; tone, key.

pure –, positive –, primary –, primitive –, complementary- colour; three primaries; spectrum, chromatic dispersion; broken –, secondary –, tertiary- colour.

local colour, colouring, keeping, tone, value, aerial perspective.

[Science of colour] chromatics, spectrum analysis; prism, spectroscope.

pigment, colouring matter, paint, dye, wash, distemper, stain; medium; mordant; oil-paint &c. (*painting*) 556.

**V.** colour, dye, tinge, stain, tint, tinct, tone, paint, wash, ingrain, grain, illuminate, emblazon, imbue; paint &c. (*fine art*) 556; daub.

**Adj.** coloured &c. *v.*; colorific, tingent, tinctorial; chromatic, prismatic; full-, high-, deep-coloured; doubly-dyed; polychromatic.

bright, vivid, intense, deep; fresh, unfaded; rich, gorgeous; highly coloured; gay; variegated &c. 440.

gaudy, florid; garish; showy, flaunting, flashy; raw, crude; glaring, flaring; discordant, inharmonious.

mellow, harmonious, pearly, sweet, delicate, tender, refined.

**429.** [Absence of colour.] **Achromatism.—N.** achromatism; de-, discoloration; pall-or, -idity; paleness &c. *adj.*; etiolation; neutral tint, monochrome, black-and-white.

**V.** lose -colour &c. 428; fade, fly, go; become -colourless &c. *adj.*; turn pale, pale, whiten.

deprive of colour, decolorize, bleach, tarnish, achromatize, blanch, etiolate, wash out, tone down.

**Adj.** uncoloured &c. (*see* colour &c. 428); colourless, achromatic, hueless, pale, pallid; pale-, tallow-faced; faint, dull, cold, muddy, leaden, dun, wan, sallow, dead, dingy, ashy, ashen, ghastly, cadaverous, glassy, lack-lustre; discoloured &c. *v.*

light-coloured, fair, *blond*; white &c. 430.

pale as -death, – ashes, – a witch, – a ghost, – a corpse.

**430. Whiteness.—N.** whiteness &c. *adj.*; argent.

albification, albescence, albinism, etiolation.

snow, paper, chalk, milk, lily, ivory, silver, alabaster; white lead, chinese –, flake –, ivory –, zinc- white, white-wash, -ning, whiting.

**V.** be -white &c. *adj.*

render -white &c. *adj.*; whiten-bleach, blanch, etiolate, whitewash, silver, frost.

**Adj.** white; milky, milk-, snow-white; snowy, niveous, candid, chalky; hoar,

**431. Blackness.—N.** blackness &c. *adj.*; darkness &c. (*want of light*) 421; swarthness, lividity, dark colour, tone, colour; *chiaroscuro* &c. 420.

nigrification, infuscation, denigration.

jet, ink, ebony, coal, pitch, soot, smudge, charcoal, sloe, raven, crow; negro, blackamoor, man of colour, nigger, darky, Ethiopian, black.

[Pigments] lamp –, ivory –, blue-black; writing –, printing –, printer's –, Indian- ink.

**V.** be -black &c. *adj.*

-y; frosted, silvery; argent, -ine; incanescent.

whitish, creamy, pearly, ivory, fair, *blond*, ash-blond, platinum blond; blanched &c. *v.*; high in tone, light.

white as -a sheet, – driven snow, – a lily – silver; like -ivory &c. *n.*

---

render -black &c. *adj.*; blacken, infuscate, denigrate; blot, -ch; smutch; smirch; darken &c. 421.

**Adj.** black, sable, swarthy, sombre, dark, inky, ebon, atramentous, jetty; coal-, jet-black; fuliginous, pitchy, sooty, swart, dusky, dingy, murky, Ethiopic; low-toned, low in tone; of the deepest dye.

black as -jet &c. *n.*, – my hat, – a shoe, – a tinker's pot, – November, – thunder, – midnight; nocturnal &c. (*dark*) 421; nigrescent; gray &c. 432; obscure &c. 421.

**Adv.** in mourning.

**432. Gray.—N.** gray &c. *adj.*; neutral tint, silver, pepper and salt, *chiaroscuro*, *grisaille*, grayness.

[Pigments] Payne's gray; black &c. 431.

**Adj.** gray, grey; steel –, iron- gray, dun, drab, dingy, leaden, livid, sombre, sad, pearly; silver, -y, -ed; ash-en, -y; ciner-eous, -itious; grizzl-y, -ed; dove-, slate-, stone-, mouse-, ash-coloured; mole; cool.

---

**433. Brown.—N.** brown &c. *adj.*

[Pigments] bistre, ochre, sepia, Vandyke brown.

**Adj.** brown, adust, bay, dapple, auburn, chestnut, nutbrown, cinnamon, hazel, fawn, puce, *écru*, russet, tawny, fuscous, chocolate, maroon, foxy, tan, brunette, whitey-brown; snuff-, liver-coloured; brown as -a berry, – mahogany; reddish brown; copper-, rust- coloured; henna, bronze, khaki; roan, sorrel.

sun-burnt; tanned &c. *v.*

**V.** render -brown &c. *adj.*; tan, embrown, bronze.

*Primitive Colours**

**434. Redness.—N.** red, scarlet, vermilion, cardinal, Post Office red, carmine, crimson, pink, lake, *cerise*, cherry red, maroon, carnation, *couleur de rose*, *rose du Barry*; magenta, damask; flesh -colour, – tint; colour; fresh –, high-colour; warmth; gules.

ruby, garnet, carbuncle; rose; rust, iron-mould.

[Dyes and pigments] cinnabar, cochineal; fuchsine; ruddle, madder, red-lead; Indian –, light –, Venetian- red; red ink, annotto.

redness &c. *adj.*; rub-escence, -icundity, -ification; erubescence, blush.

**V.** be –, become- -red &c. *adj.*; blush, flush, colour up, mantle, redden.

render -red &c. *adj.*; redden, rouge; rub-ify, -ricate; incarnadine; ruddle.

**Adj.** red &c. *n.*, -dish; rufous, ruddy, florid, incarnadine, sanguine, bloody, gory; ros-y, -eate; blowz-y, -ed; burnt; rubi-cund, -form;

*Complementary Colours*

**435. Greenness.—N.** green &c. *adj.*; blue and yellow; vert.

emerald, verd antique, verdigris, malachite, beryl, aquamarine, reseda.

[Pigments] *terre verte*, verditer, bice-chlorophyl.

greenness, verdure, verdancy; viridity, -escence.

**Adj.** green, verdant; glaucous, olive; porraceous; green as grass.

emerald –, pea –, grass –, apple –, sea –, olive –, bottle –, leaf- green.

greenish; vir-ent, -escent.

---

* The author's classification of colours has been retained, though it does not entirely accord with the theories of modern science: Complete lists of shades or pigments are beyond the scope of this work.

lurid, stammel, blood-red; russet, murrey, carroty, sorrel, lateritious.
rose-, ruby-, cherry-, claret-, wine-, plum-, flame-, flesh-, peach-, salmon-, brick-, brickdust-coloured, reddish brown &c. 433.
blushing &c. *v.*; erubescent; reddened &c. *v.*
red as -fire, – blood, – scarlet, – a turkeycock, – a lobster; warm, hot; foxy.

**436. Yellowness.**—**N.** yellow &c. *adj.*; or.
[Pigments] gamboge; cadmium –, chrome –, Indian –, lemon- yellow; orpiment, yellow ochre, Claude tint, aureolin.
crocus, saffron, topaz, gold.
jaundice; London fog; yellowness &c. *adj.*
**Adj.** yellow, aureate, gold, golden, gilt, gilded, flavous, citrine, fallow; fulv-ous, -id; sallow, luteous, tawny, creamy, sandy; xanth-ic, -ous; jaundiced.
gold-, citron-, saffron-, lemon-, sulphur-, amber-, straw-, primrose-, cream-coloured; flaxen, yellowish, buff.
yellow as a -quince, – guinea, – crow's foot.

**437. Purple.**—**N.** purple &c. *adj.*; blue and red, bishop's purple; aniline dyes, gridelin, amethyst; purpure.
livid-ness, -ity.
**V.** empurple.
**Adj.** purple, violet, plum-coloured. lavender, lilac, puce, *mauve*; livid.

**438. Blueness.**—**N.** blue &c. *adj.*; garter-blue; watchet.
[Pigments] ultramarine, smalt, cobalt, cyanogen; Prussian –, syenite-blue; bice, indigo, woad.
*lapis lazuli*, sapphire, turquoise.
blue-, bluish-ness; bloom.
**Adj.** blue, azure, cerulean; sky-blue, -coloured, -dyed; navy-blue, aquamarine, electric blue, royal blue, cyanic; bluish; atmospheric, retiring; cold.

**439. Orange.**—**N.** orange, red and yellow; gold; or; flame &c. colour, *adj.*
[Pigments] ochre, Mars orange, cadmium.
**V.** gild, warm.
**Adj.** orange; ochreous; orange-, gold-, flame-, copper-, brass-, apricot-coloured; warm, hot, glowing.

**440. Variegation.**—**N.** variegation; di-, tri-chroism; iridescence, irisation, play of colours, polychrome, maculation, spottiness, striæ.
spectrum, rainbow, iris, tulip, peacock, chameleon, butterfly, tortoiseshell; mackerel, – sky; zebra, leopard, mother-of-pearl, nacre, opal, marble, batik.
check, plaid, tartan, patchwork; mar-, par-quetry; mosaic, *tesseræ*, tesselation, chess-board, checkers, chequers; harlequin; Joseph's coat; tricolour; patches, bands, stripes, spots &c. of colour.
**V.** be -variegated &c. *adj.*; variegate, stripe, streak, checker, chequer; be-, speckle, fleck; be-, sprinkle; stipple, maculate, dot, bespot; tattoo, inlay, tesselate, damascene; embroider, braid, quilt.
**Adj.** variegated &c. *v.*; many-coloured, -hued; divers-, parti-coloured; di-, poly-chromatic; bi-, tri-, versi-colour; of all -the colours of the rainbow, – manner of colours; kaleidoscopic.
iridescent; opal-ine, -escent; prismatic, nacreous, pearly, shot, *gorge de pigeon*, *chatoyant*, irisated.
pied, piebald, skewbald; motley; mottled, marbled; pepper and salt, paned, dappled, clouded, cymophanous.
mosaic, tesselated, chequered, plaid; tortoiseshell &c. *n.*
spott-ed, -y; punctated, powdered; speckled &c. *v.*; freckled, flea-

bitten, studded; fleck-ed, -ered; striated, barred, veined; brind-ed, -led; tabby; watered; grizzled; listed; embroidered &c. *v.*; dædal.

(iii.) Perceptions of Light

**441. Vision.**—**N.** vision, sight, optics, eye-sight.

view, look, espial, glance, ken, *coup d'œil*; glimpse, peep, glint; gaze, stare, leer; perlustration, contemplation; conspect-ion, -uity; regard, survey; in-, intro-spection; *reconnaissance*, speculation, watch, espionage, *espionnage*, autopsy; ocular -inspection, – demonstration; sight-seeing.

macrography, micrography.

point of view; view-, stand-point; gazebo, loop-hole, *belvedere*, watch-tower.

field of view; theatre, amphitheatre, arena, vista, horizon; commanding –, bird's eye –, panoramic- view; periscope.

visual organ, organ of vision; eye; naked –, unassisted- eye; eye-ball, retina, pupil, iris, cornea, white; optics, orbs; saucer –, goggle –, gooseberry- eyes.

short sight &c. 443; clear –, sharp –, quick –, eagle –, piercing –, penetrating- -sight, – glance, – eye; perspicacity, discernment; catopsis.

eagle, hawk; cat, lynx; Argus.

evil eye; basilisk, cockatrice.

spectacles, telescope &c. 445.

**V.** see, behold, discern, perceive, have in sight, descry, sight, make out, discover, distinguish recognize, spy, espy, ken; get –, have –, catch- a -sight, – glimpse- of; command a view of; witness, contemplate, speculate; cast –, set- the eyes on; be a -spectator &c. 444- of; look on &c. (*be present*) 186; see sights &c. (*curiosity*) 455; see at a glance &c. (*intelligence*) 498.

look, view, eye; lift up the eyes, open one's eye; look -at, – on, – upon, – over, – about one, – round; survey, scan, inspect; run the eye -over, – through; reconnoitre, glance -round, – on, – over; turn –, bend- one's looks upon; direct the eyes to, turn the eyes on, cast a glance, make eyes at.

observe &c. (*attend to*) 457; watch &c. (*care*) 459; see with one's own eyes; watch for &c. (*expect*) 507; peek, peep, peer, pry, take a peep; play at bo-peep.

look -full in the face, – hard at, – intently; strain one's eyes; fix –, rivet- the eyes upon; stare, gaze; pore over, gloat -over, – on; leer, ogle, glare; goggle; cock the eye, squint, gloat, look askance; give the glad eye.

**Adj.** seeing &c. *v.*; visual, ocular, -al; ophthalmic.

far-, clear-sighted &c. *n.*; eagle-, hawk-, lynx-, keen-, Argus-eyed visible &c. 446.

**442. Blindness.**—**N.** blindness, anopsia, cecity, excecation, *amaurosis*, cataract, ablepsy, prestriction; dim-sightedness &c. 443.

**V.** be -blind &c. *adj.*; not see; lose sight of; have the eyes bandaged; grope in the dark.

not look; close –, shut –, turn away –, avert- the eyes; look another way; wink &c. (*limited vision*) 443; shut the eyes –, be blind- to; wink –, blink- at.

render -blind &c. *adj.*; blind, -fold; hoodwink, dazzle; put one's eyes out; throw dust into one's eyes; *jeter de la poudre aux yeux*; screen from sight &c. (*hide*) 528.

**Adj.** blind; eye-, sight-, vision-less; dark; stone-, sand-, stark-blind; undiscerning; dim-sighted &c. 443.

blind as -a bat, – a buzzard, – a beetle, – a mole, – an owl; wall-eyed.

blinded &c. *v.*

**Adv.** blind-ly, -fold; darkly.

---

**Adv.** visibly &c. 446; in sight of, with one's eyes open.
at -sight, – first sight, – a glance, – the first blush; *primâ facie.*
**Int.** look! &c. (*attention*) 457.
**Phr.** the scales falling from one's eyes.

**443.** [Imperfect vision.] **Dim-sightedness.** [Fallacies of vision.]—**N.** dim –, dull –, half –, short –, near –, long –, double –, astigmatic –, failing- sight; dim &c. -sightedness; snow blindness; purblindness, lippitude; my-, presby-opia; confusion of vision; astigmatism, nystagmus; colour-blindness, dichromism, chromato-pseudo-blepsis, Daltonism; nyctalopy; *strabismus*, strabism, squint, cast in the eye, swivel eye, goggle eyes; obliquity of vision.

winking &c. *v.*; nictitation; blinkard, albino.

dizziness, swimming, scotomy; cataract; ophthalmia.

[Limitation of vision] eye shade, blinker, blinder; screen &c. (*hider*) 530.

[Fallacies of vision] *deceptio visûs*; refraction, distortion, illusion, false light, *anamorphosis*, virtual image, *spectrum, mirage*, looming, phasma; phant-asm, -asma, -om; vision; spectre, apparition, ghost; *ignis fatuus* &c. (*luminary*) 423; spectre of the Brocken; magic mirror; magic lantern &c. (*show*) 448; mirror, lens &c. (*instrument*) 445.

**V.** be -dim-sighted &c. *n.*; see double; have a -mote in the eye, – mist before the eyes, – film over the eyes; see through a -prism, – glass darkly; wink, blink, nictitate; squint; look ask-ant, -ance; screw up the eyes, glare, glower.

dazzle, glare, blur, swim, loom.

**Adj.** dim-sighted &c. *n.*; my-, presby-opic; astigmatic; moon-, mope-, blear-, goggle-, gooseberry-, one-eyed; blind of one eye, monoculous; half-, pur-, colour-blind; dichromatic.

blind as a bat &c. (*blind*) 442; winking &c. *v.*

**444. Spectator.**—**N.** spectator, beholder, observer, inspector, viewer, looker-on, onlooker, witness, eye-witness, bystander, passer by; sight-seer.

spy, scout; sentinel &c. (*warning*) 668.

**V.** witness, behold &c. (*see*) 441; look on &c. (*be present*) 186.

**445. Optical Instruments.**—**N.** optical instruments; lens, meniscus, magnifier, reading –, burning- glass; micro-, mega-, teino-scope; spectacles, glasses, barnacles, goggles, giglamps, eyeglass, *pince-nez*, monocle; periscopic lens; telescope, glass, lorgnette, binocular; spy-, opera-, field-glass, periscope, range finder.

mirror, reflector, speculum; looking-, pier-, cheval-, hand-glass.

prism; camera, *camera-lucida, -obscura*; projector, stereopticon, magic lantern &c. (*show*) 448; chro-, thau-matrope; stereo-, pseudo-, poly-, kaleido-scope.

photo-, opto-, erio-, actino-, luci-, radio-, spectro-meter; polari-, polemo-, spectro-scope, diffraction grating.

optics, optician, optometry, optometrist; microscop-y, -ist; photometry, photography; photographer.

**446. Visibility.**—**N.** visibility, perceptibility; conspicuousness, distinctness &c. *adj.*; conspicuity; appearance &c. 448; exposure; manifestation &c. 525; ocular -proof, – evidence, – demonstration; field of view &c. (*vision*) 441.

**447. Invisibility.**—**N.** invisibility, non-appearance, imperceptibility; indistinctness &c. *adj.*; mystery, delitescence.

concealment &c. 528; latency &c. 526.

V. be –, become- -visible &c. *adj.*; appear, emerge, open to the view; meet –, catch- the eye; present –, show –, manifest –, produce –, discover –, reveal –, expose –, betray- itself; stand -forth, – out; show; arise; peep –, peer –, crop- out; start –, spring –, show –, turn –, crop- up; glimmer, glitter, glow, loom; glare; burst forth, scintillate; burst upon the -view, – sight; heave in sight; come -in sight, – into view, – out, – forth, – forward; see the light of day; break through the clouds; make its appearance, show its face, materialize, appear to one's eyes, come upon the stage, enter; float before the eyes, speak for itself &c. (*manifest*) 525; attract the attention &c. 457; reappear; live in a glass house.

expose to view &c. 525.

**Adj.** visible, perceptible, perceivable, discernible, apparent; in -view, – full view, – sight; exposed to view, *en évidence*; unclouded.

obvious &c. (*manifest*) 525; plain, clear, distinct, definite; well-defined, -marked; in focus; recognizable, palpable, autoptical; glaring, staring, conspicuous; stereoscopic; in -bold, – strong, – high- relief.

periscopic, panoramic.

before –, under- one's eyes; before one, *à vue d'œil*, in one's eye, *oculis subjecta fidelibus*.

**Adv.** visibly &c. *adj.*; in sight of; before one's eyes &c. *adj.*; *veluti in speculum.*

V. be -invisible &c. *adj.*; be hidden &c. (*hide*) 528; lurk &c. (*lie hidden*) 526; escape notice.

render -invisible &c. *adj.*; conceal &c. 528; put out of sight.

not see &c. (*be blind*) 442; lose sight of.

**Adj.** invisible, imperceptible; un-, in-discernible; un-, non-apparent; out of –, not in- sight; *à perte de vue*; behind the -scenes, – curtain; view-, sight-less; in-, un-conspicuous; unseen &c. (*see* see &c. 441); covert &c. (*latent*) 526; eclipsed, under an eclipse.

dim &c. (*faint*) 422; mysterious, dark, obscure, confused; indistin-ct, -guishable; shadowy, indefinite, undefined; ill-defined, -marked; blurred, fuzzy, out of focus; misty &c. (*opaque*) 426; veiled &c. (*concealed*) 528; delitescent.

---

**448. Appearance.—N.** appearance, phenomenon, sight, spectacle, show, premonstration, scene, species, view, *coup d'œil*; look-out, out-look, prospect, vista, perspective, bird's-eye view, scenery, landscape, picture, *tableau*; display, exposure, *mise en scène*; scenery, *décor*; rising of the curtain.

phant-asm, -om &c. (*fallacy of vision*) 443.

pageant, *spectacle*; peep-, raree-, gallanty-show; *ombres chinoises*; projector, optical –, magic- lantern, phantasmagoria, dissolving views; cinema, -tograph; bio-scope, -graph; moving pictures, movies, film, screen &c.; pan-, di-, cosm-, ge-orama; *coup* –, *jeu- de théâtre*; pageantry &c. (*ostentation*) 882; insignia &c. (*indication*) 550.

aspect, phase, *phasis*, seeming; shape &c. (*form*) 240; guise, look,

**449. Disappearance.—N.** disappearance, evanescence, eclipse, occultation.

departure &c. 293; exit, vanishing point; dissolving views.

**V.** disappear, vanish, dissolve, fade, melt away, pass, go, avaunt; be -gone &c. *adj.*; leave -no trace, – 'not a rack behind'; go off the stage &c. (*depart*) 293; suffer –, undergo- an eclipse; be lost to –, retire from- -sight, – view.

lose sight of.

efface &c. 552.

**Adj.** disappearing &c. *v.*; evanescent; missing, lost; lost to -sight, – view; gone; *spurlos versenkt*.

**Int.** vanish! disappear! avaunt! &c. (*ejection*) 297.

---

complexion, colour, image, mien, air, cast, carriage, port, demeanour; presence, expression, first blush, face of the thing; point of view, light.

lineament, feature, trait, lines; out-line, -side; contour, *silhouette*, face, countenance, physiognomy, visage, phiz, mug, cast of countenance, profile, *tournure*, cut of one's jib, metoposcopy; outside &c. 220.

**V.** appear; be –, become- visible &c. 446; seem, look, show; present –, wear –, carry –, have –, bear –, exhibit –, take –, take on –, assume- the -appearance, – semblance- of; look like; cut a figure, figure; present to the view; show &c. (*make manifest*) 525.

**Adj.** apparent, seeming, ostensible; on view.

**Adv.** apparently; to all -seeming, – appearance; ostensibly, seemingly, as it seems, on the face of it, *primâ facie*; at the first blush, at first sight; in the eyes of; to the eye.

# CLASS IV

## WORDS RELATING TO THE INTELLECTUAL FACULTIES

## DIVISION (I.) FORMATION OF IDEAS

### Section I. OPERATIONS OF INTELLECT IN GENERAL

**450. Intellect.—N.** intellect, mind, understanding, reason, thinking principle; rationality; cogitative –, cognitive –, intellectual- faculties; faculties, senses, consciousness, observation, percipience, apperception, mentality, intelligence, intellection, intuition, association of ideas, instinct, flair, conception, judgement, wits, parts, capacity, intellectuality, reasoning power, brains, genius; wit &c. 498; ability &c. (*skill*) 698; wisdom &c. 498.

soul, spirit, ghost, inner man, heart, breast, bosom, *penetralia mentis, divina particula auræ*, heart's core; ego, psyche, pneuma, subconsciousness, subconscious, subliminal self; dual personality.

organ –, seat- of thought; *sensorium*, sensory, brain, gray matter; head, -piece; pate, noddle, skull, scull, *pericranium, cerebrum, cranium*, brain-pan, -box; sconce, upper story.

[Science of mind] metaphysics; psychics, psycho-logy, -metry, -genesis, -analysis, -physics, psychi-atry, -cal research, thought reading &c. 992; ideology; mental –, moral- philosophy; philosophy of the mind; pneumat-, phren-ology; no –, cranio-logy, -scopy.

ideal-ity, -ism; transcendental-, spiritual-ism; immateriality &c. 317.

metaphysician, psychologist &c.

**V.** note, notice, mark; take -notice, – cognizance- of; be -aware, - conscious- of; realize; appreciate; ruminate &c. (*think*) 451; fancy &c. (*imagine*) 515; conceive, reason, understand.

**Adj.** [Relating to intellect] intellectual, mental, rational, subjective, metaphysical, nooscopic, spiritual; ghostly; psych-ical, -ological; cerebral.

immaterial &c. 317; endowed with reason.

**Adv.** *in petto.*

**450a. Absence or want of Intellect.—N.** absence –, want- of -intellect &c. 450; imbecility &c. 499; brutality; brute -instinct, – force.

**Adj.** unendowed with reason.

---

**451. Thought.—N.** thought; exercitation –, exercise- of the intellect; reflection, cogitation, consideration, meditation, study, lucubration, speculation, deliberation, pondering; head-,

**452.** [Absence or want of thought.] **Incogitancy.—N.** incogitancy, vacancy, inunderstanding; inanity, fatuity &c. 499; thoughtlessness &c. (*inattention*) 458.

brain-work; cerebration; mentation, deep reflection; close study, application &c. (*attention*) 457.

abstract thought, abstraction, contemplation, musing; brown study &c. (*inattention*) 458; reverie, Platonism; depth of thought, workings of the mind, thoughts, inmost thoughts; self-counsel, -communing, -consultation.

association –, succession –, flow –, train –, current- of -thought, – ideas.

after –, mature- thought; reconsideration, second thoughts; retrospection &c. (*memory*) 505; excogitation; examination &c. (*inquiry*) 461; invention &c. (*imagination*) 515.

thoughtfulness &c. *adj.*

**V.** think, reflect, reason, cogitate, excogitate, consider, deliberate; bestow -thought, – consideration- upon; speculate, contemplate, meditate, ponder, muse, dream, ruminate; brood –, con- over; animadvert, study; bend –, apply- the mind &c. (*attend*) 457; digest, discuss, hammer at, weigh, perpend; realize, appreciate; fancy &c. (*imagine*) 515; trow.

take into consideration; take counsel &c. (*be advised*) 695; commune with –, bethink- oneself; collect one's thoughts; revolve –, turn over –, run over- in the mind; chew the cud –, sleep- upon; take counsel of –, advise with- one's pillow.

rack –, ransack –, crack –, beat –, cudgel- one's brains; set one's -brain, – wits- to work.

harbour –, entertain –, cherish –, nurture- an -idea &c. 453; take into one's head; bear in mind; reconsider.

occur; present –, suggest- itself; come –, get- into one's head; strike one, flit across the view, come uppermost, run in one's head; enter –, pass in –, cross –, flash on –, flash across –, float in –, fasten itself on –, be uppermost in –, occupy- the mind; have in one's mind.

make an impression; sink –, penetrate- into the mind; engross the thoughts.

**Adj.** thinking &c. *v.*; thoughtful, pensive, meditative, reflective, cogitative, museful, wistful, contemplative, speculative, deliberative, studious, sedate, introspective, Platonic, philosophical.

lost –, engrossed –, rapt –, absorbed- in thought &c. (*inattentive*) 458; deep musing &c. (*intent*) 457.

in the mind, under consideration, in contemplation.

**Adv.** all things considered; taking everything into account.

**Phr.** the mind being on the stretch; the -mind, – head- -turning, running- upon.

**V.** not -think &c. 451; not think of; dismiss from the -mind, – thoughts &c. 451.

indulge in reverie &c. (*be inattentive*) 458.

put away thought; unbend –, relax –, divert- the mind.

**Adj.** vacant, unintellectual, unideal, unoccupied, unthinking, inconsiderate, thoughtless; absent &c. (*inattentive*) 458; diverted; irrational &c. 499; narrow-minded &c. 481.

un-thought of, -dreamt of, -considered; off one's mind; incogitable, not to be thought of, inconceivable.

---

**453.** [Object of thought.] **Idea.—N.** idea, notion, conception, thought, apprehension, impression, perception, image, sentiment, reflection, observation, consideration; abstract idea, principle; archetype.

view &c. (*opinion*) 484; theory &c.

**454.** [Subject of thought.] **Topic.—N.** subject of –, material for- thought; food for the mind, mental *pabulum.*

subject, -matter; matter, theme, topic, what it is about, *thesis*, text, business, affair, matter in hand, argument; motion, resolution; head, chap-

514; conceit, fancy; phantasy &c. (*imagination*) 515.

point of view &c. (*aspect*) 448; field of view.

ter; case, point; proposition, theorem; field of inquiry; moot point, problem, &c. (*question*) 461.

**V.** float –, pass- in the mind &c. 451.

**Adj.** thought of; uppermost in the mind; *in petto*.

**Adv.** under -discussion, – consideration, – advisement; in -question, – the mind; on -foot, – the carpet, – the *tapis*; before the house, relative to &c. 9.

## Section II. Precursory Conditions and Operations

**455.** [The desire of knowledge.] **Curiosity.** — **N.** interest thirst for knowledge; curi-osity, -ousness; inquiring mind; inquisitiveness.

sight-seer, quidnunc, newsmonger, Paul Pry, peeping Tom, eavesdropper; gossip &c. (*news*) 532; questioner, *enfant terrible*.

**V.** be -curious &c. *adj.*; take an interest in, stare, gape; prick up the ears, see sights, lionize; pry, speer; dig up.

**Adj.** curious, inquisitive, burning with curiosity, overcurious, nosey; inquiring &c. 461; prying; inquisitorial; agape &c. (*expectant*) 507; attentive &c. 457.

**Phr.** what's the matter? what next?

**456.** [Absence of curiosity.] **Incuriosity.**—**N.** incuriosity; incuriousness &c. *adj.*; *insouciance* &c. 866; indifference, apathy.

**V.** be -incurious &c. *adj.*; have no -curiosity &c. 455; take no interest in &c. 823; mind one's own business.

**Adj.** incurious, uninquisitive, uninterested, indifferent, bored; impassive &c. 823.

**457. Attention.**—**N.** attention; mindfulness &c. *adj.*; intent-ness, -iveness; thought &c. 451; adverten-ce, -cy; observ-ance, -ation; consideration, reflection, perpension; heed; particularity; notice, regard &c. *v.*; circumspection &c. (*care*) 459; study, scrutiny, once-over; in-, intro-spection; revision, -al.

active –, diligent –, exclusive –, minute –, close –, intense –, deep –, profound –, abstract –, laboured –, deliberate- -thought, – attention, – application, – study.

minuteness, attention to detail &c. 459.

absorption of mind &c. (*abstraction*) 458.

indication, calling attention to &c. *v.*

**V.** be -attentive &c. *adj.*; attend, advert to, observe, look, see, view, remark, notice, regard, take notice, mark; give –, pay- -attention, – heed- to; listen in, incline –, lend- an ear to; trouble one's head about: give a

**458. Inattention.**—**N.** in-attention, -consideration; inconsiderateness &c. *adj.*; oversight; inadverten-ce, -cy; non-observance, disregard.

supineness &c. (*inactivity*) 683; *étourderie*; want of thought; heedlessness &c. (*neglect*) 460; *insouciance* &c. (*indifference*) 866.

abstraction; absence –, absorption- of mind; preoccupation, distraction, reverie, brown study, deep musing, fit of abstraction, woolgathering.

**V.** be -inattentive &c. *adj.*; overlook, disregard; pass by &c. (*neglect*) 460; not -observe &c. 457; think little of;

close –, shut- one's eyes to; wink at; pay no attention to; dismiss –, discard –, discharge- from one's -thoughts, – mind; drop the subject, think no more of; set –, turn –, put- aside; turn -away from, – one's attention from, – a deaf ear to, – one's back upon.

abstract oneself, dream, indulge in reverie.

escape -notice, – attention; come in

thought –, animadvert- to; occupy oneself with; contemplate &c. (*think of*) 451; look -at, – to, – after, – into, – over; see to; turn –, bend –, apply –, direct –, give- the -mind, – eye, – attention- to; have -an eye to, – in one's eye; bear in mind; take into -account, – consideration; keep in -sight, – view; have regard to, heed, mind, take cognizance of, be engaged in, entertain, recognize; make –, take- note of; note.

examine cursorily; glance -at, – upon, – over; cast –, pass- the eyes over; run over, turn over the leaves, dip into, perstringe; skim &c. (*neglect*) 460; take a cursory view of.

examine, – closely, – intently; scan, scrutinize, consider; give –, bend- one's mind to; overhaul, revise, pore over; inspect, review, pass under review; take stock of; fix –, rivet –, focus –, devote- the -eye, – mind, – thoughts, – attention- on *or* to; hear –, think- out; mind one's business.

revert –, hark back- to; watch &c. (*expect*) 507, (*take care of*) 459; hearken –, listen- to; prick up the ears; have –, keep- the eyes open; come to the point.

meet with attention; fall under one's -notice, – observation; be -under consideration &c. (*topic*) 454.

catch –, strike- the eye; attract notice; catch –, awaken –, wake –, invite –, solicit –, attract –, claim –, excite –, engage –, occupy –, strike –, arrest –, fix –, engross –, absorb –, rivet- the-attention, – mind, – thoughts; be -present to, – uppermost in- the mind.

bring under one's notice; point -out, – to, – at, – the finger at; lay the finger on, indigitate, indicate; direct –, call- attention to; show; put a -mark &c. (*sign*) 550- upon; call soldiers to 'attention'; bring forward &c. (*make manifest*) 525.

**Adj.** attentive, mindful, heedful, observant, regardful; alive –, awake- to, alert; observing &c. *v.*; taken up –, occupied- with; engaged –, engrossed –, interested –, wrapped- in; absorbed, rapt; breathless; pre-occupied &c. (*inattentive*) 458; watchful &c. (*careful*) 459; intent on, open-eyed, undistracted, upon the stretch; on the watch &c. (*expectant*) 507.

steadfast.

**Int.** see! look, – here, – out, – alive, – you, – to it! mark! lo!

at one ear and go out at the other; forget &c. (*have no remembrance*) 506.

call off –, draw off –, call away –, divert –, distract- the -attention, – thoughts, – mind; put out of one's head; dis-concert, -compose; put out, confuse, perplex, bewilder, moider, fluster, muddle, dazzle; throw a sop to Cerberus.

**Adj.** inattentive; un-observant, -mindful, -heeding, -discerning; inadvertent; mind-, regard-, respect-less; listless &c. (*indifferent*) 866; blind, deaf; flighty, hand over head; cur-, percur-sory; giddy-, scatter-, hare-brained; unreflecting, *écervelé*, inconsiderate, off-hand, thoughtless, dizzy, muzzy, brainsick; giddy, – as a goose; wild, harum-scarum, rantipole, high-flying; heed-, care-less &c. (*neglectful*) 460.

absent, absent-minded, abstracted, *distrait*; lost; lost –, wrapped- in thought, woolgathering; rapt, in the clouds, bemused; dreaming –, musing- on other things; pre-occupied; engrossed &c. (*attentive*) 457; in a -reverie &c. *n.*; off one's guard &c. (*inexpectant*) 508; napping; dreamy.

disconcerted, put out &c. *v.*; rattled.

**Adv.** inattentively, inadvertently &c. *adj.*; *per incuriam, sub silentio.*

**Int.** stand -at ease, – easy!

**Phr.** the attention wanders; one's wits gone a -woolgathering, – bird's nesting; it never entered into one's head; the mind running on other things; one's thoughts being elsewhere; had it been a bear it would have bitten you.

---

behold! soho! hark, – ye! mind! halloo! observe! lo and behold! attention! *nota bene*; N.B.; *, †; I'd have you to know; notice! take notice! O yes! *Oyez!*

**Phr.** this is –, these are- to give notice.

**459. Care.** [Vigilance.]—**N.** care, solicitude, heed; heedfulness &c. *adj.*; scruple &c. (*conscientiousness*) 939.

watchfulness &c. *adj.*; vigilance, *surveillance*, eyes of Argus, watch, vigil, look out, watch and ward, *l'œil du maître*.

alertness &c. (*activity*) 682; attention &c. 457; prudence &c., circumspection &c. (*caution*) 864; forethought &c. 510; precaution &c. (*preparation*) 673; tidiness &c. (*order*) 58, (*cleanliness*) 652; accuracy &c. (*exactness*) 494; minuteness, attention to detail; meticulousness, nicety, circumstantiality.

**V.** be -careful &c. *adj.*; reck; take care &c. (*be cautious*) 864; pay attention to &c. 457; take care of; look –, see- -to, – after; keep -an eye, – a sharp eye- upon; keep -watch, – watch and ward; mount guard, set watch, watch; keep in -sight, – view; chaperon, play gooseberry; mind, – one's business.

look -sharp, – about one; look with one's own eyes; keep a -good, – sharp- look-out; have all one's -wits, – eyes- about one; watch for &c. (*expect*) 507; stand to; keep one's eyes –, have the eyes –, sleep with one eye- open.

take precautions &c. 673; protect &c. (*render safe*) 664.

do one's best &c. 682; mind one's Ps and Qs, speak by the card, pick one's steps.

**Adj.** care-, regard-, heed-ful; taking care &c. *v.*; particular; prudent &c. (*cautious*) 864; considerate; thoughtful &c. (*deliberative*) 451; provident &c. (*prepared*) 673; alert &c. (*active*) 682; sure-footed.

guarded, on one's guard; on the -*qui vive*, – alert, – watch, – look-out; awake, broad awake, vigilant; watch-, wake-, wist-ful; Argus-, lynx- eyed; wide awake &c. (*intelligent*) 498; on the watch for &c. (*expectant*) 507.

tidy &c. (*orderly*) 58, (*clean*) 652; accurate &c. (*exact*) 494; scrupulous

**460. Neglect.**—**N.** neglect; carelessness &c. *adj.*; trifling &c. *v.*; negligence; omission, laches, default; remissness, slackness, procrastination; supineness &c. (*inactivity*) 683; inattention &c. 458; *nonchalance* &c. (*insensibility*) 823; imprudence, recklessness &c. 863; slovenliness &c. (*disorder*) 59, (*dirt*) 653; improvidence &c. 674; non-completion &c. 730; inexactness &c. (*error*) 495.

paraleipsis [in rhetoric].

trifler, slacker, waster, waiter on Providence; Micawber.

**V.** be -negligent &c. *adj.*; take no care of &c. (take care of &c. 459); neglect; let -slip, – go; lay –, set –, cast –, put- aside; keep –, leave- out of sight; lose sight of.

overlook, disregard; pass -over, – by; let pass; blink; wink –, connive- at; gloss over; take no -note, – notice, – thought, – account- of; pay no regard to; *laisser aller*; allow to lie on the table.

scamp; trifle, fribble; do by halves; skimp; cut; slight &c. (*despise*) 930; play –, trifle- with; slur; skim, – the surface; *effleurer*; take a cursory view of &c. 457.

slur –, slip –, skip –, jump- over; pretermit, miss, skip, jump, omit, give the go-by to, push aside, throw into the background, shelve, sink; ignore, shut one's eyes to, refuse to hear, turn a deaf ear to; leave out of one's calculation; not -attend to &c. 457, – mind; not trouble -oneself, – one's head- -with, – about; forget &c. 506; be caught napping &c. (*not expect*) 508; leave a loose thread; let the grass grow under one's feet.

render -neglectful &c. *adj.*; put –, throw- off one's guard.

**Adj.** neglecting &c. *v.*; unmindful, negligent, neglectful; heedless, careless, thoughtless; perfunctory, remiss, slack.

inconsiderate; un-, in-circumspect;

&c. (*conscientious*) 939; *cavendo tutus* &c. (*safe*) 664.

**Adv.** carefully &c. *adj.*; with care, gingerly.

**Phr.** *quis custodiet ipsos custodes?*

---

off one's guard; un-wary, -watchful, -guarded; offhand.

supine &c. (*inactive*) 683; inattentive &c. 458; *insouciant* &c. (*indifferent*) 823; imprudent, reckless &c. 863; slovenly &c. (*disorderly*) 59, (*dirty*) 653; inexact &c. (*erroneous*) 495; improvident &c. 674.

neglected &c. *v.*; un-heeded, -cared for, -perceived, -seen, -observed, -noticed, -noted, -marked, -attended to, -thought of, -regarded, -remarked, -missed; shunted, shelved.

un-examined, -studied, -searched, -scanned, -weighed, -sifted, -explored.

abandoned; buried in a napkin, hid under a bushel.

**Adv.** negligently &c. *adj.*; hand over head, anyhow; in an unguarded moment &c. (*unexpectedly*) 508; *per incuriam*.

**Int.** never mind, no matter, let it pass; it will be all the same a hundred years hence.

**461. Inquiry.** [Subject of Inquiry. Question.]—**N.** inquiry; request &c. 765; search, research, quest; pursuit &c. 622.

examination, review, scrutiny, investigation, indagation; per-quisition, -scrutation, -vestigation; inqu-est, -isition; exploration; *exploitation*, ventilation.

sifting; calculation, analysis, dissection, resolution, induction; Baconian method.

strict –, close –, searching –, exhaustive· inquiry; narrow –, strict- search; study &c. (*consideration*) 451.

*scire facias*, *ad referendum*; trial.

questioning &c. *v.*; interroga-tion, -tory; third degree; interpellation; challenge, examination, cross-examination, catechism; feeler, Socratic method, zetetic philosophy; leading question; discussion &c. (*reasoning*) 476; questionnaire, questionary.

reconnoitering, *reconnaissance*; prying &c. *v.*; espionage, *espionnage*; domiciliary visit, peep behind the curtain; lantern of Diogenes.

question, query, problem, *desideratum*, point to be solved, porism; subject –, field- of -inquiry, – controversy; point –, matter- in dispute; moot-point; issue, question at issue; bone of contention &c. (*discord*) 713; plain –, fair –, open- question; enigma &c. (*secret*) 533; knotty point &c. (*difficulty*) 704; *quodlibet*; threshold of an inquiry.

inquirer, investigator, experimenter, inquisitor, inspector, querist,

**462. Answer.**—**N.** answer, response, reply, replication, *riposte*, rejoinder, surrejoinder, rebutter, surrebutter, counter-evidence &c. 468, countercharge, defence, plea; retort, repartee; contradiction &c. 536; rescript, -ion; antiphon, -y; acknowledgment; password; echo.

discovery &c. 480*a*; solution &c. (*explanation*) 522; rationale &c. (*cause*) 153; clue &c. (*indication*) 550.

Œdipus; oracle &c. 513; return &c. (*record*) 551.

**V.** answer, respond, reply, rebut, retort, rejoin; give –, return for- answer; acknowledge, echo.

explain &c. (*interpret*) 522; solve &c. (*unriddle*) 522; discover &c. 480*a*; fathom, hunt out &c. (*inquire*) 461; satisfy, set at rest, determine.

**Adj.** answering &c. *v.*; respon-sive, -dent; oracular; antiphonal; conclusive.

**Adv.** because &c. (*cause*) 153; on the -scent, – right scent.

**Int.** *eureka!*

---

examiner, catechist; scrut-ator, -ineer; analyst; quidnunc &c. (*curiosity*) 455.

**V.** make -inquiry &c. *n.*; inquire, seek, search, frisk, speer, look -for, – about for, – out for; scan, reconnoitre, explore, sound, rummage, ransack, pry, peer, look round; look –, go- -over, – through; spy, over-haul.

scratch the head, slap the forehead.

look –, peer –, pry- into every hole and corner; look behind the scenes; trace up; hunt –, fish –, dig –, ferret- out; unearth; leave no stone unturned.

seek a -clue, – clew; hunt, track, trail, shadow, mouse, dodge, trace; follow the -trail, – scent; pursue &c. 622; beat up one's quarters; fish for; feel for &c. (*experiment*) 463.

investigate; take up –, institute –, pursue –, follow up –, conduct –, carry on –, prosecute- -an inquiry &c *n.*; look -at, – into; pre-examine; discuss, canvass, agitate.

examine, study, consider, calculate; dip –, dive –, delve –, go deep- into; make sure of, probe, sound, fathom; probe to the -bottom, – quick; scrutinize, analyze, anatomize, dissect, parse, resolve, sift, winnow; view –, try- in all its phases; thresh out.

bring in question, subject to examination; put to the proof &c. (*experiment*) 463; audit, tax, pass in review; take into consideration &c. (*think over*) 451; take counsel &c. 695.

ask, question, demand; put –, pop –, propose –, propound –, moot –, start –, raise –, stir –, suggest –, put forth –, ventilate – grapple with –, go into- a question.

put to the question, interrogate, catechize, pump, grill; cross-question, -examine; dodge; require an answer; pick –, suck- the brains of; feel the pulse.

be -in question &c. *adj.*; undergo examination.

**Adj.** inquiring &c. *v.*; inquisitive &c. (*curious*) 455; requisit-ive, -ory; catechetical, inquisitorial, analytic; in -search, – quest- of; on the look-out for, interrogative, zetetic: all-searching.

un-determined, -tried, -decided; in -question, – dispute, – issue, – course of inquiry; under -discussion, – consideration, – investigation &c. *n.*, *sub judice*, moot, proposed; doubtful &c. (*uncertain*) 475.

**Adv.** what? why? wherefore? whence? whither? where? *quære?* how -comes, – happens, – is- it? what is the reason? what's -the matter, – up, – in the wind? what on earth? when? who?

**463. Experiment.**—**N.** experiment; essay &c. (*attempt*) 675; **research** &c. (*investigation*) 461; trial, tentative method, *tâtonnement*.

verification, probation, *experimentum crucis*, proof, criterion, **diagnostic**, test, tryout, crucial test, acid test.

crucible, reagent, check, touchstone, pix; assay, ordeal; ring.

empiricism, rule of thumb.

feeler; pilot –, messenger- balloon, *ballon d'essai*; pilot engine; scout; straw to show the wind.

speculation, random shot, leap in the dark.

analy-zer, -st; adventurer, explorer, sourdough, prospector; experiment-er, -ist, -alist; assayer.

**V.** experiment; essay &c. (*endeavour*) 675; try, assay, sample; make -an experiment, – trial of; give a trial to; put upon –, subject to- trial; experiment upon; rehearse; put –, bring –, submit- to the -test, – proof; prove, verify, test, touch, practise upon, try one's strength.

grope; feel –, grope- -for, – one's way; fumble; *tâtonner, aller à tâtons*; put –, throw- out a feeler; send up a pilot balloon; see how the -land lies, – wind blows; consult the barometer; feel the pulse; fish –, bob- for; cast –, beat- about for; angle, trawl, cast one's net, beat the bushes.

venture, try one's fortune &c. (*adventure*) 675; explore &c. (*inquire*) 461.

**Adj.** experimental; probat-ive, -ory, -ionary; analytic, docimastic; tentative; empirical; speculative.

under probation, on one's trial, on trial, on approval.

**464. Comparison.—N.** comparison, collation, contrast; identification.

sim-ile, -ilitude; allegory &c. (*metaphor*) 521.

**V.** compare -to, – with; collate, confront; place side by side &c. (*near*) 197; set –, pit- against one another; contrast, balance.

identify, draw a parallel, parallel.

compare notes; institute a comparison; *parva componere magnis.*

**Adj.** comparative, relative; metaphorical &c. 521.

compared with &c. *v.*; comparable.

**Adv.** relatively &c. (*relation*) 9; as compared with &c. *v.*

**465. Discrimination.—N.** discrimination, distinction, differentiation, diagnosis, diorism; nice perception; perception –, appreciation- of difference; acuteness; estimation &c. 466; nicety, refinement; taste &c. 850; *critique*, judgement, tact; insight, discernment &c. (*intelligence*) 498; *nuances.*

**V.** discriminate, distinguish, differentiate, severalize; separate; draw the line, sift; separate –, winnow- the chaff from the wheat; split hairs.

estimate &c. (*measure*) 466; know -which is which, – one's stuff, – one's way about, – what is what, – 'a hawk from a handsaw.'

take into -account, – consideration; give –, allow- due weight to; weigh carefully.

**Adj.** discriminating &c. *v.*; dioristic, discriminative, critical, distinctive; nice.

**Phr.** *il y a fagots et fagots*; *rem acu tetigisti.*

**465a. Indiscrimination.—N.** indiscrimination; promiscuity; indistinctness, -ion; uncertainty &c. (*doubt*) 475; obtuseness.

**V.** not -indiscriminate &c. 465; overlook &c. (*neglect*) 460- a distinction; con-found, -fuse, jumble; swallow whole.

**Adj.** indiscriminate, undiscriminating, promiscuous; undistinguish-ed, -able, -ing; unmeasured.

**466. Measurement.—N.** measurement, admeasurement, mensuration, survey, valuation, appraisement, assessment, assize; estim-ate, -ation; dead reckoning; reckoning &c. (*numeration*) 85; gauging &c. *v.*

metrology, weights and measures, compound arithmetic.

measure, yard measure, standard, rule, foot-rule, chain, tape, staff, compass, callipers; dividers; gage, gauge, planimeter; meter, line, rod, check.

volt, kilowatt, ampere, candle power; horse power; axle load; foot pound.

flood –, high water- mark; Plimsoll mark; index &c. 550.

scale; gradu-ation, -ated scale; nonius; vernier &c. (*minuteness*) 193; pedo (*length*)- 200, sounding line &c. (*depth*)- 208, thermo (*heat* &c. 389)-, baro (*air* &c. 338)-, dynamo (*power*)- 276, anemo (*wind* 349)-

gonio (*angle* 244)- meter; landmark &c. (*limit*) 233; balance &c. (*weight*) 319; optical instruments &c. 445.

co-ordinates, ordinate and abscissa, polar co-ordinates, latitude and longitude, declination and right ascension, altitude and azimuth.

geo-, stereo-, hypso-metry; metage; surveying, land surveying; geo-desy, -detics, -desia; ortho-, alti-metry; *cadastre.*

astrolabe, armillary sphere.

land, -surveyor; geometer, topographer, cartographer, hydrographer.

**V.** measure, meter, mete; value, assess, rate, appraise, estimate, form an estimate, set a value on; appreciate; standardize.

span, pace, step; apply the -compass &c. *n.*; gauge, plumb, probe, calliper, sound, fathom &c. 208; heave the -log, – lead; weigh &c. 319; survey.

take an average &c. 29; graduate.

**Adj.** measuring &c. *v.*; metric, -al; measurable; geodetical, cadastral, topographical.

## Section III. Materials for Reasoning

**467. Evidence** [on one side.]—**N.** evidence; facts, premises, *data, præcognita,* grounds.

indication &c. 550; criterion &c. (*test*) 463.

testi-mony, -fication; attestation; deposition &c. (*affirmation*) 535; examination.

admission &c. (*assent*) 488; authority, warrant, credential, diploma, voucher, certificate, docket; record &c. 551; document, muniments; *pièce justificative*; deed, warranty &c. (*security*) 771; signature, seal &c. (*identification*) 550; exhibit, citation, reference.

witness, indicator; eye-, ear-witness; deponent; sponsor.

oral –, documentary –, hearsay –, external –, extrinsic –, internal –, intrinsic –, circumstantial –, cumulative –, *ex parte* –, presumptive –, collateral –, constructive- evidence; proof &c. (*demonstration*) 478; evidence in chief; finger prints, dactylogram.

secondary evidence; confirmation, corroboration, adminicle, support; ratification &c. (*assent*) 488; authentication, verification; compurgation, wager of law, comprobation.

citation, reference.

**V.** be -evidence &c. *n.*; evince, show, betoken, tell of; indicate &c. (*denote*) 550; imply, involve, argue, bespeak, breathe.

have –, carry- weight; tell, speak

**468.** [Evidence on the other side, on the other hand.] **Counter-evidence.—N.** counter-evidence; evidence on the other -side, – hand; disproof; refutation &c. 479; negation &c. 536; conflicting evidence.

plea &c. 617; vindication &c. 937; counter-protest; *tu quoque* argument; other side –, reverse- of the shield.

**V.** countervail, oppose; run counter; rebut &c. (*refute*) 479; subvert &c. (*destroy*) 162; check, weaken; contravene; contradict &c. (*deny*) 536; tell another story, turn the -tables, – scale; alter the case; cut both ways; prove a negative.

*audire alteram partem.*

**Adj.** countervailing &c. *v.*; contradictory, in rebuttal.

un-attested, -authenticated, -supported by evidence; supposititious, trumped up.

**Adv.** *per contra,* conversely, on the other hand.

**469. Qualification.—N.** qualification, limitation, modification, colouring.

allowance, grains of allowance, consideration, extenuating circumstances.

condition, proviso, exception; exemption; salvo, saving clause; discount &c. 813.

**V.** qualify, limit, modify, affect, temper, leaven, give a colour to, introduce new conditions.

allow –, make allowance- for; ad-

volumes; speak for itself &c. (*manifest*) 525.

rest –, depend- upon; repose on.

bear -witness &c. *n.*; give -evidence &c. *n.*; testify, depose, witness, vouch for; sign, seal, undersign, set one's hand and seal, sign and seal, deliver as one's act and deed, certify, attest; acknowledge &c. (*assent*) 488.

make absolute, confirm, ratify, corroborate, endorse, countersign, support, bear out, vindicate, uphold, warrant.

adduce, attest, cite, quote; refer –, appeal- to; call, – to witness; bring -forward, – into court; allege, plead; produce –, confront- witnesses; collect –, bring together –, rake up- evidence.

have –, make out- a case; establish, circumstantiate, authenticate, substantiate, verify, make good, quote chapter and verse; bring -home to, – to book.

**Adj.** showing &c. *v.*; evidential, indica-tive, -tory; deducible &c. 478; grounded –, founded –, based- on; first hand, authentic, verifiable; corroborative, confirmatory; significant, conclusive.

**Adv.** by inference; according to, witness, *a fortiori*; still -more, – less; *raison de plus*; in corroboration &c. *n.* of; *valeat quantum*; under -seal, – one's hand and seal.

mit exceptions, take into account; take exception, object.

**Adj.** qualifying &c. *v.*; conditional; extenuatory; exceptional &c. (*unconformable*) 83.

hypothetical &c. (*supposed*) 514; contingent &c. (*uncertain*) 475.

**Adv.** provided, – always; if, unless, but, yet; according as; conditionally, admitting, supposing; on the supposition of &c. (*theoretically*) 514; with the understanding, even, although, though, for all that, after all, at all events.

with grains of allowance, *cum grano salis*; *exceptis excipiendis*; wind and weather permitting; if possible &c. 470.

subject to; with this -proviso &c. *n.*

---

*Degrees of Evidence*

**470. Possibility.—N.** possibility, potentiality; what -may be, – is possible &c. *adj.*; compatibility &c. (*agreement*) 23.

practicability, feasibility; practicableness &c. *adj.*

contingency, chance &c. 156.

**V.** be -possible &c. *adj.*; stand a chance, have a leg to stand on; admit of, bear.

render -possible &c. *adj.*; put in the way of.

**Adj.** possible; on the -cards, – dice; *in posse*, within the bounds of possibility, conceivable, credible, imaginable; compatible &c. 23.

practicable, feasible, workable, performable, achievable; within -reach, – measurable distance; accessible, superable, surmountable; at-, ob-tainable; contingent &c. (*doubtful*) 475.

**Adv.** possibly, by possibility; perhaps, -chance, -adventure; may be, haply, mayhap.

**471. Impossibility.—N.** impossibility &c. *adj.*; what -cannot, – can never- be; sour grapes; infeasibility, impracticability, hopelessness &c. 859.

**V.** be -impossible &c. *adj.*; have no chance whatever.

attempt impossibilities; square the circle; discover the -philosopher's stone, – elixir of life, – secret of perpetual motion; wash a blackamoor white; skin a flint; make -a silk purse out of a sow's ear, – bricks without straw; have nothing to go upon; weave a rope of sand, build castles in the air, *prendre la lune avec les dents*, extract sunbeams from cucumbers, set the Thames on fire, milk a he-goat into a sieve, catch a weasel asleep, *rompre l'anguille au genou*, be in two places at once.

**Adj.** impossible; not -possible &c. 470; absurd, contrary to reason; unlikely, at variance with facts; unreasonable &c. 477; incredible &c. 485; beyond the bounds of -reason, – possi-

if possible, wind and weather permitting, God willing, *Deo volente*, D.V.

---

bility; from which reason recoils; visionary; inconceivable &c. (*improbable*) 473; prodigious &c. (*wonderful*) 870; un-, in-imaginable, unthinkable, not a Chinaman's chance.

impracticable, unachievable; un-, in-feasible; insuperable; un-, in-surmountable; unat-, unob-tainable; out of -reach, – the question; not to be -had, – thought of; beyond control; desperate &c. (*hopeless*) 859; incompatible &c. 24; inaccessible, uncomeatable, impassable impervious, innavigable, inextricable.

out of –, beyond one's -power, – depth, – reach, – grasp; too much for; *ultra crepidam*.

**Phr.** the grapes are sour; *non possumus*; *non nostrum tantas componere lites*.

**472. Probability.**—**N.** probability, likelihood; likeliness &c. *adj.*

*vraisemblance*, verisimilitude, plausibility; colour, semblance, show of; presumption; presumptive –, circumstantial- evidence; credibility.

reasonable –, fair –, good –, favourable- -chance, – prospect; prospect, well-grounded hope; chance &c. 156.

**V.** be -probable &c. *adj.*; give –, lend- colour to; point to; imply &c. (*evidence*) 467; bid fair &c. (*promise*) 511; stand fair for; stand –, run- a good chance.

presume, infer, suppose, take for granted.

think likely, dare say, flatter oneself; expect &c. 507; count upon &c. (*believe*) 484.

**Adj.** probable, likely, hopeful, to be expected, in a fair way.

plausible, specious, ostensible, colourable, *ben trovato*, well-founded, reasonable, credible, easy of belief, presumable, presumptive, apparent.

**Adv.** probably &c. *adj.*; belike; in all -probability, – likelihood; very –, most- likely; as likely as not; like enough; ten &c. to one; apparently, seemingly, according to every reasonable expectation; *primâ facie*; to all appearance &c. (*to the eye*) 448.

**Phr.** the -chances, – odds- are; appearances –, chances- are in favour of; there is reason to -believe, – think, – expect; I dare say; all Lombard Street to a China orange.

**473. Improbability.**—**N.** improbability, unlikelihood; unfavourable –, bad –, little –, small –, poor –, scarcely any –, no –, not a ghost of a- chance; bare possibility; long odds; incredibility &c. 485.

**V.** be -improbable &c. *adj.*; have a -small chance &c. *n.*

**Adj.** improbable, unlikely, contrary to all reasonable expectation, implausible.

rare &c. (*infrequent*) 137; unheard of inconceivable; un-, in-imaginable; in credible &c. 485; more than doubtful

**Int.** not likely! no fear!

**Phr.** the chances are against.

---

**474. Certainty.**—**N.** certainty; necessity &c. 601; certitude, certainness, surety, assurance, sureness; dead –, moral- certainty; infallibleness &c. *adj.*; infallibility, reliability.

gospel, scripture, church, pope, court of final appeal; *res judicata, ultimatum*.

positiveness; dogmat-ism, -ist, -izer; *doctrinaire*, know-all, bigot, -ry; opin-

**475. Uncertainty.**—**N.** uncertainty, incertitude, doubt; doubtfulness &c. *adj.*; dubi-ety, -tation, -tancy, -ousness.

hesitation, suspense; perplexity, embarrassment, dilemma, quandary, Morton's fork, bewilderment; timidity &c. (*fear*) 860; indecision, vacillation &c. 605; *diaporesis*, indetermination.

vagueness &c. *adj.*; haze, fog; ob-

ionist, Sir Oracle; *ipse dixit*; zealot.

fact; positive –, matter of- fact; *fait accompli*.

**V.** be -certain &c. *adj.*; stand to reason.

render -certain &c. *adj.*; in-, en-, assure; clinch, make sure; determine, decide, set at rest, 'make assurance double sure'; know &c. (*believe*) 484; dismiss all doubt.

dogmatize, lay down the law.

**Adj.** certain, sure; assured &c. *v.*; solid, well-founded.

unqualified, absolute, positive, determinate, definite, clear, unequivocal, categorical, unmistakable, decisive, decided, ascertained.

inevitable, unavoidable, ineluctable, avoidless.

unerring, infallible; unchangeable &c. 150; to be depended on, trustworthy, reliable, bound.

un-impeachable, -deniable, -questionable; in-disputable, -contestable, -controvertible, -defeasible, -dubitable; irrefutable &c. (*proven*) 478; conclusive, without power of appeal, final.

indubious; without –, beyond a –, without a shade or shadow of- -doubt – question; past dispute; beyond all -question, – dispute; un-doubted, -contested, -questioned, -disputed; question-, doubt-less.

bigoted, fanatical, dogmatic, opinionat-ed, -ive, *doctrinaire*.

authoritative, authentic, official.

sure as -fate, – death and taxes, – a gun.

evident, self-evident, axiomatic; clear, – as day, – as the sun at noonday; obvious.

**Adv.** certainly &c. *adj.*; for certain, certes, sure, no doubt, doubtless, and no mistake, *flagrante delicto*, sure enough, to be sure, of course, as a matter of course, *à coup sur*, to a certainty, undoubtedly; in truth &c. (*truly*) 494; at -any rate, – all events; without fail; *coûte que coûte*; whatever may happen, if the worst come to the worst; come –, happen- what -may, – will; sink or swim; rain or shine.

**Phr.** *cela va sans dire*; there is -no question, – not a shadow of doubt;

scurity &c. (*darkness*) 421; ambiguity &c. (*double meaning*) 520; contingency, double contingency, possibility upon a possibility; conjecture; open question &c. (*question*) 461; *onus probandi*; blind bargain, pig in a poke, leap in the dark, something or other; needle in a bottle of hay; roving commission.

fallibility, unreliability, untrustworthiness, precariousness.

**V.** be -uncertain &c. *adj.*; wonder whether.

lose the -clue, – clew, – scent; miss one's way.

not know -what to make of &c. (*unintelligibility*) 519, – which way to turn, – whether one stands on one's head or one's heels; float in a sea of doubt, hesitate, flounder; lose -oneself, – one's head, – one's way, wander aimlessly; muddle one's brains.

render -uncertain &c. *adj.*; put out, pose, puzzle, perplex, embarrass; confuse, -found; bewilder, mystify, bother, moider, nonplus, addle the wits, throw off the scent; *spargere voces in vulgum ambiguas*; keep in suspense.

doubt &c. (*disbelieve*) 485; hang –, tremble- in the balance; depend.

**Adj.** uncertain; casual; random &c. (*aimless*) 621; changeable &c. 149.

doubtful, dubious; indecisive; unsettled, -decided, -determined; in suspense, open to discussion; controvertible; in question &c. (*inquiry*) 461; insecure, unstable.

vague; in-determinate, -definite; ambiguous, equivocal; undefin-ed, -able; confused &c. (*indistinct*) 447; mystic, mysterious, veiled, obscure, cryptic, oracular.

perplexing &c. *v.*; enigmatic, paradoxical, apocryphal, problematical, hypothetical; experimental &c. 463.

fallible, questionable, precarious, slippery, ticklish, debatable, disputable; un-reliable, -trustworthy.

contingent, – on, dependent on; subject to; dependent on circumstances; occasional; provisional.

unauth-entic, -enticated, -oritative; un-ascertained, -confirmed; undemonstrated; un-told, -counted.

in a -state of uncertainty, – cloud.

the die is cast &c. (*necessity*) 601.

---

- maze; ignorant &c. 491; on the horns of a dilemma; afraid to say; out of one's reckoning, astray, adrift; at -sea, – fault, – a loss, – one's wit's end, – a *nonplus*; puzzled &c. *v.*; lost, abroad, *désorienté*; dis-tracted, -traught.

**Adv.** *pendente lite*; *sub spe rati.*

**Phr.** Heaven knows; who can tell? who shall decide when doctors disagree?

## Section IV. Reasoning Processes

**476. Reasoning. — N.** reasoning; ratio-cination, -nalism; dialectics, induction, generalization.

discussion, comment; ventilation; inquiry &c. 461.

argumentation, controversy, debate; polemics, wrangling; contention &c. 720; logomachy; dis-putation, -ceptation; paper war.

art of reasoning, logic.

process –, train –, chain- of reasoning; de-, in-duction; synthesis, analysis.

argument; case, plea, *plaidoyer*, opening; *lemma*, proposition, terms, premises, postulate, *data*, starting point, principle; inference &c. (*judgment*) 480.

pro-, syllogism; enthymeme, sorites, dilemma, *perilepsis*, *a priori* reasoning, *reductio ad absurdum*, horns of a dilemma, *argumentum ad hominem*, comprehensive argument.

reasoner, logician, dialectician; disputant; controver-sialist, -tist; wrangler, arguer, debater, polemic, casuist, rationalist; scientist.

logical sequence; good case; correct –, just –, sound –, valid –, cogent –, logical –, forcible –, persuasive –, persuasory –, consectary –, conclusive &c. 478 –, subtle- reasoning; force of argument; strong -point, – argument.

arguments, reasons, pros and cons.

**V.** reason, argue, discuss, debate, dispute, wrangle; bandy -words, – arguments; chop logic; hold –, carry on- an argument; controvert &c. (*deny*) 536; canvass; comment –, moralize- upon; consider &c. (*examine*) 461.

open a -discussion, – case; join –, be at- issue; moot; come to the point; stir –, agitate –, ventilate –, torture- a question; try conclusions; take up a -side, – case.

**477.** [The absence of reasoning.] **Intuition.** [False or vicious reasoning; show of reason.] **Sophistry.—N.** intuition, instinct, association; presentiment; rule of thumb.

sophistry, paralogy, perversion, casuistry, jesuitry, equivocation, evasion, mental reservation; chicane, -ry; quiddit, quiddity; mystification; special pleading; speciousness &c. *adj.*; nonsense &c. 497; word-, tongue-fence.

false –, vicious- reasoning; *petitio principii*, *ignoratio elenchi*; *post hoc ergo propter hoc*; *non sequitur*, *ignotum per ignotius.*

misjudgment &c. 481; false teaching &c. 538.

sophism, solecism, paralogism; quibble, quirk, *elenchus*, elench, fallacy, *quodlibet*, subterfuge, subtlety, quillet; inconsistency, antilogy; 'a mockery, a delusion and a snare'; claptrap, mere words; 'lame and impotent conclusion.'

meshes –, cobwebs- of sophistry; flaw in an argument; weak point, bad case.

over-refinement; hair-splitting &c. *v.*

sophist, casuist, paralogist.

**V.** judge -intuitively, – by intuition; hazard a proposition, talk at random.

reason -ill, – falsely &c. *adj.*; paralogize; misjudge &c. 481.

pervert, quibble; equivocate, mystify, evade, elude; gloss over, varnish; misteach &c. 538; mislead &c. (*error*) 495; cavil, refine, subtilize, split hairs; misrepresent &c. (*lie*) 544.

beg the question, reason in a circle, cut blocks with a razor, beat about the bush, play fast and loose, blow hot and cold, prove that black is white and white black, travel out of the record, *parler à tort et à travers*, put oneself out of court, not have a leg to stand on.

**Adj.** intuitive, instinctive, impulsive;

contend, take one's stand upon, insist, lay stress on; infer &c. 480.

follow from &c. (*demonstration*) 478.

**Adj.** rational; reasoning &c. *v.*; rationalistic; argumentative, controversial, dialectic, polemical; discursory, -ive; disputatious.

debatable, controvertible.

logical; in-, de-ductive; synthetic, analytic; relevant &c. 23.

**Adv.** for, because, hence, whence, seeing that, since, sith, then, thence, so; for -that, – this, – which- reason; for-, inasmuch as; whereas, *ex concesso*, considering, in consideration of; there-, where-fore; consequently, *ergo*, thus, accordingly; *a fortiori*.

in -conclusion, – fine; finally, after all, *au bout du compte*, on the whole, taking one thing with another.

rationally &c. *adj.*

independent of –, anterior to- reason; gratuitous, hazarded; unconnected.

unreasonable, illogical, false, unsound, invalid; unwarranted, not following; inconsequent, -ial; inconsistent, incongruous; abson-ous, -ant; unscientific; untenable, inconclusive, incorrect; fall-acious, -ible; groundless, unproved.

deceptive, sophistical, sophisticated, casuistical, jesuitical; illus-ive, -ory; specious, hollow, plausible, *ad captandum*, evasive; irrelevant &c. 10.

weak, feeble, poor, flimsy, loose, vague, irrational; nonsensical &c. (*absurd*) 497; foolish &c. (*imbecile*) 499; frivolous, pettifogging, quibbling; finespun, over-refined.

at the end of one's tether, *au bout de son latin*.

**Adv.** intuitively &c. *adj.*; by intuition; illogically &c. *adj.*

**Phr.** *non constat*; that goes for nothing.

**478. Demonstration.—N.** demonstration, proof; conclusiveness &c. *adj.*; *apodixis*, probation, comprobation.

logic of facts &c. (*evidence*) 467; *experimentum crucis* &c. (*test*) 463; argument &c. 476; irrefragability.

**V.** demonstrate, prove, establish, make good; show; evince &c. (*be evidence of*) 467; verify &c. 467; settle the question, reduce to demonstration, set the question at rest.

make out, – a case; prove one's point, have the best of the argument; draw a conclusion &c. (*judge*) 480.

follow, – of course; stand to reason; hold -good, – water.

**Adj.** demonstra-ting &c. *v.*, -tive, -ble; probative, unanswerable, conclusive; apodictic, -al; irre-sistible, -futable, -fragable, undeniable.

categorical, decisive, crucial.

demonstrated &c. *v.*; proven; unconfuted, -answered, -refuted; evident &c. 474.

deducible, consequential, consectary, inferential, following.

**Adv.** of course, in consequence, consequently, as a matter of course.

**Phr.** *probatum est*; there is nothing more to be said, Q.E D., it must follow.

**479. Confutation.—N.** con-, re-futation; answer, complete answer; disproof, conviction, redargution, invalidation; expos-ure, -ition; clincher; retort; *reductio ad absurdum*; knock down –, *tu quoque*- argument.

**V.** con-, re-fute; parry, negative, disprove, redargue, expose, show the fallacy of, rebut, defeat; demolish &c. (*destroy*) 162; over-throw, -turn; scatter to the winds, explode, invalidate; silence; put –, reduce- to silence; clinch -an argument, – a question; give one a set down, stop the mouth, shut up; have, – on the hip; get the better of; confound, convince.

not leave a leg to stand on, cut the ground from under one's feet.

be confuted &c.; fail; expose –, show- one's weak point.

**Adj.** confut-ing, -ed &c. *v.*; capable of refutation; re-, con-futable.

condemned -on one's own showing, – out of one's own mouth.

**Phr.** the argument falls to the ground, *cadit quæstio*, it does not hold water, '*suo sibi gladio hunc jugulo.*'

## Section V. Results of Reasoning

**480. Judgement.** [Conclusion.]—**N.** result, conclusion, upshot; deduction, inference, ergotism, illation; corollary, porism; moral.

estimation, valuation, appreciation, judication; di-, ad-judication; arbitrament, -ement, -ation; assessment, ponderation.

award, estimate; review, criticism, *critique*, notice, report.

decision, determination, judgment, finding, verdict, sentence, decree, – nisi, – absolute, – interlocutory; *dictum*; *res judicata*.

*plébiscite*, referendum, voice, casting vote; vote &c. (*choice*) 609; opinion &c. (*belief*) 484; good judgment &c. (*wisdom*) 498.

judge, jurist, umpire; arbi-ter, -trator; assessor, referee; censor, reviewer, critic; *connoisseur*; commentator &c. 524; inspector, inspecting officer.

**V.** judge, conclude; come to –, draw –, arrive at- a conclusion; ascertain, determine, make up one's mind.

deduce, derive, gather, collect, draw an inference, make a deduction, weet, ween.

form an estimate, estimate, size up, appreciate, value, count, assess, rate, rank, account; regard, consider, think of; look upon &c. (*believe*) 484.

settle; pass –, give- an opinion; decide, try, pronounce. rule; pass -judgment, – sentence; sentence, doom; find; give –, deliver- judgment; adjud-ge, -icate; arbitrate, award, report; bring in a verdict; make absolute, set a question at rest; confirm &c. (*assent*) 488.

comment, criticize; review, pass under review &c. (*examine*) 457; investigate &c. (*inquire*) 461.

hold the scales, sit in judgment; try –, hear- a cause.

**Adj.** judging &c. *v.*; judicious &c. (*wise*) 498; determinate, conclusive, censorious, critical &c. 932.

**Adv.** on the whole, all things considered.

---

**481. Misjudgment.** — **N.** misjudgment, obliquity of –, warped- judgment; mis-calculation, -computation, -conception &c. (*error*) 495; hasty conclusion.

prejud-gment, -ication, -ice; foregone conclusion; pre-notion, -vention, -conception, -dilection, -possession, -apprehension, -sumption, -sentiment; fixed –, preconceived- idea; *idée fixe*; *mentis gratissimus error*; fool's paradise.

*esprit de corps*, party spirit, race –, class- prejudice, partisanship, clannishness, *prestige*.

bias, warp, twist; hobby, fad, whim, craze, quirk, crotchet, partiality, infatuation, blind side, mote in the eye.

one-sided –, partial –, narrow –, confined –, superficial- -views, – ideas, – conceptions, – notions; narrow mind; bigotry &c. (*obstinacy*) 606; *odium theologicum*; pedantry; hypercriticism.

*doctrinaire* &c. (*positive*) 474.

**V.** mis-judge, -estimate, -think, -conjecture, -conceive &c. (*error*) 495; fly in the face of facts; mis-calculate, -reckon, -compute.

overestimate &c. 482; underestimate &c. 483.

pre-, fore-judge; pre-suppose, -sume, -judicate; dogmatize; have a -bias &c. *n.*; have only one idea; *jurare in verba magistri*, run away with the notion; jump –, rush- to a conclusion; look only at one side of the shield; view -with jaundiced eye, – through distorting spectacles; not see beyond one's nose; *dare pondus fumo*; get the wrong sow by the ear &c. (*blunder*) 699.

give a -bias, – twist; bias, warp, twist; pre-judice, -possess.

**Adj.** misjudging &c. *v.*; ill-judging, wrong-headed; prejudiced, prejudicial, &c. *v.*; jaundiced; short-sighted, purblind; partial, one-sided, superficial.

narrow-minded; confined, insular, provincial, parochial, illiberal, intolerant, narrow, besotted, infatuated, fanatical, cracked, warped, *entêté*, positive, dogmatic, dictatorial; conceited; opin-, opini-ative; opinion-ed, -ate, -ative, -ated; self-opinioned, wedded to an opinion, *opiniâtre*; bigoted &c. (*obstinate*) 606; crotchety, fussy, impracticable; unreason-able, -ing; stupid &c. 499; credulous &c. 486.

misjudged &c. *v.*

**Adv.** *ex parte.*

**Phr.** nothing like leather; the wish the father to the thought.

**480a.** [Result of search or inquiry.] **Discovery.—N.** discovery, invention, detection, disenchantment, disclosure, find, ascertainment, revelation.

trover &c. 775.

**V.** discover, find, determine, evolve; fix upon; find –, trace –, make –, hunt –, fish –, worm –, ferret –, root- out; fathom; bring –, draw- out; educe, elicit, bring to light, invent; dig –, grub –, fish- up; unearth, disinter.

solve, resolve; un-riddle, -ravel, -lock; pick –, open- the lock; find a -clue, – clew- to; interpret &c. 522; disclose &c. 529.

trace, get at; hit it, have it; lay one's -finger, – hands- upon; spot; get –, arrive- at the -truth &c. 494; put the saddle on the right horse, hit the right nail on the head.

be near the truth. burn; smoke, scent, sniff, smell a rat.

open the eyes to; see -through, – daylight, – in its true colours, – the cloven foot; detect; catch, – tripping.

pitch –, fall –, light –, hit –, stumble –, pop- upon; come across; meet –, fall in- with.

recognize, realize, verify, make certain of, identify.

**Int.** *eureka!*

**482. Overestimation.—N.** overestimation &c. *v.*; exaggeration &c. 549; vanity &c. 880; optim-, pessim-ism, -ist; megalomania.

much -cry and little wool, – ado about nothing; storm in a teacup; fine talking, rodomontade, gush, hot air, gas, bombast.

egotism &c. 880; boasting &c. 884.

**V.** over-estimate, -rate, -value, -prize, -weigh, -reckon, -strain, -praise; estimate too highly, attach too much importance to, make mountains of molehills, catch at straws; strain, magnify; exaggerate &c. 549; set too high a value upon; think –, make- -much, – too much- of; outreckon.

extol, – to the skies; make the -most, – best, – worst- of, eulogize, panegyrize, gush, puff, boost; make two bites of a cherry.

have too high an opinion of oneself &c. (*vanity*) 880.

**Adj.** overestimated &c. *v.*; oversensitive &c. (*sensibility*) 822; inflated, puffed up, exaggerated &c. 549.

**Phr.** all his geese are swans; *parturiunt montes.*

**483. Underestimation.—N.** underestimation; depreciation &c. (*detraction*) 934; pessim-ism, -ist; undervaluing &c. *v.*; modesty &c. 881.

**V.** under-rate, -estimate, -value, -reckon; depreciate; disparage &c. (*detract*) 934; not do justice to; mis-, dis-prize; ridicule &c. 856; slight &c. (*despise*) 930; neglect &c. 460; slur over, under-state.

make -light, – little, – nothing, – no account- of; minimize, belittle, run down, think nothing of; set -no store by, – at naught; shake off as dewdrops from the lion's mane.

**Adj.** depreciat-ing, -ed, -ive, -ory, &c. *v.*; un-appreciated, -valued, -prized; pejorative.

**484. Belief.—N.** belief; credence; credit; assurance; faith, trust, troth, confidence, presumption, sanguine expectation &c. (*hope*) 858; dependence on, reliance on.

persuasion, conviction, convincement, plerophory, self-conviction; certainty &c. 474; opinion, mind, view; conception, thinking; impression &c. (*idea*) 453; surmise &c. 514; conclusion &c. (*judgment*) 480.

tenet, dogma, principle, way of thinking; popular belief &c. (*assent*) 488.

firm –, implicit –, settled –, fixed –, rooted –, deep-rooted –, staunch –, unshaken –, steadfast –, inveterate –, calm –, sober –, dispassionate –, impartial –, well-founded- -belief, – opinion &c.; *uberrima fides.*

system of opinions, school, doctrine, articles, canons; declaration –, profession- of faith; tenets, *credenda*, creed; thirty-nine articles &c. (*orthodoxy*) 983*a*; catechism; assent &c. 488; *propaganda* &c. (*teaching*) 537.

credibility &c. (*probability*) 472.

**V.** believe. credit; give -faith, – credit, – credence- to; see, realize; assume, receive; set down –, take- for; have –, take- it; consider, esteem, presume.

count –, depend –, calculate –, pin one's faith –, reckon –, lean –, build –, rely –, rest- upon; lay one's account for; make sure of.

make oneself easy -about, – on that score; take on -trust, – credit; take for -granted, –gospel; allow –, attach- some weight to.

know, – for certain; have –, make- no doubt; doubt not; be – rest- -assured &c. *adj.*; persuade –, assure –, satisfy- oneself; make up one's mind.

give one credit for; confide –, believe –, put one's trust- in; place –, repose- implicit confidence in; take -one's word for, – at one's word; place reliance on, rely upon, swear by, pay regard to.

think, hold; take, – it; opine, be of opinion, conceive, trow, ween, fancy, apprehend; have –, hold –, possess –, entertain –, adopt –, imbibe –, embrace

**485. Unbelief. Doubt.—N.** un-, dis-, mis-belief; discredit, miscreance; infidelity &c. (*irreligion*) 989; dissent &c. 489; change of -opinion &c. 484; retraction &c. 607.

doubt &c. (*uncertainty*) 475; skepticism, misgiving, demur; dis-, mis-trust; misdoubt, suspicion, jealousy, scruple, qualm; *onus probandi.*

incredib-ility, -leness; incredulity; unbeliever &c. 487.

**V.** dis-believe, -credit; not -believe &c. 484; misbelieve; refuse to admit &c. (*dissent*) 489; refuse to believe &c. (*incredulity*) 487.

doubt; be -doubtful &c. (*uncertain*) 475; doubt the truth of; be -skeptical as to &c. *adj.*; diffide; dis-, mis-trust; suspect, smoke, scent, smell a rat; have –, harbour –, entertain- -doubts, – suspicions; have one's doubts.

demur, stick at, pause, hesitate, scruple, waver, stop and consider.

hang in -suspense, – doubt.

throw doubt upon, raise a question; bring –, call- in question; question, challenge, query; dispute; deny &c. 536; cavil; cause –, raise –, start –, suggest –, awake- a -doubt, – suspicion; ergotize.

startle, stagger; shake –, stagger- one's faith, – belief.

**Adj.** unbelieving; incredulous –, skeptical- as to; distrustful –, shy –, suspicious- of; doubting &c. *v.*

doubtful &c. (*uncertain*) 475; disputable; unworthy –, undeserving- of -belief &c. 484; questionable; sus-pect, -picious; open to -suspicion, – doubt; staggering, hard to believe, incredible, not to be believed, inconceivable.

fallible &c. (*uncertain*) 475; undemonstrable; controvertible &c. (*untrue*) 495.

**Adv.** *cum grano salis.*

**Phr.** *fronti nulla fides*; *nimium ne crede colori*; '*timeo Danaos et dona ferentes*'; *credat Judæus Apella*; let those believe who may.

–, get hold of –, hazard –, foster –, nurture –, cherish- -a belief, – an opinion &c. *n.*

view –, consider –, take –, hold –, conceive –, regard –, esteem –, deem –, look upon –, account –, set down- as; surmise &c. 514.

get –, take- it into one's head; come round to an opinion; swallow &c. (*credulity*) 486.

cause to -be believed &c. *v.*; satisfy, persuade, have the ear of, gain the confidence of, assure; con-vince, -vict, -vert; put across, sell; wean, bring round; bring –, put –, win- over; indoctrinate &c. (*teach*) 537; cram down the throat; produce –, carry- conviction; bring –, drive- home to.

go down, find credence, pass current; be -received &c. *v.*, – current &c. *adj.*; possess –, take hold of –, take possession of- the mind.

**Adj.** believing &c. *v.*; certain, sure, assured, positive, cocksure, satisfied, confident, unhesitating, convinced, secure.

under the impression; impressed –, imbued –, penetrated- with.

confiding, trustful, suspectless; unsusp-ecting, -icious; void of suspicion; credulous &c. 486; wedded to.

believed &c. *v.*; accredited, putative; unsuspected.

worthy of –, deserving of –, commanding- -belief, – confidence; credible, reliable, trusted, trustworthy, to be depended on, undoubted; satisfactory; probable &c. 472; fiduci-al, -ary; persuasive, impressive.

relating to belief, doctrinal.

**Adv.** in the -opinion, – eyes- of; *me judice*; me-seems, -thinks; to the best of one's belief; I -dare say, – doubt not, – have no doubt, – am sure; in my opinion; sure enough &c. (*certainty*) 474; depend –, rely- upon it; be –, rest- assured; I'll warrant you &c. (*affirmation*) 535.

**486. Credulity.—N.** credul-ity, -ousness &c. *adj.*; gull-, cull-ibility; gross credulity, infatuation; self-delusion, -deception; blind reasoning; superstition; one's blind side; bigotry &c. (*obstinacy*) 606; hyper-orthodoxy &c. 984; misjudgment &c. 481.

credulous person &c. (*dupe*) 547.

**V.** be -credulous &c. *adj.*; *jurare in verba magistri*; follow implicitly; swallow, – whole, gulp down; take on trust; take for -granted, – gospel; run away with -a notion, – an idea; jump –, rush- to a conclusion; think the moon is made of green cheese; take –, grasp- the shadow for the substance; catch at straws.

impose upon &c. (*deceive*) 545.

**Adj.** credulous, gullible; easily -deceived &c. 545; simple, green, soft, childish, silly, stupid; over-credulous, -confident; infatuated, superstitious; confiding &c. (*believing*) 484.

**Phr.** the wish the father to the thought; *credo quia impossibile.*

**487. Incredulity.—N.** incredul-ousness, -ity; skepticism, pyrrhonism; want of faith &c. (*irreligion*) 989.

suspiciousness &c. *adj.*; scrupulosity; suspicion &c. (*unbelief*) 485; dissent &c. 489.

unbeliever, skeptic, aporetic; atheist, agnostic, infidel, disbeliever, misbeliever, pyrrhonist &c. 989; heretic &c. (*heterodox*) 984.

**V.** be -incredulous &c. *adj.*; distrust &c. (*disbelieve*) 485; refuse to believe; shut one's -eyes, – ears- to; turn a deaf ear to; hold aloof; ignore; *nullius jurare in verba magistri.*

**Adj.** incredulous, skeptical, unbelieving, inconvincible; hard –, shy- of belief; suspicious, scrupulous, distrustful, heterodox &c. 984.

**488. Assent.—N.** assent, -ment; acquiescence, admission; nod; ac-, con-cord, -cordance; agreement &c. 23; affirm-ance, -ation; recognition, acknowledgment, avowal; confession, – of faith.

unanimity, common consent, *consensus*, acclamation, chorus, *vox populi*; popular –, current- -belief, – opinion; public opinion; concurrence &c. (*of causes*) 178; co-operation &c. (*voluntary*) 709.

ratification, confirmation, corroboration, approval, acceptance, *visa*; indorsement, &c. (*record*) 551; O.K.

consent &c. (*compliance*) 762.

affirmant, consenter, covenanter, subscriber, endorser, upholder.

**V.** assent; give –, yield –, nod- assent; acquiesce; agree &c. 23; receive, accept, accede, accord, concur, lend oneself to, consent, coincide, reciprocate, go with; be -at one with &c. *adj.*; go along –, chime in –, strike in –, close- with; echo, enter into one's views, agree in opinion; vote –, give one's voice- for; recognize; subscribe –, conform –, defer- to; say -yes, – ditto, – amen, – aye- to; to O.K.

acknowledge, own, admit, allow, avow, confess; concede &c. (*yield*) 762; come round to; abide by; permit &c. 760.

come to –, arrive at- -an understanding, – terms, – an agreement.

con-, af-firm; ratify, approve, endorse, countersign; visa; corroborate &c. 467.

go –, swim- with the stream, float with the current; be in the fashion, join in the chorus; be in every mouth.

**Adj.** assenting &c. *v.*; of one -accord, – mind; of the same mind, at one with, agreed, acquiescent, content; willing &c. 602.

un-contradicted, -challenged, -questioned, -controverted.

carried –, agreed- -*nem. con.* &c. *adv.*; unanimous; agreed on all hands, carried by acclamation.

affirmative &c. 535.

**Adv.** yes, yea, ay, aye, true; good; well; very -well, – true; well and good; granted; *placet*; even –, just- so; to be sure, surely, 'thou hast said'; truly, exactly, precisely,

**489. Dissent.—N.** dissent; discordance &c. (*disagreement*) 24; difference –, diversity- of opinion.

non-conformity &c. (*heterodoxy*) 984; protestantism, recusancy, schism; disaffection; secession &c. 624; recantation &c. 607.

dissension &c. (*discord*) 713; discontent &c. 832; cavilling.

protest; contradiction &c. (*denial*) 536; non-compliance &c. (*rejection*) 764; disapprobation &c. 932; hartal.

dissent-ient, -er; non-juror, -content; recusant, sectary, schismatic, protestant, non-conformist, separatist, non-co-operator, conscientious objector, passive resister.

**V.** dissent, demur; call in question &c. (*doubt*) 485; differ in opinion, disagree; say -no &c. 536; refuse -assent, – to admit, cavil, protest, raise one's voice against, make bold to differ; repudiate; contradict &c. (*deny*) 536; agree to differ.

have no notion of, differ *toto cælo*: revolt -at, – from the idea.

shake the head, shrug the shoulders; look -askance, – askant.

secede; recant &c. 607.

**Adj.** dissenting &c. *v.*; negative &c. 536; diss-ident, -entient; unconsenting &c. (*refusing*) 764; non-content, -juring; protestant, recusant; uncon-vinced, -verted.

unavowed, unacknowledged; out of the question.

discontented &c. 832; unwilling &c. 603; extorted.

sectarian, denominational, schismatic, heterodox, intolerant.

**Adv.** no &c. 536; at -variance, – issue- with; under protest; *non placet.*

**Int.** God forbid! not for the world; not on your life; I beg to differ; I'll be hanged if; never tell me; your humble servant, pardon me; tell that to the marines.

**Phr.** many men many minds; *quot homines tot sententiæ; tant s'en faut; il s'en faut bien.*

---

that's just it, indeed, certainly, certes, *ex concesso*; of course, unquestionably, assuredly, no doubt, doubtless, undoubtedly.

be it so; so -be it, – let it be, so mote it be; amen; with all my heart; willingly &c. 602.

affirmatively, in the affirmative.

with one -consent, – voice, – accord; unanimously, *unâ voce*, by common consent, in chorus, to a man, *nem. con.*; *nemine -contradicente, – dissentiente*; without a dissentient voice; as one man, one and all, on all hands.

**490. Knowledge.—N.** knowledge; cogn-izance, -ition, -oscence; acquaintance, experience, ken privity, insight, familiarity; com-, ap-prehension; recognition; appreciation &c. (*judgment*) 480; intuition; consci-ence, -ousness; perception, precognition; acroamatics.

light, enlightenment; glimpse, inkling; side light; glimmer, -ing; dawn; scent, suspicion; impression &c. (*idea*) 453; discovery &c. 480*a*.

system –, body- of knowledge; science, philosophy, pansophy; theory, etiology; circle of the sciences; pandect, doctrine, body of doctrine; cy-, ency-clopædia; school &c. (*system of opinions*) 484.

tree of knowledge; republic of letters &c. (*language*) 560.

erudition, learning, lore, scholarship, reading, letters; literature; booklearning, bookishness; biblio-mania, -latry; information, general information; store of -knowledge &c.; education &c. (*teaching*) 537; culture, attainments; acqui-rements, -sitions; accomplishments, proficiency; practical knowledge &c. (*skill*) 698; higher education, liberal education; dilettantism; rudiments &c. (*beginning*) 66.

deep –, profound –, solid –, accurate –, acroatic –, acroamatic –, vast –, exensive –, encyclopædical- -knowledge, – learning; omniscience, pantology.

march of intellect; progress –, advance- of -science, – learning; schoolmaster abroad.

**V.** know, ken, scan, wot; wot –, be aware &c. *adj.*- of; ween, weet, trow, have, possess.

conceive; ap-, com-prehend; take, realize, understand, appreciate; fathom, make out; recognize, discern, perceive, see, get a sight of, experience.

**491. Ignorance. — N.** ignorance, nescience, *tabula rasa*, crass ignorance, *ignorance crasse*; unacquaintance; unconsciousness &c. *adj.*; dark-, blindness; incomprehension, inexperience, simplicity.

unknown quantities, $x, y, z$.

sealed book, *terra incognita*, virgin soil, unexplored ground; dark ages.

[Imperfect knowledge] smattering, superficiality, half-learning, sciolism, glimmering; bewilderment &c. (*uncertainty*) 475; incapacity.

[Affectation of knowledge] pedantry; charlatan-ry, -ism.

**V.** be -ignorant &c. *adj.*; not -know &c. 490; know -not, – not what, – nothing of; have no -idea, – notion, – conception; not have the remotest idea; not know chalk from cheese.

ignore, be blind to; keep in ignorance &c. (*conceal*) 528.

see through a glass darkly; have a -film over the eyes, – glimmering &c. *n.*; wonder whether; not know what to make of &c. (*unintelligibility*) 519; not pretend –, not take upon oneself- to say.

**Adj.** ignorant, nescient; un-knowing, -aware, -acquainted, -apprized, -witting, -weeting, -conscious; wit-, weetless; a stranger to; unconversant.

un-informed, -cultivated, -versed, -instructed, -taught, -initiated, -tutored, -schooled, -guided, -enlightened; Philistine; behind the age.

shallow, superficial, green, rude, empty, half-learned, illiterate; un-read, -informed, -educated, -learned, -lettered, -bookish; empty-headed; lowbrow; pedantic.

in the dark; be-nighted, -lated; blind-ed, -fold; hoodwinked; misinformed; *au bout de son latin*, at the

know full well; have –, possess- some knowledge of; be *-au courant* &c. *adj.*; have -in one's head, – at one's fingers' ends; know by -heart, – rote; be master of; *connaître le dessous des cartes*, know what's what &c. 698.

see one's way; learn, discover &c. 480*a*.

come to one's knowledge &c. (*information*) 527.

**Adj.** knowing &c. *v.*; cognitive; acroamatic.

aware –, cognizant –, conscious- of; acquainted –, made acquainted- with; privy –, no stranger- to; *au -fait*, *– courant*; in the secret; up –, alive- to; sensible of; behind the scenes, – curtain; let into; apprised –, informed- of; undeceived.

proficient –, versed –, read –, forward –, strong –, at home- in; conversant –, familiar- with.

erudite, instructed, learned, lettered, educated; high-brow; well-conned, -informed, -read, -grounded, -educated; enlightened, shrewd, insightful, *savant*, blue, bookish, scholastic, solid, profound, deep-read, book-learned; accomplished &c. (*skilful*) 698; omniscient; self-taught, -educated.

known &c. *v.*; ascertained, well-known, recognized, received, notorious, noted; proverbial; familiar, – as household words, to every schoolboy; hackneyed, trite, commonplace.

knowable, cogn-oscible, -izable.

**Adv.** to –, to the best of- one's knowledge.

**Phr.** one's eyes being opened &c. (*disclosure*) 529.

end of his tether; at fault; at sea &c. (*uncertain*) 475; caught tripping.

un-known, -apprehended, -explained, -ascertained, -investigated, -explored, -heard of, -perceived; concealed &c. 528; novel.

**Adv.** ignorantly &c. *adj.*; unawares; for -anything, – aught- one knows; not that one knows.

**Int.** God –, Heaven –, the Lord –, nobody- knows.

**Phr.** a little learning is a dangerous thing.

---

**492. Scholar—N.** scholar, *connoisseur*, *savant*, pundit, schoolman, professor, graduate, wrangler, moonshee; academ-ician, -ist; fellow, don, post graduate, advanced student; master –, bachelor- of arts; doctor, licentiate, gownsman; philo-sopher, -math; scientist, clerk; soph, -ist, -ister; linguist, classicist; glosso-, etymo-, philologist; philologer; lexico-, glosso-grapher; scholiast, commentator, annotator, grammarian; *littérateur*, *literati*, *dilettanti*, *illuminati*; Mezzofanti, admirable Crichton, Mæcenas.

book-worm, *helluo librorum*, biblio-phile, -maniac; blue-stocking, *bas-bleu*; big-wig, learned Theban.

learned –, literary- man; *homo multarum literarum*; man of -learning, – letters, – education; high-brow, intelligentsia.

antiquar-ian, -y; archæologist; sage &c. (*wise man*) 500.

pedant, *doctrinaire*; pedagogue, Dr. Pangloss; pantologist.

teacher &c. 540; schoolboy &c. (*learner*) 541.

**Adj.** learned &c. 490; brought up at the feet of **Gamaliel**.

**493. Ignoramus.—N.** ignoramus, illiterate, moron, dunce, numskull, wooden spoon; no scholar.

sciolist, smatterer, dabbler, half-scholar; *charlatan*; wiseacre.

novice, griffin; greenhorn &c. (*dupe*) 547; tyro &c. (*learner*) 541.

lubber &c. (*bungler*) 701; fool &c. 501; pedant &c. 492.

**Adj.** bookless, shallow, simple, dense, dumb, thick, dull, ignorant &c. 491.

**494.** [Object of knowledge.] **Truth.** —**N.** fact, reality &c. (*existence*) 1; plain matter of fact; nature &c. (*principle*) 5; truth, verity; gospel; orthodoxy &c. 983*a*; authenticity; veracity &c. 543.

accuracy, exactitude; exact-, precise-ness &c. *adj.*; precision, delicacy; rigour, mathematical precision, punctuality; clockwork precision &c. (*regularity*) 80.

orthology; *ipsissima verba*; letter of the law, realism.

plain –, honest –, sober –, naked –, unalloyed –, unqualified –, stern –, exact –, intrinsic- truth; *nuda veritas*; the very thing; not an -illusion &c. 495; real Simon Pure; unvarnished tale; the truth, the whole truth and nothing but the truth; just the thing.

**V.** be -true &c. *adj.*, – the case; stand the test; have the true ring; hold -good, – true, – water; conform to rule.

render –, prove- -true &c. *adj.*; substantiate &c. (*evidence*) 467.

get at the truth &c. (*discover*) 480*a*.

**Adj.** real, actual &c. (*existing*) 1; veritable, true; certain &c. 474; substantially –, categorically- true &c.; true -to the letter, – to life, – to scale, – the facts, – as gospel; unimpeachable; veracious &c. 543; unre-, uncon-futed; un-ideal, -imagined; realistic.

exact, accurate, definite, precise, well defined, just, right, correct, strict, severe; close &c. (*similar*) 17; literal; rigid, rigorous; scrupulous &c. (*conscientious*) 939; religiously exact, punctual, mathematical, scientific; faithful, constant, unerring; curious, particular, punctilious, meticulous, nice, delicate, fine.

genuine, authentic, legitimate, pukka; orthodox &c. 983*a*; official, *ex officio*.

pure, natural, sound, sterling; unsophisticated, -adulterated, -varnished, -coloured; in its true colours.

well-grounded, -founded; solid, substantial, tangible, valid; undis-torted, -guised; un-affected, -exaggerated, -romantic, -flattering.

**Adv.** truly &c. *adj.*; verily, indeed, in reality; as a matter of fact; beyond

**495. Error.**—**N.** error, fallacy; misconception, -apprehension, -understanding; inexactness &c. *adj.*; laxity; misconstruction &c. (*misinterpretation*) 523; miscomputation &c. (*misjudgment*) 481; *non-sequitur* &c. 477; misstatement, -report; anachronism; malapropism.

mistake; miss, fault, blunder, boner, bloomer, howler, *quid pro quo*, cross purposes, oversight, misprint, *erratum*, *corrigendum*, slip, blot, flaw, loose thread; trip, stumble &c. (*failure*) 732; botchery &c. (*want of skill*) 699; slip of the -tongue, – pen; *lapsus -linguæ*, *– calami*, clerical error; bull &c. (*absurdity*) 497.

il-, de-lusion; false -impression, – idea; bubble; self-deceit, -deception; warped notion; mists of error; superstition, exploded notion.

heresy &c. (*heterodoxy*) 984; hallucination &c. (*insanity*) 503; false light &c. (*fallacy of vision*) 443; dream &c. (*fancy*) 515; fable &c. (*untruth*) 546; bias &c. (*misjudgment*) 481; misleading &c. *v.*

**V.** be -erroneous &c. *adj.*

cause error; mis-lead, -guide; lead -astray, – into error; beguile, misinform &c. (*misteach*) 538; delude; give a false -impression, – idea; falsify, garble, misstate; deceive &c. 545; lie &c. 544.

err; be -in error &c. *adj.*, – mistaken &c. *v.*; be deceived &c. (*duped*) 547; mistake, receive a false impression, deceive oneself; fall into –, lie under –, labour under- -an error &c. *n.*; be in the wrong, blunder; mis-apprehend, -conceive, -understand, -reckon, -count, -calculate &c. (*misjudge*) 481.

play –, be- at cross purposes &c. (*misinterpret*) 523.

trip, stumble; lose oneself &c. (*uncertainty*) 475; go astray; fail &c. 732; take the wrong sow by the ear &c. (*mismanage*) 699; put the saddle on the wrong horse; reckon without one's host; take the shadow for the substance &c. (*credulity*) 486; dream &c. (*imagine*) 515.

**Adj.** erroneous, untrue, false, devoid of truth, fallacious, faulty, apocryphal.

-doubt, – question; with truth &c. (*veracity*) 543; certainly &c. (*certain*) 474; actually &c. (*existence*) 1; in effect &c. (*intrinsically*) 5.

exactly &c. *adj.*; *ad amussim*; *verbatim*, – *et literatim*; word for word, literally, *literatim*, *totidem verbis*, *sic*, to the letter, chapter and verse, *ipsissimis verbis*; *ad unguem*; to an inch; to a -nicety, – hair, – tittle, – turn, – T; *au pied de la lettre*; neither more nor less; in -every respect, – all respects; *sous tous les rapports*; at -any rate, – all events; strictly speaking.

**Phr.** the -truth, – fact- is; *rem acu tetigisti.*

unreal, ungrounded, groundless; unsubstantial &c. 4; heretical &c. (*heterodox*) 984; unsound; illogical &c. 477; wrong.

in-, un-exact; in-accurate, -correct; indefinite &c. (*uncertain*) 475.

illus-ive, -ory; delusive; mock; ideal &c. (*imaginary*) 515; spurious &c. 545; deceitful &c. 544; perverted.

controvertible, unsustain-able, -ed; unauthenticated, untrustworthy.

exploded, refuted, discarded.

in –, under an- error &c. *n.*; mistaken &c. *v.*; tripping &c. *v.*; out, – in one's reckoning; aberrant; beside –, wide of the- -mark, – truth; astray &c. (*at fault*) 475; on -a false, – the wrong-scent; in the wrong box; at cross purposes, all in the wrong, all abroad, at sea.

**Adv.** more or less.

**496. Maxim.**—**N.** maxim, aphorism; apo-, apoph-thegm; *dictum*, saying, gnome, adage, saw, proverb, epigram; sentence, *mot*, motto, word, by-word, precept, moral, phylactery, *protasis*, brocard.

axiom, postulate, theorem, *scholium*, truism.

reflection &c. (*idea*) 453; conclusion &c. (*judgment*) 480; golden rule &c. (*precept*) 697; principle, *principia*; profession of faith &c. (*belief*) 484; formula.

wise –, sage –, received –, admitted –, recognized- maxim &c.; true –, common –, hackneyed –, trite –, commonplace- saying &c.

**Adj.** aphoristic, proverbial, phylacteric; axiomatic, gnomic.

**Adv.** as -the saying is, – they say.

**497. Absurdity.**—**N.** absurd-ity, -ness &c. *adj.*; imbecility &c. 499; alogy, nonsense, paradox, inconsistency; stultiloqu-y, -ence, futility.

blunder, muddle, bull; Irish-, Hibernic-ism; slip-slop; anticlimax, bathos; sophism &c. 477.

farce, burlesque, *galimatias*, *amphigouri*, rhapsody; farrago &c. (*disorder*) 59; extravagance, romance; sciomachy.

joke, catch, sell, pun, verbal quibble, macaronic.

jargon, fustian, twaddle &c. (*no meaning*) 517; exaggeration &c. 549; moonshine, stuff; mare's nest.

vagary, tomfoolery, mummery, monkey trick, practical joke, *boutade*, *escapade*.

**V.** play the fool &c. 499; stultify, blunder, muddle; joke; talk nonsense, *parler à tort et à travers*; *battre la campagne*; be -absurd &c. *adj.*

**Adj.** absurd, nonsensical, preposterous, egregious, senseless, farcical, inconsistent, ridiculous, extravagant, quibbling, futile; macaronic, punning, paradoxical.

foolish &c. 499; sophistical &c. 477; unmeaning &c. 517; without rhyme or reason; fantastic.

**Int.** fiddle-de-dee! pish! pish and tush! pho! stuff and nonsense! rubbish! rot! bosh! in the name of the Prophet—figs!

**Phr.** *credat Judæus Apella*; tell it to the marines.

*Faculties*

**498. Intelligence. Wisdom.**—**N.** intelligence, capacity, comprehension,

**499. Imbecility. Folly.**—**N.** want of -intelligence &c. 498, – intellect &c.

understanding; intellect &c. 450; nous, parts, sagacity, mother wit, wit, *esprit*, gumption, quick parts, grasp of intellect; acuteness &c. *adj.*; acumen, subtlety, penetration; perspica-cy, -city; discernment, long-headedness, due sense of, good judgement; discrimination &c. 465; craftiness, cunning &c. 702; refinement &c. (*taste*) 850.

head, brains, gray matter, headpiece, upper story, long head, eagle -eye, – glance; eye of a -lynx, – hawk.

wisdom, sapience, sense; good –, common –, plain –, horse- sense; clear thinking; rationality, reason; reasonableness &c. *adj.*; judgement; solidity, depth, profundity, calibre; enlarged views; reach –, compass- of thought; enlargement of mind.

genius, inspiration, *Geist*, fire of genius, heaven-born genius, soul; talent &c. (*aptitude*) 698.

[Wisdom in action] prudence &c. 864; vigilance &c. 459; tact &c. 698; foresight &c. 510; sobriety, self-possession, *aplomb*, ballast, mental -poise, – balance.

a bright thought, inspiration, brainwave, not a bad idea.

**V.** be -intelligent &c. *adj.*; have all one's wits about one; understand &c. (*intelligible*) 518; catch –, take in- an idea; take a -joke, – hint.

see -through, – at a glance, – with half an eye, – far into, – through a millstone; penetrate; discern &c. (*descry*) 441; foresee &c. 510.

discriminate &c. 465; know what's what &c. 698; listen to reason.

**Adj.** [Applied to persons] intelligent, quick of apprehension, keen, acute, alive, brainy, awake, bright, quick, sharp; quick-, keen-, clear-, sharp- -eyed, -sighted, -witted; wide awake; canny, shrewd, astute; clear-headed; far-sighted &c. 510; discerning, perspicacious, penetrating, piercing; argute; nimble-, needle-witted; sharp as a needle; alive to &c. (*cognizant*) 490; clever &c. (*apt*) 698; arch &c. (*cunning*) 702; *pas si bête* &c. 682.

wise, sage, sapient, sagacious, reasonable, rational, sound, in one's right

450; shallow-, silli-, foolish-ness &c. *adj.*; imbecility, incapacity, vacancy of mind, poverty of intellect, clouded perception, poor head, apartments to let; stup-, stol-idity; hebetude, dull understanding, meanest capacity; short-sightedness; incompetence &c. (*unskilfulness*) 699.

one's weak side; bias &c. 481; infatuation &c. (*insanity*) 503.

simplicity, puerility, babyhood; dotage, anility, second childishness, senile dementia, fatuity; idio-cy, -tism; drivelling.

folly, frivolity, desipience, irrationality, trifling, ineptitude, nugacity, inconsistency, lip-wisdom, conceit; sophistry &c. 477; giddiness &c. (*inattention*) 458; eccentricity &c. 503; extravagance &c. (*absurdity*) 497; rashness &c. 863.

act of folly &c. 699.

**V.** be -imbecile &c. *adj.*; have no -brains, – sense &c. 498.

trifle, drivel, *radoter*, dote; ramble &c. (*madness*) 503; play the -fool, – monkey, – goat, take leave of one's senses; not see an inch beyond one's nose; stultify oneself &c. 699; talk nonsense &c. 497.

**Adj.** [Applied to persons] un-intelligent, -intellectual, -reasoning; mind-, wit-, reason-, brain-less; having no -head &c. 498; not -bright &c. 498; inapprehensible.

weak-, addle-, puzzle-, blunder-, muddle-, muddy-, pig-, beetle-, maggoty-, gross-headed; beef-, fat- -witted, -headed.

weak-, feeble-minded; dull-, shallow-, rattle-, lack-brained; half-, nit-, short-, dull-, blunt-witted; shallow-, clod-, addle-pated; dim-, short-sighted; thick-skulled; weak in the upper story.

shallow, *borné*, weak, wanting, soft, nutty, sappy, spoony; dull, – as a beetle; stupid, heavy, insulse, obtuse, blunt, stolid, doltish, asinine; inapt &c. 699; prosaic &c. 843.

child-ish, -like; infant-ine, -ile; baby-bab-ish; puerile, anile; simple &c. (*credulous*) 486.

fatuous, idiotic, imbecile, moronic

mind, sensible, *abnormis sapiens*, judicious, strong-minded.

un-prejudiced, -biassed, -bigoted, -prepossessed; un-dazzled, -perplexed; of unwarped judgment, impartial, equitable, fair, broad-minded.

cool; cool-, long-, hard-, strong-headed; long-sighted, calculating, thoughtful, reflecting; solid, deep, profound.

oracular; heaven-directed, -born.

prudent &c. (*cautious*) 864; sober, staid, solid; considerate, politic, wise in one's generation; watchful &c. 459; provident &c. (*prepared*) 673; in advance of one's age; wise as -a serpent, – Solomon, – Solon.

[Applied to actions] wise, sensible, reasonable, judicious; well-judged, -advised; prudent, politic; expedient &c. 646.

---

**500. Sage.—N.** sage, wise man; pundit; master -mind, – spirit of the age; longhead, thinker, philosopher.

authority, oracle, mentor, luminary, shining light, *esprit fort*, *magnus Apollo*, Solon, Solomon, Nestor, Magi, 'second Daniel.'

man of learning &c. 492; expert &c. 700; wizard &c. 994.

[Ironically] wiseacre, bigwig.

**Adj.** wise, learned; authoritative, oracular; erudite &c. 490; venerable, reverenced, revered, *emeritus*.

drivelling; blatant, babbling; vacant; sottish; bewildered &c. 475.

blockish, unteachable; Bœot-ian, -ic; bovine; un-gifted, -discerning, -enlightened, -wise, -philosophical; apish.

foolish, silly, senseless, irrational, insensate, nonsensical, inept; maudlin.

narrow-minded &c. 481; bigoted &c. (*obstinate*) 606; giddy &c. (*thoughtless*) 458; rash &c. 863; eccentric &c. (*crazed*) 503.

[Applied to actions] foolish, unwise, indiscreet, injudicious, improper, unreasonable, without reason, ridiculous, silly, stupid, asinine; ill-imagined, -advised, -judged, -devised; inconsistent, irrational, unphilosophical; extravagant &c. (*nonsensical*) 497; sleeveless, idle; useless &c. 645; inexpedient &c. 647; frivolous &c. (*trivial*) 643; absurd &c. 497.

**Phr.** *Davus sum non Œdipus.*

**501. Fool.—N.** fool, idiot, tomfool, wiseacre, simpleton, Simple Simon, nit-wit, witling, dizzard, donkey, ass; ninny, -hammer; moron, dolt, booby, Tom Noddy, looby, hoddy-doddy, noddy, nonny, noodle, nizy, owl; goose, -cap; *imbécile*; gaby, *radoteur*, nincompoop, *badaud*, zany; trifler, babbler; pretty fellow; natural, *niais*.

child, baby, infant, innocent, milksop, sop.

oaf, lout, loon, lown, dullard, doodle, calf, colt, buzzard, block, put, stick, stock, numps, tony.

---

bull-, dunder-, addle-, block-, dull-, logger-, jolt-, jolter-, beetle-, gross-, thick-, giddy-head; num-, thickskull; lack-, shallow-brain; half-, lack-wit; dunder-pate; fat-head, poor stick.

sawney, gowk; clod, -hopper; clod-, clot-poll, -pate; bull-calf; men of Bœotia, wise men of Gotham.

*un sot à triple étage*, sot; jobbernowl, changeling, mooncalf, *gobemouche*.

dotard, driveller; old -fogey, – woman; crone, grandmother.

greenhorn &c. (*dupe*) 547; dunce &c. (*ignoramus*) 493; lubber &c. (*bungler*) 701; madman &c. 504.

one who -will not set the Thames on fire, – did not invent gunpowder; *qui n'a pas inventé la poudre*; no conjuror.

**502. Sanity.—N.** sanity; soundness &c. *adj.*; rationality, normality, sobriety, lucidity, lucid interval; senses, sober senses, sound mind, *mens sana*.

**503. Insanity.—N.** disordered -reason, – intellect; diseased –, unsound –, abnormal- mind; derangement, unsoundness.

**V.** be -sane &c. *adj.*; retain one's senses, – reason.

become -sane &c. *adj.*; come to one's senses, sober down.

render -sane &c. *adj.*; bring to one's senses, sober.

**Adj.** sane, rational, reasonable, *compos mentis*, of sound mind; sound, -minded.

self-possessed; sober, -minded.

in one's -sober senses, – right mind; in possession of one's faculties.

**Adv.** sanely &c. *adj.*

---

insanity, lunacy; madness &c. *adj.*; mania, *rabies*, *furor*, mental alienation, paranoia, aberration; *amentia*, dementation, -tia, -cy; *dementia præcox*; *morosis*, idiocy, phrenitis, frenzy, raving, incoherence, wandering, delirium, calenture of the brain, delusion, hallucination; lycanthropy, brain storm, *delirium tremens*, D.T's.

vertigo, dizziness, swimming; sunstroke, *coup de soleil*, siriasis.

fanaticism, infatuation, craze; oddity, eccentricity, twist, monomania; klepto-, dipso-mania; hypochondriasis &c. (*low spirits*) 837; *melancholia*, hysteria.

screw –, tile –, slate- loose; bee in one's bonnet, rats in the upper story;

dotage &c. (*imbecility*) 499.

**V.** be –, become- -insane &c. *adj.*; lose one's senses, – reason, – faculties, – wits; go –, run- mad, run amuck; rave, dote, ramble, wander; drivel &c. (*be imbecile*) 499; have a -screw loose &c. *n.*, – devil; *avoir le diable au corps*; lose one's head &c. (*be uncertain*) 475.

derange, render –, drive- -mad &c. *adj.*; madden, dementate, addle the wits, derange the head, infatuate, befool; turn -the brain, – one's head.

**Adj.** insane, mad, lunatic; crazy, crazed, *aliéné*, *non compos mentis*; not right, cracked, touched; bereft of reason; unhinged, deranged, unsettled in one's mind; insensate, reasonless, beside oneself, demented, daft; phren-, fren-zied, -etic; possessed, – with a devil; far gone, maddened, moonstruck; shatterpated; barmy; mad-, scatter-, shatter-, crack-brained; off one's head; bug-house, *loco*.

maniacal; manic, manic-depressive; delirious, light-headed, incoherent, rambling, doting, wandering; frantic, raving, stark staring mad, amok, amuck, berserk.

corybantic, dithyrambic; rabid, giddy, vertiginous, dizzy, wild, haggard, mazed; flighty; distr-acted, -aught; bewildered &c. (*uncertain*) 475.

mad as a -March hare, – hatter; of -unsound mind &c. *n.*; touched –, wrong –, not right- in one's -head, – mind, – wits, – upper story; out of one's -mind, – senses, – wits; not in one's right mind.

fanatical, infatuated, odd, eccentric; hipp-ed, -ish.

imbecile, silly &c. 499.

**Adv.** like one possessed.

**Phr.** the mind having lost its balance; the reason under a cloud; *tête -exaltée, -montée.*

**504. Madman.—N.** madman, lunatic, maniac, bedlamite, candidate for Bedlam, raver, madcap; energumen; paranoiac; auto-, mono-, pyro-, megalo-, dipso-, klepto-maniac; hypochondriac &c. (*low spirits*) 837.

dreamer &c. 515; rhapsodist, seer, high-flier, enthusiast, crank, eccentric, nut, fanatic, *fanatico*; *exalté*; knight errant, Don Quixote.

idiot &c. 501.

## Section VI. Extension of Thought

### 1°. *To the Past*

**505. Memory.—N.** memory, remembrance; reten-tion, -tiveness; tenacity; *veteris vestigia flammæ*; tablets of the memory; readiness.

reminiscence, recognition, recurrence, recollection, rememoration; retrospect, -ion; after-thought.

suggestion &c. (*information*) 527; prompting &c. *v.*; hint, reminder, token of remembrance, *memento*, *souvenir*, keepsake, relic, *memorandum*; remembrancer, flapper; memorial &c. (*record*) 551; commemoration &c. (*celebration*) 883.

things to be remembered, *memorabilia*.

art of –, artificial- memory; *memoria technica*; mnemo-nics, -technics; phrenotypics; Mnemosyne; memorandum-, note-, engagement-, prompt-book.

retentive –, tenacious –, green –, trustworthy –, capacious –, faithful –, correct –, exact –, ready –, prompt- memory.

**V.** remember, mind; retain the -memory, – remembrance- of; keep in view.

have –, hold –, bear –, carry –, keep –, retain- in *or* in the -thoughts, – mind, – memory, – remembrance; be in –, live in –, remain in –, dwell in –, haunt –, impress- one's -memory, – thoughts, – mind.

sink in the mind; run in the head; not be able to get it out of one's head; be deeply impressed with; rankle &c. (*revenge*) 919.

recur to the mind; flash -on the mind, – across the memory.

recognize, recollect, bethink oneself, recall, call up, conjure up, retrace; look –, trace- -back, – backwards; think –, look back- upon; review; call –, recall –, bring- to mind; remembrance; carry one's thoughts back; rake up the past.

suggest &c. (*inform*) 527; prompt; put –, keep- in mind; remind; fan the embers; call –, summon –, rip- up; renew; *infandum renovare dolorem*; task –, tax –, jog –, flap –, refresh –, rub up –, awaken- the memory; pull by the sleeve; bring back to the memory, put in remembrance, memorialize.

get –, have –, learn –, know –, say –, repeat- by -heart – rote; drive –, get- into -one's head; say one's lesson; repeat, – as a parrot; have at one's fingers' ends.

**506. Oblivion.—N.** oblivion; forgetfulness &c. *adj.*; obliteration &c. 552, of –, insensibility &c. 823 to- the past.

short –, treacherous –, loose –, slippery –, failing- memory; decay –, failure –, lapse- of memory; memory like a sieve; waters of -Lethe, – oblivion, *amnesia*.

pardon, acquittal, amnesty, oblivion; absolution.

**V.** forget; be -forgetful &c. *adj.*; fall –, sink- into oblivion; have -a short memory &c. *n.*, – no head.

forget one's own name, have on the tip of one's tongue, come in at one ear and go out at the other.

slip –, escape –, fade from –, die away from- the memory; lose, – sight of.

unlearn; efface &c. 552 –, discharge- from the memory; consign to -oblivion, – the tomb of the Capulets; think no more of &c. (*turn the attention from*) 458; cast behind one's back, wean one's thoughts from; let bygones be bygones &c. (*forgive*) 918.

**Adj.** forgotten &c. *v.*; unremembered, past recollection, bygone, out of mind; buried –, sunk- in oblivion; clean forgotten; gone out of one's -head, – recollection.

forgetful, oblivious, mindless, heedless, Lethean; insensible &c. 823- to the past.

**Phr.** *non mi ricordo*; the memory -failing, – deserting one, – being at (*or* in) fault.

commit to memory; memorize; con, – over; fix –, rivet –, imprint –, impress –, stamp –, grave –, engrave –, store –, treasure up –, bottle up –, embalm –, enshrine- in the memory; load –, store –, stuff –, burden- the memory with.

redeem from oblivion; keep the memory -alive, – green; *tangere ulcus*; keep up the memory of; commemorate &c. (*celebrate*) 883.

make a note of &c. (*record*) 551.

**Adj.** remember-ing, -ed &c. *v.*; mindful, reminiscential; retained in the memory &c. *v.*; pent up in one's memory; fresh; green, – in remembrance, still vivid; unforgotten, present to the mind; within one's -memory &c. *n.*; indelible; not to be forgotten, unforgettable, enduring; uppermost in one's thoughts; memorable &c. (*important*) 642.

**Adv.** by -heart, – rote; without book, *memoriter*.

in memory of; *in memoriam*; suggestive.

**Phr.** *manet altâ mente repostum*; *forsan et hæc olim meminisse juvabit.*

2°. *To the Future*

**507. Expectation.—N.** expect-ation, -ance, -ancy; anticipation, reckoning, calculation; contingency; foresight &c. 510.

contemplation, prospection, look out; prospect, perspective, horizon, vista; destiny &c. 152.

suspense, waiting, abeyance; curiosity &c. 455; anxious –, ardent –, eager –, breathless –, sanguine- expectation; torment of Tantalus.

presumption, hope &c. 858; trust &c. (*belief*) 484; prognostication, auspices &c. (*prediction*) 511.

**V.** expect; look -for, – out for, – forward to; hope for, anticipate; have in -prospect, – contemplation; keep in view; contemplate, promise oneself; not -wonder &c. 870 -at, – if.

wait –, tarry –, lie in wait –, watch –, bargain- for; keep a -good, – sharp- look-out for; await; stand at 'attention,' abide, bide one's –, mark- time, watch.

foresee &c. 510; prepare for &c. 673; forestall &c. (*be early*) 132; count upon &c. (*believe in*) 484; think likely &c. (*probability*) 472; make one's mouth water.

lead one to expect &c. (*predict*) 511; have in store for &c. (*destiny*) 152.

prick up one's ears, hold one's breath.

**Adj.** expectant; expecting &c. *v.*; in -expectation &c. *n.*; on the watch &c. (*vigilant*) 459; open -eyed, -mouthed;

**508. Inexpectation.—N.** in-, non-expectation; false expectation &c. (*disappointment*) 509; miscalculation &c. 481; unforeseen contingency, the unforeseen, the unexpected.

surprise, sudden burst, thunderclap, blow, shock; bolt out of the blue; eye-opener; wonder &c. 870.

**V.** not -expect &c. 507; be taken by surprise; start; miscalculate &c. 481; not bargain for; come –, fall- upon.

be -unexpected &c. *adj.*; come -unawares &c. *adv.*; turn up, pop, drop from the clouds; come –, burst –, flash –, bounce –, steal –, creep- upon one; come –, burst- like a thunderclap, -bolt; take –, catch- -by surprise, – unawares, – napping.

pounce –, spring a mine- upon.

surprise, startle, take aback, electrify, stun, stagger, take away one's breath, throw off one's guard; astonish &c. (*strike with wonder*) 870.

**Adj.** non-expectant; surprised &c. *v.*; un-warned, -aware; off one's guard; inattentive &c. 458.

un-expected, -anticipated, -prepared for, -looked for, -foreseen, -hoped for; dropped from the clouds; beyond –, contrary to –, against- expectation; out of one's reckoning; unheard of &c. (*exceptional*) 83; startling; sudden &c. (*instantaneous*) 113.

**Adv.** abruptly, unexpectedly, plump, pop, *à l'improviste*, unawares; without-

agape, gaping, all agog; on -tenter-hooks, – tiptoe, – the tiptoe of expectation; *aux aguets*; ready; curious &c. 455; looking forward to; prepared for; on the rack.

expected &c. *v.*; long expected, foreseen; in prospect &c. *n.*; prospective; in -one's eye, – view, – the horizon; impending &c. (*destiny*) 152.

-notice, – warning, – saying 'by your leave'; like a -thief in the night, – thunderbolt; in an unguarded moment; suddenly &c. (*instantaneously*) 113.

**Int.** heyday! &c. (*wonder*) 870.

**Phr.** little did one -think, – expect; nobody would ever -suppose, – think, – expect; who would have thought?

---

**Adv.** expectantly; in the event of; on the watch &c. *adj.*; with -breathless expectation &c. *n.*, – bated breath, – eyes, – ears strained; *erectis auribus*; on edge.

**Phr.** we shall see; *nous verrons.*

**509.** [Failure of expectation.] **Disappointment.—N.** disappointment, disillusionment; blighted hope, balk; blow; slip 'twixt cup and lip; non-fulfilment of one's hopes; sad –, bitter- disappointment; trick of fortune; afterclap; false –, vain- expectation; miscalculation &c. 481; fool's paradise; much cry and little wool.

**V.** be disappointed; look -blank, – blue; look –, stand- -aghast &c. (*wonder*) 870; find to one's cost; laugh on the wrong side of one's mouth; find one a false prophet.

disappoint; crush –, dash –, balk –, disappoint –, blight –, falsify –, defeat –, not realize- one's -hope, – expectation; balk, jilt, bilk; play one -false, – a trick; dash the cup from the lips; tantalize; dumb-found, -founder; disillusion, -ize; dissatisfy, disgruntle.

**Adj.** disappointed &c. *v.*; disconcerted, aghast; out of one's reckoning; disgruntled.

**Phr.** the mountain brought forth a mouse; *nascitur ridiculus mus; parturiunt montes; dis aliter visum,* the bubble burst; one's countenance falling.

**510. Foresight.—N.** foresight, prospicience, prevision, longsightedness; anticipation; providence &c. (*preparation*) 673.

fore-thought, -cast; pre-deliberation, -surmise; foregone conclusion &c. (*prejudgment*) 481; prudence &c. (*caution*) 864.

foreknowledge; *prognosis*; pre-cognition, -science, -notion, -sentiment; second sight; sagacity &c. (*intelligence*) 498.

prospect &c. (*expectation*) 507; foretaste; prospectus &c. (*plan*) 626.

**V.** foresee; look -forwards to, – ahead, – beyond; scent from afar; feel in one's bones; look –, pry –, peep- into the future.

see one's way; see how the -land lies, – wind blows, – cat jumps.

anticipate; expect &c. 507; be beforehand &c. (*early*) 132; predict &c. 511; fore-know, -judge, -cast; surmise; have an eye to the -future, – main chance; *respicere finem*; keep a sharp look-out &c. (*vigilance*) 459; forewarn &c. 668.

**Adj.** foreseeing &c. *v.*; prescient; anticipatory; far-seeing, -sighted; sagacious &c. (*intelligent*) 498; weather-wise; provident &c. (*prepared*) 673; prospective &c. 507.

**Adv.** against the time when.

**511. Prediction.—N.** prediction, announcement; program, programme &c. (*plan*) 626; premonition &c. (*warning*) 668; *prognosis,* prophecy, vaticination, mantology, prognostication, premonstration, augur-y, -ation; a-, ha-riolation; fore-, a-boding; bode-, abode-ment; omin-ation,

-ousness; auspices, forecast; sign, presage, prognostic; omen &c. 512; horoscope, nativity; sooth, -saying; fortune-telling; divination; crystal gazing, necromancy &c. 992; prophet &c. 512.

[Divination by the stars] astrology, horoscopy, astromancy, judicial astrology.*

[Place of prediction] *adytum.*

prefigur-ation, -ement; prototype, type.

**V.** predict, prognosticate, prophesy, vaticinate, divine, foretell, soothsay, augurate, tell fortunes; cast a -horoscope, – nativity; advise; forewarn &c. 668.

presage, augur, bode; a-, fore-bode, -cast; fore-, be-token; prefigure, -show; portend; fore-show, -shadow, shadow forth, typify, ominate, signify, point to, precurse.

usher in, herald, premise, announce; lower.

hold out –, raise –, excite- -expectation, – hope; bid fair, promise, lead one to expect; be the -precursor &c. 64.

**Adj.** predicting &c. *v.*; predictive, prophetic, fatidical, vaticinal, oracular, Sibylline, haruspical, weatherwise.

ominous, presageful, portentous; augur-ous, -al, -ial; auspici-al, -ous; prescious, monitory, extispicious, premonitory, precursory, significant of, pregnant with, big with the fate of.

**Phr.** 'coming events cast their shadows before.'

**512. Omen.—N.** omen, portent, presage, prognostic, augury, auspice; sign &c. (*indication*) 550; herald, forerunner, harbinger &c. (*precursor*) 64.

bird of ill omen; signs of the times; gathering clouds; warning &c. 668.

prefigurement &c. 511.

**513. Oracle.—N.** oracle; prophet, -ess; seer, soothsayer, augur, fortune-teller, palmist, medium, clairvoyant, crystal gazer, witch, geomancer, *aruspex*; a-, ha-ruspice; Sibyl; Python, -ess; Pythia; Pythian –, Delphian- oracle; Monitor, Sphinx, Tiresias, Cassandra, Sibylline leaves; Zadkiel, Old Moore; sorcerer &c. 994; interpreter &c. 524.

## Section VII. Creative Thought

**514. Supposition.—N.** supposition, assumption, postulation, condition, pre-supposition, hypothesis, postulate, *postulatum*, theory, *data*; pro-, position; *thesis*, theorem; proposal &c. (*plan*) 626.

* The following terms, expressive of different forms of divination, have been collected from various sources, and are here given as a curious illustration of bygone superstitions:

Divination *by oracles*, Theomancy; *by the Bible*, Bibliomancy; *by ghosts*, Psychomancy; *by spirits seen in a magic lens*, Cristallomantia; *by shadows or manes*, Sciomancy; *by appearances in the air*, Aeromancy, Chaomancy; *by the stars at birth*, Genethliacs; *by meteors*, Meteoromancy; *by winds*, Austromancy; *by sacrificial appearances*, Aruspicy (*or* Haruspicy), Hieromancy, Hieroscopy; *by the entrails of animals sacrificed*, Hieromancy; *by the entrails of a human sacrifice*, Anthropomancy; *by the entrails of fishes*, Ichthyomancy; *by sacrificial fire*, Pyromancy; *by red-hot iron*, Sideromancy; *by smoke from the altar*, Capnomancy; *by mice*, Myomancy; *by birds*, Orniscopy, Ornithomancy; *by a cock picking up grains*, Alectryomancy (*or* Alectoromancy); *by fishes*, Ophiomancy; *by herbs*, Botanomancy; *by water*, Hydromancy; *by fountains*

bare –, vague –, loose- -supposition, – suggestion; conceit; conjecture; guess, – work; rough guess, shot; conjecturality; surmise, suspicion, inkling, suggestion, suggestiveness, association of ideas, hint; presumption &c. (*belief*) 484; divination, speculation.

theorist, speculator, doctrinarian, hypothesist.

**V.** suppose, conjecture, surmise, suspect, guess, divine; theorize; pre-sume, -surmise, -suppose; assume, fancy, wis, take it; give a guess, speculate, believe, dare say, take it into one's head, take for granted.

put forth; pro-pound, -pose; moot; hypothesize; start, put a case, submit, move, make a motion; hazard –, throw out –, put forward- a - suggestion, – conjecture.

allude to, suggest, hint, put it into one's head.

suggest itself &c. (*thought*) 451; run in the head &c. (*memory*) 505; marvel –, wonder- -if, – whether.

**Adj.** supposing &c. *v.*; given, mooted, postulatory; assumed &c. *v.* supposit-ive, -itious; gratuitous, speculative, conjectural, hypothetical, suppositional, theoretical, academic, supposable, presumptive, putative.

suggestive, allusive, stimulating.

**Adv.** if, – so be; an; on the -supposition &c. *n.*; *ex hypothesi*; in -case, – the event of; *quasi*, as if, provided; perhaps &c. (*by possibility*) 470; for aught one knows.

**515. Imagination.—N.** imagination; originality; invention; fancy; inspiration; *verve*; empathy.

warm –, heated –, excited –, sanguine –, ardent –, fiery –, boiling –, wild –, bold –, daring –, playful –, lively –, fertile- -imagination, – fancy.

'mind's eye'; 'such stuff as dreams are made of.'

ideal-ity, -ism; romanticism, utopianism, castle-building; dreaming; frenzy; ecs-, ex-tasy; calenture &c. (*delirium*) 503; reverie, brown study, trance; somnambulism.

conception, *vorstellung*, excogitation, 'a fine frenzy,' poetic frenzy, divine afflatus; cloud-, dream-land; flight –, fumes- of fancy; 'thick-coming fancies'; creation –, coinage- of the brain; imagery, word painting.

conceit, maggot, figment, myth, dream, vision, shadow, chimera; phan-tasm, -tasy; fantasy, fancy; whim, -sey; vagary, rhapsody, romance, *extravaganza*; air-drawn dagger, bugbear, nightmare; flying Dutchman, great sea-serpent, man in the moon, castle in the air, *châteaux en Espagne*; Utopia, Atlantis, happy valley, millennium, fairy land; land of Prester John, kingdom of Micomicon; work of fiction &c. (*novel*) 594; poetry &c. 597; drama &c. 599; Arabian nights; *le pot au lait*; dream of Alnaschar &c. (*hope*) 858; day –, golden- dream.

illusion &c. (*error*) 495; phantom &c. (*fallacy of vision*) 443; *Fata*

Pegomancy; *by a wand*, Rhabdomancy; *by dough of cakes*, Crithomancy; *by meal*, Aleuromancy, Alphitomancy; *by salt*, Halomancy; *by dice*, Cleromancy; *by arrows*, Belomancy; *by a balanced hatchet*, Axinomancy; *by a balanced sieve*, Coscinomancy; *by a suspended ring*, Dactyliomancy; *by dots made at random on paper*, Geomancy; *by precious stones*, Lithomancy; *by pebbles*, Pessomancy; *by pebbles drawn from a heap*, Psephomancy; *by mirrors*, Catoptromancy; *by writings in ashes*, Tephramancy; *by dreams*, Oneiromancy; *by the hand*, Palmistry, Chiromancy; *by nails reflecting the sun's rays*, Onychomancy; *by finger rings*, Dactylomancy; *by numbers*, Arithmancy; *by drawing lots*, Sortilege; *by passages in books*, Stichomancy; *by the letters forming the name of the person*, Onomancy, Nomancy; *by the features*, Anthroposcopy; *by the mode of laughing*, Geloscopy; *by ventriloquism*, Gastromancy; *by walking in a circle*, Gyromancy; *by dropping melted wax into water*, Ceromancy; *by currents*, Bletonism.

*Morgana* &c. (*ignis fatuus*) 423; vapour &c. (*cloud*) 353; stretch of the imagination &c. (*exaggeration*) 549.

idealist, romanticist, visionary; mopus; romancer, dreamer; somnambulist; rhapsodist &c. (*fanatic*) 504.

**V.** imagine, fancy, conceive; ideal-, real-ize; dream, – of; 'give to airy nothing a local habitation and a name.'

create, originate, devise, invent, coin, fabricate; improvise, strike out something new.

set one's wits to work; strain –, crack- one's invention; rack –, ransack –, cudgel- one's brains; excogitate.

give -play, – the reins, – a loose- to the -imagination, – fancy; empathize; indulge in reverie.

conjure up a vision; fancy –, represent –, picture –, figure- to oneself; envisage.

float in the mind; suggest itself &c. (*thought*) 451.

**Adj.** imagined &c. *v.*; *ben trovato*; air-drawn, -built.

imagin-ing &c. *v.*, -ative; original, inventive, creative, fertile, productive; ingenious.

romantic, high-flown, flighty, extravagant, fanatic, enthusiastic, Utopian, Quixotic; preposterous, rhapsodical.

ideal, unreal; in the clouds, *in nubibus*; unsubstantial &c. 4; illusory &c. (*fallacious*) 495; fictitious, theoretical, hypothetical.

fabulous, legendary; myth-ic, -ological; chimerical; imagin-, visionary; notional; fan-cy, -ciful, -tastic, -tastical; whimsical; fairy, -like.

dreamy, entranced, vaporous.

---

## Division (II.) COMMUNICATION OF IDEAS

### Section I. Nature of Ideas Communicated

**516.** [Idea to be conveyed.] **Meaning.** [Thing signified.]—**N.** meaning; signific-ation, -ance; sense, expression; im-, pur-port; drift, tenor, implication, connotation, essence, force, spirit, bearing, colouring; scope.

matter; subject, -matter; argument, text, sum and substance; gist &c. 5.

general –, broad –, substantial –, colloquial –, literal –, plain –, simple –, accepted –, natural –, unstrained –, true &c. (*exact*) 494 –, honest &c. 543 –, *primâ facie* &c. (*manifest*) 525- meaning.

literality; literal interpretation; after acceptation; allusion &c. (*latency*) 526; suggestion &c. (*information*) 527; synonym; figure of speech &c. 521; acceptation &c. (*interpretation*) 522.

**V.** mean, signify, express, connote, denote; im-, pur-port; convey, imply, breathe, indicate, bespeak, bear a sense; tell –, speak- of; touch on; point –, allude- to; drive at; involve &c. (*latency*) 526; declare &c. (*affirm*) 535.

**517.** [Absence of meaning.] **Unmeaningness.**—**N.** unmeaningness &c. *adj.*; scrabble, scribble, scrawl, daub, (*painting*), strumming (*music*).

empty sound, dead letter, *vox et præterea nihil*; 'a tale told by an idiot, full of sound and fury, signifying nothing'; 'sounding brass and a tinkling cymbal.'

nonsense, jargon, gibberish, jabber, mere words, hocus-pocus, fustian, rant, bombast, balderdash, palaver, patter, flummery, verbiage, babble, *bavardage*, *baragouin*, platitude, *niaiserie*; inanity; rigmarole, rodomontade; truism; *nugæ canoræ*; twaddle, twattle, fudge, trash; stuff, – and nonsense; bosh, rubbish, rot, drivel, moonshine, wish-wash, fiddle-faddle, flapdoodle; absurdity &c. 497; vagueness &c. (*unintelligibility*) 519.

**V.** mean nothing; be -unmeaning &c. *adj.*; twaddle, quibble, rant, gabble, scrabble &c. *n.*

**Adj.** unmeaning; meaning-, sense-less;

understand by &c. (*interpret*) 522.

**Adj.** meaning &c. *v.*; expressive, suggestive, meaningful, allusive; signific-ant, -ative, -atory; pithy; full of –, pregnant with- meaning.

declaratory &c. 535; intelligible &c. 518; literal, metaphrastic; synonymous; tantamount &c. (*equivalent*) 27; implied &c. (*latent*) 526; explicit &c. 525; literal &c. 562.

**Adv.** to that effect; that is to say &c. (*being interpreted*) 522.

literally; evidently, from the context.

**518. Intelligibility.—N.** intelligibility, clearness, clarity, explicitness &c. *adj.*; lucidity, perspicuity; legibility, plain speaking &c. (*manifestation*) 525; precision &c. 494; a word to the wise.

**V.** be -intelligible &c. *adj.*; speak -for itself, – volumes; tell its own tale, lie on the surface.

render -intelligible &c. *adj.*; popularize, simplify, clear up; elucidate &c. (*explain*) 522.

understand, comprehend; take, – in; catch, grasp, recognize, follow, collect, master, make out; see -with half an eye, – daylight, – one's way; enter into the ideas of; come to an understanding.

**Adj.** intelligible; clear, – as -day, – crystal, – noonday; lucid; per-, transpicuous; luminous, transparent; comprehensible.

easily understood, easy to understand, for the million, intelligible to the meanest capacity, popularized.

plain, distinct, explicit, clear-cut; positive; definite &c. (*precise*) 494.

graphic, vivid, telling; expressive &c. (*meaning*) 516; illustrative &c. (*explanatory*) 522.

un-ambiguous, -equivocal, -mistakable &c. (*manifest*) 525, -confused; legible, recognizable; obvious &c. 525.

**Adv.** in plain -terms, – words, – English.

**Phr.** he that runs may read &c. (*manifest*) 525.

nonsensical; void of -sense &c. 516.

in-, un-expressive; vacant, fatuous; not significant; insignificant.

trashy, washy, inane, vague, trumpery, trivial, fiddle-faddle, twaddling, quibbling.

unmeant, not expressed; tacit &c. (*latent*) 526.

inexpressible, undefinable, incommunicable.

**Int.** rubbish! &c. 497.

---

**519. Unintelligibility.—N.** unintelligibility, incomprehensibility, imperspicuity; inconceivableness, vagueness &c. *adj.*; obscurity; ambiguity &c. 520; doubtful meaning; uncertainty &c. 475; perplexity &c. (*confusion*) 59; spinosity; *obscurum per obscurius*; mystification &c. (*concealment*) 528; latency &c. 526; transcendentalism.

paradox; enigma, riddle &c. (*secret*) 533; *dignus vindice nodus*; sealed book; steganography, Freemasonry.

*pons asinorum*, asses' bridge; double –, high- Dutch, Greek, Hebrew; jargon &c. (*unmeaning*) 517.

obscurantist.

**V.** be -unintelligible &c. *adj.*; require -explanation &c. 522; have a doubtful meaning, pass comprehension.

render -unintelligible &c. *adj.*; conceal &c. 528; darken &c. 421; confuse &c. (*derange*) 61; perplex &c. (*bewilder*) 475.

not -understand &c. 518; lose, – the clue; miss; not know what to make of, be able to make nothing of, give it up; not be able to -account for, – make either head or tail of; be at sea &c. (*uncertain*) 475; wonder &c. 870; see through a glass darkly &c. (*ignorance*) 491.

not understand one another; play at cross purposes &c. (*misinterpret*) 523.

**Adj.** un-intelligible, -accountable, -decipherable, -discoverable, -knowable, -fathomable; in-cognizable, -explicable, -scrutable; inap-, incomprehensible; insol-vable, -uble; impenetrable.

illegible, indecipherable, as Greek to one, unexplained, paradoxical; enigmatic, -al; puzzling, baffling.

obscure, dark, muddy, clear as mud, seen through a mist, dim, nebulous, shrouded in mystery; undiscernible &c. (*invisible*) 447; misty &c. (*opaque*) 426; hidden &c. 528; latent &c. 526.

indefinite &c. (*indistinct*) 447; perplexed &c. (*confused*) 59; undetermined, vague, loose, ambiguous; mysterious; mystic, -al; transcendental; occult, recondite, esoteric, abstruse, crabbed.

incon-ceivable, -ceptible; searchless; above –, beyond –, past- comprehension; beyond one's depth; unconceived.

inexpressible, undefinable, incommunicable, unutterable, ineffable, unpronounceable.

**520.** [Having a double sense.] **Equivocalness.—N.** equivocalness &c. *adj.*; double -meaning &c. 516; ambiguity, *double entendre*, pun, paragram, *calembour*, quibble, *équivoque*, anagram; conundrum &c. (*riddle*) 533; word-play &c. (*wit*) 842; homonym, -y; amphibo-ly, -logy; ambiloquy.

Sphinx, Delphic oracle.

equivocation &c. (*duplicity*) 544; white lie, mental reservation &c. (*concealment*) 528.

**V.** be -equivocal &c. *adj.*; have two -meanings &c. 516; equivocate &c. (*palter*) 544.

**Adj.** equivocal, ambiguous, amphibolous, homonymous; double-tongued &c. (*lying*) 544.

**521. Metaphor.—N.** figure of speech; *façon de parler*, way of speaking, colloquialism.

phrase &c. 566; figure, trope, metaphor, tralatition, metonymy, enallage, *catachresis*, *synecdoche*, *antonomasia*; irony, satire, figurativeness &c. *adj.*; image, -ry; *metalepsis*, type, anagoge, simile, personification, *prosopopœia*, allegory, apologue, parable, fable; allusion, adumbration; application; euphemism; euphuism.

**V.** employ -metaphor &c. *n.*; personify, allegorize, adumbrate, shadow forth, apply, allude –, refer- to.

**Adj.** metaphorical &c. *n.*; figurative, catachrestical, typical, tralatitious, parabolic, allegorical, allusive, anagogical; ironical; colloquial.

**Adv.** so to -speak, – say, – express oneself; as it were.

**Phr.** *mutato nomine de te fabula narratur.*

**522. Interpretation.—N.** interpretation, definition; explan-, explic-ation; solution, answer; rationale; plain –, simple –, strict- interpretation; meaning &c. 516.

translation; rend-ering, -ition; reddition; literal –, free- translation; key, crib; secret; clew &c. (*indication*) 550; Rosetta stone.

*exegesis*; ex-pounding, -position; Hermeneutics; comment, -ary; inference &c. (*deduction*) 480; illustration, exemplification; gloss, annotation, *scholium*, note; e-, di-lucidation, enucleation; *éclaircissement*, *mot de l'énigme*.

symptomat-, semei-ology; metoposcopy, physiognomy; diagnosis, prog-

**523. Misinterpretation. — N.** mis-interpretation, -apprehension, -understanding, -acceptation, -construction, -application; *catachresis*; cross -reading, – purposes; mistake &c. 495.

misrepresentation, perversion, exaggeration &c. 549; false -colouring, – construction; abuse of terms; parody, travesty; falsification &c. (*lying*) 544.

**V.** mis-interpret, -apprehend, -understand, -conceive, -judge, -doubt, -spell, -translate, -construe, -apply; mistake &c. 495.

misrepresent, pervert; garble &c. (*falsify*) 544; distort, detort; travesty, play upon words; stretch –, strain –, wrest- the -sense, – meaning; explain

nosis; paleography &c. (*philology*) 560;

accept-ion, -ation, -ance; light, reading, lection, construction, version.

equivalent, – meaning &c. 516; synonym; para-, meta-phrase; convertible terms, apposition; dictionary &c. 562; polyglot.

**V.** interpret, explain, define, construe, translate, render; do –, turn- into; transfuse the sense of.

find out &c. 480*a*- -the meaning &c. 516- of; read; spell –, figure –, make- out; decipher, decode, unravel, disentangle, puzzle out; find the key of, enucleate, resolve, solve; read between the lines.

account for; find –, tell- the cause &c. 153- of; throw –, shed- -light, – new light, – a fresh light- upon; clear up, elucidate.

illustrate, exemplify; unfold, expound, comment upon, annotate; popularize &c. (*render intelligible*) 518.

take –, understand –, receive –, accept- in a particular sense; understand by, put a construction on, be given to understand.

**Adj.** explanatory, expository; explica-tive, -tory; exegetical; hermeneutic, interpretive, illustrative, elucidative, annotative scholiastic.

polyglot; literal; para-, meta-phrastic; cosignificative, synonymous; equivalent &c. 27.

**Adv.** in -explanation &c. *n.*; that is to say, *id est, videlicet,* to wit, namely, in other words.

literally, strictly speaking; in -plain, – plainer- -terms, – words, – English; more simply.

away; put a -bad, – false- construction on; give a false colouring, look through rose coloured –, – dark – spectacles; be –, play- at cross purposes.

**Adj.** misinterpreted &c. *v.*; untrans-lat-ed, -able.

**Adv.** at cross purposes.

---

**524. Interpreter.—N.** interpreter, translator, ex-positor, -pounder, -ponent, -plainer; demonstrator.

scholiast, commentator, annotator; meta-, para-phrast.

spokesman, speaker, mouthpiece, prolocutor; diplomat &c. 758.

guide, courier, dragoman, *valet de place, cicerone,* showman; oneirocritic; Œdipus; oracle &c. 513.

## Section II. Modes of Communication

**525. Manifestation.—N.** manifestation; unfolding; plainness &c. *adj.*; plain speaking; expression; showing &c. *v.*; exposition, demonstration, *séance*; exhibition, production; display, showing off &c. 882, premonstration. [Thing shown] exhibit, show.

indication &c. (*calling attention to*) 457; publicity &c. 531; disclosure &c. 529; openness &c. (*honesty*) 543, (*artlessness*) 703; *épanchement,* prominence.

**V.** make –, render- -manifest &c. *adj.*; bring -forth, – forward, – to the front, – into view; give notice; express; represent, set forth, exhibit; show, – up; expose; produce; hold up –, expose- to view; set –, place –, lay-

**526. Latency.—N.** latency, inexpression; hidden –, occult- meaning; occultness, occultism, mysticism, mystery, cabala, symbolism, anagoge; silence &c. (*taciturnity*) 585; concealment &c. 528; more than meets the -eye, – ear; Delphic oracle; *le dessous des cartes,* undercurrent.

allusion, insinuation, implication; innuendo &c. 527; adumbration; 'something rotten in the state of Denmark.'

snake in the grass &c. (*pitfall*) 667; secret &c. 533.

darkness, invisibility, imperceptibility.

latent influence, power behind the throne; friend at court, wire puller.

before -one, – one's eyes; tell to one's face; trot out, put through one's paces, unfold, show off, show forth, unveil, bring to light, display, demonstrate, unroll; lay open; draw –, bring- out; bring out in strong relief; call –, bring- into notice; hold up the mirror; wear one's heart upon his sleeve; show one's -face, – colours; manifest oneself; speak out; make no -mystery, – secret- of; unfurl the flag; proclaim &c. (*publish*) 531.

indicate &c. (*direct attention to*) 457; disclose &c. 529; elicit &c. 480*a*; interpret &c. 522.

be -manifest &c. *adj.*; appear &c. (*be visible*) 446; transpire &c. (*be disclosed*) 529; speak for itself, stand to reason; stare one in the face; loom large, appear on the horizon, rear its head; give -token, – sign, – indication of; tell its own tale &c. (*intelligible*) 518; go without saying.

**Adj.** manifest, apparent; salient, striking, demonstrative, prominent, in the foreground, notable, pronounced.

flagrant; notorious &c. (*public*) 531; arrant; stark staring; unshaded, glaring.

defin-ed, -ite; distinct, conspicuous &c. (*visible*) 446; obvious, evident, incontestable, unmistakable, not to be mistaken, plain, clear, palpable, self-evident, autoptical; intelligible &c. 518; clear as -day, – daylight, – noonday; plain as -a pikestaff, – the sun at noonday, – the nose on one's face, – the way to the parish church.

ostensible; open, – as day; overt, patent, express, explicit; naked, bare, literal, downright, undisguised, exoteric.

**V.** be -latent &c. *adj.*; lurk, smoulder, underlie, make no sign; escape -observation, – detection, – recognition; lie hid &c. 528.

laugh in one's sleeve; keep back &c. (*conceal*) 528.

involve, imply, implicate, connote, import, understand, allude to, infer, leave an inference; symbolize; whisper &c. (*conceal*) 528.

**Adj.** latent; lurking &c. *v.*; secret &c. 528; occult, symbolic, mystic; implied &c. *v.*; dormant.

un-apparent, -known, -seen &c. 441; in the background; invisible &c. 447; indiscoverable, dark; impenetrable &c. (*unintelligible*) 519; un-spied, -suspected.

un-said, -written, -published, -breathed, -talked of, -told &c. 527, -sung, -exposed, -proclaimed, -disclosed &c. 529, -pronounced, -mentioned, -expressed; not expressed, tacit.

un-developed, -solved, -explained, -traced, -discovered &c. 480*a*, -tracked. -explored, -invented.

indirect, crooked, inferential; by -inference, – implication; implicit; constructive; allusive, covert, muffled; steganographic; under-stood, -hand, -ground; concealed &c. 528; delitescent.

**Adv.** by a side wind; *sub silentio*; in the background; behind -the scenes, – one's back, – the veil; below the surface; on the tip of one's tongue; secretly &c. 528; between the lines; by a mutual understanding.

**Phr.** 'thereby hangs a tale.' 'that is another story.'

---

unreserved; frank, plain spoken &c. (*artless*) 703; barefaced, brazen, bold, shameless, daring, flaunting, loud.

manifested &c. *v.*; disclosed &c. 529; expressible, capable of being shown, producible; in-, un-concealable.

**Adv.** manifestly, openly &c. *adj.*; before one's eyes, under one's nose, to one's face, face to face, above board, *cartes sur table*, on the stage, in plain sight, in open court, in the open, – streets; at the cross roads; in market overt; in the face of -day, – heaven; in -broad –, open- daylight; without reserve; at first blush, *primâ facie*, on the face of; in set terms.

**Phr.** *cela saute aux yeux*; he that runs may read; you can see it with half an eye; it needs no ghost to tell us; the meaning lies on the surface; *cela va sans dire*; *res ipsa loquitur*.

**527. Information.**—**N.** information, enlightenment, acquaintance, knowledge &c. 490; publicity &c. 531.

communication, intimation; not-ice, -ification; e-, an-nunciation; announcement; representation, round robin, presentment.

case, estimate, specification, report, advice, monition; news &c. 532; return &c. (*record*) 551; account &c. (*description*) 594; statement &c. (*affirmation*) 535.

mention; acquainting &c. *v.*; instruction &c. (*teaching*) 537; outpouring; intercommunication, communicativeness.

informant, authority, teller, announcer, annunciator, harbinger, herald, intelligencer, commentator, columnist, reporter, exponent, mouthpiece; informer, keek, eavesdropper, delator, detective, sleuth; *mouchard*, spy stool pigeon, newsmonger; messenger &c. 534; *amicus curiæ*.

*valet de place*, *cicerone*, pilot, guide; guide-, hand-book; *vade mecum*; manual; map, plan, chart, gazetteer; itinerary &c. (*journey*) 266.

hint, suggestion, wrinkle, innuendo, inkling, whisper, passing word, word in the ear, subaudition, cue, by-play; gesture &c. (*indication*) 550; gentle – broad- hint; *verbum sapienti*; word to the wise; insinuation &c. (*latency*) 526.

**V.** tell; inform, – of; acquaint, – with; impart, – to; make acquainted with, bring to the ears of, apprise, advise, enlighten, awaken.

let fall, mention, express, intimate, represent, communicate, make known; publish &c. 531; notify, signify, specify, convey the knowledge of.

let one –, have one to- know; serve notice, give one to understand; give notice; set –, lay –, put- before; point out, put into one's head; put one in possession of; instruct &c. (*teach*) 537; direct the attention to &c. 457.

an-nounce, -nunciate; report, – progress; bring –, send –, leave –, write- word; tele-graph, -phone; ring –, call- up; wire; retail, render an account; give an account &c. (*describe*) 594; state &c. (*affirm*) 535.

**528. Concealment.**—**N.** concealment; hiding &c. *v.*; occultation, mystification.

seal of secrecy; screen &c. 530; disguise &c. 530; masquerade; masked battery; hiding place &c. 530; cipher, code, crypt-, stegan-ography; invisible –, sympathetic- ink; palimpsest; Freemasonry.

stealth, -iness; obreption; slyness &c. (*cunning*) 702.

latit-ancy, -ation; seclusion &c. 893; privacy, secrecy, secretness; *incognita*.

reticence; reserve; mental –, reservation, aside; *arrière pensée*, suppression, evasion, white lie, misprision; silence &c. (*taciturnity*) 585; suppression of truth &c. 544; underhand dealing; close-, secretive-ness &c. *adj.*; mystery.

latency &c. 526; snake in the grass; secret &c. 533.

**V.** conceal, hide, secrete, stow away, put out of sight; lock –, seal –, bottle- up.

cover, screen, cloak, veil, shroud; screen from -sight, – observation; draw the veil; draw –, close- the curtain; curtain, shade, eclipse, throw a veil over; be-cloud, -fog, -mask; mask, disguise; ensconce, muffle, smother; whisper.

keep -from, – back, – to oneself; keep -snug, – close, – secret, – dark; bury; sink, suppress; keep -from, – out of- -view, – sight; keep in –, throw into- the -shade, – background; cover up one's tracks; stifle, hush up, withhold, reserve; fence with a question; ignore &c. 460.

code, codify, use a cipher.

keep -a secret, – one's own counsel; hold one's tongue &c. (*silence*) 585; make no sign, not let it go further; not breathe a -word, – syllable- about; not let the right hand know what the left is doing; hide one's light under a bushel, bury one's talent in a napkin.

keep –, leave- in -the dark, – ignorance; blind, – the eyes; blindfold, hoodwink, mystify; puzzle &c. (*render uncertain*) 475; bamboozle &c. (*deceive*) 545.

be -concealed &c. *v.*; suffer an eclipse;

disclose &c. 529; show cause; explain &c. (*interpret*) 522.

hint; give an inkling of; give –, drop –, throw out- a hint; insinuate; allude –, make allusion- to; glance at; tip off, tip the wink &c. (*indicate*) 550; suggest, prompt, give the cue, breathe; whisper, – in the ear.

give a bit of one's mind; tell one plainly, – once for all; speak volumes.

un-deceive, -beguile; set right, correct, open the eyes of, disabuse.

be -informed of &c.; know &c. 490; learn &c. 539; get scent of, gather from; awaken –, open one's eyes- to; become -alive, – awake- to; keep posted; hear, overhear, understand.

come to one's -ears, – knowledge; reach one's ears.

**Adj.** informed &c. *v.*; *communiqué*; reported &c. *v.*; published &c. 531; advisory.

expressive &c. 516; explicit &c. (*open*) 525, (*clear*) 518; plain-spoken &c. (*artless*) 703.

declara-, nuncupa-, exposi-tory; declarative, enunciative, communicat-ive, -ory; oral.

**Adv.** from information received; according to -rumour, – report; in the air; from what one can gather.

**Phr.** a little bird told me.

---

retire from sight, couch; hide oneself; lie -hid, – in ambush, – low, – *perdu*, – snug, – close; seclude oneself &c. 893; lurk, sneak, skulk, slink, pussyfoot, prowl; steal -into, – out of, – by, – along; play at -bopeep, – hide and seek; hide in holes and corners.

**Adj.** concealed &c. *v.*; hidden; veiled, secret, recondite, mystic, cabalistic, occult, dark; cryptic, -al; private, privy, *in petto*, auricular, clandestine, close, inviolate.

behind a -screen &c. 530; under -cover, – an eclipse; in -ambush, – hiding, – disguise; in a -cloud, – fog, – mist, – haze, – dark corner; in the -shade, – dark; clouded, wrapt in clouds; invisible &c. 447; buried, underground, *perdu*; incommunicado; secluded &c. 893.

un-disclosed &c. 529, -told &c. 527; covert &c. (*latent*) 526; mysterious &c. (*unintelligible*) 519.

irrevealable, inviolable; confidential; esoteric; not to be spoken of.

obreptitious, furtive, stealthy, feline; skulking &c. *v.*; surreptitious, underhand, hole and corner; sly &c. (*cunning*) 702; secretive, evasive, non-committal, reserved, reticent, uncommunicative, buttoned up; close, – as wax; taciturn &c. 585.

**Adv.** secretly &c. *adj.*; in -secret, – private, – one's sleeve, – holes and corners; in the dark &c. *adj.*

*januis clausis*, with closed doors, *à huis clos*; hugger-mugger, *à la dérobée*; under the -cloak of, – rose, – table; *sub rosâ, en tapinois*, in the background, aside, on the sly, with bated breath, *sotto voce*, in a whisper, without beat of drum, *à la sourdine*.

in –, strict- confidence; confidentially &c. *adj.*; between -ourselves, – you and me; *entre nous, inter nos*, under the seal of secrecy; in -code, – cipher.

underhand, by stealth, like a thief in the night; stealthily &c. *adj.*; behind -the scenes, – the curtain, – one's back, – a screen &c. 530; *incognito*; *in camerâ*.

**Phr.** it -must, – will- go no further; 'tell it not in Gath,' nobody the wiser.

**529. Disclosure.—N.** disclosure; retection; unveiling &c. *v.*; deterration, revealment, revelation; divulgence, expos-ition, -ure; *exposé*; whole truth; tell-tale &c. (*news*) 532.

acknowledgment, avowal; confession, -al; shrift.

**530. Ambush.** [Means of concealment.]—**N.** hiding-place; secret -place. – drawer; recess, hole, funk hole, holes and corners; closet, crypt, *adytum*, abditory, *oubliette*, safe, – deposit; cache; am-bush, -buscade; stalking horse; lurking-hole, -place; secret path,

bursting of a bubble; *dénouement*.

**V.** dis-close, -cover, -mask; draw –, draw aside –, lift –, raise –, lift up –, remove –, tear- the -veil, – curtain; un-mask, -veil, -fold, -cover, -seal, -kennel; take off –, break- the seal; lay -open, – bare; expose; open, – up; bare, bring to light; evidence; make - clear, – evident, – manifest; evince.

divulge, reveal, break; let into the secret; reveal the secrets of the prison-house; tell &c. (*inform*) 527; breathe, utter, blab, peach; let -out, – fall, – drop, – the cat out of the bag; betray; tell tales, – out of school; come out with; give -vent, – utterance- to; open the lips, blurt out, vent, whisper about; speak out &c. (*make manifest*) 525; make public &c. 531; unriddle &c. (*find out*) 480*a*; split; blow the gaff; break the news.

acknowledge, allow, concede, grant, admit, own, confess, avow, throw off all disguise, turn inside out, make a clean breast; show one's -hand, – cards; unburden –, disburden- one's -mind, – conscience, – heart; open –, lay bare –, tell a piece of- one's mind; unbosom oneself, own to the soft impeachment; say –, speak- the truth; turn -King's, –Queen's, –State's- evidence.

raise –, drop –, lift –, remove –, throw off- the mask; expose; debunk; lay open; un-deceive, -beguile; disabuse, set right, correct, open the eyes of; *désillusionner*.

be -disclosed &c.; transpire, come to light; come in sight &c. (*be visible*) 446; become known, escape the lips; come –, ooze –, creep –, leak –, peep –, crop- out; show its -face, – colours; discover &c. itself; break through the clouds, flash on the mind.

**Adj.** disclosed &c. *v.*

**Int.** out with it!

**Phr.** the murder is out; a light breaks in upon one; the scales fall from one's eyes; the eyes are opened.

backstairs; retreat &c. (*refuge*) 666.

screen, cover, shade, blinker; veil, curtain, blind, *purdah*, cloak, cloud.

mask, vizor, visor, disguise, masquerade dress, domino; *camouflage*.

pitfall &c. (*source of danger*) 667; trap &c. (*snare*) 545.

**V.** ambush, ambuscade, lie in ambush &c. (*hide oneself*) 528; lie in wait for; set a trap for &c. (*deceive*) 545.

**Adv.** *aux aguets*.

**531. Publication.**—**N.** publication; public -announcement &c. 527; promulgation, propagation, proclamation, pronouncement, encyclical, *pronunciamento*; circulation, indiction, edition, imprint, impression, printing; hue and cry.

publicity, notoriety, currency, flagrancy, cry, *bruit*; *vox populi*; report &c. (*news*) 532.

the Press, fourth estate, public press, newspaper, periodical, journal, gazette; house organ, trade publication, tabloid; daily, weekly, monthly, quarterly, annual, magazine, monograph, book; review; news sheet, special edition, supplement, feature, rotogravure, comic strips; leaflet, pamphlet; telegraphy; publisher &c. *v.*

circular, – letter; manifesto, advertisement, puff, placard, bill, *affiche*, broadside, poster; notice &c. 527; programme.

**V.** publish; make -public, – known &c. (*information*) 527; speak –, talk- of; broach, utter; put forward; circulate, propagate, promulgate; spread –, abroad; rumour, diffuse, disseminate, evulgate; put –, give –, send- forth; emit, edit, get out; issue; cover, report; bring –, lay –, drag- before the public; give -out, – to the world; put –, bandy –, hawk –, buzz –, whisper –, bruit –, blaze- about; drag into the -open day, – limelight; voice.

proclaim, herald, blazon; blaze –, noise- abroad; sound a trumpet; trumpet –, thunder- forth; give tongue; announce with -beat of drum, – flourish of trumpets; proclaim -from the housetops, – at Charing Cross, at the cross roads; declare, declaim.

advertise, placard; post, – up; *afficher*, publish in the Gazette, send round the crier.

raise a -cry, – hue and cry, – report; set news afloat.

telegraph, cable, wireless, broadcast.

be -published &c.; be –, become- public &c. *adj.*; come out; go –, fly –, buzz –, blow- about; get -about, – abroad, – afloat, – wind; find vent; see the light; go forth, take air, acquire currency, pass current; go -the rounds, – the round of the newspapers, – through the length and breadth of the land; *virum volitare per ora*; pass from mouth to mouth; spread; run –, spread- like wildfire.

**Adj.** published &c. *v.*; current &c. (*news*) 532; in circulation, public; notorious; flagrant, arrant; open &c. 525; trumpet-tongued; encyclical, promulgatory; exoteric.

**Adv.** publicly &c. *adj.*; in open court, with open doors; in the limelight.

**Int.** *Oyez!* O yes! notice!

**Phr.** notice is hereby given; this is –, these are- to give notice.

**532. News.**—**N.** news; information &c. 527; piece –, budget- of -news, – information; report, story, yarn, copy, filler, intelligence, tidings; stop press news.

word, advice, *aviso,* message; dis-, des-patch; radio, telegram, cablegram, wireless telegram, radiogram, marconigram, communication, errand, embassy; *bulletin, petit bleu.*

rumour, hearsay, *on dit,* flying rumour, news stirring, cry, buzz, *bruit,* fame; talk, *ouï-dire,* scandal, eavesdropping; town –, table- talk; tittle-tattle; *canard,* topic of the day, idea afloat.

fresh –, stirring –, old –, stale- news; glad tidings; old –, stale- story.

narrator &c. (*describe*) 594; news-, scandal-monger; tale-bearer; tell-tale, gossip, tattler, busy-body, chatterer; informer.

**V.** transpire &c. (*be disclosed*) 529; rumour &c. (*publish*) 531.

**Adj.** many-tongued; rumoured; publicly –, currently- -rumoured, – reported; rife, current, floating, afloat, going about, in circulation, in everyone's mouth, all over the town.

**Adv.** as the story -goes, – runs; as they say, it is said.

**533. Secret.**—**N.** secret; dead –, profound- secret; *arcanum,* mystery; latency &c. 526; Asian mystery; sealed book, secrets of the prison-house; *le dessous des cartes.*

enigma, riddle, puzzle, nut to crack, conundrum, charade, rebus, logogriph; mono-, ana-gram; acrostic, cross-word puzzle; Sphinx; *crux criticorum.*

maze, labyrinth, Hyrcynian wood.

problem &c. (*question*) 461; paradox &c. (*difficulty*) 704; unintelligibility &c. 519; *terra incognita* &c. (*ignorance*) 491.

**Adj.** secret &c. (*concealed*) 528.

---

**534. Messenger.**—**N.** messenger, envoy, emissary, legate; nuncio, internuncio; intermediary; ambassador &c. (*diplomatist*) 758.

marshal, flag-bearer, herald, crier, trumpeter, bellman, pursuivant, *parlementaire, apparitor.*

courier, runner, dawk, *estafette*; Hermes, Mercury, Iris, Ariel.

postman, letter carrier, telegraph boy, messenger boy, district messenger; despatch rider, commissionaire, errand-boy.

mail; post, -office; letter-bag; mail -boat, – train, – coach, – van, air mail; tele-graph, -phone; cable, wire; carrier-pigeon; wireless tele-graph, -phone; radiotele-graph, -phone.

journalist, newspaperman, reporter; gentleman –, representative- of the press; sob sister; penny-a-liner; special –, war –, own- correspondent; spy, scout; informer &c. 527.

**535. Affirmation.—N.** affirm-ance, -ation; statement, allegation, assertion, predication, declaration, word, averment.

asseveration, adjuration, swearing, oath, affidavit; deposition &c. (*record*) 551; avouchment, assurance; protest, -ation; profession; acknowledgment &c. (*assent*) 488; pledge.

vote, voice, suffrage, ballot.

remark, observation; position &c. (*proposition*) 514; saying, *dictum*, sentence, *ipse dixit*.

emphasis, positiveness, peremptoriness; dogmatism &c. (*certainty*) 474; dogmatist &c. 887.

**V.** assert; make -an assertion &c. *n.*; have one's say; say, affirm, predicate, declare, state, represent; protest, profess.

put -forth, – forward; advance, allege, propose, propound, enunciate, enounce, broach, set forth, hold out, maintain, contend, pronounce, pretend.

depose, depone, aver, avow, avouch, asseverate, swear; make –, take one's- oath; make –, swear –, put in- an affidavit; take one's Bible oath, kiss the book, vow, *vitam impendere vero*; swear till -one is black in the face, – all's blue; be sworn, call Heaven to witness; vouch, warrant, certify, assure, swear by bell, book and candle.

swear by &c. (*believe*) 484; insist –, take one's stand- upon; emphasize, lay stress on; assert -roundly, – positively; lay down, – the law; raise one's voice, dogmatize, have the last word; rap out; repeat; re-assert, -affirm.

announce &c. (*information*) 527; acknowledge &c. (*assent*) 488; attest &c. (*evidence*) 467; adjure &c. (*put to one's oath*) 768.

**Adj.** asserting &c. *v.*; declaratory, predicatory, pronunciative, affirmative, *soi-disant*; positive; certain &c. 474; express, explicit &c. (*patent*) 525; absolute, emphatic, flat, broad, round, pointed, marked, distinct, decided, confident, assertive, insistent, trenchant, dogmatic, definitive, formal, solemn, categorical, peremptory; unretracted; predicable, affirmable.

**536. Negation.—N.** ne-, abne-gation; denial; dis-avowal, -claimer; abjuration; contra-diction, -vention; recusation, protest; rebuttal; recusancy &c. (*dissent*) 489; flat –, emphatic- -contradiction, – denial; *démenti*.

qualification &c. 469; repudiation &c. 610; retractation &c. 607; confutation &c. 479; refusal &c. 764; prohibition &c. 761.

**V.** deny; contra-dict, -vene; controvert, give denial to, gainsay, negative, shake the head.

dis-own, -affirm, -claim, -avow; recant &c. 607; revoke &c. (*abrogate*) 756.

dispute, impugn, traverse, rebut, join issue upon; bring –, call- in question &c. (*doubt*) 485.

deny -flatly, – peremptorily, – emphatically, – absolutely, – wholly, – entirely; give the lie to, belie.

repudiate &c. 610; set aside, ignore &c. 460; rebut &c. (*confute*) 479; qualify &c. 469; refuse &c. 764.

**Adj.** denying &c. *v.*; denied &c. *v.*; contradictory; negat-ive, -ory; revocatory; recusant &c. (*dissenting*) 489; at issue upon.

**Adv.** no, nay, not, nowise; not a -bit, – whit, – jot; not -at all, – in the least, – so; no such thing; nothing of the -kind, – sort; quite the contrary, *tout au contraire*, far from it; *tant s'en faut*; on no account, in no respect; by -no, – no manner of- means; negatively.

**Phr.** there never was a greater mistake; I know better; *non hæc in fœdera*.

**Adv.** affirmatively &c. *adj.*; in the affirmative.

with emphasis, *ex cathedrâ*, without fear of contradiction.

I must say, indeed, i' faith, let me tell you, why, give me leave to say, marry, you may be sure, I'd have you to know; upon my -word, – honour; by my troth, egad, I assure you; by -jingo, – Jove, – George, – &c.; troth, seriously, sadly; in –, in sober- -sadness, – truth, – earnest; of a truth, truly, pardi, perdy; in all conscience, upon oath; be assured &c. (*belief*) 484; yes &c. (*assent*) 488; I'll -warrant, – warrant you, – engage, – answer for it, – be bound, – venture to say, – take my oath; in fact, as a matter of fact, forsooth, joking apart; so help me God; not to mince the matter.

**Phr.** quoth he; *dixi*.

**537. Teaching.—N.** teaching &c. *v.*; instruction; edification; education; pedagogy; tuition; tutor-, tutel-age; direction, guidance.

qualification, preparation; train-, school-ing &c. *v.*; discipline; exer-cise, -citation; drill, practice.

persuasion, proselytism, propagandism, *propaganda*; in-doctrination, -culcation, -oculation.

explanation &c. (*interpretation*) 522; lesson, lecture, sermon, homily; apologue, parable; discourse, prelection, preachment, disquisition.

exercise, task; *curriculum*; course, – of study; grammar, three R's, initiation, A. B. C. &c. (*beginning*) 66.

elementary –, primary –, secondary –, grammar school –, high school –, college –, university –, technical –, liberal –, classical –, religious –, denominational –, moral –, secular- education; technical –, vocational- training; university extension lectures; propædeutics, moral tuition; evening classes, correspondence course.

physical education, gymnastics, calisthenics, eurythmics; *sloyd*.

**V.** teach, instruct, edify, school, tutor; cram, prime, coach; enlighten &c. (*inform*) 527.

in-culcate, -doctrinate, -oculate, -fuse, -stil, -fix, -graft, -filtrate; imbue, -pregnate, -plant; graft, sow the seeds of, disseminate, propagandize.

give an idea of; put -up to, – in the way of; set right.

sharpen the wits, enlarge the mind; give new ideas, open the eyes, bring forward, 'teach the young idea how to shoot'; improve &c. 658.

**538. Misteaching.—N.** mis-teaching, -information, -intelligence, -guidance, -direction, -persuasion, -instruction, -leading &c. *v.*; perversion, false teaching; sophistry &c. 477; college of Laputa; the blind leading the blind.

**V.** mis-inform, -teach, -direct, -guide, -instruct, -correct; pervert; put on a false –, throw off the- scent; deceive &c. 545; mislead &c. (*error*) 495; misrepresent; lie &c. 544; *spargere voces in vulgum ambiguas*, preach to the wise, teach one's grandmother to suck eggs.

render unintelligible &c. 519; bewilder &c. (*uncertainty*) 475; mystify &c. (*conceal*) 528; unteach.

**Adj.** misteaching &c. *v.*; unedifying.

**Phr.** *piscem natare doces*.

**539. Learning.—N.** learning; acquisition of -knowledge &c. 490, – skill &c. 698; acquirement, attainment; edification, scholarship, erudition; lore; information; self-instruction; study, reading, perusal; inquiry &c. 461.

ap-, prenticeship; pupil-age, -arity; tutelage, novitiate, matriculation.

docility &c. (*willingness*) 602; aptitude &c. 698.

**V.** learn; acquire –, gain –, receive –, take in –, drink in –, imbibe –, pick up –, gather –, get –, obtain –, collect –, glean- -knowledge, – information, – learning.

acquaint oneself with, master; make oneself -master of, – acquainted with; grind, cram; get –, coach- up; learn by -heart, – rote.

read, spell, peruse; con –, pore –, thumb- over; wade through; dip into;

expound &c. (*interpret*) 522; lecture; prelect; read –, give- a -lesson, – lecture, – sermon, – discourse; hold forth, preach; sermon-, moral-ize; point a moral.

train, discipline; bring up, – to; educate, form, ground, prepare, qualify, drill, exercise, practice, habituate, familiarize with, nurture, dry-nurse, breed, rear, take in hand; break, – in; tame; pre-instruct; initiate; inure &c. (*habituate*) 613.

put to nurse, send to school.

direct, guide; direct attention to &c. (*attention*) 457; impress upon the -mind, – memory; beat into, – the head; convince &c. (*belief*) 484.

**Adj.** teaching &c. *v.*; taught &c. *v.*; educational; scholastic, academic, doctrinal; disciplinal; instructive, didactic, hortative, pedagogic, tutorial.

**Phr.** the schoolmaster abroad.

run the eye -over, – through; turn over the leaves.

study; be -studious &c. *adj.*; consume the midnight oil, mind one's book.

go to -school, – college, – the university; serve -an (*or* one's) apprenticeship, – one's time; learn one's trade; be -informed &c. 527; be -taught &c. 537.

**Adj.** studious; schol-astic, -arly; teachable; docile &c. (*willing*) 602; apt &c. 698, industrious &c. 682; learned, erudite.

**Adv.** at one's books; *in statu pupillari* &c. (*learner*) 541.

———

**540. Teacher.**—**N.** teacher, trainer, instructor, institutor, master, tutor, don, director, Corypheus, dry nurse, coach, grinder, crammer; governor, bear-leader; governess, duenna; disciplinarian.

professor, lecturer, reader, prelector, prolocutor, preacher; Boanerges; pastor &c. (*clergy*) 996; schoolmaster, dominie, usher, pedagogue, abecedarian; schoolmistress, dame, monitor, proctor, pupil-teacher.

expositor &c. 524; preceptor, guide; mentor &c. (*adviser*) 695; pioneer, apostle, missionary, propagandist, moonshee; example &c. (*model for imitation*) 22.

professorship &c. (*school*) 542.

tutelage &c. (*teaching*) 537.

**Adj.** professorial, tutorial &c. 537.

**541. Learner.**—**N.** learner, scholar, student, *alumnus*, *élève*, pupil; apprentice; articled clerk; school-boy, -girl, beginner, tyro, abecedarian, alphabetarian.

recruit, novice, neophyte, tenderfoot, inceptor, *débutant*, catechumen, probationer; undergraduate; freshman, frosh; sophomore, junior, senior; junior –, senior- soph; sophister, questionist, fellow-, commoner, pensioner, exhibitioner, sizar, scholar, fellow, advanced –, post graduate –, research- student.

class, form, grade, standard, remove; pupilage &c. (*learning*) 539.

disciple, follower, apostle, proselyte; fellow student, school-mate, -fellow, class mate, condisciple.

**Adj.** *in statu pupillari*, in leading strings, sophomoric.

**542. School.**—**N.** school, academy, university, *alma mater*, college, seminary, Lyceum; instit-ute, -ution, *conservatoire*; *palæstra*, *gymnasium*.

day –, boarding –, public –, preparatory –, elementary –, primary –, infant –, dame's –, grammar –, middle class –, Board –, County –, Council –, parochial –, denominational –, Sunday –, National –, British and Foreign –, collegiate –, secondary –, continuation –, night –, correspondence –, secretarial –, military –, law –, medical –, business –, technical- school; technical –, training- college; Polytechnic; training ship; *Kindergarten*, nursery, *crèche*, reformatory.

pulpit, desk, reading desk, ambo, class-, lecture-room, theatre, amphitheatre, forum, stage, rostrum, platform, hustings, tribune.

school –, horn –, text- book; grammar, primer, abecedary, rudiments, manual, *vade mecum*, Lindley Murray, Cocker.

professor-, lecture-, reader-ship; chair; schoolmaster &c. 540.

School Board, Council of Education; *propaganda*.

**Adj.** scholastic, academic, collegiate; educational.

**Adv.** *ex cathedrâ*.

**543. Veracity.**—**N.** veracity; truthfulness, frankness &c. *adj.*; truth, sooth, sincerity, candour, honesty, fidelity; plain dealing, *bona fides*; love of truth; probity &c. 939; ingenuousness &c. (*artlessness*) 703.

the truth the whole truth and nothing but the truth; honest –, sober- truth &c. (*fact*) 494; unvarnished tale; light of truth.

**V.** speak –, tell- the truth; speak by the card; paint in its –, show oneself in one's-true colours; make a clean breast &c. (*disclose*) 529; speak one's mind &c. (*be blunt*) 703; not -lie &c. 544, – deceive &c. 545.

**Adj.** truthful, true; ver-acious, -edical; scrupulous &c. (*honourable*) 939; sincere, candid, frank, open, straightforward, unreserved; open-, true-, simple- hearted; honest, trustworthy; undissembling &c. (dissemble &c. 544); guileless, pure; unperjured, true blue, as good as one's word; unaffected, unfeigned, *bonâ fide*; outspoken, ingenuous &c. (*artless*) 703; undisguised &c. (*real*) 494.

**Adv.** truly &c. (*really*) 494; on oath; in plain words &c. 703; in –, with –, of a –, in good –, very- truth; as the -dial to the sun, – needle to the pole; honour bright; troth; in good -sooth, – earnest; unfeignedly, with no nonsense, in sooth, sooth to say, *bonâ fide*, *in foro conscientiæ*; without equivocation; *cartes sur table*, from the bottom of one's heart; by my troth &c. (*affirmation*) 535.

**544. Falsehood.** — **N.** false-hood, -ness; fals-ity, -ification; misrepresentation; deception &c. 545; untruth &c. 546; guile; bad faith; lying &c. *v.*; misrepresentation; mendacity, perjury, false swearing; forgery, invention, fabrication; subreption; covin.

perversion –, suppression- of truth; *suppressio veri*; perversion, distortion, false colouring; exaggeration &c. 549; prevarication, equivocation, shuffling, fencing, evasion, fraud; *suggestio falsi* &c. (*lie*) 546; mystification &c. (*concealment*) 528; simulation &c. (*imitation*) 19; dis-simulation, -sembling; deceit.

sham; pretence, pretending, malingering.

lip -homage, – service; mouth honour; hollowness; mere -show, – outside, eye-wash, window dressing; duplicity, double dealing, insincerity, hypocrisy, cant, humbug, casuistry; jesuit-ism, -ry; pharisaism; Machiavellism, 'organized hypocrisy'; crocodile tears, mealy-mouthedness, quackery; charlatan-ism, -ry; gammon; bun-kum, -come; flam, bam, flim-flam, cajolery, flattery; Judas kiss; perfidy &c. (*bad faith*) 940; *il volto sciolto i pensieri stretti*.

unfairness &c. (*dishonesty*) 940; artfulness &c. (*cunning*) 702; misstatement &c. (*error*) 495.

**V.** be -false &c. *adj.*, – a liar &c. 548; speak -falsely &c. *adv.*; tell -a lie &c. 546; lie, fib; lie like a trooper; swear falsely, forswear, perjure oneself, bear false witness.

mis-state, -quote, -cite, -report, -represent; belie, falsify, pervert, distort; put a false construction upon &c. (*misinterpret*) 523.

prevaricate, equivocate, quibble; palter, – to the understanding; *répondre en Normand*; trim, shuffle, fence, mince the truth, beat about the bush, blow hot and cold, play fast and loose.

garble, gloss over, disguise, give a colour to; give –, put- a -gloss, – false colouring- upon; colour, varnish, cook, dress up, embroider; varnish right and puzzle wrong, exaggerate &c. 549.

invent, fabricate; trump –, get- up; forge, hatch, concoct; romance &c. (*imagine*) 515; cry 'wolf!'

dis-semble, -simulate; feign, assume, put on, pretend, make believe; play -false, – a double game; coquet; act –, play- a part; affect &c. 855; simulate, pass off for; counterfeit, fake, sham, make a show of; malinger; swing the lead; say the grapes are sour.

cant, play the hypocrite, sham Abraham, *faire pattes de velours*, put on the mask, clean the outside of the platter, lie like a conjuror; hang out –, hold out –, sail under- false colours; 'commend the poisoned chalice to the lips'; *spargere voces in vulgum ambiguas*; deceive &c. 545.

**Adj.** false, deceitful, mendacious, unveracious, fraudulent, untruthful, dishonest; faith-, truth-, troth-less; un-fair, -candid; evasive; un-, dis-ingenuous; hollow, insincere, *Parthis mendacior*; forsworn.

canting; hypocrit-, jesuit-, pharisa-ical; tartuffish; Machiavelian; double-tongued, -faced, -handed, -minded, -hearted, -dealing; two-faced, bare-faced; Janus-faced; smooth-faced, -spoken, -tongued; plausible; mealy-mouthed; affected &c. 855.

collus-ive, -ory; artful &c. (*cunning*) 702; perfidious &c. 940, spurious &c. (*deceptive*) 545; untrue &c. 546; falsified &c. *v.*; covinous.

**Adv.** falsely &c. *adj.*; *à la Tartufe*, with a double tongue; out of whole cloth; slily &c. (*cunning*) 702.

**545. Deception.—N.** deception; falseness &c. 544; untruth &c. 546; impos-ition, -ture; fraud, deceit, guile; fraudulen-ce, -cy; covin; knavery &c. (*cunning*) 702; misrepresentation &c. (*falsehood*) 544.

delusion, gullery, bluff, spoof, *blague*; juggl-ing, -ery; sleight of hand, legerdemain; presti-giation, -digitation; magic &c. 992; conjur-ing, -ation; hocus-pocus, jockeyship; trickery, coggery, hanky-panky, chicanery, pettifogging, sharp practice; *supercherie*, cozenage, circumvention, ingannation, collusion; treachery &c. 940; practical joke.

trick, cheat, wile, ruse, blind, feint, plant, bubble, fetch, catch, chicane, juggle, reach, hocus, bite; thimble-rig, card-sharping, artful dodge, machination, swindle, hoax; tricks upon travellers; confidence trick; stratagem &c. (*artifice*) 702; theft &c. 791.

snare, trap, pitfall, decoy, gin; sprin-ge, -gle; noose, hook; bait, decoy-duck, tub to the whale, baited trap, *guet-à-pens*; cobweb, net, meshes, toils, mouse-trap, bird-lime; ambush &c. 530; trap-door, sliding panel, false bottom; spring-net, -gun; mask, -ed battery; mine booby trap.

Cornish hug; wolf in sheep's clothing &c. (*deceiver*) 548; disguise, -ment; false colours, masquerade, mummery, borrowed plumes; *pattes de velours*.

mockery &c. (*imitation*) 19; copy &c. 21; counterfeit, sham, Brummagem, make-believe, forgery, fraud, fake; lie &c. 546; 'a mockery, a delusion, and a snare,' hollow mockery.

whited –, painted- sepulchre; tinsel, paste, false jewellery, scagliola, ormolu, German silver, Britannia metal, paint; jerry building; man of straw.

illusion &c. (*error*) 495; *ignis fatuus* &c. 423; *mirage* &c. 443.

**V.** deceive, take in; defraud, cheat, jockey, do, cozen, diddle, nab, gyp, chouse, double cross, play one false, bilk, cully, jilt, bite, pluck, swindle, victimize; abuse; mystify; blind one's eyes; blindfold, hoodwink, spoof, bluff; throw dust into the eyes, 'keep the word of promise to the ear and break it to the hope,' 'draw a herring across the trail.'

impose –, practise –, play –, put –, palm –, foist- upon; snatch a verdict.

circumvent, overreach; out-reach, -wit, -manœuvre; steal a march upon, give the go-by to, leave in the lurch.

set –, lay- a -trap, – snare- for; bait the hook, forelay, spread the toils, lime; decoy, waylay, lure, beguile, delude, inveigle; tra-, tre-pan; kidnap; let-, hook-in; trick; en-, in-trap, -snare, entoil, benet; nick, springe; catch, – in a trap; sniggle, entangle, illaqueate, hocus, practise on one's credulity, dupe, gull, hoax, fool, befool, bamboozle; hum, -bug; gammon, stuff up, dope, sell; play a -trick, – practical joke- upon one; balk, trip up, throw a tub to a whale; fool to the top of one's bent, send on -a wild goose chase, – a fool's errand; make -game, – a fool, – an April fool, – an ass- of; trifle with, cajole, flatter; come over &c. (*influence*) 615; gild the pill, make things pleasant, divert, put a good face upon; dissemble &c. 544.

cog, – the dice, play with marked cards; live by one's wits, play at hide and seek; obtain money under false pretences &c. (*steal*) 791; conjure, juggle, practise chicanery; gerrymander.

play –, palm –, foist –, fob- off.

lie &c. 544; misinform &c. 538; mislead &c. (*error*) 495; betray &c. 940; be -deceived &c. 547.

**Adj.** deceived &c. *v.*; deceiving &c. *v.*; cunning &c. 702; prestigi-ous, -atory; decept-ive, -ious; deceitful, covinous; delus-ive, -ory; illus-ive, -ory; elusive, insidious, *ad captandum vulgus*.

untrue &c. 546; mock, sham, make-believe, counterfeit, faked, pseudo, spurious, so-called, pretended, feigned, trumped up, bogus, scamped, fraudulent, tricky, factitious, artificial, bastard; surreptitious, illegitimate, contraband, adulterated, sophisticated; unsound, rotten at the core; colourable; disguised; meretricious; tinsel, pinchbeck, plated; catch-penny; Brummagem; simulated &c. 544.

**Adv.** under -false colours, – the garb of, – cover of; over the left.

**Phr.** *fronti nulla fides.*

**546. Untruth.—N.** untruth, falsehood, lie, story, thing that is not, fib, bounce, crammer, taradiddle, whopper.

forgery, fabrication, invention; mis-statement, -representation; perversion, falsification, gloss, *suggestio falsi*; exaggeration &c. 549.

fiction; fable, nursery tale; romance &c. (*imagination*) 515; untrue –, false –, trumped up- -story, – statement; thing devised by the enemy; *canard*; shave, sell, hum, yarn, traveller's tale, Canterbury tale, cock and bull story, fairy tale, clap-trap.

myth, moonshine, bosh, all my eye, -and Betty Martin, mare's nest, farce.

irony; half truth, white lie, pious fraud; mental reservation &c. (*concealment*) 528.

pretence, pretext; false -plea &c. 617; subterfuge, evasion, shift, shuffle, make-believe; sham &c. (*deception*) 545.

profession, empty words; Judas kiss &c. (*hypocrisy*) 544; disguise &c. (*mask*) 530.

**V.** have a false meaning; not ring true.

pretend, sham, feign, counterfeit, make believe.

**Adj.** untrue, false, trumped up; void of –, without- foundation; far from the truth, false as dicer's oaths; unfounded, *ben trovato*, invented, fabulous, fabricated, forged; fict-, fact-, supposit-, surrept-itious; e-, il-lusory; ironical; satirical; evasive; *soi-disant* &c. (*misnamed*) 565.

**Phr.** *se non è vero è ben trovato.*

**547. Dupe.**— **N.** dupe, gull, gudgeon, *gobemouche*, cull, cully, victim, sucker, pigeon, April fool; laughing stock &c. 857; Cyclops, simple Simon, flat, mug, greenhorn; fool &c. 501; puppet, cat's paw.

**V.** be -deceived &c. 545, – the dupe of; fall into a trap; swallow –, nibble at- the bait; bite; catch a Tartar.

**Adj.** credulous &c. 486; mistaken &c. (*error*) 495.

**548. Deceiver.**—**N.** deceiver &c. (deceive &c. 545); dissembler, hypocrite; sophist, Pharisee, Jesuit, Mawworm, Pecksniff, Joseph Surface, Tartufe, Janus; serpent, snake in the grass, cockatrice, Judas, wolf in sheep's clothing; Molly Maguire; jilt; shuffler.

liar &c. (lie &c. 544); story-teller, perjurer, false-witness, *menteur*, -*à triple etage*, -*à payer patente*; Scapin.

impostor, pretender, capper, decoy, fraud, *soi-disant*, humbug; adventurer; Cagliostro, Fernam Mendez Pinto; ass in lion's skin &c. (*bungler*) 701; actor &c. (*stage player*) 599.

quack, *charlatan*, mountebank, saltimbanco, *saltimbanque*, empiric, quacksalver, medicaster.

conjuror, juggler, magician, necromancer, trickster, prestidigitator, medium, jockey; crimp; decoy-duck, stool pigeon; rogue, knave, cheat; swindler &c. (*thief*) 792; jobber.

**549. Exaggeration.**—**N.** exaggeration; expansion &c. 194; hyperbole, stretch, strain, colouring; high colouring, caricature, *caricatura*; extravagance &c. (*nonsense*) 497; Baron Munchausen; men in buckram, yarn, fringe, embroidery, traveller's tale; Ossa upon Pelion.

storm in a teacup; much ado about nothing &c. (*over-estimation*) 482; puffery &c. (*boasting*) 884; rant &c. (*turgescence*) 577.

figure of speech, *façon de parler*; stretch of -fancy, – the imagination; flight of fancy &c. (*imagination*) 515.

false colouring &c. (*falsehood*) 544; aggravation &c. 835.

**V.** exaggerate, magnify, pile up, aggravate; amplify &c. (*expand*) 194; overestimate &c. 482; hyperbolize; over-charge, -state, -draw, -lay, -shoot the mark, -praise; make -much, – the most- of; strain, – a point; stretch, – a point; go great lengths; spin a long yarn; draw –, shoot with- a long-bow; deal in the marvellous.

out-Herod Herod, run riot, talk at random.

heighten, overcolour; colour -highly, – too highly; embroider, *broder*; flourish; colour &c. (*misrepresent*) 544; puff &c. (*boast*) 884.

**Adj.** exaggerated &c. *v.*; overwrought; bombastic &c. (*magniloquent*) 577; hyperbolical, on stilts; fabulous, extravagant, preposterous, egregious, *outré*, high-flying.

**Adv.** hyperbolically &c. *adj.*

## Section III. Means of Communicating Ideas

### 1.° *Natural Means*

**550. Indication.**—**N.** indication; symbol-ism, -ization; semeio-logy, -tics; sign of the times.

lineament, feature, *trait*, characteristic, trick, diagnostic; divining-rod; cloven hoof; footfall; means of recognition; earmark.

sign, symbol; ind-ex, -ice, -icator; point, -er; marker; exponent, note, token, symptom.

type, figure, emblem, cipher, device; representation &c. 554; epigraph, motto, posy.

gest-ure, -iculation; pantomime; wink, glance, leer; nod, shrug, beck; touch, nudge; grip; dactylo-logy, -nomy; Freemasonry, telegraphy, chirology, by-play, dumb-show; cue; hint &c. 527; clue, clew, key, scent, track &c. 551.

signal, -post; rocket, blue light; watch-fire, -tower; telegraph, semaphore, flag-staff; cresset, fiery cross; calumet; heliograph, signal-, flash-lamp.

mark, line, stroke, dash, score, stripe, streak, scratch, tick, dot, point, notch, nick, blaze; asterisk, red letter, italics, heavy type, inverted commas, quotation marks, sublineation, underlining, jotting; print; impr-int, -ess, -ession; note, annotation, mark of exclamation.

[For identification] badge, criterion; counter-check, -mark, -sign, -foil; duplicate, tally; label, tab, ticket, stub, billet, letter, counter, *tessera*, card, bill, check; witness, voucher; stamp; *cachet*; trade –, hall- mark; broad arrow; signature; address –, visiting- card; *carte de visite*; credentials &c. (*evidence*) 467; passport, indentity book, *carte d' identité*; attestation; hand, – writing, sign-manual; cipher; monogram, – mark, seal, sigil, signet; autograph, -y; paraph, brand; superscription; in-, en-dorsement; title, heading, rubric, docket; *mot -de passe, – du guet*; *passe-parole*; shibboleth; watch-, catch-, pass-word; *open sesame!*

insignia; banner, -et, -ol; bandrol; flag, colours, streamer, standard, eagle, labarum, oriflamb, *oriflamme*; figure-head; ensign; pen-non, -nant, -dant; burgee, blue Peter, jack, ancient, gonfalon, Union jack; tricolour, stars and stripes; bunting, Jolly Roger, *drapeau*, *pavillon*.

heraldry, crest; coat of –, arms; armorial bearings, hatchment; e-, scutcheon; shield, supporters; livery, uniform; cockade, *epaulette*, brassard, chevron; garland, chaplet, love-knot, fillet, favour.

[Of locality] beacon, cairn, post, staff, flagstaff, hand, pointer, vane, cock, weathercock; guide-, hand-, finger-, directing-, sign-post; pillars of Hercules, pharos, signal fire; bench-, land-, sea-mark; lighthouse, balize; pole-, load-, lode-star; cynosure, guide; address, direction, name; sign, -board.

[Of the future] warning &c. 668; omen &c. 512; prefigurement &c. 511. [Of the past] trace record &c. 551. [Of danger] warning &c. 668; alarm &c. 669. [Of authority] sceptre &c. 747. [Of triumph] trophy &c. 733. [Of quantity] gauge &c. 466. [Of distance] mile-stone, -post. [Of disgrace] brand, fool's cap, stigma, mark of Cain. [For detection] check, tell-tale; test &c. (*experiment*) 463.

notification &c. (*information*) 527; advertisement &c. (*publication*) 531.

word of command, call; bugle-, trumpet-call; reveille, taps; bell, alarum, cry; battle –, rallying- cry.

church, bell, angelus, sacring bell; muezzin.

exposition &c. (*explanation*) 522; proof &c. (*evidence*) 467; pattern &c. (*prototype*) 22.

V. indicate; be the -sign &c. *n.*- of; denote, betoken; argue, testify &c. (*evidence*) 467; bear the -impress &c. *n.*- of; con-note, -notate.

represent, stand for; typify &c. (*prefigure*) 511; symbolize.

put -an indication, – a mark, – &c. *n.*; note, mark, tick, blaze, stamp, earmark; set one's seal upon; label, ticket, docket; dot, spot, score, dash, trace, chalk; print; im-print, -press, surprint; engrave, stereotype. electrotype.

make a -sign &c. *n.*; signalize; give –, hang out- a signal; beck, -on; gesture; nod; wink, glance, leer, nudge, shrug, tip the wink; gesticulate; raise –, hold up- the -finger, – hand; saw the air, suit the action to the word.

wave –, unfurl –, hoist –, hang out- a banner &c. *n.*; wave -the hand, – a kerchief; give the cue &c. (*inform*) 527; show one's colours; give –, sound- an alarm; beat the drum, sound the trumpets, raise a cry.

sign, seal, attest &c. (*evidence*) 467; underline &c. (*give importance to*) 642; call attention to &c. (*attention*) 457; give notice &c. (*inform*) 527.

**Adj.** indicat-ing &c. *v.*, -ive, -ory; de-, con-notative; diacritical, representative, typical, symbolic, pantomimic, pathognomonic, symptomatic, ominous, characteristic, demonstrative, diagnostic, exponential, emblematic, armorial; individual &c. (*special*) 79.

known –, recognizable- by; indicated &c. *v.*; pointed, marked.

[Capable of being denoted] denotable; indelible.

**Adv.** in token of; symbolically &c. *adj.*; in dumb show.

**Phr.** *ecce signum*; *ex ungue leonem, ex pede Herculem.*

**551. Record.—N.** trace, vestige, relic, remains; scar, *cicatrix*; foot-step, -mark, -print; track, mark, wake, trail, spoor, scent, *piste.*

monument, hatchment, escutcheon, slab, tablet, trophy, achievement; obelisk, pillar, column, monolith, cromlech, dolmen; memorial; *memento* &c. (*memory*) 505; testimonial, medal, ribbon, order; commemoration &c. (*celebration*) 883.

record, note, minute; *dossier*; register, -try; census, roll &c. (*list*) 86; cartulary, diptych, Domesday book; entry, memorandum, indorsement, inscription, copy, duplicate, docket; notch &c. (*mark*) 550; muniment, deed &c. (*security*) 771; document; deposition, *procès-verbal*; affidavit; certificate &c. (*evidence*) 467.

note-, memorandum-, pocket-, commonplace-book; portfolio; scoring-board, -sheet; bulletin board; card index, file; pigeon-holes, *excerpta, adversaria,* jottings, dottings.

gazette, -er; newspaper, magazine &c. 531; alman-ac, -ack; calendar, ephemeris, noctuary, diary, log, journal, account-, cash-, day-book, ledger.

archive, scroll, state-paper, Congressional Record, return, blue-book; statistics &c. 86; *compte rendu*; Acts –, Transactions –, Proceedings- of; Hansard's Debates; chronicle, annals; legend; history, biography &c. 594.

registration; en-, in-rolment; tabulation; entry, booking; signature &c. (*identification*) 550; recorder &c. 553; journalism.

drawing, photograph &c. 554; phonograph –, gramophone- record; music roll.

**552.** [Suppression of sign.] **Obliteration.—N.** obliteration; erasure, rasure; effacement; cancel, -lation; cassation; circumduction; deletion, blot; *tabula rasa.*

**V.** efface, obliterate, erase, rase, expunge, cancel; blot –, take –, rub –, scratch –, strike –, wipe –, wash –, sponge- out; wipe –, rub- off; wipe away; deface, render illegible; draw the pen through, apply the sponge.

be -effaced &c.; leave no -trace &c. 449; 'leave not a rack behind.'

**Adj.** obliterated &c. *v.*; out of print; printless; leaving no trace; intestate; un-recorded, -registered, -written.

**Int.** *dele*; out with it!

---

**V.** record; put –, place- upon record; go on record; chronicle, calendar, hand down to posterity; keep up the memory of &c. (*remember*) 505; commemorate &c. (*celebrate*) 883; report &c. (*inform*) 527; commit to –, reduce to- writing; put –, set down- -in writing, – in black and white; put –, jot –, take –, write –, note –, set- down; note, minute, put on paper; take –, make- a -note, – minute, – memorandum; make a return.

mark &c. (*indicate*) 550; sign &c. (*attest*) 467.

enter, book; post, – up; insert, make an entry of; mark –, tick-off; register, list, docket, enroll, inscroll; file &c. (*store*) 636.

**Adv.** on record.

**553. Recorder.—N.** recorder, notary, clerk; regis-trar, -trary, -ter; prothonotary; amanuensis, secretary, scribe, stenographer, remembrancer, book-keeper, *custos rotulorum*, Master of the Rolls.

annalist; histori-an, -ographer; chronicler, journalist, reporter, columnist; biographer &c. (*narrator*) 594; antiquary &c. (*antiquity*) 122; memorialist.

draughtsman &c. 559; engraver 558; photographer, cinematographer, camera man.

Recording instrument, recorder, camera, phonograph, gramophone, dictaphone, telegraphone, telautograph, printing telegraph, tape machine, ticker, time recorder, cash register, turnstile, speedometer, voting machine, seismograph, photostat.

**554. Representation.—N.** represent-ation, -ment; imitation &c. 19; illustration, delineation, depictment, portrayal; imagery, portraiture, iconography; design, -ing; art, fine arts; painting &c. 556; sculpture &c. 557; engraving &c. 558; photography, radiography, skiagraphy.

person-ation, -ification; impersonation; drama &c. 599.

picture, drawing, sketch, draught, draft; tracing; copy &c. 21; photo-, helio-graph; daguerreo-, talbo-, calo-, helio-type; cabinet, *carte-de-visite*, snapshot; X-ray photograph; radio-gram, -graph, skia-graph, -gram.

image, likeness, icon, portrait; striking –, speaking- likeness; very image; effigy, fac-simile.

figure, – head; puppet, doll, *figurine*, aglet, manikin, lay-figure, model, *marionnette*, *fantoccini*, bust; waxwork, statue, -tte, automaton, Robot.

hieroglyphic, anaglyph; dia-, mono-gram, -graph.

map, plan, chart; ground plan, projection, elevation; ichno-, carto-graphy; atlas; outline, scheme; view &c. (*painting*) 556.

artist, draughtsman &c. 559.

**V.** represent, delineate; depict, -ure; portray; picture; take –, catch- a likeness &c. *n.*; hit off, photograph, daguerreotype; figure; shadow -forth, – out; adumbrate; body forth; describe &c. 594; trace, copy; mould.

dress up; illustrate, symbolize.

paint &c. 556; carve &c. 557; engrave &c. 558.

person-ate, -ify; impersonate; assume a character; pose as; act;

**555. Misrepresentation.—N.** misrepresentation, distortion, exaggeration; daubing &c. *v.*; bad likeness, daub, sign-painting; scratch, caricature; *anamorphosis*.

**V.** misrepresent, distort, overdraw, travesty, parody, burlesque, exaggerate, caricature, daub.

**Adj.** misrepresented &c. *v.*

play &c. (*drama*) 599; mimic &c. (*imitate*) 19; hold the mirror up to nature.

Adj. represent-ing &c. *v.*, -ative; illustrative; represented &c. *v*; imitative, figurative.

like &c. 17; graphic &c. (*descriptive*) 594.

**556. Painting.—N.** painting; depicting; drawing &c. *v.*; design; perspective, skiagraphy; *chiaroscuro* &c. (*light*) 420; composition; treatment, values, atmosphere, tone, technique.

historical –, portrait –, miniature –, battle -, *genre* -, landscape –, marine –, fruit and flower –, scene- painting; scenography.

school, style; the grand style, high art, *genre*, portraiture; ornamental art &c. 847.

mono-, poly-chrome; *grisaille.*

pallet, palette; easel; brush, pencil, stump; blacklead, charcoal, crayons, chalk, pastel; paint &c. (*colouring matter*) 428; water-, body-, oil-colour; oils, oil-paint; varnish &c. 356*a*; *gouache*, tempera, distemper, fresco; enamel; encaustic painting; *graffito*, *gesso*; mosaic; tapestry.

picture, painting, piece, *tableau*, canvas; oil &c.- painting; cartoon; easel –, cabinet- picture; drawing, draught, draft; pencil &c. –, water-colour- drawing; sketch, outline; study.

portrait &c. (*representation*) 554; whole –, full –, half- length; kitcat, head; miniature; shade, *silhouette*; profile.

landscape, sea-piece, -scape; view, scene, prospect; interior; bird's-eye view; pan-, di-orama; still life.

picture –, art- gallery; studio, *atelier*.

**V.** paint, design, limn, draw, sketch, pencil, scratch, shade, stipple, hatch, dash off, chalk out, square up; colour, dead-colour, wash, varnish; draw in -pencil &c. *n.*; paint in -oils &c. *n.*; stencil; depict &c. (*represent*) 554.

**Adj.** painted &c. *v.*; pictorial, graphic, picturesque, decorative; classical, romantic, pre-Raphaelite, modern, cubist, futurist, vorticist, post-, impressionist.

pencil, oil &c. *n.*

**Adv.** in -pencil &c. *n.*

**Phr.** *fecit, delineavit, pinxit.*

**557. Sculpture.—N.** sculpture, insculpture; carving &c. *v.*; statuary, ceramics, plastic arts.

high –, low –, bas- relief; relievo; *basso-*, *alto-*, *mezzo-rilievo*; *intaglio*, anaglyph; medal, -lion; *cameo*.

marble, bronze, terracotta; ceramic ware, pottery, porcelain, china, earthenware, faïence, enamel, *cloisonné*.

statue &c. (*image*) 554; cast &c. (*copy*) 21; glyptotheca.

**V.** sculpture, carve, cut, chisel, model, mould; cast.

**Adj.** sculptured &c. *v.*; in relief, anaglyptic, ceroplastic, ceramic; parian; marble &c. *n.* **Phr.** *sculpsit.*

**558. Engraving.—N.** engraving, chalcography; line –, mezzotint –, stipple –, chalk- engraving; dry-point, bur; etching, aquatinta; plate –, copper-plate –, steel –, wood-, process-, photo-engraving; xylo-, ligno-, glypto-, cero-, litho-, chromolitho-, photolitho-, zinco-, glypho- -graphy, -graph.

impression, print, engraving, plate; steel-, copper-plate; etching; mezzo-, aqua-, litho-tint; cut, woodcut, block; stereo-, grapho-, auto-, helio-type; half-tone; *photogravure, rotogravure.*

graver, *burin*, etching-point, style; plate, stone, wood-block, negative; die, punch, stamp.

printing; plate –, copper-plate –, intaglio –, anastatic –, lithographic –, colour –, three or four colour- printing; type-printing &c. 591.

illustr-, illumin-ation; *vignette*, initial letter, *cul de lampe*, tail-piece.

**V.** engrave, grave, stipple, scrape, etch; bite, – in; lithograph &c. *n.*; print.

**Adj.** insculptured; engraved &c. *v.*

**Phr.** *fecit, sculpsit, imprimit, incisit.*

**559. Artist.—N.** artist; painter, limner, drawer, sketcher, delineator; cartoon-, caricatur-ist, designer, engraver; draughtsman; copyist; enamel-ler, -list.

historical –, landscape –, battle-, *genre* –, marine –, fruit and flower –, portrait –, miniature –, scene –, sign- painter; engraver; Apelles; sculptor, carver, chaser, modeller, lapidary, *figuriste*, statuary; Phidias, Praxiteles; Royal Academician.

photographer, retoucher.

### 2°. *Conventional Means*

### 1. *Language generally*

**560. Language.—N.** language; phraseology &c. 569; speech &c. 582; tongue, lingo, vernacular, slang; mother –, vulgar –, native- tongue; household words; King's *or* Queen's English; idiom; dialect &c. 563.

Volapuk, Esperanto, Ido, occidental, Ro.

confusion of tongues, Babel, *pasigraphie*; pantomime &c. (*signs*) 550; *onomatopœia.*

phil-, gloss-, glott-ology; linguistics, chrestomathy; paleo-logy; -graphy; comparative grammar.

literature, letters, polite literature, *belles lettres*, muses, humanities, *literæ humaniores*, republic of letters, dead languages, classics; genius of a language; scholarship &c. (*knowledge*) 490.

linguist &c. (*scholar*) 492.

**V.** speak, say, express by words &c. 566.

**Adj.** lingu-al, -istic; dialectic; vernacular, current, colloquial, slangy; bilingual, polyglot; literary.

**561. Letter.—N.** letter; character; hieroglyphic &c. (*writing*) 590; type &c. (*printing*) 591; capitals; majus-, minus-cule; alphabet, ABC, abecedary, Christ-cross-row.

consonant, vowel, diphthong; mute, surd; sonant, liquid, labial, dental, palatal, guttural.

syllable; mono-, dis-, poly-syllable; affix, prefix, suffix.

spelling, orthography; phon-ography, -etic spelling; ana-, meta-grammatism.

cipher, monogram, anagram; double –, acrostic.

**V.** spell.

**Adj.** literal; alphabetical, abecedarian; syllabic; uncial &c. (*writing*) 590; phonetic, voiced, mute &c. *n.*

**562. Word.—N.** word, term, vocable; name &c. 564; phrase &c. 566; root, etymon; derivative; part of speech &c. (*grammar*) 567.

dictionary, vocabulary, word book,

**563. Neology.—N.** neolo-gy, -gism; new-fangled expression; barbarism; caconym; archaism, black letter, monkish Latin; corruption; missaying, antiphrasis.

lexicon, index, glossary, thesaurus, *gradus*, *delectus*, concordance.

etymology, lexicology, derivation; phonology, orthoepy; gloss-, termin-, orism-ology; paleology &c. (*philology*) 560; comparative philology.

lexicograph-er, -y; glossographer &c. (*scholar*) 492; etymologist; logolept.

verbosity, verbiage, loquacity &c. 584.

**Adj.** verbal, literal; titular, nominal. [Similarly derived] conjugate, paronymous; derivative.

**Adv.** verbally &c. *adj.*; *verbatim* &c. (*exactly*) 494.

---

*paronomasia*, play upon words; word play &c. (*wit*) 842; pun; *double-entendre* &c. (*ambiguity*) 520; palindrome, paragram, clinch; abuse of -language, – terms.

dialect, brogue, *patois*, provincialism, broken English, *lingua franca*; Brit-, Gall-, Scott-, Hibern-icism; Americanism; Gipsy lingo, Romany, pidgin English.

dog Latin, macaronics, gibberish, confusion of tongues, Babel; jargon.

colloquialism &c. (*figure of speech*) 521; by-word; technicality, lingo, slang, cant, *argot*, St. Giles's Greek, thieves' Latin, peddler's French, flash tongue, Billingsgate, Wall Street slang.

pseudonym &c. (*misnomer*) 565; Mr. So-and-so; what d'ye call 'em, what's his name; N. N.; *Monsieur Un Tel*; thingum-my, -bob; gadget, dooflicker, do-funny, *oo-ja-ka-pi-vi*; *je ne sais quoi*.

neologist, coiner of words.

**V.** coin words.

**Adj.** neologic, -al; rare; archaic; obsolete &c. (*old*) 124; colloquial, dialectic, slang, cant.

**Phr.** *Il a passé par Marseille.*

**564. Nomenclature.** — **N.** nomenclature; naming &c. *v.*; nuncupation, nomination, baptism; orismology; *onomatopœia*; antonomasia.

name; appella-tion, -tive; designation; title; head, -ing, caption; denomination; by-name, epithet.

style, proper name; præ-, ag-, cognomen; patronymic, surname; cognomination; compellation, description; empty -title, – name; handle to one's name; namesake, eponym.

synonym, antonym.

term, expression, noun; by-word; convertible terms &c. 522; technical term; cant &c. 563.

**V.** name, call, term, denominate, designate, style, entitle, intitule, clepe, dub, christen, baptize, nickname, characterize, specify, define, distinguish by the name of; label &c. (*mark*) 550.

be -called &c. *v.*; take –, bear –, go (*or* be known) by –, go (*or* pass) under –, rejoice in- the name of.

**Adj.** named &c. *v.*; hight, yclept, known as; what one may -well, – fairly, – properly, – fitly- call.

nuncupa-tory, -tive; cognominal, titular, nominal; orismological.

**565. Misnomer.**—**N.** misnomer; *lucus a non lucendo*; Mrs. Malaprop; what d'ye call 'em &c. (*neologism*) 563.

nickname, *sobriquet*, by-name, handle, moniker; assumed -name, – title; *alias*; *nom de -guerre*, – *plume*, – *théâtre*; pseudonym, pen name, stage name.

**V.** mis-name, -call, -term; nickname; assume -a name, – an alias.

**Adj.** misnamed &c. *v.*; pseudonymous; *soi-disant*; self-called, -styled, -christened; so-called.

nameless, anonymous; without a –, having no- name; innominate, unnamed.

**Adv.** in no sense.

---

**566. Phrase.**—**N.** phrase, expression, set phrase; sentence, paragraph; figure of speech &c. 521; idi-om, -otism; turn of expression.

paraphrase &c. (*synonym*) 522; periphrase &c. (*circumlocution*) 573; motto &c. (*proverb*) 496; phraseology &c. 569.

**V.** express, phrase; word, – it; give -words, – expression- to; voice; arrange in –, clothe in –, put into –, express by- words; couch in terms; find words to express; speak by the card.

**Adj.** expressed &c. *v.*; idiomatic.

**Adv.** in -round, – set, – good, set- terms; in set phrases.

**567. Grammar.**—**N.** grammar, accidence, syntax, *praxis*, analysis, paradigm, punctuation; parts of speech; inflexion, case, declension, conjugation; *jus et norma loquendi*; Lindley Murray &c. (*school-book*) 542; correct style; philology &c. (*language*) 560.

**V.** parse, analyze; decline, conjugate; punctuate.

**Adj.** grammatical; syntactic; inflexional.

**568. Solecism.**—**N.** solecism; bad –, false –, faulty- grammar; slip, error; slip of the -pen, – tongue; *lapsus calami-*, – *linguæ*; *faux pas*; slip-slop; bull.

**V.** use -bad, – faulty- grammar; solecize, commit a solecism; murder the -King's, – Queen's- English; break Priscian's head.

**Adj.** ungrammatical; in-correct, -accurate; faulty, improper, incongruous, abnormal.

---

**569. Style.**—**N.** style, diction, phraseology, wording; manner, strain; composition; mode of expression, choice of words, literary power, ready pen, pen of a ready writer; command of language &c. (*eloquence*) 582; authorship; *la morgue littéraire*.

**V.** express by words &c. 566; write.

*Various Qualities of Style*

**570. Perspicuity.**—**N.** perspicuity &c. (*intelligibility*) 518; plain speaking &c. (*manifestation*) 525; defin-iteness, -ition; exactness &c. 494; perspicuousness, logical acuteness.

**Adj.** lucid &c. (*intelligible*) 518; explicit &c. (*manifest*) 525; exact &c. 494.

**571. Obscurity.**—**N.** obscurity &c. (*unintelligibility*) 519; involution; hard words; ambiguity &c. 520; vagueness &c. 475, inexactness &c. 495; what d'ye call 'em &c. (*neologism*) 563; cloudiness, confusion.

**Adj.** obscure &c. *n.*; crabbed, involved, confused.

**572. Conciseness.**—**N.** conciseness &c. *adj.*; brevity, 'the soul of wit,' laconism; Tacitus; ellipsis; syncope; abridgment &c. (*shortening*) 201; compression &c. 195; epitome &c. 596; monostitch; portmanteau word, telescope word, protogram.

**V.** be -concise &c. *adj.*; condense &c. 195; abridge &c. 201; abstract &c. 596; come to the point.

**Adj.** concise, brief, short, terse, close; to the point, exact; neat, compact, condensed, pointed; laconic, curt, pithy, trenchant, summary; pregnant; compendious &c. (*compendium*) 596; succinct; elliptical, epigrammatic, crisp, sententious.

**Adv.** concisely &c. *adj.*; briefly,

**573. Diffuseness.**—**N.** diffuseness &c. *adj.*; amplification &c. *v.*; dilating &c. *v.*; verbosity, verbiage, wordiness, cloud of words, *copia verborum*; flow of words &c. (*loquacity*) 584.

poly-, tauto-, batto-, perisso-logy; pleonasm, exuberance, redundance; thrice-told tale; prolixity; circumlocution, *ambages*; periphra-se, -sis; roundabout phrases; episode; expletive; penny-a-lining; padding, drivel, twaddle, rigmarole; richness &c. 577.

**V.** be -diffuse &c. *adj.*; run out on, descant, expatiate, enlarge, dilate, amplify, expand, inflate, pad; launch –, branch- out; rant.

maunder, prose; harp upon &c. (*repeat*) 104; dwell on, insist upon.

summarily; in -brief, – short, – a word, – few words, – a nutshell; for shortness sake; to -come to the point, – make a long story short, – cut the matter short, – be brief; it comes to this, the long and the short of it is.

digress, ramble, *battre la campagne*, beat about the bush, perorate, spin a long yarn, protract; spin –, swell –, draw- out, drivel.

**Adj.** dif-, pro-fuse; wordy, verbose, largiloquent, copious, exuberant, effusive, pleonastic, lengthy; long, -some, -winded, -spun, -drawn out; diffusive, spun out, protracted, prolix, prosing, maundering; circumlocutory, periphrastic, ambagious, roundabout; digressive; dis-, ex-cursive; rambling, episodic; flatulent, frothy.

**Adv.** diffusely &c. *adj.*; at large, *in extenso*; about it and about it.

**574. Vigour.**—**N.** vigour, power, force; boldness, raciness &c. *adj.*; spirit, point, antithesis, piquancy; *verve*, glow, fire, warmth, ardour, enthusiasm; 'thoughts that breathe and words that burn'; strong language; punch; gravity, sententiousness; elevation, loftiness, sublimity.

eloquence; command of -words, – language.

**Adj.** vigorous, nervous, powerful, forcible, trenchant, mordant, biting, incisive, impressive; sensational.

spirited, lively, glowing, sparkling, racy, bold, slashing; pungent, *piquant*, full of point, pointed, pithy, antithetical; sententious.

lofty, elevated, sublime, grand, weighty, ponderous; eloquent; vehement, petulant, impassioned; poetic.

**Adv.** in -glowing, – good set, – no measured- terms.

**575. Feebleness.**—**N.** feebleness &c. *adj.*

**Adj.** feeble, bald, tame, meagre, insipid, nerveless, jejune, vapid, trashy, cold, frigid, poor, dull, dry, languid; pros-ing, -y, -aic; unvaried, monotonous, weak, frail, washy, wishy-washy, sloppy; sketchy, slight; careless, slovenly, loose, lax; slip-shod, -slop; inexact; dis-jointed, -connected; puerile, childish; flatulent; rambling &c. (*diffuse*) 573.

**576. Plainness.**—**N.** plainness &c. *adj.*; simplicity, severity; plain -terms, – English; Saxon English; household words.

**V.** speak plainly; call a spade 'a spade'; plunge *in medias res*; come to the point.

**Adj.** plain, simple; un-ornamented, -adorned, -varnished; home-ly, -spun; neat; severe, chaste, pure, Saxon; commonplace, matter of fact, natural, prosaic, sober, unimaginative.

dry, unvaried, monotonous &c. 575.

**Adv.** in plain -terms, – words, – English, – common parlance; point blank.

**577. Ornament.** — **N.** ornament; floridness &c. *adj.*; turg-idity, -escence; altiloquence &c. *adj.*; orotundity; declamation, teratology; well-rounded periods; elegance &c. 578.

inversion, antithesis, alliteration, *paronomasia*; figurativeness &c. (*metaphor*) 521.

flourish; flowers of -speech, – rhetoric; euph-uism, -emism.

big-, high-sounding words; macrology, *sesquipedalia verba*, sesquipedalianism; Alexandrine; inflation, pretension; rant, bombast, fustian, bunkum, balderdash, prose run mad; fine writing; Minerva press.

phrasemonger; euph-uist, -emist.

**V.** ornament, overlay with ornament, overcharge; smell of the lamp.

**Adj.** ornamented &c. *v.*; beautified &c. 847; ornate, florid, rich, flowery; euph-uistic, -emistic; sonorous; high-, big-sounding; inflated, swelling, tumid; turg-id, -escent; pedantic, pompous, stilted;

high-flown, -flowing; sententious, rhetorical, declamatory; grandiose; grand-, magn-, alt-iloquent; sesquipedal, -ian; Johnsonian, mouthy; bombastic; fustian; frothy, flashy, flaming, flamboyant.

antithetical, alliterative; figurative &c. 521; artificial &c. (*inelegant*) 579.

**Adv.** *ore rotundo*; with rounded phrase.

**578. Elegance.—N.** elegance, purity, grace, ease, felicity, distinction, gracefulness, refinement, readiness &c. *adj.*; concinnity, euphony, numerosity, balance, rhythm, symmetry, proportion; restraint; good taste, propriety.

well rounded –, well turned –, flowing- periods; the right word in the right place; antithesis &c. 577.

purist, stylist.

**V.** point an antithesis, round a period.

**Adj.** elegant, polished, classical, Attic, correct, Ciceronian, artistic; chaste, pure, Saxon, academical.

graceful, easy, readable, fluent, flowing, tripping; unaffected, natural, unlaboured; mellifluous; euph-onious, -emistic; rhythmical, balanced, symmetrical.

felicitous, happy, neat; well –, neatly- -put, – expressed.

**579. Inelegance. — N.** inelegance; vulgarity, bad taste; stiffness &c. *adj.*; unlettered Muse; barbarism; slang &c. 563; solecism &c. 568; mannerism &c. (*affectation*) 855; euphuism; fustian &c. 577; cacophony; want of balance; words that -break the teeth, – dislocate the jaw.

**V.** be -inelegant &c. *adj.*

**Adj.** inelegant, graceless, ungraceful, unpolished; harsh, abrupt; dry, stiff, cramped, formal, *guindé*; forced, laboured, awkward; artificial, mannered, ponderous; turgid &c. 577; affected, euphuistic; barbarous, uncouth, grotesque, rude, crude, halting; vulgar, offensive to ears polite.

---

## 2. *Spoken Language*

**580. Voice.—N.** voice; vocality; organ, lungs, bellows; good –, fine –, powerful &c. (*loud*) 404 –, musical &c. 413- voice; intonation; tone &c. (*sound*) 402- of voice.

vocalization; cry &c. 411; strain, utterance, prolation; exclam-, ejacul-, vocifer-ation; enunci-, articul-ation; articulate sound, distinctness; clearness, – of articulation; stage whisper; delivery; attack.

accent, -uation; emphasis, stress; broad –, strong –, pure –, native –, foreign- accent; pronunciation.

[Word similarly pronounced] homonym.

orthoepy; euphony &c. (*melody*) 413.

gastri-, ventri-loquism; ventriloquist; polyphon-ism, -ist.

[Science of voice] phonology &c. (*sound*) 402.

**V.** sing, speak, utter, breathe, voice; give -utterance, – tongue; cry &c.

**581. Aphony.—N.** aphony, *aphonia*; dumbness &c. *adj.*; obmutescence; absence –, want- of voice; dysphony; silence &c. (*taciturnity*) 585; raucity; harsh &c. 410 –, unmusical &c. 414- voice; *falsetto*, 'childish treble'; mute, dummy, deaf mute.

**V.** keep silence &c. 585; speak -low, – softly; whisper &c. (*faintness*) 405.

silence; render -mute, – silent &c. 403; muzzle, muffle, suppress, smother, gag, strike dumb, dumb-found, -founder; drown the voice, put to silence, stop one's mouth, cut one short; stick in the throat.

**Adj.** aphon-ous, -ic, dumb, mute; deaf-mute, – and dumb; mum; tongue-tied; breath-, tongue-, voice-, speech-, word-less; mute as a -fish, – stockfish, – mackerel; silent &c. (*taciturn*) 585; muzzled; in-articulate, -audible.

croaking, raucous, hoarse, husky,

(*shout*) 411; ejaculate, rap out; vocalize, prolate, articulate, enunciate, enounce, pronounce, accentuate, aspirate, deliver, mouth; emit, murmur, whisper, – in the ear, croon, yodel.

**Adj.** vocal, phonetic, oral; ejaculatory, articulate, distinct, stertorous; enunciative; accentuated, aspirated; euphonious &c. (*melodious*) 413.

dry, hollow, sepulchral, hoarse as a raven.

**Adv.** with -bated breath, – the finger on the lips; *sotto voce*; in a -low tone, – cracked voice, – broken voice; in an aside.

**Phr.** *vox faucibus hæsit.*

---

**582. Speech.—N.** speech, faculty of speech; locution, talk, parlance, verbal intercourse, prolation, oral communication, word of mouth, *parole*, palaver, prattle; effusion.

oration, recitation, delivery, say, address, speech, lecture, harangue, sermon, *tirade*, screed, formal speech, salutatory, peroration; prelection; speechifying; soliloquy &c. 589; allocution &c. 586; interlocution &c. 588.

oratory; elo-cution, -quence; rhetoric, declamation; grandi-, multiloquence; burst of eloquence; facundity; talkativeness; flow –, command- of -words, – language; *copia verborum*; power of speech, gift of the gab; *usus loquendi.*

speaker &c. *v.*; spokesman; pro-, inter-locutor; mouthpiece, Hermes; ora-tor, -trix, -tress; Demosthenes, Cicero; rhetorician; stump –, platform-orator, tub-thumper; elocutionist; speech-maker, patterer, *improvisatore.*

**V.** speak, – of; say, utter, pronounce, deliver, give utterance to; utter –, pour- forth; breathe, let fall, come out with; rap –, blurt- out; have on one's lips; have at the -end, – tip- of one's tongue.

break silence; open one's -lips, – mouth; lift –, raise- one's voice; give –, wag the- tongue; talk, outspeak; put in a word or two.

hold forth; make –, deliver- -a speech &c. *n.*; speechify, harangue, declaim, stump, flourish, spout, rant, recite, lecture, preach, sermonize, discourse, be on one's legs; have –, say- one's say; expatiate &c. (*speak at length*) 573; speak one's mind.

soliloquize &c. 589; tell &c. (*inform*) 527; speak to &c. 586; talk together &c. 588.

be -eloquent &c. *adj.*; have -a tongue in one's head, – the gift of the gab &c. *n.*

pass –, escape- one's lips; fall from the -lips, – mouth.

**Adj.** speaking &c., spoken &c. *v.*; oral, lingual, phonetic, not written, unwritten, outspoken; elo-quent, -cutionary; orat-, rhetorical; declamatory; grandiloquent &c. 577; talkative &c. 584.

**583.** [Imperfect Speech.] **Stammering.—N.** inarticulateness; stammering &c. *v.*; hesitation &c. *v.*; impediment in one's speech; aphasia, titubancy, traulism; whisper &c. (*faint sound*) 405; lisp, drawl, tardiloquence; nasal -tone, – accent; twang; *falsetto* &c. (*want of voice*) 581; broken -voice, – accents, – sentences.

brogue &c. 563; slip of the tongue, *lapsus linguæ.*

**V.** stammer, stutter, hesitate, falter, hammer; balbu-tiate, -cinate; haw, hum and haw, be unable to put two words together.

mumble, mutter; maund, -er; whisper &c. 405; mince, lisp; jabber, gabble, gibber; sp-, spl-utter; muffle, mump; drawl, mouth; croak; speak -thick, – through the nose; snuffle, clip one's words; murder the -language, – King's (*or* Queen's) English; mis-pronounce, -say.

**Adj.** stammering &c. *v.*; inarticulate, guttural, nasal; tremulous.

**Adv.** *sotto voce* &c. (*faintly*) 405.

---

**Adv.** orally &c. *adj.*; by word of mouth, *vivâ voce*, from the lips of.
**Phr.** quoth –, said- he &c.

**584. Loquacity. — N.** loquac-ity, -iousness; talkativeness &c. *adj.*; garrulity; multiloquence, much speaking, effusion, wordiness.

jaw; gab, -ble; jabber, chatter; prate, prattle, cackle, clack; twaddle, twattle, rattle; *caquet*, *-terie*; blabber, *bavardage*, bibble-babble, gibble-gabble; small talk &c. (*converse*) 588.

fluency, flippancy, volubility, flowing tongue; flow, – of words; *flux de -bouche*, *– mots*, *– paroles*; *copia verborum*, *cacoëthes loquendi*; verbosity &c. (*diffuseness*) 573; gift of the gab &c. (*eloquence*) 582.

talker; chatter-er, -box; babbler &c. *v.*; rattle; ranter; sermonizer, proser, driveller; windbag; gossip &c. (*converse*) 588; magpie, jay, parrot, poll, Babel; *moulin à paroles*.

**V.** be -loquacious &c. *adj.*; talk glibly, pour forth, patter; prate, palaver, prose, chatter, prattle, clack, jabber, jaw; rattle, – on; twaddle, twaddle; babble, gabble; out-talk; talk oneself -out of breath, – hoarse; maunder, gush, blather; talk a donkey's hind leg off; expatiate &c. (*speak at length*) 573; gossip &c. (*converse*) 588; din in the ears &c. (*repeat*) 104; talk -at random, – nonsense &c. 497; be hoarse with talking.

**Adj.** loquacious, talkative, conversational, garrulous, linguacious, multiloquous; chattering &c. *v.*; chatty &c. (*sociable*) 892; declamatory &c. 582; open-mouthed.

fluent, voluble, glib, flippant; long-tongued, -winded &c. (*diffuse*) 573.

**Adv.** trippingly on the tongue; glibly &c. *adj.*
**Phr.** the tongue running -fast, – loose, – on wheels.

**585. Taciturnity.—N.** silence, muteness, obmutescence; taciturnity, pauciloquy, costiveness, curtness; reserve, reticence &c. (*concealment*) 528; *aposiopesis*.

man of few words.

**V.** be -silent &c. *adj.*; keep silence; hold one's -tongue, – peace, – jaw; not speak &c. 582; say nothing; seal –, close –, put a padlock on- the -lips, – mouth; put a bridle on one's tongue; keep one's tongue between one's teeth; make no sign, not let a word escape one; keep a secret &c. 528; not have a word to say; lay –, place- the finger on the lips; render mute &c. 581.

stick in one's throat.

**Adj.** silent, mute, mum; silent as -a post, – a stone, – the grave &c. (*still*) 403; dumb &c. 581.

taciturn, sparing of words; close, – mouthed, – tongued; laconic, costive, inconversable, curt; reserved; reticent &c. (*concealing*) 528.

**Int.** tush! silence! mum! hush! *chut!* hist! tut! &c. 403.

**586. Allocution. — N.** allocution, alloquy, address; speech &c. 582; apostrophe, interpellation, appeal, invocation, salutation; word in the ear.

[Feigned dialogue] dialogism.

platform &c. 542; audience &c. (*interview*) 588.

**V.** speak to, address, accost, make up to, apostrophize, appeal to, invoke; hail, salute; call to, halloo.

take -aside, – by the button, button-hole; talk to in private.

lecture &c. (*make a speech*) 582.

**Int.** soho! halloo! hey! hist! hi!

**587. Response &c.,** *see* Answer 462.

**588. Interlocution.—N.** interlocution; collocution, colloquy, converse, conversation, confabulation, talk, discourse, verbal intercourse; communion, oral communication, commerce; dia-, duo-, tria-logue.

*causerie*, chat, chit-chat; small –, table –, tea-table –, town –, village –, idle- talk; tattle, gossip, tittle-tattle; babble, -ment; *tripotage*, cackle, prittle-prattle, *on dit*; talk of the -town, – village.

conference, parley, interview, audience, *pourparler*; *tête-à-tête*; reception, *conversazione*; congress &c. (*council*) 696; pow-wow.

hall of audience, *durbar*, coliseum, assembly hall, auditorium.

palaver, debate, logomachy, war of words, controversy.

talker, gossip, tattler; Paul Pry; tabby; chatterer &c. (*loquacity*) 584; interlocutor &c. (*spokesman*) 582; conversation-ist, -alist; dialogist.

'the feast of reason and the flow of soul'; *mollia tempora fandi*.

**V.** talk together, converse, confabulate; hold –, carry on –, join in –, engage in- a conversation; put in a word; shine in conversation; bandy words; parley; palaver; chat, gossip, tattle; prate &c. (*loquacity*) 584.

discourse –, confer –, commune –, commerce- with; hold -converse, – conference, – intercourse; talk it over; be closeted with; talk with one -in private, – *tête-à-tête*.

**Adj.** conversing &c. *v.*; interlocutory; convers-ational, -able; discursive, -coursive; chatty &c. (*sociable*) 892; colloquial, *tête-à-tête*, confabulatory.

**589. Soliloquy.—N.** soliloquy, monologue, apostrophe.

solilo-quist, -quizer, monologist.

**V.** soliloquize; say –, talk- to oneself; say aside, think aloud, apostrophize.

**Adj.** soliloquizing &c. *v.*

**Adv.** aside.

---

### 3. *Written Language*

**590. Writing.—N.** writing &c. *v.*; chiro-, stelo-, cero-graphy, graphology; stylography; pen-craft, -script, -manship; quill-driving; typewriting.

writing, manuscript, MS., *literæ scriptæ*; these presents.

stroke –, dash- of the pen; *coup de plume*; line; pen and ink.

letter &c. 561; uncial writing, cuneiform character, arrow-head, Ogham, Runes, futhorc; hieroglyphic, hieratic, demotic; script; contraction.

short-hand; steno-, brachy-, tachygraphy; secret writing, writing in cipher; crypt-, stegan-ography; phono-, pasi-, poly-, logo-graphy.

copy; tran-, re-script; draft, rough –, fair- copy; handwriting; signature. sign-manual; auto-, mono-, holo-graph; hand, fist; mark.

calligraphy; good –, running –,

**591. Printing.—N.** printing; block –, type- printing, lino-, mono-type; plate printing &c. (*engraving*) 558; the press &c. (*publication*) 531; composition.

print, letterpress, text, matter, standing type; context, note, page, column; over-running; head-, foot-line, title.

typography; stereo-, electro-, apro-type; type, black letter, heavy type, font, fount; pi, pie; capitals &c. (*letters*) 561; diamond, pearl, nonpareil, minion, brevier, bourgeois, long primer, small pica, pica, english, great primer.

folio &c. (*book*) 593; copy, impression, pull, proof, galley –, author's –, page- proof, revise.

printer, compositor, reader; printer's devil.

**V.** print; compose; put –, go- to press; pass –, see- through the press:

flowing –, cursive –, legible –, copper-plate –, round –, bold- hand.

cacography, *griffonage*, *barbouillage*; bad –, cramped –, crabbed –, illegible-hand; scribble &c. *v.*; *pattes de mouche*; ill-formed letters; pot-hooks and hangers.

publish &c. 531; bring out; appear in –, rush into- print.

**Adj.** printed &c. *v.*; in type; typographical &c. *n.*

---

stationery; pen, quill, goose-quill, reed; stylographic-, fountain-pen; pencil, style, stylus; paper, foolscap, parchment, vellum, papyrus, pad, tablet, block, note-book, slate, marble, pillar, table, black board.

ink-bottle, -pot, -stand, -well, -horn; typewriter.

transcription &c. (*copy*) 21; inscription &c. (*record*) 551; superscription &c. (*indication*) 550.

composition, authorship; *cacoëthes scribendi.*

writer, scribe, amanuensis, scrivener, secretary, clerk, penman, copyist, transcriber, quill-driver; writer for the press &c. (*author*) 593.

shorthand writer, stenographer; typewriter, typist.

**V.** write, pen; copy, engross; write out, – fair; transcribe; scribble, scrawl, scrabble, scratch; interline; stain paper; write down &c. (*record*) 551; sign &c. (*attest*) 467; take down, – in shorthand; typewrite, type.

compose, indite, draw up, redact, draft, formulate; dictate; inscribe, throw on paper, dash off; concoct.

take -up the pen, – pen in hand; shed –, spill –, dip one's pen in- ink.

**Adj.** writing &c. *v.*; written &c. *v.*; in -writing, – black and white; under one's hand.

uncial, Runic, cuneiform, hieroglyphical &c. *n.*

**Adv.** *currente calamo*; pen in hand.

**592. Correspondence.** — **N.** correspondence, letter, epistle, note, *billet*, post-, letter-card, missive, circular, form letter; favour, *billet-doux*; des-, dis-patch; *bulletin*, communication &c. 532; these presents; rescript, -ion; post &c. (*messenger*) 534; letter writer, correspondent.

**V.** correspond, – with; write –, send a letter- to; keep up a correspondence; drop a line to; despatch; communicate with; circularize.

**Adj.** epistolary.

---

**593. Book.**—**N.** book, -let; writing, work, volume, tome, opuscule; tract, -ate; *livret*; *brochure*, *libretto*, handbook, treatise, text-book, codex, manual, pamphlet, monograph, enchiridion, circular, publication; book of poems; novel; chap-book.

part, issue, number, *livraison*; album, portfolio; periodical, serial, magazine, ephemeris, annual, journal.

paper, bill, sheet, broadsheet, screed; leaf, -let; fly-leaf, page; quire, ream.

chapter, section, head, article, paragraph, passage, clause, supplement, appendix; *feuilleton*.

folio, quarto, octavo; duo-, sexto-, octo-decimo.

en-, cyclopædia, dictionary, lexicon, thesaurus, concordance, anthology, bibliography; compilation, compendium, catalogue &c. 86; library, bibliotheca; the press &c. (*publication*) 531.

writer, author, *litterateur*, *homme de lettres*, essayist, journalist, publicist; scribe, penman, war –, special –, correspondent; pen, scribbler, the scribbling race; ghost, hack, literary hack, Grub-street writer; writer for –, gentleman of –, representative of- the press; reporter, penny-a-liner; editor, sub-editor; literary agent; playwright &c. 599; poet &c. 597.

bookseller, publisher; biblio-pole, -polist, -grapher; librarian, book -collector, – worm.

book -shop, – club, circulating –, lending –, public- library; publishing house.

knowledge of books, bibliography; book-learning &c. (*knowledge*) 490.

**594. Description.**—**N.** description, account, statement, report; *exposé* &c. (*disclosure*) 529; specification, particulars, scenario, plot; state –, summary- of facts; brief &c. (*abstract*) 596; return &c. (*record*) 551; *catalogue raisonné* &c. (*list*) 86; guide-book &c. (*information*) 527.

delineation &c. (*representation*) 554; sketch, vignette; monograph; minute –, detailed –, particular –, circumstantial –, graphic- account; narration, recital, rehearsal, relation.

histori-, chron-ography; historic Muse, Clio; history; bi-, autobi-ography; necrology, obituary.

narrative, history; memoir, memorials; annals &c. (*chronicle*) 551; tradition, legend, saga, epic, epos, story, tale, historiette; personal narrative, journal, letters, life, adventures, fortunes, experiences, confessions; anecdote, ana, *trait*.

work of fiction, short story, novelette, novel, romance, penny dreadful, shilling shocker, Minerva press; fairy –, nursery- tale; fable, allegory, parable, apologue.

relator &c. *v.*; *raconteur*; historian &c. (*recorder*) 553; biographer, fabulist, novelist, story teller, romancer, teller of tales, spinner of yarns, anecdotist.

**V.** describe; set forth &c. (*state*) 535; draw a picture, picture; portray &c. (*represent*) 554; characterize, particularize; narrate, relate, recite, recount, sum up, run over, recapitulate, rehearse, fight one's battles over again.

unfold &c. (*disclose*) 529- a tale; tell; give –, render- an account of; report, make a report, draw up a statement.

detail; enter into –, descend to- -particulars, – details.

**Adj.** descriptive, graphic, narrative, epic, suggestive, well-drawn; historic; auto-, biographical, realistic, expository, tradition-al, -ary; legendary; fabulous, mythical; anecdotic, storied; described &c. *v.*

**595. Dissertation.**—**N.** dissertation, treatise, essay; *thesis*, theme; tract, -ate, -ation, excursus; discourse, memoir, disquisition, lecture, sermon, homily, pandect.

commentary, review, *critique*, criticism, article; lead-er, -ing article, editorial; argument, running commentary.

investigation &c. (*inquiry*) 461; study &c. (*consideration*) 451; discussion &c. (*reasoning*) 476; exposition &c. (*explanation*) 522.

commentator, critic, essayist, pamphleteer; publicist, reviewer, leader writer, editor, annotator.

**V.** dissert –, descant –, write –, touch- upon a subject; dissertate; treat of –, take up –, ventilate –, discuss –, deal with –, go into –, canvass –, handle –, do justice to- a subject; comment, criticize, interpret &c. 522; argue.

**Adj.** dis-cursive, -coursive; disquisitional, disquisitionary; expository, critical.

**596. Compendium.**—**N.** compend, -ium; abstract, *précis*, epitome, *multum in parvo*, analysis, pandect, digest, sum and substance, brief, abridgment, summary, *aperçu*, draft, minute, note; synopsis, textbook, *conspectus*, outlines, syllabus, contents, heads, prospectus.

album; scrap –, note –, memorandum –, commonplace- book; extracts, *excerpta*, cuttings; fugitive -pieces, – writings; *spicilegium*, flowers, anthology, miscellany, *collectanea*, *analecta*; compilation.

recapitulation, *résumé*, review.

abbrevia-tion, -ture; contraction; shortening &c. 201; compression &c. 195.

**V.** abridge, abstract, epitomize, summarize; make –, prepare –, draw –, compile- an abstract &c. *n.*

recapitulate, review, skim, run over, sum up.

abbreviate &c. (*shorten*) 201; condense &c. (*compress*) 195; compile &c. (*collect*) 72; edit, blue pencil.

**Adj.** compendious, synoptic, analectic, analytical; abridged &c. *v.*

**Adv.** in -short, – epitome, – substance, – few words.

**Phr.** it lies in a nutshell.

**597. Poetry.—N.** poetry, poetics, poesy, Muse, Calliope, tuneful Nine, Parnassus, Helicon, Pierides, Pierian spring, afflatus, inspiration.

versification, rhyming, making verses; prosody, scansion, orthometry.

poem; epic, – poem; epopee, *epopæa*, ode, epode, idyl, lyric, eclogue, pastoral, bucolic, georgic, dithyramb, anacreontic, sonnet, roundelay, *rondel*, *rondoletto*, *rondeau*, *rondo*, triolet; madrigal, canzonet, *cento*, monody, elegy, palinode; rhapsody.

dramatic –, lyric- poetry; opera; posy, anthology.

song, ballad, lay; love –, drinking –, war –, folk –, sea- song; lullaby; music &c. 415; nursery rhymes.

[Bad poetry] doggerel, Hudibrastic verse, prose run mad; macaronics; macaronic –, leonine- verse; runes.

canto, stanza, distich, verse, line, couplet, triplet, quatrain, sestet; *strophe*, *antistrophe*, refrain, chorus, burden.

verse, rhyme, assonance, crambo, metre, measure, foot, numbers, strain, rhythm; accentuation &c. (*voice*) 580; iambus, dactyl, spondee, trochee, anapæst &c.; hex-, pent-ameter; Alexandrine; blank verse, alliteration.

elegiacs &c. *adj.*; elegiac &c. *adj.* -verse, – metre, – poetry.

poet, – laureate; laureate; minor poet, bard, lyrist, scald, troubadour, *trouvère*; minstrel; minne-, meister-singer; *improvisatore*; versifier, sonneteer; ballad monger; rhym-er, -ist, -ester; poetaster.

**V.** poetize, sing, versify, make verses, rhyme, scan.

**Adj.** poetic, -al; lyric, -al; tuneful; epic; dithyrambic &c. *n.*; metrical; a-, catalectic; elegiac, iambic, trochaic, spondaic, dactylic, anapæstic; Ionic, Sapphic, Alcaic, Pindaric.

**598. Prose.—N.** prose, – writer; pros-aism, -aist, -er.

**V.** prose, write prose.

write -prose, – in prose.

**Adj.** pros-y, -aic; unpoetical.

rhymeless, unrhymed, in prose, not in verse.

---

**599. The Drama.—N.** the -drama, – stage, – theatre, – play; theatricals, dramaturgy, histrionic art, buskin, sock, *cothurnus*, Melpomene and Thalia, Thespis.

play, drama, stage-play, piece, five-act play, tragedy, comedy, opera, comic opera, *vaudeville*, *comedietta*, *lever de rideau*, curtain raiser, interlude, afterpiece, exode, farce, *divertissement*, *extravaganza*, burletta, harlequinade, pantomime, mimodrama, burlesque, *opéra bouffe*, musical comedy, review, revue, intimate revue, variety, cabaret entertainment, *ballet*, *spectacle*, masque, *drame*, *comédie drame*; melo-drama, -drame; *comédie larmoyante*, emotional drama, sensation drama, tragi-, farcical-comedy; mono-drame, -logue; duologue; trilogy; charade, *proverbe*; mystery, miracle –, morality- play.

act, scene, *tableau*; in-, intro-duction; pro-, epi-logue, curtain; *libretto*, book, script.

performance, representation, show, *mise en scène*, stagery, *jeu de théâtre*, stage-craft; acting; gesture &c. 550; impersonation &c. 554; stage business, gag, patter, buffoonery.

theatre; play-, opera-house; house; music hall; *cabaret*; amphitheatre, circus, hippodrome; puppet-show, *fantoccini*; *marionnettes*, Punch and Judy.

cinema, -tograph-, picture –, theatre, the pictures, the movies, the talkies.

auditory, *auditorium*, front of the house, stalls, boxes, balcony, dress –, upper- -circle, – boxes, amphitheatre, pit, gallery; *foyer*; green-room; dressing rooms, *coulisses*.

flat; drop, – scene; wing, screen, side-scene; transformation scene, curtain, act-drop, safety –, fire- curtain; *proscenium*, forestage.

stage, revolving stage, scene, the boards; star –, grave –, trap, mezzanine floor; flies; gridiron, floats, battens, footlights; lime –, spot –, flood –, bunch-lights; scenery, set, *décor*; orchestra;

theatrical -costume, – properties, props.

part, *rôle*, character, cast, *dramatis personæ*; *répertoire*.

actor, player; stage –, strolling- player; old –, stager, performer; mime, -r; *artiste*; com-, trag-edian, straight man; *tragédienne*, Thespian, Roscius, star.

pantomimist, clown, harlequin, *buffo*, buffoon, *farceur*, *grimacier*, pantaloon, columbine; *Pierrot*, *Pierrette*; punch, -inello; *pulcinell-o*, *-a*; mute, *figurante*, general utility; super, -numerary, extra.

mummer, guiser, guisard, gysart, masque.

mountebank, Jack Pudding; tumbler, posture-master, acrobat, equilibrist, juggler, contortionist; *danseuse*, *ballerina*, ballet -dancer, – girl, *coryphée*; *bayadère*, *geisha*; chorus -singer, – girl.

company; first tragedian, *prima donna*, lead, leading lady, protagonist; *jeune premier*; juvenile lead, *débutant*, *-e*; light –, genteel –, low- -comedy, – comedian; *soubrette*, walking gentleman, *amoroso*, heavy, heavy father, *ingénue*, *jeune veuve*, *commère*, *compère*.

property man, *costumier*, machinist, stage hand, electrician, prompter, call-boy; director, manager; stage –, acting –, business- manager; *entrepreneur*, *impresario*, producer, press agent.

dramatic -author, – writer; play-writer, -wright; dramatist, mimographer; dramatic critic.

**V.** act, play, perform; stage, produce, put on the stage; personate &c. 554; mimic &c. (*imitate*) 19; enact; play –, act –, go through –, perform- a part; rehearse, spout, gag, rant; 'strut and fret one's hour upon a stage'; tread the -stage, – boards; come out; star.

**Adj.** dramatic; theatric, -al; scenic, histrionic, comic, tragic, buskined, farcical, tragi-comic, melodramatic, operatic; stagey, spectacular; stagestruck.

**Adv.** on the -stage, – boards; before -the floats, – an audience; in the limelight, behind the footlights; behind the scenes.

# CLASS V

## WORDS RELATING TO THE VOLUNTARY POWERS*

## DIVISION (I.) INDIVIDUAL VOLITION

### Section I. VOLITION IN GENERAL

#### 1°. *Acts of Volition*

**600. Will.—N.** will, volition, conation†, velleity; will and pleasure, free-will; freedom &c. 748; discretion; choice, inclination, intent, purpose, option &c. (*choice*) 609; voluntariness; spontane-ity, -ousness; originality.

pleasure, wish, desire, mind; frame of mind &c. (*inclination*) 602; intention &c. 620; predetermination &c. 611; self-control &c. determination &c. (*resolution*) 604; will-power.

**V.** will, list; see –, think- fit; determine &c. (*resolve*) 604; settle &c. (*choose*) 609; volunteer.

have a will of one's own; do what one chooses &c. (*freedom*) 748; have it all one's own way; have one's -will, – own way.

use –, exercise- one's discretion; take -upon oneself, – one's own course, – the law into one's own hands; do -of one's own accord, – upon one's own -responsibility, – authority; take the bit between one's teeth; take responsibility; originate &c. (*cause*) 153.

**Adj.** voluntary, volitive, volitional, wilful; free &c. 748; optional; discretion-al, -ary; volitient; dictatorial.

minded &c. (*willing*) 602; prepense &c. (*predetermined*) 611; intended &c. 620; autocratic; unbidden &c. (bid &c. 741); spontaneous; original &c. (*causal*) 153.

**Adv.** voluntarily &c. *adj.*; at -will, – pleasure; *à -volonté*, – *discrétion*; *al piacere*; *ad -libitum*, – *arbitrium*; as -one thinks proper, – it seems good to.

**601. Necessity.—N.** involuntariness; instinct, blind –, natural- impulse; inborn –, innate- proclivity; the force of circumstances.

necessi-ty, -tation, necessarianism; obligation; compulsion &c. 744; subjection &c. 749; stern –, hard –, dire –, imperious –, inexorable –, iron –, adverse- -necessity, – fate; what must be.

desti-ny, -nation; fatality, fate, *kismet*, doom, foredoom, election, predestination; pre-, fore-ordination; lot, fortune; fatalism, determinism; inevitableness &c. *adj.*; spell &c. 993.

star, -s; planet, -s; astral influence; sky, Fates, Norns, *Parcæ*, Sisters three, Clotho, Lachesis, Atropos; book of fate; God's will, will of Heaven; wheel of Fortune, Ides of March, Hobson's choice.

last -shift, – resort; *dernier ressort*; *pis aller* &c. (*substitute*) 147; necessaries &c. (*requirement*) 630.

necess-arian, -itarian; fatalist, determinist; automaton.

**V.** lie under a necessity; be -fated, – doomed, – destined &c., – in for, – under the necessity of; have no -choice, – alternative; be- obliged –, forced –, driven –, one's -fate &c. *n.*- to; be -pushed to the wall, – driven into a corner, – unable to help- – drawn irresistibly.

destine, doom, foredoom, devote; pre-destine, -ordain; cast a spell &c. 992; necessitate; compel &c. 744.

* Conative powers or faculties (Hamilton). †Hamilton.

of one's own -accord, – free will; *proprio* –, *suo* –, *ex mero- motu*; out of one's own head; by choice &c. 609; purposely &c. (*intentionally*) 620; deliberately &c. 611.

**Phr.** *stet pro ratione voluntas*; *sic volo sic jubeo.*

---

**Adj.** necessary; needful &c. (*requisite*) 630.

fated; destined &c. *v.*; fateful; elect; spell-bound.

compulsory &c. (*compel*) 744; uncontrollable, inevitable, unavoidable, irresistible, irrevocable, inexorable, binding; avoid-, resist-less; written in the book of fate.

involuntary, instinctive, automatic, blind, mechanical; un-conscious, -witting, -thinking; unintentional &c. (*undesigned*) 621; impulsive &c. 612.

**Adv.** necessarily &c. *adv.*; of -necessity, – course; *ex necessitate rei*; needs must; perforce &c. 744; *nolens volens*; will he nil he, willy nilly, *bon gré mal gré*, willing or unwilling, *coûte que coûte*, forcefully, *faute de mieux*; by stress of; if need be.

**Phr.** it cannot be helped; there is no- help for, – helping- it; it -will, – must, – must needs- be, – be so, – have its way; the die is cast; *jacta est alea*; *che sarà sarà*; 'it is written'; one's- days are numbered, – fate is sealed; *Fata obstant*; *dis aliter visum.*

**602. Willingness.—N.** willingness, voluntariness &c. *adj.*; willing mind, heart.

disposition, inclination, leaning, *animus*; frame of mind, humour, mood, vein; bent &c. (*turn of mind*) 820; *penchant* &c. (*desire*) 865; aptitude &c. 698.

doc-ility, -ibleness, tractability; persuasi-bleness, -bility; pliability &c. (*softness*) 324.

geniality, cordiality; goodwill; alacrity, readiness, earnestness, forwardness, enthusiasm; zeal, eagerness &c. (*desire*) 865.

assent &c. 488; compliance &c. 762; pleasure &c. (*will*) 600.

labour of love, self-appointed task; volunteer, -ing, gratuitous service; unpaid worker, amateur.

**V.** be -willing &c. *adj.*; incline, lean to, mind, propend; had as lief; lend –, give –, turn- a willing ear; have -a, – half a, – a great- mind to; hold –, cling- to; desire &c. 865.

see –, think- -good, – fit, – proper; acquiescence &c. (*assent*) 488; comply with &c. 762.

swallow –, nibble at- the bait; gorge the hook; swallow hook, line and sinker; have –, make- no scruple of; make no bones of; jump –, catch- at; meet half way; volunteer, offer oneself &c. 763.

**603. Unwillingness.—N.** unwillingness &c. *adj.*; indispos-ition, -edness; disinclination, aversation, aversion; nolleity, nolition; renitence; reluctance; indifference &c. 866; backwardness &c. *adj.*; slowness &c. 275; want of -alacrity, – readiness; indocility &c. (*obstinacy*) 606.

scrupul-ousness, -osity; qualms of conscience, delicacy, demur, scruple, qualm, shrinking, recoil; hesitation &c. (*irresolution*) 605; fastidiousness &c. 868.

averseness &c. (*dislike*) 867; dissent &c. 489; refusal &c. 764.

slacker, scrimshanker, *embusqué*, unwilling worker, forced labour.

**V.** be -unwilling &c. *adj.*; nill; dislike &c. 867; grudge, begrudge; not be able to find it in one's heart to, not have the stomach to.

demur, stick at, scruple, stickle; hang fire, run rusty, slack, shirk, scamp, give up, fight shy of, not pull fair; recoil, shrink, swerve; hesitate &c. 605; avoid &c. 623.

oppose &c. 708; dissent &c. 489; refuse &c. 764.

**Adj.** unwilling; not in the vein, loth, shy of, disinclined, indisposed, averse, reluctant, not content; adverse &c. (*opposed*) 708; laggard, backward, remiss, slack, slow to; renitent; indifferent &c. 866; scrupulous; squeamish

**Adj.** willing, minded, fain, disposed, inclined, favourable; favourably-minded, -inclined, -disposed; nothing loth; in the -vein, – mood, – humour, – mind.

ready, forward, enthusiastic, earnest, eager; bent upon &c. (*desirous*) 865; predisposed, propense.

docile; persua-dable, -sible; suasible, easily persuaded, facile, easy-going; amenable; tractable &c. (*pliant*) 324; genial, gracious, cordial, hearty; content &c. (*assenting*) 488.

voluntary, gratuitous, spontaneous; unasked &c. (ask &c. 765); unforced &c. (*free*) 748.

**Adv.** willingly &c. *adj.*; fain, freely, as lief, heart and soul; with -pleasure, – all one's heart, – open arms; with -good, – right good- will; *de bonne volonté, ex animo*; *con amore*, heart in hand, nothing loth, without reluctance, of one's own accord, graciously, with a good grace, without demur.

*à la bonne heure*; by all -means, – manner of means; to one's heart's content; yes &c. (*assent*) 488.

**Int.** sure, -ly! of course!

&c. (*fastidious*) 868; repugnant &c. (*dislike*) 867; rest-iff, -ive; demurring &c. *v.*; unconsenting &c. (*refusing*) 764; involuntary &c. 601; grudging, irreconcilable.

**Adv.** unwillingly &c. *adj.*; grudgingly, with a heavy heart; with -a bad, – an ill- grace; against –, sore against- -one's wishes, – one's will, – the grain; *invitâ Minervâ*; *à contre cœur*; *malgré soi*; in spite of -one's teeth, – oneself; *nolens volens* &c. (*necessity*) 601; perforce &c. 744; under protest; no &c. 536; not for the world, far be it from me; not if I can help it; if I must I must.

---

**604. Resolution.—N.** determination, will; iron –, unconquerable- will; will of one's own, decision, resolution, backbone, grit; strength of -mind, – will; resolve &c. (*intent*) 620; *intransigeance*; firmness &c. (*stability*) 150; energy, manliness, vigour; game, pluck; resoluteness &c. (*courage*) 861; zeal &c. 682; *aplomb*; desperation; devot-ion, -edness.

mastery over self; self-control, -command, -mastery, -possession, -reliance, -government, -restraint, -conquest, -denial; moral -courage, – strength, – fibre; perseverance &c. 604*a*; tenacity; obstinacy &c. 606; bull-dog; British lion.

**V.** have -determination &c. *n.*; know one's own mind; be -resolved &c. *adj.*; make up one's mind, will, resolve, determine; decide &c. (*judgment*) 480; form –, come to- a -determination, – resolution, – resolve; conclude, fix, seal, determine once for all, bring to a crisis, drive matters to an extremity; take a decisive step &c. (*choice*) 609; take upon oneself &c. (*undertake*) 676.

devote oneself –, give oneself up- to; throw away the scabbard, kick down

**605. Irresolution.—N.** irresolution, infirmity of purpose, indecision; in-, un-determination, loss of will power; unsettlement; uncertainty &c. 475; demur, suspense; hesi-tating &c. *v.*, -tation, -tancy; vacillation; ambivalence; changeableness &c. 149; fluctuation; alternation &c. (*oscillation*) 314; caprice &c. 608; lukewarmness.

fickleness, levity, *légèreté*; pliancy &c. (*softness*) 324; weakness; timidity &c. 860; cowardice &c. 862; half measures.

waverer, ass between two bundles of hay; shuttlecock, butterfly; time-server, opportunist, turn coat.

**V.** be -irresolute &c. *adj.*; hang –, keep- in suspense; leave '*ad referendum*'; think twice about, pause; dawdle &c. (*inactivity*) 683; remain neuter; dilly-dally, hesitate, boggle, hover, wobble, shilly-shally, hum and haw, demur, not know one's own mind; debate, balance; dally –, coquet- with; will and will not, *chasser-balancer*; go half-way, compromise, make a compromise; be thrown off one's balance, stagger like a drunken man; be afraid &c. 860; let 'I dare not' wait upon 'I would': falter, waver.

the ladder, nail one's colours to the mast, set one's back against the wall, set one's teeth, put one's foot down, burn one's bridges, take one's stand; stand firm &c. (*stability*) 150; steel oneself; stand no nonsense, not listen to the voice of the charmer.

buckle to; put –, lay –, set- one's shoulder to the wheel; put one's heart into; run the gauntlet, make a dash at, take the bull by the horns; beard the lion in his den; rush –, plunge- *in medias res*; go in for; insist upon, make a point of; set one's heart, – mind- upon.

stick at nothing; make short work of &c. (*activity*) 682; not stick at trifles; go -all lengths, – the whole hog; persist &c. (*persevere*) 604*a*; go down with colours flying, die game; go through fire and water, ride in the whirlwind and direct the storm.

**Adj.** resolved &c. *v.*; determined; strong-willed, -minded; resolute &c. (*brave*) 861; self-possessed, plucky, tenacious; decided, definitive, peremptory; un-hesitating, -flinching, -shrinking; firm, cast iron, indomitable, game to the backbone; inexorable relentless, not to be -shaken, – put down; *tenax propositi*; inflexible &c. (*hard*) 323; obstinate &c. 606; steady &c. (*persevering*) 604*a*; unbending, unyielding, irrevocable; firm as a rock; grim.

earnest, serious; set –, bent –, intent- upon.

steeled –, proof- against; *in utrumque paratus*.

**Adv.** resolutely &c. *adj.*; in –, in good- earnest; seriously, joking apart, earnestly, heart and soul; on one's metal; manfully, like a man, with a high hand; with a strong hand &c. (*exertion*) 686.

at any -rate, – risk, – hazard, – price, – cost, – sacrifice; at all -hazards, – risks, – events; cost what it may; *coûte que coûte*; *à tort et à travers*; once for all; neck or nothing; rain or shine; with colours nailed to the mast.

**Phr.** *spes sibi quisque*.

vacillate &c. 149; change &c. 140; retract &c. 607; fluctuate; alternate &c. (*oscillate*) 314; keep off and on, play fast and loose; blow hot and cold &c. (*caprice*) 608.

shuffle, palter, blink; trim.

**Adj.** irresolute, infirm of purpose, double-minded, half-hearted; un-decided, -resolved, -determined; drifting; shilly-shally; fidgety, tremulous; wobbly; hesitating &c. *v.*; off one's balance; at a loss &c. (*uncertain*) 475.

vacillating &c. *v.*; unsteady &c. (*changeable*) 149; unsteadfast, fickle, unreliable, irresponsible, unstable, without ballast; capricious &c. 608; volatile, frothy; light, -some, -minded; giddy; fast and loose.

weak, feeble-minded, frail; timid &c. 860; cowardly &c. 862; facile; pliant &c. (*soft*) 324; unable to say 'no,' easy-going.

revocable, reversible.

**Adv.** irresolutely &c. *adj.*; irresolvedly; in faltering accents; off and on; from pillar to post; see-saw &c. 314.

**Int.** 'how happy could I be with either!'

---

**604a. Perseverance.—N.** perseverance; continuance &c. (*inaction*) 143; permanence &c. (*absence of change*) 141; firmness &c. (*stability*) 150.

constancy, steadiness; singleness –, tenacity- of purpose; persistence, plodding, patience; sedulity &c. (*industry*) 682; pertina-cy, -city, -ciousness; iteration &c. 104.

bottom, game, pluck, stamina, backbone, grit; indefatiga-bility, -bleness; bulldog courage.

**V.** persevere, persist; hold -on, – out; die in the last ditch, be in at the death; stick –, cling –, adhere- to; stick to one's text, keep on; keep to –, maintain- one's -course, – ground; bear –, keep –, hold-up; plod; stick to work &c. (*work*) 686; continue &c. 143; follow up; die -in harness, – at one's post.

**Adj.** persevering, constant; stead-y, -fast; un-deviating, -wavering, -faltering, -swerving, -flinching, -sleeping, -flagging, -drooping; steady as time; uninter-, un-remitting; plodding; industrious &c. 682; strenuous &c. 686; pertinacious; persist-ing, -ent.

solid, sturdy, staunch, stanch, true to oneself; unchangeable &c. 150; unconquerable &c. (*strong*) 159; indomitable, game to the last, indefatigable, untiring, unwearied, never tiring.

**Adv.** through -evil report and good report, – thick and thin, – fire and water; *per fas et nefas*; without fail, sink or swim, at any price, *vogue la galère*; in sickness and in health.

**Phr.** never say die; *vestigia nulla retrorsum.*

**606. Obstinacy.—N.** obstinateness &c. *adj.*; obstinacy, tenacity; perseverance &c. 604*a*; immovability; old school; inflexibility &c. (*hardness*) 323; obdur-acy, -ation; dogged resolution; resolution &c. 604; ruling passion; blind side.

self-will, contumacy, perversity; pervica-cy, -city; indocility.

bigotry, intolerance, dogmatism; opinia-try, -tiveness; fixed idea &c.; intractability, incorrigibility; (*prejudgment*) 481; fanaticism, zealotry, infatuation, monomania, opinionativeness.

mule; opin-ionist, -ionatist, -iator, -ator; stickler, dogmatist, die-hard, bitter-ender; bigot; zealot, enthusiast, fanatic.

**V.** be -obstinate &c. *adj.*; stickle, take no denial, fly in the face of facts; opinionate, be wedded to an opinion, hug a belief; have one's own way &c. (*will*) 600; persist &c. (*persevere*) 604*a*; have –, insist on having- the last word.

die -hard, – fighting, fight -against destiny, – to the last ditch; not yield an inch, stand out.

**Adj.** obstinate, tenacious, stubborn, obdurate, case-hardened; inflexible &c. (*hard*) 323; immovable, not to be moved; inert &c. 172; unchangeable &c. 150; inexorable &c. (*determined*) 604; mulish, obstinate as a mule, pig-headed.

dogged; sullen, sulky; un-moved, -influenced, -affected.

wilful, self-willed, perverse; res-ty, -tive, -tiff; pervicacious, wayward, refractory, unruly; head-y, -strong; *entêté*; contumacious; cross-grained.

**607. Tergiversation.—N.** change of -mind, – intention, – purpose; afterthought.

tergiversation, recantation; palinode, -ody; renunciation; abjur-ation, -ement; defection &c. (*relinquishment*) 624; going over &c. *v.*; apostasy; retract-ion, -ation; withdrawal, disavowal &c. (*negation*) 536; revo-cation, -kement; reversal; repentance &c. 950; *redintegratio amoris.*

coquetry, flirtation; vacillation &c. 605; back-sliding, recidivation.

turn-coat, -tippet; rat, apostate, renegade, mugwump; con-, per-vert; proselyte, deserter; backslider, recidivist; black leg.

time-server, -pleaser; timist, Vicar of Bray, trimmer, ambidexter; weathercock &c. (*changeable*) 149; Janus.

**V.** change one's -mind, – intention, – purpose, – note; abjure, renounce; withdraw from &c. (*relinquish*) 624; wheel –, turn –, veer- round; turn a *pirouette*; go over –, pass –, change –, skip- from one side to another; go to the right about; box the compass, shift one's ground, go upon another tack; back down, crawl, crawfish.

apostatize, change sides, go over, rat; recant, retract; revoke; rescind &c. (*abrogate*) 756; recall, forswear, abjure, unsay; come -over, – round- to an opinion.

draw in one's horns, eat one's words; eat –, swallow- the leek; swerve, flinch, back out of, retrace one's steps, think better of it; come back –, return- to one's first love; turn over a new leaf &c. (*repent*) 950.

arbitrary, dogmatic, opinionated, positive, bigoted; prejudiced &c. 481; prepossessed, infatuated; stiff-backed, -necked, -hearted; hard-mouthed, hidebound; unyielding; im-pervious, -practicable, -persuasible; unpersuadable; in-, un-tractable; incorrigible, deaf to advice, impervious to reason; crotchety &c. 608.

**Adv.** obstinately &c. *adj.*

**Phr.** *non possumus*; no surrender.

trim, shuffle, play fast and loose, blow hot and cold, coquet, flirt, hold with the hare but run with the hounds; straddle; *nager entre deux eaux*; wait to see how the -cat jumps, – wind blows.

**Adj.** changeful &c. 149; irresolute &c. 605; ductile, slippery as an eel, trimming, ambidextrous, timeserving; coquetting &c. *v.*

revocatory, reactionary.

**Phr.** 'a change came o'er the spirit of my dream.'

---

**608. Caprice.—N.** caprice, fancy, humour; whim, -sey, -wham; crotchet, *capriccio*, quirk, freak, maggot, fad, vagary, prank, fit, flimflam, *escapade, boutade*, wild-goose chase; capriciousness &c. *adj.*; kink.

**V.** be -capricious &c. *adj.*; have a maggot in the brain; take it into one's head, strain at a gnat and swallow a camel; blow hot and cold; play -fast and loose, – fantastic tricks.

**Adj.** capricious; erratic, eccentric, fitful, hysterical; full of -whims &c. *n.*; maggoty; inconsistent, fanciful, fantastic, whimsical, crotchety, particular, humoursome, freakish, skittish, wanton, wayward; contrary; captious; arbitrary; unrestrained, undisciplined; not amenable to reason; uncomfortable &c. 83; penny wise and pound foolish; fickle &c. (*irresolute*) 605; frivolous, sleeveless, giddy, volatile.

**Adv.** by fits and starts, without rhyme or reason, at one's own sweet will.

**Phr.** *nil fuit unquam sic impar sibi*; the deuce is in him.

**609. Choice.—N.** choice, option; discretion &c. (*volition*) 600; preoption; alternative; dilemma; *embarras de choix*; adoption, co-optation; novation; decision &c. (*judgment*) 480.

election, poll, ballot, vote, voice, suffrage, plumper, cumulative vote; *plebiscitum, plébiscite, vox populi*; *referendum*, electioneering; voting &c. *v.*; franchise; ballot box; slate, ticket.

selection, excerption, gleaning, eclecticism; *excerpta*, gleanings, cuttings, scissors and paste; pick &c. (*best*) 650.

preference, prelation; predilection &c. (*desire*) 865.

**V.** offer for one's choice, set before; hold out –, present –, offer- the alternative; put to the vote.

use –, exercise –, one's- -discretion, – option; adopt, take up, embrace, espouse; choose, elect, co-opt; take –, make- one's choice; make choice of, fix upon.

vote, poll, hold up one's hand; divide.

settle; decide &c. (*adjudge*) 480; list

**609a. Absence of Choice.—N.** no –, Hobson's- choice; first come, first served; necessity &c. 601; not a pin to choose &c. (*equality*) 27; any, the first that comes.

neutrality, indifference; indecision &c. (*irresolution*) 605.

**V.** be -neutral &c. *adj.*; have no choice; waive, not vote; abstain –, refrain- from voting; leave undecided; make a virtue of necessity.

**Adj.** neu-tral, -ter; indifferent; undecided &c. (*irresolute*) 605.

**Adv.** either &c. (*choice*) 609.

**610. Rejection.—N.** rejection, repudiation, exclusion; declination; refusal &c. 764.

**V.** reject; set –, lay- aside; give up; decline &c. (*refuse*) 764; exclude, except, eliminate; pluck, spin; cast.

repudiate, scout, set at naught; fling –, cast –, thrown –, toss- -to the winds, – to the dogs, – overboard, – away; send to the right about; dis-

&c. (*will*) 600; make up one's mind &c. (*resolve*) 604.

select; pick, – and choose; pick –, single- out, excerpt; cull, glean, winnow; sift –, separate –, winnow- the chaff from the wheat; pick up, pitch upon; pick one's way; indulge one's fancy.

set apart, reserve, mark out for; mark &c. 550.

prefer; have -rather, – as lief; fancy &c. (desire) 865; be persuaded &c. 615.

take a -decided, – decisive- step; commit oneself to a course; pass –, cross- the Rubicon; cast in one's lot with; take for better or for worse.

**Adj.** optional; co-optative; discretional &c. (*voluntary*) 600; on approval.

eclectic; choosing &c. *v.*; preferential; chosen &c. *v.*; choice &c. (*good*) 648.

**Adv.** optionally &c. *adj.*; at pleasure &c. (*will*) 600; either, – the one or the other; or; at the option of; whether or not; once for all; for one's money.

by -choice, – preference; in preference; rather, before.

claim &c. (*deny*) 536; discard &c. (*eject*) 297, (*have done with*) 678.

**Adj.** rejected &c. *v.*; reject-aneous, -itious; not -chosen &c. 609, – to be thought of; out of the question.

**Adv.** neither, – the one nor the other; no &c. 536.

**Phr.** *non hæc in fœdera.*

---

**611. Predetermination.** — **N.** premeditation, -deliberation, -determination, -destination; foreordination; foregone conclusion; *parti pris*; resolve, propendency; intention &c. 620; project &c. 626.

**V.** pre-determine, -destine, -meditate, -resolve, -concert; foreordain; resolve beforehand.

**Adj.** pre-pense, -meditated &c. *v.*, -designed; advised, studied, designed, calculated; aforethought; intended &c. 620; foregone.

well-laid, -devised, -weighed; maturely considered; cut and dried; cunning.

**Adv.** advisedly &c. *adj.*; with premeditation, deliberately, all things considered, with eyes open, in cold blood; intentionally &c. 620.

**612. Impulse.**—**N.** impulse, sudden thought; *impromptu*, improvisation; inspiration, hunch, flash, spurt.

*improvisatore*, *improvisatrice*, improviser, extemporizer; creature of impulse.

**V.** flash on the mind.

say what comes uppermost; improvise, extemporize; rise to the occasion; spurt.

**Adj.** extemporaneous, impulsive, indeliberate; improvis-ed, -ate, -atory; un-, unpre-meditated; *improvisé*; unprompted, -guided; natural, unguarded; spontaneous &c. (*voluntary*) 600; instinctive &c. 601.

**Adv.** extem-pore, -poraneously; offhand, *impromptu*, *à l'improviste*; improviso; on the spur of the -moment, – occasion.

**613. Habit.**—**N.** habit, -ude; assuetude, -faction; wont; run, way.

common –, general –, natural –, ordinary –, habitual- -course, – run, – state- of things; matter of course; beaten -path, – track, – ground.

prescription, custom, use, usage, immemorial usage, practice; tradition; prevalence, observance; conventional-

**614. Desuetude.**—**N.** desuetude, disusage; disuse &c. 678; want of -habit, – practice; inusitation; newness to; new brooms.

infraction of usage &c. (*unconformity*) 83; non-prevalence; 'a custom more honoured in the breach than the observance.'

**V.** be -unaccustomed &c. *adj.*; leave

ism, -ity; mode, fashion, vogue; *etiquette* &c. (*gentility*) 852; order of the day, cry; conformity &c. 82.

*habitué*, addict.

one's old way, old school, consuetude, *veteris vestigia flammæ*; *laudator temporis acti*.

rule, standing order, precedent, routine; red-tape, -tapism; pipe-clay; rut, groove.

*cacoëthes*; bad –, confirmed –, inveterate –, intrinsic &c. 5- habit; addiction, trick.

training &c. (*education*) 537; seasoning, hardening, inurement; radication; second nature, acclimatization; knack &c. (*skill*) 698.

**V.** be -wont &c. *adj.*

fall into a custom &c. (*conform to*) 82; tread –, follow- the beaten -track, – path; *stare super antiquas vias*; move in a rut, run on in a groove, go round like a horse in a mill, go on in the old jog-trot way.

habituate, inure, harden, season, caseharden; accustom, familiarize; naturalize, acclimatize; keep one's hand in; train &c. (*educate*) 537.

get into the -way, – knack- of; learn &c. 539; cling –, adhere- to; repeat &c. 104; acquire –, contract –, fall into- a -habit, – trick; addict oneself –, take- to; accustom oneself to.

be -habitual &c. *adj.*; prevail; come into use, become a habit, take root; gain –, grow- upon one.

**Adj.** habitual; ac-, customary; prescriptive; accustomed &c. *v.*; traditional; of -daily, – every-day- occurrence; wonted, usual, general, ordinary, common, frequent, every-day, household, jog-trot; well-trodden, -known; familiar, vernacular, trite, commonplace, banal, bromidic, conventional, regular, set, stock, officinal, established, stereotyped; pre-vailing, -valent; current, received, acknowledged, recognized, accredited; of course, admitted, understood.

conformable &c. 82; according to -use, – custom, – routine; in vogue, – fashion; fashionable &c. (*genteel*) 852.

wont; used – given – addicted –, attuned –, habituated &c. *v.*- to; in the habit of; *habitué*; at home in &c. (*skilful*) 698; seasoned; permeated –, imbued- with; devoted –, wedded- to; never free from.

hackneyed, fixed, rooted, deep-rooted, ingrafted, permanent, inveterate, besetting; naturalized; ingrained &c. (*intrinsic*) 5.

**Adv.** habitually &c. *adj.*; always &c. (*uniformly*) 16.

as -usual, – is one's wont, – things go, – the world goes, – the sparks fly upwards; *more -suo, – solito*.

as a rule, for the most part; generally &c. *adj.*; most often, – frequently.

**Phr.** *cela s'entend.*

off –, cast off –, break off –, wean oneself of –, violate –, break through –, infringe- -a habit, – a custom, – a usage; break one's fetters; disuse &c. 678; wear off.

**Adj.** un-accustomed, -used, -wonted, -seasoned, -inured, -habituated, -trained; new; green &c. (*unskilled*) 699; fresh, original, unhackneyed.

unusual &c. (*unconformable*) 83; unconventional, non-observant; disused &c. 678.

**Adv.** just for once.

---

## 2°. *Causes of Volition*

**615. Motive.—N.** motive, springs of action.

reason, ground, call, principle; main-

**615a. Absence of Motive.—N.** absence of motive; caprice &c. 608; chance &c. (*absence of design*) 621.

spring, *primum mobile*, key-stone; the why and the wherefore; *pro* and *con*, reason why; secret –, ulterior- motive, *arrière-pensée*; intention &c. 620.

inducement, consideration; attraction &c. 288; loadstone; magnet, -ism, -ic force; allect-ation, -ive; temptation, enticement, *agacerie*, allurement, witchery; bewitch-ment, -ery; charm; spell &c. 993; fascination, blandishment, cajolery; seduc-tion, -ement; honeyed words, voice of the tempter, song of the Sirens; forbidden fruit, golden apple.

persuasi-bility, -bleness; attractability; impress-, suscept-ibility; softness; persuas-, attract-iveness; tantalization.

influence, prompting, dictate, instance; impuls-e, -ion; incit-ement, -ation; press, instigation; provocation &c. (*excitation of feeling*) 824; inspiration; per-, suasion; encouragement, advocacy; exhortation, advice &c. 695; solicitation &c. (*request*) 765; lobbying.

incentive, stimulus, spur, fillip, whip, goad, rowel, provocative, whet, dram.

bribe, lure; decoy, – duck; bait, trail of a red herring; bribery and corruption; sop, – for Cerberus.

prompter, tempter; seduc-er, -tor; suggester, coaxer, wheedler; instigator, firebrand, incendiary; Siren, Circe; *agent provocateur*; lobbyist.

**V.** induce, move; draw, – on; bring in its train, give an -impulse &c. *n.*- to; inspire; put up to, prompt, call up; attract, beckon.

stimulate &c. (*excite*) 824; spirit up, inspirit; a-, rouse; ecphorize; animate, incite, provoke, instigate, set on, actuate; act –, work –, operate- upon; encourage; pat –, clap- on the -back, – shoulder.

influence, weigh with, bias, sway, incline, dispose, predispose, turn the scale, inoculate; lead, – by the nose; have –, exercise- influence- -with, – over, – upon; go –, come- round one; turn the head, magnetize.

persuade; prevail -with, – upon; overcome, carry; bring -round, – to one's senses; draw –, win –, gain –, come –, talk- over; procure, enlist, engage; invite, court.

tempt, seduce, overpersuade, entice, allure, captivate, fascinate, intrigue, bewitch, carry away, charm, conciliate, wheedle, coax, lure, suggest; inveigle; tantalize; cajole &c. (*deceive*) 545.

tamper with, bribe, suborn, grease the palm, bait with a silver hook, gild the pill, make things pleasant, put a sop into the pan, throw a sop to, bait the hook.

**V.** have no motive; scruple &c. (*be unwilling*) 603.

**Adj.** without rhyme or reason; aimless &c. (*chance*) 621.

**Adv.** capriciously; out of mere caprice.

**616. Dissuasion.**—**N.** dissuasion, dehortation, expostulation, remonstrance; deprecation &c. 766.

discouragement, damper, wet blanket; warning.

cohibition &c. (*restraint*) 751; curb &c. (*means of restraint*) 752; check &c. (*hindrance*) 706.

reluctance &c. (*unwillingness*) 603; contraindication.

**V.** dissuade, dehort, cry out against, remonstrate, expostulate, warn, contraindicate.

disincline, indispose, shake, stagger; dispirit; dis-courage, -hearten, -enchant; deter; hold –, keep- back &c. (*restrain*) 751; render -averse &c. 603; repel; turn aside &c. (*deviation*) 279; wean from; act as a drag &c. (*hinder*) 706; throw cold water on, damp, cool, chill, blunt, calm, quiet, quench; deprecate &c. 766.

**Adj.** dissuading &c. *v.*; dissuasive; dehortatory, expostulatory; monit-ive, -ory.

dissuaded &c. *v.*; uninduced &c. (induce &c. 615); unpersuadable &c. (*obstinate*) 606; averse &c. (*unwilling*) 603; repugnant &c. (*dislike*) 867.

enforce, force; impel &c. (*push*) 276; propel &c. 284; whip, lash, goad, spur, prick, urge; egg –, hound –, hurry- on; drag &c. 285; exhort; advise &c. 695; call upon &c., press &c. (*request*) 765; advocate.

set -an example, – the fashion; keep in countenance; back up.

be -persuaded &c.; yield to temptation, come round; concede &c. (*consent*) 762; obey a call; follow -advice, – the bent, – the dictates of; act on principle.

**Adj.** impulsive, motive; suas-, persuas-, hortat-ive, -ory; protreptical; inviting, tempting &c. *v.*; seductive, attractive, irresistible; fascinating &c. (*pleasing*) 829; provocative &c. (*exciting*) 824.

induced &c. *v.*; disposed; persuadable &c. (*docile*) 602; spellbound; instinct –, smitten- with; inspired &c. *v.*- by.

**Adv.** because, therefore &c. (*cause*) 155; from -this, – that- motive; for -this, – that- reason; for; by reason –, for the sake –, on the score –, on account- of; out of, from, as, forasmuch as.

for all the world; on principle.

**617.** [Ostensible motive, ground, or reason assigned.] **Plea.—N** plea, pretext; allegation, advocation; ostensible -motive, – ground, – reason; excuse &c. (*vindication*) 937; colour; gloss, guise.

loop-, starting-hole; how to creep out of, salvo, come off.

handle, peg to hang on, room, *locus standi*; stalking-horse, *cheval de bataille*, cue.

pretence &c. (*untruth*) 546; put off, subterfuge, dust thrown in the eyes; blind; moonshine; mere –, shallow- pretext; lame -excuse, – apology; tub to a whale; false plea, sour grapes; makeshift, shift, white lie; special pleading &c. (*sophistry*) 477; soft sawder &c. (*flattery*) 933.

**V.** plead, allege; shelter oneself under the plea of; excuse &c. (*vindicate*) 937; gloss over; lend a colour to; furnish a -handle &c. *n.*; make a -pretext, – handle- of; use as a plea &c. *n.*; take one's stand upon, make capital out of; pretend &c. (*lie*) 544.

**Adj.** ostensible &c. (*manifest*) 525; excusing; alleged, apologetic; pretended &c. 545.

**Adv.** ostensibly; under -colour, – the plea, – the pretence- of.

### 3°. *Objects of Volition*

**618. Good.—N.** good, benefit, advantage; improvement &c. 658; interest, service, behoof, behalf; weal; main chance, *summum bonum*, common weal; 'consummation devoutly to be wished'; gain, boot; profit, harvest.

boon &c. (*gift*) 784; good turn; blessing, benison; world of good; piece of good -luck, – fortune; nuts, prize, windfall, godsend, waif, treasure trove.

good fortune &c. (*prosperity*) 734; happiness &c. 827.

[Source of good] goodness &c. 648; utility &c. 644; remedy &c. 662; pleasure-giving &c. 829.

**Adj.** commendable &c. 931; useful &c. 644; good &c., beneficial &c. 648.

**619. Evil.—N.** evil, ill, harm, hurt, mischief, nuisance; machinations of the devil, Pandora's box, ills that flesh is heir to.

blow, buffet, stroke, scratch, bruise, wound, gash, mutilation; mortal -blow, – wound; *immedicabile vulnus*; damage, loss &c. (*deterioration*) 659.

disadvantage, prejudice, drawback;

disaster, accident, casualty; mishap &c. (*misfortune*) 735; bad job, devil to pay; calamity, bale, woe, catastrophe, tragedy; ruin &c. (*destruction*) 162; adversity &c. 735.

mental suffering &c. 828. [Evil spirit] demon &c. 980. [Cause of evil] bane &c. 663. [Production of evil]

**V.** benefit, profit, advantage, serve, help, avail; do good to, gain, prosper, flourish.

**Adv.** well, aright, satisfactorily, favourably, not amiss; all for the best; to one's -advantage &c. *n.*; in one's -favour, – interest &c. *n.*

**Phr.** so far so good.

badness &c. 649; painfulness &c. 830; evil doer &c. 913.

outrage, wrong, injury, foul play; bad –, ill- turn; disservice; spoliation &c. 791; grievance, crying evil.

**V.** be in trouble &c. (*adversity*) 735; harm, injure, hurt, do disservice to.

**Adj.** disastrous, bad &c. 649; awry, out of joint; disadvantageous, injurious, harmful.

**Adv.** amiss, wrong, ill, to one's cost.

## Section II. Prospective Volition*

### 1°. *Conceptional Volition*

**620. Intention.—N.** intent, -ion, -ionality; purpose; *quo animo*; project &c. 626; undertaking &c. 676; predetermination &c. 611; design, ambition.

contemplation, mind, *animus*, view, purview, proposal; study; look out.

final cause; *raison d'être*; *cui bono*; object, aim, end; 'the be all and the end all'; drift &c. (*meaning*) 516; tendency &c. 176; destination, mark, point, butt, goal, target, bull's-eye, quintain; prey, quarry, game.

decision, determination, resolve; set –, settled- purpose; *ultimatum*; resolution &c. 604; wish &c. 865; *arrière-pensée*; motive &c. 615.

[Study of final causes] teleology.

**V.** intend, purpose, design, mean; have to; propose to oneself; harbour a design; have in -view, – contemplation, – one's eye, – *petto*; have an eye to.

bid –, labour- for; be –, aspire –, endeavour- after; be –, aim –, drive –, point–, level - at; take aim; set before oneself; study to.

take upon oneself &c. (*undertake*) 676; take into one's head; meditate, contemplate; think – dream –, talk- of; premeditate &c. 611; compass, calculate; dest-ine, -inate; propose.

project &c. (*plan*) 626; have a mind to &c. (*be willing*) 602; desire &c. 865; pursue &c. 622.

**Adj.** intended &c. *v.*; intentional, advised, express, determinate; prepense &c. 611; bound for; intending &c. *v.*; minded, disposed, inclined;

**621.** [Absence of purpose in the succession of events.] **Chance.†—N.** chance &c. 156; lot, fate &c. (*necessity*) 601; luck; good luck &c. (*good*) 618; bad luck &c. 735; wheel of fortune; mascot; swastika.

speculation, venture, stake, flutter, flier, gamble, game of chance; mere –, random- shot; blind bargain, leap in the dark; pig in a poke &c. (*uncertainty*) 475; fluke, pot-luck.

drawing lots; sorti-legy, -tion; ***sortes***, – *Virgilianæ*, *-biblicæ*; *rouge et noir*, hazard, *roulette*, pitch and toss, chuck-farthing, cup-tossing, heads or tails, cross and pile, wager; bet, -ting; risk, stake, plunge; gambling; the turf.

stock exchange, bourse, board of trade (U.S.A.), curb exchange.

gaming-, gambling-, betting-house; hell; betting ring, totalisator; dice, – box; dicer; gam-bler, -ester, plunger, stock operator, manipulator, punter; man of the turf; adventurer, speculator; bookmaker, layer, backer.

**V.** chance &c. (*hap*) 156; stand a chance &c. (*be possible*) 470.

toss up; cast –, draw- lots; leave –, trust- -to chance, – to the chapter of accidents; tempt fortune; chance it, take one's chance; run –, incur –, encounter- the -risk, – chance; stand the hazard of the die.

speculate, try one's luck, set on a cast, raffle, put into a lottery, buy a pig in a poke, shuffle the cards.

risk, venture, hazard, stake; lay, – a wager; make a bet, wager, bet, gamble,

* That is, volition having reference to a future object. † See note on 156.

bent upon &c. (*earnest*) 604; at stake, on the -anvil, – *tapis*; in -view; – prospect, – the breast of; *in petto*; teleological.

**Adv.** intentionally &c. *adj.*; advisedly, wittingly, knowingly, designedly, purposely, on purpose, by design, studiously, pointedly; with -intent &c. *n.*; deliberately &c. (*with premeditation*) 611; with one's eyes open, in cold blood.

for; with -a view, – an eye- to; in order -to, – that; to the end –, with the intent- that; for the purpose –, with the view –, in contemplation –, on account- of.

in pursuance of, pursuant to; *quo animo*; to all intents and purposes.

game, play for; play at chuck-farthing.

**Adj.** fortuitous &c. 156; unintentional, -ded; accidental; not meant; un-designed, -purposed; unpremeditated &c. 612; never thought of.

indiscriminate, promiscuous; undirected, random; aim-, drift-, design-, purpose-, cause-less; without purpose.

possible &c. 470.

**Adv.** casually &c. 156; unintentionally &c. *adj.*; unwittingly.

*en passant*, by the way, incidentally; as it may happen; at -random, – a venture, – haphazard; as luck would have it, by -chance, – good fortune; un-, -luckily.

---

**622.** [Purpose in action.] **Pursuit.**—**N.** pursuit; pursuing &c. *v.*; prosecution; pursuance; enterprise &c. (*undertaking*) 676; business &c. 625; adventure &c. (*essay*) 675; quest &c. (*search*) 461; scramble, hue and cry, game; hobby.

chase, hunt, *battue*, race, steeple-chase, hunting, coursing; ven-ation, -ery; fox-chase; sport, -ing; shooting, angling, fishing, hawking.

pursuer; hunt-er, -sman; sportsman, Nimrod, the field; hound &c. 366.

**V.** pursue, prosecute, follow; run –, make –, be –, hunt –, prowl- after; shadow; carry on &c. (*do*) 680; engage in &c. (*undertake*) 676; set about &c. (*begin*) 66; endeavour &c. 675; court &c. (*request*) 765; seek &c. (*search*) 461; aim at &c. (*intention*) 620; follow the trail &c. (*trace*) 461; fish for &c. (*experiment*) 463; press on &c. (*haste*) 684; run a race &c. (*velocity*) 274.

chase, give chase, course, dog, hunt, hound, stalk; tread –, follow- on the heels of &c. (*sequence*) 281.

rush upon; rush headlong &c. (*violence*) 173; ride –, run- full tilt at; make a leap –, jump –, snatch- at; run down; start game.

tread a path; take –, hold- a course; shape –, direct –, bend- one's -steps, – course; play a game; fight –, elbow- one's way; follow up; take -to, – up; go in for; ride one's hobby.

**Adj.** pursuing &c. *v.*; in quest of &c.

**623.** [Absence of pursuit.] **Avoidance.**—**N.** abst-ention, -inence; forbearance; refraining &c. *v.*; inaction &c. 681; neutrality.

avoidance, evasion, elusion; seclusion &c. 893.

avolation, flight; escape &c. 671; retreat &c. 287; recoil &c. 277; departure &c. 293; rejection &c. 610

shirker &c. *v.*; slacker; truant; fugitive, refugee; runa-way, -gate; renegade; deserter.

**V.** abstain, refrain, spare, not attempt; not do &c. 681; maintain the even tenor of one's way.

eschew, keep from, let alone, have nothing to do with; keep –, stand –, hold- -aloof, – off; take no part in, have no hand in.

avoid, shun; steer –, keep- clear of; fight shy of; keep -one's, – at a respectful- distance; keep –, get- out of the way; evade, elude, turn away from; set one's face against &c. (*oppose*) 708; deny oneself.

shrink; hang –, hold –, draw- back; recoil &c. 277; retire &c. (*recede*) 287; flinch, blink, blench, shy, shirk, dodge, parry, make way for, give place to.

beat a retreat; turn -tail, – one's back; take to one's heels; run, -away, – for one's life; cut and run; be off, – like a shot; fly, flee; fly –, flee –, run away- from; take –, take to- flight; desert, elope; make –, scamper –, sneak –, shuffle –, sheer- off; break –,

(*inquiry*) 461; in -pursuit, – full cry, – hot pursuit; on the scent.

**Adv.** in pursuance of &c. (*intention*) 620; after.

**Int.** tally-ho! yoicks! so-ho!

---

burst –, tear oneself –, slip –, slink –, steal- -away, – away from; slip cable, part company, turn on one's heel; sneak out of, play truant, give one the go by, give leg bail, take French leave, slope, decamp, flit, bolt, abscond, levant, skedaddle, absquatulate, cut one's stick, walk one's chalks, show a light pair of heels, make oneself scarce; escape &c. 671; go away &c. (*depart*) 293; abandon &c. 624; reject &c. 610.

lead one a -dance, – a merry chase, – pretty dance; throw off the scent, play at hide and seek.

**Adj.** unsought, unattempted; avoiding &c. *v.*; neutral; shy of &c. (*unwilling*) 603; elusive, evasive, distant; fugitive, runaway; shy, wild.

**Adj.** lest, in order to avoid.

**Int.** forbear! keep –, hands- off! *sauve qui peut!* devil take the hindmost!

**624. Relinquishment.—N.** relinquish-, abandon-ment; desertion, defection, secession, withdrawal; cave of Adullam; *nolle prosequi.*

discontinuance &c. (*cessation*) 142; renunciation &c. (*recantation*) 607; abrogation &c. 756; resignation &c. (*retirement*) 757; desuetude &c. 614; cession &c. (*of property*) 782.

**V.** relinquish, give up, abandon, desert, forsake, leave in the lurch; depart –, secede –, withdraw- from; back – out of, – down from, leave, go back on one's word, quit, take leave of, bid a long farewell; vacate &c. (*resign*) 757.

renounce &c. (*abjure*) 607; forego, have done with, drop; write off; disuse &c. 678; discard &c. 782; wash one's hands of; drop all idea of; *nolle-pros.*; lose interest in.

break –, leave- off; desist; stop &c. (*cease*) 142; hold –, stay- one's hand; quit one's hold; give over, shut up shop.

throw up the -game, – cards; give up the -point, – argument; pass to the order of the day, move the previous question, table the motion.

**Adj.** unpursued; relinquished &c. *v.*; relinquishing &c. *v.*

**Int.** avast &c.! (*stop*) 142.

**625. Business.—N.** business, occupation, employment; pursuit &c. 622; what one is doing-, – about; affair, concern, matter, case, undertaking.

matter in hand, irons in the fire; thing to do, *agendum*, task, work, job, chore, errand, transaction, commission, mission, charge, care; duty &c. 926.

part, *rôle*, cue; province, function, look-out, department, capacity, sphere, orb, field, line; walk, – of life; beat, round, routine; race, career.

office, place, post, incumbency, living; situation, appointment, billet, berth, employ; service &c. (*servitude*) 749; engagement; undertaking &c. 676.

vocation, calling, profession, *métier*, cloth, faculty; industry, art; industrial arts; craft, mystery, handicraft; trade &c. (*commerce*) 794.

exercise; work &c. (*action*) 680; avocation; press of business &c. (*activity*) 682.

**V.** pass –, employ –, spend- one's time in; employ oneself -in, – upon;

occupy –, concern- oneself with; make it one's -business &c. *n.*; undertake &c. 676; enter a profession; betake oneself to, turn one's hand to; have to do with &c. (*do*) 680.

drive a trade; carry on –, do –, transact- -business, – a trade &c. *n.*; keep a shop; ply one's task, – trade; labour in one's vocation; pursue the even tenor of one's way; attend to -business, – one's work.

officiate, serve, act; act –, play- one's part; do duty; serve –, discharge –, perform- the -office, – duties, – functions- of; hold –, fill- -an office, – a place, – a situation; hold a portfolio.

be -about, – doing, – engaged in, – employed in, – occupied with, – at work on; have one's hands in, have in hand; have on one's -hands, – shoulders; bear the burden; have one's hands full &c. (*activity*) 682.

be -in the hands of, – on the stocks, – on the anvil; pass through one's hands.

**Adj.** business-like; work-a-day; professional; official, functional; busy &c. (*actively employed*) 682; on –, in- -hand, – one's hands; afoot; on -foot, – the anvil; going on; acting.

**Adv.** in the course of business, all in a day's work; professionally &c. *adj.*

**626. Plan.**—**N.** plan, scheme, design, project; propos-al, -ition; suggestion; resolution, motion; precaution &c. (*provision*) 673; deep-laid &c. (*premeditated*) 611- plan &c.; racket.

system &c. (order) 58; organization &c. (*arrangement*) 60; germ &c. (*cause*) 153; Five Year Plan.

sketch, skeleton, outline, draught, draft, *ébauche*, *brouillon*; rough -cast, – draft, – draught, – copy; copy; proof, revise.

forecast, *programme*, prospectus, scenario; *carte du pays*; card; bill, protocol; order of the day, list of agenda, *memorandum*; bill of fare &c. (*food*) 298; base of operations; platform, plank.

*rôle*; policy &c. (*line of conduct*) 692.

contrivance, invention, expedient, receipt, nostrum, artifice, device, gadget; stratagem &c. (*cunning*) 702; trick &c. (*deception*) 545; alternative, loophole, shift &c. (*substitute*) 147; last shift &c. (*necessity*) 601.

measure, step; stroke, – of policy; master stroke; trump-, court-card; *cheval de bataille*, great gun; *coup*, – *d'état*; clever –, bold –, good- -move, – hit, – stroke; bright -thought, – idea, great idea.

intrigue, cabal, plot, frame-up, conspiracy, complot, machination; under-, counter-plot.

schem-ist, -atist; strategist, machinator, schemer; projector, author, builder, artist, promoter, designer &c. *v.*; conspirator; *intrigant* &c. (*cunning*) 702.

**V.** plan, scheme, design, frame, contrive, project, forecast, sketch; conceive, devise, invent &c. (*imagine*) 515; set one's wits to work &c. 515; spring a project; fall –, hit- upon; strike –, chalk –, cut –, lay –, map-out; lay down a plan; shape –, mark- out a course; predetermine &c. 611; concert, preconcert, preestablish; prepare &c. 673; hatch, – a plot; concoct; take -steps, – measures.

cast, recast, systematize, organize; arrange &c. 60; digest, mature.

plot; counter-plot, -mine; dig a mine; lay a train; intrigue &c. (*cunning*) 702.

**Adj.** planned &c. *v.*; strategic, -al; planning &c. *v.*; in course of preparation &c. 673; under consideration; on the *-tapis*, – carpet, – table.

**627. Method.** [Path.]—**N.** method, way, manner, wise, gait, form, mode, fashion, tone, guise; *modus operandi*; procedure &c. (*line of conduct*) 692.

path, road, route, course; line of -way, – road; trajectory, orbit, track, beat, tack.

steps; stair, -case; flight of stairs, ladder, stile.

bridge, viaduct, gauntry, pontoon, stepping stone, plank, gangway, catwalk, drawbridge; pass, ford, ferry, tunnel, subway, elevated; pipe &c. 260.

door; gateway &c. (*opening*) 260; channel, passage, avenue, means of access, approach, perron, adit, entrance; artery, lane, alley, aisle, lobby, corridor, cloister; back- door, -stairs; secret passage; covert-way.

road-, path-, stair-way; thoroughfare; highway, pike, turnpike, trail, parkway, *boulevard*; turnpike –, royal –, coach- road; broad –, King's –, Queen's- highway; beaten -track, – path; horse –, bridle- road, – track, – path; pathway; walk, *trottoir*, foot-path, pavement, flags, side-walk; by –, cross- -road, – path, – way; cut; short -cut &c. (*mid-course*) 628; *carrefour*; private –, occupation- road; highways and byways; rail-, tram-road, -way; funicular, ropeway, causeway; defile, cutting; canal &c. (*conduit*) 350; street &c. (*abode*) 189.

**Adv.** how; in what -way, – manner; by what mode; so, in this way, after this fashion, on these lines.

one way or another, anyhow; somehow or other &c. (*instrumentality*) 631; by way of; *viâ*; *in transitu* &c. 270; on the high road to.

**Phr.** *hæ tibi erunt artes.*

**628. Mid-course.**—**N.** middle-, mid-course; moderation, mean &c. 29; middle &c. 68; *juste milieu*, *mezzo termine*, golden mean, *aurea mediocritas*.

straight &c. (*direct*) 278 -course, – path; short –, cross- cut; short-circuit; great circle sailing.

neutrality; half –, half and half-measures; compromise.

**V.** keep in –, steer –, preserve- -a middle, – an even- course; go straight &c. (*direct*) 278.

go half way, compromise, make a compromise.

**Adj.** neutral, average, even, impartial, moderate, straight &c. (*direct*) 278.

**629. Circuit.**—**N.** circuit, roundabout way, digression, divagation, *détour*, circum-ambience, -ambulation, -bendibus, *ambages*, loop; winding &c. (*circuition*) 311; zigzag &c. (*deviation*) 279.

**V.** perform –, make- a circuit; go -round about, – out of one's way; make a *détour*; meander &c. (*deviate*) 279; circumambulate.

lead a pretty dance; beat about, – the bush; make two bites of a cherry.

**Adj.** circuitous, indirect, roundabout; zig-zag &c. (*deviating*) 279; circum-ambient, -ambulatory.

**Adv.** by -a side wind, – an indirect course; in a roundabout way; from pillar to post.

**630. Requirement.**—**N.** requirement, need, wants, necessities; necessaries, – of life; stress, exigency, pinch, *sine quâ non*, matter of necessity; case of -need, – life or death.

needfulness, essentiality, necessity, indispensability, urgency, prerequisite.

requisition &c. (*request*) 765, (*exaction*) 741; run upon; demand –, call- for.

*desideratum* &c. (*desire*) 865; want &c. (*deficiency*) 640.

charge, claim, command, injunction, requisition, mandate, order, *ultimatum*.

**V.** require, need, want, have occasion for, entail; not be able to -do without, - dispense with; prerequire.

render necessary, necessitate, create a necessity for, call for, put in requisition; make a requisition &c. (*ask for*) 765, (*demand*) 741.

stand in need of; lack &c. 640; desiderate; desire &c. 865; be -necessary &c. *adj.*

**Adj.** required &c. *v.*; requisite, needful, necessary, imperative, essential, indispensable, prerequisite; called for; in -demand, - request.

urgent, exigent, pressing, instant, crying, absorbing.

in want of; destitute of &c. 640.

**Adv.** *ex necessitate rei* &c. (*necessarily*) 601; of -, out of stern- necessity; at a pinch.

**Phr.** there is no time to lose; it cannot be -spared, - dispensed with.

2° *Subservience to Ends*

1. *Actual Subservience*

**631. Instrumentality.—N.** instrumentality; aid &c. 707; subservien-ce, -cy; mediation, inter-vention, -mediacy, medium, inter-medium, -mediary, vehicle, hand; agency &c. 170.

minister, handmaid, servant, slave, maid, valet; midwife, *accoucheur*, obstetrician; go-between; cat's paw; stepping-stone.

key; master -, pass -, latch- key; 'open sesame'; passport, *passepartout*, safe-conduct; influence.

instrument &c. 633; expedient &c. (*plan*) 626; means &c. 632.

**V.** subserve, minister, tend, mediate, intervene; come -, go- between, interpose; pull the strings; be -instrumental &c. *adj.*; pander to.

**Adj.** instrumental; useful &c. 644; ministerial, subservient, mediatorial; inter-mediate, -vening; conducive.

**Adv.** through, by, *per*; where-, there-, here-by; by the -agency &c. 170- of; by dint of; by -, in- virtue of; through the -medium &c. *n.*- of; along with; on the shoulders of; by means of &c. 632; by -, with- -the aid &c. (*assistance*) 707- of.

*per fas et nefas.* by fair means or foul; somehow, - or other; by hook or by crook.

**632. Means.—N.** means, resources, revenue, wherewithal, ways and means, income; capital &c. (*money*) 800; stock in trade &c. 636; provision &c. 637; a shot in the locker; appliances &c. (*machinery*) 633; means and appliances; conveniences; cards to play; expedients &c. (*measures*) 626; two strings to one's bow; sheet anchor &c. (*safety*) 666; aid &c. 707; medium &c. 631.

**V.** find -, have -, possess- means &c. *n.*; provide the wherewithal.

**Adj.** instrumental &c. 631; mechanical &c. 633.

**Adv.** by means of, with; by -what, - all, - any, - some- means; where-, here-, there-with; wherewithal.

how &c. (*in what manner*) 627; through &c. (*by the instrumentality of*) 631; with -, by- the aid &c. (*assistance*) 707- of; by the -agency &c. 170- of.

**633. Instrument.—N.** machinery, mechanism, engineering.

instrument, organ, tool, implement, utensil, contrivance, machine, motor, engine, lathe, gin, mill, pump.

gear; tack-le, -ling, trice, rigging, gear, apparatus, appliances; plant, *matériel*; harness, trappings, fittings, accoutrements; equip-ment, -age:

appointments, furniture, upholstery; chattels; paraphernalia &c. (*belongings*) 780; *impedimenta*.

mechanical powers; lever, -age; mechanical advantage; crow, -bar; handspike, gavelock, jemmy, arm, limb, wing; oar, paddle; pulley, sheave; parbuckle; wheel and axle; wheel-, clock-work; wheels within wheels; pinion, gear wheel, spur –, bevel- gearing, chains, belting, crank, winch, capstan, windlass, crane, derrick, hoist, lift &c. 307; cam; pedal; wheel &c. (*rotation*) 312; inclined plane; wedge; screw; jack; spring, mainspring.

handle, hilt, haft, shaft, heft, shank, blade, trigger, tiller, helm, treadle, key; turnscrew, screwdriver, spanner, wrench.

hammer &c. (*impulse*) 276; edge tool &c. (*cut*) 253; borer &c. 262; vice, teeth &c. (*hold*) 781; nail, rope &c. (*join*) 45; peg &c. (*hang*) 214; support &c. 215; spoon &c. (*vehicle*) 272; arms &c. 727; oar &c. (*navigation*) 267.

**Adj.** instrumental &c. 631; mechanical, machinal, automatic, self-acting; brachial.

**634. Substitute.—N.** substitute &c. 147; deputy &c. 759; proxy, alternative, understudy.

**635. Materials.—N.** material, raw material, stuff, stock, staple; building materials, bricks and mortar; metal; stone; clay, brick; crockery &c. 384; compo, -sition; reinforced –, ferro-, concrete; cement; wood, ore, timber; gravel, cobbles, macadam, asphalt, tarmac.

materials; supplies, munition, fuel, grist, household stuff; *pabulum* &c. (*food*) 298; ammunition &c. (*arms*) 727; contingents; relay, reinforcement; baggage &c. (*personal property*) 780; means &c. 632.

**Adj.** raw &c. (*unprepared*) 674; wooden &c. *n.*

**636. Store.—N.** stock, fund, mine, vein, lode, quarry; spring; fount, -ain; well, -spring; milch cow

stock in trade, supply; heap &c. (*collection*) 72; treasure; reserve, *corps de réserve*, reserve fund, nest-egg, savings, *bonne bouche*.

crop, harvest, mow, vintage; yield, product, gleanings.

store, accumulation, hoard, rick, stack; lumber; relay &c. (*provision*) 637.

store-house, -room, -closet; depository, depot, *cache*, safe deposit, vault, pantechnicon, re-pository, -servatory, -pertory; *repertorium*; promptuary, warehouse, *entrepôt*, magazine, dump, buttery, larder, pantry, panary, lanary, still-room, spence; crib, garner, granary, silo, barn; bunker; thesaurus; bank &c. (*treasury*) 802; armoury; arsenal; dock; gallery, museum, library, conservatory, hot-house; menag-ery, -erie, aquarium, zoological gardens.

reservoir, cistern, tank, sump, pond, mill-pond; gasometer.

budget, quiver, bandolier, portfolio; coffer &c. (*receptacle*) 191.

conservation; storing &c. *v.*; storage.

dictionary &c. 562; list &c. 86.

**V.** store; put –, lay –, set- by; stow away; set –, lay- apart; store –, hoard –, treasure –, lay –, heap –, put –, garner –, save- up; *cacher*; accumulate, amass, hoard, fund, garner, save, bank.

conserve, reserve; keep –, hold- back; husband, – one's resources.

deposit; stow, stack, load, dump; harvest; heap, collect &c. 72; lay -in, – down, – by, store &c. *adj.*; keep, file [papers]; lay in &c. (*provide*) 637; preserve &c. 670; put by for a rainy day.

Adj. stored &c. *v.*; in -store, – reserve, – ordinary; spare, supernumerary.

**637. Provision.**—**N.** provision, supply; grist, – to the mill; subvention &c. (*aid*) 707; resources &c. (*means*) 632.

providing &c. *v.*; purveyance; reinforcement; commissary, commissariat.

rations; iron –, emergency- rations; provender &c. (*food*) 298; *viaticum*; ensilage.

caterer, purveyor, commissary, quartermaster, steward, housekeeper, manciple, feeder, batman, victualler, storekeeper, provision merchant, green-, grocer, *comprador*, *restaurateur*; sutler &c. (*merchant*) 797; innkeeper, publican, confectioner, baker, butcher, wine merchant, vintner.

**V.** provide; make -provision, – due provision for; lay in, – a stock, – a store.

sup-ply, -peditate; furnish; find, – one in; arm.

cater, victual, provision, purvey, forage; beat up for; stock, – with; make good, replenish; fill, – up; recruit, feed, ration.

have in -store, – reserve; keep, – by one, – on foot; have to fall back upon; store &c. 636; provide against a rainy day &c. (*economy*) 817.

**638. Waste.**—**N.** consumption, expenditure, exhaustion; dispersion &c. 73; ebb; leakage &c. (*exudation*) 295; loss &c. 776; wear and tear; waste; prodigality &c. 818; misuse &c. 679; wasting &c. *v.*; rubbish &c. (*useless*) 645.

mountain in labour.

**V.** spend, expend, use, consume, swallow up, exhaust, deplete; impoverish; spill, drain, empty; disperse &c. 73.

cast –, throw –, fling –, fritter- away; burn the candle at both ends, waste; squander &c. 818.

'waste its sweetness on the desert air'; cast -one's bread upon the waters, – pearls before swine; employ a steam hammer to crack a nut, waste powder and shot, break a butterfly on a wheel; labour in vain &c. (*useless*) 645; cut a whetstone with a razor, pour water into a sieve; tilt at windmills.

leak &c. (*run out*) 295; run to waste; ebb; melt away, run dry, dry up.

**Adj.** wasted &c. *v.*; at a low ebb.

wasteful &c. (*prodigal*) 818; penny wise and pound foolish.

**Phr.** *magno conatu magnas nugas*; *le jeu n'en vaut pas la chandelle.*

**639. Sufficiency.**—**N.** sufficiency, adequacy, enough, withal, *quantum sufficit*, satisfaction, competence; no less.

mediocrity &c. (*average*) 29.

fill; fulness &c. (*completeness*) 52; plen-itude, -ty; abundance; copiousness &c. *adj.*; amplitude, galore, lots, profusion; full measure; 'good measure pressed down, shaken together and running over.'

luxuriance &c. (*fertility*) 168; affluence &c. (*wealth*) 803; fat of the land; a land flowing with milk and honey'; cornucopia; horn of -plenty, – Amalthæa; mine &c. (*stock*) 636.

outpouring; flood &c. (*great quantity*) 31; tide &c. (*river*) 348; repletion &c. (*redundance*) 641; satiety &c. 869; rich man &c. 803.

**640. Insufficiency.**—**N.** insufficiency; inadequa-cy, -teness; incompetence &c. (*impotence*) 158; deficiency &c. (*incompleteness*) 53; imperfection &c. 651; shortcoming &c. 304; paucity; stint; scantiness &c. (*smallness*) 32; none to spare; bare subsistence.

scarcity, dearth; want, need, lack, poverty, exigency; inanition, starvation, famine, drought.

dole, pittance, mite; short -allowance, – commons; half-rations; banyan –, fast- day, Lent.

emptiness, poorness &c. *adj.*; depletion, vacancy, flaccidity; ebb-tide; low water; 'a beggarly account of empty boxes'; indigence &c. (*poverty*) 804; insolvency &c. (*non-payment*) 808; poor man &c. 804; bankrupt &c. 808.

**V.** be -insufficient &c. *adj.*; not -suf-

**V.** be -sufficient &c. *adj.*; suffice, do, just do, satisfy, pass muster; have -enough &c. *n.*; eat –, drink –, have- one's fill; roll –, swim- in; wallow in &c. (*superabundance*) 641.

abound, exuberate, teem, flow, stream, rain, shower down; pour, – in; swarm; bristle with.

render -sufficient &c. *adj.*; replenish &c. (*fill*) 52.

**Adj.** sufficient, enough, adequate, up to the mark, commensurate, competent, satisfactory, valid, tangible.

measured; moderate &c. (*temperate*) 953.

full &c. (*complete*) 52; ample; plen-ty, -tiful, -teous; plenty as blackberries; copious, abundant; abounding &c. *v.*; replete, enough and to spare, flush; choke-full; well-stocked, -provided; liberal; unstint-ed, -ing; stintless; without stint; un-sparing, -measured; lavish &c. 641; wholesale.

rich; luxuriant &c. (*fertile*) 168; affluent &c. (*wealthy*) 803; wantless; big with &c. (*pregnant*) 161.

un-exhausted, -wasted; exhaustless, inexhaustible.

**Adv.** sufficiently, amply &c. *adj.*; full; in -abundance &c. *n.*; with no sparing hand; to one's heart's content, *ad libitum*, without stint.

**Phr.** cut and come again.

---

fice &c. 639; come short of &c. 304; run dry.

want, lack, need, require; *caret*; be in want &c. (*poor*) 804; live from hand to mouth.

render- insufficient &c. *adj.*; drain of resources; impoverish &c. (*waste*) 638; stint &c. (*begrudge*) 819; put on short -commons, – allowance.

do -insufficiently &c. *adv.*; scotch the snake.

**Adj.** insufficient, inadequate; too -little &c. 32; not -enough &c. 639; unequal to; incompetent &c. (*impotent*) 158; 'weighed in the balance and found wanting'; perfunctory &c. (*neglect*) 460; deficient &c. (*incomplete*) 53; wanting &c. *v.*; imperfect &c. 651; ill-furnished, -provided, -stored, -off.

slack, at a low ebb; empty, vacant, bare; short –, out –, destitute –, devoid –, bereft &c. 776 –, denuded- of; dry, drained.

un -provided, -supplied, -furnished; un-replenished, -fed; un-stored, -treasured; empty-handed.

meagre, poor, thin, scrimp, sparing, spare, stinted, stunted; skimpy; starv-ed, -eling; half-starved, emaciated, famine-stricken, famished, underfed, undernourished; jejune.

scant &c. (*small*) 32; scarce; not to be had, – for love or money, – at any price; scurvy; stingy &c. 819; at the end of one's tether; without -resources &c. 632; in want &c. (*poor*) 804; in debt &c. 806.

**Adv.** insufficiently &c. *adj.*; in default –, for want- of; failing.

**641. Redundance.—N.** redundance; too -much, – many; superabundance, -fluity, -fluence, -saturation; nimiety, transcendency, exuberance, profuseness; profusion &c. (*plenty*) 639; repletion, enough in all conscience, *satis superque*, lion's share; more than -enough &c. 639; plethora, engorgement, congestion, load, surfeit, sickener; turgescence &c. (*expansion*) 194; over-dose, -measure, -supply, -flow; inundation &c. (*water*) 348; *avalanche*.

accumulation &c. (*store*) 636; heap &c. 72; drug, – in the market, glut; crowd; burden.

excess; sur-, over-plus, epact; margin; remainder &c. 40; duplicate; surplusage, expletive; work of –, supererogation; *bonus*, *bonanza*.

luxury; intemperance &c. 954; extravagance &c. (*prodigality*) 818; exorbitance, lavishment.

pleonasm &c. (*diffuseness*) 573; too many irons in the fire; embarrassment of riches; money to burn.

**V.** super-, over-abound; know no bounds, swarm; meet one at every turn; creep –, bristle- with; overflow; run –, flow –, well –, brim-over; run riot; over-run, -stock, -lay, -charge, -dose, -feed, burden. -load. -do, -whelm, -shoot the mark &c. (*go beyond*) 303; surcharge, supersaturate, gorge, glut, load, drench, whelm, inundate, deluge, flood; drug, – the market.

choke, cloy, accloy, suffocate; pile up, lay it on, – with a trowel, lay on thick; impregnate with; lavish &c. (*squander*) 818.

send –, carry coals to Newcastle, – owls to Athens; teach one's grandmother to suck eggs; *pisces natare docere*; kill the slain, 'gild refined gold,' 'paint the lily'; butter one's bread on both sides, put butter upon bacon; employ a steam-hammer to crack a nut &c. (*waste*) 638.

exaggerate &c. 549; wallow in; roll in &c. (*plenty*) 639; remain on one's hands, hang heavy on hand, go a begging.

**Adj.** redundant; too -much, – many; exuberant, inordinate, superabundant, excessive, overmuch, replete, profuse, lavish; prodigal &c. 818; exorbitant; overweening; extravagant; overcharged &c. *v.*; supersaturated, drenched, overflowing; running -over, – to waste, – down.

crammed –, filled- to overflowing; gorged, stuffed, ready to burst; dropsical, turgid, plethoric, full-blooded; obese &c. 194; voluminous.

superfluous, unnecessary, needless, supervacaneous, uncalled for, to spare, in excess; over and above &c. (*remainder*) 40; *de trop*; adscititious &c. (*additional*) 37; supernumerary &c. (*reserve*) 636; on one's hands, spare, duplicate, supererogatory, expletive; *un peu fort.*

**Adv.** over, too, over and above; over –, too- much; too far; without –, beyond –, out of- measure; with . . . to spare; over head and ears; up to one's -eyes, – ears; *extra*; beyond the mark &c. (*transcursion*) 303; over one's head.

**Phr.** it never rains but it pours.

## 2. *Degree of Subservience*

**642. Importance.—N.** importance, consequence, moment, prominence, consideration, mark, materialness.

import, significance, concern; emphasis, interest.

greatness &c. 31; superiority &c. 33; notability &c. (*repute*) 873; weight &c. (*influence*) 175; value &c. (*goodness*) 648; usefulness &c. 644.

gravity, seriousness, solemnity; no -joke, – laughing matter; pressure, urgency, stress; matter of life and death.

*memorabilia, notabilia*, great doings; red-letter day.

great -thing, – point; main chance, 'the be all and end all,' cardinal point, outstanding feature; substance, gist &c. (*essence*) 5; sum and substance, *gravamen*, head and front; important –, principal –, prominent –, essential- part; half the battle; *sine quâ non*; breath of one's nostrils &c. (*life*) 359; cream, salt, core, kernel, heart, nucleus:

**643. Unimportance.—N.** unimportance, insignificance, nothingness, immateriality.

triviality, trivia, fribble, levity, frivolity; paltriness &c. *adj.*; poverty; smallness &c. 32; vanity &c. (*uselessness*) 645; matter of -indifference &c. 866; no object; side issue.

nothing, – to signify, – worth speaking of, – particular, – to boast of, – to speak of; small –, no great –, trifling &c. *adj.* -matter; mere -joke, – nothing; hardly –, scarcely- anything; nonentity, cipher, figurehead; no great shakes, *peu de chose*; child's play; small beer.

toy, plaything, popgun, paper pellet, gimcrack, gewgaw, bauble, trinket, *bagatelle*, kickshaw, knicknack, whim-wham, trifle, 'trifles light as air.'

trumpery, trash, rubbish, stuff, *fatras*, frippery; 'leather or prunello'; chaff, drug, froth, bubble, smoke, cob-

key, -note, -stone; corner stone; trump-card &c. (*device*) 626; salient points.

top-sawyer, first fiddle, *prima donna*, chief, big-wig; triton among the minnows.

**V.** be -important &c. *adj.*, – somebody, – something; import, signify, matter, be an object; carry weight &c. (*influence*) 175; make a figure &c. (*repute*) 873; be in the ascendant, come to the front, lead the way, take the lead, play first fiddle, throw all else into the shade; lie at the root of; deserve –, merit –, be worthy- -of notice, – regard, – consideration.

attach –, ascribe –, give- importance &c. *n.*- to; value, care for; set store -upon, – by; mark &c. 550; mark with a white stone, underline; write –, put –, print- in -italics, – capitals, – large letters, – large type, – letters of gold; accentuate, emphasize, lay stress on.

make -a fuss, – a stir, – a piece of work, – much ado- about; make -of, – much of.

**Adj.** important; of -importance &c. *n.*; momentous, material; to the point; not to be -overlooked, – despised, – sneezed at; egregious; weighty &c. (*influential*) 175; of note &c. (*repute*) 873; notable, prominent, salient, signal; memorable, remarkable; worthy of -remark, – notice; never to be forgotten; stirring, eventful.

grave, serious, earnest, noble, grand, solemn, impressive, commanding, imposing.

urgent, pressing, critical, instant.

paramount, essential, vital, all-absorbing, radical, cardinal, chief, main, prime, primary, principal, leading, capital, foremost, overruling; of vital &c. importance.

in the front rank, first-rate, A1; superior &c. 33; considerable &c. (*great*) 31; marked &c. *v.*; rare &c. 137.

significant, telling, trenchant, emphatic, pregnant; *tanti*.

**Adv.** materially &c. *adj.*; in the main; above all, *par excellence*, to crown all.

---

web; weed; refuse &c. (*inutility*) 645; scum &c. (*dirt*) 653.

joke, jest, snap of the fingers; fudge &c. (*unmeaning*) 517; fiddlestick, – end; pack of nonsense, mere farce.

straw, pin, fig, continental, button, rush; bulrush, feather, halfpenny, farthing, brass farthing, doit, peppercorn, jot, rap, pinch of snuff, old song.

*minutiæ*, details, minor details, small fry; dust in the balance, feather in the scale, drop in the ocean, flea-bite, molehill; fingle-fangle.

nine days' wonder, *ridiculus mus*; flash in the pan &c. (*impotence*) 158; much ado about nothing &c. (*overestimation*) 482; storm in a teacup.

**V.** be -unimportant &c. *adj.*; not -matter &c. 642; go for –, matter –, signify- -little, – nothing, – little or nothing; not matter a -straw &c. *n.*

make light of &c. (*underestimate*) 483; catch at straws &c. (*overestimate*) 482.

**Adj.** unimportant; of -little, – small, – no- -account, – importance &c. 642; immaterial; un-, non-essential; not vital; irrelevant, incidental, indifferent.

subordinate &c. (*inferior*) 34; *médiocre* &c. (*average*) 29; passable, fair, respectable, tolerable, commonplace; uneventful, mere, common; ordinary &c. (*habitual*) 613; inconsiderable, so-so, insignificant, inappreciable, nugatory.

trifling, trivial; slight, slender, light, flimsy, frothy, idle; puerile &c. (*foolish*) 499; airy, shallow; weak &c. 160; powerless &c. 158; frivolous, petty, niggling; pid-, ped-dling; fribble, inane, ridiculous, farcical; fini-cal, -kin; fiddle-faddle, namby-pamby, wishy-washy, milk and water.

poor, paltry, pitiful; contemptible &c. (*contempt*) 930; sorry, mean, meagre, shabby, miserable, wretched, vile, scrubby, scrannel, weedy, niggardly, scurvy, putid, beggarly, worthless, twopenny-halfpenny, cheap, trashy, catchpenny, gimcrack, trumpery, one-horse; toy.

not worth -the pains, – while, – mentioning, – speaking of, – a thought, – a curse, – a straw, – rap &c. *n.*; beneath –, unworthy of- -notice, – regard, – consideration, – contempt; *de lanâ caprinâ*; vain &c. (*useless*) 645.

Adv. slightly &c. *adj.*; rather, somewhat, pretty well, fairly well, tolerably.

for aught one cares.

Int. no matter! pish! tush! tut! pshaw! pugh! pooh, -pooh! fudge! bosh! humbug! fiddle-stick, – end! fiddlededee! never mind! *n'importe!* what -signifies, – matter, – boots it, – of that, –'s the odds! a fig for! stuff! nonsense! stuff and nonsense!

Phr. *magno conatu magnas nugas*; *le jeu n'en vaut pas la chandelle*; it -matters not, – does not signify; it is of no -consequence, – importance.

**644. Utility.**—N. utility; usefulness &c. *adj.*; efficacy, efficiency, adequacy; service, use, stead, avail; help &c. (*aid*) 707; applicability &c. *adj.*; subservience &c. (*instrumentality*) 631; function &c. (*business*) 625; value; worth &c. (*goodness*) 648; money's worth; productiveness &c. 168; *cui bono* &c. (*intention*) 620; utilization &c. (*use*) 677; step in the right direction.

common weal, public good; utilitarianism &c. (*philanthropy*) 910.

V. be -useful &c. *adj.*; avail, serve; subserve &c. (*be instrumental to*) 631; conduce &c. (*tend*) 176; answer –, serve- -one's turn, – a purpose.

act a part &c. (*action*) 680; perform –, discharge- -a function &c. 625; do –, render- -a service, – good service, – yeoman's service; bestead, stand one in good stead; be the making of; help &c. 707.

bear fruit &c. (*produce*) 161; bring grist to the mill; profit, remunerate; benefit &c. (*do good*) 648.

find one's -account, – advantage- in; reap the benefit of &c. (*be better for*) 658.

render useful &c. (*use*) 677.

Adj. useful; of -use &c. *n.*; serviceable, usable, proficuous, good for; subservient &c. (*instrumental*) 631; conducive &c. (*tending*) 176; subsidiary &c. (*helping*) 707.

advantageous &c. (*beneficial*) 648; profitable, gainful, remunerative, worth one's salt; in-, valuable; prolific &c. (*productive*) 168.

adequate; ef-ficient, -ficacious; ef-fect-ive, -ual; practicable, expedient &c. 646.

**645. Inutility.**—N. inutility; uselessness &c. *adj.*; inefficacy, futility; inep-, inap-titude; unsubservience; inadequacy &c. (*insufficiency*) 640; inefficiency &c. (*incompetence*) 158; unskilfulness &c. 699; disservice; unfruitfulness &c. (*unproductiveness*) 169; labour -in vain, – lost, – of Sisyphus; lost -trouble, – labour; work of Penelope; sleeveless errand, wild goose chase, mere farce.

tautology &c. (*repetition*) 104; supererogation &c. (*redundance*) 641.

*vanitas vanitatum*, vanity, inanity, worthlessness, nugacity; triviality &c. (*unimportance*) 643.

*caput mortuum*, waste paper, dead letter; blunt tool.

litter, rubbish, lumber, odds and ends, cast-off clothes; button-top; shoddy; rags, orts, trash, refuse, sweepings, scourings, off-scourings, dross, slag, waste, rubble, dottle, drast, *débris*; stubble, leavings; broken meat; dregs &c. (*dirt*) 653; weeds, tares; rubbish heap, dust hole; *rudera*, deads.

*fruges consumere natus* &c. (*drone*) 683.

V. be -useless &c. *adj.*; go a begging &c. (*redundant*) 641; fail &c. 732.

seek –, strive- after impossibilities; use vain efforts, labour in vain, roll the stone of Sisyphus, beat the air, lash the waves, *battre l'eau avec un bâton, donner un coup d'épée dans l'eau*, fish in the air, milk the ram, drop a bucket into an empty well, sow the sand; bay the moon; preach –, speak- to the winds; whistle jigs to a milestone; kick against the pricks, *se battre contre des moulins*; lock the stable door

applicable, available, ready, handy, at hand, tangible; commodious, adaptable; of all work.

**Adv.** usefully &c. *adj.*; *pro bono publico.*

---

when the steed is stolen &c. (*too late*) 135; hold a farthing candle to the sun; cast pearls before swine &c. (*waste*) 638; carry coals to Newcastle &c. (*redundance*) 641; wash a blackamoor white &c. (*impossible*) 471.

render -useless &c. *adj.*; dis-mantle, -mast, -mount, -qualify, -able; unrig; cripple, lame &c. (*injure*) 659; spike guns clip the wings; put out of gear.

**Adj.** useless, inutile, inefficacious, futile, unavailing, bootless; inoperative &c. 158; inadequate &c. (*insufficient*) 640; in-, un-sub-servient; inept, inefficient &c. (*impotent*) 158; of no -avail &c. (*use*) 644; ineffectual &c. (*failure*) 732; incompetent &c. (*unskilful*) 699; 'stale, flat and unprofitable'; superfluous &c. (*redundant*) 641; dispensable; thrown away &c. (*wasted*) 638; abortive &c. (*immature*) 674.

worth-, value-less; unsaleable; not worth a straw &c. (*trifling*) 643; dear at any price.

vain, empty, inane; gain-, profit-, fruit-less; un-serviceable, -profitable; ill-spent; unproductive &c. 169; *hors de combat*; barren, sterile, impotent, unproductive; effete, past work &c. (*impaired*) 659; obsolete &c. (*old*) 124; fit for the -dust-hole, - wastepaper basket; good for nothing; of no earthly use; not worth -having - powder and shot; leading to no end, uncalled for; un-necessary, -needed, superfluous.

**Adv.** uselessly &c. *adj.*; to -little, - no, - little or no- purpose.

**Int.** *cui bono?* what's the good!

**646.** [Specific subservience.] **Expedience.—N.** expedien-ce, -cy; desirableness, -bility &c. *adj.*; fitness &c. (*agreement*) 23; utility &c. 644; propriety; advantage; opportunism, pragmatism.

high time &c. (*occasion*) 134.

**V.** be -expedient &c. *adj.*; suit &c. (*agree*) 23; befit; suit -, befit- the -time, - season, - occasion.

conform &c. 82.

**Adj.** expedient; desir-, advis-, acceptable; convenient; worth while, meet; fit, -ting; due, proper, eligible, seemly, becoming; befitting &c. *v.*; opportune &c. (*in season*) 134; *in loco*; suitable &c. (*accordant*) 23; applicable &c. (*useful*) 644; practical, effective, pragmatical; suitable, handy; appropriate.

**Adv.** in the right place; conveniently &c. *adj.*; in the nick of time.

**Phr.** *operæ pretium est.*

---

**647. Inexpedience.—N.** inexpedien-ce, -cy; undesira-bleness, -bility &c. *adj.*; discommodity, impropriety; unfitness &c. (*disagreement*) 24; inutility &c. 645; inconvenience, inadvisability; disadvantage.

**V.** be -inexpedient &c. *adj.*; come amiss &c. (*disagree*) 24; embarrass &c. (*hinder*) 706; put to inconvenience; pay too dear for one's whistle.

**Adj.** inexpedient, undesirable; un-, in-advisable; objectionable; troublesome, in-apt, -eligible, -admissible, -convenient; in-, dis-commodious; disadvantageous; inappropriate, unsuitable, unfit &c. (*inconsonant*) 24.

ill-contrived, -advised; unsatisfactory; unprofitable &c., unsubservient &c. (*useless*) 645; inopportune &c. (*unseasonable*) 135; out of -, in the wrong- place; improper, unseemly.

clumsy, awkward; cum-brous, -bersome; lumbering, unwieldy, hulky; unmanageable &c. (*impracticable*) 704; impedient &c. (*in the way*) 706; unnecessary &c. (*redundant*) 641.

**Phr.** it will never do.

**648.** [Capability of producing good. Good qualities.] **Goodness.—N.** goodness &c. *adj.*; excellence, merit; virtue &c. 944; value, worth, price.

super-excellence, -eminence; superiority &c. 33; perfection &c. 650; *coup de maître*; master-piece, *chef d'œuvre*, prime, flower, cream, *élite*, pick, A1, none such, *nonpareil*, *crême de la crême*, flower of the flock, cock of the roost, salt of the earth; champion.

tid-bit; gem, – of the first water; *bijou*, precious stone, jewel, pearl, diamond, ruby, brilliant, treasure; good thing; *rara avis*, one in a thousand.

beneficence &c. 906; good man &c. 948.

**V.** be -beneficial &c. *adj.*; produce –, do- -good &c. 618; profit &c. (*be of use*) 644; benefit; confer a -benefit &c. 618.

be the making of, do a world of good, make a man of.

produce a good effect; do a good turn, confer an obligation; improve &c. 658.

do no harm, break no bones.

be -good &c. *adj.*; excel, transcend &c. (*be superior*) 33; bear away the bell

stand the -proof, – test; pass -muster, – an examination.

challenge comparison, vie, emulate, rival.

**Adj.** harm-, hurt-less; unobnoxious; in-nocuous, -nocent, -offensive.

beneficial, valuable, of value; serviceable &c. (*useful*) 644; advantageous, profitable, edifying; salutary &c. (*healthful*) 656.

favourable; propitious &c. (*hope-giving*) 858; fair.

good, – as gold; excellent; better; superior &c. 33; above par; nice, fine; genuine &c. (*true*) 494.

best, choice, select, picked, elect, eximious, *recherché*, rare, priceless; unpara-goned, -lleled &c. (*supreme*) 33; superlatively &c. 33; good; superfine, -excellent; bonzer; of the first water; first-rate, -class; high-wrought; exquisite, very best, crack, prime, tip-top, gilt-edged, capital, cardinal; standard &c. (*perfect*) 650; inimitable.

admirable, estimable; praiseworthy &c. (*approve*) 931; pleasing &c. 829; *couleur de rose*, precious, of great price;

**649.** [Capability of producing evil. Bad qualities.] **Badness.—N.** hurtfulness &c. *adj.*; virulence

evil doer &c. 913; bane &c. 663; plague-spot &c. (*insalubrity*) 657; evil star, ill wind; snake in the grass, skeleton in the closet; *amari aliquid*, thorn in the side; Jonah, jinx, hoodoo.

malignity; malevolence &c. 907; tender mercies [ironically].

ill-treatment, annoyance, molestation, abuse, oppression, persecution, outrage; misusage &c. 679; injury &c. (*damage*) 659.

badness &c. *adj.*; peccancy, abomination; painfulness &c. 830; pestilence &c. (*disease*) 655; guilt &c. 947; depravity &c. 945.

**V.** be -hurtful &c. *adj.*; cause –, produce –, inflict –, work –, do- evil &c. 619; damnify, endamage, hurt, harm, scathe; injure &c. (*damage*) 659; pain &c. 830.

wrong, aggrieve, oppress, persecute; trample –, tread –, bear hard –, put-upon; overburden; weigh -down, - heavy on; victimize; run down; molest &c. 830.

maltreat, abuse; ill-use, -treat; thwart, buffet, bruise, scratch, maul; smite &c. (*scourge*) 972; do -violence, – harm, – a mischief; stab, pierce, outrage.

do –, make- mischief; bring –, get into trouble.

destroy &c. 162.

**Adj.** hurt-, harm-, scath-, bane-, baleful; injurious, deleterious, detrimental, noxious, pernicious, mischievous, full of mischief, mischief-making, malefic, malignant, nocuous, noisome; prejudicial; dis-serviceable, -advantageous; wide-wasting.

unlucky, sinister; obnoxious, untoward, disastrous.

oppressive, burdensome, onerous; malign &c. (*malevolent*) 907.

corrupting &c. (corrupt &c. 659); virulent, venomous, envenomed, corrosive; poisonous &c. (*morbific*) 657; deadly &c. (*killing*) 361; destructive &c. (*destroying*) 162; inauspicious &c. 859.

bad, ill, arrant, as bad as bad can be, dreadful; hor-rid, -rible; dire; rank.

costly &c. (*dear*) 814; worth -its weight in gold, – a Jew's eye, – a king's ransom; matchless, peerless, invaluable, inestimable, precious as the apple of the eye.

tolerable &c. (*not very good*) 651; up to the mark, un-exceptionable, -objectionable; satisfactory, tidy.

in -good, – fair- condition; fresh; unspoiled; sound &c. (*perfect*) 650.

**Adv.** beneficially &c. *adj.*; well &c. 618.

peccant, foul, fulsome; rotten, – at the core.

vile, base, villainous; mean &c. (*paltry*) 643; injured &c., deteriorated &c. 659; unsatisfactory, exception, -able, indifferent; below par &c. (*imperfect*) 651; ill-contrived, -conditioned; wretched, sad, grievous, deplorable, lamentable; piti-ful, -able, woeful &c. (*painful*) 830.

evil, wrong; depraved &c. 945; shocking; reprehensible &c. (*disapprove*) 932.

hateful, – as a toad; abominable, detestable, execrable, cursed, accursed, confounded; damn-ed, -able; infernal; diabolic &c. (*malevolent*) 907.

inadvisable &c. (*inexpedient*) 647; unprofitable &c. (*useless*) 645; incompetent &c. (*unskilful*) 699; irremediable &c. (*hopeless*) 859.

**Adv.** badly &c. *adj.*; wrong, ill; to one's cost; where the shoe pinches.

**Phr.** bad is the best; the worst come to the worst.

**650. Perfection.** — **N.** perfection; perfectness &c. *adj.*; indefectibility; impecc-ancy, -ability.

pink, *beau idéal*, phœnix, paragon; pink –, acme- of perfection; *ne plus ultra*; summit &c. 210.

*cygne noir*; philosopher's stone; chrysolite, Koh-i-noor, black tulip.

model, standard, pattern, mirror, admirable Crichton; trump; very prince of.

master-piece, -stroke, super-excellence &c. (*goodness*) 648; transcendence &c. (*superiority*) 33.

**V.** be -perfect &c. *adj.*; transcend &c. (*be supreme*) 33.

bring to perfection, perfect, ripen, mature; consummate, complete &c. 729; put in trim &c. (*prepare*) 673; put the finishing touch to.

**Adj.** perfect, faultless, ideal; indefective, -ficient, -fectible; immaculate, spotless, impeccable; free from -imperfection &c. 651; un-blemished, -injured &c. 659; sound, – as a roach; in perfect condition; scathless, intact, harmless; seaworthy &c. (*safe*) 644; right as a trivet; *in seipso totus teres atque rotundus*; consummate &c. (*complete*) 52; finished &c. 729; complete in itself.

best &c. (*good*) 648; model, standard; inimitable, unparagoned, unparalleled &c. (*supreme*) 33; superhuman, divine;

**651. Imperfection.**—**N.** imperfection; imperfectness &c. *adj.*; deficiency; inadequacy &c. (*insufficiency*) 640; peccancy &c. (*badness*) 649; immaturity &c. 674.

fault, defect, weak point; screw loose; rift within the lute; fly in the ointment; flaw &c. (*break*) 70; gap &c. 198; twist &c. 243; taint, attainder; bar sinister, hole in one's coat; blemish &c. 848; weakness &c. 160; half-blood, touch of the tar brush; shortcoming &c. 304; drawback; seamy side.

mediocrity; no great -shakes, – catch; not much to boast of.

**V.** be -imperfect &c. *adj.*; have a -defect &c. *n.*; lie under a disadvantage; spring a leak.

not –, barely- pass muster; fall short &c. 304.

**Adj.** imperfect; not -perfect &c. 650; de-ficient, -fective; faulty, unsound, mutilated, tainted; out of -order, – tune; cracked, leaky; sprung; warped &c. (*distort*) 243; lame; injured &c. (*deteriorated*) 659; peccant &c. (*bad*) 649; frail &c. (*weak*) 160; inadequate &c. (*insufficient*) 640; crude &c. (*unprepared*) 674; incomplete &c. 53; found wanting; below par; short-handed; below –, under- its full -strength, – complement.

indifferent, middling, ordinary, medi-

beyond all praise &c. (*approbation*) 931; *sans peur et sans reproche*.

**Adv.** to perfection, to the limit; perfectly &c. *adj.*; *ad unguem*; clean, – as a whistle.

---

ocre; average &c. 29; so-so; *così-così*, milk and water; tolerable, fair, passable, pretty -well, – good; rather –, moderately-good; good –, well-enough; decent; not -bad, – amiss; unobjectionable, admissible, bearable, only better than nothing.

secondary, inferior; second-rate, -best, one-horse.

**Adv.** almost &c.; to a limited extent, rather &c. 32; pretty, moderately; only; considering, all things considered, enough.

**Phr.** *surgit amari aliquid.*

**652. Cleanness.—N.** cleanness &c. *adj.*; purity; cleaning &c. *v.*; purification, defecation &c. *v.*; purgation, lustration; de-, abs-tersion; epuration, mundation, ablution, lavation, colature; disinfection &c. *v.*; drain-, sewerage.

lavatory, bath, -room; swimming pool, natatorium; public baths; hot –, cold –, Turkish –, Swedish –, Russian –, vapour- bath; *hammam*, laundry, wash-house; washerwoman, laundress, laundryman; scavenger, cleaner, sweeper, goody; crossing sweeper, white wings, dustman, sweep.

brush; broom, besom, carpet-sweeper, vacuum-cleaner, mop, squilgee, rake, shovel, sieve, riddle, screen, filter; scraper, strigil.

napkin, *serviette*, cloth, table-, carving-cloth, table-linen, napery, maukin, handkerchief, towel, sudary; doyley, doily, duster, sponge, mop, swab.

cover, drugget, mat, doormat.

soap, wash, lotion, detergent, cathartic, purgative; purifier &c. *v.*; dentifrice, tooth-powder, -paste; mouth wash; disinfectant.

**V.** be –, render- clean &c. *adj.*

clean, -se; mundify, rinse, wring, flush, full, wipe, mop, sponge, scour, swab, scrub, holystone, brush up.

wash, shampoo, lave, launder, buck; abs-, de-terge; clear, purify; de-purate, -spumate, -fecate; purge, expurgate; Bowdlerize; elutriate, lixiviate, edulcorate, clarify, refine, rack; fil-ter, -trate; drain, strain.

disinfect, sterilize, pasteurize, fumigate, ventilate, deodorize; whitewash.

sift, winnow, screen, riddle, pick, weed, comb, rake, brush, sweep.

**653. Uncleanness.—N.** uncleanness &c. *adj.*; impurity; immundi-ty, -city; impurity &c. [of mind] 961.

defilement, contamination &c. *v.*; defœdation; soil-ure, -iness; abomination; leaven; taint, -ure; fetor &c. 401.

decay; putre-scence, -faction; corruption; mould, must, mildew, dry-rot, *mucor*, rubigo, caries.

slovenry; slovenliness &c. *adj.*; squalor.

dowdy, drab, slut, malkin, slattern, sloven, slammerkin, scrub, draggletail, mudlark, dustman, sweep; beast.

dirt, filth, soil, slop; dust, cobweb, flue; smoke, soot, smudge, smut, grime, raff.

*sordes*, dregs, grounds, lees; sedi-, settle-ment; heel-tap; dross, -iness; mother, precipitate, *scoriæ*, ashes, cinders, recrement, slag; scum, froth.

hog-wash, swill, ditch-, dish-, bilge-water; rinsings, cheese-parings; sweepings &c. (*useless refuse*) 645; off-, out-scourings; off-scum; *caput mortuum*, *residuum*, sprue, feculence, clinker, draff; scurf, -iness; *exuviæ*, morphew; fur, -fur; dandruff; tartar.

riffraff; vermin, louse, cootie, flea, bug.

mud, mire, quagmire, *alluvium*, silt, sludge, slime, slush, slosh.

spawn, offal, garbage, carrion; *excreta* &c. 299; slough, peccant humour, pus, matter, suppuration, *lienteria*; *fæces*, excrement, ordure, dung; sew-, sewer-age; muck, coprolite; guano, manure, compost.

dunghill, *colluvies*, mixen, midden, bog, laystall, sink, w.c., water-, earth-closet, latrine, privy, jakes, John's; cess, -pool; sump, sough, *cloaca*, drain,

rout –, clear –, sweep &c.- out; make a clean sweep of.

Adj. clean, -ly; pure; immaculate; spot-, stain-, taint-less; without a stain, un-stained, -spotted, -soiled, -sullied, -tainted, -infected, -adulterated; aseptic; sweet, – as a nut.

neat, spruce, tidy, trim, gimp, clean as a new penny, like a cat in pattens; cleaned &c. *v.*; kempt.

Adv. neatly &c. *adj.*; clean as a whistle.

---

sewer, common sewer; Cloacina; dust-hole.

sty, pig-sty, lair, den, Augean stable, sink of corruption; slum, rookery.

**V.** be –, become- unclean &c. *adj.*; rot, putrefy, fester, rankle, reek; stink &c. 401; mould, -er; go -bad &c. *adj.*

render -unclean &c. *adj.*; dirt, -y; soil, smoke, tarnish, slaver, spot, smear, daub, blot, blur, smudge, smutch, smirch; d-, dr-abble, -aggle; spatter, slubber; be-smear &c., -mire, -slime, -grime, -foul; splash, stain, distain, maculate, sully, pollute, defile, debase, contaminate, taint, leaven; corrupt &c. (*injure*) 659; cover with -dust &c. *n.*; drabble in the mud.

wallow in the mire; slob-, slab-ber.

**Adj.** unclean, dirty, filthy, grimy; soiled &c. *v.*; not to be handled with kid gloves; dusty, snuffy, smutty, sooty, smoky; thick, turbid, dreggy; slimy.

uncleanly, slovenly, untidy, sluttish, dowdy, slatternly, draggle-tailed; un-combed, -kempt, -scoured, -swept, -wiped, -washed, -strained, -purified; squalid.

nasty, coarse, foul, impure, offensive, abominable, beastly, reeky, reechy; fetid &c. 401.

mouldy, lentiginous, musty, mildewed, rusty, moth-eaten, mucid, rancid, bad, gone bad, touched, fusty, reasty, rotten, corrupt, tainted, high, fly-blown, maggoty; putr-id, -escent, -efied; purulent, carious, peccant, fec-al, -ulent; stercoraceous, excrementitious; scurfy, impetiginous; gory, bloody; rotting &c. *v.*; rotten as -a pear, – cheese.

crapulous &c. (*intemperate*) 954; gross &c. (*impure in mind*) 961.

**654. Health.—N.** health, sanity; soundness &c. *adj.*; vigour; good –, perfect –, excellent –, rude –, robust- health; bloom, *mens sana in corpore sano*; Hygeia; incorrupti-on, -bility; good state –, clean bill- of health, eupepsia.

**V.** be in health &c. *adj.*; bloom, flourish.

keep -body and soul together, – on one's legs; enjoy -good, – a good state of- health; have a clean bill of health.

return to health; recover &c. 660; get better &c. (*improve*) 658; take a -new, – fresh- lease of life; convalesce, be convalescent, recruit; restore to health; cure &c. (*restore*) 660.

**Adj.** health-y, -ful; in -health &c. *n.*; well, sound, strong, fit, hearty, hale, fresh, blooming, green, whole; florid, flush, hardy, stanch, staunch,

**655. Disease.*—N.** disease; illness, sickness &c. *adj.*; ailing &c. *v.*; 'the ills that flesh is heir to'; morb-idity, -osity; infirmity, ailment, indisposition; complaint, disorder, malady; distemper, -ature.

visitation, attack, seizure, stroke, fit, epilepsy, apoplexy, shock, shell-shock.

delicacy, loss of health, valetudinarianism, invalidism, cachexy; *cachexia*, atrophy, *marasmus*; indigestion, *dyspepsia*; decay &c. (*deterioration*) 659; malnutrition, decline, consumption, palsy, paralysis, prostration; occupational diseases.

taint, pollution, infection, contagion, septicity, septicæmia, blood poisoning, pyæmia, epi-, en-demic; murrain, plague, pestilence, virus, pox.

sore, ulcer, abscess, fester, boil; pimple &c. (*swelling*) 250; carbuncle,

* Extended lists of different diseases are beyond the scope of this work.

brave, robust, vigorous, weather-proof; convalescent.

un-scathed, -injured, -maimed, -marred, -tainted; sound of wind and limb, safe and sound; without a scratch.

on one's legs; sound as a -roach, - bell; fresh as -a daisy, - a rose, - April; picture of health; bursting with health; fit as a fiddle; hearty as a buck; in -fine, - high- feather, in -good case, - full bloom; in fine fettle; pretty bobbish, tolerably well, as well as can be expected.

sanitary &c. (*health-giving*) 656; sanatory &c. (*remedial*) 662.

---

gathering, whitlow, imposthume, peccant humour, issue; rot, canker, cancer, *carcinoma*, *caries*, mortification, corruption, gangrene, *sphacelus*, leprosy, eruption, rash, breaking out, venereal disease.

fever, calenture; inflammation.

fatal &c. (*hopeless*) 859- -disease &c.; dangerous illness, galloping consumption, churchyard cough; general breaking up, break up of the system.

[Disease of mind] neurasthenia; idiocy &c. 499; insanity &c. 503.

martyr to disease; cripple; 'the halt, the lame and the blind'; valetudinar-y, -ian; invalid, patient, case; sick-room, -chamber, hospital &c. 662.

[Science of disease] path-, eti-, nos-ology, therapeutics, diagnosis, prognosis.

**V.** be -ill &c. *adj.*; ail, suffer, labour under, be affected with, complain of; droop, flag, languish, halt; sicken, peak, pine, waste away, fail, lose strength; gasp.

keep one's bed; feign sickness &c. (*falsehood*) 544, malinger.

lay -by, - up; take -, catch- -a disease &c. *n.*, - an infection; be stricken by; break out.

**Adj.** diseased; ailing &c. *v.*; ill, - of; taken ill, seized with; indisposed, unwell, sick, squeamish, poorly, seedy; affected -, afflicted- with illness; laid up, confined, bed-ridden, invalided, in hospital, on the sick list; out of -health, - sorts; valetudinary.

un-sound, -healthy; sickly, morbose, healthless, infirm, chlorotic, unbraced, drooping, flagging, lame, halt, crippled, halting.

morbid, tainted, vitiated, peccant, contaminated, poisoned, septic, tabid, mangy, leprous, cankered; rotten, - to, - at- the core; withered, palsied, paralytic, tuberculous; dyspeptic.

touched in the wind, broken-winded, spavined, gasping; *hors de combat* &c. (*useless*) 645.

weak-ly, -ened &c. (*weak*) 160; decrepit; decayed &c. (*deteriorated*) 659; incurable &c. (*hopeless*) 859; in declining health; cranky; in a bad way, in danger, prostrate; moribund &c. (*death*) 360.

morbific, epidemic &c. 657.

**656. Salubrity.—N.** salubrity, salubriousness; healthiness &c. *adj.*

fine -air, - climate; eudiometer.

[Preservation of health] *hygiène*; valetudinarian, -ism, preventorium, sanitarian; *sanitarium*, *sanitorium*, immunity.

**V.** be -salubrious &c. *adj.*; agree with, be good for; assimilate &c. 23.

**Adj.** salu-brious, -tary, -tiferous, wholesome; health-y, -ful; sanitary, prophylactic, benign, bracing, tonic,

**657. Insalubrity.—N.** insalubrity; unhealthiness &c. *adj.*; non-naturals; plague spot; malaria &c. (*poison*) 663; death in the pot, contagion.

**Adj.** insalubrious; un-healthy, -wholesome; noxious, noisome, foul; morbi-fic, -ferous; mephitic, septic, azotic, deleterious; pesti-lent, -ferous, -lential; virulent, venomous, envenomed, poisonous, toxic, narcotic.

contagious, infectious, catching, taking, communicable, epidemic, zymotic;

invigorating, good for, nutritious, hyg-eian, -ienic.

in-noxious, -nocuous, -nocent; harmless, uninjurious, uninfectious; immune.

sanative &c. (*remedial*) 662; restorative &c. (*reinstate*) 660; useful &c. 644.

**658. Improvement.—N.** improvement; a-, melioration; betterment; mend, amendment, emendation; mending &c. *v.*; advancement; advance &c. (*progress*) 282; ascent &c. 305; promotion, preferment; elevation &c. 307; increase &c. 35.

cultiv-, civiliz-ation; menticulture, culture, march of intellect; eugenics, euthenics, meliorism, telesis.

reform, -ation; revision, radical reform; second thoughts, correction, *limæ labor*, refinement, elaboration; purification &c. 652; repair &c. (*restoration*) 660; recovery &c. 660.

revise; revised -, new- edition.

reformer, radical, progressive.

**V.** improve; be -, become -, get- better; mend, amend.

advance &c. (*progress*) 282; ascend &c. 305; increase &c. 35; fructify, ripen, mature; pick up, come about, rally, take a favourable turn; turn -over a new leaf, - the corner; raise one's head, sow one's wild oats; recover &c. 660.

be -better &c. *adj.*, - improved by; turn to -right, - good, - best- account; profit by, reap the benefit of; make -good use of, - capital out of; place to good account; take advantage of.

render better, improve, emend, make over, better; a-, meliorate; correct.

improve -, refine- upon; rectify; enrich, mellow, elaborate, fatten.

promote, cultivate, advance, forward, enhance; bring -forward, - on; foster &c. 707; invigorate &c. (*strengthen*) 159.

touch -. rub -, brush -, furbish -, bolster -, vamp -, brighten -, warm- up; polish, cook, make the most of, set off to advantage; prune; repair &c. (*restore*) 660; put in order &c. (*arrange*) 60.

review, revise, edit, redact: make -corrections, - improvements &c. *n.*; doctor &c. (*remedy*) 662; purify &c. 652.

sporadic, endemic, pandemic, epizoötic.

innutritious, indigestible, ungenial; uncongenial &c. (*disagreeing*) 24.

deadly &c. (*killing*) 361.

---

**659. Deterioration.—N.** deterioration, debasement; want, ebb; recession &c. 287; retrogradation &c. 283; decrease &c. 36.

degenera-cy, -tion, -teness; degradation; deprav-ation, -ement; depravity &c. 945; demoralization, retrogression.

impairment, inquination, injury, damage, loss, detriment, delaceration, outrage, havoc, inroad, ravage, scath; perversion, prostitution, vitiation, discoloration, oxidation, pollution, defœdation, poisoning, venenation, leaven, contamination, canker, corruption, adulteration, alloy.

decl-ine, -ension, -ination; decadence, -cy; falling off &c. *v.*; caducity, decreptitude, senility.

decay, dilapidation, ravages of time, wear and tear; cor-, e-rosion; mouldi-, rotten-ness; moth and rust, dry-rot, blight, marasmus, atrophy, collapse; disorganization; *délabrement* &c. (*destruction*) 162.

wreck, mere wreck, honeycomb, *magni nominis umbra.*

**V.** be -, become- -worse, - deteriorated &c. *adj.*; have seen better days, deteriorate, degenerate, fall off; wane &c. (*decrease*) 36; ebb; retrograde &c. 283; decline, droop; go down &c. (*sink*) 306; go -downhill, - on from bad to worse, - farther and fare worse; jump out of the frying pan into the fire.

run to -seed, - waste; swale, sweal; lapse, be the worse for; break, - down; spring a leak, crack, start; shrivel &c. (*contract*) 195; fade, go off, wither, moulder, rot, rankle, decay, go bad; go to -, fall into- decay; 'fall into the sear and yellow leaf,' rust, crumble, shake; totter, - to its fall; perish &c. 162; die &c. 360.

[Render less good] deteriorate; weaken &c. 160; put back; taint, infect, contaminate, poison, empoison,

relieve, refresh, revive, infuse new blood into, recruit, re-invigorate, renew, revivify, freshen, build -afresh, – anew; uplift, inspire.

re-form, -model, -organise; new model, civilize.

view in a new light, think better of, appeal from Philip drunk to Philip sober.

palliate, mitigate; lessen &c. 36- an evil.

**Adj.** improving &c. *v.*; progressive, improved &c. *v.*; better, – off, – for; all the better for; better advised.

reform-, emend-atory; reparatory &c. (*restorative*) 660; remedial &c. 662.

corrigible, improvable, curable, accultural.

**Adv.** on -consideration, – reconsideration, – second thoughts, – better advice; *ad melius inquirendum*; on the -mend, – up grade.

---

envenom, canker, corrupt, exulcerate, pollute, vitiate, inquinate; de-, embase; denaturalize, leaven; de-flower, -bauch, -file, -prave, -grade; stain &c. (*dirt*) 653; discolour; alloy, adulterate, sophisticate, tamper with, prejudice.

pervert, prostitute, demoralize, brutalize; render vicious &c. 945; compromise.

embitter, ex-, acerbate, aggravate.

injure, impair, labefy, damage, harm, hurt, shend, scathe, spoil, mar, despoil, dilapidate, waste; overrun; ravage; pillage &c. 791.

wound, stab, pierce, maim, lame, surbate, cripple, hough, hamstring, hit between wind and water, scotch, mangle, mutilate, disfigure, blemish, deface, warp.

blight, rot; cor-, e-rode, eat away; wear -away, – out; gnaw, – at the root of; sap, mine, undermine, shake, sap the foundations of, break up; dis-organize, -mantle, -mast; destroy &c. 162.

damnify &c. (*aggrieve*) 649; do one's worst; knock down; deal a blow to; play -havoc, – sad havoc, – the mischief, – the deuce, – the very devil- -with, – among; decimate.

**Adj.** unimproved &c. (improve &c. 658); deteriorated &c. *v.*; altered, – for the worse; injured &c. *v.*; sprung; withering, spoiling, &c. *v.*; on the -wane, – decline; tabid; degenerate; worse; the –, all the- worse for; out of -repair, – tune; imperfect &c. 651; the worse for wear; battered; weather-ed, -beaten; stale, *passé*, shaken, dilapidated, frayed, faded, wilted, shabby, second-hand, second-rate, threadbare; worn, – to- -a thread, – a shadow, – the stump, rags; reduced, – to a skeleton, skeletonized; far gone.

decayed &c. *v.*; moth-, worm-eaten; mildewed, rusty, mouldy, spotted, seedy, time-worn, moss-grown; discoloured; effete, wasted, crumbling, mouldering, rotten, cankered. blighted, tainted; depraved &c. (*vicious*) 945; decrep-id, -it; broken down; done, – for, – up; worn out, used up; fit for the -dust-hole, – wastepaper basket; past work &c. (*useless*) 645.

at a low ebb, in a bad way, on one's last legs, washed -up, – out; undermined, deciduous; nodding to its fall &c. (*destruction*) 162; tottering &c. (*dangerous*) 665; past cure &c. (*hopeless*) 859; fatigued &c. 688; backward, retrograde &c. (*retrogressive*) 283; deleterious &c. 649; behind the times.

**Adv.** on the down grade; beyond hope.

**Phr.** out of the frying pan into the fire; *ægrescit medendo.*

**660. Restoration.**—**N.** restor-ation, -al; re-instatement, -placement, -habilitation, -establishment, -construction; reproduction &c. 163; re-novation, -newal; reviv-al, -escence; refreshment

**661. Relapse.**—**N.** relapse, lapse; falling back &c. *v.*; retrogradation &c. (*retrogression*) 283; deterioration &c. 659.

[Return to, or recurrence of a bad

&c. 689; re-suscitation, -animation, -vivification, -viction; Phœnix; reorganization.

*renaissance*, renascence, rebirth, second youth, rejuvenation, rejuvenescence, new birth; regenera-tion, -cy, -teness; palingenesis, reconversion, resurgence, resurrection.

redress, retrieval, reclamation, recovery; convalescence; resumption, *résumption*.

recurrence &c. (*repetition*) 104; *réchauffé*, *rifacimento*.

cure, recure, sanation; healing &c. *v.*; redintegration; rectification, instauration.

repair, reparation, mending; recruiting &c. *v.*; cicatrization; disinfection; tinkering.

reaction; redemption &c. (*deliverance*) 672; restitution &c. 790; relief &c. 834.

mender, repairer, renewer; tinker, cobbler; doctor &c. 662; *vis medicatrix* &c. (*remedy*) 662.

curableness.

**V.** return to the original state; recover, rally, revive; come -to, – round, – to oneself; pull through, weather the storm, be oneself again; get -well, – round, – the better of, – over, – about; rise from -one's ashes, – the grave; resurge, resurrect; survive &c. (*outlive*) 110; resume, reappear; come to, – life again; live –, rise- again; relive.

heal, skin over, cicatrize; right itself.

restore, put back, place *in statu quo*; re-instate, -place, -seat, habilitate, -establish, -estate, -install.

re-construct, -build, -organize, -constitute; reconvert; re-new, -novate; recondition; regenerate; rejuvenate.

re-deem, -claim, -cover, -trieve; rescue &c. (*deliver*) 672.

redress, recure; cure, heal, remedy, doctor, physic, medicate; break of; bring round, set on one's legs.

re-suscitate, -vive, -animate, -vivify, -call to life; reproduce &c. 163; warm up; reinvigorate, refresh &c. 689.

redintegrate, make whole; recoup &c. 790; make -good, – all square; rectify; put –, set- -right, – to rights, – straight; set up, correct; put in order &c. (*arrange*) 60; refit, recruit; fill up, – the ranks; reinforce.

repair, mend; put in -repair, – thorough repair, – complete repair; retouch, botch, vamp, tinker, doctor, cobble; do –, patch –, plaster –, vamp- up; darn, fine-draw, heel-piece; stop a gap, stanch, staunch, caulk, calk, careen, splice, bind up wounds.

**Adj.** restored &c. *v.*; *redivivus*, convalescent; in a fair way; none the worse; rejuvenated, renascent.

restoring &c. *v.*; restorative, recuperative; sana-, repara-tive, -tory; curative, remedial.

restor-, recover-, san-, remedi-, retriev-, cur-able.

**Adv.** *in statu quo*; as you were.

**Phr.** *revenons à nos moutons.*

state] backsliding, recidivation, recrudescence.

**V.** relapse, lapse; fall –, slide –, sink- back; have a relapse; return; retrograde &c. 283; recidivate; fall off &c. 659 again.

---

**662. Remedy.—N.** remedy, help, redress; antidote, anti-toxin, anti-,

**663. Bane.—N.** bane, curse, thorn in the -side, -flesh, bugbear, *bête noire*

counter-poison, prophylactic, antiseptic, germicide, bactericide, corrective, restorative, stimulant, pick-me-up, tonic; sedative &c. 174; palliative; febrifuge; alter-ant, -ative; specific; emetic, carminative; narcotic &c. *adj.*; Nepenthe, Mithridate.

cure; radical –, perfect –, certain-cure; sovereign remedy.

physic, medicine, patent medicine, Galenicals, simples, drug, potion, draught, dose, pill, bolus, lozenge, tablet, tabloid, capsule; electuary; linct-us, -ure; medicament.

nostrum, receipt, recipe, prescription; catholicon, panacea, elixir, *elixir vitæ*, philosopher's stone; balm, balsam, cordial, theriac, ptisan.

salve, ointment, cerate, oil, lenitive, lotion, cosmetic; plaster; epithem, embrocation, liniment, cataplasm, sinapism, arquebusade, traumatic, vulnerary, pepastic, poultice, collyrium, depilatory.

compress, pledget; bandage &c. (*support*) 215.

treatment, medical treatment, regimen; diet-ary, -etics; *vis medicatrix, naturæ*; *medicine expectante*; seton, blood-letting, bleeding, venesection, phlebotomy, cupping, leeches; operation, surgical operation; tonsillectomy, appendectomy; injection, electrolysis, massage.

pharma-cy, -cology, -ceutics; acology; materia medica, pharmacopœia, therapeutics, therapy, posology, pathology &c. 655; homœ-, heter-, all-, hydr-opathy; cold water –, open air- cure; dietetics; sur-, chirur-gery, osteopathy; healing art, leechcraft, practice of medicine; ortho-pædy, -praxy; dentistry, midwifery, obstetrics, gynæcology.

faith -cure, – healing; psycho-therapy, -analysis, psychiatry.

hospital, infirmary, clinic; pest-, lazar-house; lazaretto, lazaret; lock hospital; *maison de santé*; *ambulance*; dispensary; *sanatorium, sanitarium*, spa, baths, pump-room, well; *hospice*; Red Cross; nursing home; asylum.

doctor, physician, surgeon; medical –, general- practitioner, consultant, specialist; medical attendant; medical student, medico; chemist, apothecary, pharmacopolist, druggist; leech; Æsculapius, Hippocrates, Galen; *accoucheur*, gynæcologist, midwife, oculist, aurist, dentist; operator; osteopath, bonesetter; nurse, monthly nurse, sister, dresser; *masseur, masseuse*.

V. apply a -remedy &c. *n.*; doctor, dose, physic, nurse, minister to, attend, dress the wounds, plaster, bandage, poultice; heal, cure, work a cure, kill or cure, remedy, stay (disease), snatch from the jaws of death; prevent &c. 706; relieve &c. 834; palliate &c. 658:

evil &c. 619; hurtfulness &c. (*badness*) 649; painfulness &c. (*cause of pain*) 830; scourge &c. (*punishment*) 975; *damnosa hereditas*; white elephant.

sting, fang. thorn, tang, bramble, brier, nettle.

poison, leaven, virus, venom; intoxicant; arsenic, Prussic acid, antimony, tartar emetic, strychnine, nicotine, cyanide of potassium, corrosive sublimate; curare; hyoscine &c.; poison-, mustard-, tear-gas; carbon di-, monoxide; ptomaine poisoning, botulism; miasm, mephitis, malaria, azote, sewer gas; pest, stench &c. 401.

rust, worm, moth, moth and rust, fungus, mildew; dry-rot; canker, -worm; cancer; torpedo; viper &c. (*evil-doer*) 913; demon &c. 980.

hemlock, hellebore, nightshade, *belladonna*, henbane, aconite; Upas tree.

drugs, dope, opium, morphia, morphine, cocaine, heroin, hashish, bhang.

[Science of poisons] Toxicology.

Adj. baneful &c. (*bad*) 649; poisonous &c. (*unwholesome*) 657.

---

restore &c. 660; drench with physic; consult, operate, extract, deliver; bleed, cup, let blood, transfuse; electrolyse; psycho-analyse.

**Adj.** remedial; restorative &c. 660; corrective, palliative, healing; sana-tory, -tive; prophylactic; salutiferous &c. (*salutary*) 656; medic-al, -inal; therapeutic, surgical, chirurgical, orthopedic, epulotic, paregoric, tonic, corroborant, analeptic, balsamic, anodyne, hypnotic, neurotic, narcotic, sedative, lenitive, demulcent, emollient; depuratory; deter-sive, -gent; abstersive, disinfectant, febrifugal, alternative; traumatic, vulnerary.

dietetic, alimentary; nutrit-ious, -ive; peptic; alexi-pharmic, -teric; remedi-, cur-able.

### 3. *Contingent Subservience*

**664. Safety.—N.** safety, security, impregnability; invulnera-bility, -bleness &c. *adj.*; danger -past, – over; storm blown over; coast clear; escape &c. 671; means of escape, safety-valve; safeguard, palladium, sheet anchor, rock, tower of strength.

guardian-, ward-, warden-ship; tutelage, custody, safe keeping; preservation &c. 670; protection, auspices.

safe-conduct, escort, convoy; guard, shield &c. (*defence*) 717; guardian angel, tutelary -god, – deity, – saint; *genius loci.*

protector, guardian; ward-en, -er; preserver, custodian, *duenna, chaperon,* third person.

watch-, ban-dog; Cerberus; watch-, patrol-, police-man, constable, peeler, bobby, copper, cop, bull, flat-foot, detective, armed guard; sentinel, sentry, scout &c. (*warning*) 668; garrison; guard-ship.

[Means of safety] refuge &c., anchor &c. 666; precaution &c. (*preparation*) 673; quarantine, *cordon sanitaire.* [Sense of security] confidence &c. 858.

**V.** be -safe &c. *adj.*; keep one's head above water, tide over, save one's bacon; ride out –, weather- the storm; light upon one's feet; bear a charmed life; escape &c. 671; possess nine lives.

make –, render- -safe &c. *adj.*; protect, watch over; take care of &c. (*care*) 459; preserve &c. 670; cover, screen, shelter, shroud, flank, ward; guard &c. (*defend*) 717; secure &c. (*restrain*) 751; intrench, fence round &c. (*circumscribe*) 229; house, nestle, ensconce; take charge of.

**665. Danger.—N.** danger, peril, insecurity, jeopardy, risk, hazard, venture, precariousness, slipperiness; instability &c. 149; defencelessness &c. *adj.*

exposure &c. (*liability*) 177; vulnerability; vulnerable point, heel of Achilles; forlorn hope &c. (*hopelessness*) 859.

[Dangerous course] leap in the dark &c. (*rashness*) 863; road to ruin, *facilis descensus Averni,* hair-breadth escape.

cause for alarm; source of danger &c. 667. [Approach of danger] rock –, breakers- ahead; storm brewing; clouds -in the horizon, – gathering; warning &c. 668; alarm &c. 669. [Sense of danger] apprehension &c. 860.

**V.** be -in danger &c. *adj.*; be exposed to –, run into –, incur –, encounter- -danger &c. *n.*; run a risk; lay oneself open to &c. (*liability*) 177; lean on –, trust to- a broken reed; feel the ground sliding from under one, have to run for it; have the -chances, – odds- against one.

hang by a thread, totter; tremble on the -verge, – brink; sleep –, stand -on a volcano; sit on a barrel of gunpowder, live in a glass house.

bring –, place –, put- in -danger &c. *n.*; endanger, expose to danger, imperil; jeopard, -ize, compromise; sail too near the wind &c. (*rash*) 863; put one's head in the lion's mouth.

adventure, risk, hazard, venture, stake, set at hazard; run the gauntlet &c. (*dare*) 861; engage in a forlorn hope.

threaten &c. 909- danger; run one

escort, convoy; garrison; watch, mount guard, patrol, scout, spy.

make assurance double sure &c. (*caution*) 864; take up a loose thread; take precautions &c. (*prepare for*) 673; take in a reef; double reef topsails.

seek safety; take –, find- shelter &c. 666; run into port.

**Adj.** safe, secure, sure; in -safety, – security; have an anchor to windward; on the safe side; under the -shield of, – shade of, – wing of, – shadow of one's wing; under -cover, – lock and key; out of -danger, – the meshes, – harm's way; in -harbour, – port; on sure ground, at anchor, high and dry, above water, on *terra firma*; unthreatened, -molested; protected &c. *v.*; *cavendo tutus*; panoplied &c. (*defended*) 717.

snug, sea-, air-worthy; weather-, water-, fire-, bomb-proof.

defensible, tenable, proof against, invulnerable; un-assailable, -attackable; im-pregnable, -perdible; founded on a rock; inexpugnable.

safe and sound &c. (*preserved*) 670; harmless; scathless &c. (*perfect*) 650; unhazarded; not -dangerous &c. 665.

protecting &c. *v.*; guardian, tutelary; preservative &c. 670; trustworthy &c. 939.

**Adv.** *ex abundanti cautelâ*; with impunity.

**Phr.** all's well; all clear; *salva res est*; *suave mari magno*; safety first.

---

hard; lay a trap for &c. (*deceive*) 545.

**Adj.** in -danger &c. *n.*; endangered &c. *v.*; fraught with danger; danger-, hazard-, peril-, parl-, pericul-ous; unsafe, unprotected &c. (safe, protect &c. 664); insecure, untrustworthy, unreliable; built upon sand, on a sandy basis.

defence-, fence-, guard-, harbourless; unshielded; vulnerable, expugnable, unsheltered, exposed; open to &c. (*liable*) 177.

*aux abois*, at bay; on -the wrong side of the wall, – a lee shore, – the rocks.

at stake, in question; precarious, aleatory, critical, ticklish; slip-pery, -py; hanging by a thread &c. *v.*; with a halter round one's neck; between -the hammer and the anvil, – Scylla and Charybdis, – two fires; on the -edge, – brink, – verge of a- -precipice, – volcano; in the lion's den, on slippery ground, under fire; not out of the wood.

un-warned, -admonished, -advised; unprepared &c. 674; off one's guard &c. (*inexpectant*) 508.

tottering; un-stable, -steady; shaky, top-heavy, tumble-down, ramshackle, crumbling, waterlogged; help-, guideless; in a bad way; reduced to –, at- the last extremity; trembling in the balance; nodding to its fall &c. (*destruction*) 162.

threatening &c. 909; ominous, ill-omened; alarming &c. (*fear*) 860; explosive; poisonous &c. 657.

adventurous &c. (*rash*) 863, (*bold*) 861.

**Int.** stop! look out! beware! take care!

**Phr.** *incidit in Scyllam qui vult vitare Charybdim*; *nam tua res agitur paries dum proximus ardet.*

**666.** [Means of safety.] **Refuge.—N.** refuge, sanctuary, retreat, fastness; stronghold, keep, last resort; ward; prison &c. 752; asylum, ark, home, almshouse, refuge for the destitute; hiding-place &c. (*ambush*) 530; *sanctum sanctorum* &c. (*privacy*) 893; cache.

roadstead, anchorage; breakwater, mole, port, haven; harbour, – of refuge; sea-port; pier, jetty, embankment, quay.

**667.** [Source of danger.] **Pitfall.—N.** rocks, reefs, coral reef, sunken rocks, snags; sands, quicksands, Goodwin sands, sandy foundation; slippery ground; breakers, shoals, shallows, bank, shelf, flat, lee shore, iron-bound coast; rock –, breakers- ahead; derelict.

precipice; abyss, chasm, pit, crevasse; maelstrom, whirlpool, eddy, vortex, rapids, current, bore, tidal wave; storm, squall, hurricane, whirl-

covert, shelter, abri, screen, lee-wall, wing, shield, umbrella; splash-, dash-board, mudguard.

wall &c. (*inclosure*) 232; fort &c. (*defence*) 717.

anchor, kedge; grap-nel, -pling iron; sheet-, mushroom-anchor, main-stay; support &c. 215; check &c. 706; ballast.

jury-mast; vent-peg; safety -valve, - lamp; lightning conductor.

means of escape &c. (*escape*) 671; life-boat, swimming belt, cork jacket; life preserver, breeches buoy; parachute, plank, stepping-stone.

safeguard &c. (*protection*) 664.

**V.** seek -, take -, find- refuge &c. *n.*; seek -, find- safety &c. 664; throw oneself into the arms of; claim sanctuary; take to the -hills, - woods; make port, reach shelter, bar -, bolt -, lock -the door, - gate; let the portcullis down; raise the drawbridge.

wind; volcano; ambush &c. 530; pitfall, trap-door; trap &c. (*snare*) 545.

sword of Damocles; wolf at the door, snake in the grass, viper in one's bosom, death in the pot; latency &c. 526.

ugly customer, dangerous person, *le chat qui dort*; firebrand, hornet's nest.

**Phr.** *latet anguis in herbâ*; *proximus ardet Ucalegon.*

---

**668. Warning.—N.** warning, caution, *caveat*; notice &c. (*information*) 527; premoni-tion, -shment; prediction &c. 511; contraindication; symptom; lesson, dehortation; admonition, monition; alarm &c. 669.

handwriting on the wall, *tekel upharsin*, yellow flag; fog-signal, -horn; siren; monitor, warning voice, Cassandra, signs of the times, Mother Carey's chickens, stormy petrel, bird of ill omen, gathering clouds, clouds in the horizon, cloud no bigger than a man's hand, death-watch.

watch-tower, beacon, signal-post; light-house &c. (*indication of locality*) 550.

sent-inel, -ry; watch, -man; watch and ward; watch-, ban-, house-dog; patrol, vedette, picket, bivouac, scout, spy, spial; advanced -, rear-guard, lookout, flagman.

cautiousness &c. 864.

**V.** warn, caution; fore-, pre-warn; ad-, pre-monish; give -notice, - warning; menace &c. (*threaten*) 909; put on one's guard; sound the alarm &c. 669; croak.

beware, ware; take -warning, - heed at one's peril; watch out for; keep watch and ward &c. (*care*) 459.

**Adj.** warning &c. *v.*; premonitory, monitory, cautionary; admonitory, -tive; ominous, threatening, lowering, minatory, symptomatic.

warned &c. *v.*; on one's guard &c. (*careful*) 459, (*cautious*) 864.

**Adv.** *in terrorem* &c. (*threat*) 909.

**Int.** beware! ware! take care! mind -, take care-what you are about; mind! look out!

**Phr.** *ne reveillez pas le chat qui dort*; *fœnum habet in cornu.*

**669.** [Indication of danger.] **Alarm.—N.** alarm; alarum, larum, alarm bell, tocsin, *alerte*, beat of drum, sound of trumpet, note of alarm, hue and cry, signal of distress, S.O.S.; blue-lights; war-cry, -whoop; warning &c. 668; fog-signal, -horn; siren; yellow flag; danger signal; red -light, - flag; fire -bell, - alarm; burglar alarm, police whistle, watchman's rattle.

false alarm, cry of wolf; bugbear, -aboo.

**V.** give -, raise -, sound -, beat- the *or* an -alarm &c. *n.*; alarm; warn &c. 668; ring the tocsin; *battre la générale*; cry wolf.

**Adj.** alarming &c. *v.*

**Int.** *sauve qui peut! qui vive?* who goes there?

**670. Preservation.—N.** preservation; safe keeping; conservation &c. (*storage*) 636; maintenance, upkeep, support, sustentation, conservatism; *vis conservatrix*; salvation &c. (*deliverance*) 672; drying &c. *v.*

[Means of preservation] prophylaxis; preserv-er, -ative; canned goods; cold pack; hygi-astics, -antics; cover, drugget; *cordon sanitaire.*

[Superstitious remedies] charm &c. 993.

**V.** preserve, maintain, keep, sustain, support; keep -up, – alive; not willingly let die; shore –, bank- up; nurse; save, rescue; be –, make- -safe &c. 664; take care of &c. (*care*) 459; guard &c. (*defend*) 717.

*stare super antiquas vias*; hold one's own; hold –, stand- -one's ground &c. (*resist*) 719.

embalm, dry, cure, smoke, salt, pickle, season, kyanize, bottle, pot, tin, can; husband &c. (*store*) 636.

**Adj.** preserving &c. *v.*; conservative; prophylactic; preserva-tory, -tive; hygienic.

preserved &c. *v.*; un-impaired, -broken, -injured, -hurt, -singed, -marred; safe, – and sound; intact, with a whole skin, without a scratch.

**Phr.** *nolumus leges Angliæ mutari.*

**671. Escape.—N.** escape, scape; avolation, elopement, flight, getaway; evasion &c. (*avoidance*) 623; retreat; narrow –, hairbreadth- escape; close –, near- shave; come off, impunity.

[Means of escape] loophole &c. (*opening*) 260; path &c. 627; secret -door, – passage; refuge &c. 666; vent, – peg; safety-valve; drawbridge, fire-escape.

reprieve &c. (*deliverance*) 672; liberation &c. 750.

refugee &c. (*fugitive*) 623.

**V.** escape, scape; make –, effect –, make good- one's escape, make a get-away; get -off, – clear off, – well out of; *échapper belle*, save one's bacon; weather the storm &c. (*safe*) 664; escape scot-free.

elude &c., make off &c. (*avoid*) 623; march off &c. (*go away*) 293; give one the slip; slip through the -hands, – fingers; slip the collar, wriggle out of; break -loose, – from prison; break –, slip –, get- away; find -vent, – a hole to creep out of.

**Adj.** escap-ing, -ed &c. *v.*; stolen away, fled.

**Phr.** the bird has flown.

**672. Deliverance.—N.** deliverance, extrication, rescue; repriev-e, -al; respite; ransom; liberation &c. 750; truce, armistice; redemption, salvation; riddance; gaol delivery; exemption, day of grace; redeemableness.

**V.** deliver, extricate, rescue, save, redeem, ransom, free, liberate, release, set free, redeem, emancipate; bring -off, – through; *tirer d'affaire*, get the wheel out of the rut; snatch from the jaws of death. come to the rescue; rid; retrieve &c. (*restore*) 660; be –, get- rid of.

**Adj.** saved &c. *v.*; extric-, redeem-, rescu-able.

**Phr.** to the rescue!

### 3°. *Precursory Measures*

**673. Preparation.—N.** preparation; providing &c. *v.*; provi-sion, -dence; anticipation &c. (*foresight*) 510; precaution, -concertation, -disposition;

**674. Non-Preparation. — N.** non-, absence of –, want of- preparation; unpreparedness; inculture, inconcoction, improvidence.

forecast &c. (*plan*) 626; rehearsal, note of preparation.

[Putting in order] arrangement &c. 60; clearance; adjustment &c. 23; tuning; equipment, outfit, accoutrement, armament, array.

ripening &c. *v.*; maturation, evolution; elaboration, concoction, digestion; gestation, hatching, incubation, sitting.

groundwork, datum, first stone, cradle, stepping-stone; foundation, scaffold &c. (*support*) 215; scaffolding, *échafaudage*.

[Preparation -of men] training &c. (*education*) 537; inurement &c. (*habit*) 613; novitiate; [– of food] cook-ing, -ery; brewing, culinary art; [– of the soil] till-, plough-, sow-ing; semination, cultivation.

[State of being prepared] prepared-, readi-, ripe-, mellow-ness; maturity; *un impromptu fait à loisir*.

[Preparer] preparer, teacher, coach, trainer, pioneer; *avant-courrier*, *-coureur*; sappers and miners, paviour, navvy; packer, stevedore; warming-pan; precursor &c. 64.

**V.** prepare; get –, make- ready; make preparations, settle preliminaries, get up, sound the note of preparation; address oneself to.

set –, put- in order &c. (*arrange*) 60; forecast &c. (*plan*) 626; prepare –, plough –, dress- the ground; till –, cultivate- the soil; predispose, sow the seed, lay a train, dig a mine; lay –, fix- the -foundations, – basis, -groundwork; dig the foundations, erect the scaffolding; lay the first stone &c. (*begin*) 66.

rough-hew; cut out work; block –, hammer- out; lick into shape &c. (*form*) 240.

elaborate, mature, ripen, mellow, season, bring to maturity; nurture &c. (*aid*) 707; hatch, cook, brew; temper; anneal, smelt; dry, cure &c. 670.

equip, arm, man; fit-out, -up; furnish, rig, dress, garnish, betrim, accoutre, array, fettle, fledge; dress –, furbish –, brush –, vamp- up; refurbish; sharpen one's tools, trim one's foils, set, prime, attune; whet the -knife, – sword; wind –, screw- up; adjust &c. (*fit*) 27; put in -trim, – train, – gear, – working order, – tune, – a groove for, – harness; pack, stow away, store.

immaturity, crudity; rawness &c. *adj.*; abortion; disqualification.

[Absence of art] nature, state of nature; virgin soil, unweeded garden; rough diamond, neglect &c. 460.

rough copy &c. (*plan*) 626; germ &c. 153; raw material &c. 635.

improvisation &c. (*impulse*) 612.

**V.** be -unprepared &c. *adj.*; want –, lack- preparation; lie fallow; *s'embarquer sans biscuits*; live from hand to mouth.

[Render unprepared] dismantle &c. (*render useless*) 645; undress &c. 226.

extemporize, improvise.

surprise, pay a surprise visit, take by surprise, drop in upon, take unawares; take pot-luck.

**Adj.** un-prepared &c. [prepare &c. 673]; without -preparation &c. 673; incomplete &c. 53; rudimental, embryonic, abortive; immature, unripe, raw, green, crude; coarse; rough, -cast, -hewn; in the rough; un-hewn, -formed, -fashioned, -wrought, -laboured, -blown, -cooked, -boiled, -concocted, -cut, -polished.

callow, un-hatched, -fledged, -nurtured, -licked, -taught, -educated, -cultivated, -trained, -tutored, -drilled, -exercised; precocious, premature; un-, in-digested; un-mellowed, -seasoned, -leavened.

fallow; un-sown, -tilled; natural, in a state of nature; undressed; in dishabille, *en déshabillé*, *en négligé*.

un-, dis-qualified; unfitted; ill-digested; un-begun, -ready, -arranged -organized, -furnished, -provided -equipped, -trimmed; out of -gear – order; dismantled &c. *v.*

shiftless, improvident, unthrifty thoughtless, unguarded; happy-go-lucky; caught napping &c. (*inexpectant*) 508; unpremeditated &c. 612.

**Adv.** extempore &c. 612.

---

train &c. (*teach*) 527; inure &c. (*habituate*) 613; breed; prepare &c.- for; rehearse; make provision for; take -steps, – measures, – precautions; provide, – against; beat up for recruits; open the door to &c. (*facilitate*) 705.

set one's house in order, make all snug; clear -decks, – for action; close one's ranks; shuffle the cards.

prepare oneself; serve an apprenticeship &c. (*learn*) 539; lay oneself out for, get into harness, gird up one's loins, buckle on one's armour, *reculer pour mieux sauter*, prime and load, shoulder arms, get the steam up, put the horses to.

guard –, make sure- against; forearm, make sure, prepare for the evil day, have a rod in pickle, provide against a rainy day, feather one's nest; lay in provisions &c. 637; make investments; keep on foot.

be -prepared, – ready &c. *adj.*; hold oneself in readiness, watch and pray, keep one's powder dry; lie in wait for &c. (*expect*) 507; anticipate &c. (*foresee*) 510; *principiis obstare*; *veniente occurrere morbo.*

**Adj.** preparing &c. *v.*; in -preparation, – course of preparation, – agitation, – embryo, – hand, – train; afoot, afloat; on -foot, – the stocks, – the anvil; under consideration &c. (*plan*) 626; brewing, hatching, forthcoming, brooding; in -store for, – reserve.

precautionary, provident; prepara-tive, -tory; provisional, inchoate, under revision; preliminary &c. (*precedent*) 62.

prepared &c. *v.*; in readiness; ready, – to one's hand, – made, cut and dried; ready for use, reach me down; made to one's hand, handy, on the table, made to order; in gear; in working -order, – gear; snug; in practice.

ripe, mature, mellow; practised &c. (*skilled*) 698; laboured, elaborate, highly-wrought, smelling of the lamp, worked up.

in -full feather, – best bib and tucker; in –, at- harness; in – the saddle, – arms, – battle array, – war paint; up in arms; armed -at all points, – to the teeth, – *cap-à-pie*; sword in hand; booted and spurred.

*in utrumque* –, *semper- paratus*; on the alert &c. (*vigilant*) 459; at one's post.

**Adv.** in -preparation, – anticipation of; afoot, astir, abroad; abroach.

**675. Essay.—N.** essay, trial, endeavour, aim, attempt; venture, adventure, speculation, *coup d'essai*, *début*; probation &c. (*experiment*) 463.

**V.** try, essay; experiment &c. 463; endeavour, strive; tempt, tackle, take on, attempt, make an attempt; venture, adventure, speculate, take one's chance, tempt fortune; try one's -fortune, – luck, – hand; use one's endeavour; feel –, grope –, pick- one's way.

try hard, push, make a bold push, use one's best endeavour; do one's best &c. (*exertion*) 686.

**Adj.** essaying &c. *v.*; experimental &c. 463; tentative, empirical, probationary.

**Adv.** experimentally &c. *adj.*; on trial, at a venture; by rule of thumb. if one may be so bold.

**676. Undertaking.—N.** undertaking; compact &c. 769; engagement &c. (*promise*) 768; enter-, em-prise; venture &c. 675; pilgrimage; matter in hand &c. (*business*) 625; move; first move &c. (*beginning*) 66.

**V.** undertake; engage -, embark- in; launch -, plunge- into; volunteer; apprentice oneself to; engage &c. (*promise*) 768; contract &c. 769; take upon -oneself, - one's shoulders; devote oneself to &c. (*determination*) 604.

take -up, - in hand; tackle; set -, go- about; set -, fall- -to, - to work; launch forth; set up shop; put in -hand, - execution; set forward; break the neck of a business, be in for; put one's hand to; betake oneself to, turn one's hand to, go to do; begin &c. 66; broach, institute, &c. (*originate*) 153; put -, lay- one's -hand to the plough, - shoulder to the wheel.

have in hand &c. (*business*) 625; have many irons in the fire &c. (*activity*) 682.

**Adj.** undertaking &c. *v.*; on the anvil &c. 625; adventurous, venturesome.

**Int.** here goes!

**677. Use.**—**N.** use; employ, -ment; exer-cise, -citation; appli-cation, -ance; adhibition, disposal; consumption; agency &c. (*physical*) 170; usufruct; usefulness &c. 644; recourse, resort, avail, pragmatism.

[Conversion to use] utilization, service, wear.

[Way of using] usage.

**V.** use, make use of, employ, put to use; apply, put in -action, - operation, - practice; set -in motion, - to work.

ply, work, wield, handle, manipulate; play, - off; exert, exercise, practise, avail oneself of, profit by; resort -, have recourse -, recur -, take -, betake oneself- to; take -up with, - advantage of; lay one's hands on, try.

render useful &c. 644; mould; turn to -account, - use; convert to use, utilize, administer; work up; call -, bring- into play; put into requisition; call -, draw- forth; press -, enlist- into the service; bring to bear upon, devote, dedicate, consecrate, apply, adhibit, dispose of; make a -handle, - cat's paw- of.

fall back upon, make a shift with; make the -most, - best- of.

use -, swallow- up; consume, absorb, expend; tax, task, wear, put to task.

**Adj.** in use; used &c. *v.*; well-worn, -trodden.

useful &c. 644; subservient &c. (*instrumental*) 631; utilitarian; pragmatical.

**678. Disuse.**—**N.** forbearance, abstinence; disuse; relinquishment &c 782; desuetude &c. (*want of habit*) 614

**V.** not use; do without, dispense with, let alone, not touch, forbear, abstain, spare, waive, neglect; keep back, reserve.

lay -up, - by, - on the shelf, - up in a napkin; shelve; set -, put -, lay- aside; disuse, leave off, have done with; supersede; discard &c. (*eject*) 297; dismiss, give warning.

throw aside &c. (*relinquish*) 782; make away with &c. (*destroy*) 162; cast -, heave -, throw- overboard; cast to the -dogs, - winds; dismantle &c. (*render useless*) 645.

lie -, remain- unemployed &c. *adj.*

**Adj.** not used &c. *v.*; un-employed, -applied, -disposed of, -spent, -exercised, -touched, -trodden, -essayed, -gathered, -culled; uncalled for, not required.

disused &c. *v.*; done with; run down, used up, cast off.

**679. Misuse.**—**N.** mis-use, -usage, -employment, -application, -appropriation.

abuse, profanation, prostitution, desecration; waste &c. 638.

**V.** mis-use, -employ, -apply, -appropriate.

desecrate, abuse, profane, prostitute; waste &c. 638; over-task, -tax, -work; squander &c. 818.

cut a whetstone with a razor, employ a steam-engine to crack a nut; catch at a straw.

**Adj.** misused &c. *v.*

## Section III. Voluntary Action

### 1°. *Simple Voluntary Action*

**680. Action.—N.** action, performance; doing &c. *v.*; perpetration; exercise, -citation; movement, operation, evolution, work; labour &c. (*exertion*) 686; *praxis*, execution; procedure &c. (*conduct*) 692; handicraft; business &c. 625; agency &c. (*power at work*) 170.

deed, act, overt act, stitch, touch, gest; transaction, job, doings, dealings, proceeding, measure, step, manœuvre, bout, passage, move, stroke, blow; *coup*, – *de main*, – *d'état*; *tour de force* &c. (*display*) 882; feat, exploit, stunt; achievement &c. (*completion*) 729; handiwork, workmanship. craftsmanship; manufacture; stroke of policy &c. (*plan*) 626.

actor &c. (*doer*) 690.

**V.** do, perform, execute; achieve &c. (*complete*) 729; transact, enact; commit, perpetrate, inflict; exercise, prosecute, carry on, work, practise, play.

employ oneself, ply one's task; officiate, have in hand &c. (*business*) 625; labour &c. 686; be at work; pursue a course; shape one's course &c. (*conduct*) 692.

act, operate; take -action, – steps; strike a blow, lift a finger, stretch forth one's hand; take in hand &c. (*undertake*) 676; put oneself in motion; put in practice; carry into execution &c. (*complete*) 729; act upon.

be -an actor &c. 690; take –, act –, play –, perform- a part in; participate in; have a -hand in, – finger in the pie; have to do with; be a -party to, – participator in; bear –, lend- a hand; pull an oar, run in a race; mix oneself up with &c. (*meddle*) 682.

be in action; come into operation &c. (*power at work*) 170.

**Adj.** doing &c. *v.*; acting; in action; in harness; on duty; at work; in operation &c. 170; up to one's ears in work, in the midst of things.

**Adv.** in the -act, – midst of, – thick of; red-handed, *in flagrante delicto*; while one's hand is in.

**681. Inaction.—N.** inaction, passiveness, abstinence from action; noninterference; Fabian –, conservative- policy; neglect &c. 460; stagnation, vegetation; loafing.

inactivity &c. 683; rest &c. (*repose*) 687; quiescence &c. 265; want of –, in- occupation; unemployment; idle hours, time hanging on one's hands, *dolce far niente*; sinecure.

**V.** not -do, – act, – attempt; be -inactive &c. 683; abstain from doing, do nothing, hold, spare; not -stir, – move, – lift- a -finger, – foot, – peg; fold one's -arms, – hands; leave –, let- alone; let -be, – pass, – things take their course, – it have its way, – well alone; *quieta non movere*; *stare super antiquas vias*; rest and be thankful, live and let live; lie –, rest- upon one's oars; *laisser -aller*, – *faire*; stand aloof; refrain &c. (*avoid*) 623; keep oneself from doing; remit –, relax- one's efforts; desist &c. (*relinquish*) 624; stop &c. (*cease*) 142; pause &c. (*be quiet*) 265.

wait, lie in wait, bide one's time, take time, tide it over.

cool –, kick- one's heels; loaf, while away the -time, – tedious hours; pass –, fill up –, beguile- the time; talk against time; waste time &c. (*inactive*) 683.

lie -by, – on the shelf, – in ordinary, – idle, – to, – fallow; keep quiet, slug; have nothing to do, whistle for want of thought; twiddle one's thumbs.

undo, do away with; take -down, – to pieces; destroy &c. 162.

**Adj.** not doing &c. *v.*; not done &c. *v.*; undone; passive; un-occupied, -employed; out of -employ, – work, – a job; fallow; *désœuvré*.

**Adv.** *re infectâ*, at a stand, *les bras croisés*, with folded arms; with the hands -in the pockets, – behind one's back; *pour passer le temps*.

**Int.** so let it be! stop! &c. 142; hands off!

**Phr.** nothing doing; *cunctando restituit rem*.

**682. Activity.—N.** activity; briskness, liveliness &c. *adj.*; animation, life, vivacity, spirit, verve, dash, energy, go.

nimbleness, agility; smartness, quickness &c. *adj.*; velocity &c. 274; alacrity, promptitude; des-, dis-patch; expedition; haste &c. 684; punctuality &c. (*early*) 132.

eagerness, zeal, ardour, *perfervidum ingenium*, *empressement*, earnestness, intentness; *abandon*; vigour &c. (*physical energy*) 171; devotion &c. (*resolution*) 604; exertion &c. 686.

industry, assiduity; assiduousness &c. *adj.*; sedulity; laboriousness; drudgery &c. (*labour*) 686; painstaking, diligence; perseverance &c. 604*a*; indefatigation; habits of business.

vigilance &c. 459; wakefulness; sleep-, rest-lessness; *pervigilium*, *insomnia*; racketing.

movement, bustle, hustle, stir, fuss, ado, bother, pottering; fidgets, -iness; flurry &c. (*haste*) 684.

officiousness; dabbling, meddling; inter-ference, -position, -meddling, butting in, intrusiveness; tampering with, intrigue.

press of business, no sinecure, plenty to do, many irons in the fire, great doings, busy hum of men, battle of life, thick of -things, – the action; the madding crowd.

housewife, busy bee; new brooms; sharp fellow, blade; hustler, devotee, enthusiast, fan, zealot, fanatic; meddler, intermeddler, intriguer, busybody, kibitzer, pickthank.

**V.** be -active &c. *adj.*; busy oneself in; stir, -about, – one's stumps; bestir –, rouse- oneself; speed, hasten, peg away, lay about one, bustle, fuss; raise –, kick up- a dust; push; make a -push, – fuss, – stir; go ahead, push forward; fight –, elbow- one's way; make progress &c. 282; toil &c. (*labour*) 686; drudge, plod, persist &c. (*persevere*) 604*a*; keep -up the ball, – the pot boiling.

look sharp; have all one's eyes about one &c. (*vigilance*) 459; rise, arouse oneself, get up early, hustle, push; be about, keep moving, steal a march, kill two birds with one stone; seize the opportunity &c. 134; lose no time, not

**683. Inactivity.—N.** inactivity; inaction &c. 681; inertness, inertia &c. 172; obstinacy &c. 606.

lull &c. (*cessation*) 142; quiescence &c. 265; rust, -iness.

idle-, remiss-ness &c. *adj.*; sloth, indolence, indiligence; otiosity, dawdling &c. *v.*

dullness &c. *adj.*; languor; segni-ty, -tude; lentor; sluggishness &c. (*slowness*) 275; procrastination &c. (*delay*) 133; torp-or, -idity, -escence; stupor &c. (*insensibility*) 823; somnolence; drowsiness &c. *adj.*; nodding &c. *v.*; oscit-ation, -ancy; pandiculation, hypnotism, lethargy; heaviness, heavy eye-lids, sand in the eyes.

sleep, slumber; sound –, heavy –, balmy- sleep; Morpheus, dreamland; coma, trance, catalepsy, hypnosis, *ecstasis*, dream, hibernation, nap, doze, snooze, *siesta*, wink of sleep, forty winks, snore; Hypnology.

dull work; pottering; relaxation &c. (*loosening*) 47; Castle of Indolence.

[Cause of inactivity] lullaby, *berceuse*; anæsthetic, sedative &c. 174; torpedo.

idler, drone, droil, dawdle, mopus; do-little, *fainéant*, dummy, sleeping partner; afternoon farmer; truant &c. (*runaway*) 623; lounger, *lazzarone*, floater, loafer, tramp, beggar, cadger; lub-ber, -bard; slow-coach &c. (*slow*) 275; opium –, lotus- eater; slug; lag-, slug-gard, lie-abed; slumberer, dormouse, marmot; waiter on Providence, *fruges consumere natus*.

**V.** be -inactive &c. *adj.*; do nothing &c. 681; move slowly &c. 275; let the grass grow under one's feet; take one's time, dawdle, poke, drawl, droil, lag, hang back, slouch; loll, -op; lounge, loaf, loiter; go to sleep over; sleep at one's post, *ne battre que d'une aile*.

take -it easy, – things as they come; lead an easy life, vegetate, swim with the stream, eat the bread of idleness; loll in the lap of -luxury, – indolence; waste –, consume –, kill –, lose- time; burn daylight, waste the precious hours.

idle –, trifle –, fritter –, fool- away time; spend –, take- time in; ped-, pid-dle; potter, putter, dabble, faddle,

lose a moment, make the most of one's time, not suffer the grass to grow under one's feet, improve the shining hour, make short work of; dash off; make haste &c. 684; do one's best, take pains &c. (*exert oneself*) 686; do –, work- wonders.

have -many irons in the fire, – one's hands full, – much on one's hands; have other -things to do, – fish to fry; be busy; not have a moment -to spare, – that one can call one's own.

have one's fling, run the round of; go all lengths, stick at nothing, run riot.

outdo; over-do, -act, -lay, -shoot the mark; make a toil of a pleasure.

have a hand in &c. (*act in*) 680; take an active part, put in one's oar, have a finger in the pie, mix oneself up with, trouble one's head about, intrigue; agitate.

tamper with, meddle, moil; intermeddle, -fere, -pose; obtrude; poke –, thrust- one's nose in, butt in.

**Adj.** active; brisk, – as a lark, – as a bee; lively, animated, vivacious; alive, – and kicking; frisky, spirited, stirring.

nimble, – as a squirrel; agile; light-, nimble-footed; featly, tripping.

quick, prompt, yare, instant, ready, alert, spry, sharp, smart, slick, go-ahead; fast &c. (*swift*) 274; quick as a lamplighter, expeditious; awake, broad awake; wide awake &c. (*intelligent*) 498.

forward, eager, ardent, strenuous, zealous, enterprising, pushing, in earnest; resolute &c. 604.

industrious, assiduous, diligent, sedulous, notable, painstaking; intent &c. (*attention*) 457; indefatigable &c. (*persevering*) 604*a*; unwearied; unsleeping, sleepless, never tired; plodding, hard-working &c. 686; business-like, workaday.

bustling; restless, – as a hyæna; fussy, fidgety, pottering; busy, – as a hen with one chicken.

working, labouring, at work, on duty, in harness; up in arms; on one's legs, at call; up and -doing, – stirring.

busy, occupied; hard at -work, – it; up to one's ears in, full of business, busy as a bee.

meddling &c. *v.*; meddlesome, pushing, officious, overofficious, *intrigant*.

astir, stirring; a-going, -foot; on foot; in full swing; eventful; on the alert &c. (*vigilant*) 459.

fribble, fiddle-faddle; dally, dilly-dally.

sleep, slumber, be asleep; hibernate; oversleep; sleep like a -top, – log, – dormouse; sleep -soundly, – heavily; doze, drowze, snooze, nap; take a -nap &c. *n.*; dream; snore; settle –, go –, go off- to sleep; drop off; fall –, drop- asleep; close –, seal up- -the -eyes, – eyelids; weigh down the eyelids; get sleepy, nod, yawn; go to bed, turn in.

languish, expend itself, flag, hang fire; relax.

render -idle &c. *adj.*; sluggardize; mitigate &c. 174.

**Adj.** inactive; motionless &c. 265; unoccupied &c. (*doing nothing*) 681.

indolent, lazy, slothful, idle, otiose, lusk, remiss, slack, inert, torpid, sluggish, languid, supine, heavy, dull, leaden, lumpish; exanimate, soulless; listless; dron-y, -ish; lazy as Ludlam's dog.

dilatory, laggard; lagging &c. *v.*; slow &c. 275; rusty, flagging; lackadaisical, maudlin, fiddle-faddle; pottering &c. *v.*; shilly-shally &c. (*irresolute*) 605.

sleeping &c. *v.*; asleep; fast –, dead –, sound- asleep; in a sound sleep; sound as a top, dormant, comatose; in the -arms, – lap- of Morpheus.

sleep-y, -ful; dozy, drowsy, somnolent, torpescent; lethargic, -al; heavy, – with sleep; napping; somni-fic, -ferous; sopor-ous, -ific, -iferous; hypnotic; balmy, dreamy; un-, una-wakened.

sedative &c. 174.

**Adv.** inactively &c. *adj.*; at leisure &c. 685.

**Phr.** the eyes begin to draw straws.

---

**Adv.** actively &c. *adj.*; with -life and spirit, – might and main &c. 686, – haste &c. 684, – wings; full tilt, *in mediis rebus*.

**Int.** be –, look- -alive, – sharp! move –, push- on! keep moving! go ahead! stir your stumps! *age quod agis!*

**Phr.** *carpe diem* &c. (*opportunity*) 134; *nulla dies sine lineâ*; *nec mora nec requies*; no sooner said than done &c. (*early*) 132; catch a weasel asleep.

**684. Haste.**—**N.** haste, urgency; des-, dis-patch; acceleration, spurt, spirt, forced march, rush, dash; velocity &c. 274; precipit-ancy, -ation, -ousness &c. *adj.*; impetuosity; *brusquerie*; hurry, scurry, scuttle, drive, scramble, push, hustle, bustle, fuss, fidgets, flurry, flutter, splutter.

**V.** haste, hasten; make -haste, – a dash &c. *n.*; hurry –, dash –, whip –, push –, press- -on, – forward; hurry, skurry, scuttle along, bundle on, dart to and fro, bustle, flutter, scramble; plunge, – headlong; run, race, speed; dash off; rush &c. (*violence*) 173.

bestir oneself &c. (*be active*) 682; lose -no time, – not a moment, – not an instant; make short work of; make the best of one's -time, – way.

be -precipitate &c. *adj.*; jump at; be in -haste, – a hurry &c. *n.*; have -no time, – not a moment- -to lose, – to spare; work -under pressure, – against time.

quicken &c. 274; accelerate, expedite, put on, precipitate, urge, whip, spur, flog, goad.

**Adj.** hasty, hurried, *brusque*; scrambling, cursory, precipitate, headlong, furious, boisterous, impetuous, hot-headed; feverish, fussy; pushing.

in -haste, – a hurry &c. *n.*; in -hot, – all- haste; breathless, pressed for time, hard pressed, urgent.

**Adv.** with -haste, – all haste, – breathless speed; in haste &c. *adj.*; apace &c. (*swiftly*) 274; amain; all at once &c. (*instantaneously*) 113; at short notice &c., immediately &c. (*early*) 132; posthaste; by -express, – telegraph, – wire, – wireless, – air mail.

hastily, precipitately &c. *adj.*; helter-skelter, hurry-skurry, holus-bolus; slap-dash, -bang; full-tilt, -drive; heels over head, head and shoulders, headlong, *à corps perdu*.

by -fits and starts, – spurts; hop, skip and jump.

**Phr.** *sauve qui peut*, devil take the hindmost, no time to be lost; no sooner said than done &c. (*early*) 132; a word and a blow.

**Int.** hurry up! look alive! get a move on! buck up! double march! rush! urgent!

**685. Leisure.**—**N.** leisure; spare -time, – hours, – moments; vacant hour; time, – to spare, – on one's hands; holiday &c. (*rest*) 687; *otium cum dignitate*, ease.

**V.** have -leisure &c. *n.*; take one's -time, – leisure, – ease; repose &c. 687; move slowly &c. 275; while away the time &c. (*inaction*) 681; be -master of one's time, – an idle man; *desipere in loco*.

**Adj.** leisurely; slow &c. 275; deliberate, quiet, calm, undisturbed; at -leisure, – one's ease, – a loose end.

**Phr.** time hanging heavy on one's hands.

---

**686. Exertion.**—**N.** exertion, effort, strain, tug, pull, stress, force, pressure, throw, stretch, struggle, spell, spurt, spirt; stroke –, stitch- of work.

**687. Repose.**—**N.** repose, rest, silken repose; sleep &c. 683.

relaxation, breathing time; halt pause &c. (*cessation*) 142; respite,

'a strong pull, a long pull and a pull all together'; dead lift; heft; gymnastics, sports; exer-cise, -citation; wear and tear; ado; toil and trouble; uphill –, hard –, warm- work; harvest time.

labour, work, toil, travail, manual labour, sweat of one's brow, swink, operoseness, drudgery, slavery, fagging, hammering; *limæ labor*.

trouble, pains, duty; resolution &c. 604; energy &c. (*physical*) 171.

**V.** exert oneself; exert –, tax- one's energies; use exertion.

labour, work, toil, moil, sweat, fag, drudge, slave, drag a lengthened chain, wade through, strive, strain; make –, stretch- a long arm; pull, tug, ply; ply –, tug at- the oar; do the work; take the labouring oar.

bestir oneself (*be active*) 682; take trouble, trouble oneself.

work hard; rough it; put forth -one's strength, – a strong arm; fall to work, bend the bow; buckle to, set one's shoulder to the wheel &c. (*resolution*) 604; work like a -Briton, – horse, – carthorse, – galley-slave, – coalheaver; labour –, work- day and night; redouble one's efforts; do double duty; work double -hours, – tides; sit up, burn the -midnight oil, – candle at both ends; stick to &c. (*persevere*) 604*a*; work –, fight- one's way; lay about one, hammer at.

take pains; do one's -best, – level best, – utmost; do -the best one can, – all one can, – all in one's power, – as much as in one lies, – what lies in one's power; use one's -best, – utmost- endeavour; try one's -best, – utmost; play one's best card; put one's -best, – right- leg foremost; have one's whole soul in one's work, put all one's strength into, strain every nerve; spare no -efforts, – pains; go all lengths; go through fire and water &c. (*resolution*) 604; move heaven and earth, leave no stone unturned.

**Adj.** labouring &c. *v.*

laborious, operose, elaborate; strained; toil-, trouble-, burden-, weari-some; uphill; herculean, gymnastic, athletic, palestric.

hardworking, painstaking, strenuous, energetic.

hard at work, on the stretch.

**Adv.** laboriously &c. *adj.*; lustily; with -might and main, – all one's might, – a strong hand, – sledge-hammer, – much ado; to the best of one's abilities, *totis viribus, vi et armis, manibus pedibusque*, tooth and nail, *unguibus et rostro*, hammer and tongs, heart and soul; through thick and thin &c. (*perseverance*) 604*a*.

by the sweat of one's brow, *suo Marte*.

day of rest, *dies non*, Sabbath, Lord's day, holiday, red-letter day, vacation, recess.

**V.** repose; rest, – and be thankful; take -rest, – one's ease.

relax, unbend, slacken; take breath &c. (*refresh*) 689; rest upon one's oars; pause &c. (*cease*) 142; stay one's hand.

lie down; recline, – on a bed of down, – on an easy chair; go to -rest, – bed, – sleep &c. 683.

take a holiday, shut up shop; lie fallow &c. (*inaction*) 681.

**Adj.** reposing &c. *v.*; unstrained.

**Adv.** at rest.

---

**688. Fatigue.**—**N.** fatigue; weariness &c. 841; yawning, drowsiness &c. 683; lassitude, tiredness, fatigation, exhaustion; sweat.

anhelation, shortness of breath, pant- faintness; collapse, prostration.

**689. Refreshment.**—**N.** bracing &c. *v.*; recovery of -strength &c. 159; restoration, revival &c. 660; repair, refection, refocillation, refreshment, regalement, bait; relief &c. 834.

**V.** brace &c. (*strengthen*) 159; rein-

swoon, fainting, *deliquium*, syncope, lipothymy.

**V.** be -fatigued &c. *adj.*; yawn &c. (*get sleepy*) 683; droop, sink, flag; lose -breath, – wind; gasp, pant, puff, blow, drop, swoon, faint, succumb.

fatigue, tire, weary, bore, irk, fag, jade, harass, exhaust, knock up, wear out, prostrate.

tax, task, strain; over-task, -work, -burden, -tax, -strain.

**Adj.** fatigued &c. *v.*; weary &c. 841; drowsy &c. 683; drooping &c. *v.*; haggard; toil-, way-worn; footsore, surbated, weatherbeaten; faint; done –, used –, knocked- up; exhausted, prostrate, spent; over-tired, -spent, -fatigued; forspent; unre-freshed, -stored.

worn, – out; battered, shattered, pulled down, seedy, altered.

breath-, wind-less; short of –, out of -breath, – wind; blown, puffing and blowing; short-breathed; anhelous; broken-, short-winded.

ready to drop, more dead than alive, dog -tired, – weary, walked off one's legs, tired to death, on one's last legs, played out, *hors de combat.*

fatiguing &c. *v.*; tire-, irk-, weari-some; weary; trying.

vigorate; air, freshen up, refresh, recruit; repair &c. (*restore*) 660; fan, refocillate.

breathe, respire; draw –, take –, gather –, take a long –, regain –, recover- breath; get better, raise one's head; recover –, regain –, renew- one's strength &c. 159; perk up.

come to oneself &c. (*revive*) 660; feel like a giant refreshed.

**Adj.** refreshing &c. *v.*; recuperative &c. 660.

refreshed &c. *v.*; un-tired, -wearied.

---

**690. Agent.**—**N.** doer, actor, agent, performer, perpetrator, operator; execu-tor, -trix; practitioner, worker, stager.

bee, ant, working bee, labouring oar, shaft horse, servant –, maid-of all work, general servant, factotum.

workman, artisan; crafts-, handicrafts-man; mechanic, operative; working –, labouring- man; hewers of wood and drawers of water, labourer, navvy; hand, man, day labourer, journeyman, hack; mere -tool &c. 633; porter, docker, stevedore, beast of burden, drudge, fag.

maker, artificer, artist, wright, manufacturer, architect, contractor, builder, mason, bricklayer, smith, forger, Vulcan; black-, tin-smith; carpenter; ganger, platelayer.

machinist, mechanician, engineer, electrician, plumber, gasfitter &c.

semp-, sem-, seam-stress; needle-, char-, work-woman; tailor, cordwainer.

minister &c. (*instrument*) 631; servant &c. 746; representative &c. (*commissioner*) 758, (*deputy*) 759.

co-worker, fellow-worker, party to, participator in, co-operator, colleague, associate, collaborator, *particeps criminis*, *dramatis personæ*; *personnel.*

**Phr.** '*quorum pars magna fui.*'

**691. Workshop.**—**N.** work-shop, -house; laboratory; manufactory, mill, factory, armoury, arsenal, mint, forge, loom; cabinet, studio, *bureau, atelier*; hive, – of industry; nursery; hot-house, -bed; kitchen, kitchenette; dock, -yard; slip, yard, wharf; found-ry, -ery; furnace; vineyard, orchard, farm, kitchen garden.

melting pot, crucible, alembic, caldron, mortar, *matrix.*

## 2°. *Complex Voluntary Action*

**692. Conduct.—N.** dealing, transaction &c. (*action*) 680; business &c. 625.

tactics, game, policy, polity; general-, statesman-, seaman-ship; strate-gy, -gics; plan &c. 626.

husbandry; house-keeping, -wifery; stewardship; *ménage*; regimen, *régime*; econom-y, -ics; political economy; management; government &c. (*direction*) 693.

execution, manipulation, treatment, campaign, career, life, course, walk, race.

conduct; behaviour; de-, com-portment; carriage, *maintien*, demeanour, guise, bearing, manner, mien, air, observance.

course –, line- of -conduct, – action, – proceeding; *rôle*; process, ways, practice, procedure, *modus operandi*; method &c., path &c. 627.

**V.** transact, execute; des-, dis-patch; proceed with, discharge; carry -on, – through, – out, – into effect; work out; go –, get- through; enact; put into practice; officiate &c. 625.

behave –, comport –, demean –, carry -, bear –, conduct –, acquit- oneself.

run a race, lead a life, play a game; take –, adopt- a course; steer –, shape- one's course; play one's- -part, – cards; shift for oneself; paddle one's own canoe.

conduct; manage &c. (*direct*) 693.

deal –, have to do- with; treat, handle a case; take -steps, – measures.

**Adj.** conducting &c. *v.*; strategical, business-like, practical, economic, executive.

**693. Direction.—N.** direction; manage-ment, -ry; government, gubernation, conduct, legislation, regulation, guidance; steer-, pilot-age; reins, – of government; helm, rudder, controls, joy stick, needle, compass, binnacle; guiding –, load –, lode –, pole- star; cynosure.

super-vision, -intendence; *surveillance*, oversight; eye of the master; control, charge, auspices; board of control &c. (*council*) 696; command &c. (*authority*) 737.

premier-, senator-ship; director &c. 694; chair, seat, portfolio.

statesmanship; state-, king-craft.

minis-try, -tration; administration; steward-, proctor-ship; agency.

**V.** direct, manage, govern, conduct; order, prescribe, cut out work for; head, lead; lead –, show- the way; take the lead, lead on; regulate, guide, steer, pilot; take –, be at- the helm; have –, handle –, hold –, take- the reins, handle the ribbons; drive, tool; tackle.

super-intend, -vise; overlook, control, keep in order, look after, see to, oversee, legislate for; administer, ministrate; patronize; have the -care, – charge- of; have –, take- the direction; pull the -strings, – wires; rule &c. (*command*) 737; have –, hold- -office, – the portfolio; preside, – at the board; take –, occupy –, be in- the chair; pull the stroke oar.

**Adj.** directing &c. *v.*; executive, supervisory, hegemonic.

**Adv.** at the -helm, – head of, in charge of; under the auspices of.

**694. Director.—N.** director, manager, governor, rector, comptroller; super-intendent, -visor; intendant; over-seer, -looker; foreman, boss, straw boss; supercargo, husband, inspector, visitor, ranger, surveyor, ædile, moderator, monitor, taskmaster; master &c. 745; leader, ringleader, demagogue, corypheus, conductor, fugleman, precentor, bellwether, agitator.

guiding **star &c.** (*guidance*) 693; adviser &c. 695; guide &c. (*information*) 527; **pilot;** helmsman; steers-man, -mate; man at the wheel; wire-puller;

driver, whip, Jehu, charioteer; coach-, car-, cab-man, jarvey; postilion, *vetturino*, muleteer, teamster; whipper in; engineer, engine driver, motorman, *chauffeur*.

head, – man; principal, president, speaker; chair, -man; captain &c. (*master*) 745; superior; dean; mayor &c. (*civil authority*) 745; vice-president, prime minister, premier, vizier, grand vizier; dictator.

officer, functionary, minister, official, red-tapist, bureaucrat; man –, Jack- in office; office-bearer; person in authority &c. 745.

statesman, strategist, legislator, lawgiver, politician, administrator, statist, statemonger; Minos, Draco; arbiter &c. (*judge*) 967; king maker, power behind the throne.

board &c. (*council*) 696.

secretary, – of state; Reis Effendi; vicar &c. (*deputy*) 759; steward, factor; agent &c. 758; bailiff, middleman; ganger, clerk of works; landreeve; factotum, major-domo, seneschal, housekeeper, shepherd, *croupier*; proctor, procurator, curator, librarian.

**Adv.** *ex officio*.

**695. Advice.—N.** advice, counsel, adhortation; word to the wise; suggestion, submonition, recommendation, advocacy, consultation.

exhortation &c. (*persuasion*) 615; expostulation &c. (*dissuasion*) 616; admonition &c. (*warning*) 668; guidance &c. (*direction*) 693.

instruction, charge, injunction.

adviser, prompter; counsel, -lor; monitor, mentor, Nestor, *magnus Apollo*, senator; teacher &c. 540.

guide, manual, chart &c. (*information*) 527.

physician, leech, archiater; arbiter &c. (*judge*) 967.

refer-ence, -ment; consultation, conference, parley, *pourparler* &c. 696.

**V.** advise, counsel; give -advice, – counsel, – a piece of advice; suggest, prompt, submonish, recommend, prescribe, advocate; exhort &c. (*persuade*) 615.

enjoin, enforce, charge, instruct, call; call upon &c. (*request*) 765; dictate.

expostulate &c. (*dissuade*) 616; admonish &c. (*warn*) 668.

advise with; lay heads –, consult- together; compare notes; hold a council, deliberate, be closeted with.

confer, consult, refer to, call in; take –, follow- advice; follow implicitly; be advised by, have at one's elbow, take one's cue from.

**Adj.** recommendatory; hortative &c. (*persuasive*) 615; dehortatory &c. (*dissuasive*) 616; admonitory &c. (*warning*) 668; consultative.

**Int.** go to!

**696. Council.—N.** council, committee, subcommittee, *comitia*, court, chamber, cabinet, board, bench, staff; consultation.

senate, *senatus*, parliament, House, – of Lords, – Peers, – Commons, legislature, legislative assembly, federal council, chamber of deputies, directory, *Reichsrath*, *rigsdag*, *cortes*, storthing, witenagemote, *junta*, divan, *musnud*, *sanhedrim*, Amphictyonic council; *duma*, *zemstvo*, *soviet*, *cheka*, *ogpu*; *Dail Eireann*; caput, consistory, chapter, syndicate; court of appeal &c. (*tribunal*) 966; board of -control, – works; vestry; county –, borough –, district –, parish –, town- council, local board.

cabinet –, privy- council, royal commission; cockpit, convocation, synod, congress, congregation, convention, diet, states-general, aulic council.

League of Nations, assembly, *caucus*, conclave, *clique*, conventicle; meeting, sitting, *séance*, conference, session, hearing, palaver, *pourparler*, *durbar*, pow-wow, house; *quorum*.

senator; member, – of parliament; councillor, M.P., representative of the people.

**Adj.** senatorial, curule, parliamentary.

**697. Precept.—N.** precept, direction, instruction, charge; prescript, -ion; *recipe*, receipt; golden rule; maxim &c. 496.

commandment, rule, ruling, canon, law, code, *corpus juris, lex scripta*, common –, unwritten –, canon-law; the Ten Commandments; act, statute, convention, rubric, stage direction, regulation; form, -ula, -ulary; technicality; nice point.

order &c. (*command*) 741.

**698. Skill.—N.** skill, skilfulness, address; dexter-ity, -ousness; adroitness, expertness &c. *adj.*; proficiency, competence, craft, callidity, facility, knack, trick, sleight; master-y, -ship; excellence, panurgy; ambidext-erity, -rousness; sleight of hand &c. (*deception*) 545.

sea-, air-, marks-, horse-manship; tight-, rope-dancing.

accomplish-, acquire-, attain-ment; art, science; techn-icality, -ology, -ique; practical –, technical- knowledge; technocracy; finish, technic.

knowledge of the world, world wisdom, *savoir-faire*; tact; mother wit &c. (*sagacity*) 498; discretion &c. (*caution*) 864; *finesse*; craftiness &c. (*cunning*) 702; management &c. (*conduct*) 692; *ars celare artem*; self-help.

cleverness, talent, ability, ingenuity, capacity, parts, talents, faculty, endowment, *forte*, turn, gift, genius, flair, feeling; intelligence &c. 498; sharpness, readiness &c. (*activity*) 682; invention &c. 515; apt-ness, -itude; turn –, capacity –, genius- for; felicity, capability, *curiosa felicitas*, qualification, habilitation.

proficient &c. 700.

masterpiece, *coup de maître, chef-d'œuvre, tour de force*; good stroke &c. (*plan*) 626.

**V.** be -skilful &c. *adj.*; excel in, be master of; have -a turn for &c. *n.*

know -what's what, – a hawk from a handsaw, – what one is about, – on

**699. Unskilfulness.—N.** unskilfulness &c. *adj.*; want of -skill &c. 698; incompeten-ce, -cy; in-ability, -felicity, -dexterity, -experience; clumsiness; disqualification, unproficiency; quackery.

folly, stupidity &c. 499; indiscretion &c. (*rashness*) 863; thoughtlessness &c. (*inattention*) 458, (*neglect*) 460.

mis-management, -conduct; impolicy; maladministration; mis-rule, -government, -application, -direction, -feasance.

absence of rule, rule of thumb; bungling &c. *v.*; failure &c. 732; screw loose; too many cooks.

blunder &c. (*mistake*) 495; *étourderie*, *gaucherie*, act of folly, *balourdise*; botch, -ery; bad job, sad work.

sprat sent out to catch a whale, much ado about nothing, wildgoose chase.

bungler &c. 701; fool &c. 501.

layman, amateur.

**V.** be -unskilful &c. *adj.*; not see an inch beyond one's nose; blunder, bungle, boggle, fumble, muff, botch, bitch, flounder, loppet, stumble, trip; hobble &c. 275; put one's foot in it; make a -mess, – hash, – sad work- of; overshoot the mark.

play -tricks with, – Puck; mismanage, -conduct, -direct, -apply, -send.

stultify –, make a fool of –, commit- oneself; act foolishly; play the fool; put oneself out of court; lose one's -head, – cunning.

begin at the wrong end; do things

which side one's bread is buttered, – what's o'clock, – a thing or two; have cut one's -eye, – wisdom- teeth.

see -one's way, – where the wind lies, – which way the wind blows; have -all one's wits about one, – one's hand in; *savoir-vivre; scire quid valeant humeri quid ferre recusent.*

look after the main chance; cut one's coat according to one's cloth; live by one's wits; exercise one's discretion, feather the oar, sail near the wind; stoop to conquer &c. (*cunning*) 702; play one's -cards well, – best card; hit the right nail on the head, put the saddle on the right horse.

take advantage of, make the most of; profit by &c. (*use*) 677; make a hit &c. (*succeed*) 731; make a virtue of necessity; make hay while the sun shines &c. (*occasion*) 134.

**Adj.** skilful, dexterous, adroit, expert, apt, slick, handy, quick, deft, ready, resourceful, gain; smart &c. (*active*) 682; proficient, good at, up to, at home in, master of, a good hand at, *au fait*, thoroughbred, masterly, crack, accomplished; conversant &c. (*knowing*) 490.

experienced, practised, skilled; up –, well up- in; in -practice, – proper cue; competent, efficient, qualified, capable, fitted, fit for, up to the mark, trained, initiated, prepared, primed, finished.

clever, able, ingenious, felicitous, gifted, talented, endowed, cute, inventive &c. 515; shrewd, sharp &c. (*intelligent*) 498; cunning &c. 702; alive to, up to snuff, not to be caught with chaff; discreet.

neat-handed, fine-fingered, ambidextrous, sure-footed; cut out –, fitted- for.

technical, artistic, scientific, dædalian, shipshape; workman-, business-, statesman-like.

**Adv.** skillfully &c. *adj.*; well &c. 618; artistically; with -skill, – consummate skill; *secundum artem, suo Marte*; to the best of one's abilities &c. (*exertion*) 686; like a machine.

---

by halves &c. (*not complete*) 730; make two bites of a cherry; play at cross purposes; strain at a gnat and swallow a camel &c. (*caprice*) 608; put the cart before the horse; lock the stable door when the horse is stolen &c. (*too late*) 135.

not know -what one is about, – one's own interest, – on which side one's bread is buttered; stand in one's own light, quarrel with one's bread and butter, throw a stone in one's own garden, kill the goose which lays the golden eggs, pay dear for one's whistle, cut one's own throat, burn one's fingers; knock –, run- one's head against a stone wall; fall into a trap, catch a Tartar, bring the house about one's ears; have too many -eggs in one basket (*imprudent*) 863, – irons in the fire.

mistake &c. 495; take the shadow for the substance &c. (*credulity*) 486; be in the wrong box, aim at a pigeon and kill a crow; take –, get- the wrong sow by the ear, – the dirty end of the stick; put -the saddle on the wrong horse, – a square peg into a round hole, – new wine into old bottles.

cut a whetstone with a razor; hold a farthing candle to the sun &c. (*useless*) 645; fight with –, grasp at- a shadow; catch at straws, lean on a broken reed, reckon without one's host, pursue a wildgoose chase; go on a fool's –, sleeveless- errand; go further and fare worse; loose –, miss- one's way; fail &c. 732.

**Adj.** un-skilful &c. 698; unskilled, inexpert; bungling &c. *v.*; awkward, clumsy, unhandy, lubberly, *gauche*, *maladroit*; left-, heavy-handed; slovenly, slatternly; gawky.

adrift, at fault.

in-, un-apt; inhabile; un-tractable, -teachable; giddy &c. (*inattentive*) 458; inconsiderate &c. (*neglectful*) 460; stupid &c. 499; inactive &c. 683; incompetent; un-, dis-, ill-qualified; unfit; quackish; raw, green, inexperienced, rusty, out of practice.

un-accustomed, -used, -trained &c. 537, -initiated, -conversant &c. (*ignorant*) 491; shiftless; unbusinesslike, unpractical; unstatesmanlike.

un-, ill-, mis-advised; ill-devised, -imagined, -judged, -contrived, -conducted; un-, mis-guided; misconducted, foolish, wild; infelicitous; penny wise and pound foolish &c. (*inconsistent*) 608.

**Phr.** one's fingers being all thumbs; the right hand forgets its cunning.

*il se noyerait dans une goutte d'eau.*

*incidit in Scyllam qui vult vitare Charybdim*; out of the frying pan into the fire.

**700. Proficient.**—**N.** proficient, expert, adept, dab; *connoisseur* &c. (*scholar*) 492; master, -hand; top-sawyer, *prima donna*, first fiddle, *cordon bleu*; protagonist; past master; profess-or, -ional, specialist.

picked man; medallist, prizeman.

veteran; old -stager, – campaigner, – soldier, – file, – hand; man of -business, – the world.

nice –, good –, clean- hand; practised –, experienced- -eye, – hand; marksman; good –, dead –, crack- shot; rope-dancer, funambulist, acrobat, contortionist; cunning man; conjuror &c. (*deceiver*) 548; wizard &c. 994.

genius; master-mind, – head, – spirit;

cunning –, sharp -blade, – fellow; jobber; cracksman &c. (*thief*) 792; politician, tactician, diplomat, -ist, strategist.

pantologist, admirable Crichton, Jack of all trades; prodigy of learning; walking encyclopædia; mine of information.

**701. Bungler.**—**N.** bungler; blunderer, -head; marplot, fumbler, lubber, lout, oaf, duffer, stick, clown; bad –, poor- -hand, – shot; butter-fingers.

no conjuror, flat, muff, slow coach, looby, lubber, swab; clod, yokel, hick, awkward squad, novice, greenhorn, jaywalker, *blanc-bec*.

land lubber; fresh water –, fair weather- sailor; horse-marine; fish out of water, ass in lion's skin, jackdaw in peacock's feathers; quack &c. (*deceiver*) 548; Lord of Misrule.

sloven, slattern, trapes.

**Phr.** *il n'a pas inventé la poudre*; he will never set the Thames on fire.

**702. Cunning.**—**N.** cunning, craft; cunningness, craftiness &c. *adj.*; subtlety, artificiality; manœuvring &c. *v.*; temporization; circumvention.

chicane, -ry; sharp practice, knavery, jugglery; concealment &c. 528; nigger in the woodpile; guile, duplicity &c. (*falsehood*) 544; foul play.

diplomacy, politics; Machiavellism; jobbery, back-stairs influence, gerrymandering.

art, -ifice; device, machination; plot &c. (*plan*) 626; manœuvre, stratagem, dodge, artful dodge, wile; trick, -ery &c. (*deception*) 545; *ruse*, – *de guerre*; *finesse*, side-blow, thin end of the wedge, shift, go by, subterfuge, evasion; white lie &c. (*untruth*) 546; juggle, *tour de force*; tricks -of the trade, – upon travellers; imposture, deception; *espièglerie*; net, trap &c. 545.

Ulysses, Machiavel, sly boots, fox,

**703. Artlessness.**—**N.** artlessness &c. *adj.*; nature, simplicity; innocence &c. 946; *bonhomie, naïveté, abandon*, candour, sincerity; singleness of -purpose, – heart; honesty &c. 939; plain speaking; *épanchement*.

rough diamond, matter of fact man; *le palais de vérité*; *enfant terrible*.

**V.** be -artless &c. *adj.*; look one in the face; wear one's heart upon his sleeve for daws to peck at; think aloud; speak -out, – one's mind; be free with one, call a spade a spade.

**Adj.** artless, natural, pure, native, simple, plain, inartificial, untutored, unsophisticated, *ingénue*, unaffected, *naïve*; sincere, frank; open, – as day; candid, ingenuous, guileless, unsuspicious, childlike; honest &c. 939; innocent &c. 946; Arcadian; undesigning, straightforward, unreserved, unvarnished, above-board; simple-, single-

reynard; Scotch-, Yorkshire-man; Jew, Greek, Yankee; intriguer, *intrigant*, schemer, trickster.

**V.** be -cunning &c. *adj.*; have cut one's eye-teeth; contrive &c. (*plan*) 626; live by one's wits; manœuvre; intrigue, gerrymander, *finesse*, double, temporize, stoop to conquer, *reculer pour mieux sauter*, circumvent, steal a march upon; overreach &c. 545; throw off one's guard; surprise &c. 508; outdo, get the better of, snatch from under one's nose; snatch a verdict; waylay, undermine, introduce the thin end of the wedge; play -a deep game, – tricks with; have an axe to grind; *spargere voces in vulgum ambiguas*; flatter, make things pleasant.

**Adj.** cunning, crafty, artful; skilful &c. 698; subtle, feline, vulpine; cunning as a -fox, – serpent; deep, – laid; profound; designing, contriving; intriguing &c. *v.*; strategic, diplomatic, politic, Machiavellian, time-serving; artificial; trick-y, -sy; wily, sly, slim, insidious, stealthy, foxy; underhand &c. (*hidden*) 528; subdolous; deceitful &c. 545; double-tongued, -faced; shifty; crooked; arch, pawky, shrewd, acute; sharp, – as a needle; canny, astute, leery, knowing, up to snuff, too clever by half, not to be caught with chaff.

**Adv.** cunningly &c. *adj.*; slily, on the sly, by a side wind.

**Phr.** diamond cut diamond.

minded; frank-, open-, single-, simple-hearted; open and above-board.

free-, plain-, out-spoken; blunt, downright, direct, matter of fact, unpoetical; unflattering.

**Adv.** in plain -words, – English; without mincing the matter; not to mince the matter &c. (*affirmation*) 535.

**Phr.** *Davus sum non Œdipus; liberavi animam meam.*

---

## Section IV. Antagonism

### 1°. *Conditional Antagonism*

**704. Difficulty.—N.** difficulty; hardness &c. *adj.*; impracticability &c. (*impossibility*) 471; tough –, hard –, uphill- work; hard –, Herculean –, Augean- task; task of Sisyphus, Sisyphean labour, tough job, teaser, rasper, dead lift.

dilemma, embarrassment; perplexity &c. (*uncertainty*) 475; involvement; intricacy; entanglement &c. 59; cross fire; awkwardness, delicacy, ticklish card to play, deadlock, knot, Gordian knot, *dignus vindice nodus*, net, meshes, maze; coil &c. (*convolution*) 248; crooked path.

nice –, delicate –, subtle –, knotty-point; vexed question, *vexata quæstio* poser; puzzle &c. (*riddle*) 533; paradox; hard –, nut to crack; bone to pick, *crux*, *pons asinorum*, where the shoe pinches.

nonplus, quandary, strait, pass, pinch, pretty pass, stress, brunt; criti-

**705. Facility. — N.** facility, ease; easiness &c. *adj.*; capability; feasibility &c. (*practicability*) 470; flexibility, pliancy &c. 324; smoothness &c. 255; convenience.

plain –, smooth –, straight- sailing; mere child's play, holiday task.

smooth water, fair wind; smooth – royal- road; clear -coast, – stage; *tabula rasa*; full play &c. (*freedom*) 748.

disen-cumbrance, -tanglement; deoppilation; permission &c. 760.

**V.** be -easy &c. *adj.*; go on –, run-smoothly; have -full play &c. *n.*; go –, run- on all fours; obey the helm, work well.

flow –, swim –, drift –, go- with the -stream, – tide; see one's way; have -it all one's own way, – the game in one's own hands; walk over the course, win -at a canter, – hands down; make -light of, – nothing of; be at home in &c. (*skilful*) 698.

cal situation, crisis; trial, rub, emergency, exigency, scramble.

scrape, hobble, slough, quagmire, hot water, hornet's nest; sea –, peck- of troubles; pretty kettle of fish; pickle, stew, *imbroglio*, mess, muddle, botch, fuss, bustle, ado; false position; set fast, stand; dead -lock, – set; fix, horns of a dilemma, *cul de sac*; hitch; stumbling block &c. (*hindrance*) 706.

**V.** be -difficult &c. *adj.*; run one hard, go against the grain, try one's patience, put one out; put to one's -shifts, – wit's end; go hard with –, try- one; pose, perplex &c. (*uncertain*) 475; bother, nonplus, gravel, bring to a dead lock; be -impossible &c. 471; be in the way of &c. (*hinder*) 706.

meet with –, labour under –, get into –, plunge into –, struggle with –, contend with –, grapple with- difficulties; labour under a disadvantage; be -in difficulty &c. *adj.*

fish in troubled waters, buffet the waves, swim against the stream, scud under bare poles.

have -much ado with, – a hard time of it; come to the -push, – pinch; bear the brunt.

grope in the dark, lose one's way, weave a tangled web, walk among eggs.

get into a -scrape &c. *n.*; bring a hornet's nest about one's ears; be put to one's shifts; flounder, boggle, struggle; not know which way to turn &c. (*uncertain*) 475; get -tangled up, – wound up; *perdre son latin*; stick - at, – in the mud, – fast; come to a -stand, – dead lock; hold the wolf by the ears.

render -difficult &c. *adj.*; encumber, embarrass, ravel, entangle; put a spoke in the wheel &c. (*hinder*) 706; lead a pretty dance.

**Adj.** difficult, not easy, hard, tough; trouble-, toil-, irk-some; operose, laborious, onerous, arduous, Herculean, formidable; sooner –, more easily- said than done; difficult –, hard- to deal with; ill-conditioned, crabbed; not -to be handled with kid gloves, – made with rosewater.

awkward, unwieldy, unmanageable; intractable, stubborn &c. (*obstinate*) 606; perverse, refractory, plaguy, trying, thorny, rugged; knot-ted, -ty; invious; path-, track-less; labyrinthine &c. (*convoluted*) 248; intricate, complicated &c. (*tangled*) 59; impracticable &c. (*impossible*) 471; not -feasible &c. 470; desperate &c. (*hopeless*) 859.

embarrassing, perplexing &c. (*uncertain*) 475; delicate, ticklish,

render -easy &c. *adj.*; facilitate, smooth, ease; popularize; lighten, – the labour; free, clear; dis-encumber, -embarrass, -entangle, -engage; deobstruct, unclog, extricate, unravel; untie –, cut- the knot; disburden, unload, exonerate, emancipate, free from, deoppilate; humour &c. (*aid*) 707; lubricate &c. 332; relieve &c. 834.

leave -a hole to creep out of, – a loophole, – the matter open; give -the reins to, – full play, – full swing; make way for; open the -door to, – way; prepare –, smooth –, clear- the -ground, – way, – path, – road; pave the way, bridge over; permit &c. 760.

**Adj.** easy, facile; feasible &c. (*practicable*) 470; easily -managed, – accomplished; within reach, accessible, easy of access, for the million, open to.

manageable, wieldy; towardly, tractable; submissive; yielding, ductile; pliant &c. (*soft*) 324; glib, slippery; smooth &c. 255; on -friction wheels, – velvet; convenient.

un-, dis-burdened, -encumbered, -embarrassed; exonerated; un-loaded, -obstructed, -trammelled, - impeded, -restrained &c. (*free*) 748; at ease, light.

at –, quite at- home; in -one's element, – smooth water.

**Adv.** easily &c. *adj.*; readily, smoothly, swimmingly, *ad lib.*, on easy terms, single-handed.

**Phr.** touch and go.

**Int.** all clear!

---

critical; beset with –, full of –, surrounded by –, entangled by –, encompassed with- difficulties.

under a difficulty; in -difficulty, – hot water, – the suds, – a cleft stick, – a fix, – the wrong box, – a scrape &c. *n.*, – deep water, – a fine pickle; *in extremis*; between -two stools, – Scylla and Charybdis; surrounded by -shoals, – breakers, – quicksands; at cross purposes; not out of the wood.

reduced to straits; hard –, sorely- pressed; run hard; pinched, put to it, straitened; hard -up, – put to it, – set; put to one's shifts; puzzled, at a loss &c. (*uncertain*) 475; at -the end of one's tether, – one's wit's end, – a nonplus, – a standstill; gravelled, nonplussed, stranded, aground; stuck –, set- fast; up a tree, at bay, *aux abois*, driven -into a corner, – from post to pillar, – to extremity, – to one's wit's end, – to the wall; *au bout de son latin*; out of one's -depth, – reckoning; put –, thrown -out.

accomplished with difficulty; hard-fought, -earned.

**Adv.** with -difficulty, – much ado; hardly &c. *adj.*; uphill; against the -stream, – grain; *à rebours*; *invitâ Minervâ*; in the teeth of; at –, upon- a pinch; at long odds.

**Phr.** ay there's the rub; *hic labor hoc opus*; things are come to a pretty pass.

## 2°. *Active Antagonism*

**706. Hindrance. — N.** prevention, preclusion, obstruction, stoppage; prohibition; inter-ruption, -ception, -clusion; hindrance, impedition; retardment, -ation; constriction; embarrassment. oppilation; coarctation, stricture, restriction; anchor &c. 666; restraint &c. 751 & 752; inhibition &c. 761; blockade &c. (*closure*) 261; picketing.

inter-ference, -position; obtrusion; dis-couragement, -countenance, -approval, -approbation; opposition &c. 708.

impediment, let, obstacle, obstruction, knot, knag; check, hitch, *contretemps*, *impasse*, screw loose, grit in the oil.

bar, stile, barrier; turn-stile, -pike; gate, portcullis; bulwark, parapet, barricade &c. (*defence*) 717; wall, dead wall, breakwater, groyne; bulkhead, block, buffer; stopper &c. 263; boom, dam, weir, burrock.

drawback, objection; stumbling-block, -stone; lion in the path; snag; snags and sawyers.

en-, in-cumbrance; clog, skid, shoe, spoke; brake, drag, – chain, – weight; stay, stop; preventive, prophylactic; contraception; load, burden, fardel,

**707. Aid.—N.** aid, -ance; assistance, help, opitulation, succour; support, lift, advance, furtherance, promotion; coadjuvancy &c. (*co-operation*) 709.

patronage, championship, countenance, favour, interest, advocacy, auspices.

sustentation, subvention, subsidy, bounty, alimentation, nutrition, nourishment, maintenance; manna in the wilderness; food &c. 298; means &c. 632.

ministr-y, -ation; subministration; accommodation.

relief, rescue; help at a dead lift; supernatural aid; *deus ex machinâ*.

supplies, reinforcements, succours, contingents, recruits; support &c. (*physical*) 215; adjunct, ally &c. (*helper*) 711.

**V.** aid, assist, help, succour, lend one's aid; come to the aid &c. *n.*- of; contribute, subscribe to; bring –, give –, furnish –, afford –, supply- -aid &c. *n.*; render assistance; give –, stretch –, lend –, bear –, hold out- a -hand, – helping hand; give one a -lift, – cast, – turn; take -by the hand, – in tow; help a lame dog over a stile, lend wings to.

*onus*, millstone round one's neck, *impedimenta*; dead weight; lumber, pack; nightmare, Ephialtes, incubus, old man of the sea; remora.

difficulty &c. 704; insuperable &c. 471- obstacle; estoppel; ill wind; head wind &c. (*opposition*) 708; trammel, tether &c. (*means of restraint*) 752; hold back, counterpoise; damper, wet blanket, hinderer, marplot, kill-joy, dog in the manger, interloper; trail of a red herring; opponent &c. 710.

V. hinder, impede, impedite, embarrass.

keep –, stave –, ward- off; picket; obviate; a-, ante-vert; turn aside, draw off, prevent, forefend, nip in the bud; retard, slacken, check, let; counter-act, -check; preclude, debar, foreclose, estop; inhibit &c. 761; shackle &c. (*restrain*) 751; restrict, restrain, cohibit.

obstruct, filibuster, stop, stay, bar, bolt, lock; block, – up; belay, barricade; block –, stop- the way; dam up &c. (*close*) 261; put on the -brake &c. *n.*; scotch –, lock –, put a spoke in- the wheel; put a stop to &c. 142; traverse, contravene; inter-rupt, -cept; oppose &c. 708; hedge -in, – round; cut off; interclude.

inter-pose, -fere, -meddle &c. 682.

cramp, hamper; clog, – the wheels; cumber; en-, in-cumber; handicap; choke; saddle –, load- with; over-load, -lay; lumber, trammel, tie one's hands, put to inconvenience; in-, discommode; discompose; hustle, drive into a corner; choke off.

run –, fall- foul of; cross the path of, break in upon.

thwart, frustrate, disconcert, balk, foil, baffle, snub, override, circumvent; defeat &c. 731; spike guns &c. (*render useless*) 645; spoil, mar, clip the wings of; cripple &c. (*injure*) 659; put an extinguisher on; damp; dishearten &c. (*dissuade*) 616; discountenance, throw cold water on, spoil sport; lay –, throw- a wet blanket on; cut the ground from under one, take the wind out of one's sails, undermine; be –, stand- in the way of; act as a drag; hang like a millstone round one's neck.

relieve, rescue; set -up, – agoing, – on one's legs; bear –, pull- through; give new life to, be the making of; reinforce, recruit; set –, put –, push- forward; give -a lift, – a shove, – an impulse- to; promote, further, forward, advance; speed, expedite, quicken, hasten.

support, sustain, uphold, prop, hold up, bolster.

cradle, nourish; nurture, nurse, dry nurse, suckle, put out to nurse; manure, cultivate, force; foster, cherish, foment; feed –, fan- the flame.

serve; do service to, tender to, pander to; ad-, sub-, minister to; tend, attend, wait on; take care of &c. 459; entertain; smooth the bed of death.

oblige, accommodate, consult the wishes of; humour, cheer, encourage.

second, stand by; back, – up; pay the piper, abet; work –, make interest –, stick up –, take up the cudgels- for; take up –, espouse –, adopt- the cause of; advocate, beat up for recruits, press into the service; squire, give moral support to, keep in countenance, countenance, patronize; lend -oneself, – one's countenance- to; smile –, shine- upon; favour, befriend, take up, take in hand, enlist under the banners of; side with &c. (*co-operate*) 709.

be of use to; subserve &c. (*instrument*) 631; benefit &c. 648; render a service &c. (*utility*) 644; conduce &c. (*tend*) 176.

Adj. aiding &c. *v.*; auxiliary, adjuvant, helpful; coadjuvant &c. 709; subservient, ministrant, ancillary, accessory, subsidiary.

at one's beck; friendly, amicable, favourable, propitious, well-disposed; neighbourly; obliging &c. (*benevolent*) 906.

**Adv.** with –, by- -the aid &c. *n.*- of; on –, in- behalf of; in -aid, – the service, – the name, – favour, – furtherance- of; on account of; for the sake of, on the part of; *non obstante*.

**Int.** help! save us! to the rescue! SOS! *à moi!*

---

**Adj.** hindering &c. *v.*; obstr-uctive, -uent; impedi-tive, -ent; intercipient; prophylactic &c. (*remedial*) 662.

in the way of, unfavourable; onerous, burdensome; cumb-rous, -ersome; obtrusive.

hindered &c. *v.*; wind-bound, water-logged, heavy laden; hard pressed.

unassisted &c. (*see* assist &c. 707); single-handed, alone; deserted &c. 624.

**708. Opposition.—N.** opposition, antagonism; oppug-nancy, -nation; impugnation; contravention; counteraction &c. 179; counterplot, obstacle.

cross-fire, under-current, head-wind.

clashing, collision, conflict, lack of harmony, contest.

competition, two of a trade, rivalry, emulation, race; war to the knife.

absence of -aid &c. 707; resistance &c. 719; restraint &c. 751; hindrance &c. 706.

**V.** oppose, counteract, run counter to; withstand &c. (*resist*) 719; control &c. (*restrain*) 751; hinder &c. 706; antagonize, oppugn, fly in the face of, go dead against, kick against, fall foul of; set –, pit- against; face, confront, cope with; make a -stand, – dead set- against; set -oneself, one's face- against; protest –, vote –, raise one's voice- against; disfavour, turn one's back upon; set at naught, slap in the face. slam the door in one's face.

be –, play- at cross purposes; counter-work, -mine; thwart, overthwart.

stem, breast, encounter; stem –, breast- the -tide, – current, – flood; buffet the waves; beat up –, make head- against; grapple with; kick against the pricks &c. (*resist*) 719; contend &c. 720 –, do battle &c. (*warfare*) 722- -with, – against.

contra-dict, -vene; belie; go –, run –, beat –, militate- against; come in conflict with.

emulate &c. (*compete*) 720; rival, spoil one's trade.

**Adj.** oppos-ing, -ed &c. *v.*; adverse, antagonistic; ambivalent; contrary &c. 14; at variance &c. 24; at issue, at war with; in opposition: 'agin the Government.'

un-favourable, -friendly; **hostile, inimical,** cross, unpropitious.

**709. Co-operation.—N.** co-operation; coadju-vancy, -tancy; coagency, coefficiency; concert, concurrence, complicity, participation; union &c. 43; amalgamation, combination &c. 48; collusion.

association, alliance, colleagueship, jointstock, copartnership, trust, cartel, pool, ring, combine, interlocking directorate; confederation &c. (*party*) 712; federation, coalition, fusion; a long pull, a strong pull and a pull all together; log-rolling, Freemasonry.

unanimity &c. (*assent*) 488; *esprit de corps*, party spirit; clan-, partisan-ship; reciprocity, concord &c. 714.

**V.** co-operate, co-adjute, concur; conduce &c. 178; combine, cartelize, unite one's efforts; keep –, draw –, pull –, club –, hang –, hold –, league –, band –, be banded- together; stand –, put- shoulder to shoulder; act in concert, join forces, fraternize, cling to one another, conspire, concert, lay one's heads together; confederate, be in league with; collude, understand one another, play into the hands of, hunt in couples.

side –, take side –, go along –, go hand in hand –, join hands –, make common cause –, strike in –, unite –, join –, mix oneself up – take part –, play along –, cast in one's lot- with; join –, enter into- partnership with; rally round, follow the lead of; come to, pass over to, come into the views of; be –, row –, sail- in the same boat; sail on the same tack.

be a party to, lend oneself to; participate; have a -hand in, – finger in the pie; take –, bear- part in; second &c. (*aid*) 707; take the part of, play the game of; espouse a -cause, – quarrel.

**Adj.** co-operating &c. *v.*; in -co-operation &c. *n.*, – league &c. (*party*) 712;

in hostile array, front to front, with crossed bayonets, at daggers drawn; up in arms; resistant &c. 719.

competitive, emulous.

**Adv.** against, *versus*, counter to, in conflict with, at cross purposes.

against the -grain, – current, – stream, – wind, – tide; with a head-wind; with the wind -ahead, – in one's teeth.

in spite, in despite, in defiance; in the -way, – teeth, – face- of; across; a-, over-thwart; where the shoe pinches.

though &c. 30; even; *quand même*; *per contra*.

**Phr.** *nitor in adversum*.

coadju-vant, -tant; hand and glove with.

favourable &c. 707- to; un-opposed &c. 708.

**Adv.** as one man &c. (*unanimously*) 488; shoulder to shoulder; in co-operation with.

---

**710. Opponent.—N.** opponent, antagonist, adversary; adverse party, opposition; enemy &c. 891; assailant.

oppositionist, obstructive; obscurantist; brawler, wrangler, brangler, disputant, extremist, irreconcilable, die-hard, bitter-ender.

malcontent; Jacobin, Fenian &c. 742; demagogue, reactionist.

passive resister, conscientious objector.

rival, competitor, contestant.

---

**711. Auxiliary.—N.** auxiliary; recruit; assistant; adju-vant, -tant; adjunct; help, -er, -mate, -ing hand; midwife; colleague, partner, mate, *confrère*, co-operator; coadju-tor, -trix; collaborator.

ally; friend &c. 890, confidant, *fidus Achates*, pal, chum, buddy, *alter ego*.

confederate; ac-, complice; accessory, – after the fact; *particeps criminis*.

*aide-de-camp*, secretary, clerk, associate, marshal; right-hand; candle-, bottle-holder; hand-maid; servant &c. 746; puppet, cat's-paw, stooge, dependent, creature, jackal; tool, *âme damnée*; satellite, adherent, parasite.

votary, disciple; secta-rian, -ry; seconder, backer, upholder, supporter, abettor, advocate, partisan, champion, patron, friend at court, mediator.

friend in need, Jack at a pinch, *deus ex machinâ*, guardian angel, fairy godmother; special providence, tutelary genius.

**712. Party.—N.** party, faction, side, denomination, class, communion, set, crowd, crew, band, horde, posse, phalanx; regiment &c. 726; family, clan &c. 166.

Tories, Conservatives, Unionists, Whigs, Liberals, Radicals, Labour party, Socialists, Communists &c.; Republicans, Democrats, Farmer-Labor; *Fascisti*, Revolutionaries &c. 742.

community, body, fellowship, sodality, solidarity; con-, fraternity; sorority; brother-, sister-hood.

Freemasons, Knights Templars, Odd Fellows, Ku Klux Klan, Rosicrucians; knot, gang, *clique*, ring, circle; *coterie*, club, *casino*.

corporation, corporate body, guild; establishment, company; co-partnership; firm, house; joint concern, joint-stock company, trust, investment trust, combine &c. 709.

society, association; instit-ute, -ution; union; trade-union; league, syndicate, alliance, *Verein*, *Bund*, *Zollverein*, combination; league –, alliance- offensive and defensive; coalition; federation; confedera -tion, -cy; junto, cabal, *camarilla*, *Camorra*, *brigue*; Freemasonry; party spirit &c. (*co-operation*) 709.

staff; cast, *dramatis personæ*.

V. unite, join; club together &c. (*co-operate*) 709; cement –, form- a party &c. *n.*; associate &c. (*assemble*) 72.

Adj. in -league, – partnership, – alliance &c. *n.*

bonded –, banded –, linked &c. (*joined*) 43- together; embattled; confederated, federative, joint, corporate, leagued, fraternal, Masonic, cliquish.

Adv. hand in hand, side by side, shoulder to shoulder, *en masse*, in the same boat.

**713. Discord.**—**N.** disagreement &c. 24; dis-cord, -accord, -sidence, -sonance; jar, clash, shock; jarring, jostling &c. *v.*; screw loose.

variance, difference, dissension, misunderstanding, cross purposes, odds, *brouillerie*; division, split, rupture, disruption, division in the camp, house divided against itself, rift within the lute; disunion, breach; schism &c. (*dissent*) 489; feud, faction.

quarrel, dispute, rippet, spat, tiff, *tracasserie*, squabble, altercation, words, high words; wrangling &c. *v.*; jangle, brabble, cross questions and crooked answers, snip-snap; family jars.

polemics; litigation; strife &c. (*contention*) 720; warfare &c. 722; outbreak, open rupture; breaking off of negotiations, recall of ambassadors; declaration of war.

broil, brawl, row, racket, hubbub, rixation; embroilment, embranglement, *imbroglio*, *fracas*, breach of the peace, piece of work, scrimmage, rumpus; breeze, squall; riot, disturbance &c. (*disorder*) 59; commotion &c. (*agitation*) 315; bear garden, Donnybrook Fair.

subject of dispute, ground of quarrel, battle ground, disputed point; bone -of contention, – to pick; apple of discord, *casus belli*; question at issue &c. (*subject of inquiry*) 461; vexed question, *vexata quæstio*, brand of discord.

troublous times; cat-and-dog life; contentiousness &c. *adj.*; enmity &c. 889; hate &c. 898; Kilkenny cats; disputant &c. 710; strange bedfellows.

V. be -discordant &c. *adj.*; disagree, come amiss &c. 24; clash, jar, jostle, pull different ways, conflict, have no measures with, misunderstand one another; live like cat and dog; differ; dissent &c. 489; have a -bone to pick, – crow to pluck- with.

fall out, quarrel, dispute; litigate; controvert &c. (*deny*) 536;

**714. Concord.**—**N.** concord, accord, harmony, symphony, homology; agreement &c. 23; sympathy &c. (*love*) 897; response; union, unison, unity; bonds of harmony; peace &c. 721; unanimity &c. (*assent*) 488; league &c. 712; happy family.

*rapprochement*; *réunion*; amity &c. (*friendship*) 888; reciprocity; alliance, *entente cordiale*, good understanding, conciliation, arbitration, peacemaker &c. 724.

V. agree &c. 23; accord, harmonize with; fraternize; be -concordant &c. *adj.*; go hand in hand; blend –, tone in- with; run parallel &c. (*concur*) 178; understand one another; pull together &c. (*co-operate*) 709; put up one's horses together, sing in chorus.

side –, sympathize –, go –, chime in –, fall in- with; come round; be pacified &c. 723; assent &c. 488; enter into the -ideas, – feelings- of; reciprocate.

*hurler avec les loups*; go –, swim- with the stream.

pour oil on troubled waters, keep in good humour, render accordant, put in tune; come to an understanding, meet half-way; keep the –, remain at- peace.

Adj. concordant, congenial; agreeing &c. *v.*; in- accord &c. *n.*; harmonious, united, cemented; banded together &c. 712; allied; friendly &c. 888; fraternal; conciliatory; at one with; of one mind &c. (*assent*) 488.

at peace, in still water; tranquil &c. (*pacific*) 721.

Adv. with one voice &c. (*assent*) 488; in concert with, hand in hand; on one's side, unanimously.

squabble, wrangle, jangle, brangle, bicker, nag; spar &c. (*contend*) 720; have -words &c. *n.* with; fall foul of.

split; break –, break squares –, part company- with; declare war, try conclusions; join –, put in- issue; pick a quarrel, fasten a quarrel on; sow –, stir up- -dissension &c. *n.*; embroil, estrange, entangle, disunite, widen the breach; set -at odds, – together by the ears; set –, pit- against; rub up the wrong way.

get into hot water, fish in troubled waters, brawl; kick up a -row. – dust; turn the house out of window.

**Adj.** discordant; disagreeing &c. *v.*; out of tune, dissonant, inharmonious, harsh, grating, jangling, ajar, on bad terms; dissentient &c. 489; inconsistent, contradictory, incongruous, discrepant; un- -reconciled, -pacified.

quarrelsome, unpacific; gladiatorial, controversial, polemic, disputatious; factious; liti-gious, -gant; pettifogging.

at odds, at loggerheads, at daggers drawn, at variance, at issue, at cross purposes, at sixes and sevens, at feud, at high words; up in arms, together by the ears, in hot water, embroiled.

torn, disunited.

**Phr.** *quot homines tot sententiæ*; no love lost between them, *non nostrum tantas componere lites.*

**715. Defiance.—N.** defiance; daring &c. *v.*; dare, challenge, *cartel*; threat &c. 909; war-cry, -whoop.

**V.** defy, dare, beard; brave &c. (*courage*) 861; bid defiance to; set at -defiance, – naught; hurl defiance at; dance the war dance; snap the fingers at, laugh to scorn; disobey &c. 742.

show -fight, – one's teeth, – a bold front; bluster, look big, stand akimbo; double –, shake- the fist; threaten &c. 909.

challenge, call out; throw –, fling- down the -gauntlet, – gage, – glove.

**Adj.** defiant; defying &c. *v.*; with arms akimbo; rebellious, insolent; reckless, greatly daring.

**Adv.** in -defiance, – the teeth- of; under one's very nose.

**Int.** do your worst! come if you dare! come on! marry come up! hoity toity!

**Phr.** *noli me tangere*; *nemo me impune lacessit.*

**716. Attack.—N.** attack; assault, – and battery; onset, onslaught, charge.

aggression, drive, offence; incursion, inroad, invasion; irruption; outbreak; *estrapade, ruade*; *coup de main*, sally, *sortie*, *camisade*, raid, foray; run -at, – against; dead set at.

storm, -ing; boarding, *escalade*; siege, investment, obsession, bombardment, cannonade; air raid.

fire, volley; platoon –, file –, rapid- fire; *fusillade*; sharp-shooting, sniping; broadside; raking –, cross –, machine gun- fire; volley of grapeshot, *feu d'enfer*; salvo.

cut, thrust, lunge, pass, *passado*, *carte* and *tierce*, home thrust; *coup de pied*; kick, punch &c. (*impulse*) 276.

**717. Defence.—N.** defence, protection. guard, ward; shielding &c. *v.*; propugnation; preservation &c. 670; guardianship.

self-defence, -preservation; resistance &c. 719.

safeguard &c. (*safety*) 664; screen &c. (*shelter*) 666, (*concealment*) 530; barrage; fortification; muni-tion, -ment; bulwark, fosse, moat, ditch, intrenchment, trench, dugout, gas mask; dike, dyke; parapet, parados, sunk fence, embankment, mound, mole, bank; earth- field-work, gabions; fence, wall, dead wall, contravallation; paling &c. (*inclosure*) 232; palisade, ha-ha, stockade, *stoccado*, *laager*, *sangar*; barri-er, -cade; boom; portcullis, *chevaux de*

*battue, razzia, Jacquerie, dragonnade*; devastation &c. 162.

assailant, aggressor, invader.

base of operations, point of attack.

**V.** attack, assault, assail; set –, fall- upon; charge, impugn, break a lance with, enter the lists.

assume –, take- the offensive; be –, become- the aggressor; strike the first blow, fire the first shot, throw the first stone at; lift a hand –, draw the sword- against; take up the cudgels; advance –, march- against; march upon, invade, harry; come on, show fight.

strike at, poke at, thrust at; aim –, deal- a blow at; give –, fetch- one a -blow, – kick; have a -cut, – shot, – fling, – shy- at; be down –, pounce- upon; fall foul of, pitch into, launch out against· bait, slap on the face; make a -thrust, – pass, – set, – dead set- at; dunt; bear down upon.

close with, come to close quarters, bring to bay.

ride full tilt against; let fly at, dash at, run a tilt at, rush at. tilt at, run at, fly at, hawk at, have at, let out at; make a -dash, – rush at; attack tooth and nail; strike home; drive –, press- one hard; be hard upon, run down, strike at the root of.

lay about one, run amuck.

fire -upon, – at, – a shot at; shoot at, pop at, level at, let off a gun at; open fire, pepper, bombard, shell, pour a broadside into; fire -a volley, – red-hot shot; spring a mine.

throw -a stone, – stones- at; stone, lapidate, pelt; hurl -at, – against, – at the head of.

beset, besiege, beleaguer; lay siege to, invest, open the trenches, plant a battery, sap, mine; storm, board, scale the walls.

cut and thrust, bayonet, butt; kick, strike &c. (*impulse*) 276; whip &c. (*punish*) 972.

**Adj.** attacking &c. *v.*; aggressive, offensive, obsidional.

up in arms; on the warpath; over the top.

**Adv.** on the offensive.

**Int.** 'up and at them!'

---

*frise*; aba-, abat-, abba-tis; *vallum*, circumvallation, battlement, rampart, scarp; e-, counter-scarp; glacis, casemate, obstacle.

mine, countermine.

buttress, abutment; shore &c. (*support*) 215.

breastwork, *banquette*, curtain, mantlet, bastion, demilune, redan, ravelin; advanced –, horn –, out- work, lunette; barb-acan, -ican; redoubt; fort-elage, -alice; lines; coast defence.

loop-hole, machicolation; sally-port, postern gate.

hold, stronghold, fastness; asylum &c. (*refuge*) 666; keep, donjon, fortress, citadel; capitol, castle; tower, – of strength; fort, barracoon, pah, sconce, martello tower, peel-house, block-house, rath; wooden walls; turret, barbette.

buffer, corner-stone, fender, apron, mask, gauntlet, thimble, carapace, armour, shield, buckler; target, targe, ægis, breastplate, cuirass, plastron, habergeon, mail, coat of mail, brigandine, hauberk, lorication, helmet, helm, basinet, sallet, salade, heaume, morion, murrion, armet, cabaset, vizor, casquetel, siege-cap, head-piece, casque, steel helmet, tin hat; *Pickelhaube*, csako; shako &c. (*dress*) 225; bearskin; panoply; truncheon &c. (*weapon*) 727.

garrison, picket, piquet; defender, protector; guardian &c. (*safety*) 664; trabant, body guard, champion; knight-errant, Paladin; propugner.

**V.** defend, forfend, fend; shield, screen, shroud; fence round &c. (*circumscribe*) 229; fence, intrench; guard &c. (*keep safe*) 664; guard against; take care of &c. (*vigilance*) 459; bear harmless; keep –, ward –, beat- off; hinder &c. 706.

parry, repel, propugn, put to flight; give a warm reception to [*ironical*]; hold –, keep- at -bay, – arm's length.

stand –, act- on the defensive; show fight; maintain –, stand- one's ground; stand by; hold one's own; bear –, stand- the brunt; fall back upon, hold, stand in the gap.

**Adj.** defending &c. *v.*; defensive; mural; armed, – at all points, – *cap-à-pie*, – to the teeth; panoplied, accoutred, harnessed; iron-plated, -clad; loop-holed, castellated, machicolated, casemated; defended &c. *v.*; proof against, bomb-, bullet-proof; protective.

**Adv.** defensively; on the -defence, – defensive; in defence; at bay, *pro aris et focis.*

**Int.** no surrender! *ils ne passeront pas!*

**Phr.** defence not defiance.

**718. Retaliation.** — **N.** retaliation, reprisal, retort; counter-stroke, -blast, -plot, -project; retribution, *lex talionis*; reciprocation &c. (*reciprocity*) 12.

requital, desert, tit for tat, give and take, blow for blow, *quid pro quo*, a Roland for an Oliver, measure for measure, an eye for an eye, diamond cut diamond, the biter bit, a game at which two can play; boomerang.

recrimination &c. (*accusation*) 938; revenge &c. 919; compensation &c. 30; reaction &c. (*recoil*) 277.

**V.** retaliate, retort, turn upon; pay -off, – back; pay in -one's own, – the same- coin; cap; reciprocate &c. 148; turn the tables upon, return the compliment; give -a *quid pro quo* &c. *n.*, – as much as one takes; give and take, exchange -blows, – fisticuffs; be -quits, – even- with; pay off old scores.

serve one right, be hoist on one's own petard, throw a stone in one's own garden, catch a Tartar.

**Adj.** retaliating &c. *v.*; retalia-tory, -tive; retributive, recriminatory, reciprocal.

**Adv.** in retaliation; *en revanche.*

**Phr.** *mutato nomine de te fabula narratur*; *par pari refero*; *tu quoque*; you're another; *suo sibi gladio hunc jugulo.*

---

**719. Resistance.** — **N.** resistance, stand, front, oppugnation; opposition &c. 708; renitence, reluctation, recalcitration, recalcitrance; repugnance; kicking &c. *v.*

repulse, rebuff.

insurrection &c. (*disobedience*) 742; strike; turn –, lock –, barring- out; *levée en masse*, *Jacquerie*; riot &c. (*disorder*) 59.

**V.** resist; not -submit &c. 725; repugn, reluctate, withstand; stand up –, strive –, bear up –, be proof –, make head- against; stand, – firm, – one's ground, – the brunt of, – out; hold -one's ground, – one's own, – out.

breast the -wave, – current; stem the -tide, – torrent; face, confront, grapple with; show a bold front &c. (*courage*) 861; present a front; make a –, take one's- stand.

kick, – against; recalcitrate, kick against the pricks; oppose &c. 708; fly in the face of; lift the hand against &c. (*attack*) 716; rise up in arms &c. (*war*) 722; strike, turn out; draw up a round robin &c. (*remonstrate*) 932; revolt &c. (*disobey*) 742; make a riot.

*prendre le mors aux dents*; take the bit between the teeth; sell one's life dearly, die hard, keep at bay; repel repulse.

**Adj.** resisting &c. *v.*; resist-ive, -ant; refractory &c. (*disobedient*) 742; recalcitrant, re-nitent, -pulsive, -pellant; up in arms.

proof against; unconquerable &c. (*strong*) 159; stubborn, unconquered; indomitable &c. (*persevering*) 604*a*; unyielding &c. (*obstinate*) 606.

**Int.** hands off! keep off!

**720. Contention.** — **N.** contention, strife; contest, -ation; struggle; belligerency; opposition &c. 708.

controversy, polemics; debate &c. (*discussion*) 476; war of words, logomachy, litigation; paper war, ink slinging; high words &c. (*quarrel*) 713; sparring &c. *v.*

**721. Peace.**—**N.** peace; amity &c. (*friendship*) 888; harmony &c. (*concord*) 714; tranquillity &c. (*quiescence*) 265; truce &c. (*pacification*) 723; pacificism; pipe –, calumet- of peace.

piping time of peace, quiet life; neutrality.

**V.** be at peace; keep the peace &c.

competition, rivalry; corrival-ry, -ship; agonism, *concours*, match, race, horse-racing, heat, steeple chase, point-to-point race, handicap; boat race, regatta; field-day; sham fight, Derby day; turf, sporting, bull-fight, tauromachy, *gymkhana*, rodeo, Olympiad.

wrestling, *ju-jitsu*, pugilism, boxing, fisticuffs, spar, mill, set-to, scrap, round, bout, event; prize-fighting; quarter-staff, single stick; gladiatorship, gymnastics; athletic-s. - sports; games of skill &c. 840.

shindy; *fracas* &c. (*discord*) 713; clash of arms; tussle, scuffle, broil, fray; affray, -ment; velitation; col-, luctation; brabble, *brigue*, scramble, *mêlée*, scrimmage, stramash, bush-fighting.

free –, stand up –, hand to hand –, running- fight.

conflict, skirmish; ren-, en-counter; *rencontre*, collision, affair, brush, fight; battle, – royal; combat, action, engagement, joust, tournament; tilt, -ing; tourney, list; pitched battle, guerilla warfare.

death-struggle, struggle for life or death, Armageddon; hard knocks, sharp contest, tug of war.

naval -engagement, – battle; *naumachia*, sea-fight.

duel, -lo; single combat, monomachy, satisfaction, *passage d'armes*, passage of arms, affair of honour; triangular duel; hostile meeting, digladiation; appeal to arms &c. (*warfare*) 722.

deeds –, feats- of arms; pugnacity; combativeness &c. *adj.*; bone of contention &c. 713.

**V.** contend; contest, strive, struggle, scramble, wrestle; spar, square; exchange -blows, – fisticuffs; scrap, mix with, fib, justle, tussle, tilt, box, stave, fence; skirmish; fight &c. (*war*) 722; wrangle &c. (*quarrel*) 713.

contend &c. –, grapple –, engage –, close –, buckle –, bandy –, try conclusions –, have a brush &c. *n.* –, tilt- with; encounter, fall foul of, pitch into, clapperclaw, run a tilt at; oppose &c. 708; reluct.

join issue, come to blows, be at loggerheads, set-to, come to the scratch, exchange shots, measure swords, meet hand to hand; take up the -cudgels, – glove, – gauntlet; enter the lists; couch one's lance; give satisfaction; appeal to arms &c. (*warfare*) 722.

lay about one; break the peace.

compete –, cope –, vie –, race- with; outvie, emulate, rival; run a race; contend &c. –, stipulate –, stickle- for; insist upon, make a point of.

**Adj.** contending &c. *v.*; together by the ears, at loggerheads, at war, at issue.

competitive, rival; belligerent; contentious, combative, bellicose, unpeaceful; warlike &c. 722; quarrelsome &c. 901; pugnacious; pugilistic, gladiatorial; palestric, -al; irenic.

**Phr.** *a verbis ad verbera*; a word and a blow

(*concord*) 714; make peace &c. 723.

**Adj.** pacific; peace-able, -ful; calm, tranquil, untroubled, halcyon; bloodless; neutral.

**Phr.** the storm blown over; the lion lies down with the lamb.

---

**722. Warfare.—N.** warfare; fighting &c. *v.*; hostilities; war, arms, the sword; Mars, Bellona, grim visaged war, *horrida bella*, Armageddon.

appeal to -arms, – the sword; ordeal

**723. Pacification.—N.** pacification, conciliation; reconcil-iation, -ement; shaking of hands, accommodation, arrangement, adjustment; terms, compromise; amnesty, deed of release.

–, wager- of battle; *ultima ratio regum,* arbitrament of the sword.

battle array, campaign, crusade, expedition; mobilization; state of siege; battle-field &c. (*arena*) 728; warpath.

art of war, tactics, strategy, castrametation; general-, soldier-ship; aerial –, submarine –, naval –, chemical- warfare; military evolutions, ballistics, gunnery; chivalry; poison gas; gunpowder, shot, – and shell.

battle, tug of war &c. (*contention*) 720; service, campaigning, active service, tented field; fiery cross, trumpet, clarion, bugle, pibroch, slogan; war-cry, -whoop; battle cry, beat of drum, rappel, tom-tom; word of command; pass-, watch-word.

war to the -death, – knife; *guerre à -mort, – outrance*; open –, internecine –, civil- war.

**V.** arm; raise –, mobilize- troops; rise up in arms; take up the cudgels &c. 720; take up –, fly to –, appeal to- -arms, – the sword; draw –, unsheathe- the sword; dig up the hatchet; go to –, declare –, wage –, let slip the dogs of- war; cry havoc; kindle –, light- the torch of war; raise one's banner, send round the fiery cross; hoist the black flag; throw –, fling- away the scabbard; enrol, enlist, join up; take the field; take the law into one's own hands; do –, give –, join –, engage in –, go to- battle; flesh one's sword; set to, fall to, engage, measure swords with, draw the trigger, cross swords; come to -blows, – close quarters; fight; combat; contend &c. 720; battle –, break a lance- with.

serve; see –, be on- -service, – active service; campaign; wield the sword, shoulder a musket, smell powder, be under the fire; spill –, imbrue the hands in- blood; be on the warpath.

carry on -war, – hostilities; keep the field; fight the good fight; go over the top; cut one's way through; fight -it out, – like devils, – one's way, – hand to hand; sell one's life dearly.

**Adj.** conten-ding, -tious &c. 720; armed, – to the teeth, – cap-à-pie; sword in hand; in –, under –, up in- arms; at war with; bristling with arms; in -battle array, – open arms, – the field; embattled.

unpacific, unpeaceful; belligerent, combative, armigerous, bellicose, martial, warlike; mili-tary, -tant; soldier-like, -ly; chivalrous; strategical, internecine.

**Adv.** *flagrante bello,* in the -thick of the fray, – cannon's mouth; at the -sword's point, – point of the bayonet.

**Int.** *væ victis!* to arms! to your tents O Israel!

**Phr.** the battle rages

peace-offering; olive-branch; overtures; pipe –, calumet –, preliminaries- of peace.

truce, armistice; suspension of -arms, – hostilities; breathing-time; convention; *modus vivendi*; flag of truce, white flag, *parlementaire, cartel.*

hollow truce, *pax in bello*; drawn battle.

**V.** pacify, tranquillize, compose; allay &c. (*moderate*) 174; reconcile, propitiate, placate, conciliate, meet half way, hold out the olive-branch, heal the breach, make peace, restore harmony, bring to terms.

settle –, arrange –, accommodate- -matters, – differences; set straight; make up a quarrel, *tantas componere lites*; come to -an understanding, – terms; bridge over, hush up; make -it, – matters- up; shake hands.

raise a siege; put up –, sheathe- the sword; bury the hatchet, lay down one's arms, turn swords into ploughshares; smoke the calumet of peace, close the temple of Janus; keep the peace &c. (*concord*) 714; be -pacified &c.; come round.

**Adj.** conciliatory, pacificatory; composing &c. *v.*; pacified &c. *v.*

**Phr.** *requiescat in pace.*

---

**724. Mediation.—N.** media-tion, -torship, -tization; inter-vention, -position, -ference, -meddling, -cession; parley, negotiation, arbitration; flag of truce &c. 723; good offices, peace-offering; diploma-tics, -cy; compromise &c. 774.

mediator, intercessor, peacemaker, make-peace, negotiator, go-between; diplomatist &c. (*consignee*) 758; moderator, propitiator, umpire, arbitrator.

**V.** media-te, -tize; inter-cede, -pose, -fere, -vene; step in, negotiate; meet half-way; arbitrate; *magnas componere lites.*

**Adj.** mediatory, propitiatory, diplomatic.

**725. Submission.—N.** submission, yielding, acquiescence, compliance; non-resistance; obedience &c. 743; submissiveness, deference.

surrender, cession, capitulation, resignation.

obeisance, homage, kneeling, genuflexion, courtesy, curtsy, *salaam*, *kowtow*, prostration.

**V.** succumb, submit, yield, bend, resign, defer to, accede.

lay down –, deliver up- one's arms; hand over one's sword; lower –, haul down –, strike- one's flag, – colours; deliver the keys of the city;

surrender, – at discretion; cede, capitulate, come to terms, retreat, beat a retreat; draw in one's horns &c. (*humility*) 879; give -way, – ground, – in, – up; cave in; suffer judgment by default; bend, – to one's yoke, – before the storm; reel back; bend –, knuckle- -down, – to, – under; knock under.

humble oneself; eat -dirt, – the leek, – humble pie; bite –, lick- the dust; be –, fall- at one's feet; craven; crouch before, throw oneself at the feet of; swallow the -leek, – pill; kiss the rod; turn the other cheek; *avaler des couleuvres*, gulp down.

obey &c. 743; kneel to, bow to, pay homage to, cringe to, truckle to; bend the -neck, – knee; kneel, fall on one's knees, bow submission, courtesy, curtsy, *kowtow*; make obeisance.

pocket the affront; make -the best of, – a virtue of necessity; grin and abide, shrug the shoulders, resign oneself; submit with a good grace &c. (*bear with*) 826.

**Adj.** surrendering &c. *v.*; submissive, resigned, crouching; down-trodden; down on one's marrow bones; on one's bended knee; weak-kneed, un-, non-resisting; pliant &c. (*soft*) 324; undefended.

untenable, indefensible; humble &c. 879.

**Phr.** have it your own way; it can't be helped; amen &c. (*assent*) 488.

**726. Combatant.—N.** combatant; disputant, controversialist, polemic, litigant, belligerent; competitor, rival, corrival; fighter, assailant, aggressor; champion, Paladin; moss-trooper, swashbuckler, fire-eater, duellist, bully, bludgeon-man, rough, fighter, fighting-man, prize-fighter, pugilist, pug, boxer, bruiser, the fancy, gladiator, athlete, wrestler; fighting-, game-cock; swordsman, *sabreur*.

warrior, soldier, Amazon, man-at-arms, armigerent; campaigner, veteran; red-coat, military man, *rajpoot*, brave.

armed force, troops, soldiery, military, forces, sabaoth, the army, standing army, regulars, the line, troops of the line, militia, territorials, yeomanry, volunteers, trainband, fencible; auxiliary –, reserve- forces; reserves, *posse comitatus*, national guard, *gendarme*, beefeater; guards, -man; yeoman of the guard, life guards, household troops.

janissary; myrmidon; Mama-, Mame-luke; spahee, *spahi*, Cossack,

Croat, Pandour; irregular, free lance, *franc-tireur*, *bashi-bazouk*, *guerilla*, *condottiere*; mercenary.

levy, draught, commando; *Land-wehr*, *-sturm*; conscript, recruit, rookie, cadet, raw levies.

private, – soldier; Tommy Atkins, rank and file, peon, trooper, doughboy, sepoy, *askari*, *légionnaire*, legionary, food for powder, cannon fodder; officer &c. (*commander*) 745; subaltern, ensign, shave-tail, standard bearer, non-com; spear-, pike-man; halberdier, lancer; musketeer, carabineer, rifleman, sharpshooter, yager, skirmisher; grenadier, fusileer; archer, bowman.

horse and foot; horse –, foot- soldier; cavalry, horse, artillery, horse –, field –, heavy –, mountain- artillery, infantry, light horse, *voltigeur*, *Uhlan*, mounted rifles, dragoon, hussar, trooper; light –, heavy- dragoon; heavy; *cuirassier*; gunner, cannoneer, bombardier, artilleryman, matross; sapper, – and miner; engineer; light infantry, rifles, *chasseur*, *zouave*; military train, supply and transport, coolie.

army, – corps, *corps d'armée*, host, division, column, wing, detachment, *escadrille*, garrison, flying column, brigade, regiment, *corps*, battalion, squadron, company, platoon, battery, subdivision, section, squad; piquet, picket, guard, rank, file; legion, phalanx, cohort; cloud of skirmishers; impi.

war-horse, charger, *destrier*.

armoured -train, – car; tank.

marine, man of war's man &c. (*sailor*) 269; navy, first line of defence, wooden walls; naval forces, fleet, flotilla, armada, squadron.

man-of-war, warship; H.M.S., U.S.S.; capital ship; line-of-battle ship, battle ship; super-, dreadnought, battle –, armoured –, protected – light- cruiser; scout, flotilla leader; destroyer, torpedo boat; submarine, submersible, U-boat; submarine chaser, eagle boat, mystery ship, Q-boat; mine-layer, -sweeper; ship of the line, iron-clad, turret-ship, ram, Monitor, floating battery; first-rate, frigate, sloop of war, corvette, gunboat, bomb-vessel, fire-boat; flag ship, guard ship, cruiser; aircraft carrier; privateer; tender; depot –, parent- ship; store –, troop- ship; transport, catamaran.

aircraft &c. 273, air force, scout, fighter, bomber, troop carrier, aerial patrol, seaplane, flying boat, torpedo plane; airship, Zeppelin; rigid –, semi-rigid –, non-rigid- airship; dirigible –, free –, captive –, kite –, observation- balloon.

anti-aircraft guns, searchlights, sound locators; catapult.

**727. Arms.**—**N.** arm, -s; weapon, deadly weapon; arma-ment, -ture; panoply, stand of arms; armour &c. (*defence*) 717; armoury &c. (*store*) 636.

ammunition; powder, – and shot; explosive; propellant; gun-powder, -cotton; dynam-, melin-, cord-, lydd-ite; trinitrotoluene, T.N.T., ammonal; cartridge; ball cartridge, *cartouche*, fire-ball; dud, black Maria; 'villainous saltpetre'; poison –, mustard –, lachrymatory –, tear- gas.

sword, sabre, broadsword, cutlass, falchion, scimitar, cimeter, brand, whinyard, bilbo, glaive, glave, rapier, skean, Toledo, Ferrara, tuck, claymore, creese, kris, *kukri*, dagger, dirk, hanger, poniard, stiletto, stylet, dudgeon, bayonet; sword-bayonet, -stick; side arms, foil, blade, steel; axe, bill; pole-, battle-axe; gisarm, halberd, partisan, tomahawk, bowie-knife; at-, att-, yat-aghan; yatachan; good –, trusty –, naked-sword; cold –, naked- steel.

club, mace, truncheon, staff, bludgeon, cudgel, life-preserver, shillelagh, sprig; hand-, quarter-staff; bat, cane, stick, knuckle-duster, sand bag.

gun, piece; fire-arms; artillery, ordnance; siege –, battering-train; park, battery; cannon, gun of position, heavy –, siege –, field –, mountain –, anti-aircraft –, breech loading –, quick firing- gun; field piece, mortar, trench mortar, mine thrower, howitzer, carronade, culverin, basilisk; falconet, jingal, swivel, *pederero, bouche à feu*; smooth bore, rifled cannon; Armstrong –, Lancaster –, Paixhan –, Whitworth –, Parrott –, Krupp –, Gatling –, Maxim –, Vickers –, Hotchkiss –, Lewis –, machine- gun; tommy gun, Thompson submachine gun; *mitrailleu-r, -se*; pom-pom; blow pipe.

small arms; musket, -ry, firelock, flintlock, fowling-piece, shot gun, rifle, *fusil*, caliver, carbine, blunderbuss, musketoon, Brown Bess, matchlock, harquebuss, *arquebuse*, haguebut; petronel; smallbore; breech-, muzzle-loader; Minié –, Enfield –, Westley Richards –, Snider –, Springfield –, Martini-Henry –, Lee-Metford –, Lee-Enfield –, Mauser –, Männlicher –, magazine –, repeating- rifle; needle-gun, *chassepot*; pistol, -et; revolver, automatic pistol, automatic; wind-, air-gun; flame –, gas-projector.

bow, cross-bow, arbalest, balister, catapult, sling; battering-ram &c. (*impulse*) 276; gunnery; ballistics &c. (*propulsion*) 284.

missile, bolt, projectile, shot, pellet, ball; grape; grape –, canister –, bar –, cannon –, langrel –, langrage –, round –, chain- shot; explosive; incendiary –, expanding –, soft-nosed –, dum-dum- bullet; slug, stone, brickbat; hand –, rifle- grenade; high explosive –, incendiary –, star –, gas- shell; depth –, gas –, incendiary –, stink- bomb; petard, torpedo, carcass, rocket; congreve, – rocket; shrapnel, *mitraille*; thunderbolt; mine, land mine, infernal machine.

pike, lance, spear, spontoon, javelin, assagai, throwing stick, dart, djerrid, arrow, reed, shaft, bolt, boomerang, harpoon, gaff.

**728. Arena.—N.** arena, field, platform; scene of action, theatre; walk, course; hustings; stage, boards &c. (*playhouse*) 599; amphitheatre; Coli-, Colos-seum; Flavian amphitheatre, hippodrome, circus, race-course, track, *stadium, corso*, turf, cockpit, bear-garden, playground, playing fields, *gymnasium, palæstra*, ring, lists; tilt-yard, -ing ground; *Campus Martius, Champ de Mars*; aerodrome, airport, air base, flying field.

theatre –, seat- of war; battle-field, -ground; field of -battle, – slaughter; no man's land; Aceldama, camp; the enemy's camp; trysting-place &c. (*place of meeting*) 74.

## Section V. Results of Voluntary Action

**729. Completion.—N.** completion; accomplish-, achieve-, fulfil-ment; performance, execution; des-, dis-patch; consummation, culmination, climax; finish, conclusion, effectuation; close &c. (*end*) 67; terminus &c. (*arrival*) 292; winding up; *finale, dénouement*, catastrophe, issue, upshot, result; final –, last –, crowning –, finishing- -touch, – stroke; last finish, *coup de grâce*;

**730. Non-Completion.—N.** non-completion, -fulfilment; shortcoming &c. 304; incompleteness &c. 53; drawn -battle, – game; work of Penelope, task of Sisyphus.

non-performance, inexecution; neglect &c. 460.

**V.** not -complete &c. 729; leave -unfinished &c. *adj.*, – undone; neglect &c. 460; let -alone, – slip; lose sight of,

crowning of the edifice; coping-, keystone; missing link &c. 53; superstructure, *ne plus ultra*, work done, *fait accompli*.

elaboration; finality; completeness &c. 52.

**V.** effect, -uate; accomplish, achieve, compass, consummate, hammer out; bring to -maturity, – perfection; perfect, complete; elaborate.

do, execute, make; go –, get- through; work out, enact; bring -about, – to bear, – to pass, – through, – to a head.

des-, dis-patch; knock –, finish –, polish- off; make short work of; dispose of, set at rest; perform, discharge, fulfil, realize; put in -practice, – force; carry -out, – into effect, – into execution; make good; be as good as one's word.

do thoroughly, not do by halves, go the whole hog; drive home; be in at the death &c. (*persevere*) 604*a*; carry through, play out, exhaust, deliver the goods, fill the bill.

finish, bring to a close &c. (*end*) 67; wind up, stamp, clinch, seal, set the seal on, put the seal to; give the -final touch &c. *n.* to; put the -last, – finishing- hand to; crown, – all; cap.

ripen, culminate; come to a -head, – crisis; come to its end; die -a natural death, – of old age; run -its course, – one's race; touch –, reach –, attain- the goal; reach &c. (*arrive*) 292; get in the harvest.

**Adj.** completing, final; conclu-ding, -sive; crowning &c. *v.*; exhaustive, complete, mature, perfect, consummate.

done, completed &c. *v.*; done for, sped, wrought out; highly wrought &c. (*preparation*) 673; thorough &c. 52; ripe &c. (*ready*) 673.

**Adv.** completely &c. (*thoroughly*) 52; to crown all, out of hand.

**Phr.** the race is run; *actum est*; *finis coronat opus*; *consummatum est*; *c'en est fait*; it is all over; the game is played out, the bubble has burst.

fall short of &c. 304; do things by halves; scotch the snake, not kill it; hang fire; be slow to; collapse &c. 304.

**Adj.** not completed &c. *v.*; incomplete &c. 53; uncompleted, unfinished, unaccomplished, unperformed, unexecuted; sketchy, addle.

in progress, in hand; going on, proceeding; on one's hands; on the fire; on the stocks; in preparation; lacking the finishing touch.

**Adv.** *re infectâ*.

---

**731. Success.—N.** success, -fulness; speed; advance &c. (*progress*) 282.

trump card; hit, stroke; lucky –, fortunate –, good- -hit, – stroke; bold –, master- stroke; *coup de maître*, checkmate; half the battle, prize; profit &c. (*acquisition*) 775; best seller.

continued success; good fortune &c. (*prosperity*) 734; time well spent.

advantage over; edge; upper-, whip-hand; ascendancy, mastery; expugnation, conquest, victory, subdual; subjugation &c. (*subjection*) 749.

triumph &c. (*exultation*) 884; proficiency &c. (*skill*) 698; conqueror, victor, winner, champion; master of the -situation, – position.

**V.** succeed; be -successful &c. *adj.*;

**732. Failure. — N.** failure; non-success, -fulfilment; dead failure, successlessness; abortion, miscarriage; *brutum fulmen* &c. 158; labour in vain &c. (*inutility*) 645; no go; inefficacy; inefficaciousness &c. *adj.*; vain –, ineffectual –, abortive- -attempt, – efforts; flash in the pan, 'lame and impotent conclusion'; frustration; slip 'twixt cup and lip &c. (*disappointment*) 509.

blunder &c. (*mistake*) 495; fault, omission, miss, oversight, slip, trip, stumble, claudication, footfall; false –, wrong- step; *faux pas*, titubation, *bévue*, *faute*, lurch; botchery &c. (*want of skill*) 699; scrape, jam, mess, muddle, foozle, *fiasco*, breakdown.

mishap &c. (*misfortune*) 735; split,

gain one's -end, – ends; crown with success.

gain –, attain –, carry –, secure –, win- -a point, – an object; put over; make a go of; manage to, contrive to; accomplish &c. (*effect, complete*) 729; do –, work- wonders.

come off -well, – successfully, – with flying colours; make short work of; take –, carry- by storm; bear away the bell; win -one's spurs, – the battle; win –, carry –, gain- the -day, – prize, – palm; climb on the bandwagon; have -the best of it, – it all one's own way, – the game in one's own hands, – the ball at one's feet, – one on the hip; walk over the course; carry all before one, remain in possession of the field; score a success, win hands down.

speed; make progress &c. (*advance*) 282; win –, make –, work –, find- one's way; strive to some purpose; prosper &c. 734; drive a roaring trade; make profit &c. (*acquire*) 775; reap –, gather- the -fruits, – benefit of, – harvest; make one's fortune, get in the harvest, turn to good account; turn to account &c. (*use*) 677.

triumph, be triumphant; gain –, obtain- -a victory, – an advantage; chain victory to one's car.

surmount –, overcome –, get over- -a difficulty, – an obstacle &c. 706; *se tirer d'affaire*; make head against; stem the -torrent, – tide, – current; weather -the storm, – a point; turn a corner, keep one's head above water, tide over; master; get –, have –, gain- the -better of, – best of, – upper hand, – ascendancy, – whip hand, – start of; distance; surpass &c. (*superiority*) 33.

defeat, conquer, vanquish, discomfit; over-come, -throw, -power, -master, -match, -set, -ride, -reach; out-wit, -do, -flank, -manœuvre, -general, -vote; take the wind out of one's adversary's sails; beat, – hollow; rout, lick, drub, floor, worst; put -down, – to flight, – to the rout, – *hors de combat*, – out of court.

silence, quell, nonsuit, checkmate, upset, confound, nonplus, trump; baffle &c. (*hinder*) 706; circumvent, elude; trip up, – the heels of; drive collapse, smash, blow, explosion.

repulse, rebuff, defeat, rout, overthrow, discomfiture; beating, drubbing; *quietus*, nonsuit, subjugation; check-, fool's-mate.

fall, downfall, ruin, perdition; wreck &c. (*destruction*) 162; death-blow; bankruptcy &c. (*non-payment*) 808.

losing game, *affaire flambée*.

victim, prey; bankrupt.

**V.** fail; be -unsuccessful &c. *adj.*; not -succeed &c. 731; make -vain efforts &c. *n.*; do –, labour –, toil- in vain; lose one's labour, take nothing by one's motion; bring to naught, make nothing of; wash a blackamoor white &c. (*impossible*) 471; roll the stone of Sisyphus &c. (*useless*) 645; do by halves &c. (*not complete*) 730; lose ground &c. (*recede*) 283; flunk; fall short of &c. 304.

miss, – one's aim, – the mark, – one's footing, – stays; slip, trip, stumble; make a -slip &c. *n.*, – blunder &c. 495, – mess of, – botch of; bitch it, miscarry, abort, go up like a rocket and come down like the stick, reckon without one's host; get the wrong sow by the ear &c. (*blunder, mismanage*) 699.

limp, halt, hobble, titubate; fall, tumble; lose one's balance; fall -to the ground, – between two stools; flounder, falter, stick in the mud, run aground, split upon a rock; run –, knock –, dash- one's head against a stone wall; break one's back; break down, sink, drown, founder, have the ground cut from under one; get into -trouble, – a mess, – a scrape; come to grief &c. (*adversity*) 735; go to -the wall, – the dogs, – pot; lick –, bite- the dust; be -defeated &c. 731; have the worst of it, lose the day, come off second best, lose; fall a prey to; succumb &c. (*submit*) 725; not have a leg to stand on.

come to nothing, end in smoke; fall -to the ground, – through, – dead, – still-born, – flat; slip through one's fingers; hang –, miss- fire; flash in the pan, collapse; topple down &c. (*descent*) 305; go to wrack and ruin &c. (*destruction*) 162.

go amiss, go wrong, go cross, go hard with, go on a wrong tack; go on –,

-into a corner, – to the wall; run hard, put one's nose out of joint.

settle, do for; break the -neck of, – back of; capsize, sink, shipwreck, drown, swamp; subdue; subjugate &c. (*subject*) 749; reduce; make the enemy bite the dust; victimize, roll in the dust, trample under foot, put an extinguisher upon.

answer, – the purpose; avail, prevail, take effect, do, turn out well, work well, take, tell, bear fruit; hit -it, – the mark, – the right nail on the head; nick it; turn up trumps, make a hit; find one's account in.

**Adj.** succeeding &c. *v.*; successful; prosperous &c. 734; triumphant; flushed –, crowned- with success; victorious; set up; in the ascendant; unbeaten &c. (*see* beat &c. *v.*); well-spent; felicitous, effective, in full swing.

**Adv.** successfully &c. *adj.*; with flying colours, in triumph, swimmingly; *à merveille*, beyond all hope; to some –, good- purpose; to one's heart's content.

**Phr.** *veni vidi vici*, the day being one's own, one's star in the ascendant; *omne tulit punctum*.

---

come off –, turn out –, work- ill; take -a wrong, – an ugly- turn; gang agley.

be all -over with, – up with; explode; dash one's hopes &c. (*disappoint*) 509; defeat the purpose; upset the apple cart; sow the wind and reap the whirlwind, jump out of the frying pan into the fire.

**Adj.** unsuccessful, successless; failing, tripping &c. *v.*; at fault; unfortunate &c. 735.

abortive, addle, still-born; fruitless, sterile, bootless; ineffect-ual, -ive; inefficient &c. (*impotent*) 158; inefficacious; lame, hobbling, *décousu*; insufficient &c. 640; unavailing &c. (*useless*) 645; of no effect.

aground, grounded, swamped, stranded, cast away, wrecked, foundered, capsized, shipwrecked, nonsuited; foiled; defeated &c. 731; struck –, borne –, broken- down; down-trodden; over-borne, -whelmed; all up with; beaten to a frazzle.

lost, undone, ruined, broken; bankrupt &c. (*not paying*) 808; played out; done -up, – for; dead beat, ruined root and branch, *flambé*, knocked on the head; destroyed &c. 162.

frustrated, thwarted, crossed, unhinged, disconcerted, dashed; thrown -off one's balance, – on one's back, – on one's beam ends; unhorsed, in a sorry plight; hard hit.

stultified, befooled, dished, hoist on one's own petard; victimized, sacrificed.

wide of the mark &c. (*error*) 495; out of one's reckoning &c. (*inexpectation*) 508; left in the lurch; thrown away &c. (*wasted*) 638; unattained; uncompleted &c. 730.

**Adv.** unsuccessfully &c. *adj.*; to little or no purpose, in vain, *re infectâ*.

**Phr.** the bubble has burst, the game is up, all is lost; the devil to pay; *parturiunt montes* &c. (*disappointment*) 509.

**733. Trophy.**—**N.** trophy; medal, prize, palm; ribbon, blue ribbon, *cordon bleu*; citation; cup; laurel, -s; bays, crown, chaplet, wreath, civic crown; Victoria Cross, V.C., *Croix de Guerre*, Iron Cross; Distinguished Service Cross, Medal of Honor, Congressional Medal; insignia &c. 550; feather in one's cap &c. (*honour*) 873; decoration &c. 877; garland, triumphal arch.

triumph &c. (*celebration*) 883; flying colours &c. (*show*) 882.

*monumentum ære perennius*.

**734. Prosperity.**—**N.** prosperity, welfare, well-being; affluence &c. (*wealth*) 803; success &c. 731; thrift, roaring

**735. Adversity.**—**N.** adversity, evil &c. 619; failure &c. 732; bad –, ill –, evil –, adverse –, hard- -fortune, – hap,

trade; chicken in every pot, the full dinner pail; good –, smiles of- fortune; blessings, godsend.

luck; good –, run of- luck; sunshine; fair -weather, – wind; palmy –, bright –, halcyon- days; piping times, tide, flood, high tide.

*Saturnia regna*, Saturnian age; golden -time, – age; bed of roses; fat of the land, milk and honey, loaves and fishes, fleshpots of Egypt.

made man, lucky dog, *enfant gâté*, spoiled child of fortune.

upstart, *parvenu*, *nouveau riche*, profiteer, skipjack, mushroom.

**V.** prosper, thrive, flourish; be -prosperous &c. *adj.*; drive a roaring trade; go on -well, – smoothly, – swimmingly; sail before the wind, swim with the tide; run -smooth, – smoothly, – on all fours.

rise –, get on- in the world; work –, make- one's way; look up; lift –, raise- one's head, make one's -fortune, – pile, feather one's nest.

flower, blow, blossom, bloom, fructify, bear fruit, fatten, batten.

keep oneself afloat; keep –, hold- one's head above water; light –, fall- on one's -legs, – feet; drop into a good thing; bear a charmed life; bask in the sunshine; have a -good, – fine- time of it; have a run, – of luck; have the -good fortune &c. *n.* to; take a favourable turn; live -on the fat of the land, – in clover.

**Adj.** prosperous; thriving &c. *v.*; in a fair way, buoyant; well -off, – to do, – to do in the world; set up, at one's ease; rich &c. 803; in good case; in -full, – high- feather; fortunate, lucky, in luck; born -with a silver spoon in one's mouth, – under a lucky star; on the sunny side of the hedge.

auspicious, propitious, providential.

palmy, halcyon; agreeable &c. 829; *couleur de rose*.

**Adv.** prosperously &c. *adj.*; swimmingly; as good luck would have it; beyond all -expectation, – hope, – one's wildest dreams.

**Phr.** one's star in the ascendant, all for the best, one's course runs smooth.

---

– luck, – lot; frowns of fortune; evil -dispensation, – star, – genius; ups and downs of life, broken fortunes; hard -case, – lines, – life; sea –, peck- of troubles; hell upon earth; slough of despond; jinx.

trouble, humiliation, hardship, curse, blight, blast, load, pressure, plight.

pressure of the times, iron age, evil day, time out of joint; hard –, bad –, sad- times; rainy day, cloud, dark cloud, gathering clouds, ill wind; visitation, infliction; affliction &c. (*painfulness*) 830; bitter -pill, – cup; care, trial; the sport of fortune.

mis-hap, -chance, -adventure, -fortune; disaster, calamity, catastrophe; accident, casualty, cross, reverse, check, *contretemps*, rub, pinch, setback.

losing game; falling &c. *v.*; fall, down-fall, come-down; ruin-ation, -ousness; undoing; extremity; ruin &c. (*destruction*) 162.

**V.** be -ill off &c. *adj.*; go hard with; fall on evil, – days; go on ill; not -prosper &c. 734.

go -downhill, – to rack and ruin &c. (*destruction*) 162, – to the dogs; fall, – from one's high estate; decay, sink, decline, go down in the world; have seen better days; bring down one's grey hairs with sorrow to the grave; come to grief; be all -over, – up- with; bring a -wasp's, – hornet's- nest about one's ears.

**Adj.** unfortunate, unblest, unhappy, unlucky; im-, un-prosperous; luck-, hap-less; out of luck; in trouble, in a bad way, in an evil plight; under a cloud; clouded; ill –, badly- off; in adverse circumstances; poor &c. 804; behindhand, down in the world, decayed, undone; on the road to ruin, on its last legs, on the wane; in one's utmost need.

planet-struck, devoted; born -under an evil star, – with a wooden ladle in one's mouth; ill-fated, -starred, -omened; inconspicuous, ominous, doomed, unpropitious.

adverse, untoward; disastrous, calamitous, ruinous, dire, deplorable.

**Adv.** if the worst come to the worst, as ill luck would have it, from bad to worse, out of the frying pan into the fire.

**Phr.** one's star is on the wane; one's luck -turns, – fails; the game is up, one's doom is sealed, the ground crumbles under one's feet, *sic transit gloria mundi, tant va la cruche à l'eau qu'à la fin elle se casse.*

**736. Mediocrity.**—**N.** moderate –, average- circumstances; respectability; middle classes, *bourgeoisie*; mediocrity; golden mean &c. (*mid-course*) 628, (*moderation*) 174.

**V.** jog on; go –, get on- -fairly, – quietly, – peaceably, – tolerably, – respectably; steer a middle course &c. 628.

**Adj.** middling, so-so, fair, medium, moderate, mediocre, second-, third- &c. -rate.

## Division (II). INTERSOCIAL VOLITION*

### Section I. General Intersocial Volition

**737. Authority.**—**N.** authority; influence, patronage, power, preponderance, credit, *prestige*, prerogative, jurisdiction; right &c. (*title*) 924.

divine right, dynastic rights, authoritativeness; absolut-eness, -ism; despotism, tyranny; *jus nocendi.*

command, empire, sway, rule; domin-ion, -ation; sovereignty, supremacy, suzerainty; lord-, head-ship; chiefdom; seignior-y, -ity, hegemony, patriarchate, patriarchy; master-y, -ship, -dom; government &c. (*direction*) 693; dictation, control.

hold, grasp; grip, -e; reach; iron sway &c. (*severity*) 739; fangs, clutches, talons; rod of empire &c. (*sceptre*) 747.

reign, regnancy, *régime*, dynasty; director-, dictator-ship; protector-ate, -ship; caliphate, pashalic, electorate; presiden-cy, -tship; administration; pro-, consulship; prefecture; seneschalship; magistra-ture, -cy; raj.

empire; monarchy; king-hood, -ship; royalty, regality, autocracy, monocracy, arist-archy, -ocracy; oligarchy, democracy, demogogy; republic, -anism, federalism; socialism, collectivism; communism, bolshevism, syndicalism; mob law, mobocracy, ochlocracy, ergatocracy; *vox populi, imperium in imperio*; bureaucracy; beadle-, bumble-dom; stratocracy; martial law, military -power, – government; feodality, feudal system, feudalism.

Thearchy, dinarchy, diarchy; du-, tri-, heter-archy; du-, tri-umvirate; auto-cracy, -nomy; limited monarchy; constitutional -government, – monarchy; home rule, self-government, -determination; representative government; Soviet government.

**738.** [Absence of authority.] **Laxity.**—**N.** laxity; lax-, loose-, slack-ness; toleration &c. (*lenity*) 740; freedom &c. 748.

anarchy, interregnum; relaxation; loosening &c. *v.*; remission; dead letter, *brutum fulmen*, misrule; licence, licentiousness; insubordination &c. (*disobedience*) 742; lynch law &c. (*illegality*) 964; nihilism.

[Deprivation of power] dethronement, deposition, usurpation, abdication.

**V.** be -lax &c. *adj.*; *laisser -faire, – aller*; hold a loose rein; give -the reins to, – rope enough, – a loose to; tolerate; relax; misrule.

go beyond the length of one's tether; have one's -swing, – fling; act without -instructions, – authority; act on one's own responsibility, usurp authority.

dethrone, depose; abdicate.

**Adj.** lax, loose; slack; remiss &c. (*careless*) 460; weak.

relaxed; licensed; reinless, unbridled; anarchical; unauthorized &c. (*unwarranted*) 925.

* Implying the action of the will of one mind over the will of another.

gyn-archy, -ocracy, -æocracy; petticoat government, matri-archate, matriarchy.

[Vicarious authority] commission &c. 755; deputy &c. 759; permission &c. 760.

country, state, realm, commonwealth, canton, constituency, toparchy, municipality, polity, body politic, *posse comitatus*.

person in authority &c. (*master*) 745; judicature &c. 965; cabinet &c. (*council*) 696; usurper; seat of -government, – authority; headquarters.

[Acquisition of authority] accession; installation &c. 755; usurpation.

**V.** authorize &c. (*permit*) 760; warrant &c. (*right*) 924; dictate &c. (*order*) 741; have –, hold –, possess –, exercise –, exert –, wield- -authority &c. *n.*

be -at the head of &c. *adj.*; hold –, be in –, fill an- office; hold –, occupy- a post; be -master &c. 745.

rule, sway, command, control, administer; govern &c. (*direct*) 693; lead, preside over, reign; possess –, be seated on –, occupy- the throne; sway –, wield- the sceptre; wear the crown.

have –, get- the -upper, – whip- hand; gain a hold upon, preponderate, dominate, boss, rule the roost; over-ride, -rule, -awe; lord it over, hold in hand, keep under, make a puppet of, lead by the nose, hold in the hollow of one's hand, turn round one's little finger, bend to one's will, hold one's own, wear the breeches; have -the ball at one's feet, – it all one's own way, – the game in one's own hand, – on the hip, – under one's thumb; be master of the situation; take the lead, play first fiddle, set the fashion; give the law to; carry with a high hand; lay down the law; 'ride in the whirlwind and direct the storm'; rule with a rod of iron &c. (*severity*) 739.

ascend –, mount- the throne, take the reins, – into one's hand; assume -authority &c. *n.*, – the reins of government; take –, assume the- command.

be -governed by, – in the power of; be under -the rule of, – the domination of.

**Adj.** ruling &c. *v.*; regnant, at the head, dominant, paramount, supreme, predominant, preponderant, in the ascendant, influential; gubernatorial; imperious; authoritative, executive, administrative, clothed with authority, official, *ex officio*, ministerial, bureaucratic, departmental, imperative, peremptory, overruling, absolute; hegemonic, -al; arbitrary; compulsory &c. 744; stringent.

regal, sovereign; royal, -ist; monarchical, kingly; imperial, -istic; princely; feudal; aristo-, auto-cratic; oligarchic &c. *n.*; democratic, republican, dynastic.

at one's command; in one's -power, – grasp; under control; authorized &c. (*due*) 924.

**Adv.** in the name of, by the authority of, *de par le Roi*, in virtue of; under the auspices of, in the hands of.

at one's pleasure; by a -dash, – stroke- of the pen; *ex mero motu*; *ex cathedrâ*.

**Phr.** the grey mare the better horse; 'every inch a king.'

**739. Severity.**—**N.** severity; strictness, formalism, harshness &c. *adj.*; rigour, stringency, austerity; inclem-

**740. Lenity.** — **N.** leni-ty, -ence, -ency; moderation &c. 174; toler-ance, -ation; mildness, gentleness; favour;

ency &c. (*pitilessness*) 914*a*; arrogance &c. 885.

arbitrary power; absolut-, despot-ism; dictatorship, autocracy, tyranny, domineering, oppression; assumption, usurpation; inquisition, reign of terror, martial law; iron -heel, – rule, – hand, – sway; tight grasp; brute -force, – strength; coercion &c. 744; strong –, tight- hand.

hard -lines, – measure; tender mercies [ironical]; sharp practice; bureaucracy, red tape; pipe-clay, officialism.

tyrant, disciplinarian, martinet, stickler, formalist, bashaw, despot, hard master, Draco, oppressor, inquisitor, extortioner, harpy, vulture, bird of prey.

V. be -severe &c. *adj.*

assume, usurp, arrogate, take liberties; domineer, bully &c. 885; tyrannize, inflict, wreak, stretch a point, put on the screw; be hard upon; bear –, lay- a heavy hand on; be –, come- down upon; ill-treat; deal -hardly with, – hard measure to; rule with a rod of iron, chastise with scorpions; dye with blood; oppress, override; trample –, tread- -down, – upon, – under foot; crush under an iron heel, ride roughshod over; rivet the yoke; hold –, keep- a tight hand; force down the throat; coerce &c. 744; give no quarter &c. (*pitiless*) 914*a*.

Adj. severe; strict, hard, harsh, dour, rigid, stiff, stern, rigorous, uncompromising, exacting, exigent, *exigeant*, inexorable, inflexible, obdurate, austere, relentless, Spartan, Draconian, stringent, strait-laced, puritanical, prudish, searching, unsparing, ironhanded, hard-headed, peremptory, absolute, positive, arbitrary, imperative; coercive &c. 744; tyrannical, despotic, masterful, extortionate, grinding, withering, oppressive, inquisitorial; inclement &c. (*ruthless*) 914*a*; cruel &c. (*malevolent*) 907; haughty, arrogant &c. 885.

Adv. severely &c. *adj.*; with a -high, – strong, – tight, – heavy-hand.

at the point of the -sword, – bayonet.

**Phr.** *Delirant reges plectuntur Achivi.*

indulgen-ce, -cy; clemency, mercy, forbearance, quarter; compassion &c. 914.

V. be -lenient &c. *adj.*; tolerate, bear with; *parcere subjectis*, give quarter.

indulge, allow one to have his own way, spoil.

Adj. lenient; mild, – as milk; gentle, soft; tolerant, indulgent, easy-going; clement &c. (*compassionate*) 914; forbearing; complaisant, long-suffering.

---

**741. Command.**—N. command, order, ordinance, act, *fiat*, bidding, *dictum*, hest, behest, call, beck, nod.

des-, dis-patch; message, direction, injunction, charge, instructions; appointment, fixture.

demand, exaction, imposition, requisition, claim, reclamation, revendication; *ultimatum* &c. (*terms*) 770; request &c. 765; requirement

dictation; dict-, mand-ate; *caveat*, decree, decree -nisi, – absolute, *senatus consultum*; precept; pre-, re-script; writ, ordination, bull, edict, decretal, dispensation, prescription, brevet, placet, ukase, *firman*, hatti-sheriff, warrant, passport, *mittimus*, *mandamus*, summons; subpœna, –*duces tecum*, *nisi prius*, interpellation, citation; word, – of command; *mot d'ordre*; bugle –, trumpet- call; beat of drum, tattoo; order of the day; enactment &c. (*law*) 963; *plebiscite* &c. (*choice*) 609.

V. command, order, decree, enact, ordain, dictate, direct, give orders.

prescribe, set, appoint, mark out; set –, prescribe –, impose- a task; set to work, put in requisition &c. 926.

bid, enjoin, charge, call upon, instruct; require, – at the hands of; exact, impose, tax, task; demand; insist on &c. (*compel*) 744.

claim, lay claim to, revendicate, reclaim.

cite, summon; call –, send- for; subpœna; beckon.

issue a command; make –, issue –, promulgate- -a requisition, – a decree, – an order &c. *n.*; give the -word of command, – word, – signal; call to order; give –, lay down- the law; assume the command &c. (*authority*) 737; remand.

be -ordered &c.; receive an order &c. *n.*

**Adj.** commanding &c. *v.*; authoritative &c. 737; decret-ory, -ive, -al; imperative, jussive, decisive, final.

**Adv.** in a commanding tone; by a -stroke, – dash- of the pen; by order, at beat of drum, on the first summons; at the word of command.

**Phr.** the decree is gone forth; *sic volo sic jubeo*; *le Roi le veut.*

**742. Disobedience.—N.** disobedience, insubordination, contumacy; infraction, -fringement; violation, non-compliance; non-observance &c. 773.

revolt, rebellion, mutiny, outbreak, rising, uprising, putsch, insurrection, *émeute*; riot, tumult &c. (*disorder*) 59; strike &c. (*resistance*) 719; barring out; defiance &c. 715.

mutinousness &c. *adj.*; mutineering; sedition, treason; high –, petty –, misprision of- treason; *premunire*; *lèse-majesté*; violation of law &c. 964; defection, secession, revolution, *sabotage*, bolshevism, *Sinn Fein.*

insurgent, mutineer, rebel, revolter, rioter, traitor, *carbonaro*, *sansculottes*, red republican, communist, Fenian, chartist, *frondeur*; seceder, runagate, brawler, anarchist, demagogue; suffragette; Spartacus, Masaniello, Wat Tyler, Jack Cade; bolshevist, bolshevik, maximalist, ringleader.

**V.** disobey, violate, infringe; shirk; set at defiance &c. (*defy*) 715; set authority at naught, run riot, fly in the face of, bolt, take the law into one's own hands; kick over the traces.

turn –, run- restive; champ the bit; strike &c. (*resist*) 719; rise, – in arms; secede; mutiny, rebel.

**Adj.** disobedient; uncompl-ying, -iant; unsubmissive, unruly, ungovernable; insubordinate, impatient of control; rest-iff, -ive; refractory, contumacious; recusant &c. (refuse) 764; recalcitrant; resisting &c. 719; lawless, mutinous, seditious, insurgent, riotous, revolutionary.

disobeyed, unobeyed; unbidden.

**743. Obedience.—N.** obedience; observance &c. 772; compliance; submission &c. 725; subjection &c. 749; non-resistance; passiveness, passivity, resignation.

allegiance, loyalty, fealty, homage, deference, devotion, fidelity, constancy.

submiss-ness, -iveness; ductility &c. (*softness*) 324; obsequiousness &c. (*servility*) 886.

**V.** be -obedient &c. *adj.*; obey, bear obedience to; submit &c. 725; comply, answer the helm, come at one's call; do -one's bidding, – what one is told, – suit and service; attend to orders, serve -devotedly, – loyally, – faithfully.

follow, – the lead of, – to the world's end; serve &c. 746; play second fiddle.

**Adj.** obedient; compl-ying, -iant; law-abiding, loyal, faithful, leal, devoted; at one's -call, – command, – orders, – beck and call; under -beck and call, – control.

restrainable; resigned, passive; submissive &c. 725; henpecked; pliant &c. (*soft*) 324.

unresist-ed, -ing.

**Adv.** obediently &c. *adj.*; in compliance with, in obedience to.

**Phr.** to hear is to obey; as –, if- you please; at your service.

**744. Compulsion.**—**N.** compulsion, coercion, coaction, constraint, eminent domain, duress, enforcement, press, conscription.

force; brute –, main –, physical- force; the sword, *ultima ratio*; club –, mob –, lynch- law; *argumentum ad baculum, le droit du plus fort*, martial law.

restraint &c. 751; necessity &c. 601; *force majeure*; Hobson's choice; the spur of necessity.

**V.** compel, force, make, drive, coerce, constrain, enforce, necessitate, oblige.

force upon, press; cram –, thrust –, force- down the throat; say it must be done, make a point of, insist upon, take no denial; put down, dragoon.

extort, wring from; put –, turn- on the screw; drag into; bind, – over; pin –, tie- down; require, tax, put in force; commandeer; restrain &c. 751.

**Adj.** compelling &c. *v.*; coercive, coactive; inexorable &c. 739; compuls-ory, -atory; obligatory, stringent, peremptory, binding.

forcible, not to be trifled with; irresistible &c. 601; compelled &c. *v.*; fain to.

**Adv.** by -force &c. *n.*, – force of arms; on compulsion, perforce; *vi et armis*, under the lash; at the point of the -sword, – bayonet; forcibly; by a strong arm.

under protest, in spite of one's teeth; against one's will &c. 603; *nolens volens* &c. (*of necessity*) 601; by stress of -circumstances, – weather; under press of; *de rigueur*.

**745. Master.**—**N.** master, *padrone*; lord, – paramount; command-er, -ant; captain; chief, -tain; *sahib*, sirdar, sachem, sheik, head, senior, governor, *duce*, ruler, dictator; leader &c. (*director*) 694.

lord of the ascendant; cock of the -walk, – roost; grey mare; mistress.

potentate; liege, – lord; suzerain, sovereign, monarch, autocrat, despot, tyrant, oligarch, overlord.

crowned head, emperor, king, anointed king, majesty, *imperator*, protector, president, stadtholder, judge.

cæsar, kaiser, czar, sultan, grand Turk, caliph, imaum, shah, padishah, sophi, mogul, great mogul, khan, cham; lama, tycoon, mikado, inca, cazique; domn; vaivode; wai-, way-wode; landamman; seyyid, cacique.

prince, duke &c. (*nobility*) 875; archduke, doge, elector; seignior; mar-, land-grave; rajah, emir, nizam, nawab, negus.

empress, queen, sultana, czarina, princess, infanta, duchess, margravine, begum, maharani.

regent, viceroy, exarch, palatine,

**746. Servant.**—**N.** subject, liegeman; servant, retainer, follower, henchman, servitor, domestic, menial, help, lady help, *employé, attaché*; official.

retinue, suite, *cortège*, staff, court.

attendant, squire, usher, page, buttons, donzel, footboy; dog robber; train-, cup-bearer; waiter, busboy, tapster, butler, livery servant, lackey, footman, flunkey, valet, *valet de chambre*; boots; scout, gyp; equerry, groom; jockey, hostler, ostler, tiger, orderly, messenger, cad, gillie, caddie; *wallah*; journeyman, herdsman, swineherd.

bailiff, castellan, seneschal, chamberlain, *major-domo*, groom of the chambers.

secretary; under –, assistant- secretary; clerk; clerical staff, stenographer, subsidiary; agent &c. 758; subaltern; under-ling, -strapper; man.

maid, -servant, waitress; handmaid; *confidente*, lady's maid, abigail, *soubrette*; nurse, *bonne, ayah*; nurse-, nursery-, house-, parlour-, waiting-, chamber-, kitchen-, scullery-, between –, laundry –, dairy-maid; *femme – fille- de chambre*; *camarista*; *chef de cuisine*,

khedive, hospodar, beglerbeg, three-tailed bashaw, pasha, pashaw, bashaw, bey, beg, dey, scherif, tetrarch, satrap, mandarin, subahdar, Nabob, maharajah; burgrave; laird &c. (*proprietor*) 779; High Commissioner.

the -authorities, – powers that be, – government; staff, *état major*, aga, official, man in office, person in authority.

[Naval authorities] admiral, -ty, – of the fleet; rear-, vice-, port-admiral; senior-, naval officer, S.N.O., commodore, captain, commander, lieutenant-commander, lieutenant, sub-lieutenant, midshipman, warrant –, petty- officer, leading seaman; skipper, mate, master.

[Military authorities] marshal, field-marshal, *maréchal*; general, -issimo; commander-in-chief, *seraskier*, *hetman*; lieutenant-, major-general; commandant; colonel, lieutenant-colonel, major, captain, centurion, skipper, lieutenant, second-lieutenant, officer, staff-officer, *aide-de-camp*, brigadier, brigade-major, adjutant, *jemidar*, ensign, cornet, cadet, subaltern, warrant officer, quartermaster, noncommissioned officer, N.C.O.; sergeant, -major; top-sergeant, troop-sergeant, colour sergeant; corporal, -major; lance-, acting-corporal; drum major; shavetail.

[Air authorities] air -marshal, – commodore; group captain, squadron leader, wing commander, flight lieutenant, flying –, pilot-officer.

[Civil authorities] judge &c. 967; mayor, -alty; prefect, chancellor, archon, provost, magistrate, syndic; alcalde, alcaid; burgomaster, *corregidor*, seneschal, alderman, warden, constable, portreeve; lord mayor, sheriff; officer &c. (*executive*) 965.

*cordon bleu*, cook, scullion, Cinderella; maid –, servant- of all work, tweeny, general servant, girl, slavey; laundress, bed-maker, goody, char-woman &c. (*worker*) 690.

serf, vassal, slave, negro, helot; bondsman, -woman; bondslave; *âme damnée*, *odalisque*, ryot, *adscriptus glebæ*; vill-ain, -ein; bead-, bede-sman; sizar; pension-er, -ary; client; dependant, -ent; hanger on, stooge, satellite; parasite &c. (*servility*) 886; led captain; *protégé*, ward, hireling, mercenary, puppet, creature.

badge of slavery; bonds &c. 752.

**V.** serve; minister to, wait –, attend –, dance attendance –, pin oneself- upon; squire, tend, hang on the sleeve of, char, do for; fag; valet.

**Adj.** in the train of; in one's -pay, – employ; at one's call &c. (*obedient*) 743; in bonds.

---

**747.** [Insignia of authority.] **Sceptre.—N.** sceptre, regalia, rod of empire, sword of state, mace, *fasces*, wand; staff, – of office; *bâton*, truncheon; flag &c. (*insignia*) 550; ensign –, emblem –, badge –, insignia- of authority, rank marks, brassard, badge, sash; cocked –, brass- hat.

epaulette, *aiguillette*, crown, star, eagle, bar, double bar, pip, stripe, chevron, curl, ring, anchor, shoulder-strap, tab.

throne, chair, musnud, divan, dais, woolsack.

*toga*, pall, mantle, robes of state, ermine, purple.

crown, coronet, diadem, tiara, triple crown, mitre, crozier, cardinal's hat &c.; cap of maintenance; decoration; title &c. 877; portfolio.

key, signet, seals, talisman; helm; reins &c. (*means of restraint*) 752.

**748. Freedom.—N.** freedom, liberty, independence; licence &c. (*permission*) 760; facility &c. 705.

scope, range, latitude, play; free –, full- -play, – scope; free stage and no

**749. Subjection. — N.** subjection; depend-ence, -ance, -ency; subordination; thrall, thraldom. enthralment, subjugation, bondage, serfdom; feudal- -ism, -ity; vassalage, villenage; slavery,

favour; swing, full swing, elbow-room, margin, rope, wide berth; Liberty Hall.

franchise, denization; free –, freed-, livery- man; denizen.

autonomy, self-government, home-rule, self-determination, liberalism, free trade; non-interference &c. 706.

immunity, exemption; emancipation &c. (*liberation*) 750; en-, af-franchisement; rights, privileges.

free land, freehold; allodium; frankalmoigne, mortmain.

independent, free-lance, -thinker, -trader.

**V.** be -free &c. *adj.*; have -scope &c. *n.*, – the run of, – one's own way, – a will of one's own, – one's fling; do what one -likes, – wishes, – pleases, – chooses; go at large, feel at home, paddle one's own canoe; stand on one's -legs, – rights; shift for oneself.

take a liberty; make -free with, – oneself quite at home; use a freedom; take -leave, – French leave.

set free &c. (*liberate*) 750; give the reins to &c. (*permit*) 760; allow –, give- scope &c. *n.* to; give a horse his head.

make free of; give the -freedom of, – franchise; en-, af-franchise.

*laisser -faire, – aller*; live and let live; leave to oneself; leave –, let- alone; mind one's own business.

**Adj.** free, – as air; out of harness, independent, at large, loose, scot free; left -alone, – to oneself.

in full swing; uncaught, unconstrained, unbuttoned, unconfined, unrestrained, unchecked, unprevented, unhindered, unobstructed, unbound, uncontrolled, untrammelled.

unsubject, ungoverned, unenslaved, unenthralled, unchained, unshackled, unfettered, unreined, unbridled, uncurbed, unmuzzled, unimpeded.

unrestricted, unlimited, unconditional; absolute; discretionary &c. (*optional*) 600.

unassailed, unforced, uncompelled.

unbiassed, unprejudiced, uninfluenced, spontaneous.

free and easy; at –, at one's- ease; *dégagé*, quite at home; wanton, rampant, irrepressible, unvanquished.

exempt; freed &c. 750; freeborn; autonomous, freehold, allodial; *gratis* &c. 815.

unclaimed, going a begging.

**Adv.** freely &c. *adj.*; *ad libitum* &c. (*at will*) 600.

enslavement, involuntary servitude.

service; servi-tude, -torship; tendence, employ, tutelage, clientship; liability &c. 177; constraint &c. 751; oppression &c. (*severity*) 739; yoke &c. (*means of restraint*) 752; submission &c. 725; obedience &c. 743.

**V.** be -subject &c. *adj.*; be –, lie- at the mercy of; depend –, lean –, hang- upon; fall -a prey to, – under; play second fiddle.

be a -mere machine, – puppet, – football; not dare to say one's soul is his own; drag a chain.

serve &c. 746; obey &c. 743; submit &c. 725.

break in, tame; subject, subjugate; master &c. 731; tread -down, – under foot; weigh down; drag at one's chariot wheels; reduce to -subjection, – slavery; en-, in-, be-thral; enslave, lead captive; take into custody &c. (*restrain*) 751; rule &c. 737; drive into a corner, hold at the sword's point; keep under; hold in -bondage, – leading strings, – swaddling clothes.

**Adj.** subject, dependent, subordinate; feud-al, -atory; in subjection to, under control; in -leading strings, – harness; subjected, enslaved &c. *v.*; constrained &c. 751; subservient, servile, fawning, slavish, obsequious, cringing; down-trodden; over-borne, -whelmed; under the lash, on the hip, led by the nose, henpecked; the -puppet, – sport, – plaything- of; under one's -orders, – command, – thumb; like dirt under one's feet; a slave to; at the mercy of; in the -power, – hands, – clutches- of; at the feet of; at one's beck and call &c. (*obedient*) 743; liable &c. 177; parasitical; stipendiary.

**Adv.** under.

**750. Liberation.**—**N.** liberation, disengagement, release, disenthrallment, enlargement, emancipation; af-, enfranchisement; manumission; discharge, dismissal.

deliverance &c. 672; redemption, extrication, acquittance, absolution; acquittal &c. 970; escape &c. 671.

**V.** liberate, free; set -free, – clear, – at liberty; render free, emancipate, release; en-, af-franchise; manumit; enlarge; dis-band, -charge, -miss, -enthral; let -go, – loose, – out, – slip; cast –, turn- adrift; deliver &c. 672; absolve &c. (*acquit*) 970; reprieve.

unfetter &c. 751; untie &c. 44; loose &c. (*disjoin*) 44; loosen, relax; un-bolt, -bar, -close, -cork, -clog, -hand, -bind, -latch, -chain, -harness; dis-engage, -entangle; clear, extricate, unloose.

gain –, obtain –, acquire- one's -liberty &c. 748; get -rid, – clear- of; deliver oneself from; shake off the yoke, slip the collar; break -loose, – prison; tear asunder one's bonds, cast off trammels; escape &c. 671.

**Adj.** at -liberty, – large, free, liberated &c. *v.*; out of harness &c. 748; adrift.

**Int.** unhand me! let me go!

**751. Restraint.**—**N.** restraint; hindrance &c. 706; coercion &c. (*compulsion*) 744; cohibition, constraint, repression; discipline, control, self-restraint &c. 604.

confinement; durance, duress; im-, prisonment; incarceration, coarctation, entombment, mancipation, durance vile, thrall, -dom, limbo, captivity; blockade; quarantine; detention.

arrest, -ation; custody, keep, care, charge, ward, restringency.

curb &c. (*means of restraint*) 752; *lettre de cachet.*

limitation, restriction, protection, monopoly; prohibition &c. 761; economic pressure.

prisoner &c. 754.

**V.** restrain, check; put –, lay- under restraint; en-, in-, be-thral; restrict; debar &c. (*hinder*) 706; constrain; coerce &c. (*compel*) 744; curb, control; hold –, keep- -back, – from, – in, – in check, – within bounds; hold in -leash, – leading strings; withhold.

keep under; repress, suppress; smother; pull in, rein in; hold, – fast; keep a tight hand on; prohibit &c. 761; in-, co-hibit.

enchain; fasten &c. (*join*) 43; fetter, shackle; en-, trammel; bridle, muzzle, gag, pinion, manacle, handcuff, tie one's hands, hobble, bind hand and foot; swathe, swaddle; pin –, peg- down; tether, picket; tie, – up, – down; secure; forge fetters; belay.

confine; shut –, clap –, lock –, box –, mew –, bottle –, cork –, seal –, button- up; shut –, hem –, bolt –, wall –, rail- in; impound, pen, coop; enclose &c. (*circumscribe*) 229; cage; in-, en-cage; close the door upon, cloister; imprison, immure; incarcerate, entomb; clap –, lay- under hatches; put in -irons, – a strait waistcoat; throw –, cast- into prison; put into bilboes.

arrest; take -up, – charge of, – into custody; take –, make- -prisoner, – captive; captivate; lead -captive, – into captivity; send –, commit- to prison; commit; give in -charge, – custody; subjugate &c. 749.

**Adj.** re-, con-strained; imprisoned &c. *v.*; pent up; jammed in, wedged in; under -restraint, – lock and key, – hatches; serving –, doing- time; in swaddling clothes; on *parole*; in custody &c. (*prisoner*) 754; cohibitive; coactive &c. (*compulsory*) 744.

stiff, restringent, straitlaced, hide-bound.

ice-, wind-, weather-bound; 'cabined, cribbed, confined'; in Lob's pound, laid by the heels.

**Adv.** in captivity, under arrest, behind the bars, in -prison, – jail, – durance vile.

**752.** [Means of restraint.] **Prison.—N.** prison, -house; jail, gaol, cage, coop, den, death house, condemned –, cell; stronghold, fortress, keep, donjon, dungeon, *Bastille*, *oubliette*, bridewell, house of correction, hulks, toll-booth, panopticon, penitentiary, guard-room, clink, can, stir, tronk, jug, lock-up, hold; round –, watch –, station –, sponging-house; station; house of detention, black hole, pen, fold, pound; enclosure &c. 232; penal settlement; chain gang; debtors' prison; reformatory; federal penitentiary, state prison; criminal lunatic asylum; bilboes, stocks, limbo, quod.

Dartmoor, Newgate, Fleet, Marshalsea; King's (*or* Queen's) Bench; Sing Sing, Dannemora.

bond; strap, bandage, splint, tourniquet; irons, pinion, gyve, fetter, shackle, trammel, manacle, handcuff, bracelets, darbies, strait waistcoat, strait-jacket.

yoke, collar, halter, harness; muzzle, gag, bit, brake, curb, snaffle, bridle; rein, -s; ribbons, lines, bearing-rein; martingale, leading string; tether, picket, band, guy, chain; cord &c. (*fastening*) 45.

bolt, bar, lock, padlock, rail, wall; paling, palisade; fence; barrier, barricade.

brake, drag &c. (*hindrance*) 706.

**753. Keeper.—N.** keeper, custodian, *custos*, ranger, warder, jailer, gaoler, turnkey, castellan, guard; watch, -dog, -man; Charley; sen-try, -tinel; watch and ward; *concierge*, coast-guard, *guarda costa*, gamekeeper.

escort, body guard, convoy.

protector, governor, duenna; guardian; governess &c. (*teacher*) 540; nurse, *bonne*, *ayah*, *amah*.

**754. Prisoner.—N.** prisoner, captive, *détenu*, close prisoner.

jail-bird, ticket-of-leave man.

**V.** stand committed; be -imprisoned &c. 751.

**Adj.** imprisoned &c. 751; in -prison, – quod, – durance vile, – limbo, – custody, – charge, – chains; under -lock and key, – hatches; on *parole*; detained at his Majesty's pleasure.

**755.** [Vicarious authority.] **Commission.—N.** commission, delegation; con-, as-signment; procuration; deputation, legation, mission, embassy; agency, agentship; power of attorney, proxy; clerkship.

errand, charge, *brevet*, diploma, *exequatur*, permit &c. (*permission*) 760.

appointment, nomination, return; charter; ordination; installation, inauguration, investiture; accession, coronation, enthronement.

vicegerency; regency, regentship.

viceroy &c 745; consignee &c. 758; deputy &c. 759.

**V.** commission, delegate, depute; consign, assign; charge; in-, en-trust; turn over to; commit, – to the hands of; authorize &c. (*permit*) 760.

put in commission, accredit, engage, hire, bespeak, appoint, name, nominate, return, ordain; install, induct,

**756. Abrogation.—N.** abrogation, annulment, nullification; cancelling &c. *v.*; cancel; revo-cation, -kement; repeal, rescission, defeasance.

dismissal, *congé*, demission; depos-al, -ition; sack, dethronement; disestablish-, disendow-ment; deconsecration.

aboli-tion, -shment; dissolution.

counter-order, -mand; repudiation, retractation; recantation &c. (*tergiversation*) 607.

**V.** abrogate, annul, cancel; destroy &c. 162; abolish; revoke, repeal, rescind, reverse, retract, recall; over-rule, -ride; set aside; disannul, dissolve, quash, nullify, declare null and void; dis-establish, -endow; deconsecrate.

disclaim &c. (*deny*) 536; ignore, repudiate; recant &c. 607; divest oneself, break off.

counter-mand, -order; do away with; sweep –, brush- away; throw -over-

inaugurate, invest, crown; en-roll, -list.

employ, empower; give power of attorney to; set –, place- over; send out.

be commissioned, be accredited; represent, stand for; stand in the -stead, – place, – shoes- of.

**Adj.** commissioned &c. *v.*

**Adv.** *per procuratione.*

---

board, – to the dogs; scatter to the winds, cast behind.

dismiss, discard; cast –, turn- -off, – out, – adrift, – out of doors, – aside, – away; send -off, – away, – about one's business; discharge, get rid of, fire out, fire &c. (*eject*) 297; jilt.

cashier; break; oust; set down, unseat, -saddle; un-, de-, disen-throne; depose, uncrown; unfrock, strike off the roll; dis-bar, -bench.

be -abrogated &c.; receive its quietus.

**Adj.** abrogated &c. *v.*; *functus officio.*

**Int.** get along with you! begone! go about your business! **away with!**

**757. Resignation.—N.** resignation, retirement, abdication, renunciation, abjuration, disclaimer, abandonment, relinquishment.

**V.** resign; give –, throw- up; lay down, throw up the cards, wash one's hands of, abjure, renounce, forego, disclaim, abandon, relinquish, retract, demit; deny &c. 536.

abrogate &c. 756; desert &c. (*relinquish*) 624; get rid of &c. 782.

abdicate; vacate, – one's seat; apply for –, accept- the stewardship of the Chiltern Hundreds; retire; tender –, send in –, hand in- one's resignation.

**Adj.** abdicant, renunciatory &c. *v.* **Phr.** 'Othello's occupation's gone.'

**758. Consignee.—N.** consignee, trustee, nominee, committee.

delegate; commiss-ary, -ioner; emissary, envoy, commissionaire; messenger &c. 534.

diplomatist, diplomat, *corps diplomatique*, embassy; am-, em-bassador; representative, resident, consul, legate, nuncio, internuncio, *chargé d'affaires*, *attaché*.

vicegerent &c. (*deputy*) 759; plenipotentiary.

functionary, placeman, curator; treasurer &c. 801; agent, factor, bailiff, steward, clerk, secretary, attorney, solicitor, proctor, broker, underwriter, commission agent, auctioneer, one's man of business; factotum &c. (*director*) 694; caretaker.

negotiator, go between; middleman; under agent, *employé*; servant &c. 746.

salesman; commercial, – traveller; bagman, *commis-voyageur*, touter.

newspaper –, own –, war –, special- correspondent; reporter.

**759. Deputy.—N.** deputy, substitute, vice, proxy, *locum tenens*, delegate, representative, next friend, surrogate, secondary.

regent, vicegerent, vizier, minister, vicar; premier &c. (*director*) 694; chancellor, prefect, provost, warden, lieutenant, archon, consul, proconsul; viceroy &c. (*governor*) 745; commissioner &c. 758; plenipotentiary, *alter ego.*

team, eight, eleven; champion.

**V.** be -deputy &c. *n.*; stand –, appear –, hold a brief –, answer- for; represent; stand –, walk- in the shoes of; stand in the stead of.

substitute, ablegate, accredit; commission, empower, delegate &c. 755.

**Adj.** acting; vice, -regal; accredited to.

**Adv.** in behalf of, by proxy.

## Section II. Special Intersocial Volition

**760. Permission.—N.** permission, leave; allow-, suffer-ance; toler-ance, -ation; liberty, law, licence, concession, grace; indulgence &c. (*lenity*) 740; favour, dispensation, exemption, release; connivance; vouchsafement.

authorization, warranty, accordance, admission.

permit, warrant, *brevet*, precept, sanction, authority, *firman*; pass, -port; furlough, licence, *carte blanche*, ticket of leave; grant, charter, patent.

**V.** permit; give -permission &c. *n.*, - power; let, allow, admit; suffer, bear with, tolerate, recognize; concede &c. 762; accord, vouchsafe, favour, humour, gratify, indulge, stretch a point; wink at, connive at; shut one's eyes to.

grant, empower, charter, enfranchise, privilege, confer a privilege, license, authorize, warrant; sanction; entrust &c. (*commission*) 755.

give -*carte blanche*, - the reins to, - scope to &c. (*freedom*) 748; leave -alone, - it to one, - the door open; open the -door to, - floodgates; give a loose to.

let off; absolve &c. (*acquit*) 970; release, exonerate, dispense with.

ask -, beg -, request- -leave, - permission.

**Adj.** permitting &c. *v.*; permissive, indulgent; permitted &c. *v.*; patent, chartered, permissible, allowable, lawful, legitimate, legal; legalized &c. (*law*) 963; licit; unforbid, -den; unconditional.

**Adv.** permissibly; by -, with -, on- -leave &c. *n.*; *speciali gratiâ*; under favour of; *pace*; *ad libitum* &c. (*freely*) 748, (*at will*) 600; by all means &c. (*willingly*) 602; yes &c. (*assent*) 488.

**761. Prohibition.—N.** pro-, in-hibition; *veto*, disallowance; interdict, -ion; injunction; embargo, ban, *verboten*, taboo, proscription; *index expurgatorius*; restriction &c. (*restraint*) 751; hindrance &c. 706; forbidden fruit.

**V.** pro-, in-hibit; forbid, put one's *veto* upon, disallow; bar; debar &c. (*hinder*) 706, forefend.

keep -in, - within bounds; restrain &c. 751; cohibit, withhold, limit, circumscribe, clip the wings of, restrict, narrow; interdict, taboo; put -, place under -an interdiction, - the ban; proscribe, censor; exclude, shut out; shut -, bolt -, show- the door; warn off; dash the cup from one's lips; forbid the banns.

**Adj.** prohibit-ive, -ory; interdictive; proscriptive; restrictive, exclusive; forbidding &c. *v.*

prohibited &c. *v.*; not -permitted &c. 760; unlicensed, contraband, under the ban of; illegal &c. 964; unauthorized, not to be thought of.

**Adv.** on no account &c. (*no*) 536.

**Int.** forbid it heaven! &c. (*deprecation*) 766.

hands -, keep- off! hold! stop! avast!

**Phr.** that will never do.

---

**762. Consent.—N.** consent; assent &c. 488; acquiescence; approval &c. 931; compliance, agreement, concession; yield-ance, -ingness; accession, acknowledgment, acceptance, agnition.

settlement, ratification, confirmation, adjustment.

permit &c. (*permission*) 760; promise &c. 768.

**V.** consent; assent &c. 488; yield assent, admit, allow, concede, grant, yield; come -over, - round; give in to, acknowledge, agnize, give consent, comply with, acquiesce, agree to, fall in with, accede, accept, embrace an offer, close with, take at one's word, have no objection.

satisfy, meet one's wishes, settle, come to terms &c. 488; not -refuse &c. 764; turn a willing ear &c. (*willingness*) 602; jump at; deign, vouchsafe; promise &c. 768.

**Adj.** consenting &c. *v.*; agreeable, compliant; agreed &c. (*assent*) 488; unconditional.

**Adv.** yes &c. (*assent*) 488; by all means &c. (*willingly*) 602; if –, as- you please; be it so, so be it, well and good, of course.

**763. Offer.**—**N.** offer, proffer, presentation, tender, bid, overture; propos-al, -ition; motion, invitation; candidature; offering &c. (*gift*) 784.

**V.** offer, proffer, present, tender; bid; propose, move; make -a motion, – advances; start; invite, hold out, place- at one's disposal, – in one's way, put forward.

hawk about; offer for sale &c. 796; press &c. (*request*) 765; lay at one's feet.

offer –, present- oneself; volunteer, come forward, be a candidate; stand –, bid- for; seek; be at one's service; go a begging; bribe &c. (*give*) 784.

**Adj.** offer-ing, -ed &c. *v.*; in the market, for sale, to let, disengaged, on hire.

---

**764. Refusal.**—**N.** refusal, rejection; non-, in-compliance; denial; declining &c. *v.*; declension; peremptory –, flat –, point blank- refusal; repulse, rebuff; discountenance.

recusancy, renunciation, abnegation. negation, protest, disclaimer; dissent &c. 489; revocation &c. 756.

**V.** refuse, reject, deny, decline; nill, negative; refuse –, withhold- one's assent; shake the head; close the -hand, – purse; grudge, begrudge, be slow to, hang fire.

be deaf to; turn -a deaf ear to, – one's back upon; set one's face against, discountenance, not hear of, have nothing to do with, wash one's hands of, stand aloof, forswear, set aside, cast behind one; not yield an inch &c. (*obstinacy*) 606.

resist, cross; not -grant &c. 762; repel, repulse; shut –, slam- the door in one's face; rebuff; send -back, – to the right about, – away with a flea in the ear; deny oneself, not be at home to; discard &c. (*repudiate*) 610; rescind &c. (*revoke*) 756; disclaim, protest; dissent &c. 489.

**Adj.** refusing &c. *v.*; rest-ive, -iff; recusant; uncomplying, noncompliant, unconsenting, uncomplaisant, protestant; not willing to hear of, deaf to.

refused &c. *v.*; ungranted, out of the question, not to be thought of, impossible.

**Adv.** no &c. 536; on no account, not for the world; no thank you.

**Phr.** *non possumus*; [ironically] your humble servant; *bien obligé*.

**765. Request.**—**N.** requ-est, -isition; claim &c. (*demand*) 741; petition, suit, prayer; begging letter, round-robin.

motion, overture, application, canvass, address, appeal, apostrophe; imprecation; rogation; proposal, proposition.

orison &c. (*worship*) 990; incantation &c. (*spell*) 993.

mendicancy; asking, panhandling, begging &c. *v.*; postulation, solicitation, invitation, entreaty, importunity, supplication, instance, impetration, imploration, obsecration, obtestation, invocation, interpellation.

**V.** request, ask; beg, crave, sue, pray, petition, solicit, invite, pop the question, make bold to ask; beg -leave, – a boon; apply to, call to, put to; call -upon, – for; make –, address –, prefer –, put up- a -request, – prayer, – petition;

**766.** [Negative request.] **Deprecation.**—**N.** deprecation, expostulation; remonstrance; intercession, mediation.

**V.** deprecate, protest, expostulate, enter a protest, intercede for.

**Adj.** deprecatory, expostulatory, intercessory, mediatorial.

deprecated, protested.

un-, unbe-sought; unasked &c. (*see* ask &c. 765).

**Int.** cry you mercy! God forbid! forbid it Heaven! Heaven -forefend, – forbid! far be it from! hands off! &c. (*prohibition*) 761.

---

make -application, - a requisition; ask -, trouble- one for; claim &c. (*demand*) 741; offer up prayers &c. (*worship*) 990; whistle for.

beg hard, entreat, beseech, plead, supplicate, implore, apostrophize; conjure, adjure; obtest; cry to, kneel to, appeal to; invoke, evoke; impetrate, imprecate, ply, press, urge, beset, importune, dun, tax, clamour for; cry -aloud, - for help; fall on one's knees; throw oneself at the feet of; come down on one's marrow-bones.

beg from door to door, send the hat round, go a begging; mendicate, mump, cadge, panhandle, beg one's bread.

dance attendance on, besiege, knock at the door.

bespeak, canvass, tout, make interest, court; seek, bid for &c. (*offer*) 763; publish the banns.

**Adj.** requesting &c. *v.*; precatory; suppli-ant, -cant, -catory; invoc-, imprec-, rog-atory; postulant, mendicant.

importunate, clamorous, urgent; solicitous; cap in hand; on one's -knees, - bended knees, - marrow-bones.

**Adv.** prithee, do, please, pray; be so good as, be good enough; have the goodness, vouchsafe, will you, I pray thee, if you please.

**Int.** for -God's, - heaven's, - goodness', - mercy's- sake.

**767. Petitioner.**—**N.** petitioner, solicitor, applicant; suppli-ant, -cant; suitor, candidate, claimant, postulant, aspirant, competitor, bidder; place -, pot -, mug- hunter; prizer.

beggar, mendicant, mumper, sturdy beggar, cadger, panhandler; canvasser, barker, touter &c. 758.

sycophant, parasite &c. 886.

## Section III. Conditional Intersocial Volition

**768. Promise.**—**N.** promise, undertaking, word, troth, plight, pledge, *parole*, word of honour, vow; oath &c. (*affirmation*) 535; profession, assurance, warranty, guarantee, insurance, obligation; contract &c. 769.

engagement, pre-engagement: affiance; betroth, -al, -ment; marriage -compact, - vow.

**V.** promise; give a -promise &c. *n.*; undertake, engage; make -, form- an engagement; enter -into, - on- an engagement; bind -, tie -, pledge -, commit -, take upon- oneself; vow; swear &c. (*affirm*) 535, give -, pass -, pledge -, plight- one's -word, - honour, - credit, - troth; betroth, plight faith; take the vows.

assure, warrant, guarantee, vouch for, avouch, covenant &c. 769; attest &c. (*bear witness*) 467.

hold out an expectation; contract an obligation; become -bound to, - sponsor for; answer -, be answerable- for; secure; give security &c. 771; underwrite.

adjure, administer an oath, put to one's oath, swear a witness.

**Adj.** promising &c. *v.*; promissory; votive; under hand and seal; upon -oath, - affirmation.

promised &c. *v.*; affianced, pledged, bound; committed, compromised; in for it.

**Adv.** as one's head shall answer for; upon my honour.

**Phr.** in for a penny, in for a pound.

**768a. Release from engagement.**—**N.** release &c. (*liberation*) 750.

**Adj.** absolute; unconditional &c. (*free*) 748.

**769. Compact.**—**N.** compact, contract, agreement, bargain, deal, transaction; affidation; pact, -ion; bond, covenant, indenture.

stipulation, settlement, convention; compromise, *cartel*.

protocol, treaty, *concordat*, *Zollverein*, *Sonderbund*, charter, *Magna Charta*, Pragmatic Sanction.

negotiation &c. (*bargaining*) 794; diplomacy &c. (*mediation*) 724; negotiator &c. (*agent*) 758.

ratification, completion, signature, seal, sigil, signet.

**V.** contract, covenant, agree for, engage &c. (*promise*) 768.

treat, negotiate, stipulate, make terms; bargain &c. (*barter*) 794.

make –, strike- a bargain; come to -terms, – an understanding; compromise &c. 774; set at rest; close, – with; conclude, complete, settle; confirm, ratify, clench, subscribe, underwrite; en-, in-dorse; put the seal to; sign, seal &c. (*attest*) 467; indent.

take one at one's word, bargain by inch of candle.

**Adj.** contractual, agreed &c. *v.*; conventional; under hand and seal; signed, sealed and delivered.

**Phr.** *caveat emptor*.

**770. Conditions.**—**N.** conditions, terms; articles, – of agreement.

clauses, provisions; proviso &c. (*qualification*) 469; covenant, stipulation, obligation, *ultimatum*, *sine quâ non*; *casus fœderis*.

**V.** make –, come to- -terms &c. (*contract*) 769; make it a condition, stipulate, insist upon, make a point of; bind, tie up.

**Adj.** conditional, provisional, guarded, fenced, hedged in.

**Adv.** conditionally &c. (*with qualification*) 469; provisionally, *pro re natâ*; on condition; with a reservation.

**771. Security.**—**N.** security; guaran-ty, -tee; gage, warranty, bond, tie, pledge, plight, mortgage, debenture, hypothecation, bill of sale, lien, pignus, pawn, pignoration; real security; bottomry; collateral, vadium.

stake, deposit, earnest, handsel, caution.

promissory note; bill, – of exchange; I.O.U.; personal security, covenant, specialty; *parole* &c. (*promise*) 768.

acceptance, indorsement, signature, execution, stamp, seal.

spon-sor, -sion, -sorship; surety, bail; mainpernor, hostage.

recognizance; deed –, covenant- of indemnity.

authentication, verification, warrant, certificate, voucher, docket, doquet; record &c. 551; probate, attested copy.

receipt; ac-, quittance; discharge, release.

muniment, title-deed, instrument; deed, – poll; assurance, insurance, indenture; charter &c. (*compact*) 769; charter-poll; paper, parchment, settlement, will, testament, last will and testament, codicil.

**V.** give -security, – bail, – substantial bail; go bail; pawn, impawn, hock, spout, mortgage, hypothecate, impignorate.

guarantee, warrant, assure; accept, indorse, underwrite, insure.

execute, stamp; sign, seal &c. (*evidence*) 467.

let, sett; grant –, take –, hold- a lease; hold in pledge; lend on security &c. 787.

**Adj.** secure, -ed; pledged &c. *v.*; in pawn, on deposit.

**772. Observance.**—**N.** observance, performance, compliance; obedience

**773. Non-observance.** — **N.** non-observance &c. 772; evasion, inob-

&c. 743; fulfilment, satisfaction, discharge; acquit-tance, -tal.

adhesion, acknowledgment; fidelity &c. (*probity*) 939; exact &c. 494- observance.

**V.** observe, comply with, respect, acknowledge, abide by; cling to, adhere to, be faithful to, act up to; meet, fulfil; carry -out, - into execution; execute, perform, keep, satisfy, discharge; do one's office.

perform -, fulfill -, discharge -, acquit oneself of- an obligation; make good; make good -, keep- one's -word, - promise; redeem one's pledge; keep faith with, stand to one's engagement.

**Adj.** observant, faithful, true, loyal; honourable &c. 939; true as the -dial to the sun, - needle to the pole; punct-ual, -ilious; meticulous; literal &c. (*exact*) 494; as good as one's word.

**Adv.** faithfully &c. *adj.*

servance, failure, omission, neglect, laches, laxity, informality.

infringement, infraction; violation, transgression.

retractation, repudiation, nullification; protest; forfeiture.

lawlessness; disobedience &c. 742; bad faith &c. 940.

**V.** fail, neglect, omit, elude, evade, give the go by to, cut, set aside, ignore; shut -, close- one's eyes to, avoid.

infringe, transgress, pirate, violate, break, trample under foot, do violence to, drive a coach and six through.

discard, protest, repudiate, fling to the winds, set at naught, nullify, declare null and void; cancel &c. (*wipe off*) 552.

retract, go back from, be off, forfeit, go from one's word, palter; stretch -, strain- a point.

**Adj.** violating &c. *v.*; lawless, transgressive; elusive, evasive; lax, casual; non-observant.

unfulfilled &c. (*see* fulfil &c. 772).

**774. Compromise.—N.** com-promise, -mutation, -position; middle term, *mezzo termine*; compensation &c. 30; adjustment, mutual concession.

**V.** com-promise, -mute, -pound; take the mean; split the difference, meet one half way, give and take; come to terms &c. (*contract*) 769; submit to -, abide by- arbitration; patch up, bridge over, fix up, arrange; adjust, - differences; agree; make -the best of, - a virtue of necessity; take the will for the deed.

## Section IV. Possessive Relations*

### 1°. *Property in general*

**775. Acquisition.—N.** acquisition; gaining &c. *v.*; obtainment; procuration, -ement; purchase, descent, inheritance; gift &c. 784.

recovery, retrieval, revendication, replevin; redemption, salvage, trover; find, *trouvaille*, foundling.

gain, thrift; money-making, -grubbing; lucre, filthy lucre, loaves and fishes, the main chance, pelf; emolument &c. 973; wealth &c. 803.

profit, earnings, winnings, innings, clean-up, pickings, perquisite, net profit; income &c. (*receipt*) 810; proceeds, -duce, -duct; out-come, -put;

**776. Loss.—N.** loss; de-, perdition; forfeiture, lapse.

privation, bereavement; deprivation &c. (*dispossession*) 789; riddance.

**V.** lose; incur -, experience -, meet with- a loss; miss; mislay, let slip, allow to slip through the fingers, squander; be without &c. (*exempt*) 777*a*; forfeit.

get rid of &c. 782; waste &c. 638.

be lost, lapse.

**Adj.** losing &c. *v.*; not having &c. 777*a*.

shorn of, deprived of; denuded, bereaved, bereft, *minus*, cut off; dispos-

* That is, relations which concern property.

return, fruit, crop, harvest, tilth; second crop, aftermath; benefit &c. (*good*) 618.

sweepstakes, trick, prize, pool.

[Fraudulent acquisition] subreption; theft, stealing &c. 791.

**V.** acquire, get, gain, win, earn, obtain, procure, gather, annex; collect &c. 72; pick, – up; glean, take &c. 789.

find; come –, pitch –, light- upon; scrape -up, – together; get in, reap and carry, net, bag, sack, bring home, secure, come across, derive, draw, get in the harvest.

profit; make –, draw- profit; turn to -profit, – account; make -capital out of, – money by; obtain a return, reap the fruits of; reap –, gain- an advantage; turn -a penny, – an honest penny; make the pot boil, bring grist to the mill; make –, coin –, raise- money; raise -funds, – the wind; fill one's pocket &c. (*wealth*) 803.

treasure up &c. (*store*) 636; realize, clear; produce &c. 161; take &c. 789.

get back, recover, regain, retrieve, revendicate, replevy, redeem, come by one's own.

come -by, – in for; receive &c. 785; inherit; step into, – a fortune, – the shoes of; succeed to.

get -hold of, – between one's finger and thumb, – into one's hand, – at; take –, come into –, enter into- possession.

be -profitable &c. *adj.*; pay, answer.

accrue &c. (*be received*) 785.

**Adj.** acquir-ing, -ed &c. *v.*; acquisitive; productive, profitable, advantageous, gainful, remunerative, paying, lucrative.

sessed &c. 789; rid of, quit of; out of pocket.

lost &c. *v.*; long lost; irretrievable &c. (*hopeless*) 859; irredentist; off one's hands.

**Int.** farewell to! adieu to! good riddance!

---

**777. Possession.—N.** possession, seisin; ownership &c. 780; occupancy; hold, -ing; tenure, tenancy, feodality, dependency; villenage, socage, chivalry, knight service.

exclusive possession, impropriation, monopoly, corner; retention &c. 781; pre-possession, -occupancy; nine points of the law.

future possession, heritage, inheritance, heirship, reversion, fee, seigniority, feud, fief.

bird in hand, *uti possidetis*, *chose* in possession.

**V.** possess, have, hold, occupy, enjoy; be -possessed of &c. *adj.*; have -in hand &c. *adj.*; own &c. 780; command.

inherit; come -to, – in for.

engross, monopolize, forestall, regrate, impropriate, have all to oneself, corner; have a firm hold of &c. (*retain*) 781; get into one's hand &c. (*acquire*) 775.

belong to, appertain to, pertain to; be -in one's possession &c. *adj.*; vest in.

**Adj.** possessing &c. *v.*; worth; possessed of, seized of, master of, in possession of; endowed –, blest –, instinct –, fraught –, laden –, charged –, instilled –, with.

possessed &c. *v.*; on hand, by one; in hand, in store, in stock; in one's -hands, – grasp, – possession; at one's -command, – disposal; one's own &c. (*property*) 780.

unsold; unshared.

**777a. Exemption.**—**N.** exemption; exception, immunity, privilege, release &c. 927*a*; absence &c. 187.

**V.** not -have &c. 777; be -without &c. *adj.*

**Adj.** exempt from, devoid of, without, unpossessed of, unblest with, immune from.

not -having &c. 777; unpossessed; untenanted &c. (*vacant*) 187; without an owner.

unobtained, unacquired.

**778.** [Joint possession.] **Participation.**—**N.** participation; co-, joint-tenancy; possession –, tenancy- in common; joint –, common- stock; co-, partnership; communion; community of -possessions, – goods; communalism, communism, socialism, collectivism; co-operation &c. 709; profit sharing.

snacks, co-portion, picnic, hotchpotch; co-heirship, -parceny, -parcenary; gavelkind.

participator, sharer; co-, partner; shareholder; co-, joint-tenant; tenants in common; co-heir, -parcener.

communist, socialist.

**V.** par-ticipate, -take; share, – in; come in for a share; go -shares, – snacks, – halves; share and share alike.

have –, possess –, be seized- -in common, – as joint tenants &c. *n.*

join in; have a hand in &c. (*co-operate*) 709.

**Adj.** partaking &c. *v.*; communistic, socialistic, co-operative, profit sharing.

**Adv.** share and share alike.

**779. Possessor.**—**N.** possessor, holder; occup-ant, -ier; tenant; person –, man- -in possession &c. 777; renter, lodger, lessee, under-lessee; zemindar, ryot; tenant -on sufferance, – at will, – from year to year, – for years, – for life.

owner; propriet-or, -ress, -ary; impropriator, master, mistress, lord.

land-holder, -owner, -lord, -lady; lord -of the manor, – paramount; heritor, laird, vavasour, landed gentry, mesne lord.

*cestui-que-trust*, beneficiary, mortgagor.

grantee, feoffee, relessee, devisee; legat-ee, -ary.

trustee; holder &c.- of the legal estate; mortgagee.

right –, rightful- owner.

[Future possessor] heir, – apparent; – presumptive; heiress; inheritor, -ress, -rix; reversioner, remainder-man.

**780. Property.**—**N.** property, possession, *suum cuique, meum et tuum.*

owner-, proprietor-, lord-ship; seignority; empire &c. (*dominion*) 737.

interest, stake, estate, right, title, claim, demand, holding; tenure &c. (*possession*) 777; vested –, contingent –, beneficial –, equitable- interest; use, trust, benefit; legal –, equitable- estate; seisin.

absolute interest, paramount estate, freehold; fee, – simple, – tail; estate -in fee, – in tail, – tail; estate in tail -male, – female, – general.

limitation, term, lease, settlement, strict settlement, particular estate; estate -for life, – for years, – *pur autre vie*; remainder, reversion, expectancy, possibility.

dower, dowry, *dot*, jointure, marriage portion, appanage, inheritance, heritage, patrimony, alimony; legacy &c. (*gift*) 784.

assets, belongings, means, resources, circumstances; wealth &c. 803; money &c. 800; what one -is worth, – will cut up for; estate and effects.

landed –, real- -estate, – property; realty; land, -s; subdivision; plot, site; tenements; hereditaments; corporeal –, incorporeal- hereditaments; acres; ground &c. (*earth*) 342; acquest; messuage.

territory, state, kingdom, principality, realm, empire, protectorate, margravate, dependancy, colony, sphere of influence, mandate.

manor, honour, domain, demesne; farm, ranch, plantation, *hacienda*; allodium &c. (*free*) 748; fief, feoff, feud, zemindary, dependency.

free-, copy-, lease-holds; chattels real; fixtures, plant, heirloom easement; folkland; right of -common, – user.

personal -property, – estate, – effects; personalty, chattels, goods, effects, movables; stock, – in trade; things, traps, rattle-traps, paraphernalia; equipage &c. 633.

parcels, appurtenances.

*impedimenta*; lug-, bag-gage; bag and baggage; pelf; cargo, lading.

rent-roll; income &c. (*receipts*) 810.

patent, copyright; *chose* in action; credit &c. 805; debt &c. 806.

**V.** possess &c. 777; be the -possessor &c. 779- of· own; have for one's own, – very own; come in for, inherit; enfeoff.

savour of the realty.

be one's -property &c. *n.*; belong to; ap-, pertain to.

**Adj.** one's own; landed, predial, manorial, allodial, seigniorial; free-, copy-, lease-hold; feu-, feo-dal; hereditary, entailed, personal.

**Adv.** to one's -credit, – account; to the good.

to one and -his heirs for ever, – the heirs of his body, – his heirs and assigns, – his executors, administrators and assigns.

**781. Retention.—N.** retention; retaining &c. *v.*; keep, detention, custody; tenacity, firm hold, grasp, gripe, grip, iron grip.

fangs, teeth, claws, talons, nail, hook, tentacle, *tenaculum*; bond &c. (*vinculum*) 45.

clutches, tongs, forceps, pincers, nippers, pliers, tweezers, vice.

paw, hand, finger, wrist, fist, neaf, neif.

bird in hand; captive &c. 754.

**V.** retain, keep; hold, – fast, – tight, – one's own, – one's ground; clinch, clench, clutch, grasp, gripe, hug, have a firm hold of.

secure, withold, detain; hold –, keep- back; keep close; husband &c. (*store*) 636; reserve; have –, keep- in stock &c. (*possess*) 777; entail, tie up, settle.

**Adj.** retaining &c. *v.*; retentive, tenacious.

unforfeited, undeprived, undisposed, uncommunicated.

incommunicable, inalienable; in mortmain; in strict settlement.

**Phr.** *uti possidetis.*

---

**782. Relinquishment. — N.** relinquishment, abandonment &c. (*of a course*) 624; renunciation, expropriation, dereliction; cession, surrender, dispensation; resignation &c. 757; riddance.

derelict &c. *adj.*; jetsam; waif, foundling, orphan.

**V.** relinquish, give up, surrender, yield, cede; let -go, – slip; spare, drop, resign, forego, renounce, abjure, abandon, expropriate, give away, dispose of, part with; lay -aside, – apart, – down, – on the shelf &c. (*disuse*) 678; set –, put- aside; make away with, cast behind; discard, cast off, dismiss; maroon.

give -notice to quit, – warning; supersede; be –, get- -rid of, – quit of; eject &c. 297.

rid –, disburden –, divest –, dispossess- oneself of; wash one's hands of; divorce, desert; disinherit, cut off.

cast –, throw –, pitch –, fling- -away, – aside, – overboard, – to the dogs; cast –, throw –, sweep- to the winds; put –, turn –, sweep- away; jettison.

quit one's hold.

**Adj.** relinquished &c. *v.*; cast off, derelict; unowned, unappropriated, un-

culled; left &c. (*residuary*) 40; divorced; disinherited.
**Int.** away with!

2°. *Transfer of Property*

**783. Transfer.**—**N.** transfer, conveyance, assignment, alienation, abalienation; demise, limitation; conveyancing; transmission &c. (*transference*) 270; enfeoffment, bargain and sale, lease and release; exchange &c. (*interchange*) 148; barter &c. 794; substitution &c. 147.

succession, reversion; shifting -use, – trust; devolution.

**V.** transfer, convey; alien, -ate; assign; grant &c. (*confer*) 784; consign; make –, hand- over; pass, hand, transmit, negotiate; hand down; exchange &c. (*interchange*) 148.

change -hands, – from one to another; devolve, succeed; come into possession &c. (*acquire*) 775; take over.

abalienate; disinherit; dispossess &c. 789; substitute &c. 147.

**Adj.** alienable, negotiable, transferable, reversional.

**Phr.** estate coming into possession.

**784. Giving.**—**N.** giving &c. *v.*; bestowal, donation; present-ation, -ment; accordance; con-, cession; delivery, consignment, dispensation, communication, endowment; invest-ment, -iture; award.

almsgiving, charity, liberality, generosity; philanthropy &c. 910.

[Thing given] gift, donation, present, *cadeau*; fairing; free gift, boon, favour, benefaction, grant, offering, oblation, sacrifice, immolation.

grace, act of grace, *bonus*, *bonanza*.

allowance, contribution, subscription, subsidy, tribute, subvention.

bequest, legacy, devise, will, dotation, appanage; dowry; voluntary -settlement, – conveyance &c. 783; amortization.

alms, largess, bounty, dole, sportule, donative, help, oblation, offertory, Peter's pence, *honorarium*, gratuity, Maundy money, Christmas box, Easter offering, vail, tip, *douceur*, drink money, *pourboire*, *Trinkgeld*, *backsheesh*; fee &c. (*recompense*) 973; consideration.

bribe, bait, ground-bait; peace-offering, handsel.

giver, grantor &c. *v.*; donor, feoffer, settlor; almoner; testator; investor, subscriber, contributor; fairy godmother; Santa Claus, benefactor &c. 816.

**V.** deliver, hand, pass, put into the hands of; hand –, make –, deliver –, pass –, turn- over.

present, give away, dispense, dispose of; give –, deal –, dole –, mete –, fork –, shell –, squeeze- out.

pay &c. 807; render, impart, communicate.

**785. Receiving.**—**N.** receiving &c. *v.*; acquisition &c. 775; reception &c. (*introduction*) 296; suscipiency, acceptance, admission.

re-, ac-cipient; assignee, devisee; lega-tee, -tary; grantee, feoffee, donee, relessee, lessee.

sportulary, stipendiary; beneficiary; pension-er, -ary; almsman.

income &c. (*receipt*) 810.

**V.** receive; take &c. 789; acquire &c. 775; admit.

take in, catch, touch; pocket; put into one's -pocket, – purse; accept; take off one's hands.

be received; come -in, – to hand; pass –, fall- into one's hand; go into one's pocket; fall to one's -lot, – share; come –, fall- to one; accrue; have -given &c. 784 to one.

**Adj.** receiving &c. *v.*; re-, suscipient.

received &c. *v.*; given &c. 784; second-hand.

not given, unbestowed &c. (*see* **give**, bestow &c. 784).

concede, cede, yield, part with, shed cast; spend &c. 809.

give, bestow, confer, grant, accord, award, assign.

entrust, consign, vest in.

make a present; allow, contribute, subscribe, donate, furnish its quota.

invest, endow, settle upon; bequeath, leave, devise.

furnish, supply, help; ad-, minister to; afford, spare; accommodate –, indulge –, favour- with; shower down upon; lavish, pour on, thrust upon; tip, bribe; tickle –, grease- the palm; offer &c. 763; sacrifice, immolate.

**Adj.** giving &c. *v.*; given &c. *v.*; allow-ed, -able; concessional; communicable; charitable, eleemosynary, sportulary, tributary; *gratis* &c. 815.

**786. Apportionment.**—**N.** apportion-, allot-, consign-, assign-, appointment; appropriation, dis-, pensation, -tribution; allocation, division, deal; repartition; administration.

dividend, portion, contingent, share, allotment, lot, cut, split, measure, dose; dole, meed, pittance; *quantum*, ration; ratio, proportion, quota, *modicum*, mess, allowance.

**V.** apportion, divide; cut, split, divvy; distribute, administer, dispense; billet, allot, detail, cast, share, mete; portion –, parcel –, dole out; deal, carve.

partition, assign, appropriate, appoint.

come in for one's share &c. (*participate*) 778.

**Adj.** apportioning &c. *v.*; respective.

**Adv.** respectively, each to each.

**787. Lending.**—**N.** lending &c. *v.*; loan, advance, accommodation, feneration; mortgage &c. (*security*) 771; investment.

*mont-de-piété*, pawnshop, hock shop, spout, my uncle's.

lender, pawnbroker, money-lender, usurer, Jew, Shylock.

**V.** lend, advance, loan, accommodate with; lend on security; pawn &c. (*security*) 771.

intrust, invest; place –, put- out to interest; sink, risk.

let, demise, lease, sett, under-, sublet.

**Adj.** lending &c. *v.*; lent &c. *v.*; unborrowed &c. (*see* borrowed &c. 788).

**Adv.** in advance; on -loan, – security.

**788. Borrowing.** — **N.** borrowing pledging, pawning.

borrowed plumes; plagiarism &c. (*thieving*) 791.

replevin.

**V.** borrow, desume; pawn.

hire, rent, farm; take a -lease, – demise; take –, hire- by the -hour, – mile, – year &c.

raise –, take up- money; float bonds; raise the wind; fly a kite, borrow of Peter to pay Paul; run into debt &c. (*debt*) 806.

make use of, plagiarize, pirate.

replevy.

---

**789. Taking.**—**N.** taking &c. *v.*; reception &c. (*taking in*) 296; deglutition &c. (*taking food*) 298; appropriation, prehension, prensation; capture, caption; ap-, de-prehension; abreption, seizure; ab-duction, -lation; subtraction &c. (*subduction*) 38; abstraction, ademption.

**790. Restitution.**—**N.** restitution, return; ren-, red-dition; reinstatement, restoration; reinvestment, recuperation; repatriation; rehabilitation &c. (*reconstruction*) 660; reparation, atonement, indemnity, compensation, recompense.

release, replevin, redemption; recov-

dispossession; depriv-ation, -ement; bereavement; divestment; disherison; distraint, distress; sequestration, confiscation, attachment, execution; eviction &c. 297.

rapacity, extortion, vampirism, predacity, blood-sucking; theft &c. 791.

resumption; repris-e, -al; recovery &c. 775.

clutch, swoop, wrench; grip &c. (*retention*) 781; haul, take, catch; scramble.

taker, captor, capturer; vampire; extortioner.

**V.** take, catch, hook, nab, bag, sack, pocket, put into one's pocket, scrounge; receive; accept.

reap, crop, cull, pluck; gather &c. (*get*) 775; draw.

ap-, im-propriate; assume, possess oneself of; take possession of; commandeer; lay –, clap- one's hands on; help oneself to; make free with, dip one's hands into, lay under contribution; intercept; scramble for; deprive of.

take –, carry –, bear- -away, – off; abstract; hurry off –, run away- with; abduct; steal &c. 791; ravish; seize; pounce –, spring- upon; swoop -to, – down upon; take by -storm, – assault; snatch, reave.

snap up, nip up, whip up, catch up; kidnap, crimp, capture, lay violent hands on.

get –, lay –, take –, catch –, lay fast –, take firm- hold of; lay by the heels, take prisoner; fasten upon, grip, grapple, embrace, gripe, clasp, grab, clutch, collar, throttle, take by the throat, claw, clinch, clench, make sure of; apprehend.

catch at, jump at, make a grab at, snap at, snatch at; reach, make a long arm, stretch forth one's hand.

take -from, – away from; deduct &c. 38; retrench &c. (*curtail*) 201; dispossess, ease one of, snatch from one's grasp; tear –, tear away –, wrench –, wrest –, wring- from; extort; deprive of, bereave; disinherit, cut off with a shilling.

oust &c. (*eject*) 297; divest; levy, distrain, confiscate; sequest-er, -rate, accroach; usurp; despoil, strip, fleece, shear, displume, impoverish, eat out of house and home; drain, – to the dregs; gut, dry, exhaust, swallow up; absorb &c. (*suck in*) 296; draw off; suck, – like a leech, – the blood of.

retake, resume; recover &c. 775.

**Adj.** taking &c. *v.*; privative, prehensile; pred-aceous, -al, -atory, -atorial; rap-acious, -torial; ravenous: parasitic; all-devouring, -engulfing.

bereft &c. 776.

**Adv.** at one fell swoop.

**Phr.** give an inch and take an ell.

ery &c. (*getting back*) 775; remitter, reversion.

**V.** return, restore; recondition; give –, carry –, bring- back; render, – up; give up; let go, unclutch; dis-, re-gorge; regurgitate; recoup, reimburse, repay, indemnify, reinvest, remit, rehabilitate; repair &c. (*make good*) 660.

redeem, recover &c. (*get back*) 775; take back again; revest, revert.

**Adj.** restoring &c. *v.*; recuperative &c. 660; in full restitution, to compensate for.

**Phr.** *suum cuique.*

---

**791. Stealing.**—**N.** stealing &c. *v.*; theft, thievery, robbery, latrociny, direption; abstraction, appropriation; plagiar-y, -ism; rape, kidnapping, depredation; raid, hold up.

spoliation, plunder, pillage; sack, -age; rapine, *brigandage*, highway robbery, foray, *razzia*; black-mail; piracy, privateering, buccaneering; filibuster-ing, -ism; burglary; house-breaking; cattle-stealing, -rustling, -lifting.

peculation, embezzlement; fraud &c. 545; larceny, petty larceny, pilfering, shop-lifting.

thievishness, rapacity, kleptomania, Alsatia; den of -Cacus, – thieves.

licence to plunder, letters of marque.

**V.** steal, thieve, rob, purloin, pilfer, filch, lift, prig, bag, nim, cri cabbage, palm; abstract; appropriate, plagiarize.

convey away, carry off, abduct, kidnap, shanghai, impress, crimp, make –, walk –, run- off with; run away with; spirit away; seize &c. (*lay violent hands on*) 789.

plunder, pillage, rifle, sack, loot, ransack, spoil, spoliate, despoil, strip, sweep, gut, forage, levy black-mail, pirate, pickeer, maraud, lift cattle, rustle, poach, smuggle, run.

stick –, hold- up.

swindle, peculate, embezzle; sponge, mulct, rook, bilk, pluck, pigeon, skin, fleece, diddle; defraud &c. 545; obtain under false pretences; live by one's wits.

rob –, borrow of- Peter to pay Paul; set a thief to catch a thief.

disregard the distinction between *meum* and *tuum*.

**Adj.** thieving &c. *v.*; thievish, light-fingered; fur-acious, -tive; piratical; pred-aceous, -al, -atory, -atorial; raptorial &c. (*rapacious*) 789.

stolen &c. *v.*

**Phr.** *sic vos non vobis*.

**792. Thief.**—**N.** thief, robber, *homo trium literarum*, pilferer, rifler, filcher, plagiarist.

spoiler, depredator, pillager, marauder; harpy, shark, land-shark, falcon, moss-trooper, bushranger, Bedouin, brigand, freebooter, bandit, thug, dacoit, pirate, corsair, viking, Paul Jones; buccan-eer, -ier; piqu-, pick-eerer; rover, ranger, privateer, filibuster; rapparee, wrecker, picaroon; smuggler, poacher, plunderer; racketeer.

highwayman, Dick Turpin, Claude Duval, Macheath, knight of the road, footpad, sturdy beggar; abductor, kidnapper.

cut-, pick-purse; pick-pocket, light-fingered gentry; sharper; card-, skittle-sharper; crook; thimble-rigger; rook, Greek, blackleg, leg, welsher, defaulter; Autolycus, Cacus, Barabbas, Jeremy Diddler, Robert Macaire, artful dodger, trickster; swell mob, *chevalier d'industrie*; shop-lifter.

swindler, peculator; forger, coiner, counterfeiter, shoful; fence, receiver of stolen goods, duffer; smasher.

burglar, housebreaker; cracks-, mags-man; Bill Sikes, Jack Sheppard, Jonathan Wild, Raffles, cat burglar.

**793. Booty.**—**N.** booty, spoil, plunder, prize, loot, graft, swag, pickings, boodle; *spolia opima*, prey; blackmail; stolen goods.

**Adj.** looting &c. *n.*; manubial, spoliative.

3°. *Interchange of Property*

**794. Barter.**—**N.** barter, exchange, scorse, truck system; interchange &c. 148.

a Roland for an Oliver; *quid pro quo*; com-mutation, -position.

trade, commerce, mercature, buying and selling, bargain and sale; traffic, business, nundination, custom, shopping; commercial enterprise, speculation, jobbing, stock-jobbing, *agiotage*, brokery, arbitrage.

dealing, transaction, negotiation, bargain.

free trade.

**V.** barter, exchange, truck, scorse, swop; interchange &c. 148; commutate &c. (*substitute*) 147; compound for.

trade, traffic, buy and sell, give and take, nundinate; carry on –, ply –, drive- a trade; be in -business, – the city; keep a shop, deal in, employ one's capital in.

trade –, deal –, have dealings- with; transact –, do- business with; open –, keep- an account with.

bargain; drive –, make- a bargain; negotiate, bid for; dicker, haggle, higgle; chaffer, huckster, cheapen, beat down; stickle, – for; out-, under-bid; ask, charge; strike a bargain &c. (*contract*) 769.

speculate, give a sprat to catch a herring; buy in the cheapest and sell in the dearest market; rig the market.

**Adj.** commercial, mercantile, trading; interchangeable, marketable, staple, in the market, for sale.

wholesale, retail.

**Adv.** across the counter; on 'change.

**795. Purchase.**—**N.** purchase, emption; buying, purchasing, shopping; pre-emption, refusal.

coemption, bribery; slave trade.

buyer, purchaser, *emptor*, vendee; patron, employer, client, customer, *clientèle*.

**V.** buy, purchase, invest in, procure; rent &c. (*hire*) 788; repurchase, buy in.

keep in one's pay, bribe, suborn; pay &c. 807; spend &c. 809.

make –, complete- a purchase; buy over the counter; pay cash for.

shop, market, go a shopping.

**Adj.** purchased &c. *v.*

**Phr.** *caveat emptor.*

**796. Sale.**—**N.** sale, vent, disposal; auction, roup, Dutch auction; custom &c. (*traffic*) 794.

vendi-bility, -bleness.

seller, salesman, peddler, smous; vender, vendor, consignor; merchant &c. 797; auctioneer.

**V.** sell, vend, dispose of, effect a sale; sell -over the counter, – by auction &c. *n.*; dispense, retail; deal in &c. 794; sell -off, – out; turn into money; realize; bring -to, – under- the hammer; put up to auction; auction, offer –, put up- for sale; hawk, peddle, bring to market; offer &c. 763; undersell; dump, unload.

let; mortgage &c. (*security*) 771.

**Adj.** under the hammer, in the market, for sale.

saleable, marketable, vendible, in demand, having a ready sale; unsaleable &c., unpurchased, unbought; on one's hands.

**797. Merchant.**—**N.** merchant, trader, dealer, monger, chandler, salesman; changer; regrater; shop-keeper, -man; trades-man, -people, -folk.

retailer; chapman, hawker, huckster, higgler; peddler, smous, pedlar, *colporteur*, cadger, Autolycus; sutler, *vivandière*; coster-man, -monger; market woman; cheap jack; caterer &c. 637; tallyman.

money-broker, -changer, -lender; stock-broker, -jobber; cambist, usurer, moneyer, banker.

jobber; broker &c. (*agent*) 758; buyer &c. 795; seller &c. 796.

concern; firm &c. (*partnership*) 712.

**798. Merchandise.** — **N.** merchandise, ware, commodity, effects, goods, article, stock, produce, staple commodity; stock in trade &c. (*store*) 636; cargo &c. (*contents*) 190.

**799. Mart.**—**N.** mart; market, -place, *forum*; fair, bazaar, staple; stock –, exchange; 'change, *bourse*, Wall Street, Rialto, hall, guildhall; toll-booth, custom-house; Tattersalls.

shop, stall, booth; wharf; office, chambers, counting-house, *bureau*; coun-, comp-ter.

ware-house, -room; depot, interposit, *entrepôt*, *emporium*, establishment; store &c. 636.

open market, market-overt.

4°. *Monetary Relations*

**800. Money.**—**N.** money -matters, – market; finance; accounts &c. 811; funds, treasure; capital, stock; assets &c. (*property*) 780; wealth &c. 803; supplies, ways and means, wherewithal, sinews of war, almighty dollar, needful, cash.

sum, amount; balance, -sheet; sum total; proceeds &c. (*receipts*) 810.

currency, circulating medium, specie; coin, – of the realm; piece, hard cash, dollar, sterling coin; pounds shillings and pence; £ s. d., guineas; pocket, breeches pocket, purse; money in hand; the best, ready, – money; filthy lucre, shekels, roll, jack, rhino, blunt, dust, bawbees, brass, dibs, dough, mopus, tin, salt, chink, oof, spondulics, pile, wads.

precious metals, gold, silver, copper, nickel; bullion, bar, ingot, nugget.

petty cash; pocket-, pin-money; small –, change; small coin, loose cash; doit, stiver, rap, mite, farthing, *sou*, penny, shilling, bob, tanner, tester, groat, guinea, ducat; *rouleau*; *wampum*; good –, round –, lump-sum; power –, mint –, tons- of money; plum, lac of rupees, millions, money-bags, miser's hoard, stocking, mine of wealth &c. 803.

[Science of coins] numismatics, chrysology.

paper-money; money –, postal –, Post Office- order; note, – of hand; bank –, treasury- note; Bradbury; promissory note; I O U., bond; bill, – of exchange; draft, cheque, order, warrant, coupon, debenture, exchequer bill, *assignat*, greenback, gold –, silver- certificate.

copper, nickel, dime, quarter, two bits, half a dollar, dollar, buck, simoleon, fiver, tenner, a twenty, a sawbuck, a century, a grand; eagle, double eagle.

gold standard, bimetallism, fiat money; rate of –, exchange; in-, de-flation.

remittance &c. (*payment*) 807; credit &c. 805; liability &c. 806; solvency &c. 803.

draw-er, -ee; oblig-or, -ee; moneyer, coiner, counterfeiter, forger.

false –, bad- money; base –, counterfeit- coin, flash note, slip, kite; Bank of Elegance.

*argumentum ad crumenam.*

**V.** amount to, come to, mount up to; touch the pocket; draw, – upon; endorse &c. (*security*) 771; issue, utter, circulate; discount &c. 813.

forge, counterfeit, coin, circulate –, pass- bad money.

**Adj.** monetary, pecuniary, crumenal, fiscal, financial, sumptuary, numismatical; sterling; solvent &c. 803.

**801. Treasurer.**—**N.** treasurer; bursar, -y; purser, purse-bearer; cash-keeper, banker; depositary; questor, receiver, steward, trustee, chartered –, accountant; Accountant-General, almoner, liquidator, paymaster, cashier, teller; cambist; money-changer &c. (*merchant*) 797.

financier, Chancellor of the Exchequer, minister of finance; Secretary of the Treasury, Director of the Budget, Controller of Currency.

**802. Treasury.**—**N.** treasury, thesaurus, bank, exchequer, almonry, fisc, hanaper, bursary; safe; strong-box, -hold, -room; coffer; chest &c. (*receptacle*) 191; depository &c. 636; till, -er; cash-box, -register, purse, pocket-book, wallet; money-bag, -belt, -box; *porte-monnaie.*

purse-strings; pocket, breeches pocket.

sinking fund; stocks; government –, public –, parliamentary- -stocks, – funds, – securities, bonds; gilt-edged securities; Consols, Liberty bonds, government bonds, *crédit mobilier*.

**803. Wealth.**—**N.** wealth, riches, fortune, handsome fortune, opulence, affluence; good –, easy- circumstances; independence; competence &c. (*sufficiency*) 639; solvency, soundness, solidity.

provision, livelihood, maintenance; alimony, dowry; means, resources, substance; property &c. 780; command of money.

income &c. 810; capital, money; round sum &c. (*treasure*) 800; mint of money, mine of wealth, *El Dorado*, Pactolus, Golconda, Potosi, *bonanza*; philosopher's stone.

long –, full –, well lined –, heavy- purse; purse of Fortunatus.

pelf, Mammon, lucre, filthy lucre; loaves and fishes; fleshpots of Egypt.

rich –, moneyed –, warm- man; man of substance; capitalist, millionaire, Nabob, Crœsus, Midas, Plutus, Dives, Timon of Athens; Timo-, Pluto-cracy; Danaë.

**V.** be -rich &c. *adj.*; roll –, wallow- in -wealth, – riches; have money to burn.

afford, well afford; command -money, – a sum; make both ends meet, hold one's head above water.

become -rich &c. *adj.*; fill one's -pocket &c. (*treasury*) 802; feather one's nest, clean up –, make- a fortune; make money &c. (*acquire*) 775.

enrich, imburse.

worship -Mammon, – the golden calf.

**Adj.** wealthy, rich, affluent, opulent, moneyed, monied, worth -a great deal,

**804. Poverty.**—**N.** poverty, indigence, penury, pauperism, destitution, want; need, -iness; lack, necessity, privation, distress, difficulties, wolf at the door.

bad –, poor –, needy –, embarrassed –, reduced –, straitened- circumstances; slender –, narrow- means; straits; hand to mouth existence, *res angusta domi*, low water, impecuniosity.

beggary; mendi-cancy, -city; broken –, loss of- fortune; insolvency &c. (*non-payment*) 808.

empty -purse, – pocket; light purse; beggarly account of empty boxes.

poor man, pauper, mendicant, mumper, beggar, starveling; *pauvre diable.*

**V.** be -poor &c. *adj.*; want, lack, starve, live from hand to mouth, have seen better days, go down in the world, be on one's uppers, come upon the parish; go to -the dogs, – wrack and ruin; not have a -penny &c. (*money*) 800, – shot in one's locker; beg one's bread; *tirer le diable par la queue*; run into debt &c. (*debt*) 806.

render -poor &c. *adj.*; impoverish; reduce, – to poverty; pauperize, fleece, ruin, bring to the parish.

**Adj.** poor, indigent; poverty-stricken; badly –, poorly –, ill- off; poor as -a rat, – a church mouse, – Job's turkey, – Job; fortune-, dower-, money-, penni-less; unportioned, unmoneyed; impecunious; broke, flat; out –, short- of -money, – cash; without –, not worth- a rap &c. (*money*) 800; *qui n'a pas le sou*, out of pocket, hard up; out at

- much; well -to do, - off; warm; well -, provided for.

made of money; rich as Crœsus; rolling in -riches, - wealth.

flush, - of -cash, - money, - tin; in -funds, - cash, - full feather; solvent, solid, sound, pecunious, out of debt, all straight; able to pay 20s in the £.

**Phr.** one's ship coming in.

---

elbows, down at heels; seedy, bare-foot, beggar-ly, -ed; destitute; fleeced, strapped, stripped; bereft, bereaved; reduced.

in -want &c. *n.*; needy, necessitous, distressed, pinched, straitened; put to one's -shifts, - last shifts; unable to -keep the wolf from the door, - make both ends meet; embarrassed, under hatches; involved &c. (*in debt*) 806; insolvent &c. (*not paying*) 808.

**Adv.** *in formâ pauperis.*

**Phr.** *zonam perdidit.*

**805. Credit.—N.** credit, trust, tick, score, tally, account.

letter of credit, circular note; duplicate; mortgage, lien, debenture, paper credit, floating capital; draft; securities.

creditor, lender, lessor, mortgagee; dun; usurer.

**V.** keep -, run up- an account with; entrust, credit, accredit.

place to one's -credit, - account; give -, take- credit; fly a kite.

**Adj.** credit-ing, -ed; accredited.

**Adv.** on -credit &c. *n.*; to the -account, - credit- of.

---

**806. Debt.—N.** debt, obligation, liability, indebtment, debit, score.

arrears, deferred payment, deficit, default; insolvency &c. (*non-payment*) 808; bad debt.

interest; usance, usury; premium; floating -debt, - capital.

debtor, debitor; mortgagor; defaulter &c. 808; borrower.

**V.** be -in debt &c. *adj.*; owe; incur -, contract- a debt &c. *n.*; run up -a bill, - a score, - an account; go on tick, put on the cuff; borrow &c. 788; run -, get- into debt; outrun the constable.

answer -, go bail- for; back one's note.

**Adj.** indebted; liable, chargeable, answerable for.

in -debt, - embarrassed circumstances, - difficulties; incumbered, involved; involved -, plunged -, deep -, over head and ears- in debt; deeply involved; fast tied up; insolvent &c. (*not paying*) 808; *minus*, out of pocket.

unpaid; unrequited, unrewarded; owing, due, in arrear, outstanding.

**807. Payment.—N.** pay-, defrayment; discharge; ac-, quittance; settlement, clearance, liquidation, satisfaction, reckoning, arrangement.

acknowledgment, release; receipt, - in full, - in full of all demands; voucher.

repayment, reimbursement, retribution; pay &c. (*reward*) 973; money paid &c. (*expenditure*) 809.

ready money &c. (*cash*) 800; stake, remittance, instalment.

payer, liquidator &c. 801.

**V.** pay, defray, make payment; pay -down, - on the nail, - ready money, - at sight, - in advance; cash, honour a bill, acknowledge; redeem; pay in kind.

**808. Non-payment.—N.** non-payment; default, defalcation; protest, repudiation; application of the sponge; whitewashing.

insolvency, bankruptcy, failure; overdraft, overdrawn account; insufficiency &c. 640; run upon a bank.

waste paper bonds; dishonoured -, protested- bills; bogus cheque.

bankrupt, insolvent debtor, lame duck, man of straw, welsher, stag, defaulter, absconder, levanter.

**V.** not -pay &c. 807; fail, break, stop payment; become -insolvent, - bankrupt; be gazetted; abscond.

protest, dishonour, repudiate, nullify. pay under protest; button up one's

pay one's -way, – shot, – footing; pay -the piper, – sauce for all, – costs; do the needful; come across; shell –, fork- out; come down with, – the dust; tickle –, grease- the palm; expend &c. 809; put –, lay- down.

discharge, settle, quit, acquit oneself of; account –, reckon –, settle –, be even –, be quits- with; strike a balance; settle –, balance –, square- accounts with; quit scores; foot the bill; wipe –, clear- off old scores; satisfy; pay in full; satisfy –, pay in full of- all demands; clear, liquidate; pay -up, – old debts.

disgorge, make repayment; repay, refund, reimburse, retribute; make compensation &c. 30.

**Adj.** paying &c., paid &c. *v.*; owing nothing, out of debt, all straight, clear of -debt, – encumbrance; unowed, never indebted.

**Adv.** to the tune of; on the nail; money –, cash- down; cash on delivery.

pockets, draw the purse strings; apply the sponge; pay over the left shoulder, get whitewashed; swindle &c. 791; run up bills, fly kites.

**Adj.** not paying; in debt &c. 806; behindhand, in arrear; beggared &c. (*poor*) 804; unable to make both ends meet; *minus*; worse than nothing.

insolvent, bankrupt, in the gazette, gazetted, ruined.

unpaid &c. (*outstanding*) 806; *gratis* &c. 815; unremunerated.

---

**809. Expenditure.—N.** expenditure, money going out; out-goings, -lay; expenses, disbursement; prime cost &c. (*price*) 812; circulation; run upon a bank.

[Money paid] payment &c. 807; pay &c. (*remuneration*) 973; bribe &c. 973; fee, footing, garnish; subsidy; tribute, Peter's pence; contingent, quota; donation &c. 784.

pay in advance, earnest, handsel, deposit, instalment.

investment; purchase &c. 795.

**V.** expend, spend; run –, get- through; pay, disburse; open –, loose –, untie- the purse strings; lay –, shell –, fork- out; bleed; make up a sum, invest, sink money.

fee &c. (*reward*) 973; pay one's way &c. (*pay*) 807; subscribe &c. (*give*) 784; subsidize, bribe.

**Adj.** expend-ing, -ed &c. *v.*; sumptuary, liberal &c. 816; open-handed, lavish &c. 818; expensive &c. 814.

**810. Receipt.—N.** receipt, accountable –, conditional –, binding –, return- receipt; value received, money coming in; income, incomings, innings, revenue, return, proceeds; gross receipts, net profit; earnings &c. (*gain*) 775.

rent, – roll; rent-al, -age; rack-rent.

premium, *bonus*; sweepstakes, tontine, prize, drawing.

pension, annuity; jointure &c. (*property*) 780; alimony, pittance; emolument &c. (*remuneration*) 973.

**V.** receive &c. 785; take money; draw –, derive- from; get, be in receipt of, acquire &c. 775; take &c. 789.

bring in, yield, afford, pay, return; accrue &c. (*be received from*) 785.

**Adj.** receiv-ing, -ed &c. *v.*; profitable &c. (*gainful*) 775.

---

**811. Accounts.—N.** accounts, accompts; commercial –, monetary- arithmetic; statistics &c. (*numeration*) 85; money matters, finance, budget, bill, score, reckoning, account.

books, account book, ledger; day –, cash –, pass- book; journal; debtor and creditor –, cash –, petty cash –, running- account; account- current; balance, – sheet; *compte rendu*, account settled.

book-keeping, audit; double –, single- entry; reckoning &c. 85.

chartered –, certified public –, accountant; auditor, actuary, book-keeper; financier &c. 801; accounting party.

V. keep accounts, enter, post, book, credit, debit, carry over; take stock; balance –, make up –, square –, settle –, wind up –, cast up –, add up –, tot up- accounts; make accounts square.

bring to book, audit, tax, surcharge and falsify.

falsify –, garble –, cook –, doctor- an account.

Adj. monetary &c. 800; account-able, -ing; statistical.

**812. Price.**—N. price, amount, cost, expense, prime cost, charge, figure, demand, damage, fare, hire; wages &c. (*remuneration*) 973.

dues, duty, toll, tax, impost, cess, sess, tallage, levy, capitation-, poll-, income-, sur-, sales-, super-tax; gabel, *gabelle*; gavel, *octroi*, custom, tariff, excise, assessment, taxation, benevolence, tithe, tenths, exactment, ransom, salvage; broker-, wharf-, lighter-, ton-, freight-age.

worth, rate, value, valuation, appraisement, money's worth, par value; penny &c. -worth; price current, market price, quotation; what it will -fetch &c. *v.*

bill &c. (*account*) 811; shot.

V. bear –, set –, fix- a price; appraise, assess, price, charge, demand, ask, require, exact, run up; distrain; run up a bill &c. (*debt*) 806; have one's price; liquidate.

amount to, come to, mount up to; stand one in.

fetch, sell for, cost, bring in, yield, afford.

Adj. priced &c. *v.*; to the tune of, *ad valorem*; mercenary, venal.

Phr. no penny, no paternoster; *point d'argent, point de Suisse*; no longer pipe, no longer dance; no song, no supper.

one may have it for.

**813. Discount.**—N. discount, abatement, concession, reduction, depreciation, allowance, qualification, set off, drawback, poundage, *agio*, percentage; rebate, -ment; backwardation, contango; salvage; tare and tret.

V. discount, bate; a-, re-bate; deduct, reduce, mark down, take off, allow, give, make allowance; tax, depreciate.

Adj. discounting &c. *v.*

Adv. at a discount, below par.

**814. Dearness.** — N. dearness &c. *adj.*; high –, famine –, fancy- price; overcharge; extravagance; exorbitance, extortion; heavy pull upon the purse; Pyrrhic victory.

V. be -dear &c. *adj.*; cost -much, – a pretty penny; rise in price, look up.

overcharge, bleed, fleece, skin, extort.

pay -too much, – through the nose, – too dear for one's whistle.

Adj. dear; high, -priced; of great price, expensive, costly, precious, worth a Jew's eye, dear bought; unreasonable, extravagant, exorbitant, extortionate.

at a premium; not to be had, – for love or money; beyond –, above- price; priceless, of priceless value.

Adv. dear, -ly; at great –, heavy- cost; *à grands frais*.

Phr. prices looking up; *le jeu n'en vaut pas la chandelle*.

**815. Cheapness.**—N. cheapness, low price; depreciation; bargain; good penny &c.- worth, *bon marché*.

[Absence of charge] gratuity; free -quarters, – seats, – admission, – warren; pass, Annie Oakley; run of one's teeth; nominal price, peppercorn rent; labour of love.

drug in the market.

V. be -cheap &c. *adj.*; cost little; come down –, fall- in price.

buy for -a mere nothing, – an old song; have one's money's worth; cheapen, beat down.

Adj. cheap; low, – priced; moderate, reasonable; in-, un-expensive; well –, worth the money; *magnifique et pas cher*; good –, cheap- at the price; dirt –, dog- cheap; cheap, -as dirt, – and nasty; catchpenny.

reduced, marked down, half-price, depreciated, unsaleable.

gratuitous, *gratis*, free, for love,

– nothing; cost-, expense-less; without charge, not charged, untaxed; scot –, shot –, rent- free; free of -cost, – expense; honorary, unbought, unpaid, complimentary.

Adv. for a mere song; at -cost price, – prime cost, – a reduction, – a bargain; on the cheap.

**816. Liberality.—N.** liberality, generosity, munificence; bount-y, -eousness, -ifulness; hospitality; charity &c. (*beneficence*) 906.

benefactor, free giver, Lady Bountiful.

**V.** be -liberal &c. *adj.*; spend –, bleed- freely; shower down upon; open one's purse strings &c. (*disburse*) 809; spare no expense, give -with both hands, – *carte blanche.*

**Adj.** liberal, free, generous; charitable &c. (*beneficent*) 906; hospitable; bount-iful, -eous; handsome; unsparing, ungrudging; open-, free-, full-handed; open-, large-, free-hearted; munificent, princely, unstinting.

overpaid.

**Adv.** liberally, ungrudgingly, with open hand.

**817. Economy.—N.** economy, frugality; thrift, -iness; prudence, care, husbandry, good housewifery, savingness, retrenchment.

savings; prevention of waste, save-all; cheese parings and candle ends; parsimony &c. 819.

**V.** be -economical &c. *adj.*; economize, save; retrench; cut- down expenses, – one's coat according to one's cloth, make both ends meet, keep within compass, meet one's expenses, pay one's way; keep one's head above water; husband &c. (*lay by*) 636; save –, invest- money; put out to interest; provide –, save- -for, – against- a rainy day; feather one's nest; look after the main chance.

**Adj.** economical, frugal, careful, thrifty, saving, chary, spare, sparing; parsimonious &c. 819.

underpaid.

**Adv.** sparingly &c. *adj.*; *ne quid nimis.*

**818. Prodigality.—N.** prodi-gality, -gence; unthriftiness, waste, -fulness; profus-ion, -eness; extravagance; squandering &c. *v.*; lavishness; malversation.

prodigal; spend-, waste-thrift; losel, play-boy, spender, squanderer, locust.

**V.** be -prodigal &c. *adj.*; squander, lavish, sow broadcast; pour forth like water; pay through the nose &c. (*dear*) 814; spill, waste, dissipate, exhaust, drain, eat out of house and home, overdraw, outrun the constable; run -out, – through; misspend; throw -good money after bad, – the helve after the hatchet; burn the candle at both ends; make ducks and drakes of one's money; squander one's substance, spend money like water; fool –, potter –, muddle –, fritter –, throw- away one's money; pour water into a sieve, kill the goose that lays the golden eggs; *manger son blé en herbe.*

**Adj.** prodigal, profuse, thriftless, unthrifty, improvident, wasteful, losel,

**819. Parsimony. — N.** parsimony, parcity; parsimoniousness, stinginess &c. *adj.*; stint; illiberality, avarice, tenacity, avidity, rapacity, extortion, venality, cupidity; selfishness &c. 943; *auri sacra fames.*

miser, niggard, churl, screw, tightwad, skinflint, crib, codger, muckworm, money-grubber, pinchfist, scrimp, lickpenny, hunks, curmudgeon, *Harpagon*, Silas Marner, harpy, extortioner, usurer.

**V.** be -parsimonious &c. *adj.*; grudge, begrudge, stint, skimp, pinch, gripe, screw, dole out, hold back, withhold, starve, famish, live upon nothing, skin a flint.

drive a -bargain, – hard bargain; cheapen, beat down; stop one hole in a sieve; have an itching palm, grasp, grab.

**Adj.** parsimonious, penurious, stingy, miserly, mean, shabby, peddling, scrubby, pennywise, near, niggardly,

extravagant, lavish, dissipated, over liberal; full-handed &c. (*liberal*) 816.

penny wise and pound foolish.

**Adv.** with an unsparing hand; money burning one's pocket; recklessly profuse.

**Int.** hang the expense!

---

frugal to excess; close; fast-, close-, strait-handed; close-, hard-, tight-fisted; tight, sparing; chary; grudging, griping &c. *v.*; illiberal, ungenerous, churlish, hidebound, sordid, mercenary, venal, covetous, usurious, avaricious, greedy, extortionate, rapacious.

**Adv.** with a sparing hand.

# CLASS VI

## Words relating to the SENTIENT and MORAL POWERS.

## Section I. AFFECTIONS IN GENERAL

**820. Affections.—N.** affections, character, qualities, disposition, nature, spirit, tone; temper, -ament; *diathesis*, idiosyncrasy; cast –, habit –, frame- of -mind, – soul; predilection, turn; natural –, turn of mind; bent, bias, predisposition, proneness, proclivity; propen-sity, -sedness, -sion, -dency; vein, humour, mood, grain, mettle; sympathy &c. (*love*) 897.

soul, heart, breast, bosom, inner man; heart's -core, – strings, – blood; heart of hearts, *penetralia mentis*; secret and inmost recesses of the –, cockles of one's- heart; inmost -heart, – soul; back-bone.

passion, pervading spirit; ruling –, master- passion; *furore*; fulness of the heart, heyday of the blood, flesh and blood, flow of soul, force of character.

**V.** have –, possess- -affections &c. *n.*; be of a -character &c. *n.*; be -affected &c. *adj.*; breathe.

**Adj.** affected, characterized, formed, moulded, cast; at-, tempered; framed; pre-, disposed; prone, inclined; having a -bias &c. *n.*; tinctured –, imbued –, penetrated –, eaten up- with.

inborn, inbred, ingrained, in the grain, congenital, inherent, bred in the bone; deep-rooted, ineffaceable, inveterate; pathoscopic.

**Adv.** in one's -heart &c. *n.*; at heart; heart and soul &c. 821; in the -vein, – mood.

**821. Feeling.—N.** feeling; suffering &c. *v.*; endurance, tolerance, sufferance, supportance, experience, response; sympathy &c. (*love*) 897; impression, inspiration, affection, sensation, emotion, pathos, deep sense.

fire, warmth, glow, unction, *gusto*, vehemence; ferv-our, -ency; heartiness, cordiality; earnestness, eagerness; *empressement*, ardour, zeal, passion, enthusiasm, *verve*, *furore*, fanaticism; excitation of feeling &c. 824; fulness of the heart &c. (*disposition*) 820; passion &c. (*state of excitability*) 825; ecstasy &c. (*pleasure*) 827.

blush, suffusion, flush; hectic; tingling, thrill, kick, turn, shock; agitation &c. (*irregular motion*) 315; quiver, heaving, flutter, flurry, fluster, twitter, tremor; throb, -bing; pulsation, palpitation, panting; trepid-, perturb-ation; ruffle, hurry of spirits, pother, stew, ferment.

**V.** feel; receive an -impression &c. *n.*; be -impressed with &c. *adj.*; entertain –, harbour –, cherish- -feeling &c. *n.*

respond; catch the -flame, – infection; enter the spirit of.

bear, suffer. support, sustain, endure, brook, thole, aby; abide &c.

(*be composed*) 826; experience &c. (*meet with*) 151; taste, prove; labour –, smart- under; bear the brunt of, brave, stand.

swell, glow, warm, flush, blush, change colour, mantle; turn -colour, – pale, – red, – black in the face; blench, crimson, whiten, pale, tingle, thrill, heave, pant, throb, palpitate, go pit-a-pat, tremble, quiver, flutter, twitter; stagger, reel; shake &c. 315; be -agitated, – excited &c. 824; look -blue, – black; wince, draw a deep breath.

impress &c. (*excite the feelings*) 824.

**Adj.** feeling &c. *v.*; sentient; sensuous; sensor-ial, -y; emo-tive, -tional; of –, with- feeling &c. *n.*

warm, quick, lively, smart, strong, sharp, acute, cutting, piercing, incisive; keen, – as a razor; trenchant, pungent, racy, *piquant*, poignant, caustic.

impressive, deep, profound, indelible; deep-, home-, heart-felt; swelling, soul-stirring, deep-mouthed, heart-expanding, electric, thrilling, rapturous, ecstatic.

earnest, wistful, eager, breathless; fer-vent, -vid; gushing, passionate, warmhearted, hearty, cordial, sincere, zealous, enthusiastic, glowing, ardent, burning, red-hot, fiery, flaming; boiling, – over.

pervading, penetrating, absorbing; rabid, raving, feverish, fanatical, hysterical; impetuous &c. (*excitable*) 825; overmastering.

impressed –, moved –, touched –, affected –, penetrated –, seized –, imbued &c. 820- with; devoured by; wrought up &c. (*excited*) 824; struck all of a heap; rapt; in a -quiver &c. *n.*; enraptured &c. 829.

**Adv.** heart and soul, from the bottom of one's heart, *ab imo pectore*, *de profundis*, at heart, *con amore*, heartily, devoutly, over head and ears.

**Phr.** the heart -big, – full, – swelling, – beating, – pulsating, – throbbing, – thumping, – beating high, – melting, – overflowing, – bursting, – breaking.

**822. Sensibility.** — **N.** sensi-bility, -bleness, -tiveness; moral sensibility; impress-, affect-ibility; suscepti-bleness, -bility, -vity; mobility; viva-city, -ciousness; tender-, soft-ness; sentimental-ity, -ism.

excitability &c. 825; fastidiousness &c. 868; physical sensibility &c. 375.

sore -point, – place; where the shoe pinches.

**V.** be -sensible &c. *adj.*; have a -tender, – warm, – sensitive- heart.

take to –, treasure up in the- heart; shrink.

'die of a rose in aromatic pain'; touch to the quick.

**Adj.** sensi-ble, -tive; impressi-ble, -onable; suscepti-ve, -ble; alive to, impassion-able, -ed; gushing; warm-, tender-, soft-hearted; tender –, as a chicken; soft, sentimental, romantic; enthusiastic, highflying, spirited, mettlesome, vivacious, lively, expressive, mobile, tremblingly alive; excitable

**823. Insensibility.**—**N.** insensi-bility, -bleness; moral insensibility; inertness, *inertia*, *vis inertiæ*; impassi-bility, -bleness; inappetency, apathy, phlegm, dulness, hebetude, supineness, lukewarmness, insusceptibility, unimpressibility.

cold -fit, – blood, – heart; cold-, cool-ness; frigidity, *sang-froid*; stoicism, imperturbation &c. (*inexcitability*) 826; *nonchalance*, unconcern, dry eyes; *insouciance* &c. (*indifference*) 866; recklessness &c. 863; callousness; heart of stone, stock and stone, marble, deadness.

torp-or, -idity; obstupefaction, lethargy, coma, trance; sleep &c. 683; suspended animation; stup-or, -efaction; paralysis, palsy; numbness &c. (*physical insensibility*) 376.

neutrality; quietism, vegetation.

**V.** be -insensible &c. *adj.*; have a rhinoceros hide; show -insensibility &c. *n.*; not -mind, – care, – be affected

&c. 825, over-sensitive, without skin, thin-skinned; fastidious &c. 868.

**Adv.** sensibly &c. *adj.*; to the -quick, - inmost core.

---

by; have no desire for &c. 866; have -, feel -, take- no interest in; *nil admirari*; not care a -straw &c. (*unimportance*) 643 for; disregard &c. (*neglect*) 460; set at naught &c. (*make light of*) 483; turn a deaf ear to &c. (*inattention*) 458; vegetate.

render -insensible, - callous; blunt, obtund, numb, benumb, paralyze, chloroform, deaden, hebetate, stun, stupefy; brut-ify, -alize.

inure; harden, - the heart; steel, case-harden, sear.

**Adj.** insensible, unconscious; impassi-ve, -ble; blind to, deaf to, dead to; un-, in-susceptible; unimpress-ionable, -ible; passion-, spirit-, heart-, soul-less; unfeeling, unmoral.

apathetic; leuco-, phlegmatic; dull, frigid; cold, -blooded, -hearted; unemotional; cold as charity; flat, obtuse, inert, supine, sluggish, torpid; sleepy &c. (*inactive*) 683; languid, half-hearted, tame; numb, -ed; comatose; anæsthetic &c. 376; stupefied, chloroformed, palsy-stricken.

indifferent, lukewarm; Laodicean; careless, mindless, regardless; inattentive &c. 458; neglectful &c. 460; disregarding.

unconcerned, *nonchalant*, *pococurante*, *insouciant*, *sans souci*; unambitious &c. 866.

un-affected, -ruffled, -impressed, -inspired, -excited, -moved, -stirred, -touched, -shocked, -struck; unblushing &c. (*shameless*) 885; unanimated; vegetative.

callous, thick-skinned, pachydermatous, impervious; hard, -ened; inured, case-hardened; steeled -, proof- against; imperturbable &c. (*inexcitable*) 826; unfelt.

**Adv.** insensibly &c. *adj.*; *æquo animo*; without being -moved, - touched, - impressed; in cold blood; with -dry eyes, - withers unwrung.

**Phr.** never mind; it is of no consequence &c. (*unimportant*) 643; it cannot be helped; nothing coming amiss; it is all -the same, - one- to.

**824. Excitation.**—**N.** excitation of feeling; mental -, excitement; suscitation, galvanism, stimulation, piquancy, provocation, inspiration, calling forth, infection; interest, animation, agitation, perturbation; subjugation, fascination, intoxication; en-, ravishment; entrancement, high pressure.

unction, impressiveness &c. *adj.*; emotional appeal; melodrama; psychological moment, crisis; sensationalism.

trial of temper, *casus belli*; irritation &c. (*anger*) 900; passion &c. (*state of excitability*) 825; thrill &c. (*feeling*) 821; repression of feeling &c. 826.

**V.** excite, affect, touch, move, impress, strike, interest, intrigue, animate, inspire, impassion, smite, infect; stir -, fire -, warm- the blood; set astir; a-, wake; a-, waken; call forth; e-, pro-voke; raise up, summon up, call up, wake up, blow up, get up, light up; raise; get up steam, rouse, arouse, stir, fire, kindle, enkindle, apply the torch, set on fire, inflame, illuminate.

stimulate; ex-, suscitate; inspirit; spirit up, stir up, work up; infuse life into, give new life to; bring -, introduce- new blood; quicken;

sharpen, whet; work upon &c. (*incite*) 615; hurry on, give a fillip, put on one's mettle.

fan the -fire, – flame; blow the coals, stir the embers; fan, – into a flame; foster, heat, warm, foment, raise to a fever heat; keep -up, – the pot boiling; revive, rekindle; rake up, rip up.

stir –, play on –, come home to- the feelings; touch -a string, – a chord, – the soul, – the heart; go to one's heart, penetrate, pierce, go through one, touch to the quick, open the wound; possess –, pervade –, penetrate –, imbrue –, absorb –, affect –, disturb- the soul.

absorb, rivet the attention; sink into the -mind, – heart; prey on the mind; intoxicate; over-whelm, -power; *bouleverser*, upset, turn one's head.

fascinate; enrapture &c. (*give pleasure*) 829.

agitate, perturb, ruffle, fluster, flutter, shake, disturb, faze, startle, shock, stagger; give one a -shock, – turn; strike -dumb, – all of a heap; stun, astound, electrify, galvanize, petrify.

irritate, sting; cut, – to the -heart, – quick; try one's temper; fool to the top of one's bent, pique; infuriate, madden, make one's blood boil; lash into fury &c. (*wrath*) 900.

be -excited &c. *adj.*; flash up, flare up; catch the infection; thrill &c. (*feel*) 821; mantle; work oneself up; seethe, boil, simmer, foam, fume, flame, rage, rave; run mad &c. (*passion*) 825.

**Adj.** excited &c. *v.*; wrought up, on the *qui vive*, astir, sparkling; in a -quiver &c. 821, – fever, – ferment, – blaze, – state of excitement; in hysterics; black in the face, over-wrought; hot, red-hot, flushed, feverish; all -of a twitter, – of a flutter, – of a dither, – in a pucker; with -quivering lips, – tears in one's eyes.

flaming; boiling, – over; ebullient, seething; foaming, – at the mouth; fuming, raging, carried away by passion, wild, raving, frantic, mad, distracted, distraught, beside oneself, out of one's wits, amuck, ready to burst, *bouleversé*, demoniacal.

lost, *éperdu*, tempest-tossed; haggard; ready to sink.

stung to the quick, up, on one's high ropes.

exciting &c. *v.*; impressive, warm, glowing, fervid, swelling, imposing, spirit-stirring, thrilling; high-wrought; soul-stirring, -subduing; heart-swelling, -thrilling; agonizing &c. (*painful*) 830; telling, sensational, melodramatic, hysterical; over-powering, -whelming; more than flesh and blood can bear.

*piquant* &c. (*pungent*) 392; spicy, appetizing, provocative, *provoquant*, tantalizing.

**Adv.** till one is black in the face.

**Phr.** the heart -beating high, – going pit-a-pat, – leaping into one's mouth; the blood -being up, – boiling in one's veins; the eye -glistening, – 'in a fine frenzy rolling'; the head turned.

**825.** [Excess of sensitiveness.] **Excitability.—N.** excitability, impetuosity, vehemence; boisterousness &c. *adj.*; turbulence; impatience, intolerance, non-endurance; irritability &c. (*irascibility*) 901; itching &c. (*desire*) 865; wincing; disquiet, -ude; restlessness; fidgets, fidgetiness; agitation &c. (*irregular motion*) 315.

**826.** [Absence of excitability, or of excitement.] **Inexcitability.—N.** inexcit-, imperturb-, inirrit-ability; even temper, tranquil mind, dispassion; tolerance, toleration, patience.

passiveness &c. (*physical inertness*) 172; hebet-ude, -ation; impassibility &c. (*insensibility*) 823; stupefaction.

coolness, calmness &c. *adj.*; compo-

trepidation, perturbation, ruffle, hurry, -skurry, fuss, flurry; fluster, flutter; pother, stew, ferment; whirl; thrill &c. (*feeling*) 821; state –, fever- of excitement; transport.

passion, excitement, flush, heat; fever, -heat; fire, flame, fume, blood boiling; tumult; effervescence, ebullition; boiling, – over; whiff, gust, storm, tempest; scene, breaking out, burst, fit, paroxysm, explosion; out-break, -burst; agony.

violence &c. 173; fierceness &c. *adj.*; rage, fury, *furor, furore,* desperation, madness, distraction, raving, delirium, brain storm; frenzy, hysterics; intoxication; tearing –, raging- passion, towering rage; anger &c. 900.

fascination, infatuation, fanaticism; Quixot-ism, -ry; *tête montée.*

**V.** be -impatient &c. *adj.*; not be able to -bear &c. 826; bear ill, wince, chafe, champ the bit; be in a -stew &c. *n.*; be out of all patience, fidget, fuss, not have a wink of sleep; toss, – on one's pillow.

lose one's temper &c. 900; break –, burst –, fly- out; go –, fly- -off, – off the handle, – off at a tangent; explode; flare up, flame up, fire up, burst into a flame, take fire, fire, burn; boil, – over; foam, fume, rage, rave, rant, tear; go –, run- -wild, – mad; go into hysterics; run -riot, – amuck; *battre la campagne, faire le diable à quatre,* play the deuce; raise -Cain, – the devil.

**Adj.** excitable, easily excited, in an excitable state; highly strung; irritable &c. (*irascible*) 901; impatient, intolerant.

feverish, febrile, hysterical; delirious, mad, moody, maggoty-headed.

unquiet, mercurial, electric, galvanic, hasty, hurried, restless, fidgety, fussy; chafing &c. *v.*

startlish, mettlesome, high mettled, skittish.

vehement, demonstrative, violent, wild, furious, fierce, fiery, hot-headed, mad-cap.

over-zealous, enthusiastic, impassioned, fanatical; rabid &c. (*eager*) 865.

rampant, clamorous, uproarious, turbulent, tempestuous, boisterous; tumultuous; ...

sure, placidity, indisturbance, imperturbation, *sang-froid,* tranquillity, serenity; quiet, -ude; peace of mind, mental calmness.

staidness &c. *adj.*; gravity, sobriety, Quakerism; philosophy, equanimity, stoicism, command of temper; self-possession, -control, -command, -restraint; presence of mind.

submission &c. 725; resignation; suffer-, support-, endur-, long-suffer-, forbear-ance; longanimity; fortitude; patience -of Job, – 'on a monument,' – 'sovereign o'er transmuted ill'; moderation; repression –, subjugation- of feeling; restraint &c. 751.

tranquillization &c. (*moderation*) 174.

**V.** be -composed &c. *adj.*

*laisser -faire, – aller*; take things -easily, – as they come; take it easy, run on, live and let live; take -easily, – coolly, – in good part; *æquam servare mentem.*

bear, – well, – the brunt; go through, support, endure, brave, disregard.

tolerate, suffer, stand, bide; abide, aby; bear –, put up –, abide- with; acquiesce; submit &c. (*yield*) 725; submit with a good grace; resign –, reconcile- oneself to; brook, digest, eat, swallow, pocket, stomach; make -light of, – the best of, – a virtue of necessity; put a good face on, keep one's countenance; carry -on, – through; check &c. 751- oneself.

compose, appease &c. (*moderate*) 174; propitiate; repress &c. (*restrain*) 751; render insensible &c. 823; overcome –, allay –, repress- one's -excitability &c. 825; master one's feelings.

make -oneself, – one's mind- easy; set one's mind at -ease, – rest.

calm –, cool- down; thaw, grow cool.

be -borne, – endured; go down.

**Adj.** in-, un-excitable; imperturbable; unsusceptible &c. (*insensible*) 823; un-, dis-passionate; cold-blooded, inirritable; enduring &c. *v.*; stoical, Platonic, philosophic, staid, stayed; sober, – minded; grave; sober –, grave- as a judge; sedate, demure, cool-, level-headed; steady.

easy-going, peaceful, placid, calm; quiet, – as a mouse; tranquil, serene;

bulent, tempestuous, tumultuary, boisterous.

impulsive, impetuous, passionate; uncontroll-ed, -able; ungovernable, irrepressible, stanchless, inextinguishable, burning, simmering, volcanic, ready to burst forth.

excit-ed, -ing &c. 824.

**Int.** pish! pshaw!

**Phr.** *noli me tangere.*

cool, – as -a cucumber, – custard; undemonstrative.

temperate &c. (*moderate*) 174; composed, collected; un-excited, -stirred, -ruffled, -disturbed, -perturbed, -impassioned; unoffended; unresisting.

meek, tolerant; patient, – as Job; submissive &c. 725; tame; content, resigned, chastened, subdued, lamblike; gentle, – as a lamb; *suaviter in modo*; mild, – as mother's milk; soft as peppermint; armed with patience, bearing with, clement, forbearant, long-suffering.

**Adv.** 'like patience on a monument smiling at grief'; *æquo animo*, in cold blood &c. 823; more in sorrow than in anger.

**Int.** patience! and shuffle the cards.

## Section II. PERSONAL AFFECTIONS*

### 1°. Passive Affections

**827. Pleasure.—N.** pleasure, gratification, enjoyment, fruition; ob-, delectation; relish, zest; *gusto* &c. (*physical pleasure*) 377; satisfaction &c. (*content*) 831; complacency.

well-being; good &c. 618; snugness, comfort, ease; cushion &c. 215; *sans souci*, mind at ease.

joy, gladness, delight, glee, cheer, sunshine; cheerfulness &c. 836.

treat, refreshment; frolic, fun, lark, gambol, merry-making; amusement &c. 840; luxury &c. 377; hedonism.

*mens sana in corpore sano.*

happiness, felicity, bliss; beati-tude, -fication; enchantment, transport, rapture, ravishment, ecstasy; *summum bonum*; paradise, elysium &c. (*heaven*) 981; third –, seventh- heaven; unalloyed -happiness &c.

honeymoon; palmy –, halcyon- days; golden -age, – time; *Saturnia regna*, Eden, Arcadia, happy valley, Agapemone; Cockaigne.

**V.** be pleased &c. 829; feel –, experience- pleasure &c. *n.*; joy; enjoy –, hug- oneself; be in -clover &c. 377, – elysium &c. 981; tread on enchanted ground; fall –, go- into raptures.

feel at home, breathe freely, bask in the sunshine.

be -pleased &c. 829- with; receive –, derive- pleasure &c. *n.*- from; take -pleasure &c. *n.*- in; delight in, rejoice

**828. Pain. — N.** mental suffering, pain, dolour; suffer-ing, -ance; ache, smart &c. (*physical pain*) 378; passion.

displeasure, dissatisfaction, discomfort, discomposure, disquiet; *malaise*; inquietude, uneasiness, vexation of spirit; taking; discontent &c. 832.

dejection &c. 837; weariness &c. 841.

annoyance, irritation, worry, infliction, visitation; plague, bore; bother, -ation; stew, vexation, mortification, chagrin, *esclandre*; *mauvais quart d'heure.*

care, anxiety, solicitude, trouble, trial, ordeal, fiery ordeal, shock, blow, cark, dole, fret, burden, load.

concern, grief, sorrow, distress, affliction, woe, bitterness, gloom, heartache; heavy –, aching –, bleeding –, broken- heart; heavy affliction, gnawing grief.

unhappiness, infelicity, misery, tribulation, wretchedness, desolation; despair &c. 859; extremity, prostration, depth of misery.

nightmare, *ephialtes*, incubus.

anguish, agony; throe, tor-ture, -ment; crucifixion, martyrdom; pang, twinge, stab; the rack, the stake; purgatory &c. (*hell*) 982.

hell upon earth; iron age, reign of terror; slough of despond &c. (*adversity*) 735; peck –, sea- of troubles; ills that flesh is heir to &c. (*evil*) 619;

* Or those which concern one's own state of feeling.

in, indulge in, luxuriate in; gloat over &c. (*physical pleasure*) 377; enjoy, relish, like; love &c. 897; take -to, – a fancy to; have a liking for; enter into the spirit of.

take in good part.

treat oneself to, solace oneself with.

**Adj.** pleased &c. 829; not sorry; glad, -some; pleased as Punch.

happy, blest, blessed, blissful, beatified; happy as -a king, – the day is long; thrice happy, *ter quaterque beatus*; enjoying &c. *v.*; joyful &c. (*in spirits*) 836; hedonic.

in -a blissful state, – paradise &c. 981, – raptures, – ecstasies, – a transport of delight; rapturous.

comfortable &c. (*physical pleasure*) 377; at ease; content &c. 831; *sans souci*, in clover.

overjoyed, entranced, enchanted; enraptured; en-, ravished; transported; fascinated, captivated.

with -a joyful face, – sparkling eyes.

pleasing &c. 829; ecstatic, beat-ic, -ific; painless, unalloyed, without alloy, cloudless.

**Adv.** happily &c. *adj.*; with pleasure &c. (*willingly*) 602; with -glee &c. *n.*

**Phr.** one's heart leaping with joy.

---

miseries of human life; unkindest cut of all.

sufferer, victim, prey, martyr, object of compassion, wretch, shorn lamb.

**V.** feel –, suffer –, experience –, undergo –, bear –, endure- pain &c. *n.*; smart, ache &c. (*physical pain*) 378; suffer, bleed, ail; be the victim of; bear –, take up- the cross.

labour under afflictions; quaff the bitter cup, have a bad time of it; fall on evil days &c. (*adversity*) 735; go hard with, come to grief, fall a sacrifice to, drain the cup of misery to the dregs, sup full of horrors.

sit on thorns, be on pins and needles, wince, fret, chafe, worry oneself, be in a taking, fret and fume, take -on, – to heart.

grieve; mourn &c. (*lament*) 839; yearn, repine, pine, droop, languish, sink; give way; despair &c. 859; break one's heart; weigh upon the heart &c. (*inflict pain*) 830.

**Adj.** in –, in a state of –, full of- pain &c. *n.*; suffering &c. *v.*; pained, afflicted, worried, displeased &c. 830; aching, griped, sore &c. (*physical pain*) 378; on the rack, in limbo; between hawk and buzzard.

un-comfortable, -easy; ill at ease; in a -taking, – way; disturbed; discontented &c. 832; out of humour &c. 901*a*; weary &c. 841.

heavy laden, stricken, crushed, a prey to, victimized, ill-used.

unfortunate &c. (*hapless*) 735; to be pitied, doomed, devoted, accursed, undone, lost, stranded.

unhappy, infelicitous, poor, wretched, miserable, woe-begone; cheerless &c. (*dejected*) 837; careworn.

concerned, sorry; sorrow-ing, -ful; cut up, chagrined, horrified, horror-stricken; in –, plunged in –, a prey to- grief &c. *n.*; in tears &c. (*lamenting*) 839; steeped to the lips in misery; heart-stricken, -broken, -scalded; broken-hearted; in despair &c. 859.

**Phr.** 'the iron entered into the soul'; '*hæret lateri lethalis arundo*'; one's heart bleeding.

---

**829.** [Capability of giving pleasure; cause or source of pleasure.] **Pleasurableness.—N.** pleasurable-, pleasant-, agreeable-ness &c. *adj.*; pleasure giving, jocundity, delectability; amusement &c. 840.

attraction &c. (*motive*) 615; attractiveness, -ability; invitingness &c. *adj.*; charm, fascination, captivation, en-

**830.** [Capability of giving pain; cause or source of pain.] **Painfulness.—N.** painfulness &c. *adj.*; trouble, care &c. (*pain*) 828; trial; af-, in-fliction; cross, blow, stroke, burden, load, curse; bitter -pill, – draught, – cup; waters of bitterness.

annoyance, grievance, nuisance, vexation, mortification, sickener; bore

chantment, witchery, seduction, winsomeness, winning ways, amenity, amiability, sweetness.

loveliness &c. (*beauty*) 845; sunny –, bright- side; sweets &c. (*sugar*) 396; goodness &c. 648; manna in the wilderness, land flowing with milk and honey.

treat; regale &c. (*physical pleasure*) 377; dainty; tit-, tid-bit; nuts, *sauce piquante*.

**V.** cause –, produce –, create –, give –, afford –, procure –, offer –, present –, yield- pleasure &c. 827.

please, charm, delight; gladden &c. (*make cheerful*) 836; take, captivate, fascinate; enchant, entrance, enrapture, transport, bewitch; en-, ravish.

bless, beatify; satisfy; gratify, – desire &c. 865; slake, satiate, quench; indulge, humour, flatter, tickle; tickle the palate &c. (*savoury*) 394; regale, refresh; enliven; treat; amuse &c. 840; take –, tickle –, hit- one's fancy; meet one's wishes; win –, gladden –, rejoice –, warm the cockles of- the heart; do one's heart good.

attract, allure &c. (*move*) 615; stimulate &c. (*excite*) 824; interest, intrigue.

make things pleasant, popularize, gild the pill, sweeten.

**Adj.** causing pleasure &c. *v.*; pleasure-giving; pleas-ing, -ant, -urable; agreeable, cushy; grat-eful, -ifying; leef, lief, acceptable; welcome, – as the roses in May; welcomed; favourite; to one's -taste, – mind, – liking, – heart's content; satisfactory &c. (*good*) 648.

refreshing; comfortable; cordial; genial; glad, -some; sweet, delectable, nice, dainty; delic-ate, -ious; dulcet; luscious &c. 396; palatable &c. 394; luxurious, voluptuous; sensual &c. 377.

attractive &c. 615; inviting, prepossessing, engaging; win-ning, -some; taking, fascinating, captivating, killing; seduc-ing, -tive; alluring, enticing; appetizing &c. (*exciting*) 824; cheering &c. 836; bewitching; interesting, absorbing, enchanting, entrancing, enravishing.

charming; delightful, felicitous, exquisite; lovely &c. (*beautiful*) 845;

bother, pother, hot water, sea of troubles, hornet's nest, plague, pest.

cancer, ulcer, sting, thorn; canker &c. (*bane*) 663; scorpion &c. (*evil-doer*) 913; dagger &c. (*arms*) 727; scourge &c. (*instrument of punishment*) 975; carking –, canker worm of- care.

mishap, misfortune &c. (*adversity*) 735; *désagrément*, *esclandre*, rub.

source of -irritation, – annoyance; wound, sore subject, skeleton in the closet; thorn in -the flesh, – one's side; where the shoe pinches, gall and wormwood.

sorry sight, heavy news, provocation; affront &c. 929; head and front of one's offending.

infestation, molestation; malignity &c. (*malevolence*) 907; acrimony.

**V.** cause –, occasion –, give –, bring –, induce –, produce –, create –, inflict- pain &c. 828; pain, hurt, wound.

pinch, prick, gripe &c. (*physical pain*) 378; pierce, lancinate, cut.

hurt –, wound –, grate upon –, jar upon- the feelings; wring –, pierce –, lacerate –, break –, rend- the heart; make the heart bleed; tear –, rend- the heart-strings; draw tears from the eyes.

sadden; make -unhappy &c. 828; plunge into sorrow, grieve, fash, afflict, distress; cut -up, – to the heart.

displease, annoy, incommode, discommode, discompose, trouble, disquiet, disturb, thwart, cross, perplex, molest, tease, rag, tire, irk, vex, mortify, wherret, worry, plague, bother, pester, bore, pother, harass, harry, badger, heckle, bait, beset, infest, persecute, importune, be troublesome.

wring, harrow, torment, torture; put to the -rack, – question; break on the wheel, rack, scarify; cruci-ate, -fy; convulse, agonize; barb the dart; plant a -dagger in the breast, – thorn in one's side.

irritate, provoke, sting, nettle, try the patience, pique, fret, rile, tweak the nose, chafe, gall; sting –, wound –, cut- to the quick; aggrieve, affront, enchafe, enrage, ruffle, sour the temper; give offence &c. (*resentment*) 900.

ravishing, rapturous; heartfelt, thrilling, ecstatic; beat-ic, -ific; seraphic; empyrean; elysian &c. (*heavenly*) 981.

palmy, halcyon, Saturnian.

**Phr.** *decies repetita placebit.*

---

maltreat, bite, snap at, assail, bully; smite &c. (*punish*) 972.

sicken, disgust, revolt, nauseate, disenchant, repel, offend, shock, stink in the nostrils; go against –, turn- the stomach; make one sick, set the teeth on edge, go against the grain, grate on the ear; stick in one's -throat, – gizzard; rankle, gnaw, corrode, horrify, appal, freeze the blood; chill the spine; make the -flesh creep, – hair stand on end; make the blood -curdle, – run cold; make one shudder.

haunt, – the memory; weigh –, prey- on the -heart, – mind, – spirits; bring one's grey hairs with sorrow to the grave; add a nail to one's coffin.

**Adj.** causing pain, hurting &c. *v.*; hurtful &c. (*bad*) 649; painful; dolor-ific, -ous; unpleasant; un-, dis-pleasing; disagreeable, unpalatable, bitter, distasteful; uninviting; unwelcome; undesir-able, -ed; obnoxious; unacceptable, unpopular, thankless.

unsatisfactory, untoward, unlucky, uncomfortable.

distressing; afflict-ing, -ive; joy-, cheer-, comfort-less; dismal, disheartening; depress-ing, -ive; dreary, melancholy, grievous, piteous; woeful, rueful, mournful, deplorable, pitiable, lamentable; sad, affecting, touching, pathetic.

irritating, provoking, stinging, annoying, aggravating, mortifying, galling; unaccommodating, invidious, vexatious; trouble-, tire-, irk-, weari-some; plagu-ing, -y; awkward.

importunate; teas-, pester-, bother-, harass-, worry-, torment-, cark-ing.

in-toler-, -suffer-, -support-able; un-bear-, -endur-able; past bearing; not to be -borne, – endured; more than flesh and blood can bear; enough to -drive one mad, – provoke a saint, – make a parson swear, – try the patience of Job.

shocking, terrific, grim, appalling, crushing; dreadful, fearful, frightful; thrilling, tremendous, dire; heart-breaking, -rending, -wounding, -corroding, -sickening; harrowing, rending.

odious, hateful, execrable, repulsive, repellent, abhorrent; horri-d, -ble, -fic, -fying; offensive; nause-ous, -ating; disgust-, sicken-, revolt-ing; nasty; loath-some, -ful; fulsome; vile &c. (*bad*) 649; hideous &c. 846.

sharp, acute, sore, severe, grave, hard, harsh, cruel, biting, acrimonious, caustic; cutting, corroding, consuming, racking, excruciating, searching, searing, grinding, grating, agonizing; envenomed.

ruinous, disastrous, calamitous, tragical; desolating, withering; burdensome, onerous, oppressive; cumb-rous, -ersome.

**Adv.** painfully &c. *adj.*; with -pain &c. 828; deuced.

**Int.** *hinc illæ lachrymæ!* woe is me!

**Phr.** *surgit amari aliquid*; the place being too hot to hold one; the iron entering into the soul.

**831. Content.**—**N.** content, -ment, -edness; complacency, satisfaction, entire satisfaction, ease, heart's ease, peace of mind; serenity &c. 826; cheer-

**832. Discontent.** — **N.** discontent, -ment; dissatisfaction; dissent &c. 489; labour unrest.

disappointment, mortification; cold

fulness &c. 836; ray of comfort; comfort &c. (*well-being*) 827.

re-, conciliation; resignation &c. (*patience*) 826.

waiter on Providence.

**V.** be -content &c. *adj.*; rest -satisfied, – and be thankful; take the good the gods provide, let well alone, feel oneself at home, hug oneself, lay the flattering unction to one's soul.

take -up with, – in good part; assent &c. 488; be reconciled to, make one's peace with; get over it; take -heart, – comfort; put up with &c. (*bear*) 826.

render -content &c. *adj.*; set at ease, comfort; set one's -heart, – mind- at -ease, – rest; speak peace; conciliate, reconcile, win over, propitiate, disarm, beguile; content, satisfy; gratify &c. 829.

be -tolerated &c. 826; go down, – with; do.

**Adj.** content, -ed; satisfied &c. *v.*; at -ease, – one's ease, – home; with the mind at ease, *sans souci, sine curâ*, easy-going, not particular; conciliatory; unrepining, of good comfort; resigned &c. (*patient*) 826; cheerful &c. 836.

un-afflicted, -vexed, -molested, -plagued; serene &c. 826; at rest; snug, comfortable; in one's element.

satisfactory, satisfying, ample, sufficient, adequate, tolerable.

**Adv.** to one's heart's content; *à la bonne heure*; all for the best.

**Int.** amen &c. (*assent*) 488; very well, so much the better, well and good; it –, that- will do; it cannot be helped.

**Phr.** nothing comes amiss.

comfort; regret &c. 833; repining, taking on &c. *v.*; inquietude, vexation of spirit, soreness; heart-burning, -grief; querulousness &c. (*lamentation*) 839; hypercriticism.

malcontent, grumbler, growler, croaker, *laudator temporis acti*; censurer, complainer, faultfinder, murmurer, Adullamite, Diehard, Bitter-ender.

the Opposition, cave of Adullam, indignation meeting, 'winter of our discontent.'

**V.** be -discontented &c. *adj.*; quarrel with one's bread and butter; repine; regret &c. 833; wish one at the bottom of the Red Sea; take -on, – to heart; shrug the shoulders; make a wry –, pull a long- face; knit one's brows, look -blue, – black, – black as thunder, – blank, – glum.

take -in bad part, – ill; fret, chafe, make a piece of work; grumble, croak, grouse; lament &c. 839.

cause -discontent &c. *n.*; dissatisfy, disappoint, mortify, put out, disconcert; cut up; dishearten.

**Adj.** discontented; dissatisfied &c. *v.*; unsatisfied, ungratified; dissident; dissentient &c. 489; malcontent, exigent, exacting, hypercritical.

repining &c. *v.*; regretful &c. 833; down in the mouth &c. (*dejected*) 837.

in -high dudgeon, – a fume, – the sulks, – the dumps, – bad humour; glum, sulky; sour, – as a crab; soured, sore; out of -humour, – temper.

disappointing &c. *v.*; unsatisfactory.

**Int.** so much the worse!

**Phr.** that –, it- will never do.

**833. Regret.—N.** regret, repining; home sickness, nostalgia; *mal –, maladie-du pays*; lamentation &c. 839, contrition, compunction, penitence &c. 950.

bitterness, heart-burning.

*laudator temporis acti* &c. (*discontent*) 832.

V. regret, deplore; bewail &c. (*lament*) 839; repine, cast a longing lingering look behind; rue, – the day; repent &c. 950; *infandum renovare dolorem.*

prey –, weigh –, have a weight- on the mind; leave an aching void.

Adj. regretting &c. *v.*; regretful; home-sick.

regretted &c. *v.*; much to be regretted, regrettable; lamentable &c. (*bad*) 649.

**Int.** what a pity! hang it!
**Phr.** 'tis -pity, – too true.

**834. Relief.—N.** relief; deliverance; refreshment &c. 689; easement, softening, alleviation, mitigation, palliation &c. 174; soothing, lullaby; cradle song, *berceuse.*

solace, consolation, comfort, encouragement.

lenitive, restorative &c. (*remedy*) 662; poultice &c. *v.*; cushion &c. 215; crumb of comfort, balm in Gilead; aspirin.

**V.** relieve, ease, alleviate, mitigate, palliate, soothe, addulce; salve; soften, – down; foment, stupe, poultice; assuage, allay.

cheer, comfort, console; encourage, bear up, pat on the back, give comfort, set at ease; enliven, gladden –, cheer- the heart.

remedy; cure &c. (*restore*) 660; refresh; pour -balm into, – oil on.

smooth the ruffled brow of care, temper the wind to the shorn lamb, lay the flattering unction to one's soul.

disburden &c. (*free*) 705; take off a load of care.

be relieved; breathe more freely, draw a long breath; take comfort; dry –, wipe- the -tears, – eyes.

**Adj.** relieving &c. *v.*; consolatory, soothing; assua-ging, -sive; bal-my, -samic; lenitive, palliative; anodyne &c. (*remedial*) 662; curative &c. 660.

**835. Aggravation.—N.** aggravation, heightening; exacerbation; exasperation; overestimation &c. 482; exaggeration &c. 549.

**V.** aggravate, render worse, heighten, embitter, sour; ex-, acerbate; exasperate, envenom; tease, provoke, enrage.

add fuel to the -fire, – flame; fan the flame &c. (*excite*) 824; go from bad to worse &c. (*deteriorate*) 659.

**Adj.** aggravated &c. *v.*; worse, unrelieved; aggravable; aggravating &c. *v.*

**Adv.** out of the frying pan into the fire, from bad to worse, worse and worse.

**Int.** so much the worse!

**836. Cheerfulness.—N.** cheerfulness &c. *adj.*; geniality, gaiety, *l'allegro,* cheer, good humour, spirits; high –, animal –, flow of- spirits; glee, high glee, light heart; sunshine of the -mind, – breast; *gaieté de cœur, bon naturel.*

liveliness &c. *adj.*; life, alacrity, vivacity, animation, *allégresse*; jocundity, joviality, jollity; levity; jocularity &c. (*wit*) 842.

mirth, merriment, hilarity, exhilaration; laughter &c. 838; merry-making &c. (*amusement*) 840; heyday, rejoicing &c. 838; marriage bells.

nepenthe, Euphrosyne.

optimism &c. (*hopefulness*) 858; self-complacency.

**V.** be -cheerful &c. *adj.*; have the mind at ease, smile, put a good face upon, keep up one's spirits; view -the bright side of the picture, – things *en couleur de rose*; *ridentem dicere verum,*

**837. Dejection.—N.** dejection; dejectedness &c. *adj.*; depression, prosternation; lowness –, depression- of spirits; weight –, oppression –, damp- on the spirits; low –, bad –, drooping –, depressed- spirits; heart sinking; heaviness –, failure- of heart.

heaviness &c. *adj.*; infestivity, gloom; weariness &c. 841; *tædium vitæ,* disgust of life; *mal du pays* &c. (*regret*) 833.

melancholy; sadness &c. *adj.*; *il penseroso, melancholia,* dismals, mumps, mopes, lachrymals, dumps, blues, blue devils, doldrums, vapours, megrims, spleen, horrors, hypochondriasis, pessimism; despondency, slough of Despond; disconsolateness &c. *adj.*; hope deferred, blank despondency.

prostration, – of soul; broken heart; despair &c. 859; cave of -despair, – Trophonius.

cheer up, brighten up, light up, bear up; chirp, take heart, cast away care, drive dull care away, perk up.

rejoice &c. 838; carol, chirrup, lilt; frisk, rollick, give a loose to mirth.

cheer, enliven, elate, exhilarate, gladden, inspirit, animate, raise the spirits, inspire; put in good humour; cheer –, rejoice- the heart; delight &c. (*give pleasure*) 829.

**Adj.** cheerful; happy &c. 827; cheery, -ly; of good cheer, smiling; blithe; in –, in good- spirits; in high -spirits, – feather; happy as -the day is long, – a king; gay, – as a lark; *allegro*; light, -some, -hearted; buoyant, *débonnaire*, bright, free and easy, airy; janty, jaunty, canty; spright-ly, -ful; spry; spirit-ed, -ful; lively; animated, breezy, vivacious; brisk, – as a bee; sparkling; sportive; full of -play, – spirit; all alive.

sunny, palmy; hopeful &c. 858.

merry, – as a -cricket, – grig, – marriage bell; joyful, joyous, jocund, jovial; jolly, – as a thrush, – as a sandboy; blithesome; glee-ful, -some; hilarious, rattling.

winsome, bonny, hearty, buxom.

play-ful, -some; *folâtre*, playful as a kitten, tricksy, frisky, frolicsome; gamesome; jocose, jocular, waggish; mirth-, laughter-loving; mirthful, rollicking.

elate, -d; exulting, jubilant, flushed; rejoicing &c. 838; cock-a-hoop.

cheering, inspiriting, exhilarating; cardiac, -al; pleasing &c. 829; flourishing, halcyon.

**Adv.** cheerfully &c. *adj.*

**Int.** never say die! come! cheer up! hurrah! &c. 838; 'hence loathed melancholy!' begone dull care! away with melancholy!

---

demureness &c. *adj.*; gravity, solemnity; long –, grave- face.

hypochondriac, seek-sorrow, self-tormentor, *heautontimorumenos*, *malade imaginaire*, *médecin tant pis*; croaker, pessimist; mope, mopus.

[Cause of dejection] affliction &c. 830; sorry sight; *memento mori*; damper, wet blanket, Job's comforter; death's head, skeleton at the feast.

**V.** be -dejected &c. *adj.*; grieve; mourn &c. (*lament*) 839; take on, give way, lose heart, despond, droop, sink.

lower, look downcast, frown, pout; hang down the head; pull –, make- a long face; laugh on the wrong side of the mouth; grin a ghastly smile; look -blue, – like a drowned man; lay –, take- to heart.

mope, brood over; fret; sulk; pine, – away; yearn; repine &c. (*regret*) 833; despair &c. 859.

refrain from laughter, keep one's countenance; be –, look- grave &c. *adj.*; repress a smile, keep a straight face.

depress; dis-courage, -hearten; dispirit; damp, dull, deject, lower, sink, dash, knock down, unman, prostrate, break one's heart; frown upon; cast a -gloom, – shade- on; sadden; damp –, dash –, wither- one's hopes; weigh –, lie heavy –, prey- on the -mind, – spirits; damp –, depress- the spirits.

**Adj.** cheer-, joy-, spirit-less; uncheerful, -y; unlively; unhappy &c. 828; melancholy, dismal, sombre, dark, gloomy, adust, *triste*, clouded, murky, lowering, frowning, lugubrious, Acherontic, funereal, mournful, lamentable, dreadful.

dreary, flat; dull, – as -a beetle, – ditchwater; depressing &c. *v.*

'melancholy as a gib cat'; oppressed with –, a prey to- melancholy; downcast, -hearted; down -in the mouth, – on one's luck; heavy-hearted; in the -dumps, – suds, – sulks, – doldrums; in doleful dumps, in bad humour; sullen; mumpish, dumpish; mopish, moping; moody, glum; sulky &c. (*discontented*) 832; out of -sorts, – humour, – heart, – spirits; ill at ease, low-spirited, in low spirits, a cup too low; weary &c. 841; dis-couraged, -heartened; desponding; chop-, jaw-, crest-fallen.

sad, pensive, *penseroso*, tristful; dole-some, -ful; woebegone, lachrymose, in tears, melancholic, hipped, hypochondriacal, bil ious, jaundiced, atrabilious, saturnine, splenetic; lackadaisical.

serious, sedate, staid, stayed; grave, – as -a judge, – an undertaker, – a mustard pot; sober, solemn, demure; grim; grim-faced, -visaged; rueful, wan, long-faced.

disconsolate; un-, in-consolable; forlorn, comfortless, desolate, *désolé*, sick at heart; soul-, heart-sick; *au désespoir*; in despair &c. 859; lost.

overcome; broken-, borne-, bowed-down; heart-stricken &c. (*mental suffering*) 828; cut up, dashed, sunk; unnerved, unmanned; down-fallen, -trodden; broken-hearted; care-worn.

**Adv.** with -a long face, – tears in one's eyes; sadly &c. *adj.*

**Phr.** the countenance falling; the heart -failing, – sinking within one.

**838.** [Expression of pleasure.] **Rejoicing.—N.** rejoicing, exultation, triumph, jubilation, heyday, flush, revelling; merry-making &c. (*amusement*) 840; jubilee &c. (*celebration*) 883; pæan, *Te Deum* &c. (*thanksgiving*) 990; congratulation &c. 896; applause &c. 931.

smile, simper, smirk, grin; broad –, sardonic- grin.

laughter, giggle, titter, crow, cheer, chuckle, snicker, snigger, shout; Homeric laughter, horse –, hearty- laugh; guffaw; burst –, fit –, shout –, roar –, peal- of laughter; cachinnation.

risibility; derision &c. 856.

Momus; Democritus the Abderite; rollicker; Laughter holding both his sides.

**V.** rejoice; thank –, bless- one's stars; congratulate –, hug- oneself; rub –, clap- one's hands; smack the lips, fling up one's cap; dance, skip, caleer; sing, carol, chirrup, chirp; hurrah; cry for –, leap with- joy; exult &c. (*boast*) 884; triumph; hold jubilee &c. (*celebrate*) 883; make merry &c. (*sport*) 840; sing a pæan of joy.

smile, simper, smirk; grin, – like a Cheshire cat; mock, laugh in one's sleeve; laugh, – outright; giggle, titter, snigger, crow, smicker, chuckle, snicker, cackle; burst -out, – into a fit of laughter; shout, split, roar.

shake –, split –, hold both- one's sides; roar –, die- with laughter.

raise laughter &c. (*amuse*) 840.

**Adj.** rejoicing &c. *v.*; jubilant, exultant, triumphant; flushed, elated; laughing &c. *v.*; risible; ready to -burst, – split, – die with laughter; convulsed with laughter.

**839.** [Expression of pain.] **Lamentation.—N.** lament, -ation; wail, complaint, plaint, murmur, mutter grumble, groan, moan, whine, whimper, sob, sigh, suspiration, heaving, deep sigh.

cry &c. (*vociferation*) 411; scream, howl; outcry, wail of woe, frown, scowl.

tear; weeping &c. *v.*; flood of tears, fit of crying, lachrymation, melting mood, weeping and gnashing of teeth.

plaintiveness &c. *adj.*; languishment; condolence &c. 915.

mourning, weeds, willow, cypress, crêpe, crape, deep mourning; sackcloth and ashes; knell &c. 363; dump, death-song, dirge, coronach, keen, *nenia*, requiem, elegy, *epicedium*; threne; mon-, thren-ody; jeremiad; ululation.

mourner, professional mourner, keener; grumbler &c. (*discontent*) 832; Niobe; Heraclitus.

**V.** lament, mourn, deplore, grieve, weep over; be-wail, -moan; keen; condole with &c. 915; fret &c. (*suffer*) 828; wear –, go into –, put on- mourning; wear -the willow, – sackcloth and ashes; *infandum renovare dolorem* &c. (*regret*) 833; give sorrow words.

sigh; give –, heave –, fetch- a sigh; 'waft a sigh from Indus to the pole'; sigh 'like furnace'; wail.

cry, weep, sob, greet, blubber, pipe, snivel, bibber, whimper, pule; pipe one's eye; drop –, shed- -tears, – a tear; melt –, burst- into tears; *fondre en larmes*; cry -oneself blind, – one's eyes out.

scream &c. (*cry out*) 411; mew &c. (*animal sounds*) 412; groan, moan,

laughable &c. (*ludicrous*) 853.

**Int.** hip, hip, -hurrah! huzza! aha! hail! tolderolloll! tra-la la! Heaven be praised! *io triumphe! tant mieux!* so much the better.

**Phr.** the heart leaping with joy.

---

whine, yammer; roar; roar –, bellow- like a bull; cry out lustily, rend the air, yell.

frown, scowl, make a wry face, grimace, gnash one's teeth, wring one's hands, tear one's hair, beat one's breast, roll on the ground, burst with grief.

complain, murmur, mutter, grumble, growl, clamour, make a fuss about, croak, grunt, maunder; deprecate &c. (*disapprove*) 932.

cry out before one is hurt, complain without cause.

**Adj.** lamenting &c. *v.*; in mourning, in sackcloth and ashes; crying, sorrowing, -ful &c. (*unhappy*) 828; mourn-, tear-ful; lachrymose; plaint-ive, -ful, quer-ulous, -imonious; in the melting mood.

in tears, with tears in one's eyes; with -moistened, – watery- eyes; bathed –, dissolved- in tears; 'like Niobe all tears.'

elagiac, epicedial, threnetic.

**Adv.** *de profundis*; *les larmes aux yeux.*

**Int.** heigh-ho! alas! alack! O dear! ah –, woe is- me! lackadaisy! well –, lack –, alack- a day! well-a-way! alas the day! *O tempora! O mores!* what a pity! *miserabile dictu!* O lud lud! too true!

**Phr.** tears -standing in, – starting from- the eyes; eyes -suffused. – swimming, – brimming –, overflowing- with tears.

**840. Amusement.—N.** amuse-, entertain-ment; diver-sion, -tissement; recreation, relaxation, solace; pastime, *passetemps*, sport; labour of love; pleasure &c. 827.

fun, frolic, merriment, whoopee, jollity; jovial-ity, -ness; heyday; laughter &c. 838; jocos-ity, -eness; droll-, buffoon-, tomfool-ery; mummery, masquing, pleasantry; wit &c. 842; quip, quirk.

play; game, – at romps; gambol, romp, prank, antic, rig, lark, spree, skylarking, vagary, trick, monkey trick, *gambade, fredaine, escapade, échappée*, bout, *espièglerie*; practical joke &c. (*ridicule*) 856.

dance; round –, square –, solo –, step –, tap –, clog –, skirt –, sand –, folk –, morris- dance, *pas seul*, step, turn, *chassé*, cut, shuffle, double shuffle; hop, reel, rigadoon, saraband, hornpipe, bolero, fandango, pavan, tarantella, minuet, waltz, polka; galop, -ade; schottische, *pas de quatre*, Boston, one-, two-step, rumba, tango, maxixe, fox-, turkey-trot, shimmy, ragtime, cakewalk, jazz, blues, Charleston; jig, breakdown, fling, strathspey; *alle-*

**841. Weariness.—N.** weariness, defatigation, boredom, *ennui*; lassitude &c. (*fatigue*) 688; drowsiness &c. 683.

disgust, nausea, loathing, sickness; satiety &c. 869; *tædium vitæ* &c. (*dejection*) 837.

wearisome-, tedious-ness &c. *adj.*; dull work, tedium, monotony, twice told tale.

bore, button-holer, proser, wet blanket; heavy hours, 'the enemy' [time].

**V.** weary; tire &c. (*fatigue*) 688; bore; bore –, weary –, tire- -to death, – out of one's life, – out of all patience; set –, send- to sleep; buttonhole.

pall, sicken, nauseate, disgust.

harp on the same string; drag its -slow, – weary- length along.

never hear the last of; be -tired &c. *adj.* -of, – with; yawn; die with *ennui*.

**Adj.** wearying &c. *v.*; wearing; weari-, tire-, irk-some; uninteresting, stupid, bald, devoid of interest, dry, monotonous, dull, arid, tedious, humdrum, mortal, flat; pros-y, -ing; slow; soporific, somniferous, dormitive.

disgusting &c. *v.*; unenjoyed.

weary; tired &c. *v.*; drowsy &c (*sleepy*) 683; uninterested, flagging

*mande*; gavot, -te; mazurka, morisco; quadrille, lancers, country dance, *cotillon*, polonaise, Sir Roger de Coverley, Swedish dance; *ballet* &c. (*drama*) 599; ball; *bal, – masqué, – costumé*; masquerade, fancy dress ball; *thé dansant*; Terpsichore, choreography, Russian ballet, classical dancing; eurythmics; nautch dance, *danse du ventre*, cancan.

used up, worn out, *blasé*, life-weary, weary of life; sick of.

**Adv.** wearily &c. *adj.*; *usque ad nauseam.*

**Phr.** time hanging heavily on one's hands; *toujours perdrix*; *crambe repetita.*

---

festivity, merry-making; party &c. (*social gathering*) 892; *fête*, festival, gala, *ridotto*; revel-s, -ry, -ling; carnival, brawl, saturnalia, high jinks; feast, banquet &c. (*food*) 298; regale, *symposium*, wassail; carous-e, -al; jollification, junket, wake, picnic, *fête champêtre*, garden party, gymkhana, regatta, track meet, field-day, jamboree, treat.

round of pleasures, dissipation, a short life and a merry one, racketing, holiday making, high jinks.

rejoicing &c. 838; jubilee &c. (*celebration*) 883.

bonfire, fireworks, *feu-de-joie*, rocket, Catherine wheel, roman candle &c.

holiday; gala –, red letter –, play- day; high days and holidays; high –, Bank- holiday; May –, Derby- day; Saint –, Easter –, Whit- Monday; King's birthday, Empire Day; *mi-careme*; *Bairam*; wayzgoose, beanfeast, beano.

place of amusement, theatre &c. 599; concert-, ball-, assembly-room; music-hall, cinema, movies, talkies, vaudeville; hippodrome, circus, rodeo; *casino, kursaal*; winter garden; park, pleasance, arbour; garden &c. 371; pleasure-, play-, cricket-, football-, polo-, croquet-, archery-, hunting-ground; golf links, race course, stadium, gridiron, bowl, speedway, racing track, ring; gymnasium, swimming pool; shooting gallery; tennis-, racket-court; bowling-green, -alley; croquet-lawn, rink, skating rink; roller-coaster, roundabout, carousel, merry-go-round; swing; *montagne russe*; switchback, scenic railway &c.

game, – of -chance, – skill; athletic sports, gymnastics; fencing; archery, rifle-shooting; tournament, pugilism &c. (*contention*) 720; sporting &c. 622; horse-racing, the turf; aquatics &c. 267; skating, roller skating; ski-running, -joring, -jumping, bobsleighing, luging, tobogganing, winter sports; sliding; cricket, tennis, lawn –, table –, deck- tennis, rackets, fives, squash, ping-pong, trap bat and ball, battledore and shuttlecock, badminton, *la grâce*; pall mall, tip-cat, croquet, golf, curling, hockey, basketball, soccer, football, Rugby, Association, *pallone*, polo; tent-pegging, tilting at the ring, quintain, greasy pole; quoits, *discus*; throwing the hammer, putting the -weight, – shot, tossing the caber; knurr and spell; leap-frog, hop, skip and jump; French and English, tug of war; blind man's buff, hunt the slipper, hide-and-seek, kiss in the ring; snapdragon; cross questions and crooked answers; jig-saw puzzle; rounders, base-ball, lacrosse &c.; angling; swimming, diving, water-polo.

billiards, pool, pyramids, snooker, bagatelle; bowls, skittles, ninepins, kail, American bowls.

cards; bridge, auction, contract, whist, rubber; round game, coon-can, loo, cribbage, *bésique*, pinocle, euchre, drole, *écarté*, skat, picquet, all-fours, quadrille, ombre, reverse, Pope Joan, commit;

bo-, boa-ston; *vingt-et-un*; *quinze*, thirty-one, put-and-take, speculation, connections, brag, cassino, lottery, commerce, snip-snap-snorem, lift smoke, blind hookey, Polish bank, poker, banker; faro; Earl of Coventry, Napoleon, nap, patience, pairs; old maid, fright, beggar-my-neighbour; *baccarat, chemin de fer, monte;* craps.

chess, draughts, backgammon, dominoes, checkers, mah jong, merelles, nine men's morris, go-bang, solitaire; game of –, fox and-geese; lotto; &c.*

*morra*; gambling &c. (*chance*) 621; roulette.

toy, plaything, bauble; doll &c. (*puppet*) 554; teetotum; knick-knack &c. (*trifle*) 643; magic lantern &c. (*show*) 448; peep-, puppet-, raree-, gallanty-show; marionnettes, Punch and Judy; toy-shop; 'quips and cranks and wanton wiles, nods and becks and wreathèd smiles.'

sportsman, gamester, gambler &c. 621; reveller, master of the -ceremonies, – revels; *arbiter elegantiarum.*

**V.** amuse, entertain, divert, enliven; tickle, – the fancy; titillate, raise a smile, put in good humour; cause –, create –, occasion –, raise –, excite –, produce –, convulse with- laughter; set the table in a roar, be the death of one.

recreate, solace, cheer, rejoice; please &c. 829; interest; treat, regale.

amuse oneself; game; play, – a game, – pranks, – tricks; sport, disport, toy, wanton, revel, junket, feast, carouse, banquet, make merry; drown care; drive dull care away; frolic, gambol, frisk, romp; caper; dance &c. (*leap*) 309; keep up the ball; run a rig, sow one's wild oats, have one's fling, paint the town red, take one's pleasure; see life; *desipere in loco*, play the fool.

make –, keep- holiday; go a Maying.

while away –, beguile- the time; kill time, dally.

**Adj.** amusing, entertaining, diverting &c. *v.*; recreative, lusory; pleasant &c. (*pleasing*) 829; laughable &c. (*ludicrous*) 853; witty &c. 842; fest-ive, -al; jovial, jolly, jocund, roguish, rompish; sporting; playful, – as a kitten; sportive, ludibrious.

amused &c. *v.*; 'pleased with a feather, tickled with a straw.'

**Adv.** 'on the light fantastic toe,' at play, in sport.

**Int.** *vive la bagatelle! vogue la galère!*

**Phr.** *Deus nobis hæc otia fecit*; *dum vivimus vivamus.*

**842. Wit.—N.** wit, -tiness; attic -wit, – salt; atticism; salt, *esprit*, point, fancy, whim, humour, drollery, pleasantry.

farce, buffoonery, fooling, tomfoolery; harlequinade &c. 599; broad -farce, – humour; fun, *espièglerie*; *vis comica.*

jocularity; jocos-ity, -eness; facetiousness; wagg-ery, -ishness; whimsicality; comicality &c. 853.

smartness, ready wit, banter, *badi-*

**843. Dulness.—N.** dulness, heaviness, flatness; infestivity &c. 837; stupidity &c. 499; want of originality, dearth of ideas.

prose, matter of fact; heavy book, *conte à dormir debout*; platitude.

**V.** be -dull &c. *adj.*; prose, platitudinize, take *au sérieux*, be caught napping.

render -dull &c. *adj.*; damp, depress, throw cold water on, lay a wet blanket on; fall flat upon the ear; hang fire.

* A curious list of games is given in Sir Thomas Urquhart's translation of Rabelais' *Life of Gargantua*, book i. chapter 22.

*nage, persiflage*, retort, repartee, *quid pro quo*; ridicule &c. 856.

*facetiæ*, quips and cranks; jest, joke, capital joke; standing -jest, - joke; conceit, quip, quirk, crank, quiddity, *concetto, plaisanterie*, brilliant idea; merry -, bright -, happy- thought; sally; flash, - of wit, - of merriment; scintillation; *mot, - pour rire*; witticism, smart saying, *bon mot, jeu d'esprit*, epigram; jest book; dry joke, *quodlibet*, cream of the jest.

word-play, *jeu de mots*; play -of, - upon- words; pun, -ning; *double entendre* &c. (*ambiguity*) 520; quibble, verbal quibble; conundrum &c. (*riddle*) 533; anagram, acrostic, double acrostic, *nugæ canoræ*, trifling, idle conceit, *turlupinade*.

old joke, Joe Miller, chestnut, hoary-headed jest.

**V.** joke, jest, cut jokes; crack a joke; perpetrate a -joke, - pun; make -fun of, - merry with; set the table in a roar &c. (*amuse*) 840; scintillate.

retort, flash back; banter &c. (*ridicule*) 856; *ridentem dicere verum*; joke at one's expense.

**Adj.** witty, attic, salty; quick-, nimble-witted; keen, clever, smart, brilliant, pungent, jocular, jocose, funny, waggish, facetious, whimsical, humorous, Gilbertian; playful &c. 840; merry and wise; pleasant, sprightly, *spirituel*, sparkling, epigrammatic, full of point, *ben trovato*; comic &c. 853.

**Adv.** in joke, in jest, in sport, in play.

**Adj.** dull, - as ditch water; dry, insipid, jejune; unentertaining, uninteresting, unlively, unimaginative; heavisome, heavy-gaited; insulse; dry as dust; pros-y, -ing, -aic; matter of fact, commonplace, banal, pointless; 'weary, flat, stale and unprofitable.'

stupid, slow, flat, sluggish, ponderous, humdrum, monotonous; melancholic &c. 837; stolid &c. 499; plodding.

**Phr.** *Davus sum non Œdipus.*

---

**844. Humorist.**—**N.** humorist, wag, wit, reparteeist, epigrammatist, gag-man, punster; *bel esprit*, life of the party; wit-snapper, -cracker, -worm; joker, jester, jokesmith, Joe Miller, *drôle de corps, gaillard*, spark, *persifleur*, banterer.

buffoon, *farceur*, merry-andrew, mime, tumbler, acrobat, mountebank, charlatan, posturemaster, harlequin, punch, *pulcinella*, scaramouch, clown; wearer of the -cap and bells, - motley; motley fool; pantaloon, gipsy; jack -pudding, - in the green, - a dandy; zany; mad-cap, pickle-herring, witling, caricaturist, *grimacier*.

## 2°. Discriminate Affections

**845. Beauty.**—**N.** beauty, the beautiful, *le beau idéal*, loveliness.

[Science of the perception of beauty] Callæsthetics.*

form, elegance, grace, beauty unadorned; symmetry &c. 242; comeliness, fairness &c. *adj.*; pulchritude, polish, gloss; good -effect, - looks; *belle tournure*; bloom, brilliancy, radiance, splendour, gorgeousness, magnificence; sublimi-ty, -fication.

**846. Ugliness.**—**N.** ugliness &c. *adj.*; deformity, inelegance; disfigurement &c. (*blemish*) 848; want of symmetry, inconcinnity; distortion &c. 243; squalor &c. (*uncleanness*) 653.

forbidding countenance, vinegar aspect, hanging look, wry face, '*spretæ injuria formæ*.'

eyesore, object, figure, sight, fright, spectre, scarecrow, hag, harridan, satyr, witch, toad, baboon, monster.

* Whewell, 'Philosophy of the Inductive Sciences.'

concinnity, delicacy, refinement; charm, *je ne sais quoi*, style, *chic*, swank.

Venus, – of Milo; Aphrodite, Hebe, the Graces, Peri, Houri, Cupid, Apollo, Hyperion, Adonis, Antinous, Narcissus; Helen of Troy.

peacock, butterfly; flower, flow'ret gay, rose, lily, asphodel; garden; flower of, pink of; *bijou*; jewel &c. (*ornament*) 847; work of art.

pleasurableness &c. 829.

beautifying; landscape gardening; decoration &c. 847; calisthenics.

**V.** be -beautiful &c. *adj.*; shine, beam, bloom; become one &c. (*accord*) 23; set off, grace, flatter one.

render -beautiful &c. *adj.*; beautify; polish, burnish; gild &c. (*decorate*) 847; set out.

'snatch a grace beyond the reach of art.'

**Adj.** beaut-iful, -eous; handsome; pretty; lovely, graceful, elegant; delicate, dainty, refined, exquisite; fair, personable, comely, seemly; bonny; good-looking; well-favoured, -made, -formed, -proportioned; proper, shapely; symmetrical &c. (*regular*) 242; harmonious &c. (*colour*) 428; sightly.

fit to be seen, passable, not amiss.

goodly, dapper, tight, jimp; gimp; janty, jaunty; natty, quaint, trim, tidy, neat, spruce, smart, tricksy.

bright, -eyed; rosy-, cherry-cheeked; rosy, ruddy; blooming, in full bloom.

brilliant, shining; beam-y, -ing; sparkling, swanky, splendid, resplendent, dazzling, glowing; glossy, sleek.

showy, specious; rich, gorgeous, superb, magnificent, grand, fine, sublime, imposing; majestic 873.

artistic, -al; æsthetic; pict-uresque, -orial; *fait à peindre*, paintable; well-composed, -grouped, -varied; curious.

enchanting &c. (*pleasure-giving*) 829; attractive &c. (*inviting*) 615; becoming &c. (*accordant*) 23; ornamental &c. 847.

undeformed, undefaced, unspotted; spotless &c. (*perfect*) 650.

Caliban, Æsop, '*monstrum horrendum informe ingens cui lumen ademptum.*'

**V.** be -ugly &c. *adj.*; look ill, grin horribly a ghastly smile, make faces.

render -ugly &c. *adj.*; deface; dis-, de-figure; deform, spoil, distort &c. 243; blemish &c. (*injure*) 659; soil &c. (*render unclean*) 653.

**Adj.** ugly, – as -sin, – a toad, – a scarecrow, – a dead monkey; plain, bald &c. 226; homely &c. (*unadorned*) 849; ordinary, unornamental, inartistic; unsightly, unseemly, uncomely, unshapely, unlovely; sightless, seemless; not fit to be seen; unbeaut-eous, -iful; beautiless; shapeless &c. (*amorphous*) 241; course; garish, over-decorated &c. 882.

mis-shapen, -proportioned; monstrous; gaunt &c. (*thin*) 203; dumpy &c. (*short*) 201; curtailed of its fair proportions; ill-made, -shaped, -proportioned; crooked &c. (*distorted*) 243; hard-featured, -visaged; ill-, hard-, evil-favoured; ill-looking; unprepossessing.

graceless, inelegant; ungraceful, ungainly, uncouth; stiff; rugged, rough, gross, rude, awkward, clumsy, slouching, rickety; gawky; lump-ing, -ish; lumbering; hulk-y, -ing; unwieldy.

squalid, haggard; grim, -faced, -visaged; grisly, ghastly; ghost-, deathlike; cadaverous, gruesome.

frightful, hideous, odious, uncanny, forbidding, repellant, repulsive; horri-d, -ble; shocking &c. (*painful*) 830.

foul &c. (*dirty*) 653; dingy &c. (*colourless*) 429; gaudy &c. (*colour*) 428; disfigured &c. *v.*; discoloured (*blemished*) &c. 848.

---

**847. Ornament.** — **N.** ornament, -ation, -al art; ornat-ure, -eness; adorn-ment, decoration, embellishment; architecture.

garnish, polish, varnish, French pol-

**848. Blemish.**—**N.** blemish, disfigurement, deformity; defect &c. (*imperfection*) 651; flaw; injury &c. (*deterioration*) 659; spots on the sun; eyesore.

ish, gilding, japanning, lacquer, ormolu, enamel.

cosmetics, rouge, powder, lipstick, lip salve, mascara; manicure, nail polish; permanent –, Marcel –, fingerwave.

pattern, diaper, powdering, panelling, graining, pargeting, inlay, detail; texture &c. 329; richness; tracery, moulding, beading, reeding, fillet, listel, strapwork, *coquillage*, flourish, *fleur-de-lis*, arabesque, fret, *anthemion*; egg and -tongue, – dart; *astragal*, zigzag, *acanthus*, *cartouche*; pilaster &c. (*projection*) 250; cyma, ogee.

em-, broidery, needlework; knitting, crochet, tatting, brocade, *brocatelle*, beads, bugles; galloon, lace, gimp, *guipure*, fringe, trapping, border, edging, insertion, *motif*, trimming; *passementerie*; drapery, hanging, tapestry, arras; millinery, ermine.

wreath, festoon, garland, lei, chaplet, flower, nosegay, *bouquet*, posy, 'daisies pied and violets blue.'

tassel, knot; shoulder-knot, *épaulette*, epaulet, aigulet, *aiguillette*, frog; star, rosette, bow; feather, plume, *panache*, *aigrette*.

jewel, -ry, -lery; bijoutry; *bijou*, *-terie*; diadem, tiara; pendant, trinket, locket, necklace, armilla, bracelet, bangle, armlet, anklet, ear-, nose- ring, carcanet, chain, *châtelaine*, albert, brooch, torque.

gem, precious stone; diamond, brilliant, beryl, aquamarine, alexandrite, cat's eye, emerald, calcedony, chrysoprase, cornelian, jasper, bloodstone, agate, heliotrope; girasol, -e; onyx, plasma; sard, -onyx; garnet, lapis-lazuli, opal, peridot, chrysolite, sapphire, ruby; spinel, -le; balais; oriental –, topaz; turquois, -e; zircon, jacinth, hyacinth, carbuncle, amethyst; moonstone; pearl, coral.

finery, frippery, gewgaw, gimcrack, knick-knack, tinsel, spangle, sequin, *clinquant*, pinch-beck, paste; excess of ornament &c. (*vulgarity*) 851; gaud, pride, ostentation; frills and furbelows.

illustration, illumination, *vignette*; *fleuron*; head-, tail-piece; *cul-de-lampe*; flowers of rhetoric &c. 577; work of art, article of vertu, *bric-à-brac*, curio, *bibelot*.

**V.** ornament, embellish, enrich, decorate, adorn, beautify, adonize.

smarten, furbish, polish, gild, varnish, whitewash, enamel, japan, lacquer, paint, grain.

garnish, trim, dizen, bedizen, prink, prank; trick –, fig- out; deck, bedeck, dight, bedight, array; dress, – up, preen, spruce up,

stain, blot, slur; spot, -tiness; speck, -le; blur, freckle, mole, *macula*, patch, blotch, birthmark, blain, maculation, tarnish, smudge, smear; dirt &c. 653; bruise, black eye, scar, wem; pustule; excrescence, pimple &c. (*protuberance*) 250.

**V.** disfigure &c. (*injure*) 659; speckle; render ugly &c. 846.

**Adj.** pitted, freckled, discoloured, bloodshot, bruised, disfigured; stained &c. *n.*; imperfect &c. 651; injured &c. (*deteriorated*) 659.

**849. Simplicity. — N.** simplicity; plain-, homeli-ness; undress, nudity, nakedness, beauty unadorned, chastity, chasteness.

**V.** be -simple &c. *adj.*

render -simple &c. *adj.*; simplify, chasten, strip of ornament.

**Adj.** simple, plain; home-ly, -spun; ordinary, household.

natural, unaffected; free from -affectation, – ornament; *simplex munditiis*; *sans façon, en déshabillé*, nude, naked.

chaste, inornate, severe.

un-adorned, -ornamented, -decked, -garnished, -arranged, -trimmed, -varnished.

bald, flat, dull, blank.

titivate; spangle, bespangle, powder; embroider, work; chase, tool, emboss, fret; emblazon, blazon, illuminate; illustrate.

become &c. (*accord with*) 23.

**Adj.** ornamented, beautified &c. *v.*; ornate, rich, gilt, begilt, tesselated, enamelled, inlaid; festooned; topiary.

smart, gay, tricksy, flowery, glittering; new-gilt, -spangled; fine, – as -a Mayday queen, – fivepence, – a carrot fresh scraped; pranked out, bedight, well-groomed.

in full dress &c. (*fashion*) 852; *en grande -tenue, – toilette*; in best bib and tucker, in Sunday best, *endimanché*; dressed to advantage.

showy, flashy; gaudy &c. (*vulgar*) 851; garish; gorgeous.

ornamental, decorative; becoming &c. (*accordant*) 23.

**850.** [Good taste.] **Taste.—N.** taste; good –, refined –, cultivated- taste; delicacy, refinement, fine feeling, gust, *gusto*, tact, *finesse*; nicety &c. (*discrimination*) 465; polish, elegance, grace.

*virtu*; dilettanteism, virtuosity; fine art; cul-ture, -ivation.

[Science of taste] æsthetics.

man of -taste &c.; *connoisseur*, judge, critic, *conoscente, virtuoso, amateur, dilettante*, Aristarchus, Corinthian, *arbiter elegantiarum*, stagirite, euphemist.

'caviare to the general.'

**V.** appreciate, judge, criticize, discriminate &c. 465.

**Adj.** in good taste; tasteful, tasty; unaffected, pure, chaste, classical, attic; cultivated, refined; dainty; æsthetic, artistic; elegant &c. 578; euphemistic.

to one's -taste, – mind; after one's fancy; *comme il faut*; *tiré à quatre épingles*.

**Adv.** elegantly &c. *adj.*

**Phr.** *nihil tetigit quod non ornavit.*

**852. Fashion.—N.** fashion, style, *ton, bon ton*, society; good –, polite- society; drawing room, civilized life, civilization, town, *beau monde*, high life, court; world; fashionable –, gay- world; Vanity Fair; show &c. (*ostentation*) 822.

manners, breeding &c. (*politeness*) 894; air, demeanour &c. (*appearance*) 448; *savoir-faire*; gentlemanliness, gentility, decorum, propriety, *bienséance*; conventions –, dictates- of society; Mrs. Grundy; convention, -ality; punctilio; form, -ality; etiquette, point of

**851.** [Bad taste.] **Vulgarity.—N.** vulgar-ity, -ism; barbar-, Vandal-, Gothic-ism; *mauvais goût*, bad taste; Babbittry; *gaucherie*, awkwardness, want of tact; ill-breeding &c. (*discourtesy*) 895; ungentlemanly behaviour.

coarseness &c. *adj.*; indecorum, misbehaviour.

low-, homeli-ness; low life, *mauvais ton*, rusticity; boorishness &c. *adj.*; brutality; rowdy-, ruffian-, blackguard-ism; ribaldry; slang &c. (*neology*) 563.

bad joke, *mauvaise plaisanterie*.

[Excess of ornament] gaudi-, tawdriness; false ornament; finery, frippery, trickery, tinsel, gewgaw, *clinquant*.

rough diamond, tomboy, hoyden, cub, unlicked cub; clown &c. (*commonalty*) 876; Hun, Goth, Vandal, Bœotian; vulgarian; snob, cad, bounder, gent; *parvenu* &c. 876; frump, dowdy; slattern &c. 653.

**V.** be -vulgar &c. *adj.*; misbehave; talk –, smell of the- shop.

**Adj.** in bad taste, vulgar, unrefined, gutter.

coarse, indecorous, ribald, gross; unseemly, unbeseeming, unpresentable; *contra bonos mores*; ungraceful &c. (*ugly*) 846.

dowdy; slovenly &c. (*dirty*) 653; ungenteel, shabby genteel; low &c. (*plebeian*) 876; uncourtly; uncivil &c. (*discourteous*) 895; ill-bred, -mannered; underbred; ungentleman-ly, -like; unladylike, unfeminine; wild, – as an unbacked colt.

unkempt, uncombed, untamed, unlicked, unpolished, uncouth, plebeian;

etiquette; custom &c. 613; mode, vogue, style, go; rage &c. (*desire*) 865; prevailing taste, *dernier cri*, dress &c. 225.

man –, woman- of -fashion, – the world; height –, pink –, star –, glass –, leader- of fashion; *arbiter elegantiarum* &c. (*taste*) 850; upper ten thousand &c. (*nobility*) 875; *élite* &c. (*distinction*) 873.

**V.** be -fashionable &c. *adj.*, – the rage &c. *n.*; have a run, pass current.

follow –, conform to –, fall in with- the fashion &c. *n.*; go with the stream &c. (*conform*) 82; *savoir -vivre, – faire*; keep up appearances, behave oneself.

set the –, bring into- fashion; give a tone to –, cut a figure in- society, rub shoulders with nobility, keep one's carriage.

**Adj.** fashionable; in -fashion &c. *n.*; *à la mode, comme il faut*; admitted –, admissible- in -society &c. *n.*; presentable, decorous, punctilious, conventional &c. (*customary*) 613; genteel; well-bred, -mannered, -behaved, -spoken; gentleman-like, -ly; ladylike; civil, polite &c. (*courteous*) 894.

polished, refined, thoroughbred, courtly; *distingué*, aristocratic, unembarrassed, poised, *dégagé*; ja-, jau-nty; dashing, fast, showy, high toned, toney.

modish, stylish, in the latest style, *recherché*; new-fangled &c. (*unfamiliar*) 83.

in -court, – full, – evening- dress; *en grande tenue* &c. (*ornament*) 847.

**Adv.** fashionably &c. *adj.*; for fashion's sake.

incondite; heavy, rude, awkward; home-ly, -spun, -bred; provincial, hick, countrified, rustic, uncultivated, fresh-water; boorish, clownish; savage, brutish, blackguard, rowdy, snobbish; barbar-ous, -ic; Gothic, unclassical, doggerel, heathenish, tramontane, outlandish; Bohemian.

obsolete &c. (*antiquated*) 124; unfashionable, old-fashioned, out of date; new-fangled &c. (*unfamiliar*) 83; fantastic, odd &c. (*ridiculous*) 853.

particular; affected &c. 855; meretricious; extravagant, monstrous, horrid; shocking &c. (*painful*) 830.

gaudy, tawdry, bedizened, tricked out, gingerbread; obtrusive, flaunting, loud, flashy, garish, showy.

---

**853. Ridiculousness.**—**N.** ridiculousness &c. *adj.*; comical-, odd-ity &c. *adj.*; extravagance, drollery.

farce, comedy; burlesque &c. (*ridicule*) 856; buffoonery &c. (*fun*) 840; frippery; doggerel verses; Irish bull, Hibernianism, Hibernicism; Spoonerism; absurdity &c. 497; bombast &c. (*unmeaning*) 517; anticlimax, bathos; monstrosity &c. (*unconformity*) 83; laughing stock &c. 857.

**V.** be -ridiculous &c. *adj.*; pass from the sublime to the ridiculous; make one laugh; play the fool, make a fool of oneself, commit an absurdity.

play a joke on, make a -fool of, – sucker of, – monkey of.

**Adj.** ridiculous, ludicrous; comic, -al; droll, funny, laughable, *pour rire*, grotesque, farcical, odd; whimsical, – as a dancing bear; fanciful, fantastic, queer, rum, quizzical, waggish, quaint, *bizarre*; eccentric &c. (*unconformable*) 83; strange, outlandish, out of the way, *baroque*, *rocaille*, rococo; awkward &c. (*ugly*) 846.

absurd, extravagant, *outré*, monstrous, preposterous, bombastic, inflated, stilted, burlesque, mock heroic.

drollish; serio-, tragic-comic; gimcrack, contemptible &c. (*unimportant*) 643; doggerel; ironical &c. (*derisive*) 856; risible.

**Phr.** *'risum teneatis amici?' rideret Heraclitus.*

**854. Fop.—N.** fop, fine gentleman; swell; dand-y, -iprat; exquisite, coxcomb, toff, beau, macaroni, blade, blood, buck, man about town, fast man; fribble, jemmy, spark, popinjay, puppy, prig, *petit maître*; jacka-napes, -dandy; man milliner; Jemmy Jessamy, carpet-knight, masher, Dundreary, Johnnie, dude.

belle, fine lady, *coquette*, flirt.

**855. Affectation.—N.** affectation; affectedness &c. *adj.*; acting a part &c. *v.*; pretence &c. (*falsehood*) 544, (*ostentation*) 882; boasting &c. 884.

charlatanism, quackery, shallow profundity, humbug, pretension, airs, pedantry, purism, precisianism, euphuism, prunes and prisms; teratology &c. (*altiloquence*) 577.

mannerism, *simagrée*, grimace.

conceit, foppery, dandyism, man millinery, coxcombry, puppyism.

stiffness, formality, buckram; prudery, demureness, coquetry, mock modesty, *minauderie*, sentimentalism; *mauvaise honte*, false shame.

affector, performer, actor; pedant, pedagogue, *doctrinaire*, purist, euphuist, mannerist; shoneen; *grimacier*; lump of affectation, *précieuse ridicule, bas bleu*, blue stocking, poetaster; prig, hypocrite; charlatan &c. (*deceiver*) 548; *petit maître* &c. (*fop*) 854; flatterer &c. 935; *coquette*, prude, puritan; precisian, formalist.

**V.** affect, act a part, put on; give oneself airs &c. (*arrogance*) 885; boast &c. 884; coquet; simper, mince, attitudinize, strike a pose, pose; flirt a fan; over-act, -play, -do.

**Adj.** affected, full of affectation, pretentious, pedantic, stilted, stagey, theatrical, big-sounding, *ad captandum*, canting, insincere.

not natural, unnatural; self-conscious; *maniéré*; artificial; overwrought, -done, -acted; euphuistic &c. 577.

stiff, starch, formal, prim, smug, demure, *tiré à quatre épingles*, quakerish, puritanical, prudish, pragmatical, priggish, conceited, coxcomical, foppish, dandified; fini-cal, -kin, -cky, mincing, simpering, namby-pamby, sentimental, languishing.

**856. Ridicule.—N.** ridicule, derision; sardonic -smile, – grin; irrision; snigger; scoffing &c. (*disrespect*) 929; mockery, quiz, banter, irony, *persiflage*, raillery, chaff, *badinage*; quizzing &c. *v.*

squib, satire, skit, quip, quib, grin.

parody, burlesque, travesty; farce &c. (*drama*) 599; caricature, take-off.

buffoonery &c. (*fun*) 840; practical joke, horseplay.

**V.** ridicule, deride; laugh at, grin at, smile at; snigger; laugh in one's sleeve; banter, rally, chaff, joke, twit, quiz, poke fun at, jolly, roast, rag; fleer; play –, play tricks- upon; fool, – to the top of one's bent; show up.

satirize, parody, caricature, burlesque, travesty.

turn into ridicule; make merry with; make -fun, – game, – a fool, – an April fool- of; rally; scoff &c. (*disrespect*) 929.

raise a laugh &c. (*amuse*) 840; play the fool, make a fool of oneself.

be ridiculous &c. 853.

**Adj.** deris-ory, -ive; mock; sarcastic, ironical, quizzical, burlesque, Hudibrastic; scurrilous &c. (*disrespectful*) 929.

**Adv.** in -ridicule &c. *n.*

**857.** [Object and cause of ridicule.] **Laughing-stock.—N.** laughing-, jesting-, gazing-stock; butt, game, fair game; April fool &c. (*dupe*) 547.

original, oddity; queer –, odd- fish; quiz, square-toes; old –, fogey *or* fogy.

monkey; buffoon &c. (*jester*) 844; pantomimist &c. (*actor*) 599.

jest &c. (*wit*) 842.

## 3°. Prospective Affections

**858. Hope.—N.** hope, -s; desire &c. 865; fervent hope, sanguine expectation, trust, confidence, reliance; faith &c. (*belief*) 484; affiance, assurance; secur-eness, -ity; reassurance.

good -omen, – auspices; promise, well-grounded hopes; good –, bright- prospect; clear sky.

as-, pre-sumption; anticipation &c. (*expectation*) 507.

hopefulness, buoyancy, optimism, enthusiasm, heart of grace, aspiration; optimist, utop-ian, -ist; Pollyanna.

castles in the air, *châteaux en Espagne*, hope chest, *le pot au lait*, Utopia, millennium; day –, golden- dream; dream of Alnaschar; airy hopes, fool's paradise; *mirage* &c. (*fallacies of vision*) 443; fond hope.

beam –, ray –, gleam –, glimmer –, dawn –, flash –, star- of hope; cheer; bit of blue sky, silver lining of the cloud, bottom of Pandora's box, balm in Gilead.

anchor, sheet-anchor, main-stay; staff &c. (*support*) 215; heaven &c. 981.

**V.** hope, trust, confide, rely on, put one's trust in, lean upon; pin one's -hope, – faith- upon &c. (*believe*) 484.

feel –, entertain –, harbour –, indulge –, cherish –, feed –, foster –, nourish –, encourage –, cling to –, live in- hope &c. *n.*; see land; feel –, rest- -assured, – confident &c. *adj.*

presume; promise oneself; expect &c. (*look forward to*) 507.

hope for &c. (*desire*) 865; anticipate.

be -hopeful &c. *adj.*; look on the bright side of, view on the sunny side, make the best of it, hope for the best; put -a good, – a bold, – the best- face upon; keep one's spirits up; take heart, – of grace; be of good -heart, – cheer; flatter oneself, lay the flattering unction to one's soul.

**859.** [Absence, want, or loss of hope.] **Hopelessness.—N.** hopelessness &c. *adj.*; despair, desperation; despondency &c. (*dejection*) 837; pessimism.

hope deferred, dashed hopes; vain expectation &c. (*disappointment*) 509.

airy hopes &c. 858; forlorn hope; bad -job, – business; *enfant perdu*; gloomy –, black spots in the- horizon; slough of Despond, cave of Despair.

Job's comforter; bird of -bad, – ill- omen.

**V.** despair; lose –, give up –, abandon –, relinquish- -all hope, – the hope of; give -up, – over; yield to despair; falter; despond &c. (*be dejected*) 837; *jeter le manche après la cognée.*

inspire –, drive to- despair &c. *n.*; disconcert; dash –, crush –, shatter –, destroy- one's hopes; hope against hope.

**Adj.** hopeless, desperate, despairing, in despair, *au désespoir*, forlorn; inconsolable &c. (*dejected*) 837; broken-hearted.

out of the question, not to be thought of; impracticable &c. 471; past -hope, – cure, – mending, – recall; at one's last gasp &c. (*death*) 360; given -up, – over.

incurable, cureless, immedicable, remediless, beyond remedy; incorrigible; irre-parable, -mediable, -coverable, -versible, -trievable, -claimable, -deemable, -vocable; ruined, undone; immitigable.

unpromising, unpropitious; inauspicious, ill-omened, threatening, clouded over, lowering, ominous.

**Phr.** '*lasciate ogni speranza voi ch' entrate*'; its days are numbered; the worst come to the worst.

**860. Fear.—N.** fear, timidity, diffidence, want of confidence; apprehensive-, fearful-ness &c. *adj.*; solicitude,

catch at a straw, hope against hope, count one's chickens before they are hatched.

give –, inspire –, raise –, hold out- hope &c. *n.*; raise expectations; encourage, hearten, cheer, assure, reassure, buoy up, embolden; promise, bid fair, augur well, be in a fair way, look up, flatter, tell a flattering tale.

**Adj.** hoping &c. *v.*; in -hopes &c. *n.*; hopeful, confident; secure &c. (*certain*) 484; sanguine, in good heart, buoyed up, buoyant, elated, flushed, exultant, enthusiastic; utopian.

unsus-pecting, -picious; fearless, free –, exempt from- -fear, – suspicion, – distrust, – despair; undespairing, self-reliant.

probable, on the high road to; within sight of -shore, – land; promising, propitious; of –, full of- promise; of good omen; auspicious, *de bon augure*; reassuring; encouraging, cheering, inspiriting, looking up, bright, roseate, *couleur de rose*, rose-coloured.

**Adv.** hopefully &c. *adj.*

**Int.** God speed! good luck!

**Phr.** *nil desperandum*; never say die, *dum spiro spero, latet scintillula forsan*, all is for the best, *spero meliora*; the wish being father to the thought; 'hope told a flattering tale'; *rusticus expectat dum defluat amnis.*

---

anxiety, care, apprehension, misgiving; mistrust &c. (*doubt*) 485; suspicion, qualm; hesitation &c. (*irresolution*) 605.

nervous-, restless-ness &c. *adj.*; in-, dis-quietude; flutter, trepidation, fear and trembling, perturbation, tremor, quivering, shaking, trembling, throbbing heart, palpitation, ague fit, cold sweat; abject fear &c. (*cowardice*) 862; mortal funk, heart-sinking, despondency; despair &c. 859.

fright; affright, -ment; alarm, pavor, dread, awe, terror, horror, dismay, consternation, panic, scare, stampede [of horses].

intimidation, terrorism, reign of terror.

[Object of fear] bug-bear, -aboo; scarecrow; hobgoblin &c. (*demon*) 980; daymare, nightmare, Gorgon, Medusa, mormo, ogre, Hurlothrumbo, raw head and bloody bones, fee faw fum, *bête noire, enfant terrible.*

alarmist &c. (*coward*) 862.

**V.** fear, stand in awe of; be -afraid &c. *adj.*; have -qualms &c. *n.*; apprehend, sit upon thorns, eye askance; distrust &c. (*disbelieve*) 485.

hesitate &c. (*be irresolute*) 605; falter, funk, cower, crouch; skulk &c. (*cowardice*) 862; let 'I dare not' wait upon 'I would'; take -fright, – alarm; start, wince, flinch, shy, shrink; fly &c. (*avoid*) 623.

tremble, shake; shiver, – in one's shoes; shudder, flutter; shake –, tremble- -like an aspen leaf, – all over; quake, quaver, quiver, quail; get the wind up.

grow –, turn- pale; blench, stand aghast; not dare to say one's soul is one's own.

inspire –, excite- -fear, – awe; raise apprehensions; give –, raise –, sound- an alarm; alarm, startle, scare, cry 'wolf,' disquiet, dismay; fright, -en; affright, terrify; astound; frighten from one's propriety; frighten out of one's -wits, – senses, – seven senses; awe; strike -all of a heap, – an awe into, – terror; harrow up the soul, appal, unman, petrify, horrify.

make one's -flesh creep, – hair stand on end, – blood run cold, – teeth chatter; chill one's spine; take away –, stop- one's breath; make one -tremble &c.

haunt, obsess, beset; prey –, weigh- on the mind.

put in -fear, – bodily fear; terrorize, intimidate, cow, daunt, overawe, abash, deter, discourage; browbeat, bully; threaten &c. 909.

**Adj.** fearing &c. *v.*; frightened &c. *v.*; in -fear, – a fright &c. *n.*; haunted with the -fear &c. *n.*- of.

afraid, fearful; tim-id, -orous; nervous, diffident, coy, faint-hearted, tremulous, shaky, afraid of one's shadow, apprehensive, restless, fidgety; more frightened than hurt.

aghast; awe-, horror-, terror-, panic- -struck, -stricken; frightened to death, white as a sheet; pale, – as -death, – ashes, – a ghost; breathless, in hysterics.

inspiring fear &c. *v.*; alarming; formidable, redoubtable; perilous &c. (*danger*) 665; portentous; fear-ful, -some; dread, -ful; fell; dire, -ful; shocking; terri-ble, -fic; tremendous; horri-d, -ble, -fic; ghastly; awful, awe-inspiring, eerie, weird; revolting &c. (*painful*) 830.

**Adv.** *in terrorem.*

**Int.** 'angels and ministers of grace defend us!'

**Phr.** *ante tubam trepidat*; *horresco referens*, one's heart failing one, *obstupui steteruntque comæ et vox faucibus hæsit.*

**861.** [Absence of fear.] **Courage.—N.** courage, bravery, valour; resolute-, bold-ness &c. *adj.*; spirit, daring, gallantry, intrepidity; contempt –, defiance- of danger; derring-do; audacity; rashness &c. 863; dash; defiance &c. 715; confidence, self-reliance.

man-liness, -hood; nerve, pluck, mettle, game; heart, – of grace; spunk, gameness, grit, face, virtue, hardihood, fortitude; firmness &c. (*stability*) 150; heart of oak; bottom, backbone &c. (*perseverance*) 604*a*.

resolution &c. (*determination*) 604; tenacity, bull-dog courage.

prowess, heroism, chivalry.

exploit, feat, achievement; heroic -deed, – act; bold stroke.

man, – of mettle; hero, demigod, paladin, heroine, Amazon, Hector, Joan of Arc; lion, tiger, panther, bull-dog; game-, fighting-cock; bully, fire-eater &c. 863; dare-devil.

**V.** be -courageous &c. *adj.*; dare, venture, make bold; face –, front –, affront –, confront –, brave –, defy –, despise –, mock- danger; look in the face; look -full, – boldly, – danger- in the face; face; meet, – in front; brave, beard; defy &c. 715.

take –, muster –, summon up –, pluck up- courage; nerve oneself, take heart; take –, pluck up- heart of grace; hold up one's head, screw one's courage to the sticking place; come -to, – up to- the scratch; stand, – to one's guns, – fire, – against; bear up, – against; hold out &c. (*persevere*) 604*a*.

put a bold face upon; show –

**862.** [Excess of fear.] **Cowardice.—N.** cowardice, pusillanimity; cowardliness &c. *adj.*; timidity, effeminacy.

poltroonery, baseness; dastard-ness, -y; abject fear, funk; Dutch courage; fear &c. 860; white feather, faint heart.

coward, poltroon, dastard, sneak, recreant; shy –, dunghill- cock; coistril, milksop, white-liver, nidget, cur, craven, one that cannot say 'Bo' to a goose; Bob Acres, Jerry Sneak.

alarm-, terror-, pessim-ist; runagate &c. (*fugitive*) 623; shirker.

**V.** quail &c. (*fear*) 860; be -cowardly &c. *adj.*, – a coward &c. *n.*; funk; cower, skulk, sneak; flinch, shy, fight shy, slink, turn tail; run away &c. (*avoid*) 623; show the white feather, have cold feet, show a yellow streak.

**Adj.** coward, -ly; fearful, shy; tim-id, -orous; skittish; poor-spirited, spiritless, soft, effeminate.

weak-minded; infirm of purpose &c. 605; weak-, faint-, chicken-, lily-, pigeon-hearted; yellow; white-, lily-, milk-livered; milksop, smock-faced; unable to say 'Bo' to a goose.

dastard, -ly; base, craven, sneaking, dunghill, recreant; unwar-, unsoldier-like.

'in face a lion but in heart a deer.'

unmanned; frightened &c. 860.

**Int.** *sauve qui peut!* devil take the hindmost!

**Adv.** in fear and trembling, in fear of one's life, in a blue funk.

**Phr.** *ante tubam trepidat*, one's courage oozing out.

---

present- a bold front, face the music; envisage; show fight.

bell the cat, take the bull by the horns, beard the lion in his den, march up to the cannon's mouth, go through fire and water, run the gauntlet, go over the top.

give –, infuse –, inspire- courage; reassure, encourage, embolden, inspirit, cheer, hearten, nerve, put upon one's mettle, rally, raise a rallying cry; pat on the back, make a man of, keep in countenance.

**Adj.** courageous, brave; val-iant, -orous; gallant, intrepid; spirit-ed, -ful; high-spirited, -mettled; mettlesome, game, plucky; man-ly, -ful; resolute; stout, -hearted; iron-, lion-hearted; heart of oak; Penthesilean.

bold, – spirited; daring, audacious; fear-, daunt-, dread-, awe-less; un-daunted, -appalled, -dismayed, -awed, -blenched, -abashed, -alarmed, -flinching, -shrinking, -blenching, -apprehensive; confident, self-reliant; bold as -a lion, – brass.

enterprising, adventurous; ventur-ous, -esome; dashing, chivalrous; soldierly &c. (*warlike*) 722; heroic.

fierce, savage; pugnacious &c. (*bellicose*) 720.

strong-minded, hardy, doughty; firm &c. (*stable*) 150; determined &c. (*resolved*) 604; dogged, indomitable &c. (*persevering*) 604*a*.

up to, – the scratch; upon one's mettle; reassured &c. *v.*; unfeared, undreaded.

**Phr.** one's blood being up.

**863. Rashness.—N.** rashness &c. *adj.*; temerity, want of caution, imprudence, indiscretion; over-confidence, presumption, audacity.

precipit-ancy, -ation; impetuosity; levity; foolhardi-hood, -ness; heed-, thought-lessness &c. (*inattention*) 458; carelessness &c. (*neglect*) 460; desperation; Quixotism, knight-errantry; fire-eating.

gam-ing, -bling; blind bargain, leap in the dark, fool's paradise; too many eggs in one basket.

*desperado*, rashling, mad-cap, daredevil, Hotspur, fire-eater, bully, *bravo*, Hector, scapegrace, *enfant perdu*; Don Quixote, knight-errant, Icarus; adventurer; gam-bler, -ester; dynamitard.

**V.** be -rash &c. *adj.*; stick at nothing, play a desperate game; run into danger &c. 665; play with -fire, – edge tools.

carry too much sail, sail too near the wind, ride at single anchor, go out of one's depth.

take a leap in the dark, buy a pig in a poke.

*donner tête baissée*; knock one's head against a wall &c. (*be unskilful*) 699; rush on destruction; kick against the

**864. Caution.—N.** caution; cautiousness &c. *adj.*; discretion, prudence, cautel, heed, circumspection, calculation, deliberation; safety first.

foresight &c. 510; vigilance &c. 459; warning &c. 668.

coolness &c. *adj.*; self-possession, -command; presence of mind, *sang-froid*; well-regulated mind; worldly wisdom, Fabian policy.

**V.** be -cautious &c. *adj.*; take -care, – heed, – good care; have a care; mind, – what one is about; be on one's guard &c. (*keep watch*) 459; make assurance double sure; ca' canny.

bespeak &c. (*be early*) 132.

think twice, look before one leaps, keep one's weather eye open, count the cost, look to the main chance, cut one's coat according to one's cloth; feel one's -ground, – way; see how the land lies &c. (*foresight*) 510; wait to see how the cat jumps; bridle one's tongue; *reculer pour mieux sauter* &c. (*prepare*) 673; let well alone, let sleeping dogs lie, *ne pas réveiller le chat qui dort*.

keep out of -harm's way, – troubled waters; keep at a respectful distance, stand aloof; keep –, be- on the safe side

pricks, tempt Providence, go on a forlorn hope.

count one's chickens before they are hatched; reckon without one's host; catch at straws; trust to –, lean on- a broken reed.

**Adj.** rash, incautious, indiscreet, injudicious; imprudent, improvident, temerarious; uncalculating; heedless; careless &c. (*neglectful*) 460; without ballast, heels over head; giddy &c. (*inattentive*) 458; wanton, reckless, wild, madcap; desperate, devil-may-care.

hot-blooded, -headed, -brained; head-long, -strong; break-neck; foolhardy; hare-brained; precipitate, impulsive.

over-confident, -weening; ventur-esome, -ous; adventurous, Quixotic; fire-eating, cavalier; free-and-easy.

off one's guard &c. (*inexpectant*) 508.

**Adv.** post haste, *à corps perdu*, hand over head, *tête baissée*, headforemost; happen what may.

**Phr.** neck or nothing, the devil being in one.

husband one's resources &c. 636.

caution &c. (*warn*) 668.

**Adj.** cautious, wary, guarded; on one's guard &c. (*watchful*) 459; *cavendo tutus*; *in medio tutissimus*.

care-, heed-ful; cautelous, stealthy, chary, shy of, circumspect, prudent, canny, safe, non-committal, discreet, politic; sure-footed &c. (*skilful*) 698.

unenterprising, unadventurous, cool, steady, self-possessed; over-cautious.

suspicious, leery, vigilant.

**Adv.** cautiously, gingerly &c. *adj.*

**Int.** have a care! look out! *cave canem!*

**Phr.** *timeo Danaos*; *festina lente.*

---

**865. Desire.**—**N.** desire, wish, fancy, fantasy; want, need, exigency.

mind, inclination, leaning, bent, *animus*, partiality, *penchant*, predilection; propensity &c. 820; willingness &c. 602; liking, love, fondness, relish.

longing, hankering; solicitude, anxiety; yearning, coveting; aspiration, ambition, vaulting ambition; eagerness, zeal, ardour, *empressement*, breathless impatience, over-anxiety; solicitude, impetuosity &c. 825.

appet-ite, -ition, -ence, -ency; sharp appetite, keenness, hunger, stomach, twist; thirst, -iness; drouth, mouthwatering; itch, -ing; prurience, *cacoëthes*, cupidity, lust, concupiscence.

edge of -appetite, – hunger; torment of Tantalus; sweet –, lickerish- tooth; itching palm; longing –, wistful –, sheep's- eye.

avidity; greed, -iness; covetous-, ravenous-ness &c. *adj.*; grasping, craving, canine appetite, rapacity; voracity &c. (*gluttony*) 957.

passion, rage, *furore*, mania, *manie*; inextinguishable desire; dips-, klept-, mon-omania.

[Person desiring] desirer, lover, *ama-*

**866. Indifference.**—**N.** indifference neutrality; coldness &c. *adj.*; unconcern, *insouciance*, *nonchalance*; want of -interest, – earnestness; anorexy, inappetency; apathy &c. (*insensibility*) 823; supineness &c. (*inactivity*) 683; disdain &c. 930; recklessness &c. 863; inattention &c. 458.

**V.** be -indifferent &c. *adj.*; stand neuter; take no interest in &c. (*insensibility*) 823; have no -desire &c. 865, – taste, – relish- for; not care for; care nothing -for, – about; not care a -straw &c. (*unimportance*) 643 -about, – for; not mind.

set at naught &c. (*make light of*) 483; spurn &c. (*disdain*) 930.

**Adj.** indifferent, cold, frigid, lukewarm; cool, – as a cucumber; unconcerned, *insouciant*, phlegmatic, *pococurante*, easy-going, devil-may-care, careless, listless, lackadaisical, feckless; half-hearted; un-ambitious, -aspiring, -desirous, -solicitous, -attracted.

un-attractive, -alluring, -desired, -desirable, -cared for, -wished, -valued, all one to.

insipid &c. 391; vain.

**Adv.** for aught one cares.

*teur*, votary, devotee, aspirant, solicitant, candidate; cormorant &c. 957; sycophant.

[Object of desire] *desideratum*; want &c. (*requirement*) 630; 'consummation devoutly to be wished'; attraction, magnet, allurement, fancy, temptation, seduction, lure, fascination, *prestige*, height of one's ambition, idol; whim, -sey; maggot; hobby, -horse.

Fortunatus's cap, wishing cap, love potion.

**V.** desire; wish, – for; be -desirous &c. *adj.*; have a -longing &c. *n.*; hope &c. 858.

care for, affect, like, list; take to, cling to, take a fancy to; fancy; prefer &c. (*choose*) 609.

have -an eye, – a mind- to; find it in one's heart &c. (*be willing*) 602; have a fancy for, set one's eyes upon; cast a sheep's eye –, look sweet- upon; take into one's head, have at heart, be bent upon; set one's -cap at, – heart upon, – mind upon; covet.

want, miss, need, lack, desiderate, feel the want of; would fain -have, – do; would be glad of.

be -hungry &c. *adj.*; have a good appetite, play a good knife and fork; hunger –, thirst –, crave –, lust –, itch –, hanker –, run mad- after; raven –, die- for; burn to.

desiderate; sigh –, cry –, gape –, gasp –, pine –, pant –, languish –, yearn –, long –, be on thorns –, hope- for; aspire after; catch at, grasp at, jump at.

woo, court, solicit; fish –, spell –, whistle –, put up- for; ogle.

cause –, create –, raise –, excite –, provoke- desire; whet the appetite; appetize, titillate, allure, attract, take one's fancy, tempt; hold out -temptation, – allurement; tantalize, make one's mouth water, *faire venir l'eau à la bouche*.

gratify desire &c. (*give pleasure*) 829.

**Adj.** desirous; desiring &c. *v.*; orectic, appetitive; inclined &c. (*willing*) 602; partial to; fain, wishful, optative; anxious, wistful, curious; at a loss for, sedulous, solicitous.

craving, hungry, sharp-set, peckish,

**Int.** never mind.

**867. Dislike.—N.** dis-like, -taste, -relish, -inclination, -placency.

reluctance; backwardness &c. (*unwillingness*) 603.

repugnance, disgust, queasiness, turn, nausea, loathing; avers-eness, -ation, -ion; abomination, antipathy, abhorrence, horror; mortal –, rooted- -antipathy, – horror; hatred, detestation; hate &c. 898; animosity &c. 900; hydrophobia.

sickener; gall and wormwood &c. (*unsavoury*) 395; shuddering, cold sweat.

**V.** dis-, mis-like, -relish; mind, object to; have rather not, not care for; have –, conceive –, entertain –, take- -a dislike, – an aversion- to; have no -taste, – stomach- for.

shun, avoid &c. 623; eschew; withdraw –, shrink –, recoil- from; not be able to -bear, – abide, – endure; shrug the shoulders at, shudder at, turn up the nose at, look askance at; make a -mouth, – wry face, – grimace; make faces.

loathe, nauseate, abominate, detest, abhor; hate &c. 898; take amiss &c. 900; have enough of &c. (*be satiated*) 869.

cause –, excite- dislike; disincline, repel, sicken; make –, render- sick; turn one's stomach, nauseate, wamble, disgust, shock, stink in the nostrils; go against the -grain, – stomach; stick in the throat; make one's blood run cold &c. (*give pain*) 830; pall.

**Adj.** disliking &c. *v.*; averse to, loth, adverse; shy of, sick of, out of conceit with; disinclined; heart-, dog-sick; queasy.

disliked &c. *v.*; uncared for, unpopular; out of favour; repulsive, repugnant, repellent; abhorrent, insufferable, fulsome, nauseous; loath-some, -ful; offensive; disgusting &c. *v.*; disagreeable &c. (*painful*) 830; unsavoury &c. 395.

**Adv.** *usque ad nauseam.*

**Int.** faugh! foh! ugh!

**868. Fastidiousness.—N.** fastidiousness &c. *adj.*; nicety, meticulosity,

ravening, with an empty stomach, esurient, lickerish, thirsty, athirst, parched with thirst, pinched with hunger, famished, dry, drouthy; hungry as a -hunter, - hawk, - horse, - church mouse.

greedy, - as a hog; over-eager, voracious; ravenous, - as a wolf; open-mouthed, covetous, rapacious, grasping, extortionate, exacting, sordid, *alieni appetens*; insati-able, -ate; unquenchable, quenchless; omnivorous.

unsatisfied, unsated, unslaked.

eager, avid, keen; burning, fervent, ardent; agog; all agog; breathless; impatient &c. (*impetuous*) 825; bent -, intent -, set- -on, - upon; mad after, *enragé*, rabid, dying for, devoured by desire.

aspiring, ambitious, vaulting, sky-aspiring.

desirable; popular; desired &c. *v.*; in demand; pleasing &c. (*giving pleasure*) 829; appeti-zing, -ble; tantalizing.

**Adv.** wistfully &c. *adj.*; fain.

**Int.** would -that, - it were! O for! *esto perpetua!* if only!

**Phr.** the wish being father to the thought; *sua cuique voluptas*; *hoc erat in votis*, the mouth watering, the fingers itching; *aut Cæsar aut nullus*.

---

hypercriticism, difficulty in being pleased, *friandise*, epicurism, *omnia suspendens naso*.

discrimination, discernment, good taste, perspicacity.

epicure, gourmet.

[Excess of delicacy] prudery, prudishness, primness.

**V.** be -fastidious &c. *adj.*; split hairs, discriminate, have a sweet tooth.

mince the matter; turn up one's nose at &c. (*disdain*) 930; look a gift horse in the mouth, see spots on the sun.

**Adj.** fastidious, meticulous, exacting, nice, delicate, *délicat*, finical, finicky, difficult, dainty, lickerish, squeamish, thin-skinned; s-, queasy; hard -, difficult- to please; querulous, particular, over-particular, straitlaced, prudish, prim, scrupulous; censorious &c. 932; hypercritical, discriminating, discerning, perspicacious.

**Phr.** *noli me tangere*.

**869. Satiety.—N.** satiety, satisfaction, saturation, repletion, glut, surfeit; weariness &c. 841.

spoiled child; *enfant gâté*; too much of a good thing, *toujours perdrix*; *crambe repetita*.

**V.** sate, satiate, satisfy, saturate; cloy, quench, slake, pall, glut, gorge, surfeit; bore &c. (*weary*) 841; tire &c. (*fatigue*) 688; spoil.

have -enough of, - quite enough of, - one's fill, - too much of; be -satiated &c. *adj.*

**Adj.** satiated &c. *v.*; overgorged; *blasé*, used up, sick of, heart-sick.

**Int.** enough! hold! *eheu jam satis!*

## 4°. Contemplative Affections

**870. Wonder.—N.** wonder, marvel; astonish-, amaze-, wonder-, bewilder-ment; amazedness &c. *adj.*; admiration, awe; stup-or, -efaction; stound, fascination; sensation; surprise &c. (*inexpectation*) 508; cynosure.

note of admiration; thaumaturgy &c. (*sorcery*) 992.

**V.** wonder, marvel, admire; be -surprised &c. *adj.*; start; stare; open -, rub -, turn up- one's eyes; gloar; gape, open one's mouth, hold one's breath;

**871.** [Absence of wonder.] **Expectance.—N.** expectan-ce, -cy &c. (*expectation*) 507; calmness, composure, tranquillity, serenity, coolness, imperturbability &c. 826.

nine days' wonder.

**V.** expect &c. 507; not -be surprised, - wonder &c. 870; *nil admirari*, make nothing of.

**Adj.** expecting &c. *v.*; unamazed, astonished at nothing; *blasé* &c. (*weary*) 841; unimaginative, calm, serene, im-

look –, stand- -aghast, – agog; look blank &c. (*disappointment*) 509; *tomber des nues*; not believe one's -eyes, – ears, – senses.

not be able to account for &c. (*unintelligible*) 519; not know whether one stands on one's head or one's heels.

surprise, astonish, amaze, astound; dumbfound, -er; startle, dazzle; strike, – with -wonder, – awe; electrify; stun, stupefy, petrify, confound, bewilder, flabbergast; stagger, throw on one's beam ends, fascinate, turn the head, take away one's breath, strike dumb; make one's -hair stand on end, – tongue cleave to the roof of one's mouth; make one stare.

take by surprise &c. (*be unexpected*) 508.

be -wonderful &c. *adj.*; beggar –, baffle- description; stagger belief.

**Adj.** surprised &c. *v.*; aghast, all agog, breathless, agape; open-mouthed; awe-, thunder-, moon-, planet-struck; spell-bound; lost in -amazement, – wonder, – astonishment; struck all of a heap, unable to believe one's senses, like a duck in thunder.

wonderful, wondrous; surprising &c. *v.*; unexpected &c. 508; unheard of; mysterious &c. (*inexplicable*) 519; miraculous; *foudroyant.*

in-describable, -expressible, -effable; un-utterable, -speakable.

monstrous, prodigious, stupendous, marvellous; in-conceivable, -credible; in-, un-imaginable; strange &c. (*uncommon*) 83; passing strange.

striking &c. *v.*; over-whelming; wonder-working.

**Adv.** wonderfully &c. *adj.*; fearfully; for a –, in the name of- wonder; strange to say; *mirabile -dictu, – visu*; to one's great surprise.

with -wonder &c. *n.*, – gaping mouth, – open eyes, – upturned eyes; eyes starting out of one's head.

**Int.** lo, – and behold! O! hey-day! halloo! what! indeed! really! surely! humph! hem! good -lack, – heavens, – gracious! – lord! by jove! gad so! well a day! dear me! only think! lack-a-daisy! my -stars, – goodness! gracious goodness! goodness gracious! mercy on us! heavens and earth! God bless me! bless -us, – my heart! odzookens! *O gemini!* adzooks! hoity-toity! strong! Heaven save –, bless- the mark! can such things be! zounds! 'sdeath! what -on earth, – in the world! who would have thought it! &c. (*inexpectation*) 508; fancy! did you ever? you don't say so! what do you say to that! how now! where am I? well I'm blowed! &c.

**Phr.** *vox faucibus hæsit*; one's hair standing on end.

**871. Expectance.**—... perturbable &c. 826; expected &c. *v.*; foreseen.

common, ordinary &c. (*habitual*) 613.

**Int.** no wonder; of course; why not?

---

**872. Prodigy.**—**N.** prodigy, phenomenon; wonder, -ment; genius, marvel, miracle; freak, monster &c. (*unconformity*) 83; curiosity, lion, infant prodigy, sight, spectacle; *jeu –, coup- de théâtre*; gazing-stock; sign; portent &c. 512.

bursting of a -shell, – bomb; volcanic eruption, peal of thunder; thunder-clap, -bolt.

what no words can paint; wonders of the world; *annus mirabilis*; *dignus vindice nodus.*

## 5°. Intrinsic Affections*

**873. Repute.**—**N.** distinction, mark, name, figure; repute, reputation, char-

**874. Disrepute.**—**N.** disrepute, discredit; ill-, bad- -repute, -name, -odour,

* Or personal affections derived from the opinions or feelings of others.

acter; good –, high- repute; note, notability, notoriety, *éclat*, 'the bubble reputation,' vogue, celebrity; fame, famousness; renown; popularity, *aura popularis*; esteem, approval, approbation &c. 931; credit, *succès d'estime*, *prestige*, talk of the town; name to conjure with.

glory, honour; lustre &c. (*light*) 420; illustriousness &c. *adj*.

account, regard, respect; reputableness &c. *adj*.; respectability &c. (*probity*) 939; good -name, – report; fair name.

dignity; stateliness &c. *adj*.; solemnity, grandeur, splendour, nobility, majesty, sublimity.

rank, standing, brevet rank, precedence, *pas*, station, place, *status*; position, – in society; order, degree, *locus standi*, caste, condition.

greatness &c. *adj*.; eminence; height &c. 206; importance &c. 642; pre-, super-eminence; high mightiness, primacy; top of the -ladder, – tree.

elevation; ascent &c. 305; super-, ex-altation; dignification, aggrandizement.

dedication, consecration, enthronement, canonization, apotheosis, deification, celebration, enshrinement, glorification.

hero, man of mark, great card, celebrity, champion, worthy, lion, *rara avis*, notability, somebody; man of rank &c. (*nobleman*) 875; pillar of the -state, – society, – church.

chief &c. (*master*) 745; first fiddle &c. (*proficient*) 700; scholar &c. 492; cynosure, mirror; flower, pink, pearl; paragon &c. (*perfection*) 650; choice and master spirits of the age; *élite*; star, sun, constellation, galaxy.

ornament, honour, feather in one's cap, halo, aureole, nimbus; halo –, blaze- of glory; blushing honours; laurels &c. (*trophy*) 733.

memory, posthumous fame, niche in the temple of fame; immor-tality, -tal name; *magni nominis umbra*.

**V.** be conscious of glory; be proud of &c. (*pride*) 878; exult &c. (*boast*) 884; be vain of &c. (*vanity*) 880.

be -distinguished &c. *adj*.; shine &c. -favour; disapprobation &c. 932; ingloriousness, derogation; a-, de-basement; abjectness &c. *adj*.; degradation, dedecoration; 'a long farewell to all one's greatness'; odium, obloquy, opprobrium, ignominy.

dishonour, disgrace; shame, humiliation; scandal, baseness, vileness; perfidy, turpitude &c. (*improbity*) 940; infamy.

tarnish, taint, defilement, pollution.

stain, blot, spot, blur, stigma, brand, reproach, imputation, slur.

crying –, burning- shame; *scandalum magnatum*, badge of infamy, blot in one's escutcheon; bend –, bar- sinister; champain, point champain; by-word of reproach; Ichabod.

*argumentum ad verecundiam*; sense of shame &c. 879.

**V.** be -inglorious &c. *adj*.; incur -disgrace &c. *n*.; have –, earn- a bad name; put –, wear- a halter round one's neck; disgrace –, expose- oneself.

play second fiddle; lose caste; pale one's ineffectual fire; recede into the shade; fall from one's high estate; keep in the background &c. (*modesty*) 881; be conscious of disgrace &c. (*humility*) 879; look -blue, – foolish, – like a fool; cut a -poor, – sorry- figure; laugh on the wrong side of the mouth; make a sorry face, go away with a flea in one's ear, slink away.

cause -shame &c. *n*.; shame, disgrace, put to shame, dishonour; throw –, cast –, fling –, reflect- dishonour &c. *n*. upon; be a -reproach &c. *n*. to; derogate from.

tarnish, stain, blot, sully, taint; discredit; degrade, debase, defile; beggar; expel &c. (*punish*) 972.

impute shame to, brand, post, stigmatize, vilify, defame, slur, cast a slur upon, hold up to shame, send to Coventry; tread –, trample- under foot; show up, drag through the mire, heap dirt upon; reprehend &c. 932.

bring low, put down, snub; take down a peg, – lower, – or two.

obscure, eclipse, outshine, take the shine out of; throw –, cast- into the shade; overshadow; leave –, put- in the background; push into a corner,

(*light*) 420; shine forth, figure; make –, cut- a -figure, – dash, – splash.

rival, surpass; out-shine, -rival, -vie, -jump; emulate, vie with, eclipse; throw –, cast- into the shade; overshadow.

live, flourish, glitter, scintillate, flaunt; gain –, acquire- honour &c. *n.*; play first fiddle &c. (*be of importance*) 642; bear the -palm, – bell; lead the way; take -precedence, – the wall of; gain –, win- -laurels, – spurs, – golden opinions &c. (*approbation*) 931; graduate, take one's degree, pass one's examination, win a -scholarship, – fellowship.

make -a, – some- -noise, – noise in the world; leave one's mark, exalt one's horn, star, have a run, be run after; enjoy popularity, come -into vogue, – to the front; raise one's head.

enthrone, signalize, immortalize, deify, exalt to the skies; hand one's name down to posterity.

consecrate; dedicate to, devote to; enshrine, inscribe, blazon, lionize, blow the trumpet, crown with laurel.

confer –, reflect- honour &c. *n.* on; shed a lustre on; redound to one's honour, ennoble.

give –, do –, pay –, render- honour to; honour, accredit, pay regard to, dignify, glorify; sing praises to &c. (*approve*) 931; look up to; exalt, aggrandize, elevate, nobilitate.

**Adj.** distinguished, *distingué*, noted; of -note &c. *n.*; honoured &c. *v.*; popular; fashionable &c. 852.

in good odour; in –, in high- favour; reput-, respect-, credit-able.

remarkable &c. (*important*) 642; notable, notorious; celebrated, renowned, in every one's mouth, talked of; fam-ous, -ed; farfamed; conspicuous, to the front; foremost; in the -front rank, – ascendant.

imperishable, deathless, immortal, never fading, *ære perennius*; time-honoured.

illustrious, glorious, splendid, brilliant, radiant; bright &c. 420; full-blown; honorific.

eminent, prominent; high &c. 206; in the zenith; at the -head of, – top of the tree; peerless, of the first water; superior &c. 33; super-, pre-eminent.

great, dignified, proud, noble, honourable, worshipful, lordly, grand, stately, august, princely, imposing, solemn, transcendent, majestic, sacred, sublime, heaven-born, heroic, *sans peur et sans reproche*; sacrosanct.

**Int.** hail! all hail! *ave! viva! vive!* long life to! glory –, honour- be to!

put one's nose out of joint; put out, – of countenance.

upset, throw off one's centre; discompose, disconcert; put to the blush &c. (*humble*) 879.

**Adj.** disgraced &c. *v.*; blown upon; shorn of -its beams, - one's glory; overcome, down-trodden; loaded with -shame &c. *n.*; in -bad repute &c. *n.*; out of -repute, – favour, – fashion, – countenance; at a discount; under -a cloud, – an eclipse; unable to show one's face; in the -shade, – background; out at elbows, down in the world, down and out.

inglorious; nameless, renownless, obscure, unknown to fame; un-noticed, -noted, -honoured, -glorified.

shameful; dis-graceful, -creditable, -reputable; despicable; questionable; unbecoming, unworthy; derogatory; degrading, humiliating, *infra dignitatem*, dedecorous; scandalous, infamous, too bad, unmentionable; ribald, opprobrious; arrant, shocking, outrageous, notorious, shady.

ignominious, scrubby, dirty, abject, vile, beggarly, pitiful, low, mean, shabby; base &c. (*dishonourable*) 940.

**Adv.** to one's shame be it spoken.

**Int.** fie! shame! for shame! *pro pudor! O tempora! O mores!* ough! *sic transit gloria mundi!*

**Phr.** one's name -being in every mouth, – living for ever; *sic itur ad astra, fama volat, aut Cæsar aut nullus*; not to know him argues oneself unknown; none but himself could be his parallel, *palmam qui meruit ferat.*

**875. Nobility.—N.** nobility, rank, condition, distinction, optimacy, blood, *pur sang*, birth, high descent, order; quality, gentility; blue blood of Castile; *ancien régime.*

high life, *haut monde*; upper -classes, – ten thousand; *élite*, aristocracy, great folks; fashionable world &c. (*fashion*) 852; salariat.

peer, -age; House of -Lords, – peers; lords, – temporal and spiritual; *noblesse*; baronage, knightage; noble, -man; lord, -ling; grandee, *magnifico*, *hidalgo*; don, -ship; aristocrat, swell, three-tailed bashaw; gentleman, squire, squireen, patrician, laureate.

gentry, gentlefolk; squirarchy, better sort, *magnates*, *primates*, *optimates.*

king &c. (*master*) 745; prince, crown prince, *Dauphin*; duke; marquis, -ate; earl, viscount, baron, thane, banneret; baronet, -cy; knight, -hood; count, armiger, laird; sig-, seig-nior; esquire, boyar, margrave, vavasour, sheik, emir, ameer, scherif, *pasha*, effendi, sahib.

queen &c. 745; princess, begum, duchess, marchioness; countess &c.; lady, dame.

personage –, man- of -distinction, – mark, – rank; nota-bles, -bilities; celebrity, big-wig, magnate, great man, star; *magni nominis umbra*; 'every inch a king'; grand Panjandrum.

**V.** be -noble &c. *adj.*

**Adj.** noble, exalted; of -rank &c. *n.*; princely, titled, patrician, aristocratic; high-, well-born; of gentle blood; genteel, *comme il faut*, gentlemanlike, courtly &c. (*fashionable*) 852; highly respectable.

**Adv.** in high quarters.

**877. Title.—N.** title, honour; knighthood &c. (*nobility*) 875.

royal –, serene- highness, excellency, grace; lordship, worship, Rt. Hon., rever-ence, -end; esquire, sir; madam, *madame*; master, mistress, Mr., Mrs., *signor*, *señor*, *Mein Herr*, *mynheer*;

**876. Commonalty.—N.** commonalty, democracy; obscurity; low -condition, – life, – society, – company; *bourgeoisie*; mass of -the people, – society; Brown, Jones, and Robinson; Tom, Dick, and Harry; lower –, humbler- -classes, – orders; vulgar –, common- herd; rank and file, *hoc genus omne*; the -many, – general, – crowd, – people, – populace, – multitude, – million, – masses, – mobility, – peasantry; king Mob; proletariat, *fruges consumere nati*, great unwashed; man in the street.

mob; rabble, – rout; chaff, rout, horde, *canaille*; scum –, *residuum* –, dregs- of -the people, – society; swinish multitude, *fæx populi*; *profanum* –, *ignobile- vulgus*; vermin, riff-raff, tag-rag and bobtail; small fry.

commoner, one of the people, democrat, plebeian, republican, proletary, *prolétaire*, *roturier*, Mr. Snooks, *bourgeois*, *épicier*, Philistine, cockney; *grisette*, *demi-mondaine.*

peasant, countryman, boor, carle, churl; vill-ain, -ein; serf, kern, tyke, tike, chuff, ryot, fellah; long-shoreman; swain, clown, hind; clod, -hopper; hobnail, yokel, hick, rube, cider squeezer, bog-trotter, bumpkin; ploughman, -boy; rustic, chawbacon, tiller of the soil; hewers of wood and drawers of water, groundling; gaffer, loon, put, cub, Tony Lumpkin, looby, lout, underling; *gamin*, guttersnipe, street arab, mudlark; rough, rowdy, ruffian, roughneck; pot-wallopper, slubberdegullion; vulgar –, low- fellow; cad, curmudgeon.

upstart, *parvenu*, *nouveau-riche*, skipjack; nobody, – one knows; *hesterni quirites*, *pessoribus orti*; *bourgeois gentilhomme*, *novus homo*, snob, gent, mushroom, no one knows who, adventurer; man of straw.

beggar, panhandler, gaberlunzie, muckworm, mudlark, *sans-culotte*, raff, tatterdemalion, caitiff, ragamuffin, Pariah, outcast of society, tramp, weary Willie, bum, vagabond, *chiffon*

your –, his- honour; handle to one's name.

decoration, laurel, palm, wreath, garland, bays, medal, ribbon, riband, blue ribbon, *cordon*, cross, crown, coronet, star, garter; feather, – in one's cap; chevron, epaulet, *épaulette*, colours, cockade; livery; order, arms, armorial bearings, shield, scutcheon, crest, reward &c. 973.

---

*nier*, rag-picker, Cinderella, cinder-wench, scrub, jade; boots, gosscon.

Goth, Vandal, Hottentot, savage, barbarian, Yahoo; unlicked cub, rough diamond.

barbar-ousness, -ism; Bœotia.

**V.** be -ignoble &c. *adj.*, – nobody &c. *n.*

**Adj.** ignoble, common, mean, low, base, vile, sorry, scrubby, beggarly, below par; no great shakes &c. (*unimportant*) 643; home-ly, -spun; vulgar, low-minded; snobbish, *parvenu*.

plebeian, proletarian; of -low, – mean- -parentage, – origin, extraction; low-, base-, earth-born, low bred; mushroom, dunghill, risen from the ranks: unknown to fame, obscure, untitled.

rustic, uncivilized; lout-, boor-, clown-, churl-, brut-, raff-ish; rude, unlicked, unpolished.

barbar-ous, -ian, -ic, -esque; cockney, born within sound of Bow bells.

underling, menial, servile, subaltern.

**Adv.** below the salt.

**878. Pride.—N.** dignity, self-respect, *mens sibi conscia recti*.

pride; haughtiness &c. *adj.*; high notions, *hauteur*; vainglory, crest; arrogance &c. (*assumption*) 885; pomposity &c. 882.

proud man, highflier; fine -gentleman, – lady; *grande dame*.

**V.** be -proud &c. *adj.*; put a good face on; look one in the face; stalk abroad, perk oneself up; presume, swagger, strut; rear –, lift up –, hold up- one's head; hold one's head high, look big, take the wall, 'bear like the Turk no rival near the throne,' carry with a high hand; ride the –, mount on one's- high horse; set one's back up, bridle, toss the head; give oneself airs &c. (*assume*) 885; boast &c. 884.

pride oneself on; glory in, take a pride in; pique –, plume –, hug- oneself; stand upon, be proud of; put a good face on; not -hide one's light under a bushel, – put one's talent in a napkin; not think small beer of oneself &c. (*vanity*) 880.

**Adj.** dignified; stately; proud, -crested; lordly, baronial; lofty-minded; high-souled, -minded, -mettled, -handed, -plumed, -flown, -toned.

**879. Humility.—N.** hum-ility, -bleness; meek-, low-ness; lowli-ness, -hood; abasement, self-abasement, -effacement; submission &c. 725; resignation.

condescension; affability &c. (*courtesy*) 894.

modesty &c. 881; verecundity, blush, suffusion, confusion; sense of -shame, – disgrace; humiliation, mortification; let –, set- down.

**V.** be -humble &c. *adj.*; deign, vouchsafe, condescend; humble –, demean- oneself; stoop, – to conquer; carry coals; submit &c. 725; submit with a good grace &c. (*brook*) 826; yield the palm.

lower one's -tone, – note; sing small, draw in one's horns, sober down; hide one's -face, – diminished head; not dare to show one's face, take shame to oneself, not have a word to say for oneself; feel –, be conscious of- -shame, – disgrace; drink the cup of humiliation to the dregs; eat -humble pie, – one's words, – dirt; be humiliated, receive a snub.

blush -for, – up to the eyes; redden, change colour; colour up; hang one's head, look foolish, feel small.

render humble; humble, humiliate;

haughty, paughty, insolent, lofty, high, mighty, swollen, puffed up, flushed, blown; vain-glorious; purse-proud, fine; proud as -a peacock, Lucifer; bloated with pride.

supercilious, disdainful, bumptious, magisterial, imperious; high -handed, - and mighty; overweening, consequential; arrogant &c. 885; unblushing &c. 880.

stiff, -necked; starch; perked -, stuck- up; in buckram, straitlaced; prim &c. (*affected*) 855.

on one's -high horses, - tight ropes, - high ropes; on stilts; *en grand seigneur*.

**Adv.** with head erect, with one's nose in the air.

**Phr.** *odi profanum vulgus et arceo.*

---

let -, set -, take -, tread -, frown-down; snub, abash, abase, make one sing small, strike dumb; teach one -his distance, - his place; take down a peg, - lower; throw -, cast- into the shade &c. 874; stare -, put- out of countenance; put to the blush; confuse, ashame, mortify, disgrace, crush; send away with a flea in one's ear.

get a set down.

**Adj.** humble, lowly, meek; modest &c. 881; humble-, sober-minded; unoffended; submissive &c. 725; servile &c. 886.

condescending; affable &c. (*courteous*) 894.

humbled &c. *v.*; bowed down, resigned; abashed, ashamed, dashed; out of countenance; down in the mouth; down on one's -knees, - marrow-bones; humbled in the dust, brow-beaten; chap-, crest-fallen; dumbfoundered, flabbergasted, struck all of a heap.

shorn of one's glory &c. (*disrepute*) 874.

**Adv.** with -downcast eyes, - bated breath, - bended knee; on all fours, on one's feet.

under correction, with due deference.

**Phr.** I am your -obedient, - very humble- servant; my service to you.

**880. Vanity.**—**N.** vanity; conceit, -edness; self-conceit, -complacency, -confidence, -sufficiency, -esteem, -love, -approbation, -praise, -glorification, -laudation, -gratulation, -applause, -admiration; *amour-propre*; selfishness &c. 943.

airs, pretensions, mannerism; egotism; prigg-ism, -ishness; coxcombry, gaudery, vainglory, elation; pride &c. 878; ostentation &c. 882; assurance &c. 885.

*vox et præterea nihil*; *cheval de bataille.*

ego-ist, -tist; peacock, coxcomb &c. 854; Sir Oracle &c. 887.

**V.** be -vain &c. *adj.*, - vain of; pique oneself &c. (*pride*) 878; lay the flattering unction to one's soul.

have -too high, - an overweening- opinion of -oneself, - one's talents; blind oneself as to one's own merit; not think -small beer, - *vin ordinaire*- of oneself; put oneself forward; fish

**881. Modesty.**—**N.** modesty; humility &c. 879; diffidence, timidity; retiring disposition, unobtrusiveness, bashfulness &c. *adj.*; *mauvaise honte*; blush, -ing; verecundity; self-knowledge.

reserve, constraint; demureness &c. *adj.*; blushing honours.

**V.** be -modest &c. *adj.*; retire, reserve oneself; give way to; draw in one's horns &c. 879; hide one's face.

keep -private, - in the background, - one's distance; pursue the noiseless tenor of one's way, 'do good by stealth and blush to find it fame,' hide one's light under a bushel, cast a sheep's eye.

**Adj.** modest, diffident; humble &c. 879; timid, timorous, bashful; shy, nervous, skittish, coy, sheepish, shamefaced, blushing, over-modest.

unpreten-ding, -tious; un-obtrusive, -assuming, -ostentatious, -boastful, -aspiring; poor in spirit.

for compliments; give oneself airs &c. (*assume*) 885; boast &c. 884.

render -vain &c. *adj.*; inspire with -vanity &c. *n.*; inflate, puff up, turn up, turn one's head.

**Adj.** vain, – as a peacock; conceited, assured, overweening, pert, forward, perky; vain-glorious, high-flown; ostentatious &c. 882; puffed up, inflated, flushed.

self-satisfied, -confident, -sufficient, -flattering, -admiring, -applauding, -glorious, -opinionated; *entêté* &c. (*wrong-headed*) 481; wise in one's own conceit, pragmatical, overwise, pretentious, priggish; egotistic, -al; *soi-disant* &c. (*boastful*) 884; arrogant &c. 885.

un-abashed, -blushing; un-constrained, -ceremonious; free and easy.

**Adv.** vainly &c. *adj.*

**Phr.** how we apples swim!

out of countenance &c. (*humbled*) 879.

reserved, constrained, demure.

**Adv.** humbly &c. *adj.*; quietly, privately; without -ceremony, – beat of drum; *sans façon.*

---

**882. Ostentation.—N.** ostentation, display, show, flourish, parade, *étalage*, pomp, array, state, solemnity; dash, splash, glitter, strut, swank, side, swagger, pomposity; preten-se, -sions; showing off; fuss.

magnificence, splendour; *coup d'œil*; grand doings.

*coup de théâtre*; stage -effect, – trick; clap-trap; *mise en scène*; *tour de force*; *chic*.

demonstration, flying colours; tomfoolery; flourish of trumpets &c. (*celebration*) 883; pageant, -ry; spectacle, exhibition, procession; turn –, set- out; grand function; *fête*, gala, field-day, review, march past, promenade, insubstantial pageant.

dress; court –, full –, evening –, ball –, fancy- dress; tailoring, millinery, man-millinery, frippery; foppery, equipage.

ceremon-y, -ial; ritual; form, -ality; etiquette; punct-o, -ilio, -iliousness; starched-, stateli-ness.

mummery, solemn mockery, mouth honour.

attitudinarian; fop &c. 854.

**V.** be -ostentatious &c. *adj.*; come –, put oneself- forward; attract attention, star it.

make –, cut- a -figure, – dash, – splash; strut, blow one's own trumpet; figure, – away; make a show, – display; glitter.

show -off, – one's paces; parade, march past; display, exhibit, put forward, hold up; trot –, hang- out; sport, brandish, blazon forth; dangle, – before the eyes.

cry up &c. (*praise*) 931; *prôner*, flaunt, emblazon, prink, set off, mount, have framed and glazed.

put a good, – smiling- face upon; clean the outside of the platter &c. (*disguise*) 544.

**Adj.** ostentatious, showy, dashing, pretentious; ja-, jau-nty; grand, pompous, palatial; high-sounding; turgid &c. (*big-sounding*) 577; garish, gorgeous; gaudy, – as a -peacock, – butterfly, – tulip; flaunting, flashing, flaming, glittering; gay &c. (*ornate*) 847; colourful.

splendid, magnificent, sumptuous.

theatrical, dramatic, spectacular, scenic, ceremonial, ritual, -istic.

solemn, stately, majestic, formal, stiff, ceremonious, punctilious, starch-ed, -y.

*en grande tenue*, in best bib and tucker, in Sunday best, *endimanché*.
**Adv.** with -flourish of trumpet, - beat of drum, - flying colours, - a brass band.
*ad captandum vulgus*.

**883. Celebration.—N.** celebration, solemnization, jubilee, diamond jubilee, commemoration, ovation, pæan, triumph, jubilation.
triumphal arch, bonfire, salute; salvo, - of artillery; *feu de joie*, flourish of trumpets, *fanfare*, colours flying, illuminations, fireworks.
inauguration, installation, presentation; *début*, coming out, birthday anniversary, bi-, ter-, centenary; silver -, golden -, diamond-wedding, -day; coronation; Lord Mayor's show; harvest home, red letter day, festival; trophy &c. 733; *Te Deum* &c. (*thanksgiving*) 990; fête &c. 882; holiday &c. 840.
**V.** celebrate, keep, signalize, do honour to, commemorate, solemnize, hallow, mark with a red letter, hold high festival, maffick.
pledge, drink to, toast, hob and nob.
inaugurate, install, instate, induct, chair.
rejoice &c. 838; kill the fatted calf, hold jubilee, roast an ox, fire a salute.
**Adj** celebrating &c. *v.*; commemorative, celebrated, immortal.
**Adv.** in -honour, - commemoration, - celebration of.
**Int.** hail! all hail! *io -pæan*, - *triumphe!* 'see the conquering hero comes!'

**884. Boasting.—N.** boasting &c. *v.*; boast, vaunt, crake; preten-ce, -sions; puff, -ery; flourish, *fanfaronnade*; gasconade; bluff, swank, brag, -gardism; bravado, bunkum, Buncombe; highfalutin; jact-itation, -ancy; bounce, rant, bluster; venditation, vapouring, rodomontade, bombast, fine talking, tall talk, magniloquence, teratology, heroics; jingoism, Chauvinism; exaggeration &c. 549; gas, hot air.
vanity &c. 880; *vox et præterea nihil*; much cry and little wool, *brutum fulmen*.
exultation; glorification; flourish of trumpets; triumph &c. 883.
boaster; bragg-art, -adocio; hot air merchant; Gascon, *fanfaron*, pretender, fourflusher, *soi-disant*; windbag, blowhard, bluffer; chauvinist; blusterer &c. 887; charlatan, jack-pudding, trumpeter; puppy &c. (*fop*) 854.
**V.** boast, make a boast of, brag, vaunt, puff, show off, flourish, crake, crack, trumpet, strut, swagger, vapour, bluff; draw the long bow.
exult, crow over, neigh, chuckle, triumph; glory, gloat, jubilate; throw up one's cap; talk big, *se faire valoir*, *faire claquer son fouet*, take merit to oneself, make a merit of, sing *Io triumphe*, holloa before one is out of the wood.
**Adj.** boasting &c. *v.*; magniloquent, flaming, Thrasonic, stilted, gasconading, braggart, boastful, pretentious, *soi-disant*; vain-glorious &c. (*conceited*) 880.
elate, -d; jubilant, triumphant, exultant; in high feather; flushed, - with victory; cock-a-hoop; on stilts.
vaunted &c. *v.*
**Adv.** vauntingly &c. *adj.*; with a brass band.
**Phr.** 'let the galled jade wince.'

**885.** [Undue assumption of superiority.] **Insolence.—N.** insolence; haughtiness &c. *adj.*; arrogance, airs; overbearance, brashness, bumptiousness, contumely, disdain; domineering &c. *v.*; tyranny &c. 739.

impertinence; cheek, nerve, sauce; sauciness &c. *adj.*; flippancy, dicacity, petulance, procacity, bluster; swagger, -ing &c. *v.*; bounce; terrorism; jingoism, chauvinism.

as-, pre-sumption; beggar on horseback; usurpation.

impudence, assurance, audacity, self-assertion, hardihood, front, face, brass; shamelessness &c. *adj.*; effrontery, hardened front, face of brass.

assumption of infallibility.

malapert, saucebox &c. (*blusterer*) 887.

**V.** be -insolent &c. *adj.*; bluster, vapour, swagger, swell, give oneself airs, snap one's fingers, kick up a dust; swear &c. (*affirm*) 535; rap out oaths; roister.

arrogate; as-, pre-sume; make -bold, – free; take a liberty, give an inch and take an ell.

domineer, bully, dictate, hector; lord it over, bulldoze; *traiter de haut, regarder de haut en bas*; exact; snub, huff, beard, fly in the face of; put to the blush; bear –, beat- down; browbeat, intimidate; trample –, tread- -down, – under foot; dragoon, ride roughshod over, terrorize.

out-face, -look, -stare, -brazen, -brave; stare out of countenance; brazen out; lay down the law; teach one's grandmother to suck eggs; assume a lofty bearing; talk –, look- big; put on big looks, act the *grand seigneur*; mount –, ride- the high horse; toss the head, carry with a high hand.

tempt Providence, want snuffing.

**Adj.** insolent, haughty, arrogant, imperious, magisterial, dictatorial, arbitrary; high-handed, high and mighty; contumelious, supercilious, overbearing, intolerant, domineering; overweening, high-flown.

flippant, pert, cavalier, saucy, forward, impertinent, fresh, malapert.

precocious, assuming, would-be, bumptious.

bluff; brazen-, -browed, -faced, shameless, aweless, unblushing, unabashed; bold-, bare-faced; dead –, lost- to shame.

**886. Servility.—N.** servility; slavery &c. (*subjection*) 749; obsequiousness &c. *adj.*; subserviency; abasement; pros-tration, -ternation; genuflexion &c. (*worship*) 990; fawning &c. *v.*; tuft-hunting, time-serving, flunkeyism; sycophancy &c. (*flattery*) 933; humility &c. 879.

sycophant, parasite, yes-man; toad, -y, -eater; tuft-hunter; snob, flunkey, lap-dog, spaniel, lickspittle, smell-feast, *Græculus esuriens*, hanger on, stooge, *cavaliere servente*, led captain, carpet knight; time-server, fortune-hunter, Vicar of Bray, Sir Pertinax Mac Sycophant, pick-thank; flatterer &c. 935; doer of dirty work; *âme damnée*, tool; reptile; slave &c. (*servant*) 746; courtier; sponge, jackal; truckler.

**V.** cringe, bow, stoop, kneel, bend the knee; fall on one's knees, prostrate oneself; worship &c. 990.

sneak, crawl, crouch, cower, truckle to, grovel, fawn, toady, lick the feet of, kiss the hem of one's garment.

pay court to; feed –, fatten –, batten- on; dance attendance on, pin oneself upon, hang on the sleeve of, *avaler des couleuvres*, keep time to, fetch and carry, do the dirty work of.

go with the stream, follow the crowd, worship the rising sun, hold with the hare and run with the hounds.

**Adj.** servile, obsequious; supple, – as a glove; soapy, oily, pliant, cringing, fawning, slavish, grovelling, snivelling, mealy-mouthed; beggarly, sycophantic, parasitical; abased, abject, prostrate, down on one's marrow-bones; base, mean, sneaking; crouching &c. *v.*

**Adv.** hat –, cap- in hand.

impudent, audacious, presumptuous, free and easy, devil-may-care, rollicking; janty, jaunty; roistering, blustering, hectoring, swaggering, vapouring; thrasonic, fire-eating, 'full of sound and fury.'

**Adv.** insolently, with a high hand; *ex cathedrâ*.

**Phr.** one's bark being worse than his bite.

**887. Blusterer.**—**N.** bluster-, swagger-, vapour-, roister-, brawl-er; brazen-face; *fanfaron*; braggart &c. (*boaster*) 884; bully, terrorist, rough, rough-neck; hooligan, hoodlum, larrikin, ruffian; Mo-hock, -hawk; drawcansir, swashbuckler, Captain Boabdil, Sir Lucius O'Trigger, Thraso, Pistol, Parolles, Bombastes Furioso, Hector, Chrononhotonthologos; jingo; desperado, dare-devil, fire-eater; fury &c. (*violent person*) 173; rowdy.

puppy &c. (*fop*) 854; prig; Sir Oracle, dogmatist, *doctrinaire*, stump orator, jack-in-office; saucebox, malapert, jackanapes, minx; bantam-cock.

## Section III. SYMPATHETIC AFFECTIONS

### 1°. Social Affections

**888. Friendship.** — **N.** friendship, amity; friendliness &c. *adj.*; brotherhood, fraternity, sodality, confraternity, sorosis, sisterhood; harmony &c. (*concord*) 714; peace &c. 721.

firm –, staunch –, intimate –, familiar –, bosom –, cordial –, tried –, devoted –, lasting –, fast –, sincere –, warm –, ardent- friendship.

cordiality, fraternization, *entente cordiale*, good understanding, *rapprochement*, sympathy, fellow-feeling, response, welcomeness; *camaraderie*.

affection &c. (*love*) 897; favouritism; goodwill &c. (*benevolence*) 906; partiality.

acquaintance, familiarity, intimacy, intercourse, fellowship, knowledge of; introduction.

**V.** be -friendly &c. *adj.*, – friends &c. 890, – acquainted with &c. *adj.*; know; have the ear of; keep company with &c. (*sociality*) 892; hold communication –, have dealings –, sympathize- with; have a leaning to; bear good will &c. (*benevolence*) 906; love &c. 897; make much of; befriend &c. (*aid*) 707; introduce to.

set one's horses together; hold out –, extend- the right hand of friendship, – fellowship; become -friendly &c. *adj.*; make -friends &c. 892 with; break the ice, be introduced to; make –, pick –, scrape- acquaintance with; get into favour, gain the friendship of.

shake hands with, fraternize, embrace; receive with open arms, throw oneself into the arms of; meet half way, take in good part.

**Adj.** friendly; amic-able, -al; well affected, unhostile, neighbourly, brotherly, fraternal, sisterly, sympathetic, harmonious, hearty, cordial, warm-hearted, devoted

**889. Enmity.**—**N.** enmity, hostility, unfriendliness &c. *adj.*; discord &c. 713.

alienation, estrangement; dislike &c. 867; hate &c. 898; antagonism.

heartburning; animosity &c. 900; malevolence &c. 907.

**V.** be -inimical &c. *adj.*; keep –, hold- at arm's length; be at loggerheads; bear malice &c. 907; fall out; take umbrage &c. 900; harden the heart, alienate, estrange.

**Adj.** inimical, unfriendly, hostile; at -enmity, – variance, – swords points, – daggers drawn, – open war with; up in arms against; in bad odour with.

on bad –, not on speaking- terms; cool; cold, -hearted; estranged, alienated, disaffected, irreconcilable.

friends –, well –, at home –, hand in hand- with; on -good, -friendly, – amicable, – cordial, – familiar, – intimate- -terms, – footing; on -speaking, – visiting- terms; in one's good -graces, – books.

acquainted, familiar, intimate, thick, hand and glove, hail fellow well met, free and easy; welcome.

**Adv.** amicably &c. *adj.*; with open arms; *sans cérémonie*; arm in arm.

**890. Friend.—N.** friend, – of one's bosom, intimate acquaintance, neighbour, well-wisher; *alter ego*; best –, bosom –, fast- friend; *amicus usque ad aras*; *fidus Achates*; *persona grata.*

favourer, *fautor*, patron, backer, Mæcenas; tutelary saint, good genius, advocate, partisan, sympathiser; ally; friend in need &c. (*auxiliary*) 711.

associate, compeer, comrade, mate, companion, *confrère*, *camarade*, *confidante*, colleague; old –, crony; side-kick; chum, buddy, bunkie, roommate, pal; play-fellow, -mate; classmate, schoolfellow; bed-fellow, -mate; maid of honour.

compatriot; fellow –, countryman, – townsman.

shop-, ship-, mess-mate; fellow –, boon –, pot- companion; co-partner.

*Arcades ambo*, Pylades and Orestes, Castor and Pollux, Nisus and Euryalus, Damon and Pythias, *par nobile fratrum.*

host, Amphitryon, Boniface; guest, visitor, frequenter, *habitué*; *protegé.*

**891. Enemy.—N.** enemy; antagonist, foeman; open –, bitter- enemy; opponent &c. 710; back friend.

public enemy, enemy to society, traitor, anarchist &c. 742; *persona non grata.*

**Phr.** every hand being against one.

---

**892. Sociality.—N.** soci-ality, -ability, -ableness &c. *adj.*; social intercourse; consociation; inter-course, -community; consort-, companion-, fellow-, comrade-ship; clubbism; *esprit de corps.*

conviviality; good -fellowship, – company, *camaraderie*; joviality, jollity, *savoir-vivre*, festivity, festive board, merry-making; loving cup; hospitality, heartiness; cheer.

welcome, -ness; greeting; hearty –, warm –, welcome- reception; urbanity &c. (*courtesy*) 894; intimacy, familiarity.

good –, jolly- fellow, good mixer, Rotarian; *bon enfant.*

social –, family- circle; circle of acquaintance, *coterie*, society, company.

social -gathering, – *réunion*; assembly &c. (*assemblage*) 72; party, entertainment, reception, *levée*, at home, *conversazione*, *soirée*, *matinée*, evening –, morning –, afternoon –, garden –, dinner –, tea –, cocktail- party; symposium, sing-song; kettle-, drum; *partie carrée*, dish of tea, *ridotto*, rout, house-

**893. Seclusion. Exclusion.—N.** seclusion, privacy; retirement; concealment; reclusion, recess; snugness &c. *adj.*; delitescence; rustication, *rus in urbe*; solitude; solitariness &c. (*singleness*) 87; isolation; loneliness &c. *adj.*; estrangement from the world, anchoritism, voluntary exile; aloofness.

cell, hermitage; convent &c. 1000; *sanctum sanctorum*; study, library, den; hide-out.

depopulation, desertion, desolation; wilderness &c. (*unproductive*) 169; howling wilderness; rotten borough, Old Sarum.

exclusion, excommunication, banishment, exile, ostracism, proscription; cut, – direct; dead cut.

inhospit-ality, -ableness &c. *adj.*; un-, dis-sociability; domesticity, Darby and Joan.

recluse, hermit, eremite, cenobite; anchor-et, -ite; Simon Stylites; Troglodyte, Timon of Athens, Santon, *solitaire*, ruralist, disciple of Zimmermann, closet cynic. Diogenes; outcast, pariah.

warming; ball, prom, hop, dance, *thé dansant*; festival &c. (*amusement*) 840; wedding breakfast; 'the feast of reason and the flow of soul.'

visit, -ing; round of visits; call, morning call; interview &c. (*interlocution*) 588; assignation; tryst, -ing place; appointment.

club &c. (*association*) 712.

**V.** be -sociable &c. *adj.*; know; be -acquainted &c. *adj.*; associate –, sort –, keep company –, walk hand in hand -with; eat off the same trencher, club together, consort, bear one company, join; make acquaintance with &c. (*friendship*) 888; make advances, fraternize, embrace; intercommunicate.

be –, feel –, make oneself- at home with; make free with; crack a bottle with; take pot luck with, receive hospitality, live at free quarters.

visit, pay a visit; interchange -visits, – cards; call -at, – upon; leave a card; drop in, look in; look one up, beat up one's quarters.

entertain; give a -party &c. *n.*; be at home, see one's friends, hang out, keep open house, do the honours; receive, – with open arms; welcome; give a warm reception &c. *n.* to; kill the fatted calf.

**Adj.** sociable, companionable, clubbable, clubby, conversable, cosy, cosey, chatty, conversational; homiletical.

convivial; fest-ive, -al; jovial, jolly, hospitable.

welcome, – as the roses in May; *fêté*, entertained.

free and easy, hail fellow well met, familiar, on visiting terms, acquainted.

social, neighbourly; international, cosmopolitan, gregarious.

**Adv.** *en famille*, in the family circle; *sans -façon, – cérémonie*, arm in arm.

castaway, outsider, pilgarlic; wastrel, foundling, orphan.

**V.** be –, live- secluded &c. *adj.*; keep –, stand –, hold oneself- -aloof, – in the background; keep snug; shut oneself up; deny –, seclude- oneself; creep into a corner, rusticate, *aller planter ses choux*; retire, – from the world; hermetize, take the veil; abandon &c. 624.

cut, – dead; refuse to -associate with, – acknowledge; look cool –, turn one's back –, shut the door- upon; repel, blackball, excommunicate, exclude, exile, expatriate; banish, outlaw, maroon, ostracize, proscribe, cut off from, send to Coventry, keep at arm's length, draw a cordon round; boycott, blockade, lay an embargo on, isolate.

depopulate; dis-, un-people.

**Adj.** secluded, sequestered, retired, delitescent, private, bye; out of the -world, -way; in a backwater; 'the world forgetting by the world forgot.'

snug, domestic, stay-at-home.

unsociable; un-, dis-social; inhospitable, cynical, inconversable, unclubbable, *sauvage*, eremetic.

solitary; lone-ly, -some; isolated, single.

excluded, estranged; unfrequented; uninhabit-able, -ed; tenantless; un-tenanted, -occupied; abandoned; deserted, – in one's utmost need; unfriended; kith-, friend-, home-less; lorn, forlorn, desolate.

un-visited, -introduced, -invited, -welcome; under a cloud, left to shift for oneself, derelict, outcast, outside the gates.

banished &c. *v.*; under an embargo.

**Phr.** *noli me tangere.*

---

**894. Courtesy.**—**N.** courtesy; respect &c. 928; good -manners, – behaviour, – breeding; manners; politeness &c. *adj.*; *bienséance*, urbanity, comity, gentility; gentle –, breeding; polish, presence, cultivation, culture; civili-ty, -zation; amenity, suavity; good -temper, – humour; amiability, easy temper, complacency, soft tongue,

**895. Discourtesy.**—**N.** discourtesy; ill-breeding; ill –, bad –, ungainly-manners; insuavity; grouchiness; uncourteousness &c. *adj.*, tactlessness; rusticity, inurbanity; illiberality, incivility, displacency.

disrespect &c. 929; procacity, impudence; barbar-ism, -ity; misbehaviour, brutality, blackguardism, conduct un-

mansuetude; condescension &c. (*humility*) 879; affability, complaisance, *prévenance*, amiability, gallantry, chivalry; pink of -politeness, - courtesy.

compliment; fair -, soft -, sweet- words; honeyed phrases, flattering remarks, ceremonial; salutation, reception, presentation, introduction, *accueil*, greeting, recognition; welcome, *abord*, respects, *devoir*, regards, remembrances; kind -regards, - remembrances; love, best love, duty; deference.

obeisance &c. (*reverence*) 928; bow, courtesy, curtsy, scrape, *salaam*, *kowtow*, bowing and scraping; kneeling; genuflexion &c. (*worship*) 990; obsequiousness &c. 886; capping, shaking hands &c. *v.*, grip of the hand, embrace, hug, squeeze, *accolade*, loving cup, *vin d'honneur*, pledge; love token &c. (*endearment*) 902; kiss, buss, salute.

mark of recognition, nod; 'nods and becks and wreathed smiles'; valediction &c. 293; condolence &c. 915.

V. be -courteous &c. *adj.*; show -courtesy &c. *n.*

mind one's P's and Q's, behave oneself, be all things to all men, conciliate, speak one fair, take in good part; make -, do- the amiable; look as if butter would not melt in one's mouth; mend one's manners.

receive, do the honours, usher, greet, hail, bid welcome; welcome, - with open arms; shake hands; hold out -, press -, squeeze- the hand; bid God speed; speed the parting guest; cheer, serenade.

salute; embrace &c. (*endearment*) 902; kiss, - hands; drink to, pledge, hob and nob; move to, nod to; smile upon.

uncover, cap; touch -, take off- the hat; doff the cap; pull the forelock; present arms; make way for; bow; make one's bow; scrape, curtsy, courtesy; bob a -curtsy, - courtesy; kneel; bow -, bend- the knee; salaam, *kowtow*.

visit, wait upon, present oneself, pay one's respects, pay a visit &c. (*sociability*) 892; dance attendance on &c. (*servility*) 886; pay attentions to; do homage to &c. (*respect*) 928.

becoming a gentleman, *grossièreté*, *brusquerie*; vulgarity &c. 851.

churlishness &c. *adj.*; spinosity, perversity; moroseness &c. (*sullenness*) 901*a*.

bad-, ill-temper; sternness &c. *adj.*; austerity; moodishness, captiousness &c. 901; cynicism; tartness &c. *adj.*; acrimony, acerbity, virulence, asperity.

scowl, black looks, frown; short answer, rebuff; hard words, contumely; unparliamentary language, personality.

bear, bruin, brute, grouch, blackguard, beast; unlicked cub; frump, cross-patch; saucebox &c. 887.

V. be -rude &c. *adj.*; insult &c. 929; treat with discourtesy; take a name in vain; make -bold, - free- with; take a liberty; stare out of countenance, ogle, point at, put to the blush.

cut; turn -one's back upon, - on one's heel; give the cold shoulder; keep at -a distance, - arm's length; look -cool, - coldly, - black- upon; show the door to, send away with a flea in the ear.

lose one's temper &c. (*resentment*) 900; sulk &c. 901*a*; frown, scowl, glower, pout; snap, snarl, growl.

render -rude &c. *adj.*; brut-alize, -ify.

Adj. dis-, un-courteous; uncourtly; ill-bred, -mannered, -behaved, -conditioned; unbred; unmanner-ly, ed; im-, un-polite; un-polished, -civilized, -genteel; ungentleman-like, -ly; unladylike; blackguard; vulgar &c. 851; dedecorous; foul-mouthed, -spoken; abusive.

un-civil, -gracious, -ceremonious; cool; pert, forward, obtrusive, impudent, rude, saucy, precocious; insolent &c. 885.

repulsive; un-complaisant, -accommodating, -neighbourly, -gallant; inaffable; un-gentle, -gainly; rough, rugged, bluff, blunt, gruff; churl-, boor-, bear-ish; brutal, *brusque*; stern, harsh, austere; cavalier.

tart, sour, crabbed, sharp, short, trenchant, sarcastic, crusty, biting, caustic, virulent, bitter, acrimonious, venomous, contumelious; snarling &c. *v.*; surly, - as a bear; perverse; grim,

prostrate oneself &c. (*worship*) 990.

give –, send- one's duty &c. *n.* to.

render -polite &c. *adj.*; polish, civilize, humanize.

sullen &c. 901*a*; peevish &c. (*irascible*) 901.

**Adv.** discourteously &c. *adj.*; with -discourtesy &c. *n.*, – a bad grace.

---

**Adj.** courteous, polite, civil, mannerly, urbane; well-behaved, -mannered, -bred, -brought up, gently bred, of gentle -breeding, – manners, good-mannered, polished, civilized, cultivated; refined &c. (*taste*) 850; gentlemanlike &c. (*fashion*) 852; gallant, chivalrous, on one's good behaviour.

fine –, fair –, soft- spoken; honey-mouthed, -tongued; oily, unctuous, bland, suave; obliging, conciliatory, complaisant, complacent; obsequious &c. 886.

ingratiating, winning; gentle, mild; good-humoured, cordial, gracious, amiable, tactful, addressful, affable, genial, friendly, familiar; neighbourly.

**Adv.** courteously &c. *adj.*; with a good grace; with -open, – outstretched- arms; *à bras ouverts*; *suaviter in modo*, in good humour.

**Int.** hail! welcome! well met! *ave!* all hail! good -day, – morning &c., – morrow! God speed! *pax vobiscum!* may your shadow never be less! *chin-chin!*

**896. Congratulations.—N.** con-, gratulation; felicitation; salute &c. 894; condolence &c. 915; compliments of the season; good –, best- wishes.

**V.** con-, gratulate; felicitate, compliment; give –, wish one- joy; tender –, offer- one's congratulations; wish -many happy returns of the day, – a merry Christmas and a happy new year.

congratulate oneself &c. (*rejoice*) 838.

**Adj.** con-, gratulatory.

**897. Love.—N.** love; fondness &c. *adj.*; liking; inclination &c. (*desire*) 865; regard, dilection, admiration, fancy.

affection, sympathy, fellow-feeling; tenderness &c. *adj.*; heart, brotherly love; benevolence &c. 906; attachment.

yearning, tender passion, *affaire de cœur*, *amour*, gallantry, passion, flame, devotion, fervour, enthusiasm, transport of love, rapture, enchantment, infatuation, adoration, idolatry.

narcissism, Œdipus complex, Electra complex.

Cupid, Venus, Eros; myrtle; true lover's knot; love -token, – suit, – affair, – tale, – story; the old story, plighted love; courtship &c. 902; *amourette.*

maternal love.

attractiveness, charm; popularity; favourite &c. 899.

lover, suitor, follower, admirer, adorer, wooer, amoret, beau, sweet-

**898. Hate.—N.** hate, hatred, vials of hate; Hymn of Hate.

dis-affection, -favour; alienation, estrangement, coolness; enmity &c. 889; animosity &c. 900.

umbrage, pique, grudge; dudgeon, spleen; bitterness, – of feeling; ill –, bad- blood; acrimony; malice &c. 907; implacability &c. (*revenge*) 919.

repugnance &c. (*dislike*) 867; odium, unpopularity; loathing, detestation, antipathy; object of -hatred, – execration; abomination, aversion, *bête noire*; enemy &c. 891; bitter pill; source of annoyance &c. 830.

**V.** hate, detest, abominate, abhor, loathe; recoil –, shudder- at; shrink from, view with horror, hold in abomination, revolt against, execrate; scowl &c. 895; disrelish &c. (*dislike*) 867.

owe a grudge; bear -spleen, – a grudge, – malice &c. (*malevolence*) 907; conceive an aversion to.

heart, inamorato, swain, young man, flame, love, truelove; leman, Lothario, gallant, paramour, *amoroso*, *cavaliere servente*, captive, *cicisbeo*; *caro sposo*, Don Juan, sheik, ladies' man, squire of dames, Knave of Hearts.

inamorata, lady-love, idol, darling, duck, Dulcinea, angel, goddess, *cara sposa*; mistress.

betrothed, affianced, *fiancée*.

flirt, *coquette*; amorette; pair of turtle doves; abode of love, *agapemone*.

**V.** love, like, affect, fancy, care for, take an interest in, be partial to, sympathize with; be -in love &c. *adj.*- with; have –, entertain –, harbour –, cherish- a -love &c. *n.* for; regard, revere; take to, bear love to, be wedded to; set one's affections on; make much of, feast one's eyes on; hold dear, prize, treasure; hug, cling to, cherish, pet, caress &c. 902.

burn; adore, idolize, love to distraction, *aimer éperdument*; dote -on, – upon.

take a fancy to, fall for, be stuck on, look sweet upon; become -enamoured &c. *adj.*; fall in love with, lose one's heart; desire &c. 865.

excite love; win –, gain –, secure –, engage- the -love, – affections, – heart; take the fancy of; have a place in –, wind round- the heart; attract, attach, endear, charm, fascinate, captivate, bewitch, seduce, enamour, enrapture, turn the head.

get into favour; ingratiate –, insinuate –, worm- oneself; propitiate, curry favour with, pay one's court to, make a date with, *faire l'aimable*, set one's cap at, flirt, coquet.

**Adj.** loving &c. *v.*; fond of; taken –, struck- with; smitten, bitten; attached to, wedded to; enamoured; charmed &c. *v.*; in love; lovesick; over head and ears in love.

affectionate, tender, sweet upon, sympathetic, loving, fond, amorous, amatory; erotic, uxurious, ardent, passionate, rapturous, devoted, motherly.

loved &c. *v.*; beloved; well –, dearly- beloved; dear, precious, darling, pet, little; favourite, popular.

congenial; to –, after- one's -mind, – taste, – fancy, – own heart.

in one's good -graces &c. (*friendly*) 888; dear as the apple of one's eye, nearest to one's heart.

lovable, adorable; lovely, sweet; attractive, seductive, winning; charming, engaging, interesting, enchanting, captivating, fascinating, intriguing, bewitching; amiable, like an angel, angelic, seraphic.

excite –, provoke- hatred &c. *n.*; be -hateful &c. *adj.*; stink in the nostrils; estrange, alienate, repel, set against, sow dissension, set by the ears, envenom, incense, irritate, rile, ruffle, vex; horrify &c. 830.

**Adj.** hating &c. *v.*; abhorrent; averse from &c. (*disliking*) 867; set against.

bitter &c. (*acrimonious*) 895; implacable &c. (*revengeful*) 919.

un-loved, -beloved, -lamented, -deplored, -mourned, -cared for, -endured, -valued; disliked &c. 867.

crossed in love, forsaken, rejected, love-lorn, jilted.

obnoxious, hateful, odious, abominable, repulsive, offensive, shocking; disgusting &c. (*disagreeable*) 830.

invidious, spiteful; malicious &c. 907.

insulting, irritating, provoking.

[Mutual hate] at -daggers drawn, – swords points; not on speaking terms &c. (*enmity*) 889.

**Phr.** no love lost between.

---

**899. Favourite.—N.** favourite, pet, cosset, minion, idol, jewel, spoiled child, *enfant gâté*; led captain; crony; fondling; apple of one's eye, man after one's own heart; *persona grata*.

love, dear, darling, duck, honey, jewel; mopsey, moppet; sweetheart &c. (*love*) 897.

general –, universal- favourite; idol of the people; matinée idol, movie –, radio- star.

**900. Resentment.—N.** resentment, displeasure, animosity, anger, wrath, indignation; vexation, exasperation, bitter resentment, wrathful indignation.

pique, umbrage, huff, miff, soreness, dudgeon, acerbity, virulence, bitterness, acrimony, asperity, spleen, gall; heart-burning, -swelling; rankling.

ill –, bad- -humour, – temper; irascibility &c. 901; ill blood &c. (*hate*) 898; revenge &c. 919.

excitement, irritation; warmth, bile, choler, ire, fume, pucker, dander, ferment, ebullition; towering -passion, – rage, *acharnement*, angry mood, taking, pet, tiff, passion, fit, tantrums.

burst, explosion, paroxysm, storm, rage, fury, desperation; violence &c. 173; fire and fury; vials of wrath; gnashing of teeth, hot blood, high words.

scowl &c. 895; sulks &c. 901*a*.

[Cause of umbrage] affront, provocation, offence; indignity &c. (*insult*) 929; grudge, crow to pluck, sore subject; red rag to a bull; *casus belli*.

Furies, Erinys, Eumenides, Alecto, Megæra, Tisiphone.

buffet, slap in the face, box on the ear, rap on the knuckles.

**V.** resent; take -amiss, – ill, – to heart, – offence, – umbrage, – huff, – exception; take in -ill part, – bad part, – dudgeon; *ne pas entendre raillerie*; breathe revenge, cut up rough.

fly –, fall –, get- into a -rage, – passion; bridle –, bristle –, froth –, fire –, flare- up; open –, pour out- the vials of one's wrath.

pout, knit the brow, frown, scowl, lower, snarl, growl, gnarl, gnash, snap; redden, colour; look -black, – black as thunder, – daggers; bite one's thumb; show –, grind- one's teeth; champ the bit.

chafe, mantle, fume, kindle, fly out, take fire; boil, – over; boil with -indignation, – rage; rage, storm, foam; vent one's -rage, – spleen; lose one's temper, stand on one's hind legs, stamp the foot, kick up a row, fly off the handle, cut up rough; stamp –, quiver –, swell –, foam- with rage; burst with anger; raise Cain, breathe fire and fury.

have a fling at; bear malice &c. (*revenge*) 919.

cause –, raise- anger; affront, offend; give -offence, – umbrage anger; hurt the feelings; insult, discompose, fret, ruffle, nettle, heckle, huff, pique; excite &c. 824; irritate, stir the blood, stir up bile; sting, – to the quick; rile, provoke, chafe, wound, incense, inflame, enrage, aggravate, add fuel to the flame, fan into a flame, widen the breach, envenom, embitter, exasperate, infuriate, kindle wrath; stick in one's gizzard; rankle &c. 919.

put out of humour; put one's -monkey, – back- up; set –, get- one's back up; raise one's -gorge, – dander, – choler; work up into a passion; make -one's blood boil, – the ears tingle; throw into a ferment, madden, drive one mad; lash into -fury, – madness; fool to the top of one's bent; set by the ears.

bring a hornet's nest about one's ears.

**Adj.** angry, wrath, irate; ire-, wrath-ful; cross &c. (*irascible*) 901; sulky &c. 901*a*; bitter, virulent; acrimonious &c. (*discourteous*) &c. 895; violent &c. 173.

warm, burning; boiling, - over; fuming, raging; foaming, - at the mouth; convulsed with rage.

offended &c. *v.*; waxy, *acharné*; wrought, worked up; indignant, hurt, sore, peeved; set against.

fierce, wild, rageful, furious, mad with rage, fiery, infuriate, rabid, savage; relentless &c. 919.

flushed with -anger, - rage; in a -huff, - stew - fume, - pucker, - passion, - rage, - fury; on one's high ropes, up in arms; in high dudgeon.

**Adv.** angrily &c. *adj.*; in the height of passion; in the heat of -passion, - the moment.

**Int.** *tantæne animis cœlestibus iræ!* marry come up! zounds! 'sdeath!

**Phr.** one's -blood, - back, - monkey- being up; *fervens difficili bile jecur*; the gorge rising, eyes flashing fire; the blood -rising, - boiling; *hæret lateri lethalis arundo.*

**901. Irascibility.—N.** irascibility, temper; crossness &c. *adj.*; susceptibility, procacity, petulance, irritability, tartness, acerbity, protervity; pugnacity &c. (*contentiousness*) 720.

excitability &c. 825; bad -, fiery -, crooked -, irritable &c. *adj.*- temper; *genus irritabile*, hot blood.

ill humour &c. (*sullenness*) 901*a*; asperity &c., churlishness &c. (*discourtesy*) 895.

huff &c. (resentment) 900; a word and a blow.

Sir Fretful Plagiary; brabbler, Tartar; shrew, vixen, virago, termagant, dragon, scold, Xanthippe; porcupine; spit-fire; fire-eater &c. (*blusterer*) 887; fury &c. (*violent person*) 173.

**V.** be -irascible &c. *adj.*; have a -temper &c. *n.*, - devil in one; fire up &c. (*be angry*) 900.

**Adj.** irascible; bad-, ill-tempered; irritable, susceptible; excitable &c. 825; thin-skinned &c. (*sensitive*) 822; fretful, fidgety; on the fret.

hasty, over-hasty, quick, warm, hot, testy, touchy, techy, tetchy; like -touchwood, - tinder; huffy; pet-tish, -ulant; waspish, snapp-y, -ish, peppery, fiery, passionate, choleric, shrewish, 'sudden and quick in quarrel.'

querulous, captious, mood-y, -ish; quarrelsome, contentious, disputatious; pugnacious &c. (*bellicose*) 720; cantankerous, exceptious; restive &c. (*perverse*) 901*a*; churlish &c. (*discourteous*) 895.

cross, - as -crabs, - two sticks, - a cat, - a dog, - the tongs; like a bear with a sore head; fractious, peevish, *acariâtre.*

in a bad temper; sulky &c. 901*a*; angry &c. 900.

resent-ful, -ive; vindictive &c. 919.

**Int.** pish!

**901a. Sullenness.—N.** sullenness &c. *adj.*; morosity, spleen; churlishness &c. (*discourtesy*) 895; irascibility &c. 901.

moodiness &c. *adj.*; perversity; obstinacy &c. 606; torvity, spinosity; crabbedness &c. *adj.*

ill -, bad- -temper, - humour; sulks, dudgeon, mumps, doleful dumps, doldrums, fit of the sulks, *bouderie*, black looks, scowl; huff &c. (*resentment*) 900.

**V.** be -sullen &c. *adj.*; sulk; frown, scowl, lower, glower, grouse, grouch, crab, gloam, pout, have a hang-dog look, glout.

**Adj.** sullen, sulky; ill-tempered, -humoured, -affected, -disposed; in an ill, - a bad, - a shocking- -temper, - humour; out of -temper, -

humour; knaggy, torvous, crusty, crabbed; sore as a boil; surly &c. (*discourteous*) 895.

moody; spleen-ish, -ly; splenetic, cankered.

cross, -grained; perverse, wayward, humoursome; restive; cantankerous, refractory, intractable, exceptious, sinistrous, deaf to reason, unaccommodating, rusty, crusty, froward.

dogged &c. (*stubborn*) 606.

grumpy, glum, grim, grum, morose, frumpish; in the -sulks &c. *n.*; out of sorts; scowl-, glower-, growl-ing.

peevish &c. (*irascible*) 901.

**902.** [Expression of affection or love.] **Endearment.—N.** endearment, caress; blandish-, blandi-ment; *épanchement*, fondling, billing and cooing, dalliance.

embrace, salute, kiss, buss, smack, osculation, deosculation; amorous glances; ogle, side glance, sheep's eyes.

courtship, wooing, suit, addresses, the soft impeachment; lovemaking; an affair; serenading; caterwauling.

flirting &c. *v.*; flirtation, gallantry; coquetry, spooning.

true lover's knot, plighted love, engagement, betrothal; love -tale, - token, - letter; *billet-doux*, valentine.

honeymoon; Strephon and Chloe, 'Arry and 'Arriet.

**V.** caress, fondle, pet, dandle, nurse; pat, – on the -head, – cheek; chuck under the chin, smile upon, coax, wheedle, cosset, coddle, cocker; make -of, – much of, pamper; cherish, foster, kill with kindness.

clasp, hug, cuddle; fold –, strain- in one's arms; nestle, nuzzle, neck, embrace, kiss, buss, smack, blow a kiss; salute &c. (*courtesy*) 894.

bill and coo, spoon, toy, dally, flirt, coquet; galli-, gala-vant; philander; make love; pay one's -court, – addresses, – attentions- to; serenade; court, woo; set one's cap at; be –, look- sweet upon; ogle, cast sheep's eyes upon; *faire les yeux doux.*

fall in love with, win the affections &c. (*love*) 897; die for.

propose; make –, have- an offer; pop the question; plight one's -troth, – faith; become -engaged, – betrothed.

**Adj.** caressing &c. *v.*; 'sighing like furnace'; love-sick, spoony.

caressed &c. *v.*

**903. Marriage.—N.** marriage, matrimony, wedlock, union, intermarriage, *vinculum matrimonii*, nuptial tie, knot.

married state, coverture. bed, cohabitation.

match; betrothment &c. (*promise*) 768; wedding, nuptials, Hymen, bridal; e-, spousals; leading to the altar &c. *v.*; nuptial benediction, *epithalamium.*

torch –, temple- of Hymen; hymeneal altar; honeymoon.

bride, bridegroom; brides-maid, -man.

best –, grooms-man, page, usher.

married -man, – woman, – couple; neogamist, Benedick, partner, spouse, mate, yokemate; husband, man, con-

**904. Celibacy.—N.** celibacy, singleness, single blessedness; bachelor-hood, -ship; miso-gamy, -gyny.

virginity, *pucelage*; maiden-hood, -head.

unmarried man, bachelor, Cœlebs, agamist, old bachelor; miso-gamist, -gynist; celibate.

unmarried woman, spinster; maid, -en; virgin, *femme sole*, old maid; bachelor girl; nun &c.

**V.** live single; keep bachelor hall.

**Adj.** un-married, -wedded; wife-, spouse-less; single, virgin, celibate.

**905. Divorce.—N.** divorce, -ment; separation; judicial separation, separ-

sort, baron; old –, good- man; wife of one's bosom; help-meet, -mate, rib, better half, grey mare, old woman, good wife; *femme couverte*; squaw, lady; matron, -age, -hood; man and wife; wedded pair, Darby and Joan.

affinity, soul-mate.

mono-, bi-, di-, deutero-, tri-, poly-gamy; mormonism; poly-andry; Turk, Bluebeard.

ate maintenance; *separatio a -mensâ et thoro, – vinculo matrimonii.*

widowhood, viduage, viduity, weeds.

widow, -er; relict; dowager; *divorcée*; cuckold.

**V.** live -separately, – apart; separate, divorce, disespouse, put away; wear the horns.

---

unlawful –, left-handed –, companionate –, morganatic –, ill-assorted- marriage; *mésalliance*; *mariage de convenance*; an affair.

match-maker, marriage broker, matrimonial agent.

**V.** marry, wive, take to oneself a wife; be -married, – spliced; go –, pair- off; wed, espouse, lead to the hymeneal altar, take 'for better, for worse,' give one's hand to, bestow one's hand upon; remarry; intermarry.

marry, join, handfast; couple &c. (*unite*) 43; tie the nuptial knot; give -away, – in marriage; affy, affiance; betroth &c. (*promise*) 768; publish –, bid- the banns; be asked in church.

**Adj.** married &c. *v.*; one, – bone and one flesh.

marriageable, nubile.

engaged, betrothed, affianced.

matrimonial, marital, conjugal, connubial, wedded; nuptial, hymeneal, spousal, bridal.

**Phr.** the grey mare the better horse.

## 2°. Diffusive Sympathetic Affections

**906. Benevolence.—N.** benevolence, Christian charity; God's -love, – grace; good-will; philanthropy &c. 910; unselfishness &c. 942.

good -nature, – feeling, – wishes; kind-, kindli-ness &c. *adj.*; lovingkindness, benignity, brotherly love, charity, humanity, fellow-feeling, sympathy; goodness –, warmth- of heart; *bonhomie*; kind-heartedness; amiability, milk of human kindness, tenderness; love &c. 897; friendship &c. 888.

toleration, consideration, generosity; mercy &c. (*pity*) 914.

charitableness &c. *adj.*; bounty, alms-giving; good works, beneficence, the luxury of doing good.

acts of kindness, a good turn; good –, kind- -offices, – treatment.

good Samaritan, sympathizer, well-wisher, philanthropist, *bon enfant*; altruist.

**V.** be -benevolent &c. *adj.*; have one's heart in the right place, bear good will; wish -well, – God speed;

**907. Malevolence.—N.** malevolence; bad intent, -ion; un-, dis-kindness; ill -nature, – will, – blood; acrimony; bad blood; enmity &c. 889; hate &c. 898; malignity; malice, – aforethought, – prepense; maliciousness &c. *adj.*; spite, despite; resentment &c. 900.

uncharitableness &c. *adj.*; incompassionateness &c. 914*a*; gall, venom, rancour, rankling, virulence, mordacity, acerbity; churlishness &c. (*discourtesy*) 895.

hardness of heart, heart of stone, obduracy; cruelty; cruelness &c. *adj.*; brutality, savagery; fer-ity, -ocity; barbarity, inhumanity, immanity, truculence, ruffianism; evil eye, cloven -foot, – hoof; inquisition; torture.

ill –, bad- turn; affront &c. (*disrespect*) 929; outrage, atrocity; ill usage; intolerance, bigotry, persecution; tender mercies [ironical]; 'unkindest cut of all.'

**V.** be -malevolent &c. *adj.*; bear –, harbour- -spleen, – a grudge, – mal-

view –, regard- with an eye of favour; take in good part; take –, feel- an interest in; be –, feel- interested- in; sympathize with, feel for; fraternize &c. (*be friendly*) 888.

enter into the feelings of others, do as you would be done by, meet half-way.

treat well; give comfort, smooth the bed of death; do -good, – a good turn; benefit &c. (*goodness*) 648; render a service, be of use; aid &c. 707.

**Adj.** benevolent; kind, -ly; well-meaning; amiable; obliging, accommodating, indulgent, considerate, gracious, complacent, good-humoured.

warm-, soft-, kind-, tender-, large-, broad-hearted; merciful &c. 914; philanthropic &c. 910; charitable, beneficent, humane, benign, benignant; bount-eous, -iful &c. 816.

good-, well-natured; spleenless; sympath-izing, -etic; complaisant &c. (*courteous*) 894; kindly, well-meant, -intentioned.

fatherly, motherly, brotherly, sisterly; pat-, mat-, frat-ernal; friendly &c. 888.

**Adv.** with -a good intention, – the best intentions.

**Int.** God speed! much good may it do!

---

ice; betray –, show- the cloven foot.

hurt &c. (*physical pain*) 378; annoy &c. 830; injure, harm, wrong; do -harm, – an ill office- to; outrage; disoblige, malign, plant a thorn in the breast.

molest, worry, harass, haunt, harry, bait, tease, throw stones at; play the devil with; hunt down, dragoon, hound; persecute, oppress, grind; maltreat; ill-treat, -use.

wreak one's malice on, do one's worst, break a butterfly on the wheel; dip –, imbrue- one's hands in blood; have no mercy &c. 914*a*.

**Adj.** male-, unbene-volent; unbenign; ill-disposed, -intentioned, -natured, -conditioned, -contrived; evil-minded, -disposed.

malicious; malign, -ant; rancorous; de-, spiteful; mordacious, caustic, bitter, envenomed, acrimonious, virulent; un-amiable, -charitable; maleficent, venomous, grinding, galling.

harsh, disobliging; un-kind, -friendly, -gracious; treacherous; inofficious; invidious; uncandid; churlish &c. (*uncourteous*) 895; surly, sullen &c. 901*a*.

cold, -blooded, -hearted; hard-, flint-marble-, stony-hearted; hard of heart, unnatural; ruthless &c. (*unmerciful*) 914*a*; relentless &c. (*revengeful*) 919.

cruel; brut-al, -ish; savage, – as a -bear, – tiger; ferine, feral, ferocious; inhuman; barbarous, fell, untamed, tameless, truculent, incendiary; bloodthirsty &c. (*murderous*) 361; atrocious.

fiend-ish, -like; demoniacal; diabolic, -al; devilish, infernal, hellish, Satanic.

**Adv.** malevolently &c. *adj.*; with -bad intent &c. *n.*

**908. Malediction.**—**N.** malediction, malison, curse, imprecation, denunciation, execration, anathema, ban, proscription, excommunication, commination, thunders of the Vatican, fulmination, aspersion, vilification, vituperation, scurrility.

abuse; foul –, bad –, strong –, unparliamentary- language, Limehouse; Billingsgate, sauce, evil speaking; cursing &c. *v.*; profane swearing, oath.

threat &c. 909; more bark than bite; invective &c. (*disapprobation*) 932.

**V.** curse, accurse, imprecate, damn, swear at; slang; curse with bell, book and candle; invoke –, call down- curses on the head of; devote to destruction.

execrate, beshrew, scold; anathematize &c. (*censure*) 932; hold up to execration, denounce, proscribe, excommunicate, fulminate, thunder against; threaten &c. 909; curse up hill and down dale.

curse and swear; swear, – like a trooper; fall a cursing, rap out an oath, damn, cuss.

**Adj.** curs-ing, -ed &c. *v.*; maledictory.

**Int.** woe to! beshrew! *ruat cœlum!* ill –, woe- betide' confusion seize! damn! confound! blast! curse! devil take! hang! out with! a plague –, out- upon! aroynt! *honi soit!*

**Phr.** *delenda est Carthago.*

**909. Threat.**—**N.** threat, menace; defiance &c. 715; abuse, minacity, intimidation; fulmination; commination &c. (*curse*) 908; gathering clouds &c. (*warning*) 668.

**V.** threat, -en; menace; snarl, growl, gnarl, mutter, bark, bully.

defy &c. 715; intimidate &c. 860; keep –, hold up –, hold out- *in terrorem*; shake –, double –, clinch- the fist at; thunder, talk big, fulminate, use big words, bluster, look daggers.

**Adj.** threatening, menacing; mina-tory, -cious; comminatory, abusive; *in terrorem*; ominous &c. (*predicting*) 511; defiant &c. 715; under the ban.

**Int.** *væ victis!* at your peril! do your worst!

**910. Philanthropy.** — **N.** philanthropy; altruism, humanit-y, -arianism; universal benevolence; *deliciæ humani generis*; cosmopolitanism, utilitarianism, the greatest happiness of the greatest number, social science, sociology.

common weal, public welfare, socialism, communism.

patriotism, civism, nationality, love of country, *amor patriæ*, public spirit.

chivalry, knight errantry; generosity &c. 942.

philanthropist, altruist &c. 906; utilitarian, Benthamite, socialist, communist, cosmopolite, citizen of the world, *amicus humani generis*; knight errant; patriot.

**Adj.** philanthropic, altruistic, humanitarian, utilitarian, cosmopolitan; public-spirited, patriotic; humane, large-hearted &c. (*benevolent*) 906; chival-ric, -rous, generous &c. 942.

**Adv.** *pro -bono publico, – aris et focis.*

**Phr.** '*humani nihil a me alienum puto.*'

**911. Misanthropy.**—**N.** misanthropy, incivism; egotism &c. (*selfishness*) 943; moroseness &c. 901*a*; cynicism; defeatism.

misanthrope, misanthropist, egotist, cynic, man-hater, Timon, Diogenes.

woman-hater, misogynist.

**Adj.** misanthropic, antisocial, unpatriotic; egotistical &c. (*selfish*) 943; morose &c. 901*a*.

---

**912. Benefactor.** — **N.** benefactor, saviour, good genius, tutelary saint, patron, guardian angel, fairy godmother, good Samaritan; *pater patriæ*; salt of the earth &c. (*good man*) 948; auxiliary &c. 711.

---

**913.** [Maleficent being.] **Evil-doer.** —**N.** evil- -doer, – worker; wrong doer &c. 949; mischief maker, marplot; oppressor, tyrant; firebrand, incendiary, pyromaniac, anarchist, destroyer, Hun, *Boche*, Vandal, iconoclast; communist; terrorist, *apache*, gunman, gangster, racketeer.

savage, brute, ruffian, barbarian, semi-barbarian, caitiff, desperado; Mo-hock, -hawk; bludgeon man, bully, rough, hooligan, larrikin, dangerous classes, ugly customer; thief &c. 792.

cockatrice, scorpion, hornet; viper, adder; snake, – in the grass;

serpent, cobra, asp, rattlesnake, anaconda; canker-, wire-worm; locust, Colorado beetle; torpedo; bane &c. 663.

cannibal; Anthropophag-us, -ist; bloodsucker, vampire, ogre, ghoul, gorilla; vulture; gyr-, ger-falcon.

wild beast, tiger, hyæna, butcher, hangman; cut-throat &c. (*killer*) 361; blood-, sleuth-, hell-hound.

hag, hellhag, beldam, Jezebel.

monster; fiend &c. (*demon*) 980; homicidal maniac, devil incarnate, demon in human shape; Frankenstein's monster.

harpy, siren, vampire; Furies, Eumenides &c. 900.

Attila, scourge of the human race.

**Phr.** *fœnum habet in cornu.*

## 3°. Special Sympathetic Affections

**914. Pity.**—**N.** pity, compassion, commiseration; bowels, – of compassion; condolence &c. 915; sympathy, fellow-feeling, tenderness, yearning, forbearance, humanity, mercy, clemency, exorability; leniency &c. (*lenity*) 740; charity, ruth, long-suffering.

melting mood; *argumentum ad misericordiam*; quarter, grace, *locus pœnitentiæ.*

sympathizer, champion, partisan.

**V.** pity; have –, show –, take- pity &c. *n.*; commiserate, compassionate; condole &c. 915; sympathize; feel –, be sorry –, yearn- for; weep, melt, thaw, enter into the feelings of.

forbear, relent, relax, give quarter, wipe the tears, *parcere subjectis,* give a *coup de grâce,* put out of one's misery; be cruel to be kind.

raise –, excite- pity &c. *n.*; touch, soften; melt, – the heart; appeal to one's better feelings; propitiate, disarm.

ask for -mercy &c. *n.*; supplicate &c. (*request*) 765; cry for quarter, beg one's life, kneel; deprecate.

**Adj.** pitying &c. *v.*; pitiful, compassionate, sympathetic, touched.

merciful, clement, ruthful; humane; humanitarian &c. (*philanthropic*) 910; tender. – hearted, – as a chicken; soft, – hearted; unhardened; lenient &c. 740; exorable, forbearing; melting &c. *v.*; weak.

**Int.** for pity's sake! mercy! have –, cry you- mercy! God help you! poor -thing, – dear, – fellow! woe betide! *quis talia fando temperet a lachrymis!*

**Phr.** one's heart bleeding for; *haud ignara mali miseris succurrere disco.*

**914a. Pitilessness.**—**N.** pitilessness &c. *adj.*; inclemency; inexorability, hardness of heart; inflexibility; severity &c. 739; malevolence &c. 907.

**V.** have no –, shut the gates of- mercy &c. 914; give no quarter.

**Adj.** piti-, merci-, ruth-, bowel-less; unpitying, unmerciful, inclement; in-, un-compassionate; inexorable, inflexible; harsh &c. 739; cruel &c. 907; unrelenting &c. 919.

**915. Condolence.**—**N.** condolence; lamentation &c. 839; sympathy, consolation.

**V.** condole with, console, sympathize &c. 914, share one's misery; feel for; express –, testify- pity; afford –, supply- consolation; lament &c. 839- with; send one's condolences.

## 4°. Retrospective Sympathetic Affections

**916. Gratitude. — N.** gratitude, thankfulness, gratefulness, feeling of obligation.

acknowledgment, recognition thanksgiving, giving thanks.

thanks, praise, benediction; pæan; *Te Deum* &c. (*worship*) 990; grace, – before, – after- meat; thank-offering.

requital.

**V.** be -grateful &c. *adj.*; thank; give –, render –, return –, offer –, tender- thanks &c. *n.*; acknowledge, requite.

feel –, be –, lie- under an obligation; *savoir gré*; not look a gift horse in the mouth; never forget, overflow with gratitude; thank –, bless- one's stars; fall on one's knees.

**Adj.** grateful, thankful, obliged, beholden, indebted to, under obligation.

**Int.** thanks! many thanks! gramercy! much obliged! thank you! thank Heaven! Heaven be praised!

**917. Ingratitude.—N.** ingratitude, thanklessness, oblivion of benefits; unthankfulness.

'benefits forgot'; thankless -task, – office.

**V.** be -ungrateful &c. *adj.*; forget benefits; look a gift horse in the mouth.

**Adj.** un-grateful, -mindful, -thankful; thankless, ingrate, wanting in gratitude, insensible of benefits.

forgotten; un-acknowledged, -thanked, -requited, -rewarded; ill-requited.

**Int.** thank you for nothing! '*et tu, Brute!*'

---

**918. Forgiveness.—N.** forgiveness, pardon, condonation, grace, remission, absolution, amnesty, oblivion; indulgence; reprieve.

conciliation; reconciliation &c. (*pacification*) 723; propitiation.

excuse, exoneration, quittance, release, indemnity; bill –, act –, covenant –, deed- of indemnity; exculpation &c. (*acquittal*) 970.

longanimity, placability, forbearance; *amantium iræ*; *locus pœnitentiæ*.

**V.** forgive, – and forget; pardon, condone, think no more of, let bygones be bygones, shake hands; forget an injury, bury the hatchet; clean the slate.

excuse, pass over, overlook; wink at &c. (*neglect*) 460; bear with; allow –, make allowances- for; let one down easily, not be too hard upon, pocket the affront; blot out one's transgression.

let off, remit, absolve, give absolution, reprieve; acquit &c. 970.

beg –, ask –, implore- pardon &c. *n.*; conciliate, propitiate, placate; make up a quarrel &c. (*pacify*) 723; let the wound heal.

**919. Revenge.—N.** revenge, -ment; vengeance; avenge-ment, -ance; sweet revenge, *vendetta*, death-feud, eye for an eye, blood for blood, a Roland for an Oliver; retaliation &c. 718; day of reckoning.

rancour, vindictiveness, implacability; malevolence &c. 907; ruthlessness &c. 914*a*.

avenger, vindicator, Nemesis, Eumenides.

**V.** re-, a-venge; take –, have one's- revenge; breathe -revenge, – vengeance; wreak one's -vengeance, – anger; give no quarter.

have -accounts to settle, – a crow to pluck, – a rod in pickle; pay off old scores.

keep the wound green; harbour -revenge, – vindictive feeling; bear malice; rankle, – in the breast; have at one's mercy.

**Adj.** revenge-, venge-ful; vindictive, rancorous; pitiless &c. 914*a*; ruthless, rigorous, avenging, retaliative.

unforgiving, unrelenting; inexorable, stony-hearted, implacable; relent-, remorse-less.

*æternum servans sub pectore vulnus*; rankling, immitigable.

**Adj.** forgiving, placable, conciliatory.

forgiven &c. *v.*; un-resented, -avenged, -revenged.

**Adv.** cry you mercy.

**Phr.** *manet -cicatrix, – altâ mente repostum.*

revenge is sweet.

**Phr.** *veniam petimusque damusque vicissim*; more in sorrow than in anger.

**920. Jealousy.—N.** jealous-y, -ness; jaundiced eye, heartburning; green-eyed monster; yellows; Juno.

**V.** be -jealous &c. *adj.*; view with -jealousy, – a jealous eye.

**Adj.** jealous, – as a Barbary pigeon; jaundiced, yellow-eyed, horn-mad.

**921. Envy.—N.** envy; enviousness &c. *adj.*; rivalry; *jalousie de métier.*

**V.** envy, covet, lust after, crave, burst with envy, regard with envious eyes.

**Adj.** envious, invidious, covetous; *alieni appetens.*

## SECTION IV. MORAL AFFECTIONS

### 1°. MORAL OBLIGATIONS

**922. Right.—N.** right; what -ought to, – should- be; fitness &c. *adj.*; *summum jus.*

justice, equity; equitableness &c. *adj.*; propriety; fair play, impartiality, measure for measure, give and take, *lex talionis*, square deal.

Astræa, Nemesis, Themis.

scales of justice, even-handed justice, retributive justice, *suum cuique*; clear stage –, fair field- and no favour; Queensberry rules.

morals &c. (*duty*) 926; law &c. 963; honour &c. (*probity*) 939; virtue &c. 944.

**V.** be -right &c. *adj.*; stand to reason.

see -justice done, – one righted, – fair play; do justice to; recompense &c. (*reward*) 973; hold the scales even, give and take; serve one right, put the saddle on the right horse; give -every one, – the devil- his due; *audire alteram partem.*

deserve &c. (*be entitled to*) 924.

**Adj.** right, good; just, reasonable; fit &c. 924; equ-al, -able, -itable; even-handed, fair, – and square.

legitimate, justifiable, rightful; as it -should, – ought to- be; lawful &c. (*permitted*) 760, (*legal*) 963.

deserved &c. 924.

**Adv.** rightly &c. *adj.*; in -justice, - equity, – reason.

without -distinction of, – regard to, – respect to- persons; upon even terms.

**Int.** all right!

**923. Wrong. — N.** wrong; what -ought not to, – should not- be; *malum in se*; unreasonableness, grievance; shame.

injustice; unfairness &c. *adj.*; iniquity, foul play, partiality, leaning; favour, -itism; nepotism, party spirit, partisanship; undueness &c. 925; unlawfulness &c. 964.

robbing Peter to pay Paul &c. *v.*; the wolf and the lamb; vice &c. 945.

a custom more honoured in the breach than the observance.

**V.** be -wrong &c. *adj.*; cry to heaven for vengeance.

do -wrong &c. *n.*; be -inequitable &c. *adj.*; favour, lean towards; encroach; impose upon; reap where one has not sown; give an inch and take an ell; rob Peter to pay Paul.

**Adj.** wrong, -ful; bad, too bad; unjust, -fair; in-, un-equitable; unequal, partial, one-sided.

objectionable; un-reasonable, -allowable, -warrantable, -justifiable; not cricket, not playing the game; improper, unfit; unjustified &c. 925; illegal &c. 964; iniquitous, criminal; immoral &c. 945; injurious &c. 649.

in the wrong, – box.

**Adv.** wrongly &c. *adj.*

**Phr.** it will not do; this is too bad.

**924. Dueness.—N.** due, -ness; right, privilege, prerogative, prescription, title, claim, pretension, demand, birthright.

immunity, licence, liberty, franchise; vested -interest, – right; licitness.

sanction, authority, warranty, charter; warrant &c. (*permission*) 760; constitution &c. (*law*) 963; tenure; bond &c. (*security*) 771.

deserts, merits, dues.

claimant, appellant; plaintiff &c. 938.

**V.** be -due &c. *adj.* to, – the due &c. *n.* of; have -right, – title, – claim- to; be entitled to; have a claim upon; belong to &c. (*property*) 780.

deserve, merit, be worthy of, richly deserve.

demand, claim; call upon –, come upon –, appeal to- for; re-vendicate, -claim; exact; insist -on, – upon; challenge; take one's stand, make a point of, require, lay claim to, assert, assume, arrogate, make good; substantiate; vindicate a -claim, – right; make out a case.

give –, confer- a right; sanction, entitle; authorize &c. 760; sanctify, legalize, ordain, prescribe, allot.

give every one his due &c. 922; pay one's dues; have one's -due, – rights; stand upon one's rights.

use a right, assert, enforce, put in force, lay under contribution.

**Adj.** having a right to &c. *v.*; entitled to; claiming; deserving, meriting, worthy of.

privileged, allowed, sanctioned, warranted, authorized; ordained, prescribed, constitutional, chartered, enfranchised.

prescriptive, presumptive; absolute, indefeasible; un-, in-alienable; imprescriptible, inviolable, unimpeachable, unchallenged; sacrosanct.

due to, merited, deserved, condign, richly deserved, *emeritus*.

allowable &c. (*permitted*) 760; lawful, licit, legitimate, legal; legalized &c. (*law*) 963.

square, unexceptionable, right; equitable &c. 922; due, *en règle*; fit, -ting; correct, proper, meet, befitting, becoming, seemly; decorous; creditable, up to the mark, right as a trivet; just –, quite- the thing; *selon les règles*.

**Adv.** duly, *ex officio, de jure*; by -right, – divine right; as is -fitting, – proper, – fitting and proper; *jure divino, Dei gratiâ*, in the name of.

**Phr.** *civis Romanus sum.*

**925.** [Absence of right.] **Undueness —N.** undueness &c. *adj.*; *malum prohibitum*; impropriety; illegality &c. 964.

falseness &c. *adj.*; emptiness –, invalidity- of title; illegitimacy.

loss of right, disfranchisement, forfeiture.

usurpation, assumption, tort, violation, breach, encroachment, presumption, seizure, stretch, exaction, imposition, lion's share

usurper, pretender, Carlist; impostor.

**V.** be -undue &c. *adj.*; not be -due &c. 924.

infringe, encroach, trench on, exact; arrogate, – to oneself; give an inch and take an ell; stretch –, strain- a point; usurp, violate, do violence to; sail under false colours.

dis-franchise, -entitle, -qualify; invalidate.

relax &c. (*be lax*) 738; misbehave &c. (*vice*) 945; misbecome.

**Adj.** undue; unlawful &c. (*illegal*) 964; unconstitutional, *ultra vires*; illicit; un-authorized, -warranted, -allowed, -sanctioned, -justified; un-, dis-entitled, -qualified; un-privileged, -chartered.

illegitimate, bastard, spurious, false; usurped, tortious.

un-deserved, -merited, -earned; unfulfilled.

forfeited, disfranchised.

improper; un-meet, -fit, -befitting, -seemly; un-, mis-becoming; seemless; *contra bonos mores*; not the thing, out of the question, not to be thought of; preposterous, pretentious, would- be.

---

**926. Duty.—N.** duty, what ought to be done, moral obligation, accountableness, liability, *onus*, responsibility; bounden –, imperative- duty; call, – of duty.

allegiance, fealty, tie; engagement &c. (*promise*) 768; part; function, calling &c. (*business*) 625.

morality, morals, decalogue; case of conscience; conscientiousness &c. (*probity*) 939; conscience, inward monitor, still small voice within, sense of duty, tender conscience.

dueness &c. 924; propriety, fitness, seemliness, amenableness, decorum; the -thing, – proper thing; the -right, – proper- thing to do.

[Science of morals] eth-ics, -ology; deon-, are-tology; moral –, ethical- philosophy; casuistry, polity.

observance, fulfilment, discharge, performance, acquittal, satisfaction, redemption; good behaviour.

**V.** be -the duty of, – incumbent &c. *adj.* on, – responsible &c. *adj.*; behoove, become, befit, beseem; belong –, pertain- to; fall to one's lot; devolve on; lie -upon, – on one's head, – at one's door; rest -with, – on the shoulders of.

take upon oneself &c. (*promise*) 768; be –, become- -bound to, – sponsor for; be responsible for; incur a -responsibility &c. *n.*; be –, stand –, lie- under an obligation; have to answer for, owe it to oneself.

impose a -duty &c. *n.*; enjoin, require, exact; bind, – over; saddle with, prescribe, assign, call upon, look to, oblige.

enter upon –, perform –, observe –, fulfil –, discharge –, adhere to –, acquit oneself of –, satisfy- -a duty, – an obligation; act one's part, redeem one's pledge, do justice to, be at one's post; do duty; do one's duty &c. (*be virtuous*) 944.

be on one's good behaviour, mind one's P's and Q's.

**Adj.** obligatory, binding; imperative, peremptory; stringent &c. (*severe*) 739; behooving &c. *v.*; incumbent –, chargeable- on; under obligation; obliged –, bound –, tied- by; saddled with.

due –, beholden –, bound –, indebted- to; tied down; compromised &c. (*promised*) 768; in duty bound.

amenable, liable, accountable, responsible, answerable.

right, meet &c. (*due*) 924; moral, ethical, casuistical, conscientious, ethological.

**Adv.** with a safe conscience, as in duty bound, on one's own re-

**927. Dereliction of Duty.—N.** dereliction of duty; fault &c. (*guilt*) 947; sin &c. (*vice*) 945; non-observance, -performance, -co-operation; neglect, carelessness, laziness, incompetence, eye-service, relaxation, infraction, violation, transgression, failure, evasion, indolence; dead letter.

slacker, loafer, striker, non-cooperator.

**V.** violate; break, – through; infringe; set -aside, – at naught; trample -on, – under foot; slight, neglect, evade, renounce, forswear, repudiate; wash one's hands of; escape, transgress, fail.

call to account &c. (*disapprobation*) 932.

**927a. Exemption.—N.** exemption, freedom, irresponsibility, immunity, liberty, licence, release, exoneration, excuse, dispensation, absolution, franchise, renunciation, discharge; exculpation &c. 970; *ægrotat*.

**V.** be -exempt &c. *adj.*

exempt, release, acquit, discharge, quit-claim, remise, remit; free, set at liberty, let off, pass over, spare, excuse, dispense with, give dispensation, license; stretch a point; absolve &c. (*forgive*) 918; exonerate &c. (*exculpate*) 970; save the necessity.

**Adj.** exempt, free, immune, at liberty, scot free; released &c. *v.*; unbound, unencumbered; irresponsible, unaccountable, not answerable; excusable.

sponsibility, at one's own risk, *suo periculo*; *in foro conscientiæ*; *quamdiu se bene gesserit*; at one's post, on duty.

**Phr.** *dura lex sed lex.*

## 2°. Moral Sentiments

**928. Respect.—N.** respect, regard, consideration; courtesy &c. 894; attention, deference, reverence, honour, esteem, estimation, veneration, admiration; approbation &c. 931.

homage, fealty, obeisance, genuflexion, kneeling, prostration; obsequiousness &c. 886; salaam, *kowtow*, bow, presenting arms, salute.

respects, regards, duty, *devoirs*, *égards*.

devotion &c. (*piety*) 987.

**V.** respect, regard; revere, -nce; hold in reverence, honour, venerate, hallow; esteem &c. (*approve of*) 931; think much of; entertain –, bear- respect for; have a high opinion of; look up to, defer to; pay -attention, – respect &c. *n.*- to; do –, render- honour to; do the honours, hail; show courtesy &c. 894; salute, present arms; do –, pay- homage to; pay tribute to, kneel to, bow to, bend the knee to; fall down before, prostrate oneself, kiss the hem of one's garment; worship &c. 990.

keep one's distance, make room, observe due decorum, stand upon ceremony.

command –, inspire- respect; awe, impose, overawe, dazzle.

**Adj.** respecting &c. *v.*; respectful, deferential, decorous, reverential, obsequious, ceremonious, bare-headed, cap in hand, on one's knees; prostrate &c. (*servile*) 886.

respected &c. *v.*; in high -esteem, – estimation; time-honoured, venerable, *emeritus*.

**Adv.** in deference to; with -all, – due, – the highest- respect; with submission.

saving your -grace, – presence; *salva sit reverentia*; *pace tanti nominis*.

**Int.** hail! all hail! *esto perpetua!* may your shadow never be less!

**929. Disrespect. — N.** dis-respect, -esteem, -estimation, -favour, -repute; low estimation; disparagement &c. (*dispraise*) 932, (*detraction*) 934.

irreverence; slight, neglect; *spretæ injuria formæ*; superciliousness &c. (*contempt*) 930.

vilipendency, contumely, affront, dishonour, insult, indignity, outrage, discourtesy &c. 895; practical joking; scurrility, scoffing, sibilation; ir-, derision; mockery; irony &c. (*ridicule*) 856; sarcasm.

hiss, hoot, gibe, flout, jeer, scoff, gleek, taunt, sneer, quip, fling, wipe, slap in the face.

**V.** hold in disrespect &c. (*despise*) 930; misprize, disregard, slight, undervalue, depreciate, trifle with, set at naught, pass by, push aside, overlook, turn one's back upon, laugh in one's sleeve; be -disrespectful &c. *adj.*, – discourteous &c. 895; treat with -disrespect &c. *n.*; set down, browbeat.

dishonour, desecrate; insult, affront, outrage.

speak slightingly of; disparage &c. (*dispraise*) 932; vilipend, call names; throw –, fling- dirt; drag through the mud, point at, indulge in personalities; make -mouths, – faces; bite the thumb; take –, pluck- by the beard; toss in a blanket, tar and feather.

have –, hold- in derision; deride, scoff, sneer, laugh at, snigger, ridicule, gibe, mock, jeer, taunt, twit, niggle, gleek, gird, flout, fleer; roast, turn into ridicule; guy, burlesque &c. 856; laugh to scorn &c. (*contempt*) 930; smoke; fool; make -game, – a fool, – an April fool- of; play a practical joke; rag; lead one a dance, run the rig upon, have a fling at, scout, hiss, hoot, mob.

**Adj.** disrespectful; aweless, irreverent; disparaging &c. 934; insulting &c. *v.*; supercilious &c. (*scornful*) 930; rude, derisive, contemptuous, sarcastic; scurri-le, -lous; contumelious.

un-respected, -worshipped, -envied, -saluted; un-, dis-regarded.

**Adv.** disrespectfully &c. *adj.*

**930. Contempt.—N.** contempt, disdain, scorn, sovereign contempt, despi-sal, -ciency; vilipendency, contumely; slight, sneer, spurn, by-word.

contemptuousness &c. *adj.*; scornful eye; smile of contempt; derision &c. (*disrespect*) 929.

[State of being despised] despisedness.

**V.** despise, contemn, scorn, disdain, feel contempt for, view with a scornful eye, disregard, slight, not mind; pass by &c. (*neglect*) 460.

look down upon; hold -cheap, - in contempt, - in disrespect; think -nothing, - small beer- of; make light of; underestimate &c. 483; esteem -slightly, - of small or no account; take no account of, care nothing for; set no store by; not care a -straw &c. (*unimportance*) 643; set at naught, laugh in one's sleeve, snap one's fingers at, shrug one's shoulders, turn up one's nose at, pooh-pooh, damn with faint praise; sneeze –, whistle –, sneer- at; curl up one's lip, toss the head, *traiter de haut*; laugh at &c. (*be disrespectful*) 929.

point the finger of –, hold up to –, laugh to- scorn; scout, hoot, flout, hiss, scoff at.

turn -one's back, – a cold shoulder- upon; tread –, trample- -upon, – under foot; spurn, kick; fling to the winds &c. (*repudiate*) 610; send away with a flea in the ear.

**Adj.** contemptuous; disdain-, scorn-ful; withering, contumelious, supercilious, cynical, haughty, bumptious, cavalier; derisive.

contemptible, despicable; pitiable; pitiful &c. (*unimportant*) 643; despised &c. *v.*; down-trodden; unenvied.

**Adv.** contemptuously &c. *adj.*

**Int.** a fig for &c. (*unimportant*) 643; bah! never mind! away with! hang it! fiddle-de-dee!

**931. Approbation.—N.** approbation; approv-al, -ement; sanction, advocacy; nod of approbation; esteem, estimation, good opinion, golden opinions, admiration; love &c. 897; appreciation, regard, account, popularity, *kudos*, credit; repute &c. 873.

commendation, praise; laud, -ation; good word; meed –, tribute- of praise; encomium; eulog-y, -ium; *éloge*, panegyric; homage, hero worship; benediction, blessing, benison.

applause, plaudit, clap; clapping, – of hands; accl-aim, -amation; cheer; pæan, hosannah; shout –, peal –, chorus –, thunders- of -applause &c.; Kentish fire; Prytaneum; blurb.

**V.** approve; think -good, – much of, – well of, – highly of; esteem, value, prize; set great store -by, – on.

do justice to, appreciate; honour, hold in esteem, look up to, admire; like &c. 897; be in favour of, wish God speed; hail, – with satisfaction.

stand –, stick- up for; uphold, hold

**932. Disapprobation.—N.** disapprobation, -val; improbation; dis-esteem, -valuation, -placency; odium: dislike &c. 867; dissent &c. 489.

dis-praise, -commendation; blame, censure, obloquy; detraction &c. 934; disparagement, depreciation; denunciation; condemnation &c. 971; ostracism; boycott; black-list, -ball; *index -expurgatorius, – librorum prohibitorum.*

animadversion, reflection, stricture, objection, exception, criticism: sardonic -grin, – laugh; sarcasm, insinuation, innuendo; bad –, poor – left-handed- compliment.

satire; sneer &c. (*contempt*) 930; taunt &c. (*disrespect*) 929; cavil, carping, censoriousness; hypercriticism &c. (*fastidiousness*) 868.

reprehension, remonstrance, expostulation, reproof, reprobation, admonition, increpation, reproach; rebuke, reprimand, castigation, jobation, lecture, curtain lecture, blow up, wigging, dressing, – down; rating, scolding, trim-

up, countenance, sanction; clap –, pat- on the back; keep in countenance, endorse, give credit, recommend; mark with a white -mark, – stone.

commend, praise; be-, laud; compliment, pay a tribute, bepraise; clap, – the hands; applaud, cheer, acclaim, acclamate, encore; panegyrize, eulogize, cry up, *prôner*, puff; extol, – to the skies; magnify, glorify, exalt, boost, swell, make much of; flatter &c. 933; bless, give a blessing to; have –, say- a good word for; speak -well, – highly, – in high terms- of; sing –, sound –, chaunt –, resound- the praises of; sing praises to; cheer –, applaud- to the -echo, – very echo.

redound to the -honour, – praise, – credit- of; do credit to; deserve -praise &c. *n.*; recommend itself; pass muster.

be -praised &c.; receive honourable mention; be in -favour, – high favour- with; ring with the praises of, win golden opinions, gain credit, find favour with, stand well in the opinion of; *laudari a laudato viro.*

**Adj.** approving &c. *v.*; in favour of; lost in admiration.

commendatory, complimentary, benedictory, laudatory, panegyrical, eulogistic, encomiastic, acclamatory, lavish of praise, uncritical.

approved, praised &c. *v.*; un-censured, -impeached; popular, in good odour; in high esteem &c. (*respected*) 928; in –, in high- favour.

deserving –, worthy of- praise &c. *n.*; praiseworthy, commendable, of estimation; good &c. 648; meritorious, estimable, creditable, plausible, unimpeachable; beyond all praise.

**Adv.** commendably, with credit, to admiration; well &c. 618; with three times three.

**Int.** hear, hear! well done! *brav-o! -a! -i! bravissimo! euge! macte virtute!* so far so good, that's right, quite right; *optime!* one cheer more; may your shadow never be less! *esto perpetua!* long life to! *viva! evviva!* God speed! *valete et plaudite! encore! bis!*

**Phr.** *probatum est.*

---

ming; correction, set down, rap on the knuckles, *coup de bec*, rebuff; slap, – on the face; home thrust, hit; frown, scowl, black look.

diatribe; jeremiad; *tirade*, philippic.

clamour, outcry, hue and cry; hiss, -ing; sibilation, cat-call; execration &c. 908.

chiding, upbraiding &c. *v.*; exprobration, abuse, vituperation, invective, objurgation, contumely, personal remarks; hard –, cutting –, bitter- words.

evil-speaking; bad language &c. 908; personality.

**V.** disapprove; dislike &c. 867; lament &c. 839; object to, take exception to; be scandalized at, think ill of; view with -disfavour, – dark eyes, – jaundiced eyes; *nil admirari*, dis-value, improbate.

frown upon, look grave; bend –, knit- the brows; shake the head at. shrug the shoulders; turn up the nose &c. (*contempt*) 930; look -askance, – black upon; look with an evil eye; make a wry -face, – mouth- at; set one's face against.

dis-praise, -commend, -parage; deprecate, speak ill of, not speak well of, slate, condemn &c. (*find guilty*) 971.

blame; lay –, cast- blame upon; censure, *fronder*, reproach, pass censure on, reprobate, impugn.

remonstrate, expostulate, recriminate.

reprehend, chide, admonish; bring –, call- -to account, – over the coals, – to order; take to task, reprove, lecture, bring to book; read a -lesson, – lecture- to; rebuke, correct.

reprimand, chastise, castigate, lash, blow up, trounce, trim, *laver la tête*, overhaul; give it one, – finely; gibbet.

accuse &c. 938; impeach, denounce; hold up to -reprobation, – execration; expose, brand, gibbet, stigmatize; show –, pull –, take- up; cry 'shame' upon; be outspoken; raise a hue and cry against.

execrate &c. 908; exprobrate, speak daggers, vituperate; abuse, – like a pickpocket; scold, rate, objurgate, upbraid, fall foul of; jaw; rail, – at, – in good set terms; bark at; anathematize, call names; call by -hard, – ugly- names; a-, re-vile; vili-fy, -pend; bespatter; backbite; clapperclaw; rave –, thunder –, fulminate- against; load with reproaches; lash with the tongue.

exclaim –, protest –, inveigh –, declaim –, cry out –, raise one's voice- against.

decry; cry –, run –, frown- down; clamour, hiss, hoot, mob, ostracize; draw up –, sign- a round robin; black-ball, -list.

animadvert –, reflect- upon; glance at; cast -reflection, – reproach, – a slur- upon; insinuate, damn with faint praise; 'hint a fault and hesitate dislike'; not to be able to say much for.

scoff at, point at; twit, taunt &c. (*disrespect*) 929; sneer at &c. (*despise*) 930; satirize, lampoon; defame &c. (*detract*) 934; depreciate, find fault with, criticize, cut up; pull –, pick- to pieces; take exception; cavil; peck –, nibble –, carp- at; be -censorious &c. *adj.*; pick -holes, – a hole, – a hole in one's coat; make a fuss about.

take –, set- down; snub, snap one up, give a rap on the knuckles; throw a stone -at, – in one's garden; have a -fling, – snap- at; have words with, pluck a crow with; give one a -wipe, – lick with the rough side of the tongue.

incur blame, excite disapprobation, scandalize, shock, revolt; get a bad name, forfeit one's good opinion, be under a cloud, come under the ferule, bring a hornet's nest about one's ears.

take blame, stand corrected; have to answer for.

**Adj.** disapproving &c. *v.*; scandalized.

disparaging, condemnatory, damnatory, denunciatory, reproachful, abusive, objurgatory, clamorous, vituperative; defamatory &c. 934.

satirical, sarcastic, sardonic, cynical, dry, sharp, cutting, biting, severe, virulent, withering, trenchant, hard upon; censorious, critical, captious, carping, hypercritical; fastidious &c. 868; sparing of –, grudging- praise.

disapproved, chid &c. *v.*; in bad odour, blown upon, unapproved; unblest; at a discount, exploded; weighed in the balance and found wanting.

blameworthy, reprehensible &c. (*guilt*) 947; to –, worthy of- blame, answerable, uncommendable, exceptionable, not to be thought of, bad &c. 649; vicious &c. 945.

un-lamented, -bewailed, -pitied.

**Adv.** with a wry face; reproachfully &c. *adj.*

**Int.** it is too bad! it -won't, – will never- do! marry come up! Oh! come! 'sdeath!

forbid it Heaven! God –, Heaven- forbid! out –, fie- upon it! away with! tut! *O tempora! O mores!* shame! fie, – for shame! out on you!

tell it not in Gath!

**933. Flattery.—N.** flattery, adulation, gloze; bland-ishment, -iloquence; cajolery; fawning, wheedling &c. *v.*; captation, coquetry, sycophancy, obsequiousness, flunkeyism, toad-eating, tuft-hunting; snobbishness.

incense, honeyed words, flummery; bun-kum, -combe; blarney, *placebo*, but-

**934. Detraction.—N.** detraction, disparagement, depreciation, vilification, obloquy, scurrility, scandal, defamation, aspersion, traducement, slander, calumny, obtrectation, evil-speaking, backbiting, *scandalum magnatum*.

personality, libel, squib, lampoon, skit, pasquinade; *chronique scandaleuse*.

ter; soft –soap, – sawder; rose water.

voice of the charmer, mouth honour; lip-homage; euphemism; unctuousness &c. *adj.*

**V.** flatter, praise to the skies, puff; wheedle, cajole, glaver, coax; fawn, – upon; humour, gloze, soothe, pet, coquet, slaver, butter; be-spatter, -slubber, -plaster, -slaver; lay it on thick, overpraise; earwig, cog, collogue; truckle –, pander *or* pandar –, pay court- to; court; creep into the good graces of; curry favour with, hang on the sleeve of; fool to the top of one's bent; lick the dust.

lay the flattering unction to one's soul, gild the pill, make things pleasant.

overestimate &c. 482; exaggerate &c. 549.

**Adj.** flattering &c. *v.*; adulatory; mealy-, honey-mouthed; honeyed; smooth, – tongued; soapy, oily, unctuous, blandiloquent, specious; fine-, fair-spoken; plausible, servile, sycophantic, fulsome; courtier-ly, -like.

**Adv.** *ad captandum.*

---

**935. Flatterer.**—**N.** flatterer, adulator; eu-logist, -phemist; optimist, encomiast, *laudator*, whitewasher, booster.

toad-y, -eater; sycophant, courtier, pickthank, Sir Pertinax MacSycophant; *flâneur*, *prôneur*; puffer, touter, *claqueur*; claw-back, ear-wig, doer of dirty work; parasite, hanger on &c. (*servility*) 886.

---

**937. Vindication.**—**N.** vindication, justification, warrant; exoneration, exculpation; acquittal &c. 970; whitewashing.

extenuation; pallia-tion, -tive; softening, mitigation.

reply, defence; recrimination &c. 938.

apology, gloss, varnish; plea &c. 617; salvo; excuse, extenuating circumstances; allowance, – to be made; *locus pœnitentiæ.*

apologist, vindicator, justifier; defendant &c. 938.

justifiable charge, true bill.

sarcasm, cynicism; criticism (*disapprobation*) 932; invective &c. 932; envenomed tongue; *spretæ injuria formæ.*

detractor &c. 936.

**V.** detract, derogate, decry, depreciate, disparage; run –, cry- down; minimize, make light of; belittle, sneer at &c. (*contemn*) 930; criticize, pull to pieces, pick a hole in one's coat, asperse, cast aspersions, blow upon, bespatter, blacken; vili-fy, -pend; avile; give a dog a bad name, brand, malign, backbite, libel, lampoon, traduce, slander, defame, calumniate, bear false witness against; speak ill of behind one's back;

'damn with faint praise, assent with civil leer; and without sneering, others teach to sneer.'

fling dirt &c. (*disrespect*) 929; anathematize &c. 932; dip the pen in gall, view in a bad light.

**Adj.** detracting &c. *v.*; defamatory, detractory, derogatory; disparaging, libellous; scurril-e, -ous; abusive; foul-spoken, -tongued, -mouthed; slanderous; calumni-ous, -atory; sar-castic, -donic; satirical, cynical.

**936. Detractor.**—**N.** detractor, reprover; cens-or, -urer; cynic, critic, caviller, carper, wordcatcher.

defamer, backbiter, slanderer, knocker, Sir Benjamin Backbite, lampooner, satirist, traducer, libeller, calumniator, dearest foe, dawplucker, Thersites; Zoilus; good-natured –, candid- friend [satirically]; reviler, vituperator, castigator; shrew &c. 901.

disapprover, *laudator temporis acti.*

**938. Accusation.** — **N.** accusation, charge, imputation, slur, inculpation, exprobration, delation; crimination; in-, ac-, re-crimination; *tu quoque* argument; invective &c. 932.

de-nunciation, -nouncement; libel, challenge, citation, arraignment; im-, ap-peachment; indictment, bill of indictment, true bill; lawsuit &c. 969; condemnation &c. 971.

*gravamen* of a charge, head and front of one's offending, *argumentum ad hominem*; scandal &c. (*detraction*) 934; *scandalum magnatum.*

V. justify, warrant; be an -excuse &c. *n.*- for; lend a colour, furnish a handle; vindicate; ex-, dis-culpate; acquit &c. 970; clear, set right, exonerate, whitewash.

extenuate, palliate, excuse, soften, apologize, varnish, slur, gloze; put a -gloss, – good face- upon; mince; gloss over, bolster up, help a lame dog over a stile.

advocate, defend, plead one's cause; stand –, stick –, speak- up for; contend –, speak- for; bear out, keep in countenance, support; plead &c. 617; say in defence; plead ignorance; confess and avoid, propugn, put in a good word for.

take the will for the deed, make allowance for, do justice to; give -one, – the Devil- his due.

make good; prove -the truth of, – one's case; be justified by the event.

**Adj.** vindicat-ed, -ing &c. *v.*; vindicat-ive, -ory; palliative; exculpatory; apologetic.

excusable, defensible, pardonable; veni-al, -able; specious, plausible, justifiable.

**Phr.** '*honi soit qui mal y pense.*'

---

accuser, prosecutor, plaintiff, complainant, petitioner; relator, informer; appellant.

accused, defendant, prisoner, panel, co-, respondent; litigant.

**V.** accuse, charge, tax, impute, twit, taunt with, reproach.

brand with reproach; stigmatize, slur; cast a -stone at, – slur on; incriminate; inculpate, implicate; call to account &c. (*censure*) 932; take to -blame, – task; put in the black book.

inform against, indict, denounce, arraign; im-, ap-peach; have up, show up, pull up; challenge, cite, lodge a complaint; prosecute, bring an action against &c. 969.

charge –, saddle- with; lay to one's -door, – charge; lay the blame on, bring home to; cast –, throw- in one's teeth; cast the first stone at.

have –, keep- a rod in pickle for; have a crow to pluck with.

trump up a charge.

**Adj.** accusing &c. *v.*; accusat-ory, -ive; imputative, denunciatory; re-, criminatory.

accused &c. *v.*; suspected; under -suspicion, – a cloud, – *surveillance*; in -custody, – detention; in the -lock up, – watch house, – house of detention.

accusable, imputable; in-defensible, -excusable; un-pardonable, -justifiable; vicious &c. 945.

**Int.** look at home; *tu quoque* &c. (*retaliation*) 718.

## 3°. Moral Conditions

**939. Probity.—N.** probity, integrity, rectitude; uprightness &c. *adj.*; honesty, faith; honour; good faith, *bona fides*; purity, clean hands.

fairness &c. *adj.*; fair play, justice, equity, impartiality, principle; grace.

constancy; faithfulness &c. *adj.*; fidelity, loyalty; incorrupt-ion, -ibility.

trustworthiness &c. *adj.*; truth, candour, singleness of heart; veracity &c. 543; tender conscience &c. (*sense of duty*) 926.

punctil-iousness, -io; delicacy, nicety; scrupul-osity, -ousness &c. *adj.*; scruple; point, – of honour; punctuality.

dignity &c. (*repute*) 873; respectability, -bleness &c. *adj.*; gentleman; man of -honour, – his word; *fidus*

**940. Improbity. N.** improbity; dishon-esty, -our; deviation from rectitude; disgrace &c. (*disrepute*) 874; fraud &c. (*deception*) 545; lying &c. 544; bad –, Punic- faith; *mala* –, *Punica- fides*; infidelity; faithlessness &c. *adj.*; Judas kiss, betrayal; scrap of paper.

breach of -promise, – trust, – faith: prodition, disloyalty, divided allegiance, treason, high treason; apostasy &c. (*tergiversation*) 607; non-observance &c. 773.

shabbiness &c. *adj.*; villainy; baseness &c. *adj.*; abjection, debasement, turpitude, moral turpitude, laxity, trimming, shuffling.

perfidy; perfidiousness &c. *adj.*;

*Achates*, *preux chevalier*, *galantuomo*; truepenny, trump, brick; true Briton, white man, sportsman.

court of honour, a fair field and no favour; *argumentum ad verecundiam*.

**V.** be -honourable &c. *adj.*; deal -honourably, – squarely, – impartially, – fairly; speak the truth &c. (*veracity*) 543; tell the truth and shame the devil, *vitam impendere vero*; show a proper spirit, make a point of; do one's duty &c. 944; play the game.

redeem one's pledge &c. 926; keep –, be as good as- one's -promise, – word; keep faith with, not fail

give and take, *audire alteram partem*, give the devil his due, put the saddle on the right horse.

redound to one's honour.

**Adj.** upright; honest, – as daylight; veracious &c. 543; virtuous &c. 944; honourable; fair, right, just, equitable, impartial, even-handed, square; fair –, open- and aboveboard.

constant, – as the northern star; faithful, loyal, staunch; true, – blue, – to one's colours, – to the core, – as the needle to the pole; true-hearted, trust-y, -worthy; as good as one's word, to be depended on, incorruptible.

manly, straightforward &c. (*ingenuous*) 703; frank, candid, open-hearted.

conscientious, tender - conscienced, right-minded; high-principled, -minded; scrupulous, religious, strict; nice, punctilious, correct, punctual; respect-, reput-able; gentlemanlike.

inviol - able, - ate; un - violated, -broken, -betrayed; un-bought, -bribed.

innocent &c. 946; pure; stainless; un-stained, -tarnished, -sullied, -tainted, -perjured; uncorrupt, -ed; unde-filed, -praved, -bauched; *integer vitæ scelerisque purus*; *justus et tenax propositi*.

chivalrous, jealous of honour, *sans peur et sans reproche*; high-spirited.

supra-mundane, unworldly, over-scrupulous.

**Adv.** honourably &c. *adj.*; *bona fide*; on the square, in good faith, honour bright, *foro conscientiæ*, with clean hands; by fair means.

treachery, double-dealing; unfairness &c. *adj.*; knavery, roguery, rascality, foul-play; jobb-ing, -ery; Tammany, graft; venality, nepotism; corruption, job, shuffle, fishy transaction, barratry; sharp practice, heads I win, tails you lose; mouth-honour &c. (*flattery*) 933.

**V.** be -dishonest &c. *adj.*; play false; break one's -word, – faith, – promise; jilt, betray, forswear; shuffle &c. (*lie*) 544; live by one's wits, sail near the wind; play with marked cards.

disgrace –, dishonour –, demean –, degrade- oneself; derogate, stoop, grovel, sneak, lose caste; sell oneself, go over to the enemy; seal one's infamy.

**Adj.** dishon-est, -ourable; un-conscientious, -scrupulous; fraudulent &c. 545; knavish; disgraceful &c. (*disreputable*) 874; wicked &c. 945.

false-hearted, disingenuous; unfair, one-sided; double, -tongued, -faced; time-serving, crooked, tortuous, insidious, Machiavellian, dark, slippery; questionable; fishy; perfidious, treacherous, perjured.

infamous, arrant, foul, base, vile, low, ignominious, blackguard.

contemptible, abject, mean, shabby, little, paltry, dirty, scurvy, scabby, sneaking, grovelling, scrubby, rascally, pettifogging; beneath one; not cricket.

low-minded, -thoughted; base-minded.

undignified, indign; unbe-coming, -seeming, -fitting; de-rogatory, -grading; *infra dignitatem*; ungentleman-ly, -like; un-knightly, -chivalric, -manly, -handsome; recreant, inglorious.

corrupt, venal; debased, mongrel.

faithless, of bad faith, false, unfaithful, disloyal; untrustworthy; trust-, troth-less; lost to shame, dead to honour.

**Adv.** dishonestly &c. *adj.*; *malâ fide*, like a thief in the night, by crooked paths; by foul means.

**Int.** *O tempora! O mores!*

---

**941. Knave.**—**N.** knave, rogue, villain; Scapin, rascal; Lazarillo de Tormes; bad man &c. 949; blackguard &c. 949.

traitor, betrayer, arch-traitor, conspirator, stool pigeon, Judas, Catiline; reptile, serpent, snake in the grass, wolf in sheep's clothing, sneak, Jerry Sneak, tell-tale, squealer, mischief-maker, trimmer; renegade &c. (*tergiversation*) 607; truant, recreant; sycophant &c. (*servility*) 886.

**942. Disinterestedness.—N.** disinterestedness &c. *adj.*; generosity; liberal-ity, -ism; altruism; benevolence &c. 906; elevation, loftiness of purpose, exaltation, magnanimity; chival-ry, -rous spirit; heroism, sublimity.

self-denial, -abnegation, -effacement, -sacrifice, -immolation, -control &c. (*resolution*) 604; stoicism, devotion, martyrdom, *suttee.*

labour of love.

**V.** be -disinterested &c. *adj.*; make a sacrifice, lay one's head on the block; put oneself in the place of others, do as one would be done by, do unto others as we would men should do unto us.

**Adj.** disinterested; unselfish; self-denying, -sacrificing, -devoted; generous.

handsome, liberal, noble; noble-, high-minded; princely, great, high, elevated, lofty, exalted, spirited, stoical, magnanimous; great-, large-hearted, chivalrous, heroic, sublime.

un-bought, -bribed; uncorrupted &c. (*upright*) 939.

---

**943. Selfishness.—N.** selfishness &c. *adj.*; self-love, -indulgence, -worship, -interest; ego-tism, -ism; egocentrism, narcissism; *amour propre* &c. (*vanity*) 880; nepotism.

worldliness &c. *adj.*; world wisdom.

illiberality; meanness &c. *adj.*

time-server; tuft-, fortune-hunter; self-seeker; jobber, worldling; egotist, egoist, monopolist, nepotist, profiteer; temporizer, trimmer; dog in the manger, charity that begins at home.

**V.** be -selfish &c. *adj.*; please –, indulge –, coddle- oneself; consult one's own -wishes, – pleasure; look after one's own interest; feather one's nest; take care of number one, have an eye to the main chance, know on which side one's bread is buttered; give an inch and take an ell; wangle.

**Adj.** selfish; self-seeking, -indulgent, -interested; wrapped up –, centred- in self; egotistic, -al; egoistical; egocentric.

illiberal, mean, ungenerous, narrow-minded; mercenary, venal; covetous &c. 819.

unspiritual; earthly, -minded; mundane; worldly, -minded, -wise; time-serving.

interested; *alieni appetens sui profusus.*

**Adv.** ungenerously &c. *adj.*; to gain some private ends; from selfish –, interested- motives.

**Phr.** *après nous le déluge.*

**944. Virtue.—N.** virtue; virtuousness &c. *adj.*; morality; moral rectitude; integrity &c. (*probity*) 939; nobleness &c. 873.

morals; ethics &c. (*duty*) 926; cardinal virtues.

merit, worth, desert, excellence, credit; self-control &c. (*resolution*) 604; self-denial &c. (*temperance*) 953.

well-doing; good -actions, – behaviour; discharge –, fulfilment –, performance- of duty; well-spent life; innocence &c. 946.

**V.** be -virtuous &c. *adj.*; practise -virtue &c. *n.*; do –, fulfil –, perform –,

**945. Vice. — N.** vice; evil -doing, – courses; wrong doing; wickedness, viciousness &c. *adj.*; iniquity, peccability, demerit; sin, Adam; old –, offending- Adam.

immorality, impropriety, indecorum, scandal, laxity, looseness of morals; want of -principle, – ballast; obliquity, backsliding, infamy, demoralization, pravity, depravity, pollution; hardness of heart; brutality &c. (*malevolence*) 907; corruption &c. (*debasement*) 659; knavery &c. (*improbity*) 940; profligacy; lust &c. 961; flagrancy, atrocity; cannibalism.

discharge- one's duty; redeem one's pledge &c. 926; act well, – one's part; fight the good fight; acquit oneself well; command –, master- one's passions; keep -straight, – in the right path.

set -an, – a good- example; be on one's -good, – best- behaviour.

**Adj.** virtuous, good; innocent &c. 946; meritorious, deserving, worthy, desertful, correct; dut-iful, -eous; moral; right, -eous, -minded; well-intentioned, creditable, laudable, commendable, praiseworthy; above –, beyond- all praise; excellent, admirable; sterling, pure, noble.

exemplary; match-, peer-less; saintly, -like; heaven-born, angelic, seraphic, godlike.

**Adv.** virtuously &c. *adj.*; *e merito.*

---

infirmity; weakness &c. *adj.*; weakness of the flesh, frailty, imperfection; error; weak side; foible; fail-ing, -ure; crying –, besetting- sin; defect, deficiency, shortcoming; cloven foot.

lowest dregs of vice, sink of iniquity, Alsatian den; *gusto picaresco.*

fault, crime; criminality &c. (*guilt*) 947.

sinner &c. 949.

**V.** be -vicious &c. *adj.*; sin, commit sin, do amiss, err, transgress; misdemean –, forget –, misconduct- oneself; mis-do, -behave; fall, lapse, slip, trip, offend, trespass; deviate from the -line of duty, – path of virtue &c. 944; take a wrong course, go astray; hug a -sin, – fault; sow one's wild oats.

render -vicious &c. *adj.*; demoralize, brutalize; corrupt &c. (*degrade*) 659.

**Adj.*** vicious; sinful; sinning &c. *v.*; wicked, iniquitous, bad, immoral, unrighteous, wrong, criminal; naughty, incorrect; undut-eous, -iful.

unprincipled, lawless, disorderly, *contra bonos mores*, indecorous, unseemly, improper; dissolute, profligate, scampish; unworthy; worth-, desert-less; disgraceful, recreant; reprehensible, blameworthy, uncommendable; dis-creditable, -reputable.

base, sinister, scurvy, foul, gross, vile, black, grave, facinorous, felonious, nefarious, shameful, scandalous, infamous, villainous, of a deep dye, heinous; flag-rant, -itious; atrocious, incarnate, accursed.

Mephistophelian, satanic, diabolic, hellish, infernal, stygian, fiend-ish, -like, hell-born, demoniacal, devilish.

mis-created, -begotten; demoralized, corrupt, depraved.

evil-minded, -disposed; ill-conditioned; malevolent &c. 907; heart-, grace-, shame-, virtue-less; abandoned, lost to virtue; unconscionable; sunk –, lost –, deep –, steeped- in iniquity.

incorrigible, irreclaimable, obdurate, reprobate, past praying for; culpable, reprehensible &c. (*guilty*) 947.

unjustifiable; in-defensible, -excusable; inexpiable, unpardonable, irremissible.

weak, frail, lax, infirm, imperfect, indiscreet; demoralizing, degrading.

**Adv.** wrong; sinfully &c. *adj.*; without excuse.

**Int.** *O tempora! O mores!*

**946. Innocence.** — **N.** innocence; guiltlessness &c. *adj.*; incorruption, impeccability.

clean hands, clear conscience, *mens sibi conscia recti.*

innocent, new born babe, lamb, dove.

**V.** be -innocent &c. *adj.*; *nil conscire sibi nullâ pallescere culpâ.*

**947. Guilt.**—**N.** guilt, -iness; culpability; crimin-ality, -ousness; deviation from rectitude &c. (*improbity*) 940; sinfulness &c. (*vice*) 945; peccability.

mis-conduct, -behaviour, -doing, -deed; malpractice, fault, sin, error, transgression; dereliction, delinquency; indiscretion, lapse, slip, trip, *faux pas,*

* Most of these adjectives are applicable both to the act and to the agent.

acquit &c. 970; exculpate &c. (*vindicate*) 937.

**Adj.** innocent, not guilty; unguilty; guilt-, fault-, sin-, stain-, blood-, spotless; clear, immaculate; *rectus in curiâ*; un-spotted, -blemished, -erring; undefiled &c. 939; unhardened, Saturnian; Arcadian &c. (*artless*) 703.

in-, un-culpable; unblam-ed, -able; blameless, inerrable, above suspicion; irrepr-oachable, -ovable, -ehensible; un-exceptionable, -objectionable, -impeachable; salvable; venial &c. 937.

harmless; in-offensive, -noxious, -nocuous; dove-, lamb-like; pure, harmless as doves; innocent as -a lamb, – the babe unborn; more sinned against than sinning.

virtuous &c. 944; un-reproved, -impeached, -reproached.

**Adv.** innocently &c. *adj.*; with clean hands; with a -clear, – safe- conscience.

*peccadillo*; flaw, blot, omission; fail-ing, -ure.

offence, trespass; mis-demeanour, -feasance, -prision; tort; mal-efaction, -feasance, -versation; crime, felony.

enormity, atrocity, outrage; deadly –, mortal –, unpardonable- sin; died without a name.

*corpus delicti.*

**Adj.** guilty, to blame, culpable, peccable, in fault, censurable, reprehensible, blameworthy, uncommendable, illaudable; weighed in the balance and found wanting; exceptionable, objectionable.

**Adv.** *in flagrante delicto*; red-handed, in the very act.

**948. Good Man.** — **N.** good man, worthy.

good woman, goddess, *madonna*, virgin.

model, paragon &c. (*perfection*) 650; good example; hero, demigod, seraph, angel; innocent &c. 946; saint &c. (*piety*) 987; benefactor &c. 912; philanthropist &c. 910; Aristides.

brick, trump, rough diamond, ugly duckling.

salt of the earth; one in ten thousand; one of the best.

**Phr.** *si sic omnes!*

**949. Bad Man.**—**N.** bad man, wrongdoer, worker of iniquity; evil-doer &c. 913; sinner; the -wicked &c. 945; bad example.

rascal, scoundrel, villain, miscreant, caitiff; wretch, reptile, viper, serpent, cockatrice, basilisk, urchin; tiger, monster; devil &c. (*demon*) 980; devil incarnate; demon in human shape, Nana Sahib; hell-hound, -cat; rake-hell.

bad woman, jade, Jezebel, adultress, &c. 962.

scamp, scapegrace, rip, runagate, ne'er-do-well, reprobate, *roué*, rake; limb; one who has sold himself to the devil, fallen angel, *âme damnée*, *vaurien*, *mauvais sujet*, loose fish, sad dog; lost –, black- sheep; castaway, recreant, defaulter; prodigal &c. 818; libertine &c. 962.

rough, rowdy, ugly customer, ruffian, hoodlum, bully; Jonathan Wild; hangman; incendiary; thief &c. 792; murderer &c. 361.

culprit, delinquent, criminal, malefactor, misdemeanant; felon; convict, jail-bird, ticket-of-leave man; outlaw.

blackguard, *polisson*, loafer, sneak; raps-, ras-callion; cullion, mean wretch, varlet, kern, *âme-de-boue*, *drôle*; cur, dog, hound, whelp, mongrel; lown, loon, runnion, outcast, vagabond; rogue &c. (*knave*) 941; scum of the earth, riff-raff; *Arcades ambo*.

**Int.** sirrah!

**950. Penitence.**—**N.** penitence, contrition, compunction, repentance, remorse; regret &c. 833.

self-reproach, -reproof, -accusation,

**951. Impenitence.**—**N.** impenitence, irrepentance, recusance.

hardness of heart, seared conscience, induration, obduracy.

-condemnation, -humiliation; stings –, pangs –, qualms –, prickings –, twinge –, twitch –, touch –, voice- of conscience; compunctious visitings of nature.

acknowledgment, confession &c. (*disclosure*) 529; apology &c. 952; recantation &c. 607; penance &c. 952; resipiscence.

awakened conscience, deathbed repentance, *locus pœnitentiæ*, stool of repentance, cutty stool.

penitent, Magdalen, prodigal son, returned prodigal, a sadder and a wiser man.

**V.** repent, be sorry for; be -penitent &c. *adj.*; rue; regret &c. 833; think better of; recant &c. 607; knock under &c. (*submit*) 725; plead guilty; sing *-miserere*, – *de profundis*; cry *peccavi*; own oneself in the wrong; acknowledge, confess &c. (*disclose*) 529; humble oneself; beg pardon &c. (*apologize*) 952; turn over a new leaf, put on the new man, turn from sin; reclaim; repent in sackcloth and ashes &c. (*do penance*) 952; learn by experience.

**Adj.** penitent; repenting &c. *v.*; repentant, contrite; conscience-smitten, -stricken; self-accusing, -convicted.

penitenti-al, -ary; chastened, reclaimed; not hardened; unhardened.

**Adv.** *meâ culpâ.*

**Phr.** *peccavi*; *erubuit*; *salva res est*; *vous l'avez voulu, Georges Dandin.*

**V.** be -impenitent &c. *adj.*; steel –, harden- the heart; die -game, – and make no sign.

**Adj.** impenitent, uncontrite, obdurate; hard, -ened; seared, recusant; unrepentant; relent-, remorse-, grace-, shrift-less.

lost, incorrigible, irreclaimable.

unre-claimed, -formed; unrepented, unatoned.

---

**952. Atonement.**—**N.** atonement, reparation; compromise, composition; compensation &c. 30; quittance, quits; indemni-ty, -fication; expiation, redemption, reclamation, conciliation, propitiation.

amends, apology, *amende honorable*, satisfaction; peace –, sin –, burnt- offering; scapegoat, sacrifice.

penance, fasting, maceration, sackcloth and ashes, white sheet, shrift, flagellation, lustration; purga-tion, -tory.

**V.** atone, – for; expiate; propitiate; make -amends, – good; reclaim, redeem, repair, ransom, absolve, purge, shrive, do penance, stand in a white sheet, repent in sackcloth and ashes.

set one's house in order, wipe off old scores, make matters up; pay the -forfeit, – penalty.

apologize, beg pardon, express regret, *faire amende honorable*, give satisfaction; come –, fall- down on one's -knees, – marrow bones.

**Adj.** propitiatory, expiatory; sacrific, -ial, -atory; piacul-ar, -ous.

## 4°. Moral Practice

**953. Temperance.**—**N.** temperance moderation, sobriety, soberness.

forbearance, abnegation; self-denial, -restraint, -control &c. (*resolution*) 604.

frugality; vegetarianism, teetotalism, total abstinence, prohibition; abst-inence, -emiousness, asceticism &c. 955; system of -Pythagoras, – Cornaro; Pythagorism, Stoicism.

**954. Intemperance.**—**N.** intemperance; sensuality, animalism, carnality; pleasure; effeminacy, silkiness; luxur-y, -iousness; lap of -pleasure, – luxury.

indulgence; high-, free- living, inabstinence, self-indulgence; voluptuousness &c. *adj.*; epicur-ism, -eanism; sybaritism.

vegetarian; Pythagorean, gymnosophist; teetotaler &c. 958; abstainer.

**V.** be -temperate &c. *adj.*; abstain, forbear, refrain, deny oneself, spare; know when one has had enough; take the pledge; look not upon the wine when it is red.

**Adj.** temperate, moderate, sober, frugal, sparing; abst-emious, -inent; within compass; measured &c. (*sufficient*) 639.

Pythagorean; vegetarian; teetotal, pussy-foot.

---

dissipation; licentiousness &c. *adj.*, debauchery; crapulence.

revel-s, -ry; debauch, carousal, jollification, drinking bout, wassail, Saturnalia, orgies; excess, too much; intoxication &c. 959.

Circean cup; drug habit &c. 663.

**V.** be -intemperate &c. *adj.*; indulge, exceed; live -well, – high, – on the fat of the land; give a loose to -indulgence &c. *n.*; dine not wisely but too well; wallow in -voluptuousness &c. *n.*; plunge into dissipation.

revel, rake, live hard, run riot, sow one's wild oats; slake one's -appetite, – thirst; swill; pamper.

**Adj.** intemperate, inabstinent, intoxicated &c. 959; sensual, self-indulgent; voluptuous, luxurious, licentious, wild, dissolute, rakish, fast, debauched.

brutish, crapulous, swinish, piggish, porcine, hoggish, bestial.

Paphian, Epicurean, Sybaritical; bred –, nursed- in the lap of luxury; indulged, pampered, full-fed.

**954a. Sensualist.—N.** Sybarite, voluptuary, Sardanapalus, man of pleasure, carpet knight; epicure, -an; *gourm-et, -and*; gormandizer, gutling, glutton, pig, hog; votary –, swine- of Epicurus; sensualist; Heliogabalus; free –, hard- liver; libertine &c. 962; hedonist.

**955. Asceticism.—N.** asceticism, puritanism, sabbatarianism; cynicism, austerity; total abstinence.

mortification, maceration, sackcloth and ashes, flagellation; penance &c. 952; fasting &c. 956; martyrdom.

ascetic; anchor-et, -ite; martyr; *Heautontimorumenos*; hermit &c. (*recluse*) 893; puritan, sabbatarian, cynic.

**Adj.** ascetic, austere, puritanical; cynical; over-religious.

**956. Fasting. — N.** fasting; xerophagy; famishment, starvation; banting.

fast, *jour maigre*; fast –, banyan-day; Lent, quadragesima; Rama-dan, -zan; spare –, meagre- diet; lenten -diet, – entertainment; *soupe maigre*, short -rations, – commons; Barmecide feast; hunger strike.

**V.** fast, starve, clem, famish, perish with hunger; dine with Duke Humphrey; make two bites of a cherry.

**Adj.** lenten, quadragesimal; unfed; starved &c. *v.*; half-starved; fasting &c. *v.*; hungry &c. 865.

---

**957. Gluttony.—N.** gluttony; greed; greediness &c. *adj.*; voracity.

epicurism; good –, high- living; edacity, gulosity, crapulence; gutt-, guzz-ling; over-indulgence.

good cheer, blow out; feast &c. (*food*) 298; gastronomy.

epicure, *bon vivant*, *gourmand*; glutton, cormorant, hog, belly-god, Apicius, gastronome, gormandizer.

**V.** gormandize, gorge; over-gorge, -eat- oneself; engorge, eat one's fill, cram, stuff, stodge, glut, satiate; gutt-le, guzz-le; bolt, devour, gobble up; gulp &c. (*swallow food*) 298; raven, eat out of house and home.

have the stomach of an ostrich; play a good knife and fork &c. (*appetite*) 865.

pamper, indulge.

**Adj.** gluttonous, greedy; gormandizing &c. *v.*; edacious, omnivorous, crapulent, swinish, voracious, devouring.

pampered; over-fed, -gorged.

**958. Sobriety.**—**N.** sobriety; teetotalism, temperance &c. 953.

water-drinker; teetotal-er, -ist; abstainer, Good Templar, Rechabite, band of hope; prohibitionist, pussyfoot.

**V.** take the pledge.

**Adj.** sober, – as a judge; dry, on the water wagon.

---

**959. Drunkenness.**—**N.** drunkenness &c. *adj.*; intemperance; drinking &c. *v.*; inebri-ety, -ation; ebri-ety, -osity; befuddlement; insobriety; intoxication; temulency, bibacity, wine-bibbing; com-, potation; deep potations, bacchanals, *bacchanalia*, libations.

oino-, dipso-mania; *delirium tremens*, d.t.; alcohol, -ism.

drink; alcoholic drinks, alcohol, booze; gin, blue ruin, grog, brandy, port wine; punch, -bowl; cup, rosy wine, flowing bowl; drop, – too much; dram; beer, wine, spirits &c. (*beverage*) 298; cocktail, nip, peg; stirrup cup.

drunkard, sot, toper, tippler, bibber, wine-bibber; hard –, gin –, dram- drinker; soak, soaker, sponge, tun; love-, toss-pot; thirsty soul, reveller, carouser; Bacchanal, -ian; Bacch-al, -ante; devotee to Bacchus, dipsomaniac.

**V.** get –, be- drunk &c. *adj.*; see double; take a -drop, – glass- too much; drink, tipple, tope, booze, bouse, guzzle, swill, soak, sot, lush, bib, swig, carouse; sacrifice at the shrine of Bacchus; take to drinking; drink -hard, – deep, – like a fish; have one's swill, drain the cup, splice the main brace, take a hair of the dog that bit you.

liquor, – up; wet one's whistle, take a whet; lift one's elbow; crack a –, pass the- bottle; toss off &c. (*drink up*) 298; go to the -ale, – public-house.

make one -drunk &c. *adj.*; inebriate, fuddle, fuzzle, get into one's head.

**Adj.** drunk, tipsy; intoxicated; inebri-ous, -ate, -ated; in one's cups; in a state of -intoxication &c. *n.*; temulent, -ive; fuddled, mellow, cut, boosy, fou, fresh, merry, elevated, squiffy; plastered, befuddled, sozzled; flush, -ed; flustered, disguised, groggy, beery; topheavy; pot-valiant, glorious; potulent; over-come, -taken; whittled, screwed, tight, primed, oiled, corned, raddled, sewed up, lushy, nappy, muddled, muzzy, bosky, obfuscated, maudlin; crapulous, dead –, blind- drunk.

*inter pocula*; in –, the worse for- liquor, having had a drop too much, half seas over, three sheets in the wind; under the table, blind to the world, one over the eight.

drunk as -a piper, – a fiddler, – a lord, – Chloe, – an owl, – David's sow, – a wheelbarrow.

drunken, bibacious, bibulous, sottish; given –, addicted- to -drink, – the bottle; toping &c. *v.*; wet.

**Phr.** *nunc est bibendum.*

**960. Purity.**—**N.** purity; decency, decorum, delicacy; continence, chastity, honesty, virtue, modesty, shame; pudicity, *pucelage*, virginity.

vestal, virgin, Joseph, Hippolytus; Lucretia, Diana; prude.

**961. Impurity.**—**N.** impurity; uncleanness &c. (*filth*) 653; immodesty; grossness &c. *adj.*; indelicacy, indecency; impudicity; obscenity, ribaldry, smut, bawdry, *double entendre*, *équivoque*; Aretinism; pornography.

**Adj.** pure, undefiled, modest, delicate, decent, decorous; *virginibus puerisque*; chaste, continent, virtuous, honest, Platonic.

concupiscence, lust, carnality, flesh, salacity; pruriency, lechery lascivi-ency, lubricity, lewdness.

incontinence, intrigue, *faux pas*; *amour*, *-ette*; gallantry; debauchery, libertinism, *libertinage*, fornication; *liaison*; wenching, venery, dissipation.

seduction; defloration, defilement, abuse, violation, rape: incest.

social evil, harlotry, stupration, whoredom, concubinage, cuckoldom, adultery, advoutry, *crim. con.*; free love.

seraglio, harem, zenana; brothel, bagnio, stew, bawdy-house, *lupanar*, house of ill fame, *bordel*, kip.

**V.** be -impure &c. *adj.*; intrigue; debauch, defile, assault attack, seduce; prostitute; abuse, violate, deflower; commit -adultery &c. *n.*

**Adj.** impure; unclean &c. (*dirty*) 653; not to be mentioned to ears polite; immodest, shameless; in-decorous, -delicate, decent; loose, suggestive, *risqué*, coarse, gross, broad, free, equivocal, smutty, fulsome, ribald, obscene, bawdy, pornographic.

concupiscent, prurient, lickerish, rampant, lustful; carnal, -minded; lewd, lascivious, lecherous, libidinous, erotic, ruttish, salacious; Paphian; voluptuous; incestuous.

unchaste, light, wanton, licentious, adulterous, debauched, dissolute; of -loose character, – easy virtue; frail, gay, riggish, incontinent, meretricious, rakish, gallant, dissipated; no better than she should be; on the -town, – streets, – *pavé*, – loose.

adulterous, incestuous, bestial.

**962. Libertine.—N.** libertine; voluptuary &c. 954*a*; rake, debauchee, loose fish, rip, rake-hell, fast man; *intrigant*, gallant, seducer, fornicator lecher, satyr, goat, whoremonger, *paillard*, adulterer, gay deceiver Lothario, Don Juan, Bluebeard.

adulteress, advoutress, courtesan, prostitute, strumpet, tart, hustler, chippy, broad, harlot, whore, punk, *fille de joie*; woman, – of the town; street-walker, Cyprian, miss, piece; frail sisterhood, fallen woman demirep, wench, trollop, trull, baggage, hussy, drab, bitch, jade, skit, rig, quean, mopsy, slut, minx, harridan; woman -of easy virtue &c (*unchaste*) 961; wanton, fornicatress; Jezebel, Messalina, Delilah, Thaïs, Phryne, Aspasia, Lais, *lorette*, *cocotte*, *petite dame*, *grisette*; *demi-mondaine*; white slave.

concubine, mistress, fancy woman, kept woman, doxy, *chère amie*, *bona roba*.

pimp; pand-er, -ar; bawd, *conciliatrix*, procuress, mackerel; wittol

## 5°. Institutions

**963. Legality.—N.** legality; legitimacy, -teness, legitimization.

legislature; law, code, *corpus juris*, constitution, pandect, charter, act, enactment, statute, rule; canon &c. (*precept*) 697; ordinance, institution, regulation; by-, bye-law, rescript; decree &c. (*order*) 741; *ordonnance*;

**964.** [Absence or violation of law.] **Illegality.—N.** lawlessness; breach –, violation- of law; disobedience &c. 742; unconformity &c. 83.

arbitrariness &c. *adj.*; antinomy, violence, brute force, despotism, outlawry.

mob –, lynch –, club –, Lydford –

standing order; *plébiscite* &c. (*choice*) 609.

legal process; form, -ula, -ality; rite; arm of the law; *habeas corpus.*

[Science of law] jurisprudence, nomology; legislation, codification.

equity, common law; *lex* –, *lex non-scripta*, unwritten law; law of nations, international law, *jus gentium*; *jus civile*; civil –, criminal –, canon –, statute –, ecclesiastical- law; *lex mercatoria.*

constitutional-ism, -ity; justice &c. 922.

**V.** legalize, legitimize; enact, ordain; decree &c. (*order*) 741; pass a law; legislate; codify, formulate; authorize.

**Adj.** legal, legitimate; according to law; vested, constitutional, chartered, legalized; lawful &c. (*permitted*) 760; statut-able, -ory; legislat-orial, -ive.

**Adv.** legally &c. *adj.*; in the eye of the law; *de jure.*

martial –, drumhead- law; *coup d'état*; *le droit du plus fort*; *argumentum ad baculum.*

illegality, informality, unlawfulness, illegitimacy, bar sinister.

trover and conversion; smuggling, boot-legging, rum-running, poaching; simony.

speakeasy, speakie, blind pig.

**V.** offend against –, violate- the law; set the law at defiance, ride rough-shod over, drive a coach and six through a statute; make the law a dead letter, take the law into one's own hands.

smuggle, run, poach.

**Adj.** illegal; prohibited &c. 761; not allowed, unlawful, illegitimate, illicit, contraband, actionable.

unchartered, unconstitutional; unwarrant-ed, -able; unauthorized; informal, unofficial; in-, extra-judicial.

lawless, arbitrary; despotic, -al; summary, irresponsible; un-answerable, -accountable.

null and void; a dead letter.

**Adv.** illegally &c. *adj.*; with a high hand, in violation of law.

---

**965. Jurisdiction.** [Executive.]—**N.** jurisdiction, judicature, administration of justice, soc; executive, commission of the peace; magistracy &c. (*authority*) 737.

judge &c. 967; tribunal &c. 966; municipality, corporation, bailiwick, shrievalty; lord lieutenant; lord –, mayor, city manager, alderman &c. 745; sheriff, bailie, shrieve, chief –, constable; police, – force; constabulary, bumbledom.

officer; proctor, high –, commissioner; bailiff, tipstaff, bum-bailiff, catchpoll, beadle; police-man, -constable, -sergeant; *sbirro*, *alguazil*, *gendarme*, kavass, *lictor*, macebearer, *huissier*, bedel.

press-gang; exciseman, gauger, custom-house officer, *douanier.*

coroner, edile, ædile, portreeve, paritor; *posse comitatus.*

**V.** judge, sit in judgment.

**Adj.** executive, administrative, municipal; inquisitorial, causidical; judic-atory, -iary, -ial; juridical.

**Adv.** *coram judice.*

**966. Tribunal.**—**N.** tribunal, court, board, bench, judicatory, curia; court of -justice, – law, – arbitration; inquisition; guild.

justice –, judgement –, mercy- seat; woolsack; bar, – of justice; dock; forum, hustings, *bureau*, drum-head; jury-, witness-box.

senate-house, town-hall, theatre; House of -Lords, – Commons.

assize, eyre; ward-, burgh-mote; superior courts of Westminster; court of -record, – oyer and terminer, – assize, – appeal, – error; High court of -Judicature, – Appeal; Judicial Committee of the Privy Council; Star-Chamber; Court of -Chancery, – King's *or* Queen's Bench, – Exchequer, – Common Pleas, – Probate, – Arches, – Admiralty, – Criminal Appeal; Lords Justices' –, Rolls –, Vice-Chancellor's –,

Stannary –, Divorce –, Palatine –, ecclesiastical –, county –, police-court; sessions; quarter –, petty- sessions; court -leet, – baron, – of pie poudre, – of common council; board of green cloth.

court-martial; drum-head court-martial; *durbar*, divan; Areopagus; *rota*.

**Adj.** judicial &c. 965; appellate; curial.

**967. Judge.—N.** judge; justi-ce, -ciar, -ciary; chancellor; justice –, judge- of assize; recorder, common serjeant; puisne –, assistant – county court- judge; conservator –, justice- of the peace, J.P.; court &c. (*tribunal*) 966; grand –, petty –, coroner's- jury; panel, juror, juryman; twelve men in a box; magistrate, police magistrate, stipendiary, the great unpaid, beak; his -worship, – honour, – lordship; deemster, moderator.

Lord -Chancellor, – Justice; Master of the Rolls, Vice-Chancellor; Lord Chief -Justice, – Baron; Mr. Justice; Baron, – of the Exchequer.

jurat, assessor; arbi-ter, -trator; umpire; refer-ee, -endary; revising barrister; domesman; censor &c. (*critic*) 480; official –, receiver.

archon, tribune, prætor, *ephor*, syndic, *podestà*, mullah, ulema, mufti, cadi, kadi; Rhadamanthus.

litigant &c. (*accusation*) 938.

**V.** adjudge &c. (*determine*) 480; try a -case, – prisoner.

**Adj.** judicial &c. 965. **Phr.** 'a Daniel come to judgment.'

**968. Lawyer.—N.** lawyer, jurist, legist, civilian, pundit, publicist, jurisconsult, legal adviser, advocate; barrister, – at law; counsel, -lor; King's *or* Queen's counsel; K.C.; Q.C.; silk gown, leader; junior, – counsel; stuff gown, serjeant-at-law, bencher; tubman; judge &c. 967.

bar, legal profession, gentleman of the long robe; junior –, outer –, inner- bar; Inns of Court; equity draftsman, conveyancer, pleader, special pleader.

solicitor, attorney, proctor; notary, – public; scrivener, cursitor; writer, – to the signet; S.S.C.; limb of the law; pettifogger.

**V.** practise -at, – within- the bar; plead; call –, be called- -to, – within- the bar; take silk.

**Adj.** learned in the law; at the bar; forensic.

**969. Lawsuit.—N.** lawsuit, suit, action, cause, petition; litigation; dispute &c. 713.

citation, arraignment, prosecution, impeachment; accusation &c. 938; presentment, true bill, indictment.

apprehension, arrest; committal; imprisonment &c. (*restraint*) 751.

writ, summons, subpœna, -*duces tecum*, *latitat*, *nisi prius*; *habeas corpus*.

pleadings; declaration, bill, claim; *procès-verbal*, bill of right, information, *corpus delicti*; affidavit, state of facts; answer, replication, plea, demurrer, rebutter, rejoinder; surre-butter, -joinder.

suitor, party to a suit; litigant &c. 938; libellant.

hearing, trial; verdict &c. (*judgment*) 480; appeal, – motion; writ of error; *certiorari*.

case, decision, precedent, ruling; decided case, reports.

**V.** go to –, appeal to the- law; bring to -justice, – trial, – the bar; put on trial, pull up; accuse &c. 938; prefer –, file- a claim &c. *n.*; take the law of, inform against.

serve with a writ, cite, apprehend, arraign, sue, prosecute, bring an action against, indict, impeach, attach, distrain, commit; arrest; summon, -s; give in charge &c. (*restrain*) 751.

empanel a jury, implead, join issue; close the pleadings; set down for hearing.

try, hear a cause; sit in judgment; adjudicate &c. 480.

**Adj.** litigious &c. (*quarrelsome*) 713; *qui tam*; *coram* –, *sub judice*.

**Adv.** *pendente lite.*

**Phr.** *adhuc sub judice lis est.*

**970. Acquittal.** — **N.** acquit-tal, -ment; clearance, exculpation, exoneration; discharge &c. (*release*) 750; *quietus*, absolution, compurgation, reprieve, respite; pardon &c. (*forgiveness*) 918.

[Exemption from punishment] impunity, immunity.

**V.** acquit, exculpate, exonerate, clear; absolve, whitewash, assoil, discharge, release; liberate &c. 750.

reprieve, respite; pardon &c. (*forgive*) 918; let off, – scot free.

**Adj.** acquitted &c. *v.*; un-condemned, -punished, -chastised; recommended to mercy.

**971. Condemnation.**—**N.** condemnation, conviction proscription, damnation; death warrant; penalty &c. 974.

attain-der, -ture, -tment.

**V.** condemn, convict, cast, bring home to, find guilty, damn, doom, sign the death warrant, sentence pass sentence on, attaint, confiscate, proscribe, sequestrate; non-suit.

disapprove &c. 932; accuse &c. 938.

stand condemned.

**Adj.** condem-, dam-natory; condemned &c. *v.*; non-suited &c. (*failure*) 732; self-convicted.

**Phr.** *mutato nomine de te fabula narratur.*

**972. Punishment.** — **N.** punishment, punition; chast-isement, -ening; correction, castigation.

discipline, infliction, trial; judgement; penalty &c. 974; retribution; thunderbolt, Nemesis; requital &c. (*reward*) 973; penology; retributive justice.

lash, scaffold &c. (*instrument of punishment*) 975; imprisonment &c. (*restraint*) 751; chain gang; transportation, banishment, expulsion, deportation, exile, involuntary exile, ostracism; penal servitude, hard labour; galleys &c. 975; beating &c. *v.*; flagellation, fustigation, ga-ntlet, *strappado, estrapade, bastinado, argumentum ad baculum*, stick law, rap on the knuckles, box on the ear; blow &c. (*impulse*) 276; stripe, cuff, kick, buffet, pummel; slap, – in the face; wipe, douse; *coup de grâce*; torture, rack; picket, -ing; *dragonnade*; capital punishment, extreme penalty; execution; hanging &c. *v.*; de-capitation, -collation; *garrotte*; electrocution, lethal chamber; crucifixion, impalement; martyrdom, *auto-da-fé*; *noyade*; *hara-kiri*, happy despatch.

**V.** punish; chast-ise, -en; castigate, correct, inflict punishment, administer correction, deal retributive justice.

visit upon, pay; pay –, serve- out; settle with, get even with, get one's own back; do for; make short work of, give a lesson to, strafe, serve one right, make an example of; have a rod in pickle for; give it one.

strike &c. 276; deal a blow to, administer the lash, smite; slap, – the face; smack, cuff, box the ears, spank, thwack, thump, beat, lay on, swinge, buffet; thresh, thrash, pummel, drub, leather, trounce, baste, belabour; lace, – one's jacket; dress, give a -dressing, – down; trim, warm, wipe, tund, cob, bang, strap, comb, lash, lick, larrup, whallop, whop, flog, scourge, whip, birch, cane, give the stick, switch, flagellate, horsewhip, *bastinado*, towel, rub down with an oaken towel, rib roast, dust one's jacket, fustigate, pitch into, lay about one, beat black and blue; beat to a -mummy, – jelly; give a black eye; hit on the head; sandbag.

tar and feather; pelt, stone, lapidate; mast-head, keelhaul.

execute; bring to the -block, – gallows; behead; de-capitate, -collate; guillotine; hang, turn off, gibbet, bowstring, hang, draw and quarter; shoot; decimate; burn; electrocute; break on the wheel, crucify; em-, im-pale; flay; lynch; put to death.

torture; put -on, – to the rack; picket.

banish, exile; trans-, de-port; expel, ostracize; rusticate; drum out; dismiss, -bar, -bench; strike off the roll, unfrock; post.

suffer, – for, – punishment; be -flogged, – hanged &c.; come to the gallows, dance upon nothing, die in one's shoes; be rightly served.

**Adj.** punishing &c. *v.*; penal; puni-tory, -tive; inflictive, castigatory; punished &c. *v.*

**Int.** *à la lanterne!*

**973. Reward.—N.** reward, recompense, remuneration, prize, meed, guerdon, reguerdon; indemni-ty, -fication, price; quittance; compensation; reparation, *ersatz*, assythment, redress; retribution, reckoning, acknowledgment, requital, amends, sop; atonement; consideration, return, *quid pro quo*; salvage, perquisite; vail &c. (*donation*) 784; *douceur*, bribe, bait, baksheesh, tip; hush-, smart-money; blackmail; carcelage; *solatium*.

allowance, salary, stipend, wages; pay, -ment; emolument; tribute; batta, shot, scot; premium, fee, *honorarium*; hire.

crown &c. (*decoration of honour*) 877.

**V.** re-ward, -compense, -pay, -quite; re, munerate; compensate; fee, tip, bribe; pay one's footing &c. (*pay*) 807; make amends, indemnify, atone; satisfy, acknowledge.

get for one's pains, reap the fruits of.

**Adj.** remunerat-ive, -ory; munerary, compensatory, retributive, reparatory.

---

**974. Penalty.—N.** penalty; retribution &c. (*punishment*) 972; pain, pains and penalties; *peine forte et dure*; penance &c. (*atonement*) 952; the devil to pay.

fine, mulct, amercement; forfeit, -ure; escheat, damages, deodand, sequestration, confiscation, *premunire*.

**V.** penalize, fine, mulct, amerce, sconce, confiscate; sequest-rate, -er; escheat; estreat, forfeit.

**975.** [Instrument of punishment.] **Scourge.—N.** scourge, rod, cane, stick; ra-, rat-tan; birch, – rod; rod in pickle; switch, ferule, cudgel, truncheon; rubber hose.

whip, lash, strap, thong, cowhide, knout; cat, – o'-nine-tails, *sjambok*, quirt; rope's end.

pillory, stocks, whipping-post; cuck-, duck-ing stool; brank; triangle, wooden horse, maiden, thumbscrew, boot, rack, wheel, iron heel; treadmill, crank, galleys.

scaffold; block, axe, *guillotine*; stake; cross; gallows, gibbet, Tyburn tree; drop, noose, rope, halter, bowstring; electric chair, lethal chamber.

house of correction &c. (*prison*) 752.

gaol-, jail-er; executioner; hang-, heads-man; Jack Ketch; lyncher.

## Section V. RELIGIOUS AFFECTIONS

### 1°. Superhuman Beings and Regions

**976. Deity.—N.** Deity, Divinity; God-head, -ship; Omnipotence, Providence.

[Quality of being divine] divin-eness, -ity.

God, Lord, Jehovah, *Deus*; The -Almighty, – Supreme Being, – First Cause; *Ens Entium*; Author –, Creator- of all things; Author of our being; The -Infinite, – Eternal; The All-powerful, -wise, -merciful, -holy; The Omni-potent, -scient.

[Attributes and perfections] infinite -power, – wisdom, – goodness, – justice, – truth, – love, – mercy; omni-potence, -science, -presence; unity, immutability, holiness, glory, majesty, sovereignty, infinity, eternity.

The -Trinity, – Holy Trinity, – Trinity in Unity, – Triune God, Three in One and One in Three.

God the Father; The -Maker, – Creator, – Preserver.

[Functions] creation, preservation, divine government; The-ocracy, -archy; providence; ways –, dealings –, dispensations –, visitations- of Providence.

God the Son, Jesus, Christ; The -Messiah, – Anointed, – Saviour, – Redeemer, – Mediator, – Intercessor, – Advocate, – Judge; The Son of -God, – Man, – David; The Only Begotten; The Lamb of God, The Word; Em-, Im-manuel; The -King of Kings and Lord of Lords, – King of Glory, – Prince of Peace, – Good Shepherd, – Way, – Truth, – Life, – Bread of Life, – Light of the World; The -Lord our, – Sun of- Righteousness.

The -Incarnation, – Hypostatic Union, – Word made Flesh.

[Functions] salvation, redemption, atonement, propitiation, mediation, intercession, judgment.

God the Holy Ghost, The Holy Spirit, Paraclete; The -Comforter, – Consoler, – Spirit of Truth, – Dove.

[Functions] inspiration, unction, regeneration, sanctification, consolation.

eon, æon, special providence, *Deus ex machinâ*; *Avatar*.

**V.** create, uphold, preserve, govern &c.

atone, redeem, save, propitiate, mediate &c.

predestinate, elect, call, ordain, bless, justify, sanctify, glorify &c.

**Adj.** almighty, holy, hallowed, sacred, divine, heavenly, celestial; messianic; sacrosanct; all-powerful, -wise, -seeing, -knowing; omnipotent, omniscient; supreme.

super-human, -natural; ghostly, spiritual, hyperphysical, unearthly; the-istic, -ocratic, deistic; anointed.

**Adv.** *jure divino*, by divine right; *Deo volente*, D.V.

**977.** [Beneficent spirits.] **Angel.—N.** angel, archangel; heavenly host, choir invisible, host of heaven, sons of God; Michael, Gabriel &c.; seraph, -im; cherub, -im; ministering spirit, morn-

**978.** [Maleficent spirits.] **Satan.—N.** Satan, the Devil, Lucifer, Ahrimanes, Belial; Sammael, Zamiel, Beelzebub, the Prince of the Devils; Mephistopheles, his satanic majesty.*

* The slang expressions 'the -deuce, – dickens, – old Gentleman; old -Nick, – Scratch, – Horny, – Harry, – Gooseberry,' have not been inserted in the text.

ing star; saint, *Madonna*; Our Lady, the Blessed Virgin, the Virgin Mary.

**Adj.** angelic, seraphic, cherubic.

---

the tempter; the evil -one, – spirit; the -author of evil, – wicked one, – old Serpent; the Prince of -darkness, – this world, – the power of the air: the -foul, – arch- fiend; the devil incarnate; the -common enemy, – angel of the bottomless pit; Abaddon, Apollyon, Mammon.

fallen angels, unclean spirits, devils; the -rulers, – powers- of darkness; inhabitants of Pandemonium; demon &c. 980.

diabolism; devil-ism, -ship, -dom, -ry, -worship; *diablerie*; satanism, manicheism; the cloven foot; black magic &c. 992.

**Adj.** satanic, diabolic, devilish, infernal, hell-born.

*Heathen, Mythological and other fabulous Deities and Powers**

**979. Jupiter.**—**N.** god, -dess; heathen gods and goddesses; Pantheon; Jupiter, Jove, Zeus, Apollo, Mars, Mercury, Neptune, Vulcan, Bacchus, Pluto, Saturn, Cupid, Eros, Pan; Juno, Ceres, Proserpina, Diana, Minerva, Pallas Athene, Venus, Aphrodite, Vesta; The Fates &c. 601.

Allah, Brahma, Vishnu, Siva, Shiva, Krishna, Juggernaut, Buddha; Ra, Isis, Osiris; Belus, Bel, Baal, Asteroth &c.; Thor, Odin; Mumbo Jumbo; good –, tutelary- genius; demiurge, familiar, – spirit; Sibyl; fairy, fay; sylph, -id; Ariel, peri, nymph, nereid, dryad, oread, sea-maid, Banshee, Benshie, Ormuzd; Oberon, Titania, Mab, hamadryad, naiad, mermaid, kelpie, Ondine, nix, nixie, sprite; denizens of the air; pixy &c. (*bad spirit*) 980.

mythology; heathen –, fairy- mythology; Lemprière, folklore.

**Adj.** fairy-, sylph-like; sylphic.

---

**980. Demon.**—**N.** demon, -ry, -ism, -ology; evil genius, fiend, familiar, – spirit, devil; bad –, unclean- spirit; cacodemon, incubus, Frankenstein's monster, succubus and succuba, Titan, Shedim, Mephistopheles, Asmodeus, Moloch, Belial, Ahriman, fury, The Furies &c. 900; harpy; Friar Rush.

vampire, ghoul; af-, ef-freet; afrite; ogre, -ss; gnome, gin, djinn, imp, deev, *lamia*; bo-gie, -gle; nis, kobold, flibbertigibbet, fairy, brownie, pixy, elf, dwarf, urchin, Puck, Robin Goodfellow; lepre-, cluri-chaune; troll, dwerger, sprite, oaf, changeling, bad fairy, nixe, pigwidgeon, Will-o'-the-wisp; Erl King.

[Supernatural appearance] ghost, spectre, apparition, genie, spirit, shade, shadow, vision, phantom &c. 443; materialization (*spiritualism*) 992; hob-, goblin; wraith, spook, werwolf, boggart, banshee, *loup-garou*, *lemures*; evil eye.

nisse, necks; mer-man, -maid, -folk; siren, Lorelei; satyr, faun.

**Adj.** supernatural, weird, uncanny, unearthly, spectral; ghost-ly, -like; elf-in, -like; fiend-ish, -like; impish, demoniacal; haunted.

**981. Heaven.**—**N.** heaven; kingdom of -heaven, – God; heavenly kingdom; throne –, presence- of God; inheritance of the saints in light.

Paradise, Eden, abode of the blessed; Holy City, New Jerusalem; celestial bliss, glory.

[Mythological -heaven] Olympus; [– paradise] Elysium, Elysian fields, Arcadia, bowers of bliss, garden of the Hesperides, Islands of the Blessed;

**982. Hell.**—**N.** hell, bottomless pit, place of torment; habitation of fallen angels; Pandemonium, Abaddon, Domdaniel.

hell fire; everlasting -fire, – torment; lake of fire and brimstone; fire that is never quenched, worm that never dies.

purgatory, limbo, gehenna, abyss.

[Mythological hell] Tartarus, Hades, Avernus, Styx, Stygian creek, pit of Acheron, Cocytus, Phlegethon, Lethe;

* Only a selection of those best known to literature is included.

happy hunting-ground; third –, seventh- heaven; Valhalla (Scandinavian); Nirvana (Buddhist).

future state, eternity, eternal life, life after death, eternal home, resurrection, translation; resuscitation &c. 660; apotheosis, deification.

Adj. heavenly, celestial, supernal, unearthly, from on high, paradisiacal, beatific, elysian, Olympian, Arcadian.

infernal regions, *inferno*, shades below, realms of Pluto.

Pluto, Rhadamanthus, Erebus, Charon, Cerberus; Tophet.

Adj. hellish, infernal, stygian.

---

## 2°. Religious Doctrines

**983.** [Religious Knowledge.] **Theology.—N.** Theology (natural and revealed); Theo-gony, -sophy; Divinity; Hagio-logy, -graphy; Caucasian mystery; monotheism; religion; religious -persuasion, – sect, – denomination; cult; creed &c. (*belief*) 484; articles –, declaration –, profession –, confession- of faith.

theolog-ue, -ian; divine, schoolman, canonist, monotheist.

Adj. theological, religious; canonical; denominational; sectarian &c. 984.

**983a. Orthodoxy.—N.** orthodoxy; strictness, soundness, religious truth, true faith; truth &c. 494.

Christian-ity, -ism; Catholic-ism, -ity; 'the faith once delivered to the saints'; hyperorthodoxy &c. 984; iconoclasm.

the Holy –, the Orthodox- Church; Catholic –, Universal –, Apostolic –, Established- Church; temple of the Holy Ghost; Church –, body –, members –, disciples –, followers- of Christ; Christian, – community; true believer; canonist &c. (*theologian*) 983; Christendom, collective body of Christians, the Church Militant.

canons &c. (*belief*) 484; thirty-nine articles; Apostles' –, Nicene –, Athanasian- Creed; Church Catechism; textuary.

Adj. orthodox, sound, literal, strict, faithful, catholic, schismless, Christian, evangelical, scriptural, divine, monotheistic; true &c. 494.

High –, Low –, Broad –, Free- Church; ultramontanism; monasticism; pap-ism, -istry; papacy; Anglican-, Catholic-, Roman-ism; popery, Scarlet Lady, Church of Rome, Greek Church; Christian Science, The Church of Christ Scientist.

---

**984. Heterodoxy.** [Sectarianism.] **N.** heterodoxy; error &c. 495; false doctrine, heresy, schism; schismaticism, -alness; recusancy, backsliding, apostasy; atheism &c. (*irreligion*) 989.

bigotry &c. (*obstinacy*) 606; fanaticism, iconoclasm; hyperorthodoxy, precisianism, bibliolatry, hagiolatry, sabbatarianism, puritanism; idolatry &c. 991; superstition &c. (*credulity*) 486; dissent &c. 489.

sectar-ism, -ianism; nonconformity; secularism; syncretism, religious sects; the clash of creeds.

protestant-, advent-, Arian-, Erastian-, Calvin-, quaker-, method-, anabapt-, Pusey-, tractarian-, ritual-, Origen-, Sabellian-, Socinian-, De-, The-, mon-, material-, positiv-, latitudinarian-ism &c.

pagan-, heathen-, ethic-ism; mythology; animism; poly-, di-, tri-, pantheism; dualism; heathendom.

Juda-, Gentil-, Mahometan-, Islam-, Turc-, Brahmin-, Hindoo-, Buddh-, Lama-, Confucian-, Shinto-, Sabian-, Gnostic-, Soofee-, Hylothe-, Mormonism.

Theosophy; Spiritualism, Occultism.

heretic, antichrist; pagan, heathen; pai-, pay-nim; *giaour*; gentile; pan-, poly-theist; idolator; misbeliever, apostate, backslider.

bigot &c. (*obstinacy*) 606; fanatic, dervish, abdal, iconoclast.

latitudinarian, limitarian, Deist, Theist, Unitarian; positivist, materialist; agnostic, skeptic &c. 989.

schismatic; sectar-y, -ian, -ist; seceder, separatist, recusant, dissenter; non-conformist, -juror; Huguenot, Protestant; orthodox dissenter, Congregationalist, Independent; Episcopalian, Presbyterian; Lutheran, Calvinist, Quaker, Methodist, Wesleyan; Ana-, Baptist; Dunker; Mormon, Latter-day Saint, Irvingite, Sandemanian, Glassite, Erastian; Sub-, Supra-lapsarian; Gentoo, Antinomian, Swedenborgian, Adventist, Plymouth Brother; Theosophist &c.

Catholic, Roman Catholic, Romanist, papist, ultramontane; Old Catholic, tractarian, Anglican, Puseyite, ritualist; Puritan.

Jew, Hebrew, Rabbist; Mahometan, Mohammedan, Mussulman, Moslem, Islamite, Osmanli; Brahm-in, -an; Parsee, Sofi, Soofee; Buddhist; Zoroastrian, Magi, Gymnosophist, fire-worshipper, Sabian, Gnostic, Sadducee, &c.

**Adj.** heterodox, heretical; un-orthodox, -scriptural, -canonical; antiscriptural, apocryphal; un-, anti-christian; schismatic, recusant, iconoclastic; sectarian; dis-senting, -sident; secular &c. (*lay*) 997.

pagan; heathen, -ish; ethnic, -al; gentile, painim; pan-, polytheistic; agnostic, skeptic.

Judaical, Mohammedan, Moslem, Brahminical, Buddhist &c. *n.*; Romish, Protestant &c. *n.*

bigoted &c. (*prejudiced*) 481, (*obstinate*) 606; superstitious &c. (*credulous*) 486; fanatical; idolatrous &c. 991; visionary &c. (*imaginative*) 515.

**985. Revelation.—N.** revelation, inspiration, *afflatus*.

Word, – of God; Scripture; the -Scriptures, – Bible, – Book of Books; Holy -Writ, – Scriptures; inspired writings, Gospel.

Old Testament, Septuagint, Vulgate, Pentateuch; Octateuch; the -Law, – Jewish Law, – Prophets; major –, minor- Prophets; Hagio-grapha, -logy; Hierographa; Apocrypha.

New Testament; Gospels, Evangelists, Acts, Epistles, Apocalypse, Revelations.

Talmud; Mishna, Masorah.

prophet &c. (*seer*) 513; evangelist, apostle, disciple, saint; the –, the Apostolical- fathers; Holy Men of old, inspired -writers, – penmen.

**Adj.** scriptural, biblical, sacred, prophetic; evangel-ical, -istic; apostolic, -al; inspired, theopneustic, apocalyptic, ecclesiastical canonical, textuary.

**986. Pseudo-Revelation.*—N.** the -Koran, – Alcoran; Ly-king, Shaster, Vedas, Zendavesta, Vedidad, Purana, Edda; Go-, Gau-tama; Book of Mormon.

[False prophets and religious founders] Buddha, Zoroaster, Zerdhusht, Confucius, Mahomet.

[Idols] golden calf &c. 991; Baal, Moloch, Dagon.

* See note on page 378.

## 3°. Religious Sentiments

**987. Piety.**—**N.** piety, religion, theism, faith; religiousness, holiness &c. *adj.*; saintship; religionism; sanctimony &c. (*assumed piety*) 988; reverence &c. (*respect*) 928; humility, veneration, devotion; prostration &c. (*worship*) 990; grace, unction, edification; sancti-ty, -tude; consecration.

spiritual existence, odour of sanctity, beauty of holiness.

theopathy, beatification, adoption, regeneration, conversion, justification, sanctification, salvation, inspiration, bread of life; Body and Blood of Christ.

believer, convert, theist, Christian, devotee, pietist; the -good, – righteous, – just, – believing, – elect; Saint, *Madonna.*

the children of -God, – the kingdom, – light.

**V.** be -pious &c. *adj.*; have -faith &c. *n.*; believe, receive Christ; revere &c. 928; worship &c. 990; be -converted &c.

convert, edify, sanctify, hallow, keep holy, beatify, regenerate, inspire, consecrate, enshrine.

**Adj.** pious, religious, devout, devoted, reverent, godly, heavenly minded, humble; pure, – in heart; holy, spiritual, pietistic; saint-ly, -like; seraphic, sacred, solemn.

believing, faithful, Christian, Catholic.

elected, adopted, justified, sanctified, regenerated, inspired, consecrated, converted, unearthly, not of the earth.

**988. Impiety.**—**N.** impiety; sin &c. 945; irreverence; profan-eness &c. *adj.*, -ity, -ation; blasphemy, desecration, sacrilege; scoffing &c. *v.*

[Assumed piety] hypocrisy &c. (*falsehood*) 544; pietism, cant, pious fraud; lip-devotion, -service, -reverence; misdevotion, formalism, austerity; sanctimon-y, -iousness &c. *adj.*; pharisaism, precisianism; sabbat-ism, -arianism; *odium theologicum*, sacerdotalism; bigotry &c. (*obstinacy*) 606, (*prejudice*) 481.

hardening, backsliding, declension, perversion, reprobation, apostasy, recusancy.

sinner &c. 949; scoffer, blasphemer; sacrilegist; worldling; hypocrite &c. (*dissembler*) 548; Scribes and Pharisees; Tartufe, Maw-worm.

bigot; saint [ironically]; Pharisee, sabbatarian, formalist, methodist, puritan, pietist, precisian, religionist, devotee, ranter, fanatic, wowser.

the -wicked, – evil, – unjust, – reprobate; son of -men, – Belial, – the wicked one; children of darkness.

**V.** be -impious &c. *adj.*; profane, desecrate, blaspheme, revile, scoff; swear &c. (*malediction*) 908; commit sacrilege.

snuffle; turn up the whites of the eyes; idolize.

**Adj.** impious; irreligious &c. 989; desecrating &c. *v.*; profane, irreverent, sacrilegious, blasphemous.

un-hallowed, -sanctified, -regenerate; hardened, perverted, reprobate.

hypocritical &c. (*false*) 544; canting, pietistical, sanctimonious, unctuous, pharisaical, over-righteous, righteous over much.

bigoted, fanatical &c. 481 & 606; priest-ridden.

**Adv.** under the -mask, cloak, – pretence, – form, – guise- of religion.

**989. Irreligion.**—**N.** irreligion, indevotion; ungodliness &c. *adj.*; laxity, quietism, apathy, indifference, passivity.

scepticism, doubt; un-, dis-belief; incredul-ity, -ousness &c. *adj.*; want of -faith, – belief; pyrrhonism; doubt &c. 485; agnosticism.

atheism, deism; hylotheism; materialism; positivism; nihilism.

infidelity, freethinking, antichristianity, rationalism.

atheist, anti-christian, sceptic, unbeliever, deist, infidel, pyrrhonist; *giaour*, heathen, alien, gentile, Nazarene; *esprit fort*, freethinker, latitudinarian, rationalist; materialist, positivist, nihilist, agnostic.

V. be -irreligious &c. *adj.*; disbelieve, lack faith; doubt, question &c. 485.

dechristianize; serve Mammon, love darkness better than light.

Adj. irreligious; in-, un-devout; devout-, god-, grace-less; ungodly, -holy, -sanctified, -hallowed; atheistic, without God.

sceptical, free-thinking; un-believing, -converted; incredulous, faithless, lacking faith; deistical; un-, anti-christian.

worldly, mundane, earthly, carnal, unspiritual; worldly &c.-minded.

Adv. irreligiously &c. *adj.*

## 4°. Acts of Religion

**990. Worship.—N.** worship, adoration, devotion, aspiration, latria, homage, service, humiliation; kneeling, genuflexion, prostration.

prayer, invocation, supplication, rogation, intercession, orison, holy breathing; petition &c. (*request*) 765; collect, litany, Lord's prayer, paternoster, *Ave Maria*, rosary; bead-roll; latria, dulia, hyperdulia, vigils; revival; cult.

thanksgiving; giving –, returning- thanks; grace, praise, glorification, benediction, doxology, hosanna; h-, allelujah; *Te Deum, non nobis Domine, nunc dimittis*; pæan.

psalm, -ody; hymn, plainsong, chant, chaunt, response, anthem, motet; antiphon, -y.

oblation, sacrifice, incense, libation; burnt –, votive –, thank-offering; offertory, collection.

discipline; self-discipline, -examination, -denial; fasting.

divine service, office, duty; morning prayer; mass, matins, evensong, vespers, compline; holy day &c. (*rites*) 998.

worshipper, congregation, communicant, celebrant.

**V.** worship, lift up the heart, aspire; revere &c. 928; adore, do service, pay homage; humble oneself, kneel; bow –, bend- the knee; fall -down, – on one's knees; prostrate oneself, bow down and worship, recite the rosary.

pray, invoke, supplicate; put –, offer- up -prayers, – petitions; beseech &c. (*ask*) 765; say one's prayers, tell one's beads.

return –, give- thanks; say grace, bless, praise, laud, glorify, magnify, sing praises; give benediction, lead the choir, intone, chant, sing.

propitiate, offer sacrifice, fast, deny oneself; vow, offer vows, give alms.

work out one's salvation; go to church; attend -service, – mass; communicate &c. (*rite*) 998.

**Adj.** worshipping &c. *v.*; devout, devotional, reverent, pure, solemn; fervid &c. (*heartfelt*) 821.

**Int.** h-, allelujah! hosanna! glory be to God! O Lord! pray God that! God -grant, – bless, – save, – forbid! *sursum corda*.

**991. Idolatry.—N.** idol-atry, -ism; demon-ism, -olatry; idol –, demon –, devil –, fire- worship; zoolatry, fetishism, Mari-, Bibli-, ecclesi-, heli-olatry.

deification, apotheosis, canonization; hero worship.

sacrifices, hecatomb, holocaust; human sacrifices, immolation, mactation, infanticide, self-immolation, *suttee*.

idol, golden calf, graven image, fetish, *avatar*, Juggernaut, joss, *lares et penates*; Baal &c. 986.

idolater &c. *n.*

**V.** worship -idols, – pictures, – relics; put on a pedestal, bow down to, prostrate oneself before, make sacrifice to; deify, canonize, idolize.

**Adj.** idolatrous.

**992. Sorcery.—N.** sorcery; superstition; occult -art, – sciences; black –, magic; the black art, necromancy, theurgy, thaumaturgy; demon-ology, -omy, -ship; *diablerie*, bedevilment; witch-craft, -ery; glamour; fetis-hism, -ism; ghost dance; hoodoo, voodoo; Shamanism [Esquimaux], vampirism; conjuration; bewitchery, exorcism, enchantment, incantation, obsession, possession, mysticism, second sight, mesmerism, animal magnetism; od –, odylic- force; electro-biology, *clairvoyance*; spiritualism, spirit-rapping, table-turning; thought reading, telepathy, thought transference, automatic writing, *planchette*, ouija board; crystal gazing; spirit manifestation, materialization, astral body, ectoplasm &c.

divination &c. (*prediction*) 511; sortilege, ordeal, *sortes Virgilianæ*, *-biblicæ*, hocus-pocus &c. (*deception*) 545; oracle &c. 513.

**V.** practice -sorcery &c. *n.*; cast a -horoscope, – nativity; conjure, exorcise, charm, enchant; be-witch, -devil; overlook, look on with the evil eye; entrance, mesmerize, magnetize; fascinate &c. (*influence*) 615; taboo; wave a wand; rub the -ring, – lamp; cast a spell; call up spirits, – from the vasty deep; raise spirits from the dead; raise –, lay- ghosts; command genii.

**Adj.** magic, -al; mystic, weird, cabalistic, talismanic, phylacteric, incantatory; charmed &c. *v.*

**993. Spell.—N.** spell, charm, incantation, exorcism, weird, cabala, exsufflation, cantrap, runes, abracadabra, hocus-pocus, open *sesame*, counter-charm, Ephesian letters, bell, book and candle, Mumbo Jumbo, evil-eye, fee-faw-fum.

talisman, amulet, periapt, telesm, phylactery, philtre, wish-bone, merry-thought, mascot, scarab, swastika; fetish; *agnus Dei*.

wand, caduceus, rod, divining rod, lamp of Aladdin, magic carpet, seven-league boots; magic ring; wishing –, Fortunatus's- cap.

**994. Sorcerer.—N.** sorcerer, magician; thaumat-, the-urgist; conjuror, necromancer, seer, wizard, witch; fairy &c. 980; *lamia*, hag, warlock, charmer, exorcist, voodoo, mage, diviner, dowser; cunning –, medicine- man, witch doctor; Shaman, figure-flinger, ecstatica, medium, *clairvoyant*, mesmerist, hypnotist; *deus ex machinâ*; astrologer; soothsayer &c. 513.

Katerfelto, Cagliostro, Merlin, Comus, Mesmer; Hecate, Circe, Lilith, siren, weird sisters; witch of Endor.

## 5°. Religious Institutions

**995. Churchdom.—N.** church, -dom; ministry, apostleship, priesthood, prelacy, hierarchy, church government, christendom, pale of the church.

clerical-, sacerdotal-, episcopalian-, ultramontan-ism; Theocracy· ecclesiolog-y, -ist; priestcraft, *odium theologicum*.

monach-ism, -y; monasticism, monkhood.

[Ecclesiastical offices and dignities] pontificate, primacy, arch bishopric, archiepiscopacy; prelacy; bishop-ric, -dom; episcop-ate -acy; see, diocese; deanery, stall; canon-ry, -icate; prebend, -aryship· benefice, incumbency, glebe, advowson, living, cure, – of souls; rector ship; vicar-iate, -ship; pastor-ate, -ship; deacon-ry, -ship; -curacy· chaplain, -cy, -ship; cardinal-ate, -ship; abbacy, presbytery.

holy orders, ordination, institution, consecration, induction, reading in, preferment, translation, presentation.

popedom, papacy; the -Vatican, – apostolic see, – see of Rome; religious sects &c. 984.

council &c. 696; conclave, college of cardinals, convocation, synod, consistory, chapter, vestry, presbytery; sanhedrim, *congé d'élire* ecclesiastical courts, consistorial court, court of Arches.

**V.** call, ordain, induct, prefer, translate, consecrate, present, elect· bestow.

take -orders, – the veil, – vows.

**Adj.** ecclesi-astical, -ological; clerical, sacerdotal, priestly, prelatical pastoral, ministerial, capitular, theocratic; hierarchical, archiepiscopal· episcopal, -ian; canonical; mon-astic, -achal; monkish; abbati-al, -cal· pontifical, papal, apostolic; ultramontane, priest-ridden.

**996. Clergy.—N.** clergy, clericals, ministry, priesthood, presbytery, the cloth, the pulpit.

clergyman, divine, ecclesiastic, churchman, priest, presbyter, hierophant, pastor, shepherd, minister, clerk in holy orders; father, – in Christ; *padre, abbé, curé*; patriarch; reverend; black coat; confessor; sky pilot.

dignitaries of the church; ecclesi-, hier-arch; eminence, reverence, elder, primate, metropolitan, archimandrite, archbishop, bishop, prelate, diocesan, suffragan, dean, subdean, archdeacon, prebendary, canon, rural dean, rector, parson, vicar, perpetual curate, residentiary, beneficiary, incumbent, chaplain, curate, – in charge; deacon, -ess; preacher; lay reader, lecturer; capitular; missionary, propagandist, Jesuit, revivalist, field preacher.

churchwarden, sidesman; clerk, precentor, choir; almoner, *suisse*, verger, beadle, sexton, sacristan; acol-yth, -othyst, -yte; thurifer; chorister, choir boy.

[Roman Catholic priesthood] Pope, *Papa*, Holy Father, pontiff, high priest, cardinal; ancient –, flamen; confessor, penitentiary; spiritual director.

cenobite, conventual, abbot, prior, monk, friar, lay brother, beadsman, mendicant, pilgrim, palmer; canon-regular, -secular; Jesuit, Franciscan, Friars minor, Minorites; Observant, Capuchin, Dominican, Carmelite; Augustinian; Gilbertine; Austin-, Black-, White-, Grey-, Crossed-, Crutched-Friars; Bonhomme, Carthusian, Benedictine, Cistercian, Trappist, Cluniac, Premonstratensian, Maturine; Templar, Hospitaller.

**997. Laity.—N.** laity, flock, fold, congregation, assembly, brethren, people.

temporality, secularization.

layman, civilian; parishioner, catechumen; secularist.

**V.** secularize.

**Adj.** secular, lay, laical, civil, temporal, profane.

abb-, prior-, canon-ess; mother superior; *religieuse*, nun, sister, *béguine*, novice, postulant.

[Under the Jewish dispensation] prophet, priest, high priest, Levite; Rabbi, -n; scribe.

[Mohammedan &c.] mullah, ulema, imaum, sheik; so-fi, -phi; mufti, hadji, muezzin, dervish; fa-kir, -quir; brahmin, gooroo, druid, bonze, santon, abdal, Lama, talapoin, caloyer &c.

**V.** take orders &c. 995.

**Adj.** the –, the very –, the Right- Reverend; ordained, in orders, called to the ministry.

**998. Rite.—N.** rite; ceremon-y, -ial; ordinance, observance, function, duty; form, -ulary; solemnity, sacrament; incantation &c. (*spell*) 993; service, psalmody &c. (*worship*) 990; liturgies.

ministration; preach-ing, -ment; predication, sermon, homily, exhortation, lecture, discourse, pastoral.

baptism, christening, chrism, immersion; baptismal regeneration; font; circumcision.

confirmation; imposition –, laying on- of hands; churching, purification, ordination &c. (*churchdom*) 995; excommunication.

Eucharist, Lord's supper, communion; the –, the holy- sacrament; celebration, high celebration; *missa cantata*; offertory; introit; consecration; con-, tran-substantiation; real presence; elements, bread and wine; mass; high –, low –, dry- mass.

matrimony &c. 903; burial &c. 363; visitation of the sick.

seven sacraments, impanation extreme unction, last rites, *viaticum*, invocation of saints, canonization, transfiguration, auricular confession; fasting; maceration, flagellation, sackcloth and ashes; penance &c. (*atonement*) 952; absolution; telling of beads, reciting the rosary, processional; thurification, incense, holy water, aspersion.

relics, rosary, beads, reliquary, host, cross, rood, crucifix, pax, pix, pyx, *agnus Dei*, censer, thurible, patera, urceole; chalice, patten, Holy Grail, sangrail; seven-branch candle stick, monstrance, sacring bell.

ritual, rubric, canon, ordinal; liturgy, prayer-book, book of common prayer, pietas, euchology, litany, lectionary; missal, breviary, mass-book, bead-roll.

psalter; psalm –, hymn- book; hymn-al, -ology; psalmody.

ritual-, ceremonial-ism; sabbat-ism, -arianism; ritualist, sabbatarian.

holyday, feast, fast; Sabbath, Passover, Pentecost; Advent, Christmas, Noël, Epiphany, Lent, Shrove Tuesday, Ash Wednesday, Maundy Thursday; Passion –, Holy- week; Good Friday, Easter, Ascension Day, Whitsuntide; Trinity Sunday, Corpus Christi; All-Saints' –, – Souls'- Day; Candle-, Lam-, Martin-, Michael-mas; hogmanay; Rama-dan, -zan; Bairam &c. &c.

**V.** perform service, do duty, minister, officiate, baptize, dip, sprinkle; confirm. lay hands on; give –, administer –, take –, receive –. attend –, partake of- the -sacrament, – communion; communicate; celebrate mass; administer –, receive- extreme unction; anele, shrive, absolve, confess; do penance; genuflect; cross oneself, make the sign of the cross.

excommunicate, ban with bell, book and candle.

preach, sermonize, predicate, lecture.

**Adj.** ritual, -istic; ceremonial, liturgic; baptismal, eucharistical; paschal.

**999. Canonicals.—N.** canonicals, vestments; robe, gown, Geneva gown, frock, pallium, surplice, cassock, dalmatic, scapulary, cope. scarf, tunicle, chasuble, alb, *alba*, stole; fan-on, -nel; tonsure, cowl, hood; calo-te, -tte; bands; capouch, amice, orarium, ephod; apron, lawn sleeves, pontificals, pall; mitre, tiara, triple crown; shovel –, cardinal's-hat; biretta; crosier; pastoral staff; costume &c. 225.

**1000. Temple.—N.** place of worship; house of -God, – prayer.

temple, cathedral, minster, church, kirk, chapel, meeting-house, bethel, tabernacle, conventicle, *basilica*, fane, holy place, chantry, oratory.

synagogue; mosque; marabout; pantheon; pagoda; joss-house; dagobah, tope; kiosk.

parsonage, rectory, vicarage, manse, deanery, glebe, church house; Vatican; bishop's palace; Lambeth.

altar, shrine, sanctuary, Holy of Holies, *sanctum sanctorum*, sacrarium, -isty; communion –, holy –, Lord's- table; table of the Lord; pyx; baptistery, font; piscina, stoup; aumbry; sedile; reredos; rood -loft, – screen; jube.

chancel, quire, choir, nave, aisle, transept, lady chapel, vestry, crypt, cloisters, porch; triforum, clerestory, churchyard, *golgotha*, calvary, Easter sepulchre; stall, pew, sitting; pulpit, ambo, lectern, reading-desk, confessional, prothesis, credence, baldachin, *baldacchino*; jesse, apse, belfry; chapter-house; presbytery.

monastery, priory, abbey, friary, convent, nunnery, cloister.

**Adj.** claustral, cloistered; monast-ic, -erial; conventual.

# INDEX

N.B.: The numbers refer to the headings under which the words or phrases occur. When the same word or phrase may be used in various senses, the several headings under which it, or its synonyms, will be found, according to those meanings, are indicated by the words printed in Italics. These words in Italics are not intended to explain the meaning of the word or phrase to which they are annexed, but only to assist in the required reference.

When the word given in the Index is itself the title or heading of a category, the number of reference is printed in blacker type, thus: abode **189.**

---

*relevant* 23
*receivable* 296
*tolerable* 651
– in society 852
**admit**
*composition* 54
*include* 76
*let in* 296
*assent* 488
*acknowledge* 529
*permit* 760
*concede* 762
*accept* 785
– exceptions 469
– of 470
**admitted**
*customary* 613
– maxim &c. 496
**admixture 41**
**admonish**
*warn* 668
*advise* 695
*reprove* 932
**ado** *activity* 682
*exertion* 686
*difficulty* 704
make much – about 642
much – about nothing
*overestimate* 482
*unimportant* 643
*unskilful* 699
**adolescence 131**
**Adonis 845**
**adonize 847**
**adopt**
*naturalize* 184
*choose* 609
– a cause *aid* 707
– a course 692
– an opinion 484
**adoption**
*religious* 987
**adore** 897, 990
**adorn** 847
**adown** 207
**adrift** *unrelated* 10
*disjoined* 44
*dispersed* 73
*uncertain* 475
*unapt* 699
*free* 750
go – *deviate* 279
turn – *disperse* 73
*liberate* 750
*dismiss* 756
**adroit** 698
**adscititious**
*extrinsic* 6
*added* 37
*redundant* 641
**adscriptus glebæ** 746
**adulation** 933
**adulator** 935
**Adullam, cave of –** 624, 832
**Adullamite** 832
**adult** 131
**adulterate** *mix* 41
*deteriorate* 659
**adulterated** 545
**adulterer** 962
**adultery** 961
**adumbrate**
*darkness* 421
*allegorize* 521
*represent* 554
**adumbration**
*semblance* 21
*allusion* 526
**aduncity** 244, 245
**adust**
*colour* 433
*gloomy* 837
**adustion** 384
**advance** *increase* 35
*course* 109
*progress* 282
*assert* 535
*improve* 658
*aid* 707
*succeed* 731
*lend* 787
in – *precedence* 62
*front* 234
*precession* 280
in – of 33
in – of one's age 498
– against 716
– of learning &c. 490
**advanced** 282
– in life 128
– guard 234
– student 541
– work 717
**advances, make –**
*offer* 763
*social* 892
**advantage**
*superiority* 33
*influence* 175
*good* 618
*expedience* 646
mechanical – 633
dressed to – 847
find one's – in 644
gain an – 775
set off to – 658
take – of 677, 698
– over *success* 731
**advantageous**
*beneficial* 648
*profitable* 775
**advene** 37
**advent**
*futurity* 121
*event* 151
*approach* 286
*arrival* 292
**Advent** 998
**adventism** 984
**adventitious** 6, 156
**adventive** 156
**adventure** *event* 151
*chance* 156
*pursuit* 622
*danger* 665
*trial* 675
the great – 360
**adventurer**
*traveller* 268
*deceiver* 548
*experimenter* 463
*gambler* 621
*rash* 863
*ignoble* 876
**adventures** 594
**adventurous**
*undertaking* 676
*bold* 861
*rash* 863
**adversaria** 551
**adversary** 710
**adverse**
*contrary* 14
*opposed* 708
*unprosperous* 735
*disliking* 867
– party 710
**adversity 735**
**advert** 457
**advertise** 531
**advice** *notice* 527
*news* 532
*counsel* **695**
**advisable** 646
**advise** *predict* 511
*inform* 527
*counsel* 695
– with one's pillow 451
**advised** *predetermined* 611
*intended* 620
better – 658
**adviser** 540, 695
**advocacy** 931
**advocate**
*prompt* 615
*recommend* **695**
*aid* 707
*auxiliary* **711**
*friend* 890
*vindicate* 937
*counsellor* 968
**Advocate, the – 976**
**advocation** 617
**advoutress** 962
**advoutry** 961
**advowson** 995
**adynamic** 160
**adytum** *room* **191**
*prediction* 511
*secret place* **530**
**adze** 253
**adzooks** 870
**ædile** 965
**ægis** 717
**ægrescit medendo** 659
**ægrotat** 927*a*
**æolian** 349
– harp 417
**æon** 976
**æquam servare mentem** 826
**æquo animo 823,** 826
**aerate** 334, 353
**ære perennius 873**
**aerial** 273
*elevated* 206
*flying* 267
*gas* 334
*air* 338
– navigation **267**
– navigator **269**
– mail 534
– patrol 726
– perspective **428**
– warfare 722
**aerie** 189
**aerify** 334
**aerodonetics 267**
**aerodrome** 728
**aerodynamics 267** 334, 349
**aerolite** 318
**aerology** 338
**aeromancy** 511
**aeromechanics 267**
**aerometer** 338
**aeronaut** 269
**aeronautical 273**
**aeronautics 267,** 338
**aeroplane** 273
**aerostat** *balloon* **273**
**aerostatics** 267, **334**
**aerostation 338**

**aery** 317
**Æsculapius** 662
**Æsop** 846
**æsthetic**
*sensibility* 375
*beauty* 845
*taste* 850
**æstival** 125
**æternum servans sub pectore vulnus** 919
**ætiology** [*see* etiology]
**afar** 196
**affable** 879, 894
**affair** *event* 151
*topic* 454
*business* 625
*battle* 720
*love* 902, 903
– of honour 720
**affaires, chargé d'** – 758
**affaire de cœur** 897
**affect** *relate to* 9
*tend to* 176
*qualify* 469
*feign* 544
*touch* 824
*desire* 865
*love* 897
**affectation** **855**
**affected with**
*feeling* 821
*disease* 655
**affectibility** 822
**affecting** 830
**affection** 821, 897
**affections** **820**
**affettuoso** 415
**affiance** 768, 858
**affianced** 897, 903
**affiche** 531
**affidation** 769
**affidavit**
*affirmation* 535
*record* 551
*lawsuit* 969
**affiliation**
*relation* 9
*kindred* 11
*attribution* 155
**affine** 11
**affinitive** 9
**affinity** 9, 17
*mate* 903
**affirmation** **535**, 488
**affix** *add* 37
*sequel* 39
*fasten* 43
*letter* 561
**afflation** 349
**afflatus** 349, 597, 985
**afflict** 830
– with illness 655
**affliction** *pain* 828
*infliction* 830
*adversity* 735
**affluence**
*sufficiency* 639
*prosperity* 734
*wealth* 803
**affluent** *river* 348
**afflux** 286
**afford** *supply* 784
*wealth* 803
*yield* 810
*sell for* 812
– aid &c. 707
**afforestation** 371
**affranchise**
*make free of* 748
*liberate* 750
**affray** 720
**affreet** 980
**affriction** 331
**affright** 860
**affront** *molest* 830
*provocation* 900
*insult* 929
– danger 861
**affuse** 337
**afield** 186
**afire** 382
**afloat** *extant* 1
*unstable* 149
*going on* 151
*ship* 273
*navigation* 267
*ocean* 341
*news* 532
*preparing* 673
keep oneself – 734
set – *publish* 531
**afoot** *on hand* 625
*preparing* 673
*astir* 682
**afore** 116
**aforementioned** 116
**aforesaid**
*preceding* 62
*repeated* 104
*prior* 116
**aforethought** 611
**aforetime** 116
**afraid** 860
be – *irresolute* 605
– to say *uncertain* 475
**afresh** 104, 123
**Afric heat** 382
**Afrikander** 57
**afrite** 980
**aft** 235
**after** *in order* 63
*in time* 117
*too late* 135
*rear* 235
*pursuit* 622
be – *intention* 620
*pursuit* 622
go – *follow* 281
– all *for all that* 30
*qualification* 469
*on the whole* 476
– time 133
**after acceptation** 516
**after-age** 124
**after-clap** 509
**after-crop** 65, 168
**after-dinner** 117
**after-glow** 40, 65, 420
**after-growth** 65
**after-life** 152
**aftermath**
*sequel* 65
*fertile* 168
*profit* 775
**aftermost** 235
**afternoon** 126
– farmer 683
**after-part** 65, 235
**after-piece** 599
**after-taste** 65, 390
**after-thought**
*thought* 451
*memory* 505
*change of mind* 607
**after-time** 121
**afterwards** 117
**aga** 745
**agacerie** 615
**again** 90, 104
– and again 136
come – *periodic* 138
fall off – 661
live – 660
**against**
*counteraction* 179
*anteposition* 237
*provision* 673
*voluntary opposition* 708
chances – 473
declaim – 932
false witness – 934
go – 708
set – *actively* 898
set one's face – 764, 932
stand up – *resist* 719
raise &c. one's voice – 489
– one's will 744
– one's expectation 508
– the grain *difficult* 704
*painful* 830
*dislike* 867
– the stream **704**
– the time when 510
– one's will **744**
– one's wishes **603**
**agamist** 904
**agape** *open* 260
*curious* 455
*expectant* 507
*wonder* 870
**Agapemone** **827**, 897
**agate** 847
**age** *time* 106
*period* 108
*long time* 110
*era* 114
*present time* **118**
*oldness* 124
*advanced life* **128**
of – 131
from age to – 112
**age quod agis!** 682
**agency**
*physical* **170**
*instrumentality* 631
*means* 632
*employment* 677
*voluntary action* 680
*direction* 693
*commission* 755
**agenda** 625, 626
**agent** *physical* 153
*intermediary* 228
*voluntary* **690**
*consignee* 758
– provocateur **615**
**agentship** 755
**ages:** for – 110
– ago 122
**agglomerate** 46, **72**
**agglutinate** 46
**aggrandize**
*in degree* 35
*in bulk* 194
*honour* 873
**aggravate**

*increase* 35
*vehemence* 173
*exaggerate* 549
*render worse* 659
*distress* 835
*exasperate* 900
**aggravating** 830
**aggravation** **835**
**aggregate** 50, 72, 84
**aggregation** 46
**aggression** 716
**aggressor** 726
**aggrieve** 649, 830
**aggroup** 72
**aghast**
*disappointed* 509
*fear* 860
*wonder* 870
**agile** 274, 682
**agio** 813
**agiotage** 794
**agitate** *move* 315
*inquire* 461
*activity* 682
*excite the feelings* 824
– a question 476
**agitation** [*see* agitate]
*changeableness* 149
*energy* 171
*motion* **315**
in – *preparing* 673
**agitator** *leader* 694
**aglet** 554
**agley, gang** – 732
**aglow** 382, 420
**agnate** 11
**agnition** 762
**agnomen** 564
**agnostic** 487
**agnosticism** 984, 989
**agnus Dei** 993, 998
**ago** 122
not long – 123
**agog** *expectant* 507
*desire* 865
*wonder* 870
**agoing** 682
set – 707
**agonism** 720
**agonizing** 824, 830
**agony** 378, 828
– of death 360
– of excitement 825
**agrarian** 371
**agree** *accord* 23
*concur* 178
*assent* 488
*concord* 714
*consent* 762
*compact* 769
*compromise* 774
– in opinion 488
– with *salubrity* 656
**agreeable**
*comfortable* 82
*physically* 377
*mentally* 829
**agreeably to** 82
**agreement** **23** [*see* agree]
*compact* 769
**agrestic** 371
**agriculture** **371**
**agronomy** 371
**aground** *fixed* 150
*in difficulty* 704
*failure* 732
**ague-fit** 860
**aguets, aux** –
*expectation* 507
*ambush* 530
**aguish** *cold* 383
**ah me!** 839
**aha!** *rejoicing* 838
**ahead** 234, 280
go – *progression* 282
shoot – *transcursion* 303
*activity* 682
rock – 665, 667
**Ahrimanes** 978, 980
**aid** **707**, 906
by the – of 631, 632
**aide-de-camp** 711, 745
**aidless** 160
**aigrette** 847
**aiguille** 253
**aiguillette** 747, 847
**aigulet** 847
**ail** 655, 828
**aileron** 267, 273
**ailment** 655
**aim** 278, 620, 675
– a blow at 716
**aimable** 894
faire l' – 897
**aimer éperdument** 897
**aimless** *without motive* 615a
*chance* 621
**air** *unsubstantial* 4
*broach* 66
*lightness* 320
*gas* 334
*atmospheric* **338**
*wind* 349
*tune* 415
*appearance* 448
*refresh* 689
*demeanour* 692
*fashionable* 852
beat the – 645
fill the – 404
fine – *salubrity* 656
fish in the – 645
fowls of the – 366
in the – 527
rend the – 404
take – 531
**air-balloon** 273
**air base** 728
**air-commodore** 745
**aircraft** 273, 726
**air-drawn** 515
**airdrome** 273
**air-force** 726
**air-gun** 727
**airing** 266
**air-mail** 273
**airman** 269
**airmanship** 698
**air-marshal** 745
**air-passage** 351
**air-pipe** **351**
**airport** 273, 292, 728
**air-pump** 349
**air-raid** 716
**airs** *affectation* 855
*pride* 878
*vanity* 880
*arrogance* 885
**air-shaft** 351
**air service** 267
**airship** 273, 726
**air-tight** 261
**airways** 267
**airworthy** 273, 664
**airy** [*see* air]
*windy* 349
*unimportant* 643
*gay* 836
– hopes 858, 859
give to – nothing a local habitation &c. 515
**aisle** *passage* 260
*way* 627
*in a church* 1000
**ait** 346
**ajar** *open* 260
*discordant* 713
**ajee** 217
**ajutage** 260, 350
**akimbo** *angular* 244
stand – 715
**akin** *related* 9
*consanguineous* 11
*similar* 17
**al fresco** 220
**alabaster** *white* **430**
**alack!** 839
**alacrity** *willing* 602
*active* 682
*cheerful* 836
**Aladdin's lamp** **993**
**alar** 267
**alarm** *warning* 668
*notice of danger* **669**
*fear* 860
cause for – 665
give an – *indicate* 550
**alarmist** 862
**alarum** 114, 550, **669**
**alas!** 839
**alate** 267
**alb** 999
**albeit** 30
**albert**
*chain* 847
**albification** 430
**albinescence** 430
**albinism** 430
**albino** 443
**album** 593, 596
**albumen**
*semi-liquid* **352**
*protein* 357
**Alcaic** 597
**alcaid** 745
**alcalde** 745
**alcazar** 189
**alchemy** 144
**alcohol** 959
**Alcoran** 986
**alcove** 191, 252
**Aldebaran** 423
**alderman** 745
**ale** 298
**alea, jacta est** – **601**
**aleatory** 665
**Alecto** 173
**alectryomancy** **511**
**alehouse** 189
go to the – **959**
**alembic**
*conversion* **144**
*vessel* 191
*furnace* 386
*laboratory* **691**
**alentours** 197
**alert** *watchful* **457**,

459
*active* 682
**alerte** 669
**aleuromancy** 511
**Alexandrine**
*ornate style* 577
*verse* 597
**alexandrite** 847
**alexipharmic** 662
**alexiteric** 662
**algebra** 85
**algid** 383
**algology** 369
**algorithm** 85
**alguazil** 965
**alias**
*otherwise* 18
*pseudonym* 565
**alibi** 187
**alien** *irrelevant* 10
*foreign* 57
*transfer* 783
*gentile* 989
**alienable** 783
**alienate**
*transfer* 783
*estrange* 44, 889
*set against* 898
**alienation**
mental – 503
**alieni appetens**
*grasping* 865
*envious* 921
*selfish* 943
**alienism** 57
**alight** *stop* 265
*arrive* 292
*descend* 306
*on fire* 382
**align** 278
**alike** 17
share and share – 778
**aliment** *food* 298
**alimentary** 662
– canal 350
**alimentation**
*aid* 707
**alimony**
*property* 780
*provision* 803
*income* 810
**aliquot** 51, 84
**aliter visum, dis** – 601
**alive**
*living* 359
*intelligent* 498
*active* 682
*cheerful* 836
be – with 102
keep – *continue* 143
keep the memory – 505
look – 684
– to *attention* 457
*cognizant* 490
*informed* 527
*able* 698
*sensible* 822
**alkahest** 335
**all** *whole* 50
*complete* 52
*generality* 78
– absorbing 642
in – ages 112
– abroad 495
– agog 865
– in all 50
– along 106
– along of 154
– but 32
– colours 440
– considered 451, 480
– day long 110
– devouring 789
in – directions 278
– engulfing 789
at – events *compensation* 30
*qualification* 469
*true* 494
*resolve* 604
– fours *easy* 705
*cards* 840
– in good time 152
– hail! *welcome* 292
*honour to* 873
*celebration* 883
*courtesy* 894
– hands *everybody* 78
on – hands 488
– of a dither 824
– of a heap 72
– knowing 976
– manner of *difference* 15
*multiform* 81
with – one's might 686
– at once 113
– one 27, 866
– out 52
– over *end* 67
*universal* 78
*destruction* 162
*space* 180
at – points 52
– in one's power 686
– powerful
*mighty* 159
*God* 976
in – quarters 180
with – respect 928
in – respects 52, 494
– right! 922
– Saints' day 998
– searching 461
– seeing 976
on – sides 227
– sorts *diverse* 16a
*mixed* 41
*multiform* 81
– talk 4
– things to all men 894
– the time 106
at – times 136
– together 50
– ways 243, 279
– wise 976
– the world and his wife 78
of – work
*useful* 644
*maid* - 746
**Allah** 979
**allay**
*moderate* 174
*pacify* 723
*relieve* 834
– excitability 826
**allective** 615
**allege** *evidence* 467
*assert* 535
*plea* 617
**allegiance** 743, 926
**allegory** 464, 521, 594
**allegro** *music* 415
*cheerful* 836
**allelujah** 990
**allemande** 840
**all-embracing** 76
**alleviate** 174, 834
**alley** *court* 189
*passage* 260
*way* 627
**alliance** *relation* 9
*kindred* 11
*physical co-operation* 178
*voluntary co-operation* 709
*party* 712
*union* 714
**allied to** *like* 17
**alligation** 43
**allign** 278
**alliteration**
*similarity* 17
*style in writing* 577
*poetry* 597
**allocation** 60, 786
**allocution** 586
**allodium** *free* 748
*property* 780
**allopathy** 662
**alloquy** 586
**allot** *arrange* 60
*distribute* 786
*due* 924
**allow** *assent* 488
*admit* 529
*permit* 760
*consent* 762
*give* 784
– to have one's own way 740
**allowable** 760, 924
**allowance**
*qualification* 469
*gift* 784
*allotment* 786
*discount* 813
*salary* 973
with grains of – 485
make – for *forgive* 918
*vindicate* 937
**alloy** *mixture* 41
*combination* 48
*debase* 659
**allude** *hint* 514
*mean* 516
*refer to* 521
*latent* 526
*inform* 527
**allure** *move* 615
*create desire* 865
**alluring** 829
**allusive**
*relative* 9
**alluvial** *level* 213
*land* 342
*plain* 344
**alluvium**
*deposit* 40
*land* 342
*soil* 653
**ally** *combine* 48
*auxiliary* 711
*friend* 890
**alma mater** 542
**almanac**
*list* 86
*chronometry* 114

*record* 551
**almighty** 157
**Almighty, the** – 976
**almoner**
*treasurer* 801
*giver* 784
*church officer* 996
**almonry** 802
**almost** *nearly* 32
*not quite* 651
– all 50
– immediately 132
**alms** *gift* 784
*benevolence* 906
*worship* 990
**almshouse** 189, 666
**almsman** 785
**Alnaschar's dream** 515, 858
**aloes** 395
**aloft** 206
**alogy** 497
**alone** *single* 87
*unaided* 706
let – *not use* 678
*not restrain* 748
**along** 200
get – *progress* 282
go – *depart* 293
go – with *concur* 178
*assent* 488
*co-operate* 709
– of *caused by* 154
– with *added* 37
*together* 88
*by means of* 631
**alongside** *near* 197
*parallel* 216
*laterally* 236
**aloof** *distant* 196
*high* 206
*secluded* 893
stand – *inaction* 681
*refuse* 764
*cautious* 864
**alopecia** 226
**aloud** 404
think – 589
*naïveté* 703
**Alp** 206
**alpenstock** 215
**Alpha** 66
– and Omega 50
**alphabet**
*beginning* 66
*letters* 561
**alphabetarian** 541
**alphabeticize** 60
**Alphitomancy** 511
**alpine** *high* 206
**Alpine Club** 268, 305
**already**
*antecedently* 116
*even now* 118
*past time* 122
**Alsatia** 791, 945
**also** 37
**altar** 903, 1000
**alter** 140
– the case 468
– one's course 279
**alter ego** *similar* 17
*auxiliary* 711
*deputy* 759
*friend* 890
**alterable** 149
**alteram partem, audire** – 468, 922
**alterative**
*substitute* 634
*remedy* 662
**altercation** 713
**altered** *worn* 688
– for the worse 659
**alternate**
*reciprocal* 12
*sequence* 63
*discontinuous* 70
*periodic* 138
*changeable* 149
*oscillate* 314
**alternative**
*substitute* 147
*choice* 609
*plan* 626
**although**
*compensation* 30
*counteraction* 179
*unless* 469
**altiloquence** 577
**altimetry**
*height* 206
*angle* 244
*measurement* 466
**altitude** *height* 206
– and azimuth 466
**alto** 410, 416
– part 415
**alto-rilievo** 250, 557
**altogether** 50, 52
*nude* 226
**altruism** 910, 942
**altruist** 906
**alum** 397
**alumnus** 541
**alveolus** 252
**always**
*uniformly* 16
*generally* 78
*during* 106
*perpetually* 112
*habitually* 613
**a.m.** 114, 125
**amah** 753
**amain** 173, 684
**amalgam, -ate** 41, 48
**amalgamation** 709
**Amalthæa's horn** 639
**amantium iræ** 918
**amanuensis** 553, 590
**amaranthine** 112
**amari aliquid**
*bad* 649
*imperfect* 651
*painful* 830
**amaritude** 395
**amass** *whole* 50
*collect* 72
*store* 636
**amateur** *volunteer* 602
*layman* 699
*taste* 850
*votary* 865
**amatory** 897
**amaurosis** 442
**amaze** 870
**amazingly** 31
**Amazon**
*woman* 374
*warrior* 726
*courage* 861
**ambages**
*convolutions* 248
*circumlocution* 573
*circuit* 629
**ambagious** 573
**ambassador**
*messenger* 534
*representative* 758
recall of –s 713
**amber** 356*a*
– colour 436
**ambidexter**
*right and left* 238
*fickle* 607
*clever* 698
**ambient** 227
**ambigu** 41
**ambiguas spargere voces**
*uncertain* 475
*misteach* 538
*false* 544
*cunning* 702
**ambiguous**
*uncertain* 475
*unintelligible* 519
*equivocal* 520
*obscure* 571
**ambiloquy** 520
**ambit** 230
**ambition** 620, 865
**ambivalence** 605, 708
**amble** 266
**ambo** *school* 542
*pulpit* 1000
**ambo, Arcades** –
*alike* 17
*friends* 890
*bad men* 949
**ambrosia** 298
**ambrosial** 394, 490
**ambulance**
*vehicle* 272
*hospital* 662
**ambulation** 266
**ambuscade** 530
**ambush** 530, 667
lie in – 528
**âme – de boue** 949
– damnée
*catspaw* 711
*servant* 746
*servile* 886
*bad man* 949
– qui vive 101, 187
**ameer** 875
**ameliorate** 658
**amen** *assent* 488
*submission* 725
*content* 831
**amenable** 177, 602, 926
not – to reason 608
**amend** 658
**amendatory** 20
**amende honorable** 952
**amends**
*compensation* 50
*atonement* 952
*reward* 973
**amenity** 829, 894
**amentia** 503
**amerce** 974
**American organ** 417
**Americanism** 563
**amethyst**
*purple* 437
*jewel* 847
**amiable**
*courteous* 894
*loving* 897
*kind* 906
**amiability** 829, 894
**amicable** 707, 888

**angular** 244
– velocity 264
**angularity 244**
**angusta domi, res** – 804
**angustation** 203
**anhelation** 688
**anhydrate** 340
**anhydrous** 340
**aniline dyes** 437
**anility** 128, 499
**animadvert**
*consider* 451
*attend to* 457
*reprehend* 932
**animal 366**
female – 374
– cries 412
– economy 359
– gratification 377
– life 364
– physiology 368
– spirits 836
– and vegetable kingdom 357
**animalcule** 193, 366
**animalism**
*sensuality* 954
**animality 364**
**animate**
*induce* 615
*excite* 824
*enliven* 836
**animation**
*life* 359
*animality* 364
*activity* 682
*vivacity* 836
suspended – 823
**animism** 984
**animo,** ex – 602
quo – 620
**animosity**
*dislike* 867
*enmity* 889
*hatred* 898
*anger* 900
**animus**
*willingness* 602
*intention* 620
*desire* 865
**ankle** 244
– deep 208, 209
**anklet** 847
**ankylosis** 150
**annalist** 114, 553
**annals**
*chronology* 114
*record* 551
*account* 594
**anneal** 673
**annex**
*addition* 37
*adjunct* 39
*junction* 43
*acquire* 775
**Annie Oakley** 815
**annihilate** 2, 162
**anniversary** 138
**anno** 106
**Anno Domini**
*era* 106
*old age* 124
**annotation** 522, 550
**annotator** 524
*scholar* 492
*interpreter* 524
*editor* 595
**annotto** 434
**announce**
*predict* 511
*inform* 527
*publish* 531
*assert* 535
**announcer** 527
**annoy**
*molest* 649, 907
*disquiet* 830
**annoyance** 828
source of – 830
**annual** *periodic* 138
*plant* 367
*book* 593
**annuity** 810
**annul** 162, 756
**annular** 247
**annunciate** 527
**annus magnus** 108
**anodyne**
*lenitive* 174
*remedial* 662
*relief* 834
**anoint** *coat* 223
*lubricate* 332
*oil* 355
**anointed**
*deity* 976
*king* 745
**anomaly**
*disorder* 59
*irregularity* 83
**anon** 132
**anonymous** 565
**anopsia** 442
**anorexy** 866
**another**
*different* 15
*repetition* 104
– story 468, 526
go upon – tack 607
– time 119
**answer**
*to an inquiry* **462**
*confute* 479
*solution* 522
*succeed* 731
*pecuniary profit* 775
*pleadings* 969
require an – 461
– for *deputy* 759
*promise* 768
*go bail* 806
I'll – for it 535
– the helm 743
– the purpose 731
– to *correspond* 9
– one's turn 644
**answerable**
*agreement* **23**
*liable* 177
*bail* 806
*duty* 926
*censurable* **932**
**ant** 690
**Antæus** 159, 192
**antagonism**
*difference* 14
*physical* 179
*voluntary* 708
*enmity* 889
**antagonist** 710, 891
**antagonistic** 24
**antarctic** 237
**antecedence** 62, 116
**antecedent** 64
**antechamber** 191
**ante Christum** 106
**antedate** 115
**antediluvian** 124
**antelope** 274
**antemundane** 124
**antenna** 379
**anteposition** 62
**anterior**
*in order* 62
*in time* 116
*in place* 234
– to reason 477
**anteroom** 191
**antevert** 706
**anthem** 990
**anthemion** 847
**anthology**
*book* 593
*collection* 596
*poem* 597
**anthracite** 388
**anthropoid** 372
**anthropology**
*zoology* 368
*mankind* 372
**anthropomancy 511**
**anthropophagi** 913
**anthroposcopy** 511
**anthroposophy** 372
**anti-aircraft gun** 564, 727
**antic** 840
**antichambre,** faire – 133
**antichristian 984,** 989
**antichronism 115**
**anticipate**
*anachronism* **115**
*priority* 116
*future* 121
*early* 132
*expect* **507**
*foresee* 510
*prepare* **673**
*hope* 858
*in* – 116
**anticlimax**
*decrease* **36**
*bathos* 497, **853**
**anticlinal** 217
**anticyclone** 265
**antidote** 662
**antigropelos** 225
**antilogarithm** 84
**antilogy** 477
**antimony** 663
**Antinomian** 984
**antinomy** 964
**Antinous** 845
**antiparallel** 217
**antipathy** 867, **898**
**antiphon** *music* **415**
*answer* 462
*worship* 990
**antiphrasis** 563
**antipodes**
*difference* 14
*distance* 196
*contraposition* 237
**antipoison** 662
**antiquary**
*past times* 122
*scholar* 492
*historian* 553
**antiquas vias,** stare super – 613, 670
**antiquated** 128
**antique** 124
**antiquity** 122
**antiscriptural** 984
**antiseptic** 652, **662**
**antisocial** 911
**antistrophe 597**

*chapter* 593
*review* 595
*goods* 798
**articled clerk** 541
**articles**
thirty-nine – 983*a*
– of agreement 770
– of faith 484, 983
**articulate** 366
**articulation**
*junction* 43
*speech* 580
**articulo, in –**
*transient* 111
*dying* 360
**artifice** 626, 702
**artificer** 690
**artificial**
*fictitious* 545
*cunning* 702
*affected* 855
– language 579
**artillery**
*explosion* 404
*arms* 727
**artilleryman** 726
**artisan** 690
**artist** *painter* &c. **559**
*contriver* 626
*agent* 690
**artiste** *music* 416
*drama* 599
**artistic** *skilful* 698
*beautiful* 845
*taste* 850
– language 578
**artlessness** **703**
**arundo, hæret**
lateri lethalis – 828
**aruspex** 513
**aruspicy** 511
**as** *motive* 615
– broad as long 27
– can be 52
– good as 27
– if *similar* 17
*suppose* 514
– little as may be 32
– it may be
*circumstance* 8
*event* 151
*chance* 156
– much again 90
– soon as 120
– they say 496, 532
– things are 7
– things go 151, 613
– to 9
– usual 82
– it were 17, 521
– you were 141, 283
– well as 37
– the world wags 151
**ascend** *be great* 31
*increase* 35
*rise* 305
*improve* 658
**ascendancy**
*power* 157
*influence* 175
*success* 731
**ascendant**
lord of the – 745
in the –
*influence* 175
*important* 642
*success* 731
*authority* 737
*repute* 873
one's star in the –
*prosperity* 734
**ascension**
[*see* ascend]
*calefaction* 384
– Day 998
**ascent**
[*see* ascend]
*gradient* 217
*rise* **305**
*glory* 873
**ascertain** *fix* 150
*determine* 480
**ascertained** 474, 490
**ascertainment** 480*a*
**asceticism** **955**
**ascititious**
*intrinsic* 6
*additional* 37
*supplementary* 52
**ascribe** 155
**aseptic** 652
**ash** 384
– coloured 432
– blond 430
**Ash Wednesday** 998
**ashamed** 879
**ashen** 429
**ashes** *corpse* 362
*dirt* 653
lay in – 162
pale as – 429, 860
rise from one's – 660
**ashore** 342
go – *arrive* 292
**ashy** 429
**Asian mystery** 533
**aside** *laterally* 236
*whisper* 405
*private* 528
say – 589
set &c. – *displace* 185
*neglect* 460
*negative* 536
*reject* 610
*disuse* 678
*abrogate* 756
*discard* 782
step – 279
**asinine** *ass* 271
*fool* 499
**ask** *inquire* 461
*request* 765
*for sale* 794
*price* 812
– leave 760
**askance** 217
eye – *fear* 860
look – *vision* 441, 443
*dissent* 489
*dislike* 867
*disapproval* 932
**askari** 726
**asked in church** 903
**askew** 217, 243
**aslant** 217
**asleep** 683
**aslope** 217
**Asmodeus** 980
**asomatous** 317
**asp** *animal* 366
*evil-doer* 913
**Aspasia** 962
**aspect** *feature* 5
*state* 7
*situation* 183
*appearance* 448
**aspen leaf**
shake like an – 315, 860
**asperity**
*roughness* 256
*discourtesy* 895
*anger* 900
*irascibility* 901
**asperse** 934
**aspersion**
*malediction* 908
*rite* 998
**asphalt**
*smooth* 255
*resin* 356*a*
*material* 635
**asphodel** 845
**asphyxia** 360
**asphyxiate** 361
**aspic** 352
**aspirant** 767, 865
**aspirate** 580
**aspirator** 349
**aspire** *rise* 305
*hope* 858
*desire* 865
*worship* 990
**aspirin** 834
**asportation** 270
**asquint** 217
**ass** *beast of burden* 271
*fool* 501
make an – of
*delude* 545
– between two bundles of hay 605
–'s bridge 519
– in lion's skin
*cheat* 548
*bungler* 701
**assafœtida** 401
**assagai** 727
**assail** 716, 830
**assailant** 710, 726
**assassin, -ate** 361
**assault** 716, 961
take by – 789
**assay** 463
**asseguay** 727
**assemblage** **72**
**assembly**
*council* 696
*society* 892
*religious* 997
**assembly hall** 588
**assembly room** 189
**assent** *belief* 484
*agree* **488**
*willing* 602
*consent* 762
*content* 831
**assert** 535, 924
**assess** *measure* 466
*determine* 480
*tax* 812
**assessor**
*judge* 967
**assets** 780, 800
**asseverate** 535
**assiduity** 110
**assiduous** 682
**assign**
*commission* 755
*transfer* 270, 783

**autoptical** 446, 525
**autotype** 558
**autumn** 126
**auxiliary** 711
*additional* 37
*helpful* 707
– forces 726
**avail** *benefit* 618
*useful* 644
*succeed* 731
of no – 645
– oneself of 677
**avalanche** *fall* 306
*snow* 383
*redundance* 641
**avaler des couleuvres** 725, 886
**avant-coureur** 64, 673
**avant-propos** 64
**avarice** 819
**avast!** *stop* 142, 265
*desist* 624
*forbid* 761
**avatar** *change* 140
*deity* 976
*idol* 991
**avaunt!** 297, 449
**ave!** *honour* 873
*courtesy* 894
**Ave maria** 990
**avenge** 919
**avenue**
*plantation* 371
*way* 627
**aver** 535
**average** *mean* 29, 628
*médiocre* 651
– circumstances 736
take an – 466
**Averni, facilis descensus** – 217, 665
**Avernus** 982
**averruncate** 297, 301
**aversion** *unwillingness* 603
*dislike* 867
*hate* 898
**avert** 706
– the eyes 442
**aviary** 370
**aviation** 267
**aviator** 269
**avidity** *avarice* 819
*desire* 865
**aviette** 273
**avile** 932, 934
**avion** 273
**aviso** 532
**avocation** 625
**avoidance** 623
**avoidless** 474, 601
**avoirdupois** 319
**avolation** 623, 671
**avouch** 535, 768
**avow** *assent* 488
*disclose* 529
*assert* 535
**avulsion** 44, 301
**avuncular** 11
**await** *future* 121
*be kept waiting* 133
*impend* 152
*expect* 507
**awake** *attentive* 457
*careful* 459
*intelligent* 498
*active* 682
– to life immortal 360
**awaken** *inform* 527
*excite* 824
– the attention 457
– the memory 505
**award** *adjudge* 480
*give* 784
**aware** 490
**away** 187, 196
break – 623
fly – 293
move – 287
take – from 789
get &c. – 671
throw &c. –
*eject* 297
*reject* 610
*waste* 638
*relinquish* 782
– from *unrelated* 10
– with! 930, 932
do – with *undo* 681
*abrogate* 756
**awe** *fear* 860
*wonder* 870
*respect* 928
**aweless** *fearless* 861
*insolent* 885
*disrespectful* 929
**awful** 31, 860
– silence 403
**awhile** 111
**awkward**
*inelegant* 579
*inexpedient* 647
*unskilful* 699
*difficult* 704
*painful* 830
*ugly* 846
*vulgar* 851
*ridiculous* 853
– squad 701
**awl** 262
**awn** 253
**awning** 223, 424
**awry** *oblique* 217
*distorted* 243
*evil* 619
**axe** *edge tool* 253
*impulse* 276
*weapon* 727
*for beheading* 975
have an – to grind 702
**Axinomancy** 511
**axiom** 496
**axiomatic** 474
**axis** *support* 215
*centre* 222
*rotation* 312
**axle** 312
wheel and – 633
**axle load** 466
**axletree** 215
**ay** 488
**ayah** 746, 753
**aye** *ever* 112
*yes* 488
**azimuth**
*horizontal* 213
*direction* 278
*measurement* 466
– circle 212
**azoic** 358
**azote** 663
**azotic** 657
**azure** 438
**azygous** *single* 87

## B

**Baal** 979, 986
**Babbittry** 851
**babble** *rivulet* 348
*faint sound* 405
*unmeaning* 517
*talk* 584, 588
**babbler** 501
**babbling**
*foolish* 499
**babe** 129
innocent as the – unborn 946
**Babel** *confusion* 59
*discord* 414
*tongues* 560
*jargon* 563
*loquacity* 584
**baboon** 846
**baby** *infant* 129
*fool* 501
– linen 225
**babyhood** 127
**babyish** 499
**baccarat** 840
**bacchanals** 959
**Bacchus** 979
*drink* 959
**bachelor** 904
– of arts 492
– girl 374
**bacillus** 193
**back** *rear* 235
*shoulder* 250
*aid* 707
behind one's –
*latent* 526
*hidden* 528
come – 292
give – 790
fall – *relapse* 661
go – 283
go – from *retract* 773
have at one's – 215
hold – *avoid* 623
keep – *reserve* 636
look – 505
on one's – *impotent* 158
*horizontal* 213
*failure* 732
pat on the –
*incite* 615
*encourage* 861
*approve* 931
pay – *retaliate* 718
put – *deteriorate* 659
*restore* 660
send – 764
take – again 790
carry one's thoughts – 505
some time – 122
spring – 277
trace – 505
turn – 283
turn one's – 283
turn one's – upon
*repel* 289
*inattention* 458
*avoid* 623
*oppose* 708
*seclusion* 893
*discourtesy* 895
*disrespect* 929
*contempt* 930
set one's – against

**bazaar** 799
**B.C.** 106
**be** 1
– all and end all
*whole* 50
*intention* 620
*importance* 642
– off *depart* 293
*eject* 297
*retract* 773
– it so 488
– that as it may 30
**beach** 231, 342
**beach comber** 268
**beacon** 550, 663
**bead** 249
**beadle** *janitor* 263
*law officer* 965
*church* 996
**beadledom** 737
**beadroll** *list* 86
*prayers* 990
*ritual* 998
**beads**
*ornament* 847
tell one's – 990, 998
**beadsman**
*servant* 746
*clergy* 996
**beagle** 366
**beak** *face* 234
*nose* 250
*magistrate* 967
**beaker** 191
**beam** *support* 215
*side* 236
*weigh* 319
*light* 420
on – ends
*powerless* 158
*horizontal* 213
*side* 236
*fail* 732
*wonder* 870
**beaming**
*beautiful* 845
**bean** 276
**beanfeast** 840
**bear** *produce* 161
*sustain* 215
*carry* 270
*admit of* 470
*suffer* 821
*endure* 826
bring to – 677
more than flesh and blood can – 824
unable to –
*excited* 825
*dislike* 867
– away 789
– away the bell 648, 731
– the brunt 704, 717
– the burden 625
– the cross 828
– company 88
– down 173, 885
– down upon 716
– false witness 544
– fruit *produce* 161
*useful* 644
*success* 731
*prosper* 734
– a hand 680
– hard upon 649
– harmless 717
– ill 825
– off *deviate* 279
– on 215
– oneself 692
– out *evidence* 467
*vindicate* 937
– pain 828
– the palm 33
– a sense 516
– through 707
– up *approach* 286
*persevere* 604a
*relieve* 834
*cheerful* 836
– up against 719, 861
– upon
*relevant* 9, 23
*influence* 175
– with
*tolerate* 740
*permit* 760
*take coolly* 826
*forgive* 918
**bear**
*savage* 907
*surly* 895
had it been a – it would have bitten you 458
– garden
*disorder* 59
*discord* 713
*arena* 728
– leader 540
– pit 370
– skin *cap* 225
*helmet* 717
– with a sore back 901
**bearable** 651
**beard** *hair* 205
*prickles* 253
*rough* 256
*defy* 715
*brave* 861
*insolence* 885
pluck by the –
*disrespect* 929
– the lion 604
**beardless** 127, 226
**bearer** 271, 363
**bearing** *relation* 9
*support* 215
*direction* 278
*meaning* 516
*demeanour* 692
– rein 706, 752
**bearings**
*circumstances* 8
*situation* 183
armorial – 550
**beast** *animal* 366
*unclean* 653
*discourteous* 895
– of burden 271, 690
**beat** *be superior* 33
*periodic* 138
*region* 181
*impulse* 276
*surpass* 303
*oscillate* 314
*agitation* 315
*crush* 330
*sound* 407
*line of pursuit* 625
*path* 627
*overcome* 731
*strike* 972
– about
*circuit* 629
– the air 645
– against 708
– one's breast 839
– about the bush
*try for* 463
*evade the point* 477
*prevaricate* 544
*diffuse style* 573
– down *destroy* 162
*cheapen* 794, 819
*insolent* 885
– of drum
*music* 416
*publish* 531
*alarm* 669
*war* 722
*command* 741
*pomp* 882
without – of drum 528
– into *teach* 537
– off 717
– a retreat
*retire* 283
*avoid* 623
*submit* 725
– time *clock* 114
*music* 416
– up *churn* 352
– up against
*oppose* 708
– up for *cater* 637
– up one's quarters
*seek* 461
*visit* 892
– up for recruits
*prepare* 673
*aid* 707
**beaten track**
*habit* 613
*way* 627
leave the – 83
tread the – 82
**beatic** 827
**beatific** 829, 981
**beatification** 827, 987
**beating high**
the heart – 824
**beatitude** 827
**beau** *man* 373
*fop* 854
*admirer* 897
– idéal 650, 845
– monde 852
**beautify** 845, 847
**beautiless** 846
**beauty** 845
**beaver** *hat* 225
**becalm** 265
**because** *cause* 153
*attribution* 155
*answer* 462
*reasoning* 476
*motive* 615
**bechance** 151
**beck** *rill* 348
*sign* 550
*mandate* 741
at one's – *aid* 707
*obey* 743
**beckon** *sign* 550
*motive* 615
*call* 741
**becloud** *dark* 421
*hide* 528
**become**
*accord with* 23
*change to* 144
*behove* 926
– of 151
**becoming**

**belike** 472
**belittle**
*decrease* 36
*underestimate* 482
*disparage* 934
**bell** 417, 550
alarm – 669
bear away the –
*goodness* 648
*success* 731
*repute* 873
church – 550
cracked – 408*a*
passing – 363
– book and candle
*swear* 535
*curse* 908
*spell* 993
*rite* 998
– the cat 861
– shape 249, 252
**belladonna** 663
**belle** 374, 854
**a** la – étoile 220, 338
**belles-lettres** 560
**belli, casus** – 824
**bellicose** 720, 722
**bellied** 250
**belligerent**
*contentious* 720
*warlike* 722
*combatant* 726
**belling** 412
**bellman** 534
**bello, flagrante** – 722
**Bellona** 722
**bellow** *loud* 404
*cry* 411
*animal cry* 412
*wail* 839
**bellows** 349, 580
**bells, peal of** – 407
**bellwether** 64, 694
**belly** *receptacle* 191
*inside* 221
*convex* 250
–ful 52
– god 957
– timber 298
**belomancy** 511
**belong to** *related* 9
*component* 56
*included* 76
*attribute* 157
*property* 777, 780
*duty* 926
**beloved** 897
**below** 207
here – 318
– the mark 32
– par 34, 207
*bad* 649
*indifferent* 651
*discount* 813
*ignoble* 876
– its full strength 651
– stairs 207
**belt** *outline* 230
*ring* 247
*strait* 343
swimming – 666
**belting** 633
**Belus** 979
**belvedere** 441
**bemask** 528
**bemingle** 41
**bemire** 653
**bemoan** 839
**bemused** 458
**bench** *support* 215
*council* 696
*tribunal* 966
**Bench, King's** – 752
**bencher** 968
**bend** *oblique* 217
*angle* 244
*curve* 245
*incline* 278
*deviate* 279
*depression* 308
*circuit* 311
*give* 324
*submit* 725
– backwards 235
– the bow 686
– the brows 932
– one's course 27
– the knee
*bow down* 308
*submit* 725
*humble* 879
*servile* 886
*courtesy* 894
*respect* 928
*worship* 990
– one's looks upon 441
– the mind 457
– over 250
– to rules &c. 82
– sinister 874
– one's steps 622
– to *tend* 176
– towards 278
– to one's will 737
**beneath** 207
– one 940
– notice 643
**Benedick** 903
**Benedictine** 996
**benediction**
*gratitude* 916
*approval* 931
*worship* 990
nuptial – 903
**benefaction** 784
**benefactor** 816, **912**
**benefice** 995
**beneficent** 906
**beneficial** 648
– interest 780
**beneficiary**
*possessor* 779
*receive* 785
*clergy* 996
**benefit** *good* 618
*use* 644
*do good* 648
*aid* 707
*acquisition* 775
*property* 780
*benevolence* 906
reap the – of 658
**benefits forgot** 917
**bene gesserit, quamdiu se** – 926
**benet** 545
**benevolence**
*tax* 812
*love* 897
*kindness* **906**
universal – 910
**Bengal heat** 382
**benighted**
*dark* 421
*ignorant* 491
**benign** 656, 906
**benignant** 906
**benison** 618, 931
**Benjamin's mess** 33, 50
**Benshie** 979
**bent** *tendency* 176
*angle* 244
*turn of mind* 820
*desire* 865
fool to the top of one's – 856
– on *willing* 602
*resolved* 604
*intention* 620
*desirous* 865
**Benthamite** 910
**ben trovato**
*likely* 472
*imagination* 515
*untruth* 546
*wit* 842
**benumb**
*insensible* **376**
*cold* 385
*deaden affections* 823
**beplaster** 933
**bepraise** 931
**bequest** 270
*gift* 784
**bereavement**
*death* 360
*loss* 776
*take away* 789
**bereft** *poor* 804
– of life 360
– of reason **503**
**béret** 225
**berg, ice** – 383
**bergamot** 400
**berlin** 272
**berserk** 173, 503
**berth** *lodging* 189
*bed* 215
*office* 625
**beryl** *green* 435
*jewel* 847
**beseech** 765, 990
**beseem** 926
**beset** *surround* **227**
*follow* 281
*attack* 716
*entreat* 765
*annoy* 830
*haunt* 860
– with difficulties 704
**besetting** 78, 613
– sin 945
**beshrew** 908
**beside** *except* 83
*near* 197
*alongside* 236
– the mark 10, 495
– oneself 503, 824
**besides** 37
**besiege**
*surround* 227
*attack* 716
*solicit* 765
**bésique** 840
**beslaver** 933
**beslime** 653
**beslubber** 933
**besmear** 223, 653
**besom** 652
**besotted** 481
**bespangle** 847
**bespatter** *dirt* 653
*disapprove* 932
*flatter* 933
*detract* 934

**bespeak** *early* 132
*evidence* 467
*indicate* 516
*engage* 755
*ask for* 765
**bespeckle** 440
**bespot** 440
**besprinkle** 41, 440
**best** 648, 650
all for the –
*good* 618
*prosper* 734
*content* 831
*hope* 858
bad is the – 649
do one's –
*care* 459
*try* 675
*activity* 682
*exertion* 686
have the – of it 731
make the – of it
*over-estimate* 482
*use* 677
*submit* 725
*compromise* 774
*take easily* 826
*hope* 858
the – 800
to the – of one's belief 484
– bib and tucker
*prepared* 673
*ornament* 847
*ostentation* 882
– friends 890
– intentions 906
– man 903
– part 31, 50
– seller 731
make the – of one's time 684
**bestead** 644
**bestial** 954, 961
**bestir oneself**
*activity* 682
*haste* 684
*exertion* 686
**bestow** 784
– one's hand 903
– thought 451
**bestraddle** 215
**bestrew** 73
**bestride** 206, 215
**bet** 621
**betake oneself to**
*journey* 266
*business* 625
*use* 677
**bête, pas si** – 498
**bête noire** *bane* 663
*fear* 860
*hate* 898
**bethel** 1000
**bethink** 451, 505
**bethral** 749, 751
**betide** 151
**betimes** 132
**betoken**
*evidence* 467
*predict* 511
*indicate* 550
**betray** *disclose* 529
*deceive* 545
*dishonour* 940
– itself *visible* 446
**betrayer** 941
**betrim** 673
**betroth** 768, 903
**betrothed** 897
**better** *good* 648
*improve* 658
appeal to one's – feelings 914
get – *health* 654
*improve* 658
*refreshment* 689
*restoration* 660
get the – of, 479, 702, 731
think – of 658, 950
seen – days
*deteriorate* 659
*adversity* 735
*poor* 804
– half 903
only – than nothing 651
– sort 875
for – for worse
*choice* 609
*marriage* 903
**between** 228
– cup and lip 111
far – 198
lie – 228
– the lines 526
vibrate – two extremes 149
– ourselves 528
– two fires 665
– maid 746
**betwixt** 228
**bevel** 217
– gearing 633
**bever** 298
**beverage** 298
**bévue** 732
**bevy** 72, 102
**bewail** *regret* 833
*lament* 839
**beware** 665, 668
**bewilder**
*put out* 458
*uncertainty* 475
*astonish* 870
**bewitch**
*fascinate* 615
*please* 829
*excite love* 897
*exorcise* 992
**bey** 745
**beyond** *superior* 33
*distance* 196
go – 303
– compare 31, 33
– control 471
– one's depth 208, 519
– expression 31
– one's grasp 471
– hope 731, 534
– the mark 303, 641
– measure 641
– possibility 471
– praise
*perfect* 650
*approbation* 931
*virtue* 944
– price 814
– question 474, 494
– reason 471
– remedy 859
– seas 57
**bezel** 217
**bhang** 663
**bias** *influence* 175
*tendency* 176
*slope* 217
*prepossession* 481
*disposition* 820
**bib** *pinafore* 225
*drink* 959
**bibber** *weep* 839
*toper* 959
**bibble-babble** 584
**bibelot** 847
**bibendum, nunc est** – 959
**Bible** 985
– oath 535
**biblioclasm** 162
**bibliography** 593
**bibliolatry**
*learning* 490
*heterodoxy* 984
*idolatry* 991
**bibliomancy** 511
**bibliomania** 490
**bibliomaniac** 492
**bibliophile** 492
**bibliopole** 593
**bibliotheca** 593
**bibulous** 298, 959
**bicameral** 90
**bicapital** 90
**bice** 435, 438
**bicentenary** 98, 138, 883
**bicker** *flutter* 315
*quarrel* 713
**bicolour** 440
**biconjugate** 91
**bicuspid** 91
**bicycle** 272
**bid** *order* 741
*offer* 763
– the banns 903
– defiance 715
– fair *tend* 176
*probable* 472
*promise* 511
*hope* 858
– a long farewell 624
– for *intend* 620
*offer* 763
*request* 765
*bargain* 794
**bidder** 767
**bide** *wait* 133
*remain* 141
*take coolly* 826
– one's time 133
*watch* 507
*inactive* 681
**bidet** 271
**biennial**
*periodic* 138
*plant* 367
**bienséance** 852, 894
**bier** 363
**bifacial** 90
**bifarious** 90
**bifid** 91
**bifold** 90
**biform** 90
**bifurcate** 91, 244
**big** *in degree* 31
*in size* 192
*wide* 194
look – *defy* 715
*proud* 878
*insolent* 885
talk – 885, 909
– sounding
*loud* 404
*words* 577
*affected* 855
– swollen 194
– with 161
– with the fate of 511

**bigamy** 903
**biggin** 191
**bight** 343
**bigot** *positive* 474
*prejudice* 481
*obstinate* 606
*heterodox* 984
*impious* 988
**bigotry** 907
**bigwig** *scholar* 492
*sage* 500
*nobility* 875
**bijou** *goodness* 648
*beauty* 845
*ornament* 847
**bilander** 273
**bilateral** 90, 236
**bilbo** 727
**bilboes** 752
put into – 751
**bile** 900
**bilge** *base* 211
*convex* 250
*yawn* 260
– water 653
**bilingual** 560
**bilious** 837
**bilk**
*disappoint* 509
*cheat* 545
*steal* 791
**bill** *list* 86
*hatchet* 253
*placard* 531
*ticket* 550
*paper* 593
*plan* 626
*weapon* 727
*money order* 800
*money account* 811
*charge* 812
*in law* 969
true – 969
– and coo 902
– of exchange 771
– of fare *food* 298
*plan* 626
– of indictment 938
–s of mortality 360
– of sale 771
**billet** *locate* 184
*ticket* 550
*apportion* 786
**billet** *epistle* 592
– doux 902
**billfold** 191
**billhook** 253
**billiard** – ball 249
– room 191
– table *flat* 213
**billiards** 840
**Billingsgate** 563, 908
**billion** 98
**billow** *sea* 348
*river* 341
**billy-cock** 225
**billy-goat** 373
**bimetallism** 800
**bin** 191
**binary** 89
**bind** *connect* 43
*cover* 223
*compel* 744
*condition* 770
*obligation* 926
– hand and foot 751
– oneself 768
– over 744
– up wounds 660
**binding** 744
**bine** 367
**binnacle** 693
**binocular** 445
**binomial** 89
**biogenesis** 161
**biograph** 448
**biography** 594
**biology** 357, 359
**bioscope** 448
**biota** 357
**biparous** 89
**bipartite** 44, 91
**biplane** 273
**biplicity** 89
**biquadrate** 96
**birch** *flog* 972
– rod 975
**bird** 366
kill two –s with one stone 682
–'s eye view 441, 448
–s of a feather 17
the – has flown 187, 671
– in hand 777, 781
– of ill omen
*omen* 512
*warning* 668
*hopeless* 859
– of passage 268
– of prey 739
a little – told me 527
**birdcage** 370
**birdlime** *glue* 45
*trap* 545
**biretta** 999
**birth** *beginning* 66
*production* 161
*paternity* 166
*nobility* 875
– place 153
– right 924
**birthday** 138, 883
– suit 226
**birthmark** 848
**bis** *repeat* 104
*approval* 931
**biscuits, s'embarquer sans** – 674
**bise** 349
**bisection** 68, 91
**bishop** *punch* 298
*clergy* 996
–'s palace 1000
–'s purple 437
**bishopric** 995
**bisque** 33
**bissextile** 138
**bistoury** 253
**bistre** 433
**bisulcate** 259
**bit**
*small quantity* 32
*part* 51
*interval* 106
*curb* 752
just a – 26
– by bit
*by degrees* 26
*by instalments* 51
*in detail* 79
*slowly* 275
– between the teeth 600, 719
**bitch** *animal* 366
*female* 374
*clumsy* 699
*fail* 732
*impure* 962
**bite** *eat* 298
*physical pain* 378
*cold* 385
*cheat* 545
*dupe* 547
*etch* 558
*mental pain* 830
– the dust 725
– in 259
– the thumb 900, 929
– the tongue 392
**biter bit** 718
**biting** *pain* 378
*cold* 383
*pungent* 392
*painful* 830
*discourteous* 895
*censorious* 932
**bitten** 897
**bitter** *beer* 298
*cold* 383
*taste* 392, 395
*painful* 830
*acrimonious* 895
*hate* 898
*angry* 900
*malevolent* 907
– end 67
– ender 606, 710,
832
– pill 735
– words 932
**bitterly** *greatly* 31
**bitterness**
[*see* bitter]
*pain* 828
*regret* 833
**bitumen** 356*a*
**bituminous coal** 388
**bivouac**
*encamp* 184
*camp* 189
*repose* 265
*watch* 668
**bi-weekly** 138
**bizarre** 83, 853
**blab** 529
**blabber** 584
**black** *colour* 431
*crime* 945
look – *feeling* 821
*discontent* 832
*angry* 900
– art 992
– and blue
*beat* 972
– board 590
– book 938
– eye 848, 972
– in the face
*swear* 535
*excitement* 821, 824
– flag 722
– hole *crowd* 72
*prison* 752
– lead 556
– letter *old* 124
*barbarism* 563
*print* 591
– list 932
– looks
*discourteous* 895
*sullen* 901*a*
*disapprove* 932
*magic* 992
– mail *theft* 791

*severe* 739
hands in – *cruel* 907
in the – 5
life – 359
new – 658, 824
spill – *war* 722
– for blood 919
– boil *excite* 824, 825
*anger* 900
– run cold 830, 860
– heat 382
– horse 271
– hound 913
– letting 297, 662
– poisoning 655
– red 434
– stained 361
– sucker 789, 913
– thirsty
*murderous* 361
*cruel* 907
– up *excited* 824
*angry* 900
bloodless 160
*peace* 721
*virtue* 946
bloody [*see* blood]
*red* 434
*unclean* 653
*cruel* 907
bloom *youth* 127
*flower* 367
*blue* 438
*health* 654
*prosperity* 734
bloomer 495
bloomers 225
blooming 654, 845
blossom
*flower* 154, 161, 367
*prosperity* 734
blot *blacken* 431
*error* 495
*obliterate* 552
*dirty* 653
*blemish* 848
*disgrace* 874
*guilt* 947
– out *destroy* 162
*forgive* 918
blotch 848
blouse 225
blow *expand* 194
*knock* 276
*wind* 349
*unexpected* 508
*disappointment* 509
*evil* 619
*action* 680
*get wind* 688
*failure* 732
*prosper* 734
*pain* 828, 830
come to –s 720, 722
deal a – at 716
deal a – to 972
death – 360, 361
– for blow 718
– one's brains out 361
– the coals 824
– down 162
– the fire 384
– the gaff 529
– hole 351
– the horn 416
– hot and cold
*lie* 544
*irresolute* 605
*tergiversation* 607
*caprice* 608
– a kiss 902
– off *disperse* 73
– out *food* 298
*darken* 421
*gorge* 957
– over *past* 122
– pipe 349, 727
– the trumpet 873
– one's own trumpet 882
– up *destroy* 162
*eruption* 173
*inflate* 194
*wind* 349
*excite* 824
*objurgate* 932, 934
blower 349
blowhard 884
blown [*see* blow]
*fatigued* 688
*proud* 878
storm – over 664, 721
– upon 874, 932
blow-out 406
blowzy *swollen* 194
*red* 434
blubber *fat* 356
*cry* 839
Blücher boot 225
bludgeon 727
– man 726, 913
blue *sky* 338
*colour* 438
*learned* 490
bit of – hope 858
look –
*disappointed* 509
*feeling* 821
*discontent* 832
*disrepute* 874
out of the – 508
swear till all's – 535
true – 543, 939
– book 86, 551
– blood 875
– devils 837
– jacket 269
– light 550, 669
– pencil 174, 596
– moon 110
– Peter 293, 550
– and red 437
– ribbon 733, 877
– ruin 959
– stocking
*scholar* 492
*affectation* 855
– and yellow 435
Bluebeard
*marriage* 903
*libertine* 962
blueness 438
blues 837, 840
bluff *violent* 173
*high cliff* 206
*blunt* 254
*deceive* 545
*boasting* 884
*insolent* 885
*discourteous* 895
blunder *error* 495
*absurdity* 497
*awkward* 699
*failure* 732
– upon 156
blunderbuss 727
blunderhead 701
blunderheaded 499
blunt *weaken* 160
*inert* 172
*moderate* v. 174
*obtuse* 254
*benumb* 376
*damp* v. 616
*plain-spoken* 703
*cash* 800
*deaden* 823
*discourteous* 895
– tool 645
– witted 499
bluntness 254
blur
*imperfect vision* 443
*dirt* 653
*blemish* 848
*stigma* 874
blurb 931
blurred
*invisible* 447
blurt out 529, 582
blush *flush* 382
*redden* 434
*feel* 821
*humbled* 879
*modest* 881
at first – *see* 441
*appear* 448
*manifest* 525
put to the –
*humble* 897
*browbeat* 885
*discourtesy* 895
blushing honours 873, 881
bluster *violent* 173
*defiant* 715
*boasting* 884
*insolent* 885
*threaten* 909
blusterer 887
blustering [*see* bluster]
*windy* 349
Bo to a goose, not say – 862
boa 225
Boanerges 540
boar 366, 373
board *layer* 204
*support* 215
*food* 298
*hard* 323
*council* 696
*attack* 716
*tribunal* 966
festive – 892
go by the – 158, 162
go on – 293
on – 186, 273
preside at the – 693
– of trade 621
– school 542
boarder 188
boarding-house 189
boards 599, 728
boast 884
not much to – of 651
boasting 884
boaston 840
boat 273

in the same – 88
– race 720
**boating** 267
**boatman** 269
**boatswain** 269
**bob** *depress* 308
*leap* 309
*oscillate* 314
*agitate* 315
*money* 800
– a curtsy 894
– for *fish* 463
**Bobadil, Captain** – 887
**bobbed**
*hair* 53
**bobbin** 312
**bobbing** *fuel* 388
**bobbish** 654
**bobby** *police* 664
**bobsleigh** 272
**bobsleighing** 840
**bobtailed** 53
**bocage** 367
**bocca, per amusare** la – 394
**Boche** 913
**boddice** 225
**bode** 511
**bodega** 189
**bodily**
*substantially* 3
*wholly* 50
*material* 316
– enjoyment 377
– fear 860
– pain 378
**bodkin**
*go between* 228
*perforator* 262
**body** *substance* 3
*whole* 50
*assemblage* 72
*frame* 215
*matter* 316
*party* 712
in a – *together* 88
– and blood of Christ 987
– clothes 225
– colour 556
– of doctrine 490
– forth 554
– guard 717, 753
– of knowledge 490
– politic
*mankind* 372
*authority* 737
keep – and soul together 654
– of water 438
**Bœotian** *rustic* 371
*stupid* 499
*fool* 501
*vulgar* 851
*ignoble* 876
**Boer** 371
**bog** 345, 653
– trotter 876
**boggart** 980
**boggle** *hesitate* 605
*awkward* 699
*difficulty* 704
**bogie** 980
*truck* 272
**bogle** 980
**bogus** 545
**Bohemian**
*unconventional* 83
*nomad* 268
*ungenteel* 851
**boil** *violence* 173
*effervesce* 315
*bubble* 353
*heat* 382, 384
*ulceration* 655
*excitement* 824, 825
*anger* 900
– down 195
**boiler** 386
**boisterous**
*violent* 173
*hasty* 684
*excitable* 825
**bold** *prominent* 250
*unreserved* 525
*vigorous* 574
*brave* 861
make – with 895
show a – front 715, 861
– faced 885
– push *essay* 675
– relief *visible* 446
– stroke *plan* 626
*success* 731
**bole** 50
**bolero** 840
**bollard** 45
**bolshevik** 146, 742
**bolshevist** 737, 742
**bolster** *support* 215
*repair* 658
*aid* 707
– up *vindicate* 937
**bolt** *sift* 42
*fasten* 43
*fastening* 45
*close* 261
*move rapidly* 274
*propel* 284
*run away* 623
*escape* 671
*hindrance* 706
*shaft* 727
*disobey* 742
*shackle* 752
thunder – 872
– the door 761
– food 298, 957
– in 751
– upright 212
**bolthead** 191
**bolus** *mouthful* 298
*remedy* 662
**bomb** 404, 727
– proof 664, 717
– vessel 726
**bombard** 716
**bombardier** 726
**bombardon** 417
**bombast**
*unmeaning* 517
*magniloquence* 577
*ridiculous* 853
*boasting* 884
*exaggeration* 549
**Bombastes Furioso** 887
**bomber**
*aeroplane* 726
**bombilation** 404
**bon – de augure** 858
– enfant *social* 892
*kindly* 906
– gré mal gré 601
– marché 815
– mot 842
– naturel 836
– ton 852
– vivant 957
– voyage 293
**bona** – fides
*veracity* 543
*probity* 939
– roba 962
**bonanza** 641, 784
*wealth* 803
**bonbon** 396
**bond** *relation* 9
*tie* 45
*compact* 769
*security* 771
*money* 800
*right* 924
– of union 9, 45
government – 802
Liberty – 802
**bondage** 749
**bonded together** 712
**bonds** [*see* bond]
*fetters* 752
*funds* 802
in – *service* 746
tear asunder one's – 750
– of harmony **714**
**bondsman** 746
**bone** *strength* 159
*dense* 321
*hard* 323
bred in the – **5**
feel it in one's – 510
– of contention 713, 720
one – and one flesh 903
– to pick *difficulty* 704
*discord* 713
– setter 662
**bonehouse** 363
**boner** 495
**bones** [*see* bone]
*corpse* 362
*music* 417
break no – 648
make no – 602, 705
**boneyard** 363
**bonfire** 382
*festivity* 840
*celebration* 883
make a – of 384
**bonhomie** 703, 906
**bonhomme** 996
**Boniface** 890
**bonne** 746, 753
– bouche *end* 67
*pleasant* 377
*savoury* 394
*saving* 636
à la – heure 602, 831
de – volonté 602
**bonnet** 225
**bonny** 836, 845
**bono:** cui –
*intention* 620
*utility* 644
*inutility* 645
pro – publico **644**, 910
**bonus** *extra* 641
*gift* 784
*money* 810
**bony** 323
**bonze** 996

**bonzer** 648
**booby** 501
– trap 545
**boodle** 793
**book** *register* 86
**publication** 531
*record* 551
*volume* **593**
*script* 599
*enter accounts* 811
at one's –s 539
bring to –
*evidence* 467
*account* 811
*reprove* 932
mind one's – 539
school – 542
without –
*by heart* 505
– of Books 985
– club 593
– of fate 601
– learning 490
– shop 593
**book-case** 191
**booked** *dying* 360
**bookish** 490
**bookkeeper** 553
**bookkeeping** 811
**bookless**
*unlearned* 493
**bookmaking** 156
**bookseller** 593
**bookworm** 492, 593
**boom**
*support* 215
*sail* 267
*rush* 274
*impulse* 276
*sound* 404
*obstacle* 706
*defence* 717
**boomerang**
*recoil* 277
*retribution* 718
*weapon* 727
**boon** 784
beg a – 765
– companion 890
**boor** *clown* 876
**boorish** 851, 895
**boost** 276, 482, 931
**booster** 935
**boot** *box* 191
*dress* 225
*advantage* 618
*punishment* 975
to – *added* 37
– legging 964
**booted and spurred** 673
**booth** 189, 799
**bootless** 645, 732
**boots** *dress* 225
*servant* 746
*low person* 876
what – it? 643
**booty** **793**
**booze** 959
**bo-peep** 441, 528
**bordel** 961
**border** *edge* 231
*limit* 233
*flower bed* 371
*ornament* 847
– upon 197, 199
**bore** *diameter* 202
*hole* 260
*tide* 348, 667
*fatigue* 688
*trouble* 828
*plague* 830
*weary* 841
**bored** 456
**boreal**
*Northern* 237
*cold* 383
**Boreas** 349
**boredom** 841
**borer** 262
**born** 359
– so 5
– under an evil star 735
– under a lucky star 734
**borne** 826
– down *failure* 732
*defection* 837
**borné** 499
**borough** 181, 189
rotten – 893
– council 696
**borrow** 19, 788
– of Peter &c. 147
**borrowed plumes**
*deception* 545
**borrower** 806
**borrowing** 788
**bosh** *absurdity* 497
*unmeaning* 517
*untrue* 546
*trifling* 643
**bosky** 959
**bosom** *breast* 221
*mind* 450
*affections* 820
in the – of 229
– of one's family 221
– friend 890
**boss** 250, 694, **737**
straw – 694
**Boston** 840
**botanic garden** 369, 371
**Botanomancy** 511
**Botany** 367, **369**
**botch** *bungle* 59
*mend* 660
*unskilful* 699
*difficulty* 704
*fail* 732
**both** 89
listen with – ears 418
burn the candle at – ends 638
butter one's bread on – sides 641
**bother**
*uncertainty* 475
*bustle* 682
*difficulty* 704
*trouble* 828
*harass* 830
**bothy** 189
**bottle**
*receptacle* 191
*preserve* 670
bee in a – 407
crack a – 298
pass the – 959
smelling – 400
– green 435
– holder
*auxiliary* 711
*mediator* 724
– up *remember* 505
*hide* 528
*restrain* 751
**bottom**
*lowest part* 211
*support* 215
*posterior* 235
*combe* 252
*ship* 273
*pluck* 604*a*
*courage* 861
at – 5
at the – of
*cause* 153
go to the – 310
probe to the – 461
from the – of one's heart *veracity* 543
*feeling* 821
– upwards 218
– land 180, 207
**bottomless** 208
– pit 982
angel of the – **pit** 978
**bottomry** **771**
**botulism** 663
**bouche:**
bonne – *end* **67**
*savoury* 394
*saving* 636
*pleasant* 829
– à feu 727
**bouderie** 901*a*
**boudoir** 191
**bouffe, opera** **599**
**bouge** 250
**bough** *part* 51
*curve* 245
*tree* 367
**bought** *flexure* **245**
**bougie** 423
**boulder** 249
**boulevards** 227
**bouleversement**
*revolution* 146
*destruction* 162
*excite* 824
**bouillabaisse** 298
**bouillon** 298
**bounce** *violence* **173**
*jump* 309
*lie* 546
*boast* 884
*insolence* 885
– upon 292, 508
**bouncing** *large* 192
**bound**
*circumscribe* **229**
*swift* 274
*leap* 309
*certain* 474
I'll be – 535
– back *recoil* **277**
– by 926
– for *direction* **278**
*destination* 620
– to *promise* 768
*responsible* 926
**boundary** 233
**bounden duty** **926**
**bounder** 851
**boundless** 105, 180
**bounds** 230, 235
keep within –
*moderation* 174
*shortcoming* 304
*restrain* 751
*prohibit* 761
– of possibility **470**
**bountiful** 816, **906**
Lady – 816
**bounty** *gift* **784**
**bouquet**

*fragrant* 400
*beauty* 847
**bourdon** 215
**bourgeois**
*middle class* 29
*type* 591
*commoner* 876
**bourgeon** 194
**bourn** 233
**bourse** 621, 799
**bouse** 959
**bout** *turn* 138
*job* 680
*fight* 720
*prank* 840
drinking – 954
**bout**
au – du compte 476
au – de son latin
*sophistry* 477
*ignorance* 491
*difficulty* 704
**boutade** 497, 608
**boutonnière** 400
**bovine** 366, 499
**bow** *be inferior* 34
*fore part* 234
*curve* 245
*projection* 250
*stoop* 308
*fiddlestick* 417
*weapon* 727
*ornament* 847
*servility* 886
*reverence* 894
*respect* 928
bend the – 686
draw the long – 884
– down *worship* 990, 991
– out 297
– submission 725
– window 260
**Bow bells**
born within sound of – 876
**Bowdlerize** 652
**bowed down** 837, 879
**bowelless** 914*a*
**bowels** *inside* 221
– of compassion 914
– of the earth 208
**bower** 189, 191
–s of bliss 981
**bowery** 424
**bowie knife** 727
**bowl** *vessel* 191
*rotate* 312
*stadium* 840
flowing – 959
– along *walk* 266
*swift* 274
**bowlder** 249
**bowline** 45
**bowler** *hat* 225
**bow-legged** 243
**bowling-green** 213, 840
**bowls** 840
**bowman** 726
**bowshot** 197
**bowsprit** 234
**bowstring** *execution* 972, 975
**box** *house* 189
*chest* 191
*seat* 215
*theatre* 599
*fight* 720
horse – 272
musical – 417
wrong – *error* 495
*unskilful* 699
*dilemma* 704
– the compass
*direction* 278
*rotation* 312
*change of mind* 607
– the ear 900, 972
– up 751
**boxer** 726
**boy** 129
– scout 534
**boyar** 875
**boycott** 55, 297, 893
**boyhood** 127
**brabble** 713, 720
**brabbler** 901
**brace** *tie* 43
*fasten* 45
*two* 89
*strengthen* 159
*support* 215
*music* 413
*refresh* 689
**bracelet** *circle* 247
*handcuff* 752
*ornament* 847
**bracer** 392
**braces** 45
**brachial** 633
**Brachygraphy** 590
**bracing** 656
**bracken** 367
**bracket** *tie* 43, 45
*couple* 89
*support* 215
**brackish** 392
**brad** 45
**bradawl** 262
**Bradbury** 800
**Bradshaw** 266
**brae** 206
**brag** *cards* 840
*boast* 884
**Braggadocio** 884
**braggart** 884
**Brahma** 979
**Brahmin** 984, 996
**braid** *tie* 43
*ligature* 45
*net* 219
*variegate* 440
**brain** *kill* 361
*intellect* 450
*skill* 498
blow one's –s out 361
coinage of the – 515
suck one's –s 461
rack one's –s 451, 515
**brainless** 499
**brainpan** 450
**brainsick** 458
**brain-storm** 503, 825
**brainwork** 451
**brainy** 498
**brake** *carriage* 272
*copse* 367
*hindrance* 706
*curb* 752
apply the – 275
**brakeman** 268
**bramble** *thorn* 253
*bane* 663
**bran** 330
**brancard** 272
**branch** *member* 51
*class* 75
*posterity* 167
*fork* 244
*tree* 367
– off 91, 291
– out *ramify* 91
*diffuse style* 573
**branching**
*symmetry* 242
**brand** *burn* 384
*fuel* 388
*torch* 423
*mark* 550
*sword* 727
*disrepute* 874
*censure* 932
*stigmatize* 934
– of discord 713
– new 123
– with reproach 938
**brandish**
*oscillate* 314
*flourish* 315
*display* 882
**brandy** 959
**brangle** 713
**brangler** 710
**brank** 975
**bras**
les – croisés 681
à – ouverts 894
**brashness** 885
**brasier** 386
**brass** *alloy* 41
*money* 800
*insolence* 885
bold as – 861
– band 417, 884
with a – 884
– coloured 439
– hat 747
– farthing 643
**brassard** 550, 747
**brat** 129
**brattice** 224, 228
**bravado** 884
**brave** *confront* 234
*healthy* 654
*defy* 715
*warrior* 726
*bear* 821, 826
*courage* 861
– a thousand years 110
**bravo**
*assassin* 361
*desperado* 863
*applause* 931
**bravura** 415
**brawl** *cry* 411
*discord* 713
*revel* 840
**brawler**
*disputant* 710
*rioter* 742
*blusterer* 887
**brawny** 159, 192
**bray** *grind* 330
*cry* 412
**Bray, Vicar of** – 607, 886
**braze** 43
**brazen** 525, 885
– browed 885
– faced 885
**brazier**
[*see* brasier]

**breach** *crack* 44
*gap* 198
*quarrel* 713
*violation* 925
custom honoured in the – 614
– of faith 940
– of law 83, 964
– of the peace 713
**bread** 298
beg – 765
*selfish* 943
quarrel with – and butter 699
– of idleness 683
– of life *Christ* 976
*piety* 987
– upon the waters 638
– and wine 998
**breadbasket** 191
**breadth** 202
*chiaroscuro* 420
**break**
*fracture* 44
*discontinuity* 70
*change* 140
*gap* 198
*carriage* 272
*crumble* 328
*disclose* 529
*cashier* 756
*violate* 773, 927
*bankrupt* 808
– away 623
– bread 298
– bulk 297
– camp 293
– of day *morning* 125
*twilight* 422
– down *destroy* 162
*fall short* 304
*decay* 659
*fail* 732
*dance* 840
– one's fetters 614
– forth 295
– ground 66
– a habit 614
– the heart *pain* 828, 830
*dejection* 837
– the ice 888
– in *ingress* 294
*domesticate* 370
*teach* 537
*tame* 749
– in upon *derange* 61
*inopportune* 135
*hinder* 706
– a lance 716, 722
– a law 83
– loose 671, 750
– one's neck
*powerless* 158
*die* 360
– the neck of
*task* 676
*success* 731
– the news 529
– no bones 648
– of 660
– off *cease* 142
*relinquish* 624
*abrogate* 756
– out *begin* 66
*violent* 173
*disease* 655
*excited* 825
– the peace 173, 720
– Priscian's head 568
– prison 750
– the ranks 61
– short 328
– silence 582
– the teeth 579
– the thread 70
– through the clouds *visible* 446
*disclose* 529
– through a custom 614
– up *disjoin* 44
*decompose* 49
*end* 67
*revolution* 146
*destroy* 162
– up of the system, 360, 655
– on the wheel
*physical pain* 378
*mental pain* 830
*punishment* 972
– with 713
– with the past 146
– word *deceive* 545
*improbity* 940
**breaker**
*of horses* 268
*reef* 346
*wave* 348
**breakers** 348, 667
surrounded by – 704
– ahead 665
**breakfast** 298
**breakneck**
*precipice* 217
*rash* 863
**breakwater**
*refuge* 666
*obstruction* 706
**breast** *interior* 221
*confront* 234
*convex* 250
*mind* 450
*oppose* 708
*soul* 820
at the – 129
in the – of 620
– the current 719
– high 206
**breastplate** 717
**breastwork** 717
**breath** *instant* 113
*breeze* 349
*life* 359
*animality* 364
*faint sound* 405
with bated – 581
hold – *quiet* 265
*expect* 507
*wonder* 870
not a – of air 265, 382
out of – 688
in the same – 120
shortness of – 688
take – 265, 689
take away one's –
*unexpected* 508
*fear* 860
*wonder* 870
**breathe** *exist* 1
*blow* 349
*live* 359
*faint sound* 405
*evince* 467
*mean* 516
*inform* 527
*disclose* 529
*utter* 580
*speak* 582
*refresh* 689
– freely 827, 834
– one's last 360
not – a word 528
**breathing time** 687, 723
**breathless**
*voiceless* 581
*out of breath* 688
*feeling* 821
*fear* 860
*eager* 865
*wonder* 870
– attention 457
– expectation 507
– impatience 865
– speed 684
**bred in the bone** 820
**breech** 235
– loader 727
**breeches** 225
wear the – 737
– buoy 666
– maker 225
– pocket
*money* 800, 802
**breed** *kind* 75
*multiply* 161
*progeny* 167
*animals* 370
*rear* 537
**breeding** 161, 852, 894
**breeze** *wind* 349
*discord* 713
**breezy** 836
**brethren** 997
**breve** 413
**brevet**
*warrant* 741
*commission* 755
*permit* 760
– rank 873
**breviary** 998
**brevier** 591
**brevity** 201, 572
**brew** 41, 673
**brewing**
*impending* 152
storm – 665
**bribe** *equivalent* 30
*tempt* 615
*offer* 763
*gift* 784
*buy* 795
*expenditure* 809
*reward* 973
**bric-à-brac** 847
**brick** *hard* 323
*pottery* 384
*material* 635
*trump* 939, 948
make -s without straw 471
– colour 434
**brickbat** 727
**bricklayer** 690
**bride** 903
**bridewell** 752
**bridge** 45, 627
– over *join* 43
*facilitate* 705
*make peace* 723
*compromise* 774

## C

**cataclysm**
*convulsion* 146
*destruction* 162
*deluge* 348
**catacomb** 363
**catacoustics** 402
**catadupe** 348
**catafalque** 363
**catalectic** 597
**catalepsy** 265, 376, 683
**catalogue** 60, 86
**catalysis** 49, 140
**catamaran** 273, 726
**catamenial** 138, 299
**cataphonics** 402
**cataplasm** 662
**catapult** 284, 726, 727
**cataract**
*waterfall* 348
*blindness* 442, 443
**catarrh** 299
**catastrophe**
*disaster* 619
*finish* 729
*misfortune* 735
*end* 67
**catch** *imitate* 19
*fastening* 45
*song* 415
*detect* 480a
*joke* 497
*gather the meaning* 518
*cheat* 545
*receive* 785
*take* 789
by –es 70
no great – 651
– at *willing* 602
*desire* 865
– the attention 457
– one's death 360
– a disease 655
– the ear 418
– the eye 446
– fire 384
– a glimpse of 441
– an idea 498
– the infection
*excitation* 824
– a likeness 554
– a sound 418
– at straws
*overrate* 482
*credulous* 486
*unskilful* 699
*rash* 863
– by surprise 508
– a Tartar *dupe* 547
*retaliate* 718
– in a trap 545
– tripping 480a
– up 789
**catching**
*infectious* 657
**catchpenny**
*deceiving* 545
*trumpery* 643
*cheap* 815
**catchpoll** 965
**catchword** 550
**catechism** 461, 484
church – 983a
**catechize** 461
**catechumen** 541, 997
**categorical**
*positive* 474
*demonstrative* 478
*affirmative* 535
**categorically true** 494
**category** 7, 75
in the same – 9
**catena** 69
**catenary** 245
**catenation** 69
**cater** 298, 637
**caterpillar tractor** 271
**caterwaul**
*cat-cry* 412
*discord* 414
*courting* 902
**cates** 298
**catgut** 417
– scraper 416
**cathartic** 652
**cathedrâ, ex** –
*affirm* 535
*school* 542
*authority* 737
*audacity* 885
**cathedral** 1000
**Catherine wheel** 840
**catholic**
*universal* 78
*religious* 987
– church 983a
Roman – 984
**catholicon** 662
**Catiline 941**
**catopsis** 441
**catoptrics** 420
**catoptromancy** 511
**cattle** 271. 366
– truck 272
**catwalk** 273, 627
**Caucasian mystery** 983
**caucus** 696
**caudal** 67, 235
**caudate** 214
**caudex** 215
**Caudine forks** 162
**cauf** 370
**caught tripping** 491
**caulk** 660
**cause** *source* **153**
*law-suit* 969
final – 620
take up the – of 707
tell the – of 522
–d by 154
**causeless**
*casual* 156
*aimless* 621
**causerie** 588
**causeway** 627
**causidical** 965
**caustic**
*energetic* 171
*feeling* 821
*painful* 830
*gruff* 895
*malevolent* 907
– curve 245
**cautel** 864
**cautelâ, ex abundanti** – 664
**cautery** 384
**caution** *warn* 668
*prudence* 864
*security* 771
want of – 863
**cavalcade** 69, 266
**cavalier**
*horseman* 268
*rash* 863
*insolent* 885
*discourteous* 895
*contemptuous* 930
**cavaliere servente**
*servile* 886
*lover* 897
**cavalry** 726
**cavatina** 415
**cave** *dwelling* 189
*cell* 191
*cavity* 252
– canem 864
– of Adullam 624, 832
– in *hollow* 252
*submit* 725
**caveat**
*warning* 668
*command* 741
– emptor 769
**cavendo tutus 664**, 864
**cavern** [*see* cave]
**cavernous** 252
**caviare** 392, 393
– to the general 850
**cavil** *sophistry* **477**
*dissent* 489
*censure* 932
**caviller** 936
**cavity** 252
**caw** 412
**cayak** 273
**cayenne** 392, **393**
**cazique** 745
**cease** 142
– to breathe **360**
– to exist 2
**ceaseless** 112
**cecity** 442
**cede** *submit* 725
*relinquish* 782
*give* 784
**ceiling** 206, 210, 223
**celare artem, ars** – 698
**cela va sans dire**
*conformity* 82
*consequence* 154
**celebrant** 990
**celebration 883, 998**
**celebrity** 873, 875
**celerity** 274
**celeste** 417
**celestial**
*physical* 318
*religious* 976
*heaven* 981
**celibacy 904**
**cell** *abode* 189
*receptacle* 191
*cavity* 221, **252**
*prison* 752
*hermitage* **893**
**cellar** 191
**cellaret** 191
**cello** 417
**cellular** 191, 252
**cement**
*medium* 45
*unite* 43, 46, 48
*covering* 223
*hard* **323**
*material* 635
– a party 712
**cemented**
*concord* 714

**cemetery** 363
**cenobite** 893, 996
**cenotaph** 363
**censer** 998
**censor**
*moderate* 174
*critic* 480
*ban* 761
*detractor* 936
**censorious** 480, 932
**censurable** 947
**censure** 932
**censurer** 936
**census** 85, 86
*record* 551
**centaur** 83, 366
**centenarian** 130
**centenary**
*hundred* 98
*period* 138
*celebration* 883
**centesimal** 99
**cento** 597
**centrality** 222
**centralize**
*combine* 48
**centre** 68, 222
– round 72, 290
**centrifugal** 291
**centripetal** 290
**centroidal** 222
**centuple** 98
**centurion** 745
**century**
*hundred* 98
*period* 108
*long time* 110
*money* 800
**ceramic**
*bake* 384
– ware 557
**cerate** 662
**Cerberus**
*janitor* 263
*custodian* 664
*hades* 932
sop for – 615
**cereal** 298
**cerebration** 451
**cerebrum** 450
**cere-cloth** 363
**cerement**
*covering* 223
*wax* 356
*burial* 363
**ceremonious** 928
**ceremony**
*parade* 882
*courtesy* 894
*rite* 998
**Ceres** 979
**cerise** 434
**cerography** 558, 590
**Ceromancy** 511
**ceroplastic** 557
**certain** *special* 79
*indefinite number* 100
*sure* 474
*belief* 484
*true* 494
make – of 480*a*
of a – age 128
to a – degree 32
**certainly** *yes* 488
**certainness** 474
**certainty** **474**
**certes** 474, 488
**certificate**
*evidence* 467
*record* 551
*security* 771
**certify** 467, 535
**certiorari** 969
**certitude** 474
**cerulean** 438
**cess** *tax* 812
*sewer* 653
**cessation** **142**
**cession**
*surrender* 725
*of property* 782
*gift* 784
**cesspool** 653
**cestui-que trust** 779
**cestus** 45, 247
**chafe**
*physical pain* 378
*warm* 384
*irritate* 825
*mental pain* 828, 830
*discontent* 832
*incense* 900
**chaff** *trash* 643
*ridicule* 856
*vulgar* 876
not to be caught with – 698, 702
winnow – from wheat 609
**chaffer** 794
**chafing-dish** 386
**chagrin** 828
**chain** *fasten* 43
*vinculum* 45
*series* 69
*measure* 200
*interlinking* 219
*measure* 466
*gearing* 633
*imprison* 752
*ornament* 847
drag a – 749
drag a lengthened – 686
in –s 754
**chain gang** 752, 972
**chain-shot** 727
**chair** *support* 215
*vehicle* 272
*professorship* 542
*throne* 747
*celebration* 883
*president* 694
in the – 693
**chairman** 694
**chaise** 272
**chalcography** 558
**chalet** 189
**chalice** 191, 998
**chalk** *earth* 342
*white* 430
*mark* 550
*drawing* 556
– from cheese 14, 491
– out *plan* 626
**challenge**
*question* 461
*doubt* 485
*claim* 924
*defy* 715
*accuse* 938
– comparison 648
**cham** 745
**chamber** *room* 191
*council* 696
*mart* 799
sick – 655
**chamberlain** 746
**chambermaid** 746
**chameleon** 149, 440
**chamfer** 259
**chamois** 309
**champ** 298
– the bit *disobedient* 742
*chafe* 825
*angry* 900
**champagne** 298
**champaign** 344
**Champ de Mars** 728
**champêtre, fête** – 840
**champion**
*best* 648
*auxiliary* 711
*defence* 717
*combatant* 726
*representative* **759**
*sympathizer* 914
**championship** 707
**chance** **156, 621**
be one's – 151
game of – 840
great – 472
small – 473
stand a – 177, 470
take one's – 675
–s against one 665
whirligig of – 156
as – would have it 152
**chancel** 1000
**chancellor**
*president* **745**
*deputy* 759
*judge* 967
– of the exchequer 801
**chancery**
court of – 966
– suit *delay* 133
**chandelier** 214, 423
**chandelle, le jeu n'en vaut pas la** – 638, 643
*dear* 814
**chandler** 797
**change**
*alteration* **140**
*mart* 799
*small coin* 800
inter– 148
radical – 146
sudden – 146
– about 149
– colour 821
– for 147
– hands 783
– of mind 607
– of opinion 485
– of place 264
**changeableness** 149, 605
**changeful**
*fickle* 607
**changeling**
*substitute* 147
*fool* 501
**changeless** 16
**changer** 797
**channel**
*furrow* 259
*opening* 260
*conduit* 350
*way* 627
**chant** *song* 415
*sing* 416
*worship* 990

**chant du cygne** 360
**chanter** 416
**chanticleer** 366
**chantry** 1000
**chaomancy** 511
**chaos** 59
**chap** *crack* 198
*jaw* 231
*fellow* 373
– book 593
**chapel** 1000
**chaperon**
*accompany* 88
*watch* 459
*protect* 664
**chapfallen** 878
**chaplain** 995, 996
**chaplet** *circle* 247
*garland* 550
*trophy* 733
*ornament* 847
**chapman** 797
**chapter** *part* 51
*topic* 454
*book* 593
*council* 696
*church* 995
– of accidents 156, 621
– house 1000
– and verse 467, 494
**char** *burn* 384
*serve* 746
**char-à-banc** 272
**character**
*nature* 5
*state* 7
*class* 75
*oddity* 83
*letter* 561
*drama* 599
*disposition* 820
*reputation* 873
**characteristic**
*intrinsic* 5
*special* 79
*tendency* 176
*mark* 550
**characterize** 564, 594
**characterized** 820
**charade** 533, 599
**charcoal** *fuel* 384, 388
*black* 431
*drawing* 556
**charge** *fill* 52
*contents* 190
*business* 625
*requisition* 630
*direction* 693
*advice* 695
*precept* 697
*attack* 716
*order* 741
*custody* 751
*commission* 755
*bargain for* 794
*price* 812
*accusation* 938
in – prisoner 754
justifiable – 937
take – of 664
take in – 751
– on *attribute* 155
– with 155, 777
**chargé d'affaires** 758
**chargeable** *debt* 806
– on *duty* 926
**charger**
*carrier* 271
*fighter* 726
**Charing Cross, proclaim at** – 531
**chariot** 272
drag at one's – wheels 749
**charioteer** 268, 694
**charity** *give* 784
*liberal* 816
*beneficent* 906
*pity* 914
Christian – 906
cold as – 823
– that begins at home 943
**charivari** 404, 407
**charlatan**
*ignoramus* 493
*impostor* 548
*mountebank* 844
*boaster* 884
**charlatanism**
*ignorance* 491
*falsehood* 544
*affectation* 855
**Charles's wain** 318
**Charleston** 840
**Charley** 753
**charm** *motive* 615
*please* 829
*beauty* 845
*love* 897
*conjure* 992
*spell* 993
bear a –ed life 664, 734
**charmer** 994
voice of the – 933
not listen to voice of – 604
**charnel-house** 363
**Charon** 982
**chart** 527, 554
**charter**
*commission* 755
*permit* 760
*compact* 769
*security* 771
*privilege* 924
**chartered**
*legal* 963
– accountant 801, 811
– libertine 962
**Chartist** 742
**charwoman** 690, 746
**chary**
*economical* 817
*stingy* 819
*cautious* 864
**Charybdis** 312, 665
**chase** *emboss* 250
*furrow* 259
*drive away* 289
*killing* 361
*forest* 367
*pursue* 622
*ornament* 847
wild goose – 645
**chaser** 559
**chasm** *interval* 198
*opening* 260
**chassé** 840
**chassemarée** 273
**chassepot** 727
**chasser** 297
– balancer 605
**chasseur** 726
**chassis** 215
**chaste**
*shapely* 242
*language* 576, 578
*simple* 849
*good taste* 850
*pure* 960
**chasten**
*moderate* 174
*punish* 972
**chastened**
*subdued spirit* 826
*penitent* 950
**chastise** 932, 972
– with scorpions 739
**chasuble** 999
**chat** 588
**chat qui dort** 667, 668
**château** 189
– en Espagne **858**
**chatelaine** 847
**chatoyant** 440
**chattels** 633, 780
**chatter** 314, 584
**chatterbox** 584
**chattering of teeth**
*cold* 383
**chatty** 584, 892
**chauffeur** 268
**chaunt**
*song* 415
*sing* 416
*worship* 990
**chaussé** 225
**chauvinism** 884, 885
**chawbacon** 876
**cheap** 643, 815
hold – 930
– jack 797
**cheapen** *haggle* **794**
*begrudge* 819
**cheapness** **815**
**cheat** 545, 548
**check**
*numerical* 85
*stop* 142
*moderate* 174
*counteract* 179
*slacken* 275
*plaid* 440
*experiment* **463**
*measure* 466
*evidence* 468
*ticket* 550
*dissuade* 616
*hinder* 706
*misfortune* **735**
*restrain* 751
*money order* **800**
– the growth **201**
– oneself 826
**checkered** 149
**checkers** 440, **840**
**checkmate**
*stop* 142
*success* 731
*failure* 732
**check-roll** 86
**check-string**
pull the – 142
**cheek** *side* 236
*impertinence* **885**
– by jowl *with* **88**
*near* 197
**cheeks** *dual* 89
**cheep** 412
**cheer** *repast* 298

*cry* 411
*aid* 707
*pleasure* 827
*relief* 834
*mirth* 836
*rejoicing* 838
*amusement* 840
*courage* 861
*sociality* 892
*welcome* 894
*applaud* 931
good – *hope* 858
*high living* 957
**cheerfulness 836**
**cheerless** 830, 837
**cheeseparings**
*remains* 40
*dirt* 653
*economy* 817
**chef de cuisine**
*servant* 746
**chef-d'œuvre** 648, 698
**cheka** 696
**chemin**
– de fer
*game* 840
– faisant 270
**chemise** 225
**chemist** 662
**Chemistry** 144
organic – 357
**cheque** 800
**chequer** 440
– roll 86
**cherchez la femme** 155
**chère amie** 962
**cherish** *aid* 707
*love* 897
*endearment* 902
– a belief 484
– feelings &c. 821
– an idea &c. 451
**cheroot** 392
**cherry**
– red 434
two bites of a –
*overrate* 482
*roundabout* 629
*clumsy* 699
**cherry-cheeked** 845
**cherry-coloured** 434
**cherub** 977
**Cheshire cat** 838
**chess** 840
**chessboard** 440
**chest** 191, 802
**chestnut-colour** 433
**cheval-de-bataille**
*plea* 617
*plan* 626
*vanity* 880
**cheval-glass** 445
**chevalier** 875
– d'industrie 792
**chevaux de frise** 253, 717
**chevron**
*angle* 217
*indication* 550
*badge* 747
*decoration* 877
**chew** 298
– the cud 451
– tobacco 392
**chiaroscuro**
*light* 420
*grey* 432
*painting* 556
**chiasma** 43
**chic** 845, 882
**chicane**
*sophistry* 477
*deceit* 545
*cunning* 702
**chicken** 129, 366
– in every pot 733
count –s before hatched 858, 863
tender as a – *soft* 324
*sensitive* 822
*compassionate* 914
**chickenhearted** 862
**chide** 932
**chief** *principal* 642
*master* 745
evidence in – 467
– constable 765
– part 31
**Chief Justice** 967
**chiefdom** 737
**chieftain** 745
**chiffonnier** 876
**chiffonnière** 191
**chignon** 225
**chilblain** 383
**child**
*infant* 129
*offspring* 167
*fool* 501
– of God 987
–'s play 643, 705
with – 161
**childbirth** 161
**childhood** 127
**childish**
*credulous* 486
*foolish* 499
*feeble* 575
– treble 581
**childlike** 703
**chiliad** 98
**chill** *cold* 383
*render cold* 385
*indispose* 616
– the spine 830, 860
**chillies** 393
**Chiltern Hundreds** 757
**chime**
*repetition* 104
*roll* 407
*resonance* 408
*melody* 413
– in with *agree* 23
*conform* 82
*assent* 488
*concord* 714
**chimera** 83, 515
**chimney** 260, 351
– corner 189
– pot 249
**china** 384, 557
**China to Peru** 180
**chine** 235
**chinese white** 430
**chink** *gap* 198
*sound* 408
*money* 800
**chip** *small* 32
*detach* 44
*bit* 51
*reduce* 195
– of the old block
*similar* 17
*copy* 21
*offspring* 167
**chippy** 962
**Chirography** 590
**Chirology** 550
**Chiromancy** 511
**chirp**
*bird-note* 412
*sing* 416
*cheerful* 836
*rejoice* 838
**chirrup** [*see* chirp]
**chirurgery** 662
**chisel**
*fabricate* 161
*form* 240
*sharp* 253
*sculpture* 557
**chit** 129, 193
**chit-chat** 588
**chitterlings** 221
**chivalry** *war* 722
*tenure* 777
*courage* 861
*courtesy* 894
*philanthropy* **910**
*honour* 939
*generosity* 942
**chlamys** 225
**chloroform** 376, **823**
**chlorophyl** 435
**chlorotic** 655
**chock full** 52
**chocolate**
*food* 298
*colour* 433
**choice** *will* 600
*election* 609
*excellent* 648
absence of – **609a**
by – 600
– spirits 873
– of words 569
**choir** *sing* 416
*church music* **996**
*church* 1000
– boy 996
– invisible **360**, 977
**choke** *close* 261
*stifle* 361
*redundant* 641
*hinder* 706
–full *complete* **52**
*replete* 639
–off 706
**choler** 900
**choleric** 901
**choose** 609
do what one –s **748**
**chop** *disjoin* 44
*change* 140
– logic 476
– up 201
**chopfallen** 837
**chopper** 330
**chopping**
*large* 192
– sea 348
**chops** *mouth* 66
*jaws* 231
*food* 298
**chorale** 415
**chord** 413
**chore** 625
**choreography** 840
**chorister** 416, 996
**chorography** 183
**chorus**
*shout* 411
*song* 415
*singers* 416

*defence* 717
line of – 233
**circumvent**
*environ* 227
*move round* 311
*cheat* 545
*cunning* 702
*hinder* 706
*defeat* 731
**circumvest** 225
**circumvolution**
*winding* 248
*rotation* 312
**circus**
*buildings* 189
*drama* 599
*arena* 728
*amusement* 840
**cirrus** 353
**cistern**
*receptacle* 191
*store* 636
**Cistercian** 996
**cit** 188
**citadel** 717
**citation** 467, 733
**cite**
*quote as example* 82
*as evidence* 467
*summon* 741
*accuse* 938
*arraign* 969
**cithern** 417
**citizen** 188
– of the world 910
**citriculture** 371
**citrine** 436
**city** 189
in the – 794
**city manager** 965
**civet** 400
**civic** 372
**civil** *courteous* 894
*laity* 997
– authorities 745
– crown 733
– law 963
– war 722
**civilian** *lawyer* 968
*layman* 997
**civilization**
*improvement* 658
*fashion* 852
*courtesy* 894
**civilized life** 852
**civism** 910
**clack** *clatter* 407
*animal cry* 412
*talkative* 584
**clad** 225
**claim** *requisition* 630
*demand* 741
*property* 780
*right* 924
*lawsuit* 969
– the attention 457
**claimant**
*petitioner* 767
*right* 924
**clair-obscur** 420
**clairvoyance** 992
**clairvoyant** 513, 994
**clamant** 411
**clamber** 305
**clammy** 352
**clamorous**
[*see* clamour]
*loud* 404
*excitable* 825
**clamour** *cry* 411
*wail* 839
– against 932
– for 765
**clamp** *fasten* 43
*fastening* 45
**clan** *race* 11
*class* 75
*family* 166
*party* 712
**clandestine** 528
**clangor** 404
**clank** 410
**clannishness** 481
**clanship** 709
**clap** *explosion* 406
*applaud* 931
thunder –
*prodigy* 872
– the hands
*rejoice* 838
– on 37
– on the shoulder 615
– together 43
– up *imprison* 751
**clapperclaw**
*contention* 720
*censure* 932
**claptrap**
*pretence* 546
*display* 882
**claquer** 935
faire – son fouet 884
**clarence** 272
**claret colour** 434
**clarify** 652
**clarinet** 417
**clarion** *music* 417
*war* 722
**clarity** 518
**clash** *disagree* 24
*cross* 179
*concussion* 276
*sound* 406
*oppose* 708
*discord* 713
– of arms 720
**clasp** *fasten* 43
*fastening* 45
*stick* 46
*come close* 197
*belt* 230
*embrace* 902
**class** *arrange* 60
*category* 75
*learners* 541
*party* 712
– prejudice 481
– room 542
**classic** *old* 124
*symmetry* 242
**classical**
*elegant writing* 578
*taste* 850
– art 556
– dancing 840
– education 537
– music 415
**classicist** 492
**classics** 560
**classify** 60
**classmate** 890
**clatter** 404, 407
**claudication**
*slowness* 275
*failure* 732
**clause** *part* 51
*passage* 593
*condition* 770
**clausis, januis** – 528
**claustral** 110
**clavate** 250
**clavichord** 417
**clavier** 417
**claw** *hook* 781
*grasp* 789
– back 935
**clay** *soft* 324
*earth* 342
*corpse* 362
*material* 635
– pipe 392
**clay-cold** 383
**claymore** 727
**clean**
*entirely* 52
*perfect* 650
*unstained* 652
– bill of health 654
– breast
*disclose* 529
– forgotten 506
– hand
*proficient* 700
with – hands
*honesty* 939
*innocence* 946
– out *empty* 297
– shaven 226
– sweep
*revolution* 146
*destruction* 162
**clean-up** 775
**clear** *simple* 42
*sound* 413
*light* 420
*transparent* 425
*visible* 446
*certain* 474
*intelligible* 518
*manifest* 525
*easy* 705
*liberate* 750
*profit* 775
*vindicate* 937
*innocent* 946
*acquit* 975
all – 664, 705
coast – 664
get – off 671
keep – of 623
make – 529
– for action
*prepare* 673
– articulation 580
– conscience 946
– the course 30
– cut 518
– the ground
*facilitate* 705
– of *distant* 196
– off *pay* 807
– out *empty* 297
*clean* 652
– sighted
*vision* 441
*shrewd* 498
– sky *hope* 858
– stage
*occasion* 134
*easy* 705
*right* 922
– thinking 498
– the throat 297
– up *light* 420
*intelligible* 518
*interpret* 522
**clearheaded** 498

**clear-obscure** 420
**cleat** 45
**cleavage**
*cutting* 44
*structure* 329
**cleave** *sunder* 44
*adhere* 46
*bisect* 91
**cleaver** 253
**cledge** 342
**clef** 413
**cleft** *divided* 44
*bisected* 91
*chink* 198
in a – stick
*difficulty* 704
**clem** 956
**clement**
*lenient* 740
*long-suffering* 826
*compassionate* 914
**clench** *compact* 769
*retain* 781
*take* 789
**clepe** 564
**clepsydra** 114
**clerestory** 191, 1000
**clergy** **996**
**clerical** 995, 996
– error 495
– staff 746
**clerk** *scholar* 492
*recorder* 553
*writer* 590
*helper* 711
*servant* 746
*agent* 758
*clergy* 996
articled – 541
– in holy orders 995
– of works 694
**clerkship**
*commission* 755
**cleromancy** 511
**clever**
*intelligent* 498
*skilful* 698
*smart* 842
too – by half 702
**clew** *ball* 249
*interpretation* 522
*indication* 550
seek a – 461
**click** 406
**client**
*dependant* 746
*customer* 795
**clientship**
*subjection* 749
**cliff** *height* 206
*vertical* 212
*steep* 217
*land* 342
**climacteric** 128
**climate** *region* 181
*weather* 338
fine – 656
**climatology** 338
**climax**
*supremacy* 33
*summit* 210
*culmination* 729
**climb** 305
– on the band-wagon 731
**clime** 181
**clinal** 217
**clinch** *fasten* 43
*close* 261
*certify* 474
*pun* 563
*complete* 729
*clutch* 781
*snatch* 789
– an argument 47
– the fist at 909
**clincher** 479
**cling** *adhere* 46
– to *near* 197
*willing* 602
*persevere* 604a
*habit* 613
*observe* 772
*desire* 865
*love* 897
– to hope 858
– to one another 709
**clinic** 662
**clink**
*resonance* 408
*stridor* 410
*prison* 752
**clinker** *brick* 384
*dirt* 653
**clinometer**
*oblique* 217
*angle* 244
**clinquant**
*ornament* 847
*vulgar* 851
**Clio** 594
**clip** *shorten* 201
– the wings
*powerless* 158
*speed* 264
*slow* 275
*useless* 645
*hinder* 706
*prohibit* 761
– one's words 583
**clipper** 273
**clipping**
*small piece* 51
**clique** *conclave* 696
*party* 712
**cloaca** *conduit* 350
*foul* 653
**Cloacina** 653
**cloak** *dress* 225
*conceal* 528
*disguise* 530
**cloaked** 223
**cloche** 371
**clock** 114
**clockwork** 633
by – *uniform* 16
*order* 58
*regular* 80
**clod** *lump* 192
*earth* 342
*fool* 501
*bungler* 701
**clodhopper** 876
**clodpated**
*stupid* 499
**clog** *shoe* 225
*hinder* 706
– dance 840
**cloison** 228
**cloisonné** 557
**cloister** *arcade* 189
*way* 627
*restraint* 751
*convent* 1000
**close** *similar* 17
*tight* 43
*end* 67
*field* 181
*court* 189
*near* 197
*narrow* 203
*shut* 261
*dense* 321
*warm* 382
*hidden* 528
*concise* 572
*taciturn* 585
*complete* 729
*stingy* 819
examine –ly 457
keep – *hide* 528
*retain* 781
tread – upon 281
– the door upon
*restrain* 751
– the ears 419
– the eyes
*die* 360
*not see* 442
– one's eyes to
*not attend* 458
*set at naught* **773**
– at hand
*to-morrow* 121
*imminent* 152
*near* 197
– the hand
*refuse* 764
– in upon 290
– inquiry 461
–ly packed 72
– prisoner 754
– quarters 197
*approach* 286
*attack* 716
*battle* 722
– one's ranks **673**
– study
*thought* 451
*attention* 457
– up 197, 290
– with *cohere* **46**
*assent* 488
*attack* 716
*contend* 720
*consent* 762
*compact* 769
**close-mouthed** **585**
**closet**
*receptacle* 191
*ambush* 530
**closeted with**
*conference* 588
*advice* 695
**close-up** 197
**closure** 142, **261**
**clot** *solidify* 321
*earth* 342
**cloth** *vocation* **625**
*napkin* 652
*clergy* 996
**clothes** 225
grave – 363
– basket 191
**clothier** 225
**Clotho** 601
**clotpoll** 501
**clotted** 352
**cloud**
*assemblage* 72
*multitude* 102
*mist* 353
*shade* 424
*screen* 530
break through the –s 446
drop from the – 508
in a – 475, 528
in the –s

**Colosseum** 728
**colossus** 192, 206
**colour** *hue* **428**
*tone* 431
*appearance* 448
*probability* 472
*disguise* 544
*paint* 556
*plea* 617
*be angry* 900
all –s 440
change –
*shame* 879
give a – to
*change* 140
*qualify* 469
*probable* 472
*falsehood* 544
lend a – to
*plea* 617
*vindicate* 937
man of – 431
show in true –s 543
– blindness 443
– printing 558
– sergeant 745
–ed spectacles 424
– too highly 549
– up *redden* 434
*blush* 879
**colourable**
*ostensible* 472
*deceptive* 545
**colourful** 882
**colouring**
[*see* colour]
*meaning* 516
false – 523
– matter 428
**colourless**
*weak* 160
*pale* 429
**colours**
*ensign* 550
*decoration* 877
with – flying
*resolution* 604
false – 544, 545
flying –
*display* 882
*celebration* 883
lower one's – 735
nail one's – to the mast 604
show one's –
*manifest* 525
*disclose* 529
true to one's – 939
**colporteur** 797
**colstaff** 215
**colt** *young* 129
*horse* 271
*fool* 501
**columbine** 599
**columella** 215
**column** *series* 69
*height* 206
*support* 215
*cylinder* 249
*caravan* 266
*monument* 551
*printing* 591
*troop* 726
**columnist** 527, 553
**colures** 318
**coma** *inactive* 683
*insensible* 376, 823
**comb** *teeth* 253
*clean* 652
*punish* 972
**combat** 720, 722
**combat, hors de –**
*useless* 645
*tired* 688
**combatant** **726**
**combe** 252
**comber** 348
**combination** **48**
*arithmetical* 84
*party* 712
**combine** *unite* 48
*co-operate* 709
**combustible** 388
**combustion** 384
**come** *happen* 151
*approach* 286
*arrive* 292
*cheer up!* 836
*out upon!* 932
to – *future* 121
*destiny* 152
– about 658
– across
*discover* 480*a*
*acquire* 775
*pay up* 807
– after
*sequence* 63
*posterior* 117
– between 631
cut and – again 639
– of age 131
– amiss
*disagreeable* 24
*ill-timed* 135
– back 283
– before 116
– by 775
– at one's call 743
– to a determination 604
– down with 807
– into existence
*be* 1
*begin* 66
– first *superior* 33
*precede* 62
– forth
*egress* 295
*appear* 446
– forward 763
– from 154
– to the front 303
– and go 314
– to hand 785
– to a head
*climax* 33
*complete* 52
– in *ingress* 294
*receipt* 785
– in for
*property* 778, 780
– to one's knowledge 527
– to life 359
– what may 474
– near 286
– to nothing
*unproductive* 169
*fail* 732
– of 154
– off *event* 151
*disjoin* 44
*loop-hole* 617
*escape* 671
– on *future* 121
*destiny* 152
*I defy you* 715
*attack* 716
– to oneself 660
– into operation 170
– out
*disclosure* 529
*publication* 531
*on the stage* 599
– out of *effect* 154
*egress* 295
– out with
*disclose* 529
*speak* 582
– over
*influence* 615
*consent* 762
– to pass *state* 7
*event* 151
– to pieces 44
– to the point
*speciality* 79
*attention* 457
*concise* 572
– to the rescue 672
– round
*period* 138
*conversion* **144**
*belief* 484
*assent* 488
*change of mind* 607
*influence* 615
*restoration* 660
*be pacified* 723
*consent* 762
– to the same thing 27
– short of
*inferior* 34
*fall short* 304
– to one's senses 502
– to a stand **142**
– to terms
*assent* 488
*contract* 769
it –s to this
*concisely* 572
– to *equal* 27
*whole* 50
*arithmetic* 85
*become* 144
*effect* 154
*inherit* 777
*money* 800
*price* 812
– together
*assemble* 72
*converge* 290
– under 76
– upon
*unexpected* 508
*acquire* 775
*claim* 924
– into use 613
– into view 446
– into the views of
*co-operate* 709
– off well 731
– into the world 359
**come-down** 306, 735
**comedy**
*drama* 599
*comic* 853
**comely** 845
**comestible** 298
**comet**
*wanderer* 268
*star* 318
**cometary** 111

**compages**
*whole* 50
*structure* 329
**compagination** 43
**companion** *match* 17
*accompaniment* 88
*ladder* 305
*friend* 890
**companionable** 892
**companionship** 892
**companionway** 305
**company**
*assembly* 72
*actors* 599
*party, partnership* 712
*troop* 726
*sociality* 892
bear – 88
in – with 88
**comparable** 9
**comparative** 464
*degree* 26
– anatomy 368
**comparatively** 32
**compare** 464
– notes 695
**comparison** **464**
**compartition** 44
**compartment**
*part* 51
*region* 181
*place* 182
*cell* 191
*carriage* 272
**compass**
*degree* 26
*space* 180
*surround* 227
*measure* 466
*intend* 620
*guidance* 693
*achieve* 729
box the –
*direction* 278
*rotation* 312
keep within –
*moderation* 174
*fall short* 304
*economy* 817
points of the – 236
in a small – 193
– about 229
– of thought 498
**compassion** 914
object of – 828
**compatible**
*consentaneous* 23
*possible* 470
**compatriot**
*inhabitant* 188
*friend* 890
**compeer** *equal* 27
*friend* 890
**compel** 744
**compellation** 564
**compendency** 43
**compendious** 201
**compendium** **596**
*book* 593
**compensate**
*make up for* 30
*requite* 973
**compensation** **30**
**compère** 599
**competence**
*power* 157
*sufficiency* 639
*skill* 698
*wealth* 803
**competition**
*opposition* 708
*contention* 720
**competitor**
*opponent* 710
*combatant* 726
*candidate* 767
**compilation**
*collect* 72
*book* 593
*compendium* 596
**compile** 54
**complacent**
*pleased* 827
*content* 831
*courteous* 894
*kind* 906
**complain** 839
**complainant** 938
**complaint**
*illness* 655
*murmur* 839
lodge a – 938
– without cause 839
**complaisant**
*lenient* 740
*courteous* 894
*kind* 906
**complement**
*adjunct* 39
*remainder* 40
*part* 52
*arithmetic* 84
**complementary**
*correlation* 12
*colour* 428
**complete**
*entire* 52
*accomplish* **729**
*compact* 769
– answer 479
– circle 311
in a – degree 31
**completeness** **52**
**completion** **729**
**complex** 59
**complexion**
*state* 7
*colour* 428
*appearance* 448
**compliance**
*conformity* 82
*obedience* 743
*consent* 762
*observance* **772**
**complicate**
*derange* 61
**complicated**
*disorder* 59
*convolution* 248
**complice** 711
**complicity** 709
**compliment**
*courtesy* 894, 896
*praise* 931
poor – 932
–s of season 896
**complimentary**
*free* 815
**complot** 626
**comply** [*see* compliance]
**compo** *coating* 223
*material* 635
**component** **56**
**componere lites** 723, 724
**comport**
– oneself 692
– with 23
**compos mentis** 502
**compose**
*make up* 54, 56
*produce* 161
*moderate* 174
*music* 416
*write* 590
*printing* 591
*pacify* 723
*assuage* 826
**composed**
*self-possessed* 826
**composer**
*music* 413
**composite** 41
**composition** **54**
[*see* compose]
*combination* 48
*piece of music* 415
*picture* 556
*style* 569
*writing* 590
*building material* 635
*compromise* **774**
*barter* 794
*atonement* 952
**compositor**
*printer* 591
**compost** 653
**composure** 826, 871
**compotation** 959
**compote** 298
**compound**
*mix* 41
*combination* 48
*limited space* 182
*enclosure* 232
*compromise* 774
– arithmetic 466
– for *substitute* **147**
*barter* 794
**comprador** 637
**comprehend**
*compose* 54
*include* 76
*know* 490
*understand* 518
**comprehension** [*see* comprehend]
*intelligence* 498
**comprehensive** 76
*complete* 50
*general* 78
*wide* 192
– argument 476
**compress**
*contract* 195
*curtail* 201
*condense* 321
*remedy* 662
**compressible** 322
**comprise** 76
**comprobation**
*evidence* 467
*demonstration* **478**
**compromise**
*dally with* 605
*mid-course* 628
*taint* 659
*danger* 665
*pacify* 723
*compact* 769
*compound* **774**
*atone* 952
**compromised**
*promised* 768
**compter** 799
**compte rendu**
*record* 551
*accounts* 811

**comptroller** 694
**compulsion** **744**
**compunction** 833, 950
**compurgation**
*evidence* 467
*acquittal* 970
**compute** 85
**comrade** 890
**comradeship** 892
**con** *think* 451
*get by heart* 505
*learn* 539
**conation** 600
**conatu magnas nugas, magno –**
*waste* 638
*unimportance* 643
**conatus** 176
**concamerate** 245
**concatenation**
*junction* 43
*continuity* 69
**concavity** **252**
**conceal**
*invisible* 447
*hide* 528
*cunning* 702
**concealment** **528**, 893
**concede**
*assent* 488
*admit* 529
*permit* 760
*consent* 762
*give* 784
**conceit** *idea* 453
*folly* 499
*supposition* 514
*imagination* 515
*wit* 842
*affectation* 855
*vanity* 880
**conceited**
*dogmatic* 481
**conceivable** 470
**conceive** *begin* 66
*beget* 161
*teem* 168
*believe* 484
*understand* 490
*imagine* 515
*plan* 626
**concent** 413
**concentrate**
*assemble* 72
*centrality* 222
*converge* 290
**concentric** 216, 222
**conception**
[*see* conceive]
*intellect* 450
*idea* 453
**concern**
*relation* **9**
*event* 151
*business* 625
*importance* 642
*firm* 797
*grief* 828
– oneself with 625
**concert**
*agreement* 23
*synchronism* 120
*music* 415
act in – 709
in – *musical* 413
*concord* 714
– measures 626
**concertina** 417
**concerto** 415
**concert-room** 840
**concession**
*permission* 760
*consent* 762
*compromise* **774**
*giving* 784
*discount* 813
**concesso, ex –**
*reasoning* 476
*assent* 488
**concetto** 842
**conchoid** 245
**conchology** 223
**concierge** 263, 753
**conciliate**
*talk over* 615
*pacify* 723
*satisfy* 831
*courtesy* 894
*atonement* 952
**conciliatory** [*see* conciliate]
*concord* 714
*forgiving* 918
**conciliatrix** 962
**concinnity**
*agreement* 23
*style* 578
*beauty* 845
**conciseness** **572**
**concision** 201
**conclave**
*assembly* 72
*council* 696
*church* 995
**conclude**
*end* 67
*infer* 480
*resolve* 604
*complete* 729
*compact* 769
**conclusion**
[*see* conclude]
*sequel* 65
*germination* 161
*judgment* 480
try –s 476
forgone – 611
hasty – 481
**conclusive**
[*see* conclude]
*answer* 462
*evidence* 467
*certain* 474
*proof* 478
– reasoning 476
**concoct** *lie* 544
*write* 590
*plan* 626
*prepare* 673
**concomitant**
*accompany* 88
*same time* 120
*concurrent* 178
**concord** *agree* 23
*music* **413**
*assent* 488
*harmony* **714**
**concordance** 562
*book* 593
**concordant** 173
**concordat** 769
**concordia discors** 24, 59
**concours** 720
**concourse**
*assemblage* 72
*convergence* 290
**concremation** 384
**concrete** *existent* 3
*mass* 46
*definite* 79
*density* 321
*hardness* 323
*materials* 635
**concubinage** 961
**concubine** 926
**concupiscence** 865, 961
**concur**
*co-exist* 120
*causation* 178
*converge* 290
*assent* 488
*concert* 709
**concurrence** **178**, 216
**concussion** 276
**condemnation** 932, **971**
**condemned cell** 752
**condense**
*compress* **195**
*dense* 321
**condensed**
*concise* 572
**condescend** 879
**condign** 924
**condiment** **393**
**condisciple** 541
**condition** *state* **7**
*modification* 469
*supposition* **514**
*term* 770
*repute* 873
*rank* 875
in – *plump* 192
in good – 648
on – 770
in perfect – 650
physical – 316
**conditional** 8
**conditions** **770**
**condolence** 914, **915**
**condone** 918
**condottiere**
*traveller* 268
*fighter* 726
**conduce**
*contribute* **153**
*tend* 176
*concur* 178
*avail* 644
**conducive** 631
**conduct**
*transfer* 270
*music* 416
*procedure* **692**
*lead* 693
safe –
*passport* 631
*safety* 664
– a funeral 363
– an inquiry **461**
– to 278
**conduction** 264
**conductor** 268
*conveyer* 271
*director* 694
lightning – 666
**conduit** **350**
**conduplicate** 89
**condyle** 250
**cone** *round* 249
*pointed* 253
**confabulation** 588
**confection** 396
*confectionery* **396**
**confectioner** 637
**confederacy**
*co-operation* **709**
*party* 712
**confederate** **711**

**construction** 161
*form* 240
*structure* 329
*meaning* 522
put a false – upon 523
**constructive**
*latent* 526
– evidence 467
**constructor** 164
**construe** 522
**consubstantiation** 998
**consuetude** 613
**consul** 758, 759
**consulship** 737
**consult** 695
– one's pillow 133
– one's own wishes 943
– the wishes of 707
**consultant** 662
**consultation** 695, 696
**consume**
*destroy* 162
*waste* 638
*use* 677
– away 36
– time
*time* 106
*inactivity* 683
**consumere natus, fruges** – 683
**consuming** 830
**consummate**
*great* 31
*complete* 52
*completed* 729
– skill 698
**consummation**
*end* 67
*completion* 729
– devoutly to be wished
*good* 618
*desire* 865
**consumption** [*see* consume]
*decrease* 36
*shrinking* 195
*disease* 655
**contact** 199
come in –
*arrive* 292
**contagion**
*transfer* 270
*disease* 655
*unhealthy* 657
**contain**
*be composed of* 54
*include* 76
**container** 191
**contaminate**
*soil* 653
*spoil* 659
**contaminated**
*diseased* 655
**contango** 133, 813
**contemn** 930
**contemper** 174
**contemplate**
*view* 441
*think* 451
*expect* 507
*purpose* 620
**contemporary** 120
**contemporation** 174
**contempt** **930**
– of danger 861
**contemptible**
*unimportant* 643
*dishonourable* 940
**contend**
*reason* 476
*assert* 535
*fight* 720
– with difficulties 704
– for
*vindicate* 937
**content**
*assenting* 488
*willing* 602
*calm* 826
*satisfied* **831**
to one's heart's –
*sufficient* 639
*success* 731
**contention** **720**
**contentious** 901
**contents**
*ingredients* 56
*list* 86
*components* **190**
*synopsis* 596
**conterminate**
*end* 67
*limit* 233
**conterminous** 199
**contesseration** 72
**contest** 708, 720
**contestant** 710
**context** 591
from the – 516
**contexture** 329
**contiguity** **199**
**continence** 960
**continent**
*land* 342
**continental** 643
**contingency**
*event* 151
*uncertainty* 475
*expectation* 507
**contingent**
*conditional* 8
*casual* 156
*liable* 177
*possible* 470
*uncertain* 475
*supply* 635
*aid* 707
*allotted* 786
*donation* 809
*unforeseen* 508
– duration **108a**
– interest 780
**continual**
*perpetual* 112
*frequent* 136
**continuance** **143**
**continuation**
*adjunct* 39
*sequence* 63
*sequel* 65
– school 542
**continue**
*endure* 106, 110
*persist* 143
**continued** 69
– success 731
**continuity** **69**
*uniformity* 16
**contortion**
*distortion* 243
*convolution* 248
**contortionist** 599, 700
**contour**
*outline* 230
*appearance* 448
**contra** 14
per – 708
– bonos mores
*vulgar* 851
*improper* 925
*vice* 945
**contraband**
*deceitful* 545
*prohibited* 761
*illicit* 964
**contrabasso** 417
**contraception** 706
**contract**
*shrink* 195
*narrow* 203
*promise* 768
*bargain* 769
*bridge* 840
– a debt 806
– a habit 613
– an obligation 768
**contractility** 195
**contraction** **195**
*short-hand* 590
*compendium* **596**
**contractor** 690
**contradict**
*contrary* 14
*answer* 462
*dissent* 489
*deny* 536
*oppose* 708
**contradictory**
*disagreement* **24**
*evidence* 468
*discord* 713
**contradistinction** **15**
**contraindicate**
*dissuade* 616
*warning* 668
**contraire, tout au** – 536
**contralto** 408, **416**
**contraposition**
*inversion* 218
*reversion* **237**
**contrapuntist** **413**
**contrariety** **14**
**contrary**
*opposite* 14
*antagonistic* **179**
*captious* 608
*opposing* 708
quite the – 536
– to expectation
*improbable* 473
*unexpected* 508
– to reason **471**
**contrast**
*contrariety* 14
*difference* 15
*comparison* 464
**contravallation** **717**
**contravene**
*contrary* 14
*counterevidence* 468
*deny* 536
*hinder* 706
*oppose* 708
**contre cœur, à** – 603
**contre-coup** **277**
**contretemps**
*ill-timed* 135
*hindrance* 706
*misfortune* **735**
**contribute**
*cause* 153
*tend* 176
*concur* 178

– fire *interchange* 148
*difficulty* 704
*opposition* 708
*attack* 716
–ed in love 898
– the mind 451
– the path of 706
– and pile 621
– purposes 14
*disorder* 59
*error* 495
*misinterpret* 523
*unskilful* 699
*difficulty* 704
*opposition* 708
*discord* 713
– oneself 998
– questions
*inquiry* 461
*discord* 713
*game* 840
– road 627
– the Rubicon 609
– sea 348
– swords 722
**crossbow** 727
**cross-examine** 461
**cross-grained** 256
*obstinate* 606
*sulky* 901*a*
**crossing** 219
– sweeper 652
**crosspatch** 895
**crossroads** 8
**cross-word puzzle** 533
**crotch** 244
**crotchet**
*eccentric* 83
*music* 413
*misjudgment* 481
*obstinacy* 606
*caprice* 608
**crouch** *lower* 207
*stoop* 308
*fear* 860
*servile* 886
– before 725
**croup** 235
**croupier** 694
**crow** *cry* 412
*black* 431
*rejoice* 838
*boast* 884
pluck a – with 932
as the – flies 278
–'s foot (*age*) 128
–'s nest 210
– to pluck
*discord* 713

*anger* 900
*accuse* 938
**crowbar** 633
**crowd** 72
*multitude* 102
*close* 197
*redundance* 641
*party* 712
*vulgar* 876
in the – *mixed* 41
madding – 682
**crown** *top* 210
*circle* 247
*complete* 729
*trophy* 733
*sceptre* 747
*install* 755
*decoration* 877
*reward* 973
to – all 33, 642
–ed head 745
– with laurel 873
– with success 731
**crowning**
[*see* crown]
*superior* 33
*end* 67
– point 210
**cruche à l'eau &c.**
tant va la – 735
**crucial**
*crossing* 219
*proof* 478
– test 463
**cruciate**
*physical pain* 378
*mental pain* 830
**crucible**
*dish* 191
*conversion* 144
*furnace* 386
*experiment* 463
*laboratory* 691
put into the – 163
**crucifix** 219, 998
**crucifixion** 828
**cruciform** 219
**crucify**
*physical torture* 378
*mental agony* 830
*execution* 972
**crucis, experimentum** – 463
**crude** *colour* 428
– *style* 579
*unprepared* 674
**cruel**
*painful* 830
*inhuman* 907
– to be kind 914

**cruelly** *much* 31
**cruet** 191
**cruise**
*vessel* 191
*navigation* 267
**cruiser** 726
**cruising** 267
**crumb** *small* 32
*powder* 330
– of comfort 834
**crumble**
*decrease* 36
*weak* 160
*destruction* 162
*brittle* 328
*pulverize* 330
*spoil* 659
– into dust
*decompose* 49
– under one's feet 735
**crumbling**
[*see* crumble]
*dangerous* 665
**crumenal** 800
**crump**
*distorted* 243
*curved* 245
**crumple**
*ruffle* 256
*fold* 258
– up *destroy* 162
*crush* 195
**crunch**
*shatter* 44
*chew* 298
*pulverize* 330
**crupper** 235
**crusade** 722
**crush** *crowd* 72
*destroy* 162
*compress* 195
*pulverize* 330
*humble* 879
– under an iron heel 739
– one's hopes
*disappoint* 509
*hopeless* 859
**crushed** 828
**crushing** 830
**crust** 223
**crustacean** 366
**crusty** 895, 901*a*
**crutch**
*support* 215
*angle* 244
–ed Friars 996
**crux** 219, 704
– criticorum 533
**cry** *human* **411**

*animal* 412
*publish* 531, **532**
*call* 550
*voice* 580
*vogue* 613
*weep* 839
far – to 196
full – *loud* 404
raise a – 550
– aloud
*implore* 765
– out against
*dissuade* 616
*censure* 932
– down 932, **934**
– for 865
– before hurt **839**
– for joy 838
– you mercy
*deprecate* 766
*pity* 914
*forgive* 918
– shame 932
– to *beseech* 765
– up 931
– for vengeance 923
– wolf *false* 544
*alarm* 669
– and little wool
*overrate* 482
*boast* 884
*disappoint* 509
**crying** [*see* cry]
*urgent* 630
*weary* 841
– evil 619
– shame 874
– sin 945
**crypt** *cell* 191
*grave* 363
*ambush* 530
*altar* 1000
**cryptic** 475, 528
**cryptography**
*hidden* 528
*writing* 590
**crystal** *hard* 323
*transparent* 425
snow – 383
– gazer 513
– gazing 511, 992
– oil 356
clear as – 518
**crystalline**
*dense* 321
*hard* 323
*transparent* 425
**crystallization** 321, 323
**csako** 225, 717

*rotation* 312
*wind* 349
**cyclopædia**
*knowledge* 490
*book* 593
**Cyclopean**
*strong* 159
*huge* 192
**Cyclops**
*monster* 83
*mighty* 159
*huge* 192
*dupe* 547
**cygne**
chant du – 360
– noir 650
**cylindric** 249
**cyma** 847
**cymbal** 417
**cymbalo** 417
**cymophanous** 440
**cynic**
*misanthrope* 911
*detractor* 936
*ascetic* 955
closet – 893
**cynical**
*contemptuous* 930
*censorious* 932
*detracting* 934
**cynicism**
*discourtesy* 895
*contempt* 930
**cynosure** *sign* 550
*direction* 693
*wonder* 870
*repute* 873
**Cynthia of the minute** 149
**cypher** [*see* cipher]
**cypress**
*interment* 363
*mourning* 839
**Cyprian** 962
**cyst** 191
**czar** 745

**D**

**da capo** 104
**dab** *small* 32
*paint* 223
*slap* 276
*clever* 700
**dabble** *water* 337
*dirty* 653
*meddle* 682
*fribble* 683
**dabbled** *wet* 339
**dabbler** 493
**dachshund** 366
**dacoit** 792
**dactyl** 597
**dactylogram** 467
**dactyliomancy** 511
**dactylonomy**
*numeration* 85
*symbol* 550
**dad** 166
**daddy** 166
**dado** 211
**dædal**
*variegated* 440
**dædalian**
*convoluted* 248
*artistic* 698
**daft** 503
**dagger** 727
look –s *anger* 900
*threat* 909
air drawn – 515
plant – in breast
*give pain* 830
speak –s 932
at –s drawn
*opposed* 708
*discord* 713
*enmity* 889
*hate* 898
**daggle** *hang* 214
*dirty* 653
**dagobah** 1000
**Dagon** 986
**daguerreotype**
*represent* 554
*paint* 556
**dahabeah** 273
**Dail Eireann** 696
**daily**
*frequent* 136
*periodic* 138
– occurrence
*normal* 82
*habitual* 613
– paper 531
**dainty** *food* 298
*savoury* 394
*pleasing* 829
*delicate* 845
*tasty* 850
*fastidious* 868
**dairy** 191, 370
– maid 746
**dais** *support* 215
*throne* 747
**daisy**
fresh as a – 654
– pied 847
**dale** 252
**dally** *delay* 133
*irresolute* 605
*inactive* 683
*amuse* 840
*fondle* 902
**dalmatic** 999
**Daltonism** 443
**dam** *parent* 166
*close* 261
*pond* 343
*obstruct* 706
**damage** *evil* 619
*injure, spoil* 659
*price* 812
**damages** 974
**damascene** 440
**damask** 434
**dame**
*woman* 374
*teacher* 540
*lady* 875
**damn**
*malediction* 908
*condemn* 971
– with faint praise 932, 934
**damnable** 649
**damnatory**
*disapprove* 932
*condemn* 971
**damnify**
*damage* 649
*spoil* 659
**damnosa hereditas** 663
**Damocles**
sword of – 667
**Damon and Pythias** 890
**damozel** 129
**damp**
*moderate* 174
*moist* 339
*cold* 385
*sound* 405
*dissuade* 616
*hinder* 706
*depress* 837
*dull* 843
– the sound 408*a*
**damper** 387
**damsel**
*youth* 129
*female* 374
**Dan to Beersheba** 52, 180
**Danaë** 803
**Danaos, timeo –**
*doubt* 485
*caution* 864
**dance**
*jump* 309
*oscillate* 314
*agitate* 315
*rejoice* 838
*sport* 840
*sociality* 892
lead the – 175
lead one a –
*run away* 623
*circuit* 629
*difficult* 704
*practical joke* 929
St. Vitus' – 315
– attendance
*waiting* 133
*follow* 281
*servant* 746
*petition* 765
*servility* 886
– the back step 283
– upon nothing 972
– the war dance 715
**dance-band** 417
**dance-music** 415
**dander** 900
**Dandie Dinmont** 366
**dandiprat** 193
**dandle** 902
**dandruff** 653
**dandy**
*ship* 273
*fop* 854
**dandyism** 855
**danger** 665
in – *liable* 177
source of – 667
– past 664
– signal 669
**dangerous**
[*see* danger]
– classes 913
– illness 655
– person 667
**dangle** *hang* 214
*swing* 314
*display* 882
**dangler** 281
**Daniel** *sage* 500
*judge* 967
**dank** 339
**Dannemora** 752
**danseuse** 599
**dapper**
*little* 193
*elegant* 845
**dapple** 433
**dappled** 440
**darbies**
*handcuffs* 752

**Darby and Joan**
*secluded* 893
*married* 903
**dare** *defy* 715
*face danger* 861
– not 860
– say *probable* 472
*believe* 484
*suppose* 514
**dare-devil**
*courage* 861
*rash* 863
*bluster* 887
**daring** 861
*unreserved* 525
– imagination 515
**dark**
*obscure* 421
*dim* 422
*black* 431
*blind* 442
*invisible* 447
*unintelligible* 519
*latent* 526
*joyless* 837
*insidious* 940
in the –
*ignorant* 491
leap in the –
*experiment* 463
*chance* 621
*rash* 863
keep – *hide* 528
– ages 491
– cloud 735
view with – eyes 932
– lantern 423
**darkly**
see through a glass – 443
**darkness** [*see* dark] 421
children of – 988
love – better than light 989
powers of – 978
**darky** 431
**darling** *beloved* 897
*favourite* 899
**darn** 660
**dart** *swift* 274
*propel* 284
*missile* 727
– to and fro 684
**Dartmoor** 752
**Darwinism** 357
**dash**
*small quantity* 32
*mix* 41
*swift* 276
*fling* 284
*mark* 550
*courage* 861
cut a – *repute* 873
*display* 882
– at *resolution* 604
*attack* 716
– board 666
– cup from lips 761
– down 308
– hopes
*disappoint* 509
*fail* 732
*dejected* 837
*despair* 859
– on 274
– off *paint* 556
*write* 590
*active* 682
*haste* 684
– of the pen 590
**dashed** [*see* dash]
*humbled* 879
**dashing**
*fashionable* 852
*brave* 861
*ostentatious* 882
**dastard** 862
**data** *evidence* 467
*reasoning* 476
*supposition* 514
**date** *time* 106
*chronology* 114
**datum** 673
**daub** *cover* 223
*paint* 428
*misrepresent* 555
*dirt* 653
**daughter** 167
**daunt** 860
**dauntless** 861
**Dauphin** 875
**davenport** 191, 215
**davit** 214
**Davus sum non Œdipus**
*unintelligent* 499
*artless* 703
*dull* 843
**Davy Jones' locker** 310
**dawdle** *tardy* 133
*slow* 275
*inactive* 683
**dawk** 534
**dawn**
*precursor* 64
*begin* 66
*priority* 116
*morning* 125
*light* 420
*dim* 422
*glimpse* 490
**dawplucker** 936
**day**
*period* 108
*present time* 118
*light* 420
all – 110
clear as –
*certain* 474
*intelligible* 518
*manifest* 525
close of – 126
decline of – 126
denizens of the – 366
good old –'s 122
have had its – 124
one fine – 119
open as – 703
order of the – 613
red letter – 642
see the light of – 446
– after day
*diuturnal* 110
*frequent* 136
– by day
*repeatedly* 104
*time* 106
*periodic* 138
– after the fair 135
–s gone by 122
– of judgment 121
happy as the – is long 827, 836
– and night
*frequent* 136
labour – and night 686
–s numbered
*transient* 111
*death* 360
– one's own 731
– of rest 687
– star 423
– after to-morrow 121
– before yesterday 122
–s of week 138
all in –'s work 625
**daybed** 215
**daybook** *record* 551
*accounts* 811
**daybreak**
*morning* 125
*dim* 422
**day-dream**
*fancy* 515
*hope* 858
**day-labourer** 690
**daylight** 125, 420
see – *intelligible* 518
– saving 114
**daymare** 859
**daze** 420
**dazed** 376
**dazzle**
*light* 420
*blind* 422, 443
*put out* 458
*astonish* 870
*awe* 928
**dazzling**
[*see* dazzle]
*beautiful* 845
**de:** – die in diem
*time* 106
*periodic* 138
– facto 1
– fond en comble 52
– novo 104
– omnibus rebus 81
– profundis 821
**deacon** 996
**deaconry** 995
**dead** *complete* 52
*inert* 172
*colourless* 429
*lifeless* 360
*insensible* 376
– against
*contrary* 14
*oppose* 708
more – than alive 688
– asleep 683
– beat
*powerless* 158
– certainty 474
– colour 556
– cut 893
– drunk 959
– failure 732
– flat 213
– heat 27
– languages 560
– letter
*impotent* 158
*unmeaning* 517
*useless* 645
*laxity* 738
*exempt* 927
*illegal* 964
– level 16
– lift *exertion* 686
*difficulty* 704, 706

*kill* 361
*play havoc* 659
*punish* 972
**decipher** 522
**decision**
*judgment* 480
*resolution* 604
*intention* 620
*law case* 969
**decisive**
*certain* 474
*proof* 478
*commanding* 741
take a – step 609
**deck** *floor* 211
*beautify* 847
**declaim** 531, 582
– against 932
**declamatory**
*style* 577
*speech* 582
**declaration**
*affirmation* 535
*law pleadings* 969
– of faith
*belief* 484
*theology* 983
– of war 713
**declaratory**
*meaning* 516
*inform* 527
**declare**
*publish* 531
**declension**
[*see* decline]
*grammar* 567
*backsliding* 988
**declensions** 5
**declination**
[*see* decline]
*deviation* 279
*measurement* 466
*rejection* 610
**decline** *decrease* 36
*old* 124
*weaken* 160
*descent* 306
*grammar* 567
*be unwilling* 603
*reject* 610
*disease* 655
*become worse* 659
*adversity* 735
*refuse* 764
– of day 126
– of life 128
**declivity** *slope* 217
*descent* 306
**decoction** 335, 384
**decode** 522
**decollate** 972
**décolleté** 226
**decoloration** 429
**decomposition** 49
**deconsecrate** 756
**decontrol** 158
**décor** 448, 599
**decoration**
*insignia* 747
*ornament* 847
*title* 877
**decorative** 556
**decorous**
[*see* decorum]
*fashionable* 862
*proper* 924
*respectful* 928
**decorticate** 226
**decorum**
*fashion* 852
*duty* 926
*purity* 960
**décousu**
*discontinuous* 70
*failure* 732
**decoy** *attract* 288
*deceive* 545
*deceiver* 548
*entice* 615
**decrease** 36, 195
**decree**
*judgment* 480
*order* 741
*law* 963, 969
**decrement**
*decrease* 36
*thing deducted* **40a**
*contraction* 195
**decrepit** *old* 128
*weak* 158, 160
*disease* 655
*decayed* 659
**decrepitate** 406
**decrescendo** 36
**decretal** 741
**decry** *underrate* 483
*censure* 932
*detract* 934
**decumbent** 213
**decuple** 98
**decursive** 306
**decurtation** 201
**decussation** 219
**dedecorous**
*disreputable* 874
*discourteous* 895
**dedicate** *use* 677
*inscribe* 873
**deduce** *deduct* 38
*infer* 480
**deducible**
*evidence* 467
*proof* 478
**deduct** *retrench* 38
*deprive* 789
*subtract* 813
**deduction**
[*see* deduce]
*decrement* 40a
*reasoning* 476
**deed** *evidence* 467
*record* 551
*act* 680
*security* 771
–s of arms 720
– without a name 947
**deem** 484
**deemster** 967
**deep** *great* 31
*profound* 208
*sea* 341
*sonorous* 404
*cunning* 702
plough the – 267
– colour 428
– in debt 806
– game 702
– knowledge 490
– mourning 839
– note 408
– potations 959
– reflection 451
– sense 821
– sigh 839
– study 457
in – water 704
**deepen** 35
**deep-dyed**
*intense* 171
*black* 431
*vicious* 945
**deep-felt** 821
**deep-laid** *plan* 626
**deep-mouthed**
*resonant* 408
*bark* 412
*thrilling* 821
**deep-musing** 458
**deep-read** 490
**deep-rooted**
*stable* 150
*strong* 159
*belief* 484
*habit* 613
*affections* 820
**deep-sea** 208
**deep-seated** 208, 221
**deer** 366
in heart a – 862
**deev** 980
**deface**
*destroy form* **241**
*obliterate* 552
*injure* 659
*render ugly* **846**
**defalcation**
*incomplete* **53**
*contraction* 195
*shortcoming* 304
*non-payment* **808**
**defame** *shame* **874**
*censure* 932
*detract* 934
**defamer** 936
**defatigation** 841
**default**
*incomplete* **53**
*shortcoming* **304**
*neglect* 460
*insufficiency* **640**
*debt* 806
*non-payment* **808**
in – of 187
judgment by – **725**
**defaulter** *thief* **792**
*non-payer* 808
*rogue* 949
**defeasance** 756
**defeat**
*confute* 479
*succeed* 731
*failure* 732
– one's hope **509**
**defeatism** 911
**defecate** 652
**defecation** 299
**defect**
*decrement* **40a**
*incomplete* **53**
*imperfect* 651
*failing* 945
**defection**
*relinquishment* 624
*disobedience* **742**
**defective**
*incomplete* **53**
*insufficient* **640**
*imperfect* 651
**defence**
*plea* 462
*resist* **717**
*vindication* **937**
first line of – **726**
**defenceless**
*impotent* 158
*weak* 160
*exposed* 665
**defendant** 938
**defensible** *safe* **664**
*excusable* 937
**defensive alliance**

712
**defer** 133
– to *assent* 488
*submit* 725
*respect* 928
**deference**
*obedience* 743
*humility* 879
*courtesy* 894
*respect* 928
**defiance 715**, 909
*threat* 909
in – *opposition* 708
set at – *disobey* 742
– of danger 861
**deficiency**
[*see* deficient]
*vice* 945
**deficient**
*inferior* 34
*incomplete* 53
*shortcoming* 304
*insufficient* 640
*imperfect* 651
**deficit**
*incompleteness* 53
*debt* 806
**defigure** 846
**defile**
*interval* 198
*march* 266
*dirt* 653
*spoil* 659
*shame* 874
*impure* 961
**define**
*specify* 79
*limit* 233
*explain* 522
*name* 564
**definite**
[*see* define]
*visible* 446
*certain* **474**
*exact* 494
*intelligible* 518
*manifest* 525
*perspicuous* 570
**definition**
*interpretation* 522
**definitive** *final* 67
*affirmative* 535
*decided* 604
**deflagration** 384
**deflate** 195
**deflation**
*currency* 800
**deflect**
*curve* 245
*deviate* 279
**deflower**
*spoil* 659
*violate* 961
**defluxion**
*egress* 295
*flowing* 348
**defœdation** 653, 659
**deform** 241
**deformity**
*distortion* 243
*ugliness* 846
*blemish* 848
**defraud** *cheat* **545**
*swindle* 791
**defray** 807
**deft** *suitable* 23
*clever* 698
**defunct** 360, 362
**defy** 715
*disobey* 742
*threaten* 909
– danger 861
**dégagé** *free* 748
*fashion* 852
**degenerate** 659
**deglutition** 298
**degradation**
*deterioration* 659
*shame* 874
*dishonour* 940
**degree 26**
*term* 71
*honour* 873
by –s 26
by slow –s 275
**degustation** 390
**dehiscence** 260
**dehort**
*dissuade* 616
*advise* 695
**dehydrate** 340
**Dei gratiâ** 924
**deification** 873, 981
**deify**
*honour* 873
*idolatry* 991
**deign**
*condescend* 762
*consent* 879
**Deism**
*heterodoxy* 984
*irreligion* 989
**Deity 976**
tutelary – 664
**dejection**
*excretion* 299
*melancholy* **837**
**déjeuner** 298
**délabrement** 162
**delaceration** 659
**delation** 938
**delator** 527
**delay** 133
**dele** 552
**delectable**
*savoury* 394
*agreeable* 829
**delectation** 827
**delectus** 562
**delegate**
*transfer* 270
*commission* 755
*consignee* 758
*deputy* 759
**delenda est Carthago**
*destroy* 162
*curse* 908
**delete** 162
**deleterious**
*pernicious* 649
*unwholesome* 657
**deletion** 552
**deletory**
*destructive* 162
**deliberate**
*slow* 275
*think* 451
*attentive* 457
*leisure* 685
*advise* 695
*cautious* 864
**deliberately**
[*see* deliberate]
*late* 133
*with premeditation* 611
**delicacy** *weak* 160
*slender* 203
*dainty* 298
*brittleness* 328
*texture* 329
*savoury* 394
*colour* 428
*exact* 494
*scruple* 603
*ill health* 655
*difficult* 704
*pleasing* 829
*beauty* 845
*taste* 850
*fastidious* 868
*honour* 939
*pure* 960
*delicate ear* 418
**délice** 377
**delicious** *taste* 394
*pleasing* 829
**delicti, corpus** –
*guilt* 947
*lawsuit* 969
**delicto, in flagrante** – **947**
**delight**
*pleasure* 827
*pleasing* 829
**Delilah** 962
**delimit** 233
**delineate**
*outline* 230
*represent* **554**
*describe* 594
**delineator** 559
**delineavit** 556
**delinquency 304**, 947
**delinquent** 949
**deliquation** 335
**deliquesce** 36
**deliquescence 335**
**deliquium**
*paralysis* 158
*fatigue* 688
**delirant reges plectuntur Achivi** 739
**delirium**
*raving* 503
*passion* 825
– tremens **503**, 959
**delitescence**
*invisible* 447
*latency* 526
*seclusion* **893**
**deliver**
*transfer* 270
*utter* 580, 582
*birth* 662
*rescue* 672
*liberate* 750
*give* 784
*relieve* 834
– as one's act and deed 467
– the goods 729
– judgment 480
– a speech 582
**deliverance 672**
**delivery**
[*see* deliver]
*bring forth* 161
cash on – 807
**dell** 252
**Delphic oracle**
*prophetic* 513
*equivocal* 520
*latent* 526
**delta** 342
**delude** *error* 495
*deceive* 545
**deluge** *crowd* **72**
*water* 337

*flood* 348
*redundance* 641
**delusion**
[*see* delude]
*insane* 503
self – *credulous* 486
**delve** *dig* 252
*till* 371
– into *inquire* 461
**demagogue**
*director* 694
*malcontent* 710
*rebel* 742
**demagogy** 737
**demand**
*inquire* 461
*order* 741
*ask* 765
*price* 812
*claim* 924
in – *require* 630
*desire* 865
*saleable* 796
**demarcation** 233
**dematerialize** 317
**demean oneself**
*conduct* 692
*humble* 879
*dishonour* 940
**demeanour**
*aid* 448
*conduct* 692
*fashion* 852
**demency** 503
**démenti** 536
**dementia** 503
**demerit** 945
**demesne**
*abode* 189
*property* 780
**demi-** 91
**demigod** *hero* 861
*angel* 948
**demigration** 266
**demijohn** 191
**demi-jour** 422
**demi-lune** 717
**demi-mondaine**
*plebeian* 876
*licentious* 962
**demirep** 962
**demise** *death* 360
*transfer* 783
*lease* 787
**demisemiquaver** 413
**demission** 756
**demit** 757
**demiurge**
*deity* 979
**demivolt** 309
**demobilize** 73
**democracy** *rule* 737
*commonalty* 876
**Democrats**
*party* 712
**Democritus** 838
**demoiselle** 129
**demolish** 479
**demon** *violent* 173
*bane* 663
*devil* **980**
– in human shape 913, 949
– worship 991
**demoniacal**
*malevolent* 907
*furious* 824
*wicked* 945
**demonology**
*demons* 980
*sorcery* 992
**demonstration**
*number* 85
*proof* **478**
*manifest* 525
*ostentation* 882
ocular – 441, 446
**demonstrative**
*manifest* 525
*indicative* 550
*vehement* 825
**demonstrator** 524
**demoralize**
*unnerve* 158
*spoil* 659
*vicious* 945
**Demosthenes** 582
**demotic** 590
**demulcent**
*mild* 174
*soothing* 662
**demur**
*disbelieve* 485
*dissent* 489
*unwilling* 603
*hesitate* 605
without – 602
**demure**
*grave* 826
*sad* 837
*affected* 855
*modest* 881
**demurrage** 133
**demurrer** 969
**den** *abode* 189
*study* 191, 893
*sty* 653
*prison* 752
– of thieves 791
**denary** 98
**denaturalize**
*corrupt* 659
**denaturalized**
*abnormal* 83
**dendriform** 242, 367
**dendrology** 369
**denial**
*negation* 536
*refusal* 764
self– 953
**denigrate** 431
**denization** 748
**denizen**
*inhabitant* 188
*freeman* 748
–s of the air 979
–s of the day 366
**Denmark, rotten in the state of** – 526
**denomination**
*class* 75
*name* 564
*sect* 712
religious – 983
**denominational**
*dissent* 489
*theological* 983
– education 537
**denominator** 84
**denote**
*specify* 79
*mean* 516
*indicate* 550
**dénouement**
*end* 67
*result* 154
*disclosure* 529
*completion* 729
**denounce**
*curse* 908
*disapprove* 932
*accuse* 938
**dense**
*crowded* 72
*ignorant* 493
**density** **321**
**dent** 252, 257
**dental** 561
**denticulated** 253, 257
**dentifrice** 652
**dentistry** 662
**denude** 226
**denuded** *loss* 776
– of
*insufficient* 640
**denunciation**
[*see* denounce]
**deny** *dissent* 489
*negative* **556**
*refuse* 764
– oneself
*avoid* 623
*seclude* 893
*temperate* **953**
*ascetic* 990
**Deo volente** **470**, 976
**deobstruct** 705
**deodand** 974
**deodorize** 399
*clean* 652
**deontology** 926
**deoppilation** 705
**deorganization** 61
**deosculation** 902
**depart** 293
– from
*deviate* 15, 279
*relinquish* 624
– this life 360
**departed**
*non-existent* **2**
**department**
*class* 75
*region* 181
*business* 625
**departure** 293
new – 66
point of – 293
**depend** *hang* 214
*contingent* 475
– upon
*be the effect of* **154**
*evidence* 467
*trust* 484
– on circumstances 475
**depended on, to be** –
*certain* 474
*reliable* 484
*honourable* 939
**dependency** **777**, 780
**dependent**
*effect* 154
*liable* 177
*hanging* 214
*puppet* 711
*servant* 746
*subject* 749
**deperdition** 776
**dephlegmation** **340**
**depict** 554, 556
*describe* 594
**depilation** 226
**depilatory** 662
**depletion** 638, 640
**deplorable** *bad* **649**

*disastrous* 735
*painful* 830
**deplore** *regret* 833
*complain* 839
*remorse* 950
**deploy** 194
**depone** 535
**deponent** 467
**depopulate**
*eject* 297
*desert* 893
**deportation**
*removal* 270
*emigration* 297
*expulsion* 972
**deportment** 692
**depose**
*evidence* 467
*declare* 535
*dethrone* 738, 756
**deposit** *place* 184
*precipitate* 321
*store* 636
*security* 771
*payment* 809
**depositary** 801
**deposition**
[*see* depose, deposit]
*record* 551
**depository** 636
**depot** *terminal* 292
*store* 636
*shop* 799
– ship 726
**deprave** *spoil* 659
**depraved** *bad* 649
*vicious* 945
**deprecation** **766**
*pity* 914
*disapprove* 932
**depreciation**
*decrease* 36
*underestimate* 483
*discount* 813
*cheap* 815
*disrespect* 929
*censure* 932
*detraction* 934
*accusation* 938
**depredation** 791
**depredator** 792
**deprehension** 789
**depression**
*lowness* 207
*depth* 208
*concavity* 252
*lowering* **308**
*dejection* 837
*dulness* 843
**depressing**
*painful* 830
**deprive** *subduct* 38
*take* 789
– of life 361
– of power 158
– of property 789
– of strength 160
**deprived of** 776
**depth** *physical* **208**
*mental* 498
out of one's – 304, 310
– bomb 727
– of misery 828
– of thought 451
– of winter 383
**depurate** *clean* 652
*improve* 658
**depuratory** 662
**deputation** 755
**depute** 755
**deputies, chamber of** – 696
**deputy** **759**
**dequantitate** 36
**derangement** **61**
mental – 503
**Derby day** 720
**derelict** *land* 342
*danger* 667
*relinquish* 782
*outcast* 893
**dereliction**
*relinquishment* 624, 782
*guilt* 947
– of duty **927**
**deride**
*ridicule* 856
*disrespect* 929
*contempt* 930
**derivation**
*origin* 153, 154, 155
*verbal* 562
**derive**
*attribute* 155
*deduce* 480
*acquire* 775
*income* 810
**dermal** 223
**dermatology** 223
**dernier**
– cri 850
– ressort 601
**dérobée, à la** – 528
**derogate**
*underrate* 483
*disparage* 934
*dishonour* 940
– from 874
**derogatory**
*shame* 874
*dishonour* 940
**derrick** 307, 633
**derring-do** 861
**dervish** 996
**désagrément** 830
**descant** *music* 415
*diffuseness* 573
*loquacity* 584
*dissert* 595
**descend** *slope* 217
*go down* 306
– to particulars
*special* 79
*describe* 594
**descendant** 167
**descensus Averni, facilis** – 665
**descent** *lineage* 166
*fall* **306**
*inheritance* **775**
**description**
*kind* 75
*name* 564
*narration* **594**
**descriptive music** 415
**descry** 441
**desecrate**
*misuse* 679
*disrespect* 929
*profane* 988
**desert**
*unproductive* 169
*empty* 187
*plain* 344
*run away* 623
*relinquish* 624, 782
*merit* 944
waste sweetness on – air 638
**deserted**
*outcast* 893
**deserter** 144, 607, 623
**desertless** 945
**deserts** 924
**deserve**
*be entitled to* 924
*merit* 944
– notice 642
– belief 484
**désespoir, au** –
*dejected* 837
*hopeless* 859
**déshabillé, en** –
*not dressed* 226
*unprepared* 674
*simplicity* 849
**desiccate** 340
**desiccator** 340
**desiderate** *need* **630**
*desire* 865
**desideratum**
*inquiry* 461
*requirement* **630**
*desire* 865
**design**
*prototype* 22
*form* 240
*delineation* **554**
*painting* 556
*intention* 620
*plan* 626
**designate**
*specify* **79**
*call* 564
**designation** **75**
**designed**
*aforethought* 611
**designer** 164, 559
**designing**
*cunning* 702
**designless** 621
**désillusioner** 529
**desinence** *end* 67
*discontinuance* 142
**desipience** 499
**desipere in loco** 840
**desirable** 646
**desire** **865**
*will* 600
have no – for **866**
**desist**
*discontinue* **142**
*relinquish* 624
*inaction* 681
**desk** *box* 191
*support* 215
*school* 542
*pulpit* 1000
**désobligeant** 272
**désœuvré** 681
**desolate** *alone* **87**
*ravage* 162
*afflicted* 828
*dejected* 837
*secluded* 893
**desolating**
*painful* 830
**désorienté** 475
**despair** *grief* 828, 859
**despatch** *eject* **297**
*kill* 361
*news* 532
*epistle* 592
*expedition* **682**
*haste* 684

*conduct* 692
*complete* 729
*command* 741
happy – 972
– case 191
– food 298
– rider 534
**desperado**
*rash* 863
*blusterer* 887
*evil-doer* 913
**desperate** *great* 31
*violent* 173
*impossible* **471**
*resolved* 604
*difficult* 704
*excitable* 825
*hopeless* 859
*rash* 863
*anger* 900
**despicable**
*trifling* 643
*shameful* 874
*contemptible* 930
**despise** 930
– danger 861
**despite** 30, 907
in – 708
**despoil** *injure* 659
*take* 789
*rob* 791
**despond** 837, 860
**despot** 745
**despotism**
*authority* **737**
*severity* 739
*arbitrary* 964
**despumate** 652
**desquamation** 226
**dessert** 298
**dessous des cartes**
*cause* 153
*latent* 526
*secret* 533
connaître le – 490
**dessus dessous**
sens – 218
**destination** *end* 67
*arrival* 292
*intention* 620
**destiny** *chance* **152**
*fate* 601
fight against – 606
**destitute**
*insufficient* 640
*poor* 804
refuge for – 666
**destrier** 726
**destroy**
*demolish* 162
*injure* 659
– hopes 859
– life 361
**destroyed**
[*see* destroy]
*inexistent* 2
*failure* 732
**destroyer** **165**
*warship* 726
*evil-doer* 913
**destructive**
*bad* 649
**destructor** 383
**desuetude** **614**
*disuse* 678
**desultory**
*disordered* **59**
*fitful* 70
*multiform* 81
*irregular in time* 139
*changeable* 149
*deviating* 279
*agitated* 315
**desume** 788
**detach** 44
**detached**
*irrelated* **10**
*loose* 47
**detachment**
*part* 51
*army* 726
**detail** *describe* 594
*special portions* 79
*allot* 786
*ornament* **847**
attention to – 457, 459
in – 51
**details**
*minutiæ* 32
*unimportant* 643
**detain** 781
**detect** 480*a*
**detective** 527, 664
**detention** 133, 751, 781
house of – 752
in house of – 938
**détenu** 754
**deter** *dissuade* 616
*alarm* 860
**deterge** *clean* 652
**detergent**
*remedy* 662
**deterioration** **659**
**determinate**
*special* 79
*exact* 474
*conclusive* 480
*intended* 620
**determine** *end* **67**
*define* 79
*cause* 153
*direction* 278
*satisfy* 462
*make sure* **474**
*judge* 480
*discover* 480*a*
*resolve* 604
**determined**
*resolute* 604
**determinism** 601
**deterration** 529
**detersion** 652
**detersive** 662
**detest** *dislike* 867
*hate* 898
**detestable** 649
**dethronement**
*anarchy* 738
*abrogation* **756**
**detonate**
*explode* **173**
*sound* 406
**detortion** *form* 243
*meaning* 523
**détour** *curve* 245
*circuit* 629
**detract** *subduct* 38
*underrate* 483
*defame* 934
*slander* 938
**detraction** 934
**detractor** 936
**detrain** 292
**detriment**
*evil* 619
*deterioration* 659
**detrimental** 649
**detrition** 330
**detritus**
*fragments* 51
*deposit* 270
*powder* 330
**detrude**
*cast out* 297
*cut down* 308
**detruncate** 38
**deuce** *two* 89
*devil* 978
play the – 825
– is in him 608
**deuced** *great* 31
*painful* 830
**deus** 976
– ex machinâ
*aid* 707
*auxiliary* **711**
*deity* 976
*sorcerer* 994
**deuterogamy** **903**
**devastate**
*destroy* **162**
*havoc* 659
**develop**
*increase* **35**
*produce* 161
*expand* 194
*evolve* 313
**development** **144,** 154
**devexity**
*bending* 217
*curvature* 245
**deviate** *vary* **20*a***
*change* 140
*turn* 279
*diverge* 291
*circuit* 629
– from 15
– from rectitude 940
– from virtue **945**
**deviation** **279**
**device** *motto* **550**
*expedient* 626
*artifice* 702
**devil**
*seasoned food* **392**
*evil-doer* 913
*bad man* 949
*Satan* 978
*demon* 980
fight like –s **722**
have a – 503
machinations of the – 619
play the – with
*injure* 659
*malevolent* **907**
printer's – 591
raise the – 825
– may care
*rash* 863
*indifferent* **866**
*insolent* 885
give the – his due
*right* 922
*vindicate* **937**
*fair* 939
– in one
*headstrong* **863**
*temper* 901
– to pay
*disorder* **59**
*violence* **173**
*evil* 619
*failure* 732
*penalty* 974
– take 908
– take the hindmost

*run away* 623
*haste* 684
*cowardice* 862
–'s tattoo 407
**devilish** *great* 31
*bad* 649
*malevolent* 907
**devious** *curved* 245
*deviating* 279
*circuitous* 311
**devisable** 270
**devise** *imagine* 515
*plan* 626
*bequeath* 784
**devised by the enemy** 546
**devisee** *possess* **779**
*receive* 785
**deviser** 164
**devitalize** 158
**devoid** *absent* 187
*empty* 640
*not having* 777*a*
**devoir** *courtesy* 894
*respect* 928
**devolve** 783
– on 926
**devote** *destine* 601
*employ* 677
*consecrate* 873
– to destruction 908
– the mind to 457
– oneself to 604
**devoted**
*habit* 613
*ill-fated* 735
*obedient* 743
*undone* 828
*friendship* 888
*love* 897
**devotee**
*zealot* 682
*aspirant* 865
*pious* 987
*fanatic* **988**
**devotion** [*see* devotee, devoted]
*love* 897
*piety* 987
*worship* 990
self – 942
**devour**
*destroy* 162
*eat* 298
*gluttony* 957
**devoured by**
*feeling* 821
**devouring element** 382
**devout** 987, 990
**devoutless** 989
**devoutly** 821
**dew** 339
shake as –drops from lion's mane 483
**dewy eve** 126
**dexterous** 238, 698
**dextrality** **238**
**dey** 745
**dhow** 273
**diable**:
avoir le – au corps 503
– à quatre
*disorder* 59
*violence* 173
*loud* 404
*excitement* 825
tirer le – par la queue 804
**diablerie** 978, 992
**diabolic**
*bad* 649
*malevolent* 907
*wicked* 945
*Satanic* 978
**Diacoustics** 402
**diacritical** 550
**diadem** 747, 847
**diaeresis** 49
**diagnosis** 465, 655
**diagnostic**
*special* 79
*experiment* 463
*indication* 550
(*intrinsic* 5)
**diagonal** 217
**diagram** 554
**dial** 114
as the – to the sun
*veracious* 543
*faithful* 772
**dialect** 563
**dialectic**
*argument* 476
*language* 560
**dialogism** 586
**dialogue** 588
**diameter** 202
**diametrically opposite**
*contrariety* 14
*contraposition* 237
**diamond**
*lozenge* 244
*type* 591
*goodness* 648
*ornament* 847
rough – 703
– cut diamond
*cunning* 702
*retaliation* 718
– jubilee 883
– wedding 883
**Diana** *moon* 318
*chaste* 960
*goddess* 979
**diapason** 413
**diaper** 847
**diaphanous** 425
**diaphonics** 402
**diaphoresis** 299
**diaphragm** 68, 228
**diaporesis** 475
**diarchy** 737
**diarrhœa** 299
**diary** 114, 551
**diastole** 194
**diatessaron** 413
**diathermancy** 384
**diathesis**
*nature* **5**
*state* 7
*temperament* 820
**diatonic** 413
**diatribe** 932
**dibble**
*perforator* 262
*till* 371
**dibs** *money* 800
**dicacity** 885
**dice** 156, 621
on the – 470
**dicer** 621
false as –'s oaths 546
**dichotomy**
*bisect* 91
*angle* 244
**dichroism** 440
**dichromatic** 443
**dickens** 978
**dicker** 794
**dicky** 215, 225
**dictaphone** 553
**dictate**
*write* 590
*enjoin* 615
*advise* 695
*authority* 737
*command* 741
–s of society 852
**dictator** 694, 745
**dictatorial**
*dogmatic* 481
*wilful* 600
*insolent* 885
**dictatorship** 737, 739
**diction** 569
**dictionary**
*list* 86
*words* 562
*book* 593
**dictum**
*judgment* 480
*maxim* 496
*affirmation* **535**
*command* 741
**didactic** 537
**didder** 383
**diddle** 545, 791
**Diddler, Jeremy** – 792
**diduction** 44
**die** *mould* 22
*expire* 360
*engraving* 558
hazard of the – 621
never say – 604*a*
not willingly let – 670
– away
*vanish* 4
*decrease* 36
*cease* 142
the – is cast 601
– with ennui 841
– for *desire* 865
*endearment* 902
– game 951
– hard
*obstinate* 606
*resist* 719
– in harness **143**, 604*a*
– in the last ditch 604*a*
– with laughter 838
– from the memory 536
– and make no sign 951
– out 2, 4
– of a rose in aromatic pain 822
– in one's shoes 972
– a violent death 361
– hard 710, 832
**dies non** *never* **107**
*rest* 687
**diet** *food* 298
*council* 696
spare – 956
**dietetics** 662
**differ** 15
*discord* **713**

*punish* 972
– from the mind 452, 458
**dismount**
*arrive* 292
*descend* 306
*render useless* 645
**disnest** 185
**disobedience** **742**
*non-observance* 773
**disoblige** 907
**disorder**
*confusion* **59**
*derange* 61
*turbulent* 173
*disease* 655
–ed intellect 503
**disorderly**
*unprincipled* 945
**disorganize**
*derange* 61
*destroy* 162
*spoil* 659
**disorganized** 59
**disown** 536
**dispair** 44
**disparage**
*underrate* 483
*disrespect* 929
*dispraise* 932
*detract* 934
**disparity**
*different* 15
*dissimilar* 18
*disagreeing* 24
*unequal* 28
*isolated* 44
**dispart** 44
**dispassionate** 826
– opinion 484
**dispatch**
[*see* despatch]
**dispel** *scatter* 73
*destroy* 162
*displace* 185
*repel* 289
**dispensable**
*useless* 645
**dispensary** 662
**dispensation**
[*see* dispense]
*command* 741
*licence* 760
*relinquishment* 782
*exemption* 927*a*
–s of Providence 976
**dispense**
*disperse* 73
*give* 784
*apportion* 786
*retail* 796
– with
*disuse* 678
*permit* 760
*exempt* 927*a*
cannot be –d with 630
**dispeople**
*eject* 297
*expatriate* 893
**disperse**
*separate* 44
*scatter* 73
*diverge* 291
*waste* 638
**dispersion** **73**
– of light 420
chromatic – 428
**dispirit**
*discourage* 616
*sadden* 837
**displacement**
*derange* 61
*remove* **185**
*transfer* 270
**displacency**
*dislike* 867
*incivility* 895
*disapprobation* 932
**displant** 185
**display** *appear* 448
*show* 525
*parade* 882
**displease** 830
**displeasure** 828
*anger* 900
**displosion** 173
**displume** 789
**disport** 840
**disposal**
[*see* dispose]
at one's – 763, 777
**dispose**
*arrange* 60
*tend* 176
*induce* 615
– of *use* 677
*complete* 729
*relinquish* 782
*give* 784
*sell* 796
**disposed** 620
**disposition**
*nature* 5
*order* 58
*arrangement* 60
*inclination* 602
*mind* 820
**dispossess**
*transfer* 783
*take away* 789
– oneself of 782
**dispraise** 932
**dispread** 73
**disprize** 483
**disproof**
*counter-evidence* 468
*confutation* 479
**disproportion**
*irrelation* 10
*disagreement* 24
**disprove** 479
**disputable** 475, 485
**disputant** 710, 726
**disputatious** 901
**dispute**
*discuss* 476
*doubt* 485
*deny* 536
*discord* 713
in – 461
**disqualification**
*incapacitate* 158
*useless* 645
*unprepared* 674
*unskilful* 699
*disentitle* 925
**disquiet**
*changeable* 149
*agitation* 315
*excitement* 825
*uneasiness* 828
*give pain* 830
**disquietude**
*apprehension* 860
**disquisition** 539, 595
**disregard**
*overlook* 458
*neglect* 460
*make light of* 483
*insensible to* 823, 826
*disrespect* **929**
*contempt* 930
– of time 115
**disrelish** 867, 898
**disreputable** 874
*vicious* 945
**disrepute** **874**, 929
**disrespect** **929**
*despise* 930
**disrobe** 226
**disruption**
*disjunction* 44
*destruction* 162
*discord* 713
**dissatisfaction**
*disappointment* 509
*sorrow* 828
*discontent* 832
**dissect**
*anatomize* **44**, **49**
*investigate* 461
**dissemblance** 18
**dissemble** 544
**dissembler** 548
**disseminate**
*scatter* 73
*pervade* 186
*publish* 531
*teach* 537
**dissension** **713**
sow – 898
**dissent**
*disagree* **489**
*refuse* 764
*heterodoxy* 984
**dissentient** 15
**dissentious** 24
**dissertation** **595**
**disservice**
*disadvantage* 619
*useless* 645
**disserviceable** 649
**dissever** 44
**dissidence**
*disagreement* 24
*dissent* 489
*discord* 713
*discontent* 832
*heterodoxy* 984
**dissilience** 173
**dissimilarity** **18**
**dissimulate** 544
**dissipate** *scatter* **73**
*destroy* 162
*pleasure* 377
*prodigality* 818
*amusement* 840
*intemperance* **954**
*dissolute* 961
**dissocial** 893
**dissociate** 44
**dissociation**
*irrelation* 10
*separation* **44**
**dissolute** 961
*profligate* 945
*intemperate* **954**
**dissolution**
[*see* dissolve]
*decomposition* **49**
*destruction* 162
*death* 360
**dissolve** *vanish* **2**, **4**
*liquefy* 335
*disappear* **449**

*abrogate* 756
**dissolving views** 448, 449
**dissonance**
*disagreement* 24
*unmusical* 414
*discord* 713
**dissuasion** **616**
**dissyllable** 561
**distaff**
– side 374
**distain** *dirty* 653
*ugly* 846
**distal** 196
**distance** **196**
*overtake* 282
*go beyond* 303
*defeat* 731
angular – 244
keep at a –
*discourtesy* 895
keep one's –
*avoid* 623
*modest* 881
*respect* 928
teach one his – 879
– of time
*long time* 110
*past* 122
**distaste** 867
**distasteful** 830
**distemper** 299, 428
*colour* 428
*painting* 556
*disease* 655
**distend** 194
**distended** 192
**distich** 89, 597
**distil** *come out* 295
*extract* 301
*evaporate* 336
*drop* 348
**distinct**
*disjoined* 44
*audible* 402
*visible* 446
*intelligible* 518
*manifest* 525
*express* 535
*articulate* 580
**distinction**
*difference* 15
*discrimination* 465
*style* 578
*fame* 873
*rank* 875
– without a difference 27
**distinctive** 15
– feature 79
**distinctness** 15
**distingué** 852, 873
**distinguish**
*perceive* 441
*discriminate* 465
– by the name of 564
**distinguishable** 15
**distinguished**
*superior* 33
*repute* 873
**Distinguished Service Cross** 733
**distortion**
*obliquity* **217**
*twist* **243**
*of vision* 443
*misinterpret* 523
*falsehood* 544
*misrepresent* 555
*ugly* 846
**distract** 458
**distracted**
*confused* 475
*insane* 503
*excited* 824
**distraction**
*passion* 825
love to – 897
**distrain** *take* 789
*appraise* 812
*attach* 969
**distrait** 458
**distraught** 824
**distress**
*distraint* 789
*poverty* 804
*affliction* 828
*cause pain* 830
signal of – 669
**distressingly**
*excessively* 31
**distribute**
*arrange* 60
*disperse* 44, 73
*allot* 786
**district** 181
– council 696
**distrust**
*disbelief* 485
*fear* 860
**distrustful** 487
**disturb**
*derange* 61
*change* 140
*agitate* 315
*excite* 824
*distress* 828, 830
**disturbance** 59
**disunion**
*discord* 24
*separation* 44
*disorder* 59
*discord* 713
**disuse**
*desuetude* 614
*relinquish* 624
*unemploy* **678**
**disused**
*old* 124
**disvalue** 932
**ditch**
*inclosure* 232
*trench* 259
*water* 343
*conduit* 350
*defence* 717
to the last – 606
**ditch-water** 653
**ditheism** 984
**dither** 315
**dithyramb**
*music* 415
*poetry* 597
**dithyrambic** 503
**ditto** 13, 104
say – to 488
**ditty** 415
– box 191
**diurnal** 138
**diuturnity** **110**
**diva** 416
**divagate** 279, 629
**divan** *sofa* 215
*council* 696
*throne* 747
*tribunal* 966
**divaricate** *differ* 15
*bifurcate* 91
*diverge* 291
**dive** *swim* 267
*fly* 267
*plunge* 306, 310
– into *inquire* 461
**divellicate** 44
**diver** 208
**divergence**
*difference* 15
*variation* 20a
*disagreement* 24
*deviation* 279
*separation* **291**
**divers** *different* 15
*multiform* 81
*many* 102
– coloured 440
**diverse** 15
**diversify**
*very* 20a
*change* 140
**diversion**
*change* 140
*deviation* **279**
*pleasure* **377**
*amusement* **840**
**diversity**
*difference* **15**
*irregular* 16c
*dissimilar* 18
*multiform* 81
– of opinion 489
**divert** *turn* 279
*deceive* 545
*amuse* 840
– the mind 452, 458
**divertissement**
*diversion* 377
*drama* 599
*amusement* 840
**Dives** 803
**divest** *denude* **226**
*take* 789
– oneself of
*abrogate* 756
*relinquish* 782
**divestment** **226**
**divide** *differ* 15
*separate* **44**
*part* 51
*arrange* 60
*arithmetic* 85
*bisect* 91
*vote* 609
*apportion* 786
**dividend** *part* **51**
*number* 84
*portion* 786
**divina particula auræ** 450
**divination**
*prediction* 511
*sorcery* 992
**divine** *predict* **511**
*guess* 514
*perfect* 650
*of God* 976, 983, 983a
*clergyman* 996
**divine afflatus** 515
– right
*authority* **737**
*due* 924
– service 990
**diving** 840
**diving-bell** 208
**divining-rod** 550, 993
**Divinity** *God* **976**
*theology* 983
**divisible**
*number* 84

**division**
[*see* divide]
*part* 51
*class* 75
*arithmetic* 85
*discord* 713
*military* 726
**divisor** 84
**divorce**
*separation* 44
*relinquish* 782
*matrimonial* 905
**Divorce Court** 966
**divulge** 529
**divulsion** 44
**divvy** 786
**dixi** 535
**dizen** 847
**dizzard** 501
**dizzy**
*dimsighted* 443
*confused* 458
*vertigo* 503
– height 206
– round 312
**djerrid** 727
**djinn** 980
**do** *fare* 7
*suit* 23
*produce* 161
*cheat* 545
*act* 680
*complete* 729
*succeed* 731
*I beg* 765
all one can – 686
plenty to – 682
thing to – 625
– away with
*destroy* 162
*eject* 297
*abrogate* 756
– battle 722
– one's bidding 743
– business 625
– to death 361
– as done by 906, 942
– for *destroy* 162
*kill* 361
*conquer* 731
*serve* 746
*punish* 972
– good 906
– harm 907
– honour 873
– into
*translate* 522
– justice to 595
– like 19
– little 683
– no harm 648
– nothing 681
– nothing but 136
– one's office 772
– as others do 82
– over 223
– as one pleases 748
– a service
*useful* 644
*aid* 707
– up 660
have to – with 680, 692
– without 678
– the work 686
– wrong 923
**docere, pisces natare** – 641
**docile** *domesticated* 370
*learning* 539
*willing* 602
**docimastic** 463
**dock** *diminish* 36
*cut off* 38
*port* 189
*shorten* 201
*edge* 231
*store* 636
*tribunal* 966
**docked**
*incomplete* 53
**docker** 690
**docket**
*list* 86
*evidence* 467
*note* 550
*record* 551
*security* 771
**dockyard** 691
**doctor**
*learned man* 492
*restore* 660
*remedy* 662
after death the – 135
– accounts 811
when –s disagree 475
**doctrinaire**
*positive* 474
*pedant* 492
*affectation* 855
*blusterer* 887
**doctrinal** 537
**doctrinarian** 514
**doctrine** *tenet* 484
*knowledge* 490
**document** 551
**documentary**
evidence 467
**dodder** 315
**doddering** 128
**dodecahedron** 244
**dodge** *change* 140
*shift* 264
*deviate* 279
*oscillate* 314
*pursue* 461
*avoid* 623
*stratagem* 702
**dodger, artful** – 792
**dodo** 366
extinct as the – 122
**Doe, John** 4
**doe** *swift* 274
*deer* 366
*female* 374
**doer**
*originator* 164
*agent* 690
**doff** 226
– the cap 894
**dog** *follow* 281
*animal* 366
*male* 373
*pursue* 622
*wretch* 949
cast to the –s
*reject* 610
*disuse* 678
*abrogate* 756
*relinquish* 782
fire – 386
go to the –s
*destruction* 162
*fail* 732
*adversity* 735
*poverty* 804
sea – 269
watch –
*safety* 664
*warning* 668
*keeper* 753
hair of – that bit you 959
let sleeping –s lie 141
– in manger 706, 943
–tired 688
–s of war 722
**dog-cart** 272
**dog-cheap** 815
**dog-days** 382
**doge** 745
**dogged**
*obstinate* 606
*valour* 861
*sullen* 901*a*
**dogger** 273
**doggerel**
*verse* 597
*ridiculous* 851, 853
**dog-hole** 189
**dog Latin** 563
**dogma** *tenet* 484
*theology* 983
**dogmatic**
*certain* 474
*positive* 481
*assertion* 535
*obstinate* 606
**dogmatist** 887
**dog's ear** 258
**dog robber** 746
**dog-sick** 867
**dog-star** 423
**dog-trot** 275
**dog-weary** 688
**doily** 652
**doing**
up and – 682
what one is – 625
**doings**
*events* 151
*actions* 680
*conduct* 692
**doit** *trifle* 643
*coin* 800
**dolce far niente** 681
**doldrums**
*dejection* 837
*sulks* 901*a*
**dole**
*small quantity* 32
*scant* 640
*give* 784
*allot* 786
*parsimony* 819
*grief* 828
**doleful** 837
– dumps 901*a*
**doll** *small* 193
*image* 554
**dollar** 800
**dolman** 225
**dolmen** 363, 551
**dolorem, infandum renovare** – 833
**dolorous** 830
**dolour**
*physical* 378
*moral* 828
**dolphin** 341
**dolt** 501
**doltish** 499
**domain**
*class* 75

*region* 181
*property* 780
**Domdaniel** 982
**dome** *high* 206
*roof* 223
*curvature* 245
*convex* 250
**Domesday book**
*list* 86
*record* 551
**domesman** 967
**domestic**
*inhabitant* 188
*home* 189
*interior* 221
*servant* 746
*secluded* 893
– animals 366
**domesticate**
*locate* 184
*acclimatize* 613
– animals 370
**domicile** 189
**domiciled** 186
**domiciliary** 188
– visit 461
**dominant** 175
*note in music* 413
**domination** 737
**dominical** 998
**domineer**
*tyrannize* 739
*insolence* 885
**Domini, anno** – 106
**Dominican** 996
**Dominie** 540
**dominion** 181, 737
**domino** *dress* 225
*mask* 530
*game* 840
**domn** 745
**don** *put on* 225
*scholar* 492
*teacher* 540
*noble* 875
**Don Juan** 897
**donation** 784
**done** *finished* 729
work – 729
– for *spoilt* 659
*failure* 732
– up
*impotent* 158
*tired* 688
have – with
*cease* 142
*relinquish* 624
*disuse* 678
**donee** 785
**donjon** 717, 752
**donkey** *ass* 271
*fool* 501
talk a –'s hind leg off 584
**donna** 374
**Donnybrook Fair**
*disorder* 59
*discord* 713
**donor** 784
**donzel** 746
**doodle** 501
**doom** *end* 67
*fate* 152
*destruction* 162
*death* 360
*judgment* 480
*necessity* 601
*sentence* 971
– sealed
*death* 360
*adversity* 735
**doomed** 735, 828
**doomsday**
*end* 67
*future* 121
till – 112
**door** *entrance* 66
*cover* 223
*brink* 231
*barrier* 232
*opening* 260
*passage* 627
at one's – 197
beg from door to – 765
bolt the – 666
close the – upon 751
death's – 360
keep within –s 265
lie at one's – 926
lock the – 666
open a – to
*liable* 177
open the – to
*receive* 296
*facilitate* 705
*permit* 760
show the – to
*eject* 297
*discourtesy* 895
– mat 652
**doorkeeper** 263
**doorway** 260
**dope** 376, 545, 663
**doquet**
*security* 771
**Dorado, El** – 803
**Doric mode** 413
**dormant**
*inert* 172
*latent* 526
*asleep* 683
**dormer** 260
**dormeuse** 272
**dormir debout,** conte à – 843
**dormitive** 841
**dormitory** 191
**dormouse** 683
**dorp** 189
**dorsal** 235
**dorser** 191
**dorsum** 235, 250
**dory** 273
**dose** *quantity* 25
*part* 51
*medicine* 662
*apportion* 786
**dosser** 191
**dossier** *bundle* 72
*record* 551
**dossil** 223, 263
**dot** *small* 32
*place* 182
*little* 193
*variegate* 440
*mark* 550
*dowry* 780
on the – 113
**dotage** 128, 499
**dotard** 130, 501
**dotation** 784
**dottle** 40, 645
**dote** *drivel* 499, 503
– upon 897
**douanier** 965
**double**
*similar* 17
*increase* 35
*duplex* 90
*substitute* 147
*fold* 258
*turn* 283
*finesse* 702
march at the – 274
see –
*dim sight* 443
*drunk* 959
– acrostic
*letters* 561
*wit* 842
– dutch 519
– entry 811
– the fist 909
– march 684
– meaning 520
– a point 311
in – quick time 274
– reef topsails 664
– sure 474
work – tides 686
– up
*render powerless* 158
**double bar** 747
**double-bass** 417
**doublecross** 545
**double-dealing**
*lie* 544
*cunning* 940
**double-distilled** 171
**double-dyed** 428
**double-eagle** 800
**double-edged** 90, 171
**double entendre**
*ambiguity* 520
*impure* 961
**double-faced**
*lie* 544
*cunning* 702, 940
**double-headed** 90
**double-minded** 605
**double-shotted** 171
**doublet** 225
**double-tongued**
*lie* 544
*cunning* 702, 940
**doubt**
*uncertain* 475
*disbelieve* 485
*sceptic* 989
**doubtful** 475
more than – 473
– meaning
*unintelligible* 519
**doubtless**
*certain* 474
*belief* 484
*assent* 488
**douceur** 784, 973
**douche** 337
**dough** 324, 354, 800
**doughty** 861
**dour** 739
**douse**
*immerse* 310
*splash* 337
*blow* 972
**Dove**
*Holy Ghost* 976
**dove**
*innocent* 946
roar like sucking · 174
**dovecote** 189
**dovetail**
*agree* 23
*join* 43
*intersect* 219
*intervene* 228
*angle* 244

## E

**economic pressure** 751
**economy**
*order* 58
*conduct* 692
*frugality* **817**
animal – 359
**écorcher les oreilles** 410
**ecphorize** 615
**écru** 433
**ecstasis** 683
**ecstasy**
*frenzy* 515
*transport* 821
*rapture* 827
**ecstatic** 829
**ecstatica** 994
**ectoplasm** 992
**ectype** 21
**ecumenical** 78
**edacity** 957
**Edda** 986
**eddy**
*whirlpool* 348
*current* 312
*danger* 667
**Eden** 827
**edge** *energy* 171
*height* 206
*brink* **231**
*sidle* 279
*advantage* 731
cutting – 253
on – 256, 507
take the – off 174
– of hunger 865
– in 228
– one's way 282
**edge-tools** 253
play with – 863
**edgewise** 217
**edging**
*obliquity* 217
*border* 231
*ornament* 847
**edible** 298
**edict** 741
**edification**
*building* 161
*teaching* 537
*learning* 539
*piety* 987
**edifice** 161
**edifying** *good* 648
**edile** 965
**edit**
*publication* 531
*condense* 596
*revise* 658
**edition, new** – 658
**editor** 593
**educate** 537
**educated** 490
self – 490
**education**
*teaching* 537
*knowledge* 490
man of – 492
higher – 490
**educational** 537, 542
**educe** *extract* 301
*discover* 480*a*
**educt** 40
**eduction** 40*a*
**edulcorate** 396, 652
**eel** 248
wriggle like an – 315
**eerie** 860
**efface**
*delete* 162
*disappear* 449
*obliterate* 552
– from the memory 506
**effect**
*consequence* **154**
*product* 161
*impression* 375
*complete* 729
carry into – 692
with crushing – 162
in – 5
take – 731
to that – 516
**effective**
*capable* 157
*useful* 644
**effectuation** 729
**expedient** 646
**effects** 780, 798
**effectual** 731
**effectually** 52
**effectuate** 729
**effeminate**
*weak* 160
*womenlike* 374
*timorous* 862
*sensual* 954
**effeminize** 158
**effendi** 875
**effervesce**
*energy* 171
*violence* 173
*agitate* 315
*bubble* 353
*excited* 825
**effervescent** 338
**effete** *old* 128
*weak* 160
*useless* 645
*spoiled* 659
**efficacious**
[*see* efficient]
**efficient**
*power* 157
*agency* 170
*utility* 644
*skill* 698
**effigy** 21, 554
**effleurer** *skim* 267, 460
**efflorescence** 330
**effluxion of time** 109
**effluence** *egress* 295
*flow* 348
**effluvium** 334, 398
**efflux** 295
**effomation** 240
**effort** 686
**effreet** 980
**effrontery** 885
**effulgence** 420
**effuse**
*pour out* 295, 297
*excrete* 299
*speech* 582
*loquacity* 584
**effusion of blood** 361
**effusive** 573
**eft** 366
**eftsoons** 117
**egad** 535
**égards** 928
**egesta** 299
**egestion** 297
**egg** *beginning* 66
*cause* 153
*food* 298
walk among –s 704
too many –s in one basket
*unskilful* 699
(*imprudent* 863)
– and dart
*ornament* 847
– on 615
**egg-shaped** 247, 249
**ego** *intrinsic* 5
*speciality* 79
*immaterial* 317
non – 6
**egocentrism** 943
**egotism**
*vanity* 880
*cynicism* 911
*selfishness* **943**
**egregious**
*exceptional* 83
*absurd* 497
*exaggerated* 549
*important* 642
**egregiously** 31, **33**
**egress** **295**
**Egyptian darkness** 421
**eheu! fugaces labuntur anni** 111
**eiderdown** 223
**eidouranion** 318
**Eiffel tower** 206
**eight** *number* 98
*boat* 273
*representative* **759**
**eisteddfod** 72, **416**
**eighty** 98
**either** *choice* 609
happy with – **605**
**ejaculate**
*propel* 284
*utter* 580
**ejection** 185, **297**
**ejecta** 299
**ejector** 349
**eke** *also* 37
– out *complete* **52**
*spin out* 110
**ekka** 272
**El Dorado** 803
**elaborate**
*improve* 658
*prepare* 673
*laborious* 686
*work out* 729
**elaine** 356
**élan** 276
**elapse** 109, **122**
**elastic fluid** **334**
**elasticity**
*power* 157
*strength* 159
*energy* 171
*spring* **325**
**elate** *cheer* 836
*rejoice* 838
*hope* 858
*vain* 880
*boast* 884
**elbow** *angle* 244
*projection* 250
*push* 276
at one's –
*near* 197
*advice* 695
lift one's –

**emboss** *convex* 250
*ornament* 847
**embouchure** 260
**embowel** 297
**embrace**
*cohere* 46
*compose* 54
*include* 76
*enclose* 227
*choose* 609
*take* 789
*friendship* 888
*sociality* 892
*courtesy* 894
*endearment* 902
– an offer 762
**embrangle** 61
**embranglement** 713
**embrasure** 257, 260
**embrocation** 662
**embroider**
*variegate* 440
*lie* 544
*ornament* 847
**embroidery**
*adjunct* 39
*exaggeration* 549
**embroil** *derange* 61
*discord* 713
**embroilment** 59
**embrown** 433
**embryo**
*beginning* 66
*cause* 153
in – *destined* 152
*preparing* 673
**embryology** 357
**embryonic** 193, 674
**embus** 293
**embusqué** 603
**emendation** 658
**emerald** *green* 435
*jewel* 847
**emerge** 295, 446
**emergency**
*circumstance* 8
*event* 151
*difficulty* 704
**emeritus** 500, 928
**emersion** 295, 446
**emery**
*sharpener* 253
– paper
*smooth* 255
**emetic** *remedy* 662
**émeute** 742
**emication** 420
**emigrant** 57, 268
**emigrate** 266, 295
**emigré** 268, 295
**eminence**
*height* 206
*fame* 873
*church dignitary* 996
**eminent domain** 744
**eminently** 33
**emir** 745, 875
**emissary**
*messenger* 534
*consignee* 758
**emission** 297
**emit** *eject* 297
*publish* 531
*voice* 580
– vapour 336
**Emmanuel** 976
**emmet** 193
**emollient** 662
**emolument**
*acquisition* 775
*receipt* 810
*remuneration* 973
**emotion** 821
–al appeal 824
–al drama 599
**empale** 260, 972
**empanel** 86, 969
**empathy** 515
**emperor** 745
**emphasis** 580
**emphatic** 535, 642
**emphatically** 31
**empierce**
*perforate* 260
*insert* 300
**empire** 737, 789
– day 840
**empiric** 548
**empirical** 463, 675
**empiricism** 463
**emplane** 293
**employ**
*business* 625
*use* 677
*servitude* 749
*commission* 755
in one's – 746
– one's capital in 794
– oneself 680
– one's time in 625
**employé**
*servant* 746
*agent* 758
**employer** 795
**empoison** 659
**emporium** 799
**empower**
*power* 157
*commission* 755
*accredit* 759
*permit* 760
**empress** 745
**empressement**
*activity* 682
*emotion* 821
*desire* 865
**emprise** 676
**emption** 795
**emptor** 795
caveat – 769
**empty** *clear* 185
*vacant* 187
*deflate* 195
*drain* 297
*ignorant* 491
*waste* 638
*deficient* 640
*useless* 645
beggarly account of – boxes
*poverty* 804
– one's glass 298
– purse 804
– sound 517
– stomach 865
– title *name* 564
*undue* 925
– words 546
**empty-handed** 640
**empty-headed** 491
**empurple** 437
**empyrean** *sky* 318
*blissful* 829
**empyreuma** 41
**empyrosis** 384
**emulate** *imitate* 19
*goodness* 648
*rival* 708
*compete* 720
*glory* 873
**emulsion** 352
**emunctory** 350
**en** – bloc 50
– masse 50
– passant
*parenthetical* 10
*transient* 111
*à propos* 134
– rapport 9
– règle *order* 58
*conformity* 82
– route
*journey* 266
*progress* 282
**enable** 157
**enact** *drama* 599
*action* 680
*conduct* 692
*complete* 729
*order* 741
*law* 963
**enallage** 521
**enamel** *coating* 223
*painting* 556
*ornament* 847
**enameller** 559
**enamour** 897
**encage** 751
**encamp** 184, 189
**encampment** 184
**encaustic** 556
**enceinte**
*with child* 161
*region* 181
*inclosure* 232
**enchafe** 830
**enchain** 751
**enchant** *please* 829
**enchanted** 827
**enchanting** 845, 897
**enchantment**
*sorcery* 992
**enchase** 43, 259
**enchiridion** 593
**enchorial** 188
**encincture** 229
**encircle** 76, 227, 311
**enclave** *close* 181
*boundary* 233
**enclose** 227, 229
**enclosure**
*region* 181
*envelope* 232
*fence* 752
**encomiast** 935
**encomium** 931
**encompass** 227, 233
–ed with difficulties 704
**encore** 104, 931
**encounter**
*undergo* 151
*clash* 276
*meet* 292
*withstand* 708
*contest* 720
– danger 665
– risk 621
**encourage**
*animate* 615
*aid* 707
*comfort* 834
*hope* 858
*embolden* 861
**encroach**
*transcursion* 303
*do wrong* 923

*infringe* 925
**encumber** 704, 706
**encumbrance**
clear of – 807
**encyclical** 531
**encyclopædia** 490, 593
walking – 700
**encyclopædical**
*general* 78
– knowledge **490**
**encysted** 229
**end**
*termination* **67**
*effect* 154
*object* 620
at an – 142
come to its – 729
one's journey's – 292
on – 212
put an – to
*destroy* 162
*kill* 361
begin at the wrong – 699
– one's days 360
–s of the earth 196
– to end *space* 180
*touching* 199
*length* 200
– of life 360
– in smoke 732
– of one's tether
*sophistry* 477
*ignorant* 491
*insufficient* **640**
*difficult* 704
**endamage** 649
**endanger** 665
**endear** 897
**endearment** **902**
**endeavour**
*pursuit* 622
*attempt* 675
use one's best – 686
– after 620
**endemic**
*special* 79
*interior* 221
*disease* 657
**endimanché** 847, 882
**endless**
*multitudinous* 102
*infinite* 105
*perpetual* 112
**endlessly** 16
**endlong** 200
**endocrine** 221
**endogenous** 367
**endorse**
*evidence* 467
*assent* 488
*compact* 769
– *a bill* 800
*approve* 931
**endorsement** 550
**endosmose** 302
**endow**
*confer power* 157
**endowed with**
*possessed of* **777**
**endowment**
*intrinsic* **5**
*power* 157
*talent* 698
*gift* 784
**endrogynous** **83**
**endue** 157
**endure** *time* **106**
*last* 110
*persist* **143**
*continue* 141
*undergo* 151
*feel* 821
*submit to* **826**
unable to – 867
– for ever 112
– pain 828
**enduring**
*indelible* 505
**endwise** 212
**enemy** *time* 841
*foe* 891
the common – 978
thing devised by the – 546
– to society 891
**energumen** 504
**energy** *power* 157
*strength* 159
*physical* **171**
*resolution* 604
*activity* 682
**enervate** 158, 160
**enfant, bon** – 906
– gâté
*prosperity* 734
*satiety* 869
*favourite* 899
– perdu
*hopeless* 859
*reckless* 863
– terrible
*curiosity* 455
*artless* 703
*object of fear* 860
**enfeeble** 160
**enfeoff** 780, 783
**Enfield rifle** **727**
**enfilade**
*lengthwise* 200
*pierce* 260
*pass through* 302
**enfold** 229
**enforce** *urge* 615
*advise* 695
*compel* 744
*require* 924
**enfranchise**
*free* 748
*liberate* 750
*permit* 760
**enfranchised** 924
**engage**
*bespeak* 132
*induce* 615
*undertake* 676
*do battle* 722
*commission* 755
*promise* 768
*compact* 769
I'll –
*affirmation* 535
– the attention 457
– with 720
**engaged**
*marriage* 903
be – 135
– in *attention* 457
**engagement**
*business* 625
*battle* 720
*betrothal* 902
**engaging**
*pleasing* 829
*amiable* 897
**engender** 161
**engine** 153, 633
**engine-driver** 268
**engineer** 690, 694, 726
**engineering** 633
**engird** 227
**English** 188
broken – 563
king's – 560
murder the king's – 568
plain –
*intelligible* 518
*interpreted* 522
*style* 576
– horn 417
**engorge**
*swallow* 296
*gluttony* 957
**engorgement**
*too much* 641
**engrail** 256
**engrave**
*furrow* 259
*mark* 550
– in the **memory** 505
**engraver** 559
**engraving** 21, 22, **558**
**engross** *write* **590**
*possess* 777
– the thoughts
*thought* 451
*attention* 457
**engrossed in thought** **451**
**engulf**
*destroy* 162
*plunge* 310
*swallow up* 296
**enhance**
*increase* 35
*improve* 658
**enharmonic** 413
**enigma**
*question* 461
*secret* 533
**enigmatic**
*uncertain* 475
*unintelligible* **517**
*obscure* 519
**énigme, mot d'** – 522
**enjoin** *advise* **695**
*command* 741
*prescribe* 926
**enjoy**
*physically* **377**
*possess* **777**
*morally* 827
– health 654
– popularity **873**
– a state 7
**enkindle** *heat* **384**
*excite* 824
**enlarge**
*increase* 35
*swell* 194
*in writing* 573
*liberate* 750
– the mind 537
**enlarged views** **498**
**enlighten**
*illumine* 420
*inform* 527
*teach* 537
**enlightened**
*knowledge* 490
**enlist** *engage* 615
*war* 722
*commission* **755**

under the banners of 707
– into the service 677
**enliven**
*delight* 829
*cheer* 836
*amuse* 840
**enmity 889**
**ennoble** 873
**ennui** 841
**enormity**
*crime* 947
**enormous** *great* 31
*big* 192
– number 102
**enough** *much* 31
*no more!* 142
*sufficient* 639
*moderately* 651
*satiety* 869
know when one has had – 953
– in all conscience 641
– to drive one mad 830
– and to spare 639
**enounce** 535, 580
**enrage** 830, 900
**enragé** 865
**enrapture**
*excite* 824
*beatify* 829
*love* 897
**enraptured** 827
**enravish** 829
**enravished** 827
**enravishment** 824
**enrich**
*improve* 658
*wealth* 803
*ornament* 847
**enrobe** 225
**enroll** *list* 86
*record* 551
– troops 722
*commission* 755
**ens** *essence* 1
**Ens Entium** 976
**ensample** 22
**ensanguined** 361
**ensconce**
*conceal* 528
*safety* 664
**ensconced**
*located* 184
**ensemble** 50
**enshrine**
*circumscribe* 229
*repute* 873
*sanctify* 987
– in the memory 505
**ensiform 253**
**ensign**
*standard* **550**
*officer* 726
*master* 745
– of authority **747**
**ensilage** 637
**enslave** 749
**ensnare** 545
**ensue** *follow* **63, 117**
*happen* 151
**ensure** 474
**entablature** 210
**entail** *cause* 153
*tie up property* 781
**entangle**
*interlink* 43
*derange* 61
*ravel* 219
*entrap* 545
*embroil* 713
**entangled**
*disorder* 59
– by difficulties 704
**entend, cela s'** – 613
**entente**
*agreement* 23
*alliance* 714
*friendship* 888
**enter** *go in* 294
*appear* 446
*note* 551
*accounts* 811
– into the composition of 56
– into details
*special* 79
*describe* 594
– into an engagement 768
– into the feelings of 914
– into the ideas of
*understand* 518
*concord* 714
– in *converge* 290
– the lists
*attack* 716
*contention* 720
– the mind 451
– a profession 625
– into the spirit of
*feel* 821
*delight* 827
– upon 66
– into one's views 488
**enterprise**
*pursuit* 622
*undertaking* 676
commercial – 794
**enterprising**
*active* 171, 682
*courageous* 861
**entertain**
*bear in mind* 457
*support* 707
*amuse* 840
*sociality* 892
– doubts 485
– feeling 821
– an idea 451
– an opinion 484
**entertainment** 840
*pleasure* 377
*repast* 298
**entêté** 481, 606
**enthral**
*subjection* 749
*restraint* 751
**enthrone** 873
**enthronement** 755
**enthusiasm**
*language* 574
*willingness* 602
*feeling* 821
*hope* 858
*love* 897
**enthusiast**
*madman* 504
*obstinate* 606
*active* 682
**enthusiastic**
*imaginative* 515
*sensitive* 822
*excitable* 825
*sanguine* 858
**enthymeme** 476
**entice** 615
**enticing** 829
**entire** *whole* 50
*complete* 52
*continuous* 69
– horse 373
**entirely** *much* 31
**entitle** *name* 564
*give a right* 924
**entity** 1
**entoil** 545
**entomb** *inter* 363
*imprison* 751
**Entomology** 368
**entourage** 88, 183, 227
**entozoon** 193
**entrails** 221
**entrain** 293
**entrammel 751**
**entrance**
*beginning* 66
*ingress* 294
*way* 627
*enrapture* **827,** 829
*magic* 992
give – to 296
**entranced** 515
**entrancement 824**
**entrap** 545
**entre nous** 528
**entreat** 765
**entrée**
*reception* 296
*dish* 298
give the – 296
have the – 294
– dish 191
**entremet** 298
**entrepôt** 636, 799
**entrepreneur** 599
**entresol** 191
**entrust**
*commission* **755**
*give* 784
*credit* 805
**entry** *beginning* **66**
*ingress* 294
*record* 551
**entwine** *join* 43
*intersect* 219
*convolve* 248
**enucleate** 522
**enumerate** 85
– among 76
**enumeration 86**
**enunciate**
*inform* 527
*affirm* 535
*voice* 580
**envelop** 225
**envelope** 223, 232
**envenom**
*deprave* 659
*exasperate* **835**
*hate* 898
*anger* 900
**envenomed**
*bad* 649
*insalubrious* **657**
*painful* 830
*malevolent* **907**
– tongue 934
**environ** 227
**environment** 183
**environs** 197
in such and such – 183
**envisage** 515, 861

**envoy**
*messenger* 534
*consignee* 758
**envy 921**
enwrap 225
enzyme 320
Eolian harp 417
Eolus 349
eon 976
épanchement
*manifest* 525
*artless* 703
*endearment* 902
epact 641
épaulette
*badge* 550, 747
*ornament* 847
*decoration* 877
éperdu 824
épergne 191
ephemeral 111
ephemeris
*calendar* 114
*record* 551
*book* 593
Ephesian letters 993
ephialtes
*physical pain* 378
*hindrance* 706
*mental pain* 828
ephod 999
ephor 967
epic 594, 597
epicedium 839
epicene 81, 83
epicier 876
epicure
*fastidious* 868
*sybarite* 954*a*
*glutton* 957
epicurean 954
Epicurus, system of – 954
epicy-cle, -cloid 247
epidemic
*general* 78
*disease* 655
*insalubrity* 657
epidermis 223
epigenesis 161
epigram 496, 842
epigrammatic 572
epigrammatist 844
epigraph 550
epilepsy 315, 655
epilogue
*sequel* 65
*end* 67
*drama* 599
èpingles, tiré à quatre – 855
Epiphany 998
episcopal 995
Episcopalian 984
episcopate 995
episode
*adjunct* 39
*discontinuity* 70
*interjacence* 228
episodic
*irrelative* 10
*style* 573
epistle 592
Epistles 985
epistrophe 104
epistyle 210
epitaph 363
epithalamium 903
epithem 662
epithet 564
epitome
*miniature* 193
*short* 201
*concise* 572
epizoötic 657
epoch *time* 106
*instant* 113
*date* 114
*present time* 118
epode 597
eponym 564
epopœa 597
epos 594
epulation 298
epulotic 662
epuration 652
equable 16, 922
equal *even* 27
*equitable* 922
– chance 156
– times 120
– to *power* 157
equality 13, **27**
equalize 213
equanimity 826
equate 27, 30
equations 85
equator 68, 318
equatorial 68, 236
equerry 746
equestrian 268
equibalanced 27
equidistant 68
equilibration 27
equilibrist 599
equilibrium 27
equine *carrier* 271
*horse* 366
equinox 125, 126
equip 225, 673
equipage
*vehicle* 272
*instruments* 633
*display* 882
equiparent 27
equipment 633
equipoise &c. 27, 30
equiponderate 30
equitable *wise* 498
*just* 922
*due* 924
*honourable* 939
– interest 780
equitation 266
equity *right* 922
*honour* 939
*law* 963
in – 922
– draftsman 968
equivalent
*identical* 13
*equal* 27
*compensation* 30
*substitute* 147
*translation* 522
equivocalness
*dubious* 475
*double meaning* **520**
*impure* 961
equivocate
*sophistry* 477
*palter* 520
*lie* 544
equivocation
[*see* equivocate]
without – 543
équivoque
*double meaning* 520
*impure* 961
era *time* 106, **108**
*date* 114
eradicate
*destroy* 162
*extract* 301
erase *destroy* 162
*obliterate* 331, 552
Erastian 984
erasure 552
Erato 416
ere 116
– long 132
– now 116
*past* 122
Erebus *dark* 421
*hell* 982
erect *build* 161
*vertical* 212
*raise* 307
with head – 878
– the scaffolding 673
erewhile 116, 122
ergatocracy 737
ergo 476
ergotism 480
ergotize 485
eriometer 445
Erinys 900
Erl King 980
ermine
*badge of authority* 747
*ornament* 847
erode 36, 659
Eros 897, 979
erosion 36
erotic 897, 961
err – *in opinion* **495**
– *morally* 945
errand
*message* 532
*business* 625
*commission* 755
errand-boy 534
errant 279
erratic
*irregular* 139
*changeable* 149
*wandering* 279
*capricious* 608
erratum 495
erroneous 495
error *fallacy* **495**
*vice* 945
*guilt* 947
court of – 966
writ of – 969
ersatz 973
erst 122
erubescence 434
erubuit salva res est 95
eruct 297
eructate 297
erudition 490, 539
eruption
*upheaval* 146
*violence* 173
*egress* 295, 297
*disease* 655
volcanic – 872
escadrille 726
escalade
*mounting* 305
*attack* 716
escalator 307
escalop 248
escapade
*absurdity* **497**
*freak* 608

*prank* 840
**escape 671**
*liberate* 750
*evade* 927
means of – 664, 666
– the lips
*disclosure* 529
*speech* 582
– the memory 506
– notice &c.
*invisible* 447
*inattention* 458
*latent* 526
**escarp** 717
**escarpment**
*stratum* 204
*height* 206
*oblique* 217
**escharotic**
*caustic* 171
*pungent* 392
**eschatology** 67
**escheat** 145, 974
**eschew**
*avoid* 623
*dislike* 867
**esclandre** 828, 830
**escort**
*accompany* 88
*safeguard* 664
*keeper* 753
**escritoire** 191
**esculent** 298
**escutcheon** 550
**esoteric**
*private* 79
*concealed* 528
**Espagne, château** en – *fancy* 515
*hope* 858
**espalier** 232
**especial** 79
**especially** 33
**Esperanto** 560
**espial** 441
**espièglerie**
*cunning* 702
*fun* 840
*wit* 842
**espionnage** 441, 461
**esplanade**
*houses* 189
*flat* 213
**espouse**
*choose* 609
*marriage* 903
– a cause *aid* 707
*co-operate* 709
**esprit**
*shrewdness* 498
*wit* 842
bel – 844
– de corps
*bias* 481
*co-operation* 709
*sociality* 892
(*party* 712)
– fort
*thinker* 500
*irreligious* 989
**espy** 441
**esquire** 875, 877
**essay**
*experiment* 463
*dissertation* 595
*endeavour* **675**
**essayist** 593, 595
**esse** 1
**essence**
*nature* 5
*scent* 398
**essential**
*intrinsic* 5
*great* 31
*required* 630
*important* 642
**essentially**
*intrinsically* 5
*substantially* 3
**essential stuff** 5
**establish**
*settle* 150
*create* 161
*place* 184
*evidence* 467
*demonstrate* 478
– equilibrium 27
**established**
*permanent* 141
*habit* 613
– church 983*a*
**establishment**
*party* 712
*shop* 799
**estafette** 534
**estaminet** 189
**estate** *condition* 7
*property* 780
come to man's – 131
**esteem**
*believe* 484
*repute* 873
*approve* 931
in high – 928
**estimable** 648
**estimate**
*measure* 466
*adjudge* 480
*information* 527
– too highly 482
**estimation**
[*see* esteem, estimate]
**estime**
succès d' – 873
**estival** 382
**esto perpetua!**
*perpetuity* 112
*permanence* 141
*desire* 865
**estop** 706
**estrade** 213
**estrange**
*alienate* 44, 889
*discord* 713
*hate* 898
**estranged**
*secluded* 893
**estrapade**
*attack* 716
*punishment* 972
**estreat** 974
**estuary** 343
**estuation** 384
**esurient** 865
**et – cætera**
*add* 37
*include* 76
*plural* 100
– hoc genus omne
*similar* 17
*include* 76
*multiform* 81
**étalage** 882
**état major** 745
**etch** *furrow* 259
*engraving* 558
**eternal** 112
– home 981
**Eternal, the** – 976
**eterne** 112
**eternify** 112
**eternity** 112
an – 110
launch into – 360, 361
**ether**
*lightness* 320
*rarity* 322
*vapour* 334
*anæsthetic* 376
**ethereal** 4
**ethicism** 984
**ethics** 926
**Ethiopian** 431
–'s skin 150
**Ethiopian's skin**
*unchangeable* 150
**ethnology** 372
**ethnic** 984
**ethology** 926
**ethos** 5
**etiolate** 429, 430
**etiology** *causes* 155, 359
*knowledge* 490
*disease* 655
**etiquette**
*custom* 613
*fashion* 852
*ceremony* 882
**étoile, à la belle –**
*out of doors* 220
*in the air* 338
**Eton jacket** 225
**étourderie**
*inattention* 458
*unskilfulness* 699
**etymological** 560
**etymology** 562
**etymon** *origin* **153**
*verbal* 562
**Eucharist** 998
**euchology** 998
**euchre** 840
**eudiometer**
*air* 338
*salubrity* 656
**euge!** 931
**eugenics** 658
**eulogist** 935
**eulogize** 482
**eulogy** 931
**Eumenides** *fury* 900
*evil-doers* 913
*revenge* 919
**eunuch** 158
**eupepsia** 654
**euphemism**
*metaphor* 521
*style* 577, 578
*flattery* 933
**euphemist**
*man of taste* 850
*flatterer* 935
**euphony** 413, 578
**Euphrosyne** 836
**euphuism**
*metaphor* 521
*elegant style* 577
*affected style* **579**
*affectation* 855
**Eurasian** 41
**eureka!** 462, 480*a*
**Euripus** 343
**Eurus** 349
**eurythmics** 537, 840
**eurythmy** 242
**Euterpe** 416

**euthanasia** 360
**euthenics** 658
**evacuate**
*quit* 293
*excrete* 295
*emit* 297
**evacuation** 299
**evade** *sophistry* 477
*avoid* 623
*not observe* 773
*exempt* 927
**evagation** 279
**evanescent**
*small* 32
*transient* 111
*little* 193
*disappearing* 449
**evangelical** 983*a*, 985
**Evangelists** 985
**evanid** 160
**evaporable** 334
**evaporate**
*unsubstantial* 4
*transient* 111
*vaporize* 336
**evaporation** 340
**evasion**
*sophistry* 477
*concealment* 528
*falsehood* 544
*untruth* 546
*avoidance* 623
*escape* 671
*cunning* 702
*non-observance* 773
*dereliction* 927
**eve** 126
on the – of
*transient* 111
*prior* 116
*future* 121
**evection** 61
**even**
*uniform* 16
*equal* 27
*still more* 33
*regular* 138
*level* 213
*straight* 246
*flat* 251
*smooth* 255
*although* 469
*in spite of* 708
– course 628
– now 118
– so
*for all that* 30
*yes* 488
– temper 826
– terms 922
– tenor
*uniform* 16
*order* 58
*continuity* **58**
pursue the – tenor
*continue* **143**
*avoid* 623
*business* 625
be – with
*retaliate* 718
*pay* 807
get – with 972
**even-handed** 922, 939
**evening** **126**
shades of – 422
– classes 537
– star 423
**evenness** 16
**evensong** 126, 990
**event** 151
*bout* 720
in the – of
*circumstance* 8
*expectation* 507
*supposition* 514
justified by the – 937
**eventful** 151
*remarkable* 642
*stirring* 682
**eventide** 126
**eventual** 121
**eventuality** **151**
**eventually**
*effect* 154
**ever** 16, 112
did you – ? 870
– and anon 136
– changing 149
– recurring 104
**ever so** 31
– little 32
– long 110
– many 102
**evergreen**
*continuous* 69
*lasting* 110
*always* 112
*fresh* 123
**everlasting** 112
– life 152
– fire 982
**evermore** 112
**eversion** 218
**evert** 140
**every** 78
– hand against one 891
– day
*conformity* 82
*frequent* 136
*habit* 613
– description 81
– inch 50
in – mouth
*assent* 488
*news* 532
*repute* 873
– other 138
in – quarter 180
in – respect 494
on – side 227
at – turn 186
– whit 52
**everybody** 78
**everyone** 78
– his due 922
– in his turn **148**
**everywhere** 180, 186
**evict** 297
**evidence** **467**
*disclose* 529
ocular – 446
**évidence, en** – **446**
**evident**
*concrete* **3**
*visible* 446
*certain* 474
*manifest* 525
**evidently** 516
**evil** *harm* **619**
*badness* 649
*impious* 988
– day
*prepare for* – 673
*adversity* 735
– eye *vision* 441
*malevolence* 907
*disapprobation* 932
*demon* 980
*sorcery* 992
*spell* 993
– favoured 846
– fortune 735
– genius 980
– hour 135
– one 978
– plight 735
through – report &c. 604*a*
– star 649
**evil-doer** **913**
**evil-doing** 945
**evil-minded** 907, 945
**evil-speaking**
*malediction* 908
*censure* 932
*detraction* **934**
**evince** *show* **467**
*prove* 478
*disclose* 529
**eviscerate** 297, **301**
**eviscerated** 4
**evoke** *cause* **153**
*call upon* **765**
*excite* 824
**evolution**
*numerical* 85
*production* 161
*motion* 264
*extraction* 301
*circuition* 311
*turning out* **313**
*organization* **357**
*training* 673
*action* 680
military –s **722**
**evolve**
*discover* 480*a*
**evolved from** **154**
[*and see* evolution]
**evulgate** 531
**evulsion** 301
**evivva!** 931
**ewe** 366, 374
– lamb 366
**ewer** 191
**ex**
– animo 602
– cathedra 542
– officio 494, **924**
– parte 467
– pede Herculem 82
– post facto **122**, 133
– tempore
*instant* 113
*occasion* 134
**exacerbate**
*increase* 35
*exasperate* **173**
*aggravate* **659**, 835
**exact** *similar* **17**
*special* 79
*true* 494
*style* 572
*require* 741
*tax* 812
*insolence* 885
*claim* 924, 926
– meaning 516
– memory 505
– observance **772**
– truth 494

*mean* 516
*declare* 525
*inform* 527
*journal* 531
*intentional* 620
by – *haste* 684
– train 272
– by words 566
**expressed, well –** 578
**expressible** 525
**expression** [*see* express]
*musical* 416
*aspect* 448
*nomenclature* 564
*phrase* 566
mode of – 569
new fangled – 563
**expressive**
*meaning* 516
*sensibility* 822
**exprobation** 932, 938
**expropriation** 782
**expugnable** 665
**expugnation** 731
**expulsion** 55 [*see* expel]
**expunge** 162, 552
**expurgate** 38, 652
**expurgatorius,** index – 761
**exquisite**
*savoury* 394
*excellent* 648
*pleasurable* 829
*beautiful* 845
*fop* 854
**exquisitely** 31
**exsiccate** 340
**exsudation** 299
**exsufflation** 993
**exsuscitate** 824
**extant 1**
**extasy** [*see* ecstasy]
**extemporaneous** [*see* extempore]
*transient* 111
**extempore**
*instant* 113
*early* 132
*occasion* 134
*off-hand* 612
*unprepared* 674
**extend**
*expand* 194
*prolong* 200
– to 196
**extended** 202
**xtensibility** 324
**extensile** 324
**extension** [*see* extend] 35, 142, 180
– of time 110
**extensive** 31, 180
– knowledge 490
**extenso, in –**
*whole* 50
*diffuse* 573
**extent** 26, 180, 200, 202
**extenuate**
*decrease* 36
*weaken* 160
*excuse* 937
**extenuated** 203
**extenuating circumstances** 469, 937
**extenuatory** 469
**exteriority 220**
**exterminate** 162
**extermination** 301
**external** 57, 220
– evidence 467
– senses 375
**extinct**
*inexistent* **2**
*past* 122
*destroyed* 162
*darkness* 421
become – 4
**extincteur** 385
**extinction of life** 360
**extinguish**
*destroy* 162
*blow out* 385
*darken* 421
**extinguisher** 385
put an – upon
*hinder* 706
**extirpate** 301
**extispicious** 511
**extol**
*over-estimate* 482
*praise* 931
**extort** *extract* 301
*compel* 744
*despoil* 789
**extorted**
*dissent* 489
**extortion** 814, 819
**extortionate** 739, 865
**extra** 37, 599, 641
ab – 220
**extract**
*draw off* 297
*take out* 301
*quotation* 596
*remedy* 662
**extraction 301**
*paternity* 166
– of roots 85
**extractor** 301
**extradition** 270, 297
**extrajudicial** 964
**extramundane** 317
**extramural** 220
**extraneous**
*extrinsic* 6
*not related* 10
*foreign* 57
*outside* 220
**extraneousness 57**
**extraordinary**
*great* 31
*exceptional* 83
**extraregarding** 220
**extravagant**
*inordinate* 31
*violent* 173
*absurd* 497
*foolish* 499
*fanciful* 515
*exaggerated* 549
*excessive* 641
*high-priced* 814
*prodigal* 818
*vulgar* 851
*ridiculous* 853
**extravaganza**
*fanciful* 515
*drama* 599
**extravagation** 303
**extravasate** 295, 297
**extreme**
*inordinate* **31**
*end* 67
– unction 998
**extremis, in –**
*dying* 360
*difficulty* 704
**extremist** 710
**extremity** *end* 67
*adversity* 735
*tribulation* 828
drive matters to an – 604
at the last – 665
**extricate**
*take out* 301
*deliver* 672
*facilitate* 705
*liberate* 750
**extrinsicality 6**
**extrinsic evidence** 467
**extrusion** 297, 299
**exuberant**
– *style* 573
*redundant* 639
**exudation** 295, **299**
**exulcerate** 659
**exult** 838, 884
**exultant** 858
**exulting** 836
**exunge** 356
**exuviæ** 653
**eye** *circle* **247**
*opening* 260
*organ of sight* **44**
all my – and Betty Martin 546
appear to one's – 446
before one's **–s**
*front* 234
*visible* 446
*manifest* 525
cast the –s on
*see* 441
cast the –s over
*attend to* 457
catch the – **457**
close the –s
*blind* 442
*death* 360
*sleep* 683
dry –s 823
fix the –s on **457**
have an – to
*attention* 457
*intention* 620
*desire* 865
in one's –
*visible* 446
*expectant* **507**
in the –s of
*appearance* **448**
*belief* 484
keep an – upon 459
look with one's own –s 459
make –'s at 441
mind's – 515
with moistened –s 839
open the –s to 480*a*
with open –s 870
set one's –s upon 865
shut one's –s to
*inattention* **458**
*permit* 760
to the –s 448
under the –s of

186
up to one's -s 641
have one's -s about one 459
- askance 860
-s draw straws 683
an - for an - 718, 919
- glistening 824
in the - of the law 963
- of the master 693
- of a needle 260
-s open
*attention* 457
*care* 459
*intention* 620
-s opened
*disclosure* 529
-s out 442
**eye-ball** 441
**eyebrows** 256
**eyeglass** 445
**eyelashes** 256
**eyeless** 442
**eyelet** 260
**eyelid** 223
**eye-shade** 443
**eye-sight** 441
**eyesore** 846, 848
**eye-teeth**
have cut one's -
*adolescence* 131
*skill* 698
*cunning* 702
**eye-wash** 544
**eye-witness**
*spectator* 444
*evidence* 467
**eyot** 346
**eyre** 966
**eyry** 189

F

**Fabian policy**
*delay* 133
*inaction* 681
*caution* 864
**fable** *error* 495
*metaphor* 521
*fiction* 546
*description* 594
**fabric** *state* 7
*effect* 154
*texture* 329
**fabricate**
*composition* 54
*make* 161
*invent* 515
*falsify* 544
**fabrication** *lie* 546
**fabula narratur, de te** - *retaliate* 718
*condemn* 971
**fabulist** 594
**fabulous**
*enormous* 31
*imaginary* 515
*untrue* 546
*exaggerated* 549
**faburden** 413
**façade** 234
**face** *exterior* 220
*covering* 223
*front* 234
*aspect* 448
*oppose* 708
*resist* 719
*brave* 861
*impudence* 885
change the - of 146
fly in the - of
*disobey* 742
put a good - upon
*sham* 545
*calm* 826
*cheerful* 836
*hope* 858
*pride* 878
*display* 882
*vindicate* 93
in the - of
*presence* 186
*opposite* 708
look in the -
*see* 441
*proud* 878
make -s
*distort* 243
*ugly* 846
*disrespect* 929
on the - of
*manifest* 525
show -
*present* 186
*visible* 446
not show -
*disreputable* 874
*bashful* 879
to one's - 525
wry - 378
- about 279
set one's - against 708
- of the country 344
on the - of the
earth
*space* 180
*world* 318
- to face *front* 234
*contraposition* 237
*manifest* 525
- of the thing
*appearance* 448
**facet** 220
**facetiæ** 842
**facetious** 842
**facia** 234
**facile** *willing* 602
*irresolute* 605
*easy* 705
**facile princeps** 33
**facilis descensus Averni**
*sloping* 217
*danger* 665
**facilitate** 705
**facility** *skill* 698
*easy* **705**
**facing** *covering* 223
**facinorous** 945
**façon de parler** 521, 549
**fac-simile** 21, 554
**fact** *existence* 1
*event* 151
*certainty* 474
*truth* 494
in - 535
**faction** 712, **713**
**factious** 24
**factitious** 545, **546**
**factor**
*numerical* 84
*director* 694
*consignee* 758
**factory** 691
**factotum**
*agent* 690
*manager* 694
*employé* 758
**facts** *evidence* 467
summary of - 594
at variance with - 471
**facula** 420
**faculties** 450
in possession of one's - 502
**faculty**
*power* 157
*profession* **625**
*skill* 698
**facundity** 582
**fad** 481, 608
**faddle** 683
**fade** *vanish* **4**
*transient* 111
*become old* **124**
*droop* 160
*grow dim* 422
*lose colour* **429**
*disappear* **449**
*spoil* 659
- from the memory **506**
**fade** 391
**fadge** 23
**fæces** 299, 653
**fæx populi** 876
**fag** *cigarette* 392
*labour* 686
*fatigue* 688
*drudge* 690, **746**
- end
*remainder* **40**
*end* 67
**faggot** 72, 388
**fagots et fagots** 15, 465
**faïence** 557
**fail** *droop* 160
*shortcoming* **304**
*be confuted* 479
*illness* 655
*not succeed* **732**
*not observe* **773**
*not pay* 808
*dereliction* 927
**failing** [*see* fail]
*incomplete* **53**
*insufficient* **640**
*vice* 945
*guilt* 947
- heart **837**
- luck 735
- memory **506**
- sight 443
- strength **160**
**failure** **732**
heart - 360
**fain** *willing* 602
*compulsive* **744**
*wish* 865
**fainéant** 683
**faint** 32
*impotent* **158**
*weak* 160
*sound* 405
*dim* 422
*colour* 429
*swoon* 688
- heart *fear* 860
*cowardice* 862
damn with - praise 930, **932, 934**

– plea *untruth* 546
*plea* 617
– position 704
– pretences 791
– prophet
*disappoint* 509
*pseudo-revelation* 986
– reasoning 477
– scent 495, 538
– shame 855
– statement 546
– step 732
– teaching 538
– witness
*deceiver* 548
*detraction* 934
**falsehood 544,** 546
**falsetto** *squeak* 410
*want of voice* 581
**falsify** *error* 495
*falsehood* 544, 546
– accounts 811
– one's hope 509
**falter** *slow* 275
*stammer* 583
*hesitate* 605
*slip* 732
*hopeless* 859
*fear* 860
**faltering accents** 605
**fame** *greatness* 31
*news* 532
*renown* 873
**familiar**
*known* 490
*habitual* 613
*sociable* 892
*affable* 894
– *spirit* 979, 980
on – terms 888
**familiarize**
*teach* 537
*habit* 613
**famille, en** – 892
**family**
*kin* 11
*class* 75
*ancestors* 166
*posterity* 167
*party* 712
in the bosom of one's – 221
happy – 714
– circle 892
– jars 713
– likeness 17
– tie 11
in the – way 161
**famine** 640
– price 814
**famine-stricken** 640
**famish**
*stingy* 819
*fasting* 956
**famished**
*insufficient* 640
*hungry* 865
**famous** 873
**famously** 31
**fan** *blow* 349
*cool* 385
*refresh* 689
*stimulate* 824
flirt a – 855
– the embers 505
– the flame
*violence* 173
*heat* 384
*aid* 707
*excite* 824
– into a flame
*anger* 900
–shaped 194
**fanatic**
*madman* 504
*imaginative* 515
*zealot* 682
*religious* – 988
**fanatical**
*misjudging* 481
*insane* 503
*emotional* 821
*excitable* 825
*heterodox* 984
*over-righteous* 988
**fanaticism** 606
**fanciful**
*imaginative* 515
*capricious* 608
*ridiculous* 853
**fancy** *think* 451
*idea* 453
*believe* 484
*suppose* 514
*imagine* 515
*caprice* 608
*choice* 609
*pugilism* 726
*wit* 842
*desire* 865
*wonder* 870
*love* 897
after one's – 850
indulge one's – 609
take a – to
*delight in* 827
*desire* 865
take one's –
*please* 829
– dog 366
– dress 840
– price 814
– woman 962
**fandango** 840
**fandi, mollia tempora** – 588
**fane** 1000
**fanfare** *loudness* 404
*celebration* 883
**fanfaron** 887
**fanfaronnade** 884
**fangs** *venom* 663
*rule* 737
*retention* 781
**fan-light** 260
**fan-like** 202
**fannel** 999
**fanon** 999
**fantasia** 415
**fantastic** *odd* 83
*absurd* 497
*imaginative* 515
*capricious* 608
*unfashionable* 851
*ridiculous* 853
**fantasy**
*imagination* 515
*desire* 865
**fantoccini** 554, 599
**faquir** 996
**far** – away 196
– be it from
*unwilling* 603
*deprecation* 766
– between
*disjunction* 44
*few* 103
*interval* 198
– from it
*unlike* 18
*shortcoming* 304
*no* 536
– from the truth 546
– and near 180
– off 196
– and wide 31, 180, 196
**farce**
*absurdity* 497
*untruth* 546
*drama* 599
*wit* 842
*ridiculous* 853
mere –
*unimportant* 643
*useless* 645
**farceur**
*actor* 599
*humorist* 844
**fardel**
*bundle* 72
*hindrance* 706
**fare** *state* 7
*food* 298
*price* 812
bill of –
*list* 86
**farewell**
*departure* 293
*relinquishment* 624
*loss* 776
– to greatness 874
**far-famed** 873
**far-fetched** 10
**far-flung** 73
**far-gone**
*much* 31
*insane* 503
*spoiled* 654
**farinaceous** 330
**farm** *till* 371
*property* 780
*rent* 788
**farmer** 188, 342, 371
afternoon – 683
**farm-house** 189
**Farmer-Labor** 712
**faro** 840
**farrago** 59
**farrier** 370
**farrow**
*produce* 161
*litter* 167
*multitude* 102
**far-sighted** 442, 510
**farther** 196
[*and see* further]
**farthing**
*quarter* 97
*worthless* 643
*coin* 800
– candle 422
**farthingale** 225
**fasces** 747
**fascia** 205, 247
**fascicule** 51
**fasciculated** 72
**fascinate**
*influence* 615
*excite* 824
*please* 829
*astonish* 870
*love* 897
*conjure* 992
**fascinated**

**fire-ball** *fuel* 388
*arms* 727
**fire-balloon** 273
**fire-barrel** 388
**fire-bell** 669
**fire-boat** 726
**fire-brand**
*fuel* 388
*instigator* 615
*dangerous man* 667
*incendiary* 913
**fire-brigade** 385
**fire-curtain** 599
**fire-drake** 423
**fire-eater**
*fighter* 726
*blusterer* 887
**fire-eating**
*rashness* 863
*insolence* 885
**fire-engine** 348
**fire-escape** 671
**fire-extinguisher** 385
**fire-fly** 423
**fireless cooker** 386
**fire-light** 422
**firelock** 727
**fireman** *stoker* 268
*extinguisher* 385
**fire-place** 386
**fire-proof** 385
**fireside** 189
**firewood** 388
**firework**
*fire* 382
*luminary* 423
*celebration* 883
*amusement* 840
**fire-worship** 991
**fire-worshipper** 984
**firing** *fuel* 388
*explosion* 406
**firkin** 191
**firm**
*junction* 43
*stable* 150
*hard* 323
*resolute* 604
*partnership* 712
*merchant* 797
*brave* 861
stand – 719
– as a rock 604
– belief 484
– hold 781
**firmament** 318
**firman** 741, 760
**first** 66
– blush
*morning* 125
*leading* 280
*vision* 441
*appearance* 448
*manifest* 525
– blow 716
– cause 976
– that comes 609*a*
– fiddle
*importance* 642
*proficient* 700
*authority* 737
– come first served 609*a*
– and foremost 66
– impression 66
– and last 87
– line 234
come back to – love 607
– move 66
– opportunity 132
at – sight 448
– stage 66
– stone
*preparation* 673
*attack* 716
on the – summons 741
of the – water
*best* 648
*repute* 873
**first-born** 124, 128
**first-fruits** 154
**first-hand** 20, 467
**firstlings** 128, 154
**first-rate**
*important* 642
*excellent* 648
*man-of-war* 726
**firth** 343
**fisc** 802
**fiscal** 800
**fish** *food* 298
*sport* 361, 622
*animal* 366
food for –es 362
other – to fry
*ill-timed* 135
*busy* 682
queer – 857
– in the air 645
– for compliments 880
– for *seek* 4
*experiment* 463
*desire* 865
– hatchery 370
– out *inquire* 461
*discover* 480*a*
– in troubled waters
*difficult* 704
*discord* 713
– up *raise* 307
*find* 480*a*
– out of water
*disagree* 24
*unconformable* 83
*displaced* 185
*bungler* 701
**fisherman** 361
**fishery** 370
**fishing** *kill* 361
*pursue* 622
**fishing-boat** 273
**fishpond** 343, 370
**fish-tail** 267
**fishy transaction** 940
**fisk** 266, 274
**fissile** 328
**fission** 44
**fissure** 44
*chink* 198
**fist**
*handwriting* 590
*grip* 781
shake the –
*defy* 715
*threat* 909
**fisticuffs** 720
**fistula** 260
**fit** *state* 7
*agreeing* 23
*equal* 27
*paroxysm* 173
*agitation* 315
*caprice* 608
*expedient* 646
*healthy* 654
*disease* 655
*excitement* 825
*anger* 900
*right* 922
*due* 924
*duty* 926
in –s 315
think – 600
– of abstraction 458
– of crying 839
– for 698
– out *dress* 225
*prepare* 673
– to be seen 845
by –s and starts
*irregular* 59
*discontinuous* 70
*agitated* 315
*capricious* 608
*haste* 684
**fitful**
*irregular* 139
*changeable* 149
*capricious* 608
**fittings** 633
**five** 98
division by – 99
– act play 599
– and twenty 98
**Five Year Plan** 626
**fiver** 800
**fives** *game* 840
**fix** *join* 43
*arrange* 60
*establish* 150
*place* 184
*immovable* 265
*solidify* 321
*resolve* 604
*difficulty* 704
– the eyes upon 441
– the foundations 673
– the memory 505
– the time 114
– the thoughts 457
– up 774
– upon *discover* 480*a*
*choose* 609
**fixed** *intrinsic* 5
*permanent* 141
*stable* 150
*quiescent* 265
*habitual* 613
– idea 481
– opinion 484
– periods 138
**fixity** 141
**fixity of purpose** 141
**fixture**
*appointment* 741
*property* 780
**fizgig** 423
**fizz** 409
**fizzle** 353
– out 304
**flabelliform** 194
**flabbergast** 870, 879
**flabby** 324
**flabbiness** 324
**flaccid** *weak* 160
*soft* 324
*empty* 640
**flag** *weak* 160
*flat stone* 204
*floor* 211

*smoothness* 255
*slow* 275
*leaf* 367
*sign* 550
*path* 627
*infirm* 655
*inactive* 683
*tired* 688
*weary* 841
lower one's – 725
red – *alarm* 669
yellow –
*warning* 668
*alarm* 669
– man 668
– ship 726
– of truce 723
**flag-bearer 534**
**flagellation**
*penance* 952
*asceticism* 955
*flogging* 972
*rite* 998
**flagelliform 205**
**flageolet 417**
**flagitious 945**
**flagon 191**
**flagrant**
*great* 31
*manifest* 525
*notorious* 531
*atrocious* 945
**flagrante**
– bello 722
– delicto
*sure enough* 474
*act* 680
*guilt* 947
**flagration 384**
**flagstaff** *tall* 206
*signal* 550
**flail** 276
**flair** 450, 698
**flake** 204
snow – 383
– white 430
**flam** 544
**flambé** 732
**flambeau** 423
**flamboyant** 577
**flame** *fire* 382
*light* 420
*luminary* 423
*passion* 824, 825
*love* 897
catch the –
*emotion* 821
consign to the –s
384
add fuel to the –
173
in –s 382
– up 825
–coloured
*red* 434
*orange* 439
**flame-projector** 727
**flamen** 996
**flaming** *violent* 173
*feeling* 821
*excited* 824
*ostentatious* 882
*boasting* 884
**flâneur** 935
**flange** *support* 215
*rim* 231
*projection* 250
**flank** *side* 236
*protect* 664
**flannel** 384
**flap** *adjunct* 39
*hanging* 214
*move to and fro*
315
– the memory 505
**flapdoodle** 517
**flapper** *girl* 129
**flapping** *loose* 47
**flare** *violent* 173
*glare* 420
*light* 423
– up
*excited* 824, 825
*angry* 900
**flaring** *colour* 428
**flash** *instant* 113
*violent* 173
*fire* 382
*light* 420
eyes – fire 900
– lamp 550
– light 423
– across the memory 505
– on the mind
*thought* 451
*disclose* 529
*impulse* 612
– note 800
– in the pan
*unsubstantial* 4
*transientness* 111
*impotent* 158
*unproductive* 169
*failure* 732
– tongue 563
– up *excited* 824
– upon
*unexpected* 508
– of wit 842
**flashing**
*ostentatious* 882
**flashy**
*gaudy colour* 428
*style* 577
*ornament* 847
*vulgar* 851
**flask** 191
**flat** *inert* 172
*abode* 189
*story* 191
*low* 207
*horizontal* 213
*vapid* 391
*low tone* 408
*musical note* 413
*positive* 535
*dupe* 547
*back-scene* 599
*shoal* 667
*bungler* 701
*poor* 804
*insensible* 823
*dejected* 837
*weary* 841
*dull* 843
*simple* 849
fall – 732
– contradiction
536
– iron 255
– refusal 764
**flatfoot** 664
**flatness** **251**
**flatter** *deceive* 545
*cunning* 702
*please* 829
*grace* 845
*encourage* 858
*approbation* 931
*adulation* 933
– oneself
*probable* 472
*hope* 858
– the palate 394
**flatterer** **935**
**flattering**
– remarks 894
– tale
*hope* 858
– unction to one's
soul
*content* 831
*vain* 880
*flattery* 933
**flattery** 544, **933**
**flatulent**
*gaseous* 334
*air* 338
*wind* 349
- *style* 573, 575
**flatus** 334, 349
**flaunt** 873, 882
**flaunting** *vulgar* **851**
*gaudy* 428
*unreserved* **525**
**flautist** 416
**Flavian amphitheatre** 728
**flavour** 390
**flavouring** 393
**flavous** 436
**flaw** *break* 70
*crack* 198
*error* 495
*imperfection* **651**
*blemish* 848
*fault* 947
– in an argument
477
**flaxen** 436
**flay** *divest* 226
*punish* 972
**flea** *jumper* **309**
*dirt* 653
– in one's ear
*repel* 289
*eject* 297
*refuse* 764
*disrepute* 874
*abashed* 879
*discourteous* **895**
*contempt* 930
**flea-bite** 643
**flea-bitten** 440
**fleck** 32
**flecked** 440
**flection** 279
**fled** *escaped* **671**
**fledge** 673
**fledgling** 123
**flee** *avoid* 623
**fleece** *tegument* **223**
*strip* 789
*rob* 791
*impoverish* 804
*surcharge* 814
**fleet** *ridicule* 856
*insult* 929
**fleet** *ships* 273
*swift* 274
*navy* 726
**Fleet** *prison* 752
**fleeting** 4, 111
**flesh** *bulk* 192
*animal* 364
*mankind* 372
*carnal* 961
gain – 194
ills that – is heir
to *evil* 619
*disease* 655
in the – 359
one – 903

**way of all – 360**
weakness of the – 945
– and blood
*substance* 3
*materiality* 316
*animality* 364
*affections* 820
make the – creep
*pain* 830
*fear* 860
**flesh-colour** 434
**flesh-pots** 298
– of Egypt 734, 803
**fleshly** 316
**fleur-de-lis** 847
**fleuron** 847
**flexible** 324, 705
**flexion**
*curvature* 245
*fold* 258
*deviation* 279
**flexuous** 248
**flexure** 245, 258
**flibbertigibbet** 980
**flicker**
*changing* 149
*waver* 314
*flutter* 315
*light* 420
*dim* 422
**flickering** 139
**flier** 621
**flies** *theatre* 599
**flight** *flock* 102
*volitation* 267
*swiftness* 274
*departure* 293
*avoidance* 623
*escape* 671
– lieutenant 745
put to –
*propel* 284
*repel* 717
*vanquish* 731
– of fancy 515
– of stairs 305, 627
– of time 109
**flighty** *inattentive* 458
*mad* 503
*fanciful* 515
**flim-flam** 544, 608
**flimsy** *unsubstantial* 4
*weak* 160
*rarity* 322
*soft* 324
*sophistical* 477

*trifling* 643
**flinch** *swerve* 607
*avoid* 623
*fear* 860
*cowardice* 862
**fling** *propel* 284
*jig* 840
*jeer* 929
have one's –
*active* 682
*laxity* 738
*freedom* 748
*amusement* 840
– aside 782
have a – at
*attack* 716
*resent* 900
*disrespect* 929
*censure* 932
– away *reject* 610
*waste* 638
*relinquish* 782
– down 308
– to the winds
*destroy* 162
*not observe* 773
**flint** *hard* 323
**flint-hearted** 907
**flintlock** 727
**flip** *beverage* 298
**flippant** *fluent* 584
*pert* 885
**flipper** *paddle* 267
**flirt** *propel* 284
*coquet* 607, 854
*love* 897
*endearment* 902
– a fan 855
**flit** *elapse* 109
*changeable* 149
*move* 264
*travel* 266
*swift* 274
*depart* 293
*run away* 623
**flitter**
*small part* 32
*changeable* 149
*flutter* 315
**flitting** 111
**float** *establish* 150
*navigate* 267
*boat* 273
*buoy up* 305
*lightness* 320
before the –s
*on the stage* 599
– on the air 405
– before the eyes 446
– bonds 788

– in the mind
*thought* 451
*imagination* 515
**floater** 683
**floating**
[*see* float]
*rumoured* 532
– battery 726
– capital 805
– debt 806
– dock 189
**flocculent**
*woolly* 256
*soft* 324
*pulverulent* 330
**flock**
*assemblage* 72
*multitude* 102
*laity* 997
–s and herds 366
– together 72
**floe** *ice* 383
**flog** 972
*hasten* 684
**flood** *much* 31
*crowd* 72
*river* 348
*abundance* 639
*redundance* 641
*prosperity* 734
stem the – 708
– of light 420
– of tears 839
**flood-gate**
*limit* 233
*egress* 295
*conduit* 350
open the –s
*eject* 297
*permit* 760
**flood-light** 423, 599
**flood-mark** 466
**flood-tide**
*increase* 35
*complete* 52
*height* 206
*advance* 282
*water* 337
**floor** *level* 204
*base* 211
*horizontal* 213
*support* 215
*overthrow* 731
ground – 191
**flop** 315
**Flora** 369
**floral** 367
**florescence** 154
**floriculture** 371
**florid** *colour* 428

*red* 434
– *style* 577
*health* 654
**florist** 371
**floss** 256
**flotilla** 273, 726
**flotsam and jetsam** 73
**flounce**
*trimming* 231
*jump* 309
*agitation* 315
**flounder**
*change* 149
*toss* 315
*uncertain* 475
*bungle* 699
*difficulty* 704
*fail* 732
**flour** 330
**flourish**
*brandish* 314, 315
*exaggerate* 549
*language* 577
*speech* 582
*prosper* 618
*healthy* 654
*prosperous* 734
*ornament* 847
*repute* 873
*display* 882
*boast* 884
– of trumpets
*loud* 404
*cheerfulness* 836
*publish* 531
*ostentation* 882
*celebrate* 883
*boast* 884
**flout** 929, 936
**flow** *course* 109
*hang* 214
*motion* 264
*stream* 348
*murmur* 405
*abundance* 639
– from
*result* 154
– of ideas 451
– in 294
– into *river* 348
– out 295
– over 641
– of soul
*conversation* 588
*affections* 820
*cheerful* 836
*social* 892
– with the tide 705
– of time 109

- implicitly 486, 695
- the lead of
*co-operate* 709
- suit *imitate* 19
- the trail 461
- up
*continue* 143
*persevere* 604*a*
**follower**
[*see* follow]
*successor* 65
*learn* 541
*servant* 746
*lover* 897
**folly**
*building* 189
*irrationality* 499
act of –
*mismanagement* 699
**foment**
*stimulate* 173
*warm* 384
*promote* 707
*excite* 824
*relieve* 834
**fond** 897
- hope 858
**fondle** 902
**fondling** 899, 902
**fondness**
*desire* 865
**fondre en larmes** 839
**fons et origo** 153
**font** *origin* 153
*type* 591
*rite* 998
*altar* 1000
**food** 298
preparation of – 673
- for the mind 454
- for powder 726
**fool** 501
*pudding* 354
*deceive* 545
*ridicule* 856
*disrespect* 929
make a – of oneself
*bungle* 699
motley – 844
play the –
*folly* 499
*amusement* 840
-'s errand
*deceived* 545
*unskilful* 699
-'s mate 732
-'s paradise
*unsubstantial* 4
*misjudgment* 481
*disappoint* 509
*hope* 858
*rash* 863
- to the top of one's bent
*excite* 824
*anger* 900
*flatter* 933
- away money 818
- away time 683
**foolhardy** 863
**fooling** 842
**foolish** 499
act -ly 699
look –
*disrepute* 874
*shame* 879
**foolscap** 550, 559
**foot**
*length* 200
*stand* 211
*metre* 597
at the – of 207
keep on –
*continue* 143
*support* 251
*provide* 637
*prepare* 673
not stir a – 681
on – *existing* 1
*during* 106
*journey* 266
*topic* 454
*business* 625
*preparing* 673
*active* 682
put one's – down
*resolved* 604
put one's – in
*undertake* 676
*bungle* 699
set – on land 342
trample under – 930
- the bill 807
- by foot 51
one – in the grave
*age* 128
*death* 360
it *journey* 266
*dance* 309
at -'s pace 275
**foot-ball**
*subjection* 749
*game* 840
**footboy** 746
**footfall**
*motion* 264
*indication* 550
*stumble* 732
**footing**
*circumstances* 8
*rank* 71
*influence* 175
*situation* 183
*foundation* 211
*support* 215
*payment* 809
friendly – 888
get a –
*location* 184
be on a –
*state* 7
pay one's – 807
**footlights** 599
**footman** 746
**footmark** 551
**footpad** 792
**foot-passenger** 268
**footpath** 627
**foot pound** 466
**footprint** 551
**foot-soldier** 726
**foot-warmer** 386
**footsore** 688
**footstep** 551
**footstool** 215
**foozle** 732
**fop** 854
**foppery** 882
**foppish** 855
**for** *cause* 155
*tendency* 176
*reason* 476
*motive* 615
*intention* 620
*preparation* 673
have –
*price* 812
- all that
*notwithstanding* 30
*qualification* 469
- all the world like 17
- aught one knows 156
- better for worse 78
- ever 112
- example 82
- form's sake 82
- good
*complete* 52
*diuturnity* 110
*permanence* 141
- the most part
*great* 31
*general* 78
*special* 79
- the nonce 118
- nothing 815
- a season 106
- a time 111
- the time being 106
**forage**
*food* 298
*provision* 637
*steal* 791
**forage-cap** 225
**foramen** 260
**foraminous** 260
**forasmuch as**
*relating to* 9
*cause* 155
*reason* 476
*motive* 615
**foray** *attack* 716
*robbery* 791
**forbear**
*avoid* 623
*spare* 678
*lenity* 740
*sufferance* 826
*pity* 914
*abstain* 953
*forbearance* 918
**forbid** 761
God –
*dissent* 489
*deprecation* 766
*censure* 932
*prayer* 990
**forbidden fruit**
*seduction* 615
*prohibition* 761
**forbidding**
*ugly* 846
**force** *corps* 72
*power* 157
*strength* 159
*agency* 170
*energy* 171
*violence* 173
*cultivate* 371, 707
*cascade* 348
- *of style* 574
*urge* 615
*exertion* 686
*compulsion* 744
armed – 726
brute – 964
put in – 924
- of argument 476
- of arms 744
- of character 820
- down the throat
*severe* 739
*compel* 744

**frankincense** 400
**frantic**
*violent* 173
*delirious* 503
*excited* 824
**fraternal**
*brother* 11
*concord* 714
*friendly* 888
**fraternity**
[*see* fraternal]
*party* 712
**fraternize**
*co-operate* 48, 709
*agree* 714
*sympathize* 888
*associate* 892
**fratricide** 361
**Frau** 374
**fraud**
*falsehood* 544
*deception* 545
*pretender* 548
*dishonour* 940
pious – 988
**fraught** *full* 52
*pregnant* 161
*possessing* 777
– with danger 665
**fray** *rub* 331
*battle* 720
in the thick of the – 722
**frayed** 659
**frazzle**
beaten to a – 732
**freak** 608, 872
– of Nature 83
**freckle** 848
**freckled** 440
**fredaine** 840
**free**
*detached* 44
*unconditional* 52
*liberate* 672
*unobstructed* 705
*at liberty* 748, 750
*gratis* 815
*liberal* 816
*insolent* 885
*exempt* 927*a*
*impure* 961
– balloon 273
– and easy
*cheerful* 836
*adventurous* 863
*vain* 880
*insolent* 885
*friendly* 888
*sociable* 892
– fight 720
– from
*simple* 42
never – from 613
– gift 784
– from imperfection 650
– lance 726
– land 748
– liver 954*a*
– love 961
make – of 748
– play 170, 748
– quarters
*cheap* 815
*hospitality* 892
– space 180
– stage 748
– trade
*commerce* 794
– translation 522
– will 600
make – with
*frank* 703
*take* 789
*sociable* 892
*uncourteous* 895
**freebooter** 792
**freeborn** 748
**freedman** 748
**freedom** **748**
**free-handed** 816
**freehold** 780
**freely**
*willingly* 602
**freeman** 748
**freemasonry**
*unintelligible* 519
*secret* 528
*sign* 550
*co-operation* 709
*party* 712
**free-spoken** 703
**freethinker** 989
**freeze**
*benumb* 381
*cold* 385
– the blood 830
**freezing** 383
– mixture 387
**freight** *lade* 184
*cargo* 190
*transfer* 270
**freightage** 812
**freighter** 273
**freight train** 272
**French**
peddler's – 563
– and English 840
– horn 417
– leave *avoid* 623
*freedom* 748
– polish 847
**frenetic** 503
**frenzy**
*madness* 503
*imagination* 515
*excitement* 825
**frequency** **136**
**frequent**
*in number* 104
*in time* 136
*in space* 186
*habitual* 613
*visit* 892
**fresco** *cold* 383
*painting* 556
al –
*out of doors* 220
*in the air* 338
**fresh** *additional* 37
*new* 123
*flood* 348
*cold* 383
*colour* 428
*remembered* 505
*unaccustomed* 614
*good* 648
*healthy* 654
*impertinent* 885
*tipsy* 959
– breeze 349
– colour 434
– news 532
**freshen** 658, 689
**freshet** 348
**freshman** 541
**freshwater** 851
**freshwater sailor** 701
**fret** *suffer* 378
*grieve* 828
*gall* 830
*discontent* 832
*sad* 837
*ornament* 847
*irritate* 900
– and fume 828
**fretful** 901
**fret-work** 219
**friable** 328, 330
**friandise** 868
**friar** 996
–'s lantern 423
– Rush 980
Black –s 996
**friary** 1000
**fribble**
*slur over* 460
*trifle* 643
*dawdle* 683
*fop* 854
**fricassee** 298
**frication** 331
**friction** *force* **157**
*obstacle* 179
*rubbing* **331**
on – wheels 705
**friend** 711, **890**
candid – 936
next – 759
**friendless** 893
**friendly** 714, 894
**friends, be** – 888
see one's – 892
**friendship** 9, **888**
**frieze** 210
**frigate** 726
**fright**
*cards* 840
*alarm* 860
**frightful** 31, 830, 846
**frightfully** 31
**frightfulness** 860
**frigid**
*cold* 383
- *style* 575
*callous* 823
*indifferent* 866
**frigidarium** 387
**frigorific** 385
**frill** 231, 248
*frills and furbelows* 847
**fringe**
*border* 231
*lace* 256
*exaggeration* **549**
*ornament* 847
**frippery**
*trifle* 643
*ornament* 847
*finery* 851
*ridiculous* 853
*ostentation* 882
**frisk** *prance* 266
*leap* 309
*search* 461
*gay* 836
*amusement* **840**
**frisky** 682, 836
**frith** *chasm* 198
*strait* 343
*forest* 367
**fritinancy** 412
**fritter** *small* 32
– away *lessen* 36
*waste* 638
– away time 683
**fritters** 298
**frivolous**
*unreasonable* **477**
*foolish* 499

*capricious* 608
*trivial* 643
**frizz** *curve* 245, 248
*fold* 258
**frock** *dress* 225
*canonicals* 999
– coat 225
**frog** *fastening* 45
*leaper* 309
*ornament* 847
**frolic** 827, 840
**frolicsome** 836
**from** *motive* 615
– this cause 155
– day to day 106, 138
– end to end 52
– that time 117
– time immemorial 122
– time to time 136
**frond** 367
**fronder**
*censure* 932
**frondeur**
*disobey* 742
**front** *foremost* 66
*wig* 225
*fore part* **234**
*resist* 719
*insolence* 885
bring to the –
*manifest* 525
come to the –
*surpass* 303
*important* 642
*repute* 873
in – 280
present a – 719
– danger 861
– to front 708
– of the house 599
– rank 234
in the – rank
*important* 642
*repute* 873
**frontage** 234
**frontal** 220
**fronti nulla fides**
*doubt* 485
*deception* 545
**frontier** 199, 233
**fronting** 237
**frontispiece** 64
**frost** 383
**frosted** 430
- glass 427
**frostbite** 383
**froth**
*bubble* 353
*trifle* 643
*dirt* 653
– up *angry* 900
**frothy** 320, 353
- *style* 573, 577
*irresolute* 605
**frounce** 258
**frouzy** 401
**froward** 901*a*
**frown** *lower* 837
*scowl* 839
*discourteous* 895
*angry* 900
*sulky* 901*a*
*disapprove* 932
– down
*abash* 879
–s of fortune 735
**frozen** 383, 385
**fructify**
*produce* 161
*be productive* 168
*improve* 658
*prosper* 734
**frugal** 817, 953
– to excess 819
**fruges consumere natus** *drone* 683
*peasant* 876
**frugivorus** 298
**fruit** *result* 154
*produce* 161
*food* 298
*profit* 775
forbidden – 615
reap the –s
*succeed* 731
*reward* 973
– tree 367
**fruitful** 168
**fruition** 161, 827
**fruitless**
*unproductive* 169
*useless* 645
*failure* 732
**frump** 851, 895
**frumpish** 901*a*
**frustrate** 179, 706
**frustrated** 732
**frustum** 51
**fry** *shoal* 102
*child* 129
*heat* 384
small –
*unimportant* 643
*commonalty* 876
**frying-pan** 386
out of – into fire
*worse* 659
*clumsy* 699
*failure* 732
*misfortune* 735
*aggravation* 835
**fuddled** 959
**fudge** 517, 643
**fuel** **388**, 638
add – to the flame 835
– oil 388
*increase* 35
*heat* 384
*aggravate* 835
*anger* 900
**fugaces labuntur anni** 111
**fugacious** 111
**fugitive**
*transient* 111
*emigrant* 268
*avoiding* 623
– writings 596
**fugleman**
*pattern* 22
*director* 694
**fugue** 415
**fulciment** 215
**fulcrum** 215
**fulfil**
*complete* 729
– a duty 926
– an obligation 772
**fulgent** 420
**fuliginous**
*dim* 422
*opaque* 426
*black* 431
**full** *much* 31
*complete* 52
*large* 192
*loud* 404
*abundant* 639
*cleanse* 652
hands –
*active* 682
receipt in – 807
– blooded 641
– bloom 131
*health* 654
*beauty* 845
– blown 131
*expanded* 194
*glorious* 873
– of business 682
– coloured 428
– cry *loud* 404
*bark* 412
*pursuit* 622
– dinner pail 734
*dress* 225
*ornament* 847
*fashion* 852
*show* 882
– drive 274
– feather
*prepared* 673
– force 159
– gallop 274
– heart 820
– of incident **151**
– many 102
– of meaning **516**
– measure 639
– of people 186
– play
*facility* 705
*freedom* 748
– of point 842
– scope 748
– score 415
– size 912
– of sound and fury &c.
*unmeaning* **517**
– speech 274
– stop
*cease* 142
*rest* 265
– swing
*strong* 159
*active* 682
*successful* **731**
*free* 748
– as a tick 52
– tide 348
– tilt *active* 682
*haste* 684
– view 446
– of whims 608
**full-fashioned** 240
**full-fed** 954
**full-flavoured** 392
**full-grown** 131, 192
**full-handed** 816, 818
**full-length** 556
**full-mouthed** 412
**full-toned** 413
**fully** 31
**fulminate**
*violent* 173
*propel* 284
*loud* 404
*malediction* **908**
*threat* 909
– against
*accuse* 932
**fulness**
[*see* full]
in the – of time 109
**fulsome**
*nauseous* 395

*fetid* 401
*bad* 649
*abhorrent* 867
*adulatory* 933
*impure* 961
**fulvid** 436
**fulvous** 436
**fumble**
*derange* 61
*handle* 379
*grope* 463
*awkward* 699
**fumbler** 701
**fume**
*violent* 173
*exhalation* 334, 336
*froth* 353
*heat* 382
*odour* 398
*excitement* 824, 825
*anger* 900
in a –
*discontented* 832
–s of fancy 515
**fumid** 426
**fumigate**
*vaporize* 336
*cleanse* 652
**fumigator** 388
**fumo, dare pondus** – 481
**fun** 827, 840, 842
make – of 856
**funambulist** 700
**function**
*algebra* 84
*office* 170
*business* 625
*utility* 644
*pomp* 882
*rite* 998
*duty* 926
**functionary**
*director* 694
*consignee* 758
**functus officio** 756
**fund** *store* 636
sinking – 802
**fundamental**
*intrinsic* 5
*base* 211
*support* 215
– bass 413
– note 413
**fundamentally** 31
**funds** 800
in – 803
public – 802
**funebrial** 363
**funeral** 363
– pace 275
– march 415
**funereal**
*interment* 363
*dismal* 837
**fungiform** 249
**fungology** 369
**fungosity** 250
**fungus**
*projection* 250
*vegetable* 367
*fœtor* 401
*bane* 663
**funicle** 205
**funicular** 627
**funk** 860, 862
– hole 530
**funnel** *opening* 260
*conduit* 350
*air-pipe* 351
**funnel-shaped** 252
**funny** *odd* 83
*boat* 273
*humorous* 842
*comic* 853
**fur** *covering* 223
*hair* 256
*warm* 384
*dirt* 653
**furacious** 791
**furbelow** 231
**furbish**
*improve* 658
*prepare* 673
*adorn* 847
**furcated** 244
**furcation** 91
**furcular** 244
**furfur** 653
**furfuraceous** 330
**Furies** *anger* 900
*evil-doers* 913
*demons* 980
**furious** *violent* 173
*haste* 684
*passion* 825
*anger* 900
**furiously** 31
**furl** 312
**furlong** 200
**furlough** 760
**furnace** **386**
*workshop* 691
like a – *hot* 382
sighing like –
*lament* 839
*in love* 902
**furnish**
*provide* 637
*prepare* 673
*give* 784
– aid 707
– a handle **617**
– its quota 784
**furniture** 633
– van 272
**furor**
*insanity* 503
*passion* 825
**furore**
*emotion* 820, 821
*passion* 825
*desire* 865
**furrow** **259**
**further**
*added* 37
*distant* 196
*aid* 707
go – and fare worse
*worse* 659
*bungle* 699
not let it go – 528
**furthermore** 37
**furtive**
*clandestine* 528
*stealing* 791
**furuncle** 250
**fury** *violence* 173
*excitation* 825
*anger* 900
*demon* 980
**furze** 367
**fuscous** 433
**fuse** *join* 43
*combine* 48
*heat* 382, 384
*torch* 388
**fuselage** 215
**fusel oil** 356
**fusiform** 244, 253
**fusil** 727
**fusileer** 726
**fusillade** 361, 716
**fusion** *union* 48
*heat* 384
*co-operation* 709
**fuss** *agitation* 315
*activity* 682
*haste* 684
*difficulty* 704
*excitement* 825
*ostentation* 882
kick up a – 173
make a – about
*importance* 642
*lament* 839
*disapprove* 932
**fussy** *crotchety* 481
*bustling* 682
*excitable* 825
**fustian**
*absurd* 497
*unmeaning* **517**
- *style* 577, **579**
**fustigate** 972
**fusty** 124, 401, **653**
**futhorc** 590
**futile** 497, 645
**future** 121
eye to the – **510**
– possession **777**
– state
*destiny* 152
*heaven* 981
**futurity** **121**
**fuzzle** 959
**fuzzy** 447

## G

**gab** 584
gift of the – **582**
**gabardine** 225
**gabble** 517, 583
**gabelle** 812
**gaberlunzie** 876
**gabion** 717
**gable** *side* 236
– end 67
**Gabriel** 977
**gaby** 501
**gad**
*about* 266, 268
**gadget** 626
**gad-so** 870
**gaff** 727
**gaffer** *old* 130
*man* 373
*clown* 876
**gag**
*closure* 261
*render mute* **403**, 581
*dramatic* 599
*muzzle* 751
*imprison* 752
**gage** *measure* 466
*security* 771
throw down the – 715
**gaggle** 412
**gag-man** 844
**gaieté de cœur** 836
**gaiety**
[*see* gay] 836
**gaillard** 844
**gain**
*increase* 35
*advantage* 618
*skilful* 698

– to sleep 683
– through
*meet with* 151
*pass* 302
*explore* 461
*perform* 599
*conduct* 692
*complete* 729
*endure* 826
– to *extend* 196
*travel* 266
*direction* 278
*remonstrance* 695
– up 305
– to war 722
– with
*assent* 488
*concord* 714
– with the stream
*conform* 82
*servile* 886
– from one's word 773
**goad** 615
*hasten* 684
**goal** *end* 67
*reach* 292
*object* 620
reach the –
*complete* 729
**goat** *substitute* 147
*jumper* 309
*lecher* 962
he – *male* 373
play the – 499
**gob** 269
**gobang** 840
**gobbet**
*small piece* 32
*food* 298
**gobble** *cry* 412
*gormandize* 957
*eat* 298
**gobemouche** 501, 547
**go-between** 758
**goblet** 191
**goblin** 980
**go-cart** 272
**GOD** 976
house of – 1000
kingdom of – 981
sons of – 977
–'s acre 363
– bless me! 870
– bless you
*farewell* 293
– forbid 766
–'s grace 906
– grant 990
– knows 491
–'s love 906
for –'s sake 765
–'s will 601
– willing 470
**god** 979
household –s 189
tutelary – 664
**goddess** *love* 897
*good woman* 948
*heathen* 979
**Godhead** 976
**godlike** 944
**godly** 987
**godsend** *good* 618
*prosperity* 734
**Godspeed**
*farewell* 293
*hope* 858
*courtesy* 894
*benevolence* 906
*approbation* 931
**goer** *horse* 271
**goes** [*see* go]
as one – 270
here – 676
**Gog and Magog** 192
**goggle** 441
– eyes 443
**goggles** 445
**going** [*see* go]
*general* 78
*rumour* 532
– to happen 152
– on
*incomplete* 53, 730
*current* 151
*transacting* 625
**goitre** 250
**Golconda** 803
**gold** *yellow* 436
*orange* 439
*money* 800
write in letters of – 642
worth its weight in – 648
**gold certificate** 800
**golden** [*see* gold]
– age
*prosperity* 734
*pleasure* 827
– apple 615
– calf
*wealth* 803
*idol* 986
*idolatry* 991
– dream
*imagination* 515
*hope* 858
– mean
*moderation* 174
*mid-course* 628
– opinions 931
– opportunity 134
– rule
*precept* 697
– season of life 127
– wedding 883
**golf** 840
**Golgotha** 363, 1000
**Goliath** 159, 192
**goloshes** 225
**gondola** 273
**gondolier** 269
**gone** [*see* go]
*past* 122
*absent* 187
*dead* 360
– bad 653
– by 122
*antiquated* 124
– out of one's recollection 506
**gonfalon** 550
**gong** 417
**goniometer** 244, 466
**good**
*complete* 52
*palatable* 394
*assent* 488
*benefit* **618**
*beneficial* 648
*right* 922
*virtuous* 944
*pious* 987
as – as 197
be so – as 765
do – 906
for –
*diuturnal* 110
*permanent* 141
make –
*evidence* 467
*provide* 637
*restore* 660
*complete* 729
*substantiate* 924
*vindicate* 937
*atone for* 952
so far so – 931
think – 931
to the – 780
turn to – account 731
what's the – 645
– actions 944
– at 698
– auspices 858
– behaviour
*contingent* **108a**
*duty* 926
*virtue* 944
in one's – books 888
– bye 293
in – case 192
– chance 472
– cheer *food* 298
*cheerful* 826
– circumstances 803
– condition 192
– day
*arrival* 292
*departure* 293
*courtesy* 894
– effect
*goodness* 648
*beauty* 845
– enough
*not perfect* 651
be – enough 765
put a – face upon
*cheerful* 836
*proud* 878
– fellow 892
– fight *war* 722
*virtue* 944
– for
*useful* 644
*salubrious* 656
– fortune 734
– Friday 998
– genius
*friend* 890
*benefactor* 912
*god* 979
in one's – graces 888
– hand 700
– humour
*concord* 714
*cheerfulness* 836
*amuse* 840
*courtesy* 894
*kindly* 906
– intention 906
– judgment 498
– lack! 870
– living
*food* 298
*gluttony* 957
– look-out 459
– looks 845
– luck 734
– man *man* 373
*husband* 903
*worthy* **948**
– manners 894
much – may it do

942
(*important* 642)
- bear 318
- circle sailing 628
- coat 225
- doings
*importance* 642
*bustle* 682
- folks 875
- gun 626
- hearted 942
- Mogul 745
- number 102
- primer 591
- quantity 31
**greater** 33
- number 102
- part 31
*nearly all* 50
**greatest** 33
**greatness** 31
**greave** 225
**greed**
*desire* 865
*gluttony* 957
**greedy**
*avaricious* 819
**Greek**
*unintelligible* 519
*sharper* 792
St. Giles's – 563
- Church 984
- Kalends 107
**green**
*new* 123
*young* 127
*lawn* 344
*grass* 367
*unripe* 397
*colour* 435
*credulous* 486
*novice* 491
*unused* 614
*healthy* 654
*immature* 674
*unskilled* 699
board of – cloth 966
- memory 505
- old age 128
**greenback** 800
**green-eyed monster** 920
**greenhorn**
*novice* 493
*dupe* 547
*bungler* 701
**greenhouse**
*receptacle* 191
*horticulture* 371
**greenness** 435
**green-room** 599
**greensward** 344
**Greenwich time** 114
**greenwood** 367
**greet** *weep* 839
*hail* 894
**greeting**
*sociality* 892
–'s! 292
**gregarious** 892
**grenade** 727
**grenadier**
*tall* 206
*soldier* 726
**grey** 432
- beard 130
- friar 996
- hairs 128
bring – hairs to the grave
*adversity* 735
*harass* 830
- mare
*ruler* 737
*master* 745
*wife* 903
- matter
*brain* 498
–hound
*swift* 274
*animal* 366
ocean –hound 273
**gridelin** 437
**gridiron**
*flatness* 213
*crossing* 219
*stove* 386
*stage* 599
*stadium* 840
**grief** 828
come to – 735
**grievance**
*evil* 619
*painful* 830
*wrong* 923
**grieve** *mourn* 828
*pain* 830
*dejected* 837
*complain* 839
**grievous** 649, 830
**grievously** 31
**griffin** 83, 366, 493
**griffo** 41
**griffonage** 590
**grig** *merry* 836
**grill** 382, 384, 461
- room 189
**grille** 219
**grim**
*resolved* 604
*painful* 830
*doleful* 837
*ugly* 846
*discourteous* 895
*sullen* 901a
–visaged war 722
**grimace** 243, 839, 855
**grimacier**
*actor* 599
*humorist* 844
*affected* 855
**grimalkin** 366
**grime** 653
**grin** *laugh* 838
*ridicule* 856
- and abide 725
- a ghastly smile
*dejected* 837
*ugly* 846
**grind**
*reduce* 195
*sharpen* 253
*pulverize* 330
*pain* 378
*learn* 539
*oppress* 907
- the organ 416
- one's teeth 900
**grinder**
*teacher* 330
*noise* 404
**grinding** 739, 830
**grindstone** 253, 330
**grip**
*indication* 550
*power* 737
*retention* 781
*clutch* 789
- of the hand 894
**gripe** [*see* grip]
*pain* 378
*parsimony* 819
**grisaille**
*grey* 432
*painting* 556
**grisette**
*woman* 374
*commonalty* 876
*libertine* 962
**grisly** 846
**grist**
*materials* 635
*provision* 637
- to the mill
*useful* 644
*acquire* 775
**gristle** 321, 327
**grit**
*strength* 159
*powder* 330
*stamina* 604a
*courage* 861
- in the oil
*hindrance* 706
**gritty** 323
**grizzled**
*grey* 432
*variegated* 440
**groan** 411, 839
**groat** 800
**grocer** 637
**grocery** 396
**grog** 298, 959
**groin** 244
**groom** 370, 746
- well
- of the chambers 746
–'s man 903
**groove**
*furrow* 259
*habit* 613
in a – 16
move in a – 82
put in a – for 673
**grope**
*feel* 379
*experiment* 463
*try* 675
in the dark 442, 704
**gross**
*great* 31
*whole* 50
*number* 98
*ugly* 846
*vulgar* 851
*vicious* 945
*impure* 961
- credulity 486
- receipts 810
**grosshead** 501
**grossheaded** 499
**grossièreté** 895
**grot** [*see* grotto]
**grotesque**
*odd* 83
*distorted* 243
- *style* 579
*ridiculous* 853
**grotto**
*alcove* 191
*hollow* 252
**grouch** 895, 901a
**ground**
*cause* 153
*region* 181
*base* 211
*lay down* 213
*support* 215
*coating* 223

*land* 342
*plain* 344
*evidence* 467
*teach* 537
*motive* 615
*plea* 617
above – 359
down to the – 52
dress the – 371
fall to the – 732
get over the – 274
go over the – 302
level with the – 162
maintain one's –
*persevere* 604*a*
play– 840
prepare the – 673
stand one's –
*defend* 717
*resist* 719
– bait 784
– cut from under one 732
– floor
*chamber* 191
*low* 207
*base* 211
– on
*attribute* 155
– plan 554
– of quarrel 713
– sliding from under one 665
– swell
*agitation* 315
*waves* 348
**grounded**
*stranded* 732
well– 490
– on *basis* 211
*evidence* 467
**groundless**
*unsubstantial* 4
*illogical* 477
*erroneous* 495
**groundling** 876
**grounds**
*dregs* 653
**groundwork**
*precursor* 64
*cause* 153
*basis* 211
*support* 215
*preparation* 673
**group**
*marshal* 60
*cluster* 72
– captain 745
**grouping** 60
**grouse** 832, 901*a*

**grout** 45
**grove**
*street* 189
*glade* 252
*wood* 367
**grovel**
*below* 207
*move slowly* 275
*cringe* 886
*base* 940
**grow**
*increase* 35
*become* 144
*expand* 194
– from
*effect* 154
– into 144
– less 195
– taller 206
– together 46
– up 194
– upon one 613
**grower** 164
**growl** *cry* 412
*complain* 839
*discourtesy* 895
*anger* 900
*threat* 909
**growler** *cab* 272
*discontented* 832
*sulky* 901*a*
**grown up** 131
**growth** [*see* grow]
*development* 161
– *in size* 194
*tumour* 250
*vegetation* 367
**groyne** 706
**grub**
*small animal* 193
*food* 298
– up
*eradicate* 301
*discover* 480*a*
**Grub-street writer** 593
**grudge**
*unwilling* 603
*refuse* 764
*stingy* 819
*hate* 898
*anger* 900
bear a – 907
owe a – 898
**grudging** 603
– praise 932
**gruel** 298
**gruesome** 846
**gruff**
*harsh sound* 410
*discourteous* 895

**grum**
*harsh sound* 410
*morose* 901*a*
**grumble**
*cry* 411
*complain* 832, 839
**grume** 321, 354
**grumous** 321, 354
**grumpy** 901*a*
**Grundy, Mrs.** 852
**grunt** 412
*complain* 839
**guano** 653
**guarantee** 768, 771
**guard**
*travelling* 268
*safety* 664
*defence* 717
*soldier* 726
*sentry* 753
advanced – 668
mount –
*care* 459
*safety* 664
off one's –
*inexpectant* 508
throw off one's –
*cunning* 702
on one's –
*careful* 459
*cautious* 864
rear – 668
– against
*prepare* 673
*defence* 717
– ship 664, 726
**guarda costa** 753
**guarded**
*conditions* 770
**guardian**
*safety* 664
*defence* 717
*keeper* 753
– angel
*helper* 711
*benefactor* 912
**guardless** 665
**guard-room** 752
**gubernation** 693
**gubernatorial** 737
**gudgeon** 547
**guerdon** 973
**guernsey** 225
**guerre:**
nom de – 565
– à outrance &c. 722
**guerilla** 726
– warfare 720
**guess** 514

**guesswork** 514
**guest** 890
paying – 188
**guet:**
mot de – 550
–à-pens 545
**guffaw** 838
**guggle**
*gush* 348
*bubble* 353
*resound* 408
*cry* 412
**guide**
*pattern* 22
*courier* 524
*teach* 537
*teacher* 540
*indicate* 550
*direct* 693
*director* 694
*advise* 695
**guide-book** 527
**guided by, be** – 82
**guideless** 665
**guide-post** 550
**guiding star** 693
**guild** 712, 966
**guildhall** 799
**guile**
*deceit* 544, 545
*cunning* 702
**guileless** 543, 703
**guillotine** 972, 975
**guilt** 947
**guiltless** 946
**guilty:**
find – 971
plead – 950
**guindé** 579
**guinea** 800
**guipure** 847
**guisard** 599
**guise**
*state* 7
*dress* 225
*appearance* 448
*plea* 617
*mode* 627
*conduct* 692
**guiser** 599
**guitar** 417
**gulch** 198
**gules** 434
**gulf**
*interval* 198
*deep* 208
*lake* 343
**gull** 545, 547
**gullet** *throat* 260
*rivulet* 348
**gullible** 486

**gully** *gorge* 198
*hollow* 252
*opening* 260
*conduit* 350
**gulosity** 957
**gulp** *swallow* 296
*take food* 298
– down
*credulity* 486
*submit* 725
**gum** *fastening* 45
*fasten* 46
*resin* 356*a*
– elastic 325
– tree 367
**gumbo** 298
**gummy** 352
**gumption** 498
**gun** *report* 406
*weapon* 727
great – 626
blow great –s 349
sure as a – 474
**gunboat** 726
**gunfire** 404
**gunlayer** 284
**gunman** 361
**gunner** 726
**gunnery**
*warfare* 722
*cannon* 727
**gunpowder**
*warfare* 722
*ammunition* 727
not invent – 665
sit on barrel of – 501
**gunroom** 191
**gun-shot** 197
**gunwale** 232
**gurge** 312, 348
**gurgle**
*flow* 348
*bubble* 353
*faint sound* 405
*resonance* 408
**gurgoyle** 350
**gush**
*flow out* 295
*flood* 348
*exaggeration* 482
*talk* 584
**gushing**
*emotional* 821
*impressible* 822
**gusset** 43
**gust** *wind* 349
*physical taste* 390
*passion* 825
*moral taste* 850
**gustation** 390
**gustful** 394
**gustless** 391
**gusto** [*see* gust]
*physical pleasure* 377
*emotion* 821
**gut** *destroy* 162
*opening* 260
*strait* 343
*eviscerate* 297
*sack* 789
*steal* 791
**gutling** 954*a*
**guts** *inside* 221
**guttapercha** 325
**gutter** *groove* 259
*conduit* 350
*vulgarity* 851
**guttersnipe** 876
**guttle** 957
**guttural**
*letter* 561
*inarticulate* 583
**guy**
*fastening* 45, 752
*fellow* 373
*disrespect* 929
*grotesque* 853
**guzzle**
*gluttony* 957
*drunkenness* 959
**gybe** [*see* jibe]
**gymkhana** 720, 840
**gymnasium** 189
*school* 542
*arena* 728, 840
**gymnast** 159
**gymnastics**
*training* 537
*exercise* 686
*contention* 720
*sport* 840
**gymnosophist**
*abstainer* 953
*sectarian* 984
**gynander** 83
**gynarchy** 727
**gynecæum** 374
**gynecology** 662
**gyniatrics** 374
**gynics** 374
**gyp** 545, 746
**gyre** 311
**gyrate** 312
**gyrfalcon** 913
**gyromancy** 511
**gyrostat** 312
**gysart** 599
**gyve** 752

## H

**habeas corpus** 963, 969
**haberdasher** 225
**habergeon** 717
**habiliment** 225
**habilitation** 698
**habit**
*essence* 5
*coat* 225
*custom* **613**
want of – 614
–s of business 682
– of mind 820
**habitant** 188
**habitat** 189
**habitation** 189
**habit-maker** 225
**habitual**
*unvariable* 16
*orderly* 58
*ordinary* 82
*customary* 613
**habituate** 537, 613
**habitude**
*state* 7
*habit* 613
**habitué** 613
**hacienda** 189, 780
**hack** *cut* 44
*shorten* 201
*horse* 271
*writer* 593
*worker* 690
literary – 593
**hackle** 44
**hackney-coach** 272
**hackneyed**
*known* 490
*trite* 496
*habitual* 613
**Hades** 982
**Hadji**
*traveller* 268
*priest* 996
**hæ tibi erunt artes** 627
**hæret lateri lethalis arundo**
*displeasure* 828
*anger* 900
**haft** 633
**hag** *age* 130
*ugly* 846
*wretch* 913
*witch* 994
**haggard**
*insane* 503
*tired* 688
*wild* 824
*ugly* 846
**haggis** 298
**haggle** *cut* 44
*chaffer* 794
**Hagiographa** 985
**Hagiolatry** 984
**Hagiology** 983, 985
**haguebut** 727
**ha-ha** *trench* 198, 717
**haik** 225
**hail** *welcome* 292
*ice* 383
*call* 586
*rejoicing* 838
*honour to* 873
*celebration* 883
*courtesy* 894
*salute* 928
*approve* 931
–fellow well met
*friendship* 888
*sociality* 892
**hailstone** 383
**hair** *small* 32
*filament* 205
*roughness* 256
to a – 494
–'s breadth
*near* 197
*narrow* 203
–breadth escape
*danger* 665
*escape* 671
–s on the head
*multitude* 102
make one's – stand on end
*distressing* 830
*fear* 860
*wonder* 870
**hairless** 226
**hairy** *rough* 256
**halberd** 727
**halberdier** 726
**halcyon** *calm* 174
*peace* 721
*prosperous* 734
*joyful* 827, 829
**hale** 654
**half** 91
– the battle
*important* 642
*success* 731
– distance 68
– a dozen *six* 98
*several* 102
see with – an eye
*intelligent* 498
*intelligible* 518
*manifest* 525

– a gale 349
– and half
*equal* 27
*mixed* 41
*incomplete* 53
– a hundred 98
– light 422
– measures
*incomplete* 53
*vacillating* 605
*mid-course* 628
– moon 245
– price 815
– rations 640
– scholar 493
– seas over 959
– sight 443
– speed
*moderate* 174
*slow* 275
– truth 546
**half-blind** 443
**half-blood**
*mixture* 41
*unconformity* 83
*imperfect* 651
**half-frozen** 352
**half-hearted**
*irresolute* 605
*insensible* 823
*indifferent* 866
**half-learned** 491
**half-melted** 352
**halfpenny**
*trifle* 643
**half-starved**
*insufficient* 640
*fasting* 956
**half-way**
*small* 32
*middle* 68
*between* 228
go – *irresolute* 605
*mid-course* 628
meet –
*willing* 602
*compromise* 774
**half-witted** 499, 501
**hall** *house* 189
*lobby* 191
*mart* 799
music – 599
– of audience 588
– mark 550
**hallelujah** 990
**halliard** 45
**halloo** *cry* 411
*look here!* 457
*call* 586
*wonder* 870
**hallow**
*celebrate* 883
*respect* 928
**hallowed** 976
**hallucination**
*error* 495
*insanity* 503
**halo** *light* 420
*glory* 873
**Halomancy** 511
**halser** 45
**halt** *cease* 142
*weak* 160
*rest* 265
*go slowly* 275
*lame* 655
*fail* 732
at the – 265
**halter** *rope* 45
*restraint* 752
*punishment* 975
wear a – 874
with a – round one's neck 665
**halting**
*style* 579
– place 292
**halve** [*see* half]
**halves**
do by –
*neglect* 460
*not complete* 730
not do by – 729
go – 778
**ham** *house* 189
**hamadryad** 979
**hamlet** 189
**hammam** 386, 652
**hammer**
*repeat* 104
*knock* 276
*stammer* 583
under the –
*auction* 796
between the – and the anvil 665
– at *think* 451
*work* 686
– out *form* 240
*prepare* 673
*complete* 729
**hammock** 215
**hamper** *basket* 191
*obstruct* 706
**hamstring** 158, 659
**hanaper** 802
**hand**
*measure of length* 200
*side* 236
*transfer* 270
*man* 372
*organ of touch* 379
*indicator* 550
*writing* 590
*medium* 631
*agent* 690
*grasp* 781
*transfer* 783
at – *future* 121
*destined* 152
*near* 197
*useful* 644
bad – 590
bird in – 781
come to – 292, 785
fold one's –s 681
give one's – to
*marry* 903
good –
*writing* 590
*skill* 698
*proficiency* 700
helping – 707, 711
hold in – 737
hold out the – 894
hold up the –
*vote* 609
in –
*incomplete* 53
*business* 625
*preparing* 673
*not finished* 730
*possessed* 777
*money* 800
in the –s of
*authority* 737
*subjection* 749
lay –s on
*discover* 480*a*
*use* 677
*take* 789
*rite* 998
much on one's –s 682
on one's –s
*business* 625
*redundant* 641
*not finished* 730
*for sale* 796
on the other – 468
no – in 623
poor – 701
put into one's –s 784
put one's – to 676
ready to one's – 673
shake –s 918
stretch forth one's – 680
take by the – 707
take in –
*teach* 537
*undertake* 676
time hanging on one's –s
*inaction* 681
*leisure* 685
*weary* 841
try one's – 675
turn one's – 675
turn one's – to 625
under one's –
*in writing* 590
*promise* 768
*compact* 769
– back 683
– cart 272
– of death 360
– down
*record* 551
*transfer* 783
have one's –s full 682
– gallop 274
– glass 445
– and glove 709, 888
– in hand
*joined* 43
*accompanying* 88
*same time* 120
*concur* 178
*co-operate* 709
*party* 712
*concord* 714
*friend* 888
*social* 892
– to hand
*touching* 199
*transfer* 270
*fight* 720, 722
– over head
*inattention* 458
*neglect* 460
*reckless* 863
have a – in
*cause* 153
*act* 680
*co-operate* 709
have one's – in
*skill* 698
keep one's – in 613
live from – to mouth
*insufficient* 640
*unprepared* 674
*poor* 804
–s off! *avoid* 623
*leave alone* 681
*prohibition* 761

– cash 800
– earned 704
– and fast rule 80
– fought 704
– frost 383
– of hearing 419
– heart
*malevolent* 907
*vicious* 945
*impenitent* 951
– hit 732
– knocks 720
– life 735
– lines
*adversity* 735
*severity* 739
– liver 954*a*
– lot 735
– master 739
– measure 739
– names 932
– necessity 601
– nut to crack 704
– to please 868
– pressed
*haste* 684
*difficulty* 704
*hindrance* 706
– put to it 704
– set 704
– tack 298
– task 703
– time 704
– up 704, 804
– upon
*attack* 716
*severe* 739
*censure* 932
– winter 383
– words
*obscure* 571
*rude* 895
*censure* 932
– work 686
– at work 682
**harden** [*see* hard]
*strengthen* 159
*accustom* 613
– the heart
*insensible* 823
*enmity* 889
*impenitence* 951
**hardened**
*impious* 988
– front
*insolent* 885
**hardening**
*habit* 613
**hard-featured** 846
**hard-fisted** 819
**hard-headed** 498, 739
**hardihood** 861, 885
**hardly**
*scarcely* 32
deal – with 739
– any *few* 103
– anything
*small* 32
*unimportant* 643
– ever 137
**hard-mouthed** 606
**hardness** 323
– of heart 914*a*
**hardship** 735
**hardy**
*strong* 159
*healthy* 654
*brave* 861
**hare** 274
hold with the – and run with the hounds
*fickle* 607
*servile* 886
**hare-brained** 458, 863
**harem** 961
**hariolation** 511
**hark** 418, 457
– back 283
**harl** 205
**harlequin**
*changeable* 149
*nimble* 274
*motley* 440
*pantomimic* 599
*humorist* 844
**harlequinade** 599
**harlot** 962
**harlotry** 961
**harm**
*evil* 619
*badness* 649
*malevolence* 907
**harmattan** 349
**harmless**
*impotent* 158
*good* 648
*perfect* 650
*salubrious* 656
*safe* 664
*innocent* 946
bear – 717
**harmonica** 417
**harmonics** 413
**harmonist** 413
**harmonium** 417
**harmonize** 178, 416
**harmony**
*agreement* 23
*order* 58
*music* 413
*colour* 428
*concord* 714
*peace* 721
*friendship* 888
**harness**
*fasten* 43
*fastening* 45
*accoutrement* 225
*yoke* 370
*instrument* 633
*restraint* 752
in –
*prepared* 673
*in action* 680
*active* 682
*subjection* 749
– up 293
**harp**
*repeat* 104
*musical instrument* 417
*weary* 841
**Harpagon** 819
**harper** 416
**harpist** 416
**harpoon** 727
**harpsichord** 417
**harpy**
*relentless* 739
*thief* 792
*miser* 819
*evil-doer* 913
*demon* 980
**harquebuss** 727
**harridan** 846, 962
**harrier** 366
**harrow**
*agriculture* 371
– up the soul 860
**harrowing** 830
**harry** *pain* 830
*attack* 716
*persecute* 907
**Harry, old** – 978
**harsh**
*acrid* 171
*sound* 410
*style* 579
*discordant* 713
*severe* 739
*disagreeable* 830
*morose* 895
*malevolent* 907
– voice 581
**hart** 366, 373
**hartal** 142, 489
**harum-scarum** 59, 458
**haruspice** 513
**Haruspicy** 511
**harvest**
*effect* 154
*profit* 618
*store* 636
*acquisition* 775
get in the –
*complete* 729
*succeed* 731
– home
*celebration* 883
– time
*autumn* 126
*exertion* 686
**has been** 122
**hash** *mix* 41
*cut* 44
*confusion* 59
*food* 298
make a – 699
**hashish** 663
**hasp** 43, 45
**hassock** 215
**hastate** 253
**haste**
*velocity* 274
*activity* 682
*hurry* 684
**hasten**
*promote* 707
**hasty**
*transient* 113
*hurried* 684
*impatient* 825
*irritable* 901
– pudding 298
**hat** 225
cardinal's – 999
send round the – 765
shovel – 999
– in hand 886
**hatch**
*produce* 161
*gate* 232
*opening* 260
*chickens* 370
*fabricate* 544
*shading* 556
*plan* 626
*prepare* 673
– a plot 626
**hatches, under** –
*restraint* 751
*prisoner* 754
*poor* 804
**hatchet**
*cutting* 253
bury the – 918
dig up the – 722
throw the helve after the – 818

*height* 206
*projection* 250
**headlong**
*hurry* 684
*rush* 863
rush –
*violence* 173
**headman** 694
**headmost**
*front* 234
*precession* 280
**head-piece**
*summit* 210
*intellect* 450
*helmet* 717
*ornament* 847
**headquarters**
*focus* 74
*abode* 189
*authority* 737
**head-race** 350
**heads**
*compendium* 596
– or tails 156, 621
lay – together
*advice* 695
*co-operate* 709
– I win tails you lose
*unfair* 940
**headship** 737
**headsman** 975
**head-stone** 363
**headstrong**
*violent* 173
*obstinate* 606
*rash* 863
**headway** *space* 180
*navigation* 267
*progression* 282
**headwind** 708
**headwork** 451
**heady** 606
**heal** *restore* 660
*remedy* 662
let the wound –
*forgive* 918
– the breach
*pacify* 723
**healing art** 662
**health 654**
picture of – 654
**healthiness** 655
**health resort** 189
**healthy** 656
**heap** *quantity* 31
*collection* 72
*store* 636
*too many* 641
**heaps** 102
rubbish – 645
**hear**
*audition* 418
*be informed* 527
not – of (refuse) 764
– a cause
*adjudge* 480
*lawsuit* 969
– hear! 931
– and obey **743**
– out 457
**hearer** 418
**hearing 418**, 696
[*see* hear]
gain a – 175
give a – 418
hard of – 419
out of – 196
within – 197
**hearken** 457
**hearsay** 532
– evidence **467**
**hearse** 363
**heart**
*intrinsicality* **5**
*interior* 221
*centre* 222
*mind* 450
*willingness* 602
*essential* 642
*affections* 820
*courage* 861
*love* 897
man after one's own – 899
with all one's – 438, 602
at – 820, 821
from bottom of – 543
beating – 821, 824
break the – 830
by –
*memory* 505
go to one's – 824
in good – 858
with a heavy – 603
know by – 490
lay to – 837
learn by – 539
lift up the – 990
lose – 837
lose one's – 897
nearest to one's – 897
not find it in one's – 603
have a place in the – 897
put one's – into 604
set one's – upon 604
take –
*content* 831
*hope* 858
*courage* 861
take to –
*sensibility* 822
*discontent* 832
*dejection* 837
*anger* 900
warm – 822
wind round the – 897
– bleeding for 914
to one's –'s content
*willing* 602
*enough* 639
*success* 731
*pleasure* 829
–'s core
*mind* 450
*affections* 820
– expanding 821
– failing one 837, 860
do one's – good 829
– of grace 858
– in hand 602
– leaping with joy 827, 838
– leaping into one's mouth 824
– of oak
*strong* 159
*hard* 323
– in right place 906
– sinking *fear* 860
– and soul
*completely* 52
*willing* 602
*resolute* 604
*exertion* 686
*feeling* 821
– of stone 823, 907
– swelling 824
**heartache** 828
**heart-breaking** 821, 830
**heart-broken** 828
**heartburning**
*discontent* 832
*regret* 833
*enmity* 889
*anger* 900
*jealousy* 920
**hearten** 858, 861
**heartfelt** 821, **829**
**hearth**
*home* 189
*fireplace* 386
**heartless** 823, **945**
**heart-rending** 830
**heartsease** 831
**heart-shaped** 245
**heart-sick**
*dejection* 837
*dislike* 867
*satiety* 869
**heart-stricken** 828
**heart-strings, tear the** – 830
**hearty**
*willing* 602
*healthy* 654
*feeling* 821
*cheerful* 836
*friendly* 888
*social* 892
– laugh 838
– meal 298
– reception 892
**heat** *warmth* **382**
*make hot* 384
*contest* 720
*excitement* 824, 825
dead – 27
– of passion **900**
– wave 382
**heated imagination** 515
**heater** 386
**heath** *moor* 344
*plant* 367
**heathen** 984, 989
– mythology 979
**heathenish** 851
**heather** *moor* 344
*plant* 367
**heaume** 717
**heautontimorumenos** 837, **955**
**heave** *raise* 307
*emotion* 821
– the lead 208, 466
– a sigh 839
– in sight 446
– to 265
**heaven** 827, **981**
call – to witness 535
in the face of – 525
light of – 420
move – and earth 686

hemispheric 250
hemlock 663
hemorrhage 299
hemp 205
hen 366
*female* 374
– with one chicken
*busy* 682
henbane 663
hence
*arising from* 155
*departure* 293
*deduction* 476
– loathed melancholy 836
henceforth 121
henchman 746
hencoop 370
hendiadys 91
henna 433
henpecked 743, 749
heptagon 244
heptarchy 98
Heraclitus 839
rideret – 853
herald
*precursor* 64
*precession* 280
*predict* 511
*forerunner* 512
*proclaim* 531
*messenger* 534
heraldry 550
herb 367
herbage 365
herbal 369
herbivorous 298
herborize 369
herculean
*strong* 159
*exertion* 686
*difficult* 704
Herculem, ex pede – 550
Hercules 159, 215
pillars of – 233, 550
herd 72, 102
herdsman 746
here
*situation* 183
*presence* 186
*arrival* 292
come –! 286
– below 318
– goes 676
– and there
*dispersed* 73
*few* 103
*place* 182, 183
– there and everywhere
*diversity* 16*a*
*space* 180
*omnipresence* 186
– to-day and gone to-morrow 111
hereabouts 183, 197
hereafter 121, 152
hereby 631
hereditament 780
hereditary
*intrinsic* 5
*derivative* 154, 167
heredity 167
herein 221
heresy 495, 984
heretic 984
heretofore 122
hereupon 106
herewith 88, 632
heritage
*futurity* 121
*possession* 777
*property* 780
heritor 779
hermaphrodite 83
– brig 273
hermeneutics 522
Hermes 534, 582
hermetically 261
hermit 893, 955
hermitage
*house* 189
*cell* 191
*seclusion* 893
hero *brave* 861
*glory* 873
*good man* 948
– worship 931, 991
Herod, out-Herod – 549
heroic [*see* hero]
*magnanimous* 942
mock – 853
heroics 884
heroin 663
heroine 861
herpetology 368
Herr 373
herring
*pungent* 392
– pond 341
draw a – across the trail 545
trail of a red – 615, 706
herring-gutted 203
hesitate
*uncertain* 475
*sceptical* 485
*stammer* 583
*reluctant* 603
*irresolute* 605
*fearful* 860
Hesperian 236
Hesperides, garden of the – 981
Hesperus 423
Hessian boot 225
hest 741
hesterni quirites 876
heterarchy 737
heteroclite 83
heterodoxy 489, 984
heterogeneous
*unrelated* 10
*different* 15
*mixed* 41
*multiform* 81
*exceptional* 83
heterogeneity 15, 16*a*
heteromorphism 16*a*
hetman 745
hew *cut* 44
*shorten* 201
*fashion* 240
– down 308
hewers of wood
*workers* 690
*commonalty* 876
hexagon 98, 244
hexahedron 244
hexameter 98, 597
hey! 586
heyday
*exultation* 838
*festivity* 840
*wonder* 870
– of the blood 820
– of youth 127
hiation 260
hiatus 198
hibernal 383
hibernate 683
Hibernicism 497, 563
hic:
– jacet 363
– labor hoc opus 704
hick 701, 851, 876
hiccup 349
hid under a bushel 460
hidalgo 875
hidden 528
– meaning 526
hide *skin* 223
*conceal* 528
– diminished hea
*inferior* 34
*decrease* 36
*humility* 879
– one's face
*modesty* 881
– and seek
*deception* 545
*avoid* 623
*game* 840
hide-bound 751, 819
hideous 846
hide-out 893
hiding-place
*abode* 189
*ambush* 530
*refuge* 666
hie 264, 274
– to 266
hiemal 126
hierarch 996
hierarchy 995
hieratic 590
hieroglyphic
*representation* 554
*letter* 561
*writing* 590
hierographa 985
hieromancy 511
hierophant 996
hieroscopy 511
higgle 794
higgledy piggledy 59
higgler 797
high *much* 31
*lofty* 206
*fetid* 401
*treble* 410
*foul* 653
*noted* 873
*proud* 878
from on – 981
on – 206
think –ly of 931
– art 556
– celebration 998
– colour
*colour* 428
*red* 434
*exaggerate* 549
– commissioner 745
– days and holi-

**H.M.S.** 726
**hoar** *aged* 128
*white* 430
– frost 383
**hoard** 636
**hoarse**
*husky* 405
*harsh* 410
*voiceless* 581
talk oneself – 584
**hoary** [*see* hoar]
**hoax** 545
**hob** *support* 215
*stove* 386
– and nob
*celebration* 883
*courtesy* 894
**hobble**
*limp* 275
*awkward* 699
*difficulty* 704
*fail* 732
*shackle* 751
– skirt 225
**hobbledehoy** 129
**hobby**
*crotchet* 481
*pursuit* 622
*desire* 865
**hobby-horse** 272
**hobgoblin**
*fearful* 860
*demon* 980
**hobo** 268
**hobnail** 876
**Hobson's choice**
*necessity* 601
*no choice* 609a
*compulsion* 744
**hoc genus omne** 876
**hock** 771
**hock shop** 787
**hockey** 840
**hockey rink** 213
**hocus** 545
**hocus-pocus**
*interchange* 148
*unmeaning* 517
*cheat* 545
*conjuration* 992
*spell* 993
**hod**
*receptacle* 191
*support* 215
*vehicle* 272
**hoddy-doddy** 501
**hodge-podge** 41
**hoe** 272, 371
**hog** *animal* 366
*sensualist* 954a
*glutton* 957
greedy as a – 865
go the whole – 604
**hog's back** 206
**hogmanay** 998
**hogshead** 191
**hog-wash** 653
**hoist** 307
– the black flag 722
– a flag 550
– on one's own petard
*retaliation* 718
*failure* 732
**hoity-toity!** 815, 870
**hold** *cohere* 46
*contain* 54
*remain* 141
*cease* 142
*go on* 143
*happen* 151
*receptacle* 191
*cellar* 207
*base* 211
*support* 215
*halt* 265
*believe* 484
*be passive* 681
*defend* 717
*power* 737
*restrain* 751
*prison* 752
*prohibit* 761
*possess* 777
*retain* 781
*enough!* 869
have a firm – 781
have a – upon 175
gain a – upon 737
get – of 789
quit one's – 782
take – 175
– aloof
*stay away* 187
*distrust* 487
*avoid* 623
– an argument 476
– authority 737
– back *avoid* 623
*store* 636
*hinder* 706
*restrain* 751
*retain* 781
*miserly* 819
– one's breath
*wonder* 870
– converse 588
– a council 695
– fast 751, 781
– forth *teach* 537
*speak* 582
– good 478, 494
– one's ground 141
– in hand 737
– one's hand
*cease* 142
*relinquish* 624
– hard 265
– up one's head 861
– a lease 771
– a meeting 72
– off 623
– office 693
– on
*continue* 141, 143
*persevere* 604a
– out [*see below*]
– one's own
*preserve* 670
*defend* 717
*resist* 719
– oneself in readiness 673
– in remembrance 505
– both one's sides 838
– a situation 625
– in solution 335
– to 602
– together 43, 709
– one's tongue 403, 585
– up [*see below*]
– oneself up 307
**hold out**
*endure* 106
*affirm* 535
*persevere* 604a
*resist* 719
*offer* 763
*brave* 861
– expectation
*predict* 511
*promise* 768
– temptation 865
**hold up**
*continue* 143
*support* 215
*not rain* 340
*aid* 707
*rob* 791
*display* 882
*extol* 931
– one's hand
*sign* 550
*threat* 609
– to execration
*cures* 908
*censure* 932
– the mirror 525
– to scorn 930
– to shame 874
– to view 525
**holder** 779
**holdfast** 45
**holding**
*tenancy* 777
*property* 780
**hole** *place* 182
*hovel* 189
*receptacle* 191
*opening* 260
*ambush* 530
– in one's coat 651
– and corner
*place* 182
*peer into* – 461
*hiding* 528, 530
– to creep out of
*plea* 617
*escape* 671
*facility* 705
**holiday** *leisure* 685
*repose* 687
*amusement* 840
– task *easy* 705
**holiness** *God* 976
*piety* 987
**holloa** 411
– before one is out of the wood 884
**hollow**
*unsubstantial* 4
*completely* 52
*incomplete* 53
*depth* 208
*concavity* 252
*channel* 350
- *sound* 408
*specious* 477
*false* 544
*voiceless* 581
beat – 731
– truce 723
**holm** 346
**holocaust**
*kill* 361
*sacrifice* 991
(*destruction* 162)
**holograph** 590
**holster** 191
**holt** 367
**holus bolus** 684
**Holy** *of God* 976
*pious* 987
keep – 987
– breathing 990

- Church 983*a*
- City 981
- day 998
- Ghost 976
temple of the -
Ghost 983*a*
- men of old 985
- orders 995
- place 1000
- Scriptures 985
- Spirit 976
- water 998
- week 998
**holystone** 652
**homage**
*submission* 725
*fealty* 743
*reverence* 928
*approbation* 931
*worship* 990
**home** *focus* 74
*habitation* 189
*near* 197
*interior* 221
*arrival* 292
*refuge* 666
at - *party* 72
*present* 186
*within* 221
*at ease* 705
*social gathering* 892
be at -
- *to visitors* 892
feel at -
*freedom* 748
*pleasure* 827
*content* 831
look at -
*accusation* 938
make oneself at -
*free* 748
*sociable* 892
not be at - 764
stay at - 265
at - in
*knowledge* 490
*skill* 698
at - with
*friendship* 888
bring - to
*evidence* 467
*belief* 484
*accuse* 938
*condemn* 971
come - 292
eternal - 981
from - 187
get - 292
go - 283
go from - 293
long - 363
strike -
*energy* 171
*attack* 716
- stroke 170
- thrust
*attack* 716
*censure* 932
**home-bred** 851
**home-felt** 821
**home-rule** 737, 748
**homeless**
*unhoused* 185
*banished* 893
**homely**
*language* 576
*unadorned* 849
*common* 851, 876
**Homeric**
- laughter 838
**home-sick** 833
**home-spun**
*texture* 329
**home-stall** 189
**homestead** 189
**homeward bound** 292
**homicidal maniac** 913
**homicide** 361
**homiletical** 892
**homily**
*teaching* 537
*advice* 595
*sermon* 998
**hominem, argumentum ad** - 938
**homœopathic**
*small* 32
*little* 193
**Homœopathy** 662
**homogeneity**
*relation* 9
*identity* 13
*uniformity* 16
*simplicity* 42
**homogenesis** 161
**homologous** 23
**homology**
*relation* 9
*uniformity* 16
*equality* 27
*concord* 714
**homonym**
*equivocal* 520
*vocal sound* 580
**homophony** 413
**homunculus** 193
**Hon.** 817
**hone** 253
**honest**
*veracious* 543
*honourable* 939
*pure* 960
- meaning 516
turn an - penny 775
- truth 494
**honey**
*sweet* 396
*favourite* 899
milk and - 734
**honeycomb**
*concave* 252
*opening* 260
*deterioration* 659
**honeyed**
- phrases 894
- words
*allurement* 615
*flattery* 933
**honeymoon**
*pleasure* 827
*endearment* 902
*marriage* 903
**honey-mouthed** 894, 933
**honeysuckle** 396
**honorarium** 784, 973
**honorary** 815
**honour**
*demesne* 780
*glory* 873
*title* 877
*respect* 928
*approbation* 931
*probity* 939
affair of - 720
do - to 883
do the -s
*sociality* 892
*courtesy* 894
*respect* 928
his - *judge* 967
in - of 883
man of - 939
upon my - 535, 768
word of - 768
- be to 873
- a bill 807
- in the breach 923
- bright
*veracity* 543
*probity* 939
**honte, mauvaise** - 881
**hood** 225, 999
**hooded** 223
**hoodlum** 887
**hoodoo** 649
**hoodwink**
*ignore* 491
*blind* 442
*hide* 528
*deceive* 545
**hoof** 211
cloven - 907
**hook** *fasten* 43
*fastening* 45
*hang* 214
*curve* 245
*deceive* 545
*retain* 781
*take* 789
by - or by crook 631
**hookah** 392
**hooker** *ship* 273
**hookey, blind - 840**
**hooks, go off the** 360
**hooligan** 887, 913
**hoop** *circle* 247
*cry* 411
**hoot** *cry* 411, 412
*deride* 929
*contempt* 930
*censure* 932
**hop** *leap* 309
*dance* 840, 892
- off 293
- skip and jump
*leap* 309
*agitation* 315
*haste* 684
*game* 840
- the twig 360
**hope 858**
band of - 958
beyond - 658, **734**
dash one's -s **837**
excite - 511
foster - 858
well-grounded - 472
- against hope **859**
- for the best **858**
- deferred
*dejection* 837
*lamentation* **859**
- for *expect* 507
*desire* 865
hope chest 858
**hopeful** *infant* **129**
*probable* 472
*hope* 858
**hopelessness 471, 859**
**Hop-o'-my-thumb** 193

the same a – years hence 460
**hundredth** 99
**hundredweight** 319
**hunger** 865
**hunger-strike** 956
**hunks** 819
**hunt** *inquiry* 461
*pursuit* 622
– after 622
– in couples 709
– down 907
– out *inquiry* 461
*discover* 480*a*
– slipper 840
**hunter** *horse* 271
*killer* 361
*pursuer* 622
place &c. – 767
**hunting** 361, 622
**hunting-ground** 840
happy – 981
**hurdle** 272
**hurdy-gurdy** 417
**hurl** 284
– against 716
– defiance 715
**hurler avec les loups** 82, 714
**Hurlothrumbo** 860
**hurly-burly** 315
**hurrah** 411, 836, 838
**hurricane** 349, 667
– deck 210
**hurry** *haste* 684
*excite* 825
– forward 684
– off with 789
– on 615
– of spirits 821
– up 684
**hurst** 367
**hurt**
*physical pain* 378
*evil* 619
*maltreat* 649
*injure* 659
more frightened than – 860
– the feelings
*pain* 830
*anger* 900
**hurtful** 649
**hurtle** 276
**hurtless** 648
**husband**
*store* 636
*director* 694
*spouse* 903
**husbandman** 371
**husbandry**
*agriculture* 371
*conduct* 692
*economy* 817
**hush** *moderate* 174
*stop* 265
*silence* 403
*taciturn* 585
– up
*conceal* 528
*pacify* 723
**hush-money** 30, 973
**husk** 223, 226
**husky** *strong* 159
*dry* 340
*faint sound* 405
*hoarse* 581
**hussar** 726
**hussy** 962
**hustings**
*school* 542
*arena* 728
*tribunal* 966
**hustle**
*perturb* 61
*push* 276
*agitate* 315
*activiiy* 682
*hinder* 706
**hustler** 682, 962
**hut** 189
**hutch** 189
**huzza** 838
**hyacinth**
*jewel* 847
**hyæna** 913
**hyaline** 425
**hybrid**
*mixture* 41
*exception* 83
**hydra**
*monster* 83, 366
*productive* 168
– headed 163
**hydrant** 348, 385
**hydraulics** 333, 348
**hydroplane** 273
**hydrodynamics** 333, 348
**hydrography** 341
**hydrology** 333
**hydrolysis** 49
**hydromancy** 511
**hydromel** 396
**hydropathy** 662
**hydrophobia** 867
**hydrostatics** 333
**hyemal** 383
**hyetology** 348
**hygeian** 656
**hygiantics** 670
**hygienic** 656, 670
**hygre** 348
**hygrometry** 339
**hyle** 316
**hylism** 316
**hylotheism** 984, 989
**Hymen** 903
**hymeneal** 903
**hymn** *song* 415
*worship* 990
– of hate 898
**hymn-book** 998
**hyoscine** 663
**hypallage** 218
**hyperbaton** 218
**hyperbola** 245
**hyperbole** 549
**hyperborean**
*far* 196
*cold* 383
**hypercriticism**
*misjudgment* 481
*discontent* 832
*fastidiousness* 868
*censure* 932
**hyperdulia** 990
**Hyperion** 423, 845
– to a satyr 14
**hyperorthodoxy** 984
**hyperphysical** 976
**hypertrophy** 194
**hyphen** 45
**hypnology** 683
**hypnotic**
*remedy* 662
*sleep* 683
**hypnotize** 376
**hypocaust** 386
**hypochondriac**
*madman* 504
*low spirits* 837
**hypochondriasis** 837
**hypocrisy**
*falsehood* 544
*religious* – 988
**hypocrite** 548, 855
play the – 544
**hypostasis** 1, 3
**Hypostatic union** 976
**hypothecate** 771
**hypothenuse** 217
**hypothesis** 514
**hypothesize** 514
**hypothetical** 475, 514
**hypped** *insane* 503
*dejected* 837
**hypsometer** 206
**Hyrcynian wood** 533
**hysteria**
*insanity* 503
**hysteric** *violent* 173
**hysterical**
*spasmodic* 608
*emotional* 821
*excitable* 825
**hysterics** 173
in – *excited* 824
*frightened* 860
**hysteron proteron** 218

## I

**I** 79
**iambic** 597
**ibidem** 13
**Icarus**
*navigator* 269
*rash* 863
fate of – 306
**ice** *cold* 383
*refrigerate* 385
**iceberg** 383
**ice-bound** 383
*restraint* 751
**ice-chest** 387
**ice-house** 387
**ice-yacht** 273
**Ichabod** 874
**ichnography** 554
**ichor** 333
**ichthyology** 368
**ichthyomancy** 511
**ichthyophagous** 298
**icicle** 383
**icon** 554
**iconoclasm** 983*a*, 984
**iconoclast** 165, 913
**iconography** 554
**icosahedron** 244
**id est** 522
**idea**
*small quantity* 32
*notion* 453
give an – of 537
**ideal** *unreal* 2
*completeness* 52
*erroneous* 495
*imaginary* 515
*perfect* 650
**ideality** 450, 515
**idée fixe** 481

**imaum** 745, 996
**imbecile** 158, 499
**imbécile** 501
**imbecility** **499**
**imbed** [*see* embed]
**imbedded** 229
**imbibe** 296
- learning 539
**imbrangle** 61
**imbricated** 223
**imbroglio**
*disorder* 59
*difficulty* 704
*discord* 713
**imbrue**
*impregnate* 300
*moisten* 339
- one's hands in blood
*killing* 361
*war* 722
- the soul 824
**imbue** *mix* 41
*impregnate* 300
*moisten* 339
*tinge* 428
*teach* 537
**imbued**
*affections* 820
- with
*belief* 484
*habit* 613
*feeling* 821
**imburse** 803
**imitation**
*copying* **19**
*copy* 21
*representation* 554
**immaculate**
*perfect* 650
*clean* 652
*innocent* 946
**immanent** 5
**immanity** 907
**Immanuel** 976
**immaterial**
*unsubstantial* 4
**immateriality**
*spiritual* **317**
*trifling* 643
**immature** 123, 674
**immeasurable** 31, 105
**immediate**
*continuous* 69
**immediately** 113, 132
**immedicabile vulnus** 619
**immedicable** 859
**immelodious** 414
**immemorial** 124
from time - 122
- usage 613
**immense** *great* 31
*infinite* 105
- *size* 192
**immerge**
**immerse**
*introduce* 300
*dip* 337
**immersed in** 229
**immethodical** 59
**immigrant** *alien* 57
*entering* 294
**immigration** 266, 294
**imminent** 132, 152, 286
**immiscible** 47
**immission** 296
**immitigable**
*hopeless* 859
*revenge* 919
**immix** 41
**immobility** 150, 265
**immoderately** 31
**immodest** 961
**immolation**
*killing* 361
*giving* 784
*sacrifice* 991
**immoral** 923, 945
**immortal**
*perpetual* 112
*glorious* 873
*celebrated* 883
**immotile** 265
**immovable**
*stable* 150
*quiescent* 265
*obstinate* 606
**immundicity** 653
**immunity**
*health* 656
*freedom* 748
*right* 924
*exemption* 777*a*, 927*a*
**immure** 751
**immutable**
*stable* 150
*deity* 976
**imo pectore, ab** - 821
**imp** 980
**impact** *contact* 43
*impulse* 276
*insertion* 300
**impair** 659
**impale** *transfix* 260
*execute* **972**
**impalpable**
*small* 193
*powder* 330
*intangible* 381
**impanation** 998
**impar sibi** 608
**imparity** 28
**impart** *inform* 527
*give* 784
**impartial**
*judicious* 498
*neutral* 628
*just* 922
*honourable* 939
- opinion 484
**impassable**
*closed* 261
*impossible* **471**
**impasse** 706
**impassible** 823
**impassion** 824
**impassionable** 822
**impassioned**
- *language* 574
*excited* 825
**impassive** 823
**impatient** 825
- of control 742
**impawn** 771
**impeach**
*censure* 932
*accuse* 938
*go to law* 969
**impeachment,**
soft - 902
**impeccability** 650, 946
**impecunious** 804
**impede** 706
**impediment** 706
- in speech 583
**impedimenta** 633, 780
**impel** *push* 276
*induce* 615
**impend**
*future* 121
*imminent* 132
*destiny* 152
*overhang* 206
**impenetrable**
*closed* 261
*solid* 321
*unintelligible* 519
*latent* 526
**impenitence** **951**
**imperative**
*require* 630
*command* 737, 741
*severe* **739**
*duty* 926
**imperator** 745
**imperceptible**
*small* 32
*minute* 193
*slow* 275
*invisible* **447**
*latent* 526
**impercipient** 376
**imperdible** 664
**imperfect**
*incomplete* **53**
*failing* 651
*vicious* 945
**imperfection** **651**
*inferiority* **34**
*vice* 945
**imperfectly** 32
**imperforate** 261
**imperial**
*trunk* 191
*beard* 256
*authority* **737**
**imperil** 665
**imperious**
*command* **737**
*proud* 878
*arrogant* 885
- necessity 601
**imperishable** 112
*stable* 150
*glorious* 873
**imperium in imperio** 737
**impermanent** 111
**impermeable**
*closed* 261
*dense* 321
**impersonal**
*general* 78
*neuter* 316
**impersonate** 19, 554
**impersonator** 19
**imperspicuity** 519
**impersuasible** 606
**impertinent**
*irrelevant* 10
*insolent* 885
**imperturbable** **823**, 826
**impervious**
*closed* 261
*impossible* **471**
*insensible* 823
- to light 426
- to reason 606
**impetiginous** 653
**impetrate** 765
**impetuous**

*boisterous* **173**
*hasty* 684
*excitable* 825
*rash* 863
*eager* 865
impetus 276
impi 726
impiety **988**
impignorate **771**
impinge 276
implacable 848, 919
implant *insert* 300
*teach* 537
implanted
*adventitious* 6
implausible 473
implead 969
implement 633
impletion 52
implex 41
implicate *involve* 54, 526
*accuse* 938
implicated *related* 9
*component* 56
implication
*disorder* 59
*meaning* 516
*latency* 526
implicit 526
– belief 484
implore 765
imply *evidence* **467**
*mean* 516
*involve* 526
impolicy 699
impolite 895
imponderable **4**, 320
imporous 261, 321
import
*put between* 228
*ingress* 294
*take in* 296
*insert* 300
*mean* 516
*imply* 526
*be of consequence* 642
importance **642**
*greatness* 31
attach – to 642
attach too much – to 482
of no – 643
importune 765, 830
impose *order* 741
*awe* 928
– upon
*credulity* 486
*deceive* 545
*be unjust* **923**
imposing
*important* 642
*exciting* 824
*glorious* 873
imposition [*see* impose]
*undue* 925
– of hands 998
impossibile, credo quia – 486
impossibilities, seek after – 645
impossibility **471**
impossible 471
*refusal* 764
– quantity
*algebra* 84
impost 812
imposthume 655
impostor 548, 925
imposture 545
impotence **158**
impotent conclusion 732
impound 751
impoverish
*weaken* 160
*waste* 638
*despoil* 789
*render poor* 804
impracticable
*impossible* 471
*misjudging* 481
*obstinate* 606
*difficult* 704
imprecation
*prayer* 765
*curse* 908
impregnable 159, 664
impregnate *mix* 41
*combine* 48
*fecundate* 161, 168
*insert* 300
*teach* 537
– with 641
impresario 599
imprescriptible 924
impress *cause*
*sensation* 375
*mark* 550
*steal* 791
*excite feeling* 824
– upon the mind
*memory* 505
*teach* 537
impressed with
*belief* 484
*feeling* 821
impressible
*motive* 615
*sensibility* 822
impression
*sensation* **375**
*idea* 453
*belief* 484
*printing* 531
*mark* 550
*engraving* 558
*print* 591
*emotion* 821
make an –
*act* 171
*thought* 451
impressionable 375, 822
impressive
*language* 574
*important* 642
*feeling* 821, 824
imprimis 66
imprimit 558
imprint
*publisher* 531
*indication* 550
– in the memory 505
imprison
*circumscribe* 229
*restrain* 751
*punish* 972
improbability **473**
improbate 932
improbity **940**
impromptu 612
– fait à loisir 673
improper
*incongruous* 24
*foolish* 499
*solecism* 568
*inexpedient* 647
*wrong* 923
*unmeet* 925
*vicious* 945
– time 135
impropriate **777**, 789
impropriator **779**
improve 658
– the occasion 134
– the shining hour 682
– upon 658
improvement **658**
improvident
*careless* 460
*not preparing* 674
*prodigal* 818
*rash* 863
improvisation
*music* 415
improvisatore
*speech* 582
*poetry* 597
*impulse* 612
improvise
*imagination* **515**
*impulse* 612
*unprepared* **674**
improviste, à l'– 508, 612
improvisatrice 612
imprudent 460, **863**
impudent 885, **895**
impudicity 961
impugn *deny* **536**
*attack* 716
*blame* 932
impugnation 708
impuissance 158
impulse *push* **276**
*sudden thought* **612**
*motive* 615
blind – 601
creature of – **612**
give an – to
*propel* 284
*aid* 707
impulsive [*see* impulse]
*intuitive* 477
*excitable* 825
*rash* 863
impunity *escape* **671**
*acquittal* 970
with – *safely* 664
impurity 653, **961**
imputation
*ascribe* 155
*slur* 874
*accuse* 938
in 221
go – 294
– as much as
*relation* 9
*degree* 26
– the circumstances 8
– doors 221
– durancevile **751**
– for
– force 1
*undertake* 676
*promise* 768
– re 9
– and out 314
–s and outs 182
in: – articulo 111
– extenso *whole* **50**

870
**indesinent** 112
**indestructible** 150
**indeterminate**
*indefinite* 78
*chance* 156
*uncertain* 475
*irresolute* 605
**indevotion** 989
**index**
*arrangement* 60
*exponent* 84
*list* 86
*sign* 550
*words* 62
**index expurgatorius** 761, 932
**indexterity** 699
**Indian:**
- file 69
- rubber 325
- summer 126
- weed 392
**indicate**
*specify* 79
*direct attention to* 457
*mean* 516
*mark* 550
**indication** **550**
**indicative**
*evidence* 467
**indict** *accuse* 938
*arraign* 969
**indiction** 108, 531
**indifference**
*incuriosity* 456
*unwillingness* 603
*no choice* 609a
*insensibility* 823
*unconcern* **866**
*irreligion* 989
matter of – 643
**indifferent**
[*see* indifference]
*unimportant* 643
*bad* 649
**indigence**
*insufficiency* 640
*poverty* 804
**indigenous** 5, 188
**indigested** 674
**indigestible** 657
**indigestion** 655
**indigitate** 457
**indign** 940
**indignation** 900
– meeting 832
**indignity** 900, 929
**indigo** 438
**indiligence** 683
**indirect**
*oblique* 217
*devious* 279
*latent* 526
*circuitous* 629
**indiscernible** 447
**indiscerptible**
*whole* 50
*unity* 87
*dense* 321
**indiscoverable** 526
**indiscreet** 499, 863, 945
**indiscretion**
*guilt* 947
**indiscriminate**
*mixed* 41
*unarranged* 59
*multiform* 81
*casual* 621
**indiscrimination** **465a**
**indispensable** 630
**indispose**
*dissuade* 616
**indisposed**
*unwilling* 603
*sick* 655
**indisputable** 474
**indissoluble, indissolvable**
*joined* 43
*whole* 50
*stable* 150
*dense* 321
**indistinct** 447
**indistinction** 465*a*
**indistinguishable**
*identical* 13
*invisible* 447
**indisturbance** 265, 826
**indite** 590
**individual**
*whole* 50
*special* 79
*unity* 87
*person* 372
**indivisible** *whole* 50
*dense* 321
**indocility** 158, 606
**indoctrinate** 537
**indolence** 683, **927**
**indomitable**
*strong* 159
*determined* 604
*persevering* 604*a*
*resisting* 719
*courage* 861
**indoor** 221
**indorse** **769, 771**
**indorsement** 550, 551
**indraught** 343, 348
**indubitable** 474
**induce** *cause* 153
*power* 157
*produce* 161
*motive* 615
**induct** 883
**induction**
*inquiry* 461
*reasoning* 476
*drama* 599
*appointment* 755
- *of a priest* 995
**indulge** *lenity* 740
*allow* 760
*please* 829
*intemperance* 954
*gluttony* 957
– one's fancy 609
– in 827
– oneself 943
– in reverie
*inattention* 458
*fancy* 515
– with *give* **784**
**indulgence**
[*see* indulge]
*absolution* 918
**indulgent** *kind* 906
**induration**
*hardening* 323
*impenitence* 951
**Indus to the pole, from** – 180
**industry** 625, 682
hive of – 691
**indweller** 188
**indwelling** 5
**inebriety** 959
**inedible** 395
**ineffable** *great* 31
*inexpressible* 519
*wonderful* 870
**ineffaceable** 820
**ineffectual**
*incapable* 158
*useless* 645
*failing* 732
– attempt 732
pale its – fire 422
**inefficacious**
*incapable* 158
*useless* 645
*failing* 732
**inefficient** 158
**inelastic** *soft* 324
– fluid 333
**inelasticity** **326**
**inelegance** **579,** 846
**ineluctable** **474**
**inept** 24, 158, **645**
**inequality** **28**
**inequitable** 923
**ineradicable**
*intrinsic* **5**
*stable* 150
**inerrable** 946
**inertia** 172
**inertness**
*physical* **172**
*inactive* 683
*moral* 823
**inestimable** 648
**inevitable** 474, **601**
**inexact**
*erroneous* 495
*feeble* 575
**inexcitability** **826**
**inexcusable**
*accusable* 938
*vicious* 945
**inexecution** 730
**inexhaustible** 105 639
**inexistence** **2**
**inexorable**
*unavoidable* 601
*resolved* 604
*stern* 739
*compelling* **744**
*pitiless* 914*a*
*revengeful* 919
**inexpectation** **508**
**inexpedience** **647**
**inexpensive** 815
**inexperience** **491,** 699
**inexpert** 699
**inexpiable** 945
**inexplicable** 519
**inexpressible**
*great* 31
*unmeaning* **517**
*unintelligible* **519**
*wonderful* 870
**inexpressibles** 225
**inexpression**
*latency* 526
**inexpensive** 517
**inexpugnable** 664
**inextension** **180a**
*littleness* 193
*immateriality* **317**
**inextinguishable**
*stable* 150
*strong* 159
*excitable* 825
– desire 865
**inextricable**
*coherent* 46

*disorder* 59
*impossible* 471
**infallibility** 474
assumption of – 885
**infamy** *shame* 874
*dishonour* 940
*vice* 945
**infancy** 66, 127
**infandum renovare dolorem** 505, 833
**infant** **129**
*fool* 501
– prodigy 872
**Infanta** 745
**infanticide** 361, 991
**infantine** 129
*foolish* 499
**infantry** 726
**infarction** 261
**infatuation**
*misjudgment* 481
*credulity* 486
*folly* 499
*insanity* 503
*obstinacy* 606
*passion* 825
*love* 897
**infeasible** 471
**infect** *mix with* 41
*contaminate* 659
*excite* 824
**infectâ, re –**
*shortcoming* 304
*non-completion* 730
*failure* 732
**infection**
*transference* 270
*disease* 655
**infectious** 270, 657
**infecund** 169
**infelicity**
*inexpertness* 699
*misery* 828
**infelicitous** 24
**infer** 472
**inference** 476, 480
by – 467
**inferential**
*demonstrative* 478
*latent* 526
**inferiority**
*in degree* **34**
*in size* 195
*imperfection* 651
personal – 34
**infernal** *bad* 649
*malevolent* 907
*wicked* 945
*satanic* 978
– machine 727
– regions 982
**infertility** 169
**infest** 830
**infestivity** 837, 843
**infibulation** 43
**infidel** 487, 989
**infidelity**
*dishonour* 940
*irreligion* 989
**infiltrate** *mix* 41
*intervene* 228
*interpenetrate* 294
*moisten* 337, 339
*teach* 537
**infiltration**
*passage* 302
**Infinite, the –** **976**
**infinite** 105
– goodness 976
**infinitely** *great* 31
**infinitesimal**
*small* 32
*little* 193
– calculus 85
**infinity** **105**
**infirm** *weak* 160
*disease* 655
*vicious* 945
– of purpose 605
**infirmary** 662
**infirmity**
[*see* infirm]
**infix** 537
**inflame**
*render violent* 173
*burn* 384
*excite* 824
*anger* 900
**inflamed** 382
**inflammable** 384, 388
**inflammation**
*heating* 384
*disease* 655
**inflate** *increase* 35
*expand* 194
*blow* 349
**inflated**
*overestimation* 482
*style* 573, 577
*ridiculous* 853
*vain* 880
**inflation**
[*see* inflate]
*rarefaction* 322
*currency* 800
**inflect** 245
**inflexible** *hard* 323
*resolved* 604
*obstinate* 606
*stern* 739
*inexorable* 914*a*
**inflexion**
*change* 140
*curvature* 245
*grammar* 567
**inflict** *act upon* 680
*severity* 739
– evil 649
– pain
*bodily pain* 378
*mental pain* 830
– punishment 972
**infliction**
*adversity* 735
*mental pain* 828, 830
*punishment* 972
**influence** 153
*change* 140
*physical* – **175**
*inducement* 615
*instrumentality* 631
*authority* 737
absence of – **175a**
sphere of – 780
make one's – felt 631
**influx** 294
**infold** 232
**inform** 527
– against
*accuse* 938
*go to law* 969
**informal** 83, 964
**informality** 773
**informant** 527
**information**
*knowledge* 490
*communication* **527**
*learning* 539
*lawsuit* 969
pick up – 539
**informer** 532
**informity** 241
**infra dignitatem** 874, 940
**infraction**
*trespass* 303
*disobedience* 742
*non-observance* 773
*exemption* 927
– of usage &c.
*unconformity* 83
*desuetude* 614
**infrangible**
*combined* 46
*dense* 321
**infra-red rays** **420**
**infrequency** **137**
**infrigidation** 385
**infringe**
*transgress* 303
*disobey* 742
*not observe* 773
*undueness* 925
*dereliction* 927
– a law &c. 83
**infundibular** 252, 269
**infuriate**
*violent* 173
*excite* 824
*anger* 900
**infuscate** 431
**infuse** *mix* 41
*insert* 300
*teach* 537
– courage 861
– life into 824
– new blood 658
**infusible** 321
**infusion** [*see* infuse]
*liquefaction* 335
**infusoria** 193
**ingannation** 545
**ingathering** 72
**ingemination** 90
**ingenerate** 5
**ingenious** 515, 698
**ingenite** 5
**ingenium, perfervidum** – 682
**ingénu** *artless* 703
**ingénue** *actress* 599
**ingenuity** 698
**ingenuous** 703
**ingesta** 298
**ingestion** 296
**ingle** 388
**inglorious** 874, **940**
**ingluvies** 191
**ingot** 800
**ingraft** *add* 37
*join* 43
*insert* 300
*teach* 537
**ingrafted**
*extrinsic* 6
*habit* 613
**ingrain**
*insinuate* 228
*colour* 428
**ingrained**
*intrinsic* **5**
*combined* **48**
*habit* 613

*character* 820
**ingrate** 917
**ingratiate** 897
**ingratiating** 894
**ingratitude** **917**
**ingredient** 51, 56
**ingress** **294**
forcible – 300
**ingurgitate** 296
**ingustible** 391
**inhabile** 699
**inhabit** 186
**inhabitant** **188**
**inhale** *receive* 296
*breathe* 349
*smell* 398
**inharmonious**
*discord* 713
– colour 428
– sound 414
**inhere** 1
**inherent** 5, 820
**inherit** 775, 777
**inheritance** 780
– of the saints 981
**inherited**
*intrinsic* 5
**inheritor** 779
**inhesion** 5
**inhibit** *hinder* **706**
*restrain* 751
*prohibit* 761
**inhospitable** 893
**inhuman** 907
**inhume** 363
**inimaginable**
*impossible* 471
*improbable* 473
*wonderful* 870
**inimical** 708, 889
**inimitable**
*non-imitation* 20
*supreme* 33
*very good* 648
*perfect* 650
**iniquity** 923, 945
worker of – 949
**inirritability** 826
**initial** 66
– letter 558
**initiate** *begin* **66**
*admit* 296
*teach* 537
**initiated** *skilful* 698
**initiative** 66
**inject** 300, 337
**injection** 662
**injudicial** 964
**injudicious** 499, 863
**injunction**
*acquirement* 630
*advice* 695
*command* 741
*prohibition* 761
**injure** *evil* 619
*damage* 659
*spite* 907
**injuria formæ, spretæ** – 846, 930
**injury** *evil* 619
*badness* 649
*damage* 659
**injustice** 923
**ink** 431
pen and – 590
before the – is dry 132
– slinging **720**
**inkle** 45
**inkling**
*knowledge* 490
*supposition* 514
*information* 527
**inkstand** 590
**inland** 221
**inlay** 440, 847
**inlet** *beginning* **66**
*interval* 198
*opening* 260
*ingress* 294
- *of the sea* **343**
**inly** 221
**inmate** 188
**inmost** 221
to the – core 822
– soul 820
– thoughts **451**
**inn** 189
– s of Court 968
**innate** 5, 601
**innavigable** 471
**inner** 221
– coating 224
– man *intellect* 450
*affections* 820
**innermost recesses** 221
**innings** *land* 342
*acquisition* 775
*receipt* 810
**innkeeper** 601
**innocence** **946**
**innocent** *fool* 501
*good* 648
*healthy* 656
*artless* 703
*guiltless* 946
**innocuous** *good* 648
*healthy* 656
*innocent* 946
**innominate** 565
**innovation**
*variation* 20*a*
*new* 123
*change* 140
**innoxious**
*salubrious* 656
*innocent* 946
**innuendo** *hint* 527
*censure* 932
**innumerable** 105
**innutritious** 657
**inobservance** 773
**inoccupation** 681
**inoculate**
*insert* 300
*teach* 537
*influence* 615
**inodorous** **399**
**inoffensive** 648, 946
**inofficious** 907
**inoperative**
*powerless* 158
*unproductive* 169
*useless* 645
**inopportune**
*untimely* 135
*inexpedient* 647
**inordinate** 31, 641
**inorganization** **358**
**inornate** 849
**inosculate** *join* 43
*intersect* 219
*convoluted* 248
**inquest** 461
**inquietude**
*changeable* 149
*uneasy* 828
*discontent* 832
*apprehension* 860
**inquinate** 659
**inquire** 461
– into 595
**inquirer** 461
**inquiring mind** 455
**inquiry** **461**
**inquisition**
*inquiry* 461
*severity* 739
*torture* 907
*tribunal* 966
**inquisitive** 455
**inquisitorial**
*prying* 455
*inquiry* 461
*severe* 739
*jurisdiction* 965
**inroad** *ingress* 294
*devastation* 659
*invasion* 716
**inrolment** 551
**insalubrity** **657**
**insanity** **503**
**insatiable** 865
**inscribe** 590, **873**
**inscription** 551
**inscroll** 551
**inscrutable** 519
**insculpture** 557
**insculptured** 558
**insecable** 43, 87
**insect** *minute* **193**
*animal* 366
– cry 412
**insecure**
*uncertain* **475**
*danger* 665
**insensate**
*foolish* 499
*insane* 503
**insensibility**
*slow* 275
*physical* **376**
*moral* **823**
– of benefits **917**
– to the past **506**
**inseparable** 43, **46**
**insert** *locate* 184
*interpose* 228
*enter* 294
*put in* 300
*record* 551
– itself 300
**insertion** **300**
*adjunct* 39
*ornament* **847**
**inservient** 645
**inseverable** 43, **87**
**inside** 221
– out 218
turn – out 529
**insidious**
*deceitful* 545
*cunning* 702
*dishonourable* **940**
**insight** 465, 490
**insignia** 550
– of authority **747**
**insignificant**
*unmeaning* 517
*unimportant* 643
**insincere** 544, **855**
**insinuate**
*intervene* 228
*ingress* 294
*insert* 300
*latency* 526
*hint* 527
*ingratiate* **897**
*blame* 932
**insipid**
*style* **575**

*prejudice* 481
*dissent* 489
*obstinacy* 606
*impatience* 825
*insolence* 885
*malevolence* 907
**intomb** 363
**intonation**
*sound* 402
*musical* 413
*voice* 580
**intone** 416, 990
**intort** 248
**intoxicant** 663
**intoxication**
*excitement* 824, 825
*inebriation* 959
**intra, ab** – 221
**intractable**
*obstinate* 606
*difficult* 704
*sullen* 901*a*
**intramural** 221
**intransient** 110
**intransigeance** 604
**intransitive** 110
**intransmutable** 110, 150
**intrap** 545
**intraregarding** 221
**intrench** 717
– on 303
**intrepid** 861
**intricate**
*confused* 59
*convoluted* 248
*difficult* 704
**intrigant**
*meddlesome* 682
*cunning* 702
*libertine* 962
**intrigue** *fascinate* 615, 897
*plot* 626
*activity* 682
*cunning* 702
*excite* 824
*interest* 829
*licentiousness* 961
**intrinsic** 5
– evidence 467
– habit 613
– truth 494
**intrinsicality** **5**
**introception** 296
**introduce** *lead* 62
*interpose* 228
*precede* 280
*insert* 300
– new blood 140
– new conditions 469
– to 888
**introduction**
[*see* introduce]
*preface* 64
*reception* 296
*drama* 599
*friendship* 888
*courtesy* 894
**introductory**
*precursor* 64
*beginning* 66
*priority* 116
**introgression** 294
**introit** 998
**intromission** 228
**intromit**
*discontinue* 142
*receive* 296
**introspection** 441, 457
**introspective** 451
**introvert** 218
**intrude**
*interfere* 24
*inopportune* 135
*intervene* 228
*enter* 294
*encroach* 303
**intruder** 57
**intrusiveness** 682
**intrust** 755, 787
**intuition** *mind* 450
*unreasoning* **477**
*knowledge* 490
**intumescence** 194, 250
**intwine** 43, 248
**inunction** 223
**inundate**
*effusion* **337**
*flow* 348
*redundance* 641
**inunderstanding** 452
**inurbanity** 895
**inure** 613, 673
**inured**
*insensible* 823
**inusitation** 614
**inutility** **645**
**invade** *ingress* 294
*encroach* 303
*attack* 716
**invalid**
*powerless* 158
*illogical* 477
*diseased* 655
*undue* 925
**invalidate**
*disable* 158
*weaken* 160
*confute* 479
**invaluable** 648
**invariable**
*intrinsic* 5
*uniform* 16
*conformable* 82
*stable* 150
**invasion**
*ingress* 294
*attack* 716
**invective** 932
**inveigh** 932
**inveigle** 545, 615
**invent**
*discover* 480*a*
*imagine* 515
*lie* 544
*devise* 626
**invented**
*untrue* 546
**invention** 480*a*
**inventive**
*skilful* 698
**inventor** 164
**inventory** 86
**inverse** 14, 218
**inversion**
*derangement* 61
*change* 140
*of position* **218**
*contraposition* 237
*reversion* 145
*language* 577
**invertebrate** 158
**invest**
*empower* 157
*clothe* 225
*besiege* 227, 716
*commission* 755
*give* 784
*lend* 787
*expend* 809
– in *locate* 184
*purchase* 795
– money 817
– with *ascribe* 155
**investigate** 461
**investment** **225**
– trust 712
make –s 673
**inveterate** *old* 124
*established* 150
*inborn* 820
– belief 484
– habit 613
**invidious**
*painful* 830
*hatred* 898
*spite* 907
*envy* 921
**invigorate**
*strengthen* **159**
**invigorating**
*healthy* 656
**invincible** 159
**inviolable**
*secret* 528
*right* 924
*honour* 939
**inviolate**
*permanent* **141**
*secret* 528
*honourable* **939**
**invious** *closed* **261**
*pathless* 704
**invisibility** **447**
**invisible** *small* **193**
*not to be seen* **447**
*concealed* 526
– ink 528
become – 4
**invitâ Minervâ 603**, 704
**invite** *induce* **615**
*offer* 763
*ask* 765
– the attention 457
**inviting**
[*see* invite]
*pleasing* 829
**invoice** 86
**invoke** *address* **586**
*implore* 765
*pray* 990
– curses 908
– saints 998
**involucrum** **223**
**involuntary**
*necessary* 601
*unwilling* 603
– servitude **749**
**involution** [*see* involve]
*algebra* 85
**involve** *include* **54**
*derange* 61
*wrap* 225
*evince* 467
*mean* 516
*latency* 526
**involved**
*disorder* 59
*convoluted* 248
*obscure style* **571**
*in debt* 806
**involvement** 704
**invulnerable** 664
**inward** *intrinsic* **5**

**itinerary** 266, 527
**itur ad astra, sic –** 360
**ivory** 430
**Ixion** 312

## J

**jab** 276
**jabber**
*unmeaning* 517
*stammer* 583
*chatter* 584
**jacent** 213
**jacet, hic –** 363
**jacinth** 847
**jack**
*rotation* 312
*ensign* 550
*instrument* 633
*money* 800
**Jack** – Cade 742
– Ketch 975
– o' lantern 423
– in office
*director* 694
*bully* 887
– at a pinch 711
– Pudding
*actor* 599
*humorist* 844
*boaster* 884
before one can say ' – Robinson' 132
– tar 269
– of all trades 700
**jack-a-dandy** 844, 854
**jackal**
*auxiliary* 711
*servility* 886
**jackanapes** 854, 887
**Jackass** 271
**jack-boot** 225
**jackdaw in peacock's feathers** 701
**jacket** 225
cork – 666
**Jacobin** 710
**Jacquerie** 716, 719
**jacta est alea** 601
**jactitation**
*tossing* 315
*boasting* 884
**jaculation** 284
**jade** *horse* 271
*fatigue* 688
*low woman* 876
*scamp* 949
*drab* 962
**jag** 257
**jagged** 244
**jail** 752
– bird
*prisoner* 754
*bad man* 949
**jailer** 753, 975
**jakes** 653
**jalousie de métier** 921
**jam** *squeeze* 43
*crowd* 72
*food* 298
*pulp* 354
*sweet* 396
*scrape* 732
– in *interpose* 228
**jamb** 215
**jamboree** 840
**jammed in** 751
**jangle**
*harsh sound* 410
*quarrel* 713
**janissary** 726
**janitor** 263
**janty** *gay* 836
*pretty* 845
*stylish* 852
*showy* 882
*insolent* 885
**January** 138
**januis clausis** 528
**Janus** *deceiver* 607
*tergiversation* 607
close the temple of – 723
**Janus-faced** 544
**japan** *coat* 223
*resin* 356*a*
*ornament* 847
**jar** *clash* 24
*vessel* 191
*agitation* 315
*stridor* 410
*discord* 713
– upon the feelings 830
**jardinière** 191
**jargon**
*absurdity* 497
*no meaning* 517
*unintelligible* 519
*neology* 563
**jarvey** 694
**jasper** 847
**jaundiced**
*yellow* 436
*prejudiced* 481
*dejected* 837
*jealous* 920
view with – eyes
*disapprove* 932
**jaunt** 266
**jaunting car** 272
**jaunty** [*see* janty]
**javelin** 727
**jaw** *chatter* 584
*scold* 932
**jaw-fallen** 837
**jaws** *mouth* 231
*eating* 298
– of death 360
**jay** 584
**jaywalker** 701
**jazz** 415, 840
– band 417
**jealous of honour** 939
**jealousy 920**
*suspicion* 485
**jecur, difficili bile –** 900
**jeer** 929
**Jehovah** 976
**Jehu** 268, 694
**jejune** *insipid* 391
*style* 575
*scanty* 640
*dull* 843
**jell** 352
**jelly** 298, 352
beat to a – 972
**jemidar** 745
**jemmy** *lever* 633
*dandy* 854
**je ne sais quoi**
*exceptional* 83
*what d'ye call 'em* 563
*beauty* 845
**jennet** 271
**jeopardy** 665
**jerboa** 309
**jeremiad**
*lament* 839
*invective* 932
**Jericho, send to –** 297
**jerk** *start* 146
*throw* 284
*pull* 285
*agitate* 315
**jerkin** 225
**jerks, by –** 70
**Jerry Sneak** 862, 941
**jersey** 225
**Jerusalem**
the new – 981
**Jessamy, Jemmy** 854
**jesse** 1000
**jest** *trifle* 643
*wit* 842
**jest-book** 842
**jester** 844
**jesting-stock** 857
**Jesuit** *deceiver* 548
*priest* 996
**jesuitical** 477, 544
**Jesus** 976
**jet** *stream* 348
– black 431
**jetsam** 73, 782
**jettison** 782
**jetty** *protection* 250
*harbour* 666
**jeu**
le – n'en vaut pas la chandelle
*waste* 638
*unimportant* 643
*dear* 814
– d'esprit 842
– de mots 842
– de théâtre 599
**jeune**
– premier 599
– veuve 599
**jewel** *gem* 648
*ornament* 847
*favourite* 899
**jewellery, false –** 545
**Jezebel** *wicked* 913
*wretch* 949
*courtesan* 962
**jib** *front* 234
*regression* 283
cut of one's –
*form* 240
*appearance* 448
**jibe** 140
**jiffy** 113
**jig** 840
**jig-saw puzzle** 840
**jilt** *disappoint* 509
*deceive* 545
*deceiver* 548
*cast off* 756
*dishonour* 940
**jilted** 898

## K

– one's promise 772
– quiet 265
– a secret 528
– a shop 625
– in sight 459
– silence 585
– straight 944
– in suspense
*uncertainty* 475
*irresolution* 605
– in the thoughts 505
– time
*punctual* 132
*music* 416
– to 604*a*
– together 709
– under
*authority* 737
*subjection* 749
*restraint* 751
– up [*see below*]
– in view
*attend to* 457
*remember* 505
*expect* 507
– waiting 133
– watch 459
– one's word 939
**keep up**
*continue* 143
*preserve* 670
*stimulate* 824
– appearances 852
– the ball 682, 840
– a correspondence 592
– the memory of 505
– one's spirits 836
– with 274
**keeper** 370, **753**
**keeping**
*congruity* 23
in – 82
safe – *safety* 664
*preservation* 670
**keepsake** 505
**keg** 191
**kelpie** 979
**kelson** 211
**kempt** 652
**ken** 441, 490
beyond mortal – 360
**kennel**
*assemblage* 72
*hovel* 189
*ditch* 259
*conduit* 350
**Kentish fire 931**
**képi** 225
**kerb-stone** 233
**kerchief** 225
wave a – 550
**kern** *quern* 330
*low fellow* 876
*varlet* 949
**kernel** *heart* **5**
*cause* 153
*central* 222
*important* 642
**kerosene** 356
**ketch**
*ship* 273
**Ketch, Jack – 975**
**kettle** *vessel* 191
*caldron* 386
– drum *music* 417
*tea-party* 892
– of fish
*disorder* 59
*difficulty* 704
**key** *cause* 153
*opener* 260
*music* 413
*colour* 428
*interpretation* 522
*indication* 550
*instrument* 631, 633
*emblem of authority* 747
deliver the –s of the city 725
**key-hole** 260
**key-note** *model* 22
*rule* 80
*music* 413
**key-stone**
*support* 215
*motive* 615
*importance* 642
*completion* 729
**khaki** 225, 433
**khan** *inn* 189
*governor* 745
**khedive** 745
**kibitka** 272
**kibitzer** 682
**kick** *impulse* 276
*recoil* 277
*assault* 716
*thrill* 821
*spurn* 930
*punish* 972
– against
*oppose* 708
*resist* 719
– against the pricks
*useless* 645
*rash* 863
*unequal* 28
*superior* 33
– up a dust
*active* 682
*discord* 713
*insolent* 885
– a row 900
– one's heels
*kept waiting* 133
*nothing to do* 681
– off 62
– up a row
*violent* 173
*discord* 713
– over the traces 742
**kicking, alive and – 359**
**kickshaw** *food* 298
*trifle* 643
**kid** *child* 129
*progeny* 167
*leather* 223
not to be handled with – gloves
*dirty* 653
*difficult* 704
**kidnap**
*deceive* 545
*take* 789
*steal* 791
**kidney** *class* 75
**kilderkin** 191
**Kilkenny cats** 713
**kill** 361
– or cure 662
– the fatted calf 883
– the goose with golden eggs 699
– with kindness 902
– the slain 641
– time 106
*inactivity* 683
*amusement* 840
– two birds with one stone 682
**killing 361**
*delightful* 829
**kill-joy** 706
**kiln** 386
**kilowatt** 466
**kilt** 225
**kimbo** 244
**kimono** 225
**kin** 75
**kind** *class* 75
*benevolent* 906
– regards 894
**kinder-garten 542**
**kindle** *cause* 153
*produce* 161
*quicken* 171
*inflame* 173
*set fire to* 384
*excite* 824
*incense* 900
**kindling wood 388**
**kindred** 9, 11
**kine** 366
**kinematics** 264
**kinetic energy 157**
**king** 745
every inch a –
*authority* 737
*rank* 875
–maker 694
**King –'s Bench** 752, 966
–'s birthday 268
–'s counsel 968
– Death 360
–'s English **560**
–'s evidence 529
–'s highway 627
–'s ransom 648
– of Kings 976
**kingcraft** 693
**kingdom**
*region* 181
*property* 780
– of heaven **981**
**kingly** 737
**king-post** 215
**kink** 248, 378, **608**
**kiosk** 189, 1000
**kip** 961
**kirk** 1000
**kirtle** 225
**kismet** 601
**kiss** *touch* 199
*courtesy* 894
*endearment* 902
– the book 535
– the hem of one's garment 928
– in the ring 840
– the rod 725
**kit** *class* 75
*equipment* 191
*fiddle* 417
–bag 191
**kitcat** 556
**kitchen** 191, 691
– maid 746
– range 386
**kitchener** 386
**kitchenette** 691
**kite** *fly* 273

*bill* 800
fly a – *credit* 805
*insolvency* 808
– balloon 273, 726
**kith** 11
**kithless** 87
**kitten** *animal* 366
*young* 129
*bring forth* 161
playful as a – 836, 840
**kleptomania**
*insanity* 503
*stealing* 791
*desire* 865
**kleptomaniac** 504
**knack** 698
get into the – 613
**knacker** 361
**knag** 706
**knaggy** 901*a*
**knap** 206
**knapsack** 191
**knave** 548, **941**
– of hearts 897
**knavery**
*deception* 545
*cunning* 702
*improbity* 940
*vice* 945
**knead** *mix* 41
*mould* 240
*soften* 324
*stroke* 379
**knee** *angle* 244
bend the –
*stoop* 308
*submission* 725
down on one's –s
*humble* 879
on one's –s
*beg* 765
*respect* 928
*atone* 952
on the –s of the gods 121, 152
**knee-deep** 208, 209
**kneel** *stoop* 308
*submit* 725
*beg* 765
*servility* 886
*courtesy* 894
*ask mercy* 914
*respect* 928
*worship* 990
**knell** 363
strike the death – 361
**knickerbockers** 225
**knicknack** 643, 847
**knife** 253
play a good – and fork *eat* 298
*appetite* 865
war to the – 708
**knight** 875
– errant
*madman* 504
*defender* 717
*rash* 863
*philanthropist* 910
–'s move 279
– service 777
– of the road 792
– Templar 712
**knit** 43
well – 159
– the brow
*discontent* 832
*anger* 900
*disapprobation* 932
**knitting** 847
**knob** *pendency* 214
*ball* 249
*protuberance* 250
**knock** *blow* 276
*sound* 406
hard –s 720
– at the door
*death* 360
*request* 765
– down
*destroy* 162
*lay flat* 213
*lower* 308
*injure* 659
*dishearten* 837
– on the head
*kill* 361
– one's head against 699
– off *complete* 729
– out 162
– over 162
– under 725
– up 688
**knock-down argument** 479
**knocked**
– to atoms 162
– on the head
*failure* 732
**knocker** 936
**knock-kneed** 243, 244
**knoll** 206
**knot** *ligature* 45
*entanglement* 59
*group* 72
*intersection* 219
*round* 249
*dense* 321
*difficulty* 704
*hindrance* 706
*junto* 712
*ornament* 847
*marriage* 903
true lover's – *love* 897
*endearment* 902
tie the nuptial – 903
**knotted** *rough* 256
**knout** 975
**know** *believe* 484
*knowledge* 490
*friendly* 888
*associate* 892
I'd have you to – 457, 535
not that one –s 491
– what one is about 698
– all 474
I – better 536
– no bounds
*great* 31
*infinite* 105
*redundance* 641
– for certain 484
– by heart 505
– one's own mind 604
– one's stuff 465
– one's way about 465
– nothing of 491
– what's what 698
– which is which 465
**knowing** 702
**knowingly** 620
**knowledge** **490**
[*and see* know]
acquire – 539
come to one's – 527
practical – 698
– of the world 698
**known:**
become – 529
make – *inform* 527
*publish* 531
well – 490
*habitual* 613
– as 564
– by 550
**knuckle** 244
– down 725
**knuckle-duster** 727
**knurl** 256
**knurr and spell 840**
**kobold** 980
**Koh-i-noor** 650
**kopje** 206
**Koran** 986
**kotow** *bow* 308
*submission* **725**
*courtesy* 894
*respect* 928
**kraal** 189, 232
**kraken** 83
**kris** 727
**Krishna** 979
**kudos** 931
**Ku klux klan 712**
**Kursaal** 840
**kyanize** 670
**kyles** 343

## L

**laager** 717
**labarum** 550
**labefy** 659
**label** 39, 550
**labent** 306
**labial** *lip* 231
*letter* 561
**labitur et labetur** 112, 143
**labor hoc opus, hic** – 704
**laboratory** 691
**laborious**
*active* 682
*exertion* 686
*difficult* 704
**labour**
*parturition* **161**
*work* 680
*exertion* 686
hard –
*punishment* **972**
mountain in – **638**
– for 620
– of love
*willing* 602
*amusement* 840
*disinterested* **942**
– party 712
– under *state* **7**
*disease* 655
*difficulty* 704
*feeling* 821
*affliction* 828
– in vain
*fall short* 304
*useless* 645
– in one's voca-

tion 625
– unrest 832
**laboured** - *style* 579
*prepared* 673
– study 457
**labourer** 690
**labouring**
– man 690
– oar 686
**labyrinth**
*disorder* 59
*convolution* 248
*secret* 533
**lac** *number* 98
*resin* 356a
– of rupees 800
**lace** *stitch* 43
*netting* 219
*ornament* 847
– one's jacket 972
**lacerable** 328
**lacerate** 44
– the heart 830
**laches** 460, 773
**Lachesis** 601
**lachrymæ, hinc illæ** – 830
**lachrymatory gas** 727
**lachrymis, quis temperet a** – 914
**lachrymose** 837
**lack** *require* 630
*insufficient* 640
*destitute* 804
*desire* 865
– faith 989
– harmony 708
– preparation 674
– wit 501
**lackadaisical**
*inactive* 683
*melancholy* 837
*indifferent* 866
**lackadaisy!** 839, 870
**lack-brain** 499, 501
**lacker** [*see* lacquer]
**lackey** 746
**lack-lustre** 422, 429
**laconic** 572
**lacquer**
*covering* 223
*resin* 356a
*adorn* 847
**lacrosse** 840
**lacteal** 352
**lacuna** 198, 252
**lacustrine** 343
**lad** 129
**ladder** 305, 627
kick down the – 604
**lade** *load* 184
*transfer* 185
*contents* 190
*dip* 270
– out 297
**laden** 52
heavy – 828
– with 777
**ladies' man** 897
**lading** 190, 780
bill of – *list* 86
**ladle** *receptacle* 191
*transfer* 270
*vehicle* 272
**lady** *woman* 374
*rank* 875
*wife* 903
our – 977
– day 138
– help 746
–'s maid 746
**lady chapel** 1000
**ladylike**
*womanly* 374
*fashionable* 852
**lady-love** 897
**lag** *linger* 275
*follow* 281
*dawdle* 683
– behind 133
**laggard** 603, 683
**lager** *beer* 298
**lagoon** 343
**laical** 997
**laid:** – on one's back 158
– by the heels 751
– low 160
– up 655
**lair** 189, 653
**laird** *master* 745
*proprietor* 779
*nobility* 875
**Lais** 962
**laisse manger, cela se** – 394
**laisser:** – aller, – faire
*permanence* 141
*neglect* 460
*inaction* 681
*laxity* 738
*freedom* 748
*inexcitable* 826
**laity** **997**
**lake** *water* **343**
*pink* 434
– of fire and brimstone 982
**Lama** 745, 99
**Lamaism** 984
**Lamarkism** 357
**lamb** *infant* 129
*animal* 366
*gentle* 826
*innocent* 946
go out like a – 174
lion lies down with – 721
**Lamb of God** 976
**lambent**
*touching* 379
– flame *heat* 382
*light* 420
**Lambeth** 1000
**lame** *incomplete* 53
*impotent* 158
*weak* 160
*imperfect* 651
*disease* 655
*injury* 659
*failing* 732
– conclusion
*illogical* 477
*failure* 732
help a – dog over a stile *aid* 707
*vindicate* 937
– duck 808
– excuse 617
**lamellar** 204
**lamentable** *bad* 649
*painful* 830
*sad* 837
**lamentably** *very* 31
**lamentation** **839**
**lamia** 980, 994
**lamina** 51, 204
**lamination** 204
**Lammas** 998
**lamp** 423
rub the – 992
safety – 666
smell of the –
*style* 577
*prepared* 673
**lamplighter**
*quick* 682
**lampoon** 932, 934
**lampooner** 936
**lanâ caprinâ, de** – 643
**lanary** 636
**lanate** 255, 256
**lance** *pierce* 260
*throw* 284
*spear* 727
break a – with
*attack* 716
*warfare* 722
couch one's – **720**
– corporal 745
**lancer** 726
–'s *dance* 840
**lancet** 253, 262
**lancinate** 378, 830
**land** *arrive* 292
*ground* **342**
*estate* 780
gone to a better – 360
hug the – 286
make the – 286
on – 342
see – 858
– covered with water 343
– flowing with milk and honey 168
how the – lies
*circumstances* 8
*experiment* 463
*foresight* 510
in the – of the living 359
**landamman** **745**
**landau** 272
**landed**
– gentry 779
– estate 780
**landgrave** 745
**landholder** 779
**landing field** 273
**landing-place** 215, 292
**landlady** 779
**land-locked** 229, 343
**landloper** 268
**landlord** 779
**land-lubber** 343, 701
**landmark**
*limit* 233
*indication* 550
**land-mine** 727
**landreeve** 694
**landscape**
*prospect* 448
– gardening
*agriculture* 371
*beauty* 845
– painting 556
– painter 559
**land-shark** 792
**land-slip** 306
**landsman** 342
**Landsturm** 726
**land-surveying** 466
**Landwehr** 726

*pioneer* 64
*influence* 175
*tend* 176
*soundings* 208
- *in motion* 280
*heavy* 319
*rôle* 599
*induce* 615
*direct* 693
*authority* 737
heave the – 466
red – 434
take the –
*influence* 175
*importance* 642
*authority* 737
white – 430
– to the altar 903
– astray 495
– captive
*subject* 749
*restraint* 751
– a merry chase 623
– the choir 990
– a dance
*run away* 623
*circuit* 629
*difficulty* 704
*disrespect* 929
– the dance 280
– one to expect 511
– a life 692
– on 693
– to no end 645
– by the nose 737
– off 62
– the way
*precedence* 62
*begin* 66
*precession* 280
*importance* 642
*direction* 693
*repute* 873
**leaden** *dim* 422
*colourless* 429
*grey* 432
*inactive* 683
**leader**
*precursor* 64
*dissertation* 595
*director* 694
*counsel* 968
– writer 595
**leading**
*beginning* 66
*important* 642
– article 595
– lady 599
– note *music* 413
– part 175
– question 461
– seaman 745
– strings
*childhood* 127
*child* 129
*pupil* 541
*subject* 749
*restraint* 751, 752
**leads** 223
**leaf** *part* 51
*layer* 204
*plant* 367
- *of a book* 593
turn over a new – 658
– green 435
**leafless** 226
**leaflet** 531
**leafy** 256
**league** *length* 200
*co-operation* 709
*party* 712
– of Nations 696
**leak** *crack* 198
*dribble* 295
*waste* 638
spring a –
*injury* 659
– out
*disclosure* 529
**leaky** *imperfect* 651
**leal** 743
**lean** *thin* 203
*oblique* 217
– on 215
– to *shed* 191
*willing* 602
– towards 923
– upon *belief* 484
*subjection* 749
*hope* 858
**leaning**
*tendency* 176
*willingness* 602
*desire* 865
*friendship* 888
*favouritism* 923
**leap**
*sudden change* 146
*ascent* 305
*jump* **309**
–s and bounds 274
make a – at 622
– in the dark
*experiment* 463
*uncertain* 475
*chance* 621
*rash* 863
– with joy 838
– year 138
**leap-frog** 840
**learn** 490, 539
– by experience 950
– by heart 505
**learned** 490
**learner** **541**
**learning** 490, **539**
**lease** *property* 780
*lending* 787
grant a – 771
take a new – of life 654
– and release 783
**leasehold** 780
**leash** *lie* 43
*three* 92
hold in – 751
**least**
– *in quantity* 34
– *in size* 193
at the – 32
**leather** *skin* 223
*tough* 327
*beat* 972
nothing like – 481
– bottle 191
– or prunello 643
**leave** *remainder* 40
*part company* 44
*relinquish* 624
*permission* 760
*bequeathe* 784
French – 623
take – *depart* 293
*freedom* 748
– alone
*inaction* 681
*freedom* 748
*permit* 760
– the beaten track 83
– to chance 621
– an inference 526
– a loophole 705
– in the lurch
*pass* 303
*decisive* 545
– no trace
*be no more* 2
*disappear* 449
*obliterate* 552
– it to one 760
– to oneself 748
– off *cease* 142
*desuetude* 614
*relinquish* 624
*disuse* 678
– out 55
– out of one's calculation **460**
– a place 293
– ad referendum 605
give me – to say 535
– undecided **609a**
– undone 730
– a void *regret* **839**
– word 527
**leaven**
*component* 56
*cause* 153
*lighten* 320
*qualify* 469
*unclean* 653
*deterioration* **659**
*bane* 663
**leavings**
*remainder* **40**
*useless* 645
**lecher** 962
**lechery** 961
**lectern** 1000
**lection** *special* 79
*interpretation* **522**
**lectionary** 998
**lecture** *teach* 537
*speak* 582
*dissertation* 595
*censure* 932
*sermon* 998
– room 542
**lecturer**
*teacher* 540
*preacher* 996
**lectureship** 542
**led** – captain
*follower* 746
*servile* 886
*favourite* 899
– by the nose **749**
**ledge** *height* 206
*horizontal* 213
*shelf* 215
*projection* 250
**ledger** *list* 86
*record* 551
*accounts* 811
**lee** 236
**leech** 662, 695
**leef** 829
**leek** eat the –
*recant* 607
*submit* 725
**Lee-Metford**
*rifle* 727
**leer** *stare* 441
*dumb-show* **550**
**leery** 702, 864
**lees** 653

**lee-shore** 665, 667
**leet, court** – 966
**lee-wall** 666
**leeward** 236
**lee-way** *space* 180
*tardy* 133
*navigation* 267
*deviation* 279
*progression* 282
*shortcoming* 304
**left** *residuary* 40
*sinistral* 239
over the – 545
– alone 748
– in the lurch 732
– to shift for oneself 893
pay over the – shoulder 808
**left-handed**
*clumsy* 699
– compliment 932
– marriage 903
**leg** *support* 215
*walker* 266
*thief* 792
best – foremost 686
fast as –s will carry 274
have a – to stand on 470
keep on one's –s 654
last –s *spoiled* 659
*fatigue* 688
light on one's –s 734
make a – 894
not a – to stand on
*illogical* 477
*confuted* 479
*failure* 732
off one's –s
*propulsion* 284
on one's –s
*upright* 212
*elevation* 307
*speaking* 582
*in health* 654
*active* 682
*free* 748
set on one's –s 660
– bail 623
**legacy** 270, 780, 784
**legal** *permitted* 760
*legitimate* 924
*relating to law* 963
– adviser 968
– estate 780
**legality** **963**
**legate** 534
**legatee** 779, 785
**legation** 755
**legato** 415
**legend** 551, 594
**legendary**
*imaginary* 515
**legerdemain** 146, 545
**légèreté** 605
**leggings** 225
**leghorn hat** 225
**legible** 518
– hand 590
**legion**
*multitude* 102
*army* 726
**legionary** 726
**legislation** 693, 963
**legislative assembly** 696
**legislator** 694
**legislature** 693, 696
**legist** 968
**legitimate** *true* 494
*permitted* 760
*right* 922
*due* 924
*legal* 963
**legume** **367**
**lei** 847
**leisure** **685**
at one's – *late* 133
**leisurely** 275
**leman** 897
**lemma** 476
**lemon** *colour* 436
**Lemprière** 979
**lemures** 980
**lend** 787
– aid 707
– countenance **707**
– a hand 680
– oneself to
*assent* 488
*co-operate* 709
– on security 789
– wings to 707
**lender** *creditor* 805
**lending** **787**
**length** **200**
go all –s
*resolution* 604
*activity* 682
*exertion* 686
at – *in time* 133
full – *portrait* 556
go great –s 549
– and breadth of 50
– and breadth of the land
*space* 180
*publication* 531
– of time 110
**lengthen** 35, 200
– out
*diuturnity* 110
*late* 133
**lengthwise** 200
**lengthy** *long* 200
*diffuse* 573
**lenient**
*moderate* **174**
*mild* 740
*compassionate* 914
**lenify** 174
**lenitive**
*moderating* 174
*remedy* 662
*relieving* 834
**lenity** **740**
**lens** 445
**Lent** 956, 998
**lenten** 956
**lenticular** 245, 250
**lentor** *slowness* 275
*spissitude* 352
*inactivity* 683
**lentous** 352
**leonem, ex ungue** – 550
**leonine verses** 597
**leopard**
*variegated* 440
–'s spots
*unchanging* 150
**leprechaune** 980
**leprosy** 655
**lerret** 273
**lèse-majesté** 742
**less** *inferior* 34
*subduction* 38
– than no time 113
**lessee**
*possessor* **779**
*receiver* 785
**lessen**
– in quantity or degree 36
– in size 195
– an evil 658
**lesson** *teaching* 537
*warning* 668
give a – to
*punish* 972
read a – to
*censure* 932
say one's –
*memory* **505**
**lessor** 805
**lest** 623
**let** *hindrance* **706**
*permit* 760
*lease* 771
*lend* 787
*sell* 796
apartments to –
*fool* 499
to – 763
– alone *besides* **37**
*permanence* 141
*quiescence* 265
*avoid* 623
*disuse* 678
*inaction* 681
*not complete* **730**
*free* 748
– be
*permanence* 141
*continuance* **143**
*inaction* 681
– blood 297
– 'I dare not' wait upon 'I would' 605
– down
*depress* 308
*humble* 879
– down easily
*forgive* 918
– fall *drop* 308
*inform* 527
*speak* 582
– fly *violence* **173**
*propel* 284
– fly at 716
– go *neglect* 460
*liberate* 750
*relinquish* 782
*restitution* 790
– in *interpose* 228
*admit* 296
*trick* 545
– into *inform* **490**
*disclose* 529
– one know **527**
– off *violent* 173
*propel* 284
*permit* 760
*forgive* 918
*exempt* 927*a*
*acquit* 970
– out *disperse* **73**
*lengthen* 200
*eject* 297
*disclose* 529
*liberate* 750
– out at 716
– pass 460

*freedom* 748
*inexcitability* 826
– in the memory 505
– upon nothing 819
– on 298
– separately 905
– by one's wits 545
livelihood 803
livelong 110
lively *keen* 375
- *style* 574
*active* 682
*acute* 821
*sensitive* 822
*sprightly* 836
– imagination 515
– pace 274
liver 83; hard – 954*a*
white – 862
liver-coloured 433
livery *suit* 225
*colour* 428
*badge* 550
*decoration* 877
– servant 746
liveryman 748
live wire 171
livid *dark* 431
*grey* 432
*purple* 437
living *life* 359
*business* 625
*benefice* 995
good – 957
– beings 357
–room 191
– soul 372
– thing 366
livraison 593
livret 593
lixiviate 335, 652
lixivium 335
llama 271
lo! 457, 870
load *quantity* 31
*fill* 52
*lade* 184
*cargo* 190
*weight* 319
*store* 636
*redundance* 641
*hindrance* 706
*adversity* 735
*anxiety* 828
*oppress* 830
prime and – 673
take off a – of care 834
– the memory 505
– with 706
– with reproaches 932
loads 102
loadstar 288, 350, 693
loadstone 288, 615
loaf *mass* 192
*do nothing* 681
*dawdle* 683
loafer
*stroller* 268
*inactive* 683
*neglect* 927
*bad man* 949
loam 342
loan 787
loathe 867, 898
loathing
[*see* loathe]
*weariness* 841
*hate* 898
loathsome
*unsavoury* 395
*painful* 830
*dislike* 867
loaves and fishes
*prosperity* 734
*acquisition* 775
*wealth* 803
Lob's pound, in – 751
lobby 191, 615, 627
lobbying 615
lobe 51
local
– habitation 184, 189
– board 966
locale 183
locality 182, 183
localize 184
location 184
loch 343
loci, genius – 664
lock *fasten* 43
*fastening* 45
*tuft* 256
*canal* 350
*hindrance* 706
*prison* 752
dead – 265
in the –up 938
under – and key
*safe* 664
*restraint* 751
*prisoner* 754
– hospital 662
–out 55, 719
– the stable door
*too late* 135
*useless* 645
*unskilful* 699
–, stock and barrel 50
– up *hide* 528
*imprison* 751
locker 191
locket 847
lock-up *prison* 752
loco, in –
*agreeing* 23
*situation* 183
*expedience* 646
locofoco 388
locomotion 264
– by air 267
– by land 266
– by water 267
locomotive 266, 271
locular 191
locum tenens
*substitute* 147
*inhabitant* 188
*deputy* 759
locus:
– pœnitentiæ 937
– standi
*support* 215
*plea* 617
*social rank* 873
locust *prodigal* 818
*evil-doer* 913
swarm like –s 102
locution 582
lode 636
lodestar
*attraction* 288
*indication* 550
*direction* 693
lodestone 288, 615
lodge *place* 184
*presence* 186
*dwelling* 189
– a complaint 938
lodgement 184
lodger
*inhabitant* 188
*possessor* 779
lodging 189
loft 191, 210
lofty *high* 206
- *style* 574
*proud* 878
*insolent* 885
*magnanimous* 942
log *velocity* 274
*fuel* 388
*record* 551
heave the – 466
sleep like a – 683
logarithm 84
loggerhead 501
at –s *discord* 713
*contention* 720
*enmity* 889
loggia 191
logic 476
– of facts 467
logician 476
logical acuteness 570
logography 590
logogryph 533
logolept 562
logomachy
*discussion* 476
*words* 588
*dispute* 720
logometer 85
logometric 84
log-rolling 709
loin 235, 236
gird up one's –s
*strong* 159
*prepare* 673
– cloth 225
loisir, impromptu fait à – 673
loiter *tardy* 133
*slow* 275
*inactive* 683
loll *sprawl* 213
*recline* 215
*inactive* 683
lollipop 396
lollop 683
Lombard Street to a China orange 472
lone 87
lonesome 893
long - *in time* 110
- *in space* 200
*diffuse* 573
go to one's – account 360
– ago 122
make a – arm
*exertion* 686
*seize* 789
–boat 273
draw the – bow 549
take a – breath
*refreshment* 689
*relief* 834
– clothes 129
– drawn out 573
– duration 110
–expected 507

– face 832, 837
– for 865
–headed *wise* 498
– life to *glory* 873
*approval* 931
–lived 110
– odds *chance* 156
*improbability* 473
*difficulty* 704
– pending 110
– primer 591
– pull and strong pull 285
– range 196
– robe 968
– run *average* 29
*whole* 50
*destiny* 152
– sea 348
– and the short
*whole* 50
*concise* 572
–sighted
*dim-sighted* 443
*wise* 498
*foresight* 510
– since 122
– spun 573
– standing
*diuturnal* 110
*old* 124
–suffering
*lenient* 740
*inexcitable* 826
*pity* 914
– time 110
–winded 573
**longanimity**
*inexcitable* 826
*forgiving* 918
**longevity** 110, 128
**longhead** 500
**longing** 865
– lingering look behind 833
**longinquity** 196
**longitude**
*situation* 183
*length* 200
*measurement* 466
**longitudinal** 200
**longo intervallo**
*discontinuity* 70
*diuturnity* 110
*distance* 196
*interval* 198
**longshore-man**
*waterman* 269
*plebeian* 876
**longways** 217
**loo** 840

**looby** *fool* 501
*bungler* 701
*clown* 876
**look** *small degree* 32
*see* 441
*appearance* 448
*attend to* 457
– about 459, 461
– after 459, 693
– ahead 510
– alive 457, 684
– another way 442
– back 122
– beyond 510
– black *or* blue
*feeling* 821
*discontent* 832
*dejection* 837
– down upon 930
– in the face
*sincerity* 703
*courage* 861
*pride* 878
– foolish 874
– for 461, 507
– forwards 121, 510
– here 457
– into 457, 461
– before one leaps 864
– like 17, 448
– on 186
– out *view* 448
*attention* 457
*care* 459
*seek* 461
*expect* 507
*intention* 620
*business* 625
*danger* 665
*warning* 668
*caution* 864
– over *examine* 461
– round *seek* 461
– sharp 682
– to 459, 926
– through 461
– up *prosper* 734
*high price* 814
*hope* 858
*visit* 892
– up to *repute* 873
*respect* 928
*approbation* 931
– upon as 480, 484
**looker-on** 444
**looking-glass** 445
**loom** *destiny* 152
*dim* 422

*dim sight* 443
*come in sight* 446
*weave* 691
– of the land 342
– up 31
**loon** *fool* 501
*clown* 876
*rascal* 949
**loop** 245, 247, 629
– the loop 245
**loop-hole**
*opening* 260
*vista* 441
*plea* 617
*device* 626
*escape* 671
*fortification* 717
**loose** *detach* 44
*incoherent* 47
*pendent* 214
*desultory* 279
*illogical* 477
*vague* 519
– *style* 575
*lax* 738
*free* 748
*liberate* 750
*debauched* 961
give a – to
- *imagination* 515
*laxity* 738
*permit* 760
*indulgence* 954
let – 750
on the – 961
screw – 713
– character 961
at a – end 685
– fish 949, 962
– morals 945
– rein 738
– suggestion 514
– thread 495
*leave a* - 460
*take up a* - 664
**loosen** 47, 750
**loot** 791, 793
**lop** 201
– and top 371
**lopped**
*incomplete* 53
**loppet** 699
**lop-eared** 53
**lop-sided** 28
**loquacity** 584
**loquendi**
cacoëthes – 584
jus et norma – 567
usus – 582
**lorcha** 273
**Lord, lord**

*ruler* 745
*nobleman* 875
*God* 976
O – *worship* 990
– Chancellor 967
– of the creation 372
–'s day 687
–s Justices 966, 967
the – knows 491
– lieutenant 965
– of Lords 976
– of the manor 779
– it over 737, 885
–'s prayer 990
–'s supper 998
–'s table 1000
**lordling** 875
**lordly** 873, 878
**Lord Mayor** 745, 965
–'s show 883
**lordship**
*authority* 737
*property* 780
*title* 877
*judge* 967
**lore** 490, 539
**Lorelei** 980
**lorette** 962
**lorgnette** 445
**lorication**
*armour* 717
**loricated**
*clothed* 223
**lorn** 893
**lorry** 272
**lose** *forget* 506
*unintelligible* 519
*fail* 732
*loss* 776
no time to – 684
– one's balance 732
– breath 688
– caste 874, 940
– the clew 475, 519
– colour 429
– one's cunning 699
– the day 732
– flesh 195
– ground
*slow* 275
*regression* 283
*shortcoming* 304
– one's head
*bewildered* 475

– heart 837
– one's heart 897
– hope 859
– interest in 624
– labour 732
– one's life 360
– no time 682, 684
– oneself 475
– an opportunity 135
– one's reason 503
– sight of
*blind* 442
*disappear* 449
*neglect* 460
*oblivion* 506
*not complete* 730
– one's temper 900
– time 683
– one's way
*wander* 279
*uncertainty* 475
*unskilful* 699
*difficulty* 704
**losel** 818
**losing game** 732, 735
**loss** *decrement* 40*a*
*death* 360
*evil* 619
*deterioration* 659
*privation* **776**
at a –
*uncertain* 475
at a – for
*desiring* 865
– of fortune 804
– of health 655
– of life 360
– of right 925
– of strength 160
**lost** *non-existing* 2
*absent* 187
*invisible* 449
*abstracted* 458
*uncertain* 475
*failure* 732
*loss* 776
*over-excited* 824
*pain* 828
*dejection* 837
*impenitent* 951
– in admiration 931
– in astonishment 870
– in iniquity 945
– labour 645
– to shame
*insolent* 885
*improbity* 940
*bad man* 949
– to sight 449
– in thought 458
– to virtue 945
**lot** *state* 7
*quantity* 25
*group* 72
*multitude* 102
*necessity* 601
*chance* 621
*sufficient* 639
*allotment* 786
be one's – 151
cast –s 621
cast in one's – with 609, 709
fall to one's – 156
in –s 51
where one's – is cast 189
**loth** 603, 867
**Lothario** 897, 962
**lotion** *liquid* 337
*clean* 652
*remedy* 662
**loto** 840
**lottery** 156, 840
put into a – 621
**lotus-eater** 683
**loud** 404, 525
*vulgar* 851
**lough** 343
**lounge** 191, 683
– suit 225
**loup**
hurler avec les –s 714
–garou 980
**louse** 653
**lout** 501, 701, 876
**louvre** 351
**lovable** 897
**love** *desire* 865
*courtesy* 894
*affection* **897**
*favourite* 899
abode of – 897
labour of –
*willing* 602
*inexpensive* 815
*amusement* 840
*disinterested* 942
God's – 906
make – 902
no – lost 713
– affair 897
– of country 910
– lock 256
not for – or money 640, 814
**love-knot** *token* 550
**love-lorn** 898
**lovely** 845, 897
**love-making** 902
**love-pot** 959
**love-potion** 865
**lover** [*see* love]
**love-sick** 897, 902
**love-story** 897, 902
**love-token** 897, 902
**loving-cup** 892, 894
**loving-kindness** 906
**low** *small* 32
*not high* 207
- *sound* 405
*moo* 412
*vulgar* 851
*disreputable* 874
*common* 876
*base* 940
bring – 308
– condition 876
– comedy 599
at a – ebb
*small* 32
*inferior* 34
*depressed* 308
*waste* 638
*deteriorated* 659
– fellow 876
– life 851
– note 408
– origin 876
– price 815
– spirits 837
– tide 207
– tone *black* 431
*mutter* 581
– water *low* 207
*dry* 340
*insufficient* 640
*poor* 804
**low-born** 876
**low-brow** 491
**low-lands** 207
**low-minded** 876, 940
**lower** *inferior* 34
*decrease* 36
*overhang* 214
*depress* 308
*dark* 421
*dim* 422
*predict* 511
*sad* 837
*irate* 900
*sulky* 901*a*
– one's flag 725
– one's note 879
– orders 876
**lowering** 668, 859
**lowly** 879
**lown** 501, **949**
**lowness** [*see* **low**] **207**
*humility* **879**
**loy** 272
**loyal** *obedient* **743**
*observant* 772
*honourable* 939
**lozenge** 244, 662
**L. s. d.** 800
**lubbard** [*see* **lubber**]
**lubber** 683, 701
**lubberly** 192, 699
**lubricant** 332
**lubrication** 255, **332**
**lubricity**
*slippery* 255
*unctuous* 355
*impure* 961
**lucent** 420
**lucid**
*luminous* 420
*transparent* 425
*intelligible* 518
- *style* 570
– interval 502
**lucidus ordo** 58
**lucifer** 388
**Lucifer** 423, 978
**lucimeter** 445
**luck** *chance* 156, 621
*prosperity* 734
good – 858
**luckless** 735
**lucky** 134, 734
**lucrative** 775
**lucre** 775, 803
**Lucretia** 960
**luctation** 720
**lucubration** 451
**luculent** 420
**lucus a non lucendo** 18, 565
**lud! O** – 839
**ludibrious** 840
**ludicrous** 853
**luff** 267
**lug** *pull* 285
*ear* 418
**luge** 272
**luggage** 270, **780**
– van 272
**lugger** 273
**lugubrious** 837
**lukewarm**
*temperate* 382
*irresolute* 605
*torpid* 823
*indifferent* 866
**lull** *cessation* 142

*mitigate* 174
*silence* 403
– to sleep 265
lullaby
*moderate* 174
*song* 415
*verses* 597
*inactivity* 683
*relief* 834
lumbago 378
lumbar 235
lumber *disorder* 59
*slow* 275
*store* 636
*useless* 645
*hindrance* 706
lumbering 647, 846
lumber-room 191
lumbriciform 249
luminary *star* 318
*light* 423
*sage* 500
luminescence 420
luminous *light* 420
*intelligible* 518
– paint 423
lump *whole* 50
*chief part* 51
*amass* 72
*mass* 192
*projection* 250
*weight* 319
*density* 321
in the – 50
– of affectation 855
– sum 800
– together *join* 43
*combine* 48
*assemble* 72
lumpish [*see* lump]
*inactive* 683
*ugly* 846
Luna 318
lunacy 503
lunar 318
– caustic 384
lunatic 503, 504
luncheon 298
lune avec les dents, prendre la – 158, 471
lunette 717
lunge 276, 716
lungs *wind* 349
*loudness* 404
*shout* 411
*voice* 580
luniform &c. 245
lupanar 961
lurch *incline* 217
*sink* 306
*oscillation* 314
*failure* 732
leave in the –
*outstrip* 303
*deceive* 545
*relinquish* 624
left in the –
*defeated* 732
lure *attraction* 288, 865
*deceive* 545
*entice* 615
lurid *dark* 421
*dim* 422
*red* 434
lurk *unseen* 447
*latent* 526
*hidden* 528
lurking-place 530
luscious 394, 829
lush *vegetation* 365
*drunkenness* 959
lushy 959
lusk 683
lusory 840
lust 865, 961
– after 921
lustily 404, 686
cry out – 839
lustless 158
lustration 652, 952
lustre
*brightness* 420
*chandelier* 423
*glory* 873
lustrum 108
lusty 159, 192
lusus naturæ 83
lute *cement* 45, 46
*guitar* 417
luteous 436
Lutheran 984
luxation 44
luxuriant 168, 639
luxuriate in 377, 827
luxurious
*pleasant* 377
*delightful* 829
*intemperate* 954
luxury
*physical* - 377
*redundance* 641
*enjoyment* 827
*sensuality* 954
lycanthropy 503
Lyceum 542
Lydford law 964
Lydian measure 415
lyddite 727
lying
*decumbent* 213
*deceptive* 544
*faithless* 986
Ly-king 986
lymph *fluid* 333
*water* 337
*transparent* 425
lymphatic 337
lynch 972
– law 964
lyncher 975
lynching 361
lynx-eyed 441, 498
lyre 417
lyric 415
– poetry 597
lyrist 597

## M

Mab 979
macadamize 255, 635
Macaire, Robert – 792
macaroni 854
macaronic
*absurdity* 497
*neology* 563
*verses* 597
Macchiavel [*see* Machiavellism]
mace
*weapon* 727
*sceptre* 747
mace-bearer 965
maceration
*saturation* 337
*atonement* 952
*asceticism* 955
*rite* 998
Macheath 792
Machiavellism
*falsehood* 544
*cunning* 702
*dishonesty* 940
machicolation 257, 717
machination
*trick* 545
*plan* 626
*cunning* 702
–s of the devil 619
machinator 626
machine 633
like a – 698
– gun 407, 727
be a mere – 749
machinist
*theatrical* - 599
*workman* 690
macilent 203
mackerel
*mottled* 440
*procuress* 962
– sky 349, 353
mackintosh 225
macrobiotic 110
macrocosm 318
macrography 441
macrology 577
Mac Sycophant, Sir Pertinax - 886, 935
mactation 991
macte virtute 931
macula 848
maculate
*unclean* 653
maculation 440, 848
mad *insane* 503
*excited* 824
drive one – 900
go – 825
– after 865
– with rage 900
madam 374
mad-brained 503
madcap
*violent* 173
*lunatic* 504
*excitable* 825
*buffoon* 844
*rash* 863
madder *colour* 434
made
– to one's hand 673
– man 734
– to order 673
madefaction 339
madman 504
Madonna
*good* 948
*angel* 977
*pious* 987
madrigal *musi.* 415
*verses* 597
Mæcenas 492, 800
maelstrom
*whirl* 312
*water* 348
*pitfall* 667
maestro 415
maffick 883
magazine
*periodical* 531
*record* 551
*book* 593

**marquetry** 440
**marquis** 875
**marriage 903**
companionate – 903
ill-assorted – 903
– bells 836
– portion 780
**marriageable** 131, 903
**marrow** *essence* 5
*interior* 221
*central* 222
chill to the – 385
**marrow-bones, on one's –**
*submit* 725
*beg* 765
*humble* 879
*servile* 886
*atonement* 952
**marrowless** 158
**marry** *combine* 48
*assertion* 535
*wed* 903
– come up
*defiance* 715
*anger* 900
*censure* 932
**Mars** 722, 979
– orange 439
**marsh 345**
**marshal**
*arrange* 60
*messenger* 534
*auxiliary* 711
*officer* 745
**Marshalsea** 752
**marsupial** 191, 366
**mart** 799
**Marte, suo –**
*exertion* 686
*skill* 698
**martello tower** 717
**martial** 722
court– 966
– law 737, 739
*compulsory* 744
*illegal* 964
– music 415
**martinet** 739
**martingale** 752
**Martinmas** 998
**martyr**
*bodily pain* 378
*mental pain* 828
*ascetic* 955
– to disease 655
**martyrdom**
*killing* 361
*agony* 378, 828
*unselfish* 942
*punishment* 972
**marvel** 870, 872
– whether 514
**marvellous** 31, 870
deal in the – 549
**Masaniello** 742
**mascaro** 847
**mascot** 993
**masculine** 159, 373
**mash** *mix* 41
*disorder* 59
*soft* 324
*semiliquid* 352
*pulpify* 354
**masher** 854
**mask** *dress* 225
*shade* 424
*concealment* 528
*ambush* 530
*deceit* 545
*shield* 717
put on the – 544
**mason** 690
**Masorah** 985
**masque** 599
**masqué, bal** – 840
**masquerade**
*dress* 225
*concealment* 528
*disguise* 530
*frolic* 840
**mass** *quantity* 25
*much* 31
*whole* 50
*heap* 72
*size* 192
*gravity* 319
*density* 321
*worship* 990
*rite* 998
attend – 990
in the – 50
– book 998
– of society 876
**massacre** 361
**massage** 324, 331, 379
**masse, en** – 712
**masses, the** – 876
**massive** *large* 31
*huge* 192
*heavy* 319
*dense* 321
**mast** 206
**master**
*boy* 129
*influence* 175
*man* 373
*know* 490
*understand* 518
*learn* 539
*teacher* 540
*director* 694
*proficient* 698, 700
*succeed, conquer* 731
*ruler* **745**
*possession* 777
*possessor* 779
*title* 877
eye of the – 693
hard – 739
past – 700
– of Arts 492
– one's feelings 826
– hand 700
– key *open* 260
*instrument* 631
– mariner 269
– mind *sage* 500
*proficient* 700
– passion 820
– one's passions 944
– of the position 731
– of the revels 840
– of the Rolls 553, 967
– of self 604
– of the situation 731, 737
– spirit of the age 500, 873
– of one's time 685
**masterdom** 737
**masterpiece**
*good* 648
*perfect* 650
*skill* 698
**master-stroke** 626, 731
**mastery** 731, 737
get the – over 175
**masthead**
*punish* 972
**mastic** *viscid* 352
*resin* 356*a*
**masticate** 298
**mastiff** 366
**mat** *support* 215
*woven* 219
*misty* 427
*cover* 652
**matador** 361
**match** *coincide* 13
*similar* 17
*copy* 19
*equal* 27
*fuel* 388
*contest* 720
*marriage* **903**
**matchless**
*supreme* 33
*excellent* 648
*virtuous* 944
**matchlock** 727
**mate** *similar* **17**
*equal* 27
*duplicate* 89
*mariner* 269
*auxiliary* **711**
*master* 745
*friend* 890
*wife* 903
check– 732
**maté** 298
**mater alma – 542**
–familias 166
**materia medica 662**
**material**
*substance* 316
*stuff* 635
*important* 642
– for thought **45**
– point 32
**materialism**
*matter* 316
*heterodoxy* 984
*irreligion* 989
**materiality 316**
**materialize 446**
**materials 635**
**matériel** 633
**maternal**
*parental* 166
*benevolent* **906**
– love 897
**maternity** 166
**mathematical**
*precise* 494
– point 193
**mathematics 25**
**mathesis** 25
**matin** 125
**matinée** 892
**matins** 990
**matrass** 191
**matriarch** 11, **166**
**matriarchate** 737
**matriculate** 86
**matriculation** 539
**matrilinear** 11, **166**
**matrimony**
*mixture* 41
*wedlock* 903
**matrix** *mould* 22
*workshop* 691
**matron** 374, 903
**matronly** 128, **131**

**matross** 726
**matter** *substance* **3**
*material world* 316
*topic* 454
*meaning* 516
*type* 591
*business* 625
*importance* 642
*pus* 653
no – 460
what – 643
what's the – 455, 461
– of course
*conformity* 82
*certain* 474
*habitual* 613
– in dispute 461
– of fact *event* 151
*certainty* 474
*truth* 494
*language* 576
*artless* 703
*dull* 843
– in hand 454, 625
– of indifference 866
– nothing 643
**mattock** 253
**mattress** 215
**mature** *old* 124
*adolescent* 131
*conversion* 144
*scheme* 626
*perfect* 650
*improve* 658
*prepare* 673
*complete* 729
– thought 451
**maturely considered** 611
**maturine** 996
**maturity** [*see* mature]
bring to – 729
**matutinal** 125
**matzoon** 298
**maudlin**
*inactive* 683
*drunk* 959
**maugre** 30
**maukin** 652
**maul** *hammer* 276
*hurt* 649
**maulstick** 215
**maund** *basket* 191
*mumble* 583
**maunder**
*diffuse style* 573
*mumble* 583
*talk* 584
*lament* 839
**maundy**
– money 784
– Thursday 988
**Mauser rifle** 727
**mausoleum** 363
**mauvais**
– goût 851
– quart d'heure 828
– sujet 949
– ton 851
**mauvaise:**
– honte
*affectation* 855
*modesty* 881
– plaisanterie 851
**mauve** 437
**maw** 191
**mawkish** 391
**Mawworm**
*deceiver* 548
*sham piety* 988
**maxim** 80, **496**
**Maxim gun** 727
**maximal** 33
**maximalist** 742
**maximum** 33, 210
**maxixe** 840
**may be** 470
as it – 156
**May-day** 138, 840
**May-fly** 111
**mayhap** 470
**mayonnaise** 298
**mayor** 745, 965
**maypole** 206
**May-queen** 847
**mazard** 298
**maze**
*disorder* 59
*convolution* 248
*enigma* 533
*difficulty* 704
in a –
*uncertain* **475**
**mazed** 503
**mazurka** 840
**me** 317
**me judice** 484
**meâ culpâ** 950
**mead** *plain* 344
*sweet* 396
**meadow** *plain* 344
*grass* 367
– land 371
**meagre** *small* 32
*incomplete* 53
*thin* 203
– *style* 575
*scanty* 640
*poor* 643
– diet 956
**meal** *repast* 298
*powder* 330
**mealy-mouthed**
*falsehood* 544
*servile* 886
*flattering* 933
**mean** *average* **29**
*small* 32
*middle* 68, 228
*signify* 516
*intend* 620
*contemptible* 643
*stingy* 819
*shabby* 874
*ignoble* 876
*sneaking* 886
*base* 940
*selfish* 943
golden – 174
take the – 774
– nothing 517
– parentage 876
– time 114
– wretch 949
**meander**
*convolution* 248
*deviate* 279
*circuition* 311
*river* 348
– around Robin Hood's barn 279
**meandering**
*diffuse* 573
**meanest capacity** 499
intelligible to the – 518
**meaning** **516**
**meaningless** 517
**means**
*appliances* **632**
*property* 780
*wealth* 803
by all – 602
by any – 632
by no – 536
– of access 627
**meantime** 106
**meanwhile** 106
**measurable** 466
within – distance 470
**measure** *extent* 25
*degree* 26
*moderation* **174**
*music* 413
*compute* 466
*verse* 597
*proceeding* **626**
*action* 680
*apportion* **786**
angular – 244
full – 639
out of – 641
without – 641
– of inclinatio 217
**measured**
*moderate* **174**
*sufficient* 639
*temperate* **953**
**measureless** 105
**measurement** **25, 466**
**measures**
have no – with **713**
take – *plan* 626
*prepare* 673
*conduct* 692
– of length **200**
**meat** 298
broken – 645
one man's – **is another man's poison** 15
**mechanic** 690
**mechanical** 601, 633
– warfare 722
– powers 633
**mechanician** 690
**mechanism** 633
**medal**
*record* 551
*sculpture* 557
*palm* 733
*decoration* 877
– of Honor **733**
**medallion** 557
**medallist** 700
**meddle** 682
**médecin tant pis** 837
**médecine expectante** 133, 662
**Medes and Persians, law of the** – 80, 141
**mediæval** 124
**mediævalism** 122
**medial** 29, 68
**median** 228
**mediant** 413
**medias res, in** – 68
plunge – 300, 576
**mediation**—*instrumentality* 631
*intercession* **724**
*deprecation* **766**

above –ed 104
not worth –ing 643
mentis gratissimus error 481
mentor *sage* 500
*teacher* 540
*adviser* 695
menu 86, 298
Mephistopheles 980
Mephistophelian 945
mephitic 401, 657
mephitis 663
meracious 392
mercantile 794
mercatoria, lex – 963
mercature 794
mercenary
*soldier* 726
*servant* 746
*price* 812
*parsimonious* 819
*selfish* 943
mercer 225
merchandise 798
merchant 797
merchantman 273
merciful 914
merciless 914*a*
mercurial
*changeable* 149
*mobile* 264
*quick* 274
*excitable* 825
Mercury 979
*traveller* 268
*quick* 274
*messenger* 534
mercy *lenity* 740
*pity* 914
at the – of
*liable* 177
*subject* 749
cry you – 766
have at one's – 919
have no – 914*a*
– on us! 870
for –'s sake 765
– seat 966
mere *simple* 32
*lake* 343
*trifling* 643
– nothing
*small* 32
*trifle* 643
buy for a – nothing 815
– pretext 617
– words 477
– wreck 659
merelles 840
meretricious
*false* 495
*vulgar* 851
*licentious* 961
merfolk 980
merge *combine* 48
*include* 76
*insert* 300
*plunge* 337
– in 56
– into *become* 144
merged 228
meridian
*region* 181
*room* 125
*summit* 210
*light* 420
– of life 131
merit
*goodness* 648
*due* 924
*virtue* 944
make a – of 884
– notice 642
merito, e – 944
meritorious 931
Merlin 994
mermaid 341
*monster* 83
*mythology* 979, 980
merman 341
mero motu, ex – 600
merriment
*cheerful* 836
*amusement* 840
merry *cheerful* 836
*drunk* 959
make – *sport* 840
make – with
*wit* 842
*ridicule* 856
wish a – Christmas &c. 896
– and wise 842
merry-andrew 844
merry-go-round 312, 840
merry-making 827, 840, 892
merry-thought 842
mersion 337
meruit ferat, palmam qui – 873
merveille, à – 731
mesa 344
mésalliance 24, 903
meseems 484
mesh 198, 219
meshes *trap* 545
*difficulty* 704
– of sophistry 477
meshwork 219
mesial
*middle* 68
mesmerism 992
mesmerist 994
mesne lord 779
mess *mixture* 41
*disorder* 59
*barracks* 191
*meal* 298
*difficulty* 704
*portion* 786
make a –
*unskilful* 699
*fail* 732
message
*intelligence* 532
*command* 741
Messalina 962
messenger 271
*envoy* 534
*servant* 746
– balloon 463
Messiah 976
messianic 976
messmate 890
messuage 189
messy 59
metabolism 140
metacentre 222
metachronism 115
metage 466
metagenesis 140
metagrammatism 561
metal 635
Brittania – 545
metallic *sound* 410
metalepsis 521
metallurgy 358
metamorphosis 140
metaphor
*comparison* 464
*figure* 521
(*analogy* 17)
metaphrase 522
metaphrast 524
metaphrastic 516
metaphysics 450
metastasis, metathesis
*change* 140
*inversion* 218
*displacement* 270
mete *measure* 466
*distribute* 786
– out *give* 784
metempsychosis 140
meteor 318, 423
meteoric 173, 420
meteorology 338
meteoromancy 511
meter 466
metheglin 396
methinks 484
method *order* 58
*way* 627
want of – 59
methodical 60
Methodist 984
methodist
*journalist* 988
methodize 60
Methuselah 130
old as – 124
since the days of – 124
methylated spirit 388
meticulous 772
métier 625
métis 83
metonymy 521
metoposcopy
*front* 234
*appearance* 448
*interpret* 522
metre
*length* 200
*poetry* 597
metrical
*measured* 466
*verse* 597
metrology 466
*moderation* 174
*mid-course* 628
metropolis 189
metropolitan
*archbishop* 996
mettle *spirit* 820
*courage* 861
man of – 861
on one's –
*resolved* 604
put on one's –
*excite* 824
*encourage* 861
mettlesome
*energetic* 171
*sensitive* 822
*excitable* 825
*brave* 861
mettre de l'eau dans son vin 160
meum et tuum 780

misfit 24
misfortune
*adversity* 735
*unhappiness* 830
misgiving 485, 860
misgovern 699
misguide 495, 538
misguided 699
mishap *evil* 619
*failure* 732
*misfortune* 735
*painful* 830
Mishna 985
misinform 538
misinformed 491
misinstruct 538
misintelligence 538
misinterpretation **523**
misjoined 24
misjudgment
*sophistry* 477
*misjudge* **481**
*misinterpretation* 523
mislay *derange* 61
*lose* 776
mislead *error* 495
*misteach* 538
*deceive* 545
mislike 867
mismanage 699
mismatch 15, 24
misname 565
misnomer **565**
misogamist 904
misogynist 911
misogyny 904
mispersuasion 538
misplace
*derange* 61
misplaced
*intrusive* 24
*unconformable* 83
*displaced* 185
misprint 495
misprision
*concealment* 528
*guilt* 947
– of treason 742
misprize 483, 929
mispronounce 583
misproportioned 243, 846
misquote 544
misreckon 481, 495
misrelish 867
misreport 495, 544
misrepresent
*misinterpret* 523
*misteach* 538
*lie* 544
misrepresentation **555**
*untruth* 544, 546
misrule
*misconduct* 699
*laxity* 738
Lord of – 701
miss *girl* 129
*neglect* 460
*error* 495
*unintelligible* 519
*fail* 732
*lose* 776
*want* 865
*courtesan* 962
– one's aim 732
– fire 732
– stays 304
– one's way
*uncertain* 475
*unskilful* 699
missa cantata 998
missal 998
missay 563, 583
missend 699
misshapen 243, 846
missile 727
missing
*non-existent* 2
*absent* 187
*disappear* 449
– link 53, 83, 729
mission 625, 755
missionary 540, 996
missive 592
misspell 523
misspend 818
misstate 495, 544
misstatement 495, 546
mist 353, 424
in a – 528
seen through a – 519
–s of error 495
– before the eyes 443
mistake *error* 495
*misconstrue* 523
*mismanage* 699
*failure* 732
never was a greater – 536
misteaching **538**
mister 373
misterm 565
misthink 481
mistime 135
mistral 349
mistranslate 523
mistress *lady* 374
*master* 745
*possessor* 779
*title* 877
*love* 897
*concubine* 962
mistrust 485
misty [*see* mist]
*semi-transparent* 427
misunderstand
*misinterpret* 523
misunderstanding 495, 713
misuse **679**
mite *bit* 32
*small* 193
*insufficiency* 640
*money* 800
little – 129
Mithridate 662
mitigate *abate* 174
*improve* 658
*relieve* 834
mitigation
[*see* mitigate]
*extenuation* 937
mitraille 727
mitrailleur 727
mitre *junction* 43
*angle* 244
*crown* 747, 999
mitten 225
mittimus 741
mix 41
– oneself up with
*meddle* 682
*co-operate* 709
– with 720
mixen 653
mixture **41**
mere – 59
mix-up 59
mizzen 235
mizzle 348
mnemonics 505
Mnemosyne 505
moa 366
moan 405
*cry* 411
*lament* 839
moat *enclosure* 232
*ditch* 259
*canal* 350
*defence* 717
mob *crowd* 72
*multitude* 102
*vulgar* 876
*hustle* 929
*scold* 932
king – 876
– cap 225
– law
*authority* 737
*illegality* 964
mobile
*inconstant* 149
*movable* 264
*sensitive* 822
mobility, the – 876
mobilize
*assemblage* 72
*render movable* 264
– troops 722
mobocracy 737
mobster 361
moccasin 225
mock *imitate* 17, **19**
*repeat* 104
*erroneous* 495
*deceptive* 545
*chuckle* 838
*ridicule* 856
*disrespect* 929
– danger 861
– modesty 855
– sun 423
mockery
[*see* mock]
*unsubstantial* **4**
solemn – 882
– delusion and snare
*sophistry* 477
*deception* 545
mocking-bird 19
modal 6, 7, 8
mode *state* **7**
*music* 413
*habit* 613
*method* 627
*fashion* 852
– of expression **56**
mode, à la – 852
model *copy* 21
*prototype* 22
*rule* 80
*form* 240
*representation* 554
*sculpture* **557**
*perfection* **650**
*good man* **948**
new – 658
– after 19
– condition **80**
modeller 559
moderate
*average* 29
*small* 32
*allay* **174**

*destroy* 162
**moxa** 384
**M.P.** 696
**Mr.** 373, 877
**Mrs.** 374
**MS.** 22, 590
**much** 31
make – of
*importance* 642
*friends* 888
*love* 897
*endearment* 902
*approval* 931
not say – for 932
think – of 928, 931
– ado *exertion* 686
*difficulty* 704
– ado about nothing
*over-estimate* 482
*exaggerate* 549
*unimportant* 643
*unskilful* 699
– cry and little wool 884
– the same
*identity* 13
*similarity* 17
*equality* 27
– speaking 584
**mucid** 352, 653
**mucilage** 352
**muck** 653
run a – *kill* 361
*attack* 716
*excitement* 825
**muckle** 31
**muckworm** 819, 876
**mucor** 653
**mucosity** 352
**mucronate** 253
**muculent** 352
**mud** *marsh* 345
*semiliquid* 352
*dirt* 653
clear as – 519
stick in the – 704
– guard 666
**muddle** *disorder* 59
*derange* 61
*inattention* 458
*absurd* 497
*difficulty* 704
*failure* 732
– one's brains 475
**muddled** 959
**muddle-headed** 499
**muddy** *moist* 339
*dim* 422
*opaque* 426
*colour* 429
*stupid* 499
**mudlark** *dirty* 653
*commonalty* 876
**muezzin** 550, 996
**muff** *incapable* 158
*dress* 225
*bungle* 699
*bungler* 701
**muffettee** 225
**muffle** *wrap* 225
*silent* 403
*deaden* 408*a*
*conceal* 528
*voiceless* 581
*stammer* 583
**muffled** *faint* 405
*latent* 526
– drums
*funeral* 363
*non-resonance* 408*a*
**muffler** 225, 384
**mufti** *undress* 225
*judge* 967
*priest* 996
**mug** *cup* 191
*face* 234, 448
*pottery* 384
*dupe* 547
**muggy** *moist* 339
*dim* 422
*opaque* 426
**mug-house** 189
**mugient** 412
**mugwump** 607
**mulatto**
*mixture* 41
*exception* 83
**mulct** *steal* 791
*fine* 974
**mule** *mongrel* 83
*beast of burden* 271
*obstinate* 606
**muleteer** 694
**muliebrity** 374
**mull**
*prominence* 250
*sweeten* 396
**mullah** 967, 996
**muller** 330
**mullion** 215
**mullioned** 219
**multifarious**
*irrelevant* 10
*diverse* 16*a*
*multiform* 81
**multiferous** 102
**multifid**
*divided* 51
**multifold** 81
**multiformity** 81
**multigenerous** 81
**multilateral** 236, 244
**multilocular** 191
**multiloquence** 582, 584
**multinomial** 102
**multiparous** 168
**multipartite** 44
**multiple** 84, 102
**multiplex** 81
**multiplicand** 84
**multiplicate** 81
**multiplication**
*increase* 35
*arithmetic* 85
*multitude* 102
*reproduction* 163
*productiveness* 168
**multiplicator** 84
**multiplicity** 102
**multiplier** 84
**multiply** 35
**multipotent** 157
**multisonous** 404
**multitude** 72, **102**
the – 876
**multum in parvo** 596
**multure** 330
**mum** 581, 585
–'s the word 403
**mumble** *chew* 298
*mutter* 583
**Mumbo Jumbo** 979, 993
**mummer** 599
**mummery**
*absurdity* 497
*imposture* 545
*masquerade* 840
*parade* 882
**mummify** 363
**mummy** *dry* 340
*corpse* 362
beat to a – 972
**mump** *mutter* 583
*beg* 765
**mumper** 767, 804
**mumpish** *sad* 837
**mumps** 837, 901*a*
**munch** 298
**Munchausen** 549
**mundane**
*world* 318
*selfish* 943
*irreligious* 989
**mundation** 652
**mundivagant** 266
**munerary** 973
**munerate** 973
**municipal** 965
**municipality** 737
**munificent** 816
**muniment**
*evidence* 467
*record* 551
*defence* 717
*security* 771
**munition**
*materials* 635
*defence* 717
**mural** 717
**murder** 361
– the King's English
*solecism* 568
*stammering* 583
the – is out 529
**murderer** 361
**muricated** 253
**murky** *dark* 421
*opaque* 426
*black* 431
*gloomy* 837
**murmur** *purl* 348
*sound* 405
*voice* 580
*complain* 839
**murmurer** 832
**murrain** 655
**Murray** *travel* 266
Lindley – 542
**murrey** 434
**murrion** 717
**mus, nascitur ridiculus** – 509, 643
**muscadine** 400
**muscle** 159
**muscular** 159
**muse** 451
[*and see* **musing**]
**Muse** *poetry* 597
historic – 594
unlettered – 579
**musette** 417
**Muses, the** – 416
**museum**
*collection* 72
*store* 636
**mush** 354
**mushroom**
*new* 123
*fungus* 367
*upstart* 734
*low-born* 876
spring up like –s 163
– anchor 666

**music 415**
face the – 861
set to – 416
– of the spheres
*order* 58
*universe* 318
**musical 413, 415,**
416
– comedy 599
– ear
*musician* 416
*hearing* 418
– instruments **417**
– note 413
– voice 580
**music-hall** 599, 840
**musician 416**
**musing** 451
– on other things
458
**musk** 400
**musket** 727
shoulder a – 722
**musketeer** 726
**musketry** 727
**muslin**
*semi-transparent*
427
**musnud**
*support* 215
*council* 696
*sceptre* 747
**muss** 59
**Mussulman** 984
**must** *necessity* 601
*mucor* 653
*compulsion* 744
it – follow 478
I – say 535
**mustachio** 256
**mustard** 392, 393
after meat – 135
– gas 663, 727
**mustard-seed** 193
**muster** 72, 85
pass – 639
not pass – 651
– courage 861
**muster-roll** 86
**musty** 401, 653
**mutable** 149
**mutation** 140
**mutatis mutandis**
*correlation* 12
*change* 140
*interchange* 148
**mutato nomine de**
**te &c.**
*parable* 521
*retaliation* 718
**mute** *funeral* 363
*silent* 403
*sordine* 405,
408*a*, 417
*letter* 561
*speechless* 581
*taciturn* 585
*dramatis persona*
599
deaf – 419
render – 581
**mutilate**
*retrench* 38
*deform* 241
*injure* 659
**mutilated** 53
**mutilation** 619
**mutineer** 742
**mutiny** 742
**mutt** 366
**mutter**
*faint sound* 405
*mumble* 583
*grumble* 839
*threaten* 909
**mutton-chop**
*whiskers* 256
**mutual** 12, 148
**mutualize** 12
**mutual under-**
**standing 23**
**muzzle**
*powerless* 158
*edge* 231
*opening* 260
*silence* 403
*render speechless*
581
*restrain* 751
*gag* 752
**muzzle-loader 727**
**muzzy** 458
*in liquor* 959
**my:** all – eye 546
– stars! 870
**mycology** 369
**mynheer** 877
**myology** 329
**myomancy** 511
**myopia** 443
**myriad** 98, 102
**myrmidon** 726
**myrrh** 400
**myrtle** 897
**myself** *I* 79
*immateriality*
317
**mysterious**
*invisible* 447
*uncertain* 475
*obscure* 519
*concealed* 528
**mystery**
[*see* mysterious]
*latency* 526
*secret* 533
*play* 599
*craft* 625
– ship 726
**mystic**
*uncertain* 475
*obscure* 519
*latent* 526
*concealed* 528
*sorcery* 992
*puzzle* 475
**mystify** *falsify* 477
*hide* 528
*misteach* 538
*deceive* 545
**myth** 515, 546
**mythology** 979, 984

## N

**nab** *deceive* 545
*seize* 789
**Nabob** 745, 803
**nacelle** 273
**nacre** 440
**nadir** 211
**nag** *horse* 271
*quarrel* 713
**nager entre deux**
**eaux** 607
**Naiad** 341, 979
**nail** *fasten* 43
*fastening* 45
*measure of length*
200
*peg* 214
*sharp* 253
*hard* 323
*retain* 781
on the –
*present* 118
*pay* 807
hit the right – on
the head
*discover* 480*a*
*skill* 698
– polish 847
**naïveté** 703
**naked** *denuded* 226
*manifest* 525
*simplicity* 849
– eye 441
– fact 151
– steel 727
– sword 727
– truth 494
**namby-pamby** 643,
855
**name**
*indication* 550
*appellation* 564
*appoint* 755
*celebrity* 873
assume a – 565
call –s
*disrespect* 929
*disapprobation*
932
fair – 873
good – 873
in the – of
*aid* 707
*authority* **737**
*due* 924
– to conjure with
873
**nameless** 565, 874
**namely** 79, 522
**namesake** 564
**Nana Sahib** 949
**Nanny-goat** 374
**nap** *down* 256
*texture* 329
*sleep* 683
*cards* 840
**nape** *back* 235
**napery** 652
**Napier's bones 85**
**napkin** 652
buried in a – 460
lay up in a – 678
**napless** 226
**Napoleon** *food* 298
*cards* 840
**napping**
*inattentive* 458
*inexpectant* 508
*dull* 843
**nappy** *frothy* 353
*tipsy* 959
**narcissism** 897, **943**
**Narcissus** 845
**narcosis** 376
**narcotic** 657, 662
**nard** 356
**narration** 594
**narrow**
*contract* 195
*thin* 203
*intolerant* 481
*restrict* 761
– down 42
– end of the **wedge**
66
– escape 671
– house 363
– means 804
– search 461

**narrow-minded** 481, 943
**narrowness 203**
**narrows** 343
**nasal accent** 583
**nascent** 66
**nascitur:** – **ridiculus mus** 509
– **a** sociis 82
**naso, omnia suspendens** – 868
**nasty**
*unsavoury* 395
*foul* 653
*offensive* 830
cheap and – 815
**natâ, pro re** – 770
**natal** *birth* 66
*indigenous* 188
**natation** 267
**natatorium** 652
**nathless** 30
**nation** 372
**national** 188, 372
– guard 726
**nationality** 372, 910
**nations, law of** 963
**native**
*inhabitant* 188
*artless* 703
– accent 580
– land 189
– soil 189
– tongue 560
**nativity** *birth* 66
cast a –
*predict* 511
*sorcery* 992
**natty** 845
**natura il fece e poi roppe la stampa** 87
**naturæ, vis medicatrix** – 662
**natural** *intrinsic* 5
*musical note* 413
*true* 494
*fool* 501
- *style* 576, 578
*spontaneous* 612
*not prepared* 674
*artless* 703
*simple* 849
– course of things 613
– death *death* 360
*completion* 729
– impulse 601
– meaning 516
– order of things 82
– state 80
– turn 820
**Natural – History** 357
– Philosophy 316
– Theology 983
**naturalist** 357
**naturalization**
*conformity* 82
*conversion* 144
*location* 184
**naturalize**
*habit* 613
**naturalized**
*inhabitant* 188
**naturally** 154
**nature** *essence* 5
*rule* 80
*tendency* 176
*world* 318
*reality* 494
*artlessness* 703
*affections* 820
animated – 357
organized – 357
second – 613
state of –
*naked* 226
*raw* 674
in –'s garb 226
**naught** *nothing* 4
*zero* 101
bring to – 732
set at –
*make light of* 483
*opposition* 708
*disobey* 742
*not observe* 773
*disrespect* 929
*contempt* 930
**naughty** 945
**naumachia** 720
**nausea** 841, 867
**nauseate** 395, 830
**nauseous**
*unsavoury* 395
*unpleasant* 830
*disgusting* 867
**nautch dancer** 840
**nautical** 267
**naval** 267
– authorities 745
– engagement 720
– forces 726
**nave** *middle* 68
*centre* 222
*church* 1000
**navel** 68, 222
**navigation 267**
**navigator** 269
**navvy** 673, 690
**navy** 273, 726
– blue 438
**nay** 536
– rather 14
**Nazarene** 989
**naze** 250
**N.C.O.** 745
**ne plus ultra**
*supreme* 33
*complete* 52
*distance* 196
*summit* 210
*limit* 233
*perfection* 650
*completion* 729
**neaf** 781
**neap** 195, 207
– tide 36, 340
**near** *like* 17
- *in space* 197
- *in time* 121
*soon* 132
*impending* 152
*approach* 286
*stingy* 819
bring – 17
draw – 197
come – 286
– one's end 360
– at hand 132
– the mark 32
– run 32
– side 239
– sight 443
– the truth 480*a*
– upon 3
sail – the wind
*skilful* 698
*rash* 863
**nearly** 32
**nearness 197**
**neat** *simple* 42
*order* 58
*in writing* 572, 576, 578
*clean* 652
*spruce* 845
–'s foot oil 356
– as a pin 58
**neat-handed** 698
**neatherd** 370
**neb** 250
**nebula** *stars* 318
*mist* 353
**nebular** *dim* 422
**nebulous** *misty* 353
*obscure* 519
**necessarian** 601
**necessaries** 630
**necessarily** 154
**necessitate** 630
**necessity** *fate* **601**
*requirement* 630
*compulsion* 744
*indigence* 804
make a virtue of – 698
**neck**
*contraction* **195**
*narrow* 203
*make love* 902
break one's – **360**
– and crop
*completely* 52
*turn out* - 297
– of land 342
– and neck **27**
– or nothing
*resolute* 604
*rash* 863
**neckcloth** 225
**necklace** 247, 847
**necks** 980
**necrology** 360, 594
**necromancer** 548, 994
**necromancy** 992
**necropsy** 363
**necroscopic** 363
**necrosis** 49
**nectar** 394, 396
**need** *necessity* 601
*requirement* 630
*insufficiency* 640
*indigence* 804
*desire* 865
friend in – 711
in one's utmost – 735
**needful**
*necessary* 601
*requisite* 630
*money* 800
do the – *pay* 807
**needle** *sharp* 253
*perforator* 262
*compass* 693
as the – to the pole
*veracity* 543
*observance* 772
*honour* 939
– in a bottle of hay 475
**needle-gun** 727
**needle-shaped** 253
**needless** 641
**needle-witted** 498
**needlewoman** 690
**needlework** 847
**ne'er-do-well** 949
**nefarious** 945

**negation 536, 764**
**negative**
*inexisting* 2
*contrary* 14
*prototype* 22
*quantity* 84
*confute* 479
*deny* 536
*photograph* 558
*refuse* 764
prove a – 468
**neglect 460**
*disuse* 678
*leave undone* 730
*omit* 773
*evade* 927
*disrespect* 929
– of time 115
**négligé** 225, 674
**negligence** 460
**negotiable** 270
**negotiate**
*mediate* 724
*bargain* 769
*transfer* 783
*traffic* 794
**negotiations**
breaking off – 713
**negotiator** 724, 758
**negro** 431, 746
**negus**
*drink* 298
*king* 745
**neif** 781
**neigh** *cry* 412
*boast* 884
**neighbour** 197, 890
**neighbourhood** 183, 197, 227
**neighbourly**
*aid* 707
*friendly* 888
*social* 892
*courteous* 894
**neither** 610
– here nor there
*irrelevant* 10
*absent* 187
– more nor less
*equal* 27
*true* 494
– one thing nor another 83
**nem. con.** 488
**Nemesis**
*vengeance* 919
*justice* 922
*punishment* 972
**nemine contradicente** 488
**nemo me impune** lacessit 715
**nenia** 839
**neogamist** 903
**neologism** 123
**neology 563**
**neophyte** 144, 541
**neoteric** 123
**nepenthe** 662, 836
**nephelogy** 353
**nephew** 11
**nepotism**
*nephew* 11
*wrong* 923
*dishonest* 940
*selfish* 943
**Neptune** 341
**Nereid** 341, 979
**nerve** 159, 861, 885
exposed – 378
**nerveless** 158
**nervous** *weak* 160
*style* 574
*timid* 860
*modest* 881
**nescience** 491
**nest**
*multitude* 102
*cradle* 153
*lodging* 189
– of boxes 204
**nest-egg** 636
**nestle** *lodge* 186
*safety* 664
*endearment* 902
**nestling** 129
**Nestor** *veteran* 130
*sage* 500
*advice* 695
**net** *remainder* 40
*receptacle* 191
*intersection* 219
*inclosure* 232
*snare* 545
*difficulty* 704
*gain* 775
– profit *gain* 775
*receipt* 810
**nether** 207
**nethermost** 211
**netting** 219
**nettle** *bane* 663
*sting* 830
*incense* 900
**network**
*disorder* 59
*crossing* 219
**neuralgia** 378
**neurasthenia** 655
**neuritis** 378
**neurology** 329
**neurotic** 662
**neuter** *matter* 316
*no choice* 609a
remain –
*irresolute* 605
stand –
*indifferent* 866
**neutral** *mean* 29
*no choice* 609a
*avoidance* 623
– tint
*colourless* 429
*grey* 432
*peace* 721
**neutrality**
*mid-course* 628
*peace* 721
*insensibility* 823
*indifference* 866
**neutralize**
*compensate* 30
*counteract* 179
**névé** 383
**never** 107
– say die
*persevere* 604a
*cheerful* 836
*hope* 858
it will – do
*inexpedient* 647
*prohibit* 761
*discontent* 832
*disapprobation* 932
–dying 112
–ending 112
–fading
*perpetual* 112
*glory* 873
– forget 916
– to be forgotten 642
– indebted 807
– hear the last of 841
– mind
*neglect* 460
*unimportant* 643
*insensible* 823
*indifferent* 866
*contempt* 930
– more 107
– a one 4
– otherwise 16
– to return 122
– was seen the like 83
– so 31
– tell me 489
– thought of 621
– tired *active* 682
– tiring
*persevering* 604a
**neverness 107**
**nevertheless** 30
**new** *different* 18
*additional* **37**
*novel* 123
*unaccustomed* **614**
– birth 660
– blood *change* **140**
*improve* 658
*excite* 824
– brooms 614, **682**
– comer 57
– conditions 469
– departure 66
– edition
*repetition* 104
*reproduction* 163
*improvement* 658
– ideas 537
turn over a – leaf
*change* 140
*repent* 950
give – life to **707**, 824
view in a – light 658
put on the – man 950
**New Year's Day** 138
**new-born** 123, 129
**Newcastle, carry coals to** – 641
**new-fangled**
*unfamiliar* 83
*change* 140
*neology* 563
**new-fashioned** 123
**new-fledged** 129
**Newfoundland dog** 366
**Newgate** 752
**new-gilt** 847
**new-model**
*convert* 144
*revolutionize* **146**
*improve* 658
**newness 123**
**news 532**
– sheet 531
**newsmonger**
*curious* 455
*informant* 527
*news* 532
**newspaper** 531, 551
– correspondent 758
**newspaperman** 534
**newt** 366

*snare* 545
*gallows* 975
**norma loquendi 567**
**normal**
*intrinsic* **5**
*mean* 29
*regular* 82
*perpendicular* 212
– condition
*rule* 80
**normality 80, 502**
**Normand, répondre en – 544**
**Norns 601**
**North 278**
– and South **237**
**Northern 237**
– light 423
– star 939
**North-west passage 311**
**noscitur a sociis 82**
**nose** *prominence* 250
*smell* 398
with one's – in the air 878
lead by the – 615, 737
led by the – 749
not see beyond one's –
*misjudge* 481
*folly* 499
*unskilful* 699
speak through the – 583
thrust one's – in
*interjacence* 228
*busy* 682
under one's –
*present* 186
*near* 197
*manifest* **525**
*defy* 715
put one's – out of joint *defeat* 731
*disrepute* 874
– ring 847
**nose-dive 306**
**nosegay 400, 847**
**nosey 455**
**nosology 655**
**nostalgia 833**
**nostril 351**
breath of one's –s 359
stink in the –s 401
**nostrum 626, 662**
**not** *negation* 536
what is – 546
what ought – 923
– at all 32
– allowed 964
– amiss 618, 651, 845
– any 101
– bad 651
– bargain for **508**
– a bit 536
– to be borne 830
– a Chinaman's chance 471
– come up to **34**
– cricket 923
– to be despised 642
it will – do 923
– of the earth 987
– expect 508
– fail 939
– far from **197**
– a few 102
– fit to be seen 846
– following **477**
– grant 764
– guilty 946
– to be had **471**, 640
– having 187, **777*a***
– hardened 950
– hear of 764
– included 55
– know what to make of 519
– a leg to stand on 158
– likely **473**
– a little 31
– matter 643
– to mention **37**
– mind 823, 930
– often 137
– on your life 489
– one 101
– a particle **4**
– particular 831
– pay 808
– a pin to choose 27
– playing the game 923
– within previous experience 137
– to be put down 604
– quite **32**
– reach 304
– right 503
– sorry 827
– a soul 101
– on speaking terms 889
– the thing 925
– to be thought of
*incogitancy* 452
*impossible* 471
*refusal* 764
*hopeless* 859
*undue* 925
*disapprobation* 932
– trouble oneself about 460
– understand 519
– vote 609*a*
– wonder 871
– for the world 603, 764
– worth
*trifling* 643
*useless* 645
**nota bene 457**
**notabilia 642**
**notabilities 875**
**notable**
*manifest* 525
*important* 642
*active* 682
*distinguished* 873
**notables 875**
**notably 31**
**notary 553, 968**
**notation 85**
**notch 198, 257, 550**
**note** *cry* 412
*music* 413
*take cognizance* 450
*remark* 457
*explanation* 522
*sign* 550
*record* 551
*printing* 591
*epistle* 592
*minute* 596
*money* 800
*fame* 873
change one's – 607
make a – of 551
of – 873
take – of 457
– of admiration 870
– of alarm 669
– of preparation 673
**note-book**
*memorandum* 505
*record* 551
*compendium* 569
*writing* 590
**noted 490, 873**
**noteworthy**
*great* 31
*exceptional* **83**
*important* 642
**nothing** *nihility* **4**
*zero* 101
*trifle* 643
come to – 304, **732**
do – 681
for – 815
go for – 643
good for – **646**
make – of
*under-estimate* 483
*fail* 732
take – by 732
think of – 930
worse than – 808
– comes amiss **831**
– to do 681
– to do with **764**
– doing 681
– to go upon **471**
– in it 4
– of the kind **18**, 536
– loth 602
– on 226
– more to be said 478
– to signify **643**
**nothingness 2**
**notice** *intellect* **450**
*observe* 457
*review* 480
*information* **527**
*warning* 668
bring into – **525**
deserve – 642
give –
*manifest* **525**
*inform* 527
*indicate* 550
short – 111
take – of 450
this is to give – 457
worthy of – 642
– is hereby given
*publication* 531
– to quit 782
**noticeable 31**
**notification 527**
**notion** *idea* **453**
**notional 515**
**notoriety 531, 873**
**notorious**
*known* 490
*public* 531
*famous* 873

*infamous* 874
**notturno** 415
**notwithstanding** 30
**nought** [*see* naught]
**noun** 564
**nourish** 707
**nourishment**
*food* 298
**nous** 498
**nous avons changé tout cela** 140
**nouveau riche** 123, 734, 876
**Nova Zembla** 383
**novation** 609
**novel**
*dissimilar* 18
*new* 123
*unknown* 491
*tale* 594
**novelette** 594
**novelist** 594
**novice**
*ignoramus* 493
*learner* 541
*bungler* 701
*religious* 996
**novitiate** 539, 673
**novocaine** 376, 381
**novus homo** 57, 876
**now** 118
– and then 136
– or never 134
**noways** 32
**nowhere** 187
**nowise** 32, 536
**noxious** 649, 657
**noyade** 361, 972
**noyerait dans une goutte d'eau, il se –** 699
**nozzle**
*projection* 250
*opening* 260
*air-pipe* 351
**nuance** 15, 465
**nubibus, in –** 2, 515
**nubiferous** 353, 426
**nubile** 131, 903
**nucleus** *middle* 68
*cause* 153
*centre* 222
*kernel* 642
**nuda veritas** 494
**nude** 226, 849
**nudge** 550
**nudity** 226
**nugacity** 499, 645
**nugæ canoræ** 517, 842
**nugas, magno conatu magnas –** 643
**nugatory** 158
*unimportant* 643
**nuggar** 273
**nugget** *mass* 192
*money* 800
**nuisance** 619, 830
**null** 4
– and void
*inexistence* 2
*powerless* 158
*unproductive* 169
*illegal* 964
declare – and void
*abrogation* 756
*non-observance* 773
**nulla dies sine lineâ** 682
**nullâ pallescere culpâ, nil conscire sibi –** 946
**nullah** 198
**nulli secundus** 33
**nullibiety** 187
**nullify** *inexistence* 2
*compensate* 30
*destroy* 162
*abrogate* 756
*not observe* 773
*not pay* 808
**nullity** 2, 4
**nullius jurare in verba magistri** 487
**numb**
*physically insensible* 376, 381
*morally insensible* 823
–skull 493
**number**
*part* 51
*abstract* - **84**
*count* 85
*plural* 100
- *of a magazine &c.* 593
– among 76
take care of – one 943
– of times 104
**numbered: days –**
*kill* 360
*necessity* 601
*hopeless* 859
– with the dead 360
**numberless** 105
**numbers** *many* 102
*verse* 597
**numbness** 375, **381**
**numerable** 85
**numeral** 84, 85
**numeration** **85**
**numerator** 84
**numerical** 85
**numerose**
*many* 102
**numerous** 102
**numismatics** 800
**numps** 501
**numskull** 501
**nun** 996
**nunc dimittis** 990
**nuncio** 534, 758
**nuncupation**
*naming* 564
**nuncupatory**
*informing* 527
**nundination** 794
**nunnery** 1000
**nuptials** 903
**nurse** *remedy* 662
*preserve* 670
*help* 707
*servant* 746
*custodian* 753
*fondle* 902
put to – 537
**nurseling** 129
**nursery** *infancy* 127
*nest* 153
*room* 191
*garden* 371
*school* 542
*workshop* 691
– rhymes 597
– tale 546, 594
**nursing home** 493
**nurture** *feed* 298
*educate* 537
*prepare* 673
*aid* 707
– a belief 484
– an idea 451
**nut**
– to crack
*fanatic* 504
*riddle* 533
*difficulty* 704
– oil 365
**nut-brown** 433
**nutmeg** 393
**nutmeg-grater** 330
**nuts** 618, 829
**nutshell** *small* 32
lie in a – 572
*little* 193
*compendium* 596
**nutation** 314
**nutriment** 298
**nutrition** 707
**nutritious** *food* 298
*healthy* 656
*remedy* 662
**nutty** 499
**nuzzle** 902
**nyctalopy** 443
**nymph** *girl* 129
*woman* 374
*mythology* 979
sea – 341
**nystagmus** **443**

## O

**O!** *wonder* 870
*discontent* 932
– for *desire* 865
**oaf** *fool* 501
*bungler* 701
*changeling* 980
**oak** *strong* 159
heart of –
*hard* 323
*brave* 861
**oakum** 205
**oar** *paddle* 267
*oarsman* 269
*instrument* 633
labouring – 686
lie upon one's –s 681
ply the –
*navigate* 267
*exert* 686
pull an – 680
put in an – 228, 682
rest on one's –
*cease* 142
*quiescence* 265
*repose* 687
stroke – 693
**oarsman** 269
**oasis** *separate* 44
*exceptional* 83
*land* 342
**oast-house** 386
**oath**
*assertion* 535
*bad language* **908**
on – 543
rap out –s 885
upon – 768
**oatmeal** 298
**obbligato** 88, **415**
**obduction** 223

– to be met with 136
**ogee** 847
**Ogham** 590
**ogive** 215
**ogle** *look* 441
*desire* 865
*rude* 895
*endearment* 902
**ogpu** 696
**ogre** *bugbear* 860
*evil-doer* 913
*demon* 980
**oil** *lubricate* 332
*grease* 355, **356**
pour – on
*relieve* 834
– on the troubled waters 174, 714
– lamp 423
– stove 386
**oilcloth** 223
**oiled** *drunk* 959
**oilskin** 386
**oil-painting** 556
**oily** *smooth* 255
*greasy* 355
*servile* 886
*courteous* 894
*flattery* 933
**oinomania** 959
**ointment**
*grease* 356
*remedy* 662
**O.K.** 488
**old** 124
of – 122
– age 128
die of – age 729
– bachelor 904
– clothes 225
– fashioned 851
– fogey 501, 857
– joke 842
– maid *cards* 840
*spinster* 904
– man *veteran* 130
*husband* 903
– man of the sea 706
– Nick 978
– school 124
*obstinate* 606
*habit* 613
pay off – scores 718
– song
*repetition* 104
*trifle* 643
*cheap* 815
– stager
*veteran* 130
*actor* 599
*proficient* 700
– story
*repetition* 104
*stale news* 532
*love* 897
– times 122
one's – way 613
– woman *fool* 501
*wife* 903
**Oldbuck** 122
**olden** 124
**older** 128
**oldest inhabitant**
not in memory of – 137
**old-fashioned** 124, 851
**oldness** **124**
**oleagine** 356
**oleaginous** 355
**oleomargarine** 356
**oleum addere camino** 35, 173
**olfactory** 398
**olid** 401
**oligarch** 745
**oligarchy** **737**
**olio** 41
**olive-branch**
*infant* 129
*offspring* 167
*pacification* 723
**olive-green** 435
**olla podrida** 41
**Olympiad** 720
**Olympus** 981
**ombre** 840
**ombres chinoises** 448
**omega** *end* **67**
**omelet** 298
**omen** **512**
**ominate** 511
**ominous**
*predicting* 511
*indicating* 550
*danger* 665
*hopeless* 859
**omission**
*incomplete* 53
*exclusion* 55
*neglect* 460
*failure* 732
*non-observance* 773
*guilt* 947
**omitted** 2, 187
**omne tulit punctum** 731
**omnibus** 272
**omnifarious** 81
**omnific** 168
**omniform** 81
**omnigenous** 81
**omnipotence** 157, 976
**omnipresence** 186, 976
**omniscience** 490, 976
**omnium gatherum**
*mixture* 41
*confusion* 59
*assemblage* 72
**omnivorous**
*eating* 298
*desire* 865
*gluttony* 957
**omphalos** 68
**on** *forwards* 282
– account of 155
– all accounts 52
– that account 155
– approval 463
– an average 29
– the brink of 32
– the cards 152
– foot *duration* 106
*event* 151
*doing* 170
– the fire 730
– all fours 13, 23
– the other hand 30
– one's head 218
– the increase 35
– a large scale 31
– these lines 627
– the move 264
– the nail 118
– no account 32
– no occasion 107
– a par 27
– the part of 9
– the point of 111
– the present occasion 118
– trial 463
– the whole 50
**on dit** 532, 588
**once** *past* 119, 122
*seldom* 137
at – 113, 132
– for all *final* 67
*infrequency* 137
*tell one* - 527
*determine* - 604
*choose* 609
– in a blue moon 137
– more 90, 104
– over 457
– upon a time
*time* 106
*different time* **119**
*formerly* 122
– in a way **137**
**Ondine** 979
**one** *identical* **13**
*whole* 50
*unity* 87
*somebody* **372**
*married* 903
all – to 823
at – with *agree* **23**
*concur* 178
*concord* 714
make – of 186
neither – nor the other 610
of – accord 488
– and all
*whole* 50
*general* 78
*unanimous* 488
from – to another
*transfer* 783
– thing with another 476
– of the best **948**
– bone and one flesh 903
– consent 178, 488
– of these days 121
– fell swoop 113, 173
– fine morning 106
– and a half 87
– horse 643
– idea 481
– jump 113
– leg in the grave 160
as – man 488, 709
– mind 178, 488
– by one
*separately* 44
*respectively* 79
*unity* 87
both the – and the other 89
the – or the other 609
– over the eight 959
– and the same 13
on – side 217, 236
– step 840
– in ten thousand 648, 948
– at a time 87

melancholy 837
**oppressive** *hot* 382
*painful* 830
**oppressor** 739, 913
**opprobrium** 874
**oppugnation** 708, 719
**optative** 865
**optical** 441
– instruments **445**
– lantern 448
**optician** 445
**optics** *light* 420, 445
**optics** *sight* 441
**optimacy** 875
**optimates** 875
**optime!** 931
**optimism** 482, 858
**optimist** 858
*flatterer* 935
**option** 609
**optional** 600
**optometer** 445
**optometry** 445
**opulence** 803
**opuscule** 593
**or** *yellow* 436
*orange* 439
*alternative* 609
**oracle** 500, **513**
**Oracle, Sir –**
*positive* 474
*vanity* 880
*blusterer* 887
**oracular**
*answering* 462
*ambiguous* 475
*wise* 498
*prediction* 511
**oral** *information* 527
*voice* 580
*speech* 582
– communication 588
– evidence 467
**orange** *round* 249
*colour* **439**
**orangery** 371
**orarium** 999
**oration** 582
funeral – 363
**orator** 582
**oratorio** 415
**oratory**
*speaking* 582
*place of prayer* 1000
**orb** *region* 181
*circle* 247
*luminary* 423
*eye* 441
*sphere of action* 625
– of day *sun* 318
*luminary* 423
– of night 318
**orbicular** 247
**orbit** *circle* 247
*heavens* 318
*path* 627
**orchard** 371
**orchestra**
*music* 415
*musicians* 416
*instruments* 417
*theatre* 599
**orchestral** 415
**orchestrate** 60, 413, 416
**orchestration** 413
**orchestrelle** 417
**ordain**
*command* 741
*commission* 755
*due* 924
*legal* 963
*God* 976
*church* 995
**ordained** *due* 924
*clergy* 996
**ordeal**
*experiment* 463
*trouble* 828
*sorcery* 992
– of battle 722
**order**
*regularity* **58**
*arrangement* 60
*class* 75
*record* 551
*requisition* 630
*direct* 693
*command* 741
*money* 800
*rank* 873
*quality* 875
*decoration* 877
*law* 963
at one's – 743
call to – 932
in – 620
keep in – 693
money – 800
out of – 651
put in – 60
recur in regular – 138
set in – 60
set one's house in – 673
standing – 613
in working – 673
– of the day
*conformity* 82
*events* 151
*habit* 613
*plan* 626
*command* 741
pass to the – of the day 624
**orderless** 59
**orderly**
*regular* 58, 80
*arrange* 60
*conformable* 82
*servant* 746
– of succession 63
– of things 80
**orders, holy** – 995
in – 996
**ordinal** 998
**ordinance**
*command* 741
*law* 963
*rite* 998
**ordinary** *usual* 82
*meal* 298
*habitual* 613
*imperfect* 651
*ugly* 846
*simple* 849
in – *store* 636
lie in – 681
– condition
*rule* 80
– course of things 613
**ordinate** 466
**ordination**
*measurement* 466
*command* 741
*commission* 755
*church* 995
*rite* 998
**ordnance** 727
**ordonnance** 963
**ordure** 653
**ore** 635
**ore rotundo** 577
**oread** 979
**orectic** 865
**organ** *music* 417
*voice* 580
*instrument* 633
internal –s 221
– point 413
**organic** *state* 7
*structural* 329
*protoplastic* 357
– change 146
– chemistry 357
– remains 357
*dead* 329
**organism** 329
**organist** 416
**organization** 60
*production* 161
*structure* 329
*animated nature* 357
**organize**
*arrange* 60
*produce* 161
*plan* 626
**organized hypocrisy** 544
**organology** 329
**orgasm** 173
**orgies** 954
**oriel** *recess* 191
*corner* 244
*window* 260
*chapel* 1000
**Orient** 236, 420
**orifice**
*beginning* **66**
*opening* 260
**oriflamme** 550
**Origenism** 984
**origin** 66, 153
derive its – **154**
**original**
*dissimilar* 18
*not imitated* **20**
*model* 22
*initial* 66
*individual* **79**
*exceptional* 83
*cause* 153
*invented* 515
*unaccustomed* **614**
*laughing-stock* 857
return to – state 660
**originality** 600
want of – 843
**originate** *begin* **66**
*cause* 153
*invent* 515
– in 154
**originator** 164
**originative** 168
**Orion's belt** 318
**orismology** 562, **564**
**orison** *request* 765
*worship* 990
**orlop deck** 211
**ormolu**
*sham* 545
*ornament* **847**
**Ormuzd** 979
**ornament**

*secluded* 893
get – the way 623
go – one's way 629
– one's wits 824
– work 681
– the world
*dead* 360
*secluded* 893
**outbalance** 30, 33
**outbid** 794
**outbrave** 885
**out-brazen** 885
**outbreak**
*beginning* 66
*violence* 173
*egress* 295
*discord* 713
*attack* 716
*revolt* 742
*passion* 825
**outburst**
*violence* 173
*egress* 295
*revolt* 825
**outcast**
*unconformable* 83
*pariah* 876
*secluded* 893
*bad man* 949
**outcome** *effect* 154
*egress* 295
*produce* 775
**outcry** *noise* 411
*complaint* 839
*censure* 932
**outdo** *superior* 33
*transcursion* 303
*activity* 682
*cunning* 702
*conquer* 731
**outdoor** 220
**outer** 220
**outermost** 220
**outface** 885
**outfit** 225, 673
**outflank** *flank* 236
*defeat* 731
**outgate** 295
**outgeneral** 731
**outgo** 303
**outgoing** 295
**outgoings** 809
**outgrow** 194
**outgrowth** 154
**out-Herod** 33, 173
**outhouse** 191
**outing** 266
**outjump**
*transcursion* 303
*repute* 873
**outlander** 57
**outlandish**
*foreign* 10
*extraneous* 57
*irregular* 83
*barbarous* 851
*ridiculous* 853
**outlast** 110
**outlaw** *irregular* 83
*secluded* 893
*reprobate* 949
**outlawry** 964
**outlay** 809
**outleap** 303
**outlet** *opening* 260
*egress* 295
**outline** *contour* 230
*form* 240
*features* 448
*sketch* 554
*painting* 556
*plan* 626
**outlines**
*rudiments* 66
*principles* 596
**outlive** 110, 141
**outlook** *view* 448
*outstare* 885
**outlying**
*remaining* 40
*exterior* 220
**outmanœuvre**
*trick* 545
*defeat* 731
**outnumber** 102
**outpost**
*distant* 196
*circumjacent* 227
*front* 234
**outpouring**
*egress* 295
*information* 527
*abundance* 639
**output** *egress* 295
*produce* 775
**outrage**
*violence* 173
*evil* 619
*badness* 649
*injury to* 659
*malevolence* 907
*disrespect* 929
*guilt* 947
**outrageous**
*excessive* 31
*violent* 173
*scandalous* 874
**outrance: à –**
*great* 31
*complete* 52
*violent* 173
guerre – 722
**outrank** 33, 62
**outré**
*exceptional* 83
*exaggerate* 549
*ridiculous* 853
**outre mer** 196
**outreach** 545
**outreckon** 482
**outride** 303
**outrider** 64
**outrigger**
*support* 215
*boat* 273
**outright** 52
**outrival**
*superior* 33
*surpass* 303
*fame* 873
**outrun** 303
– the constable
*debt* 806
*prodigal* 818
**outscourings** 653
**outset** 66, 873
**outshine** 873, 874
**outside**
*extraneous* 57
*exterior* 220
*appearance* 448
– the gates 893
mere – 544
– car 272
clean the – of the platter
*ostentation* 882
**outsider** 57, 893
**outskirts** 196, 227
**outspan** 292
**outspeak** 582
**outspoken** *say* 582
*artless* 703
be – *censure* 932
**outspread** 202
**outstanding**
*remaining* 40
*outside* 220
– debt 806
– feature 642
**outstare** 885
**outstep** 303
**outstretched** 202
with – arms 894
**outstrip** 303
**outtalk** 584
**outvie** 720, 873
**outvote** 731
**outward** 220
– bound 295
**outweigh** 33, 175
**outwit** 545, 731
**outwork**
*defence* 717
**outworn** 124
**oval** 247
**ovate** 247
**ovation** 883
**oven** 386
like an – *hot* 382
**over** *more* 33
*remainder* 40
*end* 67
*past* 122
*high* 206
*too much* 641
all – *completed* 729
all – with
*destroyed* 162
*dead* 360
*failure* 732
*adversity* 735
danger – 664
get – 660
fight one's battles – again 594
hand – 783
make – 784
set – 755
turn – 218
– and above
*superior* 33
*added* 37
*remainder* 40
*redundance* 641
– again 104
– against 237
– the border 196
– head and ears
*complete* 52
*height* 206
*feeling* 821
– the hills and far away 196
– the mark 33
– one's head 208, 641
– the way 237
**overabound** 641
**overact** *bustle* 682
*affect* 855
**overalls** 225
**over-anxiety** 865
**overarch** 223
**overawe** *sway* 737
*intimidate* 860
*respect* 928
**overbalance**
*unequal* 28
*compensation* 30
*superior* 33
**overbear** 175
**overbearing** 885
**overboard, throw –**

## P

**below** – *low* 207
*imperfect* 651
– excellence 33
– nobile fratrum
*alike* 17
*friends* 890
de – le roi 737
– parenthèse 134
– pari refero 718
– value 812
**parable**
*metaphor* 521
*teaching* 537
*description* 594
**parabola** *curve* 245
**parabolic**
*metaphorical* 521
**paracentesis** 297
**parachronism** 115
**parachute**
*balloon* 273
*means of safety* 666
– light 423
**Paraclete** 976
**parade** *procession* 69, 266
*walk* 189
*ostentation* 882
**paradigm** 22, 567
**Paradise** *bliss* 827
*heaven* 981
in – 827
**parados** 717
**paradox**
*absurdity* 497
*obscurity* 519
*difficulty* 704
**paradoxical** 475, 519
**paraffin** 356
**paragon**
*perfect* 650
*glory* 873
*good man* 948
**paragram**
*ambiguous* 520
*neology* 563
**paragraph** *part* 51
*phrase* 566
*article* 593
**paraleipsis** 460
**parallax** 196
**parallel**
*similarity* 17
*imitate* 19
*harmonious* 178
- *position* 216
*symmetry* 242
draw a – 464
none but himself can be his – 873
run – 178
**parallelism** 216
*agreement* 23
**parallelogram** 244
**parallelopiped** 244
**paralogism** 477
**paralogize** 477
**paralysis**
*impotence* 158
*physical insensibility* 376
*disease* 655
*moral insensibility* 823
**paralyse** 158, 376, 823
**paramount**
*supreme* 33
*important* 642
*authority* 737
lord – *master* 745
*possessor* 779
– estate 780
**paramour** 897
**paranoia** 503, 504
**parapet** 717
**paraph** 550
**paraphernalia**
*machinery* 633
*belonging* 780
**paraphrase**
*imitation* 19
*copy* 21
*synonym* 522
*phrase* 566
**paraphrast** 524
**paraphrastic** 19, 522
**parasite** *auxiliary* 711
*servile* 886
*flatterer* 935
**parasitic**
*subjection* 749
*grasping* 789
*servile* 886
**parasol** *covering* 223
*shade* 424
**paratus**:
in utrumque –
*resolved* 604
*ready* 673
semper – 673
**parboil** 384
**parbuckle** 633
**Parcæ** 601
**parcel** *part* 51
*group* 72
part and – 56
– out *arrange* 60
*allot* 786
**parcels**
*property* 780
**parcere subjectis** 740, 914
**parch** *dry* 340
*heat* 382
*bake* 384
**parched with thirst** 865
**parchment**
*writing* 590
*security* 771
**parcity** 819
**pardi** 535
**pardon** 506, 918
beg – 952
– me 489
**pardonable** 937
**pare** *cut* 38
*reduce* 195
*peel* 204
*divest* 226
– down
*shorten* 201
**paregoric** 662
**parenchyma** 316, 329
**parent** 166
– ship 726
**parentage** 11, 166
**parenthesis**
*discontinuity* 70
*inversion* 218
*interjacence* 228
by way of – 134
**parenthetical**
*irrelative* 10
**pargeting** 847
**parhelion** 423
**pari passu** 27, 120
**Pariah**
*outlaw* 83
*commonalty* 876
*outcast* 893
**parian**
*sculpture* 557
**parietal** 236
**parietes** 224
**paring** 32
**parish** 181
bring to the – 804
come upon the – 804
– council 696
**parishioner** 997
**paritor** 965
**parity** 17, 27
**park** *house* 189
*plain* 344
*trees* 367
*artillery* 727
*pleasure ground* 840
– paling 232
**parkway** 627
**parlance** 582
in common – 576
**parlante** 415
**parlementaire** 534, 723
**parler**:
facon de – 521
– à tort et à travers
*illogical* 477
*nonsense* 497
**parley** *talk* 588
*conference* 695
*mediation* 724
**parliament** 696
**parliamentary securities** 802
**parlour** 191
**parlour-maid** 746
**parlous** 665
**Parnassus** 597
**parochial** 181, 189
*prejudiced* 481
**parody**
*imitation* 19
*copy* 21
*misinterpret* 523
*misrepresent* 555
*travesty* 856
**parole** *speech* 582
on – *restraint* 751
*prisoner* 754
*promise* 768
**Parolles** 887
**paronomasia**
*neology* 563
*ornament* 577
**paronymous** 562
**paroxysm**
*violence* 173
*agitation* 315
*emotion* 825
*anger* 900
**parquetry** 440
**Parr, Old** – 130
**parricide** 361
**parrot**
*imitation* 19
*repetition* 104
*loquacity* 584
repeat as a – 505
**parry** *confute* 479
*avert* 623
*defend* 717
**pars magna fui, quorum** – 690

**peevish** 895, 901
**peg** *grade* 71
*hang* 214
*project* 250
*drink* 298, 959
come down a – 306
let down a – 308
not stir a – 265, 681
– away 682
– to hang on 617
– on *journey* 266
– out *die* 360
**Pegasus** 271
**pegomancy** 511
**pegs** *legs* 266
**peignoir** 225
**peindre, fait à –** 845
**peine forte et dure** 974
**pejorative** 483
**pelagic** 341
**pelerine** 225
**pelf** *gain* 775
*property* 780
*money* 803
**pelisse** 225
**Pelion, Ossa on –** 72, 319
**pellet** 249, 727
paper – 643
**pellicle** 204, 223
**pell-mell** 59
**pellucid** 425
**pelote** 249
**pelt** *skin* 223
*dress* 225
*throw* 276
*attack* 716
*punish* 972
**peltry** 223
**pemmican** 298
**pen** *inclosure* 232
*write* 590
*writer* 593
*restrain* 751
*imprison* 752
ready – 569
slip of – 495, 568
stroke of the –
*write* 590
*authority* 737
*command* 741
– in hand 590
– and ink 590
– name 565
draw the – through **552**
**penal 972**
– servitude **972**
– settlement 752
**penalty 974**
extreme – 972
**penance** 952, 974
do – 998
**penates, lares et –** 189, 991
**penchant**
*willing* 602
*desire* **865**
*love* 897
**pencil** *bundle* 72
– *of light* 420
*write* 590
**pencil-drawing** 556
**pencraft** 590
**pendant** *match* 17
*flag* 550
*ornament* 847
**pendency** *time* 106
*hanging* **214**
**pendente lite** 106
*uncertain* 475
*lawsuit* 969
**pendule** 114
**pendulous** 214, 314
**pendulum** 114, 214
motion of a – 314
**Penelope, work of –** 645, 730
**penetralia** 221
– mentis 450, 820
**penetrate**
*ingress* 294
*passage* 302
*sagacity* 498
– the soul 824
**penetrated with** 484, 821
**penetrating**
*sagacious* 498
*feeling* 821
– glance 441
**penfold** 232
**peninsula** 342
**penitence 950**
**penitentiary** 752, 996
**pen-knife** 253
**penman** 590
inspired – 985
**penmanship** 590
**pennant** 550
**pennate** 267
**penniless** 804
**pennon** 550
**penny** 800
not have a – 804
cost a pretty – 814
turn a – 775
no – no paternoster 812
in for a – in for a pound 768
– dreadful 594
– trumpet 410
– whistle 410
**penny-a-liner** 534, 593
**penny-a-lining** 573
**pennyweight** 319
**penny-wise** 819
– and pound foolish *caprice* 608
*waste* 638
*prodigal* 818
**pennyworth** 812
**penology** 972
**penscript** 590
**pensée, arrière –** 528
**penseroso** 837
**pensile** 214
**pension** *income* 810
**pensioner**
*student* 541
*servant* 746
*receiver* 785
**pensive** 451, 837
**penstock** 350
**pent up** 751
– in one's memory 505
**pentagon** 98, 244
**pentahedron** 244
**pentameter** 98, 597
**Pentateuch** 98, 985
**Pentecost** 998
**Penthesilean** 861
**penthouse** 189, 191
**pentile** 223
**penultimate** 67
**penumbra** 421
**penurious** 819
**penury** 804
**peon** 726
**people**
*kinsfolk* 11
*multitude* 102
*inhabit* 186
*mankind* 372
*commonalty* 876
*laity* 997
**pep** 171
– up 171
**pepastic** 662
**pepper** *pungent* 392
*condiment* 393
*attack* 716
– and salt 432, 440
**peppercorn 643**
– rent 815
**peppery**
*irascible* **901**
**peptic** 662
**per** 631
– contra
*contrariety* **14**
*counter-evidence* 468
*opposition* 708
– procuratio **755**
– saltum 70, **113**
– se 87
**peradventure 470**
**peragrate** 266
**perambulate** 266
**perambulator**
*measure of length* 200
*vehicle* 272
**perceivable 446**
**perceive**
*be sensible of* **375**
*see* 441
*know* 490
**percentage** 84, **813**
**perceptible** 446
**perception** 453, **490**
**perceptive** 375
**perch** *location* **184**
*abide* 186
*habitation* **189**
*length* 200
*height* 206
*support* **215**
– up 307
**perchance** 156, **470**
**percipience** 450
**percolate** 295, **348**
**percolator** 191
**percursory** 458
**percussion** 276
centre of – 222
**percussive** 277
**perdition**
*destruction* **162**
*ruin* 732
*loss* 776
**perdre son Latin** 704
**perdrix, toujours –** 841
**perdu** 528
enfant – 859, **863**
**perdurable** 110
**perdy** 535
**peregrination 266**
**peregrinator 268**
**peremptory**
*assertion* **535**

*firm* 604
*authoritative* **737**
*rigorous* 739
*compulsory* 744
*duty* 926
– denial 536
– refusal 764
**perennial**
*continuous* 69
*diuturnal* 110
- *plants* 367
**perennius, ære –**
873
**pererration** 266
**perfect**
*great* 31
*entire* 52
*excellent* 650
*complete* 729
**perfection 650**
bring to – 729
**perfervidum ingenium** 682
**perfidy** 874, 940
**perflate** 349
**perforate** 260
**perforator 262**
**perforce** 601, 744
**perform**
*produce* 161
*do* 170
- *music* 416
*action* 680
*achieve* 729
*fulfil* 772
– a circuit 629
– a duty 926
– the duties of 625
– a function 644
– an obligation
772
– a part 599, 680
– a service 998
**performable** 470
**performance**
[*see* perform]
*effect* 154
**performer**
*musician* 416
*stage-player* 599
*agent* 690
*affectation* 855
**perfume** 400
**perfunctory** 53, 460
**pergola** 191
**perhaps** 470, 514
**peri** 845, 979
**periapt** 993
**pericranium** 450
**periculous** 665
**peridot** 847
**perihelion** 197
**peril** 665
at your – 909
take heed at
one's – 668
**perilepsis** 476
**perimeter** 230
**period** *end* 67
*point* 71
- *of time* 106, **108**
*recurrence* 138
at fixed –s 138
well rounded –s
577, 578
**periodical**
*recurring* 138
*book* 593
**periodicity 138**
**peripatetic** 266, 268
**periphery** 230
**periphrase** 566, 573
**periplus** 267
**periscope** 441, 445
**periscopic** 446
– lens 445
**perish**
*cease to exist* 2
*be destroyed* 162
*die* 360
*decay* 659
– with cold 383
– with hunger 956
**perishable** 111
**perissology** 573
**peristaltic** 248
**peristyle** 189
**periwig** 225
**perjured** 940
**perjurer** 548
**perjury** 544
**perk** *dress* 225
– up *elevate* 307
*revive* 689
**perked up**
*proud* 878
**perky** 880
**perlustration** 441
**permanence**
*durability* 110
*unchanging* **141**
*unchangeable* 150
**permanent**
*habitual* 613
**permeable** 260
**permeate**
*insinuate* 228
*pervade* 186
*pass through* 302
–d with 613
**permissible** 760
**permission 760**
**permissive 760**
**permit** 760
**permitting**
weather &c. – 469,
470
**permutation**
*numerical* - 84
*change* 140
*interchange* 148
**pernicious** 649
**pernicity** 274
**perorate**
*diffuse style* **573**
**peroration**
*sequel* 65
*end* 67
*speech* 582
**perpend** *think* 451
**perpendicular** 212
**perpension**
*attention* 457
**perpetrate** 680
– a pun &c. 842
**perpetrator** 690
**perpetua, esto –**
928, 931
**perpetual** 112
*frequent* 136
– curate 996
– motion 467
**perpetuate** 112
*continue* 143
*establish* 150
**perpetuity** 69, **112**
**perplex** *derange* 61
*distract* 458
*uncertainty* **475**
*bother* 830
**perplexed** 59, 248
**perplexity**
*disorder* 59
*uncertainty* 475
*unintelligibility*
519
*difficulty* 704
**perquisite** 775, 973
**perquisition** 461
**perron** 627
**perscrutation** 461
**persecute**
*oppress* 649
*annoy* 830
*malevolence* 907
**perseverance** 143,
604a
**Persides** 215
**persiflage** 842, 856
**persifleur** 844
**persist** *duration* 106
*permanence* 141
*continue* 143
*persevere* **604a**
**persistence**
*diuturnity* 110
**person** 3, 372
without distinction of –s 922
**persona grata** 890,
899
**personable** 845
**personæ, dramatis**
– 599, 690
**personage** 372
**personal**
[*see* person]
*special* 79
*subjective* 317
– narrative 594
– property 780
– remarks 932
– security 771
**personality**
[*see* personal]
*discourtesy* 895
*disrespect* 929
*censure* 932
*detraction* 934
**personalty** 780
**personate** 19, 554
**personify** 521, 554
**personnel** 56, 590
**perspective**
*view* 448
*expectation* **507**
*painting* 556
aerial – 428
in – 200
**perspicacity**
*sight* 441
*intelligence* 498
*fastidiousness* **868**
**perspicuity**
*intelligibility* **518**
*style* **570**
**perspiration** 295,
299
in a – 382
**perstringe** 457
**persuadable** 602
**persuade** *belief* **484**
*induce* 615
**persuasibility**
*willingness* 602
**persuasion**
*class* 75
*opinion* 484
*teaching* 537
*inducement* 615
religious – 983
**persuasive**
**reasoning 476**
**pert**

**photogravure** 558
**photolysis** 49
**photometer** 445
**photosphere** 318
**photostat** 553
**phrase** *part* 51
*music* 413
*language* **566**
**phrasemonger** 577
**phraseology** 569
**phrenetic** 503
**phrenitis** 503
**phrenology** 450
**phrenotypics** 505
**Phryne** 962
**phthisozoics** 361
**phylacteric**
*sorcery* 992
**phylactery**
*maxim* 496
*spell* 993
**physic**
*cure* 660
*remedy* 662
**physical** 316
– education
*material* 316
*teaching* 537
– force
*strength* 159
*compulsion* 744
– nature 3
– pleasure **377**
– pain **378**
– science 316
**physician**
*remedy* 662
*advice* 695
**Physics** 316
**physiognomy**
*face* 234
*appearance* 448
*interpret* 522
**Physiology**
*organization* 357
*life* 359
Vegetable – 369
**physique**
*strength* 159
*animality* 364
**phytivorous** 298
**Phytology** 369
**pi** 591
**piacere, al** – 600
**piacular** 952
**pianino** 417
**pianissimo** 415
**pianist** 416
**piano** *gentle* 174
*music* 415
– organ 417
– player 417
**pianoforte** 417
**pianola** 417
**piazza** 189, 191
**pibroch** *music* 415
*war* 722
**pica** 591
**picaresco, gusto** – 945
**picaroon** 792
**piccolo** 410, 417
**pick** *axe* 253
*eat* 298
*select* 609
*best* 648
*clean* 652
*gain* 775
– a-back 215
- the brains of 461
– holes
*censure* 932, 934
– the lock 480*a*
– me up 662
– out *extract* 301
*select* 609
– to pieces
*separate* 44
*destroy* 162
*find fault* 932
– a quarrel 713
– one's steps 459
– up *learn* 539
*get better* 658
*gain* 775
– one's way 675
**pickaninny** 129
**pickaxe** 253
**picked** 648
– men 700
**pickeer** 791
**pickeerer** 792
**Pickelhaube**
*armour* 717
**picket** *join* 43
*locate* 184
*fence* 229
*guard* 668
*defence* 717
*soldiers* 726
*restrain* 751
*imprison* 752
*torture* 972
– boat 273
**pickings** 775, 793
**pickle** *condition* 7
*macerate* 337
*pungent* 392
*condiment* 393
*preserve* 670
*difficulty* 704
have a rod in – 673
**pickle-herring** 844
**pickpocket** 792
abuse like a – 932
**pickthank** *busy* 682
*servile* 886
*flatterer* 935
**picnic** *food* 298
*participation* 778
*amusement* 840
**picquet** 840
**pictorial**
*painting* 556
*beauty* 845
**picture**
*appearance* 448
*representation* 554
*painting* 556
*description* 594
– to oneself 515
**picture-gallery** 556
**picture-theatre** 599
**picturesque**
*painting* 556
*beauty* 845
**piddle** *dawdle* 683
**piddling** *trivial* 643
**pidgin English** 563
**pie** *food* 298
*sweet* 396
*printing* 591
**piebald** 440
**piece** *adjunct* 39
*bit* 31
*painting* 556
*drama* 599
*cannon* 727
*coin* 800
*courtesan* 962
fall to –s 162
go to –s 162
in –s 330
of a – 42
pull to –s 162
give a – of advice 695
– of good fortune 618
– of music 415
– of news 532
– out 52
– together 43
– of work 713
make a – of work about 642
**pièce**
– justificative 467
– de résistance 298
**piecemeal** 51
**pied** *variegated* 440
**pied de la lettre,** au – 494
**pie-poudre, court** of – 966
**pier** 189, 666
**pierce**
*perforate* 260
*bodily pain* **378**
*chill* 385
*hurt* 649
*wound* 659
*affect* 824
*mental pain* **830**
– the head 410
– the heart 830
**piercer** 262
**piercing** *cold* **383**
*loud* 404
*shrill* 410
*intelligent* 498
*feeling* 821
– eye 441
– pain 378
**pier-glass** 445
**Pierian spring** **597**
**pierre fendre, à** – 383
**Pierrot** 599
**pietas** 998
**piété, mont de** – 787
**pietism** 988
**pietist** 987, 988
**piety** **987**
**pig** *animal* 366
*sensual* 954*a*
– in a poke
*uncertain* **475**
*chance* 621
*rash* 863
– together **72**
**pigeon**
*dupe* 547
*steal* 791
gorge de – 440
**pigeon-hearted** **862**
**pigeon-hole** 191, 260
**piggin** 191
**piggish** 954
**pig-headed** 499, **606**
**pigment** 428
**pigmy** 193
**pignoration** **771**
**pignus** 771
**pig-sticking** **361**
**pigsty** 653
**pigtail** 214
**pigwidgeon** **193**, 980
**pike** *hill* 206
*sharp* **253**

*highway* 627
*weapon* 727
**pikeman** 726
**pikestaff** *tall* 206
*plain* 525
**pilaster**
*support* 215
*projection* 250
*ornament* 847
**pile** *stake* 45
*heap* 72
*edifice* 161
*post* 215
*velvet* 256
*money* 800
funeral – 363
– up 549, 641
**pile-driver** 276
**pilfer** *steal* 791
**pilferer** 792
**pilgarlic**
*outcast* 893
**pilgrim** 268, 996
**pilgrimage** 266, 676
**pill** *sphere* 249
*medicine* 662
bitter – 735
**pillage** 659, 791
**pillager** 792
**pillar** *stable* 150
*lofty* 206
*support* 215
*monument* 551
*tablet* 590
–s of Hercules 550
– of the state &c. 873
from – to post
*transfer* 270
*agitation* 315
*irresolute* 605
*circuit* 629
**pillion** 215
**pillory** 975
**pillow**
*support* 215
*soft* 324
consult one's –
*temporize* 133
*reflect* 451
**pilot** *mariner* 269
*inform* 527
*guide* 693
*director* 694
**pilot-balloon** 463
**pilot-boat** 273
**pilot-officer** 745
**pilot-jacket** 225
**pilous** 256
**pimp** 962
**pimple** 250, 848
**pin** *fasten* 43
*fastening* 45
*locate* 184
*sharp* 253
*axis* 312
*trifle* 643
might hear a – drop 403
point of a – 193
not a – to choose 27, 609*a*
– down 744, 751
– one's faith upon 484
– oneself upon 746, 886
**pinafore** 225
**pince-nez** 445
**pincers** 781
**pinch** *emergency* 8
*contract* 195
*pain* 378
*chill* 385
*need* 630
*difficulty* 704
*adversity* 735
*grudge* 819
*hurt morally* 830
at a – 630, 704
jack at a – 711
where the shoe –s 830
– of snuff 643
**pinchbeck** 545, 847
**pinched** [*see* pinch]
*thin* 203
*poor* 804
– with hunger 865
**pinching** 383, 819
**Pindaric** 597
**pine** *disease* 655
*dejection* 837
*suffer in mind* 828
– away 837
– for 865
**pinery** 371
**ping-pong** 840
**pinguid** 355
**pin-hole** 260
**pinion** *fasten* 43
*wing* 267
*instrument* 633
*restrain* 751
*fetter* 752
**pink** *notch* 257
*pierce* 260
*thrust* 276
*colour* 434
*perfection* 650
*glory* 873
**pink of** *beauty* 845
– fashion 852
– perfection 650
– politeness 894
**pinnace** 273
**pinnacle** 210
**pinocle** 840
**pin-prick** 180*a*
**pins** *legs* 266
– and needles
*bodily pain* 378
*numb* 381
*mental pain* 828
**pinscher** 366
**Pinto, Fernam Mendez** – 548
**pioneer**
*precursor* 64
*leader* 234
*teacher* 540
*prepare* 673
**pious** 987
– fraud 546, 988
**pip** 747
**pipe** *tube* 260
*conduit* 350
*vent* 351
*tobacco* 392
*sound* 410
*cry* 411
*music* 416, 417
*weep* 839
no – no dance 812
– one's eye 839
– of peace 721, 723
**pipeclay** *habit* 613
*strictness* 739
**piper** 416
pay the – 707, 807
**piping** – hot 382
– time 721, 734
**pipkin** 191
**piquant**
*pungent* 392
- *style* 574
*impressive* 821
**piquante, sauce** – 393, 829
**pique** *fly* 267
*excite* 824
*pain* 830
*hate* 898
*anger* 900
– oneself
*pride* 878
**piqueerer** 792
**piquet** 717, 726
**pirate** 773, 791, 792
**pirogue** 273
**pirouette** 218, 312
turn a – 607
**Pisa, tower of** – 271
**pis-aller** 147
**piscatorial** 366
**pisces natare docere** 538, 641
**pisciculture** 370
**piscina** 350, 1000
**pish!** *absurd* 497
*trifling* 643
*excitable* 825
*irascible* 901
**piste** 551
**Pistol** 887
**pistol** 727
**pistol-shot** 197
**piston** 263
**pit** *deep* 208
*hole* 252
*opening* 260
*extract* 301
*grave* 363
*theatre* 599
*danger* 667
bottomless – 982
– of Acheron 982
– against 708, 713
– against one another 464
**pit-a-pat**
*agitation* 315
*rattle* 407
*feeling* 821
*excitation* 824
**pitch** *degree* 26
*term* 71
*location* 184
*height* 206
*summit* 210
*erect* 212
*throw* 284
*descent* 306
*depression* 308
*reel* 314
*resin* 356*a*
*musical* - 413
*black* 431
absolute – 416
– of one's breath 411
– dark 421
– into *attack* 716
*contend* 720
*punish* 972
– overboard 782
– one's tent 292
– and toss 621
– upon *reach* 292
*discover* 480*a*
*choose* 609
*get* 775

*safety* 664
*preparation* 673
**precede**
*superior* 33
- *in order* 62
- *in time* 116
- *in motion* 280
**precedence** 873
**precedent**
[*see* precede]
*prototype* 22
*precursor* 64
*habit* 613
*legal decision* 969
follow –s 82
**precentor** 694, 996
**precept** *adage* 496
*maxim* **697**
*order* 741
*permit* 760
**preceptor** 540
**precession** 62, **280**
**précieuse ridicule** 855
**precinct** *region* 181
*place* 182
*environs* 227
*boundary* 233
**precious** *great* 31
*excellent* 648
*valuable* 814
*beloved* 897
– metals 800
– stone 648, 847
**precipice**
*vertical* 212
*slope* 217
*dangerous* 667
on the verge of a – 665
**precipitancy** 684, 863
**precipitate**
*early* 132
*sink* 308
*consolidate* 321
*refuse* 653
*haste* 684
*rash* 863
– oneself 306
**precipitous** 217
**précis** 596
**precise** *exact* 494
**preciosity** 578
**precisely**
*literally* 19
*assent* 488
**precisianism**
*affectation* 855
*heterodoxy* 984
*over-religious* 988
**preclude** 55, 706
**precocious**
*early* 132
*immature* 674
*pert* 885
*rude* 895
**precognition**
*forethought* 490
*knowledge* 510
**preconceived idea** 481
**preconception** 481
**preconcert** 611, 626
**preconcertation** 673
**precursor**
- *in order* 62, **64**
- *in time* 116
*predict* 511
**predatory** 789, 791
**predecessor** 64
**predeliberation** 510, 611
**predella** 215
**predesigned** 611
**predestination**
*fate* 152
*necessity* 601
*predetermination* 611
*Deity* 976
**predetermination** **611**
**predial**
*land* 342
*agriculture* 371
*manorial* 780
**predicament** 8, 75
**predicate**
*affirm* 535
*preach* 998
**prediction** **511**
**predilection**
*bias* 481
*affection* 820
*desire* 865
**predispose** 615, 673
**predisposed**
*willing* 602
**predisposition** 176, 820
**predominant** 175, 737
**predominate** 33
**pre-eminent** 33, 873
**pre-emption** 795
**preen** 847
**pre-engage** 132
**pre-engagement** 768
**pre-establish** 626
**pre-examine** 461
**pre-exist** 1, 116
**preface** 62, 64
**prefect** 745, 759
**prefecture** 737
**prefer** *choose* 609
– a claim 969
– a petition 765
**preference** 62
**preferment**
*improvement* 658
*ecclesiastical* - 995
**prefigure** 511
**prefix** 62, 64
*letter* 561
**pre-glacial** 124
**pregnable** 158
**pregnant**
*producing* 161
*productive* 168
*predicting* 511
- *style* 572
*important* 642
– with meaning 516
**prehensile** 789
**prehension** 789
**pre-historic** 124
**pre-instruct** 537
**prejudge** 481
**prejudicate** 481
**prejudice**
*misjudge* 481
*evil* 619
*detriment* 659
**prejudicial** 481, 649
**prelacy** 995
**prelate** 996
**prelation** 609
**prelection** 537, 582
**prelector** 540
**preliminaries:**
settle – 673
– of peace 723
**preliminary** 62, 64
**prelude** 62, 64
*beginning* 66
*music* 415
**premature** 132, 674
**premeditate** 611, 620
**prémices** 154
**premier** 694, 759
– pas 66
**premiership** 693
**premise** *prefix* 62
*precede* 116
*announce* 511
**premises**
*precursor* 64
*prior* 116
*ground* 182
*evidence* 467
*logic* 476
**premium**
*debt* 806
*receipt* 810
*reward* 973
at a – 814
**premonish** 668
**premonitory** 511, 668
**Premonstratensian** 996
**premonstration**
*appearance* 448
*prediction* 511
*manifestation* 525
**premunire** 742, 974
**prendre la balle au bond** 134
**prenotion**
*misjudgment* 481
*foresight* 510
**prensation** 789
**prentice** 541
**prenticeship** 539
**preoccupancy**
*possession* **777**
**preoccupation**
*inattention* 458
**preoption** 609
**preordain** 152, 601
**preparation** **673**
*music* 413
*instruction* **537**
in – 730
in course of – **626**
**preparatory**
*preceding* 62
**prepare the way**
*facilitate* 705
**prepared** *expectant* 507
*ready* 698
**preparing**
*destined* 152
**prepense**
*spontaneous* 600
*predetermined* 611
*intended* 620
malice – 907
**prepollence** 157
**preponderance**
*superiority* 33
*influence* 175
*dominance* **737**
**prepossessed**
*obstinate* 606

*receipt* 810
*love* 897
*approve* 931
*reward* 973
win the – 731
– open 173
**prizer** 767
**prize-fighter** 726
**prize-fighting** 720
**prizeman** 700
**pro:** – and con 476, 615
– formâ 82
– hâc vice
*special* 79
*present time* 118
*occasion* 134
*seldom* 137
– rata 23
– re natâ
*circumstances* 8
*relation* 9
*special* 79
*occasion* 134
*conditions* 770
– tanto 26, 32
– tempore 111
**proa** 273
**probability** 156, **472**
**probable** 858
**probate** 771
**Probate Court** 966
**probation**
*trial* 463
*demonstration* 478
**probationary** 463, 675
**probationer** 541
**probative** 478
**probatum est** 478, 931
**probe** *depth* 208
*perforator* 262
*investigate* 461
*measure* 466
**probity** **939**
**problem** *topic* 454
*question* 461
*enigma* 533
**problematical** 475
**proboscis** 250
**procacity**
*insolence* 885
*rudeness* 895
*irascibility* 901
**procedure**
*method* 627
*action* 680
*conduct* 692
**proceed** *time* 109
*advance* 282
– from 154
– with 692
**proceeding**
*incomplete* 53
*event* 151
*action* 680
*not finished* 730
course of – 692
**proceedings** 551
**proceeds** *gain* 775
*money* 800
*receipts* 810
**procerity** 206
**procès-verbal**
*record* 551
*law proceeding* 969
**process**
*projection* 250
*conduct* 692
legal – 963
– engraving 558
– of time 109
in – of time 117
**procession**
*continuity* 69
*march* 266
*ceremony* 882
**processional**
*rite* 998
**prochronism** 115
**proclaim** 531
**proclivity** 176, 820
**proconsul** 759
**proconsulship** 737
**procrastination** 133, 460, 683
**procreant** 168
**procreate** 161, 168
**procreator** 166
**procrustean** 82
– law 80
**Procrustes:**
stretch on the bed of – 27
**proctor** *teacher* 540
*officer* 694, 965
*consignee* 758
*lawyer* 968
**proctorship** 693
**procumbent** 213
**procurator** 694
**procuration** 170, 755
**procure** *cause* 153
*induce* 615
*get* 775
*buy* 795
**procuress** 962
**procurement** 170
**prod** 276
**prodigal** 641, 818
**prodigality** **818**
**prodigious** 31, 870
**prodigy** 83, **872**
– of learning 700
**prodition** 940
**prodrome** 64
**produce**
*increase* 35
*cause* 153
*effect* 154
*create* 161
*prolong* 200
*show* 525
*stage* 599
*fruit* 775
*merchandise* 798
– itself 446
**producer** **164**
**product**
*multiple* 84
*effect* 154
*harvest* 636
*gain* 775
finished – 154
**production** 54, **161**
[*and see* produce]
**productive**
*cause* 153
*power* 157
*inventive* 515
*profitable* 775
**productiveness** **168**
**proem** 64
**proemial**
*preceding in order* 62
*beginning* 66
**profane**
*desecrate* 679
*impious* 988
*laical* 997
– swearing 908
**profanum vulgus** 876
**profession**
*assertion* 535
*pretence* 546
*business* 625
*promise* 768
enter a – 625
– of faith 484, 983
**professional** 700
– mourner 363, 839
**professor** 492, 540, 700
**professorship** 542
**proffer** 763
**proficient**
*knowledge* **490**
*skill* 698
*adept* **700**
**proficuous** **644**
**profile**
*outline* 230
*side* 236
*appearance* **448**
*portraiture* **556**
**profit**
*increase* 35
*advantage* 618
*utility* 644
*acquisition* **775**
– by *use* 677
– sharing **778**
**profitable**
*useful* 644
*good* 648
*gainful* 775
**profitless** 645
**profligacy** 945
**profluent**
*progressive* **282**
*stream* 348
**profound**
*great* 31
*deep* 208
*learned* 490
*wise* 498
*sagacious* **702**
*feeling* 821
– attention **457**
– knowledge **490**
– secret 533
**profundis, de** – 839, 950
**profuse**
*diffuse style* **573**
*redundant* 641
*prodigal* 818
**profusion** 102, **639**
**prog** 298
**progenerate** 161
**progenitive** 163
**progenitor** 166
**progeny** 167
**prognosis** 510, **511**, 522, 655
**prognostic** 511, **512**
**prognosticate** 511
**prognostication** **507**
**programme**
*catalogue* 86
*publication* **531**
*plan* 626
**progress**
*growth* 144
*motion* 264
*advance* 282

in – *incomplete* 53, 730
make – 282
in mid – 270
– of science 490
– of time 109
**progression**
*gradation* 58
*series* 69
*numerical* – 84
*motion* **282**
**progressive**
*continuous* 69
*course* 109
*advancing* 282
*improving* 658
**prohibition 761**
*exclusion* 55
*stoppage* 706
*teetotalism* 953, 958
**project** *bulge* 250
*impel* 284
*intend* 620
*plan* 626
**projectile** 727
**projection** *map* **554**
**projector**
*lantern* 423
*film* 445
*designer* 626
**prolation** 580, 582
**prole, sine** – 169
**prolegomena** 64
**prolepsis** 64, 115
**proletarian** 876
**prolific** 168
**prolix** 573
**prolocutor**
*interpreter* 524
*teacher* 540
*speaker* 582
**prologue**
*precursor* 64
*drama* 599
**prolong**
*protract* 110
*late* 133
*continue* 143
*lengthen* 200
**prolongation** 63, 143
**prolusion** 64
**prom** 892
**promenade** 266
*display* 882
*on pier* 189
**Promethean** 359
**prominent**
*convex* 250
*manifest* 525
*important* 642
*eminent* 873
**prominently** 31, 33
**promiscuous**
*mixed* 41
*irregular* 59
*indiscriminate* 465a
*casual* 621
**promise**
*predict* 511
*engage* **768**
*hope* 858
keep one's – 939
keep – to ear and break to hope 545
– oneself 507, 858
**promissory** 768
– note 771, 800
**promontory**
*height* 206
*projection* 250
*land* 342
**promote** 153, 658, 707
**promoter** 626
**promotion** 658
**prompt** *early* 132
*remind* 505
*tell* 527
*induce* 615
*active* 682
*advise* 695
– memory **505**
**prompter**
*drama* 599
*motive* 615
*adviser* 695
**promptuary** 636
**promulgate** 531
– a decree 741
**pronation and supination** 218
**prone**
*horizontal* 213
**proneness**
*tendency* 176
*disposition* 820
**prôner** 882, 931
**prôneur** 935
**prong** 91
**pronounce**
*judge* 480
*assert* 535
*voice* 580
*speak* 582
**pronounced** 525
**pronouncement** 531
**pronunciamento** 531
**pronunciation** 580
**pronunciative** 535
**proof** *hard* 323
*insensible* 376
*test* 463
*demonstration* 478
*printing* 591
*draft* 626
ocular – 446
– against
*strong* 159
*resolute* 604
*safe* 664
*defence* 717
*resistance* 719
*insensible* 823
**prop** 215, 707
**propædeutics** 537
**propagable** 168
**propaganda** 537, 542
**propagandism** 537
**propagandist** 540, 996
**propagate**
*produce* 161
*be productive* 168
*publish* 531
**propel** 284
**propellant** 727
**propeller** 267, 312
**propend** 602
**propendency**
*predetermination* 611
*inclination* 820
**propense** 602
**propension** 820
**propensity** 176, 820
**proper** *special* 79
*expedient* 646
*handsome* 845
*due* 924
– name 564
in its – place 58
show a – spirit 939
the – thing 926
– time 134
**properties**
theatrical – 225, 599
**property** *power* 157
*possessions* **780**
*wealth* 803
**property-man** 599
**prophecy** 511
**prophet** 513, 996
false –s 986
in the name of the – figs! 497
**prophetic** 511, **985**
**Prophets, the** – **985**
**prophylactic**
*healthful* 656
*remedy* 662
*preservative* **670**
*hindrance* 706
**prophylaxis** 670
**propinquity** 197
**propitiate**
*pacify* 723, **724**
*calm* 826
*content* 831
*love* 897
*pity* 914
*forgive* 918
*atone* 952
*worship* **990**
**propitious**
*timely* 134
*beneficial* 648
*helping* 707
*prosperous* **734**
*auspicious* **858**
**proplasm** 22
**proportion**
*relation* 9
*degree* 26
*mathematical* **84**
*symmetry* 242
*style* 578
*allotment* 786
**proportionate**
*agreeing* 23
**proportions** 180, 192
**proposal** *plan* **626**
**propose**
*suggest* 514
*broach* 535
*intend* 620
*offer* 763
*offer marriage* 902
– a question **461**
**proposition**
*supposition* **454**
*reasoning* 476
*project* 626
*suggestion* 514
*offer* 763
**propound** 514, **535**
– a question 461
**propriâ personâ**
in – *speciality* **79**
*presence* 186
**proprietary** 779
**proprietor** 779
**proprietorship 780**
**propriety**

**proximate**
*next* 63
*near* 197
– cause 153
**proximity** *near* 197
*adjacent* 199
**proximo** 121
**proximus ardet**
*danger* 665, 667
**proxy** 634, 759
**prude** *affected* 855
*chaste* 960
**prudent**
*careful* 459
*wise* 498
*economical* **817**
*cautious* 864
**prudery** 855, 868
**prudish** 739
**prune**
*take away* 38
*lop* 201, 371
*repair* 658
**prunes and prisms** 855
**prunello, leather or** – 643
**prurience** 865, 961
**Prussian blue** 438
**Prussic acid** 663
**pry** *look* 441
*curiosity* 455
*inquire* 461
– into the future 510
**Prytaneum** 931
**psalm** 415, 990
**psalm-book** 998
**psalmody** 415, 998
**psalter** 998
**psaltery** 417
**psephomancy** 511
**pseudo** 17, 545
**pseudoblepsis** 443
**pseudonym** 565
**pseudo-revelation** **986**
**pseudoscope** 445
**pshaw**
*trifling* 643
*excitement* 825
**psychiatry** 662
**psychical** 450
**psycho-analysis** 662
**psychological moment** 824
**Psychology** 450
**Psychomancy** 511
**psycho-therapy** 662
**ptisan** 662
**ptomaine poisoning** 663
**puberty** 127
**pubescent** 131
**public, general** – 372
make – 531
– enemy 891
– good 644
– opinion 488
– press 531
– school 542
– spirit 910
– welfare 910
**publican** 637
**publication** **531**
*production* 161
*book* 593
**public-house** 189
go to the – 959
**publicist** 593, 595, 968
**publicity** 531
**publicly rumoured** 532
**publico, pro bono** – 644, 910
**publish** 531
– the banns **765**, 903
**publisher** 593
**puce** 433, 437
**pucelage** *youth* 127
*celibacy* 904
*purity* 960
**Puck** 980
play – 699
**pucker** *fold* 258
*anger* 900
in a – 824
**pudder**
*disorder* 59
**pudding** *food* 298
*soft* 324
*pulpy* 354
*sweets* 396
in – time 132
**Pudding, Jack** – **599**
**puddle** 343
**pudicity** 960
**pudor, proh** – 874
**puerile** *boyish* 129
*foolish* 499
*feeble* 575
*trifling* 643
**puerperal** 161
**puff** *inflate* 194
*wind* 349
*tartlet* 396
*exaggerate* 482
*advertisement* 531
*pant* 688
*boast* 884
*praise* 931
*flatter* 933
– of smoke 330
– out 194
– up *vanity* 880
**puffed up**
*exaggerated* 482
*pride* 878
**puffer** 935
**puffery** 884
**puffy** 194
**pug** *short* 201
*dog* 366
*pugilist* 726
**pugh!** 643
**pugilism** 720
**pugilist** 726
**pugilistic** 720
**pugnacity** 720, 901
**puisné**
*posterior* 117
*young* 127
**puissant** 157, 159
**puke** 297
**pukka** 494
**pulchritude** 845
**pulcinella** 599, 844
**pule** *cry* 411, 412
*weep* 839
**pull** *superiority* 33
*influence* 175
*row* 267
*draw* 285
*printing* 591
a long and a strong – 709
strong – 636
– the check string 142
– different ways 713
– down 162, 308
– about one's ears 308
– in 751
– an oar 680
– out 301
– to pieces
*separate* 44
*destroy* 162
*censure* 932
*detract* 934
– upon the purse 814
– by the sleeve 505
– the strings 631
– through **660**, 707
– together **709**
– towards 288
– up *stop* 142
*rest* 265
*root out* 301
*reprimand* **932**
*accuse* 969
– the wires 693
**pulled down** 160, 688
**pullet** 129
**pulley** 633
**Pullman car** **272**
**pullulate**
*produce* 161
*multiply* 168
*grow* 194
**pulmonary** 349
**pulmotor** 349
**pulp** 354
**pulpiness** **354**
**pulpit** *rostrum* **542**
*church* 1000
the – 996
**pulsate**
*periodic* 138
*oscillate* 314
*agitate* 315
**pulsation**
*feeling* 821
**pulse** [*see* pulsate]
*vegetable* 367
feel the –
*inquire* 461
*test* 463
**pulsion** 276
**pultaceous** 354
**pulverize** 330
*destroy* 162
*dust* 358
**pulverulence** **330**
**pulvil** 400
**pummel**
[*see* pommel]
**pump** *shoe* 225
*water supply* **348**
*inquire* 461
– up 349
**pump-room**
*house* 189
*remedy* 662
**pun** *similarity* **17**
*absurdity* 497
*ambiguity* 520
*wit* 563, 842
**punce** 276
**punch** *mould* 22
*perforate* 260
*perforator* 262

*end* 67
*stop* 142
*destroy* 162
- *oneself* 361
- in force
*complete* 729
*compel* 744
- forth
*expand* 194
*suggest* 514
*publish* 531
*assert* 535
- *a question* 461
- *strength* 686
- forward
*suggest* 514
*publish* 531
*ostentation* 882
one's hand to 676
the horses to 673
in [*see below*]
- to inconvenience 647
- a mark upon 457
- one's nose out of joint 33
- off *late* 133
*divest* 226
*depart* 293
*plea* 617
- on *clothe* 225
*deceive* 544
*hasten* 684
*affect* 855
- out [*see below*]
- on paper 551
- over 484, 731
- a question 461
- right 660
- the saddle on the right horse 155
- the seal to 729, 769
- to [*see below*]
- together *join* 43
*combine* 48
*assemble* 161
- one's trust in 484
- up [*see below*]
- upon 545, 649
**put in** *arrive* 292
*insert* 300
- an affidavit 535
- hand 676
- one's head 514
- mind 505
- motion 264
- order 60
- the place of 147
- one's pocket 785
- practice 692
- remembrance 505
- shape 60
- trim 60, 673
- the way of 470
- a word 582, 588
**put out**
*destroy* 162
*outside* 220
*extinguish* 385
*darken* 421
*distract the attention* 458
*uncertain* **475**
*difficult* 704
*discontent* 832
- of countenance 874
oneself - of court
*sophistry* 477
*bungling* 699
- of gear 158
- of one's head 458
- of joint 61
- of one's misery 914
- to nurse 707
- of order 59
**put to** *attribute* 155
*request* 765
- the blush 879
- death 361
- the door 261
- it 704
- one's oath 768
- press 591
- the proof 463
- the question 830
- the rack 830
- rights 60
- sea 293
- shame 874
- silence 581
- the sword 361
- task 677
- use 677
- the vote 609
**put up** *assemble* 72
*locate* 184
*store* 636
- to auction 796
- for 865
- a petition } 765
- a prayer } 990
- for sale 796
- a shutter 424
- the sword 723
- to 615
- with 147, 826
**putative**
*attributed* 155
*believed* 484
*supposed* 514
**putid** 643
**putrefy** 653
**putrescence** 49
**putrid** 653
**putsch** 742
**puttee** 225
**putter** 683
**putting the weight** 840
**putty** 45
**puzzle** *uncertain* 475
*conceal* 528
*enigma* 533
- out 522
**puzzled** 475, 533
**puzzle-headed** 499
**puzzling** 519
**pyæmia** 655
**pyjamas** 225
**Pylades and Orestes** 890
**pylon** 206
**pyramid** *heap* 72
*height* 206
*point* 253
**pyramids**
*billiards* 840
**pyre** 363
**pyriform** 249
**pyrology** 382
**pyromaniac** 384, 504, 913
**pyromancy** 511
**pyrometer** 389
**pyrotechnics** 423
**pyrotechny** 382
**Pyrrhic victory** 814
**pyrrhonism** 487, 989
**Pythagorean** 953
**Pythia** *oracle* 513
**Python, -ess** 513
**pyx** *vessel* 191, 998
*temple* 1000

## Q

**Q-boat** 726
**Q.C.** 968
**Q.E.D.** 478
**quack** *cry* 412
*imposter* 548
**quackery**
*falsehood* 544
*want of skill* **699**
*affectation* 855
**quacksalver** 548
**quad** 189
**quadragesima** **956**
**quadrangle**
*four-sided* 95
*precinct* 182
*house* 189
*angular* 244
**quadrant** 244, **247**
**quadrate with** 23
**quadratic** 95
**quadrature**
*four* 95
*angle* 244
**quadrennial** 95
**quadrible** 96
**quadrifid** 97
**quadriga** 95, **272**
**quadrilateral**
*sides* 236
*angles* 244
**quadrille** 840
**quadripartition** **97**
**quadrisection** **97**
**quadrivalent** 95
**quadroon** 41
**quadruped** 366
**quadruplet** 95
**quadruplex** 96
**quadruplication** **96**
**quære** 461
**quaff** 298
- the bitter cup 828
**quaggy** 345
**quagmire**
*marsh* 345
*dirty* 653
*difficult* 704
**quail** 860, 862
**quaint** *odd* 83
*pretty* 845
*ridiculous* 853
**quake** *oscillate* **314**
*shake* 315
*cold* 383
*fear* 860
**quakery** 826, 855
**Quakerism** 984
**qualification**
[*see* qualify]
*power* 157
*modification* **469**
*skill* 698
*discount* 813
**qualify** *change* **140**
*modify* 469

## R

*wrath* 900
the battle –s 722
**ragged** 226
**ragoût** 41, 298
**rag-picker** 876
**rags** *clothes* 225
*useless* 645
do to – 384
tear to – 162
worn to – 659
**ragtime** 415, 473
**raid** 716, 791
**rail** *inclosure* 232
*prison* 752
– at 932
– in
*circumscribe* 229
*restrain* 751
**railing** 232
**raillerie, ne pas entendre** – 900
**raillery** 856
**railway** 627
– speed 274
– station 292
**raiment** 225
**rain** *stream* 348
*sufficient* 639
– or shine 474, 604
**rainbow** 440
**raincoat** 225
**rainless** 340
**rains but it pours, never** – 641
**rainy day** 735
provide against a – 673, 817
**rainy season** 348
**raise** *increase* 35
*produce* 161
*erect* 212
*elevate* 307
*excite* 824
– alarm 860
– anger 900
– one's banner 722
– a cry 531
– a dust 682
– expectations 858
– the finger 550
– funds 775
– one's head
*improve* 658
*refresh* 689
*prosperity* 734
*repute* 873
– ghosts 992
– hope 511
– a hue and cry against 932
– a laugh 840
– the mask 529
– money 788
– a question 461, 485
– a report 531
– a siege 723
– the spirits 836
– spirits from the dead 992
– a storm 173
– troops 722
– up 212, 824
– the voice 411
– one's voice 535, 932
– the wind 775, 788
**raised** *convex* 250
**raison:**
– d'être 620
– de plus 467
**raj** 737
**rajah** 745
**rajpoot** 726
**rake** *drag* 285
*gardening* 371
*clean* 652
*profligate* 949
*intemperance* 954
*libertine* 962
– out 301
– up *collect* 72
*extract* 301
*recall* 505
*excite* 824
– up evidence 467
**rake-hell** 949, 962
**raking-fire** 716
**rakish**
*intemperate* 954
*licentious* 961
**rallentando** 415
**rally** *arrange* 60
*improve* 658
*restore* 660
*ridicule* 856
*encourage* 861
– round *order* 58
*co-operate* 709
**rallying:** – cry 550, 861
– point 74
**ram** *impulse* 276
*sheep* 366
*male* 373
*man-of-war* 726
milk the – 645
– down 261, 321
– in 300
**Ramadan** 956, 998
**ramage** 367
**ramble** *stroll* 266
*wander* 279
*folly* 499
*delirium* 503
*digress* 573
**rambler** 268
**rambling** 139
**ramification** *part* 51
*bisection* 91
*posterity* 167
*filament* 205
*symmetry* 242
*divergence* 291
**rammer** 263, 276
**ramose** 242
**ramp** *slope* 217
*climb* 305
*leap* 309
**rampage** 173
**rampant**
*violent* 173
*prevalent* 175
*vertical* 212
*raised* 307
*free* 748
*vehement* 825
*licentious* 961
**rampart** 717
**ramrod** 263
**ramshackle** 665
**ranch** 780
**rancid** 401, 653
**rancour** 907, 919
**randan** 273
**random** *casual* 156
*carriage* 272
*uncertain* 475
*airless* 621
talk at –
*sophistry* 477
*exaggerate* 549
*loquacity* 584
- *experiment* 463
*chance* 621
**range** *extent* 26
*collocate* 60
*series* 69
*term* 71
*class* 75
*space* 180
*distance* 196
*roam* 266
*direction* 278
*stove* 386
*freedom* 748
out– 196
long – 196
within – 197
–finder 200
– itself 58
– under, – with 76
**ranger**
*director* 694
*keeper* 753
*thief* 792
**rank** *have place* 1
*degree* 26
*thorough* 31
*collocate* 60
*row* 69
*term* 71
*vegetation* 365
*fetid* 401
*estimate* 480
*bad* 649
*soldiers* 726
*glory* 873
*nobility* 875
man of – 875
– and file
*continuity* 69
*soldiers* 726
*commonalty* 876
– marks 747
**rankle** *unclean* 653
*corrupt* 659
*painful* 830
*animosity* 900
*malevolence* 907
*revenge* 919
**ranks**
fill up the – 660
risen from the – 876
**ransack** *seek* 461
*deliver* 672
*plunder* 791
*price* 812
*atonement* 952
– one's brains 451, 515
**ransom** 672
**rant**
*unmeaning* 517
*exaggeration* 549
*diffuse style* 573
*turgescence* 577
*speech* 582
*acting* 599
*excitement* 825
*boasting* 884
**ranter** *talker* 584
*false piety* 988
**rantipole** 458
**rap** *blow* 276
*sound* 406
*trifle* 643
*money* 800
not worth a – 804
– on the knuckles

*angry* 900
*censure* 932
*punish* 972
– out *affirm* 535
*voice* 580
*speak* 582
– out oaths 885, 908
**rapacity**
*taking* 789
*stealing* 791
*avarice* 819
*greed* 865
**rape** 791, 961
– oil 356
**rapid** 274
– slope 217
– strides
*progress* 282
*velocity* 274
– succession 136
**rapids** 348
**rapier** 727
**rapine** 791
**rapparee** 792
**rappel** 722
**rapping, spirit** – 992
**rapport** 9
**rapports, sous tous les** – 494
**rapprochement** 714, 888
**rapscallion** 949
**rapt** *attention* 457
*inattention* 458
*emotion* 821
– in thought 451
**raptorial** 789, 791
**rapture** 827, 897
**rapturous** 827
**rara avis**
*exceptional* 83
*good* 648
*famous* 873
**rare** *exceptional* 83
*few* 103
*infrequent* 137
*light* 322
*excellent* 648
**raree show** 448, 840
**rarefaction** 194, 322
**rari nantes** 103
**rarity** 322
**rasa, tabula** – 552
**rascal** 941, 949
**rascality** 940
**rase** *obliterate* 552
**rash**
*skin disease* 655
*reckless* 863
**rasher** 204
**rashness** 863
**rasp** 330, 331
**rasper** *difficult* 704
**rasure** 552
**rat** *recant* 607
smell a –
*discover* 480*a*
*doubt* 485
**rataplan** 407
**rat-a-tat** 407
**ratchet** 253
**rate** *degree* 26
*motion* 264
*measure* 466
*estimation* 480
*price, tax* 812
*abuse* 932
at a great – 274
**rath** *early* 132
*fort* 717
**rather** 32, 643
have – 609
– good 651
have – not 867
**ratification**
*confirm* 467
*affirm* 488
*consent* 762
*compact* 769
**ratio** *relation* 9
*degree* 26
*proportion* 84
*apportionment* 786
**ratiocination** 476
**ration** *quantity* 25
*food* 298
*provisions* 637
*allotment* 786
*short* –s 956
**rational**
– *quantity* 84
*intellectual* 450
*judicious* 498
*sane* 502
**rationale** *cause* 153
*attribution* 155
*answer* 462
*interpretation* 522
**rationalism** 476, 989
**rationalization** 60
**rats in the upper story** 503
**rattan** 975
**ratten** 158
**rattle** *noise* 407
*music* 417
*prattle* 584
death – 360
watchman's – 669
– on 584
**rattle-snake** 913
**rattle-traps** 780
**rattling** 836
– pace 274
**raucity** 405, 410
**raucous** *hoarse* 581
**ravage** 162, 659
**ravages of time** 659
**rave** *madness* 503
*excitement* 824, 825
– against 932
**ravel** *untwist* 60
*derange* 61
*entangle* 219
*difficulty* 704
**ravelin** 717
**ravelled** 59
**raven** *black* 431
*hoarse* 581
*gorge* 957
– for 865
**ravening** 173, 865
**ravenous** 789, 865
**raver** 504
**ravine** *interval* 198
*narrow* 203
*dike* 259
*channel* 350
**raving** *mad* 503
*feeling* 821
*excitement* 824, 825
**ravish** *seize* 789
*please* 829
**ravished**
*pleased* 827
**ravishment** 824
**raw** *immature* 123
*sensitive* 378
*cold* 383
*colour* 428
*unprepared* 674
*unskilled* 699
– head and bloody bones 860
– levies 726
– material 635
**raw-boned** 203
**ray** 420
– of comfort 831
**rayah** 745
**rayless** 421
**raze** 162
– to the ground 308
**razor** 253
cut a whetstone with a – 638
*misuse* 679
*unskilful* 699
keen as a – 821
**razzia**
*destruction* 162
*attack* 716
*plunder* 791
**re, in** – 9
**reabsorb** 296
**reach** *degree* 26
*equal* 27
*distance* 196
*fetch* 270
*arrive at* 292
*river* 348
*deceive* 545
*grasp* 737
*take* 789
within – *near* 197
*possible* 470
– the ear
*hearing* 418
*information* 527
– of thought 498
– to *distance* 196
*length* 200
**reach-me-down** 673
**reaction**
*compensation* 30
*reversion* 145
*counteraction* 179
*recoil* 277
*restoration* 660
**reactionary** 145, 607
**reactionist** 710
**read** 522, 539
well – 490
– a lecture 537
**readable** 578
**reader** *teacher* 540
*printer* 591
*clergyman* 996
**readership** 542
**readily** 705
**reading**
*speciality* 79
*knowledge* 490
*interpretation* 522
*learning* 539
– glass 445
– in 995
**reading-desk** 1000
**readjust** 23, 27
**readmit** 296
**ready**
*expecting* 507
*willing* 602
*useful* 644
*prepare* 673

*assent* 488
*concord* 714
*retaliate* 718
**reciprocity** 709
**recision** 38
**recital** 415
**recitativo** 415
**recite**
*enumerate* 85
*speak* 582
*narrate* 594
**reck** 459
**reckless**
*careless* 460
*defiant* 715
*rash* 863
**recklessly profuse** 818
**reckon** *count* 85
– among 76
– upon 484, 507
– with 807
– without one's host
*unskilful* 699
*fail* 732
*rash* 863
**reckoning**
*numeration* 85
*measure* 466
*expectation* 507
*payment* 807
*accounts* 811
*reward* 973
day of – 919
out of one's – 704
**reclaim** *restore* 660
*command* 741
*due* 924
*atonement* 952
**reclaimed**
*penitent* 950
**recline** *lie flat* 213
*depress* 308
*repose* 687
– on 215
**recluse** 893
**recognition**
[*see* recognize]
*courtesy* 894
*thanks* 916
means of – 550
**recognizable** 446, 518
– by 550
**recognizance** 771
**recognize** *see* 441
*attention* 457
*discover* 480a
*assent* 488
*know* 490
*remember* 505
*understand* 518
*permit* 760
**recognized**
*influential* 175
*customary* 613
– maxim 496
**recoil** *reaction* 179
*repercussion* 277
*reluctance* 603
*shun* 623
from which reason –s 471
– at *hate* 898
– from *dislike* 867
**recollect** 505
**recommence** 66
**recommend** 695, 931
– itself
*approbation* 931
**recompense** 790, 973
**reconcile** *agree* 23
*pacify* 723
*content* 831
*forgive* 918
– oneself to 826
**recondite** 519, 528
**recondition** 660, 790
**reconnaissance** 441
**reconnoitre** 441, 461
**reconsideration** 451
on – 658
**reconstitute** 660
**reconstruct** 660
**reconvert** 660
**record** 551
break the – 33
court of – 966
gramophone – 551
**recorder** 553
*judge* 967
**recount** 594
**recoup** 30, 790
**recourse** 677
**recovery**
*improvement* 658
*reinstatement* 660
*getting back* 775
*restitution* 790
– of strength 689
**recreant**
*coward* 862
*base* 940
*knave* 941
*vicious* 945
*bad man* 949
**recreation** 840
**recrement** 653
**recriminate** 932
**recrimination** 938
**recrudescence** 661
**recruit** *strength* 159
*learner* 541
*provision* 637
*health* 654
*repair* 658
*reinstate* 660
*refresh* 689
*aid* 707
*auxiliary* 711
*soldier* 726
beat up for –s 673, 707
**rectangle** 244
**rectangular** 212, 244
**rectify**
*straighten* 246
*improve* 658
*re-establish* 660
**rectilinear** 246
**rectitude** 939, 944
**rector** 694, 996
**rectorship** 995
**rectory** 1000
**rectus in curiâ** 946
**reculer pour mieux sauter** 673, 702
**reculons, à** – 283
**recumbent** 213, 217
**recuperation** 790
**recuperative** 660
**recur**
*repeat* 104
*frequent* 136
*periodic* 138
– to the mind 505
– to 677
**recure** 660
**recursion** 292
**recurvity** 245
**recusant**
*dissenting* 489
*denying* 536
*disobedient* 742
*refusing* 764
*impenitent* 951
*heterodox* 984
**red** 434
paint the town – 840
turn – *feeling* 821
– book *list* 86
– coat 726
– cross 662
– flag 669
– hot *great* 31
*violent* 173
*hot* 382
*emotion* 821
*excited* 824
– letter 550, 883
–letter day
*important* 642
*rest* 687
*amusement* 840
*celebration* 883
– light 669
– rag to a bull 900
– republican 742
– tape 613
– tapist 694
– and yellow 439
**redact** 590, 658
**redan** 717
**redargue** 479
**red cap** 271
**redden** *colour* 434
*humble* 879
*angry* 900
**reddition**
*interpretation* 522
*restitution* 790
**redeem**
*compensate* 30
*substitute* 147
*reinstate* 660
*deliver* 672
*regain* 775
*restore* 790
*pay* 807
*atone* 952
– from oblivion 505
– one's pledge 772, 926
**Redeemer** 976
**redemption**
[*see* redeem]
*liberation* 750
*duty* 926
*salvation* 976
**red-handed**
*murder* 361
*in the act* 680
*guilty* 947
**redict** 905
**redingote** 225
**redintegrate** 660
**redintegratio amoris** 607
**redivivus** 660
**redness** 434
**redolence**
*odour* 398
*fragrance* 400
**redouble**
*increase* 35
*duplication* 90

**reliquary** 191, 998
**reliquiæ** 362
**relish** *pleasure* 377
*savour* 390
*condiment* 393
*savoury* 394
*delight* 827
*desire* 865
**relive** 660
**relucent** 420
**reluct** 720
**reluctance**
*dissuasion* 616
*unwilling* 603
*dislike* 867
**reluctation** 719
**relume** 384, 420
**rely** 484, 858
**rem acu tetigisti** 23
**remain** *be left* 40
*endure* 106
*long time* 110
*continue* 141
*be present* 186
*stand* 265
– firm 150
– on one's hands 641
– in one's mind 505
– neuter 605
– in possession of the field 731
**remainder** 40
*estate* 780
in – *posterior* 117
**remainder-man** 779
**remains**
*remainder* 40
*corpse* 362
*vestige* 551
organic – 357
**remand** *defer* 133
*order* 741
**remanet** 40
**remark** *observe* 457
*affirmation* 535
worthy of – 642
**remarkable**
*great* 31
*exceptional* 83
*important* 642
**remarry** 903
**Rembrandtesque** 160
**remediable, remedial** 660, 662
**remediless** 859
**remedy** 660, 662
**remembrance** 505
**remembrances** 894
**rememoration** 505
**remigration**
*regression* 283
*arrival* 292
*egress* 295
**remind** 505
that –s me 134
**reminiscence** 505
**remise** 927*a*
**remiss**
*neglectful* 460
*reluctant* 603
*idle* 683
*lax* 738
**remission**
*cessation* 142
*moderation* 174
*laxity* 738
*forgiveness* 918
*exemption* 927*a*
**remit**
[*see* remission]
– one's efforts 681
**remittance** 807
**remittent**
*periodic* 138
**remitter** 790
**remnant** 40
**remodel**
*convert* 144
*revolutionize* 146
*improve* 658
**remonstrance** 616, 766, 932
**remora** *cohere* 46
*hindrance* 706
**remorse** 950
**remorseless** 919
**remote** 10, 196
– age 122
– cause 153
– future 121
**remotest idea, not have** – 491
**remotion** 270
**remount** 147
**remove** *subduct* 38
*term* 71
*displace* 185
*transfer* 270
*recede* 287
*depart* 293
*dinner* 298
*extract* 301
*school* 541
– the mask 529
**removedness**
*distance* 196
**remugient** 412
**remunerate** 973
**remunerative** 644, 775
**renaissance** 660
**renascence** 660
**renascent** 163
**rencounter**
*contact* 199
*meeting* 292
*fight* 720
**rend** 44
– the air 404, 411, 839
– the heart-strings 830
**render** *convert* 144
*interpret* 522
*give* 784
*restore* 790
– an account
*inform* 527
*describe* 594
– *hors de combat* 645
– a service 644
**rendering**
*covering* 223
**rendezvous** 72, 74
**rendition**
*interpretation* 522
*restore* 790
**renegade**
*convert* 144
*turncoat* 607
*fugitive* 623
*apostate* 941
**renew** *twice* 90
*repeat* 104
*reproduce* 163
*recollect* 505
*improve* 658
*restore* 660
– one's strength 689
**reniform** 245
**renitence**
*counteraction* 179
*hardness* 323
*elasticity* 325
*unwillingness* 603
*resistance* 719
**renitency**
*light* 420
**renounce**
*recant* 607
*relinquish* 624
*resign* 757
*abnegate* 764
- *property* 782
*repudiate* 927
**renovare dolorem, infandum** – 833
**renovate** 163, 660
**renovated** *new* 123
**renown** 873
**renownless** 874
**rent** *tear* 44
*fissure* 198
*hire* 788
*purchase* 795
**rental** 810
**renter** 188, 779
**rent-free** 815
**rent-roll** 780, 810
**rents** *houses* 189
**renunciation**
[*see* renounce]
*exemption* 927*a*
**reorganize**
*order* 60
*convert* 144
*improve* 658
*restore* 660
**repair**
*mend* 658
*make good* 660
*refresh* 689
out of – 659
– to 266
**reparation**
[*see* repair]
*compensation* 30
*restitution* 790
*atonement* 952
*reward* 973
**repartee** 462, 842
**reparteeist** 844
**repartition** 786
**repass, pass and** – 314
**repast** 298
**repatriation** 790
**repay** 790, 807, 973
**repeal** 756
**repeat** *imitate* 19
*duplication* 90
*iterate* 104
*reproduce* 163
*affirm* 535
– by rote 505
**repeated** 104, 136
**repeater**
*watch* 114
*fire-arm* 727
**repel** *repulse* 289
*deter* 616
*defend* 717
*resist* 719
*refuse* 764
*give pain* 830
*disincline* 867
*banish* 893
*excite hate* 898
**repent** 950
**repercussion** 277

*choose* 609
*store* 636
*disuse* 678
*retain* 781
*shyness* 881
in – *destined* 152
*prepared* 673
– forces 726
– oneself 881
reservoir 636
re-shape 140
resiance 189
resiant 186
reside 1, 186
residence 189
resident
*consignee* 758
*present* 186
*inhabitant* 188
residentiary 186, 188
*clergy* 996
residue 40
residuum
*remainder* **40**
*dregs* 653
*commonalty* 876
resign 757, 782
– one's being 364
– one's breath 360
– oneself 725, 826
resignation [*see* resign]
*submission* 725
*obedience* 743
*abdication* **757**
*renunciation* 782
*endurance* 826
*humility* 879
resile 277
resilience
*regression* 283
*elasticity* 325
resin **356a**
resipiscence 950
resist *oppose* 179
*withstand* 719
*disobey* 742
*refuse* 764
resistance 719
résistance, pièce de – 298
resister
passive – **710**
resisting
*tenacious* 327
resistless 159, 601
resolute 604, 861
resolution
*decomposition* 49
*conversion* 144
*music* 413
*topic* 454
*investigation* 461
*mental energy* **604**
*intention* 620
*scheme* 626
*courage* 861
resolvable into 27, 144
resolve *change* 140
*liquefy* 335
*investigate* 461
*discover* 480*a*
*interpret* 522
*determine* 604
*predetermine* 611
*intend* 620
– into elements 49
– into *convert* 144
resonance 402, **408**
resorb 296
resort *assemble* 72
*focus* 74
*dwelling* 189
*converge* 290
last – 601
– to *be present* 186
*travel* 266
*employ* 677
resound *loud* 404
*ring* 408
– praises 931
resourceful 698
resources
*means* 632
*property* 780
*wealth* 803
respect *relation* 9
*observe* 772
*fame* 873
*salutation* 894
*deference* **928**
have – to 9
in no – 536
with – to 9
respectability
*mediocrity* 736
*repute* 873
*probity* 939
respectable
*unimportant* 643
respectful 928
– distance 623, 864
respective 79, 786
respectless 458
respects 894, 928
resperse 73
respicere finem 510
respire *breathe* 349
*live* 359
*refresh* 689
respite
*intermission* 106
*defer* 133
*pause* 142
*deliver* 672
*repose* 687
*reprieve* 970
resplendent
*luminous* 420
*splendid* 845
respond *accord* 23
*answer* 462
*feel* 821
respondent 462
*accused* 938
response
*answer* 462, **587**
*concord* 714
*feeling* 821
*friendship* 888
*worship* 990
responsible 177, 926
responsibility
upon one's own – 600
responsive 375
rest *remainder* 40
*pause* 141
*cessation* 142
*support* 215
*quiescence* 265
*death* 360
*silence* 403
*music* 413
*inaction* 681
*repose* 687
at – *repose* 687
*content* 831
home of – 189
set at –
*answer* 462
*ascertain* 474
*complete* 729
*compact* 769
set one's mind at – *calm* 826
set the question at – 478, 480
– assured 484, 858
– on *support* 215
– on one's oars 142, 687
– satisfied 831
– and be thankful 681, 687
– upon
*evidence* 467
*confide* 484
– with *duty* 926
restaurant 189
– car 272
restaurateur **637**
restful 265
resting place
*support* 215
*quiet* 265
*arrival* 292
restitution **790, 660**
restive *averse* 603
*obstinate* 606
*disobedient* 742
*refusal* 764
*perverse* 901*a*
restless
*changeable* 149
*moving* 264
*agitated* 315
*active* 682
*excited* 825
*fearful* 860
restoration **660**
restorative
*salubrious* 656
*remedial* 662
*relieving* 834
restore *reinstate* 660
*refresh* 689
*return* 790
– equilibrium **27**
– harmony 723
– to health 654
restrain 616, 706, 751
restrainable 743
restrained 751
restraint 578, **751**
self – 826, 953
restrict *hinder* **706**
*restrain* 751
*prohibit* 761
restringency 751
result *remainder* **40**
*follow* 117
*effect* 154
*conclusion* 480
*completion* 729
resultant 48, 154
resume *begin* 66
*repeat* 104
*change* 140
*restore* 660
*take* 789
résumé 596
resupination 213
resurgence 163, 660
resurrection
*reproduction* **163**
*restoration* **660**
*heaven* 981

**revision, under –** 673
**revisit** 186
**revival**
*reproduction* 163
*restoration* 660
*worship* 990
**revivalist** 996
**revive**
*reproduce* 163
*improve* 658
*resuscitate* 660
*excite* 824
**revivify**
*reproduce* 163
*life* 359
*improve* 658
*resuscitate* 660
**revocable** 605
**revoir, au –** 293
**revoke** 607, 756
**revolt** *resist* 719
*disobey* 742
*shock* 830
*disapproval* 932
– against *hate* 898
– at the idea
*dissent* 489
**revolting**
*painful* 830
**revolution**
*periodicity* 138
*change* **146**
*rotation* 312
*disobedience* 742
**revolutionize** 140, 146
**revolve**
[*see* revolution]
– in the mind 451
**revolver** 727
**revue** 599
intimate – 599
**revulsion**
*reversion* 145
*revolution* 146
*inversion* 218
*recoil* 277
**reward** **973**
**reword** 104
**Reynard**
*animal* 366
*cunning* 702
**rez-de-chaussée** 191, 207
**rhabdology** 85
**rhabdomancy** 511
**Rhadamanthus** 967, 982
**rhapsodical**
*irregular* 139
*imaginary* 515
**rhapsodist**
*fanatic* 504
**rhapsody**
*discontinuity* 70
*music* 415
*nonsense* 497
*fancy* 515
*poetry* 597
**rhetoric** *speech* 582
flowers of – 577
**rheum**
*excretion* 299
*fluidity* 333
*water* 337
**rhino** 800
**rhinoceros hide** 376, 823
**rhomb** 244
**rhumb** 278
**rhyme**
*similarity* 17
*verse* 597
without – or reason
*absurd* 497
*caprice* 608
*motiveless* 615a
**rhymeless** 598
**rhymester** 597
**rhythm**
*periodicity* 138
*melody* 413
*elegance* 578
*verse* 597
**rhythmical**
- *style* 578
**Rialto** 799
**rib** *support* 215
*ridge* 250
*wife* 903
**ribald** *vulgar* 851
*disreputable* 874
*impure* 961
**riband**
[*see* ribbon]
**ribbed** 259
**ribbon** *tie* 45
*filament* 205
*record* 551
*decoration* 877
–s *reins* 752
handle the – 693
**ribroast** 972
**rich** *savoury* 394
*colour* 428
*language* 577
*abundant* 639
*wealthy* 803
*beautiful* 845
*ornament* 847
– man 803
**riches** 803
**richesses, embarras de** – 641, 803
**richly** *much* 31
– deserve 924
**rick** 72, 636
**rickety** *weak* 160
*ugly* 846
*imperfect* 651
**rickshaw** 272
**ricochet** 277
**ricordo, non mi –** 506
**rid** *deliver* 672
get – of *eject* 297
*liberation* 750
*loose* 776
*relinquish* 782
**riddance** 672, 776, 782
good – 776
**riddle** *arrange* 60
*sieve* 260
*secret* 533
*clean* 652
**ride** *get above* 206
*move* 266
*break in* 370
– at anchor 265
– full tilt at 622, 716
– hard 274
– one's hobby 622
– rough shod
*violence* 173
*severity* 739
*insolence* 885
*illegality* 964
– out the storm 664
– and tie
*periodicity* 138
*journey* 266
– the whirlwind 604, 737
**rideau, lever de –** 599
**ridentem dicere verum** 836, 842
**rider** *appendix* 39
*equestrian* 268
**rideret Heraclitus** 853
**ridge** *narrow* 203
*height* 206
*prominence* 250
**ridicule** **856**, 929
**ridiculous**
*absurd* 497
*foolish* 499
*trifling* 643
*grotesque* 853
**ridiculousness** **853**
**riding** *district* 181
*journey* 266
**ridotto** 840, 892
**rifacimento** 104, 660
**rife** *existence* 1
*general* 78
*influence* 175
**riff-raff** *dirt* 653
*commonalty* **876**
*bad folk* 949
**rifle** *musket* 727
*plunder* 791
– shot 406
**rifled cannon** **727**
**rifleman** 726
**rifler** 792
**rifles** 726
**rifle-shooting** 840
**rift** 44, 198
– within the lute 651, 713
**rig** *dress* 225
*prepare* 673
*frolic* 840
*strumpet* 962
– the market **794**
run the – upon **929**
**rigadoon** 840
**rigging** *ropes* 45
*gear* 225
*instrument* **633**
**riggish** 961
**right** *dextral* **238**
*straight* 246
*true* 494
*property* 780
*just* **922**
*privilege* 924
*duty* 926
*honour* 939
*virtuous* 944
bill of – 969
by – 924
have a – to **924**
set – *inform* **527**
*disclose* 529
that's – 931
– about
[*see below*]
– ahead 234
– angle 212
– ascension 466
– away 133
step in the – direction 644
– hand [*see below*]
– itself 660

– and boiled 298
– an ox 883
**rob** 354, 791
**robber** 792
**robbery** 791
**robe** 225, 999
**robes** – of state 747
**Robin Goodfellow** 980
**Robinson**
say Jack – 132
**Robot** 554
**robust** *strong* 159, 654
**roc** 83
**rocaille** 853
**rock** *firm* 150
*oscillate* 314
*hard* 323
*land* 342
*safety* 664
*danger* 667
build on a – 150
founded on a – 664
split upon a – 732
– ahead 665
–bound coast 342
– oil 356
**rocket** *rapid* 274
*rise* 305
*light* 423
*signal* 550
*arms* 727
*fireworks* 840
go up like a – and come down like the stick 732
**rocking-chair** 215
**rococo** 124, 853
**rod** *support* 215
*measure* 466
*scourge* 975
*divining* 993
kiss the – 725
sounding – 208
– of empire 747
– in pickle
*prepared* 673
*accusation* 938
*punishment* 972
*scourge* 975
**rodeo** 720, 840
**rodomontade**
*exaggeration* 482
*unmeaning* 517
*boast* 884
**roe** 366, 374
**Roentgen rays** 420
**rogation**
*request* 765
*worship* 990
**rogue** *cheat* 548
*knave* 941
*scamp* 949
–'s march 297
**roguery** 940
**roguish**
*playful* 840
**Roi le veut, le** – 741
**roister** 885
**roisterer** 887
**Roland for an Oliver**
*retaliation* 718
*revenge* 919
*barter* 794
**rôle** *drama* 599
*business* 625
*plan* 626
*conduct* 692
**roll** *list* 86
*fillet* 205
*convolution* 248
*rotundity* 249
*make smooth* 255
*move* 264
*fly* 267
*rotate* 312
*rock* 314
*flow* 348
*sound* **407**
*record* 551
*money* 800
strike off the – 756, 972
– along 312
– in the dust 731
– on the ground 839
– of honour 86
– in 639, 641
– on 109
– into one 43
– in riches 803
– up 312
– up in 225
– in wealth 803
**roll-call** 85
**roller** *fillet* 45
*round* 249
*clothing* 255
*rotate* 312
**roller-coaster** 840
**rollers** *billows* 348
**rollick** 836
**rollicker** 838
**rollicking**
*frolicsome* 836
*blustering* 885
**rolling:** – pin 249
– stock 272
– stone 312
**Rolls:** Master of the –
*recorder* 553
*judge* 967
– Court 966
**Roman candle** 840
**Roman Catholic** 984
**romance**
*music* 415
*absurdity* 497
*imagination* 515
*untruth* 546
*fable* 594
**Romanism** 984
**romantic**
*imaginative* 515
*art* 556
*sensitive* 822
**romanticism** 515
**Romanus sum, civis** – 924
**Romany** 563
**Rome:** Church of 984
do at – as the Romans do 82
**romp** *violent* 173
*game* 840
**rondeau** *music* 415
*poem* 597
**rondel** 597
**rondoletto** 597
**rood** *area* 180
*cross* 998
– loft 1000
**roof** 189, 223
**roofless** 226
**rook** 791, 792
**rookie** 726
**rookery** *nests* 189
*dirt* 653
**room** *occasion* 134
*space* 180
*lodge* 186
*chamber* 191
*plea* 617
assembly – 840
in the – of 147
make – for
*opening* 260
*respect* 928
**roommate** 890
**rooms**
*lodgings* 189
**roomy** 180
**roost** 189
rule the – **737**
**rooster** 366
**root** *algebraic* - **84**
*cause* 153
*place* 184
*abide* 186
*base* 211
*etymon* 562
lie at the – of 642
pluck up by the –s 301
strike at the – of 716
take –
*influence* **175**
*locate* 184
*habit* 613
– and branch **52**
cut up – and branch 162
– out *eject* 297
*extract* 301
*discover* 480a
**rooted**
*old* 124
*firm* 150
*located* 184
*habit* 613
deep – 820
– antipathy **867**
– belief 484
**rope** *fastening* **45**
cord 205
*freedom* 748
*scourge* 975
give – enough **738**
–'s end 975
– of sand
*incoherence* **47**
*weakness* 160
*impossible* **471**
– way 627
**rope-dancer** 700
**rope-dancing** 698
**ropy** 352
**roquelaure** 225
**roric** 339
**rosâ, sub** – 528
**rosary** 990, 998
**Roscius** 599
**rose** *pipe* 350
*fragrant* **400**
*red* 434
*beauty* 845
bed of –s 377, **734**
couleur de –
*red* 434
*good* 648
*prosperity* **734**
*hope* 858
under the – 528
welcome as the –s in May 829, **892**

**roseate** *red* 434
*hopeful* 858
**rose-coloured**
*hope* 858
**Rosetta stone** 522
**rosette** 847
**rose-water**
*moderation* 174
*flattery* 933
not made with –
704
**Rosicrucian**
*order* or *party*
712
**rosin** *rub* 331
*resin* 356*a*
**Rosinante** 271
**roster** 86
**rostrum** *beak* 234
*pulpit* 542
**rosy** 434
– wine 959
**rosy-cheeked** 845
**rot** *decompose* 49
*absurdity* 497
*rubbish* 517
*putrefy* 653
*disease* 655
*decay* 659
**rota** 86, 138
**Rotarian** 892
**rotate** 138
**rotation** 312
*periodicity* 138
**rote, by** – 505
know – 490
learn – 539
**rôti** 298
**rôtisserie** 189
**rotogravure** 531,
558
**rotten** *weak* 160
*bad* 649
*foul* 653
*decayed* 659
– at the core
*deceptive* 545
*diseased* 655
– borough 893
**rotulorum, custos** –
553
**rotund** 249
**rotunda** 189
**rotundity** 249
**roturier** 876
**roué** 949
**rouge** 434, 847
**rouge-et-noir** 621
**rough** *violent* 173
*shapeless* 241
*uneven* 256
*pungent* 392
*unsavoury* 395
*sour* 397
*sound* 410
*unprepared* 674
*fighter* 726
*ugly* 846
*low fellow* 876
*bully* 887
*churlish* 895
*evil-doer* 913
*bad man* 949
cut up – 900
– copy *writing* 590
*unprepared* 674
– diamond
*uncouth* 241
*unprepared* 674
*artless* 703
*vulgar* 851
*commonalty* 876
*good man* 948
– draft 626
– guess 514
– it 686
– sea 348
– side of the
tongue 932
– and tumble 59
– weather 173, 349
**rough-cast** 256
*covering* 223
*shape* 240
*scheme* 626
*unpolished* 674
**rough-hew** 240, 673
**roughly**
*nearly* 197
**rough-neck** 876,
887
**roughness** 256
**rough-rider** 268
**roughshod over,**
ride – 739
**roulade** 415
**rouleau**
*assemblage* 72
*cylinder* 249
*money* 800
**roulette** 621, 840
**round** *series* 69
*revolution* 138
– *of a ladder* 215
*curve* 245
*circle* 247
*rotund* 249
*music* 415
*fight* 720
all – 227
bring – 660
come –
*periodic* 138
*recant* 607
*persuade* 615
dizzy – 312
get – 660
go – 311
go one's –s 266
go the –
*publication* 531
make the – of 311
run the – of 682
go the same – 104
turn – *invert* 218
*retreat* 283
*revolve* 311
– assertion 535
– a corner 311
– dance 840
– game 840
– hand 590
– like a horse in a
mill 613
– of the ladder 71
– number 84, 102
in – numbers 29,
197
– pace 274
– of pleasures
377, 840
– robin
*information* 527
*petition* 765
*censure* 932
– and round 138,
312
– sum 800
– terms 566
– trot 274
– up 370
– of visits 892
**round about**
*circumjacent* 227
*deviation* 279
*circuit* 311
*amusement* 840
– phrases 573
– way 279
**rounded periods**
577, 578
**roundelay** 597
**rounders** 840
**round-house** 752
**roundlet** 247
**round-shouldered**
243
**roup** 796
**rouse** 615, 824
– oneself 682
**rousing** 171
**rout** *crowd* 72
*agitation* 315
*overcome* 731
*discomfit* 732
*rabble* 876
*assembly* 892
put to the – 732
– out 652
**route** 627
en – 270
en – for 282
**routine**
*uniform* 16
*order* 58
*rule* 80
*periodic* 138
*custom* 613
*business* 625
**rove** *travel* 266
*deviate* 279
**rover** *traveller* 268
*pirate* 792
**roving commission**
475
**row** *disorder* 59
*series* 69
*violence* 173
*street* 189
*navigate* 267
*discord* 713
– in the same
boat 88
**rowdy** *vulgar* 851,
876
*blusterer* 887
*bad man* 949
**rowel** 253, 615
**rower** 269
**rowlock** 215
**royal** 737
– blue 438
– highness 877
– road 627, 705
**Royal Academician**
559
**royalist** 737
**royaliste que le roi**
plus 33
**royalty** 737
**Rt. Hon.** 877
**ruade** *impulse* 276
*attack* 716
**ruat cœlum** 908
**rub** *friction* 331
*touch* 379
*difficulty* 704
*adversity* 735
*painful* 830
– off corners 82
– down *lessen* 195
*powder* 330
– down with an
oaken towel 972

**saddle** 215
in the – 673
– on 37, 43
– on the right horse
*discovery* 480*a*
*skill* 698
*right* 922
*fair* 939
– with *add* 37
*attribute* 155
*quarter on* 184
*clog* 706
*impose a duty* 926
*accuse* 938
– on the wrong horse 495, 699
– up 293
**saddle-bags** 191
**Sadducee** 984
**sadness, in** – 535
**safe** *cupboard* 191
*hiding place* 530
*secure* 664
*treasury* 802
*cautious* 864
– conduct 631
– conscience 926, 946
– deposit 636
– keeping 670
– and sound 654
on the – side 864
**safety 664**
– bicycle 272
– curtain 599
– first 664, 864
– match 388
– valve 666
**saffron** *colour* 436
**sag** 214, 217, 245
**saga** 594
**sagacious** 498, 510
**sage** 498, **500**
– maxim 496
**saggar** 386
**sagittal** 253
**sagittary** 83
**sagum** 225
**Sahara** 169
**sahib** 373, 745, 875
**saick** 273
**said** *preceding* 62
*repeated* 104
*prior* 116
it is – 532
thou hast – 488
more easily – than done 704
**sail** *navigate* **267**
*ship* 273
*set out* 293
easy – 174
full – 274
press of – 274
shorten – 275
take in – 174
take the wind out of one's –s 706
too much – 863
under – 267
– before the wind 734
– near the wind 698
– too near the wind 863
**sailing**: plain – **705**
– vessel 273
**sailor** 269
fair weather – **701**
**saint** *angel* 977
*revelation* 985
*piety* 987
*false piety* 988
tutelary – 664
**Saint Monday** 840
**saintly** 944, 987
**sais quoi, je ne** – 563
**sake**:
for the – of 615, 707
for goodness – **765**
**salaam**
*bow* 308
*submit* 725
*courtesy* 894
*respect* 928
**salacity** 961
**salad** 41
– oil 356
**salade** 717
**salamander** 386
**salariat** 875
**salary** 973
**sale 796**
bill of – 771
for – *offer* 763
*barter* 794
**saleable** 796
**salebrosity** 256
**salesman** 797
**salient**
*projecting* 250
*sharp* 253
*manifest* 525
*important* 642
– angle 244
– points 642
**saline** 392
**saliva** 299, 332
**salivate** 297
**salle-à-manger** 191
**sallet** 717
**sallow**
*colourless* 429
*yellow* 436
**sally** *issue* 293
*attack* 716
*wit* 842
**sally-port** 295, **717**
**salmagundi** 41
**salmi** 298
**salmon-coloured** 434
**saloon** 189, 191
**salt** *sailor* 269
*pungent* 392
*condiment* 393
*importance* 642
*preserve* 670
*money* 800
*wit* 842
below the – 876
worth one's – 644
– of the earth 648, 948
– water 341
**saltation** 309
**saltatory** 315
**saltimbanco** 548
**saltpetre** 392, 727
**saltum, per** – 315
**salubrity 656**
**salutary** 656
**salutatory** 582
**salute**
*allocution* 586
*celebration* 883
*courtesy* 894
*kiss* 902
*respect* 928
**salutiferous** [*see* salutary]
**salva**:
– res est 664
– sit reverentia 928
**salvable** 946
**salvage**
*acquisition* 775
*tax* 812
*discount* 813
*reward* 973
**salvation**
*preservation* 670
*deliverance* 672
*religious* 976
*piety* 987
work out one's – 990
**salve** *unguent* **356**
*remedy* 662
*relieve* 834
**salver** 191
**salvo** *exception* **83**
*explosion* 406
*qualification* **469**
*plea* 617
*attack* 716
*excuse* 937
– of artillery
*celebration* 883
**Samaritan, good** – 906, 912
**same** 13
all the – to 823
in the – boat **709**
in the – breath 113, 120
go over the – ground 104
of the – mind **488**
on the – tack **709**
adds up to the – thing 27
at the – time **30,** 120
**sameness** 16
**samiel** 349
**samisen** 417
**Sammael** 978
**samovar** 191
**sampan** 273
**sample** 82, 463
**Samson** 159
**sana, mens** – 502
– in corpore sano 827
**sanation** 660
**sanative** 662
**sanatorium** 662
**sanctification** 976
**sanctify** 926, 987
**sanctimony** 988
**sanction**
*permission* **760**
*dueness* 924
*approbation* **931**
**sanctitude** 987
**sanctity** 987
**sanctuary** 666, **100**
**sanctum** 191
– sanctorum
*abode* 189
*privacy* 893
*temple* 1000
**sand** *powder* **330**
–bag 727
built upon – **665**
–dance 840
sow the – **645**

**sciolist** 493
**sciomachy** 497
**Sciomancy** 511
**scion** *part* 51
*child* 129
*posterity* 167
**scire**: – facias 461
– quid valeant humeri 698
**scission** 44
**scissors** 253
– and paste 609
**scissure** 198
**sclerotics** 195
**scobs** 330
**scoff** *ridicule* 856
*deride* 929
*impiety* 988
– at *despise* 930
*censure* 932
**scold** *shrew* 901
*malediction* 908
*censure* 932
**scollop** 248, 257
**sconce** *top* 210
*candlestick* 423
*brain* 450
*defence* 717
*mulct* 974
**scone** 298
**scoop**
*depression* 252
*perforator* 262
**scooter** 272
**scope** *degree* 26
*opportunity* 134
*extent* 180
*meaning* 516
*freedom* 748
**scorch**
*rush* 274
*heat* 382, 384
**scorching**
*violent* 173
**score**
*music* 60, 415
*count* 85
*list* 86
*twenty* 98
*notch* 257
*furrow* 259
*mark* 550
*success* 731
*credit* 805
*debt* 806
*accounts* 811
on the – of
*relation* 9
*motive* 615
**scores** *many* 102
**scoriæ** *ash* 384
*dirt* 653
**scorify** 384
**scoring board** 551
**scorn** 930
**scorpion**
*painful* 830
*evil-doer* 913
(*bane* 663)
chastise with –s 739
**scorse** 794
**scot** *reward* 973
**scot free** *free* 748
*cheap* 815
*exempt* 927*a*
escape –
*escape* 671
let off – 970
**scotch** *notch* 257
*injure* 659
– the snake
*maim* 158
*insufficient* 640
*non-completion* 730
– the wheel 706
**scotomy** 443
**Scotsman**
*canny* 702
**Scotticism** 563
**scoundrel** 913, 949
**scour** *run* 274
*rub* 331
*clean* 652
– the country 266
– the plain 274
**scourge** *bane* 663
*painful* 830
*punish* 972
*instrument of punishment* **975**
– of the human race 913
**scourings** 645
**scout** 234
*observer* 444
*feeler* 463
*messenger* **534**
*reject* 610
*warship* 726
*servant* 746
*watch* 664
*warning* 668
*disrespect* 929
*disdain* 930
(*looker* 444)
(*underrate* 483)
(*ridicule* 856)
**scow** 273
**scowl**
*complain* 839
*frown* 895
*anger* 900
*sullen* 901*a*
*disapprobation* 932
**scrabble**
*unmeaning* **517**
*scribble* 590
**scrag** 32, 203
**scraggy** *lean* **193**, 203
*rough* 256
**scramble**
*confusion* **59**
*climb* 305
*pursue* 622
*haste* 684
*difficulty* 704
*contend* 720
*seize* 789
**scranch** 330
**scrannel** 643
**scrap** 32, 720
– of paper 158, 940
**scrap-book** 596
**scrape** *subduct* 38
*reduce* 195
*pulverize* 330
*abrade* 331
*mezzotint* 558
*difficulty* 704
*mischance* 732
*bow* 894
– together
*assemble* 72
*acquire* 775
**scraper** 652
**scratch** *groove* **259**
*abrade* 331
*mark* 550
*daub* 555
*draw* 556
*write* 590
*hurt* 619
*wound* 649
come to the – 720, 861
mere – 209
old – 978
up to the – 861
without a – 654, 670
– the head **461**
– out 552
**scrawl** 590
**scrawny** 203
**screak** 411
**scream** *cry* 411, 839
**screech** 411, 412
**screech owl** 412
**screed** 582, 593
**screen** *sift* **60**
*sieve* 260
*shade* 424
*cinema* 448
*hide* 528
*hider* 530
*side-scene* **599**
*clean* 652
*safety* 664
*shelter* 666
*defence* 717
– from sight **442**
**screw** *fasten* 43
*fastening* 45
*distort* 243
*oar* 267
*rotation* 312
*instrument* **633**
*miser* 819
put on the – **739**, **744**
– one's courage to the sticking place 861
– loose *insane* **503**
*imperfect* 651
*unskilful* 699
*hindrance* 706
*attack* 713
– up *fasten* 43
*strengthen* 159
*prepare* 673
– up the eyes **443**
**screw-driver** 633
**screwed**
*drunk* 959
**screw-steamer** 273
**scribble** 517, 590
**scribbler** 593
**scribe** *recorder* **553**
*writer* 590, 593
*priest* 996
–s and Pharisees 988
**scribendi, ca-coëthes** – 580
**scrimshanker** 603
**scrimmage** 713, 720
**scrimp** *short* 201
*insufficient* 640
*stingy* 819
**scrip** 191
**script** 590, 599
**scripta, lex** – 963
**scriptæ, literæ** – 590
**scriptural** 983*a*
**Scripture**
*certain* 474
*revelation* 985
**scrivener** *writer* **590**
*lawyer* 968

in the – 490
keep a – 585
– motive 615
– passage 627, 671
– place 530
– writing 590
**secrétaire** 191
**secretary**
*recorder* 553
*writer* 590
*director* 694
*auxiliary* 711
*servant* 746
*consignee* 758
– of state 694
– of the treasury 801
**secrete** *excrete* 297
*conceal* 528
**secretion** 299
**secretive** 528
**sect** 75
religious – 983, 984
**sectarian**
*dissent* 489
*ally* 711
*heterodox* 984
**sectary** 489
**section** *division* 44
*part* 51
*class* 75
*chapter* 593
*troops* 726
**sector** *part* 51
*circle* 247
**secula seculorum,** in – 112
**secular**
*centenary* 98
*periodic* 138
*laity* 997
– education 537
**secularism** 984
**secundum artem** 82, 698
**secure** *fasten* 43
*bespeak* 132
*belief* 484
*safe* 664
*restrain* 751
*engage* 768
*gain* 775
*confident* 858
– an object 731
**securities** 802–805
**security** *safety* 664
*pledge* 771
*hope* 858
lend on – 787
**Sedan**
*disaster* 162
**sedan chair** 272
**sedate**
*thoughtful* 451
*calm* 826
*grave* 837
**sedative** 174, 662
**sedentary** 265
**sedge** 367
**sedile** 1000
**sediment** *dregs* 653
**sedimentary** 40
**sedition** 742
**seduce** *entice* 615
*love* 897
*debauch* 961
**seducer** 962
**seduction** 829, 865
**sedulous** 682, 865
**see** *view* 441
*look* 457
*believe* 484
*know* 490
*bishopric* 995
we shall – 507
– after 459
– daylight 480*a*
– double 959
– fit 600, 602
– at a glance 498
– justice done 922
– life 840
– the light
*born* 359
*published* 531
– service 722
– sights 455
– through 480*a*, 498
– to *attention* 457
*care* 459
*direction* 693
– one's way
*foresight* 510
*intelligible* 518
*skill* 698
*easy* 705
**seed** *small* 32
*cause* 153
*posterity* 167
*grain* 330
run to – *age* 128
*lose health* 659
sow the – 673
**seedling** 129
**seed-plot** 168, 371
**seed-time of life** 127
**seedy** *weak* 160
*disease* 655
*deteriorated* 659
*exhausted* 688
*needy* 804
**seeing that** 8, 476
**seek** *inquire* 461
*pursue* 622
*offer* 763
*request* 765
– safety 664
**seek-sorrow** 837
**seel** 217
**seem** 448
as it –s good to 600
**seeming** 448
**seemingly** 472
**seemless** 846, 925
**seemliness** 926
**seemly**
*expedient* 646
*handsome* 845
*due* 924
**seep** 295
**seer** *veteran* 130
*madman* 504
*oracle* 513
*sorcerer* 994
**see-saw** 12, 314
**seethe** *wet* 339
*hot* 382
*make hot* 384
*excitement* 824
**seething caldron** 386
**segar** 392
**segment** 44, 51
**segnitude** 683
**s'égosiller** 411
**segregate**
*not related* 10
*separate* 44
*exclude* 55
**segregated**
*incoherent* 47
**seigneur, grand** –
*pride* 878
*insolence* 885
**seignior** 745, 875
**seigniority**
*authority* 737
*possession* 777
*property* 780
**seigniory** 737
**seine net** 232
**seisin** 777, 780
**seismic** 314
**seismograph** 553
**seismometer** 276, 314
**seize** 789, 791
– an opportunity 134
**seized with**
*disease* 655
*feeling* 821
**seizure** 925
**sejunction** 44
**seldom** 137
**select** *choose* 609
*good* 648
**self** 13, 79
–abasement 879
–accusing 950
–admiration 880
–applause 880
–appointed task 602
–assertion 885
–called 565
–command 604, 864
–communing 451
–complacency 836, 880
–confidence 880
–conquest 604
–conscious 855
–consultation 451
–contained 52
–control 604
–conviction
*belief* 484
*penitent* 950
*condemned* 971
–counsel 451
–deceit *error* 495
–deception 486
–defence 717
–delusion 486
–denial
*disinterested* 942
*temperance* 953
*penance* 990
–discipline 990
–effacement 879, 942
–esteem 880
–evident 474, 525
–examination 990
–existing 1
–government 748
–help 698
–immolation 991
–indulgence
*selfishness* 943
*intemperance* 954
–interest 943
–knowledge 881
–love 943
–luminous 423
–mastery 604
–opinioned 481
–possession

*sanity* 502
*resolution* 604
*inexcitability* 826
*caution* 864
–praise 880
–preservation 717
–reliance
*resolution* 604
*hope* 858
*courage* 861
–reproach 950
–respect 878
–restraint 953
–sacrifice 942
–satisfied 880
–seeking 943
–styled 565
–sufficient 880
–taught 490
–tormentor 837
–will 606
**selfishness 943**
**self-same** 13
**sell** *convince* 484
*absurdity* 497
*deception* 545
*untruth* 546
*sale* 796
– for 812
– one's life dearly 719, 722
– off 796
– oneself 940
– out 796
**seller** 796
**selon les règles** 82
**selvedge** 231
**semaphore** 550
**semblance**
*similarity* 17
*imitation* 19
*copy* 21
*probability* 472
wear the – of
*appearance* 448
**semeiology** 522
**semeiotics** 550
**semester** 108
**semi-** 91
**semi-barbarian** 913
**semibreve** 413
**semicircle** 247
**semicircular** 245
**semicolon** 142
**semi-diaphanous** 427
**semi-fluid** 352
**semi-liquidity 352**
**semi-lunar** 245
**seminal** 153
**seminary 542**
**semination** 673
**semi-opaque** 427
**semi-pellucid** 427
**semiquaver** 413
**semitone** 413
**semi-transparency 427**
**sempervirent** 110
**sempiternal** 112
**sempstress** 225, 690
**senary** 98
**senate** 696
**senate-house** 966
**senator** 695, 696
**senatorship** 693
**senatus consultum** 741
**send** 270, 284
– adrift 597
– away
*repel* 289
*eject* 297
*refuse* 764
– for 741
– forth 284, 531
– a letter to 592
– off 284
– out *eject* 297
– packing 289
*commission* 755
– word 527
**senescence** 128
**seneschal**
*director* 694
*master* 745
*servant* 746
**seneschalship** 737
**senile** 128
**senility** 158, 659
**senior** *age* 128
*student* 541
*master* 745
**seniores priores** 62, 280
**seniority** 124, 128
**sennight** 108
**señor** 373, 877
**señora** 374
**sensation**
*physical sensibility* 375
*emotion* 821
*wonder* 870
**sensational** 574, 824
**sensation drama** 599
**sensations of touch 380**
**sense** 498, 516
deep – 821
horse – 498
in no – 565
accept in a particular – 522
– of duty 926
**senseless**
*insensible* 376
*absurd* 497
*foolish* 499
*unmeaning* 517
**senses**
*external* - 375
*intellect* 450
*sanity* 502
**sensibility 375, 822**
**sensible**
*material* 316
*wise* 498
**sensitive** 375, 822
**sensorial** 821
**sensorium** 450
**sensual** 377, 954
**sensualist** 954*a*
**sensuous**
*sensibility* 375
*pleasure* 377
*feeling* 821
**sentence**
*decision* 480
*maxim* 496
*affirmation* 535
*phrase* 566
*condemnation* 971
**sententious** 572, 574
**sentient** 375, 821
**sentiment** 453
**sentimental**
*sensitive* 822
*affected* 855
**sentinel** } 263
**sentry** }
*guardian* 664
*watch* 668
*keeper* 753
**separate** *disjoin* 44
*exclude* 55
*bisect* 91
*diverge* 291
*divorce* 905
– the chaff from the wheat
*discriminate* 465
*select* 609
– into elements 49
– maintenance 905
**separation** 44
**separatist** 489, 984
**sepia** 433
**seposition** 44, 55
**sepoy** 726
**sept** *kin* 11
*class* 75
*clan* 166
**Septentrional 237**
**septet** 415
**septic** 655, 657
**septicæmia** 655
**septuagenarian 98**
**Septuagint** 985
**septum** 228
**sepulchral**
*interment* 363
*resonance* 408
*stridor* 410
*hoarse* 581
**sepulchre** 363
whited – 545
**sepulture** 363
**sequacious** 63
**sequacity** *soft* 324
*tenacity* 327
**sequel** 65, 117
**sequela** 65, 154
**sequence**
- *in order* **63**
- *in time* 117
*motion* **281**
logical – 476
**sequent** 63
**sequester** 789, **974**
**sequestered** 893
**sequestrate**
*seize* 789
*condemn* 971
*confiscate* 974
**sequin** 847
**serac** 383
**seraglio** 961
**seraph** 948, **977**
**seraphic**
*blissful* 829
*virtuous* 944
*pious* 987
**seraphina** 417
**seraskier** 745
**sere and yellow leaf** 128
**serein** 339, 348
**serenade** *music* **415**
*compliment* 894
*endearment* 902
**serene**
*pellucid* 425
*calm* 826
*content* 831
*imperturbable* **871**
– highness 877
**serf** *slave* 746
*clown* 876
**serfdom** 749
**sergeant 745**

under the – of
one's wing 664
**shadowy** 4, 447
**shady** 874
**shaft** *deep* 208
*frame* 215
*pit* 260
*missile* 284
*axis* 312
*air-pipe* 351
*handle* 633
*weapon* 727
**shaggy** 256
**shagreen** 223
**shah** 745
**shake** *totter* 149
*weak* 160
*vibrate* 314
*agitation* 315
*shiver* 383
*trill* 407
*music* 416
*dissuade* 616
*injure* 659
*impress* 821
*excited* 824
*fear* 860
– one's faith 485
– hands
*pacification* 723
*friendship* 888
*courtesy* 894
*forgive* 918
– the head
*dissent* 489
*deny* 536
*refuse* 764
*disapprove* 932
– off 297
– off the yoke 750
– to pieces 162
– one's sides 838
– up 315
**shakedown** *bed* 215
**shakes, no great –**
643, 651
**shako** 225, 717
**shaky** *weak* 160
*in danger* 665
*fearful* 860
**shallop** 273
**shallow**
*not deep* 32, 209
*ignorant* 491
*ignoramus* 493
*foolish* 499
*trifling* 643
– pretext 617
– profundity 855
**shallow-brain** 501
**shallowness** 209
**shallow-pated** 499
**shallows**
*danger* 667
**sham** *imitation* 19
*falsehood* 544
*deception* 545,
546
– fight 720
**shaman** 994
**shamanism** 992
**shamble** 275, 315
**shambles** 361
**shame**
*disrepute* 874
*wrong* 923
*censure* 932
*chastity* 960
cry – upon 932
false – 855
for – 874
sense of – 879
– the devil 939
to one's – be it
spoken 874
**shamefaced** 881
**shameful**
*disgraceful* 874
*profligate* 945
**shameless**
*bold* 525
*impudent* 885
*profligate* 945
*indecent* 961
**shampoo** 652
**shandredhan** 272
**shanghai** 791
**shank** *support* 215
*instrument* 633
**Shanks's mare** 266
**shanty** 189
**shape** 240, 448
– one's course
*direction* 278
*pursuit* 622
*conduct* 692
– out a course 626
**shapeless** 241, 846
**shapely** 242, 845
**shard** 51
**share**
*part* 51
*participate* 778
*allotted portion*
786
– and share alike
778
**shareholder** 778
**shark** 792
**sharp**
*energetic* 171
*violent* 173
*acute* 253
*sensible* 375
*pungent* 392
– *sound* 410
*musical tone* 413
*intelligent* 498
*active* 682
*clever* 698
*cunning* 702
*feeling* 821
*painful* 830
*rude* 895
*censorious* 932
look – 459, 682
– appetite 865
– contest 720
– ear 418
– eye 441
– fellow 682, 700
– frost 383
– look-out 459,
507
– pain 378
– practice
*cunning* 702
*severity* 739
*improbity* 940
– set 865
**sharpen**
[*see* sharp]
*excite* 824
– one's tools 673
– one's wits 537
**sharpener** 253
**sharper** 792
**sharpness** 253
**sharpshooter** 726
**sharpshooting** 716
**Shaster** 986
**shatter** *disjoin* 44
*disperse* 73
*render powerless*
158
*destroy* 162
**shatter-brained** 503
**shattered** 160, 688
**shave** *reduce* 195
*shorten* 201
*layer* 204
*smooth* 255
*cut* 44
*lie* 546
close – 671
**shaved** 226
**shaving** *small* 32
*layer* 204
*filament* 205
**shave-tail** 726, 745
**shawl** 225
**shawm** 417
**shay** 272
**she** 374
**sheaf** 72
**shear** *reduce* 195
*shorten* 201
*sheep* 370
*take* 789
**shears** 253
**sheath** 191, 223
**sheathe** 225
*moderate* 174
– the sword 723
**sheathing** 223
**sheave** 633
**shed** *scatter* 73
*building* 189
*divest* 226
*emit* 297
*give* 784
– blood 361
– light upon 420
– a lustre on 873
– tears 839
**Shedim** 980
**sheen** 420
**sheep** 366
**sheep-dog** 366
**sheep-fold** 232
**sheepish** 881
**sheep's eye, cast a –**
*desire* 865
*modest* 881
*endearment* 902
**sheer** *simple* 42
*complete* 52
*deviate* 279
– off *avoid* 623
**sheet** *layer* 204
*covering* 223
*paper* 593
come down in –s
*rain* 348
white – 952
winding – 363
– of fire 382
– of water 343
**sheet-anchor**
*safety* 664, 666
*hope* 858
**sheet-lightning** 423
**sheik** *ruler* 745, 875
*lover* 897
*priest* 996
**shelf** 215, 667
on the –
*powerless* 158
*disused* 678
*inaction* 681
**shell** *cover* 223
*coffin* 363
*bombard* 716
*bomb* 727

– of its beams 422, 874
– lamb 828
**Short**
*not long* 201
*brittle* 328
*concise* 572
*uncivil* 895
come – of, fall – of
*inferior* 34
*shortcoming* 304
*insufficient* 640
in – 572, 596
– allowance 640
– answer 895
– breath 688
– by 201
– of cash 804
– commons
*insufficiency* 640
*fasting* 956
– circuit 279, 628
– cut *straight* 246
*mid-course* 628
– distance 197
– life and merry 840
– measure 53
at – notice 111, 132
– of *small* 32
*inferior* 34
*subtraction* 38
*incomplete* 53
*shortcoming* 304
*insufficient* 640
– sea 348
make – work of
*destroy* 162
*active* 682
*haste* 684
*complete* 729
*conquer* 731
*punish* 972
**shortage** 53
**shortcoming**
*inequality* 28
*inferiority* 34
*motion short of* 304
*non-completion* 730
*deficiency* 945
**shorten** 201
– sail 275
**shorthand** 590
**short-handed** 651
**shorthorn** 366
**short-lived** 111
**shortly** *soon* 132
**shortness** 201
for – sake 572
**shorts** 225
**short-sighted**
*myopic* 443
*misjudging* 481
*foolish* 499
**short-story** 594
**short-winded** 160, 688
**short-witted** 499
**shot** *missile* 284
*report* 406
*variegated* 440
*guess* 514
*war material* 722, 727
*price* 812
*reward* 973
bad – 701
exchange –s 720
good – 700
have a – at 716
like a – 113
off like a – 623
pistol – 406
random – 463, 621
round – 727
– in the locker 632
not have a – in one's locker 804
– and shell 722
**shot-free** 815
**shot-gun** 727
**should be:**
no better than she – 961
what – 922
**shoulder**
*support* 215
*projection* 250
*shove* 276
broad –ed 159
cold – 289
have on one's –s 625
on the –s of
*high* 206
*elevated* 307
*instrumentality* 631
shrug the –s [*see* shrug]
rest on the –s of 926
rub –s with nobility 852
take upon one's –s 676
– arms 673
– a musket 722
– to shoulder 709, 712
– to the wheel 604, 676
**shoulder-knot** 847
**shoulder-strap** 747
**shout**
*loud* 404
*cry* 411
*rejoice* 838
**shove** 276
give a – to
*aid* 707
**shovel**
*receptacle* 191
*transfer* 270
*vehicle* 272
*fire-iron* 386
*cleanness* 652
put to bed with a – 363
– away 297
**shovel-hat** 999
**show** *visible* 446
*appear* 448
*draw attention* 457
*evidence* 467
*demonstrate* 478
*manifest* 525
*entertainment* 599
*parade* 882
dumb – 550
make a – 544
mere – 544
peep– 840
– off 525
– one's cards 529
– cause 527
– one's colours, 550
– one's face
*presence* 186
*manifest* 525
*disclose* 529
– fight *defy* 715
*attack* 716
*defend* 717
*brave* 861
– forth 525
– in front 303
– one's cards 529
– one's hand 529
– a light pair of heels 623
– itself 446
– of 17, 472
– off 882, 884
– one's teeth 715
– up *visible* 446
*manifest* 525
*ridicule* 856
*degrade* 874
*censure* 932
*accuse* 938
**shower**
*assemblage* **72**
*rain* 348
– bath 386
– down
*abundance* 639
– down upon 784, 816
**showman** 524
**showy** *colour* 428
*beauty* 845
*ornament* 847
*fashion* 852
*vulgar* 851
*ostentatious* 882
**shrapnel** 727
**shred** 32, 205
**shredder** 260
**shrew** 901
**shrewd**
*knowing* 490
*wise* 498
*cunning* 702
**shriek** 410, 411
**shrievalty** 965
**shrieve** 965
**shrift**
*confession* 529
*absolution* 952
**shriftless** 951
**shrill** 410, 411
**shrimp** 193
**shrine** 363, 1000
*receptacle* 191
**shrink**
*decrease* 36
*shrivel* 195
*go back* 283, 287
*unwilling* 603
*avoid* 623
*sensitive* 822
– from *fear* 860
*dislike* 867
*hate* 898
**shrive** 952, 998
**shrivel** 195
**shrivelled** *thin* 203
**shroud** *cover* 225
*funeral* 363
*hide* 528
*safety* 664
*defend* 717
–ed in mystery 519
**shrouds** 45
**Shrove Tuesday** 998
**shrub** *plant* 367

*plantation* 371
**shrug** *sign* 550
– the shoulders
*dissent* 489
*submit* 725
*discontent* 832
*dislike* 867
*contempt* 930
*disapprobation* 932
**shrunk** 193, 195
**shudder** *cold* 383
*fear* 860
make one –
*painful* 830
– at *aversion* 867
*hate* 898
**shuffle** *mix* 41
*derange* 61
*change* 140
*interchange* 148
*changeable* 149
*move slowly* 275
*agitate* 315
*falsehood* 544
*untruth* 546
*irresolute* 605
*recant* 607
*dance* 840
*improbity* 940
the cards
*begin again* 66
*change* 140
*chance* 621
*prepare* 673
patience and – the cards 826
– off *run away* 623
– off this mortal coil 360
– on 266
**shuffler** 548
**shun** 623, 867
**shunt** 270, 279
**shunted**
*shelved* 460
**shut** 261
– the door 761
– the door in one's face 764
– the door upon 893
– one's ears 419, 487
– the eyes 442
– one's eyes to
*not attend to* 458
*neglect* 460
*not believe* 487
*permit* 760
*not observe* 773
– the gates of mercy 914*a*
– in 751
– oneself up 893
– out 55, 761
– up shop *end* 67
*cease* 142
*silence* 403
*relinquish* 624
*repose* 687
– up *close* 261
*confute* 479
*imprison* 751
**shutter** 424
**shuttle** 314
**shuttlecock** 605
**shy** *deviate* 279
*draw back* 283
*propel* 284
*avoid* 623
*fearful* 860
*cowardly* 862
*modest* 881
fight – of 623
have a – at 716
– of belief 487
– cock 862
– of *doubtful* 485
*unwilling* 603
*cautious* 864
*dislike* 867
**Shylock** 787
**Siamese twins** 89
**sib** 11
**Siberia** 383
**sibi gladio hunc jugulo, suo** – 718
**sibilation** *hiss* 409
*disrespect* 929
*disapprobation* 932
**Sibyl** *oracle* 513
*ugly* 846
**Sibylline** 511
– leaves 513
**sic** *imitation* 19
*exact* 494
si – omnes! 948
– transit gloria mundi 111
– volo sic jubeo 600
– vos non vobis 791
**siccity** 340
**sick** *ill* 655
make one – 830, 867
visitation of the – 998
– at heart 837
– of *weary* 841
*dislike* 867
*satiated* 869
in –ness and in health 604
**sick-chamber** 655
**sicken** *nauseate* 395
*disease* 655
*pain* 830
*weary* 841
*disgust* 867
**sickener**
*too much* 641
**sickle** 244, 253
**sickly** *weak* 160
**sick-room** 655
**side**
*consanguinity* 11
*edge* 231
*laterality* 236
*party* 712
*ostentation* 882
at one's – 197
on every – 227
on one – 243
on one's – 714
look only at one – of the shield 481
pass from one – to another 607
take up a – 476
wrong – up 218
– by side
*accompaniment* 88
*near* 197
*laterality* 236
*party* 712
from – to side 314
– with *aid* 707
*co-operate* 709
*concord* 714
**side-arms** 727
**side-blow** 702
**sideboard** 191
**side-car** 272
**side-dish** 298
**side-drum** 417
**side-kick** 890
**side issue** 643
**sideling** 279
**sidelong** 236
**sideration** 158
**sidereal** 318
– time 114
**siderite** 288
**Sideromancy** 511
**side-saddle** 215
**side-scene** 599
**sideslip** 267
**sidesman** 996
**side-track** 287
**sidewalk** 627
**sideways** 217, 236
**side-wind**
*oblique* 217
*circuit* 629
*cunning* 702
**sidle** *oblique* 217
*lateral* 236
*deviate* 279
**siege** 716
lay – to 716
state of – 722
**siege-train** 727
**siesta** 683
**sieve** *sort* 60
*perforate* 260
*clean* 652
memory like a – 506
pour water into a – 638, 818
stop one hole in a – 819
**sift** *simplify* 42
*sort* 60
*inquire* 461
*discriminate* 465
*clean* 652
– the chaff from the wheat 609
**sigh** 405, 839
– for 865
**sighing like furnace** 902
**sight** *much* 31
*multitude* 102
*vision* 441
*appearance* 448
*ugly* 846
*prodigy* 872
at – 132, 441
dim – 443
in – 446
in – of 197, 441
in plain – 525
keep in – 457
within – of shore 858
**sightless**
*blind* 442
*invisible* 447
*ugly* 846
**sightly** 845
**sights, see** – 455
**sightseeing** 441
**sightseer** 444, 455
**sigil** *seal* 550
*evidence* 769
**sigmoidal** 248
**sign** *attest* 467

**sobriety 958**
sobriquet 565
sob sister 534
so-called 545, 565
soc *jurisdiction* 965
socage 777
soccer 840
sociable
*carriage* 272
*sociality* 892
social *mankind* 372
*sociable* 892
– circle 892
– evil 961
– gathering 892
– science 910
socialism
*government* 737
*participation* 778
*philanthropy* 910
socialist 712
sociality **892**
society
*mankind* **372**
*party* 712
*fashion* 852
*sociality* 892
position in – **873**
Socinianism 984
sociology 910
sock *hosiery* 225
*drama* 599
socket 191, 252
socle 215
Socratic method
461
sod 344
beneath the – 363
sodality 712, 888
sodden 339, 384
sofa 215
Sofi 984, 996
soft *stop!* 142
*weak* 160
*moderate* **174**
*smooth* 255
*not hard* 324
*moist* 339
*marsh* 345
*silence!* 403
- *sound* 405
*dulcet* 413
*credulous* 486
*silly* 499
*lenient* 740
*tender* 822
*timid* 862
own to the – impeachment 529
– music 415
– pedal 405
– sawder 617, 933
– soap 356, 933
– tongue, – words
894
soften [*see* soft]
*moderate* 174
*relieve* 834
*pity* 914
*palliate* 937
softening of the
brain 158
softer sex 374
soft-hearted 914
softling 160
softness **324**
*persuasibility* **615**
soft-spoken **894**
soggy 339
soho
*attention* **457**
*parley* 586
*hunting* 622
soi-disant
*asserting* 535
*pretender* 548
*misnomer* 565
*vain* 880
*boastful* 884
soil *region* 181
*land* 342
*dirt* 653
*deface* 846
till the – 371, 673
soirée 892
sojourn 186, 189
sojourner 188
soke 181
solace *relief* 834
*recreation* 840
– oneself with
*pleasure* 827
solar 318
– system 318
– time 114
solatium 973
sold to the devil 949
soldan [*see* sultan]
solder *join* 43
*cement* 45
*cohere* 46
soldier 726
soldier-like 722,
861
sole *alone* 87
*base* 211
*support* 215
feme – 904
solecism **568**
soleil, coup de –
*hot* 384
*mad* 503
solemn
*affirmation* **535**
*important* 642
*grave* 837
*glorious* **873**
*ostentatious* 882
*religious* 987
*worship* 990
– mockery 882
– silence 403
solemnity *rite* 998
solemnization 883
sol-fa 416
solfeggio 415
solicit *induce* 615
*request* 765
*desire* 865
– the attention
457
solicitor *agent* 758
*petitioner* 767
*lawyer* 968
solicitous 865
solicitude *care* 459
*pain* 828
*anxiety* 860
*desire* 865
solid *complete* **52**
*dense* 321
*certain* 474
*learned* 490
*exact* 494
*wise* 498
*persevering* 604*a*
*solvent* 803
– angle 244
solidarity
*party* 712
solidify 321
soliloquy **589**
solitaire *game* 840
*hermit* 893
solitary } *alone*
solitude } 87
*secluded* 893
solmization 416
solo 87, 415
– dance 840
Solomon } *wise*
Solon } 498
*sage* 500
solstice 125, 126
soluble *fluid* 333
*liquefy* 335
solus 87
solution
*liquefaction* 335
*answer* 462
*explanation* 522
– of continuity 70
solve *liquefy* 335
*discover* **480*a***
*unriddle* **522**
solvent
*liquefier* **335**
*monied* 803
somatics 316
sombre *dark* **421**
*black* 431
*grey* 432
*sad* 837
sombrero 225
some *indefinite*
*quantity* 25
*small quantity* **32**
*more than one*
100
–body *person* **372**
*important or distinguished* **642**
in – degree
*degree* 26
*small* 32
at – other time **119**
in – place 182
– ten or a dozen
102
– time ago 122
– time or other
119
**somehow or other**
*cause* 155
*instrument* 631
somersault 218
something *thing* **3**
*small degree* 32
*matter* 316
– else 15
– like 17
– or other **475**
sometimes 136
somewhat
*a little* 32
*a trifle* 643
somewhere 182
– about 32
somnambulism
*walking* 266
*trance* 515
somnambulist
*walker* 268
*dreamer* 515
somniferous
*sleepy* 683
*weary* 841
somnolence 683
son 167
Son, God the – **976**
sonant 402
*letter* 561
sonata 415
Sonderbund 769

**song** *music* 415
*poem* 597
death – 360, 839
love– 597
for a mere – 815
no – no supper 812
old – 643
**songster** 416
**soniferous** 402
**sonnet** 597
**sonneteer** 597
**sonorous** *sound* 402
*loud* 404
*language* 577
**sons of:**
– Belial 988
– God 977
**Soofeeism** 984
**soon** *transient* 111
*future* 121
*early* 132
too – for 135
**sooner:** – or later
*another time* 119
*future* 121
– said than done 704
**soot** 431, 653
**sooth** 511
in good – 543
**soothe**
*allay* 174
*relieve* 834
*flatter* 933
**soothing**
*faint sound* 405
– syrup 174
**soothsay** 511
**soothsayer** 513, 994
**soothsaying** 511
**sop**
*small quantity* 32
*food* 298
*fool* 501
*inducement* 615
*reward* 973
– to Cerberus 458
– in the pan 615
**soph** 492, 541
**Sophi** 745, 996
**sophism** 477, 497
**sophist** *scholar* 492
*dissembler* 548
**sophister** 492
*student* 541
**sophistical** 477
**sophisticate** *mix* 41
*debase* 659
**sophisticated**
*spurious* 545
**sophistry** 477
**sophomore** 541
**soporific** 683, 841
**soporous** 683
**soprano** 410, 416
**sorbet** 298
**sorcerer** 994
**sorcery** 992
**sordes** 653
**sordet** 417
**sordid** *stingy* 819
*covetous* 865
**sordine** 417
**sore**
*bodily pain* 378
*disease* 655
*mental suffering* 828, 830
*discontent* 832
*anger* 900
– as a boil 901*a*
– place 822
– subject 830, 900
**sorely** *very* 31
**s'orienter** 278
**sorites** 476
**sorority** 712
**sorrel** 433, 434
**sorrow** 828
give – words 839
**sorry** *trifling* 643
*grieved* 828
*mean* 876
make a – face 874
cut a – figure 874
be – for 750, 914
in a – plight 732
– sight 830, 837
**sort** *degree* 26
*arrange* 60
*kind* 75
– with
*sociality* 892
**sortable** }
**sortance** }
*agreement* 23
**sortes**
*chance* 156, 621
– Virgilianæ
*sorcery* 992
**sortie** 716
**sortilege**
*prediction* 511
*sorcery* 992
**sortilegy** 621
**sortition** 621
**sorts, out of** –
*ill-health* 655
*sulky* 901*a*
**S.O.S.** 669, 707
**so-so** *small* 32
*trifling* 643
*imperfect* 651
**sostenuto** 415
**sot** *fool* 501
*drunkard* 959
**sot à triple étage** 501
**sotto voce**
*faint sound* 405
*conceal* 528
*voiceless* 581
**sou** *money* 800
qui n'a pas le – 804
**soubrette** 599, 746
**sough** *conduit* 350
*noise* 405
*cloaca* 653
**soul** *essence* 5
*person* 372
*intellect* 450
*genius* 498
*affections* 820
cure of –s 995
flow of – 588
not a – 187
not dare to say one's – is his own *subjection* 749
*fear* 860
– of wit 572
have one's whole – in his work 686
**soulless** 683, 823
**soul-mate** 903
**soul-sick** 837
**soul-stirring** 821, 824
**sound** *great* 31
*conformable* 82
*stable* 150
*strong* 159
*fathom* 208
*bay* 343
*noise* 402
*investigate* 461
*measure* 466
*true* 494
*wise* 498
*sane* 502
*good* 648
*perfect* 650
*healthy* 654
*solvent* 803
*orthodox* 983*a*
catch a – 418
safe and – 654, 670
– the alarm
*indication* 550
*warning* 668
*alarm* 669
*fear* 860
– asleep 683
full of – and fury
*unmeaning* 517
*insolent* 885
– the horn 416
– of limb 654
– locator 726
– mind 502
– the praises of 931
– the note of preparation 673
– reasoning 476
– a retreat 283
– sleep 683
– a trumpet
*publish* 531
*alarm* 669
– of wind 654
**sounding:** big – 577
– brass 517
**sounding-board** 417
**soundings** 208
**soundless**
*unfathomable* 208
*silent* 403
**soup** 298, 352
**soupçon** 32, 41
**soufflé** 298
**sour** *acid* 397
*discontented* 832
*embitter* 835
*uncivil* 895
*sulky* 901
– grapes
*impossible* 471
*excuse* 617
– the temper 830
**source** *beginning* 66
*cause* 153
**sourdet** 417
**sourdine** 417
à la – *noiseless* 403
*concealed* 528
**sourdough** 463
**soured** 832
**sourness** 397
**sous tous les rapports** 52
**souse** 310, 337
**South** *direction* 278
North and –
*opposite* 237
**Southern**
*antipodes* 237
– Cross 318
**souvenir** 505

**sovereign**
*superior* 33
*all-powerful* 159
*authorities* 737
*ruler* 745
– contempt 930
– remedy 662
**Soviet** 696, 737
**sow** *scatter* 73
*pig* 366
*agriculture* 371
*female* 374
get the wrong – by the ear
*misjudgment* 481
*error* 495
*mismanage* 699
*fail* 732
– broadcast 818
– dissension 713, 898
– the sand 645
– the seed
*prepare* 673
– the seeds of
*cause* 153
*teach* 537
– one's wild oats
*improve* 658
*amusement* 840
*vice* 945
*intemperance* 954
**sozzled** 959
**spa** *town* 189
*sanatorium* 662
**space** *distribute* 60
*time* 106
*extension* **180**
*musical* 413
celestial –s 318
wide open –'s 180
**spaddle** 272
**spade** 272
call a – a spade
*plain language* 576
*straightforward* 703
**spade-husbandry** 371
**spahi** 726
**span** *join* 43
*link* 45
*duality* 89
*time* 106
*transient* 111
*distance* 196
*near* 197
*length* 200
*short* 201
*measure* 466
– new 124
**spangle** *spark* 420
*ornament* 847
**spaniel** *dog* 366
*servile* 886
**spanish fly** 171
**spank** *swift* 274
*flog* 972
**spanking** *large* 192
– pace 274
**spanner** 633
**spar** *beam* 214
*quarrel* 713
*contend* 720
**spare** *extra* 37
*small* 193
*meagre* 203
*refrain* 623
*store* 636
*scanty* 640
*redundant* 641
*disuse* 678
*inaction* 681
*relinquish* 782
*give* 784
*economy* 817
*exempt* 927*a*
*temperate* 953
enough and to – 639
not a moment to – 682
to – 641
– diet 956
– no expense 816
– no pains 686
– room 180
– time 685
**spared**: be –
*live* 359
it cannot be – 630
**sparge** 337
**spargefaction**
*scatter* 73
*wet* 337
**sparing** [*see* spare]
*small* 32
*economy* 817
*parsimony* 819
*temperate* 953
with a – hand 819
with no – hand 639
– of praise 932
– of words 585
**spark** *small* 32
*heat* 382
*light* 420
*luminary* 423
*wag* 844
*fop* 854
as the –s fly upwards *habit* 613
**sparkle**
*bubble* 353
*glisten* 420
**sparkling**
*vigorous* 574
*excitement* 824
*cheerful* 836
*wit* 842
*beauty* 845
with – eyes 827
**sparse** 73
**sparsity** 103
**Spartacus** 742
**spartan** 739
**spasm**
*sudden change* 146
*violence* 173
*agitation* 315
*pain* 378
**spasmodic**
*discontinuous* 70
*irregular* 139
*changeable* 149
*violent* 173
**spat** 225, 713
**spate** 348
**spathic** 204
**spatter** *dirt* 653
**spatterdash** 225
**spatula** 191, 272
**spavined** 655
**spawn** *produce* 161
*offspring* 167
*dirt* 653
**spay** 38, 158
**speak** 560, 580, 582
– one fair 894
– for 937
– ill of 932, 934
– for itself 518, 525
– low 581
– of *meaning* **516**
*publish* 531
*speak* 582
– out *make manifest* 525
*artless* 703
– softly 581
– to 586
– up 411
– up for 937
– volumes 467
– well of 931
**speakeasy** 189, 964
**speaker**
*interpreter* 524
*chairman* 694
**speakie** 964
**speaking: much** – 584
way of – 521
– likeness 554
on – terms 888
**speaking-trumpet** 418
**spear** 260, 727
– shaped 253
**spearman** 726
**special** 79
– correspondent 593
**special pleader** **968**
**special pleading**
*sophistry* 477
**speciali gratiâ** **760**
**specialist** 662, **700**
**speciality** **79**
**specialty**
*security* **771**
**specie** 800
**species** *kind* **75**
*appearance* **448**
human – 372
**specific** *special* **79**
*remedy* 662
– gravity 321
**specification** **594**
**specify**
*particularize* **79**
*tell* 527
*name* 564
**specimen** 82
**specious**
*probable* 472
*sophistical* **477**
*beauty* 845
*flattering* 933
*pardonable* **937**
**speck** 32
**speckle** 440, **848**
**spectacle**
*appearance* **448**
*prodigy* 872
*show* 882
*drama* 599
**spectacles** 445
look through rose coloured – **523**
**spectacular** 882
**spectator** **444**
**spectral** 4, 980
**spectre**
*fallacy of vision* 443
*ugly* 846
*ghost* 980
**spectroscope**
*light* 420
*colour* 428

*optical instrument* 445
**spectrum**
*colour* 428
*variegation* 440
*optical illusion* 443
**speculate**
*view* 441
*think* 451
*suppose* 514
*chance* 621
*essay* 675
*traffic* 794
**speculation**
*experiment* 463
*cards* 840
**speculative** 463, 514
**speculum** 445
veluti in – 446
**sped** *completed* 729
**speech** 582
figure of – 521
parts of – 567
**speechify** 582
**speechless** 403, 581
**speechmaker** 582
**speed**
*velocity* 274
*activity* 682
*haste* 684
*help* 707
*succeed* 731
with breathless – 684
God – 731, 906
**speedily** *soon* 132
**speedometer** 200, 274, 553
**speedway** 840
**speer** 455, 461
**spell** *period* 106
*influence* 175
*read* 539
*letter* 561
*necessity* 601
*motive* 615
*exertion* 686
*charm* 993
cast a – 992
*wonder* 870
knurr and – 840
– for 865
– out *interpret* 522
**spell-bound** 601, 615
**spence** 636
**spencer** 225
**spend** *effuse* 297
*waste* 638
*give* 784
*purchase* 795
*expend* 809
– freely 816
– time 106
– time in 683
– one's time in 625
**spender** 818
**spendthrift** 818
**spent** 160, 688
**spermaceti** 356
**spermatic** 168
**spermatize** 168
**spero, dum spiro** – 858
**spes sibi quisque** 604
**spew** 297
**sphacelus** 655
**sphere** *rank* 26
*domain* 75
*space* 180
*region* 181
*ball* 249
*world* 318
*business* 625
– of influence 181, 780
**spheroid** 249
**spherule** 249
**sphery** 318
**Sphinx** *monster* 83
*oracle* 513
*ambiguous* 520
*riddle* 533
**spial** 668
**spice**
*small quantity* 32
*mixture* 41
*pungent* 392
*condiment* 393
**spiced** 390
**spicilegium** 72, 596
**spick and span** 123
**spiculate** 253
**spiculum** 253
**spicy** 400, 824
**spigot** 263
**spike** *sharp* 253
*pierce* 260
*plug* 263
– guns 158, 645
**spikebit** 262
**spikenard** 356
**spill** *filament* 205
*stopper* 263
*shed* 297
*splash* 348
*match* 388
*waste* 638
*lavish* 818
– blood 722
– and pelt 59
**spin** *flying* 267
*rotate* 312
*pluck* 610
– out *protract* 110
*late* 133
*prolong* 200
*diffuse style* 573
– the wheel 140
– a long yarn 549
**spindle** 312
**spindling** 203
**spindle-shanks** 203
**spindle-shaped** 253
**spindrift** 353
**spine** 222, 253
**spinel** 847
**spinet** *copse* 367
*harpsichord* 417
**spinney** 367
**spinner of yarns** 594
**spinosity**
*unintelligible* 519
*discourtesy* 895
*sullenness* 901*a*
**spinous** *prickly* 253
**spinster** 374, 904
**spiracle** 351
**spiral** 248
**spire** *height* 206
*convolution* 248
*peak* 253
*soar* 305
**spirit** *essence* 5
*immateriality* 317
*fuel* 388
*intellect* 450
*meaning* 516
*vigorous language* 574
*activity* 682
*affections* 820
*courage* 861
*ghost* 980
bad – 980
keep one's – up
*hope* 858
with life and – 682
unclean – 978
– away 791
– up 615, 824
**Spirit, the Holy** – 976
**spirited**
*language* 574
*active* 682
*sensitive* 822
*cheerful* 836
*brave* 861
*generous* 942
**spiritless**
*insensible* 823
*sad* 837
*cowardly* 862
**spirit-level** 213
**spiritoso** *music* 415
**spirit-rapping** 992
**spirits** *drink* 298, 959
*cheer* 836
**spirit-stirring** 824
**spiritual**
*immaterial* 317
*psychical* 450
*heterodoxy* 984
*divine* 976
*pious* 987
– director 996
– existence 987
**spiritualism**
*immateriality* 317
*intellect* 450
*sorcery* 992
**spiritualize** 317
*reasoning* 476
**spirituel** 842
**spirt** *eject* 297
*stream* 348
*haste* 684
*exertion* 686
**spirtle** *disperse* 73
*splash* 348
**spissitude** 321, 352
**spit** *pointed* 253
*perforate* 260
*eject* 297
*rotate* 312
*rain* 348
– fire *irascible* 901
**spite** 907
in – of
*disagreement* 24
*notwithstanding* 30
*counteraction* 179
*opposition* 708
in – of one's teeth
*unwilling* 603
*compulsion* 744
**spiteful** 898, 907
*hating* 898
**spittle** 299
**spittoon** 191
**splanchnology** 329
**splash** *affuse* 337
*stream* 348
*spatter* 653
*parade* 882
make a –
*fame* 873

*display* 882
–board 666
**splay** 291
–footed 243
**spleen**
*melancholy* 837
*hatred* 898
*anger* 900
*sullen* 901*a*
harbour – 907
**spleenless** 906
**splendour**
*bright* 420
*beautiful* 845
*glorious* 873
*display* 882
**splenetic** 837, 901*a*
**splice** *join* 43
*cross* 219
*interjacent* 228
*repair* 660
– the main brace
*tipsy* 959
**spliced, be –**
*marriage* 903
**splint** 215
**splinter**
*small piece* 32
*divide* 44
*filament* 205
*brittle* 328
**split** *divide* 44
*discontinuity* 70
*bisect* 91
*brittle* 328
*divulge* 529
*quarrel* 713
*fail* 732
*portion* 786
*laugh* 838
– the difference 29, 774
– the ears } 404
– the head } 410
– hairs
*discriminate* 465
*sophistry* 477
*fastidiousness* 868
– upon a rock 732
– one's sides 838
**splutter** *energy* 171
*spit* 297
*stammer* 583
*haste* 684
**spoil** *vitiate* 659
*hinder* 706
*lenity* 740
*plunder* 791
*booty* 793
*deface* 846
*satiate* 869
– sport 706
– trade 708
**spoiled child** 869, 899
– of fortune 734
**spoiler** 792
**spoke** *radius* 200
*tooth* 253
*obstruct* 706
put a – in one's wheel *render powerless* 158
*hinder* 706
**spokesman** 524, 582
**spolia opima** 793
**spoliate** 791
**spoliative** 793
**spondee** 597
**spondulics** 800
**sponge** *moisten* 339
*dry* 340
*pulp* 354
*clean* 652
*despoil* 791
*hanger on* 886
*drunkard* 959
apply the –
*obliterate* 552
*non-payment* 808
– out 552
**sponging-house** 752
**spongy** *porous* 252
*soft* 324
*marshy* 345
**sponsion** 771
**sponsor**
*witness* 467
*security* 771
be – for
*promise* 768
*obligation* 926
**sponsorship** 771
**spontaneous**
*voluntary* 600
*willing* 602
*impulsive* 612
**spontoon** 727
**spoof** 545
**spook** 980
**spool** 312
**spoon**
*receptacle* 191
*ladle* 272
*bill and coo* 902
born with a silver – in one's mouth 734
**Spoonerism** 218, 853
**spoonful** 25, 32
**spoon-like** 252
**spoon-meat** 298
**spoony** *foolish* 499
*lovesick* 902
**spoor** 551
**sporadic** 73, 137, 657
**spore** 330
**sport** *killing* 361
*chase* 622
*amusement* 840
*show off* 882
in – *pastime* 840
*humour* 842
the – of 749
– of fortune 735
**sporting** *killing* 361
*contention* 720
*amusement* 840
– dog 366
**sportive** 836, 840
**sports** 686
**sportsman** 361, 622, 840
**sportulary** 784, 785
**sportule** 784
**sporule** 330
**spot** *place* 182
*discover* 480*a*
*mark* 550
*dirt* 653
*blemish* 848
*blot* 874
on the –
*instantly* 113
*present time* 118
*soon* 132
*in one's presence* 186
**spotless** *perfect* 650
*clean* 652
*innocent* 946
**spot light** 423, 599
**spots in the sun,** see – *fastidious* 868
**spotted**
*variegated* 440
*damaged* 659
**spousal** 903
**spouse** 88, 903
**spouseless** 904
**spout** *egress* 295
*flow out* 348
*conduit* 350
*speak* 582
*act* 599
*pawn* 771, 787, 788
**sprag** 215
**sprain** 158, 160
**sprat to catch a:**
– herring 794
– whale 699
**sprawl** *length* 200
*horizontal* 213
*descend* 306
**spray** *sprig* 51
*vaporizer* 336
*foam* 353
**spread** *enlarge* 35
*disperse* 73
*broadcast* 78
*expanse* 180
*expand* 194
*diverge* 291
*feast* 298
*publish* 531
– abroad 531
– canvas 267
– out 194
– sail 267
– a shade 421
– to 196
– the toils 545
**spree** 840
**spretæ injuria formæ** *ugly* 846
*disrespect* 929
*detraction* 934
**sprig** *branch* 51
*child* 129
*shillelagh* 727
**sprightly** 836, 842
**spring** *early* 125
*source* 153
*strength* 159
*velocity* 274
*recoil* 277
*fly* 293
*leap* 309
*elasticity* 325
*rivulet* 348
*instrument* 633
*store* 636
–s of action 615
– back 277
– to one's feet 307
– from 154
– a leak 651, 659
– a mine
*destroy* 162
*unexpected* 508
*attack* 716
– a project 626
– up *begin* 66
*event* 151
*grow* 194
*ascend* 305
*visible* 446
hot – 382
– upon 789

**spring balance** 319
**springe** 545
**spring-gun** 545
**spring tide**
*greatness* 31
*increase* 35
*completeness* 52
*youth* 127
*high* 206
*low* 207
*wave* 348
*water* 337
**springy** 325
**sprinkle** *add* 37
*mix* 41
*scatter* 73
*wet* 337
*rain* 348
*variegate* 440
*baptize* 998
**sprinkler** 348, 385
**sprinkling**
*small quantity* 32
**sprint** 274
**sprit** *sprout* 167
*support* 215
**sprite** 979, 980
**sprout** *grow* 35
*germinate* 161
*offspring* 167
*expand* 194
– from *result* 154
**spruce** 652, 845
– up 847
**sprue** 653
**sprung** 651, 659
**spry** 682, 836
**spud** 272
**spume** 353
**spun out** 110, 573
**spunk** 861
**spur**
*pointed* 250
*sharp* 253
*incite* 615
*hasten* 684
win –s *succeed* 731
*glory* 873
on the – of the moment
*instantly* 113
*now* 118
*soon* 132
*opportune* 134
*impulse* 612
– gearing 633
the – of necessity 745
**spurious**
*erroneous* 495
*false* 544
*deceptive* 545
*illegitimate* 925
**spurlos versenkt** 2, 449
**spurn** *reject* 55
*disdain* 930
**spurred** 253
**spurt**
*transient* 111
*swift* 274
*gush* 348
*impulse* 612
*haste* 684
*exertion* 686
**sputa** 299
**sputter** *emit* 297
*splash* 348
*stammer* 583
**spy** *see* 441
*spectator* 444
*inquire* 461
*informer* 527
*emissary* 534
*watcher* 664
*warning* 668
**spy-glass** 445
**squab** *large* 192
*short* 201
*broad* 202
*bench* 215
**squabble** 713
**squad** 72, 726
**squadron** 726
– leader 745
**squalid** 653, 846
**squall** *violent* 173
*wind* 349
*cry* 411
*quarrel* 713
**squalor** 653
**squamous** 204, 223
**squander** *waste* 638
*misuse* 679
*lose* 776
*prodigal* 818
**square**
*congruous* 23
*compensate* 30
*four* 95
*limited space* 182
*houses* 189
*perpendicular* 212
*form* 244
*sparring* 720
*justice* 924
*honourable* 939
make all – 660
on the – 939
– accounts
*pay* 807
*account* 811
– dance 840
– deal 922
– the circle 471
– inches 180
– peg into a round hole 699
– up 556
– with 23
– yards 180
**square-toes** 857
**squash** *destroy* 162
*flatten* 251
*blow* 276
*soft* 324
*marsh* 345
*semiliquid* 352
*hiss* 409
*game* 840
**squashy** 345, 352
**squat** 308
*locate oneself* 184
*little* 193
*short* 201
*thick* 202
*low* 207
**squatter** 188
**squaw** *woman* 374
*wife* 903
**squeak**, **squeal** 411, 412
**squeamish** 655
*unwilling* 603
*fastidious* 868
**squeasy** 868
**squeezable** 762
**squeeze**
*contract* 195
*condense* 321
*embrace* 894
**squeeze out** 301, 784
**squelch** 162
**squib** *sound* 406
*lampoon* 856, 934
**squiffy** 959
**squilgee** 652
**squint**
*peephole* 260
*look* 441
*defective sight* 443
**squirarchy** 875
**squire** *aid* 707
*attendant* 746
*gentry* 875
– of Dames 897
**squirm** 315
**squirrel** 274, 682
**squirt** 297, 348
**S.S.C.** 968
**stab** *pierce* 260
*kill* 361
*pain* 378, 649, 828
*injure* 659
**stabilimetre** 150
**stabilizator** 150
**stability** 16, 150
**stable** *firm* 150
*house* 189
lock the – door when the steed is stolen
*too late* 135
*useless* 645
*bungling* 699
– equilibrium 150
**staccato** 415
**stack** 72, 636
**staddle** 215
**stade** 252
**stadium** 728, 840
**stadtholder** 745
**staff** *support* 215
*music* 413
*measure* 466
*signal* 550
*council* 696
*party* 712
*weapon* 727
*chief* 745
*retinue* 746
pastoral – 999
– of life 298
– of office 747
– officer 745
**stag** *deer* 366
*male* 373
*defaulter* 808
**stage** *degree* 26
*term* 71
*time* 106
*position* 183
*layer* 204
*platform* 215
*forum* 542
*drama* 599
*arena* 728
come upon the – 446
on the – 525, 599
go off the – 293
revolving – 599
– business 599
– coach 272
– craft 599
– direction 697
– effect 882
– hand 599
– manager 599
– name 565
– play 599
– player 599

– struck 599
– whisper 580
**stager** *player* 599
*doer* 690
old – 130
**stagger** *slow* 275
*totter* 314, 821
*agitate* 315
*unexpected* 508
*dissuade* 616
*affect* 824
*astonish* 870
- belief *doubt* 485
– like a drunken man 605
**staggers** 315
**stagirite** 850
**stagnant** 265
**stagnation** 681
**stagy** 599, 855
**staid** *wise* 498
*calm* 826
*grave* 837
**stain** *paint* 223
*colour* 428
*dirt* 653
*spoil* 659
*blemish* 848
*disgrace* 874
– paper *writing* 590
**stained, travel-** 266
**stainless** *clean* 652
*honourable* 939
*innocent* 946
**stair** 305, 627
**stake** *fastening* 45
*wager* 621
*danger* 665
*security* 771
*property* 780
*lay down* 807
*execution* 975
at – *intended* 620
*in danger* 665
the – *agony* 828
burn at the – 384
**stalactite** 224
**stalagmite** 224
**stale** *old* 124
*insipid* 391
*deteriorated* 659
– flat and unprofitable 645
– news 532
**stale-mate** 27, 731
**stalk** *stem* 153
*support* 215
*walk* 266
– abroad
*generality* 78
*pursue* 622
*proud* 878
**stalking-horse**
*ambush* 530
*plea* 617
**stall** *cease* 142
*abode* 189
*receptacle* 191
*support* 215
*play-house* 599
*mart* 799
*churchdom* 995
*cathedral* 1000
finger– 223
**stallion** 271, 373
**stalwart** 159, 192
**stamina** 159, 604*a*
**stammel** 434
**stammering** **583**
**stamp**
*character* 7
*prototype* 22
*kind* 75
*form* 240
*mark* 550
*engraving* 558
*complete* 729
*security* 771
– the foot
*anger* 900
– in the memory 505
– out 162, 385
**stampede** 860
**stanch** - *a flow* 348
*persevering* 604*a*
*health* 654
*reinstate* 660
**stanchion** 215
**stanchless** 825
**stand** *exist* 1
*rank* 71
*long time* 110
*permanent* 141
*support* 215
*quiescence* 265
*difficulty* 704
*resistance* 719
*brook* 821
*patience* 826
*brave* 861
at a – 681
come to a – 704
make a – 708, 719
take one's –
*resolve* 604
*resist* 719
*due* 924
take one's – upon
*reasoning* 476
*affirm* 535
*plea* 617
– aghast 870
– aloof 623, 681
– of arms 727
– at attention 507
– the brunt 717
– by *near* 197
*aid* 707
*defend* 717
– a chance 470, 472
– committed 754
– at ease 458
– to one's engagement 772
– fair for 472
– fire 861
– firm 150, 719
– first 66
– for *indicate* 550
*deputy* 759
*candidate* 763
– forth 446
– one's ground
*preserved* 670
*resist* 719
– the hazard of the die 621
– one in 812
– in need of 630
– no nonsense 604
– off 287, 623
– on 215
– out *project* 250
*visible* 446
*obstinate* 606
– over 133
– the proof 648
– to reason
*proof* 478
*manifest* 525
*right* 922
– on one's rights 748
– in the shoes of 147
– one in good stead 644
– still *remain* 141
*stop* 265
*difficulty* 704
– the test 494, 648
– up [*see below*]
– upon *pride* 878
– upon one's rights 924
– in the way of 706
– well in the opinion of 931
**stand up** 212, 307
– against 719
– fight 720
– for 931, **937**
– to 459
**standard** *model* **22**
*degree* 26
*mean* 29
*rule* 80
*measure* **466**
*flag* 550
*good* 648
*perfect* 650
gold – 800
**standard-bearer** 726
**standardize** 22, **60**, 466
**standing** *footing* **8**
*degree* 26
*long time* 110
*permanence* **141**
*situation* 183
*note* 873
– army 726
– dish *rule* 80
*permanent* 141
– jest *wit* 842
– order 613, **963**
– type 591
– water 343
**stand-pipe** 348, **385**
**stand-point** 183, 441
**Stannary Court 966**
**stanza** 597
**staple**
*fastening* **45**
*whole* 50
*peg* 214
*texture* 329
*material* 635
*trade* 794
*mart* 799
– commodity **798**
**star** *luminary* **423**
*actor* 599
*destiny* 601
*badge* 747
*ornament* **847**
*glory* 873
*noble* 875
*decoration* **877**
– in the ascendant
*success* 731
*prosperity* **734**
– of fashion 852
– in *drama* 599
*fame* 873
*display* 882
– shell 423
– trap 599
**starboard** 238

*silent* 403
– less 467
– life *matter* 316
*painting* 556
– more
*superior* 33
*evidence* 467
– small voice 405
in – water 714
**still-born** 360, 732
**stillroom** 636
**stillicidium** 348
**stilted**
*elevated* 307
- *style* 577
*ridiculous* 853
*affected* 855
*boasting* 884
**stilts** *support* 215
on – *high* 206
*elevated* 307
*hyperbolical* 549
*proud* 878
*boasting* 884
**stimulant** 662
**stimulate**
*energy* 171
*violence* 173
*incite* 615
*excite* 824
**stimulating**
*suggestive* 514
**stimulus** 615
**sting** *pain* 378
*tingle* 380
*poison* 663
*excite* 824
*mental suffering* 830
*anger* 900
**stinging**
*pungent* 392
**stingo** 298
**stingy** 819
**stink** 401
– in the nostrils
*unpleasant* 830
*dislike* 867
*hate* 898
**stink-bomb** 727
**stink-pot** 401
**stint** *degree* 26
*limit* 233
*scanty* 640
*begrudge* 819
**stintless** 639
**stipend** *salary* 973
**stipendiary**
*subject* 749
*receiving* 785
*magistrate* 967
**stipple**
*variegate* 440
*painting* 556
*engraving* 558
**stipulate** 769, 770
– for 720
**stipule** 51
**stir** *energy* 171
*move* 264
*agitation* 315
*excite* 375
*activity* 682
*jail* 752
*emotion* 824
make a – 642, 682
– about 682
– the blood 824, 900
– up dissension 713
– the embers 163, 824
– the feelings 824
– the fire 384
– a question 461, 476
– one's stumps 266, 682
– up *mix* 41
*violent* 173
*excite* 824
**stirps** *kin* 11
*source* 153
*paternity* 166
**stirring** *events* 151
*important* 642
*active* 682
– news 532
**stirrup**
*support* 215
with a foot in the – 293
**stirrup-cup** 293, 959
**stitch** *junction* 43
*pain* 378
*work* 680
– in time 132
– of work 686
**stive** 384
**stiver** 800
**stoat** 401
**stoccado** 717
**stock** *kinship* 11
*quantity* 25
*origin* 153
*paternity* 166
*collar* 225
*soup* 298
*fool* 501
*habitual* 613
*materials* 635
*store* 636
*property* 780
*merchandise* 798
*money* 800
in – 777
laughing – 857
lay in a – 637
take – *inspect* 457
*accounts* 811
– exchange 799
– still 265
– in trade
*means* 632
*store* 636
*property* 780
*merchandise* 798
– with 637
**stockade** 717
**stocked, well** – 639
**stock exchange** 621
**stock-farm** 370
**stocking** 225
*hoard* 800
**stock-jobbing** 794
**stock operator** 621
**stocks** *prison* 752
*funds* 802
*punishment* 975
on the –
*business* 625
*preparation* 673
*incomplete* 730
– and stones 316, 823
**stocky** 201
**stodge** 957
**stoicism**
*insensibility* 823
*inexcitability* 826
*disinterested* 942
*temperance* 953
**stoke** 388
**stoker** 268
**stole** 999
**stolen**: – away 671
– goods 793
**stolid** 499, 843
**stomach** *pouch* 191
*taste* 390
*brook* 826
*desire* 865
not have the – to 603
turn the – 830
– of an ostrich 957
**stomacher** 225
**stone** *heavy* 319
*dense* 321
*hard* 323
*kill* 361
*lithography* 558
*material* 635
*attack* 716
*weapon* 727
*punish* 972
corner – 642
go down like **a** – 310
cast the first – **at** 938
heart of – 823, **907**
key- 642
musical –s 417
no – unturned 461, 686
philosopher's – 662
precious – 648
stepping – 627
throw a – at
*attack* 716
*censure* 932
*accuse* 938
throw –s at 907
tomb- 363
mark with a white – 642
throw a – in one's own garden 699
– dead 360
– of Sisyphus 645
**stone-blind** 442
**stone-coloured** 432
**stone-deaf** 419
**stone's throw** 197
**stoneware** 384
**stony** 323
**stony-hearted** 907, 919
**stooge** 711, 746, 886
**stook** 72
**stool** 215
between two –s 704
– of repentance 950
– pigeon 527, 548
**stoop** *slope* 217
*lower* 308
*humble* 879
*servile* 886
*dishonourable* 940
– to conquer 702
**stop** *end* 67
*cease* 142
*close* 261
*rest* 265
*silent* 403
*danger* 665
*inaction* 681
*hinder* 706
*prohibit* 761

*long* 200
*narrow* 203
*furrow* 259
*light* 420
*stripe* 440
*mark* 550
**streaked** 219, 440
**stream** *assemble* 72
*move* 264
– *of fluid* **347**
– *of water* 348
– *of air* 349
– *of light* 420
*abundance* 639
against the – 708
with the –
*conformity* 82
*progression* 282
*assent* 488
*facility* 705
*concord* 714
*fashion* 852
*servility* 886
– of events **151**
– of time 109
**streamer** *flag* 550
**streaming** 47, 73
**streamlet** 348
**street** 189, 627
man in the – 876
**streets:**
in the open – 525
on the – 961
**street-walker** 962
**strength**
*quantity* 25
*degree* 26
*greatness* 31
*vigour* **159**
*energy* 171
*tenacity* 327
*animality* 364
put all one's – into 686
lose – 655
tower of – 717
– of mind 604
**strengthen** 35
**strengthless** 160
**strenuous**
*persevering* 604*a*
*active* 682
*exertion* 686
**Strephon and Chloe** 902
**stress** *emphasis* 580
*requirement* 630
*importance* 642
*strain* 686
*difficulty* 704
by – of 601
lay – on 476
– of circumstances
*compulsion* 744
– of weather 349
**stretch** *expanse* 180
*expand* 194
*extend* 200
*exaggerate* 549
*exertion* 686
*encroach* 925
at a – 69
mind on the – 451
on the – 686
upon the – 457
– away to 196
– forth one's hand 680, 789
– of the imagination 515, 549
– the meaning 523
– a point 83, 303
*exaggerate* 549
*severity* 739
*permit* 760
*not observe* 773
*undue* 925
*exempt* 927*a*
– to *distance* 196
*length* 200
**stretcher** 215, 272
**strew** 73
**striæ, striated** 259, 440
**stricken** *pain* 828
terror– 860
be – by 655
– in years 128
**strict**
*in conformity* 82
*exact* 494
*severe* 739
*conscientious* 939
*orthodox* 983*a*
– inquiry 461
– interpretation 522
– search 461
– settlement 780
**strictly speaking**
*literally* 19
*exact* 494
*interpreted* 522
**stricture**
*constriction* 203
*hindrance* 706
*censure* 932
**stride** *distance* 196
*motion* 264
*walk* 266
**strident** 410
**strides:** make – 282
rapid – 274
**stridor** **410**
**strife** 713, 720
**strigil** 652
**strike** *operate* 170
*hit* 276
*resist* 719
*disobey* 742
*impress* 824
*beat* 972
– at 716
– a balance
*equalize* 27
*mean* 29
*pay* 807
– a bargain 769, 794
– a blow *act* 680
– dumb *dumb* 581
*excitement* 824
*wonder* 870
*humble* 879
– the eye 457
– the first blow 716
– one's flag 725
– hard 171
– all of a heap 824, 860
– home 171
– in with
*imitate* 19
*assent* 488
*cooperate* 709
– the iron while it is hot 134
– a light 384, 420
– the lyre 416
– the mind 457
– out something new 146, 515
– off *exclude* 55
– one 451
– out *exclude* 55
*destroy* 162
*invent* 515
*obliterate* 552
*scheme* 626
– off the roll 756, 972
– at the root of 162
– root 150
– sail 275
– tents 293
– terror 860
– up 416
– with wonder 870
**striker** 927
**striking** 525
– likeness 554
**strikingly**
*greatly* 31
**string** *tie* 43
*ligature* 45
*continuity* 69
*filament* 205
*musical note* 413
– together 60, 69
**stringed instruments** 417
**stringent**
*energetic* 171
*authoritative* **737**
*strict* 739
*compulsory* 744
**strings:** *music* 417
leading – 541
pull the – 175, 693
two – to one's bow 632
**stringy** 205, 327
**strip** *adjunct* 39
*narrow* 203
*filament* 205
*divest* 226
*take* 789
*rob* 791
**stripe** *length* 200
*variegation* 440
*mark* 550
*badge* 747
*blow* 972
**stripling** 129
**stripped** *poor* 804
**strive** *endeavour* 675
*exert* 686
*contend* 720
– against 720
**stroke** *impulse* **276**
*touch* 379
*mark* 550
*evil* 619
*expedient* 626
*disease* 655
*action* 680
*success* 731
*painful* 830
at a – 113
good – 626
– of death 360
– of the pen
*writing* 590
*command* 741
– of policy 626
– of time 113
– of work 686
– the wrong way 256
**stroll** 266
**strolling player** 599

**strong** *great* 31
*powerful* 159
*energetic* 171
*tough* 327
*taste* 390
*pungent* 392
*fetid* 401
*healthy* 654
*feeling* 821
*wonderful!* 870
smell – of 398
– accent 580
– argument 476
by a – arm 744
– box 802
with a – hand
*resolution* 604
*exertion* 686
*severity* 739
– language 574
– pull 686
– point 476
**strong-headed** 498
**stronghold**
*refuge* 666
*defence* 717
*prison* 752
**strong-minded** 498, 861
**strong-scented** 398
**strong-willed** 604
**strop** 253
**strophe** 597
**strow** 73
**struck** [*see* stricken, strike]
awe– 860
– down 732
– all of a heap
*emotion* 821
*wonder* 870
*humbled* 879
– with *love* 897
**structural** *state* 7
**structure**
*production* 161
*form* 240
*texture* 329
*organization* 357
**struggle** *exert* 686
*difficulty* 704
*contend* 720
**strum** 416, 517
**strumpet** 962
**strung**
highly – 825
**strut** *walk* 266
*pride* 878
*parade* 882
*boast* 884
– and fret one's hour upon a stage 359, 599
**strychnine** 663
**stub** 40, 550
**stubbed** 201
**stubble** *remains* 40
*useless* 645
**stubborn**
*strong* 159
*hard* 323
*obstinate* 606
*resistance* 719
**stubby** 201
**stucco** 45, 223
**stuck** [*see* stick]
– fast 150, 704
be – on 897
**stuck-up** 878
**stud** *hanging-peg* 214
*knob* 250
*horses* 271
**studded** *many* 102
*spiked* 253
*variegated* 440
**student** 541
**stud-farm** 370
**studied**
*predetermined* 611
**studio** *room* 191
*painting* 556
*workshop* 691
**studious**
*thoughtful* 451
*docile* 539
*intending* 620
**study** *copy* 21
*room* 191
*thought* 451
*attention* 457
*research* 461
*learning* 539
*painting* 556
*intention* 620
*retreat* 893
brown – 515
**stuff** *substance* 3
*contents* 190
*expand* 194
*line* 224
*matter* 316
*texture* 329
*absurdity* 497
*unmeaning* 517
*material* 635
*trifle* 643
*overeat* 957
such – as dreams are made of 515
– gown 968
– in 300
– the memory with 505
– and nonsense
*unsubstantial* 4
*absurdity* 497
*unmeaning* 517
– up *close* 261
*hoax* 545
**stuffed**
*redundancy* 641
**stuffing** *contents* 190
*lining* 224
*stopper* 263
**stuffy** 321, 382
**stultified** 732
**stultify oneself** 699
**stultiloquy** 497
**stumble** *fall* 306
*flounder* 315
*error* 495
*unskilful* 699
*failure* 732
– on *chance* 156
*discover* 480a
**stumbling-block**
*difficulty* 704
*hindrance* 706
**stump**
*remainder* 40
*trunk* 51
*walk* 266
*drawing* 556
*speak* 582
stir your –s
*active* 682
worn to the – 659
– along *slow* 275
**stump orator** 582, 887
**stumpy** *short* 201
**stun** *physically insensible* 376
*loud* 404
*deafen* 419
*unexpected* 508
*morally insensible* 823
*affect* 824
*astonish* 870
**stung** [*see* sting]
– to the quick 824
**stunt** *shorten* 201
*performance* 680
**stunted** 193, 195
*insufficient* 640
**stupe** 834
**stupefaction** 826
**stupefy**
- *physically* 376
- *morally* 823
*astonish* 870
**stupendous**
*great* 31
*large* 192
*wonderful* 870
**stupid**
*unsubstantial* 4
*misjudging* 481
*credulous* 486
*unintelligent* 499
*tiresome* 841
*dull* 843
**stupor**
*insensibility* 823
*wonder* 870
**stupration** 961
**sturdy** *strong* 159
*persevering* 604a
– beggar 767, 792
**stutter** 583
**sty** *house* 189
*enclosure* 232
*dirt* 653
**Stygian** *dark* 421
*diabolic* 945
*infernal* 982
cross the – ferry
*die* 360
– shore
*death* 360
**style** *state* 7
*time* 114
*painting* 556
*graver* 558
*name* 564
*diction* 569
*writing* 590
*beauty* 845
*fashion* 852
**stylet**
*awl* 262
*dagger* 727
**stylist** 578
**Stylites, Simon** – 893
**stylographic pen** 590
**stylography** 590
**stylus** 590
**styptic** 397
**Styx** 982
**suasible** 602
**suasion** 615
**suave mari magno** 664
**suaviter in modo** 826, 894
**suavity** 894
**sub** 34
– spe rati 475
**subacid** 397

**subaction** 330
**subahdar** 745
**subalpine** 206
**subaltern**
*inferior* 34
*soldier* 726
*officer* 745
*servant* 746
*plebeian* 876
**subaqueous** 208
**subastral** 318
**subaudition** 527
**subcommittee** 696
**subconscious** 317
**subcontrary** 237
**subcutaneous** 221
**subdean** 996
**subdichotomy** 91
**subdititious** 147
**subdivide** 44
**subdivision**
*part* 51
*class* 75
*military* 726
*realty* 780
**subdolous** 702
**subdominant** 413
**subdual** 731
**subduction** **38**
**subdue** *calm* 174
*succeed* 731
**subdued**
*morally* 826
**sub-editor** 593
**subitaneous** 113
**subito** 113
**subjacent** 207
**subject** *dominate* 175
*liable* 177
*topic* 454
*meaning* 516
*servant* 746
*enthral* 749
– of dispute 713
– to examination 461
– of inquiry 461
– of thought 454
– to 469, 475
**subjection** **749**
**subjective**
*intrinsic* 5
*immaterial* 317
*intellectual* 450
**subjoin** 37
**subjugate** 731, 749
**subjugation** 732, 824
**subjunctive** 37
**sublapsarian** 984
**sublation** 38
**sublevation** 307
**sub-lieutenant** 745
**sublimate**
*elevate* 307
*lighten* 320
*vaporize* 336
**sublime** *high* 206
*language* 574
*beauty* 845
*glory* 873
*magnanimous* 942
from the – to the ridiculous 853
**subliminal** 317
**sublineation** 550
**sublunary** 318
**submarine**
*deep* 208
*ship* 273
*warship* 726
– chaser 726
– warfare 722
**submediant** 413
**submerge**
*destroy* 162
*immerse* 300
*plunge* 310
*steep* 337
**submersible** 273, 726
**submersion** 208
**subministration** 707
**submission** **725**
*obedience* 743
**submissive**
*tractable* 705
*enduring* 826
*humble* 879
**submit to arbitration** 774
**submonish** 695
**submultiple** 84
**subordinate**
*inferior* 34
*unimportant* 643
*subject* 749
**subordination** 58
**suborn** 615, 795
**subpœna** 741, 969
**subreption**
*falsehood* 544
*acquisition* 775
**subrogation** 147
**subscribe**
*assent* 488
*aid* 707
*agree to* 769
*give* 784
**subscript** 39, 65
**subscription**
*gift* 784
**subsequent**
- *in order* 63
- *in time* 117
**subserviency**
*servility* 886
**subservient**
*instrumental* 631
*aid* 707
*subject* 749
**subside** 36, 306
**subsidiary** *aid* 707
*servant* 746
**subsidy**
*assistance* 707
*gift* 784
*pay* 809
**subsist** *exist* 1
*continue* 141
*live* 359
**subsistence** 298
**subsoil** 221, 342
**substance**
*existence* 1
*thing* 3
*quantity* 25
*inside* 221
*matter* 316
*texture* 329
*important part* 642
*wealth* 803
in – 596
man of – 803
**substantial**
*existing* 1
*hypostatic* 3
*material* 316
*dense* 321
*true* 494
– meaning 516
**substantiality** **3**
**substantially**
*intrinsically* 5
– true 494
**substantiate** 467, 924
**substantive** 1, 3
**substitute**
*inferior* 34
*change* 147
*means* **634**
*deputy* 759
**substitution** **147**
**substratum**
*substance* 3
*layer* 204
*base* 211
*support* 215
*interior* 221
*materiality* 316
**substructure** 211
**subsultory** 315
**subsume** 54
**subtend** 237
**subterfuge** 617
*sophistry* 477
*lie* 546
*cunning* 702
**subterranean** 208
**subtile** *light* 320
*rare* 322
- *texture* 329
**subtilize** *rarefy* 322
*sophistry* 477
**subtle** *slight* 32
*light* 320
*cunning* 702
– point 704
– reasoning 476
**subtlety** 477, 498
**subtraction**
*subduction* 38
*arithmetic* 85
*taking* 789
**subtrahend** 38, 84
**suburb** *town* 189
*near* 197
*environs* 227
**subvention**
*support* 215
*aid* 707
*gift* 784
**subversion** 146
**subvert** *destroy* 162
*invert* 218
*depress* 308
**subway** 627
– train 272
**succedaneum** 147
**succeed** *follow* 63
*posterior* 117
*success* 731
*transfer* 783
– to *acquire* 775
**succès d'estime** 873
**success** **731**
**succession**
*sequence* 63
*continuity* 69
*repetition* 104
*posteriority* 117
*transfer* 783
in quick – 136
in regular – 138
– of ideas 451
– of time 109
**successless** 732
**successor** 65, **117**
**succinct** 572

**suo:** – periculo 926
– sibi gladio hunc jugulo
*absurdity* 479
*retaliation* 718
**sup** *small quantity* 32
*feed* 298
– full of horrors 828
**super** *theatrical* 599
**superable** 470
**superabound** 641
**superadd** 37
**superannuated** 128
**superb** 845
**supercargo** 694
**supercherie** 545
**supercilious**
*proud* 878
*insolent* 885
*disrespectful* 929
*scornful* 930
**superdreadnought** 726
**supereminence** 648, 873
**supererogation** 641, 645
**superexaltation** 873
**superexcellence** 648
**superfetation** 37, 168
**superficial**
*shallow* 209
*outside* 220
*misjudging* 481
*ignorant* 491
– extent 180
**superficies** 220
**superfine** 648
**superfluitant** 305
**superfluity** 40, 641
**superfluous** 645
**superhuman** 650, 976
**superimpose** 223
**superimposed** 206
**superincumbent** 206, 319
**superinduce**
*change* 140
*cause* 153
*produce* 161
**superintend** 693
**superintendent** 694
**superior** *greater* 33
- *in size* 194
*important* 642
*good* 648
*director* 694
**superiority** 33
**superjunction** 37
**superlative** 33
**superlatively good** 648
**superman** 33
**supernal** 206, 210, 981
**supernatant** 206, 305
**supernatural** 976, 980
– aid 707
**supernumerary**
*adjunct* 39
*theatrical* 599
*reserve* 636
*redundant* 641
**superpose** 37, 223
**supersaturate** 641
**superscription** 550, 590
**supersede**
*substitute* 147
*disuse* 678
*relinquish* 782
**supersensible** 317
**superstition**
*credulity* 486
*error* 495
*religion* 984
**superstratum** 220
**superstructure** 729
**supertax** 812
**supertonic** 413
**supervacaneous** 641
**supervene**
*extrinsic* 6
*be added* 37
*succeed* 117
*happen* 151
**supervise** 693
**supervisor** 694
**supination** 213
**supine**
*horizontal* 213
*inverted* 218
*sluggish* 683
*mentally torpid* 823
**suppeditate** 637
**supper** 298
**supplant** 147
**supple** *soft* 324
*servile* 886
**supplement**
*addition* 37
*adjunct* 39
*completion* 52
*publication* 531
*book* 593
**suppletory** 37
**suppliant** 765, 767
**supplicate** *beg* 765
*pity* 914
*worship* 990
**supplies**
*materials* 635
*aid* 707
*money* 800
**supply** *store* 636
*provide* 637
*give* 784
– aid 707
– deficiencies 52
– the place of 147
– and transport 726
**support** *perform* 170
*sustain* 215
*evidence* 467
*preserve* 670
*aid* 707
*feel* 821
*endure* 826
*vindicate* 937
– life 359
**supporter** 711
–s *heraldic* 550
**suppose** 514
**supposing** 469
**supposition** 514
**supposititious** 546
**suppress**
*destroy* 162
*conceal* 528
*silent* 581
*restrain* 751
**suppression of truth** 544
**suppuration** 653
**suppute** 85
**supralapsarian** 984
**supramundane** 939
**supremacy** 33, 737
**supreme** 33
*summit* 210
*authority* 737
in a – degree 31
**Supreme Being** 976
**surbate** 659
**surbated** 688
**surcease** 142
**surcharge** 641
– and falsify 811
**surcingle** 45
**surcoat** 225
**surd** *number* 84
*deaf* 419
*silent letter* 561
**sure** *certain* 474
*belief* 484
*safe* 664
make – against 673
make – of
*inquire* 461
*take* 789
you may be – 535
to be – *assent* 488
on – ground 664
*security* 771
**sure-footed**
*careful* 459
*skilful* 698
*cautious* 864
**surely** 488, 602, 870
**sureness** 474
**surety** 474, 664
**surf** 348, 353
**surface** *outside* 220
*texture* 329
below the – 526
lie on the – 518, 525
skim the – 460
**Surface, Joseph** – 548
**surfeit** 641, 869
**surge** *swarm* 72
*swell* 305
*rotation* 312
*wave* 348
**surgeon** 662
**surgery** 662
**surgit amari aliquid** 651
**surly** *gruff* 895
*sullen* 901a
*unkind* 907
**surmise** 514
**surmount** *be superior* 33
*tower* 206
*transcursion* 303
*ascent* 305
– a difficulty
*overcome* 731
**surmountable** 470
**surname** 564
**surpass**
*be superior* 33
*grow* 194
*go beyond* 303
*outshine* 873
**surplice** 999
**surplus** 40, 641
**surplusage** 641
**surprint** 550
**surprise**
*non-expectation*

## T

**tape** *string* 205
*measure* 466
– machine 553
**taper** *contract* 195
*narrow* 203
*candle* 423
– to a point 253
**tapestry** 556, 847
**tapinois, en** – 528
**tapis**: on the –
*event* 151
*topic* 454
*intention* 620
*plan* 626
**tap-root** 153
**taps** 550
**tapster** 746
**tar** *cover* 223
*sailor* 269
*pitch* 356*a*
– and feather 929, 972
**taradiddle** 546
**tarantass** 272
**tarantella** 840
**tarboosh** 225
**tardiloquence** 583
**tardy** 133, 275
**tare** 40*a*
– and tret 813
**tares** 645
**targe** 717
**target** 620
*shield* 717
**tariff** 812
**tarmac** 635
**tarn** 343
**tarnish**
*discoloration* 429
*soil* 653
*deface* 848
*disgrace* 874
**tarpaulin** 223
**tarry** *remain* 110, 265
*later* 133
*continue* 141
– for *expect* 507
**tart** *pastry* 298, 396
*acid* 397
*rude* 895
*irascible* 901
*harlot* 962
**tartan** 440
**tartane** 273
**Tartar** *choleric* 901
catch a – *dupe* 547
*unskilful* 699
*retaliation* 718
**tartar** *dirt* 653
– emetic 663
**Tartarus** 982
**Tartufe**
*hypocrisy* 544
*deceiver* 548
*impiety* 988
**task** *lesson* 537
*business* 625
*put to use* 677
*fatigue* 688
*command* 741
hard – 704
set a – 741
take to – 932
– the memory 505
**taskmaster** 694
**tass** 191
**tassel** 847
**taste** *sapidity* **390**
*experience* 821
*good taste* **850**
man of – 850
to one's – *savoury* 394
*pleasant* 829
*love* 897
**tasteful** 850
**tasteless** *insipid* 391
**tasty** 394, 850
**tâtonner** 463
**tatter**
*small quantity* 32
**tatterdemalion** 876
**Tattersalls** 799
**tatters** *garments* 225
tear to – 162
**tatting** 847
**tattle** 588
**tattler** 532, 588
**tattoo**
*drumming* 407
*mottled* 440
*summons* 741
**taught** [*see* teach]
*fastened* 43
**taunt** 929, 938
**tauromachy** 720
**taut** 43
**tautology** 104, 573
**tavern** 189
**tawdry** 851
**tawny** 433, 436
**tax** *inquire* 461
*employ* 677
*fatigue* 688
*command* 741
*compel* 744
*request* 765
*accounts* 811
*impost* 812
*discount* 813
*accuse* 938
– one's energies 686
– the memory 505
**taxi** 266
**taxi-cab** 272
**taxi-driver** 268
**taxidermy** 368
**taxis** 60
**taxonomy** 60
**tazza** 191
**Te Deum** 990
**te fabula narratur, de** – *retaliate* 718
*condemn* 971
**tea** 298
**teach** 537
– one's grandmother 641, 885
– one his place 879
**teachable** 539
**teacher** **540**, 673
**teaching** **537**
false – 538
**teacup, storm in a** –
*overrate* 482, 549
*exaggerate* 549
**teagown** 225
**team** *assemblage* 69, 72
**teamster** 694
**tea-party** 892
**tea-pot** 191
**tear** *separate* 44
*violence* 173
*move rapidly* 274
*excite* 825
*weeping* 839
– away from 789
– oneself away 623
– asunder one's bonds 750
– one's hair 839
– out 301
– to pieces
*separate* 44
*destroy* 162
– up *destroy* 162
**tear-gas** 663, 727
**tearful** 839
**tearing passion** 825
**tears**: draw – 830
shed – 839
– in one's eyes
*excited* 824
*sad* 837
**tease** *annoy* 830
*spite* 907
**teaser** *difficult* 704
**teasing** 830
**teat** 250
**tea-table talk** 588
**technic** 698
**technica, memoria** – 505
**technical**
*conformable* 82
*workmanlike* 698
– college 542
– education 537
– knowledge 698
– school 542
– term 564
**technicality**
*special* 79
*cant term* 563
*formulary* 697
**technique** 556, 698
**technocracy** 698
**technology** 698
**techy** 901
**tedious** 841
while away the – hours 681
**tedium** 841
**teem**
*produce* 161
*productive* 168
*abound* 639
– with *multitude* 102
**teemful** 168
**teeming** *crowd* 72
**teemless** 169
**'teens** 98
in one's – 127, 129
**teeter** 314
**teeth** 330, 781
armed to the – 673, 717, 722
between the – 405
cast in one's – 938
chattering of – 383
have cut one's eye – 698
in the – of 704, 708
grind one's – 900
the run of one's – 815
set one's – 604
show one's – 900
in spite of one's – 708, 744
make one's – chatter 385, 860
set the – on edge
*scrape* 331
*sour* 397
*stridor* 410
*pain the feelings*

830
**tee** 66
**teetotalism** 953, 958
**teetotum** 312, 840
**teg** 366
**tegument** 223
**teind** 99
**teinoscope** 445
**tekel upharsin** 668
**telautograph** 553
**telegram** 532
**telegraph**
*velocity* 274
*messenger* 534
*signal* 550
– boy 534
by – *haste* 684
**telegraphone** 553
**telegraphy**
*publication* 531
**teleology** 620
**telemeter** 200
**telepathy** 992
**telephone** 418
*inform* 527
*messenger* 534
**telescope** 445
– word 572
**telescopic** 196
**telesis** 658
**telesm** 993
**tell** *count* 85
*influence* 175
*evidence* 467
*inform* 527
*speak* 582
*describe* 594
*succeed* 731
let me – you 535
who can – 475
– one's beads 990, 998
– the cause of 522
– fortunes 511
– how 155
– a lie 544
– a piece of one's mind 529
– of 467
– off 85
– one plainly 527
– its own tale 518
– tales
*disclose* 529
– the truth 543
**teller** *treasurer* 801
– of tales 594
**telling** 175
*graphic* 518
*important* 642
*exciting* 824
with – effect 171, 175
**telltale** *news* 532
*indicator* 550
*knave* 941
**telluric** 318
**telum imbelle** 158
**temerity** 863
**temper** *nature* 5
*state* 7
*moderate* 174
*elasticity* 323
*pliability* 324
*modify* 469
*prepare* 673
*affections* 820
*irascibility* 901
command of – 826
lose one's – 900
out of – 901*a*
trial of – 824
– the wind to the shorn lamb 834
**tempera** 556
**temperament**
*nature* 5
*tendency* 176
*musical* 413
*affections* 820
**temperance** 174, **953**
**temperate**
[*see* temperance]
*mild* 826
**temperature** 382
increase of – 384
reduction of – 385
**tempest**
*violence* 173
*agitation* 315
*wind* 349
*excitement* 825
**tempestivity** 134
**tempest-tossed** 824
**tempestuous** 59
**Templar** 996
Good – 958
**temple** *house* 189
*side* 236
*church* **1000**
– of the Holy Ghost 983*a*
**templet** 22
**tempora:**
O –! O mores!
*lament* 839
*disreputable* 874
*disapprobation* 932
*improbity* 940
*vice* 945
– mutantur 140
**temporal**
*transient* 111
*laical* 997
lords – and spiritual 875
**temporality** 997
**temporary** 111
**temporize**
*protract* 110
*defer* 133
*cunning* 702
**temporizer** 943
**tempt** *entice* 615
*attempt* 675
*desire* 865
– fortune 621, 675
– Providence 863, 885
**tempter** 615
*Satan* 978
voice of the – 615
**temulency** 959
**ten** 98
– to one 472
– thousand 98
**tenable** 664
**tenacity**
*coherence* 46
*toughness* **327**
*memory* 505
*resolution* 604
*obstinacy* 606
*retention* 781
*avarice* 819
*courage* 861
– of life 359
– of purpose 604*a*
**tenaculum** 781
**tenancy** 777
**tenant**
*present* 186
*occupier* 188
*possessor* 779
**tenantless**
*absence* 187
*seclusion* 893
**tenax propositi** 204, 939
**tend** *conduce* 176
- *animals* 370
*aid* 707
*serve* 631, 746
– towards 278
**tendence** 749
**tendency** **176**
**tender** *slight* 32
*ship* 273
*soft* 324
*painful* 378
*colour* 428
*war vessel* **726**
*offer* 763
*susceptible* 822
*affectionate* **897**
*compassionate* 914
– age 127
– conscience **926**
– heart
*susceptible* 822
*kind* 906
*compassionate* 914
– mercies [ironical]
*badness* 649
*severity* 739
*cruelty* 907
– passion 897
– one's resignation 757
– to 707
**tenderfoot** 57, **541**
**tendon** 45
**tendril** *fastening* **45**
*offshoot* 51
*infant* 129
*filament* 205
*convoluted* 248
*plant* 367
**tenebrious** 421
**tenebrosity** 421
**tenement** 189, **780**
– of clay 362
**tenet** *belief* 484
**tenner** 800
**tennis** 840
– ground 213
**tenor** *course* 7
*degree* 26
*direction* 278
*high note* 410
*singer* 416
*violin* 417
*meaning* 516
pursue the noiseless – of one's way 881
**tense** *hard* 323
**tensile** 325
**tension** 159, 200
**tensure** 200
**tent** *abode* 189
*covering* 223
pitch one's –
*locate* 184
*arrive* 292
**tentacle** 781
**tentative** 463, 675
**tente d'abri** 223
**tented field** 722

**Tories 712**
**torment**
*physical* 378
*moral* 828, 830
place of – 982
**Tormes, Lazarillo de** – 941
**torn** [*see* tear]
*discord* 713
**tornado** 312, 349
**torpedo** *bane* 663
*sluggish* 683
*weapon* 727
*evil-doer* 913
– boat 726
– boat destroyer 726
– plane 276
**torpid, torpor**
*inert* 172
*inactive* 683
*insensible* 823
**torque** 847
*torrefy* 384
**torrent**
*violence* 173
*rapid* 274
*flow* 348
rain in –s **348**
**torrid** 382
**torsion** 248
**torso** 50
**tort** 925, 947
**tort et à travers, à** –
*disagreement* 24
*absurdity* 497
*resolution* 604
**tortious** 925
**tortile** 248
**tortive** 248
**tortoise** 275
**tortoise-shell** 440
**tortuous**
*twisted* 248
*dishonourable* 940
**torture**
*physical* 378
*moral* 828, 830
*cruelty* 907
*punishment* 972
– a question 476
**torvity** 901*a*
**toss** *derange* 61
*throw* 284
*oscillate* 314
*agitate* 315
– in a blanket 929
– the caber 840
– the head
*pride* 878
*insolence* 885
*contempt* 930
– off *drink* 298
– overboard 610
– on one's pillow 825
– up 156, 621
**tosspot** 959
**tot** *child* 129
**tot homines, tot sententiæ** 15
**total** 50, 84
sum – 800
– abstinence **953**, 955
– eclipse 421
**totalisator** 621
**totality** 52
**totally** 52
**totidem verbis** 19, 494
**totient** 84
**toties quoties** 136
**totis viribus** 686
**totitive** 84
**toto: in** – 52
– cœlo 52
**totter**
*changeable* 149
*weak* 160
*limp* 275
*oscillate* 314
*agitate* 315
*decay* 659
*danger* 665
– to its fall 162
**touch** *relate to* 9
*small quantity* 32
*mixture* 41
*contact* 199
*sensation* **379, 380**
*music* 416
*test* 463
*indication* **550**
*act* 680
*receive* 785
*excite* 824
*pity* 914
– and go
*instant* 113
*soon* 132
*changeable* 149
*easy* 705
– the guitar 416
– the hat 894
– the heart 824
– on 516
– to the quick 822
– up 658
– upon 595
in – with **9**
**touched** *crazy* **503**
*tainted* 653
*compassion* 914
– in the wind 655
– with *feeling* 821
**touching** 830
**touchstone** 463
**touchwood**
*fuel* 388
*irascible* 901
**touchy** 901
**tough** *coherent* **46**
*tenacious* 327
*difficult* 704
**toujours perdrix**
*repetition* 104
*weary* 841
*satiety* 869
**toupee** 256
**tour** 266
**tour de force**
*skill* 698
*stratagem* 702
*display* 882
**touring car** 272
**tourist** 268
**tournament** 720
**tourniquet** 263
**tournure** 230, 448
belle – 845
**tous les rapports, sous** – 494
**tousle** 61
**tout** *solicit* 765
**tout:** – au contraire 14
– court 265
– ensemble **50**
– le monde 78
**touter** *agent* **758**
*solicitor* 767
*eulogist* 935
**tow** 285
take in – *aid* 707
**towage** 812
**towardly** 705
**towards** 278
draw – 288
move – 286
**towel** *clean* 652
*flog* 972
**tower**
*stability* 150
*edifice* 161
*abode* 189
*height* 206
*soar* 305
*defence* 717
– of strength
*strong* 159
*influential* 175
*safety* **664**
**towering** *great* **31**
*furious* **173**
*large* 192
*high* 206
– passion **900**
– rage 900
**town** *city* 189
*fashion* 852
man about – **854**
on the – 961
all over the – **532**
talk of the – **873**
– council 696
**town-hall** 189, **966**
**township** 181
**townsman** 188
fellow – 892
**town-talk** 532, **588**
**toxic** 657
**toxicology** 663
**toxophilite** 284
**toy** *trifle* 643
*amusement* **840**
*fondle* 902
**toy-dog** 366
**toy-shop** 840
**trabant** 717
**tracasserie** 713
**trace** *inquire* **461**
*discover* 480*a*
*mark* 550
*record* 551
*delineate* **554**
– back 122
– out 480*a*
– to 155
– up 461
**tracery**
*lattice* 219
*curve* 245
*ornament* 847
**traces** *harness* **45**
**trachea** 351
**tracing** 21
**track** *trace* 461
*record* 551
*way* 627
cover up one's –s 528
in one's –s **113**
racing – 840
– meet 840
– racing 728
**trackless**
*space* 180
*difficult* 704
– trolley 272
**tract** *region* 181
*book* 593
*dissertation* **595**

*evaporate* 336
*appear* 525
*be disclosed* 529
**transplace** 270
**transplant** 270
**transplendent** 420
**transpontine** 196
**transport**
*transfer* 270
*ship* 273
*war vessel* 726
*excitement* 825
*delight* 827
*please* 829
*punish* 972
– of love 897
– plane 273
**transpose**
*exchange* 148
*displace* 185
*invert* 218
*transfer* 270
– *music* 413
**transubstantiation**
*change* 140
*sacrament* 998
**transude** 295, 302
**transume** 140
**transumption** 270
**transverse** 217, 219
**tranter** 271
**trap** *closure* 261
*gig* 272
*snare* 545
*stage* – 599
*pitfall* 667
fall into a – 547, 699
lay a – for 545
**trapan** 545
**trap bat and ball** 840
**trap-door**
*opening* 260
*snare* 545
*pitfall* 667
**trapes** 701
**trappings**
*adjunct* 39
*clothes* 225
*equipment* 633
*ornament* 847
**Trappist** 996
**traps**
*clothes* 225
*baggage* 780
**trash**
*unmeaning* 517
*trifling* 643
*useless* 645
**trashy** – style 575
**traulism** 583
**traumatic** 662
**travail** 161, 686
**trave** 215
**travel** 266
– out of the record 477
**traveller** 268
*bagman* 758
tricks upon –s 545, 702
–'s tale 546, 549
**travelling bag** 191
**traverse** *move* 266
*pass* 302
*negative* 536
*obstruct* 706
**travesty**
*imitate* 19, 21
*misinterpret* 523
*misrepresent* 555
*ridicule* 856
**travis** 215
**trawl** 285, 463
**trawler** 273
**tray** 191
**treacherous** 907, 940
– memory 506
**treachery** 545, 940
**treacle** 352, 396
**tread** 264, 266
– the beaten track 82, 613
– the boards 599
– down 739, 879
– on the heels of 281
– a path 266, 622
– the stage 599
– in the steps of 19
– under foot
*destroy* 162
*subjection* 749
*disrepute* 874
*insolence* 885
*contempt* 930
– upon 649
**treadle** 633
**treadmill** 975
**treason** 742, 940
**treasure** *cherish* 897
*store* 636
*goodness* 648
*money* 800
– trove 618
– up in the memory 505
**treasurer** 801
**treasury** 802
– note 800
**treat** *physical pleasure* 377
*manage* 692
*bargain* 769
*delight* 827, 829
*amusement* 840
– of 595
– oneself to 827
– well 906
**treatise** 593, 595
**treatment**
*painting* 556
*conduct* 692
ill – 649
medical – 662
**treaty** 769
**treble**
*three* 93
*shrill* 410
childish – 581
**tree** *pedigree* 166
*plant* 367
*gallows* 975
top of the – 210
up a – 704
as the – falls 151
– of knowledge 490
**treenail** 45
**trefoil** 92
**trek** 266
**trellis** 219
**tremble**
*fluctuate* 149
*weakness* 160
*shake* 315
*cold* 383
*emotion* 821
*fear* 860
make one – 860
**trembling:**
– in the balance 475, 665
– to its fall 162
**tremblingly alive** 822
**tremendous** 31, 830, 860
**tremendously** 31
**tremolo** 415
**tremor**
*agitation* 315
*emotion* 821
*fearful* 860
**tremulous**
*agitated* 315
– *voice* 583
*irresolute* 605
*fear* 860
**trench** *moat* 232
*furrow* 259
*concavity* 252
*defence* 717
– mortar 727
– on *near* 197
*trespass* 303
*moral trespass* 925
**trenchant**
*energetic* 171
*assertive* 535
*concise style* 572
*vigorous language* 574
*important* 642
*emotion* 821
*discourteous* 895
*censure* 932
**trench-coat** 225
**trencher** *plate* 191
*layer* 204
**trenches, open the** – 716
**trend** *tendency* 176
*bend* 278
*deviate* 279
**trennel** 45
**trepan** 260
*snare* 545
*borer* 262
**trephine** 260, 262
**trepidation**
*agitation* 315
*emotion* 821
*excitement* 825
*fear* 860
**tres juncta in uno** 92
**trespass**
*go beyond* 303
*vice* 945
*guilt* 947
**tress** 256
**trestle** 215
**trevet** 215
[*and see* **trivet**]
**trews** 225
**trey** 92
**triad** 92
**triagonal** 244
**trial** *inquiry* 461
*experiment* 463
*essay* 675
*difficulty* 704
*adversity* 735
*suffering* 828, 830
*lawsuit* 969
*punishment* 972
– of temper 824
**triality** 92
**trialogue** 588
**triangle** 92, 244

*adversity* 735
*pain* 828
*painful* 830
bring into – 649
get into – 649, 732
in – 619, 735
take – 686
– one's head about 682
– one for 765
– oneself 686
**troubled waters, fish in** – 704
**troublesome** 686, 704, 830
**troublous** 59, 173
– times 713
**trough** *hollow* 252
*trench* 259
*conduit* 350
**trounce** 932, 972
**troupe** 72
**trousers** 225
**trousseau** 225
**trouvaille** 775
**trouvère** 597
**trover** 775, 964
**trow** *think* 451
*believe* 484
*know* 490
**trowel** 191
**troy-weight** 319
**truant** *absent* 187
*runaway* 623
*idle* 682
*apostate* 941
**truce** *cessation* 142
*deliverance* 672
*peace* 721
*pacification* 723
flag of – 724
**trucidation** 361
**truck** *summit* 210
*vehicle* 272
*barter* 794
**truck driver** 268
**truck farm** 371
**truckle to**
*submit* 725
*servile* 886
*flatter* 933
**truckle-bed** 215
**truck-load** 31
**truckman** 268
**truculent** 907
**trudge** 266, 275
**truditur dies die** 109
**true** *real* 1
*straight* 246
*assent* 488
*accurate* 494
*veracious* 543
*faithful* 772
*honourable* 939
*orthodox* 983a
– bill
*vindicate* 937
*accuse* 938
*lawsuit* 969
see in its – colours 480a
– meaning 516
– to nature 17
– to oneself 604a
– saying 496
– to scale 494
**true-hearted** 543, 939
**true-love** 897
**true-lover's knot** 897, 902
**true-penny** 939
**truism** *axiom* 496
*unmeaning* 517
**trull** 962
**truly** *very* 31
*assent* 488
*really* 494
*indeed* 535
**trump** *perfect* 650
*honourable* 939
*good man* 948
turn up –s 731
– card *device* 626
*success* 731
– up *falsehood* 544
*accuse* 938
**trumped up** 468, 545, 546
**trumpery** 517, 643
**trumpet** *music* 417
*war cry* 722
*boast* 884
flourish of –s
*ostentation* 882
*celebration* 883
*boasting* 884
ear– 418
penny –
*skill* 410
sound of –
*alarm* 669
speaking – 418
– blast 404
– call 550, 741
– forth 531
**trumpeter**
*musician* 416
*messenger* 534
*boaster* 884
**trumpet-toned** 410
**trumpet-tongued** 404, 531
**truncate** 201, 241
**truncated** 53
**truncheon**
*weapon* 727
*staff of office* 747
*instrument of punishment* 975
**trundle** 284, 312
**trunk** *whole* 50
*origin* 153
*paternity* 166
*box* 191
**trunk-hose** 225
**trunnion**
*support* 215
*projection* 250
**truss** *tie* 43
*pack, packet* 72
*support* 215
**trust**
*belief* 484
*combination* 709
*property* 780
*credit* 805
*hope* 858
– to a broken reed 699
– to the chapter of accidents 621
**trustee**
*consignee* 758
*possessor* 779
*treasurer* 801
**trustful** 484
**trustless** 940
**trustworthy**
*certain* 474
*belief* 484
- *memory* 505
*veracious* 543
*honourable* 939
**truth**
*exactness* 494
*veracity* 543
*probity* 939
arrive at the – 480a
in – *certainly* 474
love of – 543
of a – 535, 543
prove the – of 937
religious – 983a
speak the – 529, 543
in very – 543
**Truth, Spirit of** – 976
**truthless** 544
**trutination** 319
**try** *experiment* 463
*adjudge* 480
*endeavour* 675
*use* 677
*lawsuit* 969
– a case 967
– a cause 480
– conclusions
*discuss* 476
*quarrel* 713
*contend* 720
– one's hand 675
– one's luck 621
– one 704
– out 463
– the patience 830
– a prisoner 967
– one's temper 824
– one's utmost 686
**trying** 688, 704
**tryst** 892
**trysting-place** 74
**tsar** [*see* czar]
**tu quoque** 718
– argument
*counter-evidence* 468
*confutation* 479
*accuse* 938
**tub** 191
– thumper 582
– to a whale 545, 617
**tuba** 417
**tubam trepidat, ante** – 860, 862
**tubby** 202
**tube** 260
test – 144
**tubercle** 250
**tuberculous** 655
**tuberosity** 250
**tubman** 968
**tubular** 260
**tubulated** 260
**tubule** 260
**tuck** *fold* 258
*dagger* 727
– in *locate* 184
*eat* 298
*insert* 300
**tucker** 225
**tuft** *collection* 72
*rough* 256
**tufted** 256
**tuft-hunter** 886, 943
**tuft-hunting** 886, 933
**tug** *ship* 273
*pull* 285

**U**

**unbesought** 766
**unbetrayed** 939
**unbewailed** 932
**unbiassed** 498, 748
**unbidden** 600, 742
**unbigoted** 498
**unbind** 44, 750
**unblamable** 946
**unblamed** 946
**unblemished** 650, 946
**unblenching** 861
**unblended** 42
**unblest** 735, 932
– with 777*a*
**unblown** 674
**uncommenced** 67
**unblushing**
*proud* 878
*vain* 880
*imprudent* 885
**unboastful** 881
**unbodied** 317
**unboiled** 674
**unbolt** 750
**unbookish** 491
**unborn** 2, 152
**unborrowed** 787, 788
**unbosom oneself** 529
**unbought**
*not bought* 796
*honorary* 815
*honourable* 939
*unselfish* 942
**unbound** 748, 927*a*
**unbounded** 105
**unbrace** 160, 655
**unbreathed** 526
**unbred** 895
**unbribed** 939, 942
**unbridled**
*violent* 173
*lax* 738
*free* 748
**unbroken**
*entire* 50
*continuous* 69
*preserved* 670
*unviolated* 939
**unbruised** 50
**unbuckle** 44
**unburden**
– one's mind 529
**unburdened** 705
**unburied** 362
**unbusinesslike** 699
**unbuttoned** 748
**uncalculating** 863
**uncalled for**
*redundant* 641
*useless* 645
*not used* 678
**uncandid** 544, 907
**uncanny** 846, 980
**uncanonical** 984
**uncared for**
*neglected* 460
*indifference* 866
*disliked* 867
*hated* 898
**uncase** 226
**uncaught** 748
**uncaused** 156
**unceasing** 112
**uncensured** 931
**unceremonious** 880, 895
**uncertain**
*irregular* 139
*not certain* 475
*doubtful* 485
in an – degree 32
**uncertainty** 475
**unchain** 44, 750
**unchained** 748
**unchallenged** 488, 924
**unchangeable** 150, 604*a*
**unchanged** 16, 141
**unchanging** 5
**uncharitable** 907
**unchartered** 925, 964
**unchaste** 961
**unchastised** 970
**unchecked** 748
**uncheckered** 141
**uncheerful** 837
**unchivalric** 940
**unchristian** 984, 989
**uncial** 590
**uncinated** 244
**uncircumscribed** 180
**uncircumspect** 460
**uncivil** 851, 895
**uncivilized** 876, 895
**unclaimed** 748
**unclassical** 851
**uncle** *kin* 11
my –'s
*pawnshop* 787
**unclean** 653
– spirit 978, 980
**uncleanness** 653
**unclipped** 50
**unclog** 705, 750
**unclose** 260, 750
**unclothe** 226
**unclouded** 420, 446
**unclubbable** 893
**unclutch** 790
**uncoif** 226
**uncoil** 313
**uncoloured**
*achromatic* 429
*true* 494
**uncombed** 653, 851
**uncombined**
*simple* 42
*incoherent* 47
**uncomeatable** 471
**uncomely** 846
**uncomfortable** 828, 830
**uncommenced** 67
**uncommendable**
*blamable* 932
*bad* 945
*guilt* 947
**uncommensurable** 24
**uncommon** 31, 83, 137
**uncommonly** 31
**uncommunicated** 781
**uncommunicative** 528
**uncompact** 322
**uncompassionate** 914*a*
**uncompelled** 748
**uncomplaisant** 764
**uncompleted**
*incomplete* 53
*unfinished* 730
*failure* 732
**uncomplying** 742, 764
**uncompounded** 42
**uncompressed** 320, 322
**uncompromising**
*conformable* 82
*severe* 739
**unconcealable** 525
**unconceived**
*uncreated* 2
*unintelligible* 519
**unconcern** 823, 866
**unconcocted** 674
**uncondemned** 970
**unconditional**
*complete* 52
*free* 748
*permission* 760
*consent* 762
*release* 768*a*
**unconducive** 175*a*
**unconfined** 748
**unconfirmed** 475
**unconformity**
*disagreement* 24
*irregularity* 83
**unconfused**
*methodical* 58
*clear* 518
**unconfuted** 478, 494
**uncongealed** 333
**uncongenial** 24, 657
**unconnected**
*irrelative* 10
*disjointed* 44
*discontinuous* 70
*illogical* 477
**unconquerable**
*strong* 159
*persevering* 604*a*
– will 604
**unconquered** 719
**unconscientious** 940
**unconscionable**
*excessive* 31
*unprincipled* 945
**unconscious**
*ignorant* 491
*insensible* 823
**unconsenting** 603, 764
**unconsidered** 452
**unconsolable** 837
**unconsolidated** 47
**unconsonant** 24
**unconspicuous** 447
**unconstitutional** 925, 964
**unconstrained** 748, 880
**unconsumed** 40
**uncontested** 474
**uncontradicted** 488
**uncontrite** 951
**uncontrollable**
*violent* 173
*necessity* 601
*emotion* 825
**uncontrolled**
*free* 748
*excitability* 825
**uncontroverted** 488
**unconventional** 83, 614
**unconversant** 491, 699
**unconverted**
*dissenting* 489
*irreligious* 989

**unforfeited** 781
**unforgettable** 505
**unforgiving** 919
**unforgotten** 505
**unformed** 241, 674
**unfortified**
*pure* 42
*powerless* 158
**unfortunate**
*ill-timed* 135
*failure* 732
*adversity* 735
*unhappy* 828
– woman 962
**unfounded** 546
**unfrequent** 137
**unfrequented** 893
**unfriended**
*powerless* 158
*secluded* 893
**unfriendly**
*opposed* 708
*hostile* 889
*malevolent* 907
**unfrock** 756, 972
**unfrozen** 382
**unfruitful** 169
**unfulfilled** 773, 925
**unfurl**
*unfold* 313
– a flag 525, 550
**unfurnished** 640, 674
**ungainly** 846, 895
**ungallant** 895
**ungarnished** 849
**ungathered** 678
**ungenerous** 819, 943
**ungenial** 657
**ungenteel** 851, 895
**ungentle** 173, 895
**ungentlemanly**
*vulgar* 851
*rude* 895
*dishonourable* 940
**ungifted** 499
**unglorified** 874
**unglue** 47
**ungodly** 989
**ungovernable**
*violent* 173
*disobedient* 742
*passionate* 825
**ungoverned** 748
**ungraceful**
- *language* 579
*ugly* 846
*vulgar* 851
**ungracious** 895, 907
**ungrammatical** 568
**ungranted** 764
**ungrateful** 917
**ungratified** 832
**ungrounded**
*unsubstantial* 4
*erroneous* 495
**ungrudging** 816
**unguarded**
*neglected* 460
*spontaneous* 612
*unprepared* 674
in an – moment
*unexpectedly* 508
**unguem, ad** – 494, 650
**unguent** 356
**unguibus et rostro** 686
**unguided**
*ignorant* 491
*impulsive* 612
*unskilled* 699
**unguilty** 946
**unhabitable** 187
**unhabituated** 614
**unhackneyed** 614
**unhallowed** 988, 989
**unhand** 750
**unhandseled** 123
**unhandsome** 940
**unhandy** 699
**unhappy**
*adversity* 735
*pain* 828
*dejected* 837
make – 830
**unharbored** 185
**unhardened**
*tender* 914
*innocent* 946
*penitent* 950
**unharmonious** 24, 414
**unharness** 750
**unhatched** 674
**unhazarded** 664
**unhealthy** 655, 657
**unheard of**
*exceptional* 83
*improbable* 473
*ignorant* 491
*wonderful* 870
**unheated** 383
**unheed, -ed** 460
**unheeding** 458
**unhesitating**
*belief* 484
*resolved* 604
**unhewn** 241, 674
**unhindered** 748
**unhinge** 61, 158
**unhinged**
*impotent* 158
*insane* 503
*failure* 732
**unhitch** 44
**unholy** 989
**unhonoured** 874
**unhook** (44)
**unhoped** 508
**unhorsed** 732
**unhostile** 888
**unhouse** 297
**unhoused** 185
**unhurt** 670
**unicorn**
*monster* 83
*carriage* 272
**unideal** *existing* 1
*no thought* 452
*true* 494
**unification** 48, 87
**uniform**
*homogeneous* 16
*simple* 42
*orderly* 58
*regular* 80
*dress* 225
*symmetry* 242
*livery* 550
**uniformity** 16
**unilluminated** 421
**unimaginable** 471, 473
*wonderful* 870
**unimaginative** 576, 843, 871
**unimagined** 1, 494
**unimitated** 20
**unimpaired** 670
**unimpassioned** 826
**unimpeachable**
*certain* 474
*true* 494
*due* 924
*approved* 931
*innocent* 946
**unimpeached** 931, 946
**unimpeded** 705, 748
**unimportance** 643
**unimpressed** 838
**unimpressible** 823
**unimproved** 659
**unincreased** 36
**unincumbered**
*easy* 705
*exempt* 927a
**uninduced** 616
**uninfected** 652
**uninfectious** 656
**uninflammable** 385
**uninfluenced**
*obstinate* 606
*unactuated* 616
*free* 748
**uninfluential** 172, 175a
**uninformed** 491
**uningenuous** 544
**uninhabit, -able, -ed** 187, 893
**uninitiated** 491, 699
**uninjured**
*perfect* 650
*healthy* 654
*preserved* 670
**uninjurious** 656
**uninquisitive** 456
**uninspired** 823
**uninstructed** 491
**unintellectual** 452, 499
**unintelligent** 499
**unintelligibility** 519
**unintelligible** 519
- *style* 571
render – 538
**unintentional**
*necessary* 601
*undesigned* 621
**uninterested** 456, 841, 843
**unintermitting**
*unbroken* 69
*durable* 110
*continuing* 143
*persevering* 604a
**uninterrupted**
*continuous* 69
*perpetual* 112
*unremitting* 143
**unintroduced** 893
**uninured** 614
**uninvented** 526
**uninvestigated** 491
**uninvited** 893
**uninviting** 830
**union**
*agreement* 23
*junction* 43
*combination* 48
*concurrence* 178
*workhouse* 189
*party* 712
*concord* 714
*marriage* 903
**unionist** 712
**union-jack** 550
**union-pipes** 417
**unique**
*dissimilar* 18

*original* 20
*exceptional* 83
*alone* 87
**unirritating** 174
**unison**
*agreement* 23
*melody* 413
*concord* 714
**unit** 51, 87
**Unitarian** 984
**unite** *join* 43
*combine* 48
*assemble* 72
*concur* 178
*converge* 290
*party* 712
– one's efforts 709
– in pairs 89
– with 709
**united** 46, 714
**unity** *identity* 13
*uniformity* 16
*whole* 50
*complete* 52
*single* **87**
*concord* 714
– of time 120
**Unity, Trinity in –** 976
**universal** 78
– Church 983*a*
– favourite 899
**universality** 52
**universe** 318
**university** 542
– education 537
– extension 537
go to the – 539
**unjust** *wrong* 923
*impious* 988
**unjustifiable**
*wrong* 923
*inexcusable* 938
*wicked* 945
**unjustified** 923
*undue* 925
**unkempt**
*unclean* 653
*vulgar* 851
**unkennel** *eject* 297
*disclose* 529
**unkind** 907
–est cut of all 828
**unknightly** 940
**unknit** (44)
**unknowable** 519
**unknowing** 491
**unknown**
*ignorant* 491
*latent* 526
– to fame
*inglorious* 874
*low-born* 876
– quantities 491
**unlaboured**
– *style* 578
*unprepared* 674
**unlace** (44)
**unlade** 297
**unladylike**
*vulgar* 851
*rude* 895
**unlamented**
*hated* 898
*disapproved* 932
**unlatch** 44, 750
**unlawful**
*undue* 925
*illegal* 964
**unlearn** 506
**unlearned** 491
**unleavened** 674
**unless**
*circumstances* 8
*except* 83
*qualification* 469
**unlettered** 491
– Muse 579
**unlicensed** 761
**unlicked**
*unprepared* 674
*vulgar* 851
*clownish* 876
– cub
*youngster* 129
*shapeless* 241
*unmannerly* 895
**unlike** 18
**unlikely** 473
**unlikeness** 15
**unlimber** 323
**unlimited**
*great* 31
*infinite* 105
*free* 748
– space 180
**unliquefied** 321
**unlively** 837, 843
**unload**
*displaced* 185
*eject* 297
*disencumber* 705
**unlock** *unfasten* 44
*discover* 480*a*
**unlooked for** 508
**unloose**
*unfasten* 44
*liberate* 750
**unloved** 898
**unlovely** 846
**unlucky**
*inopportune* 135
*bad* 649
*unfortunate* **735**
*in pain* 830
**unmade** 2
**unmaimed** 654
**unmake** 145
**unman**
*mutilate* 38
*render powerless* 158
*madden* 837
*frighten* 860
**unmanly**
*effeminate* 374
*dishonourable* 940
**unmanageable**
*unwieldy* 647
*perverse* 704
**unmanned**
*dejected* 837
*cowardly* 862
**unmannered** 895
**unmannerly** 895
**unmarked** 460
**unmarred** 654, 670
**unmarried** 904
**unmask** 529
**unmatched**
*different* 15
*dissimilar* 18
*unparalleled* 20
**unmeaningness** **517**
**unmeant** 517
**unmeasured**
*infinite* 105
*undistinguished* 465*a*
*abundant* 639
**unmeditated** 612
**unmeet** 925
**unmellowed** 674
**unmelodious** 414
**unmelted** 321
**unmentionable** 874
–s 225
**unmentioned** 526
**unmerciful** 914*a*
**unmerited** 925
**unmethodical** 59
**unmindful**
*inattentive* 458
*neglectful* 460
*ungrateful* 917
**unmingled** 42
**unmissed** 460
**unmistakable**
*certain* 474
*intelligible* 518
*manifest* 525
**unmitigable** 173
**unmitigated**
*great* 31
*complete* 52
*violent* 173
**unmixed** 42
**unmolested** 664, 831
**unmoneyed** 804
**unmoral** 823
**unmourned** 898
**unmoved**
*quiescent* 265
*obstinate* 606
*insensible* 823
**unmusical** 414
– voice 581
**unmuzzled** 748
**unnamed** 565
**unnatural**
*exceptional* **83**
*affected* 855
*spiteful* 907
**unnecessary**
*redundant* 641
*useless* 645
*inexpedient* **647**
**unneeded** 645
**unneighbourly** **895**
**unnerved**
*powerless* 158
*weak* 160
*dejected* 837
**unnoted** } 460
**unnoticed** } 874
**unnumbered** 105
**unnurtured** 674
**uno saltu** 113
**unobeyed** 742
**unobjectionable**
*good* 648
*pretty good* 651
*innocent* 946
**unobnoxious** 648
**unobscured** 420
**unobservant** 458
**unobserved** 460
**unobstructed** 705, 748
**unobtainable** 471
**unobtained** 777*a*
**unobtrusive** 881
**unoccupied**
*vacant* 187
*unthinking* 452
*doing nothing* 681
*inactive* 683
*untenanted* 893
**unoffended**
*enduring* 826
*humble* 879
**unofficial** 964
**unoften** 137

*free* 748
unretracted 535
unrevenged 918
unreversed 143
unrevoked 143
unrewarded 806, 917
unrhymed 598
unriddle 480*a*, 529
unrig 645
unrighteous 945
unrip 260
unripe
*young* 127
*sour* 397
*immature* 674
unrivalled 33
unroll *evolve* 313
*display* 525
unromantic 494
unroot 301
unruffled
*calm* 174
*quiet* 265
*unaffected* 823
*placid* 826
unruly *violent* 173
*obstinate* 606
*disobedient* 742
unsaddle 756
unsafe 665
unsaid 526
unsaleable
*useless* 645
*selling* 796
*cheap* 815
unsaluted 929
unsanctified 988, 989
unsanctioned 925
unsated 865
unsatisfactory
*inexpedient* 647
*bad* 649
*displeasing* 830
*discontent* 832
unsatisfied 832, 865
unsavouriness 395
unsay *recant* 607
unscanned 460
unscathed 654
unschooled 491
unscientific 477
unscoured 653
unscriptural 984
unscrupulous 940
seal 529
unsearched 460
unseasonable 24, 135
unseasoned 614, 674
unseat 756
unseemly
*inexpedient* 647
*ugly* 846
*vulgar* 851
*undue* 925
*vicious* 945
unseen
*invisible* 447
*neglected* 460
*latent* 526
unseldom 136
unselfish 942
unseparated 46
unserviceable 645
unsettle *derange* 61
unsettled
*mutable* 149
*displaced* 185
*uncertain* 475
– in one's mind 503
unsevered 50
unsex 146
unshaded 525
unshaken 159
– belief 484
unshapely 846
unshapen 241
unshared 777
unsheathe
– the sword 722
unsheltered 665
unshielded 665
unshifting 143
unship 185, 297
unshocked 823
unshorn 50
unshortened 200
unshrinking 604, 861
unsifted 460
unsightly 846
unsinged 670
unskilfulness 699
unslaked 865
unsleeping 604*a*, 682
unsmooth 256
unsociable 893
unsocial 893
unsoiled 652
unsold 777
unsoldierlike 862
unsolicitous 866
unsolved 526
unsophisticated
*simple* 42
*genuine* 494
*artless* 703
unsorted 59
unsought
*avoided* 623
*unrequested* 766
unsound
*illogical* 477
*erroneous* 495
*deceptive* 545
*imperfect* 651
– mind 503
unsown 674
unsparing
*abundant* 639
*severe* 739
*liberal* 816
with an – hand 818
unspeakable 31, 870
unspecified 78
unspent 678
unspied 526
unspiritual 316, 989
unspoiled 648
unspotted
*clean* 652
*beautiful* 845
*innocent* 946
unstable 218
*changeable* 149
*uncertain* 475
*irresolute* 605
*precarious* 665
– equilibrium 149
unstaid 149
unstained
*clean* 652
*honourable* 939
unstatesmanlike 699
unsteadfast 605
unsteady
*mutable* 149
*irresolute* 605
*in danger* 665
unstinted 639
unstinting 816
unstirred 823, 826
unstopped
*continuing* 143
*open* 260
unstored 640
unstrained
*turbid* 653
*relaxed* 687
– meaning 516
unstrengthened 160
unstruck 823
unstrung 160
unstudied 460
unsubject 748
unsubmissive 742
unsubservient
*useless* 645
*inexpedient* 647
unsubstantial 4
*weak* 160
*rare* 322
*erroneous* 495
*imaginary* 515
unsubstantiality 4
unsuccessful 732
unsuccessive 70
unsuitable
*incongruous* 24
(*inexpedient* 647)
– time 135
unsullied *clean* 652
*honourable* 939
(*guiltless* 946)
unsung 526
unsupplied 640
unsupported
*weak* 160
(*unassisted* 706)
– by evidence 468
unsuppressed 141
unsurmountable 471
unsurpassed 33
unsusceptible 823
unsuspected
*latent* 526
unsuspecting
*belief* 484
*hopeful* 858
unsuspicious
*belief* 484
*artless* 703
*hope* 858
unsustainable 495
unsweet 395
unswept 653
unswerving
*straight* 246
*direct* 278
*persevering* 604*a*
unsymmetric 83
unsymmetrical 59, 243
unsystematic 59
untainted *pure* 652
*healthy* 654
*honourable* 939
untalked of 526
untamed 851, 907
untarnished 939
untasted 391
untaught 491, 674
untaxed 815
unteach 538
unteachable 499,

*continue* 143
*support* 215
*evidence* 467
*aid* 707
*praise* 931
**upholder** 488, **711**
**upholstery** 633
**uplands** 180, **206,** 344
**uplift** 307, 658
**upon:**
– my honour **535**
– oath 535
– which 117, 121
**upper** 206
– boxes, – circle 599
– classes 875
– hand
*influence* 175
*success* 731
*sway* 737
– story
*summit* 210
*intellect* 450
*wisdom* 498
– ten thousand 875
be on one's –'s 804
**uppermost** 210
say what comes – 612
– in the mind
*thought* 451
*topic* 454
*attention* 457
– in one's thoughts
*memory* 505
**upraise** 307
**uprear** 307
**upright**
*vertical* 212
*honest* 939
**uprise** 305
**uprising** 742
**uproar**
*disorder* 59
*violence* 173
*noise* 404
**uproarious** 825
**uproot** 301
**ups and downs of life** 151, 735
**upset** *destroy* 162
*invert* 218
*throw down* 308
*defeat* 731
*excite* 824
*disconcert* 874
– the apple cart **732**

**upshot** *result* **154**
*judgment* 480
*completion* 729
**upside down** 218
**upstairs** 206
**upstart**
*new* 123
*prosperous* 734
*plebeian* 876
**upturn** 218
**upwards** 206
– of 33, 100
**uranology** 318
**urban** 189
**urbane** 894
**urbis conditæ, anno** – 106
**urceole** 998
**urchin**
*child* 129
*small* 193
*wretch* 949
*imp* 980
**urge** *violence* **173**
*impel* 276
*incite* 615
*hasten* 684
*beg* 765
**urgent**
*required* 630
*important* **642**
*haste* 684
*request* 765
**urn** *vase* 191
*funereal* 363
*heater* 386
cinerary – **363**
**usage** 613, **677**
**usance** 806
**use** *habit* 613
*waste* 638
*utility* 644
*employ* **677**
*property* 780
make good – of 658
in – 677
be of – to *aid* **707**
*benevolence* 906
– one's discretion 600
– one's endeavour 675
– a right 924
– up 677
**used to** 613
**used up**
*deteriorated* 659
*disuse* 678
*fatigue* 688
*weary* 841

*satiated* **869**
**useful** 644
render – **677**
**useless** 645
**user,**
right of – **780**
**usher**
*guard* 263
*receive* 296
*teacher* 540
*servant* 746
*courtesy* 894
*wedding* 903
– in *precedence* **62**
*begin* 66
*precession* 280
*announce* 511
– into the world 161
**usque ad nauseam** 841
**U.S.S.** 726
**ustulation** 384
**usual**
*general* **78**
*ordinary* 82
*customary* **613**
**usufruct** 677
**usurer**
*lender* 787
*merchant* **797**
*credit* 805
*miser* 819
**usurious** 819
**usurp** *assume* **739**
*seize* 789
*illegal* 925
– authority **738**
**usurpation**
*insolence* 885
**usurper** 737
**usury** 806
**utensil** 191, **633**
**uti possidetis**
*permanence* 141
*possession* 777
*retention* 781
**utilitarian** 677, **910**
**utility** **644**
general –
*actor* 599
**utilize** 677
**utmost** 33
do one's – 686
– height 210
in one's – need 735
deserted in one's – need 893
**Utopia** 515, 858
**utricle** 191

**utter** *extreme* **31**
*distribute* **73**
*disclose* 529
*publish* 531
*speak* 580, **582**
*money* 800
**utterly** 52
**uttermost** 31
to the – parts of the eartn **180,** 196
**uxorious** 897

## V

**va sans dire, cela** – 474, 525
**vacant** *void* 4
*absent* 187
*thoughtless* 452
*unmeaning* **517**
*scanty* 640
– hour 685
– mind *folly* **499**
**vacate** *displace* **185**
*absent* 187
*depart* 293
*resign* 757
**vacation** 687
**vaccine** 366
**vache** 191
**vacillate**
*changeable* **149**
*undulate* 314
*waver* 605
**vacuity** 187
**vacuous**
*unsubstantial* **4**
*absent* 187
**vacuum** 187
– cleaner 652
**vade mecum** **527,** 542
**vadium** 771
**væ victis!** *war* **722**
*threat* 909
**vagabond**
*wanderer* 268
*low person* 876
*rogue* 949
**vagabondage** 266
**vagary**
*absurdity* 497
*imagination* **515**
*whim* 608
*antic* 840
**vagrant**
*changeable* **149**
*roving* 266
*traveller* 268

**vindicator** 919
**vindictive** 901, 919
**vine** 367
- grower 371
**vinegar** 397
- aspect 846
**vinery** 191
**vineyard** 371, 691
**vingt et un** 840
**vintage** 371, 636
**vintner** 637
**viol** 417
**violate**
*disobey* 742
*non-observance* 773
*undue* 925
*dereliction* 927
*ravish* 961
– a law 83
– the law 964
– a usage 614
**violence** **173**
*arbitrary* 964
do – to *bad* 649
*non-observance* 773
*undue* 925
**violent** 173
*excitable* 825
– death 360, 361
in a – degree 31
lay – hands on 789
**violet** 437
**violin** 417
**violinist** 416
**violoncello** 417
**viper** *snake* 366
*bane* 663
*evil-doer* 913
*bad man* 949
– in one's bosom 667
**virago** 901
**virent** 435
**vires acquirit eundo**
*increase* 35
*energy* 171
*velocity* 274
**virescence** 435
**Virgilianæ, sortes** – 621
**virgin** *new* 123
*girl* 129
*woman* 374
*spinster* 904
*good* 948
*pure* 960
– forest 367
– soil
*ignorance* 491
*untilled* 674
the – Mary 977
**virginals** 417
**virginibus puerisque** 960
**viribus, totis** – 686
**viridity** 435
**virile**
*adolescent* 131
*strong* 159
*manly* 373
**virtu** 850
article of – 847
**virtual** 2, 5
– image 443
**virtue** *power* 157
*courage* 861
*goodness* **944**
*purity* 960
by – of 157, 631
in – of 737
make a – of necessity *no choice* 609*a*
*skill* 698
*submit* 725
*compromise* 774
*bear* 826
**virtueless** 945
**virtuoso** 416, 850
**virtuous** 944, 960
**virulence**
*energy* 171
*noxiousness* 649
*insalubrity* 657
*discourtesy* 895
*anger* 900
*malevolence* 907
**virulent** 932
**virum volitare per ora** 531
**virus** 655, 663
**vis:**
– comica 842
– conservatrix 670
– inertiæ
*power* 157
*inertness* 172
*insensibility* 823
– medicatrix 660, 662
– mortua 157
– a tergo 284
– viva 157
**visa** 488
**visage** 234, 448
**vis-à-vis** *front* 234
*opposite* 237
*carriage* 272
**viscera** 221
**viscid** 352
**viscount** 875
**viscous** 352
**vise** 781
**Vishnu** 979
**visibility** **446**
**visible** 446
be – 448
become – 448
darkness – 421
– radiation 420
**vision** *sight* **441**
*phantasm* 443
*dream* 515
*spectre* 980
organ of – 441
**visionary**
*inexistence* 2
*unsubstantial* 4
*impossible* 471
*imaginary* 515
*heterodox* 984
**visionless** 442
**visit** *arrival* 292
*social* 892
*courtesy* 894
– upon 972
pay a surprise – 674
**visitation**
*disease* 655
*adversity* 735
*suffering* 828
–s of Providence 976
– of the sick 998
**visiting:**
– card 550
on – terms 888, 892
**visitor** *incomer* 294
*director* 694
*friend* 890
**visor** 530
**vista**
*convergence* 260
*sight* 441
*appearance* 448
*expectation* 507
**visual** 441
– organ 441
**vitability** 359
**vitæ, elixir** – 662
**vital** *life* 359
*important* 642
**vitality**
*stability* 150
*strength* 159
*life* 359
**vitalize** 359
**vitals** 221
**vitam impendere vero** 535, 939
**vitamines** 298
**vitiate** 659
**vitiated** 655
**viticulture** 371
**vitreous** 323, 425
**vitrify** 323
**vituperate** 908, 932
**vituperator** 936
**viva!** 873, 931
**vivace** *music* **415**
**vivacious**
*active* 682
*sensitive* 822
*cheerful* 836
**vivamus, dum vivimus** – 840
**vivandière** 797
**vivarium** 370
**vivâ voce** 582
**vive** *glory be to* **873**
on the qui – 824
**vivendi**
modus – 723
– causa 359
**vivid** *energetic* **171**
*sensibility* **375**
*light* 420
*colour* 428
*distinct* 518
– memory **505**
**vivify** 159, 359
**vivisection** 378
**vixen** *fox* 366
*female* 374
*shrew* 901
**viz.** [*see* videlicet]
**vizier** *director* **694**
*mask* 530
*shield* 717
*deputy* 759
**vizor** 530
**vobis, sic vos non** – 791
**vocable** 562
**vocabulary** 562
**vocal** 415, 580
– training **537**
**vocalist** 416
**vocalize** 580
**vocation** 625
**voce, sotto** – **581**
**vociferation**
*loud* 404
*cry* 411
*voice* 580
**vogue** *custom* **613**
*fashion* 852
*fame* 873
**vogue la galère**

## W

*inquiry* 461
*reasoning* 476
**where** 186, 461
– am I? 870
**whereabouts** 183, 197
**whereas** 9, 476
**whereby** 631
**wherefore**
*attribution* 155
*inquiry* 461
*reasoning* 476
*motive* 615
**wherein** 221
**whereness** 186
**whereupon** 106, 121
**wherever** 180, 182
**wherewith** 632, 800
**wherret** 830
**wherry** 273
**whet** *sharpen* 253
*meal* 298
*incite* 615
*excite* 824
take a –
*tipple* 959
– the appetite 865
– the knife 673
**whether or not** 609
**whetstone, cut a –** with a razor 638
**which:**
at – time 119
know – is which 465
**whiff** 349, 825
**whiffle** 349
**Whig** 712
**while** *time* 106
in a – 132
worth – 646
– away time
*inaction* 681
*pastime* 840
– speaking of 9, 134
**whilom** 122
**whilst** 106
**whim** *fad* 481
*fancy* 515
*caprice* 608
*wit* 842
*desire* 865
**whimper** 839
**whimsey** 515, 865
**whimsical** [*see* whim] 853
**whimwham** 608, 643
**whin** 367
**whine** 411, 839
**whinyard** 727
**whip** *collect* 72
*coachman* 268
*strike* 276
*stir up* 315
*urge* 615
*hasten* 684
*director* 694
*flog* 972
*scourge* 975
– and spur 274
– away 293
– hand 731, **737**
– in 300
– on 684
– off 293
– up 789
**whipcord** 205
**whipper-in** 694
**whippersnapper** 129
**whipping-post** 975
**whipster** 129
**whir** *rotate* 312
*sound* 407
**whirl** *rotate* 312
*flurry* 825
**whirligig** 312
**whirlpool** *rotate* 312
*agitation* 315
*water* 348
*danger* 667
**whirlwind**
*disorder* 59
*agitation* 315
*wind* 349
reap the –
*product* 154
*fail* 732
ride the –
*resolution* 604
*authority* 737
**whisk** *rapid* 274
*circuition* 311
*agitation* 315
– off 297
**whisker** 256
**whisket** 191
**whisky**
*vehicle* 272
*drink* 298
**whisper**
*faint sound* 405
*tell* 527
*conceal* 528
*stammer* 583
stage – 580
– about
*disclose* 529
*publish* 531
– in the ear
*voice* 580
**whist** *hush* 403
*cards* 840
**whistle** *wind* 349
*hiss* 409
*play music* 416
*musical instrument* 417
clean as a –
*thorough* 52
*perfect* 650
*neatly* 652
pay too dear for one's –
*inexpedient* 647
*unskilful* 699
*dear* 814
police – 669
wet one's –
*drink* 298
*tipple* 959
– at 930
– for *request* 765
*desire* 865
– jigs to a milestone 645
– for want of thought
*inaction* 681
**whit** *small* 32
**whit-leather** 327
**Whit-Monday** 840
**white** 430
– of the eye 441
– feather 862
– flag 723
– frost 383
– heat 382
– horses 348
– lie *equivocal* 520
*concealment* 528
*untruth* 546
*plea* 617
– liver 862
– as a sheet 860
– slave 962
stand in a – sheet 952
mark with a – stone 642, 931
**whitechapel**
*vehicle* 272
**Whitefriars** 996
**whiteness** **430**
**whitewash**
*cover* 223
*whiten* 430
*cleanse* 652
*ornament* 847
*justify* 937
*acquit* 970
**whitewashed**
get – 808
**whitewasher** 935
**white wings** 652
**whitey-brown** 433
**whither**
*tendency* 176
*direction* 278
*inquiry* 461
**whitlow** 655
**whittle** 44, 253
**whittled**
*drunk* 959
**Whitsuntide** 998
**whiz** 409
**who** 461
– goes there? **669**
– would have thought? 508, 870
**whoa!** 265
**whole** *entire* **50**
*healthy* 654
make – 660
as a – 50
on the – 476, 480
go the – hog 729
the – time 106
– truth
*truth* 494
*disclosure* 529
*veracity* 543
**wholesale**
*large scale* 31
*whole* 50
*abundant* 639
*trade* 794
**wholesome** 656
**wholly** 50, 52
**whoop** 411
war – 715, 722
**whop** *flog* 972
**whoopee** 840
**whopper** *lie* 546
**whopping** *huge* 192
**whore** 962
**whoredom** 961
**whoremonger** 962
**whorl** 248
**why** *cause* 153
*attribution* 155
*inquiry* 461
*indeed* 535
*motive* 615
– not 868
**wibble-wabble** 314
**wick** 388, 423
**wicked** 945
the – *bad men* 949
*impious* 988
the – one 978
**wicker** 219
**wicket** 66, 260

**wing** *extension* 39
*part* 51
*side* 236
*fly* 267
*side-scene* 599
*instrument* 633
*refuge* 666
*army* 726
clip the –s 275
lend –s to 707
on the –
*motion* 264
*flying* 267
*transference* 270
*departure* 293
take – *journey* 266
*fly* 267
*depart* 293
under the – of
*safe* 664
with –s *active* 682
– one's flight 293
– one's way 267
on the –s of the wind 274
**wing-commander** 745
**winged** *swift* 274
**wink** 443, 550
tip the – 550, 527
– at
*be blind to* 442
*disregard* 458
*neglect* 460
*permit* 760
*forgive* 918
– of sleep 683
**winning** [*see* win]
*pleasing* 829
*courteous* 894
*lovable* 897
**winnings** 775
**winnow** *sift* 42
*exclude* 55
*inquire* 461
*pick* 609
*clean* 652
– the chaff from the wheat 465
**winsome** 829, 836
**winter** 126, 383
– of our discontent 832
– garden 840
– sports 840
**wintry** 126
**wipe** *dry* 340
*clean* 652
*disrespect* 929
*flog* 972
give one a –
*rebuke* 932
– away 552
– the eyes
*relieve* 834
– off old scores 807, 952
– the tears 914
**wire** *ligature* 45
*filament* 205
*telegraph* 527, 534
pull the –s 693
**wire-drawn**
*long* 200
**wireless** 531
– telegram 532
– telegraph 534
– telephone 534
**wire-puller** 526, 694
**wire-worm** 913
**wiry** *strong* 159
**wis** 514
**wisdom** **498**
have cut one's – teeth 698
worldly – 864
**wise**
*intelligent* 498
*sage* 500
*manner* 627
in such – 8
word to the – 695
– in one's own conceit 880
– after the event 135
– man 500
– maxim 496
dine not –ly but too well 953
**wiseacre** 493, 500,
**wiser, nobody the** – 528
**wish** *will* 600
*intention* 620
*desire* 865
do what one –es 748
– at the bottom of the Red Sea 832
– the father to the thought
*misjudge* 481
*credulous* 486
*hope* 858
*desire* 865
– joy 896
– well 906
**wishing-cap** 993
**wish-wash**
*unmeaning* 517
**wishy-washy**
*languid* 160
*insipid* 391
*feeble style* 575
*unimportant* 643
**wisket** 191
**wisp** 72
**wistful**
*thought* 451
*care* 459
*feeling* 821
*desire* 865
**wit** *intellect* 450
*wisdom* 498
*humour* **842**
*humorist* 844
mother – 498
soul of – 572
to – 522
at one's –'s end 475, 704
**witch** *oracle* 513
*ugly* 846
*sorceress* 994
– doctor 994
**witchcraft** 992
**witchery**
*attraction* 615
*pleasing* 829
*sorcery* 992
**witching time** 126, 421
**witenagemote** 696
**with** *added* 37
*mixed* 41
*ligature* 45
*accompanying* 88
*means* 632
go – 178
– all its parts 52
– regard to 9
– a vengeance 31, 52
– a witness 31
**withal**
*in addition* 37
*accompanying* 88
*enough* 639
**withdraw**
*subduct* 38
*absent* 187
*turn back* 283
*recede* 287
*depart* 293
– from
*recant* 607
*relinquish* 624
*dislike* 867
**withe** 45
**wither** 195, 659
– one's hopes 837
**withered** *weak* **160**
*disease* 655
**withering**
*harsh* 739
*painful* 830
*contempt* 930
*censure* 932
**withers** 250
– unwrung 159, 823
**withhold** *hide* 528
*restrain* 751
*prohibit* 761
*retain* 781
*stint* 819
– one's assent **764**
**within** 221
derived from – 5
place – 221
keep – 221
– an ace 32
– bounds
*small* 32
*shortcoming* **304**
*restraint* 751
– call 197
– compass
*shortcoming* **304**
*temperate* 953
– the mark 304
– one's memory 505
– reach 197, **705**
**without** *unless* 8
*subduction* 38
*exception* 83
*absence* 187
*exterior* 220
*circumjacent* 227
*exemption* 777*a*
derived from – 6
not be able to do .. 630
– alloy 827
– ballast 605, 863
– ceasing 136
– ceremony 881
– charge 815
– fear of contradiction 535
– a dissentient voice 488
– end 105, 112
– exception 16
– excuse 945
– fail 474, 604*a*
– God 989
– a leg to stand on 158
– limit 105
– measure 105

– notice 508
– number 105
– parallel 33
– a rap 804
– reason 499
– regard to 10
– reluctance 602
– reserve 525
– rhyme or reason 615*a*
– a shadow of turning 141
– stint 639
– warning 508
**withstand** 708, 719
**withy** 45
**witless** 491
**witling** 501, 844
**witness** [*see* 441]
*spectator* 444
*evidence* 467
*voucher* 550
call to – 467
**witness-box** 966
**wits** 450
live by one's –
*deceive* 545
*skill* 698
*cunning* 702
*steal* 791
*dishonourable* 940
set one's – to work
*think* 451
*invent* 515
*plan* 626
all one's – about one
*care* 459
*intelligence* 498
*skill* 698
one's – gone a woolgathering 458
**witsnapper** 844
**witticism** 842
**wittingly** 620
**wittol** 962
**wive** 903
**wiveless** 904
**wizard** *sage* 500
*proficient* 700
*sorcerer* 994
**wizen** *wither* 195
*throat* 260
**woad** 438
**wobble** 605
**woe** 828
– betide 908, 914
– is me 839
– to 908
**woebegone** 828, 837
**woeful** 649, 830
**woefully** *very* 31
**wold** 344
**wolf** *ravenous* 865
cry – *false* 544
*alarm* 669
*fear* 860
hold the – by the ears 704
keep the – from the door 359
unable to keep the – from the door 804
– at the door 667, 804
– and the lamb 923
– in sheep's clothing 548, 941
**woman** 131, **374**
– of the town 962
**woman-hater** 911
**womanhood** 131, 374
**womanish** 160
**womanly**
*adolescent* 131
*feminine* 374
**womb** *cause* 153
*interior* 221
– of time 121, 152
**wonder**
*exception* 83
*astonishment* **870**
*prodigy* 872
do –s 682, 731
for a – 870
nine days' – 643
not – 507
– whether
*uncertain* 475
*ignorant* 491
*suppose* 514
–s of the world 872
**wonderfully** 31
**wonder-working** 870
**wondrous** 870
**wont** *habitual* 613
**won't do, it** – 932
**woo** 865, 902
**wood** *trees* 367
*material* 635
not out of the – 665, 704
take to the –s 666
**woodcut** 558
**woodcutter** 371
**wooded, well-** 256
**wooden** 635
– horse 975
– spoon 493
– walls 717, 726
**wood engraving** 558
**woodlands** 367
**wood-note** 412
**wood pavement** 255
**woody** 367
**wooer** 897
**woof**
warp and – 329
**wool** *flocculent* 256
*warm* 382
much cry and little – 482
**woolgathering** 458
**woolly** 255, 256
**woolpack** *cloud* 353
**woolsack**
*pillow* 215
*authority* 747
*tribunal* 966
**word** *maxim* 496
*intelligence* 532
*assertion* 535
*vocable* **562**
*phrase* 566
*command* 741
*promise* 768
give the – 741
good as one's –
*veracious* 543
*complete* 729
*probity* 939
in a – 572
keep one's – 939
man of his – 939
not a – to say 585, 879
pass– 550
put in a – 582
take at one's – 484, 762
upon my – 535
watch– 722
– and a blow
*hasty* 684
*contentious* 720
*irascible* 901
– of command
*indication* 550
*military* 722
*command* 741
– in the ear 527, 586
– of honour 768
– it 566
– of mouth 582
– to the wise
*intelligible* 518
*advice* 695
– for word 19, **494**
**Word** *Deity* 976
– of God 985
**word-catcher** 936
**wordiness** 573, **584**
**wording** 569
**wordless** 581
**word-play**
*equivocal* 520
*neology* 563
*wit* 842
**words** *quarrel* **713**
bandy – 588
bitter – 932
choice of – 569
command of – **574**
express by – **566**
flow of – 582, **584**
mere – 477, 517
no – can paint **872**
play of – 842
put into – 566
war of – 588, 720
– that burn 574
– painting 515
– with 932
**wordy** 573
**work**
*product* **154**
*operation* 170
*pass and repass* 302
*book* 593
*business* 625
*use* 677
*action* 680
*exertion* 686
*ornament* **847**
at –
*in operation* **170**
*business* 625
*doing* 680
*active* 682
earth– 717
field– 717
hard – 686, **704**
piece of –
*importance* **642**
*discord* 713
stick to – 604*a*
stitch of – 686
stroke of – 686
– of art 845, **847**
– a change 140
– a cure 662
– of fiction **594**
– for 707
– hard 686, **704**
– ill 732
– in 228
– out *conduct* **692**

*complete* 729
-room 191
- out one's salvation 990
- against time 684
- up [*see below*]
- upon
*influence* 175
*incite* 615
*excite* 824
- one's way
*progress* 282
*ascent* 305
*exertion* 681
*succeed* 731
- well 705, 731
- wonders 682, 731
**work up**
*prepare* 673
*use* 677
*excite* 824
- into *form* 240
- into a passion 900
**workable** 470
**work-a-day** 625, 882
**worker** 690
**workhouse** 691
**working** *acting* 170
*active* 682
- bee 690
- man 690
- order 673
- towards 176
**workman** 690
**workmanlike** 698
**workmanship** 161, 680
**works**
board of - 696
good - 906
- of the mind 451
**workshop** 691
**workwoman** 690
**world** *great* 31
*events* 151
*space* 180
*universe* 318
*mankind* 372
*fashion* 852
all the - over 180
citizen of the - 910
come into the - 359
for all the - 615
give to the - 531
knowledge of the - 698
man of the -
*proficient* 700
*fashion* 852
not for the - 489, 764
organized - 357
Prince of this - 978
rise in the - 734
throughout the - 180
- to come 152
follow to the -'s end 743
- forgetting by the world forgot 893
as the - goes 613
- of good 618, 648
a - of 102
- and his wife 102
- without end 112
**worldling** 943, 988
**worldly** 943, 989
**world-wide**
*great* 31
*universal* 78
*space* 180
**world-wisdom**
*skill* 698
*caution* 864
*selfishness* 943
**worm** *small* 193
*spiral* 248
*animal* 366
*bane* 663
- in 228
- oneself
*ingress* 294
*love* 897
- out 480*a*
- that never dies 982
- one's way 275, 302
**worm-eaten** 659
**worms, food for** - 362
**wormwood**
gall and - 395
**worn** *weak* 160
*damage* 659
*fatigue* 688
well- *used* 677
- out 659, 841
**worry**
*vexation* 828
*tease* 830
*harass* 907
**worse** 659, 835
- for wear 160
**worship** *title* 877
*servility* 886
*religious* 990
demon - 991
idol - 991
fire - 991
his - 967
place of - 1000
- Mammon 803
- the rising sun 886
**worshipful** 873
**worst** *defeat* 731
do one's - 659, 907
do your - 715, 909
have the - of it 732
make the - of 482
worst come to the - *certain* 474
*bad* 649
*hopeless* 859
**worsted** 205
**worth** *value* 644
*goodness* 648
*possession* 777
*price* 812
*virtue* 944
penny - 815
what one is - 780
- a great deal 803
- the money 815
- much 803
- one's salt 644
- while 646
**worthless**
*trifling* 643
*useless* 645
*profligate* 945
**worthy**
*famous* 873
*virtuous* 944
*good* 948
- of 924
- of belief 484
- of blame 932
- of notice 642
- of remark 642
**wot** 490
**would**: - fain 865
- that! 865
**would-be** *pert* 885
*usurping* 925
**wound** *evil* 619
*injure* 659
*pain* 830
*anger* 900
keep the - green 919
- the feelings 830
- up 704
**woven fabrics** 219
**wowser** 988
**wrack** 162
go to - and ruin
*perish* 162
*fail* 732
*bankrupt* 804
**wraith** 980
**wrangle**
*disagreement* 24
*reason* 476
*quarrel* 713
*contend* 720
**wrangler**
*reasoner* 476
*scholar* 492
*opponent* 710
**wrap** 223, 225
**wrapped in**
*attention* 457
- clouds 528
- self 943
- thought 458
**wrapper** 223, 225
*inclosure* 232
**wraprascal** 225
**wrath** 900
**wreak** *violent* 173
*harsh* 739
- one's anger 919
- one's malice on 907
**wreath** *woven* 219
*circle* 247
*trophy* 733
*ornament* 847
*honour* 877
**wreathe** *weave* 219
**wreathy** 248
**wreck**
*remainder* 40
*destruction* 162
*damage* 659
*defeat* 732
**wrecker** 792
**wrench** *disjoin* 44
*draw* 285
*extract* 301
*twist* 311
*tool* 633
*seize* 789
**wrest** *distort* 243
- from 789
- the sense 523
**wrestle** 720
**wrestler** 726
**wretch** *sufferer* 828
*sinner* 949
**wretched**
*unimportant* 643
*bad* 649
*unhappy* 828
**wretchedly**